SOUTH AFRICA

3RD EDITION

Where to Stay and Eat
for All Budgets

Must-See Sights
and Local Secrets

Ratings You Can Trust

Fodor's Travel Publications   New York, Toronto, London, Sydney, Auckland
www.fodors.com

W9-APE-487

FODOR'S SOUTH AFRICA
Editors: Andrea Lehman, Jennifer Paull

Editorial Production: Tom Holton
Editorial Contributors: Matthew Burbidge, Sanja Cloete-Jones, Sue Derwent, Karena du Plessis, Audra Epstein, Sarah Gold, Shellee-Kim Gold, Laura Kidder, Myrna Robins, Jennifer Stern, Alice Thompson, Kate Turkington, Tara Turkington, Riaan Wolmarans
Maps: David Lindroth, *cartographer;* Bob Blake and Rebecca Baer, *map editors*
Design: Fabrizio La Rocca, *creative director;* Guido Caroti, *art director;* Moon Sun Kim, *cover designer;* Melanie Marin, *senior picture editor*
Cover Photo (Elephants, Limpopo Province): Gallo Images-Heinrich van den Berg/The Image Bank/Getty Images
Production/Manufacturing: Angela L. McLean

SPECIAL SALES
This book is available for special discounts for bulk purchases for sales promotions or premiums. Special editions, including personalized covers, excerpts of existing books, and corporate imprints, can be created in large quantities for special needs. For more information, write to Special Markets/Premium Sales, 1745 Broadway, MD 6-2, New York, New York 10019, or e-mail specialmarkets@randomhouse.com.

AN IMPORTANT TIP & AN INVITATION
Although all prices, opening times, and other details in this book are based on information supplied to us at press time, changes occur all the time in the travel world, and Fodor's cannot accept responsibility for facts that become outdated or for inadvertent errors or omissions. So **always confirm information when it matters,** especially if you're making a detour to visit a specific place. Your experiences—positive and negative—matter to us. If we have missed or misstated something, **please write to us.** We follow up on all suggestions. Contact the South Africa editor at editors@fodors.com or c/o Fodor's at 1745 Broadway, New York, New York 10019.

PRINTED IN THE UNITED STATES OF AMERICA

10 9 8 7 6 5 4 3 2 1

Be a Fodor's Correspondent

Your opinion matters. It matters to us. It matters to your fellow Fodor's travelers, too. And we'd like to hear it. In fact, we *need* to hear it.

When you share your experiences and opinions, you become an active member of the Fodor's community. That means we'll not only use your feedback to make our books better, but we'll publish your names and comments whenever possible. Throughout our guides, look for "Word of Mouth," excerpts of your unvarnished feedback.

Here's how you can help improve Fodor's for all of us.

Tell us when we're right. We rely on local writers to give you an insider's perspective. But our writers and staff editors—who are the best in the business—depend on you. Your positive feedback is a vote to renew our recommendations for the next edition.

Tell us when we're wrong. We're proud that we update most of our guides every year. But we're not perfect. Things change. Hotels cut services. Museums change hours. Charming cafés lose charm. If our writer didn't quite capture the essence of a place, tell us how you'd do it differently. If any of our descriptions are inaccurate or inadequate, we'll incorporate your changes in the next edition and will correct factual errors at fodors.com *immediately.*

Tell us what to include. You probably have had fantastic travel experiences that aren't yet in Fodor's. Why not share them with a community of like-minded travelers? Maybe you chanced upon a beach or bistro or B&B that you don't want to keep to yourself. Tell us why we should include it. And share your discoveries and experiences with everyone directly at fodors.com. Your input may lead us to add a new listing or highlight a place we cover with a "Highly Recommended" star or with our highest rating, "Fodor's Choice."

Give us your opinion instantly at our feedback center at www.fodors.com/feedback. You may also e-mail editors@fodors.com with the subject line "South Africa Editor." Or send your nominations, comments, and complaints by mail to South Africa Editor, Fodor's, 1745 Broadway, New York, NY 10019.

You and travelers like you are the heart of the Fodor's community. Make our community richer by sharing your experiences. Be a Fodor's correspondent.

Happy traveling!

Tim Jarrell, Publisher

CONTENTS

Maps

CloseUps

Our Ratings

Sometimes you find terrific travel experiences and sometimes they just find you. But usually it's up to you to select the right combination of experiences. That's where our ratings come in.

As travelers we've all discovered a place so wonderful that its worthiness is obvious. And sometimes that place is so experiential that superlatives don't do it justice: you just have to be there to know. These sights, properties, and experiences get our highest rating, **Fodor's Choice,** indicated by orange stars throughout this book.

Black stars ★ highlight sights and properties we deem **Highly Recommended,** places that our writers, editors, and readers praise again and again for consistency and excellence.

By default, there's another category: any place we include in this book is by definition worth your time, unless we say otherwise. And we will.

Disagree with any of our choices? Care to nominate a place or suggest that we rate one more highly? Visit our feedback center at www.fodors.com/feedback.

Budget Well

Hotel and restaurant price categories from ¢ to $$$$ are defined in the opening pages of each chapter. For attractions, we always give standard adult admission fees; reductions are usually available for children, students, and senior citizens. Want to pay with plastic? **AE, D, DC, MC, V** following restaurant and hotel listings indicate if American Express, Diner's Club, MasterCard, and Visa are accepted.

Restaurants

Unless we state otherwise, restaurants are open for lunch and dinner daily. We mention dress only when there's a specific requirement and reservations only when they're essential or not accepted—it's always best to book ahead.

Hotels

Hotels have private bath, phone, TV, and air-conditioning and operate on the European Plan (a.k.a. EP, meaning without meals), unless we specify that they use the Continental Plan (CP, with a Continental breakfast), Breakfast Plan (BP, with a full breakfast), or Modified American Plan (MAP, with breakfast and dinner) or are all-inclusive (including all meals and most activities). We always

list facilities but not whether you'll be charged an extra fee to use them, so when pricing accommodations, find out what's included.

Many Listings
- ★ Fodor's Choice
- ★ Highly recommended
- ⊠ Physical address
- ⊹ Directions
- ⌖ Mailing address
- ☎ Telephone
- 🖷 Fax
- ⊕ On the Web
- ✉ E-mail
- 🎫 Admission fee
- ☉ Open/closed times
- ▶ Start of walk/itinerary
- Ⓜ Metro stations
- ▭ Credit cards

Hotels & Restaurants
- 🏨 Hotel
- ↩ Number of rooms
- ♿ Facilities
- ⅋○⅋ Meal plans
- ✕ Restaurant
- 🕭 Reservations
- 🏛 Dress code
- ↘ Smoking
- 🎙 BYOB
- ✕🏨 Hotel with restaurant that warrants a visit

Outdoors
- 🏌 Golf
- ⛺ Camping

Other
- ♨ Family-friendly
- 🛈 Contact information
- ⇨ See also
- ⊠ Branch address
- ☞ Take note

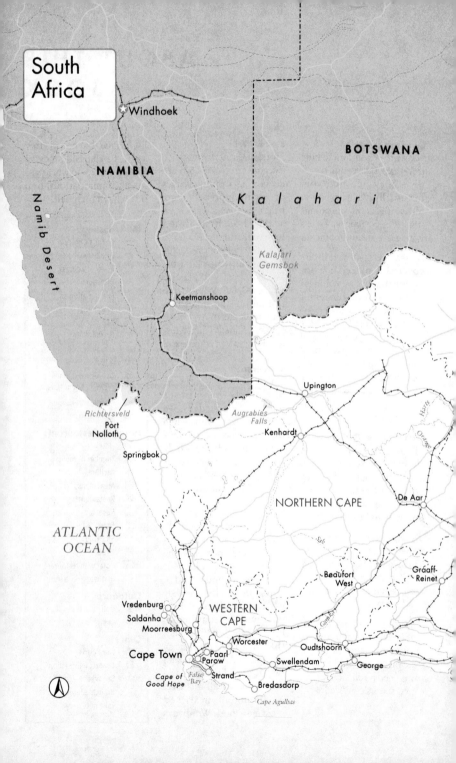

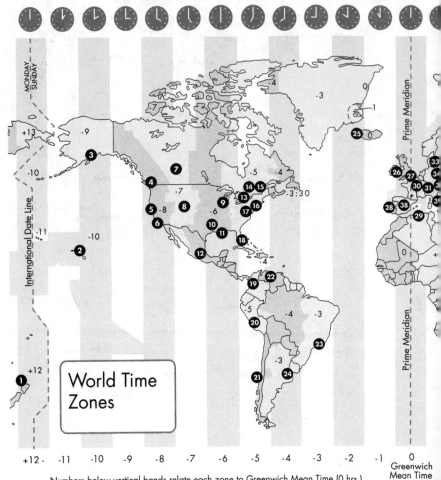

World Time Zones

Numbers below vertical bands relate each zone to Greenwich Mean Time (0 hrs.).
Local times frequently differ from these general indications,
as indicated by light-face numbers on map.

+12 - -11 -10 -9 -8 -7 -6 -5 -4 -3 -2 -1 0
Greenwich
Mean Time

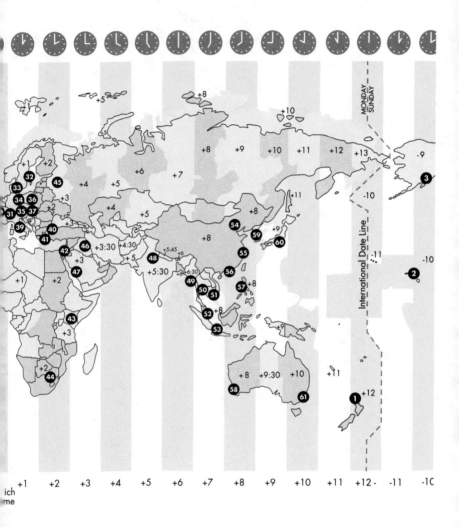

ABOUT OUR WRITERS

Matthew Burbidge, co-author of the Johannesburg & Environs chapter, was born in the Eastern Cape but now lives in Johannesburg. Trained as a photographer, he works as news editor for the *Mail & Guardian Online.* He also cooks. Though Matthew misses the sea, he lives for Johannesburg thunderstorms.

Sanja Cloete-Jones started life in the Kalahari Desert and has slept under the stars in most countries of southern, eastern, and northern Africa. Travel writing her way around Australasia, she completed guides to eight countries. She has now returned to the continent that remains her first love and lives in Zambia—the heart of Africa.

Award-winning freelance journalist **Karena du Plessis** is passionate about food, wine, and travel. When she's not exploring (and covering the Western Cape and Cape Town chapters of this book), she lives in the fishing village of Kalk Bay, just outside Cape Town; works in her micro vineyard; and spends time with her two horses. Karena is also the author of *The Overberg—Inland from the Tip of Africa.*

Globetrotting through 43 countries with a backpack, freelance journalist **Shellee-Kim Gold** has celebrated a bedouin desert wedding in Jordan, lived beyond the Arctic Circle in Finnish Lapland, and been arrested in China for traveling independently. Shellee-Kim has contributed to more than 30 publications and several guidebooks. Between writing assignments—and to prevent cabin fever—she helps build bridges between people as a South African tour guide.

Myrna Robins, who writes for various newspapers and magazines, is one of South Africa's most popular food writers. Author of several cookbooks, including *Cape Flavour—A Gastronomic Meander through the Winelands,* she divides her time between the Atlantic seaboard suburb of Blouberg and the exquisite hamlet of McGregor, beneath the Riviersonderend mountains.

Jennifer Stern is the author of *Southern Africa on a Budget* and *Guide to Adventure Travel in Southern Africa.* In the line of duty she has braved strange wayside pubs, dived pristine reefs, paddled beautiful rivers, walked with wildlife, and ridden mountain bikes, horses, camels, and elephants all over southern Africa's wilder parts.

Kate Turkington is one of South Africa's best-known journalists and broadcasters. Her live Sunday night radio show on Radio 702/Cape Talk, *Believe It or Not,* is the longest-running radio show in South Africa. She has waltzed at dawn in a Beijing square, fallen over Emperor penguins in Antarctica, lunched under a silken canopy with a rajah in Rajasthan, been winched over a raging river 9,000 feet up in the Andes, prayed with monks in Tibet's oldest monastery, and heard the stars sing in the Kalahari Desert.

Tara Turkington is a journalist and researcher who has lived in four diverse South African provinces: industrial Gauteng (she currently lives in Johannesburg), tropical KwaZulu-Natal, the desolate Northern Cape, and the majestic Western Cape. She has worked as a newspaper designer and copy editor, reporter, schoolteacher, university lecturer, heritage manager, and tourism developer. As a freelance journalist, she has written and photographed for more than 20 publications, including the *Mail & Guardian, Sowetan Sunday World,* and *True Love.*

Riaan Wolmarans, co-author of our Johannesburg & Environs chapter, is senior sub-editor of the *Mail & Guardian Online,* Africa's leading news Web site. Previously, he kept an eagle eye on South Africa's theater, arts, culture, and music as the newspaper's listings editor, and he still writes music reviews and features. He regularly spends all his savings on traveling, which takes him to seaside villages in Spain, pancake restaurants in Amsterdam, and nightclubs in New York City.

WHAT'S WHERE

(1) Cape Town & the Peninsula

Capetonians tend to look with pity on those who don't have the good fortune to live in their Eden. Their attitude is understandable—Cape Town is indeed one of the world's fairest cities. Backed by Table Mountain, the city presides over a coastline of unsurpassed beauty: mountains cascading into the sea, miles of beaches, and 17th-century wineries snoozing under giant oaks. Modern South Africa was born here, and the city is filled with historic reminders of its three centuries as the sea link between Europe and the East.

(2) The Western Cape

This diverse region serves as the weekend playground for Capetonians. The jewel of the province is the Winelands, a stunning collection of jagged mountains, vine-covered slopes, and centuries-old Cape Dutch estates that produce some of the world's finest wine. Farther afield, the Overberg is a quiet region of farms and beach resorts that ends at Cape Agulhas, the southernmost tip of Africa. The long, lonely coastline has pristine beaches and towering dunes framed by sheer, rocky mountains. The West Coast is a desolate landscape dotted with tiny fishing villages. Inland, the Cederberg mountains offer fantastic scenery and hiking.

(3) The Northern Cape

A rugged, lonely land, much of it with vistas of desert and semidesert, the Northern Cape reaches across a third of South Africa and incorporates some of the country's most unforgettable travel destinations. Along the country's northwestern seaboard lies Namaqualand, which each year produces a springtime paradise of wildflowers famous the world over. In the central north is the Kalahari, a harsh landscape of dunes and scrub that, surprisingly, offers superb game-viewing. On the province's eastern border and in the country's geographical center lies the historic city of Kimberley, where diamonds have been mined for well over a century.

(4) The Garden Route & the Little Karoo

The Garden Route is a beautiful 208-km (130-mi) stretch of coast that takes its name from the region's year-round riot of vegetation. Here you'll find some of South Africa's most inspiring scenery: forest-cloaked mountains, myriad rivers and streams, and golden beaches backed by thick, indigenous bush. You'll also find Plettenberg Bay, South Africa's glitziest beach resort, and Knysna, a charming town built around an oyster-rich lagoon. The Little Karoo, separated from the coast by the Outeniqua Mountains, is a semiarid region famous for its ostrich farms, turn-of-the-20th-century "feather palaces," and the Cango Caves, one of the world's most impressive networks of underground caverns.

(5) The Eastern Cape

The Eastern Cape is South Africa's most diverse province: small, sleepy cities, long deserted beaches, fabulous mountain wildernesses, huge game reserves, fascinating villages, and myriad wonderful cultural attractions. The Eastern Cape probably has the most interesting cultural heritage of any South African province, with a long history of resistance to colonialism and apartheid. It was here that South Africans of various hues and political persuasions first met. The British colonialists, the Boer settlers, the Xhosa tribespeople, the Khoi herders, and the San hunters all had intense clashes in this historically rich region.

6 Durban & KwaZulu-Natal

Steamy heat, the heady aroma of spices, and a polyglot of English, Hindi, and Zulu give the bustling port city of Durban a tropical feel. Some of the country's most popular swimming beaches extend north and south of the city; inland you can tour the battlefields where Boer, Briton, and Zulu struggled for control of the country. The Drakensberg is a breathtaking sanctuary of soaring beauty, crisp air, and some of the country's best hiking. In the far north Hluhluwe-Umfolozi and several private reserves have wildlife rivaling that of Mpumalanga.

7 Johannesburg & Environs

A mile high, South Africa's largest city sprawls across the highveld plateau, its soaring skyscrapers giving way to endless suburbs. Johannesburg was built—literally and figuratively—on gold, and the relentless pursuit of wealth has imbued it with a pulsing energy. Much of the antiapartheid struggle was played out in the dusty black townships ringing the city, and a tour of Soweto and the city center will give you a feel for the new South Africa.

8 Mpumalanga & Kruger National Park

Classic Africa—the Africa of heat, thorn trees, and big game—unfolds before you in Mpumalanga and the Limpopo Province on the Mozambique border. The great allure here is game watching, either in famed Kruger National Park or in an exclusive private reserve. But the area has much more to offer than animals. The Drakensberg (Afrikaans for "Dragon Mountains") divides the subtropical lowveld from the high interior plateau. Tucked away in these mountains of mists, forests, waterfalls, and panoramic views lie some of South Africa's most luxurious hotels and lodges, as well as beautiful hikes, river trips, horse trails, and historic gold-rush towns.

9 Victoria Falls

Its Makololo name, Mosi-oa-Tunya (literally, "the Smoke that Thunders") doesn't undersell this amazing natural wonder—the largest falls on the planet. Its river border location means that it's shared by two countries and two towns that serve as bases for soaking up all that water: Livingstone (named for the 19th-century explorer), in Zambia, and the even more aptly named Victoria Falls, in Zimbabwe.

10 Botswana & Namibia's Best Safari Destinations

Botswana is a natural wonder. Its variety of terrains, from vast salt pans to the waterways of the Okavango Delta to the Kalahari Desert, have a diversity seldom found in such a small area. Chobe National Park is a hot spot for both pachyderms and predators. And with so little industry blotting the sky, the stars may seem brighter than you have ever seen them. The Kalahari Bushmen say that you can hear the stars sing—listen.

Few countries have landscapes as spectacular as Namibia's. The 12.1 million-acre Namib Naukluft National Park is home to the highest sand dunes in the world, as well as eerie desertscapes and canyons filled with plants and wildlife. The numerous water holes at Etosha National Park draw lions, rhinos, antelope, zebras, and wildebeests. And the starkly beautiful, aptly named Skeleton Coast has rugged cliffs, treacherous winds and currents, and crashing seas where innumerable ships have foundered over the years.

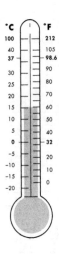

As southern Africa is in the Southern Hemisphere, its seasons are opposite to those in the Northern Hemisphere—it's summer there during the North American and European winter.

Peak tourist season is from November through March, when hotel prices rise dramatically and making a reservation can be difficult. The situation is exacerbated during major school holidays—especially December 1–January 15, the South African summer vacation—when South African families take to the roads in droves. Schools also have two weeks' vacation around Easter and a month in July or August, when the warmer parts of the region, especially KwaZulu-Natal, are particularly popular.

The most popular time to visit Cape Town is from November through January, although February and March offer the best weather. Keep in mind, however, that the shoulder months of October and April can be fabulous and uncrowded. Cape winters (May–August) are notorious for cold, windy, rainy weather, but in reality these are miserable days interspersed with glorious sunny days that rival the best summer days in Britain. This season is known as the "secret season," during which really good deals can be had. As long as you stay for a week or more, you're bound to have at least a few days of gorgeous weather.

Much of the rest of the region receives its rain in the hot summer months, which is the worst time for watching game, as the abundant standing water enables the animals to spread out over a large area and the luxuriant new growth makes it difficult to see anything. The rains usually end in about March or April, from which point the standing water starts to dry up and the vegetation to be eaten, so game-viewing improves throughout the dry season. By October there is usually very little standing water and vegetation cover, making game-viewing excellent, although the hot, humid conditions may be a bit uncomfortable. Once the rains start, usually in November, game-viewing takes a second place to bird-watching as the summer migrants arrive.

Johannesburg and the highveld enjoy glorious summers, with hot, sunny days broken by afternoon thunderstorms. Winter nights are frosty; days are generally mild and sunny but can be decidedly chilly, with rain, sleet, and even a little snow.

The coastal areas of KwaZulu-Natal are warm year-round, but summers are steamy and hot, and August sees high winds buffet the coastline. The water along the KwaZulu-Natal coast is warmest in February, but it seldom dips below 17°C (65°F) at any time of year. The Drakensberg Mountains can be bitterly cold in winter, often with snow, and are dry and brown. In summer the mountains are a bright green with new grass and warm, but spectacular thunderstorms pose a real threat to hikers in that high altitude.

Climate

The following are average daily maximum and minimum temperatures for some major cities in southern Africa.

📋 Forecasts **Weather Channel** ⊕ www.weather.com.

CAPE TOWN

Jan.	79F	26C	May	68F	20C	Sept.	66F	19C
	61	16		48	9		48	9
Feb.	81F	27C	June	64F	18C	Oct.	70F	21C
	61	16		46	8		52	11
Mar.	77F	25C	July	64F	18C	Nov.	75F	24C
	57	14		45	7		55	13
Apr.	73F	23C	Aug.	64F	18C	Dec.	77F	25C
	54	12		46	8		59	15

DURBAN

Jan.	82F	28C	May	77F	25C	Sept.	73F	23C
	70	21		57	14		59	15
Feb.	82F	28C	June	73F	23C	Oct.	75F	24C
	70	21		52	11		63	17
Mar.	82F	28C	July	73F	23C	Nov.	77F	25C
	68	20		52	11		64	18
Apr.	79F	26C	Aug.	73F	23C	Dec.	81F	27C
	63	17		55	13		68	20

JOHANNESBURG

Jan.	79F	26C	May	66F	19C	Sept.	73F	23C
	59	15		45	7		50	10
Feb.	77F	25C	June	61	16C	Oct.	75F	24C
	57	14		39	4		52	11
Mar.	75F	24C	July	63F	17C	Nov.	75F	24C
	55	13		39	4		55	13
Apr.	70F	21C	Aug.	66F	19C	Dec.	77F	25C
	50	10		43	6		57	14

KRUGER NATIONAL PARK

Jan.	91F	33C	May	82F	28C	Sept.	84F	29C
	70	21		50	10		55	13
Feb.	90F	32C	June	79F	26C	Oct.	86F	30C
	68	20		43	6		61	16
Mar.	88F	31C	July	79F	26C	Nov.	88F	31C
	66	19		43	6		64	18
Apr.	84F	29C	Aug.	81F	27C	Dec.	90F	32C
	59	15		48	9		68	20

ON THE CALENDAR

LATE SUMMER	
January	The 17-day **Cape Coon Carnival** celebrates the New Year in grand style, as thousands of coloureds dressed in bright costumes take to the streets of Cape Town to sing and dance. Run between what many people consider to be two of the most beautiful cities on earth, the **Cape to Rio Yacht Race** attracts a fair number of cruisers as well as serious competitors. It is run every three years and is due to leave Cape Town in January 2006. Even if you don't follow the whole race, the start is a fantastic spectacle, either from a boat, from Robben Island, or from the top of Table Mountain.
January or February	The **Cape Metropolitan Handicap,** run at Kenilworth, in Cape Town, is one of the most prestigious horse races on the local calendar. In summer, when the water level is high, the tough three-day, 120-km (about 75-mi) kayak **Dusi Marathon** takes place on the Msinnduzi River, which runs from Pietermaritzburg to Durban.
FALL	
February	The **Midmar Mile** is a rather tough swimming race in the freezing cold Midmar Dam, between Durban and Pietermaritzburg in the KZN Midlands. The **FNB Vita Dance Umbrella** is a three-week-long showcase of local dance at the University of the Witwatersrand, Johannesburg.
Early March	The **Argus Cycle Tour,** in Cape Town, is the largest individually timed race in the world, with about 40,000 competitors riding a scenic 108-km (67-mi) course. Just before the Argus, Cape Town's far more strenuous five-day **Giro del Capo** attracts serious cyclists, who may then just cycle the Argus as a cool-down.
Late March	The **North Sea Jazz Festival,** a showcase of international jazz, is held in Cape Town.
March or April	The **Klein Karoo Nasionale Kunstefees** takes place in Oudtshoorn; it's a celebration of Afrikaans culture, although there are performances in English as well. The annual **Nederburg Auction** is *the* event on the wine calendar. It's the place to be seen, even if you don't bid, as South Africa's finest old and new wines go under the hammer. The **Two Oceans Marathon** draws 8,000 runners for perhaps the most scenic race in the country, a grueling 56-km (35-mi) course that circumnavigates part of the Cape Peninsula.
April	**Splashy Fen,** in KwaZulu-Natal, is one of the most popular music festivals in South Africa. Originally concentrating on folk music, it is rapidly becoming more contemporary. The 100-km (60-mi) **Tour Durban** bicycle race is held on the last Sunday of April.

WINTER	
May	The **Pink Loerie Festival**, in the pretty coastal town of Knysna, is a celebration of gay pride and culture.
June	The **Comrades Marathon** is an agonizing 80-km (50-mi) double marathon and South Africa's most famous sporting event. The race, run between Pietermaritzburg and Durban, wends through the glorious scenery of the Valley of a Thousand Hills. When winter storms hit Cape Town, Dungeons—a break about a mile from shore near Hout Bay, on the Cape Peninsula—works. Big-wave surfers from all around the world gather to compete in **Big Wave Africa**. Freezing water and 20-foot-plus bone-crunching waves make this a really tough one.
June–July	The **ragged tooth sharks** are in residence on the reefs of southern KwaZulu-Natal for their annual breeding season. Divers may visit them on escorted dives. The **sardine run** should be in full swing around June or July on the Wild Coast and the KZN South Coast.
June–Sept.	Yes, it's **skiing season**. Not that it means a lot. Tiffindel, in the Eastern Cape, is South Africa's only ski resort. The skiing is far from the best in the world, but it's dependable, with snow guaranteed for three months.
July	The **Durban July** is one of the country's biggest horse races and a definite fashion love fest, where race goers compete to wear the most outrageous and glamorous attire. The **Durban Tattoo**, a 17-year tradition, is a military pageant filled with music, color, and pomp and ceremony. The **Mr. Price Pro championship**, which takes place in a number of centers along the coast, usually ending in Durban, draws the world's best to compete in the South African leg of the international surfing circuit. The **Knysna Oyster Festival** is about much more than oysters. The whole town puts on its finery. There are road races, mountain-bike races, cookouts, and—of course—oysters, oysters, and oysters. The **National Arts Festival**, in Grahamstown, is South Africa's most famous celebration of the arts, a wild and wacky 10-day extravaganza showcasing the best of South African theater, film, dance, music, and art.
SPRING	
August 2010	The **Soccer World Cup** is coming to South Africa. Start planning now if you're a follower of the beautiful game.
August	The **Imana Wild Coast Challenge**, a mountain-bike ride of about 195 km (140 mi), traverses some of the most spectacular scenery in South Africa; it skirts the beaches and cliffs of the Wild Coast and occasionally heads inland. In early August the hills around Tshwane ring with music, as some of South Africa's best bands, and best partyers, assemble for the annual **Oppikoppi Music Festival**.

August to September	The wildflowers of Namaqualand and the West Coast are one of nature's great spectacles, with bright spring blooms emerging in their millions from the seemingly barren semidesert. Several of the region's towns hold major flower festivals.
August to November	The annual whale migration of southern right whales takes place along the coast from Port Elizabeth to Cape Town and beyond along the West Coast. In Cape Town and the Overberg they come very close to shore, giving even landlubbers a great view of these graceful leviathans.
September	It's really just a big party with a bit of hectic consumerism with a whale motif, but the Hermanus Whale Festival is fun nevertheless. The Natal Witness Hilton Arts Festival showcases the pick of South African theater at Hilton College, in the KwaZulu-Natal Midlands. The Barefoot Festival is held the last week of the month in Plettenberg Bay. Look for art exhibitions, sporting and environmental events, and a whale and dolphin symposium.
October	Purple jacaranda blossoms blanket South Africa's capital city, Tshwane. The Good Food and Wine Festival, in Gauteng, is a celebration of all the good things in life.

SUMMER

November	The 94.7 Challenge is Johannesburg's biggest cycling race. It's—surprise—94.7 km (just under 60 mi), which is not that far, but it's pretty hilly. The Nedbank Golf Challenge, held at Sun City, is the richest golf tournament in the world. November is film month in Cape Town, with a whole lot of film festivals all orbiting around the Cape Town World Cinema Festival and Sithengi Film & Television Market.
Mid-November to mid-March	The Spier Arts Summer Festival is an extravaganza of music and theater performances at the Spier Estate, in Stellenbosch.
Mid-December	The Mother City Queer Project is the highlight of the social calendar for the less conservative of Cape Town's residents. With a different theme every year, this costume party is attended by both straight and gay people, but it really is about as camp as a row of pink tents.
December to January	The Ncwala, or First Fruits Ceremony, is common to many African tribes of Nguni origin and takes place in KwaZulu-Natal and elsewhere. The king blesses the harvest by ritually tasting the first fruits.

PLEASURES & PASTIMES

Air Sports & Aviation Southern Africa has some fantastic paragliding and hang-gliding venues. Cape Town, the Garden Route, and the Drakensberg are favorite spots, and the hot Northern Cape is popular for cross-country winch-launched flights. Namibia has one of the best gliding venues in the world. Hot-air ballooning is a popular getaway in the areas near Johannesburg. You can take an aerobatic flight near Cape Town or on the Garden Route, fly over Victoria Falls in a microlight, or do an aerial city tour of Johannesburg in a vintage plane. The sky's the limit.

Beaches South Africa has some of the finest beaches on earth—hundreds of miles of white, soft, sandy beaches, often without a soul on them. The surf is big, and dangerous undertows and side washes are common, although there are also some wonderful, safe swimming beaches. Beaches in major cities have lifeguards, and helicopters periodically patrol the coastline. Cape Town and the entire Western Cape have glorious beaches, but the water is extremely cold year-round, and wind can be a problem. The water is warmer along the Garden Route, with the best swimming at Plettenberg Bay. Around Durban and the resorts of KwaZulu-Natal the water is ideal for swimming. All major resort beaches in KwaZulu-Natal are protected by shark nets. For truly deserted beaches and warm water, head to Rocktail Bay Lodge, in the far north of KwaZulu-Natal.

Big-Game Adventures Southern Africa may not have the vast herds of East Africa, but it has far more species of animals—many more than the Big Five, which grab all the headlines. In fact, nowhere else on the continent do wild animals enjoy better protection than in southern Africa, and nowhere do you have a better chance of seeing Africa's big game. South Africa and Namibia have reasonably priced national parks, whereas Botswana deliberately keeps park entry fees high to minimize tourist damage. (Even the parts of Zambia and Zimbabwe around Victoria Falls offer game-viewing opportunities.) And because almost every game-viewing hot spot has luxury lodges where you can be pampered, your adventure needn't be too much of an adventure.

Bird-Watching South Africa ranks as one of the finest bird-watching destinations on the planet. Kruger National Park alone has recorded more than 500 bird species, many of breathtaking beauty. Birds in Zimbabwe, Botswana, and Namibia are spectacular as well. Look for sacred ibis, a variety of eagles and falcons and vultures, red- and yellow-billed hornbills, and the spectacularly beautiful lilac-breasted roller. The best time for bird-watching is October–April, when migrants are in residence.

Canoeing & White-Water Rafting From gentle scenic floats and short sea-kayak trips to hectic white-water or epic expeditions, southern Africa offers some of the best paddling around. Try the Orange River, on the border of South Africa and Namibia, for scenery and gentle rapids; the Kunene, on the border of Angola and Namibia, for white water, remoteness, and scenery; and the Tugela, in KwaZulu-Natal, the Usutu, in Swaziland, or the mighty Zambezi, on the border of Zimbabwe and Zambia, for white water.

Climbing

Southern Africa has some of the best rock climbing in the world—a fact hidden from the international climbing fraternity during the many years of isolation during the apartheid era. There are excellent venues all over the region, but Cape Town stands out. With literally hundreds of bolted and natural climbing routes on good-quality sandstone and granite right within the city limits, this is surely one of the most climber-friendly cities in the world.

Cricket

White South Africans are crazy about cricket—during international matches you'll often find crowds gathered in pubs around large-screen televisions. A major push is under way to introduce cricket into black communities, but it remains essentially a white sport.

Cycling

You can do a gentle cycle through the Winelands of the Cape, to the scenic Cape Point, or across the bridge at Victoria Falls, or you can hit any of the great mountain-biking trails all over South Africa. The Argus Cycle Tour, in Cape Town in March, is the biggest individually timed event in the world. It's 108 km (67 mi) long, and contestants number more than 40,000.

Dining

South Africa won't unseat France from its culinary throne anytime soon. But there are four bright spots that you should keep in mind. The first is the abundance of fresh seafood, from plump Knysna oysters to enormous Mozambican prawns to the local lobsters, known as crayfish. The second is the country's love affair with Indian cuisine, first brought to South Africa by indentured laborers in the 19th century. Samosas and curries appear on almost every menu. The third is South Africa's own Cape Malay cuisine, a centuries-old blend of recipes brought by early Dutch settlers and slaves transported from the Dutch East Indies. Most evident in the Cape, the cuisine is characterized by mild, fruity curries and the use of aromatic spices. And last is the ubiquitous *braai*. This is a South African institution of note—and it really is so much more than the average barbecue. As well as meat of all kinds, including the essential *boerewors* (sausages), there is also fish, crayfish tails, spicy *sosaties* (kebabs), *pap en sous* (cornmeal), and the inevitable *potjiekos* (stew). And, of course, no braai is complete without beer.

Fishing

South Africans are among the most avid anglers in the world. During peak holidays the long coastline is lined with surf casters trying for everything from cob to stump nose, rock cod, shad, and blacktail. Fly-fishing is a major draw. There are numerous trout dams and streams in all the high-lying areas, but the indigenous yellow fish is considered a greater challenge. In the Okavango Delta and all along the Zambezi River you can try to bag an aptly named tiger fish—an incredibly strong fighter with jaws like a bear trap. It makes a bass look like a bluegill.

Flora

South Africa's floral wealth is astounding. Many small parks in South Africa support more plant species than the entire North American continent. Nowhere is this blessing of nature more evident than in the Cape, home to the smallest and richest of the world's six floral kingdoms. More than 8,500 species of plants grow in the province, of which 5,000 are endemic. Much of the Cape vegetation consists of *fynbos* (pronounced "*feign*-boss"), hardy, thin-leaved plants ideally suited to the Cape environment. Proteas, including the magnificent king protea, are examples of fynbos. In the Northern Cape's Namaqualand, on the country's west coast, an annual show of spring flowers—including billions of orange Namaqualand daisies—is a spectacular wonder unrivaled anywhere else on earth.

Golf

The success of local heroes like Gary Player, David Frost, and Ernie Els confirms that golf in South Africa has a fervent following. The country has dozens of championship-quality courses, many designed by Gary Player himself. The stretch of coastline extending south from Durban has gone as far as to christen itself the Gold Coast, but it has serious competition from the Garden Route. You can play on almost any course in the country, and greens fees are low compared with those in the United States.

Hiking

Hiking is a major activity in South Africa, and you'll find trails almost everywhere you go. Perhaps the most exciting hikes are the wilderness trails conducted by rangers in Kruger National Park and Hluhluwe-Umfolozi, where you sleep out in the bush and spend the day tracking animals, learning about the ecology, and becoming familiar with the ways of the wild. The country's most popular route is the Otter Trail, a five-day hike that runs along the coast of the Garden Route. Other hikes, ranging in length from a couple of hours to a week, wend through the scenic splendors of the Drakensberg; the Cederberg, in the Cape; and the Mpumalanga and Limpopo Province escarpment and forests.

Rugby

Although long associated with white Afrikaners, rugby became a unifying force in South Africa during the 1995 Rugby World Cup, when South Africa's Springboks beat the New Zealand All Blacks in the final, sparking a nationwide celebration among all races. The audience is still mostly white, but it is changing. Rugby is taken very, very seriously in South Africa and inspires a devotion bordering on religion. In addition to a series of international matches staged each year, the rugby calendar is notable for the Currie Cup, played to decide the best provincial team in the country.

Scuba Diving

Diving in South Africa ranges from the icy kelp forests off Cape Town to the warm, tropical coral reefs of northern Maputaland, in KwaZulu-Natal. There are dive shops, schools, and resorts all along the coast and in Gauteng. The Holy Grail of dives, and not for the faint of heart, is to dive a baitball during the annual sardine run along the Wild Coast.

Soccer

If rugby is what gets white South African men out of bed on a weekend, soccer does the same for their black counterparts. Sure, there is an increasing overlap, but each game is still quite culture specific. And soccer is taken every bit as seriously as rugby.

Surfing

In the cult movie *Endless Summer*, globe-trotting surfers discovered the perfect wave at Cape St. Francis, near Port Elizabeth. South Africa *is* one of the major surfing countries in the world, with South Africans figuring prominently on the professional circuit. Durban is probably the center of wave mania, hosting a series of international competitions each year; other great surfing spots include Jeffrey's Bay and East London. The beaches around Cape Town and up the West Coast (Elands Bay, in particular) are popular, too, although you need a good wet suit to survive the cold water. The Wild Coast has some fantastic surf, but the best beaches are pretty remote. The water off the Namibian coast is freezing, but there are some spectacularly long breaks (of more than half a mile—no kidding).

Wine

Forgotten during the years of international sanctions, South African wines are only now getting the recognition they deserve. Visitors will be delighted by the quality and range of wines available, including pinotage, a uniquely South African blend of pinot noir and cinsault (or cinsaut) grapes (cinsault is known in South Africa as Hermitage). Equally appealing are the low, low prices: Expect to pay no more than $10 for a fantastic bottle of wine and $20 for a superb one. Unfortunately, wine prices are almost doubled in restaurants, but are still pretty reasonable. Although drinking a bottle of good wine is itself a pleasure, driving the wine routes of the Cape, touring cellars, attending tastings, and having picnics on the grounds of pastoral vineyards can't fail to delight the palate.

FODOR'S CHOICE

LODGING

$$$$	**Cape Grace, Cape Town.** On the V&A Waterfront, this hotel combines majestic views with attentive service and a sophisticated atmosphere.
$$$$	**Ellerman House, Bantry Bay.** High on a hill with fabulous sea views, this exclusive hotel built in 1912 is elegant without being too formal.
$$$$	**Le Quartier Français, Franschhoek.** It's hard to decide which is better: the classy Relais & Chateaux guesthouse or the award-winning cuisine of chef Margo Janse.
$$$$	**Mount Nelson Hotel, Cape Town.** This historic hotel has been the place to see and be seen in Cape Town for nearly a century.
$$$$	**Saxon, Johannesburg.** The beautiful grounds, impeccable service, and luxurious rooms here will make you feel that you've found an enchanted oasis.
$$$$	**Sindabezi Island, Livingstone, Zambia.** Your every desire is catered to at this small island getaway affiliated with Tongabezi.
$$$–$$$$	**Victoria Falls Hotel, Zimbabwe.** Since 1904, this has been the grande dame of the falls.
$$$	**Cleopatra Mountain Farmhouse.** This enchanting hideaway is tucked away at the foot of the Drakensberg Range.
$$$	**The Grace, Johannesburg.** Popular with businesspeople, this hotel has old-world style and a convenient location in Rosebank.
$$$	**Long Beach, Kommetjie.** This intimate hotel in a fishing village combines serenity, luxury, and knockout sea views.
$–$$$	**Royal Hotel, Durban.** The classic service at this Durban institution explains why royals have stayed here for years.
$$	**Andries Stockenström Guest House, Graaff-Reinet.** A member of Good Cooks and Their Country Houses, this simple guesthouse features great food in unusual combinations.
$$	**Rocktail Bay Lodge, Maputaland.** With miles of empty beaches, giant turtles, dune forests—nothing but nature as far as the eye can see—this tiny lodge is one of the most special places in the country.

$	**Bitou River Lodge, Plettenberg Bay.** Restful rooms overlook a tranquil garden and quiet, bird-filled river. And at the reasonable bed-and-breakfast rates you can afford to spend a week or two here just chilling.

RESTAURANTS

$$$$	**Livingstone Island Picnic, Zambia.** Savor a delicious buffet lunch perched on the edge of Victoria Falls.
$$$–$$$$	**Bosman's, Paarl.** Superb contemporary cuisine and peerless service make dinner at this elegant Winelands restaurant in the famous Grand Roche Hotel an affair to remember.
$$$–$$$$	**Linger Longer, Johannesburg.** When goose-liver pâté sets you on cloud nine before you even reach main courses of crisped duckling or boned loin of lamb with garlic and mustard, you'll know that, without a doubt, this is Johannesburg's finest.
$$–$$$$	**La Colombe, Cape Town.** The Provençal dining room of the Constantia Uitsig farm and winery is making waves on the Cape Peninsula.
$$	**La Cucina di Ciro, Parkhurst.** Johannesburg's best Italian restaurant combines a warm atmosphere with inventive cuisine.
$$	**Yum, Johannesburg.** Chef Dario De Angeli turns out innovative "new South African cuisine" that's equal to the name.
$–$$	**Reuben's, Franschhoek.** Choose from two menus—classic or contemporary. Either way, chef Reuben Riffel's rule-breaking cuisine satisfies. And since this is the heart of the Winelands, the waiters know their wine.
¢–$	**Jemima's Restaurant, Oudtshoorn.** Enjoy the best of the fruits of Cape farming in this family-run restaurant where the majority of the raw ingredients come from local farms.
¢–$	**Ile de Pain, Knysna.** You may find you can live on bread alone at this restaurant where the seasonally changing menu is bread based—but definitely not your average sandwich.

GAME LODGES

$$$$	**Sanbona Wildlife Reserve.** The first Big Five reserve in the Western Cape, Sanbona combines big and not-so-big game with beautiful flowering vegetation.
$$$$	**Serra Cafema, Namibia.** Along the Skeleton Coast near the border with Angola, this remote camp amid the dunes feels like an oasis.
$$$–$$$$	**Tswalu Kalahari Reserve, Northern Cape.** The location, in the southern Kalahari, gives this lodge an otherworldly feel and appeal. Luxurious accommodations are set amid red dunes and beneath a blue sky.

$$$	**Eagles Cragg, Shamwari Game Reserve.** Conservation-minded Shamwari's best accommodation is this sleek lodge.
$$$	**Ecca Lodge, Kwandwe Private Game Reserve.** Clean, modern lines take the place of animal skins and trophies in this game reserve in the Karoo scrub near Grahamstown.
$$–$$$	**Mala Mala, Mpumalanga.** Retaining that genuine bushveld feel of bygone days, Mala Mala, which adjoins Kruger National Park, is the largest privately owned Big Five game area in South Africa. The animal-viewing is unbeatable.
$$	**Duba Plains, Okavango Delta, Botswana.** This small, intimate camp puts you in the middle of wall-to-wall game in the heart of the delta.
$–$$	**Bushmans Kloof Wilderness Reserve & Retreat, Cederberg.** Typical Cape fauna and flora (including spectacular spring flowers) are almost eclipsed by the fantastic array of rock art. The accommodations are quiet and stylish and the food almost sinful. Absence of dangerous game makes walking and cycling a fantastic alternative to the usual game drives.

FLORA & FAUNA

Kirstenbosch National Botanic Gardens, Cape Town. Plants native to South Africa are on display in all their glory throughout the year in Newlands.

National Zoological Gardens, Tshwane. Nearly 4,300 animals represent much more than just Africa at this zoo, one of the world's best.

Two Oceans Aquarium, Cape Town. Marine life at this V&A Waterfront attraction represents the warm waters of the Indian Ocean and the cold blue of the Atlantic.

WHERE ART COMES FIRST

Owl House, Nieu-Bethesda. The fantastical animal sculptures of Helen Martins are worth a drive to this little hamlet.

South African National Gallery, Cape Town. The gems here are the South African works, many of which reflect the country's traumatic history.

AFTER HOURS

Carfax, Johannesburg. This converted factory is always hopping, from dance events to performance art.

Cinema Nouveau, Johannesburg. A far cry from your average mall multiplex, this is Jo'burg's art-house and foreign-language cinema.

Evita se Perron, Darling. Spend an evening with South Africa's favorite drag queen to learn about South Africa while splitting your sides.

Ninetysix, Johannesburg. It's a lounge. It's a bar. It's a restaurant. And it plays mainly house and jazz.

NATURAL WONDERS

Cape Point and the Cape of Good Hope. These may not be the real southernmost points on the continent, but their drama is unsurpassed.

Cederberg. This Western Cape mountain range is known for its San paintings, bizarre rock formations, and incomparable beauty.

De Hoop Nature Reserve. This huge conservation area has white-sand dunes, mountains, and rare lowland fynbos that are home to eland, bontebok, and Cape mountain zebra.

Mosi-oa-Tunya. You might think Victoria Falls is the most impressive falls in the world, and you'd be right—if you could hear yourself think over the roar of all that water. For a vintage view of the falls, take a ride in an open-cockpit biplane with Tiger Moth Flight of the Angels.

Tsitsikamma National Park & Storms River. The coastal scenery along this stretch of the Garden Route has it all: deep gorges, evergreen forests, tidal pools, and beautiful empty beaches. Explore it by hiking the Dolphin Trail, tubing a river, or sailing through the tree-tops on a zip line with Storms River Adventures.

QUINTESSENTIAL SOUTH AFRICA

A sunset picnic atop Table Mountain, Cape Town. Pack a bottle of chilled Cape wine and good bread and cheese, and take the cable car to the summit, where views stretch forever and the sunset never quits. Warning: This is *extremely* romantic.

Shining light on the shadow of apartheid. Tour the cell where Nelson Mandela was incarcerated on Robben Island (off Cape Town), or explore Johannesburg's Apartheid Museum to learn about the half century of apartheid.

Watching whales on the Cape Coast. From July to November southern right whales make their annual procession up the coast of South Africa. From the cliff-top walkways of Hermanus you look straight down on these graceful behemoths, or get a closer view from a boat in Plettenberg Bay.

A tour of the Winelands. Amid the tastings and cellar tours of the Western Cape's wine routes, Meerlust, near Stellenbosch, is the quintessential Winelands vineyard. In the same family for centuries, it boasts classic Cape Dutch architecture and spectacular wines.

Hunting for rock art. Discovering the rock engravings of native people who lived thousands of years ago can be a spiritual experience at places like Wildebeest Kuil Rock Art Tourism Centre, near Kimberley, and the Kamberg Rock Art Centre in Drakensberg.

Walking in wildflowers in spring, Namaqualand. The "garden of the gods" is an apt epithet for the annual wildflower spectacle, when the drab desert hillsides explode in a rainbow of colors.

Horseback riding on Goukamma Beach. You may feel like you're in a Calvin Klein ad as you ride along this deserted beach with Garden Route Equestrian Adventure Tours.

SMART TRAVEL TIPS

Finding out about your destination before you leave home means you won't squander time organizing everyday minutiae once you've arrived. You'll be more street-wise when you hit the ground as well, better prepared to explore the aspects of South Africa that drew you here in the first place. The organizations in this section can provide information to supplement this guide; contact them for up-to-the-minute news, and consult the A to Z sections in each chapter for facts on the various topics as they relate to the country's many regions. Happy landings!

ADDRESSES

You may have a few problems trying to find your way around South Africa, but it shouldn't be insurmountable. The newest wrinkle is the renaming of place names. Countless cities, towns, streets, parks, and other geographical features have gotten or will get new monikers, both to rid the country of names that recall the apartheid era and to honor the previously unsung.

The names in this book were accurate at time of writing, but even if names are different by the time of your trip, don't worry; all of South Africa will be coping with these large-scale changes and will undoubtedly use both names for some time.

Another problem you may encounter trying to find your way around South African cities is that geographical features, such as streets and town names, are sometimes alternately signposted in English and Afrikaans. So, for example, Wale St. and Waalst. are the same road. Note that the first floor of a building is the one between the ground floor and the second floor. Mailing addresses are pretty straightforward. If they're not a street address, they're either a P.O. Box or a Private Bag—essentially the same, just differing in size. The only vaguely tricky variation is a postnet suite, which consists of a number, followed by a private bag and then a post office (e.g., Postnet Suite 25, Private Bag X25, name of town, postal code). Even the smallest town has its own postal code, and suburbs may have different postal codes—

one for a street address and one for P.O. boxes.

AIR TRAVEL

AIRPORTS

South Africa's major airports are in Johannesburg, Cape Town, and, to a lesser extent, Durban. Most international flights arrive at and depart from Johannesburg International Airport, which lies 19 km (12 mi) from the city. The airport has a tourist information desk, a VAT refund office, and a computerized accommodations service. Several international flights departing from Cape Town are also routed via Johannesburg. Cape Town International is 20 km (12½ mi) southeast of the city, and Durban International is 16 km (10 mi) south of the city. If you are traveling to or from either Johannesburg or Cape Town airport (and, to a lesser extent, Durban) **be very aware of the time of day.** Traffic can be horrendous between 7 and 9 in the morning and between about 3:30 and 6 in the evening, so if you need to be, say, at Cape Town International at 5, it's better to leave at 3 and spend the extra time reading a book at the airport. It's less stressful than spending the same amount of time in traffic. The morning rush hour does not affect Cape Town International as much—but only if you're traveling from the city center. The Cape Town airport is much smaller than Jo'burg's and therefore much easier to get around in, although Jo'burg is quite small by international standards.

The other major cities are served by small airports that are really easy to find your way around in. Most airports are managed by the Airports Company of South Africa.
🛈 International Airports **Airports Company of South Africa** ⊕ www.acsa.co.za. **Cape Town International Airport** (CPT) ☎ 021/937-1200. **Durban International Airport** (DUR) ☎ 031/451-6667. **Johannesburg International Airport** (JNB) ☎ 011/921-6262.
🛈 Domestic Airports **Bloemfontein Airport** (BFN) ☎ 051/433-2662. **East London Airport** (ELS) ☎ 043/706-0304. **George Airport** (GRJ) ☎ 044/876-9310. **Kimberley Airport** (KIM) ☎ 053/838-3216. **Pilanesberg Airport** (NTY, next to Sun City) ☎ 014/552-1261. **Port Elizabeth Airport** (PLZ)

☎ 041/507-7348. **Umtata Airport** (UTT) ☎ 047/536-0023. **Upington Airport** (UTN) ☎ 054/332-2161.
🛈 General Information **Flight information** ☎ 086/727-7888.

BOOKING

When you book, look for nonstop flights and remember that "direct" flights stop at least once. Try to avoid connecting flights, which require a change of plane. Two airlines may operate a connecting flight jointly, so ask whether your airline operates every segment of the trip; you may find that the carrier you prefer flies you only part of the way. To find more booking tips and to check prices and make online flight reservations, log on to www.fodors.com.

CARRIERS

South African Airways (SAA) flies from New York (JFK) to Johannesburg and, at times, from Atlanta to Cape Town, sharing the route with Delta (though this is subject to change). When booking flights, **check the routing carefully,** as some are direct and some involve stopovers of an hour or two, which greatly increase the flying time. The options from Europe include SAA and most European national airlines. SAA, British Airways, and Virgin Atlantic fly nonstop between London and Johannesburg or Cape Town. At time of writing, a good, low-cost airline flying to South Africa was in the offing. Civair is planning to fly between Cape Town and London three times a week each way. You must book online.

Four major domestic airlines and two low-cost, Web-based airlines have flights connecting South Africa's principal airports. SA Airlink and SA Express are subsidiaries of SAA, and Comair is a subsidiary of British Airways. Nationwide is giving the big guys a run for their money, and the two new kids on the block, Kulula.com and 1time, are making waves with low-cost flights. One of the ways they've cut their overhead is by accepting only online bookings.
🛈 International Airlines **Civair** ⊕ www.civair.com. **Delta** ☎ 800/221-2121. **South African Airways** ☎ 800/722-9675. **Virgin Atlantic** ☎ 01293/747-747.

🛪 Domestic Airlines British Airways (operating as Comair) ☎ 011/921-0222 ⊕ www.comair.co.za. **Kulula.com** ⊕ www.kulula.com. **Nationwide** ☎ 011/390-1660 ⊕ www.flynationwide.co.za. **1time** ⊕ www.1time.aero. **South African Airways/SA Airlink/South African Express** ☎ 011/978-1111 ⊕ www.flysaa.com.

CHECK-IN & BOARDING

Always **find out your carrier's check-in policy.** As a rule, you need to get to the airport an hour before a domestic flight and three hours before an international one. In peak season (midsummer and South African school vacations), it's a good idea to give yourself at least a half hour extra for domestic flights, as the check-in lines can be horrendous—particularly on flights to the coast at the start of vacations and back to Johannesburg at the end. To avoid delays at airport-security checkpoints, try not to wear any metal. Jewelry, belt and other buckles, steel-toe shoes, barrettes, and underwire bras are among the items that can set off detectors.

Assuming that not everyone with a ticket will show up, airlines routinely overbook planes. When everyone does, airlines ask for volunteers to give up their seats. In return, these volunteers usually get a several-hundred-dollar flight voucher, which can be used toward the purchase of another ticket, and are rebooked on the next flight out. If there are not enough volunteers, the airline must choose who will be denied boarding. The first to get bumped are passengers who checked in late and those flying on discounted tickets, so get to the gate and check in as early as possible, especially during peak periods.

Always **bring a government-issued photo ID** to the airport; even when it's not required, a passport is best.

CUTTING COSTS

The least expensive airfares to South Africa are priced for round-trip travel and must usually be purchased in advance. Airlines generally allow you to change your return date for a fee; most low-fare tickets, however, are nonrefundable. It's smart to call a number of airlines and check the Internet; when you are quoted a good price,

book it on the spot—the same fare may not be available the next day, or even the next hour. Always check different routings and look into using alternate airports. Also, price off-peak flights, which may be significantly less expensive than others. Travel agents, especially low-fare specialists (⇨ Discounts & Deals), are helpful.

Consolidators are another good source. They buy tickets for scheduled flights at reduced rates from the airlines, then sell them at prices that beat the best fare available directly from the airlines. (Many also offer reduced car-rental and hotel rates.) Sometimes you can even get your money back if you need to return the ticket. Carefully read the fine print detailing penalties for changes and cancellations, purchase the ticket with a credit card, and confirm your consolidator reservation with the airline.

Many airlines, singly or in collaboration, offer discount air passes that allow foreigners to travel economically in a particular country or region. These visitor passes usually must be reserved and purchased before you leave home. Information about passes often can be found on most airlines' international Web pages, which tend to be aimed at travelers from outside the carrier's home country. Also, try typing the name of the pass into a search engine, or search for "pass" within the carrier's Web site.

🛪 Consolidators AirlineConsolidator.com ☎ 888/468-5385 ⊕ www.airlineconsolidator.com; for international tickets. **Best Fares** ☎ 800/880-1234 or 800/576-8255 ⊕ www.bestfares.com; $59.90 annual membership. **Cheap Tickets** ☎ 800/377-1000 or 800/652-4327 ⊕ www.cheaptickets.com. **Expedia** ☎ 800/397-3342 or 404/728-8787 ⊕ www.expedia.com. **Hotwire** ☎ 866/468-9473 or 920/330-9418 ⊕ www.hotwire.com. **Now Voyager Travel** ✉ 45 W. 21st St., Suite 5A, New York, NY 10010 ☎ 212/459-1616 🖷 212/243-2711 ⊕ www.nowvoyagertravel.com. **Onetravel.com** ⊕ www.onetravel.com. **Orbitz** ☎ 888/656-4546 ⊕ www.orbitz.com. **Priceline.com** ⊕ www.priceline.com. **Travelocity** ☎ 888/709-5983, 877/282-2925 in Canada, 0870/876-3876 in U.K. ⊕ www.travelocity.com.

ENJOYING THE FLIGHT

State your seat preference when purchasing your ticket, and then repeat it when you confirm and when you check in. For more legroom, you can request one of the few emergency-aisle seats at check-in, if you're capable of moving obstacles comparable in weight to an airplane exit door (usually between 35 pounds and 60 pounds)—a Federal Aviation Administration requirement of passengers in these seats. Seats behind a bulkhead also offer more legroom, but they don't have underseat storage. Don't sit in the row in front of the emergency aisle or in front of a bulkhead, where seats may not recline.

Ask the airline whether a snack or meal is served on the flight. If you have dietary concerns, request special meals when booking. These can be vegetarian, low-cholesterol, or kosher, for example. It's a good idea to pack some healthful snacks and a small (plastic) bottle of water in your carry-on bag. On long flights, try to maintain a normal routine, to help fight jet lag. At night, get some sleep. By day, eat light meals, drink water (not alcohol), and **move around the cabin** to stretch your legs. For additional jet-lag tips consult *Fodor's FYI: Travel Fit & Healthy* (available at bookstores everywhere).

Smoking policies vary from carrier to carrier. Many airlines prohibit smoking on all their flights; others allow smoking only on certain routes or certain departures. Ask your carrier about its policy. All domestic flights within South Africa are no-smoking—the longest is only two hours—and all airports are smoke-free except for designated smoking areas.

FLYING TIMES

When booking flights, **check the routing carefully.** Flights from New York to Johannesburg take approximately 15 hours direct or 17½ hours via Lagos. Atlanta to Cape Town is 15 hours direct or 18½ hours via Ilha do Sal, with a connection to Johannesburg. Atlanta to Johannesburg is 15½ hours direct, with a connection to Cape Town. The flying time between Johannesburg and Cape Town is two hours. From London the flying time is about 11 hours to Johannesburg and 11½ hours to Cape Town direct. The return flights are about a half hour longer.

HOW TO COMPLAIN

If your baggage goes astray or your flight goes awry, complain right away. Most carriers require that you **file a claim immediately.** The Aviation Consumer Protection Division of the Department of Transportation publishes *Fly-Rights,* which discusses airlines and consumer issues and is available online. You can also find articles and information on mytravelrights.com, the Web site of the nonprofit Consumer Travel Rights Center.

7 Airline Complaints Aviation Consumer Protection Division ⊠ U.S. Department of Transportation, Office of Aviation Enforcement and Proceedings, C-75, Room 4107, 400 7th St. SW, Washington, DC 20590 ☎ 202/366-2220 ⊕ airconsumer.ost.dot.gov. **Federal Aviation Administration Consumer Hotline** ⊠ For inquiries: FAA, 800 Independence Ave. SW, Washington, DC 20591 ☎ 800/322-7873 ⊕ www.faa.gov.

RECONFIRMING

Check the status of your flight before you leave for the airport. You can do this on your carrier's Web site, by linking to a flight-status checker (many Web booking services offer these), or by calling your carrier or travel agent. Always confirm international flights at least 72 hours ahead of the scheduled departure time. It is not necessary to reconfirm domestic flights if you have a confirmed booking—but, hey, it's always a good idea.

BIKE TRAVEL

Keen off-roaders will discover some fantastic mountain-bike trails in South Africa, with the Garden Route the mecca of MTB (mountain biking) in SA. You can rent mountain bikes in the major cities and near most of the good cycling spots. Bike rental usually runs R100–R150 per day. If you're short, you might want to consider bringing your own bike, as it's almost impossible to find a rental smaller than 15 inches. Bike touring is becoming more popular, but **stay off the main highways,** such as the N2, because slow vehicles—often huge trucks—have the habit of driving on the shoulder. There are some great dirt roads and off-road routes in most parts of the country—particularly the Garden Route and Mpumalanga. If you're even halfway interested in cycling, you should **consider getting to Cape Town for the Argus Cycle Tour** in early March. One of the most scenic road races in the world, it's also the largest individually timed sporting event in the world. More than 30,000 cyclists take over the streets of Cape Town for the day. Check out ⊕ www.cycletour.co.za.

BIKES IN FLIGHT

Most airlines accommodate bikes as luggage, provided they are dismantled and boxed; check with individual airlines about packing requirements. Some airlines sell bike boxes, which are often free at bike shops, for about $20 (bike bags can be considerably more expensive). International travelers often can substitute a bike for a piece of checked luggage at no charge; otherwise, the cost is about $100. Most U.S. and Canadian airlines charge $40–$80 each way.

BUSINESS HOURS

BANKS & OFFICES

Business hours in major South African cities are quite standard: weekdays from about 9 to 5. Most banks close in midafternoon, usually about 3, but dedicated currency exchange offices usually stay open longer. In addition, post offices and banks are open on Saturday morning from about 9 to noon. In rural areas and small towns things are less rigid. Post offices often close for lunch, and, in very small towns and villages banks may have very abbreviated hours.

GAS STATIONS

Almost all gas stations are open 24 hours.

MUSEUMS

Most museums are open during usual business hours, including Saturday mornings, but some stay open longer.

PHARMACIES

Most pharmacies close about 6, but there is generally an all-night pharmacy in towns of a reasonable size. If not, look for an emergency number posted on a pharmacy.

SHOPS

Most shops stick to standard business hours, including Saturday morning, but there are many, including some malls, that are open until 9 or 10 and on Sunday. It is very unusual for shops to close for lunch— the exception being Muslim-run stores, which close for prayers on Friday. All urban gas stations have 24-hour convenience stores, some of which have an impressive range of goods.

BUS TRAVEL

Greyhound, Intercape Mainliner, and Translux operate extensive bus networks that serve all major cities. The buses are comfortable, sometimes there are videos, and tea and coffee are served on board. Distances are long; for example, Cape Town to Johannesburg takes 19 hours. Johannesburg to Durban, at about seven hours, is less stressful. The Garden Route is less intense if you take it in stages, but the whole trip from Cape Town to Port Elizabeth takes 12 hours. Buses are usually pretty punctual. Greyhound and Intercape buses can be booked directly or through Computicket.

For travelers with a sense of adventure, a bit of time, and not too much money, the Baz Bus runs a daily hop-on/hop-off door-to-door service between backpackers' hostels around South Africa and other countries in the region. The rates are a bit higher than for the same distance on a standard bus, but you can break the journey up into a number of different legs, days or weeks apart, and the bus drops you off at the hostels so you don't need to find taxis, shuttles, or lifts. Tickets and reservations can be arranged directly or through almost any backpackers' hostel.

It is illegal to smoke on buses in South Africa.

🚌 **Bus Information Baz Bus** ☎ 021/439-2323 ⊕ www.bazbus.com. **Computicket** ☎ 083/909-0909 ⊕ www.computicket.co.za. **Greyhound** ☎ 011/276-8500 or 083/915-9000 ⊕ www.greyhound.co.za. **Intercape Mainliner** ☎ 021/380-4400 ⊕ www.intercape.co.za. **Translux** ☎ 0861/589-282 ⊕ www.translux.co.za.

CUTTING COSTS

The Baz Bus offers a 7-day package for R850 and a 14-day package for R1,600. Each allows unrestricted travel; you can change direction as many times as you want and travel as far as you want. It's especially useful if you're planning a long leg followed by a few short ones before returning to your starting point.

FARES & SCHEDULES

Approximate one-way prices for all three major bus lines are R450–R500 Cape Town to Tshwane, R230–R260 Cape Town to Springbok, R120–R150 Cape Town to George, R240–R260 Cape Town to Port Elizabeth, R150–R170 Johannesburg to Durban, and R460–R500 Cape Town to Durban. Baz Bus fares are higher but include intermediate stops: R1,600 Cape Town to Durban, R320 Durban to Johannesburg via the Drakensberg or R735 via Zululand and Swaziland. A loop between Johannesburg and Durban, doing both routes, costs R1,010. Shorter distances are proportionally cheaper.

CAMERAS & PHOTOGRAPHY

Use your common sense when taking photographs. Like anywhere else in the world, you may just get into trouble if you start photographing military installations. When photographing people, **be sensitive** to their moods, and ask if you're not sure. The *Kodak Guide to Shooting Great Travel Pictures* (available at bookstores everywhere) is loaded with tips.

FILM & DEVELOPING

There are camera shops and one-hour photo labs in even the smallest towns in South Africa. For properly stored professional film and high-quality processing of transparency film, the best options are listed below.

🎞 **Film & Developing ORMS Professional Photo Warehouse** ✉ Roeland Sq., Roeland St., Cape Town ☎ 021/465-3574. **Kameraz** ✉ Rosebank Mews, Rosebank, Johannesburg ☎ 011/880-2885 ⊕ www.kameraz.co.za.

🎞 **Photo Help Kodak Information Center** ☎ 800/242-2424 ⊕ www.kodak.com.

EQUIPMENT PRECAUTIONS

Don't pack film or equipment in checked luggage, where it is much more susceptible to damage. X-ray machines used to view checked luggage are extremely powerful and therefore are likely to ruin your film. Try to ask for hand inspection of film, which becomes clouded after repeated exposure to airport X-ray machines, and keep videotapes and computer disks away from metal detectors. Always keep film, tape, and computer disks out of the sun, and try to protect your equipment from dust. Carry extra batteries, especially if you're traveling to a spot where recharging batteries might prove difficult. Be prepared to turn on your camera, camcorder, or laptop to prove to airport security personnel that the device is real.

VIDEOS

The South African standard for videotape is PAL.

CAR RENTAL

Rates in South Africa begin at about R210 per day for unlimited mileage or a slightly cheaper rate for 200 km (125 mi) per day and about R1.50 for each additional kilometer. These prices are for an economy car with a 1,300-cc engine, no air-conditioning, and a stick shift. For a car with automatic transmission and a/c, you'll pay around R400 per day for unlimited kilometers and slightly less for 200 km per day plus about R3.50 per extra kilometer. When comparing prices, make sure you're getting the same thing. Some companies quote prices with no insurance, some include 80% or 90% coverage, and some quote with 100% protection.

Maui Camper Hire rents out fully equipped camper vans and four-wheel-drive vehicles, which can be totally equipped for a bush sojourn. Prices for both start at around R1,000 per day, not including insurance, which comes in at about R220–R300 per day, depending on the vehicle. The above price includes 200 km per day—additional mileage costs R3 per kilometer (about R4.50 per mile). Car rental prices include VAT and usually include 80% coverage.

You can opt for 100% coverage, which will naturally cost more.

🚗 **Local Agency Maui Camper Hire** ☎ 011/396-1445 or 021/982-5107 🌐 www.maui.co.za.

🚗 **Major Agencies Alamo** ☎ 800/522-9696 🌐 www.alamo.com. **Avis** ☎ 800/331-1084, 800/879-2847 in Canada, 0870/606-0100 in U.K., 02/9353-9000 in Australia, 09/526-2847 in New Zealand 🌐 www.avis.com. **Budget** ☎ 800/527-0700, 0870/156-5656 in U.K. 🌐 www.budget.com. **Dollar** ☎ 800/800-6000, 0800/085-4578 in U.K. 🌐 www.dollar.com. **Hertz** ☎ 800/654-3001, 800/263-0600 in Canada, 0870/844-8844 in U.K., 02/9669-2444 in Australia, 09/256-8690 in New Zealand 🌐 www.hertz.com. **National Car Rental** ☎ 800/227-7368, 0870/600-6666 in U.K. 🌐 www.nationalcar.com.

CUTTING COSTS

You can often save some money by booking a car through a broker, who will access the car from one of the main agencies. Smaller, local agencies often give a much better price but the car must be returned in the same city. This is pretty popular in Cape Town but not so much in other centers.

For a good deal, book through a travel agent who will shop around. Do look into wholesalers, companies that do not own fleets but rent in bulk from those that do and often offer better rates than traditional car-rental operations. Prices are best during off-peak periods. Rentals booked through wholesalers often must be paid for before you leave home.

🚗 **Auto Europe** ☎ 207/842-2000 or 800/223-5555 🖨 207/842-2222 🌐 www.autoeurope.com. **Car Mania** ☎ 021/447-3001 or 083/261-9834 🌐 www.carmania.co.za. **Felix Unite Vehicle Rental** ☎ 021/674-0420 🖨 021/683-6485 🌐 www.felixunite.com. **Value Car Hire** ☎ 021/696-2298 🌐 www.valuecarhire.co.za.

INSURANCE

When driving a rented car you are generally responsible for any damage to or loss of the vehicle. You also may be liable for any property damage or personal injury that you may cause while driving. Before you rent, see what coverage you already have under the terms of your personal auto-insurance policy and credit cards.

REQUIREMENTS & RESTRICTIONS

In order to rent a car you need to be 23 years or older and have held a driver's license for three years. You need to get special permission to take rental cars into neighboring countries, such as Lesotho, Swaziland, Namibia, or Botswana. You will not be allowed to take rental cars into Zimbabwe.

SURCHARGES

Before you pick up a car in one city and leave it in another, ask about drop-off charges or one-way service fees, which can be substantial. Also inquire about early-return policies; some rental agencies charge extra if you return the car before the time specified in your contract, and others give you a refund for the days not used. To avoid a hefty refueling fee, fill the tank just before you turn in the car, but be aware that gas stations near the rental outlet may overcharge. It's almost never a deal to buy the tank of gas that's in the car when you rent it; the understanding is that you'll return it empty, but some fuel usually remains. There is no charge for additional drivers, but they must be listed on the rental agreement; otherwise they won't be covered by insurance.

CAR TRAVEL

The first thing you will have to remember is that South Africans **drive on the left-hand side of the road.** That may be confusing at first, but having the steering wheel on the right might help to remind you that the driver should be closer to the middle of the road. The most dangerous maneuver is turning onto an empty road. You'll almost certainly veer to the right and stay there until you see a car coming toward you.

Although uncommon, carjackings can occur (⇨ Safety). South Africa has a superb network of multilane roads and highways, so driving can be a pleasure. Remember, though, that distances are vast, so guard against fatigue, which is an even bigger killer than alcohol. Toll roads, scattered among the main routes, charge anything from R10 to R60.

In South African parlance, traffic lights are known as "robots," and what people refer to as the "pavement" is actually the sidewalk. Paved roads are just called roads.

You can drive in South Africa for six months on any English-language license; otherwise you need an international license.

AUTO CLUBS

The Automobile Association (AA) of South Africa extends privileges to members of the American Automobile Association in the United States and the Automobile Association in Britain. Contact a local office in your home country for more information.

◪ In South Africa **Automobile Association of South Africa** ☎ 011/799-1000 in Johannesburg, 021/419-6914 in Cape Town, 031/201-5244 in Durban, 0800/01-0101 24-hr toll-free emergency ⊕ www.aa.co.za.

EMERGENCY SERVICES

If you have an accident or break down, call the AA and/or the car-rental agency. In the case of an accident you should also call the police and—perhaps—an ambulance. (From mobile phones you can call one number for police and ambulance.) If you are involved in a fender bender where no one is hurt, don't block traffic. Move the cars to the side of the road, and exchange contact details with the other driver. Then phone the rental company and **report the accident to a police station within 24 hrs.** If you break down at night in a scary or lonely place, call the AA, tell them you are alone and in an unsafe place, and then **walk away from the vehicle**—not far, just a few hundred yards, preferably off into the bush on the side of the road, where you can't be seen. Wait there until the AA arrives—recognizable by the flashing orange light—and then walk back to your car. When you get your rental car, the agency will give you a detailed outline of what to do in an emergency. Read it.

◪ **Automobile Association** ☎ 0800/01-0101. **General emergency number** ☎ 112 from mobile phone, 10111 from landline.

GASOLINE

Huge 24-hour service stations are positioned at regular intervals along all major highways in South Africa. There are no self-service stations; attendants pump the gas, check the oil and water, and wash the windows. In return, **tip the attendant R2–R3.** South Africa has a choice of unleaded or leaded gasoline, and many vehicles operate on diesel—be sure you get the right fuel. Older vehicles run on leaded fuel. Check when booking a rental car as to what fuel to use. Gasoline is measured in liters, and the cost works out to about R20 a gallon. When driving long distances, check your routing carefully, as the distances between towns—and hence gas stations—can be as much as 200 km (120 mi). It's better to fill a half-full tank than to try to squeeze the last drop out of an unfamiliar rental car.

PARKING

In the countryside parking is mostly free, but you will almost certainly need to pay for parking in cities. Coin-operated parking meters are rapidly being phased out, and exist in only a few places. Cape Town was the first city to implement rechargeable smart-card parking meters. You can buy the cards from convenience stores or traffic wardens on the street, both of whom can also recharge them for you. Some towns (e.g., Grahamstown in the Eastern Cape) have "human parking meters." An attendant notes the number of your parking spot and logs it in when you park. When you return, the attendant shows you an electronic readout detailing the amount due. At Pay and Display parking lots you pay in advance. Some parking garages expect payment at the exit, whereas others require that you pay for your parking before you return to your car, and your receipt allows you to exit. Just read the signs carefully. In most cities you will find official parking guards, who usually wear brightly colored bibs or T-shirts. They do not get paid much (in fact some pay for the privilege of working a spot) so they depend on tips. You'll get the most out of these guys if you acknowledge them when you park, ask them politely to look after your car, and then pay them a couple of rand when you return and find it is safe.

ROAD CONDITIONS

South African roads are mostly excellent, but South African drivers tend to be aggressive and reckless, thinking nothing of tailgating at high speeds and passing on blind rises. During national holidays the body count from highway collisions is staggering. The problem is compounded by widespread drunk driving.

If it's safe to do so, it's courteous for slow vehicles to **move over onto the shoulder,** which is separated from the road by a solid yellow line. (In built-up areas, however, road shoulders are occasionally marked by red lines. This is a strict "no-stopping" zone.) The more aggressive drivers expect this and will flash their lights at you if you don't. If a slower vehicle pulls onto the shoulder to allow you to pass, it's polite to flash your hazard lights a couple of times in thanks, and they'll flash their brights in acknowledgment. Where there are two lanes in each direction, **remember that the right-hand lane is for passing.** If you're not concentrating, you might end up dawdling along in the right lane, annoying faster drivers.

It's dangerous to drive at night in some rural areas, as roads are not always fenced and domestic or wild animals often stray onto the road. In very remote areas only the main road might be paved, whereas many secondary roads are of high-quality gravel. Traffic is often light in these areas, so be sure to **bring extra water and carry a spare, a jack, and a tire iron** (your rental car should come with these).

In towns, minibus taxis can be quite unnerving, swerving in and out of traffic without warning to pick up customers. Stay alert at all times, and **expect the unexpected.** Many cities use mini traffic circles that look like giant fried eggs in lieu of four-way stops. These can be dangerous, particularly if you're not used to them. In theory, the first vehicle to the circle has the right-of-way; otherwise yield to the right. In practice, keep your wits about you at all times. In most cities traffic lights are on poles at the side of the street. In Johannesburg the lights are only on the far side of each intersection, so don't stop in front of the light or you'll be in the middle of the intersection.

ROAD MAPS

Europcar supplies a good-quality map book with car rentals, whereas the other rental companies will supply you with whatever maps you ask for. You can buy really good map books from bookstores (the Map Studio series is particularly well known), and the AA (⇨ Auto Clubs) sells probably the best range of maps. Most of the fuel companies sell road maps (usually Map Studio ones with their imprint) at their stations. When buying a map book, flip through to make sure it covers the areas you want to explore in sufficient detail. Some map books include strip maps of major routes. These are particularly handy if you are planning long-distance trips.

RULES OF THE ROAD

The speed limit is 100 kmh (60 mph) or 120 kmh (about 75 mph) on the open road and usually 60 kmh (35 mph) or 80 kmh (about 50 mph) in towns. Of course, many people drive far faster than that. Wearing seat belts is required by law, and the legal blood-alcohol limit is 0.08 mg/100 ml. It is illegal to talk on a hand-held mobile phone while driving.

But the most important thing for Americans and Canadians to remember is to **drive left, and look right.**

CHILDREN IN SOUTH AFRICA

Cape Town, the Garden Route, the Wild Coast, and the KZN South Coast are great family vacation destinations. The hotels of the Wild Coast, particularly, cater to the needs of little ones—as well as the needs of people who don't necessarily want other people's little ones underfoot. Although some private game reserves are very child-friendly, most aren't, but the national parks and provincial reserves are very family-oriented. In addition, Future Nature offers children's nature programs, including safari opportunities. Depending on the ages of your children, you may want to avoid malarial areas, so stick to the Eastern Cape, Western Cape, Northern Cape, and Waterberg parks.

Distances in South Africa are long, so make sure you bring plenty of games, non-messy snacks, and comforting toys. The large fuel complexes on the highway have restaurants with children's menus, and some have small playgrounds where your little angels can let off steam for a while.

If you are renting a car, don't forget to **arrange for a car seat** when you reserve. For general advice about traveling with children, consult *Fodor's FYI: Travel with Your Baby* (available in bookstores everywhere).

🎫 Children's Program **Future Nature** 📦 Box 4752, Rivonia 2128 ☎ 083/308-0757 ✉ info@future-nature.com ⊕ www.future-nature.com.

FLYING

If your children are two or older, ask about children's airfares. As a general rule, infants under two not occupying a seat fly at greatly reduced fares or even for free. But if you want to guarantee a seat for an infant, you have to pay full fare. Consider flying during off-peak days and times; most airlines will grant an infant a seat without a ticket if there are available seats. When booking, confirm carry-on allowances if you're traveling with infants. In general, for babies charged 10% to 50% of the adult fare you are allowed one carry-on bag and a collapsible stroller; if the flight is full, the stroller may have to be checked or you may be limited to less.

Experts agree that it's a good idea to use safety seats aloft for children weighing less than 40 pounds. Airlines set their own policies: if you use a safety seat, U.S. carriers usually require that the child be ticketed, even if he or she is young enough to ride free, because the seats must be strapped into regular seats. It may be worth paying the full adult fare for the seat, especially on longer trips. Do **check your airline's policy about using safety seats during takeoff and landing.** Safety seats are not allowed everywhere in the plane, so get your seat assignments as early as possible.

When reserving, request children's meals or a freestanding bassinet (not available at all airlines) if you need them. But note that bulkhead seats, where you must sit to use the bassinet, may lack an overhead bin or storage space on the floor.

Young children often cry as the plane descends because of the pain in their ears. Getting them to suck in (giving them a bottle, tapping them on the chest) often opens up their eustachian tubes and eases the pain.

FOOD

If your children are used to eating fast food, they'll find plenty of familiar fare in South Africa, ranging from homegrown chains like Wimpy to McDonald's. Of course there's plenty of other local food to explore, much of which traveling children should like.

LODGING

Many of southern Africa's luxury lodges and private game reserves do not accept children under 10 or 12 without prior arrangement, and many other hotels require children to eat dinner at a separate, earlier seating. Some hotels and lodges allow children under a certain age to stay in their parents' room at no extra charge, or at a discount. Be sure to **find out the cutoff age for children's discounts.** Many hotels have family suites, priced differently from standard rooms. Many of the coastal hotels are particularly geared for children. In almost every case, children who occupy a separate room will pay an adult rate.

PRECAUTIONS

If you have young children, are pregnant, or are trying to conceive, stay away from malarial areas, especially the far northeast of the country, including Kruger National Park. There are excellent malaria-free game reserves and national parks in the Eastern Cape, the Northern Cape, and the Waterberg. Try hard to **keep children out of the sun around midday,** smear them with sunscreen, and beg, bribe, or bully them into wearing hats. The sun is fierce in the Southern Hemisphere.

SIGHTS & ATTRACTIONS

Places that are especially appealing to children are indicated by a rubber-duckie icon (🦆) in the margin.

SUPPLIES & EQUIPMENT

South Africa has a first-world infrastructure, enabling you to buy almost anything you need in cities and towns. If you are heading off the beaten track, stock up on essential items. Powdered infant formula and a whole range of diapers are available in supermarkets, pharmacies, and convenience stores. Expect to pay between R1.50 and R3 per diaper, depending on brand and package size. You can mix formula with bottled water or, except in very isolated areas, tap water. It is advisable, but not essential, to filter water, as all urban tap water contains chemicals but is free of harmful organisms.

COMPUTERS ON THE ROAD

You will have absolutely no problem getting service for your computer in the cities. In the smaller towns you will usually find a computer store, but it's unlikely you'll find anyone to service a Mac. It's worth bringing a long phone cord, as some hotels have only one phone jack—right next to the bed. Many Internet cafés allow you to just plug into their phone line or, in some cases, their network. **Back up all your data before leaving home.**

CONSUMER PROTECTION

Whether you're shopping for gifts or purchasing travel services, **pay with a major credit card** whenever possible, so you can cancel payment or get reimbursed if there's a problem (and you can provide documentation). If you're doing business with a particular company for the first time, contact your local Better Business Bureau and the attorney general's offices in your state and (for U.S. businesses) the company's home state as well. Have any complaints been filed? Finally, if you're buying a package or tour, always consider travel insurance that includes default coverage (⇨ Insurance).

🔳 BBBs **Council of Better Business Bureaus** ✉ 4200 Wilson Blvd., Suite 800, Arlington, VA 22203 ☎ 703/276-0100 🖷 703/525-8277 ⊕ www.bbb.org.

CUSTOMS & DUTIES

When shopping abroad, keep receipts for all purchases. Upon reentering the country, **be ready to show customs officials what you've bought.** Pack purchases together in an easily accessible place. If you think a duty is incorrect, appeal the assessment. If you object to the way your clearance was handled, note the inspector's badge number. In either case, first ask to see a supervisor. If the problem isn't resolved, write to the appropriate authorities, beginning with the port director at your point of entry.

IN AUSTRALIA

Australian residents who are 18 or older may bring home A$400 worth of souvenirs and gifts (including jewelry), 250 cigarettes or 250 grams of cigars or other tobacco products, and 1,125 ml of alcohol (including wine, beer, and spirits). Residents under 18 may bring back A$200 worth of goods. Members of the same family traveling together may pool their allowances. Prohibited items include meat products. Seeds, plants, and fruits need to be declared upon arrival.

🔳 **Australian Customs Service** 🖉 Regional Director, Box 8, Sydney, NSW 2001 ☎ 02/9213-2000 or 1300/363263, 02/9364-7222 or 1800/020-504 quarantine-inquiry line 🖷 02/9213-4043 ⊕ www.customs.gov.au.

IN CANADA

Canadian residents who have been out of Canada for at least seven days may bring in C$750 worth of goods duty-free. If you've been away fewer than seven days but more than 48 hours, the duty-free allowance drops to C$200. If your trip lasts 24 to 48 hours, the allowance is C$50. You may not pool allowances with family members. Goods claimed under the C$750 exemption may follow you by mail; those claimed under the lesser exemptions must accompany you. Alcohol and tobacco products may be included in the seven-day and 48-hour exemptions but not in the 24-hour exemption. If you meet the age requirements of the province or territory through which you reenter Canada, you may bring in, duty-free, 1.5 liters of wine *or* 1.14 liters (40 imperial ounces) of liquor *or* 24 12-ounce cans or bottles of beer or ale. Also, if you meet the local age requirement for tobacco products, you may bring in, duty-free, 200 cigarettes and 50 cigars. Check ahead of time with the Canada Customs and Revenue Agency or the Department of Agriculture for policies regarding meat products, seeds, plants, and fruits.

You may send an unlimited number of gifts (only one gift per recipient, however) worth up to C$60 each duty-free to Canada. Label the package UNSOLICITED GIFT—VALUE UNDER $60. Alcohol and tobacco are excluded.

⛵ Canada Customs and Revenue Agency ✉ 2265 St. Laurent Blvd., Ottawa, Ontario K1G 4K3 ☎ 800/461-9999 in Canada, 204/983-3500, 506/636-5064 ⊕ www.ccra.gc.ca.

IN NEW ZEALAND

All homeward-bound residents may bring back NZ$700 worth of souvenirs and gifts; passengers may not pool their allowances, and children can claim only the concession on goods intended for their own use. For those 17 or older, the duty-free allowance also includes 4.5 liters of wine or beer; one 1,125-ml bottle of spirits; and either 200 cigarettes, 250 grams of tobacco, 50 cigars, *or* a combination of the three up to 250 grams. Meat products, seeds, plants, and fruits must be declared upon arrival to the Agricultural Services Department.

⛵ New Zealand Customs ✉ Head office: The Customhouse, 17–21 Whitmore St., Box 2218, Wellington ☎ 09/300-5399 or 0800/428-786 ⊕ www.customs.govt.nz.

IN SOUTH AFRICA

Visitors may bring in new or used gifts and souvenirs up to a total value of R3,000 duty-free. For additional goods (new or used) up to a value of R12,000, a fee of 20% is levied. In addition, each person may bring up to 200 cigarettes, 20 cigars, 250 grams of tobacco, 2 liters of wine, 1 liter of other alcoholic beverages, 50 ml of perfume, and 250 ml of toilet water into South Africa or other Southern Africa Common Customs Union (SACU) countries (Botswana, Lesotho, Namibia, and Swaziland). The tobacco and alcohol allowance applies only to people 18 and over. If you enter a SACU country from or through an-

other in the union, you are not liable for any duties. You will, however, need to complete a form listing items imported.

If you buy animal products to take home, including skins or legally culled ivory, make sure you get the requisite documentation from the seller.

⛵ South African Department of Foreign Affairs ⊕ www.dfa.gov.za/foreign/Multilateral/africa/sacu.htm.

IN THE U.K.

From countries outside the European Union, including South Africa, you may bring home, duty-free, 200 cigarettes, 50 cigars, 100 cigarillos, or 250 grams of tobacco; 1 liter of spirits or 2 liters of fortified or sparkling wine or liqueurs; 2 liters of still table wine; 60 ml of perfume; 250 ml of toilet water; plus £145 worth of other goods, including gifts and souvenirs. Prohibited items include meat and dairy products, seeds, plants, and fruits.

⛵ HM Customs and Excise ✉ Portcullis House, 21 Cowbridge Rd. E, Cardiff CF11 9SS ☎ 0845/010-9000 or 0208/929-0152 advice service, 0208/929-6731 or 0208/910-3602 complaints ⊕ www.hmce.gov.uk.

IN THE U.S.

U.S. residents who have been out of the country for at least 48 hours may bring home, for personal use, $800 worth of foreign goods duty-free, as long as they haven't used the $800 allowance or any part of it in the past 30 days. This exemption may include 1 liter of alcohol (for travelers 21 and older), 200 cigarettes, and 100 non-Cuban cigars. Family members from the same household who are traveling together may pool their $800 personal exemptions. For fewer than 48 hours, the duty-free allowance drops to $200, which may include 50 cigarettes, 10 non-Cuban cigars, and 150 ml of alcohol (or 150 ml of perfume containing alcohol). The $200 allowance cannot be combined with other individuals' exemptions, and if you exceed it, the full value of all the goods will be taxed. Antiques, which U.S. Customs and Border Protection defines as objects more than 100 years old, enter duty-free, as do original works of art done entirely by hand, including paintings, drawings, and sculptures. This doesn't apply to folk art or handicrafts, which are in general dutiable.

You may also send packages home duty-free, with a limit of one parcel per addressee per day (except alcohol or tobacco products or perfume worth more than $5). You can mail up to $200 worth of goods for personal use; label the package PERSONAL USE and attach a list of its contents and their retail value. If the package contains your used personal belongings, mark it AMERICAN GOODS RETURNED to avoid paying duties. You may send up to $100 worth of goods as a gift; mark the package UNSOLICITED GIFT. Mailed items do not affect your duty-free allowance on your return.

To avoid paying duty on foreign-made high-ticket items you already own and will take on your trip, register them with Customs before you leave the country. Consider filing a Certificate of Registration for laptops, cameras, watches, and other digital devices identified with serial numbers or other permanent markings; you can keep the certificate for other trips. Otherwise, bring a sales receipt or insurance form to show that you owned the item before you left the United States.

For more about duties, restricted items, and other information about international travel, check out U.S. Customs and Border Protection's online brochure, *Know Before You Go.*

🏢 **U.S. Customs and Border Protection** ✉ For inquiries and equipment registration, 1300 Pennsylvania Ave. NW, Washington, DC 20229 🌐 www.cbp.gov ☎ 877/287-8667, 202/354-1000 ✉ For complaints, Customer Satisfaction Unit, 1300 Pennsylvania Ave. NW, Room 5.2C, Washington, DC 20229.

DISABILITIES & ACCESSIBILITY

South Africa is slowly adding facilities for travelers with disabilities, but standards vary widely from place to place. Some interesting examples include Port Elizabeth, the first city to be proactive about making its beaches accessible to people with limited mobility, and the bungee jump at the Bloukrans River, the highest bungee jump in the world, which was designed to be wheelchair accessible. Many national parks

and nature reserves have touch trails or scent trails with Braille interpretive plaques.

Eco Access has information about accessible facilities for game lodges and outdoor activities in southern Africa. Flamingo Tours, based in South Africa, specializes in customized tours for people with disabilities and can arrange for rental cars with hand controls for self-driving tours.

Most restrooms—but not all—have facilities for people in wheelchairs. All shopping malls and highway gas stations should have accessible stalls. City sidewalks can be problematic, as they'll be fine for a while and then you'll find a high curb. It's a work in progress. Most public buildings have ramps. Many supermarkets have register lanes displaying a wheelchair logo, which are wider.

🏢 **Disability Help-Line** ☎ 082/290-3764 or 041/368-3707 ✉ barndans@yebo.co.za. **Eco Access** ☎ 011/477-3676 🌐 www.eco-access.org. **Flamingo Tours** ☎ 021/557-4496, 082/450-2031, 082/920-0901 🖶 021/556-5853 🌐 www.flamingotours.co.za.

LODGING

Many large chains now offer one or more rooms in their hotels specially adapted for travelers with disabilities, and most national parks have at least one chalet for people in wheelchairs.

When discussing accessibility with an operator or reservations agent, ask hard questions. Are there any stairs, inside *or* out? Are there grab bars next to the toilet *and* in the shower/tub? How wide is the doorway to the room? To the bathroom? For the most extensive facilities meeting the latest legal specifications, opt for newer accommodations. If you reserve through a toll-free number, consider also calling the hotel's local number to confirm the information from the central reservations office. Get confirmation in writing when you can.

TRANSPORTATION

Flying presents no problem at all, as all South African airports have a PAU (passenger assistance unit) to get people on and off planes, and the airports have accessible facilities. If you are flying on SAA, use of the PAU is free, but you may be charged for its use if you fly other domestic airlines. However, the difference in ticket price might more than compensate for that, so check prices carefully when booking, and ensure that you know how much the PAU will cost—it can be as much as R1,000 for a round-trip. Other than the *Blue Train* (⇨ Train Travel), trains are not accessible. The *Blue Train* has one—rather cramped, but manageable—accessible compartment on one of its trains. Double-check when booking. There are no kneeling buses in South Africa, and access is very difficult.

You can rent cars with hand controls from most of the major agencies, but it is a lot easier—and no more expensive—to arrange your car rental through an organization like Flamingo Tours, which can also provide information about facilities on your chosen route. Almost all buildings have special disabled parking spots near the entrances. These are outlined in yellow with a big yellow wheelchair painted in the middle, and there is usually a wheelchair sign on a pole as well. In order to use these you must **bring your blue-and-white sticker or card** to hang on the rearview mirror or leave on the dash. Without this your car may be booted.

🚩 Complaints **Aviation Consumer Protection Division** (⇨ Air Travel) for airline-related problems. **Departmental Office of Civil Rights** ✉ For general inquiries, U.S. Department of Transportation, S-30, 400 7th St. SW, Room 10215, Washington, DC 20590 ☎ 202/366-4648 🖷 202/366-9371 ⊕ www.dot. gov/ost/docr/index.htm. **Disability Rights Section** ✉ NYAV, U.S. Department of Justice, Civil Rights Division, 950 Pennsylvania Ave. NW, Washington, DC 20530 ☎ ADA information line 202/514-0301, 800/ 514-0301, 202/514-0383 TTY, 800/514-0383 TTY ⊕ www.ada.gov. **U.S. Department of Transportation Hotline** ☎ For disability-related air-travel problems, 800/778-4838 or 800/455-9880 TTY.

TRAVEL AGENCIES

In the United States, the Americans with Disabilities Act requires that travel firms serve the needs of all travelers. Some agencies specialize in working with people with disabilities.

🚩 Travelers with Mobility Problems **Access Adventures/B. Roberts Travel** ✉ 206 Chestnut Ridge Rd., Scottsville, NY 14624 ☎ 585/889-9096

⊕ www.brobertstravel.com ✎ dltravel@prodigy. net, run by a former physical-rehabilitation counselor. **Flying Wheels Travel** ✉ 143 W. Bridge St., Box 382, Owatonna, MN 55060 ☎ 507/451-5005 🖷 507/451-1685 ⊕ www.flyingwheelstravel.com.

DISCOUNTS & DEALS

Be a smart shopper and compare all your options before making decisions. A plane ticket bought with a promotional coupon from travel clubs, coupon books, and direct-mail offers or purchased on the Internet may not be cheaper than the least expensive fare from a discount ticket agency. And always keep in mind that what you get is just as important as what you save.

DISCOUNT RESERVATIONS

To save money, look into discount reservations services with Web sites and toll-free numbers, which use their buying power to get a better price on hotels, airline tickets (⇨ Air Travel), even car rentals. When booking a room, always **call the hotel's local toll-free number** (if one is available) rather than the central reservations number—you'll often get a better price. Always ask about special packages or corporate rates.

When shopping for the best deal on hotels and car rentals, look for guaranteed exchange rates, which protect you against a falling dollar. With your rate locked in, you won't pay more, even if the price goes up in the local currency.

🚩 Airline Tickets **Air 4 Less** ☎ 800/AIR4LESS; low-fare specialist.

🚩 Hotel Rooms **Accommodations Express** ☎ 800/444-7666 or 800/277-1064 ⊕ www.acex. net. **Steigenberger Reservation Service** ☎ 800/ 223-5652 ⊕ www.srs-worldhotels.com. **Turbotrip. com** ☎ 800/473-7829 ⊕ www.turbotrip.com.

PACKAGE DEALS

Don't confuse packages and guided tours. When you buy a package, you travel on your own, just as though you had planned the trip yourself. Fly/drive packages, which combine airfare and car rental, are often a good deal. In cities, ask the local visitor's bureau about hotel and local transportation packages that include tickets to major museum exhibits or other special events.

EATING & DRINKING

The restaurants we list are the cream of the crop in each price category. Properties indicated by a ✕⊞ are lodging establishments whose restaurant warrants a special trip. Price categories are charted in each chapter and are based on the costs of main courses or a prix-fixe price, where there is no à la carte dining. For more information on local food, see the Dining section in Pleasures & Pastimes at the front of this book. If you really love seafood, you should make a point of visiting one of the very casual West Coast beach restaurants (⇨ Chapter 2), where you sit on the beach in a makeshift structure and eat course after course of seafood cooked on an open fire.

MEALS & MEALTIMES

In South Africa, dinner is eaten at night and lunch at noon. Breakfast is still pretty much understood to consist of something eggy and hot, but many people are moving over to muesli and fruit. South Africans may eat muffins for breakfast but draw the line at doughnuts. Most restaurants serve breakfast until about 11:30, but some pride themselves on serving breakfast all day.

If you are staying at a game lodge, your mealtimes will revolve around the game drives—usually coffee and rusks (similar to biscotti) early in the morning, more coffee and probably muffins on the first game drive, a huge brunch in the late morning, no lunch, tea and something sweet in the late afternoon before the evening game drive, cocktails and snacks on the drive, and a substantial supper, or dinner, about 8 or 8:30.

If you are particularly interested in food, plan your trip to include one or two of the guesthouses in the Good Cooks and Their Country Houses collection. All the establishments listed are owner managed and are noted for superior cuisine. In order for a guesthouse to qualify for inclusion, the chef must be the owner (or one of them).

Unless otherwise noted, the restaurants listed in this guide are open daily for lunch and dinner.

🎦 **Good Cooks and Their Country Houses**
⊕ www.goodcooks.co.za.

PAYING

Very few restaurants don't accept credit cards, but quite a few will not accept American Express and/or Diners Club.

RESERVATIONS & DRESS

Most restaurants welcome casual dress, including jeans and sneakers, but draw the line at shorts and a halter top at dinner, except for restaurants on the beach. Very expensive restaurants and old-fashioned hotel restaurants (where colonial traditions die hard) may welcome nicer dress, but other than the *Blue Train,* few require a jacket and tie.

Reservations are always a good idea; we mention them only when they're essential or not accepted. Book as far ahead as you can, and reconfirm as soon as you arrive. (Large parties should always call ahead to check the reservations policy.)

WINE, BEER & SPIRITS

South African wines are excellent. You could spend days or even weeks wandering around the Winelands, contentedly tasting cultivar after cultivar (⇨ chapters 2 and 4).

Other than a few small microbreweries, most South African beer is made by one company, previously called SA Breweries and now called SAB-Miller, after buying a major share in Miller. There is a good selection of imported beers in most drinking holes and restaurants, but the one you really should try is made just across the Orange River. Windhoek Lager is widely acknowledged to be the best beer brewed in southern Africa.

There are also a few interesting local liqueurs to try. Van der Hum is a citrus-flavored brandy-based liqueur that appeals to a slightly more mature palette than the ubiquitous, and very popular, Amarula, which is sweet and creamy. Buchenbos is not that easy to get hold of, but it's worth it. It's also brandy based and flavored with *rooibos* tea and *buchu* (a very aromatic and therapeutic wild herb). It's made in Clanwilliam (⇨ Chapter 2). Buchu brandy is becoming very popular and is also not that easy to get hold of. Mons Ruber in De Rust (⇨ Chapter 4) makes a good one. A number of small manufacturers are making *mampoer*—basically moonshine—in flavors ranging from the sublime (peach, rooibos, honeybush, and marula) to the, well, different (chili).

You can buy beer and wine in supermarkets and many convenience stores. Most restaurants are licensed to sell wine and beer, and many also sell spirits. In theory, on Sunday you can buy alcohol only in restaurants, and only if you're eating, but that rule is slowly being whittled away in practice. You may not take alcohol onto beaches, and it is illegal to walk down the street openly sipping from a bottle (street people get by this rule by keeping the bottle in a brown paper bag). You can, however, drink with a picnic or enjoy sundowners (cocktails at sunset) in almost any public place, such as Table Mountain or Kirstenbosch. The beach rule may be somewhat relaxed at sundowner time.

ELECTRICITY

To use electric-powered equipment purchased in the United States or Canada, **bring a converter and adapter.** The electrical current is 220 volts, 50 cycles alternating current (AC); wall outlets in most of the region take 15-amp plugs with three round prongs (the old British system), but some take the straight-edged three-prong plugs, also 15 amps.

If your appliances are dual-voltage, you'll need only an adapter. Don't use 110-volt outlets marked FOR SHAVERS ONLY for high-wattage appliances such as blow dryers. Most laptops operate equally well on 110 and 220 volts and so require only an adapter. In remote areas (and even in some lodges) power may be solar or from a generator; this means that delivery is erratic both in voltage and supply. In even the remotest places, however, lodge staff will find a way to charge video and camera batteries, but you will receive little sympathy if you insist on using a hair dryer or electric razor.

EMBASSIES

🇦🇺 Australia **Australian High Commission** ✉ 292 Orient St., Arcadia, Tshwane ☎ 012/342-3781 Ext. 273 🖷 012/342-4222 ⊕ www.citizenship.gov.au. 🇨🇦 Canada **Canadian Embassy** ✉ 1103 Arcadia St., Hatfield, Tshwane ☎ 012/422-3000.

🇳🇿 New Zealand **New Zealand High Commission** ✉ 2nd Floor, Block C, Hatfield Gardens, 1110 Arcadia St., Hatfield, Tshwane ☎ 012/342-8656 🖷 012/342-8640 ⊕ www.nzembassy.com. 🇬🇧 United Kingdom **British High Commission** ✉ 255 Hill St., Arcadia, Tshwane ☎ 012/483-1200 🖷 012/433-3207 ⊕ www.britishhighcommission.gov. uk. **British Consulate General** ✉ Southern Life Centre, 8 Riebeek St., Cape Town ☎ 021/405-2400 🖷 011/325-2131 ⊕ www.britishhighcommission.gov.uk. 🇺🇸 United States **U.S. Embassy** ✉ 877 Pretorius St., Arcadia, Tshwane ✉ Broadway Centre, Cape Town ☎ 021/421-4280 ⊕ wwwsouthafrica. usembassy.gov.

EMERGENCIES

If you specifically need an ambulance, you can get one by calling the special ambulance number or through the general emergency number. Europ Assistance offers professional evacuation in the event of emergency. If you intend to dive in South Africa, make sure you have DAN membership, which will be honored by Divers Alert Network South Africa (DANSA).

🚑 Ambulance ☎ 10177. Europ Assistance ☎ 011/242-1700 for inquiries, 0860/635-635 or 083/1999 for emergencies ⊕ www.europassistance.co.za. DANSA ☎ 0800/020-111 or 011/254-1112 ⊕ www. dansa.org. General emergency ☎ 10111 from landline, 112 from mobile phone). Police ☎ 10111.

ENGLISH-LANGUAGE MEDIA

There is a wide range of English-language publications in South Africa. Probably the most progressive newspaper is the national weekly the *Mail & Guardian*, which also has the most comprehensive international news coverage. In addition to the local dailies and Sunday papers, you will also find two national Sunday papers—the very worthwhile *Sunday Independent* and the somewhat less cerebral *Sunday Times*. You will find a number of English-language radio stations to keep you amused on long drives. SAFM has pretty good commentary and Radio 5 is very much a music station, but the best bet is to tune into the local stations, which are usually somewhere around 93–94 FM. Just play around. Check the press for TV programming, as you probably don't want to watch the news in Sepedi or Xhosa.

ETIQUETTE & BEHAVIOR

South Africa is a multicultural country, so though you won't fit in, you don't have to try to, either. South Africans recognize and value diversity, so they understand that other people have different cultural norms and readily accept those differences. Just be polite and friendly, accept that you are in a foreign country, and ask when you're not sure.

Americans should not be surprised to find that the policies of George W. Bush have made them extremely unpopular in most countries. However, since white South Africans spent years as the pariahs of the world for the actions of a government that was voted in by a minority of voters (yes, a minority of white voters), they are a little more understanding, and realize that individuals should not necessarily be held responsible for the actions of their government. However, if you support Bush, whatever you do, don't talk politics.

South Africans are warm, open people, and even relatively casual acquaintances greet with a hug or a kiss on the cheek—but some don't. Also, since it's a multicultural society, different sectors of society have different norms regarding personal space and touching. You'll have to play this by ear. And you know that fancy handshake where you grasp and twist and do the thumb thing? Well, it is so last week, it's really not worth trying. Only die-hard revolutionaries stuck in the '80s and a few gullible tourists ever really use it.

If you are invited to someone's home, it is—like almost anywhere—a good idea to **bring a small gift.** If you know your hosts' habits, you can bring a bottle of wine, chocolates, or flowers. But tailor the gift to the receiver, and use some common sense. If you have been invited to a very humble home—as can happen in rural areas—and your hosts are struggling to feed their children, they may prefer something a bit more pragmatic than a bunch of flowers. This is delicate territory so, when in doubt, ask a trustworthy, knowledgeable third party.

In traditional societies it is best to give and receive something with both hands—with the right hand uppermost. You can even just use your right hand but support your hand or your arm with your left. Much the same goes for shaking hands. As a rule, the closer your left hand is to your right, the greater you value the gift and the person. If you don't do this, you will certainly not offend anyone. If you do do this, many people won't notice, but some might and they will be touched. As a rule, though, it's a good idea to **always use your right hand to give or receive something.** Even more important: a little humility and a genuine smile will get you a lot further than a special handshake or greeting.

If you're visiting a house of worship, **dress modestly.** This is especially true at mosques, where women should bring scarves to cover their heads out of courtesy, wear skirts below the knees, and cover their shoulders. Men should not wear shorts. A good idea is to keep a lightweight saronglike garment at the ready to use as a skirt, scarf, or other covering.

BUSINESS ETIQUETTE

South Africans play hard and work hard—which means business is taken pretty seriously—even in the notoriously laid-back cities of Cape Town and Durban. **Arrive on time for appointments,** and hand over a business card during introductions. If it is a small meeting of between two and four people, you will probably indulge in a bit of chitchat before cutting to the chase. You'll almost certainly be asked the obvious questions, like, How was your trip? and Are you enjoying your stay? A short anecdote describing some really positive aspect of your visit, such as the beauty of South Africa or the great service at your hotel, can only help your cause.

Unless you are involved in a creative field, in which case you can get away with virtually anything, men should wear a jacket and tie to meetings, but a suit is not necessary, unless it's a really high-powered do. Women can get away with anything from a pretty floral dress to a severe suit, but take your cue from the general purpose of the meeting and who is going to be there. If it's serious, skip the floral dress and go for the power suit. Trousers are perfectly acceptable.

GAY & LESBIAN TRAVEL

The major cities of South Africa are very gay-friendly, particularly Cape Town, which has a large gay population. (Johannesburg, Durban, and Cape Town have "pink routes" that highlight gay-friendly or gay-interest establishments.) This was pretty much the case even before the new constitution enshrined the right to freedom of expression of sexual orientation. However, **be discreet.** You can walk down the road holding hands, and a quick hug or kiss is acceptable, but much more than that is frowned upon—even for heterosexual couples. Of course, it's a bit different in clubs and at parties.

If you want to attend one of the best parties of the year anywhere, try to be in Cape Town in December for the Mother City Queer Party—a real rip-roaring themed costume party that has grown to become a weeklong extravaganza. The Pink Loerie Festival, a Mardi Gras–style carnival, rocks the Garden Route town of Knysna in May. The Gay Pride March in Johannesburg every September is also a really cool event.

🎏 Celebrations **Mother City Queer Project** ⊕ www.mcqp.co.za. **Pink Loerie Festival** ⊕ www. pinkloerie.com. **Pride South Africa** ⊕ www. sapride.org.

🎏 Gay- & Lesbian-Friendly Travel Agencies **Different Roads Travel** ✉ 8383 Wilshire Blvd., Suite 520, Beverly Hills, CA 90211 ☎ 323/651-5557 or 800/429-8747 (Ext. 14 for both) 🖷 323/651-5454 ✉ lgernert@tzell.com. **Kennedy Travel** ✉ 130 W. 42nd St., Suite 401, New York, NY 10036 ☎ 212/840-8659, 800/237-7433 🖷 212/730-2269 ⊕ www. kennedytravel.com. **Now, Voyager** ✉ 4406 18th St., San Francisco, CA 94114 ☎ 415/626-1169 or 800/255-6951 🖷 415/626-8626 ⊕ www.nowvoyager. com. **Skylink Travel and Tour/Flying Dutchmen Travel** ✉ 1455 N. Dutton Ave., Suite A, Santa Rosa, CA 95401 ☎ 707/546-9888 or 800/225-5759 🖷 707/636-0951; serving lesbian travelers.

HEALTH

The most serious health problem facing travelers is malaria, which occurs in the prime South African game-viewing areas of Mpumalanga, Limpopo Province, and northern KwaZulu-Natal and in the countries farther north. The risk is medium at the height of the summer and very low in winter. All travelers heading into malaria-endemic regions should **consult a health-care professional at least one month before departure** for advice. Unfortunately, the malarial agent *Plasmodium sp.* seems to be able to develop a hardy resistance to new prophylactic drugs pretty quickly, so even if you are taking the newest miracle drug, the best prevention is to **avoid being bitten by mosquitoes** in the first place. After sunset wear light-colored, loose, long-sleeve shirts; long pants; and shoes and socks; and apply mosquito repellent. Always sleep in a mosquito-proof room or tent, and if possible, keep a fan going in your room. **If you are pregnant or trying to conceive, avoid malaria areas if at all possible.**

Generally speaking, the risk is much lower in the dry season (May–October) and peaks immediately after the first rains, which should be in November, but *El Nino* has made that a lot less predictable.

Many lakes and streams, particularly east of the watershed divide (i.e., in rivers flowing toward the Indian Ocean), are infected with *bilharzia* (schistosomiasis), a parasite carried by a small freshwater snail. The microscopic fluke enters through the skin of swimmers or waders, attaches itself to the intestines or bladder, and lays eggs. **Avoid wading in still waters** or in areas close to reeds. If you have been wading or swimming in doubtful water, dry yourself off vigorously with a towel immediately upon exiting the water, as this may help to dislodge any flukes before they can burrow into your skin. Fast-moving water is considered safe. Have a checkup once you get home. Bilharzia is easily diagnosed, and it's also easily treated in the early stages.

Like everywhere else in the world, you need to be aware of the possibility of becoming infected with HIV (which is a big problem in Africa) or hepatitis. Make sure you use a good condom during a sexual encounter; they're for sale in supermarkets, pharmacies, and most convenience stores. If you have a favorite brand, bring your own supplies. If you feel there is a possibility you have become infected, you can get anti-retroviral treatment from private hospitals. Check that your insurance covers this.

Rabies is extremely rare in domesticated animals in South Africa, but is more common in wild animals—one more reason you should not feed or tease wild animals. If you are bitten by a monkey or other wild animal, **seek medical attention immediately.** The chance of contracting rabies is extremely small, but the consequences are so horrible that you really don't want to gamble on this one.

As a foreigner, you will be expected to pay in full for any medical services, so **check your existing health plan to see whether you're covered while abroad,** and supplement it if necessary. South African doctors are generally excellent. The equipment and training in private clinics rivals the best in the world, but public hospitals tend to suffer from overcrowding and underfunding.

On returning home, if you experience any unusual symptoms, including fever, painful eyes, backache, diarrhea, severe headache, general lassitude, or blood in urine or stool, be sure to **tell your doctor where you have been.** These symptoms may indicate malaria, tick-bite fever, bilharzia, or—if you've been traveling north of South Africa's borders—some other tropical malady.

FOOD & DRINK
The drinking water in South Africa is treated and, except in rural areas (⇨ Safari Primer), is absolutely safe to drink. Many people filter it, though, to get rid of the chlorine, as that aseptic status does not come free. You can eat fresh fruits and salads and have ice in your drinks.

MEDICAL PLANS
No one plans to get sick while traveling, but it happens, so consider signing up with a medical-assistance company. Members get doctor referrals, emergency evacuation or repatriation, hotlines for medical consultation, cash for emergencies, and other assistance.

⚡ Medical-Assistance Companies **International SOS Assistance** ⊕ www.internationalsos.com ✉ 8 Neshaminy Interplex, Suite 207, Trevose, PA 19053

☏ 215/245-4707 or 800/523-6586 ⎙ 215/244-9617 ✉ Landmark House, Hammersmith Bridge Rd., 6th Floor, London, W6 9DP ☏ 20/8762-8008 ⎙ 20/8748-7744 ✉ 12 Chemin Riantbosson, 1217 Meyrin 1, Geneva, Switzerland ☏ 22/785-6464 ⎙ 22/785-6424 ✉ 331 N. Bridge Rd., 17-00, Odeon Towers, Singapore 188720 ☏ 6338-7800 ⎙ 6338-7611. International SOS Assistance, South Africa ☏ 011/541-1350 ⊕ www.internationalsos.com/countries/SouthAfrica.

OVER-THE-COUNTER REMEDIES
You can buy over-the-counter medication in pharmacies and supermarkets, and you will find the more general remedies in Clicks, a chain store selling beauty products, some OTC medication, and housewares.

PESTS & OTHER HAZARDS
In summer ticks may be a problem, even in open areas close to cities. If you intend to walk or hike anywhere, **use a suitable insect repellent.** After your walk examine your body and clothes for ticks, looking carefully for pepper ticks, which are tiny but may cause tick-bite fever. If you find a tick has bitten you, do not pull it off. If you do, you may pull the body off, and the head will remain embedded in your skin, causing an infection. Rather, smother the area with petroleum jelly, and the tick will eventually let go, as it will be unable to breathe; you can then scrape it off with a fingernail. If you are bitten, keep an eye on the bite. If the tick was infected, the bite will swell, itch, and develop a black necrotic center. This is a sure sign that you will develop tick-bite fever, which usually hits after about 8–12 days. Symptoms may be mild or severe, depending on the patient. This disease is not usually life threatening in healthy adults, but it is horribly unpleasant. Most people who are bitten by ticks suffer no more than an itchy bump, so don't panic.

Also, obviously, keep a lookout for mosquitoes. Even in nonmalarial areas they are extremely irritating. When walking anywhere in the bush, keep a lookout for snakes. Most will slither away when they feel you coming, but just keep your eyes peeled. If you see one, give it a wide berth and you should be fine. Snakes really bite only when they are taken by surprise, so you don't want to step on a napping adder.

SHOTS & MEDICATIONS

Travelers entering South Africa within six days of leaving a country infected with yellow fever require a yellow-fever vaccination certificate. (But you'd probably want to get the yellow fever shots before going to the infected country anyway.) The South African travel clinics and the U.S.'s National Centers for Disease Control and Prevention (CDC) recommend that you be vaccinated against hepatitis A and B if you intend to travel to more isolated areas. Cholera injections are widely regarded as useless, so don't let anyone talk you into having one, but the newer oral vaccine seems to be more effective. Depending on your destination, you may wish to take oral malaria prophylactic drugs. Resistance to malaria drugs develops quite rapidly, so be sure to **ask a reputable authority about the most appropriate drug for your destination.** The CDC provides up-to-date information on health risks and recommended vaccinations and medications for travelers to southern Africa. In most of South Africa you need not worry about any of the above, but if you plan to visit remote regions, check with the CDC's traveler's health line. For up-to-date, local expertise, contact SAA Netcare Travel Clinics.

Health Warnings National Centers for Disease Control and Prevention (CDC) ✉ Office of Health Communication, National Center for Infectious Diseases, Division of Quarantine, Travelers' Health, 1600 Clifton Rd. NE, Atlanta, GA 30333 ☎ 877/394-8747 international travelers' health line, 800/311-3435 other inquiries, 404/498-1600 Division of Quarantine ♨ 888/232-3299 ⊕ www.cdc.gov/travel. **SAA Netcare Travel Clinics** ☎ 0800/002-609 toll-free in South Africa ⊕ www.travelclinics.co.za. **World Health Organization (WHO)** ⊕ www.who.int.

HOLIDAYS

National holidays in South Africa are New Year's Day (January 1), Human Rights Day (March 21), Easter (sometime in March or April), Freedom Day (April 27), Workers Day (May 1), Youth Day (June 16), Heritage Day (September 24), Day of

Reconciliation (December 16), and Christmas Day (December 25).

December 26 is a general unnamed holiday. In Cape Town, January 2 is also a holiday, known as *tweede nuwe jaar* (second new year). School vacations vary with the provinces, but usually comprise about 10 days over Easter, about three weeks around June or July, and then the big summer vacation from about December 10 to January 10.

INSURANCE

The most useful travel-insurance plan is a comprehensive policy that includes coverage for trip cancellation and interruption, default, trip delay, and medical expenses (with a waiver for preexisting conditions).

Without insurance you'll lose all or most of your money if you cancel your trip, regardless of the reason. Default insurance covers you if your tour operator, airline, or cruise line goes out of business—the chances of which have been increasing. Trip-delay covers expenses that arise because of bad weather or mechanical delays. Study the fine print when comparing policies.

If you're traveling internationally, a key component of travel insurance is coverage for medical bills incurred if you get sick on the road. Such expenses aren't generally covered by Medicare or private policies. U.K. residents can buy a travel-insurance policy valid for most vacations taken during the year in which it's purchased (but check preexisting-condition coverage). British and Australian citizens need extra medical coverage when traveling overseas.

Always **buy travel policies directly from the insurance company**; if you buy them from a cruise line, airline, or tour operator that goes out of business you probably won't be covered for the agency or operator's default, a major risk. Before making any purchase, review your existing health and home-owner's policies to find what they cover away from home.

Travel Insurers In the U.S.: Access America ✉ 2805 N. Parham Rd., Richmond, VA 23294 ☎ 800/284-8300 ♨ 804/673-1491 or 800/346-9265 ⊕ www.accessamerica.com. **Travel Guard In-**

ternational ✉ 1145 Clark St., Stevens Point, WI
54481 ☎ 715/345-0505 or 800/826-1300 🖷 800/
955-8785 ⊕ www.travelguard.com.
🔲 In the U.K.: **Association of British Insurers**
✉ 51 Gresham St., London EC2V 7HQ ☎ 020/
7600-3333 🖷 020/7696-8999 ⊕ www.abi.org.uk. In
Canada: **RBC Insurance** ✉ 6880 Financial Dr., Mis-
sissauga, Ontario L5N 7Y5 ☎ 800/668-4342 or 905/
816-2400 🖷 905/813-4704 ⊕ www.rbcinsurance.
com. In Australia: **Insurance Council of Australia**
✉ Insurance Enquiries and Complaints, Level 12,
Box 561, Collins St. W, Melbourne, VIC 8007 ☎ 1300/
780808 or 03/9629-4109 🖷 03/9621-2060 ⊕ www.
iecltd.com.au. In New Zealand: **Insurance Council of
New Zealand** ✉ Level 7, 111-115 Customhouse Quay,
Box 474, Wellington ☎ 04/472-5230 🖷 04/473-3011
⊕ www.icnz.org.nz.

LANGUAGE

South Africa has a mind-numbing 11 official languages: Afrikaans, English, Ndebele,
North Sotho, South Sotho, Swati, Tsonga,
Tswana (same as Setswana in Botswana),
Venda, Xhosa, and Zulu. Happily for visitors, English is the widely spoken, unofficial
lingua franca, although road signs and
other important markers often alternate between English and Afrikaans (South African
Dutch). Be warned that street names also
often alternate between English and
Afrikaans, so, for example, "Wale Street"
and "Waalstraat" are the same. Because
South Africa is a multilingual country, restroom signs are usually graphic, but you
may come across Afrikaans signs in some
parts of the country. Ladies is pretty easy—
it's *Dames*—but you probably wouldn't
guess that *Here* is Gents.

South African English is heavily influenced
by Afrikaans and, to a lesser extent, by
some of the African languages. First-time
visitors may have trouble understanding
some regional South African accents. For a
list of local terms and definitions, *see the*
glossaries *in* Understanding South Africa.

LODGING

The Tourism Grading Council of South
Africa is the official accreditation and
grading body for accommodation in South
Africa. However, you may still find some
establishments clinging to other grading
systems. Hotels, bed-and-breakfasts, guest-

houses, and game lodges are graded on a
star rating from one to five. Grading is not
compulsory, and there are many excellent
establishments that are not graded.

Most hotel rooms come with private bathrooms that are usually en suite, but they
may, very occasionally, be across the corridor. You can usually choose between
rooms with twin or double beds. A full
English breakfast is often included in the
rate, particularly in more traditional hotels. In most luxury lodges the rate usually
covers the cost of dinner, bed, and breakfast, whereas in game lodges the rate includes everything but alcohol—and some
include that. A self-catering room is one
with kitchen facilities.

Be warned, though, that in southern Africa
words do not necessarily mean what you
think they do. The term *lodge* is a particularly tricky one. A guest lodge or a game
lodge is almost always an upmarket, full-
service facility with loads of extra attractions. But the term *lodge* when applied to
city hotels often indicates a minimum-ser-
vice hotel. These are usually very well appointed and comfortable but have no
restaurant or room service, and thus offer
very good-value bed-and-breakfast accommodations. Examples are the Protea
Lodges (as opposed to Protea Hotels), City
and Town Lodges, and Holiday Inn Garden Courts. A backpacker lodge, however,
is essentially a hostel.

The lodgings we list are the cream of the
crop in each price category. Price charts are
found in each chapter. We always list the facilities that are available—but we don't
specify whether they cost extra: when pricing accommodations, always ask what's included. Price categories are based on a
property's least expensive standard double
room at high season (excluding holidays).
Properties indicated by a ✕🗔 are lodging
establishments whose restaurant warrants a
special trip. Those indicated by a 🛆 are
campgrounds with rustic camping accommodations. (These are different from the
fairly luxurious safari tents found at many
private game lodges.) Mailing addresses follow the street address or location, where
appropriate.

Assume that hotels operate on the European Plan (EP, with no meals) unless we specify that they use the Continental Plan (CP, with a Continental breakfast daily), Breakfast Plan (BP, with a full breakfast daily), Modified American Plan (MAP, with breakfast and dinner daily), or Full American Plan (FAP, including all meals and usually all or most activities). Most game lodges have FAP. All hotels listed have private bath unless otherwise noted.

Safarinow.com and Siyabona Africa operate two of the better online booking agencies, and the Portfolio Collection is the best-known accommodation bureau.

🗐 **Grading Council of South Africa** ⊕ www.tourismgrading.co.za. **Portfolio Collection** ☎ 021/689-4020, 072/371-2472 after hours ⊕ www.portfoliocollection.com. **Safarinow.com** ⊕ www.safarinow.com. **Siyabona Africa** ⊕ www.hotelguide.com.

B&BS

There are thousands of B&Bs scattered all over the region. As in most other parts of the world, many are very small and personalized, giving the visitor an insight into the lives of locals. For more info contact BABASA (Bed and Breakfast Association of South Africa). The Portfolio Collection publishes a respected list of South Africa's best bed-and-breakfasts that may also be useful. It also offers a similar guide to small hotels and lodges.

🗐 **Reservation Services BABASA** ⌂ Box 2005, Groenkloof 0027 ☎ 072/947-8514 🖷 012/480-2041 ⊕ www.babasa.co.za. **Portfolio Collection** ☎ 021/689-4020, 072/371-2472 after hours ⊕ www.portfoliocollection.com.

FARM STAYS

Jacana Marketing and Reservations offers a range of farms, coastal and country cottages, and privately operated hiking, biking, and horse trails in country areas.

🗐 **Jacana Marketing and Reservations** ⌂ Box 95212, Waterkloof 0145 ☎ 012/346-3550 through 012/346-3552 🖷 012/346-2499 ⊕ www.jacanacollection.co.za.

GAME LODGES

Safariplan/Wild African Ventures, the Mantis Collection, CC Africa, Wilderness Sa-

faris, Safarinow.com, and Classic Safari Camps of Africa represent a number of the best and most exclusive game lodges in southern and East Africa. The Portfolio Collection has a special edition on game lodges.

🗐 **CC Africa** ☎ 011/809-4300 🖷 011/809-4400 ⊕ www.ccafrica.com. **Classic Safari Camps of Africa** ☎ 011/465-6427 🖷 011/465-9309 ⊕ www.classicsafaricamps.com. **Mantis Collection** ☎ 021/713-2230 🖷 021/713-2201 ⊕ www.mantiscollection.com. **Portfolio Collection** ☎ 021/689-4020, 072/371-2472 after hours ⊕ www.portfoliocollection.com. **Safarinow.com** ⊕ www.safarinow.com. **Wild African Ventures** ☎ 800/358-8530 ⊕ www.wildafricanventures.com. **Wilderness Safaris** ☎ 011/807-1800 ⊕ www.wilderness-safaris.com.

HOME EXCHANGES

If you would like to exchange your home for someone else's, join a home-exchange organization, which will send you its updated listings of available exchanges for a year and will include your own listing in at least one of them. It's up to you to make specific arrangements.

🗐 **Exchange Clubs HomeLink International** ⌂ Box 47747, Tampa, FL 33647 ☎ 813/975-9825 or 800/638-3841 🖷 813/910-8144 ⊕ www.homelink.org; $110 yearly for a listing, online access, and catalog; $70 without catalog. **Intervac U.S.** ⊠ 30 Corte San Fernando, Tiburon, CA 94920 ☎ 800/756-4663 🖷 415/435-7440 ⊕ www.intervacus.com; $125 yearly for a listing, online access, and a catalog; $65 without catalog.

HOSTELS

No matter what your age, you can save on lodging costs by staying at hostels. You'll find a backpackers hostel in almost every great destination—some are fabulous, some are a tad, well, scruffy. Most hostels are affiliated with BTSA (Backpacker Tourism South Africa). You can get a good overview of the hostel scene from "Coast to Coast" or "the Alternative Route," both of which are small, free booklets that are regularly updated. The Baz Bus (⇨ Bus Travel) offers a handy door-to-door service to backpacker lodgings all around the country. In some 4,500 locations in more than 70 countries around the world, Hostelling International (HI), the umbrella group for a number of national youth-hostel associations, offers single-sex, dorm-style beds and, at many hostels, rooms for couples and family accommodations. Membership in any HI national hostel association, open to travelers of all ages, allows you to stay in HI-affiliated hostels at member rates; one-year membership is about $28 for adults (C$35 for a two-year minimum membership in Canada, £14 in the U.K., A$52 in Australia, and NZ$40 in New Zealand); hostels charge about $10–$30 per night. Members have priority if the hostel is full; they're also eligible for discounts around the world, even on rail and bus travel in some countries.

🚌 **Organizations Alternative Route** ⊕ www. alternativeroute.net. **BTSA** ⊕ www.btsa.co.za. **Coast to Coast** ⊕ www.coastingafrica.com. **Hostelling International South Africa** ⊕ www.hisa.org.za. **Hostelling International–USA** ✉ 8401 Colesville Rd., Suite 600, Silver Spring, MD 20910 ☎ 301/495-1240 🖷 301/495-6697 ⊕ www.hiusa.org. **Hostelling International–Canada** ✉ 205 Catherine St., Suite 400, Ottawa, Ontario K2P 1C3 ☎ 613/237-7884 or 800/663-5777 🖷 613/237-7868 ⊕ www.hihostels.ca. **YHA England and Wales** ✉ Trevelyan House, Dimple Rd., Matlock, Derbyshire DE4 3YH, U.K. ☎ 0870/870-8808, 0870/ 770-8868, 0162/959-2600 🖷 0870/770-6127 ⊕ www.yha.org.uk. **YHA Australia** ✉ 422 Kent St., Sydney, NSW 2001 ☎ 02/9261-1111 🖷 02/9261-1969 ⊕ www.yha.com.au. **YHA New Zealand** ✉ Level 1, Moorhouse City, 166 Moorhouse Ave., Box 436, Christchurch ☎ 03/379-9970 or 0800/278-299 🖷 03/365-4476 ⊕ www.yha.org.nz.

HOTELS

Hotel rates are at their highest during peak season, November through March, when you can expect to pay anywhere from 50% to 90% more than in the off-season. International hotel groups, such as Hyatt International and Sheraton, are moderately well represented around the region. Major South African conglomerates include Protea and the Southern Sun Group, which runs Southern Sun Hotels and Holiday Inn Hotels. Southern Sun Group manages the budget French hotel chain Formule 1 and the South African Inter-Continental Hotels.

🚌 **Central Reservation Numbers Best Western** ☎ 800/528-1234 ⊕ www.bestwestern.com. **Choice** ☎ 800/424-6423 ⊕ www.choicehotels.com. **Days Inn** ☎ 800/325-2525 ⊕ www.daysinn.com. **Formule 1** ☎ 011/807-0750 ⊕ www.hotelformule1.co.za. **Hilton** ☎ 800/445-8667 ⊕ www.hilton.com. **Holiday Inn** ☎ 800/465-4329 ⊕ www.ichotelsgroup.com. **Hyatt Hotels & Resorts** ☎ 800/233-1234 ⊕ www.hyatt.com. **Inter-Continental** ☎ 800/327-0200 ⊕ www.ichotelsgroup.com. **Protea** ☎ 021/419-8800, 0800/11-9000 toll-free ⊕ www.proteahotels.com. **Radisson** ☎ 800/333-3333 ⊕ www.radisson.com. **Sheraton** ☎ 800/325-3535 ⊕ www.starwood.com/sheraton. **Southern Sun** ☎ 011/482-3500 ⊕ www.southernsun.com.

MAIL & SHIPPING

The mail service in South Africa is reasonably reliable, but mail can take weeks to arrive, and money and other valuables may be stolen from letters and packages. You can buy stamps at post offices, open weekdays 8:30–4:30 and Saturday 8–noon. Stamps for local use only, marked STANDARDISED POST, may be purchased from newsstands in booklets of 10 stamps. Postnet franchises—a combined post office, courier service, business services center, and Internet café—are in convenient places like shopping malls and are open longer hours than post offices.

OVERNIGHT SERVICES

Federal Express and several other express-mail companies offer more reliable service than regular mail, as do the new Fast Mail and Speed Courier services. Postnets also offer courier services. A parcel of up to about a pound (half a kilogram) will cost between R300 and R750 to send the United States, and a 1-kilogram parcel (2.2 pounds) will cost anything from R550 to just over R1,000.

🚌 **Major Services DHL** ☎ 0860/345-000 ⊕ www.dhl.co.za. **FedEx** ☎ 021/951-6660, 080/953-9599 toll-free in South Africa ⊕ www.fedex.com. **Postnet** ⊕ www.postnet.co.za.

POSTAL RATES

All overseas mail costs the same. A postcard is about R3.50, and a letter ranges from R4 to about R15, depending on size and weight.

RECEIVING MAIL

The central post office in each city has a *poste restante* desk that will hold mail for you. Be sure the post office's mail code and your name are prominently displayed on all letters. Most hotels also accept faxes and express-mail deliveries addressed to their guests. If you have trouble retrieving your mail, ask the clerk to check under the initial of your first name (and any other). So, for example, check under J, R, and S if your name is John Robert Smith.

A better place to receive mail is at American Express offices; for a list of offices worldwide, write for AE's "Traveler's Companion."

🗹 **Mail Service American Express** ⌦ Box 678, Canal Street Station, New York, NY 10013.

MONEY MATTERS

Because of inflation and currency fluctuations, it's difficult to give exact exchange rates. It's safe to say, though, that the region is a reasonably cheap destination for foreign visitors. You may find the cost of meals, hotels, and entertainment noticeably lower than at home.

A bottle of good South African wine costs about $6 (double or triple in a restaurant), and a meal at a prestigious restaurant won't set you back more than $40 per person. Double rooms in the country's finest hotels may cost $400 a night, but $150 is more than enough to secure high-quality lodging in most cities.

But not everything in South Africa is cheap. Expect to pay international rates and more to stay in one of the exclusive private game lodges in Mpumalanga, Limpopo Province, or KwaZulu-Natal—between $1,500 and $2,000 per couple per night. Flights to South Africa and within the country itself are also extremely expensive.

The following were sample costs in South Africa in U.S. dollars at time of writing: cup of coffee, $1.50; bottle of beer in a bar, $1.50–$2; quarter roasted chicken with salad and drink at a fast-food restaurant, $5–$7; room-service sandwich in a hotel, $5–$7; 2-km (1-mi) taxi ride, $6–$8.

Prices throughout this guide are given for adults. Substantially reduced fees are almost always available for children, students, and senior citizens. For information on taxes, *see* Taxes.

ATMS

Before leaving home, **make sure that your credit cards have been programmed for ATM use in South Africa** (most South African ATMs take five-digit PIN numbers). There are ATMs practically everywhere. All ATMs accept Cirrus, Plus, Maestro, Visa Electron, and Visa and MasterCard.

CREDIT CARDS

MasterCard and Visa are accepted almost everywhere, whereas American Express and Diners Club are not quite as widely accepted. Discover is not recognized.

Throughout this guide, the following abbreviations are used: **AE,** American Express; **DC,** Diners Club; **MC,** MasterCard; and **V,** Visa.

🗹 **Reporting Lost Cards Amex** ☎ 0800/110–929. **Diners Club** ☎ 021/794–8170 Cape Town, 011/358–8400 Johannesburg, 0860/346–377 24 hrs. **MasterCard** ☎ 0800/990–418 toll-free. **Visa** ☎ 0800/990–475 toll-free.

CURRENCY

The unit of currency in South Africa is the rand (R), with 100 cents (¢) equaling R1. Bills come in R10, R20, R50, R100, and R200 denominations, which are differentiated by color. Coins are minted in R5, R2, R1, 50¢, 20¢, 10¢, 5¢, 2¢, and 1¢ denominations.

CURRENCY EXCHANGE

At time of writing, the conversion rate for South Africa was about R6 to the US$. For the most favorable rates, **change money through banks.** Although ATM transaction fees may be higher abroad than at home, ATM rates are excellent because they're based on wholesale rates offered only by major banks. You won't do as well at exchange booths in airports or rail and bus stations, in hotels, in restaurants, or in stores. To avoid lines at airport exchange booths, get a bit of local currency before you leave home. Alternatvely, get local currency from an ATM at the airport.

To avoid administrative hassles, keep all foreign-exchange receipts until you leave the region, as you may need them as proof when changing any unspent local currency back into your own currency. You may not take more than R5,000 in cash out of South Africa. For more information you can contact the South African Reserve Bank.

Currency Information South African Reserve Bank ⌂ Box 427, Pretoria 0001 ☎ 012/313-3911 ⊕ www.reservebank.co.za.

Exchange Services International Currency Express ✉ 427 N. Camden Dr., Suite F, Beverly Hills, CA 90210 ☎ 888/278-6628 orders 🖷 310/278-6410 ⊕ www.foreignmoney.com. **Travel Ex Currency Services** ☎ 800/287-7362 orders and retail locations ⊕ www.travelex.com.

TRAVELER'S CHECKS

Do you need traveler's checks? It depends on where you're headed. If you're going to rural areas and small towns, go with cash; traveler's checks are best used in cities. Lost or stolen checks can usually be replaced within 24 hours. To ensure a speedy refund, buy your own traveler's checks—don't let someone else pay for them: irregularities like this can cause delays. The person who bought the checks should make the call to request a refund. Traveler's checks in either rand or other major denominations (U.S. dollars, euros, and sterling) are readily accepted by most lodgings, though most people use credit cards.

PACKING

In southern Africa it's possible to experience muggy heat, bone-chilling cold, torrential thunderstorms, and scorching African sun all within a couple of days. The secret is to **pack lightweight clothes that you can wear in layers,** and at least one sweater. **Take along a warm jacket,** too, especially if you're going to a private game lodge. It can get mighty cold sitting in an open Land Rover at night. It really and truly does get very cold in almost every part of southern Africa, so don't fall into the it's-Africa-so-it-must-always-be-hot trap.

South Africans tend to dress casually, donning shorts and T-shirts as soon as the weather turns pleasant. Businessmen still wear suits all over the region, but in South Africa dress standards have become less rigid and more interesting since ex-president Nelson Mandela redefined the concept of

sartorial elegance with his Madiba shirts. You can go almost anywhere in neat, clean, casual clothes, but you can still get dolled up to go to the theater or opera if you wish. Dinner on the *Blue Train* and in some of the smarter hotels is formal. An interesting development since 1994 is that invitations to social and official events prescribe dress code as "formal or traditional," so it really is quite acceptable for men to appear at the opera or the opening of parliament in skirts made of monkey tails. (But don't try it as a foreigner, although you may wear a kilt or Native American feathered headdress if it is culturally appropriate for you.)

It's easy to get fried in the strong African sun, especially in mile-high Johannesburg, where the temperature can be deceptively cool. **Pack plenty of sunscreen, sunglasses, and a hat.** An umbrella comes in handy during those late-afternoon thunderstorms but is almost useless in Cape Town in the winter, as it will get blown inside out. But do **take a waterproof coat.**

If you're heading into the bush, **bring binoculars, a strong insect repellent (with a good amount of DEET), and sturdy pants** (preferably cotton) that can stand up to the wicked thorns that protect much of the foliage. Avoid black, white, and garish clothing, which will make you more visible to animals (and insects, which tend to mistake you for a buffalo if you wear black); medium tones will make you blend in most, but you don't have to look like an extra on the set of *Out of Africa,* so don't rush out and buy a suitcase of designer khaki—you'll just look like a tourist. And **leave behind perfumes,** which mask the smell of the bush and also attract insects. Lightweight hiking boots are a good idea if you plan to set out on any of South Africa's great trails; otherwise, a sturdy pair of walking shoes should suffice. For more details on what to pack for a safari, *see* the Safari Primer chapter.

Some hotels do supply washcloths; some don't. It's always a good idea to have at least a couple of tissues in your bag in rural areas, as there may not be a restroom (and toilet paper) just when you need it.

Make copies of all your important documents and leave them with someone at home who can courier them to you if you should be unlucky enough to lose them all.

In your carry-on luggage, pack an extra pair of eyeglasses or contact lenses and enough of any medication you take to last a few days longer than the entire trip. You may also ask your doctor to write a spare prescription using the drug's generic name, as brand names may vary from country to country. In luggage to be checked, **never pack prescription drugs, valuables, or undeveloped film.** And don't forget to carry with you the addresses of offices that handle refunds of lost traveler's checks. Check *Fodor's How to Pack* (available at online retailers and bookstores everywhere) for more tips.

To avoid customs and security delays, carry medications in their original packaging. Don't pack any sharp objects in your carry-on luggage, including knives of any size or material, scissors, nail clippers, and corkscrews, or anything else that might arouse suspicion.

To avoid having your checked luggage chosen for hand inspection, don't cram bags full. The U.S. Transportation Security Administration suggests packing shoes on top and placing personal items you don't want touched in clear plastic bags.

CHECKING LUGGAGE

You're allowed to carry aboard one bag and one personal article, such as a purse or a laptop computer. Make sure what you carry on fits under your seat or in the overhead bin. Get to the gate early, so you can board as soon as possible, before the overhead bins fill up.

Baggage allowances vary by carrier, destination, and ticket class. On international flights, you're usually allowed to check two bags weighing up to 70 pounds (32 kilograms) each, although a few airlines allow checked bags of up to 88 pounds (40 kilograms) in first class. Some international carriers don't allow more than 66 pounds (30 kilograms) per bag in business class and 44 pounds (20 kilograms) in economy. On domestic flights, the limit is usually 50 to 70 pounds (23 to 32 kilograms) per bag. In general, carry-on bags shouldn't exceed 40 pounds (18 kilograms). Most airlines won't accept bags that weigh more than 100 pounds (45 kilograms) on domestic or international flights. Expect to pay a fee for baggage that exceeds weight limits. Check baggage restrictions with your carrier before you pack.

Airline liability for baggage is limited to $2,500 per person on flights within the United States. On international flights it amounts to $9.07 per pound or $20 per kilogram for checked baggage (roughly $640 per 70-pound bag), with a maximum of $634.90 per piece, and $400 per passenger for unchecked baggage. You can buy additional coverage at check-in for about $10 per $1,000 of coverage, but it often excludes a rather extensive list of items, shown on your airline ticket.

Before departure, itemize your bags' contents and their worth, and label the bags with your name, address, and phone number. (If you use your home address, cover it so potential thieves can't see it readily.) Include a label inside each bag and pack a copy of your itinerary. At check-in, make sure each bag is correctly tagged with the destination airport's three-letter code. Because some checked bags will be opened for hand inspection, the U.S. Transportation Security Administration recommends that you leave luggage unlocked or use the plastic locks offered at check-in. TSA screeners place an inspection notice inside searched bags, which are re-sealed with a special lock.

If your bag has been searched and contents are missing or damaged, file a claim with the TSA Consumer Response Center as soon as possible. If your bags arrive damaged or fail to arrive at all, file a written report with the airline before leaving the airport.

Baggage carts are widely available at South African airports.

🚩 Complaints **U.S. Transportation Security Administration Contact Center** ☎ 866/289–9673 ⊕ www.tsa.gov.

LUGGAGE ON BUSH FLIGHTS

If you are visiting a game lodge deep in the bush, you will be arriving by light plane—and you really will be restricted in what you can bring. Excess luggage can usually be stored with the operator until your return. Don't just gloss over this: charter operators take weight very seriously, and some will charge you for an extra ticket if you insist on bringing excess baggage. For more details, *see* the Safari Primer chapter.

PASSPORTS & VISAS

When traveling internationally, carry your passport even if you don't need one (it's always the best form of ID) and make two photocopies of the data page (one for someone at home and another for you, carried separately from your passport). If you lose your passport, promptly call the nearest embassy or consulate and the local police.

U.S. passport applications for children under age 14 require consent from both parents or legal guardians; both parents must appear together to sign the application. If only one parent appears, he or she must submit a written statement from the other parent authorizing passport issuance for the child. A parent with sole authority must present evidence of it when applying; acceptable documentation includes the child's certified birth certificate listing only the applying parent, a court order specifically permitting this parent's travel with the child, or a death certificate for the nonapplying parent. Application forms and instructions are available on the Web site of the U.S. State Department's Bureau of Consular Affairs (⊕ travel.state.gov).

IN SOUTH AFRICA

All Australian, New Zealand, U.S., Canadian, and U.K. citizens, even infants, need only a valid passport to enter South Africa for visits of up to 90 days. If it's due to expire within six months of your return date, you need to renew your passport in advance, as South Africa won't let you enter with a soon-to-expire passport. You also need two blank pages in your passport to enter South Africa.

PASSPORT OFFICES

The best time to apply for a passport or to renew is in fall and winter. Before any trip, check your passport's expiration date, and, if necessary, renew it as soon as possible.

🔝 Australian Citizens **Passports Australia** Australian Department of Foreign Affairs and Trade ☎ 131-232 ⊕ www.passports.gov.au.

🔝 Canadian Citizens **Passport Office** ✉ To mail in applications: 200 Promenade du Portage, Hull, Québec J8X 4B7 ☎ 819/994-3500 or 800/567-6868 ⊕ www.ppt.gc.ca.

🔝 New Zealand Citizens **New Zealand Passports Office** ☎ 0800/22-5050 or 04/474-8100 ⊕ www.passports.govt.nz.

🔝 U.K. Citizens **U.K. Passport Service** ☎ 0870/521-0410 ⊕ www.passport.gov.uk.

🔝 U.S. Citizens **National Passport Information Center** ☎ 877/487-2778, 888/874-7793 TDD/TTY ⊕ travel.state.gov.

RESPONSIBLE TOURISM

Southern Africa is a dry region, so water is a precious resource and should be used sparingly. Please **take short showers and always turn faucets off** when not in use, especially when shaving or brushing teeth. In some places you may notice that the toilets have two flush options, one small and one large. Some also have a mechanism that flushes only as long as you hold it down, so you can judge how much water you need to use. In some hotels you will find a note in your bathroom, informing you to leave any towels you want washed in the bath. It's a great system that keeps hotels from using lots of water, electricity, and soap to wash perfectly clean towels.

When outdoors, don't litter or pick flowers. When hiking, **don't take shortcuts on mountain slopes;** this exacerbates erosion, already a major problem in many parts of the region. If you're camping, don't wash with soap or shampoo in streams, springs, or lakes. Also, **avoid feeding wild animals**—at best it can make them sick; at worst it may cause them to expect food from future visitors, who may be attacked. The animal will then be killed by wildlife authorities. Also **use power sparingly,** turning off lights when not in use. Electricity is a finite resource.

Of course, responsible tourism is about more than just plants, animals, earth, and water. If you are remotely concerned about your impact on the planet, you'll want to know that the money you spend is being plowed back into the community and not just enriching some clever businessperson. FTTSA (Fair Trade in Tourism, SA) accreditation indicates a high level of commitment to responsible tourism.

🔏 **Fair Trade in Tourism SA** ✉ Box 11536, Hatfield, Pretoria 0028 ☎ 012/342-8307 🖷 012/342-8289 ⊕ www.fairtourismsa.org.za.

RESTROOMS

All fuel complexes on the major roads have large, clean, well-maintained restrooms. In cities you can find restrooms in shopping malls, at some gas stations, and in restaurants—most of which are quite happy to allow you to use them.

SAFETY

Crime is a major problem in the whole region, particularly in large cities, and all visitors should take precautions to protect themselves. **Do not walk alone at night,** and exercise caution even during the day. **Avoid wearing jewelry** (even costume jewelry), don't invite attention by wearing an expensive camera around your neck, and don't flash a large wad of cash. If you are toting a handbag, wear the strap across your body; even better, wear a money belt, preferably hidden from view under your clothing. When sitting at airports or at restaurants, especially outdoor cafés, make sure to **keep your bag on your lap** or between your legs—otherwise it may just quietly "walk off" when you're not looking. Even better, loop the strap around your leg, or clip the strap around the table or chair.

Carjacking is another problem, with armed bandits often forcing drivers out of their vehicles at traffic lights, in driveways, or during a fake accident. **Always drive with your windows closed and doors** locked, don't stop for hitchhikers, and park in well-lighted places. At traffic lights, leave enough space between you and the vehicle in front so you can pull into another lane

if necessary. Always be aware of your surroundings. In the unlikely event you are carjacked, don't argue, and don't look at the carjacker's face. Just get out of the car, or ask to be let out of the car. **Do not try to keep any of your belongings**—they are all replaceable, even that laptop with all that data on it. If you are not given the opportunity to leave the car, try to stay calm, ostentatiously look away from the hijackers so they can be sure you can't identify them, and follow all instructions. Ask again, calmly, to be let out of the car.

Do not leave anything visible in the car when parking. Stow it all in the trunk.

Make sure you know exactly where you're going. Purchase a good map and obtain comprehensive directions. Taking the wrong exit off a highway into a township could lead you straight to disaster. Many cities are ringed by "no-go" areas. Learn from your hotel or the locals which areas to avoid.

Stay aware of what's going on around you. When on foot, walk with a purposeful stride so you look like you know where you're going, and duck into a shop or café if you need to check a map or speak on your mobile phone.

Never, ever visit a township or squatter camp on your own. Unemployment is rife, and obviously affluent foreigners are easy pickings. If you wish to see a township, check with reputable companies, which run excellent tours and know which areas to avoid. Book yourself on one of these instead.

The countryside is less intense, and crime is not as common. Nevertheless, always remain alert, and don't let a false sense of security lead you into behaving foolishly. Avoid wandering alone in deserted areas. Most hiking trails and tourist areas are reasonably safe, but crime can and does happen anywhere.

WOMEN IN SOUTH AFRICA

If you carry a purse, choose one with a zipper and a thick strap that you can drape across your body; adjust the length so that the purse sits in front of you at or above hip level. (Don't wear a waist pack.) Store only enough money in the purse to cover casual spending. Distribute the rest of your cash and any valuables between deep front pockets, inside jacket or vest pockets, and a concealed money pouch.

Lone women travelers need to be particularly vigilant about walking alone and locking their rooms, but South Africa is a pretty cool place to travel in. You're not likely to get hassled just because you're alone. You know the drill. If you do attract someone who won't take a firm but polite *no* for an answer, appeal immediately to the hotel manager, bartender, or someone else who seems to be in charge.

SENIOR-CITIZEN TRAVEL

Senior citizens in South Africa often receive discounts on admission prices and tickets if they can show valid pensioner's cards, which can prove they are on a fixed income, as age itself is no indication of financial status. As a foreigner, though, you are unlikely to get a discount.

When traveling in deep rural areas where people have not been urbanized, you will find that local youths, children, and even younger adults treat senior citizens with a great deal of respect, as age is revered in Africa.

To qualify for age-related discounts, mention your senior-citizen status up front when booking hotel reservations (not when checking out) and before you're seated in restaurants (not when paying the bill). Be sure to have identification on hand. When renting a car, ask about promotional car-rental discounts, which can be cheaper than senior-citizen rates.

F **Educational Program Elderhostel** ✉ 11 Ave. de Lafayette, Boston, MA 02111-1746 ☎ 877/426-8056, 978/323-4141 international callers, 877/426-2167 TTY ☎ 877/426-2166 ⊕ www.elderhostel.org.

SHOPPING

Southern Africa isn't the sort of place to shop for high-tech consumer goods, as they are quite expensive and import duties are so high you will almost certainly get a better deal on any nonlocal goods at home. By and large, you'll find that South Africa has a lot of crafts and artifacts from through-

out Africa. If you look around, you can find some excellent clothing buys, ranging from traditional "African chic" outfits to haute couture and some very-well-made and reasonably priced outdoor goods.

Bargaining is not part of South African culture. However, some traders have learned that tourists always try to bargain them down and so have been forced to raise their asking prices. If you think a price is a bit high, you can try to bargain down, but do it with a conscience. Be aware that you may be pushing an impoverished person into a barely profitable deal because they desperately need cash right then. Think long and hard before you gleefully knock someone down R5 or R10. What is it worth to you? To them it may mean the difference between feeding their children that night or not. Play it by ear and be sensitive.

CRAFTS & SOUVENIRS

Traditional arts and crafts—whether they're made in South Africa or other African countries—are very good buys. Keep an eye out for Zulu baskets, Ndebele beaded aprons, Zimbabwean printed fabrics, Kuba cloth from Zaire, fetishes and masks from West Africa, and Mali mud cloth and wedding blankets. But arts and crafts have also moved on, and you can get fabulous items made from unexpected materials. For instance, you might find little boxes—and even briefcases—made from the overruns of soft-drink-can metal. On almost every street corner you will find chickens made from plastic bags (they look better than they sound) and fabulous beaded animals—classic chameleons and, since the movie *Finding Nemo,* Nemos and Dorys ranging from tiddler to tarpon.

LUXURY GOODS

South Africa is a great place to buy gold and diamond jewelry, which is hardly surprising. There are numerous manufacturing jewelers who will make up a special design for you in a couple of days. Ostrich-leather goods are also a great buy.

WINE

Many wineries will mail your wine purchases to your home, as will the major wineshops. You are allowed a maximum of 24 bottles per person, at a cost of US$10 a bottle. Shipping takes about two weeks. Alternatively, you can contact one of the companies in the United States and Canada that import a wide range of Cape wines. Whatever you do, get hold of a copy of *John Platter's Wine Guide*, a handy little booklet that tells you everything you need to know about wine. Wines of South Africa is the official marketing arm of the South African wine industry.

🈲 John Platter's Wine Guide ⊕ www. platteronline.com. **Vaughan Johnson's Wine Shop** ✉ Pier Head, Dock Rd., Box 50012, Waterfront, Cape Town 8002 ☎ 021/419-2121 📠 021/419-0040 ✉ vjohnson@mweb.co.za. **Wines of South Africa** ☎ 021/883-3860 📠 021/883-3861 ⊕ www.wosa. co.za.

SIGHTSEEING GUIDES

All tourist guides in South Africa have to be registered and must wear their golden SA Tourism name tags.

STUDENTS IN SOUTH AFRICA

To save money, look into deals available through student-oriented travel agencies. To qualify, you'll need a bona fide student ID card. Members of international student groups are also eligible. Students get discounts at some museums—it's worth asking.

One of the best ways to get around southern Africa, including all of South Africa, is on the Baz Bus, a budget door-to-door bus catering to the needs of backpackers. You don't have to be young, but a cool attitude helps. Some of the game farms, most notably those in the Mantis Collection, offer great student programs—either just for fun or as a credit if you're studying a relevant subject.

🈲 IDs & Services **STA Travel** ✉ 10 Downing St., New York, NY 10014 ☎ 212/627-3111, 800/777-0112 24-hr service center 📠 212/627-3387 ⊕ www.sta. com ✉ 31 Riebeeck St., Cape Town 8001 ☎ 021/418-6570 📠 021/418-4689 ⊕ www.statravel.co.za. **Travel Cuts** ✉ 187 College St., Toronto, Ontario M5T 1P7, Canada ☎ 800/592-2887 in U.S., 416/979-2406 or 866/246-9762 in Canada 📠 416/979-8167 ⊕ www.travelcuts.com.

🈲 Tour Operators **Baz Bus** ✉ 8 Rosedene Rd., Sea Point, Cape Town 8005 ☎ 021/439-2323 📠 021/

439-2343 ✉ info@buzbus.co.za ⊕ www.bazbus. co.za. **Mantis Collection** 🏠 Box 10802, Steenberg Estate, Cape Town 7945 ☎ 021/713-2222 📠 021/713-2251 ✉ info@mantiscollection.com ⊕ www. mantiscollection.com.

TAXES

HOTEL

All South African hotels pay a bed tax, which is included in quoted prices.

VALUE-ADDED TAX

In South Africa the value-added tax (VAT), currently 14%, is included in the price of most goods and services, including hotel accommodations and food. To get a VAT refund, foreign visitors must present their receipts (minimum of R250) at the airport and be carrying any purchased items with them or in their luggage. You must fill out Form VAT 255, available at the airport VAT refund office. Whatever you buy, make sure that your receipt is an original tax invoice, containing the vendor's name and address, VAT registration number, and the words *tax invoice*. Refunds are paid by check, which can be cashed immediately at an airport bank. If you have packed your purchases in luggage you intend to check, be sure you visit the VAT refund desk before you go through check-in procedures. For items in your carry-on baggage, visit the refund desk in the departures hall.

🈲 VAT Refund Office ☎ 011/394-1117 ⊕ www. taxrefunds.co.za.

TELEPHONES

The parastatal (semi-state-run) phone system in South Africa is pretty good, but not without some bugs. A major difficulty is the high cost of scrap copper, so it's not unknown for a couple of miles of telephone cable to go missing overnight, leaving large areas incommunicado—even in Johannesburg. Cell phones are ubiquitous and have quite extensive coverage. There are three cell-phone service providers in South Africa—Cell C, MTN, and Vodacom. The least complicated way to make and receive phone calls is to obtain international roaming service from your cellphone service provider before you leave home, but this can be expensive. Cell phones can be rented by the day, week, or longer from the airport on your arrival.

There are toll-free numbers in South Africa. There is also something called a share-call line, for which the cost of the call is split between both parties.

🎧 Cellular Phone Rental Cell C Rentals ☎ 021/934-1452 in Cape Town, 011/390-2922 in Johannesburg ⊕ www.cellrentals.co.za. **Cellucity/Vodashop** ☎ 021/934-0492 in Cape Town, 011/394-8834 in Johannesburg ⊕ www.cellucity.co.za. **Mobile Solutions (MTN)** ☎ 021/934-3261 in Cape Town, 011/390-2234 in Johannesburg ⊕ www.mobilesolutions.co.za.

AREA & COUNTRY CODES

The country code for South Africa is 27. When dialing from abroad, drop the initial 0 from local area codes. When dialing out from South Africa, dial 09 before the international code. So, for example, you would dial 09/1 for the United States and Canada, 09/61 for Australia, 09/64 for New Zealand, and 09/44 for the United Kingdom. Other country codes are 267 for Botswana, 264 for Namibia, 260 for Zambia, and 263 for Zimbabwe.

DIRECTORY & OPERATOR ASSISTANCE

For directory assistance in South Africa, call 1023. For operator-assisted national long-distance calls, call 1025. For international operator assistance, dial 0903. These numbers are free if dialed from a Telkom (landline) phone but are charged at normal cell-phone rates from a mobile—and they're busy call centers. Directory inquiries numbers are different for each cell-phone network. Vodacom is 111, MTN is 200, and Cell C is 146. These calls are charged at normal rates, but the call is timed only from when it is actually answered. You can, for an extra fee, get the call connected by the operator.

LOCAL CALLS

Local calls are very cheap, although all calls from hotels attract a hefty premium. South Africa has two types of pay phones: coin-operated phones, which accept a variety of coins, and card-operated phones. Coin-operated phones are being phased out, and there aren't too many left in

tourist destinations. Phone cards are the better option; they free you from the hassle of juggling handfuls of coins, and they're available in several denominations. In addition, a digital readout tells you how much credit remains while you're talking. Cards are available at newsstands, convenience stores, and telephone company offices. When making a phone call in South Africa, always use the full 10-digit number, including the area code, even if you're in the same area.

LONG-DISTANCE SERVICES

AT&T, MCI, and Sprint access codes make calling long-distance relatively convenient, but you may find the local access number blocked in many hotel rooms. First ask the hotel operator to connect you. If the hotel operator balks, ask for an international operator, or dial the international operator yourself. One way to improve your odds of getting connected to your long-distance carrier is to travel with more than one company's calling card (a hotel may block Sprint, for example, but not MCI). If all else fails, call from a pay phone.

🎧 Access Codes AT&T Direct ☎ 0800/99-0123 from South Africa. **MCI WorldPhone** ☎ 0800/990-011 from South Africa. **Sprint International Access** ☎ 0800/990-001 from South Africa.

TIME

South Africa operates on CAST (Central African Standard Time), which is two hours ahead of Universal Time (UT). That makes it seven hours ahead of North American eastern standard time (six hours ahead during eastern daylight saving time). South Africa does not follow any daylight saving time.

TIPPING

Tipping is an integral part of South African life, and it's expected that you'll **tip for services that you might take for granted at home.** Most notable among these is getting gas, as there are no self-service stations. If the attendant simply fills your tank, tip R2–R3; if he or she offers to clean your windshield, checks your tires, oil, or water, and is generally helpful, tip R4–R5. In restaurants the size of the tip should depend on the quality of service, but 10% is standard, unless, of course, a service charge has already been added to the bill. Give the same percentage to bartenders, taxi drivers, and tour guides.

Hotel porters should receive R2–R3 per bag. Check with management regarding tips for room service and housekeeping. Different lodgings handle it differently. In game lodges, for example, it's handled through management. Informal parking attendants operate in the major cities in South Africa and even in some tourist areas. Although they often look a bit seedy, they do provide a good service, so tip them a couple of rand if your car is still in one piece when you return to it.

At the end of your stay at a private game lodge, you're expected to tip both the ranger and the tracker. Tipping guidelines vary from lodge to lodge, but plan to give the local equivalents of about US$10 per person per day to the ranger and not much less to the tracker; an additional tip of US$25 for the general staff would be sufficient for a couple staying two days.

TOURS & PACKAGES

Because everything is prearranged on a prepackaged tour or independent vacation, you spend less time planning—and often get it all at a good price.

BOOKING WITH AN AGENT

Travel agents are excellent resources. But it's a good idea to collect brochures from several agencies, as some agents' suggestions may be influenced by relationships with tour and package firms that reward them for volume sales. If you have a special interest, find an agent with expertise in that area; the American Society of Travel Agents (ASTA; ⇨ Travel Agencies) has a database of specialists worldwide. You can log on to the group's Web site to find an ASTA travel agent in your neighborhood.

Make sure your travel agent knows the accommodations and other services of the place being recommended. Ask about the hotel's location, room size, beds, and whether it has a pool, room service, or programs for children, if you care about these. Has your agent been there in person or sent others whom you can contact?

Do some homework on your own, too: local tourism boards can provide information about lesser-known and small-niche operators, some of which may sell only direct.

BUYER BEWARE

Each year consumers are stranded or lose their money when tour operators—even large ones with excellent reputations—go out of business. So check out the operator. Ask several travel agents about its reputation, and try to **book with a company that has a consumer-protection program.** (Look for information in the company's brochure.) In the United States, members of the United States Tour Operators Association are required to set aside funds ($1 million) to help eligible customers cover payments and travel arrangements in the event that the company defaults. It's also a good idea to choose a company that participates in the American Society of Travel Agents' Tour Operator Program; ASTA will act as mediator in any disputes between you and your tour operator.

Remember that the more your package or tour includes, the better you can predict the ultimate cost of your vacation. Make sure you know exactly what is covered, and beware of hidden costs. Are taxes, tips, and transfers included? Entertainment and excursions? These can add up.

🖪 Tour-Operator Recommendations **American Society of Travel Agents** (⇨ Travel Agencies). **National Tour Association** (NTA) ✉ 546 E. Main St., Lexington, KY 40508 ☎ 859/226-4444 or 800/682-8886 🖷 859/226-4404 ⊕ www.ntaonline.com. **United States Tour Operators Association** (USTOA) ✉ 275 Madison Ave., Suite 2014, New York, NY 10016 ☎ 212/599-6599 🖷 212/599-6744 ⊕ www.ustoa.com.

SPECIALTY TOUR OPERATORS

The advantages of dealing with a tour operator that specializes in the area you are planning to visit include better access to special deals, specialized local knowledge, and understanding of seasonal peculiarities. For example, a local operator won't send you on a delta trip at the wrong time of year.

Local Contacts Big Five ✉ 1551 S.E. Palm Ct., Stuart, FL 34994 ☎ 800/244-3483 ⊕ www.bigfive. com. **Karibu Safaris** ☎ 031/563-9774 ⊕ www. karibu.co.za. **Fairfield Tours** ☎ 021/930-3534 🖷 021/930-1850 ⊕ www.fairfieldtours.com. **Felix Unite Tourism Group** ☎ 021/683-6433 🖷 021/683-6486 ⊕ www.felixunite.com. **Premier Tours** ✉ 1430 Walnut St., 2nd Floor, Philadelphia, PA 19102 ☎ 800/545-1910) ⊕ www.premiertours.com. **Siyabona Africa** ☎ 021/424-1037 🖷 021/424-1036 ⊕ www.siyabona.com. **Sun Tours** ☎ 0861/696-059 ⊕ www.suntourssa.co.za. **Thompson's South Africa** ☎ 031/250-3100 ⊕ www.thompsonssa.com. **Wilderness Safaris** ☎ 011/807-1800 🖷 011/807-2110 ⊕ www.wilderness-safaris.com.

TRAIN TRAVEL

Shosholoza Meyl, part of the parastatal rail network known as Spoornet, operates an extensive system of passenger trains connecting all major cities and many small towns in South Africa. Departures are usually limited to one per day, although trains covering minor routes leave less frequently. Distances are vast, so many journeys require overnight travel. The service is good and the trains are safe and well maintained, but this is far from a luxury option. The old first and second classes have been replaced by referring to the cars as four-sleeper (old first class) and six-sleeper. The only difference between four- and six-sleeper is that the four-sleeper has two double bunks, whereas the six-sleeper has two triple bunks. Don't expect air-conditioning or heat in either class, and in either case you will be using a communal toilet and shower. The compartments have a sink. Bedding can be rented. The dining car serves pretty ordinary food, but it's reasonably well cooked and inexpensive. Third class is now referred to as "sitter class," because that's what you do—up to 25 hours on a hard seat with up to 71 other people in the car, sharing two toilets and no shower. You must reserve tickets in advance for four- and six-sleeper accommodations, whereas sitter-class tickets require no advance booking. You can book up to three months in advance with travel agents, reservations offices in major cities,

and at railway stations. Note that though the classes have been officially renamed, most people still refer to them by their old numeric names.

Shosholoza Meyl ☎ 086/000-8888 ⊕ www. spoornet.co.za.

LUXURY TRAIN TRIPS

A trip aboard the famous *Blue Train* has long been a highlight of a trip to South Africa. Compartments are individually air-conditioned and have remote-operated blinds and curtains, TV, CD player, and a personal mobile phone for contacting your butler/valet or making outgoing calls. The comfortably furnished lounge car offers refreshments and drinks throughout the day and is a good place to meet fellow travelers. There are two trains: the Classic and the African theme, which, while maintaining the same very high standard, is decorated with African touches such as faux animal-skin furniture and somewhat more exotic uniforms for the staff. In the well-appointed dining car, men are required to wear jacket and tie to dinner. On the Tshwane–Cape Town route, guests are treated to sparkling wine when the train stops in Kimberley and taken by coach on a tour of the historic diamond-mining town.

In addition to its regular run between Cape Town and Tshwane, the *Blue Train* does monthly trips between Cape Town and Port Elizabeth. All meals and alcohol are included in the ticket price, which ranges from R16,330 for a double in low season between Cape Town and Tshwane to R24,675 for a deluxe double in high season between Cape Town and Port Elizabeth via the Garden Route, both one-way.

Another luxury option is Rovos Rail. Sixty beautifully restored Edwardian-era cars make up three trains, which are drawn by a steam engine on certain sections. This opulent train carries a maximum of 72 passengers, attended by up to 21 staff members, including two gourmet chefs. Regular weekly trips are run between Tshwane and Cape Town and Tshwane and Victoria Falls (both two nights). Bi-weekly overnight trips are run between Cape Town and George. Every May a

7-day trip from Cape Town to Swakopmund (and back) is run, and in July there is a 13-day epic from Cape Town to Dar es Salaam (and, of course, back again). Prices per person sharing range from about R8,000 for a deluxe suite on the Cape Town–George run to about R50,000 for the Royal Suite on the *African Collage,* which is a seven-night, eight-day trip from Tshwane to Cape Town the long way around. The single-occupancy supplement is 50%. The cost of the Cape Town–Dar es Salaam trip ranges from US$7,600 to US$9,950 one-way, with a single supplement of US$3,000. The ticket covers everything, including alcohol, meals, and scheduled excursions.

▪ *Blue Train* ⌂ Box 2671, Joubert Park 2044 ☎ 011/773-7631 🖷 011/773-7643 ⊕ www.bluetrain. co.za. **Rovos Rail** ⌂ Box 2837, Pretoria 0001 ☎ 012/323-6052 🖷 012/323-0843 ⊕ www. rovosrail.co.za.

SPECIALTY TRAIN TRIPS

A really fun way to see the country is on the Shongololo Express—a devilishly clever idea. The train is pretty basic, much like the Shosholoza Meyl trains. While you sleep at night, it heads off to a new destination. After breakfast, tour buses are loaded, and you head off to explore the surroundings. In the evening, you climb back on the train, have supper, and sleep while you head off to the next fun destination. Rates start at about R1,000 per person per night sharing. By the way, a *shongololo* is a millipede.

▪ **Shongololo Express** ☎ 011/781-4616 ⊕ www. shongololo.com.

TRAVEL AGENCIES

A good travel agent puts your needs first. Look for an agency that has been in business at least five years, emphasizes customer service, and has someone on staff who specializes in your destination. In addition, **make sure the agency belongs to a professional trade organization.** The American Society of Travel Agents (ASTA)—the largest and most influential in the field with more than 20,000 members in some 140 countries—maintains and enforces a strict code of ethics and

will step in to help mediate any agent-client disputes involving ASTA members if necessary. ASTA (whose motto is "Without a travel agent, you're on your own") also maintains a Web site that includes a directory of agents. (If a travel agency is also acting as your tour operator, *see* Buyer Beware *in* Tours & Packages.)

South African Tourism runs a training program for travel agents. Graduates are called fundis, which means "expert" in Zulu. A list of fundis can be found on the SA Tourism Web site.

▪ Local Agent Referrals **SA Tourism** ⊕ www. southafrica.net. **American Society of Travel Agents** (ASTA) ✉ 1101 King St., Suite 200, Alexandria, VA 22314 ☎ 703/739-2782 or 800/965-2782 24-hr hotline 🖷 703/684-8319 ⊕ www.astanet.com. **Association of British Travel Agents** ✉ 68-71 Newman St., London W1T 3AH ☎ 020/7637-2444 🖷 020/ 7637-0713 ⊕ www.abta.com. **Association of Canadian Travel Agencies** ✉ 130 Albert St., Suite 1705, Ottawa, Ontario K1P 5G4 ☎ 613/237-3657 🖷 613/ 237-7052 ⊕ www.acta.ca. **Australian Federation of Travel Agents** ✉ Level 3, 309 Pitt St., Sydney, NSW 2000 ☎ 02/9264-3299 or 1300/363-416 🖷 02/ 9264-1085 ⊕ www.afta.com.au. **Travel Agents' Association of New Zealand** ✉ Level 5, Tourism and Travel House, 79 Boulcott St., Box 1888, Wellington 6001 ☎ 04/499-0104 🖷 04/499-0786 ⊕ www. taanz.org.nz.

VISITOR INFORMATION

See the individual chapter A to Z sections for details on local visitor bureaus.

▪ South African Government Tourist Offices **U.S.** ✉ 500 5th Ave., Suite 2040, New York, NY 10110 ☎ 800/822-5368 🖷 212/764-1980 ✉ 9841 Airport Blvd., Suite 1524, Los Angeles, CA 90045 ☎ 800/782-9772 🖷 310/641-5812. **Canada** ✉ 4117 Lawrence Ave. E, Suite 2, Scarborough, Ontario M1E 2S2 ☎ 416/283-0563 🖷 416/283-5465. **South Africa** ☎ 011/895-3000 🖷 011/895-3001 ⊕ www. southafrica.net. **U.K.** ✉ 5-6 Alt Grove, Wimbledon SW19 4DZ ☎ 0181/944-8080 🖷 0181/944-6705.

GOVERNMENT ADVISORIES

▪ **Australian Department of Foreign Affairs and Trade** ☎ 300/139-281 travel advice, 02/6261-1299 Consular Travel Advice Faxback Service ⊕ www.dfat. gov.au. **Consular Affairs Bureau of Canada** ☎ 800/267-6788 or 613/944-6788 ⊕ www.voyage. gc.ca. **New Zealand Ministry of Foreign Affairs**

and Trade ☎ 04/439-8000 ⊕ www.mft.govt.nz.
U.K. Foreign and Commonwealth Office ✉ Travel
Advice Unit, Consular Division, Old Admiralty Building, London SW1A 2PA ☎ 0870/606-0290 or 020/
7008-1500 ⊕ www.fco.gov.uk/travel. **U.S. Department of State** ✉ Overseas Citizens Services Office,
2100 Pennsylvania Ave. NW, 4th Floor, Washington,
DC 20520 ☎ 202/647-5225 interactive hotline or
888/407-4747 ⊕ www.travel.state.gov.

WEB SITES

Do check out the World Wide Web when
planning your trip. You'll find everything
from weather forecasts to virtual tours of
famous cities. Be sure to visit Fodors.com
(⊕ www.fodors.com), a complete travel-
planning site. You can research prices and
book plane tickets, hotel rooms, rental
cars, vacation packages, and more. In addition, you can post your pressing questions in the Travel Talk section. Other
planning tools include a currency converter and weather reports, and there are
loads of links to travel resources.

The official SA Tourism Web site (⊕ www.
southafrica.net) is reasonable for general
tourism information and pretty good on
events, but you'll really struggle to find a
decent hotel or other tourism product with
its search engine. Another government-
sponsored Web site, ⊕ www.southafrica.
info, is a mine of useful information about
the country generally and is a far better
bet than the SA Tourism site.

Getaway magazine's online portal—
⊕ www.getawaytoafrica.com—offers
really good information about all of Africa
as well as tours, packages, and an online
booking system. For information about activities all over the region, your best bet is
⊕ www.africa-adventure.org. For a good
rundown on most of the museums in
South Africa, try ⊕ www.museums.org.za.

The SANParks (formerly National Parks
Board) Web site (⊕ www.parks-sa.co.za) is
excellent, outlining where the parks are,
what kinds of accommodations they have,
what kind of animals you're likely to see,
and what activities are available. A really
good, user-friendly, commercial site is
⊕ www.krugerpark.co.za. For general information about safaris, ⊕ www.safari.co.
za offers online booking and is backed by
a call center. Both of these are operated by
Siyabona Africa.

To stay abreast of news and events in
South Africa, check out ⊕ www.iol.co.za,
the online version of Independent Newspapers, which is the biggest newspaper group
in South Africa and has papers in all the
major centers. The *Mail & Guardian* online (⊕ www.mg.co.za) provides a good
selection of South African and international news and insightful comment.

If you feel like surfing, use ⊕ www.ananzi.
com, a local search engine, and ⊕ www.
goafrica.co.za, a comprehensive directory
of Web sites pertaining to the whole of
Africa. For weather information, check
out ⊕ www.weathersa.co.za.

SAFARI PRIMER

By Andrew
Barbour, Julian
Harrison, and
David Bristow
Updated by
Kate Turkington

MENTION AFRICA and most of us conjure up visions of wildlife—lions roaring in the gathering dusk, antelope skittering across the savanna, a leopard silhouetted by the setting sun. The images never fail to fascinate and draw us in, and once you experience them in the flesh, you're hooked. The look, the feel—the dusty smell—of the African bush seep into your soul, and long after you've gone, you find yourself missing it with an almost physical longing.

Do everyone a favor, though, and pass up the impulse to rush out and buy khakis and a pith helmet. The classic safari is dead. Hemingway and the great white hunters took it to their graves, along with thousands upon thousands of equally dead animals. Indeed, too many wildlife documentaries have conditioned foreign visitors into thinking that Africa is overrun with animals. The truth is far less romantic—and much safer—especially in South Africa, where fences or rivers enclose all major reserves. The African bush is no Disney-choreographed show, however; this wilderness is a real one.

In choosing to take a safari, you'll embark on one of the biggest travel adventures of your life. It's a big investment of both time and money—and planning well is crucial to ensure you have a good time. Even a basic question like "what should I wear?" is extremely important. In this safari section, we'll cover all the special considerations and lingo you'll need, with plenty of insider tips along the way. *Fodor's African Safari: From Budget to Big Spending,* available at bookstores everywhere, has more information.

GETTING STARTED

It's never too soon to start planning your safari. There are many factors to consider just regarding the destination: geography, animal migrations, weather, visa requirements, and inoculations. You must also weigh some personal factors: your budget, schedule, fitness level, and comfort requirements. Most people start planning a safari six to nine months in advance, which allows time to set a spending limit, choose an itinerary, and organize travel documents. You can wait and plan the trip over a few weeks, but doing so greatly increases your chances of being closed out of the places you really want to see. In fact, planning your trip 12 months in advance isn't unreasonable, especially if you want to travel during peak season—November through February in South Africa, July through October elsewhere—and have your heart set on a particular lodge.

Deciding where you want to go and choosing the safari operator in whose hands you'll place your trip are the most important things you need to do. Start planning for your safari the way you would any trip. Read travel books about the areas that most interest you. Talk to people who have been on a similar trip; word-of-mouth advice can be invaluable. Get inspired. Line up your priorities. And find someone you trust to help plan your trip.

Travel Agents & Safari Operators

There's no substitute for a knowledgeable tour operator or travel agent who specializes in Africa. These specialists look out for your best interests, are aware of trends and developments, and functions as indispensable backup in the rare instance when something goes wrong.

Who's Who

African safari outfitter. Also referred to as a ground operator, this type of outfitter is a company in Africa that provides logistical support to a U.S.-based tour operator by seeing to the details of your safari. An outfitter might charter flights, pick you up at the airport, and take you on game-viewing trips, for example. Some outfitters own or manage safari lodges. In addition, an outfitter communicates changing trends and developments in the region to tour operators and serves as your on-site contact in cases of illness, injury, or other unexpected situations.

African-tour operator. Based in the United States, this type of company specializes in tours and safaris to Africa and works with a safari outfitter that provides support on the ground. Start dates and itineraries are set for some trips offered by the operator, but customized vacations can be arranged. Travelers usually find out about these trips through retail travel agents.

Air consolidator. A consolidator aggressively promotes and sells plane tickets to Africa, usually concentrating on only one or a few airlines to ensure a large volume of sales with those particular carriers. The airlines provide greatly reduced airfares to the consolidator, who in turn adds a markup and resells them directly to you.

Retail travel agent. In general, a travel agent sells trip packages directly to consumers. In most cases an agent doesn't have a geographical specialty. When called on to arrange a trip to Africa, the travel agent turns to an African-tour operator for details.

Before you entrust your trip to an agent, do your best to determine the extent of his or her knowledge as well as the level of enthusiasm he or she has for the destination. There are as many travel companies claiming to specialize in Africa as there are hippos in the Zambezi, so it's especially important to determine which operators and agents are up to the challenge.

After choosing a tour operator or travel agent, it's a good idea to discuss with him or her the logistics and details of the itinerary so you know what to expect each day. Ask questions about lodging, even if you're traveling on a group tour. A lodge that is completely open to the elements may be a highlight for some travelers and terrifying for others, particularly at night when a lion roars nearby. Also inquire about the amount of time you'll spend with other travelers. If you're planning a safari honeymoon, find out how many meals will be communal and ask about honeymoon packages.

Questions to Ask a Safari Specialist

Don't forward a deposit to a safari specialist (a general term for a safari outfitter or African-tour operator) until you have considered his or her answers to these questions. Once you have paid a deposit, you're liable for a penalty if you decide to cancel the arrangements for any reason.

- Do you handle Africa exclusively?
- How many years have you been selling tours in Africa?
- Are you or any of the staff native to the continent?
- To which professional organizations do you belong? For example, the American Society of Travel Agents (ASTA) or the United States Tour Operators Association (USTOA)?
- Has your company received any accolades or awards relating to Africa?
- Can you provide a reference list of past clients?
- How often do you and your staff visit Africa?
- What sort of support do you have in Africa?
- Do you charge a fee? (Agents and operators usually make their money through commissions.)
- What is your cancellation policy?
- Can you handle arrangements from start to finish, including flights?

Internet Caveat

Although the Internet is useful for booking in Europe and other destinations with a sophisticated travel infrastructure in place, it's not an efficient option for Africa, where tangled, complicated logistics are usually the norm in trying to piece together an itinerary. The Web sites with discounted packages can be tempting, and you may be keen on bargain-hunting overall, but it's important to remember that a bargain price may get you a cut-rate experience.

You may manage to successfully put together a trip on your own, but you'll be just that—on your own—once in your safari destination. Faced with a challenge such as a canceled flight, or something more drastic— like the floods that swept through South Africa's Sabi Sands region a few years ago—you won't have anyone back home to help you with new arrangements. Well-established and well-connected safari specialists can take advantage of long-standing business relationships to secure the assistance their clients need, whether it be last-minute transportation or lodging or a way to communicate with family back home. Furthermore, many safari lodges, such as those run by Wilderness Safaris, require individuals to reserve through an African-tour operator or a travel agent.

What's Your Budget?

When setting a safari budget, you must consider how much you want to spend. You can have a low-budget self-catering trip in one of South

Africa's national parks or spend a great deal of money in one of the small, pampering, exclusive camps in Botswana. Almost every market has high-priced options as well as some economical ones. When planning your safari budget, keep in mind three main factors: your flight, the actual safari costs, and extras. For information on air travel, *see* Smart Travel Tips.

Luxury Safaris

The most popular safari-planning option is to book with a tour operator and stay in private lodges, which are owned and run by an individual or company rather than a government or country. Prices at these lodges include all meals and, in many cases, alcoholic beverages, as well as two three- to five-hour-long game-viewing expeditions a day. Occasionally high-end lodges offer extra services such as spa treatments, boat trips, or special-occasion meals served alfresco in the bush. Prices range from US$350 to US$1,200 per person per night sharing a double room. If you travel alone, you have to pay a single supplement because all safari-lodge rooms are doubles. Safari lodges with unique or especially extravagant facilities or options charge accordingly—up to US$1,500 per person per night. Those who can afford private lodges say they're worth every cent for the spectacular game-viewing, the knowledgeable guides, the well-prepared food, and the attention to detail.

Safaris on a Shoestring

Don't let a tight budget deter you from a safari adventure. There are many opportunities for big-game experiences outside the luxury lodges. Your least expensive option is to choose one of the public game parks in southern Africa—Kruger National Park in South Africa, for example—where you drive yourself and self-cater (shop for and prepare all meals yourself). The price of this type of trip is approximately one-tenth of that for private, fully inclusive lodges.

Mobile safaris are another option. On this type of trip, travel is by four-wheel-drive vehicle (often something that looks like a bus), and you sleep in tents at public or private campsites. Although self-drive safaris are popular with locals, you need to be self-sufficient and bush-savvy to travel this way.

Rates for the camps in national parks, called rest camps, start at about R220 a day for a two-bed *rondawel* (a round hut modeled after traditional African dwellings) and go up to R510 for a four-bed bungalow. Budget about R35 for breakfast, R45 for lunch, and R75 for dinner per person for each day on the trip. You also need to figure in the small entrance charges to the parks (usually a one-time fee of less than R120 per person).

If you book into a private lodge off-season, you can save a bundle of money. Many lodges, in the Sabi Sands area of South Africa, for example, usually cost about US$500 per person per night during the high season but can drop to approximately US$300 a night during the slower months of July and August.

SAFARI PLANNING TIME LINE

Six Months Ahead
- Research destinations and options and make a list of the sights you want to see.
- Start a safari file to keep track of relevant information.
- Set a budget.
- Consult guidebooks and narrow your choices.
- Search the Internet. Post questions on bulletin boards.
- Contact a travel agent to start firming up details.
- Choose your destination and make your reservations.
- Buy travel insurance.

Three to Six Months Ahead
- Find out which travel documents you need.
- Apply for a passport, or renew yours if it's due to expire within six months of travel time.
- Confirm whether your destination requires visas and certified health documents.
- Arrange vaccinations or medical clearances.
- Research malaria precautions.
- Book excursions, tours, and side trips.

One to Three Months Ahead
- Create a packing checklist.
- Fill prescriptions for antimalarial and regular medications. Buy mosquito repellent.
- Shop for safari clothing and equipment.
- Arrange for a house sitter and a kennel for pets.

One Month Ahead
- Get copies of any prescriptions and make sure you have enough of any needed medicine to last you a few days longer than your trip.
- Confirm international flights directly and lodging reservations and transfers with your travel agent.
- Buy additional guidebooks and light reading.

Three Weeks Ahead
- Using your packing list, start buying articles you don't have. Update the list as you go.
- Take care of any clothes that need mending or other chores that require attention.

Two Weeks Ahead

- *Purchase traveler's checks and some local currency. Collect small denominations of U.S. currency ($1 and $5) for tips.*

- *Dry-clean and wash clothes.*

- *Get ready to pack; remember bag size and weight restrictions.*

One Week Ahead

- *Suspend newspaper and mail delivery.*

- *List contact numbers and other details for your house sitter.*

- *Check antimalarial prescriptions to see whether you need to start taking medication now.*

- *Arrange transportation to the airport.*

- *Make two copies of your passport's data page. Leave one copy, and a copy of your itinerary, with someone at home; pack the other separately from your passport.*

A Few Days Ahead

- *Take pets to the kennel.*

- *Pack.*

- *Reconfirm flights.*

- *Buy snacks and gum for the plane.*

One Day Ahead

- *Enable your e-mail "out of office" message.*

- *Check destination weather reports.*

- *Make a last check of your house and go through your travel checklist one final time.*

The Extras

You'll have other expenses besides airfare and safari costs, including tips, medications, and film and other sundries. For ease of travel, and to help you adjust to jet lag, plan to stay at a city hotel on your first and last nights in Africa. Expect to pay from US$50 for basic accommodations to a maximum US$750 a night in the most luxurious hotels.

Plan to spend, on average, US$5 to US$15 a day (per traveler) on gratuities. In South Africa tips are on the higher end of this range and usually are paid in rand (the local currency); you may also use U.S. dollars for tips, however. Elsewhere in southern Africa, U.S. currency is preferable, but tips paid in rand may also be accepted.

A two-week course of antimalarial medication costs between US$10 and US$100, depending on your health insurance. Stock up on film before you head out into the bush; a roll of regular print film costs about US$3 to US$4 in South Africa and soars to US$8–US$12 in a safari camp. And don't forget to put some money aside for souvenirs; you'll undoubtedly want to take home reminders of your trip.

WHERE & WHEN TO GO

The countries covered in this book are in the Southern Hemisphere, and their seasons are opposite to those in the Northern Hemisphere. Winter runs from about June through September, spring from October through November, summer from December through March, and fall from April through May.

To make the most of your trip, plan to spend at least two nights at any one place—be it a private lodge or a rest camp. Game-viewing can't be rushed. Racing around from camp to camp is a waste of time and money—give yourself the pleasure of slowing down, appreciating your surroundings, and taking in the sights and sounds of the bush. It's also important to remember that the concept of time in Africa is different from Western time. Patience and good humor are often needed here.

South African safari destinations are covered in the pertinent regional chapters of this book. Safari destinations in neighboring Namibia and Botswana are discussed in Chapter 10, Botswana & Namibia's Best Safari Destinations.

Timing

No two people can agree on the best time to visit the bush. Summer (December–March) is certainly hot, with afternoon rain a good possibility, but the bush is green, the animals are sleek and glossy, and the bird-life is prolific. Unfortunately, it's the worst time of year to spot game. All the foliage makes finding game harder, and animals tend to disperse over a wide area because they are no longer reliant on water holes and rivers. Winter, on the other hand, is a superb time for game-viewing because trees are bare and animals congregate around the few remaining water sources. Because the weather's cooler, you may also see lions and leopards hunting by day. Most lodges drop their rates dramatically during winter months, often lopping as much as 30%–40% off their peak-season prices. The drawbacks to a winter visit are the cold and the fact that the bush looks dead and the animals thin.

A happy compromise may be the shoulder seasons. Overall, in October and most of November the weather is pleasant, the trees have blossoms, and migrant birds are arriving—even better, the antelope herds begin to drop their young. In April the temperature is also fine, many of the migrant birds are still around, and the annual rutting season has begun, when males compete for the right to mate with females and are much more visible.

In **South Africa,** summer—that is, November through February—is high season because that's when South Africans take their vacations. However, the weather can be hot, with temperatures frequently reaching 100°F in January and February. There's also the rain; in Kruger, the Kalahari, and Zululand, the annual rains fall from late November through February, mostly in the form of afternoon thundershowers. In many safari locations, including Kruger, summer is the high malaria season. The remainder of the year is predominantly dry and, as there are no mass migrations, the game-viewing is good almost year-round. In winter some areas stay mild (Zululand among them), but others get very cold. For instance, in July temperatures in Kruger can dip down to the freezing point, and in the Kalahari temperatures can drop to 10°F. The winter months, July and August, are considered the low season, and therefore fewer tourists frequent the private lodges. In fact, this is a superb time for game-viewing, and you can find some great deals.

In **Botswana** the tourism high season corresponds to the dry season: winter, roughly July through October. Although winter days are warm—70°F to 85°F—nights can be cold, down around 35°F. The rains arrive in late November and last through February, generally in the form of afternoon thundershowers. When these showers turn into electrical storms, the weather show can rival the most elaborate fireworks display. The threat of malaria is highest during these wet months, when mosquitoes breed. (Some 95% of malaria cases in Botswana occur December through May.) Summer days are usually in the 85°F to 100°F range. It's considered the off-season. The shoulder months of June and November are considered mostly low season, and are great times to view game at much-reduced costs.

The best time to travel to **Namibia** is winter, May through October. Winter days may be warm, but winter nights are cold to downright freezing. Rain usually falls in summer, with a short rainy season in November and the main rainy season from February to March, which is also prime malaria season. In the Namib Desert, rain sometimes doesn't fall for 10 years or more.

National Parks & Game Reserves

South Africa has more than a dozen national parks and a host of provincial reserves, but only a few contain all the indigenous species that once roamed the veld in vast herds. Good roads, plentiful and cheap accommodations, and excellent facilities are what differentiate South African parks from their East African counterparts.

But if you picture yourself bouncing in an old Land Rover through an untouched golden landscape in pursuit of big game, South Africa's national parks will disappoint you. They bear less resemblance to the Serengeti than to America's national parks: they are superbly managed, sometimes overcrowded, and bear the marks of civilization.

Take Kruger National Park, for instance, the crown jewel of South Africa's reserves and the second-largest game reserve in Africa. It's a magnificent tract of pristine wilderness that is home to an astonishing number of animals. Like all South Africa's parks, it's completely open to the public, and you can tour and view game from the comfort of your own car. In fact, you could tour Kruger in a Porsche if you so desired. Many of the park roads are paved, and rangers even set up speed traps to nail overzealous game-watchers (take your car off-road and the dung will really hit the fan). Signposts throughout the park direct visitors to everything from scenic viewpoints to picnic sites and rest areas selling soft drinks and snacks.

It's no wonder, then, that foreign visitors sometimes act like they're in a giant petting zoo. But even in parks like Kruger, one or two animals are killed each year to save visitors in harm's way. South Africa's game reserves may impose a veneer of domesticity on the wilderness, but don't let this lull you into letting your guard down or becoming blasé.

The national parks look the way they do for good reason: they are the country's natural heritage, set up for the use and enjoyment of its citizens, which until recently meant whites only. For many South African families a trip to a game reserve is an annual rite, as certain as death and taxes. On December weekends Kruger's rest camps look like they're on fire because of all the barbecue smoke. One reason for this popularity is their affordability: a couple probably won't pay more than R500 to stay in a rest camp.

South Africa's game parks are becoming more attuned to foreign travelers and their expectations. Accommodations in the park rest camps are cheap, comfortable, but numbingly institutional. In Kruger the South African National Parks symbol—the head of a kudu bull—is plastered over everything from your towel to the sheets to the bathroom walls. All camps are fenced against the animals, and some have better facilities than small towns: gas stations, mechanics, grocery stores, laundromats, cafeterias, restaurants—even a car wash. And the restaurants' food tends to be mediocre. Not surprisingly, many foreign visitors shy away from the rest camps, dreaming instead of something more remote or more glamorous. If that's you, check out the bushveld camps in Kruger, which are more expensive than the regular camps but offer excellent accommodations, exclusivity, and, as always in the park, great game-viewing.

Don't write off the public parks too quickly, though. Few people can afford to stay in the exclusive private lodges more than a few days, and the game reserves offer a chance to explore some of Africa's richest and most beautiful country at a fraction of the cost, especially if you drive yourself. Armed with a good field guide to wildlife, you can learn an enormous amount about African game from the driver's seat of a rental car.

National parks in Botswana and Namibia vary a great deal, although they're much more geared for foreign visitors than they were a few years ago. They have more facilities and a better understanding of tourists and their needs. Botswana's "low impact–high cost" tourism policy makes the national parks very pricey; park fees are more than US$20 per person *per day*. Botswana national parks have no permanent hutted camps as in Kruger, only camping sites, often in quite inaccessible places, and you will certainly need a 4×4 to get to most of them. Unless you have a lot of time and determination, stick to private lodges. Remember that the Okavango, for example, is a watery wilderness where most places are accessible only by plane or boat. Though roads between cities and towns are good (watch out for stray domestic animals and game), those in the parks are dirt roads (mud when wet) and sometimes almost impossible to drive. However, Namibia's Etosha National Park is a great place to drive yourself. There are both bush roads and paved roads between the hutted camps and excellent facilities at all the camps. And there's nothing quite like doing your own thing—stopping when you please, spending hours checking out the game at a water hole, and spotting your "very own" elephant. Namibia has an excellent tourism infrastructure, with simple but clean and comfortable accommodations in all its national parks. Road conditions vary a lot, from tarred roads to gravel and dirt roads; check out conditions on a daily basis. Always book national park accommodations well in advance.

Private Game Reserves & Concessions

In southern Africa, game areas bordering national parks and other tracts of wilderness have been sectioned into private areas and leased to safari companies who then have the exclusive right to build game lodges and traverse the area for game drives or other activities. This concession system is now being extended into the national parks themselves, as government conservation authorities let private operators handle the tourism side of the business.

Staying on a private game reserve is a much more expensive option than staying in a national park, but if you can afford it, don't miss out, because private reserves offer a wildlife experience without parallel. You can get close to the animals because, after many years of exposure, they no longer see the game vehicles as a threat. That doesn't mean they don't sometimes object to your presence: an elephant charge will clear out more than your sinuses.

The rangers know the reserves intimately, and can introduce you to sights and sounds that you would have missed on your own: a medicinal shrub, a male dung beetle busily rolling its ball of dung to a suitable site, a lion ant trapping its prey. On game drives at bigger camps, rangers stay in contact with one another via radio, so that if one group has a good sighting, other vehicles can come have a look, too. Most lodges coordinate this carefully, so that there's not too much traffic at any one sighting.

Although the quality of the game-viewing and the expertise of the staff are major attractions of a private game reserve, there's also a fantasy aspect to their appeal. The lodges on the reserves and concessions also sell exclusivity, and many of them unite shameless luxury and bush living. You'll get chic design, comfortable beds, flush toilets, running water, hot showers—even air-conditioning—but the bush still lies right outside your door. Nothing stops an elephant from joining you for dinner. For more details on the luxury lodge experience, *see* Types of Safaris, *below.*

TYPES OF SAFARIS

Do you picture yourself zipping from camp to camp in a tiny Cessna, getting a bird's-eye view of a water hole? Or inspecting an animal track up close while on a multiday walk through the bush? Since there are many kinds of safaris, you should think hard about what approach suits you best. There are high- and low-end versions of each option, and you can always mix and match options to create your ideal itinerary.

Luxury Lodge–Based Safaris

The majority of safari goers base their trips at luxury lodges, which pack the double punch of outstanding game-viewing and stylish, atmospheric accommodations. A lodge may be made up of stone chalets, thatch-roof huts, rondawels, or large suitelike tents. Mosquito nets, leather furnishings, and mounted trophies add to the ambience. Dinners are served in an open-air *boma* (traditional thatch dining enclosure). All have hot-and-cold running water, flush toilets, toiletries, laundry service, electricity, and, in most cases, swimming pools. In South African lodges rooms also have air-conditioning, telephones, hair dryers, and minibars. The most lavish places also have private plunge pools.

Make no mistake—you pay for all this pampering. Expect to spend anywhere from R2,000 to R8,000 (US$300 to US$1,300) per person per night. All meals and game drives are included. A three-night stay is ideal, but two nights are usually sufficient to see the big game.

The time you spend at a private lodge is tightly structured. With some exceptions, the lodges offer almost identical programs of events. There are usually two three- to four-hour game drives a day, one in the early morning and another in the evening. You spend a lot of time sitting and eating, and in the afternoon you can nap and relax. However, you can always opt for an after-breakfast bush walk, and many lodges now have spas and gyms. If you're tired after your night drive, ask for something to be sent to your room, but don't miss the bush *braai* (barbecue) and at least one night in the boma.

On game drives at bigger camps, rangers stay in contact with one another via radio. If one finds a rhino, for example, he relays its location to the others so they can bring their guests to have a look. It's a double-edged sword. The more vehicles you have in the field, the more wildlife everyone is likely to see. At the same time, too many vehicles create a rush-hour effect that can destroy the whole atmosphere—and the environment. Most lodges are very well disciplined with their vehicles, rarely allowing more than three or four vehicles at a sighting. As your vehicle arrives, one already there will drive away. In choosing a game lodge remember to check how much land a lodge can traverse and how many vehicles it uses. Try to go on a bush walk with an armed ranger—an unforgettable experience, as the ranger can point out fascinating details along the way.

All lodges arrange transfers from nearby airports, train stations, or drop-off points, as the case may be. In more remote areas most have their own private airstrips carved out of the bush and fly guests in on chartered aircraft at extra cost. If you're driving yourself, the lodge will send you detailed instructions, because many dirt back roads don't appear on maps and lack names.

A Day at a Luxury Lodge

You are awakened in the dark—anytime from 5 AM in summer to 7 AM in winter—by a cheerful voice. Within 15 to 30 minutes you're in the dining area, having coffee and a light breakfast with your guide. A half hour to an hour after waking, you climb into a game-drive vehicle and head off in search of animals, which are most active before the heat of the day sets in. The morning drive usually lasts three or four hours. You might see lions feasting on a kill from the previous night or zebras having a breakfast of grass, and you'll stop for coffee as the sun rises. At the end of the drive you return to the lodge for a huge cooked brunch.

Early afternoon is for napping, bird-watching around camp, and reading, with time for a dip in the pool if there is one. Some lodges offer a guided game walk or arrange visits to local villages.

In midafternoon you gather in the dining area for high tea. Then it's back into the game-drive vehicle for the evening ride to look for animals waking up from their late-day naps or getting ready for their evening hunting. This ride lasts three to four hours and usually includes a stop at sunset for cocktails, called sundowners. In addition to providing refreshment, these stops allow you to quietly savor the sounds, sights, and smells of this most magical time in the bush. On the slow drive back to camp, a powerful spotlight may be used to illuminate nocturnal animals. After a brief period for freshening up, dinner is served around 8 PM, often in a boma, followed by drinks around the campfire, and, if your hosts are amenable, fireside stories. You can turn in whenever you like, but remember that you need to be up before the sun the next day.

If you stay more than two days, most lodges will also serve a bush braai, a full barbecue spread out in the veld, with hurricane lanterns hanging in the thorn trees, a crackling fire, and the sounds of Africa all around you. Under a full moon it's incredibly romantic.

Tip: You'll be awed by the brilliance of the night skies on safari, especially if you live in a city. To add romance and interest to your stargazing, study up on the southern skies and bring a star guide.

CloseUp

SAFARI SPEAK

The following words and terms are used throughout the book.

Big Five: buffalos, elephants, leopards, lions, and rhinoceros, collectively

Boma: a fenced-in open-air eating area, usually circular

Braai: barbecue

Bush or bushveld: general safari area in South Africa, usually with scattered shrubs and trees and lots of game; also referred to as the bush or the veld

Camp: used interchangeably with lodge

Campground: a place used for camping that encompasses several campsites and often includes some shared facilities

Campsite: may or may not be part of a campground

Concession: game-area lease that is granted to a safari company and gives it exclusive access to the land

Game guide: used interchangeably with ranger; usually a man

Hides: small, partially camouflaged shelters from which to view game and birds; blinds

Kraal: traditional rural settlement of huts and houses

Lodge: accommodation in rustic-yet-stylish tents, rondawels, or lavish suites; prices at lodges usually include all meals and game-viewing

Mobile or overland safari: usually a self-sufficient, camping affair set up at a different location (at public or private campgrounds) each night

Mokoro: dugout canoe; plural mekoro

Ranger: safari guide with vast experience with and knowledge of the bush and the animals that inhabit it; used interchangeably with game guide

Rest camp: camp in a national park

Rondawel/rondavel: a traditional, round dwelling with a conical roof

Self-catering: with some kind of kitchen facilities, so you can store food and prepare meals yourself

Self-drive safari: budget-safari option in which you drive, and guide, yourself in a rented vehicle

Tracker: works in conjunction with a ranger, spotting animals from a special seat on the front of the four-wheel-drive game-viewing vehicle

Veld: a grassland; see bushveld

Vlei: wetland or marsh

Fly-In Safaris

The mode of transportation for fly-in safaris is as central to the experience as the accommodations. In places such as northern Botswana, where few roads are paved, or northern Namibia, where distances make road transfers impractical, small bush planes take you from lodge to lodge. These planes are usually six-seat Cessna 206 craft flown by bush pilots. The planes have no air-conditioning and in summer can be quite warm, especially in the afternoon. If flying in small planes makes you uncomfortable, this type of safari is not for you.

However, flying from destination to destination is a special experience. The planes stay at low altitudes, allowing you to spot game along the way; sometimes you can see, for example, elephant and buffalo herds lined up drinking along the edges of remote water holes or large numbers of zebras walking across the plains. Fly-in safaris also allow you to cover more territory than other types of safaris. In Botswana, for example, the trip between the diverse game destinations of the Moremi Wildlife Reserve in the Okavango Delta and northern Chobe National Park is 40 minutes by plane; it would take six hours by vehicle, if a road between these locations existed.

Hopping from place to place by plane is so easy and fast that many travelers make the mistake of cramming their itineraries with too many lodges. Plan your trip this way and you'll spend more time at airstrips, in planes, and shuttling to and from the airfields than tracking animals or enjoying the bush. You will glimpse animals as you travel back and forth—sometimes you'll even see them on the airstrips—but you won't have time to stop and really take in the sights. If possible, spend at least two nights at any one lodge; three nights is even better.

The best way to set up a fly-in safari is to book an all-inclusive package that includes airfare. (It's impractical to try to do it yourself.) A tour operator makes all the arrangements, and many offer standard trips that visit several of its lodges. For example, in Botswana, Orient-Express Safaris has a package that includes three camps in three very different locations.

Lighten Up

The key to fly-in safaris is to pack light. In southern Africa the maximum weight allowed for luggage is 26 pounds (South Africa is the exception to this rule). Your bag should be a soft-sided duffel or something similar, so the pilot can easily fit it into the small cargo area. Consider also that the less you bring the more time you'll save packing and unpacking every time you switch lodges.

If your bag is over the weight limit, or if you weigh more than 220 pounds, you will be required to purchase an additional plane seat (usually about US$100).

Walking Safaris

Many lodges offer walks as an optional way to view game. On a walking safari, however, you spend most, if not all, of your time in the bush on foot, accompanied by an armed guide. Because you're trekking through big-game country, there's an element of danger. But it's the proximity to wilderness that makes this type of trip so enchanting—and exciting. Of course, you can't stop every step of the way or you'd never get very far, but you will stop frequently to be shown something—from a native flower to spoor to animals—or to discuss some aspect of animal behavior or of tracking. Some walking safaris cover more distance than others, and their primary aim is to reach the next checkpoint; others move at a much slower pace in order to concentrate on gaining bush knowledge and seeing animals and wildlife. Choose the one that best suits you, or you could become frustrated.

Walking treks take place on what are known as wilderness trails, which are natural tracks made by animals and are traversed only on foot, never by vehicle, to maintain their pristine condition. These trails usually lead into remote areas that you would never see on a typical safari. In most cases porters or donkeys carry the supplies and bags. Accommodation is usually in remote camps or occasionally in tents. On "primitive trail" trips you're required to carry your own bags and sleep under the stars (primitive trails don't use tents). This is an extreme option and is not the most common type of walking safari.

The Umfolozi Wilderness Area of South Africa's Hluhluwe-Umfolozi Game Reserve, where wilderness trails were pioneered, is a popular walking safari destination. The wilderness trails in public Kruger National Park, where national-park rangers guide you, are also excellent; trails need to be reserved 13 months in advance, when bookings first become available.

If you consider a walking safari, you must factor in your physical condition. You should be in good health and be able to walk between 4 and 10 mi a day, depending on the parameters of the trip. Some trips don't allow hikers under age 12 or over age 60. Also, you shouldn't scare easily. No guide has time for people who freeze up at the sight of a beetle, spider, or something more menacing up close; guides need to keep their attention on the wilds around them and on the group as a whole. The guides are armed, and they take great caution to keep you away from trouble. Sometimes, however, trouble comes looking for you, so you are expected to shoulder a good deal of the burden in terms of your behavior. Your best insurance against getting in harm's way is to always listen to your guide and follow instructions.

Walking trails are usually three days, four nights. Expect to pay R2,150 for a national-parks walking trail.

A Day on a Walking Safari

The evening you arrive at base camp you sit around the fire after supper and establish what the walking program will be. Maybe there are birders in the group who wish to stop and start and mosey along at a slower pace than others. It's important to reach consensus. Ask the ranger what he (or she) has in mind. The trail is never intended to be a forced march; it's a back-to-nature, interpretive experience. The next morning you are wakened at dawn. After tea and coffee, you set off into the wilderness for a five- to six-hour walk, stopping by a river to watch hippos, resting under the shade of giant trees to listen to birds, or maybe tracking lions or rhinos. At the halfway point there's a drink and snack break (cheese, cookies, dried fruit), and then it's back to camp for brunch and a rest during the hottest part of the day. In late afternoon you may be driven in an open-air vehicle to a superb sunset-view site. Then it's back to a blazing campfire, tales of the wilderness and a swapping of experiences, and early to bed.

Mobile & Overland Safaris

In places such as Botswana and Namibia, where in the 1970s and '80s hunting concessions controlled the best safari areas, so-called photographic-safari operators gained access to these areas by special four-wheel-drive vehicles. And thus the mobile, or literally overland, safari was born. Travel was usually in specially adapted Land Rovers and, later, Toyota Land Cruisers that were fitted with extra seats, long-range fuel tanks, high canopies, and large windows. You'd climb aboard in Johannesburg, Windhoek, or Maun and head off into the bush with your friendly, experienced, and knowledgeable guide.

Today most mobile-safari operations are expertly run but are nevertheless budget options. Some of those twinkle-eyed young guides eventually bought out or outbid the hunting concessions and now have thriving safari businesses. Mobile excursions are mostly self-sufficient camping affairs with overnights at either public or private campgrounds, depending on the safari's itinerary and price. Sometimes you stay at basic lodges along the way. Travel is often by something that looks like a four-wheel-drive bus.

For young people, or the young at heart, mobile safaris are a great way to see the land from ground level. You taste the dust, smell the bacon cooking, stop where and when you want (within reason), and get to see the best places in the region. Many of these trips are aimed at budget-conscious travelers; prices are especially low if you book with a local operator after arriving in South Africa.

Trips usually run 14 to 21 days, although you can find shorter ones that cover fewer destinations. Prices start at US$750 and climb to US$2,500 for the trip all-inclusive. Not sure whether this is right for you? Consider combining a mobile safari with a lodge-based one, which gives you the best of both worlds. A minimum of 10 nights is recommended for such an itinerary.

A Day on a Mobile Safari

Before sunrise you wake up in a "fly camp"—a group of small tents you pitch yourself, set up in a new location at the end of every day. You have time for a steaming cup of coffee or tea before departing at dawn on a game drive. You have to pack before you leave for the morning drive because while you're out, breakfast is being prepared and the camp broken down.

A grand breakfast (you'll be amazed what can come out of a simple camping kitchen) awaits your return from the game drive, which usually takes

CloseUp

TREADING LIGHTLY

What is true ecotourism? It's difficult to say because the term is widely used but lacks a widely accepted definition. In general, however, ecotourism aims to expose travelers to natural areas, preferably those areas practicing sustainable land use while conserving these very places; to educate travelers about the physical and/or cultural environment of these areas; and to bring about positive developments for the local communities. Not every safari strives to achieve all these goals.

Definitions aside, you should, on a basic level, care and be informed about the environment and the people you visit, particularly in places where living conditions are poor. What can you do? For starters, ask your tour operator and safari outfitter for specifics about how their trips are run and what their relationship is to the local communities where the trips are held. You can also ask specific questions about ecological measures, such as whether the

lodges utilize solar power and conserve water. Don't litter, pay too much or too little for services and curios or souvenirs (ask locals for advice), or feed wild animals. If you'd like to help local conservation efforts or support local communities, ask about funds and trusts set up by safari operators, and make a donation. And try to heed the ethic of taking only photographs and leaving only your footprints—but do have fun along the way.

a few hours. Then you're off, driving leisurely through the African wilds and toward your next overnight destination, which you reach by early afternoon. Lunch is normally a snack at a scenic spot en route. Sometimes you can take a guided game walk in the afternoon; otherwise, you have an hour or two to rest before the evening game drive.

When you return, there's time to freshen up with a hot bucket shower (a pecking order quickly asserts itself as to who goes first and last), and then it's time for dinner under the stars. A proper table is laid, right down to wineglasses and chilled beer. Everyone winds down at night around the campfire, with the sounds of the night creatures, the smell of acacia-wood smoke, and the dazzling ceiling of the Milky Way.

Self-Drive Safaris

A self-drive safari, where you drive yourself in your own rental vehicle, is a great option for budget travelers and for those who feel comfortable seeing the bush without a ranger at hand to search out game or explain what you're seeing. The two most popular and easiest-to-navigate options for this kind of trip are Kruger National Park in South Africa and Etosha National Park in Namibia. These two parks have paved, well-marked roads and a wide range of accommodations that include family-size chalets, small huts, tents, and hostel-like dorms. You may buy your own groceries and cook for yourself at all of these areas; some options, especially in Kruger, have restaurants and small stores on-site.

If possible, rent a van or a four-by-four, since the higher off the ground you are the better your chances of spotting game. But a two-wheel-drive car is fine, and you can stop and start at your leisure; remember that you have to stick to marked roads. In addition to patience, you'll need drinks, snacks, and a ready camera. Keep your eyes and ears open and you may come across game at any time, in any place.

An indispensable aid is a good park map, showing not only the roads but also the location of watering holes, different ecozones, and the types of animals you can expect to find in each. It's no good driving around open grassland searching for black rhinos when the lumbering browsers are miles away in a woodland region. You can buy these maps when you enter a park or at rest-camp shops, and it would be foolish to pass them up.

When planning your day's game drive, plot your route around as many water holes and rivers as possible. Except during the height of the summer rains, most game must come to permanent water sources to drink. In winter, when the land is at its most parched, a tour of water holes is bound to reap great rewards. Even better, take a picnic lunch along and park at the same watering hole for several hours. Not only will you see plenty of animals, but you'll find yourself slipping into the drama of the bush. Has that kudu seen the huge crocodile? What's making the impala nervous? What's that sitting on my car?

GETTING READY TO GO

You've picked your safari location and firmed up your travel plans. Now it's time to start your detail planning. You need to organize your papers, create thorough packing lists, and do more homework on your destination. You also should research the currency used and international exchange rates, tipping practices, health precautions, photographic needs, and the weather. If you take the time to manage the details before you leave, the only bumps on your safari should be in your 4×4 as you traverse the African bush.

The Paper Trail

You need a valid passport to travel to any African country. If you don't have a passport, apply immediately, because the process takes approximately five to six weeks. For a greatly increased fee, the application process can be shortened to as little as one week, but leaving this detail to the last minute can be stressful. If you have a passport, check the expiration date; if it's due to expire within six months of your return date, you need to renew your passport at once. Certain countries, such as South Africa, won't let you enter with a soon-to-expire passport; you also need two blank pages in your passport to enter South Africa.

Check on what immunizations are required for the countries you're visiting. Some countries may demand an inoculation certificate if you arrive directly from a tropical area or have traveled to one prior to your safari trip.

If you're taking a self-driving safari in a national park or will be renting a car before or after your safari in countries other than South Africa and Namibia, you need an international driver's license. These licenses are valid for one year and are issued while you wait at any American Automobile Association (AAA) office in the United States; you must have a current U.S. driver's license. You need to bring two passport-type photographs with you for the license. A valid U.S. driver's license is accepted in South Africa and Namibia.

Tip: If you're planning a honeymoon safari, make sure the bride's airline ticket, passport, and visas all use the same last name. Any discrepancies, especially between a passport and an airline ticket, will result in your trip being grounded before you ever take off. Brides may want to consider waiting to change their last name until after the honeymoon. And be sure to let the lodge know in advance that you are on your honeymoon. You'll get lots of special goodies and extra-special pampering thrown in.

Travel Insurance

Get a comprehensive travel-insurance policy in addition to any primary insurance you already have. Travel insurance incorporates trip cancellation; trip interruption or travel delay; loss or theft of, or damage to, baggage; baggage delay; medical expenses; emergency medical transportation; and collision damage waiver if renting a car. These policies are offered by most travel-insurance companies in one comprehensive policy and vary in price based on both your total trip cost and your age.

Tip: Purchase travel insurance within seven days of paying your initial trip deposit. For most policies this will not only ensure your trip deposit, but also cover you for any preexisting medical conditions and default by most airlines and safari companies. The latter two are not covered if your policy is purchased after seven days.

Many travel agents and tour operators stipulate that travel insurance is mandatory if you book your trip through them. This coverage is not only for your financial protection in the event of a cancellation but also for coverage of medical emergencies and medical evacuations due to injury or illness, which often involve use of jet aircraft with hospital equipment and doctors on board and can amount to many thousands of dollars.

If you need emergency medical evacuation, most travel-insurance companies stipulate that you must obtain authorization by the company prior to the evacuation. Unfortunately, many safari camps and lodges are so remote that they don't have access to a telephone, so getting prior authorization is extremely difficult if not impossible. You should check with your insurance company before you leave to see whether it has this clause and if so, what can be done to get around it. Good travel agents and tour operators are aware of the issue and will address it.

Money Matters

Most safaris are paid for in advance, so you need money only to cover personal purchases and gratuities. (The cash you take should include small denominations, like US$1, US$5, and US$10, for tips.) If you're not on a packaged tour and are self-driving, you need to carry more money. Credit cards—MasterCard, Visa, and, to a much lesser extent, American Express and Diners Club—are accepted throughout South Africa (American Express and, for the most part, Diners Club are not accepted in Botswana) and at most group-owned lodges and hotels, but not much elsewhere. Always check in advance whether your preferred card is accepted at the lodge. If you're self-driving, note that many places prefer to be paid in the local currency, so make sure you change money where you can.

Tip: It's a good idea to notify your credit-card company that you'll be traveling to Africa, so that unusual-looking transactions aren't denied.

Health Issues

If you stick to cities and safari lodges, you won't be at an exaggerated health risk for most diseases. The real danger is malaria, but by taking the necessary precautions you should be well protected.

Malaria

Malaria is the most common parasitic infection in the world. It infects 300 to 500 million people each year in some 90 countries of the tropical and subtropical regions of the globe and kills between 1.5 million and 3 million. Malaria infects about 10,000 returning travelers each year, killing about 1% of them. However, malaria is preventable and shouldn't prevent you from going on safari.

Malaria occurs throughout the tropics and in adjacent hot and low-lying areas. The disease is spread by the female Anopheles mosquito, which is infected with the malaria parasite. She spreads it by picking it up from an already infected person and passing it on when she next feeds on the high-protein blood she needs to reproduce.

This female Anopheles mosquito is the ultimate insect Stealth fighter plane; she is shy and feeds only between dusk and dawn, usually after midnight when you are most soundly asleep. She is almost silent when she flies and she homes in mainly on your exhaled carbon dioxide and body warmth. When she locates you, this pesky little critter can spend hours searching for access to your skin through a small hole in your clothing or mosquito net. If you have been infected, you can expect to feel the effects anywhere from 7 to 90 days afterward. Typically you will feel like you have the flu, with worsening high fever, chills and sweats, headache, and muscle aches. In some cases this is accompanied by abdominal pain, diarrhea, and a cough. If it's not treated you could die.

It's possible to treat malaria after you have contracted it, but this shouldn't be your long-term strategy for dealing with the disease.

DOCUMENT CHECKLIST

- Passport
- Visas, if necessary
- Airline tickets
- Proof of yellow-fever inoculation
- Accommodation and transfer vouchers
- Car-rental reservation forms
- International driver's license
- Copy of information page of your passport
- Copy of airline tickets
- Copy of medical prescriptions
- Copy of traveler's check numbers
- List of credit-card numbers and international contact information for each card issuer

- Copy of travel insurance and medical-emergency evacuation policy
- Travel agent's contact numbers
- Notarized letter of consent from one parent if the other parent is traveling alone with their children

Tip: If you feel ill even several months after you return home, tell your doctor that you have been in a malaria-infected area. The onset of flu-like symptoms—aching joints or headache—is often the first sign that you have contracted either tick-bite fever (a bacterial infection transmitted by ticks with symptoms including fever, severe headache, and a rash consisting of small red bumps) or malaria. Take it very seriously and go for a blood test immediately.

The first malarial protection method is to practice "safe safari"—that is, avoid getting bitten in the first place. Start your precautions by treating your clothes with a mosquito-repellent spray or laundry wash before you leave home. Most of these last approximately 14 days and through several washings and contain the active ingredient permethrin, which is sold as Permanone and Duranon. This spray is specifically for clothes and shouldn't be used on skin. You can find it at camping and outdoor stores such as Eastern Mountain Sports. Bring a mosquito-repellent spray that contains DEET and light-colored clothing, as mosquitoes (and tsetse flies) are attracted to dark surfaces, where they're hard to detect. For more tips on what to do once you're on safari, see the malaria section of Health on Safari, *below*.

There's no vaccine against malaria, but there are several medications you can use to protect yourself from getting the disease. In the United States, mefloquine (known as Lariam) was the most widely used antimalarial until relatively recently. Although the active ingredient mefloquine works well against the disease, it can have strong side effects, such as depression, nightmares, and hallucinations. And it shouldn't be used by anyone on any other medication, including birth-control hormones. Chloroquine and Malarone are currently the most recommended antimalaria medications in the United States. They are easy to take and have few known side effects.

Consult a doctor who has knowledge of malarial areas to prescribe the correct medication. If you live in an area without a tropical-disease specialist, consult the Centers for Disease Control and Prevention (CDC) Web site for more information. It's vital that you take the prescribed dosage and the full course of the antimalarial medication because the incubation period for malaria can last up to four weeks after your return. Not taking even the last tablet of a multiweek course can mask the disease for several months; when it does erupt it will be more advanced and harder to detect than if you had followed the full regimen.

Where children are concerned, you cannot be too safe. The CDC recommends that parents of children traveling to a malarial area see a doctor four to six weeks prior to the trip. There are several prescription antimalaria drugs, including mefloquine and Malarone, that have been approved by the CDC for use by children. Malaria's effects on young children are much worse than they are on older people, and both the effects of malaria and the side effects of malarial prophylactics put strain on young kidneys. For this and other health reasons, it's best not to visit malarial areas with children under age 10 unless you practice stringent nonchemical preventive measures. Another, easier option is to choose a nonmalarial safari destination, including Waterberg, Pilanesberg and Sun City, or the Eastern Cape in South Africa and the Skeleton Coast or Etosha Pan in Namibia.

Other Health Issues

Yellow fever isn't inherent in any of the countries discussed in this book. Southern countries may, however, require you to present a valid yellow-fever inoculation certificate if prior to arrival you traveled to a region infected with yellow fever.

Hepatitis A can be transmitted via contaminated seafood, water, or fruits and vegetables. According to the CDC, hepatitis A is the most common vaccine-preventable disease in travelers. Immunization consists of a series of two shots received six months apart. You need have received only the first one before you travel. This should be given at least four weeks before your trip.

The CDC recommends vaccination for hepatitis B only if you might be exposed to blood (if you are a health-care worker, for example), have sexual contact with the local population, stay longer than six months, or risk exposure during medical treatment. As needed, you should receive booster shots for tetanus-diphtheria (every 10 years), measles (you're usually immunized as a child), and polio (you're usually immunized as a child).

WHAT TO PACK

If you're flying to safari destinations with regular airports where large airplanes are used—Hoedspruit or Nelspruit's Kruger Mpumalanga International Airport, both in South Africa—normal international airline baggage allowances apply. Otherwise, access to game-viewing areas is often by light aircraft, on short sandy landing strips; therefore, luggage weight restrictions are strictly enforced. You'll be allowed one duffel-type bag, approximately 36 inches by 18 inches, so that it can be easily packed into the baggage pods of a small plane. One small camera and personal-effects bag can go on your lap. Keep all your documents and money in this personal bag.

Do yourself a favor and leave breakables and valuables at home. If you'd be heartbroken if an item was broken or lost, it probably doesn't belong on a safari.

Tip: At Johannesburg International Airport you can check bags at Lock-Up Luggage, one level below international departures. The cost is approximately US$5 per bag per day.

Clothing

Just because you're going to Africa, don't think you can pack light cottons and nothing else. If you're heading to a private lodge, be sure to take a long, thigh-length padded jacket, even in midsummer (from December to March) because it can get mighty cold in an exposed, open 4×4 at dawn or after dark. All lodges provide blankets and rain ponchos in their vehicles, but that's often not enough. A couple of pairs of pants with zip-off legs are versatile and useful, as is a photographer/safari vest with lots of pockets. Don't forget sunscreen, insect repellent, Band-Aids, and medications like painkillers, indigestion pills, and eyedrops. A small flashlight is always useful.

Tip: Tinted fashion glasses are in most cases not strong enough for the harsh African sunlight. When shopping for sunglasses purchase Polaroid and UV-protected ones.

Light, neutral-colored clothes are universally worn on safari. Khaki-colored clothing was first used in Africa as camouflage by the South African Boers, and then by the British army that fought them during the South African War. The khaki color replaced the famously conspicuous red coats of the British and helped them blend into the open veld. Light colors also help to deflect the harsh sun and, unlike dark colors, are less likely to attract mosquitoes.

Start with these basics when you're packing: for summer, two pairs of shorts (skirts or sarongs are great, too); two T-shirts or short-sleeve shirts; two long-sleeve lightweight shirts for sun and bug protection; two pairs of long pants; sandals; sneakers or light boots, depending on what type of safari you're taking; a sun hat or baseball cap; and a light rain jacket or Windbreaker. Women may want to consider packing a support or sports bra, which can make things much more comfortable during a bumpy ride. On some safaris, dinners are dressy; ask your travel agent about what to expect, and pack appropriately. In winter, eliminate the shorts and add a warm jacket, a sweater or sweatshirt (lightweight and warm, fleece is an especially good choice), gloves, and a warm hat.

Tip: Because of recent guerrilla bush wars in Africa, and due to its association with hunting, jungle camouflage clothing isn't appropriate for a game-viewing safari. In some countries, including South Africa, it is banned for reasons of security.

Think twice about packing blue jeans. For one, denim is heavy and therefore takes a long time to dry if you're having laundry done in the bush. Also, in areas where tsetse flies occur, the traps used to lure the insects are a dark blue color, similar to the dye of many jeans. It's possible that in these locations your jeans could make you a tsetse-fly target.

You should need only three changes of clothing for an entire trip; almost all safaris include laundry as part of the package. If you're self-driving you can carry more, but washing is still easy and three changes of clothes should be ample if you use drip-dry fabrics that need no ironing. On mobile safaris you're expected to wear tops and bottoms more than once, and either bring enough underwear to last a week between lodges, or wash as you go in the bathroom sink. In summer, clothes dry overnight in the hot African air.

Tip: Note that in certain countries—Botswana, for example—the staff won't wash underwear because it's against their cultural custom.

For game walks, pack sturdy but light walking shoes or boots—in most cases durable sneakers suffice for this option. For a walking-based safari, you need sturdy, lightweight boots. Buy them well in advance of your trip so you can break them in. If possible, isolate the clothes used on your walk from the remainder of the clean garments in your bag. Bring a couple of large white plastic garbage bags for dirty laundry.

Toiletries & Sundries

Most hotels and game lodges provide toiletries such as soap, shampoo, and insect repellent, so you don't need to overpack these items. In the larger lodges in South Africa, in the national parks as well as the private game reserves, stores and gift shops are fairly well stocked with clothing, film, and guidebooks; in self-drive and self-catering areas, shops also carry food and drink. In Botswana, lodges that belong to groups such as Wilderness Safaris or Gametrackers have small shops with a limited selection of books, clothing, film, and trinkets. Elsewhere in Africa you're not likely to find this type of amenity on safari.

On a canoe safari you're in the relentless sun every day and have to protect your legs, especially the tops of your thighs and shins, from sunburn. Bring a towel or, even better, a sarong, and place it over your legs. Sunscreen of SPF 30 or higher is de rigueur.

Tip: The African sun is harsh, and if you're even remotely susceptible to burning, especially coming from a northern winter, don't skimp on sunscreens and moisturizers. Also bring conditioner for your hair, which can dry out and start breaking off.

Plugging In

Most of Southern Africa is on 220/240 volt alternating current (AC). The plug points are round. However, there are both large 15-amp three-prong sockets (with a ground connection) and smaller two-prong 5-amp sockets. Most lodges have adapter plugs, especially for recharging camera batteries; check before you go, or purchase a universal plug adapter before you leave home.

Safari hotels in the Serengeti, the private reserve areas outside Kruger National Park, and the less-rustic private lodges in South Africa are likely to provide you with plug points and plugs, and some offer hair dryers and electric-razor sockets as well (check this before you go). Lodges on limited generator and solar power are usually able to charge camera batteries, so long as you have the right plug.

Binoculars

The bush is teeming with life—much of it on the petite side. You'll miss thousands of birds, small meerkats, tortoises, dung beetles, and tree species without a pair of binoculars. Plus, from a greater distance you'll be able to watch larger animals behaving in a totally unhindered way.

Although your guide may have binoculars in the safari vehicle, don't count on being able to borrow them at the precise moment an African eagle takes off from its nest or when a leopard is spotted in a tree 300 yards away. One of Africa's greatest attractions is its bird-life, and sea-soned safari goers can be identified by the binoculars slung around their necks and the bird field guides in their hands. You'll gain an entirely new perspective on the bush with binoculars at hand. Many people find that when they start using binoculars and stop documenting each trip detail on film, they have a much better safari experience.

Binoculars come in many types and sizes, and you basically get what you pay for. Avoid buying a cheap pair because the optics will be poor and the lenses usually don't stay aligned for long (especially if they get bumped, which they will on safari). The most expensive binoculars have specially tinted lenses and are auto-focusing; these are a great option if they fit into your budget. For game-viewing, compact binoculars are fine, but for birds you might want a more powerful pair. Take them with you on a night drive; you'll get great visuals of nocturnal animals and birds by the light of the tracker's spotlight.

The minimum size you should consider is around 7×30 (this means the magnification is seven times and the diameter of the lens, which determines how bright the image will be, is 30mm). Up to 10×60 is good, but larger sizes can become too heavy to use for any length of time. If binoculars are not light enough to hold steady for a good while, they will start shaking and will magnify not only the image but also the shake, making them difficult to use in a moving vehicle.

CAMERA SMARTS

All the safaris included in this book are photographic (game-viewing) safaris. That said, if you spend your entire safari with one eye closed and the other peering through a camera lens, you may miss all the other sensual elements that contribute to the great show that is the African bush. And more than likely, your pictures won't look like the photos you see in books about African safaris. A professional photographer can spend a full year in the field to produce a book, so you are often better off just taking snaps of your trip and buying a book to take home.

There's no shortage of first-class coffee-table books on the African bush. Once, when asked how he was able to capture the images he did, a wildlife photographer answered "five miles." He had calculated that he'd shot five miles of 35mm film in his professional life (at a cost of around US$200,000 for the film and processing).

Tip: No matter what kind of camera you bring, be sure to keep it tightly sealed in plastic bags while you're traveling to protect it from dust. (Dust is especially troublesome in Namibia.) Tuck your equipment away when the wind kicks up. You should have one or more cloth covers while you're working, and clean your equipment every day if you can.

Learning some basics about the wildlife that you expect to see on your safari will help you capture some terrific shots of the animals. If you know something about their behavior patterns ahead of time, you'll be primed to capture action, like when the hippos start to roar. Learning from your guide and carefully observing the wildlife once you're there will also help you gauge just when to click your shutter.

Photography Pointers

For point-and-shoot cameras, you should use a 35mm camera with at least a 300mm lens and a sandbag to act as a rest (you can't set up a regular tripod on a vehicle). Light readings in glaring sunshine can be tricky, so be sure to bracket your shots. No matter what camera you use, you're bound to take an embarrassing number of bum shots—animals caught fleeing—so it pays to shoot bucketloads of film. You may want to pack a couple of disposable cameras that allow you to take panoramic shots.

The trick to taking great pictures has three components: first is always good light. An hour after sunrise and before sunset are the magic times. The light is softer; textures pop when light comes from the side and rear. For the few hours of harsh light each side of midday, you might as well put your camera away. The second component is framing. Framing a

PACKING CHECKLIST

- Two cotton T-shirts
- Two long-sleeve cotton shirts
- Two pairs shorts or two skirts in summer
- Two pairs long pants (three pairs in winter)
- Optional: sweatshirt and pants, which can double as sleepwear
- Optional: a dressy dinner outfit
- Underwear and socks
- Walking shoes or sneakers
- Sandals
- Bathing suit
- Warm thigh-length padded jacket, or sweater, in winter
- Windbreaker or rain poncho
- Camera equipment, plenty of film, and extra batteries
- Contact lenses, including extras
- Eyeglasses
- Binoculars
- Personal toiletries
- Malaria tablets
- Sunscreen and lip balm with SPF 30 or higher, moisturizer, and hair conditioner
- Antihistamine cream
- Insect repellent with minimum 30% DEET
- Basic first-aid kit (aspirin, bandages, antidiarrheal, antiseptic cream, etc.)

- Tissues and/or premoistened wipes
- Hat, scarf, and gloves (for winter)
- Sun hat and sunglasses
- Documents and money (cash, traveler's checks, credit cards), etc.
- A notebook and pens
- Travel and field guides
- A couple of large white plastic garbage bags
- U.S. dollars in small denominations ($1, $5, $10) for tipping

scene so that the composition is simple gives an image potency; with close-ups, fill the frame for maximum impact. Using objects of known size in the foreground or middle ground will help establish scale. The third component is capturing sharp images: use a tripod or a beanbag to rest the camera on while in a vehicle. When using a long lens (upward of 200mm), you cannot hand-hold a steady shot; you must have some support if you want your photos to be clear.

Take lots of film with you because it's not always available on safaris. Also, take spare batteries; two sets of spares if you're going for longer than a week.

Digital Cameras

Good digital cameras and their memory cards or sticks may be more expensive than basic 35mm cameras, but the benefits of being able to preview shots, select what you want and delete what you don't, store them, and then adjust them on a computer can outweigh the initial cost. The resolution of nonprofessional digital images is approaching that of good film. Cameras with eight megapixels of resolution can print high-quality, smooth A4 or letter-size prints; images with five-megapixel resolution are fine as well.

Invest in a telephoto lens to shoot wildlife, as you tend to be too far away from the animals to capture any detail with the zoom lens generally built into most point-and-shoot digital cameras. This may mean upgrading to a more robust camera. A tripod or beanbag is another must-have; it will stabilize your camera, especially when a zoom lens is extended.

Buy or borrow as many memory cards as you can—you'll use them. You may want to use multiple smaller memory cards to minimize the risk of losing an entire card's worth of images. And, as always, bring extra batteries.

Video Cameras

Video cameras these days are almost universally digital. The benefits of video are threefold: it's much easier to get basically pleasing results with moving images than with still photography; video cameras are much more light-sensitive than still cameras, so you can shoot in much lower light conditions; and you can edit your tapes and show them on your VCR at home. There's also the added benefit of the zoom-lens capability on most video cameras, which can give you almost as close a look at large animals as with binoculars (the zoom doesn't work as well with smaller, far-off subjects). Video cameras are hungry for batteries, however, and you may run into recharging problems in remote safari destinations.

Another problem with video cameras (but not for the person behind the lens) is that persistent videographers can become annoying to the other people in a group, so be sensitive about this. Don't go everywhere with your camera glued to your eye while simultaneously issuing nonstop commentary. Eventually someone is going to tell you to plug it, or worse.

Resist poking your lens close to strangers' faces—it looks great through the lens but these are not paid actors, and they'll appreciate being given their own space.

ON SAFARI

The pieces are falling into place, but your idea of what life is like on safari may still be a golden-tinged haze. The whos, whats, and hows still need to come into focus. If you have questions like, Where's the best place to sit in a game-drive vehicle? and Can you get near a honey badger? then read on.

Game-Viewing

This is the heart of a safari, and it has certain similarities regardless of the safari destination you've chosen. First, there's the overwhelming primeval atmosphere. You realize that you are the transient visitor in an ancient tableau of nature that has been going on since the dawn of time. Then there are the animals, from tiny rodents to the largest of land mammals, all going about their daily business: feeding, killing or avoiding being killed, and engaging in the never-ending territorial disputes that have evolved between species to ensure the maximum reproductive success of each animal group. The species you see are selected by time and nature; they are supremely adapted to their unforgiving habitats. You can move through the scene in dreamlike wonderment, but the strong scents of the bush, the birdsong, the bellows, and the roars remind you that you are very much awake, and alive.

Game Rangers & Trackers

Game rangers (sometimes referred to as guides) tend to be of two types: those who have come to conservation by way of hunting and those who are professional conservationists. In both cases they have vast experience with and knowledge of the bush and the animals that inhabit it.

For better or worse, the quality of your bush experience depends most heavily on your guide or game ranger. A ranger wears many hats while on safari: he's there to entertain you, protect you, and put you as close to the wilderness as possible while serving as bush mechanic, first-aid specialist, and host. He'll often eat meals with you, will explain animal habits and behavior while out in the bush, and, if you're on foot, will keep you alive in the presence of an excitable elephant, buffalo, hippo, or lion. This is no small feat, and each ranger has his particular strengths. Because of the intensity of the safari experience, with its exposure to potentially dangerous animals and tricky situations, your relationship with your guide or ranger is one of trust, friendliness, and respect. Misunderstandings may sometimes occur, but you're one step closer to ensuring that all goes well if you know the protocols and expectations.

On game drives, rangers work in conjunction with trackers, who sit in a special seat on the front of the four-wheel-drive vehicle, spot animals, and advise the rangers where to go. These trackers are invariably blacks who grew up in the area and know the bush intimately. Some of them become rangers, but many don't speak English well enough to communicate the extraordinary wealth of their knowledge. If the tracker speaks good English and seems comfortable talking to you, consider discussing animals with him.

The vast majority of rangers used to be white and male, but this is changing rapidly. Very often now your ranger will be local and have come up through the ranks of trackers. (They're still almost invariably men, though, hence our use of masculine pronouns.) Don't hesitate to ask him about local native cultures and their relationships with the land and its creatures—if this interests you. This link with traditional cultures adds immeasurably to an experience of Africa.

Most rangers are personable, knowledgeable, and devoted to conservation. The turnover rate is so high, however, that it's impossible in this book to recommend a particular ranger at a specific lodge. The best you can do is select a lodge that has a proven ranger-training program.

Tip: Gratuities are a fact of life on safari. In southern Africa you may tip in U.S. currency or, when South Africa's currency is strong, in rand. Plan to give the local equivalents of about US$10 per person per day to the ranger and not much less to the tracker; an additional tip of US$25 for the general staff would be sufficient for a couple staying two days. Tips are presented as a lump sum at the end of the trip. Consider including a thank-you note with the tip as a personal touch.

Wondering how to treat your ranger? Acknowledge that your guide is a professional and an expert in the field, and defer to his knowledge. Instead of trying to show how much you know, follow the example of the hunter, which is to walk quietly and take notice of all the little signs around you. Save social chatter with the guide for when you're back at camp, not out on a game drive. Rangers appreciate questions, which give them an idea of your range of knowledge and of how much detail to include in their animal descriptions. However, if you like to ask a lot of questions, save some for later, especially as several other people are likely to be in the safari vehicle with you. Carry a pocket notebook on game drives and jot down questions as they occur; you can then bring them up at dinner or around the campfire, when your ranger has more time to talk and everyone can participate in the discussion.

Wondering how your ranger will treat you? You can expect your ranger or guide to behave with respect: you are the client and he is the service provider, and you can expect delivery of that service 100% of the time. A guide should be pleasant and friendly but never too chummy or, worse, patronizing. If you believe a show-off guide or gung-ho ranger is speaking down to you, a quiet word with him should be enough to change his demeanor. (The safari world is small; a guide's reputation is built by word of mouth and can be eroded in the same fashion.)

Don't let your ranger get away with rote guiding, or "guiding by numbers"—providing only a list of an animal's attributes. Push him by politely asking questions and showing you'd like to know more. Even the best guides may experience "bush burnout" by the end of a busy safari season with demanding clients, but any guide worthy of the title always goes out of his way to give you the best possible experience. If you suspect yours has a case of burnout, or just laziness, you have a right to ask for certain things. There's never any harm in asking, and you can't expect your guide to read your mind about what you like. If, for example, you have a preference for birds, insects, or whatever, ask your guide to spend time on these subjects. You may be surprised by how happy he is to oblige.

Game-Viewing with a Ranger

When you're in the care of a professional guide or ranger, you're unlikely to be placed in a dangerous situation. If you're going for a walk or ride in risky territory, your guide will first brief you about all the possible dangers and tell you how to behave in the unlikely event of an emergency. Listen to all the safety briefings and adhere to them strictly.

At most southern African camps and lodges, open vehicles with raised, stepped seating—meaning the seats in back are higher than the ones in front—are used for game drives. There are usually three rows of seats after the driver's row; the norm at a luxury lodge is to have two people per row. In the front row you'll have the clearest conversations with the ranger, but farther back you'll have a clearer, elevated view over the front of the car. Try not to get stuck in the very back, though; in that row you spend a lot of time ducking thorny branches, you're exposed to the most dust, you feel the most bumps, and communicating with your ranger is difficult because of the rows between you. In closed vehicles, which are used by private touring companies operating in Kruger National Park, sit as close to the driver-guide as possible so you can get in and out of the vehicle more easily and get the best views.

The tracker will be busy searching out animal tracks, spoor, and other clues to nearby wildlife while the guide drives and discusses the animals and their environment. As described in Luxury Lodge–Based Safaris, *above,* rangers often communicate with each other via radio when someone has a good sighting.

Even though you're not at the wheel, when you spot an animal, observe it carefully and gauge when your presence begins to have an effect on it. Fight the urge to get as close as you can. Not all game guides and rangers are sensitive to this, their focus being on giving you the best sighting. But if you feel uncomfortable, say so.

Guided bush walks vary, but usually a maximum of eight guests walk in single file with the armed ranger up front and the tracker at the back. A bush walk is a more intimate experience than a drive. You are up close with the bush and with your fellow walkers and guides. Your guide will brief you thoroughly about where and how to walk, emergency procedures, and the like.

Game-Viewing on a Self-Drive Safari

Although most animals in popular parks are accustomed to vehicles with humans in them and will carry on unperturbed in many cases, a vehicle should still approach any animal carefully and quietly, and the driver should "feel" the response. This is for your own and the animals' safety. A delicate approach also gives you a better chance of getting as close as possible without alarming the animal. Be conservative and err on the side of caution, stopping as soon as circumstances suggest.

Human presence among wild animals never goes unnoticed. Don't get out of the vehicle, even if the animals appear friendly, and don't feed the creatures. Animals don't associate people in a vehicle with the potential food source or possible threat that they are when out of the vehicle. But for this ruse to work you must be quiet and still. The smell of the exhaust fumes and noise of a vehicle mask the presence of the human cargo, so when the engine is off you need to exercise extra caution. This is especially true when closely viewing lions and elephants—the only two animals likely to attack a vehicle or people in a vehicle. When approaching lions or elephants, never leap out of your seat or talk loudly; you want to be able to get as close as possible without scaring them off, and you want to avoid provoking an attack.

It does take time to develop your ability to find motionless game in thick bush. On the first day you're less likely to spot an animal than to run it over. All those fancy stripes and tawny colors really do work. Slowly, though, you learn to recognize the small clues that give away an animal in the bush: the flick of a tail, the toss of a horn, even fresh dung. To see any of this, you have to drive *slowly,* 15–25 kph (10–15 mph). Fight the urge to pin back your ears and tear around a park at 50 kph (30 mph) hoping to find something big. The only way to spot game at that speed is if it's standing in the road or if you come upon a number of cars already at a sighting. But remember that being the 10th car at a game sighting is less exciting than finding the animal yourself. Not only do the other cars detract from the experience, but you feel like a scavenger—a sort of voyeuristic vulture.

The best time to find game is in the early morning and early evening, when the animals are most active, although old Africa hands will tell you that you can come across good game at any time of day. Stick to the philosophy "you never know what's around the next corner," and keep your eyes and ears wide open all the time. If your rest camp offers guided night drives on open vehicles with spotlights—go for it. You'll rarely be disappointed, seeing not only big game, but also a lot of fascinating little critters that surface only at night. Book your night drive in advance or as soon as you get to camp.

Animal Kingdom

Talk to travel agents about a safari, and sooner or later they will start babbling about the Big Five. This was originally a hunting term referring to those animals that posed the greatest risk to hunters on foot—elephants, black rhinos, leopards, lions, and buffalo—yet it has now become the single-most important criterion used in evaluating a lodge or reserve. Although the Big Five label may have helped engender tourist interest in African wildlife, it can also demean the entire bush experience, turning it into a treasure hunt. You will be amazed how many visitors ignore a gorgeous animal that doesn't "rank" in the Big Five or lose interest in a species once they've checked it off their list. After you've spent a few days in the bush, you will also recognize the idiocy of racing around in search of five animals when there are another 150 equally fascinating species all around you. You get a completely different experience looking for the Little Five: the elephant shrew, lion ant, leopard tortoise, buffalo weaverbird, and rhinoceros beetle. It's up to you to tell your ranger exactly what kind of wildlife you want to see.

Until several decades ago, the Big Five were present in just about every game reserve. In many areas today, however, poaching and in some cases poor land management have brought about local extinction, mainly of elephants and rhinos. For instance, in the mid-1980s the Lower Zambezi Valley had 10,000 black rhinos, the highest concentration in the world. Today it has none.

Tip: Arm yourself with specialized books on mammals and birds rather than a more general one that tries to cover too much. Airports, lodges, and camp shops stock a good range, but try to bring one with you and do a bit of boning up in advance. Any bird guide by Ken Newman (Struik Publishers) and the *Sasol Guide to Birds* are recommended.

Wildlife Safety & Respect

Immersion in the African safari lands is a privilege. In order to preserve this privilege for future generations, it's important to view wildlife with minimal disturbance and to avoid upsetting the delicate balance of nature at all costs. Remember that you're a visitor to these animals' territories, so act like you would in someone else's home: respect their space.

Nature is neither kind nor sentimental. Nothing is wasted in the great pyramid of life in the African bush—from lion and hyena to vulture and jackal to dung beetle. Do not be tempted to interfere with these natural processes. The animals are going about the business of survival in a harsh environment, and you can unwittingly make this business more difficult. Don't get too close to the animals; you might cause alarm or influence a hunt by chasing away the prey or shielding a predator's approach. Don't even pick up a tortoise to help it across some perceived obstacle; you have no idea what it's really trying to do, or where it wants to go. If you're intrusive, you could drive animals away from feeding and, even worse, from drinking at water holes, where they are very skittish and vulnerable to predators. That time at the water hole may be their only opportunity to drink that day.

Never feed any wild creature—not a cute monkey, not an inquisitive baboon, not a baby tree squirrel, or a young bird out of its nest. When you feed wild animals you help to habituate them to humans, and the animals get closer to humans than they normally would. If an animal then feels threatened, the likelihood of a fatal attack increases. Feeding young birds can transfer your scent to them or to their nest. In either case you are ultimately signing the animal's death warrant, because problem animals will eventually have to be shot and adult birds will abandon their young if they smell of humans. Also, by giving food you

GAME-WATCHING DO'S & DON'TS

- *Observe animals silently and with a minimum of disturbance to their natural activities. Standing up in your vehicle and talking loudly on game drives can frighten animals away.*

- *Never attempt to attract an animal's attention. Don't imitate animal sounds, clap your hands, pound the vehicle, or throw objects.*

- *Show respect for your driver and guide's judgment: don't insist that he take the vehicle closer so you can get a better photograph. Getting too close may hinder a hunt or cause animals to abandon a hard-earned meal and put you in danger. Driving off-road in certain areas can cause the guide to lose his license.*

- *Don't litter—any tossed item can choke or poison animals.*

- *Never attempt to feed or approach any wild animal. This is especially important to remember near lodges and in campgrounds, where animals may have become accustomed to human visitors.*

- *Don't get out of the vehicle without permission for any reason, even if nature's calling.*

- *Refrain from smoking on game drives. The dry African bush ignites easily.*

- *Dress in neutral-toned clothes because animals pay the least attention to muted colors; if everyone in the car is wearing beige, brown, green, and tan, the animal sees one large vegetation-colored mass.*

- *Use a minimum of body fragrances for the benefit of both the animals and your fellow travelers.*

diminish that animal's ability to feed itself. In some cases, such as where lodges throw their waste into the veld, baboons and other animals can become displaced like city tramps.

In some camps and lodges animals have gotten used to being fed or stealing food. The most common animals in this category are baboons and monkeys; in some places they sneak into huts, tents, and even occupied vehicles to snatch food. If you see primates around, keep all food out of sight, and keep your windows rolled up. (If a baboon manages to get into your vehicle, he will trash the interior as he searches for food and pretty much use your car as a bathroom.) Otherwise, give them a wide berth—even vacate an area if they seem intent on being there. Like other animals, baboons and monkeys are vicious when they feel threatened or cornered, and they have huge canine teeth. A male baboon can kill a leopard, and a monkey will easily overpower you and deliver nasty wounds.

Never try to get an animal to pose with you. This is probably the biggest cause of death and injury on safaris, when visitors don't listen to or believe the warnings from their rangers or posted notices in the public parks. Regardless of how cute or harmless they may look, these animals are not tame. An herbivore impala, giraffe, or ostrich can kill you just as easily as a lion, elephant, or buffalo can. Smaller animals such as mongooses and otters are also predators that can kill or injure something much bigger than themselves, so stay clear of them as well.

Other animals may not be such active and aggressive pests, but pose problems of their own. The honey badger, for example, is an intriguing animal. It's black and white, looks like a skunk on steroids, and walks with the swaying gait of a large lizard. Although the honey badger is the size of a small dog, it's one of the fiercest animals in Africa and will stand up to a large lion. If you see one around, give it a wide berth—most people in the know would rather face just about any other animal than an enraged honey badger.

Caution is your most trusted safety measure. Keep your distance, keep quiet, and keep your hands to yourself, and you should be fine.

Nighttime Safety

At night, never sleep out in the open in any area with wildlife. If you're sleeping in a tent make sure it's fully closed; if it's a small tent, place something between you and the side of the wall to prevent an opportunistic bite from the outside. If you're in your tent and not exposed, you should be quite safe. Few people lose their lives to lions or hyenas. Malaria is a much more potent danger, so keep your tent zipped up tight at night to keep out mosquitoes.

Nearly all camps and lodges insist that an armed ranger accompany you at night, and rightly so. If, for some reason, you are walking alone, you should carry and use a flashlight—known locally as a torch—which all lodges and even tented camps supply. Shine your torch in a wide arc all around you; if there's anything lurking up ahead, you'll see its eyes shining. If you do pick up any night eyes, back off slowly in the direction you came from and call a ranger to accompany you. If you find yourself isolated and feel threatened, make a noise. But don't turn around and run; if it's a predator, it will pounce on you. If you hear the thumping footfalls of a large beast—hippopotamus, elephant, buffalo, or rhinoceros—jump off the path and out of its way. Small nocturnal creatures such as owls and bush babies have large eyes that, when caught in the light, may make you think they belong to a huge monster. Go call a ranger or member of the camp staff; it's always better to err on the side of safety.

Tip: If you're walking in the bush at night, whistle or sing to alert anything or anyone in your path. The biggest danger is that you will startle an animal by suddenly bearing down on it; it will attack as its first means of defense.

Kids on Safari

Many camps now welcome children over 12 on safari, but generally speaking kids under 6 may not take part in game activities, even if they are allowed in camp. Small children are potential take-out snacks! Certain camps offer specialized kids' programs, such as Honeyguide Khoka Moya and Ngala Main Camp, in Mpumalanga; Thanda, in KwaZulu-

Natal; and the Kwando camps in Botswana. It's a good idea to check with your tour operator, because more and more camps are offering kids' programs.

In Kruger there are no age limits, but if you have small children, don't keep them locked up and bored in a car for long stretches. You'll put them off the bush forever. Instead take short drives in the early morning and late afternoon, when it's cooler. They can spend the rest of the day playing around camp, but since not all of Kruger's camps have pools, check this out in advance.

Future Nature runs a series of dedicated programs for children and young adults in Mpumalanga and central South Africa. (For more information on this program and on children in South Africa, *see* Smart Travel Tips.) Specially trained educators teach small groups of kids, and there are plenty of options to choose from: tracking the Big Five in Mpumalanga; experiencing the wide-open spaces of the Karoo; canoeing South Africa's longest river, the Gariep; learning the traditional uses of plants; game drives; mammal, bird, and plant identification; hiking; and discovering South Africa's brilliant night skies. Kids get the opportunity to work with local kids of the same age on a number of community projects, giving your children the chance to leave their individual and positive mark on Africa. Programs are designed for kids 8–12 and 12–18, and can be tailored to fit in with parents' safaris. There are also programs for young adults 17 and up.

Health on Safari

In addition to the health hazards described below, there's a safari disease that's as well known as malaria: "khaki fever." It is part of the plotline in the film *Mogambo,* in which the married society girl (Grace Kelly) falls for the rugged, tanned game ranger (Clark Gable), who's already carrying on with a wild American (Ava Gardner). You're on safari, a magical world quite unlike the one to which you're accustomed, and in a good mood. Romantic notions fill your head, and here's this tanned, knowledgeable ranger protecting you from the wilds of Africa, chauffeuring you around, and seemingly delivering your every wish. Heavenly things may happen . . . but if they do, just make sure you're prepared for the earthbound realities. AIDS in Africa is rife; if there's even the remotest chance of having a sexual encounter on safari, carry condoms.

Dehydration & Overheating
Of all the horror stories and fantastic nightmares about meeting your end in the bush—being devoured by lions and crocodiles; succumbing to some ghastly fever like Ernest Hemingway's hero in *The Snows of Kilimanjaro*—the problem you're most likely to encounter will be of your own doing: dehydration.

The African sun is hot and the air is dry, and sweat evaporates quickly in these conditions. You might not realize how much bodily fluid you are losing as a result. Wear a hat, lightweight clothing, and sunscreen—all of which will help your body cope with high temperatures.

Drink at least two to three quarts of water a day, and in extreme heat conditions as much as three to four quarts of water or juice. Drink more if you're exerting yourself physically. If you overdo it at dinner with wine or spirits or even caffeine, you need to drink even more water to recover the fluid lost as your body processes the alcohol. Antimalarial medications are also very dehydrating, so it's important to increase your water intake while you're taking this medicine.

Don't rely on thirst to tell you when to drink; people often don't feel thirsty until they're a little dehydrated. At the first sign of dry mouth, exhaustion, or headache, drink water, because dehydration is the likely culprit.

Tip: To test for dehydration, pinch the skin on the back of your hand and see if it stays in a peak; if it does, you're dehydrated. Drink a solution of ½ teaspoon salt and 4 tablespoons sugar dissolved in a quart of water to replace electrolytes.

Advanced dehydration can lead to heat exhaustion, which can become serious. The signs include headache, profuse sweating, a weak pulse, loss of motor skills, and shivering, which occurs as the body tries to regulate its temperature. A drop in core body temperature follows overheating, and the person should be kept warm and given liquids. In extreme cases where liquids can't be kept down, a saline drip should be administered.

Heat cramps stem from a low salt level due to excessive sweating. These muscle pains usually occur in the abdomen, arms, or legs. When a child says he can't take another step, investigate whether he has cramps. When cramps occur, stop all activity and sit quietly in a cool spot and drink. Don't do anything strenuous for a few hours after the cramps subside. If heat cramps persist for more than an hour, seek medical assistance.

Malaria
See the malaria section under Getting Ready to Go, *above,* for details on antimalarial drugs.

If you're on safari in a malarial zone, be vigilant about protecting yourself. In the morning and evening cover exposed skin with strong insect repellent; dress in long pants, long-sleeve shirts, and shoes and socks; and wear clothes you've treated with a mosquito-repellent spray or laundry wash. Forget fashion statements and tuck your pants into your socks so your ankles aren't exposed. Spray insect repellent on your shoes, socks, and legs up to your knees, even if you're wearing pants, before you set off for a game walk or evening drive. Wear light-colored clothing, since mosquitoes (as well as tsetse flies) are attracted to dark surfaces. Spray all exposed skin with a mosquito-repellent spray that contains DEET, unless you're pregnant or nursing. DEET also isn't recommended for children. Citronella and other natural bug repellents can be used, but they're not as potent and require more vigilant use. If you've been out on a walk it's a good idea to take a hot shower and soap your entire body when you return.

When you go to bed, make sure you turn on any fan that's over or facing your bed, since mosquitoes can't fly well in moving air; keep it on while you sleep. Most lodges supply insect repellent. Use mosquito coils and sprays in your room (especially if you're traveling with children), and sleep under mosquito nets. Mosquito nets shouldn't have holes or gaps and can be treated in permethrin, which is the active ingredient found in mosquito-repellent spray and laundry wash and may be sold as Permanone and Duranon. Many southern Africans prefer to do all of the above rather than take strong antimalaria drugs. If you are 100% vigilant, this tactic can work.

Tip: Sleeping under a mosquito net or in an insectproof tent is customary, but it can stifle airflow. If you can't sleep, wet a sheet, wring it out, and lie under it: you'll fall asleep before you know it.

Motion Sickness

If you're prone to motion sickness, be sure to examine your safari itinerary closely. Though most landing strips for chartered planes are not paved but rather grass, earth, or gravel, landings are smooth most of the time. If you're going on safari to northern Botswana (the Okavango Delta, specifically), know that small planes and unpaved airstrips are the main means of transportation between camps; these trips can be very bumpy, hot, and a little dizzying even if you're not prone to motion sickness. The first preventive is not to go on a safari that involves flying in small planes, which immediately cuts out the Okavango Delta. If, however, you've set your heart on a trip to one of these areas, take motion-sickness pills, bite the bullet, and go for it. Most of the air transfers take an average of only 30 minutes and the rewards will be infinitely greater than the pains.

Tip: When you fly in small planes take a sun hat and a pair of sunglasses. If you sit in the front seat next to the pilot, or on the side of the sun, you will experience harsh glare that could give you a severe headache and exacerbate motion sickness.

Intestinal Upset

Natural microfauna and -flora differ in every region of Africa, so if you drink local, unfiltered water, add ice to your soda in the airport, or eat a piece of fruit from a roadside stand, you may get what's commonly referred to as traveler's diarrhea. All reputable hotels and lodges have either filtered, clean tap water or provide sterilized drinking water in jugs, and nearly all camps and lodges have adequate supplies of bottled water, in some cases including it in the cost of your trip. If you're traveling outside of organized safari camps in rural Africa or are unsure of local water supplies, carry plenty of bottled water and follow the CDC's advice for fruits and vegetables: boil it, cook it, peel it, or forget it. If you're going on a mobile safari, ask your guide whether drinking water is available.

By taking commonsense precautions, your safari will be uneventful from a health perspective but memorable in every other way.

Cape Town & the Peninsula

1

41

Updated by
Karena du
Plessis and
Myrna Robins

IF YOU VISIT ONLY ONE PLACE IN SOUTH AFRICA, MAKE IT CAPE TOWN.
Sheltered beneath the familiar shape of Table Mountain, this historic
city is instantly recognizable, and few cities in the world possess its beauty
and style.

A stroll through the lovely city center reveals Cape Town's three centuries as the sea link between Europe and the East. Elegant Cape Dutch
buildings, characterized by big whitewashed gables, often a thatch roof,
and shuttered windows, abut imposing monuments to Britain's imperial legacy. In the Bo-Kaap neighborhood the call to prayer echoes from
minarets while the sweet tang of Malay curry wafts through the cobbled streets. And everywhere, whether you're eating outdoors at one of
the country's best restaurants or sipping wine atop Table Mountain, you
sense—correctly—that this is South Africa's most urbane, civilized city.

As impressive as all this is, though, what you will ultimately recall
about Cape Town is the sheer grandeur of its setting—Table Mountain
rising above the city, the sweep of the bay, and mountains cascading into
the sea. You will likely spend more time marveling at the views than
anything else.

The city lies at the northern end of the Cape Peninsula, a 75-km (44-
mi) tail of mountains that hangs down from the tip of Africa, ending at
the Cape of Good Hope. Drive 15 minutes in any direction, and you
may lose yourself in a stunning landscape of 18th-century Cape Dutch
manors, historic wineries, and white-sand beaches backed by sheer
mountains. Francis Drake wasn't exaggerating when he said this was
"the fairest Cape we saw in the whole circumference of the earth," and
he would have little cause to change his opinion today. You could spend
a week exploring just the city and peninsula—and a lifetime discovering the nearby wonders of the Western Cape, including the Winelands,
one of the great highlights of a trip to South Africa.

Capetonians know they have it good and look with sympathy on those
unfortunate enough to live elsewhere. On weekends they hike, sail, and
bike in their African Eden. At night they congregate at the city's fine
restaurants, fortified with the Cape wine that plays such an integral role
in the city's life. Laid-back Cape Town has none of the frenetic energy
of hard-nosed Johannesburg. Maybe that's because Cape Town does-
n't need to unearth its treasures; the beauty of the place is right in front
of you as soon as you roll out of bed.

Though the city is often likened to San Francisco, Cape Town has something that the City by the Bay doesn't—Table Mountain. The mountain,
or tabletop, is key to Cape Town's identity. It dominates the city in a
way that's difficult to comprehend until you visit. In the afternoon, when
creeping fingers of clouds spill over Table Mountain and reach toward
the city, the whole town seems to shiver and hold its breath. Depending on which side of the mountain you live on, it even dictates when the
sun will rise and set.

Indeed, the city owes its very existence to the mountain. The freshwater streams running off its slopes were what first prompted early explorers

to anchor here. In 1652 Jan van Riebeeck and 90 Dutch settlers established a refreshment station for ships of the Dutch East India Company—also known by its Dutch name, the Verenigde Oostindische Compagnie (VOC)—on the long voyage east. The settlement represented the first European toehold in South Africa, and Cape Town is still sometimes called the Mother City.

Those first Dutch settlers soon ventured into the interior to establish their own farms, and 140 years later the settlement supported a population of 20,000 whites and 25,000 slaves brought from distant lands like Java, Madagascar, and Guinea. Its position on the strategic cusp of Africa, however, meant that the colony never enjoyed any real stability. The British, entangled in a global dogfight with Napoléon, occupied the Cape twice, first in 1795 and then more permanently in 1806. With them they brought additional slaves from Ceylon, India, and the Philippines. Destroyed or assimilated in this colonial expansion were the indigenous Khoekhoen (previously called Khoikhoi and Hottentots), who once herded their cattle here and foraged along the coast.

Though South Africa's more recent history is better known, it's worth remembering that between 1889 and 1902 the British and the Boers (Afrikaans for "farmers") also fought bitterly and that the conflicts that have shaped and scarred the country haven't always been between black and white. The wounds of the 20th century are largely attributable to apartheid, however. More than a decade since apartheid's demise, South Africa *is* a different country, but poverty and unemployment are still huge problems. Many among the poor feel betrayed because their lives haven't improved, but it takes years to redress social inequality. Some changes are beginning in such areas as free health care, education, and basic services. The new struggle being fought in South Africa, and the rest of the continent, is the battle against HIV/AIDS, which is decimating communities and leaving them as bereft and impoverished as they were during the grim years of apartheid.

Visitors to South Africa often find Cape Town something of an anomaly. It's a remarkably cosmopolitan city made up of a number of different races and language groups. Sit in a city café or bar, and you're likely to hear at least four languages (there are 11 official ones here). Some of this cosmopolitan character may be due to the influx of overseas tourists, but, tragically, conflict within Africa has also contributed. A widespread diaspora has brought thousands of people from Mali, Nigeria, and Senegal to call the Cape their home. A predominant group in the Cape, Cape coloureds (a local term for people of mixed, white European and black African, heritage) play an important role in shaping the city and giving it its distinct spice.

Perhaps the greatest celebration of this colored culture is the annual Coon Carnival, also known as the Cape Town Minstrel Carnival. Thousands of wild celebrants take to the streets of central Cape Town in vibrant costumes to sing *moppies* (pronounced a somewhat guttural "*more peas*," they're vaudeville-style songs), accompanied by banjos, drums, and whistles. The carnival is the most visible reminder of a way of life

Whatever activities you hope to accomplish in Cape Town, head up Table Mountain as soon as the wind isn't blowing. Cape Town wind is notorious, and the mountain can be shut for days on end when there are gales.

If you have 2 days

On your first day take an early morning city walk to see the sights or take a half-day city tour. Take in the Company's Gardens, Castle of Good Hope, District Six Museum, the Bo-Kaap, and other historical highlights. For lunch, eat at one of the outside restaurants at the V&A Waterfront if the weather's good, inside if it's not. Visit the various waterfront attractions, including the Two Oceans Aquarium, especially if you have children. Then you can dine either at the Green Dolphin, where you can listen to terrific jazz, or go uptown to one of the city's many excellent restaurants, followed by the theater, ballet, or opera at the Artscape or Baxter theater complexes. For a real taste of contemporary African music, head for pulsing marimba music at Mama Africa.

The next morning take a Robben Island tour, which takes 3½ hours. On your return go straight to the Lower Cable Station, and ride to the summit of Table Mountain (if you didn't do this first thing). Take some sandwiches with you, and hike one of the trails—for a few minutes or a few hours—until you find a glorious spot to sit and enjoy the view. When you come down from the mountain, drive to Camps Bay and kick off your shoes to stroll along the beach. To round out the evening, find a sophisticated sea-facing bar for a drink before going on to dinner.

If you have 5 or more days

Spend the first day or two exploring Cape Town. Pop in to museums and galleries, and wander around the Bo-Kaap, an old Cape Malay area with cobblestone streets and quaint buildings. One of the best ways to understand the city is to take a walking tour with Footsteps to Freedom. On the afternoon of the second day head for Table Mountain.

On the morning of Day 3 explore Robben Island, and, on your return, lunch at the Waterfront. In the afternoon you might visit the castle or have high tea at the Mount Nelson Hotel. In the evening head out to the vibey suburb of Observatory for dinner, and then wander down Lower Main Road, perhaps popping in for a drink or late-night coffee at a café. If you want something closer to the city, try de Waterkant, another exciting area for a drink and dinner. Party animals will find plenty of clubs as well.

On Day 4 drive out to the Constantia winelands. Visit the estates, enjoy the countryside, do a little wine tasting, have lunch, and then in the afternoon drive over Constantia Nek to Hout Bay. From the harbor, take an early afternoon cruise to Seal Island. For a more adventurous activity, admire the sunset from the back of a horse at Noordhoek or from a kayak out at sea. If the conditions are right, you can do a tandem paraglider flight off Lion's Head, landing just in time for cocktails overlooking the beach. Even if you don't paraglide here, have dinner on this side of the mountain, at Green Point, Sea Point, or Camps Bay.

Day 5 is penguin day. Wend your way along the False Bay coast to Boulders Beach, in the Table Mountain National Park, where you'll find African penguins in profusion. This is one of the few mainland sites where these comical little creatures live and breed. Then grab your map and follow the road to the Cape of Good Hope and Cape Point. You can take the steep walk to the point or take the funicular. It looks as if this is where the Indian and Atlantic oceans meet—sometimes there is even a line of foam stretching out to sea—but of course it's not. No matter, it's a dramatic spot. For a late lunch make your way back to the pretty fishing village of Kalk Bay, where the streets are lined with antiques shops and there are plenty of excellent restaurants to relax in. Back in Cape Town for the last night, you can have a drink at the Bascule bar at the Cape Grace (at the Waterfront) and watch the gulls wheel overhead against a backdrop of Table Mountain. Chances are, you won't ever want to leave.

---

that saw its finest flowering in District Six, a predominantly colored but truly multiracial neighborhood on the fringes of the city center whose destruction was a tragic result of apartheid. District Six was a living festival of music and soul, a vibrant community bound by poverty, hope, and sheer joie de vivre. In 1966 the Nationalist government invoked the Group Areas Act, rezoned District Six a whites-only area, and razed it. The scars of that event still run deep. The District Six Museum seeks to recapture the mood of the lost community and is not to be missed. A process of land restitution has begun but is fraught with politics and attendant delays, which means that the area is still largely a wasteland.

Other legacies of apartheid still fester, and although the city is made up of many different nationalities that mingle happily, it is still divided along racial and economic lines. Each year for decades, thousands of blacks have streamed to the Cape in search of work, food, and a better life. They end up in the squatter camps of Crossroads and Khayelitsha, names that once flickered across TV screens around the globe. Many visitors never see this side of South Africa, but as you drive into town along the N2 from the airport, you can't miss the pitiful shacks built on shifting dunes as far as the eye can see—a sobering contrast to the first-world luxury of the city center. A tour of these areas offers a glimpse of the old South Africa—and the enormous challenges facing the new one.

EXPLORING CAPE TOWN

Cape Town is surprisingly small. The area between Table Mountain and Table Bay, including Cape Town central and the nearby areas of Gardens, Oranjezicht, Tamboerskloof, and Bo-Kaap, is known as the City Bowl. In the city center an orderly street grid and the constant view of Table Mountain make it almost impossible to get lost. Major arteries running toward the mountain from the sea are Adderley, Loop, and Long streets; among the major cross streets are Strand, Longmarket, and Wale, which, be warned, is alternately written as WALE ST. (the English version) and WAALST (in Afrikaans), on signs. The heart of the historic city—where you'll find many of the museums and major buildings—is Government Avenue, a pedestrian mall at the top of Adderley Street.

St. George's Mall, another major pedestrian thoroughfare, runs the length of commercial Cape Town.

Cape Town has grown as a city in a way that few others in the world have. Take a good look at the street names. Strand and Waterkant streets (meaning "beach" and "waterside," respectively) are now far from the sea. However, when they were named, they were right on the beach. An enormous program of dumping rubble into the ocean extended the city by a good few square miles (this can, no doubt, be attributed to the Dutch obsession with reclaiming land from the sea). Almost all the city on the seaward side of Strand and Waterkant is part of the reclaimed area of the city known as the Foreshore. If you look at old paintings of the city, you will see that originally waves lapped at the very walls of the castle, now more than half a mile from the ocean.

Once you leave the city center, orienting yourself becomes trickier. As you face Table Mountain from the city, the distinctive triangular-shape mountain on your left is Devil's Peak; on the right are Signal Hill and Lion's Head. Signal Hill takes its name from a gun fired there every day at noon. If you look carefully, you will see that Signal Hill forms the rump of a reclining lion, and the maned Lion's Head looks south past Table Mountain (this is best seen from the N1 driving in to town). On the other side of Signal Hill and Lion's Head lies the fashionable Atlantic Seaboard. This stretch of coast is also known as Millionaire's Row, and is made up of the cosmopolitan Granger Bay, Green Point, and Sea Point through to the exclusive suburbs of Clifton, Camps Bay, and Llandudno. Heading the other way, around Devil's Peak, you come to Cape Town's Southern Suburbs—Rondebosch, Newlands, Claremont, and the classy Constantia. The vibrant Waterfront lies north of the City Bowl on the other side of the freeways that separate the docks from downtown, and the nearby Waterkant is another fashionable enclave. But there's a lot more to the city than these predominantly white suburbs. The infamous Cape Flats stretch over what used to be sandy flat areas (hence the name) between the city center and the northern suburbs of Panorama, Tygerberg, and Durbanville. The sprawling townships of Khayelitsha, Langa, and Gugulethu are also an integral part of Cape Town, and each year these informal settlements continue to grow, as immigrants move from the countryside, and the rest of the continent, looking for work.

The Cape Peninsula, much of which is included in Table Mountain National Park (TMNP), extends for around 40 km (25 mi) from the city through to Cape Point. The park comprises Table Mountain, most of the high-lying land in the mountain chain that runs down the center of the peninsula, the Cape of Good Hope nature reserve, and Boulders Beach. The steep mountain slopes leave little room for settlement in the narrow shelf next to the sea. On the east side the peninsula is washed by the waters of False Bay. Here, connected by a coastal road and railway line, lie the suburbs of Muizenberg, St. James, Kalk Bay, and Fish Hoek, as well as the naval base at historic Simon's Town. The western shores of the peninsula are wilder and emptier, pounded by huge Atlantic swells. In addition to the hamlets of Scarborough, Kommetjie, Noordhoek, and Llandudno, you'll find the fishing port of Hout Bay.

Table Mountain

Along with Victoria Falls on the border of Zimbabwe and Zambia, Table Mountain is one of southern Africa's most beautiful and impressive natural wonders. The views from its summit are awe-inspiring. The mountain rises more than 3,500 feet above the city, and its distinctive flat top is visible to sailors 65 km (40 mi) out to sea. In summer, when the southeaster blows, moist air from False Bay funnels over the tabletop, condensing in the colder, higher air to form a tablecloth of cloud. Legend attributes this low-lying cloud to a pipe-smoking contest between the devil and Jan van Hunks, a pirate who settled on Devil's Peak. The devil lost, and the cloud serves to remind him of his defeat.

The first recorded ascent of Table Mountain was made in 1503 by Portuguese admiral Antonio de Saldanha, who wanted to get a better sense of the topography of the Cape Peninsula. He couldn't have asked for a better view. In one direction you look down on the city, cradled between Lion's Head and Devil's Peak. In another, the crescent of sand at Camps Bay is sandwiched between the sea and the mountain range known as the Twelve Apostles. Farther south the peninsula trails off toward the Cape of Good Hope, its mountains forming a ragged spine between False Bay and the empty vastness of the Atlantic. It's a stunning panorama, no matter which way you look.

Despite being virtually surrounded by the city, Table Mountain is a remarkably unspoiled wilderness. Most of the Cape Peninsula's 2,200 species of flora—about as many plant species as there are in all of North America and Europe combined—are found on the mountain. This includes magnificent examples of Cape Town's wild indigenous flowers known as *fynbos,* Afrikaans for "fine bush," a reference to the tiny leaves characteristic of these heathlike plants. The best time to see the mountain in bloom is between September and March, although you're sure to find some flowers throughout the year. Long gone are the days when Cape lions, zebras, and hyenas roamed the mountain, but you can still glimpse *grysboks* (small antelopes), baboons, and rabbitlike *dassies* (rhymes with "fussy"). Although these creatures, also called rock hyraxes, look like oversize guinea pigs, this is where the similarities end; the dassie's closest relative is the elephant. They congregate in large numbers near the Upper Cable Station, where they've learned to beg for food. Over the years a diet of junk food has seriously compromised their health. Visitors are encouraged not to feed them tidbits—no matter how endearing they look.

Atop the mountain, well-marked trails offering 10- to 40-minute jaunts crisscross the western Table near the Upper Cable Station. Many other trails lead to the other side of Platteklip Gorge and into the mountain's catchment area, where you'll find reservoirs, hidden streams, and more incredible views. If you're feeling adventurous, try a rappel from the top—it's only about 350 feet, but you're hanging out over 3,300 feet of air (⇨ Rappelling under Sports & the Outdoors, *below*). A shop at the top of the mountain, appropriately called the Shop at the Top, sells gifts and curios.

At the Beach

Cape Town's beaches on both the Atlantic and False Bay sides are legendary. The beaches at Milnerton, Blouberg, and Long Beach (in Noordhoek) stretch endlessly, and you can walk for miles without seeing a fast-food outlet or drink stand. But you will see seagulls, dolphins, penguins, and whales (in season). Forget about swimming in the Atlantic, though; even a quick dip will freeze your toes. The "in" crowd flocks to Clifton, a must for sunbathers. If it's swimming you're into, head to the warmer waters of St. James, Kalk Bay, Fish Hoek, and Simon's Town, where the warm Benguela current sweeps along the False Bay side of the peninsula. The beaches are dotted with tidal pools, which make swimming even more comfortable and are safe for kids. Windsurfers congregate at Blouberg, where several competitions are held. At Boulders or Seaforth, you can sunbathe and snorkel in the coves and pools, sheltered by huge granite rocks. Cape Town's surfing community appreciates Muizenberg, Kommetjie, Fish Hoek, Hout Bay, and Blouberg. For kite-surfing, Strandfontein and Sunrise beaches are the places to try or to watch.

History Lesson

Cape Town is saturated with an extremely rich and fascinating history. Most of the sites worth seeing are packed into a small area, which means you can see a lot in just a few hours. At Robben Island you can stand in Mandela's old cell and learn about political and social banishment during the apartheid and colonial periods as well as about the ecological significance of the island. The District Six Museum tells the tale of the destruction of one of Cape Town's most vibrant inner-city neighborhoods, and the Bo-Kaap Museum looks down on the city center from one of the town's first settlements, originally inhabited by Muslims who settled here after the abolition of slavery. The Castle of Good Hope, former seat of the British and Dutch governments and still the city's military headquarters, is the oldest colonial building still standing in South Africa. For a taste of the city's long naval history, visit Simon's Town, and the South African Museum, alongside the Company's Gardens (what's left of Van Riebeeck's veggie patch), is also worth seeing.

Picnic Paradise

Cape Town is the ultimate picnic land. Pack a basket and head off to the top of Table Mountain to enjoy gorgeous views or to Kirstenbosch, especially on a Sunday evening in summer when there's an outdoor concert. Drive along Chapman's Peak Drive from Hout Bay and grab one of the roadside picnic sites overlooking the water, or bring your provisions to Blouberg to experience the sun dropping behind the famous picture-postcard view of the mountain. For evening beach picnics, choose Bakoven, Clifton, or Llandudno. Or try a *braai* (barbecue) in the Tokai Forest, or at the reservoir at Silvermine Nature Reserve, at the top of Ou Kaapse Weg.

To Markets, To Markets

Cape Town's markets are the best in the country—informal, creative, artistic, and with a good selection of both tatty and splendid African curios. Waterfront markets are fun, especially the Sunday Green

Point open-air market. At Greenmarket Square, look for the special rubber-tire sandals. There are other markets in Constantia, Rondebosch, and opposite the Kirstenbosch National Botanical Gardens. Read the papers for up-to-date listings on these and other ephemeral markets, such as the Observatory Holistic Lifestyle Fair, held on the first Sunday of the month.

Be aware, though, that weather on the mountain can change quickly. Even if you're making only a short visit, take a sweater. If you're planning an extended hike, carry water, plenty of warm clothing, and a mobile phone. Be aware, also, that recent muggings have made it unwise to walk alone on the mountain. It's recommended that you travel in a group or, better yet, with a guide.

need a break? During the warm summer months Capetonians are fond of taking picnic baskets up the mountain. The best time to picnic is after 5, as some say sipping a glass of chilled Cape wine while watching the sun set from Table Mountain is one of life's great joys. Otherwise, you can eat at the large self-service restaurant called, quite simply, The **Restaurant** (☎ 021/424–8181). It serves great hot breakfasts, light meals, and sandwiches and has a good salad bar. The **Cableway Cocktail Bar** (☎ 021/424–8181) dishes up a spectacular view along with cocktails and bar snacks from 2 until the last cable car. As you might expect, both offer a good wine list, with local wines predominating.

But first: To reach the top of the mountain, you either have to walk or take the Cableway.

A Good Ride

The revamped **Table Mountain Aerial Cableway** is a slick operation. Two large, wheelchair-friendly revolving cars, which provide spectacular views, take three to five minutes to reach the summit. Operating times vary from month to month according to season, daylight hours, and weather. To avoid disappointment, phone ahead for exact times. You can't prebook for the cable car, but the longest you'll have to wait is about a half hour and then only in peak season (December 15–January 15). Several tour operators include a trip up the mountain in their schedules. ⊠ *Tafelberg Rd.* ☎ *021/424–8181* ⊕ *www.tablemountain. net* ☒ *R110 round-trip, R57 one-way* ☉ *Hrs vary, but usually daily 8:30 AM–9 PM.*

The Lower Cable Station lies on the slope of Table Mountain near its western end. It's a long way from the city on foot, and you're better off traveling by car, taxi, or *rikki* (a small, low-tech minibus). To get there from the City Bowl, take Buitengracht Street toward the mountain. Once you cross Camp Street, Buitengracht becomes Kloof Nek Road. Follow Kloof Nek Road through the residential neighborhood of Gardens to a traffic circle; turn left on Tafelberg Road and follow signs to the Table Mountain Cableway. Taxis from the city center to the Lower Cable Station (one-way) cost about R50–R60, and rikkis, which operate weekdays 7–7 and Saturday 8–4, cost R9–R14 per person.

A Good Walk

More than 300 walking trails wend their way up the mountain, but the most accessible route up the front section is via Platteklip Gorge. You can start at the Lower Cable Station, but remember that you need to walk just over 1 km (about ⅔ mi) to the left (east) along Tafelberg Road before heading up at the Platteklip Gorge sign. Once on the right path, you shouldn't get lost, but this is no stroll in the park and will take two to three hours, depending on your level of fitness. There is no water along the route; you *must* take at least 2 liters (½ gallon) of water per person. Table Mountain can be dangerous if you're not familiar with the terrain. Many paths that look like good routes down the mountain end in treacherous cliffs. Do not underestimate this mountain. It may be in the middle of a city, but it is not a genteel town park. Wear sturdy shoes or hiking boots; always take warm clothes, such as a Windbreaker, and a mobile phone; and let someone know of your plans. The mountain is quite safe if you stick to known paths, but, although the paths are marked, it is easy to become disoriented, especially when there is heavy cloud cover. Look for the Table Mountain map by Peter Slingsby at most major outdoor stores or the shop at the Lower Cable Station. If you are on the mountain and the weather changes dramatically (heavy rain, mist) and you can't tell where you are, just sit tight and call Wilderness Search and Rescue (⇨ Emergencies under Cape Town A to Z, *below*) to let them know you're in trouble. You will be rescued as soon as the weather permits. Walking around in the mist is very dangerous.

If you are prepared to go the distance, there are several wonderful routes from Kirstenbosch National Botanic Gardens to the front of Table that are very scenic but fairly challenging. Two of the most popular routes are up Skeleton Gorge and Nursery Ravine. These take between four and five hours, with plenty of time to admire the views and flowers along the way. A longer route starting from Constantia Neck and running along the jeep track is more gradual but takes the better part of a day. If you just want to explore the top of the mountain, look for the sign near the Upper Cable Station. At 10 and noon, volunteers offer visitors free guided walks. How long the walk takes—from 20 minutes to an hour—is determined by the group.

City Center

Numbers in the text correspond to numbers in the margin and on the Cape Town map.

Begin your walk at the **Cape Town Tourism Information Office ❶**, on the corner of Burg and Castle streets (one block up from Strand Street). Since the city is geographically very small, at no time during the walk will you be more than 15 minutes from this starting point. Head down Castle past the fast-talking fruit and vegetable sellers, and turn right onto **Adderley Street ❷**. Turn left on Darling Street and head toward the **Castle of Good Hope ❸** and the not-so-grand **Grand Parade ❹**, a parking lot that transforms twice a week into a busy flea market. Just across the way is the majestic **City Hall** ❺. From the castle, head up Buitenkant Street toward the mountain and the **District Six Museum** ❻, where you can get a feel for the havoc and heartache apartheid caused among communities classified as nonwhite. Directly opposite the museum is the notorious Caledon Square police station, where many anti-apartheid activists were detained and died from mysterious causes.

Now make your way back toward Adderley Street, cutting toward the post office and the heady smell of flowers, which have been sold in Trafalgar Place for the last 100 years. After pausing to admire the king proteas, arum lilies, and fynbos, turn left on Adderley Street. A couple of blocks up, the austere **Groote Kerk** ❼ faces Church Square, now a parking lot, where churchgoers used to unharness their oxen. It's easy to miss, but look out for the concrete plaque on the skinny traffic island in the middle of Spin Street, which marks the place where the **Slave Tree** ❽ is supposed to have stood. Across the road, on Adderley Street, you'll see the **Slave Lodge** ❾ and an imposing statue of Jan Smuts with his back turned toward it. Had he not been defeated by the National Party in 1948, South African history would have taken a very different turn.

Speaking of turns, here Adderley swings to the right to become Wale Street (Waalstraat), but if you continue straight, you'll be walking up Government Avenue, a wide and attractive squirrel-filled, tree-lined walkway, which leads past many of the country's most important institutions and museums. Don't forget to buy a bag of nuts for the squirrels on your way in. On your right is the **National Library of South Africa—Cape Town Campus** ❿, the oldest in the country, and the tranquil **Company's Gardens** ⑪. This is a great place to sit and watch the world go by while making friends with the tame squirrels. Continue along Government Avenue, and pause to admire the imposing classical buildings that make up Parliament; here, in 1966, a parliamentary messenger, Dimitri Tsafendas, stabbed to death Hendrick Verwoerd, the chief architect of apartheid. Next you'll pass **Tuynhuys** ⑫, which serves as the president's office.

Farther up Government Avenue are the **South African National Gallery** ⑬, on the left, and, opposite it the **South African Museum** ⑭ and planetarium, where you can easily lose yourself for a few hours. The small temple in front of the South African Museum is the **Delville Wood Monument** ⑮. Walk through the alley on the left of the gallery onto Hatfield Street to reach the **Cape Town Holocaust Centre** ⑯, **South African Jewish Museum** ⑰, and the imposing **Great Synagogue** ⑱, South Africa's mother synagogue. Carry on up Hatfield toward the mountain and take the first small tree-lined lane to the right; this will lead you back to Government Avenue. Turn left to go to **Bertram House** ⑲, at the top of the avenue, and then backtrack and turn left, cutting across the front of the South African Museum to Queen Victoria Street. To experience modern Cape Town, head down Bloem into **Long Street** ⑳, full of street cafés, arty shops, and interesting characters.

The city changes once more when you turn left on Wale Street and walk four blocks to historic Bo-Kaap, where you can visit the **Bo-Kaap Museum** ㉑. After exploring cobbled streets from a bygone age, retrace your steps down Wale Street to **St. George's Cathedral** ㉒, an important religious landmark. Across Wale is the entrance to **St. George's Mall** ㉓, where you'll be greeted by the hustle and bustle of street vendors from all over Africa. Turn left onto **Church Street** ㉔, home to art galleries, African curio shops, a flea market, and a great coffee shop (Mozart's) in the short section between Burg and Long. It's worth turning left on Long to see some attractive old buildings, but if you're short on time or energy, turn right, and head to Longmarket Street, where **Greenmarket Square** ㉕ has been the center of the city since 1710. The **Old Town House** ㉖ faces the square on the mountain side.

Work your way back to Long Street and walk away from the mountain. When you reach Strand Street, turn left to see the awe-inspiring **Gold of Africa Museum** ㉗ and the **Evangelical Lutheran Church** ㉘. Retrace your route on Strand Street to reach the **Koopmans–De Wet House** ㉙. Turn right again onto Burg, and you'll be back at Cape Town Tourism.

TIMING   If you are pressed for time, you can explore the city in a day, getting the lay of the land and a feel for the people of Cape Town while visiting or skipping sights as your interests dictate. However, if you'd like to linger in various museums and galleries, you could easily fill two days. Start at about 9, when most workers have finished their commute, and then stop for a long, leisurely lunch during the hottest part of the day, finishing the tour in the late afternoon. If you have to head out of town on either the N1 or N2, make sure to finish before 4, when rush-hour congestion takes over and you can sit in traffic for a couple of hours at a stretch.

Except for the top end of Long Street and around Heritage Square, where there are lots of bars and cafés, the city center dies at night, and you are advised not to wander the streets after most Capetonians have left for home. The last commuters leave around 6. The biggest threat is groups of street children, who might mug you for your cell phone, jewelry, or money.

What to See

❷ **Adderley Street.** Originally named Heerengracht after a canal that ran the length of the avenue, this street has always been Cape Town's principal thoroughfare. It was once the favored address of the city's leading families, and its oak-shaded sidewalks served as a promenade for those who wanted to see and be seen. By the mid-19th century the oaks had all been chopped down and the canal covered, as Adderley Street became the main commercial street. By 1908 it had become so busy that the city fathers paved it with wooden blocks in an attempt to dampen the noise of countless wagons, carts, and hooves. In recent years Adderley Street has lost most of its charm. Although there are a couple of beautiful old buildings dating back to the early 1900s, they are mostly crowded out by uninspiring office buildings, and the sidewalks are packed with street hawkers selling everything from fruits and vegetables to cell-phone covers and tea towels. City management is trying to halt the urban decay, however, and there's plenty of evidence of regeneration. A lot of old office buildings are now being converted to upscale

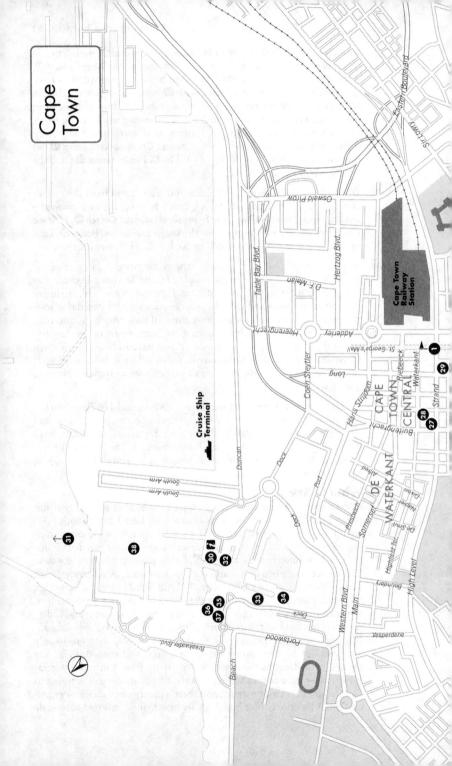

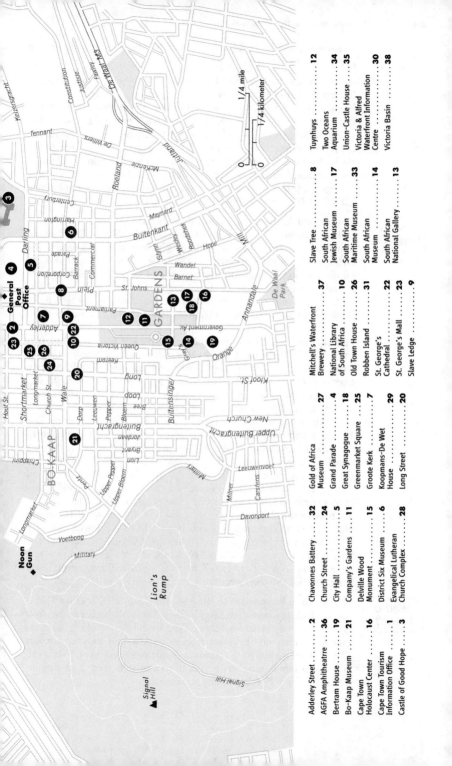

apartments, and beautiful old Art Deco buildings are getting the spit and polish they so desperately need.

19 **Bertram House.** Built around 1840, this is the only surviving Georgian brick town house in Cape Town. Once a common sight in the city, these boxlike two-story houses were a response by the English community to Cape Dutch architecture. The projecting front porch was intended to shield the house from the worst effects of the frequent southeasters. The collection of furniture, silver, jewelry, and porcelain inside recaptures the look and feel of an early-19th-century home. A catalog available at the entrance describes the entire collection. ✉ *Government Ave. and Orange St., Gardens* ☎ *021/424–9381* 🌐 *www.museums.org.za/bertram* 🎟 *R5* 🕑 *Tues.–Sat. 9:30–4:30.*

need a break?

Government Avenue ends opposite the impressive gateway to the **Mount Nelson Hotel** (✉ 76 Orange St., Gardens ☎ 021/483–1000 🌐 www.mountnelson.co.za), complete with two pith-helmeted gatekeepers. The Nellie, as it's known, was erected in 1899 to welcome the Prince of Wales on his visit to the Cape and today is one of Cape Town's most fashionable and genteel social venues. Come for the terrific high tea. The pastry selection can tempt even the most jaded palate. (Note that the Table Bay Hotel at the V&A Waterfront also provides a memorable tea.)

★ **Bo-Kaap.** You'll know you're in the Bo-Kaap when you catch the heady smell wafting from Atlas Trading Co., which is often packed with housewives stocking up on fresh spices, or when you hear the call of the muezzin from one of the many mosques in the area. You might even have to sidestep lights, cameras, and film stars, since the district is an oft-used setting for movies and magazine shoots. Bo-Kaap is the historic home of the city's Muslim population, brought from the East as slaves in the late 17th and early 18th centuries. So it's no surprise that it's also home to the Auwal Mosque, the oldest mosque in South Africa. Today the area remains strongly Muslim, and it's fascinating to wander the narrow cobbled lanes past mosques and colorful flat-roofed houses. Here you'll find the largest collection of pre-1840 architecture in South Africa, with many homes combining elements of Cape Dutch and British styles. The Bo-Kaap (Afrikaans for "on top of the Cape") is also known as the Malay quarter, even though its inhabitants originated from all over, including the Indonesian archipelago, India, Turkey, and Madagascar. Because there have been a few muggings in the Bo-Kaap, taking a guided tour is recommended (⇨ Cape Town A to Z, *below*), or stick to Buitengracht, Dorp, Rose, and Shortmarket streets.

need a break?

The **Bo-Kaap Bazaar** (✉ 46 Rose St., Bo-Kaap ☎ 021/423–9978) is a funny little tearoom-cum-restaurant in Zanie Misbach's house. You sit at tables set up in her lounge or on the veranda overlooking the street if the weather is good. She makes delicious chicken curry and crisp samosas filled with mince and fresh coriander. While you're enjoying your meal, friends and family members pop in to chat or to borrow a missing ingredient. It's a very relaxed, fun experience.

㉑ Bo-Kaap Museum. Built in the 18th century, this museum was originally the home of Abu Bakr Effendi, a well-known Turkish scholar and prominent leader in the Muslim community. He was brought here to help quell feuding between Muslim factions and is believed to have written one of the first books in Afrikaans. The house has been furnished to re-create the lifestyle of a typical Malay family in the 19th century. (Since the exhibits aren't labeled, you might do better to visit the museum as part of a guided tour of the Malay quarter.) Look for works by artist Gregoire Boonzaire, who is famous for capturing both the chaos and charm of neighborhoods such as the Bo-Kaap and District Six. ⊠ *71 Wale St., Bo-Kaap* ☎ *021/481–3939* ⊕ *www.museums.org.za/bokaap* ☎ *R5* ⊙ *Mon.–Sat. 9:30–4.*

★ **⓰ Cape Town Holocaust Centre.** This museum is both a memorial to the 6 million Jews and other victims of Nazism who were killed during the Holocaust, and an education center whose aim is to create a caring and just society in which human rights and diversity are valued. The permanent exhibit is excellent and very moving. A multimedia display, comprising photo panels, text, film footage, and music, creates a chilling reminder of the dangers of prejudice, racism, and discrimination. ⊠ *88 Hatfield St., Gardens* ☎ *021/462–5553* ⊕ *www.museums.org. za/ctholocaust* ☎ *Free* ⊙ *Sun.–Thurs. 10–5, Fri. 10–1.*

❶ Cape Town Tourism Information Office. One of the best information offices in South Africa, Cape Town Tourism is light, bright, and breezy, and filled with really helpful and knowledgeable people. It has a *bureau de change,* wineshop with tastings, Internet café, coffee shop, and loads of information, including a National Parks and Cape Nature Conservation desk and an accommodations desk. ⊠ *The Pinnacle at Burg and Castle Sts., Cape Town central* ☐ *Box 1403, 8000* ☎ *021/426–4260* ⊕ *www.tourismcapetown.co.za* ☎ *Free* ⊙ *Weekdays 9–6, Sat. 8:30–2, Sun. 9–1.*

★ **❸ Castle of Good Hope.** Despite its name, the castle isn't one of those fairytale fantasies you find perched on a cliff. It's a squat fortress that hunkers into the ground as if to avoid shellfire. Built between 1665 and 1676 by the Dutch East India Company (VOC) to replace an earthen fort constructed by Jan van Riebeeck in 1652, it's the oldest building in the country. Its pentagonal plan, with a diamond-shape bastion at each corner, is typical of the Old Netherlands defense system adopted in the early 17th century. The design was intended to allow covering fire for every portion of the castle. As added protection, the whole fortification was surrounded by a moat, and the sea nearly washed up against its walls. The castle served as both the VOC headquarters and the official governor's residence, and still houses the regional headquarters of the National Defence Force. Despite its bellicose origins, no shot has ever been fired from its ramparts, except ceremonially.

You can wander around on your own or join one of the guided tours at no extra cost. Also worth seeing is the excellent William Fehr Collection. Housed in the governor's residence, it consists of antiques, artifacts, and paintings of early Cape Town and South African history.

Conservationists should go upstairs to see John Thomas Baine's *The Greatest Hunt in Africa*, celebrating a "hunt" in honor of Prince Alfred, when nearly 30,000 animals were driven together and slaughtered. ⊠ *1 Buitenkant St., Cape Town central* ☎ *021/787–1200* ⊕ *www. castleofgoodhope.co.za* 🖘 *R18* ⊙ *Weekdays 9–3:30, Sat. 9–1; tours at 11, noon, and 2.*

need a break? **De Goewerneur Restaurant** (⊠ 1 Buitenkant St., Cape Town central ☎ 021/787–1202), in the central courtyard of the Castle of Good Hope, serves light meals and teas. From the veranda you get a pleasing view of the lawn and the buildings beyond.

㉔ Church Street. The center of Cape Town's art and antiques business, the section between Burg and Long streets is a pedestrian mall filled with art galleries, antiques dealers, and small cafés. This is the site of a daily antiques and flea market.

❺ City Hall. Though this attractive Edwardian building, which celebrates its centenary in 2005, is in need of sprucing up, it still is a commanding presence overlooking the Grand Parade. What was the seat of local administration is now home to the Cape Town Philharmonic Orchestra (the acoustics in the main hall are phenomenal) and City Library. Instead of city leaders dominating the passages, noisy schoolchildren now work on projects here, and the library has a specialized art-book collection as well as extensive clippings on local history. Some of the building's stone was imported from Bath, England, and the clock is a scaled-down replica of Big Ben. Visitors can ask at security to visit the clock tower. From a balcony overlooking Darling Street, Nelson Mandela gave his historic speech on his release from prison. ⊠ *Darling St.* ☎ *021/467–1567 library* 🖘 *Free* ⊙ *Library Mon., Wed., Fri. 10–5:30, Tues. 1–5:30, Thurs. 10–2, Sat. 9–4.*

★ ⓫ Company's Gardens. These are all that remains of a 43-acre garden laid out by Jan van Riebeeck in April 1652 to supply fresh vegetables to ships on their way to the Dutch East Indies. By 1700 free burghers were cultivating plenty of crops on their own land, and in time the VOC vegetable patch was transformed into a botanic garden. It remains a delightful haven in the city center, graced by fountains, exotic trees, rose gardens, aviaries, and a pleasant outdoor café. At the bottom of the gardens, close to Government Avenue, look for an **old well** that used to provide water for the town's residents and the garden. The old water pump, engraved with the maker's name and the date 1842, has been overtaken by an oak tree and now juts out of the tree's trunk some 6 feet above the ground. A huge **statue of Cecil Rhodes,** the Cape's prime minister in the late 19th century, looms over the path that runs through the center of the gardens. He points to the north, and an inscription reads, YOUR HINTERLAND IS THERE, a reference to Rhodes's dream of extending the British Empire from the Cape to Cairo. ⊠ *Between Government Ave. and Queen Victoria St., Cape Town central* 🖘 *Free* ⊙ *Daily 7–7.*

⓯ Delville Wood Monument. The monument honors South Africans who died in the fight for Delville Wood during the great Somme offensive of

1916. Of the 121 officers and 3,032 soldiers who participated in the three-day battle, only five officers and 750 soldiers survived unhurt. Facing the memorial is a **statue of Brigadier-General Lukin,** who commanded the South African infantry brigade during World War I. ✉ *Company's Gardens.*

★ ❻ **District Six Museum.** Housed in the Buitenkant Methodist Church, this museum preserves the memory of one of Cape Town's most vibrant multicultural neighborhoods, and of the district's destruction in one of the cruelest acts of the apartheid-era Nationalist government. District Six was proclaimed a white area in 1966, and existing residents were evicted from their homes, which were razed to make way for a white suburb. The people were forced to resettle in bleak outlying areas on the Cape Flats, and by the 1970s all the buildings, except churches and mosques, had been demolished. Huge controversy accompanied the proposed redevelopment of the area, and only a small housing component, Zonnebloem, and the campus of the Cape Technicon have been built, leaving much of the ground still bare—a grim reminder of the past. There are plans to bring former residents back into the area and reestablish the suburb; however, the old swinging District Six can never be re-created. The museum consists of street signs, photographs, life stories of the people who lived there, and a huge map, where former residents can identify the sites of their homes and record their names. This map is being used to help sort out land claims. You can arrange in advance for a two-hour walking tour of the district. ✉ *25 Buitenkant St.* ☎ *021/466–7200 or 021/461–8745* ⊕ *www.districtsix.co.za* 🖃 *R10* ⊗ *Mon. 9–3, Tues.–Sat. 9–4, Sun. by appointment.*

❷❽ **Evangelical Lutheran Church Complex.** Established as an act of defiance against the Dutch in 1779, this is the oldest church in South Africa. Not only did the Dutch East India Company exert commercial control over early Cape Town, but it also had a stranglehold on religion. The VOC recognized only the Dutch Reformed Church, and other faiths were banned. Contravention of this law brought confiscation of property, deportation, or death. The Lutherans were not content to put up with this religious bullying, however, so in 1774, when Martin Melck, a wealthy landowner, donated a barn and land in town, they started worshipping. Five years later the VOC relented slightly, and once religious freedom was granted, German sculptor Anton Anreith was commissioned to convert the barn into a church. This was also the first church that welcomed slaves to its services, as long as they occupied the designated slave pews running down either side. ✉ *98 Strand St., Cape Town central* ☎ *021/ 421–5854* 🖃 *Free* ⊗ *Weekdays 10–1.*

★ ❷❼ **Gold of Africa Museum.** Located in the historic Martin Melck House, this museum chronicles the history and artistry of African gold and houses arguably one of the best collections in the world. The exquisite exhibition upstairs—cleverly displayed in a darkened room—will leave you gasping and will dispel any myths about African art being naive and unsophisticated. Artisans from Mali, Senegal, Ghana, and the Ivory Coast certainly knew how to transform this precious metal. Downstairs is a workshop where you can watch jewelers busy at their craft. When you've taken in all the opulence you can, you can escape to the great coffee shop in a secluded courtyard and forget that you're in the center of a busy city. Ask about Wednesday's Pangolin Night Tours (R35), which include a guided flashlighted tour of the collection and a glass of wine with gold flakes. ⊠ *96 Strand St., Cape Town central* ☎ *021/405–1540* ⊕ *www.goldofafrica.com* ✍ *R20* ✆ *Mon.–Sat. 9:30–5.*

❹ **Grand Parade.** Once a military parade ground, this is now just a bleak parking lot. A statue of Edward VII serves as a parking attendant and seagull resting post. It was here, on his release on February 11, 1990, after 27 years in prison, that Nelson Mandela addressed an adoring crowd of more than 100,000 supporters. Today this is the site of South Africa's oldest flea market, which has been held on Wednesday and Saturday mornings for decades. It's not particularly tourist oriented, but it is the best place to see some of the "real" Cape Town. Pop into one of the informal food stalls for a *gatsby* (a sandwich on a long roll filled with french fries, lettuce, tomato, and a choice of fresh or pickled fish, curry, or steak), or a *salomie* (roti, a soft round bread, wrapped around a curry filling) for a cheap lunch and a genuine cultural experience. Finish it off with some delicious *koeksusters* (sweet, braided, lightly spiced, deep-fried pastries). Watch out for pickpockets, and don't wear flashy gold jewelry, as you might leave the area without it. ⊠ *Darling, Lower Plein, and Buitenkant Sts.*

❶⓼ **Great Synagogue.** Built in 1905 in the baroque style, this synagogue has notable twin towers and a dome and was apparently inspired by Florentine architecture. The Aron Kodesh, the closet in which the Torah scrolls are stored, is flanked by two beautiful mosaic panels, and light filters through an impressive stained-glass window. The synagogue is the center of a Jewish complex, which includes the South African Jewish Museum, the Jacob Gitlin Library, and the Cape Town Holocaust Centre, which is housed in the Albow Centre, next door. ⊠ *88 Hatfield St., Gardens* ☎ *021/465–1405* ⊕ *www.gardensshul.org* ✆ *Hrs vary; no tours Fri. or Sat.*

★ ❷⑤ **Greenmarket Square.** For more than a century this cobbled square served as a forum for public announcements, including the 1834 declaration abolishing slavery, which was read from the balcony of the Old Town House, overlooking the cobbled square. In the 19th century the square became a vegetable market as well as a popular watering hole, and you can still enjoy a drink at an open-air restaurant or hotel veranda while watching the crowds go by. Today the square has a fun outdoor market (⇨ Shopping, *below*), and is flanked by some of the best examples of art-deco architecture in South Africa. ⊠ *Longmarket, Burg, and Shortmarket Sts.*

❼ **Groote Kerk.** One of the most famous churches in South Africa, the Groote Kerk (Great Church) was built in 1841 on the site of an earlier Dutch Reformed church dating from 1704. The adjoining clock tower is all that remains of that earlier building. Among the building's interesting features are the enclosed pews, each with its own door. Prominent families would buy their own pews—and lock the doors—so they wouldn't have to pray with the great unwashed. The enormous pulpit is the joint work of famous sculptor Anton Anreith and carpenter Jan Jacob Graaff. The lions supporting it are carved from local stinkwood; the upper portion is Burmese teak. The organ, with nearly 6,000 pipes, is the largest in the Southern Hemisphere. Approximately 200 people are buried beneath the Batavian soapstone floor, including eight governors. There are free guided tours on request. ✉ *43 Adderley St. (enter on Parliament St.), Cape Town central* ☎ *021/422–0569* 🖃 *Free* ◷ *Weekdays 10–2; services Sun. at 10 and 7.*

㉙ Koopmans–De Wet House. Now a museum, this lovely 18th-century home with its classical facade is a haven of peace in the city center. The structure you see today dates largely from the period 1771–93. The house enjoyed its heyday under Maria de Wet (1834–1906), a Cape Town socialite who entertained most of the major figures in Cape society, including Boer presidents and British governors. The collection includes a stunning selection of antiques, carpets, paintings, and porcelain; it's worth buying the excellent guide to the museum, which describes every item in detail. The bricks at the entryway steps originally served as ballast in ships rounding the Cape. ✉ *35 Strand St., Cape Town central* ☎ *021/424–2473* 🖃 *R5* ◷ *Tues.–Sat. 9:30–4:30.*

⑳ Long Street. The section of Long between Orange and Wale streets is lined with magnificently restored Georgian and Victorian buildings. Wrought-iron balconies and fancy curlicues on these colorful houses evoke the French Quarter in New Orleans; and during the 1960s Long Street did a good imitation of the Big Easy, playing host to bars, prostitutes, and sleazy hotels. Today, antiques dealers, secondhand bookstores (Clarke's is a must), pawnshops, the Pan-African Market, and funky clothing outlets make it the best browsing street in the city. Lodgings here range from backpackers' lodges to the more exclusive Metropole. At the mountain end is Long Street Baths, an indoor swimming pool and old Turkish *hammam* (steam bath).

⑩ National Library of South Africa—Cape Town Campus. Launched as the National Library in 1999, with the amalgamation of the State Library in what was then Pretoria and the South African Library here, this library owes its existence to Lord Charles Somerset, governor of the Cape Colony. In 1818 he imposed a wine tax to fund the creation of a library that would "place the means of knowledge within the reach of the youth of this remote corner of the Globe." In 1860 the library moved into its current home, a neoclassical building modeled after the Fitzwilliam Museum in Cambridge, England. The library has an extensive collection of Africana, including the works of many 18th- and 19th-century explorers, and an impressive map collection that attracts worldwide attention. At last count the enormous postcard collection numbered more than 10,000 pieces. ✉ *5 Queen Victoria St. (enter through Company's Gardens), Cape Town central* ☎ *021/424–6320* ⊕ *www.nlsa.ac.za* 🖃 *Free* ◷ *Mon. and Tues., and Thurs.and Fri. 9–5, Wed. 10–5.*

㉖ Old Town House. For 150 years this was the most important civic building in Cape Town. Built in 1755 as a guardhouse, it also saw duty as a meeting place for the burgher senate, a police station, and from 1840 to 1905 as Cape Town's city hall. All road distances to and from Cape Town are measured from this building, which is a beautiful example of urban Cape Dutch architecture, with thick whitewashed walls, green-and-white shutters, and small-paned windows. Today it's home to the extensive Michaelis Collection of 17th-century Dutch paintings, including evocative etchings by Rembrandt, as well as changing exhibits. ⊠ *Greenmarket Sq., Cape Town central* ☏ *021/481–3922 or 021/481–3923* ⊕ *www.museums.org.za/michaelis/townhouse.htm* 🎟 *Free* ⊙ *Weekdays 10–5, Sat. 10–4.*

need a
break?

The **Ivy Garden** (⊠ Greenmarket Sq., Cape Town central ☏ 021/423–2360), in the courtyard of the Old Town House, serves light lunches and teas in a leafy, green setting. Seating on the veranda overlooks the hustle and bustle of Greenmarket Square.

㉒ St. George's Cathedral. This cathedral was once the religious seat of one of the most recognizable faces—and voices—in the fight against apartheid, Archbishop Desmond Tutu. In his position as the first black archbishop of Cape Town, he vociferously denounced apartheid and relentlessly pressed for a democratic government. It was from these steps that he led a demonstration of more than 30,000 people and coined the phrase the Rainbow People to describe South Africans in all their glorious diversity. The Anglican cathedral was designed by Sir Herbert Baker in the Gothic Revival style; construction began in 1901, using sandstone from Table Mountain. The structure contains the largest stained-glass window in the country, some beautiful examples of late-Victorian stained glass, and a 1,000-year-old Coptic cross. If you want to hear the magnificent organ, go to the choral evensong at 7 on Sunday evening, the 9:15 AM or 7 PM mass on Sunday, or the 11 AM mass on the last Sunday of every month. ⊠ *5 Wale St., Cape Town central* ☏ *021/424–7360* 🎟 *Free* ⊙ *Daily 8–5; services weekdays at 7:15 and 1:15, Sat. at 8 AM, Sun. at 7:15 AM, 8 AM, 9:15 AM, and 7 PM.*

㉓ St. George's Mall. This promenade stretches almost all the way to the Foreshore. Shops and cafés line the mall, and street vendors hawk everything from T-shirts to African arts and crafts. Street performers and dancers gather daily to entertain crowds of locals and visitors, who rub shoulders on their way to and from work or while sightseeing.

❾ Slave Lodge. Previously known as the South African Cultural History Museum, this beautiful building has a dark past. It was built in 1679 by the Dutch East India Company to house slaves, convicts, and lunatics, and from 1815 to 1914 the building housed the supreme court. Today it's a museum, which is in the process of being redeveloped to more accurately represent the diverse cultures of all South Africans, not just white settlers. As such, it hasn't yet found its place among Cape Town's top museums. Though it does have an excellent collection of colonial furniture, letters, coins, paintings, and clothes, they are not on permanent display. ⊠ *49 Wale St., Cape Town central* ☏ *021/460–8242* ⊕ *www.museums.org.za/slavelodge* 🎟 *R10* ⊙ *Weekdays 10–4:30, Sat. 10–1.*

8 **Slave Tree.** An inconspicuous concrete plaque marks the spot where slaves are purported to have been auctioned under an enormous Canadian pine tree, which once stood here. Slavery began in the Cape Colony in 1658, when free burghers petitioned the government for farmhands. The first group of 400 slaves arrived from Guinea, Angola, Batavia (modern-day Java), and Madagascar. During the first British occupation of the Cape (1795–1803), 17,000 slaves were brought from India, Ceylon, and the Philippines, swelling the total slave population to 30,000. Slavery was abolished by the British in 1834, an act that served as the final impetus for one of South Africa's great historical events, the Great Trek, when thousands of outraged Afrikaners set off in their covered wagons to establish a new state in the hinterland where they would be free from British taxation and laws. A section of the tree is on display at the District Six Museum. ⊠ *Spin St.*

17 **South African Jewish Museum.** This museum captures the story of South African Jewry from its beginnings, spanning 150 years. The Themes of Memories (immigrant experiences), Reality (integration into South Africa), and Dreams (visions) exhibits are dynamically portrayed with high-tech multimedia and interactive displays, reconstructed sets, models, and Judaica artifacts. Also here are a computerized Discovery Center with a roots bank, a temporary gallery for changing exhibits, a museum restaurant and shop, and an auditorium. The museum also screens an exclusive 20-minute documentary on Mandela throughout the day. ⊠ *88 Hatfield St., Gardens* ☎ *021/465–1546* ⊕ *www. sajewishmuseum.co.za* 🖭 *R50* ☉ *Sun.–Thurs. 10–5, Fri. 10–2.*

14 **South African Museum.** If you don't get the opportunity to see rock art in its natural setting, come to this museum, which has some excellent examples that will give you insight into the ancient Khoisan culture. The museum also has an interesting section on the fossil remains of prehistoric reptiles and other animals, and the quite spectacular Whale Well, where musical recitals are often held under suspended life-size casts of enormous marine mammals. Shark World thrills children with exhibits on the sharks that ply the oceans. The adjoining planetarium stages a variety of shows throughout the week, some of which are specifically designed for children as young as five. ⊠ *25 Queen Victoria St., Cape Town central* ☎ *021/481–3800* ⊕ *www.museums.org.za/sam* 🖭 *Museum R10, planetarium R20* ☉ *Museum daily 10–5; planetarium shows weekdays at 2, plus Tues. at 8 PM, weekends at noon, 1, and 2:30.*

13 **South African National Gallery.** This museum houses a good collection of 19th- and 20th-century European, including British, art, but what's most interesting are its South African works, many of which reflect the country's traumatic history. An excellent example of contemporary South Africa art is the ghoulish sculpture *The Butcher Boys,* by Jane Alexander. Walk around these three sitting figures with an air of foreboding and menace about them, and you'll be shocked to discover their exposed spines. This is the stuff of nightmares, recalling the torture activists suffered at the hands of the security police during the height of apartheid. The gallery owns an enormous body of work, so exhibitions

FodorśChoice
★

change regularly, but there's always something provocative—whether it's documentary photographs or a multimedia exhibit chronicling South African's struggles with HIV/AIDS. The director, Marilyn Martin, is known for innovative, brave, and sometimes controversial exhibitions and her outspoken stance on art policy and development. Photographer Peter Magubane's exhibition on Nelson Mandela runs in 2005. Free guided tours take about an hour. ⊠ *Government Ave., Gardens* ☎ *021/ 467–4660* ⊕ *www.museums.org.za/sang* ⊠ *R10* ⊙ *Tues.–Sun. 10–5; tours Tues. and Thurs. at 1.*

⓬ **Tuynhuys (Town House).** Parts of the Tuynhuys date from the late 17th and early 18th centuries. In the early 1700s, foreign dignitaries stopped being entertained at the castle for fear that state secrets would fall into the wrong hands, so the then Governors Pleasure House was converted to accommodate them. (The British royal family even stayed here in 1947.) The elegant building with its classical columns now contains the offices of the state president and is not open to the public. ⊠ *Government Ave., Cape Town central.*

Victoria & Alfred Waterfront

The Victoria & Alfred Waterfront is the culmination of a long-term project undertaken to breathe new life into the historical dockland of the city. It is one of Cape Town's most vibrant and exciting attractions, and construction is ongoing. Expensive apartments are being built at the marina, and hotel giant Sol Kerzner (of Sun City and Lost City fame) is building a hotel near the aquarium. Hundreds of shops, movie theaters, restaurants, and bars share quarters in restored warehouses and dock buildings, all connected by pedestrian plazas and promenades. It's clean, it's safe, and it's car-free.

Since this part of the city changes constantly, it makes sense to begin your walk at the main **Victoria & Alfred Waterfront Information Centre** ㉚, so you can get the absolutely latest news. There are other information kiosks dotted around the V&A, if you need help along the way. Now head down the stairs toward Clock Tower Square with its landmark brick-red Clock Tower, which used to be the port captain's office. To your right is the Nelson Mandela Gateway to Robben Island, where you can buy a ticket for a trip to **Robben Island** ㉛ and watch seals basking in the sun near the embarkation platform. Across the square past the restaurants is **Chavonnes Battery** ㉜, in the highly acclaimed Board of Executors (BoE) building. After admiring the fortifications that were built to protect the city, cross over the swing bridge toward the blue Victorian building, which was the second office of the port captain. Take a left up the North Quay and past the Victoria & Alfred Hotel on your right. Up ahead is the enormous dry dock, where you're bound to see a few ships being painted or serviced. Walk through the enormous old shed that houses the Waterfront Trading Co. to see what's for sale in the stalls. Stop in at the **South African Maritime Museum** ㉝ to get a sense of shipping's impact on South Africa, and then make your way to the unmissable **Two Oceans Aquarium** ㉞. Once you've taken in the awe-inspiring sharks and kelp forest, wander down Dock Road, but don't forget to look up at what used to be the gruesome Breakwater Prison—now the University of Cape Town's Graduate School of Business. Its students joke that they have it harder than the prisoners who were incarcerated here. Walk through the square in front of the Victoria & Alfred Hotel and the mustard-colored **Union-Castle House** ㉟, pass the National Sea Rescue Institute (NSRI) shed, and follow your ears to the **AGFA Amphitheatre** ㊱. Go on to **Mitchell's Waterfront Brewery** ㊲, where the heady smell of malt should be enough to send you into the adjoining Ferryman's Tavern. Would-be shoppers can nip over to Red Shed Craft to stock up on locally made gifts. With purchases tucked safely under your arm, make your way along Quay 5, and find a bench where you can put up your feet and gaze at the **Victoria Basin** ㊳ while boats come and go and gulls wheel overhead.

TIMING You could complete this tour in half a day, but that won't give you much time for shopping, coffee stops, or lunch, or for all that the aquarium has to offer. A more leisurely approach would be to set aside a whole day, at the end of which you could find a waterside restaurant or bar and enjoy a cold glass of wine or a sophisticated cocktail.

What to See

㊱ **AGFA Amphitheatre.** This popular outdoor space mounts performances ranging from concerts by the Cape Town Philharmonic Orchestra to gigs by jazz and rock bands. (Check with the Victoria & Alfred Waterfront Information Centre for a schedule of events.) The amphitheater stands on the site where, in 1860, teenage Prince Alfred inaugurated the construction of a breakwater to protect ships in the harbor from devastating northwesterly winds. ⊠ *Near Market Sq.* ☎ *021/408–7600 for schedule.*

㉜ **Chavonnes Battery.** The Waterfront wasn't always a chi-chi watering hole and shopping center. In 1715 the Dutch East India Company was determined to defend the southern approaches to Table Bay, and so had a fort built on the site of what are today the offices of the Board of Executors (BoE) bank. The fort's foundations, which had been covered up by subsequent construction over the years, were unearthed when the site was being developed in the late 1990s. Total reconstruction of the battery was out of the question, but a sensitive partial reconstruction has been accomplished. Walkways around the foundations give you a clear sense of what the fort must have been like when it bristled with twelve 36-pound cannons and sixteen 18-pounders ready to blast any unfriendly British or French ship that came into the bay. A guided tour is included in admission. ⊠ *BoE Bldg., Clock Tower Precinct* ☎ *021/416–6230* ☞ *R30* ☉ *Weekdays 9–5, weekends 10–4.*

㊲ **Mitchell's Waterfront Brewery.** One of a handful of microbreweries in South Africa, Mitchell's produces four beers: Foresters Draught Lager, Bosuns Bitter, Ravenstout, and Ferryman's Ale. (Foresters Draught Lager, regarded as a "healthful" beer, contains no preservatives and has a fairly light taste.) Tours, for which reservations are essential, include beer tasting and a look at the fermentation tanks. ⊠ *E. Pier Rd.* ☎ *021/418–2461* ☞ *R20* ☉ *Weekdays 7–5.*

need a break?

After a visit to the brewery next door, you won't want to wait long for a nice cool one at **Ferryman's Tavern** (⊠ E. Pier Rd. ☎ 021/419–7748), and you won't have to. In addition to Mitchell's beers, you can sample other South African beers. Constructed in 1877 of bluestone and Table Mountain sandstone, Ferryman's is one of the oldest buildings in the harbor. Before 1912 the temperance movement in Cape Town had managed to force a ban on the sale of alcohol within the docks. As a result, a host of pubs sprang up just outside the dock gates, particularly along Dock Road.

③   **Robben Island.** Made famous by its most illustrious inhabitant, Nelson
Fodor's Choice   Rolihlahla Mandela, this island, whose name is Dutch for "seals," has
★   a long and sad history. At various times a prison, leper colony, mental institution, and military base, it is finally filling a positive, enlightening, and empowering role in its latest incarnation as a museum. Robert Sobukwe and Walter Sisulu were also imprisoned here for their role in opposing apartheid. For many years the African National Congress secretary-general, Sisulu died in 2003 in his early 90s and was given a hero's burial. Sobukwe, founding president of the Pan Africanist Congress, proved to be such a thorn in the government's side that he was imprisoned under the special Sobukwe Clause, which had to be renewed every year to keep him in jail. John Voster, then the country's minister, said of Sobukwe, "He is a man with magnetic personality, great organising ability, and a divine sense of mission," and it was these very qualities that made him such a threat. He was treated slightly better than other prisoners but was kept completely isolated from them—an especially terrible punishment for a man with such a strong sense of community. In addition to these more recent prisoners, there have been some fascinating (and reluctant) inhabitants of this at once formidable and beautiful place. One of the first prisoners was Autshumato, known to the early Dutch settlers as Harry the Hottentot. He was one of the main interpreters for Jan van Riebeeck in the mid-17th century and was imprisoned for opposing British colonial rule, as was his niece Krotoa. In 1820 the British thought they could solve some of the problems they were having on the Eastern Cape frontier by banishing Xhosa leader Makhanda to the island. Both Autshumato and Makhanda (also spelled Makana) escaped by rowboat, but Makhanda didn't make it. When you go to the island, notice that the two sleek high-speed ferries are called *Autshumato* and *Makana*.

Declared a World Heritage site on December 1, 1997, Robben Island has become a symbol of the triumph of the human spirit. Each year the number of visitors to the island rises dramatically. In 1997 around 90,000 made the pilgrimage, and in 2002 more than 300,000 crossed the water to see where some of the greatest South Africans spent much of their lives. Visiting the island is a sobering experience, which begins at the modern Nelson Mandela Gateway to Robben Island, an impressive embarkation center that doubles as a conference center. Interactive exhibits display historic photos of prison life. (You can also buy one of the sought-after Mandela drawings, which he made while imprisoned.) Next make the journey across the water, remembering to watch Table

Mountain recede in the distance and imagine what it must have been like to have just received a 20-year jail sentence. Boats leave on the hour, and the crossing takes 30 minutes.

Tours of the island are organized by the Robben Island Museum. (Other operators advertise Robben Island tours but just take visitors on a boat trip *around* the island.) As a result of the reconciliation process, most tour guides are former political prisoners. During the 2½-hour tour you walk through the prison and see the cells where Mandela and other leaders were imprisoned. Many people are reduced to tears when they see Mandela's tiny cell and walk down the bleak, echoing corridors. You also tour the lime quarry, where Mandela spent so many years pounding rocks; in summer, the reflection off the rock is blinding, and Mandela's eyesight— but thankfully not his insight—was irreparably damaged by the glare. The tour also takes you past Robert Sobukwe's house and the leper church. Many of the prison buildings have been renovated, but there are also plans to upgrade unoccupied houses where the warders used to live, extend the harbor, and make it more wheelchair-friendly. During peak season (mid-December–mid-January) it can get pretty crowded, so reserve in advance, and take sunglasses and a hat. You are advised to tip your guide only if you feel that the tour has been informative. ☎ *021/419–1300 information, 021/413–4200 reservations ⊕ www.robben-island.org.za* ☞ *R150 ☉ Daily 9–3 (last ferry leaves island at 6).*

㉝ South African Maritime Museum. As this museum demonstrates, Cape history is tied to the sea. Among the exhibits about the ships of Table Bay are models of the mail ships that used to ply the oceans. A fascinating model of Cape Town harbor as it appeared in 1886 was built by two convicts with an excellent eye for detail, as is evident in the intricate rigging on the sailing ships. The museum also has photographs and negatives of the more than 9,000 ships that called at Cape Town during the 20th century. ⊠ *Dock Rd.* ☎ *021/405–2880 ⊕ www.museums.org.za/ maritime* ☞ *R10 ☉ Daily 10–5.*

㉞ Two Oceans Aquarium. This aquarium is thought to be one of the finest
Fodor'sChoice in the world. Stunning displays reveal the marine life of the warm Indian Ocean and the icy Atlantic. It's a hands-on place, with a touch pool for children and opportunities for certified divers to explore the vast, five-story kelp forest or the predator tank, where you share the water with a couple of large ragged-tooth sharks (*Carcharias taurus*) and get a legal adrenaline rush (R400, R325 with own gear). And for something completely different, you can do a copper-helmet dive with antique dive equipment in the predator tank (R650). If you don't fancy getting wet, you can still watch the feeding in the predator tank every day at 3:30, and on Sundays there's a shark feed at the same time. But there's more to the aquarium than just snapping jaws. Look for the endangered African penguins (also known as jackass penguins because of the awkward braying noise they make); pulsating moon jellies and spider crabs; and, if you're lucky, the strange and elusive sunfish, which is exhibited only when one gets trapped in the harbor. ⊠ *Dock Rd.* ☎ *021/418–3823 ⊕ www.aquarium.co.za* ☞ *R60 ☉ Daily 9:30–6.*

⑤ Union-Castle House. Designed in 1919 by famed British architect Sir Herbert Baker, this house was headquarters for the famous Union-Castle shipping line. Before World War II many English-speaking South Africans looked upon England as home, even if they had never been there. The emotional link between the two countries was symbolized most strongly by the mail steamers, carrying both mail and passengers, that sailed weekly between South Africa and England. In 1977, amid much pomp and ceremony, the last Union-Castle mail ship, the *Windsor Castle,* made its final passage to England. Even today older South Africans like to wax lyrical about the joys of a voyage on one of those steamers. Union-Castle House is now home to several banks and small businesses. Inside Standard Bank you can still see the iron rings in the ceiling from which mailbags were hung. ⊠ *Quay 4.*

㉚ Victoria & Alfred Waterfront Information Centre. This tourism office has the lowdown on everything happening in the area, including upcoming events and shows. Here you can arrange walking tours of the Waterfront, book accommodations, and get information about the whole Western Cape. ⊠ *Clock Tower Centre, South Arm Rd.* ☎ *021/405–4500* ⊕ *www.waterfront.co.za* ⊠ *Free* ⊙ *Daily 9–9.*

㊳ Victoria Basin. The basin was constructed between 1870 and 1905 to accommodate the huge increase in shipping following the discovery of diamonds at Kimberley and gold on the Witwatersrand. The South Arm was used as a debarkation point for British troops, horses, and matériel during the Second South African War (1899–1902), also called the Boer War. Much of the fodder for the British horses was shipped in from Argentina, and was catastrophically infested with rats and fleas. As a result, bubonic plague broke out in Cape Town in February 1901, causing wholesale panic and hundreds of deaths. The basin today is nothing like its grim past, however. The gorgeous Cape Grace hotel presides at the water's edge, as do privately owned penthouses and another luxury hotel currently under construction.

The Peninsula

Numbers in the text correspond to numbers in the margin and on the Cape Peninsula map.

 a good drive

This driving tour takes you south from Cape Town on a loop of the Cape Peninsula, heading through the scenic Southern Suburbs before running down the False Bay coast to Cape Point and then making the magnificent drive back to the city along the wild Atlantic coast.

Take the N2 or De Waal Drive (M3) out of the city center. The two highways merge near **Groote Schuur Hospital** ㊴ and split again soon after. Bear right, taking the M3 (signposted SOUTHERN SUBURBS/MUIZENBERG), and look up at the mountain—you should see zebras, wildebeest, and eland grazing peacefully on the lower slopes. After 1 km (½ mi) you'll pass **Mostert's Mill** ㊵ on your left, one of two remaining windmills in the Cape. On your right is the beautifully situated campus of the University of Cape Town, nestled against the slopes of Devil's Peak. To visit the **Irma Stern**

BLACK & WHITE & RED ALL OVER

In 1948 the National Party was voted into power and apartheid machinery set in motion. "Separate development," as it was euphemistically known, was deemed appropriate, and black South Africans were regarded as nothing more than "hewers of wood and drawers of water." As such, black education was accepted as inferior, whole communities were moved off desirable land, and the majority of South Africans were unable to vote. Fortunately, however, exceptional men and women—Nelson Mandela being the most famous and best-loved—were determined to change the status quo. In fact, the anti-apartheid struggle began as soon as the Nats came to power. While F. W. de Klerk was president, negotiations began, Mandela was released from prison, and the first democratic election was held in 1994. For their efforts, de Klerk and Mandela received the Nobel Peace Prize for an achievement others thought impossible.

Museum 🔴, take the Woolsack Drive exit just after Mostert's Mill. Turn left on Main Road, left again on Chapel Road, and then right on Cecil Road, where you'll find the museum. (Finding parking might be a bit harder, especially if the university is in session.) Retrace your route to the highway, and continue to the exit for the **Rhodes Memorial** 🔴, which yields an excellent view of the city. Return to the M3 and head south toward Muizenberg. After 1½ km (1 mi) exit right onto Rhodes Avenue (M63), a leafy road that winds through large trees to the **Kirstenbosch National Botanic Gardens** 🔴, one of the most beautiful spots in the Cape.

Turn right as you leave the botanic gardens. When you reach a T, turn right again, and begin the winding climb to the pass at Constantia Nek. From the traffic circle at the top you can either cut over the mountains and down into Hout Bay or turn left onto the M41 (the sign reads WYNBERG AND GROOT CONSTANTIA) and begin the snaking descent to Constantia, the domain of the suburban gentry. Plantations of pine predominate higher up, but vineyards carpet the lower slopes. The first wine farm you come to is **Groot Constantia** 🔴; after a visit, turn right on Main Road and right again on Ladies Mile Extension (a sign points to Muizenberg and Bergvliet). A right at the first traffic light puts you on Spaanschemat River Road, and yet another right funnels you onto Klein Constantia Road and on to the winery **Buitenverwachting** 🔴. Once you've tasted the wine and admired the setting, turn left out of Buitenverwachting and continue for ½ km (¼ mi) to **Klein Constantia** 🔴 wine farm. Many of these farms are good places to stop for lunch. Now head back down Klein Constantia Road, and turn right on Spaanschemat River Road. After about 3 km (2 mi), turn right at the traffic circle into Tokai Road, and drive for about 1 km (½ mi) to reach **Tokai Manor** 🔴. Retrace your route, and at the traffic circle go right past the Steenberg Hotel & Winery. On your left is Pollsmoor Prison, where Nelson Mandela stayed after he was moved from Robben Island.

Continue past the child-friendly Steenberg Farmstall, on your right; it's a good place for a snack. At the next set of traffic lights is the turnoff for Ou Kaapse Weg, but instead continue on through to Main Road (M4), where you turn right. After ½ km (¼ mi), the scenic Boyes Drive leads off the M4 and provides fantastic views and photo ops over False Bay and the Hottentots Holland Mountains. During spring, this is a good place to spot whales, who come to calve here. The M4, on the other hand, runs through **Muizenberg** ⓭, where it runs parallel to the sea. Watch for Het Post Huys, a small thatch building with rough whitewashed walls on your right; the imposing pink facade of the Natale Labia Museum, a mansion that belonged to the Italian plenipotentiary to South Africa in the '30s but is not currently worth a stop; and the Rhodes Cottage Museum.

From Muizenberg, Main Road heads down the peninsula, hugging the shore of False Bay. Strung along this coastline is a collection of small villages that long ago merged to form a thin suburban belt between the ocean and the mountains: **Kalk Bay** ⓭, **Fish Hoek** ⓭, and **Simon's Town** ⓭, the last community of any size before you reach Cape Point. As you head out of town, you can stop at tiny **Boulders Beach** ⓭ to look at the colony of African penguins and, on a hot day, have a swim among the enormous boulders that give the beach its name.

From here the road traverses a wild, windswept landscape as beautiful as it is desolate. The mountains, covered with indigenous fynbos, descend almost straight into the sea. Don't be surprised to see troops of baboons lounging beside the road as you approach **Cape Point and the Cape of Good Hope** ⓭. Close the car windows, and don't attempt to feed the baboons. They are extremely bold and will happily sit on your car or try to climb through the window if they know you have food. Before you reach the Cape Point gate, look left and you will see the almost outrageously picturesque settlement of Smitswinkel Bay—accessible only on foot via a steep and narrow path.

On leaving the nature preserve, turn left out of the Cape Point gate and take the M65 to **Scarborough** ⓭ and **Kommetjie** ⓭, where you can take a walk to the lighthouse at Slangkoppunt. Continue on the M65 to the intersection with the M6, turn left, and follow the signs to Hout Bay. The road passes through the small community of **Noordhoek** ⓭ before beginning its treacherous climb around **Chapman's Peak Drive** ⓭, arguably one of the most scenic routes in the country. Although the cliffs above this drive have been secured, there are times when it is closed due to rock instability. Check the sign at the beginning of the drive to see if it's open. If it is, you are in for an exceptional drive through to **Hout Bay** ⓭. If it's closed, retrace your route to the Noordhoek side of **Ou Kaapse Weg** ⓭, which goes over the mountain through the Silvermine section of the TMNP. (From the bottom of the mountain you would retrace your route—minus the detours for stops—back to the traffic circle at Constantia Nek, from which you can drive down into Hout Bay.)

Back on the M6 (a sign reads CITY AND LLANDUDNO), after less than 1 km (½ mi), turn right on Valley Road to the **World of Birds** ⓭. The M6 climbs past the exclusive suburb of Llandudno and then runs along the coast to **Camps Bay** ㊿. Follow Victoria Road (M6) out of Camps Bay, and turn right at the sign reading KLOOF NEK ROUND HOUSE. This road snakes up the mountain until it reaches a five-way intersection at Kloof Nek. Make a sharp left onto the road leading to **Signal Hill** ㊿. For more great views of the city, return to the Kloof Nek intersection and take **Tafelberg Road** ㊿.

TIMING Distances on the Peninsula are not that great, so it's certainly possible to drive the loop in a day, visiting a few sights of interest to you. It's equally possible, however, to spend three days on this tour, either moving slowly around the Peninsula and staying in a different guesthouse each night or returning to a central spot in the Southern Suburbs at the end of each day. If you don't have time for the Winelands but still want to experience the Cape's excellent wines, work in a visit to Constantia's excellent estates.

What to See

★ ☺ ㊾ **Boulders Beach.** This series of small coves lies among giant boulders on the outskirts of Simon's Town. Part of the Table Mountain National Park, the beach is best known for its resident colony of African penguins. You must stay out of the fenced-off breeding beach, but don't be surprised if a wandering bird comes waddling up to you to take a look. Penguin-viewing platforms, accessible from either the Boulders Beach or Seaforth side, provide close-up looks at these comical birds. When you've had enough penguin peering, you can stroll back to Boulders Beach for some excellent swimming in the quiet coves. This beach is great for children because it is so protected and the sea is warm and calm. It can get crowded in summer, though, so go early. Without traffic, it takes about 45 minutes to get here from town, less from the Southern Suburbs. ✉ *Follow signs from Bellvue Rd., Simon's Town* ☎ *021/786–5786* ⊕ *www. tmnp.co.za* ✉ *R20* ☽ *Daily 9–6.*

> **need a break?** Serving a hearty breakfast, light lunch, tea, dinner, and drinks, **Penguin Point Restaurant** (✉ Boulders Beach parking lot ☎ 021/786–1758) has a huge veranda that's great for gazing out over False Bay and watching the sun set. Even though you're facing east, False Bay sunsets are still spectacular. Consisting mostly of reflected light, they are pastel pink, pale blue, lavender, and gold.

㊺ **Buitenverwachting.** Once part of Dutch governor Simon van der Stel's original Constantia farm, Buitenverwachting (which means "beyond expectation" and is roughly pronounced "Bait-in-fur-wagh-ting") has an absolutely gorgeous setting. An oak-lined avenue leads past the Cape Dutch homestead to the thatch but modern cellar. Acres of vines spread up hillsides flanked by more towering oaks and the rocky crags of the Constantiaberg. Buitenverwachting's wine is just as good. The largest seller is the slightly dry Buiten Blanc, an easy-drinking blend of a few varietals. The best red is Christine, a blend of mostly cabernet sauvignon and merlot. The winery's eponymous restaurant is also worth a visit. ✉ *Off Klein Constantia Rd.* ☎ *021/794–5190* ✉ *Tastings free* ☽ *Weekdays 9–5, Sat. 9–1.*

need a
break?

Buitenverwachting (☎ 021/794–1012) serves great picnic lunches during the summer months (November–April) under the oaks on the estate's lawns. It's an idyllic setting and a most civilized way to cap a morning of wine tasting. Each picnic basket is packed with a selection of breads, chicken and other meat, pâtés, and cheeses. You can buy a bottle of estate wine as an accompaniment. Keep an eye out for the enormous pet pig who spends her life under the oaks; she might want to join you. The picnic costs R90 per person, and reservations are essential.

61 **Camps Bay.** With a long beach and plenty of restaurants and bars, this popular vacation resort is where Cape Town's beautiful people—models, movie stars, and the rest of the rich and famous—hang out. The craggy faces of the Twelve Apostles, huge granite buttresses reaching down to the sea from the mountains behind, loom over the town.

53 **Cape Point and the Cape of Good Hope.** Once a nature reserve on its own,
Fodor'sChoice   this section of Table Mountain National Park covers more than 19,000
★   acres. Much of the park consists of rolling hills covered with fynbos and laced with miles of walking trails, for which maps are available at the park entrance. It also has beautiful deserted beaches. Eland, baboon, ostrich, and bontebok (a colorful antelope that was hunted to near extinction in the early 20th century) are among the animals that roam the park. A paved road runs 12½ km (8 mi) to the tip of the peninsula, and a turnoff leads to the Cape of Good Hope, a rocky cape that is the southwesternmost point of the continent. A plaque marks the spot—otherwise you would never know you're standing on a site of such significance.

The opposite is true of Cape Point, a dramatic knife's edge of rock that slices into the Atlantic. Looking out to sea from the viewing platform, you feel you're at the tip of Africa, even though that honor officially belongs to Cape Agulhas, about 160 km (100 mi) to the southeast. From Cape Point the views of False Bay and the Hottentots Holland Mountains are astonishing. The walk up to the viewing platform and the old lighthouse is very steep; a funicular (R31 round-trip, R21 one-way) makes the run every three or four minutes. Take a jacket or sweater—the wind can take your breath away. It took six years, from 1913 to 1919, to build the old lighthouse, 816 feet above the high-water mark. Considering how precipitous the path is, it's surprising it didn't take a lot longer. On a clear day the old lighthouse was a great navigational mark, but when the mists rolled in, it was useless, so a new and much lower lighthouse (286 feet) was built at Dias Lookout Point. The newer, revolving lighthouse, the most powerful on the South African coast, emits a group of three flashes every 30 seconds. It has prevented a number of ships from ending up on Bellows or Albatross Rock below. You can't go into the lighthouses, but the views from their bases are spectacular.

Stark reminders of the ships that didn't make it are dotted around the Cape. You'll see their rusty remains on some of the beaches. One of the more famous wrecks is the *Thomas T. Tucker,* one of hundreds of Liberty Ships produced by the United States to enable the Allies to move vast amounts of supplies during World War II. It wasn't the U-boats patrolling the coastline that did the ship in. Rather the fog closed in, and on her maiden voyage in 1942, she ended up on Olifantsbos Point. Fortunately, all on board were saved, but the wreck soon broke up in the rough seas that pound the coast.

The park has some excellent land-based whale-watching spots. About June–November, whales return to these waters to calve. You're most likely to see the southern right whale in False Bay, but the occasional humpback and Bryde's whale also shows up. When the water is calm, you may even be lucky enough to see a school of dolphins looping their way past. The Rooikrans parking lot is good for whale-watching, but there are any number of lookout points. It's just a matter of driving around until you see the characteristic spray or a shiny black fluke.

The mast you see on the western slopes of Cape Point near the lighthouse belongs to the Global Atmosphere Watch Station (GAW). The South African Weather Bureau, together with the Fraunhofer Institute in Garmisch, Germany, maintains a research laboratory here to monitor long-term changes in the chemistry of the earth's atmosphere, which may impact climate. This is one of 20 GAWs throughout the world, chosen because the air at Cape Point is considered particularly pure most of the time.

A large sit-down restaurant has better views than food (but that is saying a lot), and a kiosk sells snacks. There are three gift shops and an Internet café, where you can send a photo of yourself with Cape Point in the distance to the folks back home. During peak season (December-January), visit Cape Point as early in the day as you can; otherwise you'll be swamped by horrendous numbers of tour buses and their occupants. Fun alternatives include an escorted bike trip to the point and an overnight hike with comfortable basic accommodations and incredible views, which is booked through South African National Parks. Be wary of baboons in the parking lot; they have been known to steal food and can be dangerous if provoked. Unfortunately the indigenous chacma baboons are increasingly under threat, and in 2004 it was estimated that only 125 (98 females and 27 males in 10 troops) remain in the Cape Peninsula. Many baboons have been shot for raiding homes and stealing food. Baboon-feeding tourists only exacerbate this serious situation. ⊠ *Off the M65 (Plateau Rd.)* ☎ *021/780–9526 or 021/780–9204* ⊕ *www.tmnp.co.za* ⊠ *R40* ⊗ *Apr.–Sept., daily 7–5; Oct.–Mar., daily 6–6; last exit 1 hr after closing.*

★ ㊲ **Chapman's Peak Drive.** After being closed for several years due to rock slides and unstable cliff faces, this fantastically scenic drive has reopened after a major reconstruction that involved state-of-the-art engineering techniques, some of which had never been used on South African roads. But that wasn't the first engineering feat for this road that clings to the mountainside. Work began on the drive in 1910, when it was considered an impossibility. Charl Marais, a mining surveyor, wasn't deterred by the task and set about surveying a route by sending a worker ahead of him to chop out footholds and create rudimentary platforms for his theodolite. There are stories of him hanging on to the side of the cliff by ropes and nearly losing his life on a number of occasions. His tenacity paid off, and, with the help of 700 convicts, dynamite, picks, and shovels, a road was chipped and blasted out of the rock. Chapman's Peak Drive officially opened in 1922. A reporter from a local newspaper waxed lyrical, writing that the road was much like a woman, "always changing, luring, and at moments giving you a quick sense of danger." You can access the drive from both Noordhoek and Hout Bay.

⑤ Fish Hoek. This popular resort town on the False Bay coast has a smooth sandy beach that is protected on the south side from the summer south-easters by Elsies Peak. The main drag is ugly for a town with such a pretty setting, as nobody gave much thought to the architecture of the commercial center. Once the preserve of retirees, and until the late 1990s the only teetotaling town in the country, Fish Hoek is facing a boom as the city of Cape Town expands south and more young people are moving to the area. It's also one of the best places to see whales during calving season—approximately August to November—though there have been whale sightings as early as June and as late as January. Jagers Walk, from the south side of Fish Hoek Beach to Sunny Cove, is a pleasant, scenic, wheelchair-friendly pathway that meanders through the rocks, providing access to some sheltered natural rock pools that are just great for swimming. The snorkeling is good, too. In 2004, however, a 77-year-old swimmer was attacked and killed by a great white shark, so be sure not to swim far out to sea. Outside of peak traffic, it takes about 30 minutes to get from Cape Town to Fish Hoek, but over Christmas and New Year's the roads get very congested, so leave early to miss the crowds.

★ ㊹ Groot Constantia. Constantia takes its name from the wine estate founded here in 1685 by Simon van der Stel, one of the first Dutch governors of the Cape. After his death in 1712 the land was subdivided, with the heart of the estate preserved at Groot Constantia. The enormous complex enjoys the status of a national monument and is by far the most commercial and touristy of the wineries. Van der Stel's magnificent homestead, the oldest in the Cape, lies at the center of Groot Constantia. It's built in traditional Cape Dutch–style, with thick whitewashed walls, a thatch roof, small-paned windows, and ornate gables. The house is a museum furnished with exquisite period pieces. The old wine cellar sits behind the manor house. Built in 1791, it is most famous for its own ornate gable, which contains a sculpture designed by Anton Anreith. The sculpture, depicting fertility, is regarded as one of the most important in the country. The cellar houses a wine museum, with displays on wine-drinking and storage vessels dating to antiquity.

In the 19th century the sweet wines of Groot Constantia were highly regarded in Europe, and especially favored by King Louis Philippe and Bismarck. Today Groot Constantia is known for its splendid red wines. The best is the excellent Bordeaux-style Gouverneurs Reserve, made mostly from cabernet sauvignon grapes with smaller amounts of merlot and cabernet franc. The pinotage is consistently good, too, reaching its velvety prime in about five years. The estate operates two restaurants: the elegant Jonkershuis and Simon's, which serves sophisticated meals in a spectacular setting. You can also bring your own picnic and relax on the lawns behind the wine cellar. ⊠ *Off Constantia Rd., Constantia* 🕿 *021/ 794–5128 winery, 021/795–5140 museum* 🖃 *Museum R10, tastings R20, cellar tour with tastings R25* ⊙ *Museum daily 10–5; winery May–Sept., daily 9–5; Oct.–Apr., daily 9–6; 7 tours per day.*

㊟ Groote Schuur Hospital. In 1967 Dr. Christian Barnard performed the world's first heart transplant at this landmark on the slopes of Table Mountain, just off Main Road below the scenic De Waal Drive. The Transplant Museum is worth a visit if you're interested in medical history or techniques. ⊠ *Old Hospital Bldg., Hospital Dr., Observatory* 🕿 *021/ 404–5232* ⊕ *www.gsh.co.za* 🖃 *R5* ⊙ *Weekdays 9–2.*

㊸ Hout Bay. Cradled in a lovely bay of the same name and guarded by a 1,000-foot peak known as the Sentinel, Hout Bay is the center of Cape Town's crayfishing industry, and the town operates several fish-processing plants. Mariner's Wharf is Hout Bay's salty answer to the Waterfront in Cape Town, a collection of bars and restaurants on the quayside. You can buy fresh fish at a seafood market and take it outside to be grilled. You should also try *snoek,* a barracudalike fish that is traditionally eaten smoked. Cruise boats (⇨ Cape Town A to Z, *below*) depart from Hout Bay's harbor to view the Cape fur seal colony on Duiker Island.

㊶ Irma Stern Museum. This museum is dedicated to the works and art collection of Stern (1894–1966), one of South Africa's greatest painters. The museum is administered by the University of Cape Town and occupies the Firs, the artist's home for 38 years. She is best known for African studies, particularly her paintings of indigenous people inspired by trips to the Congo and Zanzibar. Her collection of African artifacts, including priceless Congolese stools and carvings, is superb. ⊠ *Cecil Rd., Rosebank* 🕿 *021/685–5686* ⊕ *www.irmastern.co.za* 🖃 *R8* ⊙ *Tues.–Sat. 10–5.*

★ ⊙ ㊾ Kalk Bay. This small, fascinating harbor, which shelters a weathered fishing fleet, gets its name from the seashells that were once baked in large kilns near the shore to produce lime (*kalk*). Tiny cottages crowd the narrow cobbled streets, clinging to the mountain, and funky clothing shops, galleries, antiques shops, and cozy bistros can fill a whole day of rambling. Here gnarled fishingfolk rub shoulders with artists, writers, surfers, yuppies, New Age trendies, and genteel ladies with blue hair rinses. During whale seasons the gentle giants rub up against the harbor wall, and if you time your visit right, you can almost touch them. You can also walk up any of the steep stairways to Boyes Drive and from there up the mountain, or relax and down a few beers in the sun at the Brass Bell while local surfers strut their stuff on Kalk Bay Reef. Other possibilities on your to-do list might include buying fish so fresh it wriggles, dropping your own line off the pier (fishing supplies available from the small supermarket on the Main Road), and watching the harbor seals who loll around waiting for fishy discards when the boats come in. The lives of the fishermen are changing rapidly due to declining fish stocks, however; a window on this world is provided through Adventure Kalk Bay (⇨ Cape Town A to Z, *below*), a nonprofit group whose goal is to preserve this traditional way of life.

need a break? Part of the Adventure Kalk Bay initiative, the **Money Tree Café** (⊠ Outspan parking lot, Main Rd. ☎021/788–2242), opposite the harbor, serves simple, traditional meals prepared by fishermen's wives. Typical fare includes fish cakes with rice and tomato *bredie* (stew), grilled fish, and fish curry. Stopping here for lunch or tea after a guided walk of the village is a good way to continue your authentic experience.

Kirstenbosch National Botanic Gardens. Spectacular in each season, these world-famous gardens showcase stunning South African flora in a magnificent setting, extending up the eastern slopes of Table Mountain and overlooking the sprawling city and the distant Hottentots Holland Mountains. No wonder the gardens are photographed from every angle. They aren't just enjoyed by out-of-town visitors, however; on weekends Capetonians flock here with their families to lie on the lawns and read their newspapers while the kids run riot. Walking trails meander through the gardens, and grassy banks are ideal for a picnic or afternoon nap. The plantings are limited to species indigenous to southern Africa, including fynbos—hardy, thin-leaved plants that proliferate in the Cape. Among these are proteas, including silver trees and king proteas; ericas; and *restios* (reeds). Magnificent sculptures from Zimbabwe are displayed around the gardens, too.

Garden highlights include a large cycad garden, the Bird Bath (a beautiful stone pool built around a crystal-clear spring), and the fragrance garden, which is wheelchair-friendly and has a tapping rail and Braille interpretive boards. Those who have difficulty walking can take a comprehensive tour lasting 45 minutes to an hour (R20; hourly 10–3) in six-person (including the driver) golf carts. Another wheelchair trail leads from the main paths into the wilder section of the park, getting close to the feel of the mountain walks. Concerts featuring the best of South African entertainment—from classical music to township jazz to rock and roll—are held on summer Sundays starting an hour before sunset. A visitor center by the conservatory houses a restaurant, bookstore, and coffee shop. Unfortunately, muggings are not unheard of in the gardens' isolated areas, and women are advised not to walk alone in the upper reaches of the park far from general activity. ⊠ *Rhodes Ave., Newlands* ☎ *021/799–8783* ⊕ *www.nbi.ac.za* ☎ *R22* ☉ *Apr.–Aug., daily 8–6; Sept.–Mar., daily 8–7.*

Klein Constantia. *Klein* (rhymes with "stain") means "small" in Afrikaans and indicates the relative size of this portion of van der Stel's original Constantia estate. The winery has an impressive modern cellar, deliberately unobtrusive so as not to detract from the vine-covered mountain slopes. Its Cape Dutch homestead, visible as you drive in, was built in the late 18th century. This estate produces wines of superb quality, as awards displayed in the tasting area attest. The excellent sauvignon blanc is used as a point of reference by many South African connoisseurs and vintners. The closest you'll come to the famous Constantia wine of the 18th century is the Vin de Constance, a sweet wine made from predominantly Muscat de Frontignan grapes. The cabernet sauvignon is one of the best produced in the Cape—a collector's wine that will develop wonderfully over time. ⊠ *Klein Constantia Rd., Con-*

stantia ☎ *021/794–5188* ⊕ *www.kleinconstantia.com* ⚏ *Tastings free* ☉ *Weekdays 9–5, Sat. 9–1; cellar tours weekdays by appointment.*

🕙 ⑤⑤ **Kommetjie.** A pleasant, somewhat isolated suburb, Kommetjie has a scenic 45-minute walk down Long Beach that leads to the wreck of the *Kakapo,* a steamship that ran aground on her maiden voyage in 1900. This is a surfer's paradise, with some really big waves and a few gentler breaks. Unfortunately, because of a series of attacks on Long Beach, you are advised to walk here only in a group. If you don't have security in numbers, walk instead to the Kommetjie lighthouse, the tallest cast-iron tower on South Africa's coast, at Slangkoppunt, almost exactly midway between Robben Island and Cape Point. The lighthouse has a 5-million-candlepower light and a range of 30 nautical miles, with four flashes every 30 seconds. Nearby **Imhoff Farm** (⊠ Imhoff's Gift complex, Kommetjie Rd. ☎ 021/783–4545) is a good stop if you're traveling with children, as there are camel and horseback rides, a petting zoo, crafts shops, and a coffee shop. **Solole Game Reserve** (⊠ Wood Rd., off Kommetjie Rd., between Kommetjie and Noordhoek ☎ 021/785–3248) offers tractor rides, tame buffalo, and plenty of space for kids to let off steam.

④⓪ **Mostert's Mill.** Built in 1796, this thatch wheat mill consists of a tower with a rotating cap to which sails were attached. Mills like this were once common in the area. Inside is the original mechanism, but it's not necessarily worth pulling off the highway to see. ⊠ *Off Woolsack Ave., visible from Rhodes Dr., Mowbray* ☎ *No phone* ☉ *Daily 9–5.*

④⑧ **Muizenberg.** At the turn of the 20th century this was the premier swimming resort in South Africa, attracting many of the country's wealthy mining magnates, as the many mansions along Baden Powell Drive attest. Long gone, though, are the days when anyone thought of Muizenberg as chic. A drab complex of shops and fast-food outlets, complete with kiddie pools and miniature golf, blights the beachfront, and the flood of immigrants from the rest of Africa has brought its own set of problems. Drug dealing is not uncommon, the whole area is in a state of not-so-genteel decay, and many beautiful art-deco beachfront buildings have become slums. That doesn't stop beginner surfers and keen dog walkers from utilizing the still-wonderful beach, but they skip the area on the sea side of the railway line. Muizenberg's future looks bright, however. Property prices have risen sharply, and there are plans to restore the old beachfront beauties. A couple of trendy coffee shops and restaurants have helped give Muizenberg the boost it needs, and successful community initiatives have taken aim at crime.

There are two sights worth seeing in Muizenberg—both free and open daily. **Het Post Huys** (⊠ Main Rd. ☎ 021/788–7972), one of the oldest buildings in the country still standing, was constructed in 1673 as a lookout post and signal station. It also served as an early toll station in precolonial times but now houses an exhibition on the Battle of Muizenberg (1795) as well as more recent photos chronicling the town's heyday. **Rhodes Cottage Museum** (⊠ 246 Main Rd. ☎ 021/788–1816), the seaside home of Cecil John Rhodes (1853–1902), reflects more-recent local history. Considering the power wielded by this great empire builder, his cottage was surprisingly humble and spare, and yet this is where he chose to spend his last days in 1902, preferring the cool sea air of Muizenberg to the stifling opulence of his home at Groote Schuur. The cottage, including the bedroom where he died, has been completely restored. Other rooms display photos documenting Rhodes's life. His remains are buried in the Matopos Hills, in Zimbabwe.

56 **Noordhoek.** This popular beach community has stunning white sands that stretch forever. The small bordering village has become a retreat for the arts-and-crafts community and has a couple of galleries and boutiques. You can walk all the way to Kommetjie on the aptly named Long Beach. It's also very popular with horseback riders and surfers.

need a break? The **Red Herring Restaurant** (⊠ Noordhoek ☎ 021/789–1783) is a favorite local hangout for surfers and dogs. The upstairs bar has a fantastic view, the pizzas are good, and the beer is always cold.

★ **59** **Ou Kaapse Weg** (Old Cape Road). The shortest route between Noordhoek and Constantia is also the most scenic, with lovely flowers and distant vistas of False Bay in the east and the Atlantic in the west. Heading toward the city over Ou Kaapse Weg you get an excellent view of the sprawling Pollsmoor Prison next door to the exclusive Steenberg wine farm and golf estate—a stark illustration of the contradictions that continue to plague South Africa and make it such a confounding country.

★ **42** **Rhodes Memorial.** Rhodes served as prime minister of the Cape from 1890 to 1896. He made his fortune in the diamond rush at Kimberley, but his greatest dream was to forge a Cape–Cairo railway, a tangible symbol of British dominion in Africa. The classical-style granite memorial sits high on the slopes of Devil's Peak, on part of Rhodes's old estate, Groote Schuur. A mounted rider symbolizing energy faces north toward the continent for which Rhodes felt such passion. A bust of Rhodes dominates the temple—ironically, he's leaning on one hand as if he's about to nod off. ⊠ Off Rhodes Dr., Rondebosch 🎟 Free.

need a break? The **Rhodes Memorial Tea Garden** (⊠ Off Rhodes Dr., Rondebosch ☎ 021/689–9151), tucked under towering pines behind the memorial, is a pleasant spot that serves breakfast, tea, and a light lunch.

54 **Scarborough.** This tiny vacation community has one of the best beaches on the peninsula. Scarborough is becoming popular with artists and craftspeople, and you'll find their offerings exhibited at informal galleries. From Scarborough to Kommetjie the M65 hugs the shoreline, snaking between the mountains and the crashing surf. This part of the shore is considered unsafe for swimming, but experienced surfers and windsurfers revel in the wind and waves.

62 **Signal Hill.** Where Signal Hill Road swings around the shoulder of Lion's Head and runs along the flank of Signal Hill, the views of Table Mountain and the city below are superb. The road ends at a parking lot overlooking Sea Point and all of Table Bay. Be careful around here, especially if it's deserted. There have been incidents of violent crime.

★ **51** **Simon's Town.** Picturesque Simon's Town has many lovely old buildings and is close to what are possibly the peninsula's best swimming beaches, Seaforth and Boulders. The town has had a long association with the Royal Navy. British troops landed here in 1795 before defeating the Dutch at the Battle of Muizenberg, and the town served as a base for the Royal Navy from 1814 to 1957, when it was handed over to the South African navy. Today you are bound to see plenty of men and women decked out in crisp white uniforms.

Jubilee Square, a dockside plaza that serves as the de facto town center, is just off the main road (St. George's Road). Next to the dock wall stands a **statue of Just Nuisance,** a Great Dane adopted as a mascot by the Royal Navy during World War II. Just Nuisance apparently liked his pint of beer and would accompany sailors on the train into Cape Town. He had the endearing habit of leading drunken sailors—and only sailors—that he found in the city back to the station in time to catch the last train. The navy went so far as to induct him into the service as an able seaman attached to the HMS *Afrikander.* He died at the age of seven in April 1944 and was given a military funeral. Just below Jubilee Square is the popular Simon's Town Waterfront, with numerous shops and restaurants; a toy museum; a nearby gemstone factory, which will keep children occupied for hours; and Bear Basics, where you can buy any number of cute teddy bears and even trendier gear for them to wear, including outfits made out of traditional South African fabrics. Day cruises and deep-sea fishing trips also leave from the harbor.

need a break? At **Just Sushi Bar & Restaurant** (✉ Simon's Town Waterfront ☎ 021/786–4340), the sushi is fresh, the atmosphere is friendly and unpretentious, and the prices are welcoming.

63 **Tafelberg Road.** This road crosses the northern side of Table Mountain before ending at Devil's Peak. From the Kloof Nek intersection you can descend to Cape Town directly or return to Camps Bay and follow the coastal road back to the city. This route takes you through the beautiful seaside communities of Clifton and Bantry Bay and then along the seaside promenade in Sea Point.

47 **Tokai Manor.** Built in 1795, this is one of the finest Cape Dutch homes in the country. Famed architect Louis Michel Thibault designed its facade. The homestead is reputedly haunted by a horseman who died when he tried to ride his horse down the curving front steps during a drunken revel. You can stop for a look, but the house is not open to the public. The **Arboretum,** just behind the manor house (follow the dirt road), is a good place to walk and learn about trees, which all have name tags. After the first winter rains, the forest is full of edible mushrooms, so you're bound to come across mushroom pickers. The Arboretum also has a simple tea garden. ✉ *Tokai Rd., Tokai.*

🖑 **60** **World of Birds.** Here you can walk through aviaries housing 450 species of indigenous and exotic birds, including eagles, vultures, penguins, and flamingos. No cages separate you from most of the birds, so you can get some pretty good photographs; however, the big raptors are kept

behind fences. ⊠ *Valley Rd., Hout Bay* ☎ *021/790–2730* ⊕ *www.*
worldofbirds.org.za 🎫 *R45* ☉ *Daily 9–5.*

BEACHES

With panoramic views of mountains tumbling to the ocean, the stunning sandy beaches of the Cape Peninsula are a major draw for Capetonians and visitors alike. Beautiful as the beaches may be, don't expect
to spend hours splashing in the surf: the water around Cape Town is
very, very cold (although you get used to it). Beaches on the Atlantic are
washed by the Benguela Current flowing up from the Antarctic, and in
midsummer the water hovers around 10°C–15°C (50°F–60°F). The
water on the False Bay side is usually 5°C (9°F) warmer. Cape beaches
are renowned for their clean, snow-white powdery sand. Beachcombers
will find every kind of beach to suit them, from intimate coves to sheltered bays and wild, wide beaches stretching forever. If you are looking
for more tropical water temperatures, head for the warm Indian Ocean
waters of KwaZulu-Natal or the Garden Route.

The major factor that affects any day at a Cape beach is wind. In summer howling southeasters, known collectively as the Cape Doctor, are
all too common and can ruin a trip to the beach; during these gales you're
better off at Clifton or Llandudno, on the Atlantic side, or the sheltered
but very small St. James Beach, on the False Bay side, and maybe even
the southern corner of Fish Hoek Beach or one of the pools along
Jager's Walk. Boulders (⇨ *above*) and Seaforth are also often sheltered
from southeasters.

Every False Bay community has its own beach, but most are not reviewed
here. In comparison with Atlantic beaches, most of them are rather small
and often crowded, sandwiched between the sea and the commuter rail
line, with Fish Hoek a major exception. South of Simon's Town the
beaches tend to be wilder and less developed, except for the very popular Seaforth and Millers Point beaches. At many beaches there may be
powerful waves, a strong undertow, and dangerous riptides. Lifeguards
work the main beaches, but only on weekends and during school breaks.
Other beaches are unpatrolled. Although it is nice to stroll along a
lonely beach, remember it's risky to wander off on your own in a deserted area. Toilet facilities at beaches are limited, which is a drawback.

The beaches below are listed from north to south and are marked on
the Cape Peninsula map.

Atlantic Coast
Blouberg. Make the 25-km (16-mi) trip north from the city to the other
side of Table Bay, and you'll be rewarded with an exceptional (and the
most famous) view of Cape Town and Table Mountain. It's divided into
two parts: Big Bay, which hosts surfing and windsurfing contests, and
Little Bay, better suited to sunbathers and families. It's frequently windy
here, which is fine if you want to fly a kite but a nuisance otherwise.
(Buy a brightly colored high-tech number at the Kite Shop in Victoria
Wharf at the V&A Waterfront and relive your childhood.) For safety,

swim in front of the lifeguard club. The lawns of the Blue Peter Hotel are a favorite sunset cocktail spot, especially with tired windsurfers. ⊠ *N1 north to R27 to Milnerton and Bloubergstrand, Blouberg.*

★ **Clifton.** This is where the "in" crowd comes to see and be seen. Some of the Cape's most desirable houses cling to the slopes above the beach, and elegant yachts often anchor in the calm water beyond the breakers. Granite outcroppings divide the beach into four segments, unimaginatively known as First, Second, Third, and Fourth beaches. Fourth Beach is popular with families, whereas the others support a strong social and singles scene. Swimming is reasonably safe here, although the undertow is strong and the water, again, freezing. Lifeguards are on duty on weekends and in peak season. During holidays Clifton can be a madhouse, and your chances of finding parking at these times are nil. If you plan to visit the beaches in midsummer, consider renting a scooter or motorcycle instead of a car, taking a shuttle from your hotel, or going early in the morning, when the beautiful people are still sleeping off their champagne from the night before. ⊠ *Off Victoria Rd., Clifton* Ⓜ *Hout Bay bus from OK Bazaars on Adderley St.*

Camps Bay. The spectacular western edge of Table Mountain, known as the Twelve Apostles, provides the backdrop for this long, sandy beach that slopes gently to the water from a grassy verge. Playing Frisbee or beach volleyball is very popular on this beach. The surf is powerful, but sunbathers can cool off in a tidal pool or under cool outdoor showers. The popular bars and restaurants of Camps Bay lie only yards away across Victoria Road. One drawback is the wind, which can blow hard here. ⊠ *Victoria Rd., Camps Bay* Ⓜ *Hout Bay bus from OK Bazaars on Adderley St.*

Llandudno. Die-hard fans return to this beach again and again, and who can blame them? Its setting, among giant boulders at the base of a mountain, is glorious, and sunsets here attract their own aficionados. The surf can be very powerful on the northern side of the beach (where you'll find all the surfers, of course), but the southern side is fine for a quick dip—and in this water that's all you'll want. Lifeguards are on duty on weekends and in season. If you come by bus, brace yourself for a long walk down (and back up) the mountain from the bus stop on the M6. Parking is a nightmare, but most hotels run shuttles during summer. ⊠ *Llandudno exit off M6, Llandudno* Ⓜ *Hout Bay bus from OK Bazaars on Adderley St.*

Sandy Bay. Backed by wild dunes, Cape Town's unofficial nudist beach is also one of its prettiest. Sunbathers can hide among rocky coves or frolic on a long stretch of sandy beach. Shy nudists will appreciate its isolation, 20 minutes on foot from the nearest parking area in Llandudno. Wind, however, can be a problem: if you're caught in the buff when the southeaster starts to blow, you're in for a painful sandblasting. Sandy Bay is also popular with gay men. Getting here by bus means a very long walk going down and up the mountain, but parking, too, is very difficult. ⊠ *Llandudno exit off M6, Llandudno* Ⓜ *Hout Bay bus from OK Bazaars on Adderley St.*

Hout Bay. This beach appears to have it all: a knockout view of the mountains, gentle surf, and easy access to the restaurants and bars of Mariner's Wharf. Unfortunately, however, this is a working harbor; the beach can be polluted, and the water often has an oily film on the surface. ✉ *Off the M6, Hout Bay* Ⓜ *Hout Bay bus from OK Bazaars on Adderley St.*

Long Beach. This may be the most impressive beach on the peninsula, a vast expanse of white sand stretching 6½ km (4 mi) from the base of Chapman's Peak to Kommetjie. It's also one of the wildest and least populated, backed by a lagoon and private nature reserve. Because of the wind and the space, it attracts horseback riders and walkers rather than sunbathers, and the surfing is excellent. There are no lifeguards and there is no bus service, and as at some other beaches, there are real safety concerns. You'd do well not to visit this beach unless it is well populated. ✉ *Off M6, Noordhoek.*

False Bay

Muizenberg. Once the fashionable resort of South African high society, this long, sandy beach has lost much of its glamour and now appeals to families and beginner surfers. A tacky pavilion houses a swimming pool, waterslides, toilets, changing rooms, and snack shops. The beach is lined with colorful bathing boxes of the type once popular at British resorts. Lifeguards are on duty, and the sea is shallow and reasonably safe. ✉ *Off the M4, Muizenberg.*

🌥 **Fish Hoek.** With the southern corner protected from the southeaster by Elsies Peak, this sandy beach attracts retirees and families with young kids, who appreciate the calm, clear water—it may be the safest bathing beach in the Cape. The middle and northern end of the beach are also popular with catamaran sailors and windsurfers, who often stage regattas offshore. Jager's Walk, a pathway that runs along the rocky coastline, begins at the beach's southern end. This is also a great beach for boogie boarding. ✉ *Beach Rd., Fish Hoek.*

WHERE TO EAT

By Myrna
Robins

Cape Town is the culinary capital of South Africa. Nowhere else in the country is the populace so discerning about food, and nowhere else is there such a wide selection of restaurants. Western culinary history here dates back more than 350 years—Cape Town was founded specifically to grow food—and that heritage is reflected in the city's cuisine. A number of restaurants operate in historic town houses and 18th-century wine estates, and many include heritage dishes on their menus.

Today dining in the city and its suburbs can offer a truly global culinary experience, since Cape chefs are now showing the same enthusiasm for global trends as their counterparts worldwide. Japanese cuisine has become popular fairly recently, and a rash of sushi venues—some topnotch—have popped up in seafood restaurants. Other Asian fare, such as Vietnamese, is appearing on menus, usually at Thai restaurants. Cape Malay (not as spicy as Indian food) is a perennial favorite, especially in Bo-Kaap.

Wine lists at many restaurants reflect the enormous expansion and resurgence of the Cape wine industry since the 1990s, with some establishments compiling exciting selections of lesser-known gems. As yet, however, only a handful of the most exclusive restaurants employ a sommelier to offer guidance on wine, but at some places, the staff is well versed about both wine lists and menus. But just as prices at many restaurants have soared over the last few years, both because of price hiking and the stronger rand, corkage charges have increased as a way of discouraging diners from bringing their own wine.

During summer months, restaurants in trendier areas are geared up for late-night dining but will accept dinner orders from about 6. In winter locals tend to dine earlier, but there are venues that stay open late, particularly at the Waterfront and the strip along the main road between the city and Green Point. Other areas that are meccas for food lovers include Kloof Street (dubbed Restaurant Mile) in the City Bowl and the beachfront road in Camps Bay along the Atlantic seaboard. Many restaurants are crowded in high season, so it's best to book in advance whenever possible. With the exception of the fancier hotel restaurants—where a jacket is suggested—the dress code in Cape Town is casual (but no shorts).

For a description of South African culinary terms, see Pleasures and Pastimes in Smart Travel Tips.

WHAT IT COSTS In South African rand				
	$$$$	$$$	$$	$	¢
RESTAURANTS	over 125	100–125	75–100	50–75	under 50

Prices are per person for a main course at dinner, a main course equivalent, or a prix-fixe meal.

City Bowl

$$–$$$$ ✕ **Blue Danube.** Updated classics from western and central Europe dominate the menu at this restaurant in a former home on the city perimeter. Complimentary appetizers precede starters like smoked ostrich carpaccio with mushroom lasagne, and ham-wrapped warm goat's cheese with rocket (arugula) salad. Robust main courses include gratinéed veal kidneys with mustard sauce and slow-braised Karoo lamb shank teamed with potato puree and onion. Desserts—hazelnut praline pancakes with black-cherry ice cream or variations on Belgian chocolate—are worth every delicious calorie. Unhurried, professional service and a carefully selected wine list are hallmarks here. The shorter lunch menu is significantly cheaper. ⊠ *102 New Church St., Tamboerskloof* ☎ *021/423–3624* ☐ *AE, DC, MC, V* ⊗ *No lunch Sat.–Mon.*

$$–$$$$ ✕ **Cape Colony Restaurant.** Tall bay windows, a high domed ceiling, and a giant trompe-l'oeil mural—an inventive evocation of Table Mountain in days of yore—are a befitting setting for the city's most historic and unashamedly colonial hotel. Executive chef Stephen Templeton presents such fashionable fare as smoked crocodile paired with a spinach-and-red-onion ragout, followed by a duo of venison cuts—springbok and kudu—on mashed potato, sauced with a pinotage (local red wine) reduction. Among desserts that look as good as they taste is tarte tatin

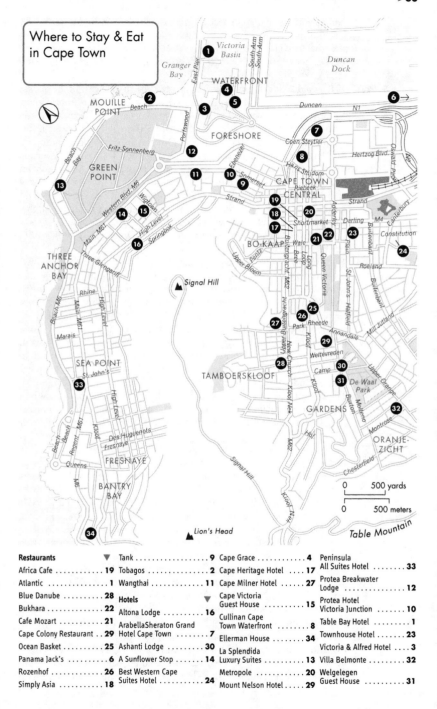

Where to Stay & Eat
in Cape Town

teamed with liqueur-spiked ice cream, pistachio cream, and toffee apple. An authoritative wine list offers the best South African vintages supplemented by French champagnes. ✉ *Mount Nelson Hotel, 76 Orange St., Gardens* ☎ *021/483–1000* ⚲ *Reservations essential* ▭ *AE, DC, MC, V* ⊘ *No lunch.*

$–$$$$ ✕ **Panama Jack's.** In this raw-timber structure in the heart of the docks, the music is loud, the tables are crowded, and the decor is nonexistent, but nowhere in town will you find bigger crayfish. Your choice, made from large open tanks, is weighed before being grilled or steamed. Expect to pay about R360 per kilogram for this delicacy and a whopping R600 a kilogram for the scarce and endangered wild abalone, which is being poached nearly to extinction. Large prawns range in price from R195 for 10 to R110 each for Mozambique tiger giants. There is plenty of less expensive seafood as well, and daily specials such as baby squid and local line fish are competitively priced. It can be difficult to find this place at night, so you may want to come for lunch if it's your first visit. ✉ *Royal Yacht Club basin, off Goliath Rd., Docks* ☎ *021/447–3992* ▭ *AE, DC, MC, V* ⊘ *No lunch Sat.*

$$$ ✕ **Africa Cafe.** Tourist oriented it may be, but it would be a pity to miss out on this vibrant restaurant in a historic 18th-century former home, with its African decor and city views. Fresh-fruit cocktails accompany a communal feast, with dishes originating from Ethiopia to Zambia, from Kenya to Angola. There are no starters or entrées, but rather a tasty series of patties, puffs, and pastries accompanied by addictive dips, along with dishes like West African shrimp-and-pepper salad, ostrich fillet in a cashew-nut sauce, and Ethiopian Doro Wat chicken, cooked in a mild *berbere* (Ethiopian spice mix) paprika sauce. Vegetarian dishes are plentiful, including the Soweto *chakalaka* (a fiery cooked vegetable relish). The cost of this colorful prix-fixe abundance is R125 a person. Wines from Cape estates are available, or you can ask for *umqomboti* beer, brewed from sorghum or millet. ✉ *108 Shortmarket St., Cape Town central* ☎*021/ 422–0221* ▭ *AE, DC, MC, V* ⊘ *Closed Sun. June–Aug. No lunch.*

$–$$$ ✕ **Atlantic.** The elegant flagship restaurant at the luxurious Table Bay Hotel holds a prime position at the city's waterfront. On balmy evenings diners seated on the terrace have stunning views of working docks against a mountain backdrop. A starter of salmon pastrami with pickled pear, ginger, cucumber, and a wasabi crème fraîche could precede sage-rubbed loin of springbok teamed with new potato, French beans, and white-bean puree. Vegetarians are limited to pasta dishes. Artistically plated desserts range from trendy lemon tart with berries to rich mango cheesecake partnered with coriander ice cream. The extensive wine list covers the best of the Cape, supplemented by a selection of New World labels. ✉ *Table Bay Hotel, Quay 6, Waterfront* ☎ *021/406–5688* ▭ *AE, DC, MC, V* ⊘ *Closed Sun. and Mon. No lunch.*

$–$$$ ✕ **Bukhara.** Set above a pedestrian mall lined with antiques shops and stalls, this popular restaurant has delectable and authentic northern Indian fare. Even red walls and dark furniture do little to minimize the cavernous interior, which also showcases an open kitchen. Delicious garlic nan bread starts the proceedings, which could include a selection from the tandoor oven, along with a choice of curries. Lamb marinated with yogurt and spices will please sensitive palates, and the chicken tikka in tomato-and-cashew gravy is an enduring classic. Prawns come in several guises: the spicy coconut curry with tamarind is a firm, if pricey, favorite. Vegetarians have a delicious and less expensive selection to contemplate, such as tandoori homemade cheese and vegetables. ⊠ *33 Church St., Cape Town central* ☎ *021/424–0000* ⌖ *Reservations essential* ☰ *AE, DC, MC, V* ⊙ *No lunch Sun.*

$–$$$ ✕ **Tank.** In a block packed with restaurants, coffee and wine bars, and delis, this trendy and striking venue is the biggest of the lot, offering courtyard seating, a cool blue bar, and an indoor dining area with a huge fish tank. This is one of the best addresses in the city for sushi fans, thanks to a huge number of variations and combinations of this voguish Japanese fare. Meat-eaters and vegetarians are provided for, but the emphasis is on line fish and shellfish, much of which is given Pacific Rim treatment. Local produce is augmented by seafood flown in from abroad. The small dessert selection is delicious and stylishly presented. ⊠ *B15 Cape Quarter, Waterkant St., de Waterkant* ☎ *021/419–0007* ☰ *AE, DC, MC, V* ⊙ *No lunch Mon.*

¢–$$$ ✕ **Ocean Basket.** On Restaurant Mile along the city fringe, this informal spot has few competitors in the field of bargain-price, ocean-fresh, well-cooked seafood. You can sit facing the street or find a table in the courtyard at the back. Calamari—stewed, grilled, pickled, or in a salad—features prominently among the starters, which include a mezes selection. The catch of the day is listed on the many blackboards lining the mustard-yellow walls, but delicately flavored hake-and-chips is the budget draw card. Standard entrées range from excellent Cajun-style grilled calamari to a huge seafood platter for two. Tartar, chili, and garlic sauces come on the side, and Greek salads are authentic. Desserts are average. ⊠ *75 Kloof St., Gardens* ☎ *021/422–0322* ⌖ *Reservations not accepted* ☰ *AE, DC, MC, V.*

$–$$ ✕ **Rozenhof.** It's always a pleasure to revisit this 18th-century town house, home of stylish fare and and an excellent wine list. Yellowwood ceilings and brass chandeliers provide historical Cape touches, and works by local artists adorn the walls. Inspiration from Asia and the Mediterranean is detectable, but cuisine here is noted more for consistently good quality served in cozy and friendly surroundings. The signature cheese soufflé with mustard cream holds its own among trendier first courses like smoked marlin on sushi rice with cucumber and wasabi dressing. Crispy roast duck with a choice of fruity sauces is a time-honored favorite. Layers of local Gorgonzola and mascarpone paired with preserved figs and a glass of port make a savory-sweet alternative to more traditional desserts. ⊠ *18 Kloof St., Gardens* ☎ *021/424–1968* ☰ *AE, DC, MC, V* ⊙ *Closed Sun. No lunch Sat.*

¢–$ ✕ **Cafe Mozart.** This Continental-style café and coffee shop is an institution, housed in a tall narrow building between antiques shops and art galleries. Its lemon-colored walls are lined with mirrors and music-themed posters, and its tables are dressed with lace tablecloths (there are also pavement tables with umbrellas). Breakfast selections can be enjoyed all day, and the menu has a good selection of sandwiches and salads. But it's the daily specials—and the soups in particular—that most diners choose. These could include black-bean soup garnished with avocado-and-tomato relish or North African chili lamb on couscous. Decadent desserts, made daily, are usually sold out by 2. ⊠ *37 Church St. Cape Town central* ☏☏ *021/424–3774* ⚑ *Reservations essential* ⊟ *AE, DC, MC, V* ☺ *Closed Sun. No dinner* ⏣ *BYOB.*

¢–$ ✕ **Simply Asia.** This was the first of a chain of affordable noodle bars to have opened across the Cape Peninsula, serving appetizing Asian dishes speedily and efficiently. Decor is fairly stark. Scarlet touches brighten black-tiled floors and gunmetal-gray walls, and a couple of tables outside are occupied early on windless days. Vegetable spring rolls with plum sauce make a popular first course, and vegetarians have a substantial choice of spicy main dishes as well. *Suki yaki goong pla-muk* (soup packed with prawns, calamari, vegetables, and glass noodles) is a chili-spiked, colorful, and fragrant concoction in a white bowl. Takeout is also available. ⊠ *Heritage Sq., 94 Shortmarket St., Cape Town central* ☏ *021/ 426–4347* ⊟ *AE, DC, MC, V.*

¢–$ ✕ **Wangthai.** Authentic flavors, consistent quality, and good value make this Thai establishment perenially popular. Top vegetarian starters include *tom yum je* (mushrooms and tofu in a spicy sour lemongrass broth), and fish cakes come curried with a cucumber chili sauce. Colorful stir-fries of beef, pork, and chicken vie with others of seafood served with sweet-and-sour, hot, and mild sauces and pungent red and green curries tempered by coconut milk and mounds of sticky rice. Steamed fish with a coconut red-curry sauce and cabbage, hints at a Vietnamese influence. The restaurant has an open kitchen and attractive Asian decor, and it occupies a prime spot on a trendy late-night strip between the city and the Atlantic seaboard. ⊠ *105 Paramount Place, Main Rd., Green Point* ☏ *021/439–6164* ⊟ *AE, DC, MC, V* ☺ *No lunch Sat.*

Atlantic Coast

$–$$$$ ✕ **Tobagos.** The restaurant is a series of intimate areas, and the terrace extends into a vast deck with panoramic views across Table Bay, an idyllic venue for cocktails and alfresco meals. Executive chef Jeffrie Siew, who has launched several top South African hotel restaurants, moves effortlessly from Asian to Western cuisines. Among the stars on the starter menu is chicken wontons with green onion and shiitake mushroom, spiced with ginger and dressed with toasted sesame seeds. Pot-roasted guinea fowl is teamed with caramelized root vegetables in a rosemary and red-wine sauce. Chocoholics will relish chocolate spring rolls partnered with espresso chocolate mousse, refreshed with orange sorbet and garnished with spun sugar. In addition to the à la carte menus, there are prix-fixe buffets for both lunch and dinner (R145). ⊠ *Radisson Hotel Waterfront, Beach Rd., Granger Bay* ☏ *021/441–3414* ⊟ *AE, DC, MC, V.*

–$$$ ✕ **Azure.** This comparative newcomer has some patrons claiming it has cornered the best spot along the Atlantic seaboard. Both restaurant and terrace enjoy mesmerizing sunsets over the ocean, and the lack of neighboring buildings enhances the impression of being aboard an ocean liner. Inside the restaurant the nautical feeling is further emphasized with a navy-and-cream color scheme and wooden walkways. Chef Roberto de Carvalho's à la carte menu is straightforward, but two additional menus—one that stars indigenous ingredients, the other using edible fynbos—are more innovative. Diners can mix and match items from these, starting perhaps with ostrich carpaccio rolled in wild rosemary, drizzled with local grapeseed oil and presented on rocket, followed by a conventional main course such as char-grilled fillet of beef served with mushroom risotto and ruby port sauce, and finished off with a Cape Malay sweet treat of *melktert* (sweet custard tart) accompanied by a mini-*koeksister* (a braided doughnut served with syrup and dried coconut). ⊠ *Victoria Rd., Camps Bay* ☎ *021/437–9029* ⊟ AE, DC, MC, V.

$–$$ ✕ **Blues.** Doors open to frame an inviting vista of palms, sand, and azure sea from the balcony of this perennially popular restaurant in Camps Bay. This remains *the* place for celebrity-spotting, the trendy vibe and good service making up for food that can disappoint. Seafood features prominently on the menu, from first-course calamari given Vietnamese treatment (marinated and dressed with peanut, chili, and mint) to the luxurious seafood platter for two, which comes in at a hefty R465. A single overpriced pasta dish is the only vegetarian main course. Popular desserts include chocolate-pecan brownie topped with vanilla ice cream and hot chocolate sauce. ⊠ *The Promenade, Victoria Rd., Camps Bay* ☎ *021/438–2040* ⌂ *Reservations essential* ⊟ AE, DC, MC, V.

¢–$$ ✕ **Mnandis.** An 18th-century cottage, found abandoned and derelict, is now home to this informal restaurant in the Solole Game Reserve overlooking the Noordhoek wetlands and beach. Profits from the restaurant are plowed back into operating costs and future development in the reserve, which has preserved some 750 acres from development. Freshly caught seafood is always on the menu, sometimes prepared with Asian spices, somethimes simply grilled in lemon-caper butter. A pizza menu is offered on certain evenings, and the wine list is both well chosen and nicely priced. The Italian treat *affogato* (honey-and-nut ice cream) is served with a shot of espresso. ⊠ *Solole Game Reserve, Wood Rd., off Kommetjie Rd. (M65), between Kommetjie and Noordhoek* ☎ *021/785–3248* ⊟ AE, DC, MC, V ☾ Closed Mon.

¢–$ ✕ **Cafe Orca.** It may be laid-back and a trifle shabby, but this tiny eatery in a former fishing village enjoys views overlooking a stretch of pristine beach. There are salads, burgers, and toasted sandwiches on the menu, but the seafood combos and baskets—which combine fish or hake with calamari, shrimp, mussels, or chicken—are the most popular items. At R159, the seafood platter is probably the best bargain of its kind. Service is friendly but can be slow. ⊠ *88 Beach Rd., Melkbosstrand* ☎ *021/553–4120* ⌂ *Reservations essential* ⊟ AE, DC, MC, V ☾ No dinner Sun. and Tues.

Southern Suburbs

★ $$–$$$$ ✕ **Buitenverwachting.** On a historic wine estate in Constantia, this gracious restaurant occupies a modern building on one side of a grassy court ringed by the manor house, wine cellar, and former slave quarters. Window-side tables have views of the vineyards in serried rows along the lower mountain slopes. Starters include quail saltimbocca with truffled *jus,* panfried polenta, and broccoli shoots in foie-gras butter. Local fish

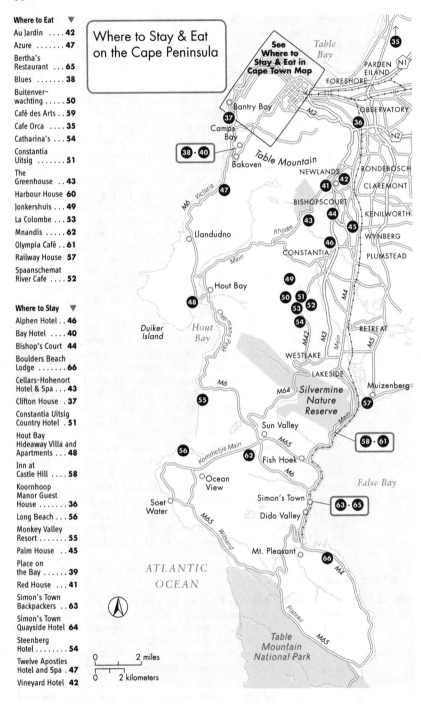

Where to Stay & Eat on the Cape Peninsula

See Where to Stay & Eat in Cape Town Map

get star treatment; yellowtail is teamed with a tomato, leek, and saffron coulis and homemade pasta with crayfish butter. The short list of meaty choices includes rack and saddle of lamb, sauced with *gremolata* (a parsley and lemon zest mix). Local fruits star in the imaginative but pricey works of dessert art. ⊠ *Klein Constantia Rd., Constantia* ☎ *021/794–3522* ⌇ *Reservations essential* ▭ *AE, DC, MC, V* ⊘ *Closed June and July; Mon. Aug.–Oct.; and Sun.*

$$–$$$$ ✕ **La Colombe.** Constantia Uitsig farm and winery is home to three ex-
Fodor$Choice cellent restaurants (all reviewed here), but it is this Provençal dining room
★ that is collecting accolades from gourmets and other devotees of southern French fare. The walls and woodwork of this small restaurant are painted sunshine yellow and sky blue, and French doors in the dining room open onto a courtyard. Chef Franck Dangereux transforms local produce into a menu that sings of his native French province: expect flavorful renderings of *pan bagna* (salad *niçoise* sandwiched into French bread), and tartare of tuna with crème fraîche and salmon caviar. Entrées include a magnificent creation of roast mustard-crusted lamb loin. Desserts range from a wicked terrine of dark chocolate to an artistic presentation of fresh figs topped with walnuts, enriched with an almond sabayon, and paired with a *tuile* (sweet, paper-thin wafer) filled with milk sorbet. ⊠ *Uitsig Farm, Spaanschemat River Rd., Constantia* ☎ *021/794–2390* ⌇ *Reservations essential* ▭ *AE, DC, MC, V* ⊘ *No dinner Sun. May–Sept.*

$$$ ✕ **Catharina's.** The original winery on this historic estate makes an elegant home for the restaurant, recently renamed for the original, feisty, and much-married 17th-century owner. At lunchtime you can opt to sit on the oak-shaded terrace. Executive chef Garth Almazan presents a global menu that includes West Coast mussels in a Thai curry broth, and crispy duck sauced with orange and ginger. Diners who enjoy pairing food and wine will appreciate the excellent selection of estate wines by the glass. ⊠ *Steenberg Hotel, Steenberg Rd., Tokai* ☎ *021/713–2222* ▭ *AE, DC, MC, V.*

$–$$$ ✕ **Constantia Uitsig.** Reserve a table on the enclosed veranda for tremendous views of the mountains at this restored famstead house. The menu is a pricey and harmonious blend of northern Italian and Provençal cuisines. Many diners start with homemade pasta before going on to such main courses as line fish served on mashed sweet potato with baby spinach and a verjuice vinaigrette or the classic *trippa alla Fiorentina* (tripe braised in tomato, carrot, and celery sauce). Desserts include iced berries with a hot white-chocolate sauce. ⊠ *Uitsig Farm, Spaanschemat River Rd., Constantia* ☎ *021/794–4480* ⌇ *Reservations essential* ▭ *AE, DC, MC, V.*

$–$$ ✕ **Au Jardin.** Tucked away in a corner of the historic Vineyard Hotel, complete with fountain and views of Table Mountain, this airy and elegant restaurant serves classic French cuisine imbued with subtle Cape and Mediterranean accents. Appetizers might include onion tarte tatin with a goat-cheese soufflé and Gruyère sauce or salmon trout in three guises: tian (gratin), tartare (raw), and panfried. Finales include coconut mousse filled with exotic fruit jelly, paired with pineapple-and-kiwi sorbet. There's a six-course chef's table menu, with a wine for each course, that costs R295. ⊠ *Vineyard Hotel, Colinton Rd., Newlands* ☎ *021/657–4545* ▭ *AE, DC, MC, V* ⊘ *Closed Mon. May–Sept. and Sun. No lunch.*

$-$$ ✕ The Greenhouse. Aptly named, this conservatorylike dining room overlooks the beautiful gardens of the Cellars-Hohenort Hotel. Chef David Godin's menu uses fresh seasonal produce, much of it organic. Creations include home-cured, oak-smoked salmon served Benedict-style, with *blini*, quails' eggs, and hollandaise; and roasted breast of free-range chicken is teamed with *rösti* (hash browns) and braised cabbage. Save room for the Irish-coffee crème brûlée, or a summery concoction of lemon poppy-seed cake with vanilla panna cotta and caramelized strawberries. ⊠ *Cellars-Hohenort Hotel, 15 Hohenort Ave., Constantia* ☎ *021/794–2137* ⌂ *Reservations essential* ▭ *AE, DC, MC, V.*

¢-$$ ✕ Jonkershuis. Classic Cape hospitality is on display at this 19th-century building adjoining the gracious manor house at Groot Constantia, the Cape's oldest wine estate. Fresh line fish and roast loin of lamb keep company on the menu with classic *bobotie* (spiced minced beef studded with dried fruit and topped with a savory baked custard) and *smoorsnoek* (a popular Cape fish braised with onion, potato, and chili). The traditional chicken pie is made from a recipe handed down through generations of Dutch settlers. To taste all these dishes, ask for a Cape sampler. ⊠ *Groot Constantia Estate, Main Rd., Constantia* ☎*021/794–6255* ⌂*Reservations essential* ▭ *AE, DC, MC, V* ✆ *No dinner Sun. and Mon.*

¢-$$ ✕ Spaanschemat River Cafe. For informal feasting on country fare in idyllic surroundings, this pretty spot is hard to beat. On peak-season weekends, cars line up waiting for the doors to open; the lavender-fringed terrace is filled with diners. Simple grilled-vegetable-and-goat-cheese salads topped with *dukkah* (a spicy nut mix), and eggs Florentine—poached eggs topped with hollandaise with creamed spinach and smoked salmon—are favorite choices. Scrumptious desserts like citron-almond-and-pine-nut tart teamed with vanilla ice cream and honey-butterscotch sauce are worth the extra calories. ⊠ *Uitsig Farm, Spaanschemat River Rd., Constantia* ☎ *021/794–3010* ▭ *AE, DC, MC, V* ✆ *No dinner.*

False Bay

$-$$$$ ✕ Harbour House. Don't be put off by the unremarkable entrance here; once you're upstairs and seated at a window table you'll be entranced by views across the bay, where fishing boats chug back and forth, and whales spout for much of the year. Bring a keen appetite; starter salads are substantial, and you can follow them with just-landed, olive oil-brushed line fish, or Mediterranean calamari with baby tomato, black olives, and giant capers. There is also a tempting and trendy dessert list. ⊠ *Kalk Bay Harbour, Main Rd., Kalk Bay* ☎ *021/788–4133* ▭ *AE, DC, MC, V.*

¢-$$$ ✕ Bertha's Restaurant. Alfresco dining at this waterfront venue offers a feast for both palate and eye. Boating activities from the naval dockyard on one side and yacht club on the other add action to a backdrop of sparkling water and mountain. The contemporary menu makes good use of local seafood, such as Atlantic black mussels and line fish, which is grilled or fried. There are also reasonably priced burgers, and yummy spiked ice-cream drinks and coffees. Lunch here is popular, so it's a good idea to reserve in advance. ⊠ *1 Wharf Rd., Simon's Town* ☎ *021/ 786–2138* ▭ *AE, DC, MC, V.*

¢–$$ ✗ **Olympia Café.** This tiny Kalk Bay landmark, furnished with mismatched tables and a counter along the window, has long been a well-kept secret among locals and regular visitors. The quality of the mostly Mediterranean fare is consistently high, and the servers are consistently sassy. (Don't dare ask for anything low-fat!) A delectable dish of eggplant rolls, filled with butternut squash, ricotta, and sweet potato and sauced with piquant tomato, is consistently popular. Penne pasta topped with fresh tuna comes in two sizes, as do other specialties chalked up daily. The chef also serves more than 12,000 delicious omelets each year, accompanied by excellent croissants and crusty loaves from the café's bakery up the road. ⊠ *134 Main Rd., Kalk Bay* ☎ *021/788–6396* ⌨ *Reservations not accepted* ☰ *AE, DC, MC, V.*

¢–$$ ✗ **Railway House.** This huge, well-proportioned room and enclosed balcony served as a tearoom when the Edwardian railway station, with its tall clock tower, was opened early in the 20th century. Today, balcony tables overlook the whitecaps curving onto Muizenberg beach, and the occasional shudder alerts diners to the arrival and departure of trains at the station below. The cuisine is unpretentious and fresh; seared game salad with basil pesto makes a meaty starter, while smoked-salmon-and-avocado salad offers a lighter first course. Among the dozen main courses is an aromatic seafood curry of line fish, calamari, and mussels in coconut sauce. Pavlova (meringue) filled with berries and whipped cream makes a calorific but delicious dessert. ⊠ *Muizenberg Station, Main Rd., Muizenberg* ☎ *021/788–3252* ☰ *AE, DC, MC, V* ☽ *Closed Mon. and Tues.*

¢ ✗ **Café des Arts.** After browsing through the antiques shops and art galleries on the mountain side of Kalk Bay's main road, pause here for a simple breakfast or lunch. The vibrantly colored handmade ceramic dishes make a pleasing contrast to the minimalist decor, and there is more art on view in the adjacent gallery. In good weather, a few tables in the little courtyard offer a quiet place to dig into hearty soups (chilled in summer) or the pasta special of the day, perhaps tagliatelle tossed with shrimp, smoked salmon, garlic, and cream. ⊠ *22 Main Rd., Kalk Bay* ☎ *021/788–3765* ☰ *AE, DC, MC, V* ☽ *Closed Mon. No dinner.*

WHERE TO STAY

Finding lodging in Cape Town can be a nightmare during high season (December–January), as many of the more reasonable accommodations are booked up. It is worth traveling between April and August, if you can, to take advantage of the "secret season" discounts. If you arrive in Cape Town without a reservation, head for the Cape Town Tourism Information Office, which has a helpful accommodations desk.

Hotels in the city center are a good option if you're here on business or are here for only a short stay. During the day the historic city center is a vibrant place. At night, though, it's shut up tight; night owls may prefer a hotel amid the nonstop action of the Waterfront. Hotels and bed-and-breakfasts in the Southern Suburbs, especially Constantia, offer unrivaled beauty and tranquillity and make an ideal base if you're exploring the

Peninsula. You'll need a car, though, and should plan on 15–30 minutes to get into town. Atlantic Coast hotels provide the closest thing in Cape Town to a beach-vacation atmosphere despite the cold ocean waters.

Keep in mind that international flights from the United States and Europe arrive in the morning and return flights depart in the evening. Because most hotels have an 11 AM checkout, you may have to wait for a room if you've just arrived; if you're leaving, you will be hauled kicking and screaming out of your room hours before your flight. Most hotels will try to accommodate you, but they often have no choice in peak season. Some of the larger hotels have residents-only lounges where you can spend the hours awaiting your flight. Note that many small luxury accommodations either do not permit children or have minimum-age restrictions. It's a good idea to inquire in advance if this will be an issue.

Cape Town is regarded as one of the top backpacker destinations in the world, with plenty of hostels to choose from. Contact **Backpacker Tourism South Africa** (BTSA; ⊕ www.btsa.co.za) for information.

The most reliable source of good B&B establishments is the **Bed & Breakfast Bureau** (☎ 021/794–0030 🖷 021/794–0031 ⊕ www.bookabed. co.za). Or try the **Portfolio of Places** (☎ 021/689–4020 🖷 021/686–5310 ⊕ www.portfoliocollection.com) brochure. If you don't like tiptoeing around someone's house or you want to save money, consider renting a fully furnished apartment, especially if you're staying two or more weeks. **CAPSOL Property & Tourism Solutions** (☎ 021/422–3521 ⊕ www.capsol.co.za) has around 800 high-quality, furnished, fully stocked villas and apartments on its books. Another good option, **Cape Stay** (☎ 021/674–3104 🖷 021/674–1058 ⊕ www.capestay.co.za), has a wide selection of accommodations to suit different needs.

The **de Waterkant Village** is Cape Town's first and only guest street, an entire little community of houses to rent. There are 30 beautifully restored, small, self-catering (with cooking facilities) houses with daily housekeeping services that are unusual, trendy, classy, and quite charming. The high-season double-occupancy rate starts at R650 per night. All are near the harbor, as the name implies. ⊠ *1 Loader St., Cape Town central 8000* ☎ *021/422–2721* 🖷 *021/426–5088* ⊕ *www.dewaterkant.com* 🖃 *AE, DC, MC, V.*

WHAT IT COSTS In South African rand				
$$$$	$$$	$$	$	¢
HOTELS over 3,000	2,000–3,000	1,000–2,000	500–1,000	under 500

Prices are for a standard double room in high season, including 12.5% tax.

Cape Town Central & City Bowl

$$$$

FodorsChoice

★

🖼 **Mount Nelson Hotel.** This distinctive pink landmark is the grande dame of Cape Town. Since it opened its doors in 1899 to accommodate passengers just off the Union-Castle steamships, it has been the focal point of Cape social life. It retains a traditional charm and gentility that other luxury hotels often lack: high tea is served in the lounge to piano accompaniment, the Planet Champagne Bar is very glam, and the staff almost outnumbers the guests. Rooms are decorated with fine antiques and fresh flowers and have an air of aristocracy about them. The hotel stands at the top of Government Avenue, but, surrounded as it is by 7 acres of manicured gardens, it might as well be in the country. Once a week the head gardener offers a guided tour through the magnificent gardens, and tea is served afterward. Very civilized! For peak season, December–March, it's advisable to book a year in advance. ⊠ *76 Orange St., Gardens 8001* ☎ *021/483–1000* 🖨 *021/483–1929* ⊕ *www.mountnelsonhotel.orient-express.com* 🛏 *145 rooms, 56 suites* 🕭 *2 restaurants, 2 tennis courts, 2 pools, gym, bar* ⊟ *AE, DC, MC, V* ❘⊙❘ *BP.*

$$$–$$$$ 🏨 **ArabellaSheraton Grand Hotel Cape Town** The super-sophisticated e-butler service in the foyer is enough to get excited about—and that's before you've even set foot in the rooms. Since the hotel is linked to the Cape Town International Convention Centre rooms are geared toward working guests, but that doesn't mean they're spartan. The decor is modern minimalist with touches of African creativity, perhaps in pillowcases or a quirky wall color. Workstations are cleverly partitioned away from the sleeping area, so even if you have to burn the midnight oil, you can do it in comfort and style. Everything glides and whirls at the touch of a button, and service is seamless. Take special note of the artworks in the lobby and foyer area. This hotel group makes it its business to collect and support local art. The spa at the top of the hotel is an experience not to be missed, as is a water-taxi ride from the hotel to the Waterfront. ⊠ *Convention Sq., Lower Long St., Cape Town central 8002* ☎ *021/412–9999* 🖨 *021/412–9001* ⊕ *www.sheraton.com/capetown* 🛏 *451 rooms, 32 suites* 🕭 *3 restaurants, gym, spa, bar* ⊟ *AE, DC, MC, V* ❘⊙❘ *BP.*

★ **$$** 🏨 **Cape Heritage Hotel.** Built as a private home in 1771, this friendly, attractive, well-run hotel is part of the Heritage Square development and as such has direct access to a host of restaurants and a couple of shops. Teak-beamed ceilings and foot-wide yellowwood floorboards echo the building's gracious past, and the spacious rooms are individually decorated. Some have four-poster beds, others exposed brickwork, but each has its own special charm. Rooms overlooking the attractive courtyard—filled with tables sheltering under what is claimed to be the oldest grapevine in South Africa—may be a little noisy, but the revelry stops at midnight sharp, when the bar stops serving. Parking is across the street in a section of a public parking lot with good security. ⊠ *90 Bree St., Cape Town central 8001* ☎ *021/424–4646* 🖨 *021/424–4949* ⊕ *www.capeheritage.co.za* 🛏 *15 rooms* 🕭 *6 restaurants, hair salon, bar, 2 lounges, shops, parking (fee)* ⊟ *AE, MC, V.*

$$ 🏨 **Cape Milner Hotel.** Tamboerskloof is an ideal location from which to explore the city and farther afield. This attractive, well-positioned hotel has been extensively refurbished and extended. The look is clean, classical, and contemporary, with rooms decorated in restful shades of gray, white, and black. Each room has a tea/coffeemaker, and there's a gym if you need to work off some of your holiday excesses. The hotel shuttle service to the Waterfront and nearby beaches is also a real plus. The terrace has wonderful views of Table Mountain. ✉ *2 Milner Rd., Tamboerskloof 8001* ☎ *021/426–1101* 📠 *021/426–1109* ⊕ *www.capemilner. com* ↴ *55 rooms, 2 suites* ⚒ *Restaurant, pool, gym, 2 bars, 2 lounges, meeting rooms, parking (fee)* ⊟ *AE, DC, MC, V.*

$$ 🏨 **Metropole.** If it's style and a very central address you're after, then the Metropole is for you. The decor is a clever mix of old and new; art-deco furniture sits comfortably alongside stunning modern pieces. Rooms are simple and pared down. There's no extraneous clutter, but the attention to detail is superb. The Veranda restaurant is also excellent, and the M Bar & Lounge is a very trendy place to get a drink. ✉ *38 Long St., Cape Town central 8001* ☎ *021/424–7247* 📠 *021/424–7248* ⊕ *www.metropolehotel.co.za* ↴ *27 rooms, 2 suites* ⚒ *Restaurant, coffee shop, bar, airport shuttle* ⊟ *AE, DC, MC, V* ⦿ *BP.*

$$ 🏨 **Villa Belmonte.** In a quiet residential neighborhood on the slopes above the city, this small five-star guesthouse offers privacy and luxury in an attractive Dutch Revival residence. The owners have sought to create the feeling of an Italian villa through the use of marbling, molded ceilings, and natural wood floors. Wide verandas have superb views of the city, Table Mountain, and Devil's Peak. Rooms have colorful draperies, luxurious finishes, wicker furniture, and small-pane windows. It's a 20-minute walk to the city center. ✉ *33 Belmont Ave., Oranjezicht 8001* ☎ *021/462–1576* 📠 *021/462–1579* ⊕ *www. villabelmontehotel.co.za* ↴ *14 rooms* ⚒ *Restaurant, room service, pool, bar* ⊟ *AE, DC, MC, V* ⦿ *BP.*

$–$$ 🏨 **Welgelegen Guest House.** In Afrikaans, *welgelegen* means "well situated," and this classy guesthouse in two beautifully restored Victorian mansions is just that: it's nestled under Table Mountain and just minutes away from city attractions. Each room is individually and stylishly decorated. The look is a mixture of African chic and romantic whimsy, and the pretty courtyard is a good place to relax after a busy day. If you want more independence, you can opt for a two-bedroom, self-catering cottage down the road. ✉ *6 Stephen St., Gardens 8001* ☎ *021/426–2373/4,* 📠 *021/426–2375,* ⊕ *www.welgelegen.co.za* ↴ *13 rooms, 1 cottage* ⚒ *Minibars, pool, airport shuttle* ⊟ *AE, DC, MC, V* ⦿ *BP.*

$ 🏨 **Best Western Cape Suites Hotel.** This village-style hotel, with low buildings and adjoining individual units, is five minutes from the center of Cape Town and a brisk 20-minute walk from the Waterfront. Rooms are spacious and pleasantly furnished in a cheerful and contemporary style, and all come with a fully equipped kitchen. Some rooms have mountain views; others look into the city. Although it's on a corner site, the hotel is well insulated, so traffic noise is not a major problem; inner rooms tend to be quieter. If you have a car, you can park it virtually outside your room. A free shuttle takes you to popular sights within about 13 km (8 mi) of the hotel. ✉ *Constitution and de Villiers Sts., Zonnebloem* ⓓ *Box 51085, Waterfront 8002* ☎ *021/461–0727* 📠 *021/462–4389* ⊕ *www.capesuites.co.za* ↴ *126 suites* ⚒ *2 restaurants, kitchens, 2 pools, bar, recreation room, free parking* ⊟ *AE, DC, MC, V.*

$ 🏨 **Townhouse Hotel.** Its proximity to government buildings and its easy-going atmosphere (not to mention extremely competitive rates) make the Townhouse a popular choice. Rooms are decorated in neutral shades and provide a restful retreat from the hubbub of the city. Request a room with a view of the mountain. ⊠ *60 Corporation St., Box 5053, Cape Town central 8000* ☎ *021/465–7050* 🖶 *021/465–3891* ⊕ *www. townhouse.co.za* 🛏 *104 rooms* ⚘ *Restaurant, room service, pool, health club, bar, airport shuttle* ▤ *AE, DC, MC, V.*

★ ¢ 🏨 **Ashanti Lodge.** A five-minute walk from the city center, Ashanti is a great place to stay if you're on a limited budget or just don't like the idea of spending a year's salary on one night's accommodation. The lodge has just about everything a backpacker or budget traveler might need—from laundry to a luggage-holding service to light meals. Rooms vary from cheerful dorms to smart doubles with private baths—great if you want more privacy. There's a communal kitchen, TV lounge, and very organized travel center, which can advise you on the rest of your stay. ⊠ *11 Hof St., Gardens 8001* ☎ *021/423–8721* 🖶 *021/423–8790* ⊕ *www.ashanti.co.za* 🛏 *20 rooms, 10 dormitories* ⚘ *Kitchen, pool, bar, lounge, laundry service, Internet, airport shuttle, travel services; no a/c, no room TVs* ▤ *MC, V.*

Waterfront

$$$$ 🏨 **Cape Grace.** The exclusive and well-appointed Cape Grace, at the V&A
Fodor'sChoice Waterfront, is a hard act to follow. Built on a spit of land jutting into a
★ working harbor, it offers views of seals frolicking in the surrounding waters and seagulls soaring above. Large, elegant guest rooms have harbor or mountain views and are decorated with a combination of French period furnishings and wonderful modern design. The attention to detail throughout is outstanding, from the antique pieces to the fresh flowers in the rooms. There's a wonderful well-stocked library for browsing, and the superb restaurant, one.waterfront, serves creative cuisine with a strong South African influence. Add to that a fantastic spa with treatments inspired by the spice route and African traditions. You also have free use of a nearby health club and the hotel's courtesy car for getting into the city and to the main beaches. The Bascule is the hotel's sophisticated watering hole. ⊠ *West Quay, Waterfront 8002* ☎ *021/ 410–7100* 🖶 *021/419–7622* ⊕ *www.capegrace.com* 🛏 *122 rooms* ⚘ *Restaurant, pool, spa, bar, library* ▤ *AE, DC, MC, V* ⦿ *BP.*

$$$$ 🏨 **Table Bay Hotel.** This glitzy hotel has a prime spot at the tip of the V&A Waterfront. The decor is sunny, with huge picture windows looking onto the mountain, marble mosaic and parquet floors, and lots of plants, including the hotel's trademark orchid arrangements. In the lounge you can browse through a selection of international newspapers as you sit by the fire, relaxing to live piano music. Rooms, although traditionally decorated with hints of dark wood, are bright and have marble-and-tile bathrooms with roomy showers. And if you have to work away from home, there's a business center full of modern conveniences, including helpful administrators who can make your life easier. The hotel has direct access to the large Waterfront mall. ⊠ *Quay 6, Waterfront 8002* ☎ *021/406–5000* 🖶 *021/406–5656* ⊕ *www.suninternational.com* 🛏 *307 rooms, 18 suites* ⚘ *3 restaurants, pool, health club, spa, 2 bars, lobby lounge, business services, meeting room* ▤ *AE, DC, MC, V.*

$$–$$$ ⊞ **Victoria & Alfred Hotel.** You couldn't find a better location for this upscale hotel, in a converted warehouse smack in the middle of the Waterfront and surrounded by shops, bars, and restaurants. Rooms are huge and luxurious, with crisp linens and elegant throws. Views from the costlier mountain-facing rooms are spectacular, encompassing not only Table Mountain but the city and docks as well. The terrace is a great place to relax. ✉ *On the Waterfront Pierhead, Box 50050, Waterfront 8002* ☎ *021/419–6677* 🖷 *021/419–8955* ⊕ *www.vahotel.co. za* ➪ *68 rooms* ☖ *Restaurant, room service, gym, bar, business services* ⊟ *AE, DC, MC, V.*

$$ ⊞ **Cullinan Cape Town Waterfront.** This sparkling white hotel is just opposite the entrance to the Waterfront. It has a spacious marble-tile lobby, huge picture windows draped in rose and gold that lead out to the pool, and an enormous double-curving gilt staircase that completes the picture. Rooms are quite restrained, with muted green carpets and floral notes, and bathrooms are well laid out, with separate showers in white tile and gray marble. But what steals the show are the views of Table Mountain and the harbor. The conveniently located hotel has an efficient shuttle service that runs 8 AM–11 PM, so you'll be able to get around easily. ✉ *1 Cullinan St., Waterfront 8002* ☎ *021/418–6920* 🖷 *021/418–3559* ⊕ *www.southernsun.com* ➪ *410 rooms* ☖ *2 restaurants, room service, pool, gym, hair salon, bar* ⊟ *AE, DC, MC, V.*

$$ ⊞ **Protea Hotel Victoria Junction.** Adjacent to the Waterfront and de Waterkant and with a distinctly funky and art deco–style decor, this hotel is popular with those looking for something different. Spacious high-ceilinged loft rooms have large double beds on an upper level; you have to be fairly nimble to climb in. Standard rooms have ordinary knee-level beds but are still quite chic. The Set, a trendy restaurant for business lunches, has a great range of salads and innovative fare, and the bar always jumps at happy hour. ✉ *Somerset and Ebenezer Rds., de Waterkant* ✑ *Box 51234, Waterfront 8002* ☎ *021/418–1234* 🖷 *021/418–5678* ⊕ *www.proteahotels.com/victoriajunction* ➪ *172 rooms* ☖ *Restaurant, coffee shop, pool, bar* ⊟ *AE, DC, MC, V.*

$–$$ ⊞ **Cape Victoria Guest House.** Only a five-minute walk from the Waterfront, this charming guesthouse is a luxurious refuge from the bustle of the city. Each room is individually decorated, and there are quirky touches throughout—from an enormous Victorian bath to an African-inspired room for those wishing they were on safari. The staff is exceptionally friendly and well informed, and the owner, Lily Kaplan, is a gem. The breakfasts are legendary; you will be fortified for the rest of the day, especially if you have a slice of the warm almond tart with a cup of strong coffee. Delicious! ✉ *13 Torbay Rd., Green Point 8012* 🖷🖷 *021/439–7721* ⊕ *www.capevictoria.co.za* ➪ *10 rooms* ☖ *Some fans, pool; no a/c in some rooms* ⊟ *AE, DC, MC, V* ⦿ *BP.*

¢–$ ⊞ **Protea Breakwater Lodge.** You won't find another hotel at the Waterfront offering rates so low. Built in a converted 19th-century prison on Portswood Ridge, the Breakwater certainly won't win any awards for charm or coziness. Its history is quite evident in the long, narrow corridors, which lead to tiny, sparsely furnished cells (sorry, rooms). Nevertheless, the rooms are clean and have TVs, phones, and tea/coffeemakers. Ask for a room with a view of Table Mountain. ⊠ *Portswood Rd., Waterfront 8001* ☎ *021/406–1911* 🖷 *021/406–1070* ⊕ *www.bwl.co.za* ⟵ *263 rooms, 102 suites* ♨ *2 restaurants, bar; no a/c* ☐ *AE, DC, MC, V.*

¢ 🖭 **A Sunflower Stop.** If your vocab is peppered with expressions such as *wicked, lethal,* and *cooool,* then this cheerful backpackers' lodge is a good stopover. It's close to the Waterfront, and the friendly staff can help you with everything you need to know about Cape Town and the surrounds. It's also a great place to meet other travelers. You can use the kitchen, braai area, and TV lounge. Rooms are small, clean, and functional, but that's okay; you aren't going to be spending much time in them. ⊠ *179 Main Rd., Green Point 8001* ☎ *021/434–6535* 🖷 *021/ 434–6501* ⊕ *www.sunflowerstop.co.za* ⟵ *15 rooms, 4 with bath; 3 dormitories,* ♨ *Kitchen, pool, bar, laundry service, airport shuttle; no a/c, no room TVs* ☐ *No credit cards.*

Atlantic Coast

$$$$ 🖭 **Ellerman House.** Without a doubt, this is one of the finest (and most
Fodor'sChoice exclusive) hotels in South Africa. Built in 1912 for shipping magnate Sir
★ John Ellerman, the hotel sits high on a hill in Bantry Bay and has stupendous views of the sea. Broad, terraced lawns fronted by elegant balustrades step down the hillside to a sparkling pool. The drawing and living rooms, decorated in Regency style, are elegant yet not forbiddingly formal. Guest rooms have enormous picture windows, high ceilings, and spacious tile bathrooms. The hotel accommodates only 22 guests, and a highly trained staff caters to their every whim. In the kitchen chefs prepare whatever guests request—whether it's on the menu or not. All drinks except wine and champagne are included in the rates. ⊠ *180 Kloof Rd., Bantry Bay* 🖃 *Box 515, Sea Point 8060* ☎ *021/430– 3200* 🖷 *021/430–3215* ⊕ *www.ellerman.co.za* ⟵ *11 rooms* ♨ *Restaurant, room service, pool, gym, sauna, bar; no kids under 14* ☐ *AE, DC, MC, V* ¶◎¶ *BP.*

★ $$$$ 🖭 **Twelve Apostles Hotel and Spa.** Fancy taking a helicopter to the airport or lazing in a bubble bath while looking out floor-to-ceiling windows at sea and mountains? If this sounds like you, then opt for this hotel and spa, formerly de Ouderkraal Hotel. The only building between Camps Bay and Llandudno and bordering the Table Mountain National Park, it was built amid controversy just before the park's status was proclaimed. The hotel has spectacular views and an enormous indigenous garden that disappears up the mountain. Each room varies, and is decorated in either cool blues and whites to reflect the colors of the ocean or warmer tones to conjure up the lifestyle of Africa's explorers. ⊠ *Victoria Rd., Box 32117, Camps Bay 8040* ☎ *021/437–9000* 🖷 *021/ 437–9001* ⊕ *www.12apostles.com* ⟵ *46 rooms, 24 suites* ♨ *Restaurant, 2 pools, gym, spa, bar, cinema, meeting room, travel services* ☐ *AE, DC, MC, V* ¶◎¶ *BP.*

$$$–$$$$ 🖭 **Bay Hotel.** This beach hotel in Camps Bay is the most relaxed and unpretentious of the luxury hotels in and around Cape Town. It's across the road from a white-sand beach and is backed by the towering cliffs of the Twelve Apostles. From the raised pool deck guests look out over

sea and sand and onto one of the coolest strips in South Africa, where all the beautiful people congregate. Decor is contemporary, clean, and bright, and the rooms are decorated in a sophisticated range of neutral shades. Service is excellent, and although you're only 10 minutes from the hurly-burly of the city, it feels like a lifetime away. Ask for a premier room if you want a sea view. ✉ *69 Victoria Rd., Box 32021, Camps Bay 8040* ☎ *021/438–4444* 🖷 *021/438–4433* ⊕ *www.thebay.co.za* ↻ *78 rooms* ⚐ *Restaurant, room service, pool, bar; no kids under 12* ▤ *AE, DC, MC, V.*

$$–$$$$ 🏨 **Place on the Bay.** These luxury self-catering apartments are on the beachfront in Camps Bay, within easy walking distance of a host of restaurants and bars. Apartments are tasteful, modern affairs that make extensive use of glass. Many units have good sea views from their balconies. If you really want to have it all, take the magnificent penthouse, which occupies the entire top floor and comes with its own plunge pool, for about R10,000 per day. All units have daily housekeeping service. ✉ *Fairways and Victoria Rds., Camps Bay 8001* ☎ *021/438–* 🖷 *021/438–2692* ⊕ *www.theplaceonthebay.co.za* ↻ *21 apartments* ⚐ *Restaurant, some fans, kitchens, pool, bar; no a/c in some rooms* ▤ *AE, DC, MC, V.*

$$$ 🏨 **Long Beach.** It's no surprise that each of the rooms is named after a **Fodor'sChoice** game fish. Kommetjie is after all a pretty lobster-fishing village, and your ★ room is a stone's throw away from the water's edge. Management pays a lot of attention to details, such as offering mobile phones with useful preprogrammed numbers, which you can borrow for your Cape Town stay. The view is spectacular, rooms are serene yet luxurious, and spa treatments are on-site. When you're not basking on the sundeck (good for whale-watching during the season), you can explore the white expanse of the Kommetjie beach. ✉ *1 Kirsten Ave., Kommetjie 7975* ☎ *021/794–6561* 🖷 *021/794–2069* ⊕ *www.thelastword.co.za* ↻ *5 rooms* ⚐ *Pool, bar, airport shuttle* ▤ *AE, DC, MC, V* ⦿ *BP.*

$$–$$$ 🏨 **Clifton House.** You'll be hard-pressed to find a better view of the Twelve Apostles and Camps Bay, and while you're lazing around the saltwater pool, you'll wonder why you didn't come here sooner. Ocean-facing rooms are stylishly decorated with excellent-quality linen, Oriental rugs, and cane furniture, and, better still, you can fling open the double doors and hear the sea in the distance. You could be on the French Riviera, but you're just five minutes from the Waterfront and a hop and a skip away from the city sights. ✉ *1 Clifton Rd,, Clifton 8005* ☎ *021/438–2308* 🖷 *021/438–3716* ⊕ *www.cliftonhouse.co.za* ↻ *5 rooms* ⚐ *Saltwater pool, 2 lounges,* ▤ *MC, V* ⦿ *BP.*

$$–$$$ 🏨 **Peninsula All Suites Hotel.** In an 11-story building just across the road from the ocean, these accommodations are ideal for families or groups of friends. You can choose from a variety of rooms that sleep from four to eight people and have incredible views of the sea. The larger suites are the most attractive, full of light and air, thanks to picture windows, sliding doors, wide balconies, and white-tile floors. Small "studio suites" are more like conventional hotel rooms. Each unit has a fully equipped kitchen with microwave oven. The hotel is a time-share property, so booking during the busy December holiday could be a problem. ✉ *313*

Beach Rd., Sea Point ✆ *Box 768, Sea Point 8060* ☎ *021/430–7777* 🖷 *021/430–7776* ⊕ *www.peninsula.co.za* ➥ *42 rooms, 68 suites* ☖ *Restaurant, room service, kitchens, 2 pools, gym, sauna, bar* ▭ *AE, DC, MC, V.*

$–$$ 🖾 **Hout Bay Hideaway Villa and Apartments.** You'll know you're in an exceptional place when you can lie in an outdoor bath surrounded by indigenous trees and an astonishing view of the mountains. Hout Bay Hideaway is a luxury retreat. All rooms are individually and beautifully decorated with original antiques and artwork. To complete the stylish picture, you can rent one of the beautifully restored Jaguars so that you can tool around Cape Town in style before returning to your extremely hip guesthouse. ⊠ *Hout Bay 7872* ☎ *021/790–8040* ⊕ *www. hout-bayhideaway.com* ➥ *5 suites* ☖ *Pool, Internet; no a/c* ▭ *AE, MC, V* ⎮⊙⎮ *CP.*

★ **$–$$** 🖾 **Monkey Valley Resort.** This secluded resort is one of the best places on the peninsula for families, and is very popular for small conferences. Built on stilts, the self-catering thatch log cottages lie in an indigenous milk-wood forest overlooking a nature reserve and the white sands of Noordhoek Beach. Cottages have two or three bedrooms, fully equipped kitchens, and large balconies. The wood interiors are attractive and rustic, brightened by floral fabrics, cottage-style furniture, and fireplaces. Rooms are similarly decorated, and some have pretty Victorian bathrooms. There's a large grocery store 5 km (3 mi) away. Owner Judy Sole runs an outstanding establishment and is a character in her own right. ⊠ *Mountain Rd., Box 114, Noordhoek 7985* ☎ *021/789–1391* 🖷 *021/ 789–1143* ⊕ *www.monkeyvalleyresort.com* ➥ *32 rooms, 15 cottages* ☖ *Restaurant, some kitchens, pool, bar, playground, convention center; no a/c* ▭ *AE, DC, MC, V* ⎮⊙⎮ *BP.*

$ 🖾 **La Splendida Luxury Suites.** Designed to look like a Miami South Beach art-deco hotel, this trendy all-suites lodging has a great location on Beach Road, Mouille Point. Ask for a sea- or mountain-facing room, either of which will have great views. Well-proportioned rooms are decorated with natural fabrics, and the overall feeling is light and airy. The hotel restaurant specializes in contemporary Italian food: great pizzas and pastas and fresh salads. The V&A Waterfront is a seven-minute walk away. You have a choice of executive or penthouse suites (slightly larger and a bit more expensive), but whichever you choose, you'll be very comfortable. ⊠ *121 Beach Rd., Mouille Point 8005* ☎ *021/439– 5119* 🖷 *021/439–5112* ⊕ *www.lasplendida.co.za* ➥ *24 suites* ☖ *Restaurant, bar* ▭ *AE, DC, MC, V.*

¢ 🖾 **Altona Lodge.** If you don't want to spend an arm and a leg on accommodations, the Altona Lodge is a good alternative. This imposing 1890s mansion has been converted into a comfortable and homey B&B. Not all rooms have private bathrooms, so be sure to state your preference when you book. Ask for a room with a view. If this is full, inquire about the Wilton Manor, Altona's sister hotel. It's a bit pricier, but nothing like other hotels on the Atlantic seaboard. ⊠ *19 Croxteth Rd., Green Point 8001* ☎ *021/434–2572* 🖷 *021/434–7879* ⊕ *www.altona.co.za,* ➥ *20 rooms, 4 with bath* ☖ *Laundry service, free parking; no a/c* ▭ *AE, MC, V* ⎮⊙⎮ *BP.*

Southern Suburbs

★ **$$$–$$$$**   🏨 **Cellars-Hohenort Hotel & Spa.** It's easy to forget the outside world at this idyllic getaway in Constantia. Set on 9 acres of gardens on the slopes of Constantiaberg, this luxury hotel commands spectacular views across Constantia Valley to False Bay. The 18th-century cellars of the Klaasenbosch wine estate and the Hohenort manor house form the heart of the hotel. Guest rooms are large and elegant, furnished in English-country style with brass beds, flowery valances, and reproduction antiques. Rooms in the manor house have the best views of the valley. The Presidential Suite sleeps a family of six. ✉ *93 Brommersvlei Rd., Box 270, Constantia 7800* ☎ *021/794–2137* 🖷 *021/794–2149* ⊕ *www. cellarshohenort.com* ⤳ *55 rooms, 1 suite ⚹ 2 restaurants, room service, tennis court, 2 pools, gym, spa, hair salon, 2 bars* ☰ *AE, DC, MC, V* ⑩ *BP.*

★ **$$$–$$$$**   🏨 **Constantia Uitsig Country Hotel.** This 200-acre winery has an enviable setting, backed by the magnificent mountains of the Constantiaberg and overlooking the vineyards of Constantia Valley. Rooms, in whitewashed farm cottages set on manicured lawns and gardens, are comfortable and inviting. Wicker headboards, timber ceilings, and bright floral patterns add a rustic feeling. The restaurant in the original farmhouse draws diners from all over the Cape. ✉ *Spaanschemat River Rd., Box 32, Constantia 7848* ☎ *021/794–6500* 🖷 *021/794–7605* ⊕ *www.constantiauitsig. co.za* ⤳ *16 rooms ⚹ 3 restaurants, room service, pool; no a/c* ☰ *AE, DC, MC, V* ⑩ *BP.*

$$$ 🏨 **Bishop's Court.** Nestled in the exclusive suburb of Bishopscourt, where the bishop of the Anglican Church still has his residence, this boutique hotel with unrivaled views over Kirstenbosch and Table Mountain is a good combination of class and homey comfort. Thanks to a friendly and attentive staff, you may end up feeling as though you're staying with wealthy cousins. After browsing through the private library you can retreat to your gorgeous room. Decor is classical, and fine touches include fluffy robes, wonderful toiletries, and brilliant baths. Better still, there's a complimentary in-house chauffer who is happy to shuttle you around. If a group of friends are traveling together, you can even rent the entire establishment. ✉ *18 Hillwood Ave., Bishopscourt 7700* ☎ *021/797–6710* 🖷 *021/794–2069* ⊕ *www.thelastword.co.za* ⤳ *5 rooms ⚹ Tennis court, pool, bar, library, airport shuttle* ☰ *AE, DC, MC, V* ⑩ *BP.*

$$–$$$ 🏨 **Alphen Hotel.** Built in the mid-1700s in Cape Dutch–style, this former manor house is now a national monument and one of the Cape's historic treasures. The owners are descendants of the distinguished Cloete family, which has farmed the land around Constantia since 1750. Cloete paintings and antiques, each with a story to tell, adorn the public rooms. Rooms range in size from compact to rather large. A small drawback is the slight traffic noise from the nearby highway in rush hour, but a health and wellness center on the grounds just might help you forget about it. Only luxury rooms have air-conditioning. ✉ *Alphen Dr., Box 35, Constantia 7848* ☎ *021/794–5011* 🖷 *021/794–5710* ⊕ *www. alphen.co.za* ⤳ *34 rooms ⚹ Restaurant, room service, pool, hair salon, gym, bar; no a/c in some rooms* ☰ *AE, DC, MC, V* ⑩ *BP.*

$$–$$$ ⊞ **Steenberg Hotel.** Originally called Swaaneweide aan den Steenberg, this is one of the oldest estates in the area. It was granted to the four-time widow Catherina Ustings by her lover, Simon van der Stel, then governor of the Cape, making her the first woman to own land in South Africa. The original buildings on this working wine estate have been painstakingly restored, the gardens manicured to perfection, and the vineyards replanted on the slopes of the Constantiaberg. The original vineyards have been converted into a championship 18-hole golf course. The spectacular buildings are all furnished with antiques, as are guest rooms, which are done in a Provençal style but with a modern touch. The hotel is exceptionally classy, as is its award-winning wine. Don't leave without buying some sauvignon blanc. ✉ *Steenberg and Tokai Rds., Tokai 7945* ☎ *021/713–2222* 🖷 *021/713–2251* ⊕ *www.steenberghotel.com* 🛏 *30 rooms, 1 suite* ♿ *Restaurant, 18-hole golf course, 2 pools, gym, hair salon, bar* ⊟ *AE, DC, MC, V* ⵑⵔ *BP.*

$$ ⊞ **Red House.** Once the hunting lodge of Lord Charles Somerset, this house, dating from 1729, is one of Cape Town's oldest surviving buildings. It's been lavishly restored, but the walls remain their signature red, the result of a former, eccentric owner, who chose the bold color to "ensure protection against the elements." You won't have to worry much about the elements here, as the elegant rooms are extremely comfortable and decorated with heavy drapes, dark mahogany furniture, chandeliers, and bold gilt-framed mirrors. What's more, the guesthouse is nestled in the leafy suburb of Newlands, just five minutes from Kirstenbosch and 10 minutes from the city center. The terrace is a good place to relax after a busy day, and you can even get an on-site massage in the garden or near the pool. ✉ *4 Hiddingh Ave., Newlands 7700* ☎ *021/683—8000* 🖷 *021/683–8006* ⊕ *www.redhouse.co.za* 🛏 *4 rooms, 1 cottage* ♿ *Pool, sauna, steam room, airport shuttle; no a/c* ⊟ *AE, DC, MC, V* ⵑⵔ *BP.*

$$ ⊞ **Vineyard Hotel.** Set on 6 acres of rolling gardens overlooking the Liesbeek River in residential Newlands, this comfortable hotel was built around the 18th-century weekend home of Lady Anne Barnard. The views of the back of Table Mountain are spectacular, but for a better rate ask for a courtyard-facing room. The hotel is 10 minutes by car from the city but within walking distance of the Newlands sports arenas and the shops of Cavendish Square. Au Jardin, the classic French restaurant, is very well regarded. ✉ *Colinton Rd., Box 151, Newlands 7725* ☎ *021/ 657–4500* 🖷 *021/683–4501* ⊕ *www.vineyard.co.za* 🛏 *173 rooms* ♿ *3 restaurants, room service, 2 pools, gym, bar* ⊟ *AE, DC, MC, V.*

$–$$ ⊞ **Palm House.** Towering palms dominate the manicured lawns of this peaceful guest house straddling the border of Kenilworth and Wynberg, a 15-minute drive from the city. The house is an enormous, stolid affair, built in the early 1920s by a protégé of Sir Herbert Baker and filled with dark-wood paneling, wood staircases, and fireplaces. Guest rooms are large and decorated with bold floral fabrics and reproduction antiques. Upstairs rooms benefit from more air and light. Guests often meet for evening drinks in the drawing room. ✉ *10 Oxford St., Wynberg 7800* ☎ *021/761–5009* 🖷 *021/761–8776* ⊕ *www.thepalmhouse.co.za* 🛏 *10 rooms* ♿ *Pool, bar; no a/c in some rooms* ⊟ *AE, DC, MC, V* ⵑⵔ *BP.*

★ ¢ 🖼 **Koornhoop Manor Guest House.** One of the best values in Cape Town, this lovely Victorian house is set in a pretty garden. Unpretentious rooms vary in size, are simply decorated in pretty florals, and have private bath and tea/coffeemakers. The hotel is very central, and is within safe walking distance of a huge range of restaurants in the vibey young suburb of Observatory, five minutes' drive from the city and convenient to the railway station. A communal area with an honor bar is a convivial meeting place. You need to book quite far in advance to take advantage of this little gem. ⊠ *Wrench and Nuttal Rds., Observatory 7925* 🕾🕾 *021/448–0595* ⊕ *www.geocities.com/koornhoop* ➡ *8 rooms, 2 three-bedroom apartments* ♢ *No a/c* ⊟ *No credit cards* �†⊙�† *BP.*

False Bay

$ 🖼 **Boulders Beach Lodge.** Just a few steps from beautiful Boulders Beach— the best swimming beach in Cape Town—this comfortable guesthouse is a winner. The understated rooms are decorated with elegant black wrought-iron furniture and snow-white linen, creating a restful, minimalist feel. The adjacent restaurant and pub are a bit more boisterous. ⊠ *4 Boulders Pl., Simon's Town 7975* 🕾 *021/786–1758* 🕾 *021/786– 1825* ⊕ *www.bouldersbeach.co.za* ➡ *12 rooms* ♢ *Restaurant, bar; no a/c, no room TVs* ⊟ *AE, DC, MC, V* �†⊙�† *BP.*

$ 🖼 **Inn at Castle Hill.** The fishing village of Kalk Bay is a vacation destination in itself. From the inn you can stroll down to the beach, walk to the restaurants, or explore the antiques shops that this bohemian village is known for. The carefully restored Edwardian villa has a wonderful view over False Bay, and the spacious rooms are individually decorated. Be sure to ask for a room that opens onto the veranda. There's a communal TV lounge, and braai facilities are available on request. ⊠ *37 Gatesville Rd., Kalk Bay 7975* 🕾 *021/788–2554* 🕾 *021/ 788–3843* ⊕ *www.castlehill.co.za* ➡ *5 rooms* ♢ *Bar; no a/c, no room TVs* ⊟ *AE, DC, MC, V* �†⊙�† *BP.*

$ 🖼 **Simon's Town Quayside Hotel.** On Jubilee Square, part of the Simon's Town Waterfront, this hotel is right in the action and has wonderful views over Simon's Bay, the harbor, and the yacht club. Almost all rooms have sea views, and all are light and airy, combining lime-washed wood with white walls and pale blue finishes. Room service can be arranged from the adjacent Bertha's Restaurant. ⊠ *Jubilee Sq., Main Rd., Simon's Town* 🕾 *021/786–3838* 🕾 *021/786–2241* ⊕ *www.quayside.co.za* ➡ *26 rooms* ♢ *Room service* ⊟ *AE, DC, MC, V* �†⊙�† *BP.*

¢ 🖼 **Simon's Town Backpackers.** Don't expect designer linen or glam furnishings at this backpackers' lodge. It's simple, cheap, cheerful, and spotlessly clean, and offers fantastic views from the upstairs balcony. Besides, Simon's Town is a great place to station yourself. It's only 45 minutes from Cape Town, it's on the railway line, and it's within walking distance of Boulders Beach and the penguin colony. You can also choose from plenty of nearby restaurants, serving everything from sushi to Nepalese fare. The historic building has been many things in its lifetime, including a whorehouse. TV is available in a communal lounge. ⊠ *66 St. George's St., Simon's Town 7975* 🕾 *021/786–1964* ⊕ *www.capepax.co.za* ➡ *4 rooms, 4 dormitories* ♢ *Bar; no a/c, no room TVs* ⊟ *No credit cards.*

NIGHTLIFE & THE ARTS

Cape etc. is a great bimonthly roundup of entertainment in Cape Town. For weekly updates try "Friday," the entertainment supplement of the *Mail & Guardian*, or the "Top of the Times" in Friday's *Cape Times*. Both are informed, opinionated, and up-to-date. The *Argus* newspaper's "Tonight" section gives you a complete daily listing of what's on, plus contact numbers. Tickets for almost every cultural and sporting event in the country (including movies) can be purchased through **Computicket** (☎ 083/909–0909 ⊕ www.computicket.co.za); the problem is that you need a credit card with a South African address. Cape Town is a very gay-friendly city. For information on the gay scene, contact **Africa Outing** (☎ 021/671–4028 or 083/273–8422 ⊕ www.afouting.com). **Gay Net Cape Town** (⊕ www.gaynetcapetown.co.za) will also keep you updated.

Nightlife

There's plenty to do in Cape Town after dark. The city's nightlife is concentrated in a number of areas, so you can explore a different one each night or move from one hub to another. After all, the city is small enough to get around quite easily. That said, however, walking from one area to another isn't advisable, as there are some parts of the city that are completely deserted and unsafe. Women, in pairs or singly, and couples should not walk alone. One of the best—and safest—places to start is the Waterfront, where you can choose from movies, restaurants, bars, and pubs and walk between them quite happily, as there are plenty of security guards and other people walking around. The top end of Long Street is another good nightlife area. Here you'll find a couple of blocks of bars, restaurants, and backpacker lodges that are open late. And the area bounded by Loop, Long, Wale, and Orange streets is the best place to get a feeling for Cape Town's always-changing nightclub scene, but ask around for the latest on the current flavor of the month. De Waterkant is very busy at night; if you're in the area, you can also take in the Green Point strip, where restaurants and bars open out onto the streets. On weekends these bars are packed, and you'll get a good idea of how Capetonians let down their hair. Heritage Square, in the city center, is another vibey place to spend an evening. Here you'll find an ever-changing mix of bars and restaurants.

A key event on Cape Town's social calendar is the MCQP (Mother City Queer Party). Party animals should definitely add this to their must-do list. It's part Mardi Gras, part Gay Pride March, and one enormous fancy dress party. Each year the party is themed, and everyone goes all out to dress up in fantastic outfits. Heterosexuals welcome!

Bars & Pubs

Built right on the water's edge adjacent to the new yacht marina, **Bascule Whisky Bar and Wine Cellar** (⊠ Cape Grace hotel, Waterfront ☎ 021/410–7238) is a very fancy watering hole for well-heeled, cigar-puffing locals. Its 451 whiskies are reputed to be the biggest selection in the Southern Hemisphere, so it's a great place to enjoy a good single-malt or glass of bubbly while the light fades behind Table Mountain. **Quay Four** (✉ Quay 4, Waterfront ☎ 021/419–2008) is a very relaxed option popular with visitors and locals, who clog picnic tables on the wooden deck overlooking the harbor before moving on to one of the many Waterfront restaurants. The **Sports Café** (✉ Victoria Wharf, Waterfront ☎ 021/419–5558) is a huge place with big-screen TVs. The food isn't going to win any awards, but if you're homesick, this is the place to head. The bar gets into the spirit of major foreign sporting events, like the Super Bowl and the FA Cup Final (England's soccer championship) and is undoubtedly the best place to watch sports in the city.

In the city center, the **Long Street Café** (✉ 259 Long St., Cape Town central ☎ 021/424–2464), an easygoing favorite with locals, serves light, tasty dishes, coffee, and, of course, cocktails. Try the Long Street iced tea, but be warned: there's no tea in it. With its dark-wood paneling and hot-red upholstery, the **M Bar & Lounge** (✉ 38 Long St., Cape Town central ☎ 021/424–7247) is home to the hip and happening. It's always busy with the after-work crowd looking for a bit of R&R. The **Planet Champagne Bar** (✉ Mount Nelson Hotel, 76 Orange St., Gardens ☎ 021/483–1000) is a sophisticated bar that carries an excellent selection of local and international wines and champagnes by the glass. The decor is an interesting mix of retro and modern and reflects some of the hotel's history—most notably as a port of call for ocean-liner travelers. Planet opens onto one of the Mount Nelson's magnificent garden terraces, and on a hot summer night it's one of the coolest places to be seen.

You can watch the sun set at the hugely popular **Café Caprice** (✉ 37 Victoria Rd., Camps Bay ☎ 021/438–8315) while rubbing shoulders with beautiful bronzed bodies just off the beach. Look out for all the pretty, young things in their cowboy boots and short, short rah-rah skirts. It's very LA, very Sunset Strip, dahlin'. **Cafe Erte** (✉ 265 Main Rd., Three Anchor Bay ☎ 021/434–6624) is very gay-friendly. **Tank Cocktail Lounge** (✉ 72 Waterkant St., de Waterkant ☎ 021/419–0007), in the trendy de Waterkant, is a must for cool customers. It's been described as "schmodelly," which in Cape Town lingo roughly translates as a place where you can schmooze with models. The cocktails are made with the freshest ingredients. Try the signature Tank cocktail, a delicious mix of homemade lemongrass syrup, fresh litchi juice, and lots of alcohol. Once you've finished with the drinks, you can move on to the sushi bar and restaurant.

Out of town in the quaint fishing village of Kalk Bay, **Polana** (✉ Kalk Bay Harbour, off Main Rd., Kalk Bay ☎ 021/788–7162) has astonishing views across the bay. You can see all the way to Cape Hangklip, and when the weather is good, they slide back the windows so you can enjoy the sea breeze while you sip a cold glass of South Africa's best.

Dance Clubs

The **Fez** (✉ 38 Hout St., Cape Town central ☎ 021/423–1456) has been around for eons in club terms. Its Moroccan theme, with cushions for lounging around on and good cocktails, makes it a favorite with the young and trendy. The **Ivory Room** (✉ 196 Loop St., Cape Town central ☎ 021/

422–3257) always cooks until late. Think African colonial with a twist of R&B, funk, hip-hop, and lots in between. It's good for "everyone from 20 to old." **Rhodes House** (✉ 60 Queen Victoria St., Cape Town central ☎ 021/424–8844) is one of the smarter places to boogie up a storm and, while you're at it, bump into a visiting celeb or two. Music varies from R&B to hip-hop, house, jazz, and funk. There are two dance floors and a cigar lounge to relax in.

Green Point also has its share of clubs. **The Bronx** (✉ 35 Somerset Rd., Green Point ☎ 021/419–9216), one of the oldest kids on the block, is gay-friendly and plays disco (remember that?), so you can make like John Travolta and pull on your shiny pants to dance the night away. **Purgatory** (✉ 8B Dixon St., Green Point ☎ 021/421–7464) combines art-deco chic with modern elegance.

Live Music Clubs

The **Drum Café** (✉ 32 Glynn St. ☎ 021/461–1305) has live performances by percussionists from all over Africa. On Monday and Wednesday starting around 9, a drum circle lets you discover your inner rhythm. Among the clubs with live African music, a good bet is **Mama Africa** (✉ 178 Long St., Cape Town central ☎ 021/424–8634). It has live music Monday through Saturday, and usually a marimba band on Monday, Wednesday, Friday, and Saturday night as well as authentic African food, authentic African music, and authentic African pulse.

Many of the mainstream jazz clubs in the city double as restaurants. Cover charges range from R15 to R30. The **Green Dolphin Jazz Restaurant** (✉ Victoria & Alfred Hotel, Waterfront ☎ 021/421–7471) attracts some of the best mainstream musicians in the country as well as a few from overseas. The cover charge is R20–R25. **Mannenberg's Jazz Café** (✉ Clock Tower Precinct, Waterfront ☎ 021/421–5639), a long-standing Cape Town favorite, showcases talented musicians from South Africa and the rest of the continent. You can enjoy a sundowner or a meal while listening. **Winchester Mansions Hotel** (✉ 221 Beach Rd., Sea Point ☎ 021/434–2351) does a mellow Sunday brunch in the courtyard (11–2; about R125) with some of the city's best jazz musicians. Other than the above, the hot venues change so quickly that it's best to get info when you're here. Cape Town Tourism has a list of good jazz venues and attempts to keep up with the frequent changes.

The Arts

The **Artscape** (✉ D. F. Malan St. and Hertzog Blvd., Foreshore ☎ 021/421–7839 ⊕ www.artscape.co.za), a huge and unattractive theater complex, is the hub of performing arts and other cultural activities. Cape Town City Ballet, the Cape Town Philharmonic Orchestra, and the city's theater and opera companies perform in the center's three theaters. Since 1994 there's been a conscious effort to make the performing arts more representative and multicultural, and today there's a palpable African-arts excitement in the air. Classics are still well represented, as are more contemporary works.

Classical Music

The **Cape Town Philharmonic Orchestra** (☎ 021/410–9809 ⊕ www.capephilharmonic.org.za) alternates performances between City Hall and Artscape. It's also relaxing to listen to the orchestra at one of its two open-air concerts at the Kirstenbosch gardens—usually the first and last concerts of the season. The orchestra has hosted several guest conductors from Europe and the United States and has an active program, which includes free concerts in the summer at the outdoor AGFA Amphitheatre, at the Waterfront. You can also make a day trip to hear the orchestra and other musical groups at the Spier Estate during the Spier Arts Summer Festival or at a music festival in Franschhoek in October (⇨ Chapter 2).

Film

Ster-Kinekor (☎ 082/16789 ⊕ www.sterkinekor.com) and **Nu Metro** (☎ 086/110–0220) screen mainstream movies at cinema complexes all over the city. The Waterfront alone has two movie houses with a total of 19 screens. Check newspaper listings for what's playing.

At two locations, the **Cinema Nouveau** (⊠ Cavendish Square shopping center, basement level, Cavendish Sq., Claremont ☎ 082/16789 ⊠ V&A Waterfront shopping center, ground floor, Waterfront ☎ 082/16789) concentrates on foreign and art films. The **Labia** (⊠ 68 Orange St., Gardens ⊠ 50 Kloof St., Gardens ☎ 021/424–5927 ⊕ www.labia.co.za) is an independent art house that screens good-quality mainstream and alternative films, including the works of some of the best European filmmakers. There are four screens at the Labia on Orange and two at the Labia on Kloof, just up the road. A small coffee bar serves snacks at both venues.

Theater

The **Baxter Theatre Complex** (⊠ Main Rd., Rondebosch ☎ 021/685–7880 ⊕ www.baxter.co.za), part of the University of Cape Town, hosts a range of productions from serious drama to wacky comedies, as well as some rather experimental stuff. The complex features a 666-seat theater, a concert hall, a smaller studio, and a restaurant and bar.

During the summer, when the weather's good, Cape Town has its own version of New York City's Central Park's Shakespeare in the Park at the excellent **Maynardville Open-Air Theatre** (⊠ Wolfe and Church Sts., Wynberg ☎ 083/909–0909 Computicket ⊕ www.artscape.co.za). Theatergoers often bring a picnic supper to enjoy before the show.

The **Theatre on the Bay** (⊠ 1 Link St., Camps Bay ☎ 021/438–3301 ⊕ www.theatreonthebay.co.za) features local and international drama and comedy, plus occasional cabaret and music. Its Act I Theatre Café is great for a preshow drink.

SPORTS & THE OUTDOORS

Cape Town is the adventure capital of the universe. Whatever you want to do—dive, paddle, fly, jump, run, slide, fin, walk, or clamber—this is the city to do it in. **Adventure Village** (☎ 021/424–1580 ⊕ www.

adventure-village.co.za) books a range of activities. **Siyabona Africa Travel** (✉ 10 Dean St., Gardens ☎ 021/424–1037 ⊕ www.siyabona.com) offers general travel advice and adventure booking.

Participant Sports

Biking

Downhill Adventures (✉ Shop 10 Overbeek Bldg., Kloof, Orange, and Long Sts., Cape Town central ☎ 021/422–0388 ⊕ www.downhilladventures.co.za) offers great cycling trips around the Peninsula. You can opt for a full day at the nature reserve at Cape Point, including a picnic lunch, or a leisurely cycle through the Constantia winelands, stopping for wine tasting along the way. Those wanting something more hard-core might like mountain biking in the Tokai forest. Expect to pay R400–R500 per trip.

Climbing

Cape Town has hundreds of bolted sport routes around the city and Peninsula, ranging from an easy 10 to a hectic 30. (To give you some idea of difficulty, a route rated a 10 in South Africa would be equivalent to a 5.5 climb in the United States. A 20 climb would register around 5.10c, while the hardest you'll find in South Africa is probably a 34, which American climbers would know as a 5.14b. The toughest climb up Table Mountain rates about 32, which is 5.14a.) Both Table Mountain sandstone and Cape granite are excellent hard rocks. There are route guides to all the major climbs and a number of climbing schools in Cape Town. A few favorite climbs include Table Mountain (from various angles), Lion's Head, du Toit's Kloof, and Muizenberg Peak.

Cape Town School of Mountaineering(✉ 24 Elizabeth Ave., Pinelands ☎ 021/531–4290) is a good bet for day excursions and escorted walks. **High Adventure** (☎ 021/689–1234) specializes in climbing in the Cape Town area but also organizes trips farther afield.

Fishing

If you're keen to take to the open ocean for some deep-sea fishing, you'll have plenty of choices, as South Africa has excellent game fish, such as dorado, yellowfin tuna, and broadbill swordfish, which keep salty sea dogs going back for more. **Big Game Fishing Safaris** (✉ Town Pier, Simon's Town ☎ 021/674–2203 ⊕ www.simonstown.com/fishing/safaris) operates a 39-foot luxury catamaran for a day of fishing. You can also spend a day with **Reel Deep Charters** (✉ Hout Bay Marina, Hout Bay ☎ 083/414–6908 or 083/258–0707 ⊕ www.reeldeep.co.za.) out on the deep blue.

You won't find any captive-bred, corn-fed trout lurking in sluggish dams near Cape Town, but in the mountains, just an hour or so away, you'll encounter wild and wily fish in wild and wonderful rivers. The season runs September–May. **Inkwazi Fly-Fishing Safaris** (☎ 083/626–0467 or 021/788–7611 ⊕ www.inkwaziflyfishing.co.za) offers escorted tours, all the equipment you'll need, and plenty of good advice.

Golf

Most golf clubs in the Cape accept visitors, but prior booking is essential. Expect to pay R350–R400 for 18 holes and between R120 and R250 to rent golf clubs. Most clubs offer equipment rental. You can also rent golf carts for around R200, but you are encouraged to employ a caddie instead, as this offers valuable employment to local communities. Expect to pay around R100 and a tip of 10%–20% for good service. **Clovelly Country Club** (✉ 178 Clovelly Rd., Clovelly ☎ 021/782–6410 ⊕ www.clovelly.co.za), near Fish Hoek, is a tight course that requires masterful shot placement from tee to green. **Milnerton Golf Club** (✉ Bridge Rd., Milnerton ☎ 021/552–1047 ⊕ www.milnertongolfclub.co.za), sandwiched between the sea and a lagoon, is the Western Cape's only links course and can be difficult when the wind blows. **Mowbray Golf Club** (✉ 1 Raapenberg Rd., Mowbray ☎ 021/685–3018 ⊕ www.mowbraygolfcourse.co.za), with its great views of Devil's Peak, is a magnificent parkland course that has hosted several major tournaments; there are a number of interesting water holes. Unfortunately, noise from the highway can spoil the atmosphere. Founded in 1885, **Royal Cape Golf Club** (✉ 174 Ottery Rd., Wynberg ☎ 021/761–6551 ⊕ www.royalcapegolf.co.za) is the oldest course in Africa and has hosted the South African Open many times. Its beautiful setting and immaculate fairways and greens make a round here a must for serious golf enthusiasts. The challenging and scenic **Steenberg Golf Estate** (✉ Steenberg and Tokai Rds., Tokai ☎ 021/713–1632 ⊕ www.steenberghotel.co.za) is the most exclusive and expensive course on the Peninsula. A round costs more than R500 per person unless you're staying at the hotel. Dress codes are strictly enforced here.

Hiking & Canyoning

Cape Town and the surrounding areas offer some of the finest hiking in the world, mostly through the spectacularly beautiful mountains. Kloofing, known as canyoning in the United States, is the practice of following a mountain stream through its gorge, canyon, or kloof by swimming, rock hopping, and jumping over waterfalls or cliffs into deep pools. There are some exceptional kloofing venues in the Cape. **Abseil Africa** (✉ 295 Long St., Cape Town central ☎ 021/424–4760 ⊕ www.abseilafrica.co.za) runs a kloofing and abseiling (rappelling) trip on the Steenbras River, better known as Kamikaze Kanyon. **Table Mountain Walks** (☎ 021/715–6136 ⊕ www.tablemountainwalks.co.za) offers various hikes, including options at Table Mountain and Silvermine Nature Reserve, with a well-informed guide.

There is a fantastic overnight hiking trail in the Cape Point section of **Table Mountain National Park** (☎ 021/701–8692 ⊕ www.tmnp.co.za), but you need to book ahead—sometimes by as much as a year.

Horseback Riding

Sleepy Hollow Horse Riding (✉ Sleepy Hollow La., Noordhoek ☎☎ 021/789–2341) offers 1½- and 2-hour rides down Long Beach, a 6-km (4-mi) expanse of sand that stretches from Noordhoek Beach to Kommetjie.

Kayaking

You don't have to be a pro to discover Cape Town by kayak. **Coastal Kayak Trails** (⊠ 179 Beach Rd., Mouille Point ☎ 021/439–1134 ⊕ www. kayak.co.za) has regular sunset and sunrise paddles off Sea Point. A two-hour paddle costs around R150. **Real Cape Adventures** (⊠ Vineyard House, 3 Green Acres Close, Hout Bay ☎ 021/790–5611 ⊕ www. seakayak.co.za) offers regular scenic paddles off Hout Bay and from Simon's Town around to Boulders. Expect to pay R150–R250.

Paragliding & Skydiving

Para-pax Tandem Paragliding (☎ 021/461–7070 ⊕ www.parapax.com) will take you flying off landmarks such as Lion's Head, Signal Hill, and Table Mountain, depending on the wind and weather conditions. Aaaagh! You can do a tandem sky dive (no experience necessary) and have a video taken of you hurtling earthward with Table Mountain in the background with **Skydive Cape Town** (☎ 082/800–6290 ⊕ www. skydivecapetown.za.net). A tandem fall costs around R1,200, R1,380 if you want a video of your madness.

Rappelling

Abseil Africa (⊠ 295 Long St., Cape Town central ☎ 021/424–4760 ⊕ www.abseilafrica.co.za) offers a 350-foot abseil (rappel) off the top of Table Mountain for about R250, not including cable car, and over a waterfall in the Helderberg mountains, about an hour's drive away, for about R550, including transportation and lunch.

Sailing

Drum Africa (☎ 021/785–5201 ⊕ www.drumafrica.co.za) launches catamarans (and you) off Fish Hoek beach, and before you know it you'll be in a trapeze harness leaning over the side of the boat like an old pro. In whale season (June–November) you're bound to see plenty of whales in the bay, which is thrilling.

Scuba Diving

The diving around the Cape is excellent, with kelp forests, cold-water corals, very brightly colored reef life, and numerous wrecks. An unusual experience is a dive in the Two Oceans Aquarium (⇨ Exploring Cape Town, *above*). CMSA, NAUI, and PADI dive courses are offered by local operators, beginning at about R1,700. **Orca Industries** (⊠ 3 Bowwood Rd., Claremont ☎ 021/671–9673 ⊕ www.orca-industries.co.za) offers dive courses and charters. **Pro Divers** (⊠ Shop 88b, Main Rd., Sea Point ☎ 021/433–0472 ⊕ www.prodiverssa.co.za) runs dive tours to some of the many ships wrecked at the infamous Cape of Storms. The friendly **Scuba Shack** (⊠ 289 Long St., Cape Town central ☎ 021/424–9368 ⊠ Shop 3 Glencairn Shopping Centre, Glencairn ☎ 021/782–7358 ⊕ www.scubashack.co.za) has two outlets: one in town and one in Glencairn, near Simon's Town. **Underwater World** (⊠ Wicht Close, off Tennant St., Zonnebloem ☎ 021/461–8290) is a city dive shop that offers PADI courses.

Surfing

Cape Town's surf is a bit erratic when compared with Durban's or the revered J-Bay's, but there are still some excellent spots. **Gary's Surf**

School (✉ 90 Beach Rd., Muizenberg ☎ 021/788–9839 ⊕ www.garysurf. com) offers surfing lessons to youngsters and the young at heart in the relatively warm and gentle waters at Muizenberg. You can also rent boards and wet suits. Lessons last two hours and cost around R380 for adults, R240 for children, including suit and board; if you still feel strong after that, you can keep the equipment for the rest of the day. You do need to be aware, however, that you'll be sharing the ocean with plenty of sharks, but that never seems to stop anyone.

Spectator Sports

It's easy to get tickets for ordinary club matches and for interprovincial games. Getting tickets to an international test match is more of a challenge; however, there's always somebody selling tickets—at a price, of course.

Cricket & Rugby

The huge sporting complex off Boundary Road in Newlands is the home of the **Western Province Cricket Association** (☎ 021/657–2003). The **Western Province Rugby Football Union** (✉ Newlands ☎ 021/659–4500) also has its headquarters at Newlands. Next door to the Newlands sporting complex, in the South African Sports Science Institute, is the **SA Rugby Museum** (☎ 021/686–2151), open weekdays 9–5.

Soccer

Soccer in South Africa is much more grassroots than cricket or rugby, and is very big in the townships. Amateur games are played from March to September at many venues all over the Peninsula. Professional games are played from October to April at Green Point Stadium, Athlone Stadium, and Newlands. Watch the press for details.

SHOPPING

When it comes to shopping, Cape Town has something for everyone—from sophisticated malls to trendy markets. Although African art and curios are obvious choices (and you will find some gems), South Africans have woken up to their own sense of style and creativity, and the results are fantastic and as diverse as the people who make up this rainbow nation. So in a morning you could bag some sophisticated tableware from Carrol Boyes, a funky wire-art object from a street vendor, and a beautifully designed handbag made by HIV-positive women who are working as part of a community development program.

Cape Town has great malls selling well-known brands, and the V&A Waterfront is an excellent place to start, followed by Cavendish Square in Claremont and Canal Walk at Century City, on the N1 heading out of town toward Paarl. But it's beyond the malls that you can get a richer shopping experience, one that will give you greater insight into the soul of the city and its people. Shopping malls usually have extended shopping hours beyond the normal 9–5 on weekdays and 9–1 on Saturdays. Most shops outside of malls (except for small grocery stores) are closed on Sunday.

Markets

Greenmarket Square. You can get good buys on clothing, T-shirts, hand-crafted silver jewelry, and locally made leather shoes and sandals, and you can find African jewelry, art, and fabrics here, too. It's lively and fun whether or not you buy anything, but it is one of the best places in town to buy gifts. More than half the stalls are owned by people not from South Africa. Here you'll find political and economic refugees from Ethiopia, Eritrea, Zimbabwe, and the Democratic Republic of Congo trying to eke out a living. Bargain, but do so with a conscience. ☒ *Long-market, Burg, and Shortmarket Sts., Cape Town central* ☉ *Mon.–Sat. 9–4:30.*

Obs Holistic Lifestyle Fair. For everything weird and wonderful, this market is an absolute winner. Cape Town is home to plenty of alternative-therapy practitioners, crystal gazers, and energy healers, and they congregate on the first Sunday of every month to sell their wares and trade spells. Food is abundant, healthful (of course), and vegetarian. Kids are not ignored; they run wild together with their parents. ☒ *Station and Lower Main Rds., Observatory* ☎ *021/782–8882* ☉ *1st Sun. of month 10–4.*

Waterfront Craft Market. This indoor market contains an assortment of handcrafted jewelry, rugs, glass, pottery, and leather sandals as well as a wellness center where you can have a shiatsu massage or some reflexology to pep you up if you're shopped out. ☒ *Dock Rd., Waterfront* ☎ *021/408–7842* ☉ *Daily 9:30–6.*

Specialty Stores

Art & Crafts

A number of stores in Cape Town sell African art and crafts, much of which comes from Zululand or neighboring countries. Street vendors, particularly on St. George's Mall and Greenmarket Square, often sell the same curios for half the price.

African Image. Look here for traditional and contemporary African art and curios, colorful cloth from Nigeria and Ghana, plus West African masks, Malian blankets, and beaded designs from southern African tribes. A variety of Zulu baskets is also available. ☒ *52 Burg St., Cape Town central* ☎ *021/423–8385* ☒ *Shop 6228, Table Bay Hotel Mall, Waterfront* ☎ *021/419–0382.*

Africa Nova. If you aren't crazy about traditional African artifacts, you might want to visit this store, which stocks contemporary African art that's quirky and interesting. Original African art is showcased for those looking for one-of-a-kind pieces. Come Christmastime, the store is transformed with beaded African Christmas decorations: gorgeous stars, divine angels, and brilliant nativity animals. Even if you aren't buying, it's worth visiting for the display. ☒ *72 Waterkant St., Cape Quarter* ☎ *021/425–5123.*

Montebello Craft & Design Centre. This old building nestled under tall, shady trees houses a number of job-creation projects. This is a good place to shop if you have only a short time, as included here are textiles, ceramics, jewelry, handbags, and sought-after Madiba dolls (soft dolls fashioned after the great South African icon; *Madiba* is a term of endearment for Mandela). For a break from shopping you can have a delicious light lunch or tea at the **Gardener's Cottage** (☎ 021/689–3158) in the complex. ⊠ *31 Newlands Ave., Newlands* ☎ *021/685–6445.*

Pan-African Market. The market, extending over two floors of a huge building, is a jumble of tiny stalls, traditional African hairdressers, tailors, potters, artists, musicians, and drummers. There is also a small, very African restaurant. If you're not going to visit countries to the north, come here for an idea of what you're missing. ⊠ *76 Long St., Cape Town central* ☎ *021/426–4478.*

Streetwires. You'll see street wire art everywhere in Cape Town, but this shop is a treasure trove of the art form, which uses a combination of wire, beads, and other recycled materials to create bowls, lights, mobiles, and expressive sculptures. You might even want to buy a working wire radio. You won't find too many of those back home. A wire sculpture of former president Nelson Mandela, created by Streetwires' Jeff Mwazha, was for sale for R45,000 to raise awareness about HIV/AIDS. The sculpture, entitled *Free Drugs for All,* depicts Mandela holding anti-retroviral drugs. ⊠ *77/79 Shortmarket St., Cape Town central* ☎ *021/426–2475.*

Books & Music

African Music Store. The staff here is passionate about African music and eager to pass on their love to anybody who lends them half an ear. You could easily spend a couple of hours listening to any- and everything in the store. You're bound to find something here that captures the heart of the country for you. ⊠ *134 Long St., Cape Town central* ☎ *021/426–0857.*

Clarke's Bookshop. At this local favorite you'll find a fantastic collection of both old and new books on southern Africa as well as general secondhand titles. ⊠ *211 Long St., Cape Town central* ☎ *021/423–5739.*

Compact Disc Wherehouse. Looking for local music—or any music, for that matter? Compact Disc Wherehouse (get the pun?) has an enormous selection of African music, and you'll find plenty of recordings from local artists as well as some from farther afield. The staff is knowledgeable and very helpful. ⊠ *Pumphouse, Dock Rd., Waterfront* ☎ *021/425–6300.*

Exclusive Books. This is one of the best all-around bookshops in the country. The chain carries a wide selection of local and international periodicals and coffee-table books on Africa. A coffee bar allows you to browse at a comfortable table with an espresso or cappuccino. Be prepared, though, to pay at least twice as much for books here as you would in the United States or Britain. ⊠ *Shop 6160, Victoria Wharf, Waterfront* ☎ *021/419–0905* ⊠ *Lower Mall, Cavendish Sq., Claremont* ☎ *021/674–3030* ⊠ *Constantia Village Shopping Centre, Constantia* ☎ *021/*

794–7800 ✉ *Tygervalley Shopping Centre, Tygervalley* ☎ *021/914–9910* ✉ *Canal Walk, Century City Shopping Centre* ☎ *021/555–3720.*

Traveller's Bookshop. South Africa is astonishingly beautiful and diverse, and there are hundreds of books that capture both these qualities. This store, one of the best places to shop for travel books, stocks more than 25,000 titles, with everything from glossy coffee-table books to intimate portraits of a changing nation. It also stocks books about other countries. This store is linked to **Wordsworth Books,** an independent all-purpose bookstore next door. ✉ *Shop 2, King's Warehouse, Waterfront* ☎ *021/425–6880.*

Clothing & Fabrics

South African designers are flexing their creative muscles and coming up with innovative designs that will look good on you. Sure, there's traditional garb, such as a pretty Shweshwe (traditional African print) skirt or a Madiba-style shirt, but also watch out for exciting interpretations on old themes.

Heartworks. This shop has people at its heart. Part of a job-creation initiative, it stocks gorgeous things to wear. Buying something here means you can do good and look good at the same time. ✉ *98 Kloof St., Gardens* ☎ *021/424–8419* ✉ *Gardens Centre, Gardens* ☎ *021/465–3289.*

Mnandi Textiles. Here you'll find a range of African fabrics, including traditional West African prints and Dutch wax prints. The store sells ready-made African clothing for adults and children, and you can also have garments made to order. ✉ *90 Station Rd., Observatory* ☎ *021/447–6814.*

N.C.M. Fashions–African Pride. This is the place to go for traditional clothing from all over Africa. One of the most striking outfits is the brightly colored *bubu,* a loose-fitting garment with a matching head wrap, or try a traditional Xhosa outfit, complete with braiding, beads, and a multilayer wraparound skirt. You can buy off the rack or order a custom outfit from a wide selection of fabrics. ✉ *152 Main Rd., Claremont* ☎ *021/683–1022.*

Housewares

Carrol Boyes Functional Art. Knives and forks need never be mundane again once you've seen Carrol Boyes's range of tableware and, more recently, leatherware. She works in pewter, aluminum, and stainless steel and weaves fluid female forms into functional items. ✉ *43 Rose St., Bo-Kaap* ☎ *021/424–8263,* ✉ *Shop 6180, Waterfront* ☎ *021/418–0595.*

LIM. The name of the shop stands for "Less Is More," and these savvy designers have come up with a range of glassware, ceramics, and custom-made furniture that reflects this philosophy. The lines are clean and unfussy and the colors bold and unusual. ✉ *86a Kloof St., Gardens* ☎ *021/423–1000.*

L'Orangerie. If knobbly imported linens, thick white ceramic bowls, and butcher blocks the size of a small car get you excited, then this is a good place to visit. The gardening shop is also enticing, and will make you want to rush home and start making things pretty. ⊠ *7 Wolfe St., Wynberg* ☎ *021/761–8355.*

Wine

Most Capetonians wouldn't dream of having supper without a glass of wine, and most supermarket chains carry a good range of affordable local wines. You shouldn't come to Cape Town without tasting and buying some of the wine the area is famous for. Your best bet is to buy directly from the wine farms, but if you don't manage to get out to the Winelands, there are some area stores that can fix you up with local or international wines.

Manuka Fine Wines. This store in the Southern Suburbs makes a point of stocking wines from the nearby Constantia Valley wine farms as well as those from the rest of the Cape. There are free wine tastings on Saturday morning and wine-tasting dinners once a month, at which winemakers introduce their wines to appreciative imbibers. ⊠ *Steenberg Village Shopping Centre, Steenberg Rd. and Reddam Ave., Tokai* ☎ *021/701–2046.*

Vaughan Johnson's Wine & Cigar Shop. This wineshop has a terrific selection and a staff who knows their stuff. They can even advise you about shipping if you decide to take a few cases home with you. And who could blame you? ⊠ *Dock Rd., Waterfront* ☎ *021/419–2121.*

CAPE TOWN A TO Z

AIR TRAVEL

Cape Town International Airport lies about 20 km (12½ mi) southeast of the city center in the Cape Flats. The recently upgraded domestic and international terminals both have booths run by Cape Town Tourism, which are open from 7:30 until the last flight comes in.

International carriers flying into Cape Town include Air Namibia, British Airways, KLM Royal Dutch Airlines, Lufthansa, Malaysia Airlines, Singapore Airlines, and South African Airways. Domestic flights are operated by British Airways/Comair/Kulula.com, Nationwide, 1time, and South African Airways/SA Airlink/SA Express.

There are no scheduled buses or trains to or from the airport, but there are plenty of private transportation operators. Shuttle services are based inside the domestic baggage hall and outside the international terminal, and can be phoned for airport drop-offs (as can other shuttle and taxi operators). Rates vary depending on the operator, the number in the group, the destination, and the time of arrival. As a single traveler, you can pay less if you're prepared to share the ride with others. One person going into the city center pays between R110 and R195, whereas the rate for a group of four is R140 to R210. A surcharge of up to 50% is usually levied from 10 PM until early morning, and some shuttles charge more for arrivals than for departures to cover waiting time. Metered taxis can also be found outside the terminals. Reports of overcharging are common, so check the fare first. A ride into the center of town costs around R160 with Dalhouzie/Touch Down and about R210 with Marine Taxis. For the ultimate luxury ride you can hire a six-seat Lincoln stretch limo from Cape Limo Services. Rates are R1,000 for the first two hours and R300 per hour thereafter (add extra for gas if you travel outside the Cape Town area).

📶 Airport **Cape Town International Airport** ☎ 021/937-1200, 086/727-7888 flight information ⊕ www.airports.co.za.

📶 Airlines **Air Namibia** ☎ 021/936-2755 ⊕ www.airnamibia.com. **British Airways/ Comair/Kulula.com** ☎ 021/936-9000 ⊕ www.britishairways.com ⊕ www.kulula.com. **KLM Royal Dutch Airlines** ☎ 086/024-7747 ⊕ www.klm.co.za. **Lufthansa** ☎ 011/ 975-0402 ⊕ www.lufthansa.com. **Malaysia Airlines** ☎ 021/934-8794 ⊕ www. malaysiaairlines.co.za. **Nationwide** ☎ 021/936-2050 ⊕ www.flynationwide.co.za. **1time** ☎ 086/134-5345 ⊕ www.1time.aero. **Singapore Airlines** ☎ 021/674-0601 ⊕ www.singaporeair.com. **South African Airways/SA Airlink/SA Express** ☎ 021/ 936-1111 ⊕ www.flysaa.com.

📶 Airport Transfers **Cape Limo Services** ☎ 021/785-3100. **City Hopper** ☎ 021/934- 4440. **Dalhouzie/Touch Down Taxis** ☎ 021/919-4659 or 021/919-2834. **Dumalisila** ☎ 021/934-1660. **Legend Tours and Transfers** ☎ 021/936-2814. **Magic Bus** ☎ 021/ 934-5455. **Marine Taxis** ☎ 021/434-0434. **Way to Go** ☎ 021/934-2503.

BUS TRAVEL

Intercape Mainliner travels to Johannesburg, Durban, towns in the southwest Cape, and Windhoek, in Namibia. Greyhound offers daily overnight service to Johannesburg and Tshwane, but for Western Cape destinations Intercape Mainliner is a better option. Translux offers luxury vehicles between major cities, and its sister company City-to-City runs to less well-serviced destinations like Umtata in addition to mainstream routes. The Baz Bus offers a hop-on/hop-off service and other flexible tours aimed mostly at backpackers who don't want to travel vast distances in one day and can't easily get to train and bus stations. The Baz Bus is more expensive than the regular bus but more convenient for covering distances in short stages. All the main bus companies operate from the bus terminal alongside the central train station on Adderley Street, and most have their offices there.

Daily overnight service to Johannesburg and Tshwane costs around R450–R500 one-way. Cape Town to Springbok is about R300–R350, to Windhoek R450–R550, to George R200, and to Durban R450–R500. Round-trip tickets are roughly double. A Baz Bus Durban hopper ticket via the Wild Coast costs about R1,600 one-way, R2,400 round-trip, and travel cards are R850 for a seven-day pass and R1,600 for a 14-day pass.

Within Cape Town, Golden Arrow runs an extensive network of routes from the main Golden Acre terminal on the Grand Parade (Castle Street side). These subsidized buses are by far the cheapest form of transportation (much to the frustration of the minibus taxi operators). You'll get to most destinations for R5–R10, and you can save by buying 10-ride clip cards. The service has a timetable, but buses often run late and you'll need a certain level of knowledge regarding its operation. Bus shelters and lamppost markers indicate stops. Route maps are not available in leaflet form, but they are displayed at all major depots. Alternatively, phone the Golden Arrow hotline, or ask people at a bus stop for info on which ones go your way.

For short trips locals generally use minibus taxis, which waste no tim getting you to your destination and, for the modest fare of R5–R20, pr vide you with some local atmosphere. You can hop on and off the *con bis* (vans) quite easily; small gatherings on the roadside usually indica a stop. However, don't expect to leave the starting point until the ta is full, which can slow you down outside of peak hours or away fro busy routes. The main minibus stop in the city center is above the tra station on Adderley Street, but you can flag combis down just abo anywhere. Most taxis are sound, but watch out for those held togeth with tape and wire (literally). There are no route maps for minibus tax ask the drivers where they're going. If you don't have the exact chang you may have to wait until the guy taking the fares gets your chang Overcharging is not that common, but it's best to discreetly ask oth passengers what the fare should be. Taxis are crowded, so watch o for pickpockets.

A few shuttle buses operate tourist-friendly routes around the city ce ter. Shuttles to Kirstenbosch (R40 per person) and the Table Mounta cableway (R30) can be obtained from the Victoria & Alfred Waterfro Information Centre. A regular bus runs from the central train stati to the V&A Waterfront (R2.50), and there's also service from the Ca Town Tourism Information Office in town.

🚌 **Bus Lines Baz Bus** ☎ 021/439-2323 ⊕ www.bazbus.co.za. **Golden Arrow** ☎ 08 121-2111. **Greyhound** ☎ 083/915-9000 ⊕ www.greyhound.co.za. **Intercape Mainlin** ☎ 0861/287-287 or 0861/287-329 ⊕ www.intercape.co.za. **Translux/City-to-C** ☎ 0861/589-282 ⊕ www.translux.co.za.

CAR & MOTORCYCLE TRAVEL

A car is by far the best way to get around Cape Town, particularly the evenings, when public transportation closes down. The Automob Association has a presence, and if you're a member of any organizati at home affiliated with AIT (Automobile International Travel), y qualify for basic benefits here, including breakdown service, towing, a transportation to the nearest provincial hospital. Fill in a form at t airport's Imperial Car Rental depot (Imperial has a rental-discount de with the AA) or at any of the city's three AA auto shops.

Cape Town's roads are excellent, but they are unusual in a few respec and can be a bit confusing. Signage is inconsistent, switching betwe Afrikaans and English, between different names for the same road (e pecially highways), and between different destinations on the sar route. Sometimes the signs simply vanish. Cape Town is also littered wi signs indicating "Cape Town" instead of "City Center." Good one-pa maps are essential and are freely available from car-rental agencies a tourism information desks. Among the hazards are pedestrians, parti ularly those looking for a quick route across highways, and speedi vehicles, especially minibus taxis as they race to drop one load of pa sengers and pick up the next. The sight of highway patrols and spe traps is no longer rare, and Cape Town just got its first digital trappi devices. Roadblocks for document and roadworthiness checks are al becoming more frequent, and there are concerted attempts to catch pe ple who drink and drive.

Parking attendants organized by municipal authorities and private business networks provide a valuable service. Most wear brightly colored vests; pay them R2–R3 for a short daytime stop and R5–R10 in the evening. Parking in the city center can be a hassle. Longer-stay parking spaces are so scarce that most hotels charge extra for them, and even then you won't be guaranteed a space. For short stays you may get lucky and find metered parking; this requires a special parking card, which you can usually buy from nearby shops or from parking attendants. Be sure to watch while details are fed into the meter. There are numerous pay-and-display (i.e., put a ticket in your windshield) and pay-on-exit parking lots around the city. For central attractions like Greenmarket Square, Parliament, the Company Gardens, museums, the South African National Gallery, and the Castle of Good Hope, park your car on the Grand Parade in Darling Street. The Sanlam Golden Acre Parking Garage, on Adderley Street, offers covered parking, as does the Parkade, on Strand Street.

The main arteries leading out of the city are the N1, which bypasses the city's Northern Suburbs en route to Paarl and, ultimately, Johannesburg, and the N2, which heads out past Khayelitsha and through Somerset West to the Overberg and the Garden Route before continuing on through the Eastern Cape to Durban. The N7 goes up to Namibia and leads off the N1. The M3 splits from the N2 at Hospital Bend, so called because of the high number of accidents and the presence of South Africa's leading teaching hospital, Groote Schuur. The M3 leads to Muizenberg via Claremont, Constantia, and Tokai, and is the main route to the False Bay suburbs on the city's south Peninsula. Expect delays in drive time from 7 to 9 and 4 to 6:30.

Most large car-rental agencies have offices in the city and major suburbs as well as at the airport, and all offer similar rates. You'll pay R200–R250 per day for a basic no-frills vehicle including standard insurance coverage (extended coverage costs more). If you want air-conditioning, power steering, or automatic transmission, you'll pay R250–R300. Rates come down by 10%–20% on longer rentals. Some companies include unlimited mileage, but more common is 200–300 km (125–187 mi) a day plus R1.50–R3 per km thereafter. Try to negotiate if it's low season or you're renting for a longer period. Some companies throw in free delivery and pickup. Expect to pay a bit more on one-way rentals. Airport rentals carry a 10% surcharge, so you may want to pick up a car elsewhere or have it delivered.

Another option is to rent a scooter or motorbike. African Buzz has scooters for around R175 a day (motorcycle license required). Motorcycles can be rented from Mitaka or Moto Berlin at R650–R800 a day for a 650-cc and R900–R1,000 for an 1100-cc machine. At Café Vespa you can rent a trendy Vespa and discuss the rental agreement over an excellent cappuccino. A much cheaper option is to rent a mountain bike from Rent 'n' Ride (which also rents scooters and cars) and do some pedal pushing, from R70 to R100 a day. Bear in mind, however, that distances between attractions can be great.

Roadside Assistance Automobile Association ☎ 0800/01-01-01 ⊕ www.aasa.co.za.

Car-Rental Companies Aroundaboutcars ☎ 021/422-4022 ⊕ www.aroundaboutcars. com. **Avis** ☎ 0861/021-111 ⊕ www.avis.co.za. **Beach Buggy Rentals** ☎ 084/428-4443 ⊕ www.beachbuggyrentals.co.za. **Budget** ☎ 0861/016-622 ⊕ www.budget.co.za. **CABS** ☎ 021/683-1932 ⊕ www.cabs.co.za. **Happy Beetle Company** ☎ 021/426-4170 ⊕ www.thehappybettleco.com. **Hertz** ☎ 0861/600-136 ⊕ www.hertz.co.za. **Imperial Car Rental** ☎ 086/113-1000 ⊕ www.imperialcarrental.co.za. **Value Car Hire** ☎ 021/696-2198 ⊕ www.valuecarhire.co.za.

Motorcycle/Scooter-Rental Companies African Buzz ✉ 202 Long St., Cape Town central ☎ 021/423-0052. **Café Vespa** ✉ 108 Kloof St., Gardens ☎ 021/426-5042 ⊕www.cafevespa.com. **Mitaka** ✉Unit 3, Chiappini Sq., Chiappini St., Green Point ☎082/577-5797 ⊕ www.mitaka.co.za. **Moto Berlin** ✉ Loop and Waterkant Sts., Cape Town central ☎ 021/421-3092. **Rent 'n' Ride** ✉ 243 Main Rd., Three Anchor Bay ☎ 082/881-1588.

DISCOUNTS

For one fee, the Cape Town Pass provides admission to 50 Cape Town–area attractions, including Table Mountain, Robben Island, the Cape of Good Hope, Kirstenbosch, and selected museums. The pass, which comes with its own guide to the attractions, costs R275 for one day, R425 for two days, R495 for three days, and R750 for six days, but covers more than R3,000 worth of entry fees. You can buy the pass from tourism offices, guesthouses and hotels, travel agents, and the Web site.

Cape Town Pass ⊕ www.capetownpass.co.za.

EMBASSIES & CONSULATES

Canada Canadian High Commission ✉ SA Reserve Bank Bldg., 19th floor, St. George's Mall, Box 683, Cape Town central 8000 ☎ 021/423-5240 🖷 021/423-4893 ⊕ www.canada.co.za.

United Kingdom British Consulate ✉ Southern Life Centre, 8 Riebeeck St., 15th floor, Box 500, Cape Town central 8000 ☎021/405-2400 🖷021/405-2447 ⊕www.britain. org.za.

United States U.S.Consulate ✉ Broadway Bldg., Heerengracht and Hertzog Blvd., Box 6773, Roggebaai 8012 ☎ 021/421-4280 🖷 021/425-4151 ⊕ www.usembassy.state. gov/southafrica.

EMERGENCIES

There are several numbers you can call for general emergencies, including Vodacom mobile networks. Metrorail has its own security/emergency number. If you get lost on Table Mountain, call Wilderness Search and Rescue (WSAR)/Metro Rescue, and for all sea emergencies, call the National Sea Rescue Institute (NSRI).

Emergency services at public hospitals are overworked, understaffed, and underfunded. They deal with a huge number of local people, most of whom cannot afford any alternative. Ambulances are provided by the state, but visitors are advised to use private hospitals, which are open 24/7 and have ambulances linked to their private hospital group (although these services can transport patients to any health facility). Most public hospitals have facilities for private patients at lower rates than the fully private hospitals. Make sure that you have medical insurance that's good in South Africa before you leave home.

A number of pharmacies are open from 8 AM to around 10 PM. Most pharmacies display telephone numbers on their door or storefront in case you have an emergency and need medicine during off-hours. (In a real emergency, head to the closest private clinic.)

▣ Emergency Services Ambulance ☎ 10177. **Metrorail** ☎ 0800/210-081. **National Sea Rescue Institute** ☎ 021/449-3500. **Police** ☎ 10111. **Police, Fire, and Ambulance services** ☎ 107 from landline. **Vodacom emergency services** ☎ 112 from mobile phone. **Weather** ☎ 082162. **Wilderness Search and Rescue** ☎ 021/948-9900.

▣ Hospitals Christiaan Barnard Hospital ⊠ 181 Longmarket St., Cape Town central ☎ 021/480-6111. **Claremont Hospital** ⊠ Harfield and Main Rds., Claremont ☎ 021/670-4300. **Constantiaberg Medi-clinic** ⊠ Burnham Rd., Plumstead ☎ 021/799-2911. **Newlands Surgical Clinic** ⊠ Pick 'n Pay Centre, Main Rd., Claremont ☎ 021/683-1220. **Panorama Medi-clinic** ⊠ Rothchild Blvd., Panorama ☎ 021/938-2111.

▣ Pharmacies Lite-Kem Pharmacy ⊠ Scotts Building, 24 Darling St., Cape Town central ☎ 021/461-8040. **Rustenberg Pharmacy** ⊠ Rondebosch Shopping Centre, Main Rd., Rondebosch ☎ 021/686-3997. **Table Bay Pharmacy** ⊠ Shop 6108, V&A Waterfront, Waterfront ☎ 021/418-4556.

HEALTH & SAFETY

There's no reason for paranoia in Cape Town, but there are a few things to look out for. Avoid the city center at night and on Saturday afternoons and Sundays, when it is very quiet. Street kids and roving teens are blamed for much of the petty crime, but sophisticated crime syndicates are often involved, and many of Cape Town's fraudsters are smartly dressed. Cell phones can be snatched from car seats through open windows and even out of people's hands while in use. Watch your pockets at busy transportation interchanges and on trains. Pick a crowded car; if you suddenly find yourself alone, move to another one. Public transportation collapses after dark. Unless you're at the Waterfront or are in a large group, use metered taxis. Better still, rent a car, but don't leave valuables visible and don't park in isolated areas. Poor signage is an issue in Cape Town, especially in the black townships, where most streets still have numbers rather than names and many streets are not signed at all. Carry a good map, and visit township attractions as part of an organized tour with a reputable operator.

As in other major cities, drugs are big in Cape Town. IV drug use carries a high risk of HIV transmission, as does the sex trade. (AIDS is a huge problem in South Africa, so exercise appropriate caution.) The drug of choice for children on the street is glue. You will undoubtedly come across many people begging in Cape Town, including kids, but you are encouraged not to give cash directly to children, as this often supports either a glue habit or adults lurking in the background. If you are concerned and wish to contribute, consider supporting people who sell *The Big Issue* magazine (a worthy organization) or giving food instead of money.

MONEY MATTERS

Most shops, restaurants, hotels, and B&Bs in Cape Town take credit cards, but you generally need cash to buy gas. Surveillance cameras cover most ATMs in the city center, but the money machines are still a magnet for fraudsters. Improvements in security in the central business district have led to increased ATM crime outside the center, so be alert wherever you withdraw cash. Keep your card in your hand, don't be distracted while using an ATM, and decline offers or requests for help. If your card gets swallowed, *stay at the ATM* and call the help line number displayed. If possible, withdraw money during the day and choose ATMs with security guards present or those inside stores.

Don't even think about changing money at your hotel. The rates at most hotels are outrageous, and the city has plenty of banks and bureaus de change offering better rates. Most suburbs have banks in the main streets and malls with currency-exchange facilities and American Express branches open business hours (weekdays and Saturday mornings). Rennies' Waterfront branch is open until 9 daily. At the airport, Trust Bank exchanges currency weekdays 9–3:30 and Saturday 8:30–10:30; it stays open later for international arrivals and departures.
🚩 **Exchange Services American Express** ⊠ Thibault Sq., Cape Town central ☎ 021/425-7991 ⊠ Shop 11A, Alfred Mall, Waterfront ☎ 021/419-3917 ⊕ www.amex.co.za. **Rennies Bank** ⊠ 2 St. George's Mall, Cape Town central ☎ 021/418-1206 ⊠ Upper Level, Victoria Wharf, Waterfront ☎ 021/418-3744.

TAXIS

Taxis are expensive compared with other forms of transportation but offer an easy, quick way to get around the city center. Don't expect to see the throngs of cabs you find in London or New York, as most people in Cape Town use public transportation or their own cars. You'll be lucky to hail one on the street. Taxis don't always use their roof lights to indicate availability, but if you flag down an occupied cab, the driver may radio for another car for you. Your best bet is to summon a cab by phone or head to one of the major taxi stands, such as at Greenmarket Square or either end of Adderley Street, near the Slave Lodge, and outside the train station. For lower rates at night, try prebooking the Backpacker Bus, a shuttle service on Adderley Street. Sea Point Taxis charges R8 per kilometer and R48 an hour for waiting time. Expect to pay R40–R60 for a trip from the city center to the Waterfront. In the Southern Suburbs try phoning Unicab and in the Northern Suburbs Bellville Taxis, or ask at your lodging for local recommendations.

Rikkis are little minivans with open sides that provide a (slow) cheap alternative to taxis. Service is door-to-door, but they may stop at several other doors to pick up additional passengers en route. Rikkis operate limited hours in a limited area. Five rikkis work from the central business district, and three are based at Simon's Town train station. Central rikkis work 7–7 weekdays and 8–4 Saturdays. They go everywhere (including the airport) and have a reasonable fare structure. For example, a one-way trip from the city center to Hout Bay for four people would cost R70. The Simon's Town rikkis (enclosed to protect you from the elements) can also take you anywhere, but the most popular trip is to Cape Point. A two-hour trip for two is about R250 including entry fees. Minibus taxis are another option (⇨ Bus Travel, *above*).
🚩 Taxi Companies **Backpacker Bus** ☎ 021/447-4991. **Bellville Taxis** ☎ 021/949-6918. **Marine Taxis** ☎ 021/434-0434. **Rikkis Central** ☎ 021/423-4888. **Rikkis Simon's**

Town ☎ 021/786-2136 or 073/387-4366 after hours. **Sea Point Taxis** ☎ 021/434-4444. **Unicab** ☎ 021/448-1720 or 021/448-1721.

TOURS

A host of companies offer guided tours of the city center, the south Peninsula, the Winelands, and anyplace else in the Cape you might wish to visit. They differ in type of transportation used and tour focus.

BIKE TOUR Baz Bus tours the south Peninsula with a trailer full of bikes. You cycle the fun parts and sit in the bus for the rest. It costs about R350. Daytrippers specializes in bike tours but uses all sorts of modes of transportation, from bus to boat to foot, to explore the area.

🚻 Tour Operator **Baz Bus** ☎ 021/439-2323 ⊕ www.bazbus.com. **Daytrippers** ☎ 021/ 511-4766 ⊕ www.daytrippers.co.za.

BOAT TOURS Until the middle of the 20th century, most travelers' first glimpse of Cape Town was from the sea, and that's still the best way to get a feeling for the city's impressive setting, with its famous mountain as a backdrop. The Waterfront Boat Company offers trips on a range of boats, from yachts to large motor cruisers. A 1½-hour sunset cruise from the V&A Waterfront costs about R170, and includes a glass of bubbly. *Tigger 2* and Drumbeat charters both run a variety of trips in the Hout Bay area, ranging from sunset cruises to full-day crayfishing expeditions. A trip from Hout Bay to Seal Island, in False Bay, with Drumbeat Charters costs R45 for adults, R20 for kids. The only boat trip to actually land on Robben Island is the museum's ferry (⇨ Exploring Cape Town, *above*).

🚻 Tour Operators **Drumbeat Charters** ☎ 021/791-4441 or 021/790-4859. *Tigger 2* **Charters** ☎ 021/790-5256 ⊕ www.tiggertoo.co.za. **Waterfront Boat Company** ☎ 021/ 418-0134 ⊕ www.waterfrontboats.co.za.

BUS & CAR Large-group bus tours are operated by Hylton Ross, Mother City Tours,
TOURS and Springbok Atlas, among many others. Expect to pay R250–R350 for a half-day trip, about R400–R500 for a full-day tour. A trip on the hop-on/hop-off Cape Town Explorer bus costs R90 for a day ticket through Hylton Ross. Paradise Touring leads tours all around the Cape Town area.

If you're a little more adventurous, contrast the upscale estates of the Winelands with a trip to a *shebeen* (an informal neighborhood bar) with Ferdinand's Tours. Exclusively gay tours are offered by Friends of Dorothy.

Quite a few cultural tours are also offered. Thuthuka Tours offers music and gospel tours of the townships. Grassroute Tours tours the townships as well, in addition to offering a walking tour of Bo-Kaap, which takes in the neighborhood's brightly colored facades and rich history. You can develop your understanding of the destruction brought on by apartheid's forced removals while touring District Six with Our Pride-Bonani. A group of MK veterans (former cadres of the ANC's armed wing, Umkhonto we Sizwe), going by the name Western Cape Action Tours, provide insight into Cape Town's experience of apartheid and resistance. Tours include scenes of struggle and other historical sites as well as development projects, township markets, and housing programs.

A half-day tour is R220 per person (minimum two people), a full-day tour including lunch costs R450 a head (minimum four people), and a customized day trip for a single individual is R800. Though these operators specialize in niche tours, most of them cover mainstream trips like Cape Point and the Winelands, too.

🎦 Tour Operators **Ferdinand's Tours and Adventures** ☎ 021/421-1660 ⊕ www. ferdinandstours.co.za. **Friends of Dorothy** ☎021/465-1871 ⊕www.friendsofdorothytours. co.za. **Grassroute Tours** ☎ 021/706-1006 ⊕ www.grassroutetours.co.za. **Hylton Ross Tours** ☎ 021/511-1784 ⊕ www.hyltonross.co.za. **Mother City Tours** ☎ 021/448-3817 ⊕ www.mctours.co.za. **Our Pride-Bonani** ☎ 021/531-4291 or 022/446-7974. **Paradise Touring** ☎ 021/713-1020 ⊕ www.paradisetouring.co.za. **Springbok Atlas** ☎ 021/460-4700 ⊕ www.springbokatlas.com. **Thuthuka Tours** ☎ 021/433-2429 or 083/979-5831 ⊕ www.townshipcrawling.com. **Western Cape Action Tours** ☎ 021/461-1371 ⊕ www. dacpm.org.za.

HELICOPTER & AIRPLANE TOURS
Helicopters fly from the V&A Waterfront and charge around R5,000 an hour for a three- or four-seater chopper. Civair and NAC/Makana offer tours of the city and surrounding area ranging in length from 20 minutes to several hours. Custom tours can be arranged. Most operators charge between R1,300 and R1,800 for a 20-minute trip and R4,900 to R5,400 for an hour in the air. Adventure Village offers trips in a variety of light aircraft, including helicopters. Flying from Cape Town International Airport, Southern Right Air Charter will fly you over Cape Point and the Winelands with lots in between and will tailor flights to suit. Prices vary according to the number of passengers, but expect to pay around R700 for a one-hour flight.

🎦 Tour Operators **Adventure Village** ☎ 021/424-1580 ⊕ www.adventure-village.co. za. **Civair Helicopters** ☎021/419-5182 ⊕www.civair.co.za. **NAC/Makana Aviation** ☎021/425-3868 ⊕ www.nacmakana.com. **Southern Right Air Charter** ☎ 021/786-1962 or 082/456-5946 ⊕ www.sr.co.za.

WALKING TOURS
Footsteps to Freedom offers two really good walking tours—one of the city and its historical sites and the other of the V&A Waterfront. The guides are friendly and well informed, offer a rare insight into the city, and can help you with tours of the Bo-Kaap and townships. They also have great maps of the city, Peninsula, and Winelands called *Serious Fun Guides,* which you can pick up at various outlets. Bo-Kaap Guided Tours conducts a walking tour that lasts just under two hours and offers an insider's look of the neighborhood. You can also do a walking tour of Langa township as part of Legend Tours' *Walk to Freedom* portfolio. The guides explain the social structures and lifestyles of Cape Town's oldest African precinct, as well as the cultural history of the area.

Take some of the mystery out of Table Mountain with a guide who can share information on the incredible diversity of flora and fauna you'll come across. Join walking and climbing tours with the Cape Town School of Mountaineering, or tag along on a group walk open to everyone (most are on weekends). Pick up a Cumhike timetable from any Cape Union Mart outdoor store (found in almost every mall). A self-guided walking tour of city center attractions was recently developed. Pamphlets can be picked up at Cape Town Tourism. Longer walking tours (four days and longer) outside Cape Town can be arranged through Active Africa, specialized birding walks through Bird-Watch Cape.

Adventure Kalk Bay, a group of concerned longtime citizens, has as its goal to promote and preserve the old fishing way of life in Kalk Bay. Toward that end it arranges for knowledgeable guides for village walks and canoe trips (including rentals) and homestays with fishing families. ⏺ **Tour Operators Active Africa** ☎ 021/461-6658 ⊕ www.active-africa.com. **Adventure Kalk Bay** ☎ 021/788-5113. **Bird-Watch Cape** ☎ 021/762-5059 ⊕ www.birdwatch. co.za. **Bo-Kaap Guided Tours** ☎ 021/422-1554 or 082/423-6932. **Cape Town School of Mountaineering** ☎ 021/531-4290 ⊕ www.ctsm.co.za. **Footsteps to Freedom** ☎ 021/426-4260 or 083/452-1112 ⊕ www.footstepstofreedom.co.za. **Legend Tours** ☎ 021/697-4056 ⊕ www.legendtourism.co.za.

TRAIN TRAVEL

Cape Town's train station is on Adderley Street, in the heart of the city, surrounded by lively rows of street vendors and a taxi stand. The station building and facilities are unattractive but functional (and about to get a major renovation), servicing local, interprovincial, and luxury lines.

Metrorail, Cape Town's commuter line, offers regular service to the Northern Suburbs, including Parow and Bellville; the Cape Flats townships Langa, Nyanga, Mitchell's Plain, and Khayelitsha; the Southern and False Bay suburbs of Observatory, Claremont, Wynberg, Muizenberg, St. James, Kalk Bay, Fish Hoek, and Simon's Town; and the Winelands towns of Paarl, Stellenbosch, and Franschoek (⇨ Chapter 2). The trip to Simon's Town takes 45–60 minutes and costs about R25 for a first-class round-trip ticket, R15 for third class. On weekends several trains carry a popular breakfast car. The train to Khayelitsha costs less than R20 round-trip first class, and a third-class ticket is around half that. The last train leaves about 7 on weekdays, and weekend service is reduced. Timetables change often. If you travel on Metrorail during off-peak periods, avoid isolated cars and compartments, and be alert to your surroundings when the train is stopped. Muggers work trains intensively, slipping on and off with ease. Train security is at best erratic. You're safer standing in a cramped third-class car than sitting comfortably in splendid isolation in an empty first-class one, but watch your pockets.

National carrier Shosholoza Meyl runs the *Trans-Karoo* daily between Cape Town and Johannesburg; the trip takes about 26 hours and costs R500 first class, R335 second class, and R200 economy. First- and second-class cars have sleeping compartments. A weekly train to Durban, *Trans-Oranjia,* takes two days and costs R645 first class. You need to make first- and second-class reservations by phone (bookings open three months before date of travel) and then pay at the station in advance (not just before departure). For a third-class ticket you can pay just before you go. The reservations office is open 8–4 weekdays and 8–10 AM weekends. Transnet's *Union Limited* steam train and Shongololo Express's *Southern Cross* also run through the Karoo and the Garden Route to Johannesburg. The *Southern Cross* is a night ride, so forget about seeing the splendors of the Garden Route en route.

The luxurious and leisurely *Blue Train* has two main routes: Cape Town–Tshwane and Cape Town–Port Elizabeth. It costs around R15,000 one-way inclusive of meals and excursions and departs once or twice a week. (Less frequently, the *Blue Train* runs to Victoria Falls and Hoedspruit, near Kruger National Park.) The Rovos Rail *Pride of Africa* runs from Cape Town to Tshwane every Monday and costs R11,000 for the two-day trip in a deluxe suite, up to R15,000 for a royal suite, including excursions, meals, and drinks. The Spier Vintage Train occasionally steams its way to the Spier Estate, near Stellenbosch, costing R100 round-trip. The schedule changes monthly.

🚆 Train Lines **Blue Train** 📞 021/449-2672 ⊕ www.bluetrain.co.za. **Metrorail** 📞 080/065-6463 ⊕ www.metrorail.co.za. **Rovos Rail** *Pride of Africa* 📞 021/421-4020 ⊕ www.rovos.co.za. **Shongololo Express** 📞 011/781-4616 ⊕ www.shongololo.com. **Shosholoza Meyl** 📞 086/000-8888 ⊕ www.spoornet.co.za/ShosholozaProject/index.jsp. **Spier Vintage Train** 📞 021/419-5222 or 021/419-5223 ⊕ www.spier.co.za. **Transnet** ⊕ www.transnetheritagefoundation.co.za.

VISITOR INFORMATION

Cape Town Tourism is the city's official tourist body and offers information on tours, hotels, restaurants, rental cars, and shops. It has a coffee shop, wineshop, and Internet café. The staff also makes hotel, tour, travel, and walking-tour reservations. It is open weekdays 9–6, Saturday 8:30–2, and Sunday 9–1.

🏢 Tourist Office **Cape Town Tourism** ✉ The Pinnacle at Burg and Castle Sts., Cape Town central 📪 Box 1403, 8000 📞 021/426-4260 📠 021/426-4266 ⊕ www.tourismcapetown.co.za.

The Western Cape

WORD OF MOUTH

"On our second day, we went to the winelands. We decided to spend the day in Franschhoek, taking a circuitous route (via Sir Lowry's Pass) to get there. The scenery was amazing. One minute you feel like you're in Spain, the next like you're in the Western U.S., and the next like you're in Provence. So varied and so spectacular. We very much enjoyed strolling through the delightful town of Franschhoek, and doing a wine tasting at Boschendal nearby."

—dlm

By Andrew
Barbour

Updated by
Karena du
Plessis and
Myrna Robins

THE WESTERN CAPE IS AN ALLURING PROVINCE, a sweep of endless mountain ranges, empty beaches, and European history dating back more than
three centuries and anchored by Cape Town in the southwest. The rich
cultures of the indigenous Khoekhoen and San people—the first inhabitants of this enormous area—also contribute to the region's richness. In
less than two hours you can reach most of the province's highlights from
Cape Town, making the city an ideal base from which to explore.

The historic Winelands, in the city's backyard, produce fine wine amid
the exquisite beauty of rocky mountains, serried vines, and elegant
Cape Dutch estates. By South African standards, this southwestern region of the Cape is a settled land, with a sense of tradition and conti-
nuity lacking in much of the rest of the country. Here farms have been
handed down from one generation to another for centuries, and old-
name families like the Cloetes and Myburghs have become part of the
fabric of the region.

Even first-time visitors may notice subtle differences between these
Cape Afrikaners and their more conservative cousins in the hinterland.
For the most part they are descendants of the landed gentry and educated classes who stayed in the Cape after the British takeover in 1806
and the emancipation of the slaves in 1834. Not for them the hard un-
certainties of the Great Trek, when ruddy-faced Boer (South Africans
of Dutch or Huguenot descent) farmers, outraged at British interven-
tion, loaded their families into ox wagons and set off into the unknown,
a rifle in one hand and a Bible in the other.

The genteel atmosphere of the southwestern Cape fades quickly the farther from Cape Town you go. The Overberg, separated from the city
by the Hottentots Holland Mountains, presides over the rocky headland of Cape Agulhas, where the Indian and Atlantic oceans meet (officially) at the southernmost tip of the continent. Unspoiled beaches and
coastal mountains are the lure of this remote area. North of Cape Town
on the West Coast, civilization drops away altogether, bar a few lonely
fishing villages and mining towns. Each spring, though, the entire region explodes in a spectacular wildflower display that slowly spreads
inland to the desiccated Namaqualand and the Cederberg.

Wildflowers are one extraordinary element of a region truly blessed by
nature. The Western Cape is famous for its *fynbos* (pronounced *feign*-
boss), the hardy, thin-leaf vegetation that gives much of the province its
distinctive look. Fynbos composes a major part of the Cape floral kingdom, the smallest and richest of the world's six floral kingdoms. More
than 8,500 plant species are found in the province, of which 5,000 grow
nowhere else on earth. The region is dotted with nature reserves where
you can hike through this profusion of flora, admiring the majesty of
the king protea or the shimmering leaves of the silver tree. When the
wind blows and mist trails across the mountainsides, the fynbos-cov-
ered landscape takes on the look of a Scottish heath.

Not surprisingly, people have taken full advantage of the Cape's natural bonanza. In the Overberg and along the West Coast, rolling wheat

Many people come to the Western Cape after getting a big-game fix in Mpumalanga. Although it's possible to explore Cape Town and the Winelands in three or four days—the area is compact enough to allow it—you need six or seven to do it justice. You can get a good sense of either the Overberg or the West Coast on a three- or four-day jaunt, but set aside a week if you plan to tackle more than one or two of the regions in this chapter.

Numbers in the text correspond to numbers in the margin and on the Western Cape and Winelands maps.

2

If you have
3 days

Spend your first morning looking around **Stellenbosch ❷**. In the afternoon head off along the R304 toward **Simonsig** and **Villiera** for some wine tasting, and continue to 🖫 **Paarl ❹** for a gourmet meal at the Grande Roche. If you feel like a second day of wine tasting, head to **Franschhoek ❺** and **Backsberg**, either before or after you visit **Fairview**, timing it for lunchtime so you can taste some goat cheese with your wine. Then make your way to **Rhebokskloof** for some wine tasting and a horseback ride through the vines. Return to Paarl via **Nelson's Creek**, and sample some of the New Beginnings wines. On your third day take a long, scenic route to Cape Town. Leave Paarl on the R45, and drive through Franschhoek and up the Franschhoek Pass toward Villiersdorp, Grabouw, and Elgin. If you're short on time, turn right on the N2 at Grabouw and head straight back to Cape Town. If you have plenty of time, turn left on the N2 at Elgin, and go over the pass that takes you into the Overberg. Turn off the N2 on the R43, and follow the signs to **Kleinmond ⑪** on the R41. Return to Cape Town via Kleinmond, Betty's Bay, Pringle Bay, and **Gordon's Bay ⑩**. The view over False Bay from this coastal road is fantastic—especially toward sunset. If you'd rather not spend Day 2 wine tasting, take a drive over Sir Lowry's Pass through Elgin to 🖫 **Greyton ⑯**, where you can wander around the village and Genadendal by day and spend the night at a charming guesthouse. Spend the morning of Day 3 in Greyton before heading back to Cape Town via the coastal road as described above.

If you have
5 days

Take the N7 north out of Cape Town to the area around 🖫 **Clanwilliam ㉑**, at the edge of the Cederberg. (The drive to the Clanwilliam area will take you through the Swartland and the beginning of the wildflower route, which is best in spring. Spend the second day here, taking in all that the inspiring local environment has to offer. On the third morning head west to the coast, and drive south through fishing villages, stopping for lunch at one of the great restaurants in **Elands Bay ⑳** or **Paternoster ⑰**. Carry on to **Langebaan ⑱** and the West Coast National Park, ending in 🖫 **Paarl ❹**, where you could spend two days. From here it is a comfortable, 90-minute drive back to Cape Town on the fifth day. Alternatively, choose one of these destinations, and combine it with the three-day itinerary, above.

If you have
7 days

Spend the first two days as described in the five-day itinerary. Then choose between the rest of that itinerary or heading through **Riebeek Kasteel ㉓** and Wellington to 🖫 **Paarl ❹**, where you can spend the next two or three days as in the three-day itinerary. If you followed the full five-day itinerary, you can then spend your last days in Paarl, or head farther south to the coast. (If you spent the middle days in Paarl, then pick up the itinerary here.) Drive through **Franschhoek** ❸ to the N2 and off on the R43. Spend your last two nights in ▣ **Hermanus** ⓬ or ▣ **Arniston** ⓮, using your days to explore the coast. If it's winter, watch whales. If you're not all wined out, taste some of the Overberg wines. Drive back to Cape Town via Betty's Bay and **Gordon's Bay** ❿ as described in the three-day itinerary.

---

fields extend to the horizon, while farther inland jagged mountain ranges hide fertile valleys of apple orchards, orange groves, and vineyards. At sea hardy fishermen battle icy swells to harvest succulent crayfish (Cape lobsters), delicate *perlemoen* (abalone), and line fish, such as the delicious *kabeljou*. Each June–November, hundreds of whales return to the Cape shores to calve, and the stretch of coastline that includes Hermanus, now referred to as the Whale Coast, becomes one of the best places for land-based whale-watching in the world.

For untold centuries this fertile region supported the Khoekhoen (Khoikhoi) and San (Bushmen), indigenous peoples who lived off the land as pastoralists and hunter-gatherers. With the arrival of European settlers, however, they were chased off, killed as vermin, or enslaved. In the remote recesses of the Cederberg and along the West Coast you can still see the fading rock paintings left by the San, whose few remaining clans have long since retreated into the Kalahari Desert. The population of the Western Cape today is largely "coloured," a catchall term to describe South Africans of mixed race and descendants of imported slaves, the San, the Khoekhoen, and European settlers.

Exploring the Western Cape

The best way to explore the Western Cape is to rent a car and take to the roads. You need to be flexible to enjoy all this region has to offer, and public transportation is too limited. Navigating your way around is not difficult. There are three main routes out of the city: the N1, N2, and N7. The N1 and N2 take you to the Winelands of Stellenbosch, Franschhoek, and Paarl, and the N7 heads up the West Coast. To reach the Overberg, take the N2 out of town and head up over Sir Lowry's Pass. To the east is the historically significant and scenic Swellendam area, nestled under the towering Langeberg Mountains. Off the main road to the south is the coast and the southern tip of Africa, Cape Agulhas. This southern coastal part of Overberg, containing the small towns and villages of Gordon's Bay, Betty's Bay, Kleinmond, Hermanus, Stanford, and Gansbaai, is usually referred to as the Overstrand. (*Strand* is Afrikaans for "beach.")

About the Restaurants

The Western Cape dining scene ranges from fine South African cuisine complete with silver service to local, laid-back, country-style cooking. Franschhoek restaurants attract some of the country's most innovative

Cape Dutch Architecture

As you travel around the region, the most visible emblems of settler culture you'll encounter are the Cape Dutch–style houses. Here 18th- and 19th-century manor houses share certain characteristics: thick whitewashed walls, thatch roofs curving around elegant gables, and small-pane windows framed by wooden shutters. It's a classic look—a uniquely Cape look—ideally suited to a land that is hot in summer and cold in winter. The Cape Dutch style developed in the 18th century from traditional long houses: simple rectangular sheds capped by thatch. As farmers became more prosperous, they added the ornate gables and other features. Several estates, most notably Vergelegen and Boschendal, have opened their manor houses as museums.

2

Glorious Golf

You shouldn't have a problem finding a course to your liking in the Western Cape. There are plenty of options within a 45-minute drive of the center of the Winelands, and the number of courses grows each year. All accept foreign visitors, most rent clubs, and they typically charge greens fees of R300–R400. Two of the best area courses are the Gary Player–designed Erinvale, in Somerset West, and the stunning Arabella Golf Club, which is part of the Western Cape Hotel & Spa, on the Bot River lagoon between Kleinmond and Hermanus.

Wine Touring

Few places in the world can match the drama of the Winelands, where mountains rise above vine-covered valleys and 300-year-old homesteads snooze in the shade of giant oaks. It's a place of such enviable beauty that you might catch yourself glancing through the local real-estate pages. With this as a backdrop, you can visit scores of wineries, which open their doors to visitors—to tour their cellars, taste their vintages, or dine at their restaurant or with a picnic basket on the grounds (with a bottle of wine, of course). Wine farms, especially the small family-run ones, can be idiosyncratic. Many owners won't charge you for a tasting as long as you're not in a group, and if they're in a good mood or take a shine to you, they might even throw in a free tour. But you can't count on it. Most wineries expect you to call in advance to arrange for cellar tours. Though the greatest concentration of wineries is in the Winelands, there are others scattered about the Overberg, Breede River Valley, and even the Cederberg and Swartland. Keep in mind that some wineries close for lunch during the week, shut at midday on Saturday, and don't open at all on Sunday.

---

chefs, who aren't afraid to experiment with unusual ingredients or food and wine combinations, and offer up a very sophisticated dining experience in a gorgeous setting. West Coast fare is not as urban as what you find in the Winelands, and coastal towns usually concentrate on seafood, especially served in open-air restaurants. Farther inland the cuisine tends to be less trendy and the portions more generous. Be sure to try some Cape Malay cuisine, characterized by mild, slightly sweet curries and aromatic spices. The only places you're likely to be disappointed in the food are in smaller agricultural towns in the Overberg or up the West Coast, where overcooked veggies and an uninspiring and indistinguishable roast are still the norm.

Country restaurants tend to serve lunch from noon and dinner from 6 and do not cater to late diners except on weekends. Because these areas rely heavily on tourists and local day-trippers, most restaurants in the Winelands and seaside towns are open on the weekends, especially for leisurely Sunday lunches, but may catch their breath on Sunday evenings or quieter Mondays. Dress code varies as much as the dining experience. Casual wear is acceptable during the day and at most restaurants in the evening. On the coast people pull shorts and T-shirts over their swimsuits before tucking into a plate of calamari and chips (fries), but some Winelands restaurants like their patrons to look as good as the cuisine they deliver. Even so, a nice pair of jeans or pants and a good shirt are usually enough; jackets and ties are rarely expected. If there's someplace you really want to eat, reserve ahead. In December and January, popular restaurants book up quickly, and reservations are advised at least a day or two in advance.

WHAT IT COSTS In South African rand					
	$$$$	$$$	$$	$	¢
RESTAURANTS	over 125	100–125	75–100	50–75	under 50

Prices are per person for a main course at dinner, a main course equivalent, or a prix-fixe meal.

About the Hotels

The Winelands are sufficiently compact that you can make one hotel your touring base. Stellenbosch and Paarl offer the most flexibility, situated close to dozens of wineries and restaurants as well as the major highways to Cape Town. Here bed-and-breakfasts and self-catering (with cooking facilities) options are often less expensive than hotels, and provide a better taste of life in the country. Franschhoek is comparatively isolated, which many visitors consider a blessing. The West Coast, Cederberg, and Overberg are a bit more spread out, so you'll want to stay in one place for a day or two and then move on. During the peak season of December–January, book well in advance, and be prepared for mandatory two-night stays on weekends. Although the winter months of June–September are usually a lot quieter and bring negotiable rates, seaside towns get really busy (and booked up) when the whales arrive to calve. The same is true up the West Coast during flower season.

WHAT IT COSTS In South African rand					
	$$$$	$$$	$$	$	¢
HOTELS	over 3,000	2,000–3,000	1,000–2,000	500–1,000	under 500

Prices are for a standard double room in high season, including 12.5% tax.

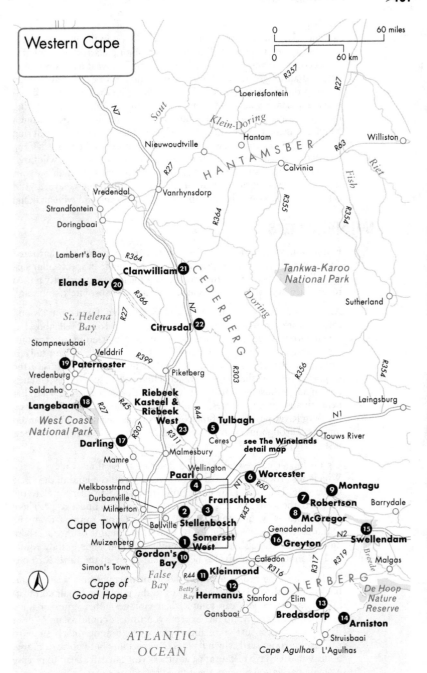

Western Cape

Loeriesfontein

N7

Sout

Klein-Doring

R357

R27

Hantam

H A N T A M S B E R

Williston

R63

Riet

Fish

Nieuwoudtville

Calvinia

R355

R34

Vredendal

Vanrhynsdorp

R364

Strandfontein

Doringbaai

R27

Tankwa-Karoo
National Park

Lambert's Bay

R364

Clanwilliam 21

C E D E R B E R G

Doring

Sutherland

Elands Bay 20

R366

St. Helena
Bay

R27

N7

Citrusdal 22

R356

Stompneusbaai

Velddrif

R399

19 Paternoster

Piketberg

R303

Laingsburg

Vredenburg

Saldanha

Langebaan 18

R27

R45

R307

**Riebeek
Kasteel &
Riebeek
West**

R44

Tulbagh 5

N1

Touws River

West Coast
National Park

R311

23

Ceres

see The Winelands
detail map

Darling 17

Mamre

Malmesbury

Wellington

Paarl 4

N1

6 Worcester

R60

9 Montagu

Melkbosstrand

Durbanville

Milnerton

Franschhoek 3

R43

7 Robertson

Barrydale

2

8 McGregor

Cape Town

Bellville

Stellenbosch

Genadendal

N2

15

Muizenberg

**1 Somerset
West**

16 Greyton

Swellendam

Simon's Town

**Gordon's
Bay 10**

False
Bay

Caledon

R317

R319

Malgas

Cape of
Good Hope

R44

Kleinmond 11

R316

O V E R B E R G

Breede

De Hoop
Nature
Reserve

Betty's
Bay

12

Stanford

Elim

13

Hermanus

Gansbaai

Bredasdorp

Arniston 14

ATLANTIC
OCEAN

Struisbaai

Cape Agulhas

L'Agulhas

0 — 60 miles

0 — 60 km

Timing

Summer (late November–January) is high season in the Western Cape, and during that time you will seldom visit major places of interest without encountering busloads of fellow visitors. The weather is warm and dry, and although strong southeasterly winds can be a nuisance, they do keep the temperature bearable. If soaking up the sun is not of primary importance, and you prefer to tour during quieter times, spring (September and October) and autumn–early winter (late March through May) are ideal. The weather is milder, and the lines are shorter. Spring also brings southern right whales close to the shores of the Western Cape to calve, and late August–October are the months to see the wildflowers explode across the West Coast. If the Winelands are high on your list of must-dos, remember that the busiest time in the vineyards and cellars is January–April, when they begin harvesting and wine making.

THE WINELANDS

Frank Prial, wine critic for the *New York Times,* wrote that he harbored "a nagging suspicion that great wines must be made in spectacular surroundings." If that's true, then the Cape Winelands are perfectly poised to produce fantastic wines, because the setting is absolutely stunning.

All of this lies only 45 minutes east of Cape Town, fanned out around three historic towns and their valleys. Founded in 1685, Stellenbosch is a gem. Its oak-lined streets bristle with historic architecture, good restaurants, and interesting galleries and shops, and it has a vibrant university community. Franschhoek, enclosed by towering mountains, is the original home of the Cape's French Huguenots, whose descendants have made a conscious effort to reassert their French heritage. Paarl lies beneath huge granite domes, its main street running 11 km (7 mi) along the Berg River past some of the country's most elegant historical monuments. Throughout the region you will find some of South Africa's best restaurants and hotels.

It's no longer entirely accurate to describe these three valleys as *the* Winelands. Today they make up only 32% of all the land in the Cape under vine. This wine-growing region is now so vast you can trek to the fringes of the Karoo Desert, in the northeast, and still find a grape. There are around 16 wine routes in the Western Cape, ranging from the Olifants River, in the north, to the coastal mountains of the Overberg and beyond. There's also a well-established Winelands brandy route, and an annual port festival is held in Calitzdorp, in the Little Karoo.

Each of the wine-producing areas has its own wine route, where member wineries throw open their estates to the public and maintain tasting rooms where you can sample their vintages either gratis or for a nominal fee. Happily, no one expects you to be a connoisseur, or even to buy the wines. Just relax and enjoy yourself, and don't hesitate to ask tasting-room staff which flavors to expect in what you're drinking. Some wineries have restaurants; at others you can call ahead to reserve a picnic basket to enjoy on the estate grounds.

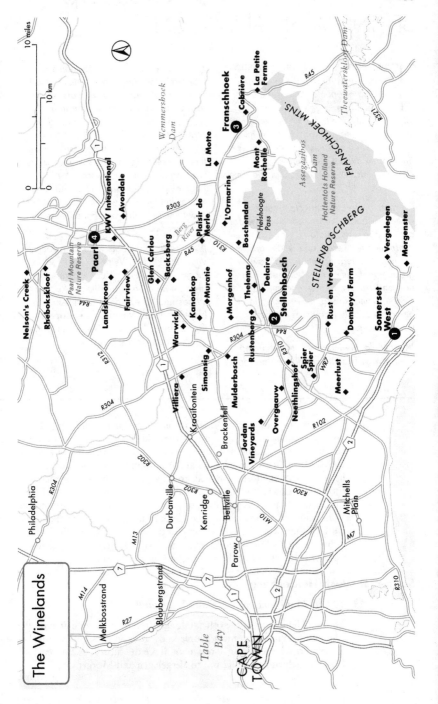

The Winelands

10 miles

10 km

Philadelphia

Melkbosstrand

Blouebergstrand

Durbanville

Kenridge

Bellville

Parow

Brackenfell

Kraaifontein

CAPE TOWN

Table Bay

Mitchells Plain

Somerset West ❶

Vergelegen

Morgenster

Paarl ❹

KWV International

Avondale

Nelson's Creek

Rhebokskloof

Landskroon

Fairview

Glen Carlou

Backsberg

Plaisir de Merle

La Motte

L'Ormarins

Boschendal

Helshoogte Pass

Mont Rochelle

Franschhoek ❸

Cabrière

La Petite Ferme

Stellenbosch ❷

Delaire

Thelema

Morgenhof

Muratie

Kanonkop

Warwick

Simonsig

Mulderbosch

Rustenberg

Overgaauw

Jordan Vineyards

Neethlingshof

Spier Spier

Meerlust

Rust en Vrede

Dombeya Farm

Villiera

Paarl Mountain Nature Reserve

Hottentots Holland Nature Reserve

Assegaaibos Dam

Wemmershoek Dam

Theewaterskloof Dam

Berg River

STELLENBOSCHBERG

FRANSCHHOEK MTNS

R45

R303

R310

R44

R304

R310

R102

R300

R312

R304

R302

R302

M13

M14

R27

M10

M7

R310

R321

CloseUp
BEHIND WINELANDS WINE

THE SOUTH AFRICAN WINE INDUSTRY is booming. Buried by sanctions during apartheid, South African wines were largely unknown internationally. But today there's enormous interest in South African reds and whites, and good-quality wines at varied prices are readily available—even in supermarkets. Wine drinking has become part of daily life.

Currently red-wine production outstrips white; the quality continually improves for both. Cape reds regularly win international awards, and whites are gaining. Pinotage, South Africa's own grape variety, is a cross between pinot noir and cinsaut (formerly hermitage). Chenin blanc is used in everything from blends to bubbly (known as Methode Cap Classique).

Meanwhile, the industry is transforming itself slowly. Though illegal, the dop (drink) system, in which farmers pay some of laborers' wages in wine, is still practiced on some outlying farms, with disastrous results, as many workers suffer from alcoholism. But things are changing. Many international companies refuse to import wine from farms that don't secure their workers' rights, and some farms are working at black empowerment. New Beginnings at Nelson's Creek and Thandi Wines in Elgin are two pioneers, but only Mont Rochelle, in Franschhoek, is solely black owned.

If you're serious about wine, arm yourself with John Platter's Wine Guide or Wine magazine, featuring local wineries. For an in-depth read and fantastic photos, get Wines and Vineyards of South Africa or New World of Wine from the Cape of Good Hope: The Definitive Guide to the South African Wine Industry.

The secret to touring the Winelands is not to hurry. Dally over lunch on a vine-shaded veranda at a 300-year-old estate, enjoy an afternoon nap under a spreading oak, or sip wine while savoring the impossible views. Of the scores of wineries and estates in the Winelands, the ones listed below are chosen for their great wine, their beauty, or their historic significance. It would be a mistake to try to cover them all in less than a week. You have nothing to gain from hightailing it around the Winelands other than a headache. If your interest is more aesthetic and cultural than wine driven, you would do well to focus on the historic estates of Stellenbosch and Franschhoek. Most Paarl wineries stand out more for the quality of their wine than for their beauty.

Somerset West (Helderberg)

❶ *40 km (25 mi) southeast of Cape Town on the N2.*

Though Helderberg is the official designation for this wine area on the edge of the Winelands, most people know it as Somerset West. Just before you reach the center of town you'll see the turnoff to Lourensford Road, which runs 3 km (2 mi) to Vergelegen and Morgenster.

★ **Vergelegen** was established in 1700 by Willem Adriaan van der Stel, who succeeded his father as governor of the Cape. His traditional Cape Dutch homestead, with thatch roof and gables, looks like something out of a fairy tale. An octagonal walled garden aflame with flowers surrounds it, and huge camphor trees, planted almost 300 years ago, stand as gnarled sentinels. The estate was purchased for Lady Florence Phillips by her husband, mining magnate Sir Lionel Phillips, in 1917, and she spent vast sums on the restoration of the homestead, library, and gardens. The homestead is now a museum and is furnished in period style. Other historic buildings include a magnificent library and the old stables, now the reception area and interpretive center. Behind the house, the Lady Phillips Restaurant serves lunch and tea, and the Rose Terrace café looks onto a formal rose garden. Much of the fresh produce is supplied by the Margaret Roberts Herb and Vegetable Garden, which is next to the reception area.

Although Vergelegen still buys grapes from neighboring farms, the vineyards that were planted in 1989, during what is described as the renaissance of the farm, are beginning to give an inkling of some very good wines to come. The flagship Vergelegen is a Bordeaux-style blend, whereas the merlot has ripe, plummy flavors. The chardonnay has touches of wood fermentation but is dominated by a fresh citrus nose. Reservations are essential for the tours. ⊠ *Lourensford Rd.* ☎ *021/847–1334* ⊕ *www.vergelegen.co.za* ⊠ *Tastings R10* ☉ *Daily 9:30–4; guided tours daily at 8:30; cellar tours daily at 10:30, 11:30, and 3.*

South Africans are beginning to produce extra-virgin olive oils that are as excellent as their wines. To learn about this fruit of the local fields, take the turnoff just before Vergelegen to **Morgenster** (Morning Star). This historic estate, part of Cape governor van der Stel's original farm, has been restored and is now producing some of the best oils in the country. Five different cultivars—frantoio, leccino, favoloza, coratina, and peranzana—are pressed individually before they're blended. You can taste the olives, the oil, and delicious olive paste. The estate also produces good Bordeaux-style reds. Watch for the flagship Morgenster label and the promising Lourens River Valley red blend, named after the river that runs past the property. ⊠ *Vergelegen Ave., off Lourensford Rd* ☎ *021/852–1738* ⊕ *www.morgenster.co.za* ⊠ *Tastings R10* ☉ *Daily 10–5.*

Nestled against the base of the Helderberg mountain and shaded by giant oaks, the peaceful **Rust en Vrede** winery looks over steep slopes of vines and roses. Owned by former Springbok rugby great Jannie Engelbrecht, it's a comparatively small estate that specializes entirely in red wine—and produces some of the very best in South Africa. Rust en Vrede Estate is the flagship wine, a blend of predominantly cabernet sauvignon, shiraz, and just over 10% merlot grapes. It has already won several awards both locally and abroad, but it would do well to mature in the bottle for another 10 years or more. Another interesting wine is the shiraz, which has an inviting, spicy bouquet with a mellowness imparted by the American oak in which it is matured, but none of the characteristic cloying sweetness; it will age from five to eight years. ⊠ *R44, between Somer-*

set West and Stellenbosch ☎ *021/881–3881* ⊕ *www.rustenvrede.com* ✉ *Tastings free* ⊘ *May–Sept., weekdays 9–5, Sat. 9–3; Oct.–Apr., weekdays 9–5, Sat. 9–4.*

Next door to Rust en Vrede is **Dombeya Farm,** one of the few places in the Western Cape to see spinning and hand weaving. The farm makes jerseys, blankets, and rugs from merino wool, all in the bright, floral patterns that are Dombeya's hallmark. The shop also sells knitting patterns and wool. A garden restaurant serves light lunches and snacks. ⊠ *Annandale Rd., between Somerset West and Stellenbosch* ☎☎ *021/881–3746* ⊕ *www.dombeyayarns.co.za* ✉ *Free* ⊘ *Daily 9–5.*

need a break?

You can't drive down the R44 between Somerset West and Stellenbosch without noticing the remarkable scarecrows at **Mooiberge Farm Stall.** They're riding bicycles, driving tractors, and working in the strawberry fields, where you can spend a morning picking the luscious red fruit. The strawberry season varies from one year to the next but usually begins in October and runs to February. You pay for what you pick, and you can also buy jams, dried fruit, and other refreshments at the farm stall. Look for the interesting display of old farm implements at the side of the building. ⊠ *R44, between Somerset West and Stellenbosch* ☎ *021/881–3222* ✉ *Free* ⊘ *Daily 8–6.*

Where to Stay & Eat

$$$$ ✕ **L'Auberge du Paysan.** This little cottage near Somerset West offers a formally presented mélange of southern and classic French cuisine that makes good use of South African game birds and venison. Tall upholstered chairs, small brass table lamps, and snowy linen create a Gallic setting for first courses like delicate *coquille de mer* (seafood in a lobster sauce topped with Parmesan cheese) or frogs' legs panfried in an herb and garlic butter. Fish entrées could include fresh kabeljou topped with a *dijonnaise* (dijon mustard seeds, sherry, and cream) sauce or bouillabaisse, and guinea fowl is given traditional cassoulet treatment. Seasonal berries—filling meringue baskets, pureed into sorbets, and teamed with spiked chantilly cream—create irresistible desserts. ⊠ *Raithby Rd., off R44 between Somerset West and Stellenbosch* ☎ *021/842–2008* ▤ *AE, DC, MC, V* ⊘ *Closed Mon. No lunch Sat.; no dinner Sun.*

$$$–$$$$ ✕ **96 Winery Road.** This relaxed venue, with its rustic decor, is always buzzing with folk from the wine industry, regulars, and up-country visitors. Inside, farm implements hang on butternut-bright walls, while outside terrace seating offers soothing mountain views. The menu tempts with such fresh and flavorful first courses as prawn tempura and salmon and line fish sashimi. Steak lovers are treated well here; dry-aged cuts of prime beef are grilled and teamed with a variety of sauces. An eggplant, tomato, and feta stack topped with hummus and fresh herbs is a meatless delight. A good cheese board makes a savory—and many think, superior—option to rich desserts. ⊠ *Zandberg Farm, Winery Rd., between Somerset West and Stellenbosch* ☎ *021/842–2020* ⚭ *Reservations essential* ▤ *AE, DC, MC, V* ⊘ *No dinner Sun.*

$$$ ✕ **Lady Phillips Restaurant.** In summer you need to reserve a table three weeks in advance at this idyllic country restaurant on the Vergelegen

Estate. As long as weather allows, ask for a table on the terrace, shaded by liquid amber trees. Consider starting with Cajun crocodile carpaccio with chili-lime sorbet before moving on to homemade crab and asparagus ravioli with sautéed leeks in white wine velouté. If you want game, try the delicious duo of warthog and eland fillet with fried sweet butternut wedges and ribbon zucchini. Of the wide dessert selection, the glazed orange ice cream wrapped in phyllo pastry, deep fried, and served with a burnt white-chocolate sauce and granadilla coulis is noteworthy. If you can't get a reservation, head to the Rose Terrace during summer for light meals. ☒ *Vergelegen Estate, Lourensford Rd.* ☎ *021/847–1346* ⌂ *Reservations essential* ☰ *AE, DC, MC, V* ☾ *No dinner.*

$$$$ ✕⌂ **Willowbrook Lodge.** This lodge makes a good base for exploring the entire southwestern Cape, including the peninsula, the Winelands, and the Overberg. The lodge lies hidden among beautiful gardens that extend down to the Lourens River; in the distance the peaks of the Helderberg are visible. It's a very peaceful place, with large, airy, comfortable rooms and sliding doors opening onto the gardens. D'Vine Restaurant ($–$$$) has equally high standards and regularly gets voted onto the country's top-100 list. The seasonally changing menu might include rabbit and apricot pie or crispy tiger prawns, and a separate vegetarian menu has delights such as cheese and celery soufflé and mushroom tortellini. ☒ *Morgenster Ave., Box 1892, 7129* ☎ *021/851–3759* 🖷 *021/851–4152* ⊕ *www.willowbrook.co.za* ⇪ *11 rooms, 1 suite* ⌂ *Restaurant, pool, bar; no kids under 12* ☰ *AE, DC, MC, V* ⦿ *BP.*

Sports & the Outdoors

The Gary Player–designed **Erinvale Golf Club** (☒ Lourensford Rd. ☎ 021/847–1144) is beautifully nestled beneath the Hottentots Holland Mountains. It costs around R495 to play 18 holes and about R330 for 9, R250–R300 to rent clubs, and approximately R210 for a golf cart (there are no caddies). You can book only one week in advance. **Somerset West Golf Club** (☒ Rue de Jacqueline ☎ 021/852–2925) is an easy course with plenty of leeway for errant tee shots, except when the wind blows. Greens fees run about R240 for 18 holes (half that for 9 holes), and club rental is around R120. Golf carts are available for around R165, but you are encouraged to make use of the caddies for around R80, excluding tip.

Stellenbosch

★ ❷ *15 km (9½ mi) north of Somerset West.*

You could easily while away a week in this small, sophisticated, beautiful, and absolutely delightful town. South Africa's second-oldest municipality, after Cape Town, Stellenbosch actually *feels* old, unlike so many other historic towns. Wandering the oak-shaded streets, which still have open irrigation furrows (known as the *lei water,* pronounced "lay vaater"), you'll see some of the finest examples of Cape Dutch, Georgian, Victorian, and Regency architecture in the country. The town was founded in 1679 by Simon van der Stel, first governor of the Cape, who recognized the agricultural potential of this fertile valley.

Wheat was the major crop grown by the early settlers, but vineyards now blanket the surrounding hills. Stellenbosch is considered the center of the Winelands, and many of the older and more established wineries are situated nearby. Wine routes fan out like spokes of a wheel, making excellent day trips if you're staying in town. The town is also home to the University of Stellenbosch, the country's first and most prestigious Afrikaner university.

A brief walking tour of the town starts at the corner of Dorp Street and the R44, where you first enter Stellenbosch. Look for street names written in yellow on curbs; they're easy to miss, so remember to look down and not up.

Stroll up oak-lined **Dorp Street,** Stellenbosch's most historic avenue. Almost the entire street is a national monument, flanked by lovely, restored homes from every period of the town's history. Redolent of tobacco, dried fish, and spices, **Oom Samie Se Winkel** is a 19th-century-style general dealer and one of Stellenbosch's most popular landmarks. In addition to the usual Cape kitsch, Oom Samie's sells some genuine South African produce, including *witblitz* and *mampoer,* both Afrikaner versions of moonshine. The shop operates a wine-export business and restaurant too. ✉ *82–84 Dorp St.* ☎ *021/887–0797* ⊘ *Weekdays 8:30–6, weekends 9–5:30.*

As you continue up Dorp Street, keep an eye out for the historic **La Gratitude home** (✉ 95 Dorp St.), built in the early 18th century in traditional Cape Dutch town-house style. The all-seeing eye of God molded on its gable was designed as a talisman to watch over the owner's property and keep him and his family safe from harm.

Voorgelegen (✉ 176 Dorp St.) and the houses on either side of it form one of the best-preserved Georgian ensembles in town. When you reach Andringa Street, turn left and then right onto Church (also called Kerk) Street. On your left is **d'Ouwe Werf** (✉ 30 Church St.). Possibly the country's oldest boardinghouse, it first took in paying guests in 1802.

At the corner of Church and Ryneveld streets, the **Stellenbosch Village Museum** comprises four dwellings scattered within a two-block radius. Dating from different periods in Stellenbosch's history, the houses have been furnished to reflect changing lifestyles and tastes. The oldest is the very basic Schreuderhuis, which dates from 1709. The others date from 1789, 1803, and 1850. ✉ *18 Ryneveld St.* ☎ *021/887–2902* ⊕ *www.museums.org.za/stellmus/village_museum.htm* ✉ *R15* ⊘ *Mon.–Sat. 9:30–5, Sun. 10–5.*

Continue down Ryneveld to Plein Street. Turn left and walk to the **Braak,** the grassy town square. Some of Stellenbosch's most historic buildings face the square, which is a national monument. At the southern end is the **Rhenish Church** (✉ Bloem St.), erected by the Missionary Society of Stellenbosch in 1823 as a training school for slaves and blacks. **St. Mary's Church** stands at the far end of the Braak. Built in 1852, it reflects the growing influence of the English in Stellenbosch. Across Bloem Street from St. Mary's is the **Burgher House,** built in 1797. Today it houses the offices of Historical Homes in South Africa.

STELLENBOSCH WINE ROUTE

Along R310. West of town, the R310 (also known locally as Baden Powell Avenue) forks to the left, but go straight on the M12; **Neethlingshof** is on your left. Next turn right on the Stellenbosch Kloof Road, where **Overgaauw** is a merlot mainstay. Follow the winding road through pretty vineyards; at the end is **Jordan**, known for its whites. Double-back to the fork, and take the R310 to your right to the touristy but fun **Spier**. Next up this road is **Meerlust** with its submerged windmill.

If you drive east on the R310 from Stellenbosch, detour up the Idasvallei Road and follow a narrow lane through cattle pastures and oak groves to **Rustenberg**, which focuses on reds. Then it's up and over the scenic Helshoogte Pass to **Thelema Mountain Vineyards**, which has knockout reds and whites. Its neighbor, **Delaire**, is a great lunch spot.

Along R44. Some important wineries are on the R44 north of Stellenbosch. At **Morgenhof** you can sip chardonnay and pinotage and linger for lunch. About a mile farther on the R44, turn right on the Knorhoek Road to reach low-frills **Muratie**, with some good reds. Back on the R44, continue to **Kanonkop**, known for terrific pinotage, and perhaps **Warwick**, with great red blends, or turn left on the Kromme Rhee Road and visit **Simonsig**, home to wonderful bubbly.

Along R304. This road shoots northwest from Stellenbosch past several wine farms. Stop at **Mulderbosch** for its excellent white wines. Cross over the Kromme Rhee Road and on to **Villiera**, known for sparkling wine and lush sauvignon blanc.

Next to the Burgher House, on a traffic island in Market Street, stands the **V.O.C. Arsenal,** also known as the V.O.C. *Kruithuis* (powder house). It took 91 years for the political council to decide that Stellenbosch needed its own magazine, and just six months in 1777 to complete the structure. Today the arsenal contains a wide selection of guns, gunpowder holders, and cannons. If the arsenal is closed, call or pop into the **Toy and Miniature Museum** (☎ 021/886–7888), on the Braak, and someone will open it up for you. ⊠ *Bloem St.* ☎ *021/886–4153* 🖼 *R5* ☉ *Sept.–May, weekdays 9–2.*

Walk down Market Street past the Tourist Information Bureau. On your left, facing a large lawn, is the **Rhenish Complex** (⊠ Bloem St.), one of the most impressive restoration projects ever undertaken in South Africa and a good example of what early Stellenbosch must have been like. The complex consists of an art center; the old Cape Dutch Rhenish parsonage (1815), which is now the Toy and Miniature Museum; the Leipoldt House, which melds elements of English and Cape architecture; and a two-story building that is typically English.

Continue down Market and turn left on **Herte Street.** The whitewashed cottages along this street were built for freed slaves after the Emancipation Act of 1834. Although they are no longer thatch, the houses are still evocative of 19th-century Stellenbosch.

Wineries

Delaire. This has to be one of the most spectacular settings of any winery in the country. Sit on the terrace of the tasting room or restaurant and look past a screen of oaks to the valley below and the majestic crags of the Groot Drakenstein and Simonsberg mountains. It's an ideal place to stop for lunch as its Green Door restaurant (open for lunch Tuesday to Saturday and for dinner Wednesday to Saturday) serves great food. You can also order a picnic basket and relax on the lawn with a bottle of estate wine. The tasting room is unpretentious and casual. The winery produces under two labels: Botmaskop (try the cabernet sauvignon or the flagship merlot) and the Delaire. There are no cellar tours. ⊠ *Helshoogte Rd. (between Stellenbosch and Franschhoek)* ☎ *021/885–1756, 021/885–1149 restaurant* ⊕ *www.delairewinery.co.za* ⊠ *Tastings R15* ⊗ *Weekdays 9–5, weekends 10–5.*

Jordan. At the end of the Stellenbosch Kloof Road, this meticulous winery, flanked by the Bottelary hills, overlooks rolling vineyards and jagged mountains. Husband-and-wife team Gary and Kathy Jordan studied at the University of California at Davis and worked at California's Iron Horse Winery. Although they produced their first vintage only in 1992, they have already established a strong reputation. The sauvignon blanc, with refreshing hints of asparagus, makes good summer drinking, and the multi-award-winning dense but fruity chardonnay is extremely popular. The two are combined in the versatile, flavorful, and well-priced Chameleon dry white. Wine critics keep their eyes on the Jordan spicy cabernet sauvignon. ⊠ *Stellenbosch Kloof Rd.* ☎ *021/881–3441* ⊕ *www.jordanwines.co.za* ⊠ *Tastings R15* ⊗ *May–Oct., weekdays 10–4:30, Sat. 9:30–12:30; Nov.–Apr., weekdays 10–4:30, Sat. 9:30–2:30; cellar tours by appointment.*

Kanonkop. In the days when ships of the Dutch East India Company used Cape Town as a refreshment station on the way to the East, a ship would fire a cannon as it entered the harbor to let farmers know provisions were needed, and a set of relay cannons, all set on hilltops, would carry the message far inland. One such cannon was on this farm, which was then called Kanonkop, Afrikaans for Cannon Hill. The beauty of Kanonkop today is not in its history or its buildings but in its wine. Winemaker Abrie Beeslaar has taken over from the legendary Beyers Truter (a very hard act to follow), but Kanonkop continues to reel in numerous awards and accolades. For example, the 1998 Paul Sauer, a blend of about 80% cabernet sauvignon with the balance made up of equal parts merlot and cabernet franc, was the grand champion at the South African Trophy Wine Show in 2002. No cellar tours are offered. ⊠ *R44, between Paarl and Stellenbosch* ☎ *021/884–4656* ⊕ *www.kanonkop. co.za* ⊠ *Tastings R10* ⊗ *Weekdays 8:30–5, Sat. 8:30–12:30.*

FodorsChoice ★ **Meerlust.** A visit to Meerlust, probably South Africa's most celebrated estate, provides an introduction to Cape history. In the same family for generations, the wine farm was bought by Johannes Albertus Myburgh in 1757. When Nicolaas Myburgh, seventh-generation Myburgh and father of Hannes (the current owner), took over the reins in 1959, he began restoring the farm's Cape Dutch buildings. (The entire complex was declared a national monument in 1987.) But Nico Myburgh did more than just renovate. He took a fresh look at red wines and broke with tradition by deciding to make a red blend. In the '70s, conventional wisdom had it that cabernet sauvignon was king, but Nico went against the grain and opted for a Bordeaux-style blend, planting both merlot and cabernet franc. The first wine, made in 1980 and released in 1983, was named Rubicon (an allusion to Julius Caesar) to symbolize the crossing of a significant barrier. Although Rubicon rakes in the awards year after year, Meerlust's other wines—chardonnay, pinot noir, and merlot—are also notably good. ☒ *Off R310* ☎ *021/843–3587* ⊕ *www.meerlust. co.za* 🖾 *Tastings R60* ☾ *Weekdays 9–5.*

Morgenhof Wine Estate. This beautiful Cape Dutch estate, with a history stretching back 300 years, lies in the lee of a steep hill covered with vines and pine trees. In 1993 Morgenhof was acquired by Anne Cointreau of Cognac, France. She has spared no expense in making this a showpiece, and the estate has a talented winemaker, Rianie Strydom, and some distinguished wines. Try the chardonnay with fresh coconut nose and hints of lime, or the smoky, somewhat Burgundian pinotage. The estate's flagship wine is the wonderful Premiere Selection, a Bordeaux blend. Morgenhof is an excellent place to stop for a simple lunch of homemade soup and freshly baked bread. Reservations are advisable in summer. ☒ *R44, between Paarl and Stellenbosch* ☎ *021/889–5510* ⊕ *www.morgenhof. com* 🖾 *Tastings R10* ☾ *May–Oct., weekdays 9–4:30, weekends 10–3; Nov.–Apr., weekdays 9–5:30, weekends 10–5; cellar tours by appointment.*

Mulderbosch Vineyards. It's widely accepted that this small estate (only 67 acres are under vine) produces some of the best white wines around, thanks to Mike Dobrovic, an extremely talented winemaker. The robust, barrel-fermented chardonnay has a complex nose and a smooth, velvety finish; a sip might have you tasting buttered toast, citrus, vanilla, and wild herbs. The 2003 vintage claimed a number of awards, so try to get hold of a bottle. The 2004 sauvignon blanc is also delicious; it's packed with gooseberry, nettle, and a touch of citrus. The Faithful Hound red blend was named after a dog who, when the current owners bought the farm in the late 1980s, refused to leave the house where he lived. A huge portion of the farm has been left to indigenous vegetation and wildlife. ☒ *R304, between Stellenbosch and Paarl* ☎ *021/865–2488,* ⊕ *www. mulderbosch.co.za* 🖾 *Fees vary* ☾ *Mon.–Thurs. 8–5, Fri. 8–4; tastings by appointment.*

Muratie. Ancient oaks and a cellar that truly seems to be more concerned with the business of making wine than with decor make this a refreshing change from the "prettier" wineries. It's a small estate, specializing in rich, earthy reds and full-bodied dessert wines. Muratie's port is an old favorite in the Cape, and the well-balanced amber is a fortified dessert wine of note, with pleasing citrus overtones to counter the sweetness. The cellar produces some fine red wines. Two worth looking out for are the pinot noir, from some of the oldest vines of this cultivar in the Cape, and Ansela van der Caab, a dry red blend of cabernet and merlot, named after the freed slave who married the first owner of the farm, Laurens Campher, and helped set up the vineyards in the early 1700s. Cellar tours are not offered. ✉ *Knorhoek Rd., off the R44, between Stellenbosch and Paarl* ☎ *021/865–2330* ⊕ *www.muratie.co.za* 🖼 *Tastings R10* ⊙ *Weekdays 9–5, weekends 10–4.*

Neethlingshof. A long avenue of pines leads to this lovely estate, which traces its origins to 1692. The magnificent 1814 Cape Dutch manor house looks out across formal rose gardens to the Stellenbosch Valley and the Hottentots Holland Mountains. The wines produced on this estate and those from its sister farm, Stellenzicht, are highly regarded, so be prepared for a rush of tour buses during high season. The Gewürztraminer is an off-dry, very elegant wine with rose-petal and spice aromas, and the Weisser Riesling Noble Late Harvest is one of the best of its kind, having scooped almost every local award since 1990. Two delicious wines worth stockpiling are the Stellenzicht Syrah and the Lord Neethling Pinotage. ✉ *M12* ☎ *021/883–8988* ⊕ *www.neetlingshof.co.za* 🖼 *Tastings R25* ⊙ *Weekdays 9–5, weekends 10–4 (stays open around 2 hrs later Dec. and Jan.); cellar tours by appointment.*

Overgaauw. Among the established estates on Stellenbosch Kloof Road, Overgaauw definitely deserves a visit. You can admire the pretty Victorian tasting room while exploring the range of big red wines. Overgaauw was the first South African estate to make a merlot, in 1982, and it's still up there with the leaders. The 2002 merlot is a wonderful, velvety wine that has rich chocolate, cherry, and raspberry flavors. It should age well. Try the Tria Corda, if you can get your hands on some; it sells out faster than it can be released. The spicy, fruity sylvaner is named for a grape of the same name. To date Overgaauw is the only Cape estate to grow this varietal, which comes from the Alsace region of France. ✉ *Stellenbosch Kloof Rd.* ☎ *021/881–3815* ⊕ *www.overgaauw.co.za* 🖼 *Tastings R10* ⊙ *Weekdays 9–12:30 and 2–5, Sat. 10–12:30.*

Rustenberg. This estate may date back to 1682, but it's been brought thoroughly up to date with a state-of-the art winery and underground vaulted maturation rooms. The estate is known for red wine, particularly its 100% cabernet Peter Barlow (named after the present owner's father), which is made from grapes from one lovely, well-tended vineyard that unfortunately suffered extensive smoke damage in the fires of 2000. The Five Soldiers chardonnay is also delicious and also made from a single vineyard, which gives it its unique character. It's named for the five tall pine trees that stand guard on top of the hill above the chardonnay grapes. ✉ *Off R310 (Rustenberg Rd.), Ida's Valley* ☎ *021/809–1200* ⊕ *www.rustenberg.co.za* 🖼 *Tastings free* ⊙ *Weekdays 9–4:30, Sat. 9–12:30; cellar tours by appointment.*

☾ **Simonsig.** Sitting in a sea of vines with tremendous views back toward Stellenbosch and the mountains, this estate has more than a dozen white and red wines of impressive range, both in terms of taste and price. Kaapse Vonkel was South Africa's first Methode Cap Classique sparkling wine, and since 1971 this classic blend of chardonnay, pinot noir, and a touch of pinot meunier has been among the best. Tiara is a great Bordeaux blend. The pinotage demonstrates how well this varietal fares with no wood aging, but the Pinotage Red Hill, from old bush vines, shows just how much good oaking can improve it. You can bring your own picnic to enjoy at tables by the small playground. ⊠ *Kromme Rhee Rd.* ☎ *021/888–4900* ⊕ *www.simonsig.co.za* ✉ *Tastings R5* ☉ *Weekdays 8:30–5, Sat. 8:30–4; cellar tours weekdays at 10 and 3, Sat. at 10.*

🐾 **Spier.** Describing Spier Home Farms as simply a wine estate is doing it an enormous disservice. The vast complex comprises a manor house, wine cellars, wine and farm shop, rose garden, restaurants, equestrian facilities (*see* Sports & the Outdoors, *below*), a conference center, an open-air amphitheater featuring a variety of performances during summer, and a cheetah park, where you can watch the animals being fed daily 1–2. (If you want to touch a cheetah or have a photograph taken, it costs around R50 per person.) It's all designed in Cape-country style, with whitewashed walls and thatch roofs, set along the verdant north bank of the Eerste River. You can even get to Spier's own little railway station by vintage train from Cape Town (R100 round-trip). So, yes, it's seriously touristy, but still delightful. The Spier wines go from strength to strength, and the estate has a successful initiative to train young black and coloured winemakers. Try the cabernet sauvignon or the consistently good and well-priced chardonnay. ⊠ *R310* ☎ *021/809–1143* ⊕ *www.spier.co.za* ✉ *Tastings R12* ☉ *Daily 9–5.*

Thelema Mountain Vineyards. On the slopes of the Simonsberg, just off the Helshoogte Pass, this is an excellent example of the exciting developments in the Cape Winelands since the early 1980s, when farmers began to eye land that hadn't traditionally been earmarked for wine farming. When Gyles and Barbara Webb bought the farm in 1983, there was nothing here but very good soil and old fruit trees. It's a testament to their efforts that the winery has regularly won prizes for both its reds and whites ever since. To cap it all off, the view of the Groot Drakenstein Mountains from the tasting room is unforgettable. This vineyard suffered quite severe damage from the fires of 2000, but it's bounced back. Be sure to taste Ed's Reserve, a dry white, and chat with Edna McLean, for whom the wine is named. She works in wine tasting, and is as refreshing as the wine. Ever the pioneers, the Webbs have also bought an old fruit farm in the Elgin area (an exciting new wine-growing area at the top of Sir Lowry's Pass), and are working on getting that up and running. ⊠ *Off R310, between Stellenbosch and Franschhoek* ☎ *021/885–1924* ⊕ *www. thelema.co.za* ✉ *Tastings free* ☉ *Weekdays 9–5, Sat. 9–1.*

Villiera. Since they started wine making in 1984, the Grier family has notched numerous successes. As John Platter, one of South Africa's foremost wine writers, says: "Other wine makers might jog or work out in the gym; Jeff Grier gets all the exercise he needs stepping up to the podium for wine industry awards." Try the Bush Vine Sauvignon Blanc, for which Grier was voted Winemaker of the Year, and you'll start to understand why it's become almost a cult wine. Then check out the range of Methode Cap Classique sparkling wines—the Tradition rosé brut, for instance, is a delicate pink bubbly with soft, creamy overtones. This is one of the wineries that is, as far as possible, producing chemical-free wines. ⊠ *R101 and R304 (Old Paarl and Stellenbosch Rds.), Koelenhof* ☎ *021/865–2002* ⊕ *www.villiera.com* ✍ *Tastings free* ☼ *Weekdays 8:30–5, Sat. 8:30–1; tours by appointment.*

Warwick. This family-run farm is all business. The tasting area is in a tiny cellar room cluttered with wine-making equipment, and the farm hubbub continues while you're tasting. The previous winemaker, Norma Ratcliffe, spent a couple of vintages in France perfecting traditional techniques, which have left their mark on Warwick's reds. The first female winemaker in South Africa, Norma pioneered the way for a new breed of young women who are now making their mark in the industry. Trilogy is a stylish and complex red made predominantly from cabernet sauvignon, with about 20% merlot and 20% cabernet franc. Another great red, the Three Cape Ladies, was named after the indomitable Ratcliffe women. It's been described as a "feminine" blend of around 40% cabernet sauvignon, 30% merlot, and 30% pinotage. The cabernet franc is undoubtedly one of the best wines made from this varietal in the Winelands. Louis Nel, formerly from Neil Ellis estate, has joined the dynamic Warwick team as their winemaker. ⊠ *R44, between Paarl and Stellenbosch* ☎ *021/884–4410* ⊕ *www.warickwine.co.za* ✍ *Tastings free* ☼ *Weekdays 10–5, weekends 10–4; cellar tours by appointment.*

Where to Stay & Eat

$$$$ ✕ **Jonkershuis at Spier.** The culinary influences that have contributed to traditional Cape cuisine—Cape Malay, Dutch, French, and German—are all celebrated here with a gargantuan R140-a-head buffet feast that you can savor under venerable oaks or inside the well-restored 18th-century homestead. Start at the cold table laden with local seafood dishes such as *snoek* (a South African game fish) pâté, smoked salmon trout, fish cakes, and excellent pickled fish. Salads complement hearty entrées of Cape chicken pie, *bobotie* (a light Malay curry of minced meat and dried fruit topped with a thin baked savory egg custard), *bredie* (lamb casserole in a tomato sauce), and Malay curries. Look for the time-honored desserts *melktert* (a sweet custard tart sprinkled with cinnamon and sugar), *koeksister* (a braided doughnut served with a gingery syrup), and brandy pudding. ⊠ *Spier Estate, Lynedoch Rd.* ☎ *021/809–1172* ▭ *AE, DC, MC, V* ☼ *No dinner Sun. and Mon.*

$–$$ ✕ **Olivello.** Be sure to book a table outside near the lily pond at this relaxed restaurant that serves Cape-meets-Mediterranean-style food in a fabulous country setting. Though the menu is fairly small, you will still be hard-pressed to make a snappy choice. Try the signature dish of lamb shank with a balsamic, rosemary, and red-wine reduction or the beef fillet with a cracked peppercorn and brandy sauce. If that sounds too rich for a hot summer's day, try the chicken salad with a lightly curried mayonnaise sauce served with almonds and apricots. On Sundays a Mediterranean table provides a huge variety of tapas and main courses from which to choose. Little ones can have pasta with a homemade tomato sauce and grated cheese. ⊠ *Marianne Wine Farm, Valley Rd., off the*

R44 ☎ *021/875–5443* ▤ *AE, DC, MC, V* ☾ *Closed Mon. and Tues. No dinner.*

★ **$–$$** ✕ **Terroir.** The setting on a golf estate and wine farm is pretty, but it's the excellent food and service that really stand out here. Chefs Michael Broughton and Nic van Wyk, both with impressive culinary credentials, do their best to honor the concept of *terroir* (from the French, *terre,* for "earth") and get as many ingredients from the surrounding area as possible. The menu changes regularly to make use of the fresh produce. Earthy and nutty cèpe mushrooms lightly fried in butter, garlic, and parsley make great starters. For the main course try the wood-roasted pork belly in honey, garlic, and chili on roasted onion mash with applesauce and sage, or roast quail served with cabbage braised with ginger, sultanas, and a Madeira sauce. Desserts include a pear and Frangelica crème brûlée. Though the wine list is small, you can sample several different (and delicious) wines by the glass. Try the barrel-fermented chenin blanc, one of the estate's best-kept secrets. ⊠ *Kleine Zalze Residential Golf Estate, R44, between Somerset West and Stellenbosch* ☎*021/880–8167* ⚲*Reservations essential* ▤ *AE, DC, MC, V* ☾ *Closed Mon. No dinner Sun.*

$$$$ ✕▥ **Lanzerac Manor.** The sense of history is almost tangible on this large working wine estate dating from 1692. The sheer beauty of the setting has not changed: a classic Cape Dutch manor house flanked by the rolling vineyards and mountains of the Jonkershoek Valley. The staff at this luxurious hotel and winery is friendly, and guest rooms are tastefully decorated. Diners can choose from casual alfresco meals at the Terrace ($–$$) or more formal fare in the Governors Hall Restaurant ($$–$$$). During summer a jazz band ups the tempo on the Terrace. At the Governors Hall you can have the ever-popular quail gratin with a juniper jus as a starter and, for an entrée, choose from medallions of springbok loin with a fynbos honey and black-pepper sauce and the ostrich served with a butternut muffin and a red-wine-butter-shallot sauce. The legendary Lanzerac cheesecake is creamy, tangy, and utterly sublime. ⊠ *Jonkershoek Rd., 1 km (½ mi) from Stellenbosch* ⛫ *Box 4, 7599* ☎ *021/887–1132* 🖷 *021/887–2310* ⊕ *www.lanzerac.co.za* ⇥ *43 rooms, 5 suites* ⚘ *2 restaurants, room service, 3 pools, bar* ▤ *AE, DC, MC, V* ⫿◯⫾ *BP.*

$$ ▥ **D'Ouwe Werf Country Inn.** A national monument, this attractive 1802 inn is thought to be the oldest in South Africa. From the street, guests enter the original living room, a beautiful space with a lofty beamed ceiling and elegant antiques. The hotel is divided into two parts: the old inn with luxury rooms on its Georgian second story and a new wing with more standard rooms. All luxury rooms are furnished with antiques, including four-poster beds, draped sash windows, and bronze bathroom fittings. The standard rooms have reproductions only. A lovely garden in a brick courtyard shaded by trellised vines is open for meals and drinks throughout the day. ⊠ *30 Church St., 7600* ☎ *021/887–4608* 🖷 *021/887–4626* ⊕ *www.ouwewerf.com* ⇥ *31 rooms* ⚘ *Restaurant, room service, pool, free parking* ▤ *AE, DC, MC, V* ⫿◯⫾ *BP.*

$$ ▥ **Village at Spier.** The innovative design of these two-story buildings grouped around six courtyards, each with its own pool and leisure area, achieves the goal of feeling like a Mediterranean village, albeit a very luxurious one. Rooms and suites are elegantly appointed, with In-donesian furniture, gas fireplaces, and stylish detail evident in the cot-ton throws and wide choice of pillows. The surrounding orchards and shade trees make the complex and walkways both verdant and private. ⊠ *Spier Estate, Lynedoch Rd., 7600* ☎ *021/809–1100* 🖷 *021/809–1134* ⊕ *www.spier.co.za* ⟿ *155 rooms* ♿ *5 restaurants, room service, 6 outdoor pools, bar* ☰ *AE, DC, MC, V* ⎮◯⎮ *BP.*

$ ▦ **Michaelhouse Guest House.** At this guesthouse in the heart of the his-toric village, the individually decorated rooms are comfortable, and the linen is crisp and white. The leafy gardens are both a great place for breakfast and a real bonus on hot summer evenings. In winter, break-fast is served in front of the fire. The friendly and knowledgeable staff is on hand to help with any arrangements. ⊠ *29 van Riebeek St., 7600* ☎☎ *021/886–6343* ⊕ *www.michaelhousegh.com* ⟿ *4 rooms* ♿ *Mini-bars, free parking* ☰ *DC, MC, V* ⎮◯⎮ *BP.*

¢ ▦ **Stumble Inn Backpackers Lodge.** Stellenbosch's original backpackers' lodging is within easy walking distance of most major town sights and is a great place to stay if you're traveling on a limited budget. You can choose from simple double rooms, dorm beds, and even limited camp-ing facilities in the gardens. Other amenities include shared kitchen fa-cilities and an on-site travel agent. The folks here will even arrange budget-minded packages that include wine tours and cheese tastings. ⊠ *12 Market St., 7600* ☎ *021/887–4049* ⊕ *www.jump.to/stumble* ⟿ *7 rooms, 6 dormitories* ♿ *Pool, lounge, Internet; no room phones, no room TVs* ☰ *AE, DC, MC, V.*

Nightlife & the Arts

NIGHTLIFE The **Dorp Street Theatre Café** (⊠ 59 Dorp St. ☎ 021/886–6107), open daily, always has a great lineup of local musicians. Take a stroll into the Church Street part of town, where shops stay open late and bars and cafés spill onto the streets. A good place to start, the **Wijnhuis** (⊠ Church and Andringa Sts. ☎ 021/887–5844) quickly fills up with trendy locals wanting to unwind.

THE ARTS Each summer performances ranging from African jazz to opera to bal-
★ let are staged at the **Oude Libertas Amphitheatre** (⊠ Oude Libertas St.), a delightful open-air venue across from and run and owned by Distell. For bookings contact **Computicket** (☎ 083/909–0909). The **Spier Arts Summer Festival** (⊠ Spier Estate ☎ 021/809–1158) runs from mid-November to mid-March and usually includes opera, classical music, and a host of other performances.

Sports & the Outdoors

GOLF **Stellenbosch Golf Club** (⊠ Strand Rd. ☎ 021/880–0103) has long tree-lined fairways that will pose a problem if you don't hit the ball straight. Greens fees are R300 for 18 holes. A caddy costs R100, club rental R200, and a golf cart R180.

HORSEBACK **Spier Equestrian Centre** (⊠ Spier Estate ☎ 021/881–3683 or 083/627–
RIDING 2282) offers a gentle amble or a quick canter through the vineyards (R150 one hour, R250 two hours). If you don't fancy getting into a saddle, you can go on a horse-drawn wagon ride (R150 per person for an hour).

> **need a
> break?**

From Thelema the **R310** runs down into the fruit orchards and vines
that mark the beginning of the Franschhoek Valley. The R310 dead ends
at the R45. To the left is Paarl, to the right Franschhoek.

Franschhoek

★ ❸ *22 km (14 mi) northeast of Stellenbosch.*

Franschhoek (French Corner) takes its name from its first white settlers,
French Huguenots who fled to the Cape to escape Catholic persecution
in France in the late 1600s. By the early 18th century about 200
Huguenots had settled in the Cape; today their descendants—with
names like de Villiers, Malan, and Joubert—number in the tens of thousands. With their experience in French vineyards, the early Huguenots
were instrumental in nurturing a wine-making culture in South Africa.

Franschhoek is the most spectacular of the three wine centers, a long
valley encircled by towering mountain ranges and fed by a single road
that runs through town. As spectacular as the valley is today, it must
have been even more so in the 17th century, when it teemed with game.
In calving season herds of elephants would migrate to the valley via the
precipitous Franschhoek Mountains. The last wild elephant in the valley died in the 1930s. Some leopards still survive high in the mountains,
but you won't see them.

What you will see today is an increasingly upmarket village with beautifully renovated cottages and gorgeous gardens. Although it can get very
busy during the summer season, you will always be able to find a quiet
spot with a view of the mountains, roses, and swathes of lavender,
which do well here. Over the last few years, Franschhoek has developed
into something of a culinary mecca, with some of the country's best restaurants and cafés lining the pretty main street. In October the village
hosts a music festival featuring many local and visiting artists. The
town is more touristy than agrarian, although you will see the occasional
wine farmer steaming into town with his dogs on the back of his *bakkie*
(pickup truck), looking for tractor tires or other essentials. It's a great
place for lunch or for a couple of days, as there are excellent small hotels and guesthouses to choose from.

The **Huguenot Monument** stands at the end of the main road through Franschhoek. It was built in 1948 to commemorate the contribution of the
Huguenots to South Africa's development. The three arches symbolize
the Holy Trinity, the sun and cross form the Huguenots' emblem, and
the female figure in front represents Freedom of Conscience. ⊠ *Lambrecht and Huguenot Sts.* ☎ *No phone (contact Huguenot Memorial
Museum)* 🎟 *R5* ☉ *Daily 9–5.*

To trace the history of the Huguenot community here, visit the **Huguenot
Memorial Museum.** Its main building is modeled after Thibault's 1791
Saasveld in Cape Town. Wall displays profile some of the early Huguenot
families. Exhibits also focus on other aspects of the region's history, such
as the development of Cape Dutch architecture and the relationship of

FRANSCHHOEK WINE ROUTE

Along R310. The drive out of Stellenbosch up the Helshoogte Pass is spectacular. In winter you'll more than likely find snow on the mountain peaks; in summer, once you top the pass you enter a verdant valley of fruit trees and ordered vineyards. Be sure to stop in at *Hillcrest Berry Farm* (✉ R310, Banhoek Valley ☎ 021/885–1629) for delicious tea and scones before moving on to **Boschendal**, one of the oldest and most established estates in the country.

Along R45. There are well over 20 estates to choose from here, and there's something for everyone—from enormous farms covering hundreds of acres to smaller, boutique vineyards producing just a few hundred bottles each year. If you turn right on R45 from the R310, **L'Ormarins** is one of the first wine farms you'll come to (off the R45 through a tunnel of trees). It's a well-established estate that's undergoing some interesting changes. Just outside town, **La Motte** is a sister farm to L'Ormarins. Closer to town the estates come thick and fast. Amid this flurry—Môreson (up the aptly named Happy Valley Road), Rickety Bridge, Agusta, Chamonix, and Dieu Donne—is **Mont Rochelle**, best known for its black ownership. Outside town and up the Franschhoek Pass toward Villiersdorp, the fabulous **Cabrière**, at Haute Cabrière, is built into the mountain. **La Petite Ferme** is worth phoning ahead for (you can't just pop in).

If you turn left on the R45 from the R310, you'll find more outstanding wine farms, including **Plaisir de Merle**, which makes a distinctive merlot and cabernet.

the Huguenots with the Dutch East India Company. Displays in the annex cover the culture and life of the Khoekhoen, or Khoikhoi, once derogatorily known as Hottentots, as well as the role of slaves and local laborers in the development of the Franschhoek Valley. ✉ *Lambrecht St.* ☎ *021/876–2532* ✉ *R5* ☉ *Mon.–Sat. 9–5, Sun. 2–5.*

Wineries
It should come as no surprise that the Franschhoek Valley produces excellent wines. After all, the original French settlers brought with them an extensive and intimate understanding of viticulture. Some of the country's oldest estates nestle at the base of the spectacular Groot Drakenstein mountains, and the wine farmers here are constantly trying to top themselves.

Boschendal. With a history that dates back three centuries, this lovely estate is one of the Cape's major attractions. You can easily spend half a day here. Cradled between the Simonsberg and Groot Drakenstein mountains at the base of Helshoogte Pass, the farm—originally called Bossendaal—was originally granted to Jean le Long, one of the first French Huguenot settlers in the late 17th century.

Boschendal runs one of the most pleasant wine tastings in the region: you can sit inside at the Taphuis, a Cape Dutch *langhuis* (longhouse) and the oldest building on the estate, or outside at wrought-iron tables under a spreading oak. In 1980 Boschendal was the first to pioneer a Cape blanc de noir, a pink wine made in a white-wine style from black grapes. The Boschendal Blanc de Noir remains the best-selling wine of this style. If you prefer sparkling wines, try the extremely popular Boschendal Brut, a blend of pinot noir and chardonnay made by the Methode Cap Classique. From the Taphuis it's a two-minute drive through vines and fruit trees to the main estate complex. The excellent Boschendal Restaurant serves a buffet of Cape specialties, Le Café serves light meals at tables under the oaks leading to the manor house, and Le Pique Nique (October–May) provides picnic baskets that you can enjoy on the lawns. During the summer months, Boschendal also hosts a formal full-moon dinner under the oak trees to the accompaniment of a string quartet. (Calling ahead is essential for the restaurant, picnic, and full-moon dinner.) The estate is wheelchair-friendly. ⊠ *R310, between Franschhoek and Stellenbosch, Groot Drakenstein* ☎ *021/870–4274* ⊕ *www.boschendal.co.za* 🖃 *Tastings R15* ⊘ *Daily 8:30–4:30.*

Cabrière. Built in 1994 on the lower slopes of the Franschhoek Mountains, Cabrière is the brainchild of Achim von Arnim, one of the Cape's most colorful winemakers. To avoid scarring the mountain, the complex hunkers into the hillside. There are five Cap Classique sparkling wines under the Pierre Jordan label, and the fruity, mouth-filling Haute Cabrière pinot noir is consistently one of the best. Also delicious is the chardonnay–pinot noir blend, an ideal, extremely quaffable wine to enjoy at lunchtime. Take a Saturday-morning cellar tour with von Arnim, and watch him perform his trademark display of *sabrage*—the dramatic decapitation of a bottle of bubbly with a saber. ⊠ *R45* ☎ *021/876–2630* ⊕ *www.cabriere.co.za* 🖃 *Tastings and cellar tour R25* ⊘ *Weekdays 9–4:30, Sat. 11–3:30; tours Sat. at 11.*

La Motte Estate. This estate is owned by a branch of the same Rupert family that owns L'Ormarins, and is a partner in Rupert & Rothschild, a vineyard closer to Paarl. The elegant and rather formal tasting room looks into the cellars through a wall of smoked glass. You sit at a long marble-top table and sample from five to seven wines. The shiraz is one of the biggest and boldest you'll taste of this variety, full of rich flavors; it needs from four to eight years to reach its peak. The Millennium is a very good blend of just over 50% cabernet sauvignon, with the balance consisting of merlot and a little cabernet franc. This wine needs time to develop, coming into its own in 5–10 years. There are no cellar tours. ⊠ *R45 (Huguenot Rd.)* ☎ *021/876–3119* ⊕ *www.la-motte.co.za* 🖃 *Tastings R15* ⊘ *Weekdays 9–4:30, Sat. 10–3.*

La Petite Ferme. You'll have to phone ahead to arrange a tasting here, but it's worth it, because then you'll know what to have with your lunch if you decide to dine here. True to its name, this is a small, family-run estate producing just enough wine for the restaurant and to keep its faithful regular customers happy. Try the chardonnay. ⊠ *Franschhoek Pass Rd. (R45)* ☎ *021/876–3016* ☉ *Sales daily noon–4; tastings and tours by appointment.*

L'Ormarins. Dating from 1811, the archetypal Cape Dutch manor house is festooned with flowers and framed by majestic peaks. In contrast, the huge tasting room is modern and slick, indicative of the estate's modern wine-making style. Using classic grape varieties, the winemakers produce big, complex red wines ready for early drinking but with excellent maturation potential. The merlot is the farm's flagship red. It has soft, ripe tannins and good aging potential (5 to 10 years). The cabernet is just as pleasing; among whites, try the pinot grigio. ⊠ *R45 (Franschhoek Rd.), Groot Drakenstein* ☎ *021/874–1026* ⊕ *www.lormarins. com* ⊠ *Tastings R20; tours R25* ☉ *Weekdays 9–4:30, Sat. 10–3.*

Mont Rochelle. This is the only fully black-owned vineyard in the country. Owner Miko Rwayitare has injected new enthusiasm into the farm, which he bought in 2001, renovating the estate and replanting the vineyards. Winemaker Justin Hoy gained experience in Bordeaux and Burgundy before coming back to Cape Town, and the estate produces an excellent range of wines. The sauvignon blanc is harvested in the cool of the morning to help capture the grapes' complexity. The aptly named Alchemy is a great blend, and the cabernet sauvignon is consistently excellent. It would be good to keep an eye on this estate's wines to see how they develop, given the recent (in wine terms) overhaul the vineyards received. ⊠ *Dassenberg Rd.* ☎ *021/876–3000* ⊕ *www. montrochelle.co.za* ⊠ *Tastings R15; cellar tour R10* ☉ *Mon.–Sat. 10–5, Sun. 10–3; cellar tours weekdays at 11, 12:30, and 3.*

Plaisir de Merle. The name means "Song of the Blackbird" and has its origins with the original French owners of the farm. This huge estate (2,500 acres) is Distell's showpiece. With its innovative architecture and conservation area, it truly feels different from the ubiquitous "oak and gable" wineries that you see all over the Cape. But forget all the frills—it really is about the wine. Don't miss the cabernet sauvignon, probably the smoothest, lowest-acid, lowest-tannin local example of this cultivar. ⊠ *R45, Simondium* ☎ *021/874–1071 or 021/874–1072* ⊕ *www.plaisirdemerle.co.za* ⊠ *Tastings R20; cellar tour with tastings R30* ☉ *Apr.–Oct., weekdays 9–5, Sat. 10–2; Nov.–Mar., weekdays 9–5, Sat. 10–4; cellar tours by appointment.*

Where to Stay & Eat

$$$$ ✕ **Boschendal Restaurant.** Reserve well in advance for the buffet lunch here at one of the Cape's most beautiful and historic wineries. A wide selection of soups, quiches, and pâtés prefaces a bewildering array of cold and hot main dishes, including pickled fish, roasts, and imaginative salads; traditional Cape dishes are well prepared. End with an excellent sampling of South African cheeses and preserves or a quintessentially Cape dessert such as malva pudding. Unobtrusive, professional, but friendly service complements the bounty, priced at R195 a head. ⊠ *R310, between Franschhoek and Stellenbosch* ☎ *021/870–4274* ⋈ *Reservations essential* ▭ *AE, DC, MC, V* ☉ *No dinner.*

$–$$ ✕ **Reuben's.** Reuben Riffel is one of a small band of talented homegrown **Fodor'sChoice** chefs who are breaking culinary rules with passion, and, more important, ★ delectable results. Formerly of the popular Monneaux, Riffel is flexing his wings and "cooking food he would like to eat." And so, it seems, people would like to eat along with him. Choose from two menus—classic or contemporary—and then have an even harder time choosing a meal. Do you opt for the chorizo, spinach, and saffron risotto with sun-dried tomatoes and basil or quail with creamed cabbage and crisped pancetta? The decor is minimalist but welcoming, with a roaring fire in winter, and the service impeccable. The waiters know their wine, and are happy to make menu recommendations. Have a drink at the trendy bar, made from an airplane wing. ✉ *19 Huguenot Rd.* ☎ *021/876–3772* ⬦ *Reservations essential* ▤ *AE, DC, MC, V.*

$–$$ ✕ **Topsi & Company.** Chef Topsi Venter, doyenne of the Cape culinary scene, is as renowned as a raconteur as she is for her innovative country fare. The decor is simple and rustic, and local art lines the white walls. Blackboard menus change daily, and only fresh, local ingredients are used. Topsi concentrates on traditional and indigenous Cape food, saying, "If somebody arrives with goat, we'll do goat. If they come with a zebra, then we'll do zebra." It's not that intimidating, however. The *biltong* (dried, spiced meat similar to jerky) pâté served with sorrel salad and home-baked bread is a good start before you move on to the kudu fillet with pine-ring mushrooms. Mussel bobotie is an unusual take on the traditional South African dish, usually made with minced beef. The preserved grapefruit with chocolate chili sauce is a taste experience, but the old-fashioned apple-almond tart is sublime. In this valley of wonderful wines, it's great to be able to BYOB. ✉ *7 Reservoir St.* ☎ *021/876–2952* ⬦ *Reservations essential* ▤ *AE, DC, MC, V* ☉ *Closed Tues.*

¢–$$ ✕ **Haute Cabrière.** Dine here atop a working winery built into the mountainside. Try to reserve a window table for views across the vine-clad valley as you select from a mix-and-match menu created to complement the estate wines maturing in the cellar beneath you. You can opt for half or full portions of renowned chef Matthew Gordon's mouthwatering seasonal fare. Selections might include tandoori-spiced Franschhoek salmon trout fish cakes or Chinese-style roasted duck leg with stir-fried Asian vegetables and a crisp melon-and-ginger wonton. Local Belgian-trained chocolatiers contribute to the luscious selection of desserts. ✉ *Franschhoek Pass Rd. (R45)* ☎ *021/876–3688* ⬦ *Reservations essential* ▤ *AE, DC, MC, V.*

¢–$ ✕ **Delicious!** If you're looking for a light lunch or quick snack, make for this fantastic deli on Franschhoek's main drag, find a spot on the sofas on the veranda, and watch the world go by while sipping a cappuccino. The sticky buns are irresistible, as is the *tremazzini* (pita-like bread) filled with smoked salmon, cream cheese, and avocado and toasted. Delicious! has become so popular that it now stays open Wednesday evenings, when chef Neil Jewell comes to cook. The menu changes each week, but starters could include a baked camembert and beetroot tart or hot smoked trout and watercress served with an apple-and-almond dressing. Entrée options are melt-in-your-mouth parsley pasta with artichokes, olives, and sweet pickled sardines, and fennel-roasted pork loin with apple marmalade and smoked crackling. In a word—it's delicious!

⊠ *38 Huguenot St.* ☎ *021/876–4004* ⚶ *Dinner reservations essential*
▤ *AE, DC, MC, V* ☺ *No dinner Thurs.–Tues.*

$$$$ ✕▣ Le Quartier Français. This classy guesthouse is a Winelands favorite
Fodor'sChoice and part of the Relais & Chateaux group. Separated from the village's main
★ drag by a courtyard bistro and a superb restaurant, the guesthouse exudes
privacy and peace. Rooms in two-story whitewashed cottages face a pool
deck and central garden exploding with flowers. Decor is vibrant, with
rustic furniture, sponge-painted walls, colorful drapes, and small fireplaces. Upstairs rooms have timber beams and mountain views, and suites
have private pools. So which awards hasn't the restaurant won? None, by
the looks of it, but chef Margo Janse and her team aren't resting on their
laurels. You can eat at the Tasting Room, a formal restaurant, or the relaxed iCi ($). Either way you won't likely be disappointed—unless you don't
make reservations. Favorites from the iCi menu include the lamb burger
with marinated tomatoes and creamed avocado, and the wood-roasted free-
range chicken for two. The Tasting Room ($$$$; closed Sunday dinner)
offers four-course meals for R240 and six courses for R300. These could
include inventive dishes like a prawn, basil, and white-anchovy risotto or
a crème fraîche mousse with shortbread and wild berries. The boldly colored decor is as contemporary as the menu. As you enter, look for the exotic candelabras, made by iThemba, an organization providing employment
for HIV-positive women. ⊠ *16 Huguenot Rd.* ⚲ *Box 237, 7690* ☎ *021/
876–2248 or 021/876–2151* 🖷 *021/876–3105* ⊕ *www.lequartier.co.za*
⤳ *15 rooms, 2 suites* ♨ *2 restaurants, pool, bar* ▤ *AE, DC, MC, V.*

$–$$ ✕▣ Résidence Klein Oliphants Hoek. Originally built as the home of a
British missionary, this lovingly restored guesthouse also once served as
a school. Now its rooms are decorated with rich fabrics and luxurious
finishes. One has its own plunge pool, and others have generous fireplaces. Guests are given preference in the restaurant ($$$$), which produces delicious meals five (changing) nights a week. Look out for
typically South African ingredients such as kudu, warthog, butternut,
and *waterblommetjies* (water flowers) prepared with a modern twist.
Choices might include duck with duck-liver sauce served with mango
and *kruidkoek* (herb cake). ⊠ *14 Akademie St., Box 470, 7690* 🖷🖷 *021/
876–2566* ⊕ *www.kleinoliphantshoek.com* ⤳ *8 rooms* ♨ *Restaurant,
pool, free parking; no a/c* ▤ *AE, DC, MC, V* ⎮◎⎮ *BP.*

$ ▣ East. Guest rooms at this early village homestead are small but well
proportioned, pretty, eclectically decorated, and comfortable. All open
onto the wraparound veranda, and some have great mountain views.
Dark-red walls make a striking statement in the entrance hall, and original art hangs everywhere. Priced to please, East is popular with city visitors year-round. ⊠ *7 Reservoir St., Box 156, 7690* ☎ *021/876–2651*
🖷 *021/876–3743* ⊕ *www.eastguesthouse.co.za* ⤳ *8 rooms* ♨ *Pool, bar,
free parking; no a/c* ▤ *AE, DC, MC, V* ⎮◎⎮ *BP.*

Paarl

❹ *21 km (13 mi) northwest of Franschhoek.*

Paarl takes its name from the granite domes of Paarl Mountain, which
looms above the town—*paarl* is Dutch for "pearl." The first farmers

settled here in 1687, two years after the founding of Stellenbosch. The town has its fair share of historic homes and estates, but it lacks the charm of its distinguished neighbor simply because it's so spread out. Main Street, the town's oak-lined thoroughfare, extends some 11 km (7 mi) along the western bank of the Berg River. You can gain a good sense of the town's history on a drive along this lovely street.

Main Street North doglegs to the right at Lady Grey Street before continuing as Main Street South. On your left, the **Paarl Museum** (formerly Oude Pastorie) occupies a gorgeous Cape Dutch home built as a parsonage in 1787. In fact, the building itself is of more interest than the collection, which includes odds and ends donated by local families, including silver, glass, and kitchen utensils. ⊠ *303 Main St.* ☎ *021/872–2651* 🖃 *R5* ☉ *Weekdays 10–5, Sat. 9–1.*

From the Paarl Museum walk about 200 yards along Pastorie Street to the **Afrikaanse Taalmuseum** (Afrikaans Language Museum), in the Gideon Malherbe House. It was from here in 1875 that the Society of True Afrikaners launched their campaign to gain widespread acceptance for Afrikaans, hitherto considered a sort of inferior kitchen Dutch. However, the museum may be of only limited interest to you because the displays are entirely in Afrikaans. ⊠ *11 Pastorie St.* ☎ *021/872–3441* 🖃 *R10* ☉ *Weekdays 8–5.*

Continue along Main Street past the Paarl Tourism Bureau to **Zeederberg Square,** a grassy park bordered by some excellent examples of Cape Dutch, Georgian, and Victorian homes. A little farther down Main Street on the left is the old **Dutch Reformed Church,** a thatch building dating from 1805. The cemetery contains the tombstones of the Malherbe family, which was instrumental in the campaign to gain official recognition for Afrikaans. The church is still active, and you can peek inside.

After the N1 bridge, a sign on your right points the way to the **Afrikaanse Taalmonument** (Afrikaans Language Monument), set high on a hill overlooking Paarl. Like the Voortrekker Monument in Pretoria, this concrete structure holds a special place in the hearts of Afrikaners, who struggled for years to gain acceptance for their language alongside English. The rising curve of the main pillar is supposed to represent the growth and potential of Afrikaans. When it was erected in 1973, the monument was as much a gesture of political victory as a paean to the Afrikaans language. Ironically, it may become the language's memorial. Under the new South Africa, Afrikaans has become just one of 11 official languages and is gradually losing its dominance, although attempts are being made to ensure that the rich culture isn't lost. The view from the top of the hill is incredible, taking in Table Mountain, False Bay, Paarl Valley, and the various mountain ranges of the Winelands. Buy a picnic basket at the monument's restaurant, and watch the sun set with a cold glass of the best. A short, paved walking trail leads around the hillside past impressive fynbos specimens, particularly proteas. ⊠ *Afrikaanse Taalmonument Rd.* ☎ *021/863–4809* 🖃 *R5* ☉ *Mon. 8–5, Tues.–Sun. 8–10.*

CloseUp

PAARL WINE ROUTE

WINERIES HERE are spread far apart, so you might want to select only a couple or take a whole day to taste at leisure. Start in Paarl, home to the impressive **KWV International**, with cellars covering 55 acres and a wide selection of wines.

Along R301/303. On its way to Franschhoek, the R301/303 runs past **Avondale Wine**, a relatively new farm with a state-of-the-art cellar, a gorgeous rose garden, and excellent wines.

Along WR1 between R44 and R45. On your way from Franschhoek to Paarl, take a quick detour down the WR1 (Simondium Road) to **Backsberg** and, a bit farther, **Glen Carlou**. Backsberg has more going on than Glen Carlou, but they both have wines that are worth tasting and buying. Continue on, and turn right on the R44. At a four-way stop, turn right onto the R101 and cross over the N1. Follow the goat signs to Suid Agter Paarl Road and Fairview.

Along Suid and Noord Agter Paarl roads. Fairview is as famous for its cheeses as it is for its wines. Leave yourself plenty of time here. From Fairview, turn right onto the Suid Agter Paarl Road and make your way to **Landskroon**, known for full-bodied reds. Turn right on the R44 and, after about 10 km (6 mi), right onto the WR8 (Noord Agter Paarl Road), and then right again to **Rhebokskloof**. If you continue on the R44 toward Wellington, you'll pass **Nelson's Creek** on your left. This farm has done a lot to empower farmworkers in the art of wine making.

Halfway down the hill from the Afrikaans Language Monument is a turnoff onto a dirt road and a sign for the Paarl Mountain Nature Reserve. The dirt road is **Jan Phillips Mountain Drive,** which runs 11 km (7 mi) along the mountainside, offering tremendous views over the valley. Along the way it passes the **Mill Water Wildflower Garden** and the starting points for several trails, including hikes up to the great granite domes of Paarl Mountain. The dirt road rejoins Main Street at the far end of Paarl.

Wineries

Avondale Wine. Although the farm was established as early as 1693, new owners Johnny and Ginny Grieve have done some serious reorganizing in the vineyards and built a state-of-the-art cellar, which is dug into a dry river bed. Avondale started producing wines only in 1999, making them one of the newer kids on the block. No matter. They have hit the ground running, and their wines are winning one award after the other. The reds are especially good, and the intense Paarl summers result in full-bodied grapes that deliver knockout flavors. Unlike many farms, which have absent owners, the Grieve family takes a hands-on approach. The casually dressed guy behind the wine-tasting counter might, in fact, be the owner. Once you've done your wine tasting and buying, be sure to visit Ginny's exquisite rose garden. ⊠ *Lustigan Rd., off R301* ☎ *021/863–1976* ⊕ *www.avondalewine.co.za* ⊠ *Tastings R8* ☉ *Weekdays 9–5, Sat. 10–4; cellar tours by appointment.*

Backsberg. Framed by the mountains of the Simonsberg, this lovely estate is run by the Back family, well known for producing great wines of good value. Backsberg has a comprehensive range of red and white wines and a very fine brandy made from chenin blanc. Among the wines to look out for are the 2002 Babylons Toren chardonnay and the Babylons Toren red blend. Backsberg is one of only a handful of estates that produce a malbec—and then only in very small quantities. It also produces kosher wines and a certified organic unwooded chardonnay that has an interesting earthiness to it. The restaurant does a lamb spit every lunch, so you can taste some excellent wines before digging in to a typical South African meal. The estate also has self-guided cellar tours and the largest living maze in South Africa. Don't enter it after drinking too much wine; you might never come out. ⊠ *WR1 (Simondium Rd.), between R44 and R45* ☎ *021/875–5141* ⊕ *www.backsberg.co.za* ⊠ *Tastings R10; cellar tours free* ☉ *Weekdays 8:30–5, Sat. 8:30–2, Sun. 11–3.*

☺ **Fairview.** This is one of the few wineries that's good for families. Children get a kick out of seeing peacocks roaming the grounds and goats clambering up a spiral staircase into a goat tower. In fact, Fairview produces a superb line of goat cheeses, all of which you can taste. But don't let Fairview's sideshows color your judgment about the wines. Charles Back, a member of the family that runs Backsberg, is one of the most successful and innovative winemakers in the Cape, and the estate's wines are top drawer and often surprising. Back does not stick to the tried-and-true Cape varietals. The zinfandel-cinsaut blend is quite unusual, as is the shiraz-mourvedre-viognier blend. The winery also makes creative use of the farm's many Rhône varieties. Perhaps it's just because the pun was irresistible, but (as claimed by the label) goats are sent into the vineyard to personally select grapes for the Goats-do-Roam, which is indeed like a young Côtes du Rhône (infuriating French winemakers). Likewise, the very popular Goat-Roti sounds awfully like Côte-Rôtie. If you care to linger, you can have a light meal and freshly baked bread at the Goatshed restaurant. ⊠ *WR3, off R101 (Suid Agter Paarl Rd.)* ☎ *021/863–2450* ⊕ *www.fairview.co.za* ⊠ *Wine/cheese tastings R10* ☉ *Weekdays 8:30–5, Sat. 8:30–1; cellar tours by appointment.*

Glen Carlou. What comes out of Glen Carlou is rather special. The chardonnay reserve is exceptional, and the shiraz is noteworthy. The winery also sells a small range of farm cheeses and olives. The cellar is undergoing a major overhaul, and an art gallery is being added. ⊠ *WR1 (Simondium Rd.), between R44 and R45, Klapmuts* ☎ *021/875–5528* ⊕ *www.glencarlou.co.za* ⊠ *Tastings R10* ☉ *Weekdays 8:45–4:45, Sat. 9–12:30.*

KWV International. Short for Ko-operatieve Wijnbouwers Vereniging (Cooperative Winegrowers' Association), KWV International regulated and controlled the Cape wine industry for decades. Though it no longer has a regulatory function, it continues to dominate the industry. Its brandies, sherries, and fortified dessert wines regularly garner gold medals at the International Wine & Spirit Competition in London, and it offers one of the most popular and crowded cellar tours in the Winelands. KWV's cellars are some of the largest in the world, covering around 55 acres. Among the highlights is the famous Cathedral Cellar, with a barrel-vaulted ceiling and giant vats carved with scenes from the history of Cape wine making. In an adjoining cellar you can see the five largest vats in the world under one roof. The tour begins with a short audiovisual presentation and ends with a tasting of some of KWV's products. ⊠ *André du Toit Bldg., Kohler St.* ☎ *021/807–3007* ⊕ *www.kwv-international.com* ☒ *Tastings R15; cellar tour with tastings R22* ⊙ *Mon.–Sat. 9–4:30; English tours at 10, 10:30, and 2:15.*

Landskroon. This venerable estate, run by the ninth generation of the de Villiers family, produces a lovely cabernet franc and a cabernet sauvignon—with hints of vanilla and oak—that's up there with the best. For a little something to sip after a long, leisurely dinner, try the Murio Muscat Jerepico—a rich, velvety fortified wine with a fresh finish. ⊠ *Suid Agter Paarl Rd., off R44, Suider Paarl* ☎ *021/863–1039* ⊕ *www.landskroonwines.com* ☒ *Tastings free* ⊙ *Weekdays 8:30–5, Sat. 9–1.*

Nelson's Creek. A huge geological fault runs through this wonderful estate and is partly responsible for the multiple soil types and microclimates here. But that's just the physical background. In 1997 owner Alan Nelson decided that land redistribution was a good idea, so he gave 24 acres of prime vineyard to the estate's farmworkers to inaugurate the New Beginnings program. From the proceeds of their first vintage, they bought another 20 acres. Mathewis Thabo, who started off as a part-time gardener, is now producing three pretty respectable wines—a red, a white, and a rosé. Nelson's Creek produces some fantastic reds, too. The cabernet sauvignon is a big, ripe blackberry-flavored wine with a hint of spice; the pinotage is unwooded and, although a bit unusual, has been well received. The best buy is probably the inexpensive, very drinkable Albenet, a cinsaut-shiraz blend. This is also a great place for a picnic or walk. ⊠ *R44, Agter Paarl* ☎ *021/869–8453* ⊕ *www.nelsonscreek.co.za* ☒ *Tastings free; cellar tour with tastings R20* ⊙ *Weekdays 8–5, Sat. 9–2; cellar tours by appointment.*

Rhebokskloof. This winery sits at the head of a shallow valley, backed by hillsides covered with vines and fynbos. It's a lovely place for lunch on a sunny day. The Victorian Restaurant serves à la carte meals and teas on an oak-shaded terrace overlooking the gardens and mountains; in inclement weather meals are served in the Cape Dutch Restaurant, as is a Sunday buffet lunch. The Chardonnay Sur Lie is the pick of the bunch, with a lovely balance and fruity, toasty overtones. You can also take horseback rides through the vineyards. ⊠ *WR8* ☎ *021/869–8386* ⊕ *www.rhebokskloof.co.za* ☒ *Tastings R8; cellar tour with tastings R15* ⊙ *Daily 9–5; cellar tours by appointment.*

Where to Stay & Eat

$$$$ ✕ **Roggeland.** For an unforgettable Cape experience, make a beeline for this glorious Cape Dutch manor house on a farm outside Paarl. Meals are long, languid rituals, whether it's an alfresco lunch in the garden or a four-course dinner in the 18th-century dining room. You might start with sweet-corn soup with cilantro cream followed by trout fillet on hand-made pasta with a basil sabayon. A main course of lamb loin comes teamed with roasted butternut and shallots in muscadel, with an indigenous malva pudding with a rooibos-tea mousse as the finale. This feast is priced at R160, and includes a different wine with each course. ⊠ *Roggeland Rd., North Paarl* ☎ *021/868–2501* ⌦ *Reservations essential* ▤ *AE, DC, MC, V.*

$$$–$$$$
Fodor's Choice
★ ✕ **Bosman's.** Set amid the heady opulence of the Grande Roche hotel, this elegant restaurant and Relais & Châteaux member ranks as one of the country's finest. The level of service is extraordinary, commensurate with that of the finest European restaurants, although some diners may find the attention a little suffocating. Having overcome the hurdle of which menu to choose—seafood, tasting (8–12 dishes), Cape specialties, vegetarian, low-fat gourmet, or à la carte—you start with a complimentary *amuse-bouche* (literally, something to entertain your palate). A first course of hot olive oil–seared peppered beef sashimi with a wasabi-scented jus could precede an entrée of cherry crêpe–wrapped springbok loin with a delicious pinotage-inspired sauce. ⊠ *Grand Roche, Plantasie St.* ☎ *021/863–2727* ▤ *AE, DC, MC, V* ☉ *Closed mid-May–July.*

¢–$$$$
✕ **Pontac Manor.** Having established a popular small hotel in a striking Cape Victorian former farmstead, the owners added a restaurant that is a Winelands favorite. The deep veranda is the place for lunch except on very hot days, when the elegant dining room makes a cooler option. All savory items can be ordered in starter or full portions. A distinct Cape accent is discernible in dishes like venison with polenta accompanied by burnt-banana quenelles. Finish with country cheeses or try the cheese-cake mille-feuille on an amaretto syrup garnished with chocolate cigars. ⊠ *16 Zion St.* ☎ *021/872–0445* 🖷 *021/872–0460* ⌦ *Reservations essential* ▤ *AE, DC, MC, V.*

¢–$
✕ **La Masseria Ruitersvlei.** The ambience is rustic Italian, hardly surprising since the restaurant name means "the farmhouse" in Italian. This is a casual eatery, where large families arrive early for meals served at long tables. Tuck into delectable antipasti: marinated vegetables, cold meats, salads, and wonderful homemade cheeses and breads. The buffet costs R80, with additional items charged separately. If you wish, choose one of the homemade pastas of the day: if gnocchi in burnt sage butter is available, don't hesitate. The restaurant is also open for breakfast. ⊠ *Ruitersvlei wine estate, Suid Agter Paarl Rd.* ☎ *021/863–3637* ⌦ *Reservations essential on weekends* ▤ *AE, MC, V* ☉ *Closed Mon.*

★ $
✕▥ **Diemersfontein Wine & Country Estate.** Set in a lush garden with rolling lawns and abundant roses and azalea bushes, this historic farmstead was built in the 19th century. It was a much-loved family home before being converted into a guesthouse, and has retained that personal touch. The comfortable sofas, bowls of fresh flowers, thick carpets, and original artwork give Diemersfontein a lived-in feeling. At the end of your stay you might have to be pried off the veranda, where you can contemplate what life would be like as a successful wine farmer. The farm has begun producing a range of noteworthy red wines, which you can taste on the

estate. Seasons restaurant ($–$$) serves, appropriately enough, seasonal meals. You must phone ahead for the six-course tasting menu. If you want something more low-key, order a picnic basket to take onto the grounds. If you're feeling energetic, try your hand at bass fishing or horseback riding on the estate. The farm has an honor bar and a self-catering cottage. ✉ *Jan van Riebeek Dr. (R301), Wellington 7655* ☎ *021/873–2671 guesthouse, 021/864–5060 restaurant* 🖷 *021/864–2095* ⊕ *www.diemersfontein.co.za* ⤳ *18 rooms, 1 cottage* ⟁ *Restaurant, pool, fishing, horseback riding, bar; no a/c in some rooms, no room TVs* ▤ *AE, DC, MC, V* ⦿❘ *BP.*

★ **$$$** 🏨 **Bartholomeus Klip Farmhouse.** For a break from a long bout of wine tasting, head to this Victorian guesthouse on a nature reserve and working farm. Its luxurious accommodations and excellent food come in the middle of 9,900 acres of rare *renosterveld* scrubland that is home to the endangered geometric tortoise. There are also plenty of eland, zebra, wildebeest, springbok, rhebok, bontebok, bat-eared fox, Cape buffalo, and bird life in and around the mountains, streams, and plains, and the farm runs a growing Cape buffalo breeding program. Watch sheep shearing in action, hike, mountain bike, swim, or paddle. The farmhouse is decorated in old African colonial style, with plenty of floral fabrics, antique silver, and botanical art. Rooms have thick comforters and crisp linens. Ask for one that opens onto the veranda, especially in summer. A wonderful self-catering house next to the farmhouse is ideal for families and has its own pool. Have high tea in the boathouse. The scones and cream are fabulous, as is the traditionally made melktert (cinnamon-sprinkled custard tart), a South African teatime institution. Rates include all meals, teas, and game drives. ✉ *Off the R44, near Bo-Hermon* ✍ *Box 36, Hermon 7308* ☎ *021/794–6561* 🖷 *021/794–2069* ⊕ *www.thelastword.co.za* ⤳ *5 rooms, 1 suite, 1 house* ⟁ *Pool, boating, fishing, mountain bikes, hiking* ▤ *AE, DC, MC, V* ⦿❘ *FAP.*

★ **$$$** 🏨 **Grande Roche.** A member of the prestigious Relais & Châteaux group, this establishment can stake a claim to being one of the best hotels in South Africa. In a gorgeous Cape Dutch manor house that dates from the mid-18th century, the hotel sits amid acres of vines beneath Paarl Mountain, overlooking the valley and the Drakenstein Mountains. Suites are either in the historic buildings—slave quarters, stables, and wine cellar—or in attractive terrace buildings constructed in traditional Cape Dutch style. Rooms are a tasteful mix of the modern and the old: reed ceilings and thatch comfortably coexist with heated towel racks and air-conditioning. The staff, many of whom trained in Europe, outnumber the guests two to one, and offer a level of service extremely rare in South Africa. ✉ *Plantasie St., Box 6038, 7622* ☎ *021/863–2727* 🖷 *021/863–2220* ⊕ *www.granderoche.co.za* ⤳ *5 rooms, 30 suites* ⟁ *Restaurant, room service, 2 tennis courts, 2 pools, gym, bar* ▤ *AE, DC, MC, V* ⦿❘ *BP* ⊘ *Closed mid-May–July.*

★ **$$$** 🏨 **Santé Winelands Hotel & Wellness Centre.** The location is great for exploring Stellenbosch, Paarl, and Franschhoek, but given the level of luxury and incredible spa treatments, you might never want to leave this 395-acre estate. Rooms, much bigger than most, are stylishly decorated with such touches as extra-huge beds and, in a manor house room, an enormous bathtub overlooking the vines. Self-catering vineyard villas, great for families or couples traveling together, comprise four double rooms, a lounge with an entertainment center, and a gourmet kitchen. Each villa also has a private pool, terrace, and garden, and costs around R13,000 for eight people. But the highlight of any stay is the spa, which offers vinotherapy—the second place in the world to use grapes and grape products to pamper and beautify. This is, after all, the Winelands. There's a shiraz grape-seed scrub, a chardonnay wrap, a Cap Classique massage, and even a cabernet sauvignon wine-casket soak. ⊠ *Off Simonsvlei Rd.* 🕾 *Box 381, Klapmuts 7625* ☎ *021/875–8100* 📠 *021/875–8111* ⊕ *www.santewellness.co.za* 🛏 *90 rooms, 7 villas* ⚒ *2 restaurants, 3 pools (1 indoors), spa, fishing, mountain bikes, hiking, horseback riding* ⊟ *AE, DC, MC, V* ⎮◎⎮ *BP.*

★ **\$\$** 🏨 **Roggeland Country House.** Dating from 1693, this farm is one of the most delightful lodgings in the Winelands. The setting in the Dal Josaphat valley is breathtaking, with stunning views of the craggy Drakenstein Mountains. Guest rooms in restored farm buildings have reed ceilings, country dressers, and mosquito nets (not just for effect). The 1779 manor house, which contains the dining room and lounge, is a masterpiece of Cape Dutch architecture. ⊠ *Roggeland Rd., Box 7210, Northern Paarl 7623* ☎ *021/868–2501* 📠 *021/868–2113* ⊕ *www.exploreafrica.com/roggeland* 🛏 *10 rooms* ⚒ *Restaurant; no a/c, no room TVs* ⊟ *AE, DC, MC, V* ⎮◎⎮ *MAP.*

\$ 🏨 **Lemoenkloof Historical Hotel.** In the heart of Paarl, this national monument is decorated in sophisticated country style, with generous throws and flouncy curtains. The rest of the house is peppered with antiques and Oriental rugs. Modern accoutrements, such as television, air-conditioning, and tea- and coffeemaking facilities in each of the guest rooms, make your stay comfortable. The swimming pool and art gallery add an element of fun, and the private garden is a great place to relax after some hectic wine tasting. ⊠ *396A Main St., 7646* ☎ *021/872–7520 or 021/872–3782* 📠 *021/872–7532* ⊕ *www.lemoenkloof.co.za* 🛏 *20 rooms* ⚒ *Pool* ⊟ *AE, DC, MC, V* ⎮◎⎮ *BP.*

Sports & the Outdoors

BALLOONING **Wineland Ballooning** (☎ 021/863–3192 ⊕ www.kaapinfo.com) makes one-hour flights over the Winelands every morning from about November through April, weather permitting. The balloon holds a maximum of five passengers, and the trip costs about R1,550 per person. After the flight there's a champagne breakfast at the Grand Roche.

GOLF **Paarl Golf Club** (⊠ Wemmershoek Rd. ☎ 021/863–1140) is surrounded by mountains, covered with trees, and dotted with water hazards. The greens fees are R285 for 18 holes, golf-club rental is around R150, caddies cost around R90, and golf carts are approximately R150.

HORSEBACK RIDING **Wine Valley Horse Trails** (⊠ Rheboksloof wine farm, WR8, off the R44 ☎ 083/226–8735 or 021/869–8687 ⊕ www.horsetrails-sa.co.za) offers scenic rides around the Rhebokskloof vineyards or up into the surrounding Paarl Mountain Nature Reserve. A longish ride of about four hours gets you to the far side of the hill, from where you have a distant view of Table Mountain. Prices range from R150 for a one-hour ride to R480 for a full day.

en route

The **Bain's Kloof Pass Road,** built by engineer Andrew Geddes Bain, was opened in 1853, linking Wellington to Ceres and Worcester. The road (an extension of the R303 from Paarl through Wellington) winds north from Wellington, through the Hawekwa Mountains, revealing breathtaking views across the valley below. On a clear day you can see as far as the coast. The road has a good tar surface, but unlike many Western Cape passes, Bain's Kloof has not been widened much since it was built, so take your time and enjoy the views. There are places where you can park and walk down to lovely, refreshing mountain pools—great on a hot summer's day. As you approach the initial slopes of Bain's Kloof, look out for the **Bovlei Winery,** on the right. Built in 1907 in traditional style, the building itself is not particularly noteworthy, but it has a vast picture window offering a stupendous view of the undulating vineyards beyond. Be sure to try their light New World–style reds and the fortified or Muscat d'Alexandrie (White Hanepoot) dessert wines. The award-winning cabernet-merlot reserve blend is an excellent buy. ⊠ *Bain's Kloof Rd., Wellington* ☎ *021/873–1567* ⊕ *www.bovlei.co.za* ☲ *Tastings free* ☉ *Weekdays 8:30–5, Sat. 8:30–12:30.*

Winelands A to Z

BUS TRAVEL

There is no regular bus service to the Winelands suitable for tourists. If you are based in Stellenbosch, however, and don't want to drive to the wineries, you can make use of the Vine Hopper, a minibus that follows a fixed route to five wine farms. Tickets cost around R135, and you'll be given a timetable so that you can get on and off as you please.
🚌 Bus Line **Vine Hopper** ☎ 021/882-8112 or 084/875-5959.

CAR TRAVEL

Driving yourself is undoubtedly the best way to appreciate the Winelands. Each wine route is clearly marked with attractive road signs, and there are complimentary maps available at the tourism bureaus and at most wine farms. Roads in the area are good, and even the dirt roads leading up to a couple of the farms are nothing to worry about.

The best way to get to the Winelands is to take the N2 out of Cape Town and then the R310 to Stellenbosch. Outside of rush hour, this will take you around 45 minutes. Expect some delays during the harvest months, when tractors ferry grapes from farms to cellars on the narrower secondary roads. On your way back to Cape Town, stick to the R310 and the N2. Avoid taking the M12, as it gets very confusing, and you'll end up in suburbs that aren't on tourist maps.

If you spend a day out in the Winelands and return at dusk or after dark, be on the lookout for pedestrians, especially on weekends, when people are likely to have been drinking. There is, unfortunately, a high incidence of pedestrian-related accidents on these roads. Also be sure to designate a driver so that you don't get caught drinking and driving.

South African drivers are erratic, and the condition of their cars varies enormously. There are lots of expensive SUVs on the roads, but also plenty of old bangers with no turn signals and dubious brakes, so watch for cars turning without warning. South African drivers tend to drive fairly fast and get very impatient when they're held up by slower vehicles. It's common practice to pull over onto the shoulder to let faster drivers pass you. If somebody flashes his or her lights behind you, that's what they're expecting you to do. If you do pull over, do so briefly and with an eye out for pedestrians. Passing drivers usually acknowledge your courtesy by putting on their hazard lights for a few seconds or with a simple wave. If an oncoming driver flashes his or her lights, it's a warning to slow down, either for traffic police or for a dangerous situation, such as an accident or slippery road.

The major car-rental agencies have offices in the smaller towns, but it's best to deal with the Cape Town offices. Besides, you'll probably want to pick up a car at the airport. If you're already in the Winelands and would like a car for the day, try Wine Route Rent-a-Car, based in Paarl, which will drop off a car at your hotel. Since driving yourself around limits the amount of wine you can taste, unless you have a designated driver, it's best to take a tour, take a taxi, or—do it in style—rent a limo. Limos cost about R400 per hour, so they're particularly cost effective if you have a group of four or five.

🚗 Rental Companies **Avis** ✉ 123 Strand St., Cape Town ☎ 021/424-1177, 021/934-0330 airport, 086/102-1111 reservations ⊕ www.avis.co.za. **Budget** ✉ 120 Strand St., Cape Town ☎ 021/418-5232, 021/980-3140 airport ⊕ www.budget.co.za. **Europcar** ✉ 49 Loop St., Cape Town ☎ 021/418-0670 or 021/934-2263 ⊕ www.europcar.co.za. **Hertz** ✉ 40 Loop St., Cape Town ☎ 021/400-9650 ⊕ www.hertz.co.za. **Wine Route Rent-a-Car** ☎ 021/872-8513 or 083/225-7089 ⊕ www.encounter.co.za/rentacar.

🚗 Limousine Company **Cape Limo Services** ☎ 021/785-3100.

EMERGENCIES

🚑 Emergency Services **Ambulance** ☎ 10177. **Police** ☎ 10111. **Police, Fire, and Ambulance** ☎ 107 from landline. **Vodacom emergency services** ☎ 112 from mobile phone.

🏥 Hospitals **Paarl Medi-Clinic** ✉ Berlyn St., Paarl North ☎ 021/807-8000. **Stellenbosch Medi-Clinic** ✉ Saffraan and Rokewood Rds., Die Boord, Stellenbosch ☎ 021/883-8571. **Strand Medi-Clini** ✉ Altena Rd., Strand ☎ 021/854-7663.

💊 Late-Night Pharmacy **Die Boord Pharmacy** ✉ 14 Saffraan Ave., Die Boord Shopping Centre, Stellenbosch ☎ 021/887-9400.

INTERNET

There are a couple of Internet cafés in the region's main towns, especially Stellenbosch. Some hotels and guesthouses also offer Internet connections, so ask at the front desk before heading into town. Where there are no Internet cafés, print shops are usually a good bet. Expect to pay around R5 for every 10 minutes of browsing.

🌐 Internet Access **Fandango** ✉ Drostdy Sq., Bird St., Stellenbosch ☎ 021/887-7501. **Stellenbosch Adventure Centre** ✉ 36 Market St., Stellenbosch ☎ 021/882-8112.

MONEY MATTERS

Changing money in the Winelands is a breeze. Hotels, restaurants, and wineries are increasingly sophisticated and only too happy to swipe your credit card through their machines. There are also plenty of ATMs, banks, and *bureaux de change,* so you won't be stuck without cash. Be careful when withdrawing money from ATMs; don't let anyone distract you while your card is in the machine or while you're punching in your PIN.

TAXIS

Paarl Radio Taxis will transport up to three people at about R7 per kilometer (R9 per mile) during the day, R8 per kilometer (R10 per mile) at night. Waiting time is around R60 per hour. Larger groups can arrange transportation by minibus. Daksi Cab, based in Stellenbosch, works on a trip rate rather than a per-kilometer basis. A trip to a local restaurant costs around R70 regardless of the number of people. Daksi also offers shuttle service to the airport.

🚖 Taxi Companies **Daksi Cab** ☎ 082/854-1541. **Paarl Radio Taxis** ☎ 021/872-5671.

TOURS

The historic area of Stellenbosch is so pretty and compact that it's a pity just to drive through. Take a walking tour with Sandra Krige from Stellenbosch on Foot. Tours last around 1½ hours and take in all the well-known sights. Sandra is a mine of information about the town and even offers an evening ghost tour. Expect to pay around R60 per person, more for the evening tour. De Omnibus Compagnie offers tours in which you are ferried around in a tractor-drawn bus that looks like an old-fashioned tram. Options include a historical tour of the town, a restaurant tour comprising a three-course meal at three different Stellenbosch restaurants, and a full-moon picnic at Zorgvliet wine estate. The historical tour (R75) departs from the Stellenbosch Tourism and Information Bureau on weekdays at 10, 2, and 3:30. The restaurant tour (about R395) takes place Tuesday and Thursday nights.

Most tours to the Winelands are operated by companies based in Cape Town, such as Ferdinand's Tours and Adventures. Easy Rider Wine Tours has a great all-day tour that's very reasonably priced (around R250, including lunch in Franschhoek). You get picked up around Stellenbosch at 10:30-ish and will visit five estates in the three regions. More conservative tour companies include reliable standbys Springbok Atlas, Welcome Tourism Services, and Hylton Ross. All companies have half- or full-day tours, but they vary by company and might include a cheese tasting or cellar tour in addition to wine tasting. Expect to pay around R350 for a half day and R450 for a full day, including all tasting fees. Though you stop for lunch, it is not included. Most tour buses stop at Spier, as the cheetahs provide a magnetic pull.

For those serious about wine, Vineyard Ventures offers the best of the Winelands tour companies. Sisters Gillian Stoltzman and Glen Christie are knowledgeable and passionate about wine and will tailor tours to your interests. The cost ranges from around R900 per person for four people to roughly R2,200 for one person and includes all tastings, museum entries, and a fabulous lunch (with wine, of course).

⚐ Tour Operators De Omnibus Compagnie ☎ 021/882-8112 or 084/875-5959. **Easy Rider Wine Tours** ☎ 021/886-4651 ⊕ www.jump.to/stumble. **Ferdinand's Tours and Adventures** ☎ 021/913-8800 or 082/708-4820 ⊕ www.fgroup.co.za. **Hylton Ross Tours** ☎ 021/511-1784 ⊕ www.hyltonross.co.za. **Springbok Atlas** ☎ 021/460-4700 ⊕ www.springbokatlas.com. **Stellenbosch on Foot** ☎ 021/887-9150 or 083/218-1310. **Vineyard Ventures** ☎ 021/434-8888 or 082/920-2825 ⊕ www.vineyardventures.co.za. **Welcome Tourism Services** ☎ 021/505-6350 ⊕ www.welcome.co.za.

TRAIN TRAVEL

Cape Metro trains run from Cape Town to Stellenbosch and Paarl, but owing to an increase in violent muggings the trains should be avoided. A far safer, more stylish, and more fun alternative is to hop on the Spier Vintage Train when it is running. Regular trips run from Spier Monument Station out to Spier, in the Winelands, at R100 for a round-trip, and also to Darling (⇨ the West Coast, *below*).

⚐ Train Line Spier Vintage Train ☎ 021/419-5222 ⊕ www.spier.co.za.

VISITOR INFORMATION

You can get almost all the information you need about the Western Cape from the very organized Cape Town Tourism offices, which are open weekdays 9–6, Saturday 8:30–2, and Sunday 9–1. Cape Town Tourism's Helderberg branch is open weekdays 8:30–5 during winter (approximately March–October) and 9:30–6 in summer (about November–February), Saturday 9–1. Franschhoek Vallée Tourisme is open weekdays 9–6, weekends 9–4. Paarl Tourism Bureau is open weekdays 8:30–5, Saturday 9–1, and Sunday 10–1. Stellenbosch Tourism and Information Bureau is open weekdays 8–6, Saturday 9–5, and Sunday 10–4.

⚐ Tourist Offices Cape Town Tourism ✉ The Pinnacle at Burg and Castle Sts., Box 1403, Cape Town 8000 ☎ 021/426-4260 ⊕ www.tourismcapetown.co.za. **Cape Town Tourism-Helderberg Branch** ✉ 186 Main Rd., Somerset West 7129 ☎ 021/851-4022 ⊕ www.tourismcapetown.co.za. **Franschhoek Vallée Tourisme** ✉ 28 Huguenot Rd., Franschhoek 7690 ☎ 021/876-3603 ⊕ www.franschhoek.org.za. **Paarl Tourism Bureau** ✉ 216 Main St., Paarl 7646 ☎ 021/872-3829 or 021/872-4842 ⊕ www.paarlonline. com. **Stellenbosch Tourism and Information Bureau** ✉ 36 Market St., Stellenbosch 7600 ☎ 021/883-3584 ⊕ www.stellenboschtourism.com.

BREEDE RIVER VALLEY

The upper and central part of the catchment of the Breede River extends over a large area. It's a beautiful part of the country, with a combination of fantastic mountain scenery, fabulous fynbos, pretty bucolic farmlands, and small towns. A short drive over any one of the scenic mountain passes is sure to bring you into a secluded valley resplendent with the greens of spring, the grape-laden vines of summer, the myriad colors of autumn, or the snowcapped peaks and crisp misty mornings of winter.

A natural climatic combination of comparatively mild but wet winters followed by long, warm summers makes this area perfectly suited for the cultivation of deciduous fruit, especially viticulture. In the summer the intense sunshine allows the wine and table grapes to develop rich ruby colors. Virtually deprived of rain in summer, the vines nurture their precious crop, irrigated from the meandering Breede River and the huge Brandvlei dam, near Worcester.

Tulbagh

⑤ *60 km (37 mi) north of Paarl.*

Founded in 1743, the town of Tulbagh is nestled in a secluded valley bounded by the Witzenberg and Groot Winterhoek mountains. A devastating earthquake in September 1969 shook the city and destroyed many of the original facades of the historic town. Much of the town is unlovely, having simply been rebuilt, often prefab style, on old foundations, but the real attraction of Tulbagh is **Church Street,** parallel to the main Van der Stel Street, where each of the 32 buildings was restored to its original form and subsequently declared a national monument.

The **Oude Kerk** (Old Church) museum stands at the entrance to Church Street, and is the logical departure point for a self-guided tour of the area, which is well marked. The church has been extensively restored and has an interesting collection of artifacts from the area, including carvings made by Boer prisoners of war. A ticket includes admission to another two buildings on Church Street, which operate as annexes of the main museum. These show a practical history of events before, during, and after the quake. The buildings have been painstakingly reconstructed. ⊠ *Church St.* ☎ *023/230–1041* ⌂ *R5* ⊙ *Weekdays 9–5, Sat. 10–4, Sun. 11–4 (opens earlier on Sat. in summer).*

need a break?   If you're feeling peckish, head to **Digby Butchery** (⊠ Station Rd. ☎ 023/230–0466) for an excellent range of biltong and *droë wors* (dried sausage), made exclusively from beef, lamb, and spices. In winter, during game-hunting season, there's a wide variety of game biltong that's quickly snapped up by regular customers.

Just 3 km (2 mi) out of town, built on high ground commensurate with its status, is the majestic **Oude Drostdy Museum.** Built by renowned Cape architect Louis Thibault in 1804, the building was badly damaged by fire in 1934 and later by the 1969 quake, but it has been carefully restored and is a fine example of neoclassical architecture. The building now houses an impressive collection of antique furniture and artifacts. Look for the gramaphone collection and the Dutch grandfather clock that has a picture of Amsterdam harbor painted on its face. As the original magistrate's house, the Drostdy had a cellar, which served as the local jail and now hosts wine tastings and sales. ☎ *023/230–0203* ⌂ *Museum R5, tastings R8* ⊙ *Weekdays 10–5, Sat. 10–2.*

If you stand in front of the church on Van der Stel Street, you will see a wine barrel indicating the road to **Twee Jonge Gezellen,** which is about 8 km (5 mi) from town. One of the finest and oldest wineries in the area, it's a family-run estate best known for its fantastic Cap Classique—Krone Borealis Brut. But many Capetonians are more familiar with the old, tried, and trusted TJ39, an easily drinkable, well-priced blend of *weisser* (white) riesling, chardonnay, chenin blanc, and sauvignon blanc that has been making a regular appearance on local tables for years. The Krone Engeltjipipi (referring to—er—a certain body waste of little angels) is a blend made from grapes naturally infected with botrytis and considered a gift from the cherubs. The grapes are harvested by hand over a number of nights at the end of the season. ☎ 023/230–0680 ⊕ *www. tjwines.co.za* ⧠ *Tastings free* ☉ *Weekdays 9–4, Sat. 10–2 cellar tours weekdays at 11 and 3, Sat. at 11.*

Where to Stay & Eat

$ ✕ **Paddagang.** Though built as a private residence in 1809, by 1821 Paddagang (Frog's Way) was already serving as one of South Africa's first tap houses (like a pub with wine on tap). Immaculately restored after the 1969 earthquake, it was turned into a restaurant and became a popular tourist destination. Although a little timeworn, the decor is authentic, as are the *riempie* (thong-upholstered) chairs. The vine-covered pergola makes a lovely place to eat in all but the hottest weather. Traditional Cape fare is your best bet here, from starters like *smoorsnoek* (local smoked fish braised with potato and onion) with grape jam on the side, to a main course of South Africa's national dish, bobotie. Though the establishment has much going for it, standards of both food and service have taken a dive recently. ⊠ *23 Church St.* ☎ *023/230– 0242* ⊟ *AE, DC, MC, V* ☉ *No dinner.*

★ ¢–$ ✕ **Readers.** The historic residence of the former church reader makes a cozy setting for this restaurant. Carol Collins's innovative fare offers sophisticated contrasts, although she keeps presentation simple and appetizing. Her small seasonal menu changes daily. Dinner could start with smoked chicken salad with papaw, nuts, and goat cheese, or a butternut squash and zucchini soup. If the springbok fillet with gooseberry and Amarula (a liquor made from the fruit of the marula tree) sauce is listed, don't miss it. Any one of the dessert trio is sure to make a memorable finale. The carefully chosen and well-priced wine list reflects regional labels. ⊠ *12 Church St.* ☎ *023/230–0087* ⊟ *AE, DC, MC, V* ☉ *Closed Tues.*

$ ▦ **Rijk's Ridge Country House.** This spot is on the outskirts of the village, on a ridge overlooking a lake where you can enjoy sweeping views of the surrounding mountains. Each suite, decorated in a plush Cape cottage style, has a private terrace leading to the poolside garden. ⊠ *Main Rd., Box 340, 6820* ☎ *023/230–1006* ⧠ *023/230–1125* ⊕ *www.rijks. co.za* ⇥ *12 suites, 3 cottages* ♿ *Restaurant, pool, billiards; no a/c* ⊟ *AE, DC, MC, V* ⎰⎱ *BP.*

$ ▦ **Tulbagh Country House.** Ginny Clarke, owner of this guesthouse, is warm, friendly, and open—just the sort of qualities you'd expect from somebody in a small country town. Ginny's a mine of information about the village, the beds are comfortable, and breakfasts are hearty. The house was built in 1809 and has been declared a national monument. There's even a resident ghost who appears periodically to make sure things are running as they should. If you don't feel like eating out, you can use the *braai* (barbecue) facilities, but there are a number of good restaurants within walking distance. Ginny will also pack you a picnic basket on request. ⊠ *24 Church St., 6820* ☎ *023/230–1171*

🏠 *023/230–0721* ⊕ *www.tulbaghguesthouse.co.za* ⤴ *3 rooms, 1 suite* ⚡ *No a/c* ▤ *MC, V* ❢❢ *BP.*

Worcester

❻ *45 km (28 mi) southeast of Tulbagh; 50 km (30 mi) east of Paarl on the N1, on the other side of the du Toits Kloof Pass or tunnel.*

Worcester is by far the largest town in the Breede River valley, often termed the region's capital by locals, and with good cause. Much of the town's burgeoning commerce and industry is connected to agriculture—viticulture, in particular—and its brandy cellars produce the highest volume of the spirit in the country.

The **Karoo National Botanical Garden** lies on the opposite side of the N1 highway from the town of Worcester, but is easy to find if you follow the signs eastward from the last set of traffic lights on High Street. Billed as one of the most important such collections in the world, this one includes several hundred species of indigenous flora, including succulents, aloes, and trees. Follow the road from the entrance to the main parking area, the starting point of three clearly marked walks. A special Braille Garden is geared for the visually impaired. If you phone ahead, you can arrange to watch a slide show and take a guided walk through the gardens and the collection houses for around R60. ☏ *023/347–0785* 🎫 *R10* ☉ *Daily 7–7.*

☸ The **Kleinplasie Living Open-Air Museum** is a welcome change from dusty artifacts in glass cases. The fascinating museum is actually a collection of original buildings from the area that have been re-erected around a working farmyard. Following a narrated slide show, venture into the farmyard and watch the museum staff, intent on keeping traditional skills alive, as they bake bread, twist tobacco, make horseshoes in a smithy, and distill witblitz. The museum also has a shop where you can buy produce from the farmyard. ✉ *Kleinplasie Agricultural Showgrounds, Traub St.* ☏ *023/342–2225* 🎫 *R12* ☉ *Mon.–Sat. 9–4:30.*

The **KWV Brandy Cellar** is the largest distillery of its kind in the world, with 120 pot stills under one roof. Informative guided tours, followed by a brandy tasting, will take you through the process of brandy making. The well-informed guide will give a layman's rundown of the various methods used, the pros and cons of pot-still distillation as compared with the continuous-still method, as well as a description of the maturation process. In the cooperage you can see traditional barrel-making. ✉ *Church and Smith Sts.* ☏ *023/342–0255* ⊕ *www.kwv-international. com* 🎫 *Tastings R15; tours R20 weekdays, R22 Sat., R25 Sun.* ☉ *Weekdays 8–4:30; English tours weekdays at 2, weekends by appointment.*

Where to Stay & Eat

$–$$ ✕ **St. Geran.** Townsfolk and the local farming community form the bulk of the clientele, and most of them like red meat and plenty of it. Neither they nor the chef-patron see any need for change, so the menu, with its wide range of steak tempered by a good selection of seafood, has varied little since the start of the new century. The most popular dishes are still peppered fillets panfried in cream and sherry or filled with ham and cheese, followed by *kingklip* (a firm, white fish) topped with shrimp and cheese sauce. Starters and desserts are run-of-the-mill. ⊠ *48 Church St.* ☎ *023/342–2800* ◻ *AE, DC, MC, V* ⊗ *Closed Sun. No lunch Sat.*

¢–$ ✕ **Pear Tree.** In a town where few examples of vernacular architecture have survived, the Beck Huis museum is an important example of a well-restored homestead. The garden and courtyard—complete with venerable pear tree—are the setting for alfresco meals. The adjoining restaurant, now part of the museum complex, seats guests in separate rooms, one with a bar and two with fireplaces. The extensive menu is geared to South African palates and includes several heritage dishes, from Cape chicken pie to char-grilled ostrich kebabs. Don't expect haute cuisine, rather generous portions of country cooking. This is also a great place to stop for breakfast, tea, or coffee. ⊠ *Beck Huis, Church and Baring Sts.* ☎ *023/ 342–0936* ◻ *DC, MC, V* ⊗ *No dinner Sun.*

$ 🏨 **Cumberland Hotel.** In a town that is, for its size, surprisingly short on hotels, this central hotel is large, convenient, and well stocked with facilities. The reception area spreads out into a courtyard, and the dining area and spa and gym facilities have been placed around a central landscaped swimming pool. Rooms—all air-conditioned against the hot Boland summer and scrupulously clean—are reasonably priced. You can opt for a plan with no meals or one with breakfast included. ⊠ *2 Stockenstrom St., 6850* ☎ *023/347–2641* ᐧ *023/347–3613* ⊕ *www. cumberland.co.za* ↰ *54 rooms, 1 suite* ↻ *Tennis court, pool, health club, sauna, squash* ◻ *AE, DC, MC, V.*

Sports & the Outdoors

The Breede River has only tiny rapids near Worcester, where it twists and turns between clumps of *palmiet* (river reeds) and the overgrown banks. **Felix Unite River Adventures** (☎ 021/670–1300) runs canoe trips that include a light breakfast, not-so-light picnic lunch, and tasting of a selection of local wines (around R450). Using two-person inflatables, **River Rafters** (☎ 021/712–5094) offers a one-day trip with wine tasting for R420 and a two-day, two-night trip for R995. **Wildthing Adventures** (☎ 021/552–7753) offers a one- or two-day canoe trip. The one-day Wine Route trip (R425) is the most popular, and is more about food and drink than paddling. The highlight is the tasting of local wines during the extensive picnic lunch.

Robertson

❼   *48 km (30 mi) southeast of Worcester.*

Robertson was founded primarily to service the surrounding farms, and it retains its agricultural and industrial character. Some effort has been made to beautify the town with tree-lined roads, but there is little for visitors here, except as a stop-off for lunch on the way to McGregor or Montagu. If you are in the area, however, you might consider visiting one of the well-known local wine farms.

Capetonians in the know have long considered **Rooiberg Winery**, between Worcester and Robertson, one of the best value-for-money wineries in the area. The red muscadel is reputedly one of the best in the world, and the shiraz, pinotage, chardonnay, and port are all good buys. Check out the pyramidlike sculpture by landscape artist Strydom van der Merwe, built to commemorate the winery's 40th anniversary. ⊠ *R60, about 10 km (6 mi) northwest of Robertson* ☎ *023/626–1663* ⊕ *www. rooiberg.co.za* 🍷 *Tastings free* ⊙ *Weekdays 8–5:30, Sat. 9–3.*

Also on the road between Worcester and Robertson, **Graham Beck, Robertson Cellar** is the sibling to a cellar of the same name in Franschhoek. This country cousin produces some sophisticated wines. The Rhona Muscadel, a New Age muscat that's fruity but not cloying, and the excellent brut rosé are two favorites, but the reds are not to be ignored. Try the Ridge Syrah, which is garnering rave reviews, as is the Cornerstone Cabernet. ⊠ *R60, about 10 km (6 mi) northwest of Robertson* ☎ *023/ 626–1214* ⊕ *www.gahambeckwines.co.za* 🍷 *Tastings free* ⊙ *Weekdays 9–5, Sat. 10–3; cellar tours by appointment.*

At **Van Loveren Winery,** between Robertson and Bonnievale, apart from sampling the unusual Fernão Pires and a very delicate shiraz *blanc de noir*—both of which are very inexpensive—make sure you visit the unusual grounds. The owner's mother has planted a garden of indigenous and exotic plants and trees, surrounding a water fountain that supplies the entire farm. Instead of visiting the usual tasting room, you sit out under the trees and the various wines are brought to you. ⊠ *Off R317, 15 km (9 mi) southeast of Robertson* ☎ *023/615–1505* ⊕ *www. vanloveren.co.za* 🍷 *Tastings free* ⊙ *Weekdays 8:30–5, Sat. 9:30–1.*

Although the cabernet has its loyal following, the innovative **Springfield Estate** winery is best known for its unusual approach to white wines, especially chardonnay. The Methode Ancienne Chardonnay is made in the original Burgundy style and is bottled only if it's perfect—which happens about two years in five. The creamy Wild Yeast Chardonnay, with its all-natural fermentation, is an unwooded version of the above and comes highly recommended. ⊠ *R317, just north of Robertson* ☎ *023/ 626–3661* ⊕ *www.springfieldestate.com* 🍷 *Tastings free* ⊙ *Weekdays 8–5, Sat. 9–4; cellar tours by appointment.*

Where to Eat

★ **$–$$**   ✕**Fraai Uitzicht.** In a deeply rural setting between Robertson and Ashton, this 200-year-old fruit and wine farm is home to a rustic restaurant where Italian chef Mario Motti whips up impressively sophisticated fare. Garden produce and herbs are transformed into a menu of culinary joy, and serious food lovers can opt for the six- or seven-course tasting menu with matching wines for each course. You might start with a fragrant steamed prawn mousse with a foamy, ginger-spiked sauce. Among the five main courses, you can expect to find Karoo lamb rendered in various delectable ways, such as deboned leg in red wine with black olives and an onion confit. Desserts are as admirable, their sauces as stellar as those of the savory variety. The wine list does not disappoint, presenting a selection of the Robertson Valley's best augmented with French champagne. ⊠ *Off the R60, Klaas Voogds East* ☎ *023/626–6156* 🔔 *Reservations essential* 🚪 *AE, DC, MC, V* ⊙ *Closed June and July and Mon. and Tues.*

¢–$ ✕ **Branewynsdraai.** You will see the sign to this restaurant as you enter Robertson; it's a superb place to have lunch under ancient pepper trees on the lawns or in the air-conditioned interior in midsummer. The menu is straightforward, but includes traditional South African fare and top-quality steaks along with lighter fare and meal salads. Portions are generous, whether you opt for deep-fried calamari or sink your teeth into a giant sirloin topped with herb butter. As official stocker of Robertson Valley wines, this is the place to shop if lack of time limits your visits to the estates. ✉ *1 Kromhout St.* ☎ *023/626–3202* ▭ *AE, DC, MC, V* ☉ *No dinner Sun.*

en route On the R60 out of Robertson you can either take the clearly marked turnoff to McGregor, which snakes between vineyards and farms—a picture of bucolic charm—or continue on toward Montagu. Before reaching the latter, you'll pass through the unlovely agricultural town of Ashton. Keep left (don't turn off to Swellendam), and enter the short but spectacular **Cogman's Kloof Pass.** On either side of the pass, which runs in a river gorge, you can see the magnificent fold mountains, which are ultimately the source for Montagu's hot springs.

McGregor

❽ *20 km (12 mi) south of Robertson.*

Saved from development as a result of a planned mountain pass that never materialized, McGregor is the epitome of the sleepy country hollow, tucked away between the mountains, and is one of the best-preserved examples of a 19th-century Cape village. As you approach McGregor from Robertson, farmsteads give way to small cottages with distinctive red-painted doors and window frames. The McGregor Co-op Winery, on the left, heralds your entry into the town with its thatch cottages in vernacular architecture.

McGregor has become popular with artists who have settled here permanently and with busy executives from Cape Town intent on getting away from it all. Frankly, this is an ideal place to do absolutely nothing, but you can take a leisurely stroll through the fynbos, watch birds from one of several blinds on the Heron Walk, or follow one of the hiking or mountain-bike trails if you are feeling more energetic. There is a great hiking trail across the Riviersonderend Mountains to Greyton.

The **McGregor Co-op Winery** is a popular attraction, with surprisingly inexpensive wines, considering their quality. Try the unwooded chardonnay and the exceptional port. The 2004 colombar has also received rave reviews and a couple of awards. ✉ *Main Rd.* ☎ *023/625–1741* ⊕ *www. mcgregorwinery.co.za* ▱ *Tastings free* ☉ *Mon.–Thurs. 8–12:30 and 1:30–5, Fri. 8–5, Sat. 9–12:30; cellar tours by appointment.*

Where to Stay

$ 🏠 **Old Mill Lodge.** This simple thatch lodge, its adjacent 19th-century waterwheel still intact, dreams on among tall trees at the far end of the village. Accommodations are in thatch cottages with antique-style beds.

Before dinner take a walk through the olive grove or a dip in the swimming pool. À la carte lunches and dinners are optional. ☞ *Box 25, 6708* 🕿 *023/625–1841* 🖷 *023/625–1941* ⊕ *www.oldmilllodge.co.za* ✍ *8 rooms ☖ Restaurant, pool; no a/c, no room phones, no room TVs* ▤ *AE, DC, MC, V* ℣ *MAP.*

Sports & the Outdoors

There are two wonderful two-day hikes through the **Vrolijkheid Nature Reserve** (⊠ *5 km [3 mi] outside McGregor* 🕿 *023/625–1621*). For each you need to get a permit from the reserve and pay R18 per person for the two days. You'll also need to book accommodations.

Montagu

⑨ *29 km (22 mi) northeast of Robertson.*

Montagu bills itself as "the Gateway to the Little Karoo," and its picturesque streets lined with Cape Victorian architecture lend this some credence. Today the town's main attraction is its natural hot springs, and many of the Victorian houses have been transformed into bed-and-breakfast guesthouses. You know you're in a special place when farmers drop off their produce at the unmanned Honesty Shop and buyers leave money for what they owe.

There are a number of resorts where you can "partake of the waters," either as a day visitor or as a guest. Popular **Avalon Springs,** the only resort open to day visitors, is not the most stylish, and the architecture leaves a lot to be desired. But if you look beyond this and the numerous signs carrying stern warnings and instructions, you'll get good insight into South African life and culture, as people float and splash around in the various pools. If you're not staying at the resort, you can rent bikes from the village and cycle to the springs, where you can spend a few hours before heading home again. ⊠ *Uitvlucht St., 3 km (2 mi) outside Montagu* 🕿 *023/614–1150* ⊕ *www.avalonsprings.co.za* ✍ *R22.50 hot springs, R15 parking* ☉ *Daily 8* AM–11 PM.

The popular three-hour **Langeberg Tractor Ride** takes you to the summit of the Langeberg (Long Mountain) and back. The tractor winds up some tortuously twisted paths, revealing magnificent views of the area's peaks and valleys. After a short stop at the summit, a similarly harrowing descent follows, but you won't be disappointed by the views or the driver's chirpy banter. If you're here in spring or summer when the flowers are in bloom, you might even get to pick some gorgeous proteas on the way down. Following your trip, you can enjoy a delicious lunch of *potjiekos* (traditional stew cooked over a fire in a single cast-iron pot) for R50. Reservations are essential. ⊠ *Protea Farm, R318* 🕿 *023/614–2471* ✍ *R50* ☉ *Wed. and Sat. at 10 and 2.*

Where to Stay & Eat

$–$$ ✕ **Jessica's Restaurant.** Pet Staffordshire bull terrier Jessica not only lends her name to this Victorian house that has been converted into a restaurant, but also features in blown-up photographs on the walls, interspersed with delightful doggy prints from previous eras. If you cannot make up your mind after perusing the menu, stay with the recommended daily specials, such as smoked venison carpaccio with an avocado and mild chili salsa. Follow that with tiger prawns and chicken breast in Thai spices and coconut cream, or roasted vegetables with a pesto and feta cheese mousse. Classic highlights are the crispy duck and satiny crème brûlée. ⊠ *47 Bath St.* ☎ *023/614–1805* ⚖ *Reservations essential* ☰ *AE, DC, MC, V* ⊘ *Closed Sun. May–Sept., and Dec. and Jan. No lunch.*

$–$$ ✕☐ **Montagu Country Hotel.** This salmon-colored hotel was built in Victorian times but was extensively remodeled in the early 1930s. Present owner Gert Lubbe highlights its many art deco features and collects furniture and artifacts from this era to complement the interior. A well-trained staff ensures efficient and personal service, inspired by the owner, a consummate professional. The hotel has a wellness center and mineral pool. The hotel's Wild Apricot restaurant (¢–$) serves an excellent breakfast, satisfying no-frills lunch, and similarly straightforward dinner, with the addition of traditional country favorites like Karoo lamb pie. ⊠ *27 Bath St., Box 338, 6720* ☎ *023/614–3125* ⚖ *023/614–1905* ⊕ *www.montagucountryhotel.co.za* ⇌ *26 rooms* ⚘ *Restaurant, room service, pool, massage, bar* ☰ *AE, DC, MC, V* ⦿| *BP.*

$ ☐ **7 Church Street.** In the heart of the village, this lovingly restored Victorian home was converted into a guesthouse in 2000. Each room is individually and stylishly decorated with hand-embroidered cotton percale linens. The Honeymoon Suite has a big wrought-iron bed and a bathroom with a claw-foot tub. Ask for the Garden Suite if you want extra privacy. The pool is set in a magnificent garden and has stunning views, the perfect place to chill out with a book after a morning at the springs or exploring town. ⊠ *7 Church St., Box 43, 6720* ☎ *023/614–1186* ⚖ *023/ 614–3442* ⊕ *www.7churchstreet.co.za* ⇌ *3 rooms, 1 suite* ⚘ *Pool; no a/c* ☰ *AE, MC, V* ⦿| *BP.*

Breede River Valley A to Z

BUS TRAVEL

Intercape Mainliner, Greyhound, and Translux have daily service throughout most of the Western Cape, stopping at bigger towns such as Worcester and Robertson on their way upcountry. Although each company's timetable varies, most have approximately four trips a day from Cape Town. The journeys are not long. From Cape Town to Worcester takes about 1½ hours, 2 hours to Robertson. A one-way trip to Worcester costs around R150, and the drop-off spot is a service station on the side of the N1. It is a little way out of town, but shuttle buses will take you into town for a small fee.

🚌 Bus Lines **Greyhound** ⊠ 1 Adderley St., Cape Town ☎ 083/909–0909 for bookings through Computicket ⊕ www.greyhound.co.za. **Intercape Mainliner** ⊠ 1 Adderley St., Cape Town ☎ 086/128–7287 or 083/909–0909 for Computicket ⊕ www.intercape. co.za. **Translux Express Bus** ⊠ 1 Adderley St., Cape Town ☎ 086/158–9282.

CAR TRAVEL

DIY is definitely the way to go when exploring the Breede River Valley and will give you the flexibility you need to discover interesting backroads or to linger at a lovely lunch spot. The roads in the Western Cape are generally good. Although you might have to navigate some dirt roads, they tend to be graded regularly and are in fine condition.

The major car-rental agencies have offices in some of the smaller towns, but it's best to deal with the Cape Town offices. An alternative is to pick up a car in Stellenbosch. For car rental agencies, *see* Winelands A to Z, *above.*

The best way to get to this area is to take the N1 from Cape Town past Paarl. You can either go through the Huguenot toll tunnel (around R25 per vehicle) or over the spectacular Bain's Kloof mountain pass to Worcester. From there take the R60 to Robertson and Montagu.

EMERGENCIES

In the event of an emergency, you'll be able to track down medical professionals without too much trouble. Although Montagu and Robertson don't have any late-night pharmacies, small-town professionals are happy to open up after hours. Robertson and Montagu have small provincial hospitals, and Worcester has three, including the privately run Medi-Clinic.

🔁 Emergency Services **Ambulance** ☎ 10177. **Police** ☎ 10111. **Police, Fire, and Ambulance services** ☎ 107 from landline. **Vodacom emergency services** ☎ 112 from mobile phone.

🔁 Hospitals **Montagu Hospital** ✉ Church and Hospital Sts., Montagu ☎ 023/614–1131. **Robertson Hospital** ✉ Van Oudtshoorn St., Robertson ☎ 023/626–8051. **Worcester Medi-Clinic** ✉ 67 Fairburn St., Worcester ☎ 023/348–1500.

INTERNET

You won't find a slew of Internet cafés in these smaller rural towns, but you won't be completely stuck without access either. Some hotels and guesthouses will let you send and receive mail, but if your hotel does not offer access, ask the local tourism bureau for suggestions. Rates vary, but expect to pay around R24 for 30 minutes and R40 for an hour.

🔁 Internet Access **Printmor** ✉ 70 Bath St., Montagu ☎ 023/614–1838. **Rob Café** ✉ Piet Retief and Swellendam Sts., Robertson ☎ 023/626–6778.

MONEY MATTERS

Changing money isn't a problem in these outlying towns. They have banks and ATMs, and credit cards are widely accepted.

TOURS

Rather than big tour companies, there are a couple of individual guides operating in Breede River towns. Because the guides are usually from the area, they provide rare insights about the towns. Your best bet is to ask at local tourism offices for names and numbers. If you wish to hike in the Montagu Mountain Reserve, where trails are not well marked, go with someone familiar with the area, such as Patti van Dyk. She charges around R50 per person for a strenuous hike lasting 6–10 hours, including the park's entrance fee.

🔁 Tour Guide **Patti van Dyk** ☎ 023/614–1501 or 084/793–8477.

VISITOR INFORMATION

Cape Town Tourism offices are a good source of info on the whole Western Cape. Offices are are open weekdays 9–6, Saturday 8:30–2, and Sunday 9–1. The Breede River Valley Tourism office is open weekdays 8–4:30. The Montagu Tourism Bureau is open weekdays 9–6 and Saturday 8–5 during high season (November–March). The Worcester Tourism Bureau is open weekdays 8–4:30 and Saturday 8:30–12:30. The Robertson Tourism Bureau is open weekdays 9–5, Saturday 9–4, and Sunday 10–2. Tulbagh Tourism is open weekdays 9–5, Saturday 10–4, and Sunday 11–4.

🖪 Tourist Offices **Breede River Valley Tourism** 🗐 Box 91, Worcester 6850 ☎ 023/347–6411. **Cape Town Tourism** ✉ The Pinnacle at Burg and Castle Sts., Box 1403, Cape Town 8000 ☎ 021/426–4260 ⊕ www.tourismcapetown.co.za. **Montagu Tourism Bureau** ✉ 24 Bath St., Montagu 6720 ☎ 023/614–2471 ⊕ www.montagu-ashton.info. **Robertson Tourism Bureau** ✉ Reitz and Voortrekker Sts. 🗐 Box 675 Robertson 6705 ☎ 023/626–4437 ⊕ www.robertsonr62.com. **Tulbagh Tourism** ✉ 4 Church St., Tulbagh 6820 ☎ 023/230–1348 ⊕ tulbaghtourism.org.za. **Worcester Tourism Bureau** ✉ 23 Baring St., Worcester 6850 ☎ 023/348–2795.

THE OVERBERG

Overberg, Afrikaans for "over the mountains," is an apt name for this remote region at the bottom of the continent, separated from the rest of the Cape by mountains. Before 19th-century engineers blasted a route over the Hottentots Holland mountain range, the Overberg developed in comparative isolation. To this day it possesses a wild emptiness far removed from the settled valleys of the Winelands.

It's a land of immense contrasts, and if you're planning a trip along the Garden Route, you would be well advised to add the Overberg to your itinerary. The coastal drive from Gordon's Bay to Hermanus unfolds a panorama of deserted beaches, pounding surf, and fractured granite mountains. Once you pass Hermanus and head out onto the windswept plains leading to Cape Agulhas, you have to search harder for the Overberg's riches. Towns are few and far between, the countryside an expanse of wheat fields and sheep pastures. The occasional reward of the drive is a coastline of sublime beauty. Dunes and unspoiled beaches extend for miles. Currently no roads run parallel to the ocean along this stretch, and you must repeatedly divert inland before heading to another part of the coast. But there are plans afoot for a major coastal highway, which has brought mixed reactions. It means economic growth for far-flung towns but threatens to destroy the peace and quiet that makes these villages so attractive.

Unfortunately, the ocean's bounty has been the undoing of communities along this coastline. *Perlemoen* (abalone) poaching is an enormous problem. These sea mollusks are being taken out and shipped to the East, where they are considered a powerful aphrodisiac, faster than they can reproduce. Violent Western Cape gangs are involved in perlemoen trafficking, and children as young as 11 are used as runners in exchange for drugs.

Naturally, the coast has plenty of good on tap. Hermanus is one of the best places in South Africa for land-based whale-watching during the annual migration of southern right whales between June and November. Spring is also the best time to see the Overberg's wildflowers, although the region's profusion of coastal and montane fynbos is beautiful year-round. The raw, rugged beauty of Africa's southernmost coastline can be found at De Hoop Nature Reserve and Marine Protected Area. The Whale Trail, a five-day hike mapped out through De Hoop, might just oust the Otter Trail as South Africa's most popular. In fact, walking is one of the Overberg's major attractions, and almost every town and nature reserve offers a host of trails.

The upper part of the Overberg, north of the N2 highway, is more like the Winelands, with 18th- and 19th-century towns sheltered in the lee of rocky mountains. Here the draws are apple orchards, inns, and hiking trails that wind through the mountains. The historic towns of Swellendam and Greyton are good places to spend a night before moving on to your next destination. Stanford, a tiny hamlet just outside of Hermanus, is also a lovely place to stay if you want to avoid the crowds that clog the streets of Hermanus on holidays.

To tour the whole area would take three to four days, but you could easily spend a week in the Overberg. For a shorter trip focus on the splendors of the coastal route from Gordon's Bay to Hermanus, and then head north toward Greyton and Swellendam.

Gordon's Bay

⑩ *70 km (44 mi) southeast of Cape Town.*

This attractive resort is built on a steep mountain slope overlooking the vast expanse of False Bay. You can often see whales and their calves in the bay in October and November.

From Gordon's Bay the road hugs the mountainside, slipping between the craggy peaks of the Hottentots Holland Mountains and the sea far below. The coastal drive, known as Clarence Drive, between Gordon's Bay and Hermanus is one of the country's best, particularly if you take the time to follow some of the dirt roads leading down to the sea from the highway. There are numerous paths down to the seashore from the road between Gordon's Bay and Rooiels. It's worth walking down to watch the waves pounding the rocky coast, but take care. If there are no other people around and the waves are quite big, stay a few yards back from the water, as this section of coast is notorious for freak waves in certain swell and wind conditions. Note the many crosses on the side of the road—each one denotes somebody who has been swept off the rocks and drowned at sea.

The road passes the tiny settlement of **Rooiels** (pronounced *roy*-els), then cuts inland for a couple of miles. A turnoff leads to **Pringle Bay,** a collection of vacation homes sprinkled across the fynbos. The village has little to offer other than a beautiful wide beach (check out the sign warning of quicksand). If you continue through Pringle Bay, the tar road soon gives way to gravel. This road, badly washboarded in patches, runs around the looming pinnacle of Hangklip and along a deserted stretch of magnificent beach and dunes to **Betty's Bay.** At time of writing, sand storms had made the road impassable, as the dunes had shifted, blocking all traffic. It was uncertain when authorities would remove the sand and reopen the road.

If you don't fancy the gravel road, return to the R44 and continue 1½ km (1 mi) to the turnoff to Stony Point, on the edge of Betty's Bay. Follow Porter Drive for 3 km (2 mi) until you reach a sign marked MOOI HAWENS and a smaller sign picturing a penguin. Follow the penguin signs to a **colony of African penguins,** one of only two mainland colonies in southern Africa (the other is at Boulders Beach in Cape Town, where it is much easier to see these endangered seabirds). The colony lies about 600 yards from the parking area along a rocky coastal path. Along the way you pass the concrete remains of tank stands, reminders of the days when Betty's Bay was a big whaling station. The African penguin is endangered, so the colony has been fenced off for protection.

★ Return to Porter Drive and turn right to rejoin the R44. Go another 2 km (1 mi) to the **Harold Porter National Botanical Garden,** a 440-acre nature reserve in the heart of the coastal fynbos, where the Cape floral kingdom is at its richest. The profusion of plants supports 78 species of birds and a wide range of small mammals, including large troops of Chacma baboons. You couldn't ask for a more fantastic setting, cradled between the Atlantic and the towering peaks of the 3,000-foot Kogelberg Range. Walking trails wind through the reserve and into the mountains via Disa and Leopard's kloofs, which echo with the sound of waterfalls. Back at the main buildings, a pleasant restaurant serves light meals and teas. Book ahead for a volunteer guide to take you around the gardens, for which a donation is welcome. ✉ *R44, Betty's Bay* ☎ *028/272–9311* 💷 *R8* ☺ *Weekdays 8–4:30, weekends 8–5.*

Kleinmond

⓫ *25 km (15½ mi) southeast of Gordon's Bay.*

The sleepy coastal town of Kleinmond (Small Mouth) presides over a magnificent stretch of shoreline, backed by the mountains of the Palmietberg. It's a favorite among retirees, but more and more city-weary baby boomers are moving here as well. A harbor development near the old slipway is bustling with restaurants and shops.

en route **Alive Alive-O-Shellfish Bar** (✉ Kleinmond harbor ☎ 028/271–3774) is one of the places where you can try abalone quite legally. At the big abalone factory the mollusks are cultivated, harvested, and packaged for local restaurants and overseas markets.

Close to town, on the Cape Town side and clearly marked with signs from the main street, is the **Kogelberg Nature Reserve,** a 66,000-acre area of fynbos that extends from the mountains almost to the sea, and includes most of the course of the Palmiet River. Take one of the well-marked nature walks through the reserve and you are sure to see some of the area's magnificent flora and bird life. ☎ *028/271–5138* ☞ *R20* ☉ *Apr.–Aug., daily 8–7; Sept.–Mar., daily 7:30–7.*

Almost as impressive are the 10 km (6 mi) of sandy beach that fringe **Sandown Bay,** at the eastern edge of town. Much of the beach is nothing more than a sandbar, separating the Atlantic from the huge lagoon formed by the Bot River. Swift currents make swimming risky, although there is a sheltered corner near the rocks close to the Beach House hotel. Keep an eye out for the famous Bot River horses that live on *vlei* (pronounced flay), or marsh. There are lots of theories about just how the horses got here. One has it that they were turned loose during the Anglo-Boer War to save them from being killed, and ended up on the vlei for safety. DNA tests show that these horses are descendants of the Kaapse Waperd (Cape Wagon Horse), a sturdy breed used to help settle the wild regions of the Overberg.

The R44 becomes the R41 and cuts inland around the Bot River lagoon. Ten km (6 mi) past Kleinmond is the junction with the R43. Hermanus is to the right, but take a quick detour to the left through the sleepy town of Bot River to the big old white gates of **Beaumont Wines.** This is a fabulous family-run winery. It's just sufficiently scruffy to create an ambience of age and country charm without actually being untidy. But, charm aside, it's the wine you come here for, and it really is worth the detour. It produces a range of dependable, notable wines, like the new-wave pinotage and the first mourvèdre to be bottled in South Africa. ☒ *R43, Bot River* ☎ *028/284–9194* ☞ *Tastings free* ☉ *Weekdays 9:30–12:30 and 1:30–4:30, Sat. morning by appointment.*

Head back toward Kleinmond, continuing on the R43 toward Hermanus and across the Bot River. The R43 swings eastward around the mountains, past the not-particularly-attractive fishing village of Hawston, one of the Overstrand communities hardest hit by abalone poaching, and the small artists' colony of **Onrus.** The Onrus lagoon is a great swimming spot for children. The water is always a couple of degrees warmer than the sea and is safe for the newly waterborne.

need a break? **The Milkwood** (☒ Atlantic Dr., Onrus ☎ 028/316–1516), overlooking the lagoon, is a great place for a languid lunch. You can sit on the deck after a quick dip and eat some fresh fish (what kind of fish depends on the day's catch), grilled and served with a lemon or garlic-butter sauce, or one of several Thai-style stir-fries.

Where to Stay

$–$$ **Beach House on Sandown Bay.** In quiet, seaside Kleinmond this comfortable hotel overlooks a 10-km (6-mi) crescent of beach and a beautiful lagoon. It's a good base for whale-watching in October and November, as well as for walks in the surrounding nature reserves. The hotel itself is attractive, the rooms simply decorated with wicker furniture and floral draperies and bedspreads. In sea-facing rooms (worth requesting), sliding doors open onto small balconies with tremendous views of Sandown Bay. The restaurant specializes in seafood fresh from the local harbor. ✉ *13 Beach Rd., 7195* ☎ *028/271–3130* 🖷 *028/271–4022* ⊕ *www.relaishotels.com* ⤳ *22 rooms, 1 suite* ♿ *Restaurant, pool, bar* ▭ *AE, DC, MC, V* ⧦ *BP.*

Sports & the Outdoors

GOLF   The setting of the **Arabella Golf Club** (✉ R43 ☎ 028/284–9383 ⊕ www. arabellagolf.co.za) is so beautiful that you'd do well to take time to admire the views at the eighth hole, with the lagoon, the mountains, and the sea in the distance. The course is fairly challenging and quite expensive. Greens fees are R550 for 18 holes. A caddy costs R110, club rental R250, and a golf cart R210.

RAFTING   The Palmiet River is a low-volume, technical white-water river of about Grade 3. In high water, **Gravity Adventures** (✉ 21 Selous Rd., Claremont 7700 ☎ 021/683–3698 or 082/574–9901 ⊕ www.gravity.co.za) offers rafting trips in four- or two-seater inflatable rafts. In low water they do the same trip but on specially designed one-person inflatable crafts called "geckos." A half-day trip costs R295, including snacks, and a full day R395 including breakfast and lunch or R350 without the food.

Hermanus

⓬ *34 km (21 mi) southeast of Kleinmond on the R43.*

Pristine beaches extend as far as the eye can see, and the Kleinriviersberg provides a breathtaking backdrop to this popular resort, the Overberg's major coastal town. Restaurants and shops line the streets, and Grotto Beach was awarded Blue Flag status (a symbol of high environmental standards as well as good sanitary and safety facilities) in 2003. Though the town has lost much of its original charm, it is still most definitely worth a visit.

Fodor'sChoice   Hermanus sits atop a long line of cliffs, which makes it one of the best
★   places in South Africa for **land-based whale-watching.** (The town is packed during the Whale Festival in late September as well as over Christmas vacation.) The 11-km (7-mi) Cliff Walk allows watchers to follow the whales, which often come within 100 feet of the cliffs as they move along the coastline. Keep an ear and an eye out for the whale crier, Wilson T. Salukazana, who does his rounds during the season. Using horns made from dried kelp, he produces different codes indicating where to catch the best sighting of these mighty giants of the deep. A long note followed by a short one signals the new harbor, for instance.

Originally, Hermanus was a simple fishing village. Its Old Harbour, the oldest original harbor in South Africa that is still intact, has been declared a national monument. The **Old Harbour Museum** bears testimony to the town's maritime past. A small building at the old stone fishing basin displays a couple of the horrific harpoons used to lance whales and sharks as well as some interesting whale bones. There are also exhibits on fishing techniques, local marine life, and angling records. The white building next to the harbor parking lot on Market Square is De Wet's Huis, which houses the Old Harbour Museum Photographic Exhibition. Here are photos of old Hermanus, and many of the town's fishermen proudly displaying their catches of fish, sharks, and dolphins— yes, dolphins. The third component is the Whale House, which currently houses a temporary exhibit of whale painting. At the time of writing, the museum was busy preparing the permanent exhibition, which will be completed in 2006. A crafts market every weekend outside De Wet's Huis is fun for browsing. ⊠ *Old Harbour, Marine Dr.* ☎ *028/312–1475* 🖃 *R3* ⊙ *Mon.–Sat. 9–4:30, Sun. noon–4.*

★ On the outskirts of town a pair of white gateposts set well back from the R43 signal the start of **Rotary Way**. This scenic drive climbs along the spine of the mountains above Hermanus, with incredible views of the town, Walker Bay, and the Hemel-en-Aarde Valley as well as some of the area's beautiful fynbos. It's a highlight of a trip to Hermanus and shouldn't be missed. The entire mountainside is laced with wonderful walking trails, and many of the scenic lookouts have benches.

West of town off the R43, the R320 (Hemel-en-Aarde Valley Road) leads through the vineyards and orchards of the scenic Hemel-en-Aarde (Heaven and Earth) Valley and over Shaw's Pass to Caledon. The gravel road is a bit potholed and washboarded but nothing terrifying. A short way down the road in thatch building overlooking a small dam, **Hamilton Russell Vineyards** produces some excellent wines. The pinot noir won loud acclaim from Frank Prial of the *New York Times,* and is one of the best produced in the country. The chardonnay comes closer to the French style of chardonnay than any other Cape wine, with lovely fruit and a touch of lemon rind and butterscotch. ⊠ *Off Hemel-en-Aarde Valley Rd. (R320), Walker Bay* ☎ *028/312–3595* 🖃 *Tastings free* ⊙ *Weekdays 9–5, Sat. 9–1.*

A short distance farther on the Hemel-en-Aarde Valley Road, **Bouchard Finlayson,** with only 44 acres under vine, nevertheless thrills critics and wine lovers year after year. Winemaker Peter Finlayson makes good use of the cool sea breeze and unique terroir of the estate to create some fantastic deep-south wines. Try the French-style Galpin Peak Pinot Noir. Finlayson, who has a great voice, maintains that pinot noir "is like opera. When it's great it is pure seduction, almost hedonistic. There is no middle road." You might wish to lay down a few bottles of the limited release Tête de Cuvée Galpin Peak Pinot Noir, which gives off an exciting whiff of truffles. A recent addition is the limited release of the Cuvée X Chardonnay. ⊠ *Off Hemel-en-Aarde Valley Rd. (R320)* ☎ *028/312–3515* ⊕ *www.bouchardfinlayson.co.za* 🖃 *Tastings free* ⊙ *Weekdays 9:30–5, Sat. 9:30–12:30.*

Where to Stay & Eat

$–$$$ ✕ **Mediterrea Seafood Restaurant.** You can't go wrong with excellent food and sweeping bay views, and Medittrea regulars know to ask for a window seat. In whale season you can hear the giants blow just below you. The restaurant's owner is Greek, and chef James Rowntree strives to combine the best of Mediterranean cuisine with all that South African food has to offer. Favorite starters include baby calamari tubes flamed with Cajun spice, capsicums, and fresh herbs and served on *tsatsiki* (Greek-style yogurt-cucumber-garlic dip), and the phyllo Mediterrea (spinach, feta, mushrooms, mozzarella, chives, and sun-dried tomatoes rolled in phyllo and served with hummus). For a main course, the lamb stuffed with garlic, rosemary, and apricots, slow roasted in red wine and fresh herbs, is out of this world, as are the medallions of ostrich fillet topped with a sweet-onion-and-chili marmalade. Or you could go straight for the ice-cream halvah (layers of phyllo and vanilla ice cream infused with pistachio halvah and drizzled with honey). ⊠ *87 Marine Dr.* ☎ *028/ 313–1685* ▤ *AE, DC, MC, V* ⊘ *No lunch Mon.*

$–$$ ✕ **Mogg's Country Cookhouse.** Don't be put off by the bumpy dirt road heading up the Hemel-en-Aarde Valley. This restaurant on a fruit farm at the top of the valley is worth any amount of dust and corrugations. The converted laborer's cottage is as pretty as a picture in a tumbledown, overgrown kind of way. Mother-and-daughters trio Jenny, Julia, and Jozi Mogg cook excellent food in a relaxed and friendly setting. The seasonal menu is scribbled on a chalkboard. For starters you could expect beef carpaccio with a caper-and-olive dressing and pecorino cheese, or pork-and-bean-sprout spring rolls with a sweet chili dipping sauce. For mains you might try chicken breast stuffed with tomatoes, olives, and feta wrapped in phyllo pastry, or homemade pasta with a creamy lemon, fennel, and seafood sauce with line fish, calamari, and mussels. For dessert there's homemade vanilla or Cointreau ice cream served with a hot chocolate sauce. ⊠ *Nuwe Pos farm, off the Hemel-en-Aarde Valley Rd. (R320)* ☎ *028/312–4321* ▤ *No credit cards* ⊘ *Closed Mon. and Tues. No dinner Sun.–Fri.*

★ **$** ✕ **Mariana's.** Mariana and Peter Esterhuizen started out selling organic vegetables at the Hermanus farmers' market before converting a house in the little village of Stanford, just 10 minutes away, into a restaurant. In just a few years they've made their mark, and Capetonians regularly make the trip for one of their memorable meals. What's the attraction? Excellent food, a relaxed setting, friendly hosts, and organic produce grown behind the restaurant. Although lots of restaurants use seasonal produce, Mariana and Peter pick their ingredients moments before you arrive. You're welcome to wander around the garden, which is as much a tapestry as it is a veggie patch. The food is Mediterranean with a South African twist. The Gruyère soufflé is a sublimely light, cheesy concoction served in a pool of tomato cream that will make you want to lick the plate. The cheese comes from a local dairy, and the eggs come from an artist down the road. There's usually a warm trout or chicken salad, but if you're really hungry, go for the *skaap en dinge* (sheep and things), an enormous lamb shank served with mashed potatoes and seasonal vegetables. ⊠ *12 du Toit St., Stanford* ☎ *028/341–0272* ⚛ *Reservations essential* ▤ *No credit cards* ⊘ *Closed Mon.–Thurs. No dinner.*

★ **$$$–$$$$** ✕▦ **The Marine.** In an incomparable cliff-top setting, this venerable hotel has sumptuously decorated rooms. The sea-facing rooms, some with private balcony and all with under-floor heating, provide whale-watchers with grandstand views over Walker Bay. The revamped orangery invites guests to linger over tea or drinks, and the two restaurants tempt with sophisticated menus. The Pavilion ($$$$), with wonderful views of Walker Bay, offers up-to-the-minute fare. Cultivated perlemoen ravioli and wilted bok-choy salad with a seafood-and-coconut-bisque dressing is a delicious first course, as is the twice-baked artichoke soufflé with toasted pine nuts and goat-cheese dressing. Mains include roast rack of lamb with hazelnut crust. Desserts are stunning. ✉ *Marine Dr., Box 9, 7200* ☎ *028/313–1000* 📠 *028/313–0160* 🌐 *www.marine-hermanus.co.za* 43 *rooms* 2 *restaurants, room service, 2 pools, spa, bar* 💳 *AE, DC, MC, V* 🍽 *BP.*

$$ **Auberge Burgundy Guesthouse.** If you want to be in the center of the village, this stylish guesthouse is an excellent choice. You're a stone's throw from the famous whale-watching cliffs and the market, and three minutes from the Old Harbour Museum. When Hermanus took off as a tourist destination, this well-run and friendly operation was one of the first lodgings to take off with it. The rooms are comfortably decorated in French Provincial style. Larger rooms with sleeper couches cost about a third more, but they're great for families or friends traveling together. Ask for a room with a balcony overlooking the bay or a suite that opens onto the pool. ✉ *16 Harbour Rd., 7200* ☎ *028/313–1201* 📠 *028/313–1204* 🌐 *www.auberge.co.za* *18 rooms* *Pool; no a/c, no kids under 12* 💳 *AE, DC, MC, V* 🍽 *BP.*

$ **Windsor.** If you come to Hermanus anytime from July to November, stay at this hotel in the heart of town. It's a family-run hostelry that offers comfort but little pretense. However, the hotel's position atop the cliffs makes it a great place to view the annual whale migration. Request one of the second-floor, sea-facing rooms, with huge sliding-glass doors and unbeatable views. ✉ *Marine Dr., Box 3, 7200* ☎ *028/312–3727* 📠 *028/312–2181* *60 rooms* *Restaurant, bar; no a/c* 💳 *AE, DC, MC, V* 🍽 *BP.*

$ **Whale Cottage, Hermanus.** Decorated in restful shades of blue and white, this is a great base from which to take long whale-watching walks. Ask for a room with a view, and put your feet up while you watch the southern right whales splashing in the bay below. Alternatively, take a stroll along the nearby whale-watching cliffs. There's an honor bar and tea and coffee available throughout the day. ✉ *38 Westcliff Dr., 7200* ☎ *028/313–0929* 📠 *028/313–0912* 🌐 *www.whalecottage.com* *6 rooms* *Pool* 💳 *AE, DC, MC, V* 🍽 *BP.*

Sports & the Outdoors

East of Hermanus the R43 hugs the strip of land between the mountains and the Klein River Lagoon. The lagoon is popular with waterskiers, boaters, and anglers.

BOATING You can take a sunset cruise up the Klein River with **Walker Bay Adventures** (✉ Prawn Flats, off R43 ☎ 028/314–0925 🌐 www.hermanus.co.za/com/walkerbayadventures/). The cost is R60, R160 for the cruise, snacks on board, and a braai afterward.

KAYAKING For a really fun outing, join a gentle paddling excursion from the Old Harbour operated by **Walker Bay Adventures** (✉ Prawn Flats, off R43 ☎ 028/314–0925 🌐 www.hermanus.co.za/com/walkerbayadventures/). You paddle in safe, stable double sea kayaks accompanied by a guide, and you pay around R200 for a two-hour morning trip. From July to December Walker Bay is a whale sanctuary, and this is the only company with a permit to operate here.

WHALE-
WATCHING &
SHARK-DIVING

Although Hermanus is great for land-based whale-watching, you get a different perspective on a boat trip into Walker Bay. Boats leave on 2½-hour whale-watching trips (around R650) from both Hermanus and Gansbaai. **Dyer Island Cruises** (⊠ Gansbaai ☎082/801–8014 or 083/402–8541) is a good bet for whale-watching.

Shark-diving is also extremely popular, and Gansbaai has a number of operators working from the small harbor, including **White Shark Diving Company** (⊠ Gansbaai ☎ 082/559–6858). A 4½-hour trip (with plenty of adrenaline) costs around R650, including breakfast and snacks on the boat. If you don't want to take the plunge, you can just stay in the boat and watch the sharks from the deck.

Shopping
Wine Village (⊠R43 and R320 ☎028/316–3988) carries a good selection of South African wines, including wines from neighboring vineyards Hamilton Russell and Bouchard Finlayson as well as Southern Right.

Bredasdorp

⑬ *89 km (55 mi) east of Hermanus; 60 km (37½ mi) east of Stanford.*

This sleepy agricultural town has a certain charm, as long as you don't catch it on a Sunday afternoon, when everything's closed and an air of ennui pervades the brassy, windswept streets. Each spring, however, the usual lethargic atmosphere is abandoned, and a radical sense of purpose takes its place when Bredasdorp hosts the Foot of Africa Marathon. Don't be lulled by the small-town, country setting into thinking that this race is a breeze and that you might give it a go. Word has it that the undulating landscape has the fittest athletes doubting their perseverance.

Housed in a converted church and rectory, the **Bredasdorp Museum** has an extensive collection of objects salvaged from the hundreds of ships that have gone down in the stormy waters off the Cape. In addition to the usual cannons and figureheads, the museum displays a surprising array of undamaged household articles rescued from the sea, including entire dining room sets, sideboards, china, and phonographs. ⊠ *6 Independent St.* ☎ *028/424–1240* ⊕ *www.capeinfo.com/bredamuseum* ⊠ *R10* ⊘ *Weekdays 9–4:45, weekends 11–4.*

en route

ELIM – Little has changed in the last hundred years in this Moravian mission village founded in 1824: simple whitewashed cottages line the few streets, and the settlement's coloured residents all belong to the Moravian Church. The whole village has been declared a national monument, and it's the only town in the country that has a monument dedicated to the freeing of the slaves in 1838. It's also home to the country's oldest working clock and biggest wooden waterwheel. Try to attend a church service on Sunday morning at 10, when just about the whole town turns out in their Sunday best and voices soar in the white church at the top of the main street. Elim is 36 km (22 mi) west of Bredasdorp and accessible only by dirt road. The easiest access is via the R317, off the R319 between Cape Agulhas and Bredasdorp.

Fodor'sChoice **De Hoop Nature Reserve** is a huge conservation area covering 88,900 acres
★ of isolated coastal terrain as well as a marine reserve extending 5 km
(3 mi) out to sea. Massive white-sand dunes, mountains, and rare lowland fynbos are home to eland, bontebok, and Cape mountain zebra,
as well as more than 250 bird species. Though it's only three hours from
Cape Town, it feels a lifetime away. Access is via the dirt road between
Bredasdorp and Malgas. It's worth planning ahead and renting a mountain bike, as there are a number of wonderfully laid-out trails. This is
also a fantastic place to watch whales from the shore—not quite as easy
as in Hermanus but much less crowded. You can also hike the enormously
popular Whale Trail, which runs through this reserve. A shuttle service
takes your bags to each new stop, so all you have to carry is a small day
pack and some water between overnight stops. You need to book up to
a year in advance to enjoy the Whale Trail, or you might get lucky and
snag a last-minute cancellation. In fact, this hike is now so popular that
it's beginning to appear on online auctions. Self-catering cottages
(R350–R535) sleep up to four people and range from basic to fully
equipped. ✍ *Private Bag X16, 7280* ☎ *028/425–5020 or 028/542–1253*
⊕ *www.capenature.org.za* ✉ *R20* ☾ *Sat.–Thurs. 7–6, Fri. 7–7.*

Past De Hoop Nature Reserve on the dirt road from Bredasdorp is the
small hamlet of **Malgas,** a major port in the 19th century before the mouth
of the Breede River silted up. In addition to a lovely village, you will
find the last hand-drawn car ferry in the country (R15 round-trip). It's
fascinating to watch the technique, as the ferry operators "walk" the
ferry across the river on a huge cable, leaning into their harnesses.

en route   From Bredasdorp it's just 41 km (26 mi) through rolling farmland to
the **Cape Agulhas** lighthouse. Although the cape is not nearly as spectacular as Cape Point (⇨ Chapter 1), it's a wild and lonely place—rather
fitting for the end of a wild and wonderful continent.

Arniston (Waenhuiskrans)

★ ⑭ *25 km (15 mi) southeast of Bredasdorp.*

Although its official name is Waenhuiskrans, and that's what you'll see
on maps, this lovely, isolated vacation village is almost always called
Arniston—after a British ship of that name that was wrecked on the nearby
reef in 1815. Beautiful beaches, water that assumes Caribbean shades
of blue, and mile after mile of towering white dunes attract anglers and
vacationers alike. Only the frequent southeasters that blow off the sea
and the chilly water are likely to put a damper on your enjoyment.

For 200 years a community of local fisherfolk has eked out a living here,
setting sail each day in small fishing boats. Today their village, **Kassies-
baai** (translation: "suitcase bay," supposedly for all the suitcases that
washed ashore from the frequent shipwrecks), is a national monument.
It's a pleasure to wander around the thatch cottages of this still-vibrant
community, although declining fish stocks have left many families vulnerable. Abalone poaching is also a problem here. The adjacent village
of Arniston has expanded enormously in the last two decades, thanks

to the construction of vacation homes. Fortunately, much of the new architecture blends well with the whitewashed simplicity of the original cottages.

Waenhuiskrans is Afrikaans for "wagon-house cliff," and the village takes its other name from a vast **cave** 2 km (1 mi) south of town, which is theoretically large enough to house several wagons and their spans of oxen. Signs point the way over the dunes to the cave, which is accessible only at low tide. You need shoes to protect your feet from the sharp rocks, and wear something you don't mind getting wet. It's definitely worth the trouble, however, to see this stunning spot.

Where to Stay & Eat

★ **$$** ✕▥ **Arniston Hotel.** You could easily spend a week here and still need to be dragged away. The setting, a crescent of white dunes, has a lot to do with its appeal, but the hotel also strikes a fine balance between elegance and beach-vacation comfort. Request a sea-facing room, where you can enjoy the ever-changing colors of the horizon and have a grandstand view of the large concentration of cow and calf pairs found here during the whaling season, between June and November. The à la carte menu ($–$$$) offers substantial variety, with few surprises, but the grilled catch of the day is as fresh as you can get. Lunch is served on the patio in fine weather, and wine lovers will rejoice at the quality of the deservedly renowned wine list. ⊠ *Beach Rd., Arniston* ✆ *Box 126, Bredasdorp 7280* ☎ *028/445–9000* 🖷 *028/445–9633* ⊕ *www.arnistonhotel.com* 🛏 *40 rooms* ⚐ *Restaurant, room service, pool, bar; no a/c* ⊟ *AE, DC, MC, V* ⏆ *BP.*

Swellendam

★ ⑮ *72 km (45 mi) north of Arniston.*

Beautiful Swellendam lies in the shadow of the imposing Langeberg. Founded in 1745, it is the third-oldest town in South Africa, and many of its historic buildings have been elegantly restored. Even on a casual drive along the main street you'll see a number of lovely Cape Dutch homes, with their traditional whitewashed walls, gables, and thatch roofs.

The centerpiece of the town's historical past is the **Drostdy Museum,** a collection of buildings dating from the town's earliest days. The Drostdy was built in 1747 by the Dutch East India Company to serve as the residence of the *landdrost,* the magistrate who presided over the district. The building is furnished in a style that was common in the mid-19th century. A path leads through the Drostdy herb gardens to Mayville, an 1855 middle-class home that blends elements of Cape Dutch and Cape Georgian architecture. Across Swellengrebel Street stand the old jail and the Ambagswerf, an outdoor exhibit of tools used by the town's blacksmiths, wainwrights, coopers, and tanners. ⊠ *18 Swellengrebel St.* ☎ *028/514–1138* 🖭 *R12* ⊙ *Daily 9–4:45.*

Swellendam's **Dutch Reformed Church** is an imposing white edifice built in 1911 in an eclectic style. The gables are baroque, the windows Gothic, the cupola vaguely Eastern, and the steeple extravagant. Surprisingly, all the elements work together wonderfully. Inside is an interesting tiered amphitheater with banks of curving wood pews facing the pulpit and organ. ✉ *7 Voortrek St.* ☎ *028/514–1225* 🖘 *R5; services free* ☉ *Weekdays 8–4; services (in Afrikaans) May–Sept., Sun. at 10; Oct.–Apr., Sun. at 9:30.*

If you'd like to stretch your legs, take a hike in the **Marloth Nature Reserve** in the Langeberg above town. Five easy walks, ranging from one to four hours, explore some of the mountain gorges. An office at the entrance to the reserve has trail maps and hiking information. There is a five-day trail, which costs R55 per person, per day, in addition to the park entrance fee. If you're doing a day walk, park outside the entrance boom. Although you can stay in the reserve until sunset, the gates close at the time advertised. ✉ *1½ km (1 mi) from Voortrek St. on Andrew White St. to golf course, and follow signs* ☎ *028/514–1410* ⊕ *www. capenature.org.za* 🖘 *R18* ☉ *Weekdays 7:30–4, weekends 7–6.*

Covering just 6,880 acres of coastal fynbos, **Bontebok National Park** is one of the smallest of South Africa's national parks. Don't expect to see big game here—the park contains no elephant, lion, or rhino. What you will see are bontebok, graceful white-face antelope nearly exterminated by hunters earlier in the last century, as well as red hartebeest, Cape grysbok, steenbok, duiker, and the endangered Cape mountain zebra. Two short walking trails start at the campsite, next to the Breede River. ✉ *Off the N2, 5 km (3 mi) from Swellendam* ☎ *028/514–2735* ⊕ *www. SANParks.org* 🖘 *R20* ☉ *May–Sept., daily 7–6; Oct.–Apr., daily 7–7.*

Where to Stay & Eat

$$ ✕🖂 **Klippe Rivier Country House.** Amid rolling farmland 3 km (2 mi) outside Swellendam, this guesthouse occupies one of the Overberg's most gracious and historic country homes. It was built around 1825 in traditional Cape style, with thick white walls, a thatch roof, and a distinctive gable. Guests stay in enormous rooms in the converted stables. The three downstairs rooms are furnished with antiques in Cape Dutch, colonial, and Victorian styles. Upstairs, raw wood beams, cane ceilings, and bold prints set the tone for less expensive Provençal-style rooms with small balconies. Some public rooms have trouble supporting the sheer volume of antique collectibles, taking on a museumlike quality. At R160, delectable three-course dinners ($$$$) are table d'hôte and prepared with fresh herbs, vegetables, fruit, and cream from surrounding farms. ✉ *On dirt road off R60 to Ashton* 🖃 *Box 483, Swellendam 6740* ☎ *028/514– 3341* 🖷 *028/514–3337* ⊕ *www.klipperivier.com* 🖘 *6 rooms, 1 cottage* 🗍 *Restaurant, saltwater pool; no room TVs, no kids under 8* 🖃 *AE, DC, MC, V* ⊙| *BP.*

★ **$** 🖂 **Adin's and Sharon's Hideaway.** The Victorian homestead and its three luxury cottages are set in a peaceful garden with literally hundreds of rosebushes. Although the setting and beautifully appointed cottages are excellent reasons to stay here, the level of hospitality sets this place above the rest. Adin and Sharon Greaves continue to win every award there is for the best South African bed-and-breakfast. Their dedication extends to providing lifts, planning routes, and presenting the best breakfast for many miles around. (There's something crazy like 38 homemade jams available.) Even at twice the cost it would be recommended; attention like this is priceless. ✉ *10 Hermanus Steyn Rd., 6740* 📠 *028/514–3316* ⊕ *www.adinbb.co.za* 🛏 *1 room, 3 cottages* ⚖ *Pool; no room TVs* ⊟ *AE, DC, MC, V* ⑩ *BP.*

¢–$ 🏨 **Coachman Guesthouse.** Dating back to the 18th century and declared a national monument in 1983, this guesthouse is in the historic heart of Swellendam, within easy walking distance of all the major sights and restaurants. A lovely garden surrounds the house; the three rooms have entrances that open onto a courtyard, and two thatch garden cottages have their own verandas and great views over the Langeberg mountains. Rooms are charmingly furnished with brass beds and comfortable throws. The pool is an absolutely necessity in summer, when temperatures soar. ✉ *14 Drostdy St., 6740* 📞 *028/514–2294* 📠 *028/514–3349* ⊕ *www.coachman.co.za* 🛏 *3 rooms, 2 cottages* ⚖ *Pool; no a/c, no room TVs* ⊟ *AE, DC, MC, V* ⑩ *BP.*

Sports & the Outdoors

You can take just a little trot or a longer excursion through the Marloth Nature Reserve on horseback with **Two Feathers Horse Trails** (✉ Koloniesbos Hut 📞 082/494–8279 ⊕ www.twofeathers.co.za). Expect to pay between R100 for an hour and R550 for a full-day ride, including a packed lunch.

en route | From Swellendam return to the N2 and turn right toward Cape Town. The road sweeps through rich, rolling cropland that extends to the base of the Langeberg. A few kilometers after the town of Riviersonderend (pronounced riff-*ear*-sonder-ent), turn right onto the R406, a good gravel road that leads to the village of Greyton, in the lee of the Riviersonderend Mountains.

Greyton

★ ⑯ *32 km (20 mi) west of Swellendam.*

The charming village of Greyton, filled with white thatch cottages and quiet lanes, is a popular weekend retreat for Capetonians as well as a permanent home for many retirees. The village offers almost nothing in the way of traditional sights, but it's a relaxing place to stop for a meal or a night, and a great base for walks into the surrounding mountains.

After Greyton the R406 becomes paved. Drive 5 km (3 mi) to the turnoff to **Genadendal** (Valley of Grace), a Moravian mission station founded in 1737 to educate the Khoekhoen and convert them to Christianity. Seeing this impoverished hamlet today, it's difficult to comprehend the major role this mission played in the early history of South Africa. In the late 18th century it was the second-largest settlement after Cape Town, and its Khoekhoen craftsmen produced the finest silver cutlery and woodwork in the country. Some of the first written works in Afrikaans were printed here, and the coloured community greatly influenced the development of Afrikaans as it is heard today. None of this went down well with the white population. By 1909 new legislation prohibited coloured ownership of land, and in 1926 the Department of Public Education closed the settlement's teachers' training college, arguing that coloueds were better employed on neighboring farms. In 1980 all the buildings on Church Square were declared national monuments (it's considered the country's most authentic church square), but despite a number of community-based projects, Genadendal has endured a long slide into obscurity and remains impoverished. In 1995, then-president Nelson Mandela renamed his official residence Genadendal. You can walk the streets and tour the historic buildings facing Church Square. Genadendal is still a mission station, and community tour guides show interested visitors around.

Of particular note is the **Genadendal Mission Museum,** spread through 15 rooms in three buildings. The museum collection, the only one in South Africa to be named a National Cultural Treasure, includes unique household implements, books, tools, and musical instruments, among them the country's oldest pipe organ. Wall displays examine mission life in the Cape in the 18th and 19th centuries, focusing on the early missionaries' work with the Khoekhoen. Unfortunately, many of the displays are in Afrikaans only. ⊠ *Off R406* ☏☏ *028/251–8582* 💷 *R7* ⊙ *Mon.–Thurs. 9–1 and 2–5, Fri. 9–1 and 2–3:30, Sat. 9–1.*

Sports & the Outdoors

To get your heart rate up, your best bet is to contact **IntrApid Adventures** (☎ 021/461–4918 or 082/324–1188 ⊕ www.raftsa.co.za), which offers full-day adventures that include anything from a gentle rafting trip on the Sonderend River to a short mountain-bike ride to a scenic rappel. Trips cost R350–R450 for a full-day trip, which includes a packed lunch and a light breakfast. Prices are based on a minimum of six people, but you can organize a trip for one or two people at a higher cost.

HIKING   In addition to day hikes and short walks, you can take the 32-km (20-mi) **Boesmanskloof Trail** through the Riviersonderend Mountains between Greyton and the exquisite hamlet of McGregor (⇨ Breede River Valley, *above*). Accommodations, in hiking huts on a private farm (R50 per person excluding bedding), can be booked through **Barry Oosthuizen** (☎ 023/625–1735), who will also buy groceries and leave them at the hut, charging you only what he pays. Hikers often book the following night's accommodation at a local B&B, and have a good meal and a good night's sleep before heading home. In McGregor the trailhead is a ways from the town, but most guesthouses will pick up and drop off. Cell-phone coverage is sporadic. In the good old days, youngsters used to walk from Greyton to McGregor for an energetic game of tennis before walking home again the same evening.

To book the **Genadendal Hiking Trail,** which costs R25 per person per day for a permit, contact the De Hoop Nature Reserve (*see* Bredasdorp, *above*). Accommodations (R30 per person) are in huts on the farm **De Hoek** (☎ 023/626–2176 or 082/400–6677), which has a gas stove, hot showers, flush toilets, a braai, and wood. If you like, you may spend a night at the **Moravian Mission Church** (☎ 028/251–8346), where the hike starts and ends.

en route

To head back toward Cape Town, follow the R406 to the N2. After the town of Bot River the road leaves the wheat fields and climbs into the mountains. It's lovely country, full of rock and pine forest interspersed with orchards. **Sir Lowry's Pass** serves as the gateway to Cape Town and the Winelands, a magnificent breach in the mountains that opens to reveal the curving expanse of False Bay, the long ridge of the peninsula, and, in the distance, Table Mountain.

Overberg A to Z

BUS TRAVEL

Intercape Mainliner, Greyhound, and Translux have daily service throughout most of the Western Cape, especially to the bigger towns on the N2. Swellendam is a major hub and a good transit point, but to enjoy smaller towns such as Greyton or those along the coast, you'll need your own transportation.

Bus Lines Greyhound ⊠ 1 Adderley St., Cape Town ☎ 083/909–0909 for bookings through Computicket ⊕ www.greyhound.co.za. **Intercape Mainliner** ⊠ 1 Adderley St., Cape Town ☎ 086/128–7287 or 083/909–0909 for Computicket ⊕ www.intercape. co.za. **Translux Express Bus** ⊠ 1 Adderley St., Cape Town ☎ 086/158–9282.

CAR TRAVEL

Driving yourself is undoubtedly the best way to appreciate this lovely and diverse area. The roads in the Western Cape are generally good. They are signposted, and major routes are paved. For the most part, you'll come across gravel roads only around Elim and Napier and from Swellendam to Malgas, and they may be a bit rutted and bumpy. A two-wheel-drive vehicle is fine, but take it easy if it's been raining, as gravel roads can get slippery. You'll need a 4x4 only if you're planning to tackle some of the more remote back roads or want to do a 4x4 route.

The major car-rental agencies have offices in the bigger towns, such as Hermanus and Swellendam. However, it's best to deal with the Cape Town offices; you'll probably want to pick up a car at the airport anyway. For car-rental agencies, *see* Winelands A to Z, *above*.

The Overberg stretches over an enormous area, so you need to decide where you're heading before planning your route. If you want to enjoy the beauty of the coast, then take the N2 from Cape Town, but, instead of heading up Sir Lowry's Pass, turn off to Gordon's Bay and follow the R44, also known as Clarence Drive, along the scenic route. Just after Kleinmond the road becomes the R41 and turns inland to bypass the Bot River Lagoon. It becomes the R43 as it makes its way toward Hermanus. If you want to explore inland, however, take the N2 over Sir Lowry's Pass and past Caledon and Swellendam. To get to the pretty hamlet of Greyton, take the R406 to your left just before Caledon.

Keep in mind that on Sunday afternnoons and in early evenings, traffic returning to the city via Sir Lowry's Pass can be very congested. Expect delays as you enter Somerset West, and be very careful if it is misty (which it often is on the pass), as this stretch of road sees numerous accidents each year. Leaving Cape Town on a Friday afternoon can also take time, so try to leave by lunchtime to avoid traffic jams.

EMERGENCIES

There are doctors and dentists in every town, as well as provincial hospitals in all but the smallest villages. Hermanus has a private hospital. Late-night pharmacies are a rarity in these small towns, but all pharmacies have emergency and after-hours numbers.

🔢 Emergency Services **Ambulance** ☎ 10177. **Police** ☎ 10111. **Police, Fire, and Ambulance services** ☎ 107 from landline. **Vodacom emergency services** ☎ 112 from mobile phone.

🔢 Hospitals **Hermanus Medi-Clinic** ✉ Hospital St., Hermanus ☎ 028/313-0168. **Otto du Plessis Hospital** ✉ Dorpsig and van Riebeek Sts., Bredasdorp ☎ 028/424-1167. **Swellendam Hospital** ✉ 18 Drostdy St., Swellendam ☎ 028/514-1142.

INTERNET

You won't find an Internet café on every corner. Remember, until a couple of years ago many of these towns were just sleepy *dorpies* (villages) servicing far-flung farming communities. You will find Internet cafés in more touristy destinations, such as Hermanus, but first inquire at your hotel or B&B, as many allow guests access for a small fee. Alternatively, print shops often have an Internet station. Expect to pay around R10 for 10 minutes, but this varies from shop to shop.

🔢 Internet Access **Comcell** ✉ Main Rd., Greyton ☎ 028/254-9161. **Hermanus Internet and Information Centre** ✉ 38 Main Rd., Hermanus ☎ 028/313-0277.

MONEY MATTERS

There are plenty of ATMs and banks throughout the region, so you won't have a problem withdrawing or exchanging money. As always, take care when getting large sums of money, and make sure you have your bank and credit cards with you at all times. You'll be able to use your credit card just about everywhere—except at some smaller farm stands.

TOURS

There are a number of individuals and small companies offering customized tours. A day trip, which would cost R350–R400 including a packed lunch, could include an excursion to De Hoop Nature Reserve, with plenty of time to admire the birds, fynbos, and whales; a ride on the ferry at Malgas; and time at Bontebok National Park. Or you could start in Swellendam, head over picturesque Tradouw Pass through the spectacular Cape Fold mountains to Barrydale, where you could do some wine tasting before heading on to Robertson. Other tours concentrate on the historic fishing village of Waenhuiskrans, Bredasdorp, and Elim.

When the Hermanus whale crier, Wilson Salukazana, is not busy blowing his horn in Hermanus, he conducts township tours. On a guided walk through the nearby township of Zwelihle, you can have a traditional Xhosa meal, visit a traditional African healer, and meet local residents.

🔢 Tour Operators **Riaan van Deventer** ✉ Swellendam ☎ 028/514-1066 or 082/376-1213. **Ruggens en Rante** ✉ Arniston ☎ 028/445-9998 or 082/747-0141. **Wilson Salukazana** ✉ Hermanus ☎ 028/312-2629 or 073/214-6949.

VISITOR INFORMATION

You can get plenty of info on the Overberg at the Cape Town Tourism offices; these are open weekdays 9–6, Saturday 8:30–2, and Sunday 9–1. The Hermanus Tourism Bureau is open in summer weekdays 8–6, Saturday 9–5, and Sunday 10–3, and in winter Monday–Saturday 9–5. The Hangklip-Kleinmond Tourism Bureau has information on Kleinmond, Betty's Bay, Pringle Bay, and Rooi Els, and is open weekdays 8–6, Saturday 8–2, and Sunday 10–3 during the summer season only. The Cape Agulhas Tourism Bureau has information for Bredasdorp, Elim, L'Agulhas, Struisbaai, and Arniston. It is open weekdays 8–5 and Saturday 9–12:30. The Swellendam Tourism Bureau is open weekdays 8–1 and 2–5, Saturday 9–noon. The Greyton Tourism Bureau is open Monday–Saturday 9–5 and Sunday 10–3. Overberg Tourism is a good information clearinghouse and source of brochures.

🔳 Tourist Offices **Cape Agulhas Tourism Bureau** ✉ Long St., Bredasdorp ☎ 028/424-2584. **Cape Town Tourism** ✉ The Pinnacle at Burg and Castle Sts., Box 1403, Cape Town 8000 ☎ 021/426-4260 ⊕ www.tourismcapetown.co.za. **Greyton Tourism Bureau** ✉ 29 Main Rd., Greyton 7233 ☎ 028/254-9414 or 254-9564 ⊕ www.greyton.net. **Hangklip-Kleinmond Tourism Bureau** ✉ Main Rd., Kleinmond 7195 ☎ 028/271-5657 ⊕ www.ecoscape.org.za. **Hermanus Tourism Bureau** ✉ Lord Robert and Mitchell Sts., Hermanus 7200 ☎ 028/312-2629 ⊕ www.hermanus.co.za. **Overberg Tourism** ✉ 22 Plein St., Caledon 7230 ☎ 028/214-1466 ⊕ www.tourismcapeoverberg.co.za. **Swellendam Tourism Bureau** ✉ Oefeningshuis, Voortrek St., Swellendam 6740 ☎ 028/514-2770 ⊕ www.swellendamtourism.co.za.

WEST COAST

The West Coast is an acquired taste. It's dry and bleak, and other than the ubiquitous exotic gum trees, nothing grows higher than your knees. It's a wild and wonderful place. An icy sea pounds long deserted beaches or rocky headlands, and the sky stretches for miles.

Historically, this area has been populated by hardy fisherfolk and tough, grizzled farmers. Over the years they have worked out a balance with the extreme elements—responding with a stoic minimalism that is obvious in the building styles, the cuisine, and the language.

Unfortunately, minimalism became fashionable, and urban refugees started settling on the West Coast. The first lot weren't bad—they bought tattered old houses and renovated them just enough to make them livable. Then came those who insisted on building replicas of their suburban homes at the coast. And then—worst of all—came the developers. They bought up huge tracts of land and cut them up into tiny little plots, popping horrid little houses onto them. Or perhaps they'd turn a whole bay into a pseudo-Greek village. As a result, the austere aesthetic that makes the West Coast so special is fast disappearing. But it's not gone—at least not yet.

Just inland from the West Coast is the Swartland (Black Ground, a reference to the fertile soil that supports a flourishing wheat and wine industry). Rolling wheat fields extend as far as the eye can see to mountains on either side. In summer the heat is relentless, and there's a sea of golden-brown grain, but in winter the landscape is a shimmery green, and when there's snow on the mountains, it's as pretty as can be. The Swartland includes Piketberg, Malmesbury, Darling (also considered the West Coast), and the twin towns of Riebeek West and Riebeek Kasteel.

To the north, the Cederberg is an absolutely beautiful and rugged range of mountains, most of which is a designated wilderness area. In South Africa that means you may hike there with a permit, but there are no laid-out trails and no accommodations or facilities of any kind. Fantastic rock formations, myriad flowering plants, delicate rock art, and crystal-clear streams with tinkling waterfalls and deep pools make this a veritable hiker's paradise.

A loop around the West Coast, Swartland, and the Cederberg, starting from Cape Town, will take a minimum of three days.

Darling

17 *82 km (51 mi) north of Cape Town via the N7 and R315.*

Darling is best known for two draws: its sensational wildflowers and its sensational performer, Pieter-Dirk Uys, otherwise known as Evita Bezuidenhout. The wildflowers are usually at their best August–October, and there's an annual Wildflower and Orchid Show held in September. Evita's at her best all year round (*see* Nightlife, *below*). When driving into Darling, ignore the rather unattractive new houses on the Cape Town side of the village, and head straight through to the Victorian section of town, where pretty period houses line up among lush gardens.

During the flower season the **Tienie Versfeld Wildflower Reserve** is just fantastic: a wonderful, unpretentious, uncommercialized little gem. ⊠ *R315, 12 km (7 mi) west of Darling* ⊡ *Free* ⊙ *Daily 24 hrs.*

Rondeberg Nature Reserve offers a more formal flower experience. The reserve is justly proud of the more than 900 species found here, including rare disas, which you aren't likely to find elsewhere as easily. All visits are via guided tours of the grounds, so you must call ahead to reserve your visit. ⊠ *R27, 25 km (16 mi) outside Darling* ☎ *022/492–3099* ⊕ *www.rondeberg.co.za* ⊡ *R50* ⊙ *Flower season, usually Mar.–Oct.*

The large, well-run, environmentally sensitive **Groote Post Vineyard** got off to a fantastic start when its maiden '99 sauvignon blanc was judged one of the best in the Cape. Since then the wine farm has continued to garner award after award. Try the chardonnay or the chocolaty, berryish merlot. The restaurant, Hilda's Kitchen, is an excellent choice for a lunch, or phone ahead and order a picnic basket to enjoy under the trees after a morning's tasting. ⊠ *Off R307 south* ☎ *022/492–2825* ⊕ *www. grootepost.com* ⊡ *Tastings free* ⊙ *Weekdays 8–5, Sat. 9–2:30.*

Large **Darling Cellars** produces wines under a number of labels. In the Onyx range, look for the 2002 pinotage-shiraz blend. Other suggestions include the pinotage and the 2004 sauvignon blanc—the cellar's flag-

PIETER-DIRK UYS: EVERYONE'S DARLING

T'S FITTING THAT PIETER-DIRK UYS and his alter ego, Evita Bezuidenhout, live in a village called Darling. He's the darling of South African satire, and his speech is peppered with dramatic and warm-hearted "dahlings." Tannie (Auntie) Evita, as she's fondly known, is as much a South African icon as braais and biltong.

But let's backtrack. Evita Bezuidenhout debuted in a newspaper column written by playwright Pieter-Dirk Uys in the 1970s. He wrote as though he was an insider at the Nationalist Party and so dished the dirt. His mysterious source's voice grew so strong that she was soon nicknamed the "Evita of Pretoria." She hit the stage in the early 1980s, when apartheid was in full swing and the ruling Nationalist Party was short on humor.

Uys's first production, Adapt or Dye, was at a small venue in Johannesburg at 11 PM, a time when he hoped the censors would be in bed (possibly with each other, he was quick to add!) and therefore unable to censor him. The titles of his shows and some characters (all of which he plays himself) are intricately wound up with South African politics and life. Adapt or Dye, for instance, was based on a speech by former prime minister P. W. Botha, who said, "South Africans have to adapt to a changing world or die." For a country ripped apart by politics based on color, it was a play on words Uys couldn't pass up. Every performance shows an intricate understanding of the country and her people. One of his characters, Nowell Fine, for instance, is named after the delicious South African phrase "Yes, no well, fine," said before saying what really has to be said.

Over the years, Uys's richest material has come from the government, especially the Groot Krokodil (big crocodile), P. W. Botha; Piet Koornhof, once U.S. ambassador; and foreign minister Pik Botha. Most politicians were happy to be lampooned; in an inhumane society, laughing at themselves made them seem more human. And, if there's any criticism leveled at Uys, it's that for all his biting remarks, he played court jester to the apartheid government and pulled back when he could have gone for the kill. He would argue that shows need a balance between punches and tickles. Too many punches don't put bums on seats; too many tickles end up being vacuous.

Uys is not just about comedy and satire, however. He's deeply committed to transforming society. Before the first democratic elections in 1994, he embarked on self-funded voter-education tours. He's now channeling his considerable energy into tackling HIV/AIDS. He travels to schools, where he uses humor and intelligence to tackle the thorny issue, which he believes the government is ignoring. As in his performances, he pulls no punches. During his talk he demonstrates how to put a condom on a banana. This he swiftly replaces with a lifelike rubber penis, "because," he explains with a twinkle, "men and boys don't have bananas between their legs. A condom on a banana on the bedside table is not going to protect you!" Of course the kids shriek with laughter and "the black teachers turn white!"

Uys is a huge fan of Nelson Mandela. Of Mandela's long imprisonment Tannie Evita said, "He's very grateful we kept him from Winnie all those years." In 2002 Uys was nominated as a national living treasure by the South African Human Sciences Research Council. Here's to you, dahling!

— Karena du Plessis

ship wine. The DC range has some stalwart old reds, including a nice, plummy merlot, and the newer Flamingo Bay range still needs to prove that it can produce more than pleasant quaffables. ⊠ *R315* ☎ *022/492–2276* ⊕ *www.darlingcellars.co.za* 🖉 *Tastings R5* ⊘ *Mon.–Thurs. 8–5, Fri. 8–4, Sat. 8–noon; cellar tours by appointment.*

Where to Stay & Eat

$ ✕▥ Trinity Guest Lodge and Restaurant. This old Victorian house has been elegantly transformed into a stylish and comfortable guest lodge. White linen and subtle furnishings create a restful atmosphere. Some bathrooms have Victorian claw-foot tubs. With a menu that changes daily, the restaurant ($) will have you coming back for more, especially for dishes such as roast beef fillet with a verjuice hollandaise sauce. ⊠ *19 Long St., 7345* ☎ *022/492–3430* ⊕ *www.trinitylodge.co.za* ⇥ *4 rooms* ⚬ *Restaurant, pool; no a/c* ▭ *MC, V* †⊙† *BP.*

¢ ▥ Darling Guest House. You'll soon be made to feel at home at this pretty Victorian B&B. The emphasis is on enjoying the peace and quiet, so there are no TVs, but you won't be at a loss for something to do. There's plenty going on in the area, and you will probably be ready for a refuge at the end of the day, perhaps in one of the claw-foot tubs. ⊠ *22 Pastorie St., 7345* ☎ *022/492–3062* 🖷 *022/492–3916* ⇥ *6 rooms* ⚬ *Pool; no, a/c, no room TVs* ▭ *No credit cards* †⊙† *BP.*

Nightlife & the Arts

Fodor'sChoice One of Darling's main attractions is **Evita se Perron** (☎ 022/492–2831
★ ⊕ www.evita.co.za), the theater and restaurant started by satirist and drag artist Pieter-Dirk Uys. The theater is on the platform of the Darling station (*perron* is the Afrikaans word for "railway platform"). Pieter-Dirk Uys has made his alter ego, Evita Bezuidenhout, a household name in South Africa. Performances are on Friday evening, Saturday afternoon and evening, and Sunday afternoon, and cost R85. Come early to enjoy a meal in the restaurant, or make it a day trip from Cape Town via the Spier Vintage Train (⇨ West Coast A to Z, *below*). A package including a picnic lunch and the performance costs R300, R210 without lunch. In the same complex, **Evita's A en C** is the gallery of an arts-and-crafts collective. Here you can see and buy works from West Coast artists. It's open daily 10–5.

Langebaan

⑱ *50 km (30 mi) northwest of Darling.*

Probably the most popular destination on the coast, Langebaan is a great base from which to explore the region, and the sheltered lagoon makes for fantastic water sports, especially windsurfing, kite-surfing, and sea kayaking. The town has a truly laid-back, beachy feel. To quote a local: "There is nowhere in Langebaan you can't go barefoot." Lots of Capetonians have weekend houses and head here on a Friday afternoon with boats, bikes, and boards in tow. If you're not into water sports and serious tanning, however, Langebaan doesn't have that much to offer. The town grew up around a slipway, yacht club, and cluster of brick-faced beach houses, and the main drag is unexciting. Though the town comes alive in summer, as youngsters crowd the beach and flex their muscles, during the off-season the town quickly reverts to a quiet settlement where people retire to fish and mess about on boats.

Even if you don't stop in **West Coast National Park,** consider driving the scenic road that runs through it rather than the R27 to Langebaan. The park is a fabulous mix of lagoon wetlands, pounding surf, and coastal fynbos. On a sunny day the lagoon assumes a magical color, made all the more impressive by blinding white beaches and the sheer emptiness of the place. Birders will have a field day identifying waterbirds, and the sandveld flowers are among the best along the West Coast. Postberg, the little mountain at the tip of the reserve where ships would drop off their mail on their trip around the Cape, is open only in flower season, which changes from year to year but usually falls between August and October, when the flowers are at their very best. It's easy to run out of superlatives when describing West Coast flowers, but imagine acres of land carpeted in multicolored blooms—as far as the eye can see. If you're lucky, you may catch glimpses of zebra, wildebeest, or bat-eared fox. ⊠ *Off the R27, 11 km (7 mi) north of the R315* ☎ *022/772–2144* 🖃 *R30 in flower season, roughly ½ price other times* ☉ *Park: Apr.–Aug., daily 7–7:30; Sept.–Mar., daily 6–8; Postberg: flower season, daily 9–5.*

Where to Stay & Eat

★ **$–$$** ✕ **Froggy's.** The food at this attractive and unpretentious establishment would be impressive even in a smart city restaurant, but in a town where most people consider steak, egg, and fries to be the height of culinary achievement, it really does stand out. The owner, Froggy, doesn't put on airs. The menu is eclectic—basically it's what Froggy likes to cook and eat. The caramelized-onion-and-brie tart is a masterpiece, and the Mediterranean salad with grilled vegetables is a Langebaan institution. Other standouts are the Moroccan lamb shank, slow baked with cinnamon, coriander, cumin, ginger, and garlic, and the Thai curries. ⊠ *29 Main Rd.* ☎ *022/772–1869* 🖃 *No credit cards* ☉ *Closed Mon. No lunch Tues, no dinner Sun.*

$–$$ ✕🏨 **Farmhouse Hotel.** Centered on a restored farmstead built in the 1860s, this hotel has thick white walls, tile floors, and timber beams. All rooms are decorated with rustic pine furniture and bright floral fabrics; some have fireplaces and views of the lagoon. The hotel's à la carte menu focuses on Cape cuisine, served in the attractive dining room ($–$$) notable for its Oregon-pine furniture, fireplace, and high ceiling. The breakfast is said to be the best in town. ⊠ *5 Egret St., Box 160, 7357* ☎ *022/772–2062* 🖷 *022/772–1980* ⊕ *www.thefarmhouselangebaan.co.za* 🛏 *18 rooms* ⚷ *Restaurant, pool, bar; no a/c* 🖃 *AE, DC, MC, V* ⴾ◍ *BP.*

$ 🏨 **Friday Island.** If you're into water sports or cycling or are generally active, then this guesthouse is a great choice. It's bright, airy, and right on the beach. Rooms are, not surprisingly, decorated in blue and white and have an outside shower for wet suits, boards, and such. Sea-facing rooms are ideal for families, with two beds downstairs and two in a loft. To top it off, the property is connected to the Cape Sports Centre complex. But Friday Island also has a lovely beachfront bar and restaurant and is a good place to stay even if you don't take to water in a big way. ⊠ *Main Rd., Langebaan Lagoon, Box 280, 7357* ☎ *022/772–2506*

🖸 022/772–1115 ⊕ *www.fridayisland.co.za* 🛏 *12 rooms* ⚜ *Restaurant, bar; no a/c, no room TVs* ▤ *MC, V* 🍴 *BP.*

¢–$ 🖼 **Langebaan Beach House.** On the beach with uninterrupted views of the lagoon and close to the nightlife of Langebaan (such as it is), this comfortable, friendly place even has dogs you can take for walks on the beach. Rooms are simply and tastefully furnished, with pine headboards and colorful comforters. Ask for a sea-facing suite; if there aren't any available, your room will look out onto the pool and garden instead. ✉ *44 Beach Rd., 7357* ☎ *022/772–2625* 🖸 *022/772–1432* ⊕ *www. langebaanbeachhouse.com* 🛏 *2 rooms, 2 suites* ⚜ *Pool; no a/c, no kids under 12* ▤ *AE, DC, MC, V* 🍴 *BP.*

Sports & the Outdoors

The sheltered Langebaan lagoon is a haven for water-sports enthusiasts, but you don't have to be energetic all the time. There are expansive stretches of beach that are good for walking, sunbathing, and kite flying. Be warned, however: the water might look calm and idyllic, but it's still cold, and the wind can blow unmercifully for days at a stretch. Great for windsurfing, but not so great if you want to spend a peaceful day under your umbrella with a book.

Cape Sports Centre (✉ Main Rd. ☎ 021/772–1115 ⊕ www.capesport. co.za) has everything you need if you want to kite surf, windsurf, kayak, or canoe or even learn how. You can rent gear or take lessons from qualified instructors, including packages consisting of a week of intensive lessons. Cape Sports Centre also rents mountain bikes.

Paternoster

⑲ *47 km (29 mi) northwest of Langebaan.*

Paternoster is a mostly unspoiled village of whitewashed thatch cottages perched on a deserted stretch of coastline. The population here consists mainly of fisherfolk, who for generations have eked out a living harvesting crayfish and other seafood. Despite the overt poverty, the village has a character and sense of identity often lacking in larger towns. It helps if you turn a blind eye to the rather opulent houses on the northern side of the village.

Along the coast just south of Paternoster, the **Columbine Nature Reserve** is a great spot for spring wildflowers, coastal fynbos, and succulents. Cormorants and sacred ibis are common here, and the population of the endangered African black oystercatcher is growing each year. You can walk anywhere you like in the 692-acre park (map provided); a round-trip through the reserve is 7 km (4 mi). It's very exposed, however, so don't plan to walk in the middle of the day, or you'll end up with some serious sunburn. Die-hard fisherfolk and their families decamp here during the Christmas holidays and revel in the isolation and abundant fish. ☎ *022/752–2718* ✉ *R9* ⊙ *Daily 7–7.*

Where to Eat

★ ¢–$ ✗ **Voorstrand.** A little West Coast gem, this old corrugated-iron shack on the beach stood empty for years, then suddenly metamorphosed into

ROOIBOS TEA

CHANCES ARE you will either love or hate rooibos (red bush) tea, which South Africans drink in vast quantities. It has an unusual, earthy taste, and is naturally sweet. People drink it hot with lemon and honey or with milk or as a refreshing iced tea with slices of lemon and a sprig of mint. It's rich in minerals, such as copper, iron, potassium, calcium, fluoride, zinc, manganese, and magnesium; contains antioxidants; and is low in tannin. Best of all, it contains no caffeine. Trendy chefs are incorporating it into their cooking; you might see rooibos-infused sauces or marinades mentioned on menus. Rooibos leaves are coarser than regular tea and look like finely chopped sticks. When they're harvested they're green; then they're chopped, bruised, and left to ferment in mounds before being spread out to dry in the baking summer sun. The fermentation process turns the leaves red—hence the name.

a really innovative seafood restaurant. Literally set on the sand, you can almost hear the ones that got away. They serve all the expected seafood and fish, but the Malay-style fish curries and fresh local crayfish are favorites. You could also splash out and try the seafood platter, which has a little bit of everything. Although it's designed to serve two people, there's always some left over. ✉ *Strandloper St.* ☎ *022/752–2038* 🖃 *MC, V.*

Elands Bay

20 75 km (46 mi) north of Paternoster.

Mention eBay auctions here, and most people will stare at you blankly. But mention the E'bay left-hand break, and you'll get nods of approval and instant admission into the inner circle of experienced surfers, who make the pilgrimage to Elands Bay to experience some of the Western Cape's best surfing.

This lovely destination is at the mouth of the beautiful Verlorevlei Lagoon. Verlorevlei (Afrikaans for "lost wetland," a testimony to its remoteness) is a birder's paradise; you're likely to see around 240 species, including white pelican, purple gallinule, African spoonbill, African fish eagle, and the goliath and purple herons. Nearby are some fantastic walks to interesting caves with well-preserved rock art that dates back to the Pleistocene Era, 10,000 years ago.

Where to Eat

$$$–$$$$ ✕ **Muisbosskerm.** For the true flavor of West Coast life, come to this open-air seafood restaurant on the beach south of Lambert's Bay. It consists of nothing more than a circular *boma* (enclosure) of packed *muisbos* (a local shrub), with benches and tables haphazardly arranged in the sandy enclosure. You'll watch food cook over blazing fires. Snoek is smoked in an old drum covered with burlap, bread bakes in a clay oven, and

everywhere fish sizzles on grills and in giant pots. Prepare to eat as much as you can, using your hands or mussel shells as spoons. Be sure to try some of the local specialties like *bokkems* (dried salty fish) and *waterblommetjiebredie* (water-flower stew). Unless you have an enormous appetite, don't order the half crayfish (it costs around R50 extra). The only drawback is high-season crowding: when the restaurant operates at full capacity, your 150 fellow diners can overwhelm the experience. ⊠ *Elands Bay Rd., 5 km (3 mi) south of Lambert's Bay* ☎ *027/432–1017* ⌂ *Reservations essential* ☰ *AE, DC, MC, V.*

Clanwilliam

㉑ *46 km (28 mi) northeast of Elands Bay.*

Although the town itself is uninspiring, it's no surprise that half the streets are named after trees or plants. Clanwilliam is at the edge of one of the natural jewels of the Western Cape—the Cederberg (sometimes spelled Cedarburg, after the trees that used to cover the mountains) Wilderness Area. In spring the town is inundated with flower-watchers. Clanwilliam is also the center of the rooibos tea industry.

The **Ramskop Wildflower Garden** is at its best in August. (This is also when the Clanwilliam Flower Show takes place at the old Dutch Reformed church, and almost every available space in town is filled with flowers.) It's a wonderful opportunity to see many of the region's flowers all growing in one place. Even in other seasons the gardens are still quite attractive, but spring is orders of magnitude prettier. ⊠ *Ou Kaapseweg* ☎ *022/482–8000* ⊠ *R12* ☉ *Daily 7:30–5.*

If you continue east on the R364, it becomes a spectacularly scenic gravel road called **Pakhuis Pass.** Fantastic rock formations glow in the early morning or late afternoon. There's even a mountain range called the Tra-Tra Mountains, a completely fantastical name for a suitably fantastical landscape. A steep, narrow road to the right leads to the mission town of **Wuppertal,** with its characteristic white-thatch houses. You can drive this road in an ordinary rental car, but be very careful in wet weather. There are no guided tours, but there is a factory where you can see and buy sturdy handmade leather shoes and boots.

Fodor'sChoice Clanwilliam is close to the northern edge of the **Cederberg,** a mountain
★ range known for its San paintings, its bizarre rock formations, and, once upon a time, its cedars. Most of the ancient cedars have been cut down, but a few specimens still survive in the more remote regions. The Cederberg is a hiking paradise—a wild, largely unspoiled area where you can disappear from civilization for days at a time. About 172,900 acres of this mountain range constitute what has been declared the Cederberg Wilderness Area, and entry permits are required if you wish to hike.

A scenic dirt road that heads south out of town, past the tourism bureau and museum, winds for about 30 km (18 mi) into the Cederberg to **Algeria,** a Cape Nature Conservation (☎ 022/931–2900 ⊕ www.capenature.org.za) campsite set in an idyllic valley. Algeria is the starting point for several excellent hikes into the Cederberg. The short, one-hour hike to a waterfall is great, but it's worth going into the mountains for a day or two, for which you will need to book and obtain a permit through Cape Nature Conservation or from one of the local farms, many of which have simple, self-catering cottages on their land.

The Cederberg might be the last place you'd expect to find a vineyard, but that's what makes **Cederberg Cellars** so unusual. It's been in the Nieuwoudt family for five generations. When old man Nieuwoudt, known to everyone as "Oom Pollie," planted the first vines in the 1970s, all his sheep-farming neighbors thought he had gone mad. Today, however, winemaker David Nieuwoudt and his viticulturist father, Ernst, are laughing all the way to the award ceremonies. At an altitude of around 3,300 feet, this is the highest vineyard in the Western Cape, and consequently is almost completely disease-free. They don't have to spray for the mildews and mealybug that are the bane of wine farmers in the Winelands and Constantia area. Try the chenin blanc, which wins one award after the other, as does the shiraz. The bukettraube is a perfect accompaniment to South African curries. The farm has self-catering accommodations and is near the Wolfberg Cracks (cracks in the mountain that lure hikers) and Malgat (a huge rock pool), both well-known Cederberg attractions. ⊠ *Dwarsrivier Farm, Algeria turnoff from the N7* ☎ *027/482–2827* ⊕ *www.cederbergwine.com* ☜ *Tastings R10* ⊗ *Mon.–Sat. 8–12:30 and 2–5.*

Where to Stay

$$$$ 🏨 **Bushmans Kloof Wilderness Reserve & Retreat.** It should come as no
Fodor'sChoice   surprise that this fantastic wilderness reserve was voted No. 5 on *Travel*
★   *+ Leisure*'s list of Top Hotels in the World in 2004. It deserves the accolades. Bushmans Kloof is in an area of rich cultural significance and a South African National Heritage site. The stark beauty of the mountains, the incredible rock formations, and the waterfalls, pools, and potholes probably were as attractive to the San of long ago as they are to visitors today. More than 130 San rock-art locations can be seen on a tour with a trained guide. The reserve used to be an overgrazed stock farm, and every attempt is being made to restore the land to a more pristine state. Only game endemic to the area has been reintroduced, including wildebeest, Cape mountain zebra, eland, genet, mongoose, blesbok, brown hyena, and the endangered bontebok. Freestanding thatch double cottages have all the modern conveniences, and the luxurious suites in the manor house are spacious and stylish. The food is exceptional, including the legendary springbok loin. Built into the rocks, the Embers site makes for a memorable place to eat. The attention to detail is astonishing; you'll find flowers floating in the toilet bowl, and the library even has titles in Arabic and Chinese. Best of all, you can fly in from Cape Town. ⊠ *Off Pakhuis Pass* ✉ *Reservations: Box 38104, Pinelands 7430* ☎ *021/685–2598* 🖷 *021/685–5210* ⊕ *www.bushmanskloof.co.za* ⟿ *7 rooms, 9 suites* ⚭ *Dining room, 4 pools, spa, fishing, mountain bikes, hiking, bar, library, airstrip; no TV in some rooms, no kids under 10* ➌ *AE, DC, MC, V* ⑩ *FAP.*

$$$ 🏨 **Karu Kareb.** Frans and Beneta Bester are old hands at the guesthouse business, and some of the best. Rooms are in a 100-year-old farmhouse surrounded by high mountains, a crystal-clear stream, and fantastic rock art. The Besters have mastered the art of excellent local cuisine, for which they were renowned at their previous lodging. Frans does incredible things with a braai or a potjie, and Beneta is surprisingly creative with dietary restrictions, cooking for vegetarians, diabetics, and lactose-intolerant people without batting an eyelid—a rarity in this part of the world. (At this writing, only overnight guests can have meals here, but they hope to open as a restaurant.) Beneta is also something of a mini–tourism bureau, with tons of information at her fingertips. ⊠ *13 km (8 mi) from Clanwilliam on Boskloof Rd., Box 273, 8135* ☎ *027/ 482–1675 or 027/482–9900* ⊕ *www.karukareb.co.za* ⤴ *5 rooms* ♿ *Dining room, pool, hiking, horseback riding; no room TVs* ⊟ *No credit cards* ⊧⊙⊧ *MAP.*

$ 🏨 **Strassberger's Hotel Clanwilliam.** On the main street, this friendly family-run hotel makes an excellent base for exploring the area. Rooms are large, decorated with rustic cane furniture and plaid country fabrics. Dinner in the hotel restaurant is a traditional four-course affair that makes use of local produce. ⊠ *Main Rd., Box 4, 8135* ☎ *027/482–1101* 🖷 *027/ 482–2678* ⊕ *www.clanwilliam.info/hotel* ⤴ *17 rooms* ♿ *2 restaurants, pool, squash, bar* ⊟ *AE, DC, MC, V* ⊧⊙⊧ *BP.*

¢ 🏨 **Traveller's Rest.** If you're on a tight budget, this is the place to stay. Basic but comfortable cottages are dotted about the farm. There are no frills, but the surrounding mountain scenery is just as spectacular as at the expensive lodge next door. You can take a guided tour, but if you prefer to explore for yourself you can get a booklet (R60) that describes all the rock art on the farm. There is also a scenic drive for which you really need four-wheel drive, although it's not an off-road challenge. ⊠ *Off Pakhuis Pass, 8135* ☎🖷 *027/482–1824* ⊕ *www.travellersrest.co.za* ⤴ *12 cottages* ♿ *Tennis court, pool, hiking, horseback riding; no a/c, no room TVs* ⊟ *No credit cards.*

Citrusdal

㉒ *53 km (33 mi) south of Clanwilliam.*

As you might guess from the name, Citrusdal is a fruit-growing town. It sits by the Olifants River valley, surrounded by the peaks of the Cederberg.

After a grueling hike, there's no better way to relax than at the **Baths,** where hot mineral water gushes from a natural spring. The waters' curative powers have been talked about for centuries, and although the formal baths were established in 1739, there's little doubt that indigenous San and Bushmen spent time here as well. In 1903 the hot springs were bought by James McGregor, and his great-grandchildren run them today. On-site are self-catering facilities and a restaurant. You can also go as as day visitor, but you must book ahead. ⊠ *16 km (10 mi) outside Citrusdal; follow signs* ☎ *022/921–8026/7* ⊕ *www.thebaths.co.za* 🎫 *Day of soaking R40* ⊙ *Daily 8–5.*

Sports & the Outdoors

At **Skydive Citrusdal** (☎ *021/462–5666 or 083/462–5666* ⊕ www. skydive.co.za) you can take a daylong first-jump course or, if you want someone to hold your hand, a tandem. As you float down under the canopy, you can see orange groves stretching out forever and the surrounding mountains; it's a particularly gorgeous sight in the late afternoon. A static-line first-jump course costs around R725, the tandem R1,100, R1,500 including a video.

Shopping

The lovely building that houses **Craig Royston Wines** (⊠ Off N7 ☎ 022/921–2963) has been a retail store continually since 1860, and has never been renovated. First it was the main trading store on the road north, and then, when the highway moved away, it sold groceries. It still maintains that basic farm-store feel, but now also stocks a selection of all the wines grown in the Cederberg region as well as a few touristy gimmicks. There is a coffee shop that serves all-day breakfasts and light lunches.

en route Once over the Piekenaarskloof Pass (aka Piekenierskloof Pass), you'll head toward the small town of Piketberg and enter the Swartland, the breadbasket of the Western Cape. On your left are the Groot Winterhoek Mountains and a road leading to the small town of Porterville. On your right is the village of Piketberg, where you can turn off for **Excelsior Farm** (⊠ Tar road off Versveld Pass ☎ 022/914–5853), a small organic peach farm on top of the Piketberg Mountains. It offers day and overnight horseback rides (R150 for two hours, R450 for a full day with lunch) through the orchards and fynbos-clad mountains, and two simple, inexpensive, self-catering cottages.

Riebeek Kasteel & Riebeek West

㉓ *104 km (65 mi) south of Citrusdal via the N7 and R311.*

Drive through the small agricultural town of Malmesbury and over the Bothman's Kloof Pass to these twin towns named after Jan van Riebeek, an early Dutch explorer of the Cape. The towns developed only a few miles apart because of a disagreement about where to build a church. In the end, two separate places of worship were built, and two distinct towns grew up around them.

Riebeek West is the birthplace of Jan Christiaan Smuts, one of the country's great politicians and leader of the United Party in the 1940s. D. F. Malan, prime minister of the Nationalist Party in 1948, was born on the farm Allesverloren, just outside Riebeek Kasteel. This wine estate produces some great red wines and an exceptional port. The *kasteel* or castle in question is the Kasteelberg (Castle Mountain), which stands sentinel behind the towns.

Today, disenchanted city dwellers have been buying up cottages here to use as weekend getaways, and others are moving out to the small towns and commuting into the city. It's not hard to understand why. Children play in the street and people keep sheep in their huge gardens—a far cry from Cape Town life. There are now a number of restaurants, some galleries, and plenty of olive products to buy, including excellent olive oils and bottled olives. (Huge groves in the area do well in the Mediterranean climate.)

You'll hear the distinctive, rolling accent of the Swartland here. Known as the "Malmesbury *brei*," it's characterized by long "grrrr" sounds that seem to run together at the back of the throat. In Afrikaans, *brei* means "to knit" or "temper," both of which make sense when listening to somebody from the Swartland.

en route | **SWARTLAND WINERY** – Because of its location in the less fashionable part of the Winelands, this large cellar a few miles outside Malmesbury has had to work hard for its place in the sun. Previously a well-kept secret among local cost- and quality-conscious wine experts, it's slowly garnering an international reputation. Try the fantastic cabernet sauvignon–merlot blend, which can hold its own in any company, or if you're just looking for something pleasant to knock back with lunch, check out the low-alcohol (9%) Fernão Pires Light. ⊠ *R45, Malmesbury* ☎ *022/482–1134 or 022/482–1135* ⊕ *www.swwines.co.za* ⊠ *Tastings free* ⊗ *Weekdays 8–5, Sat. 9–2; cellar tours by appointment.*

Where to Stay

$ 🏨 **Riebeek Valley Hotel.** At the top of town, with a great view over vineyards and mountains, this small luxury hotel is an oasis from the sweltering Swartland summer heat as well as a winter getaway. The original old farmhouse has been converted. Each room has a different color palette: refreshing lavender, peaceful cream, warm rose, and bold red, to mention just a few. In addition to a regular pool, there's an indoor pool so you can swim even if the weather is iffy. Massages are also available. The Sunday buffet draws crowds of day-trippers. ⊠ *4 Dennehof St., Riebeek West 7306* ☎ *022/461–2672* 🖶 *022/461–2692* ⊕ *www. riebeekvalley.co.za* ⇗ *11 rooms, 5 suites* ⚒ *Restaurant, 2 pools (1 indoors), bar* ⊟ *AE, DC, MC, V* 🍴 *BP.*

West Coast A to Z

BUS TRAVEL

Intercape Mainliner heads up the N7 daily. The bus stops at Malmesbury, Citrusdal, and Clanwilliam, but not coastal towns such as Langebaan and Elands Bay. Expect to pay around R85 for a one-way trip to Malmesbury, R140 to Citrusdal, and R150 to Clanwilliam. Malmesbury is only 70 km (43 mi) from Cape Town, and the trip takes 1½ hours. The journey to Clanwilliam takes about four hours.

🚍 Bus Line **Intercape Mainliner** ⊠ 1 Adderley St., Cape Town ☎ 086/128-7287 or 083/909-0909 for Computicket ⊕ www.intercape.co.za.

CAR TRAVEL

Driving is undoubtedly the best way to appreciate this area. The roads up the West Coast are generally good, but some dirt roads on the West Coast and in the Cederberg are rutted and bumpy. If you plan to head into the Cederberg mountains rather than just sticking to the small towns, consider renting a 4x4, especially in winter, when roads become muddy and you run a small risk of being snowed in.

The major car-rental agencies have offices in the smaller towns, but it's best to deal with the Cape Town offices; you'll probably want to pick up a car at the airport anyway. For car rental agencies, *see* Winelands A to Z, *above*.

To get up the West Coast and to the Cederberg, take the N1 out of Cape Town. Just before Century City shopping center, take Exit 10, which is marked GOODWOOD, MALMESBURY, CENTURY CITY DR. AND SABLE RD.) and leads to the N7, the region's major access road. Though the highway is well marked, get yourself a good map from a book-store or tourism office and explore some of the smaller roads, which offer surprising vistas or a glimpse into the rural heart of the Western Cape. The Versveld Pass, between Piketberg and the hamlet of Piket-Bo-Berg, at the top of the mountains, offers views that stretch for miles. Driving to Clanwilliam takes close to three hours without stopping, but half the fun is checking out what local farm stands have to offer and stopping to admire the scenery. In spring, this trip will take much longer, as you'll want to stop to photograph the flowers that carpet the countryside.

EMERGENCIES
There are doctors and dentists in every town, as well as provincial hospitals in Citrusdal, Clanwilliam, Malmesbury, and Vredenburg. The closest private hospital is Milnerton, a Cape Town suburb that has developed along the N7. Late-night pharmacies are a rarity in these small towns, but all pharmacies have emergency and after-hours phone numbers. If there isn't a pharmacy, head for the hospital.

⑦ Emergency Services Ambulance ☎ 10177. **Police** ☎ 10111. **Police, Fire, and Ambulance services** ☎ 107 from landline. **Vodacom emergency services** ☎ 112 from mobile phone.

⑦ Hospitals Citrusdal Hospital ✉ Vrede St., Citrusdal ☎ 022/921-2153. **Clanwilliam Hospital** ✉ Hospital St., Clanwilliam ☎ 027/482-2166. **Malmesbury Hospital** ✉ P. G. Nelson St., Malmesbury ☎ 022/482-1161. **Vredenburg Hospital** ✉ Voortrekker Rd., Vredenberg ☎ 022/709-7200.

INTERNET
There's public Internet access in several West Coast towns. For instance, you can have a cup of coffee while catching up on your e-mail at Saint du Barrys Country Lodge in Clanwilliam. You'll pay R15 for the first 15 minutes and R15 for every 30 minutes thereafter. At Lauren's Coffee Shop, in Darling, you'll pay R1 per minute.

⑦ Internet Access Compunet ✉ Burrel St., Lambert's Bay ☎ 027/432-1585. **Internet and Computer Centre** ✉ Marra's Building, Bree St., Langebaan ☎ 022/772-1760. **Lauren's Coffee Shop** ✉ 2 Arcadia St., Darling ☎ 022/492-3291. **Saint du Barrys Country Lodge** ✉ 13 Augsburg Rd., Clanwilliam ☎ 027/482-1537.

MONEY MATTERS
Credit cards are widely accepted at larger establishments, including shops and supermarkets. Smaller B&Bs and museums might operate on a cash-only basis, however, so ask ahead when you make your reservation. There are ATMs and banks in most towns on the West Coast.

TOURS

To see the exceptional rock art in the Cederberg, it's recommended that you take a tour, so that you can fully appreciate and understand this ancient art form, about which experts still have questions. The community-driven Clanwilliam Living Landscape Project has trained locals to act as guides. Expect to pay around R50 for a one-hour tour that includes a visit to two sites, R80 for five sites, which takes about four hours. If you don't have your own vehicle, the guide can pick you up, but you'll be charged a little extra for gas.

Rooibos tea is a big part of this region's economy, and a rooibos tour with Elandsburg Eco-Tourism should fill you in on all you need to know about it. The shorter tour, around 1½ hours, costs R35, and the three- to four-hour tour costs around R50. Because the tour is out on a farm, they will arrange to pick you up in town.

During the orange-harvest season (April–September), you can gain insight into the fruit industry with an hour-long tour through the packing sheds at Goedehoop Citrus Ltd. These tours meet at the Citrusdal Tourism Bureau.

If you're feeling energetic, 180 Degrees hosts a four-day mountain-biking experience in the scenic Cederberg. You're picked up in Cape Town, but the real fun begins in Algeria, where you spend the first night. From there you do a big circle through Wuppertal and then head back home. The trip costs around R4,000 per person with a group of four, and gets cheaper with each additional person.

🄵 Tour Operators **Clanwilliam Living Landscape Project** ✉ Clanwilliam ☎ 027/482-1911. **Elandsberg Eco-Tourism** ✉ Clanwilliam ☎ 027/482-2002 ⊕ www.africandawn. com. **Goedehoop Citrus Tour** ✉ Clanwilliam ☎ 022/921-3210. **180 Degrees** ☎ 022/462-0992 ⊕ www.180.co.za.

TRAIN TRAVEL

The Spier Vintage Train makes a few trips each month from Spier Monument Station, which is at the Cape Town station in Cape Town, out to Evita se Perron, in Darling, specifically for a Pieter-Dirk Uys performance. The trip costs from R210 to R300.

Although there is public train service to major West Coast towns, this isn't a recommended way to travel, as there have been regular on-board muggings. The train service is working hard to overcome these problems, but to date hasn't found a lasting solution.

🄵 Train Line **Spier Vintage Train** ☎ 021/419-5222 ⊕ www.spier.co.za.

VISITOR INFORMATION

You can get almost all the information you need about the Western Cape from the very organized Cape Town Tourism offices in Cape Town, which are open weekdays 9–6, Saturday 8:30–2, and Sunday 9–1. There are also tourist offices in most small towns along the West Coast, but the West Coast Regional Tourism Organisation has information on the entire area. Visit its Web site to get a good overview of the area. The Citrusdal Tourism Bureau is open weekdays 8:30–12:30 and 1–5, and Saturday 9–1. The Clanwilliam Tourism Bureau is open daily in the flower season 8:30–6. During the rest of the year it is open weekdays 8:30–5 and Saturday 8:30–12:30. The Darling Tourism Bureau is based at the museum and is open weekdays 9–1 and 2–4, Saturday 10–3, and Sunday 11–3. During the flower season, the Lambert's Bay Tourism Bureau is open weekdays 8–6 and Saturday 9–3. Off-season it is open weekdays 9–1 and 2–5 and Saturday 9–12:30. The Langebaan Tourism Bureau is open weekdays 9–5 and weekends 9–1. Piketberg Tourism is open weekdays 8:30–4:30. The Riebeek Valley Information Centre is open Monday to Saturday 9–4 and Sunday 11–3.

The **Flowerline** (☎ 083/910–1028) is a central hotline that offers details about where the flowers are best seen each day. It is open August–October, daily 8–4:30.

❼ Tourist Offices Cape Town Tourism ✉ The Pinnacle at Burg and Castle Sts., Box 1403, Cape Town 8000 ☎ 021/426-4260 ⊕ www.tourismcapetown.co.za. **Citrusdal Tourism Bureau** ✉ 39 Voortrekker St., Citrusdal 7340 ☎ 022/921-3210 ⊕ www.citrusdal.info. **Clanwilliam Tourism Bureau** ✉ Main Rd. ☏ Box 5, Clanwilliam 8135 ☎ 027/482-2024 ⊕ www.clanwilliam.info. **Darling Tourism Bureau** ✉ Pastorie and Hill Sts., Darling 7345 ☎ 022/492-3361 ⊕ www.darlingtourism.co.za. **Lambert's Bay Tourism Bureau** ✉ 5 Medical Centre, Main Rd., Lambert's Bay ☎ 027/432-1000 ⊕ www.lambertsbay.com. **Langebaan Tourism Bureau** ✉ Municipal Bldg., Langebaan 7357 ☎ 022/772-1515 ⊕ www.langebaaninfo.co.za. **Piketberg Tourism** ✉ 14 Church St., Piketberg 7320 ☎ 022/913-2063 ⊕ www.piketberg.com. **Riebeek Valley Information Centre** ✉ 7 Main St., Riebeek Kasteel ☎ 022/448-1584 ⊕ www.capewestcoast.org/Towns/RiebMiddel.htm. **West Coast Regional Tourism Organisation** ⊕ www.capewestcoast.org.

The Northern Cape

3

"In the spring, you may be lucky enough to be in time for the Namaqualand daisies. It's a bit of a drive out from Cape Town, but is a spectacular sight—endless fields of colorful daisies as far as you can see in the middle of a desert."

—traci

Updated by
Shellee-Kim
Gold

IT MAY BE SOUTH AFRICA'S LARGEST PROVINCE, covering almost a third of the country, but the Northern Cape is also its least populated and least understood. Its deserts and semideserts—the Karoo, Kalahari, Namaqualand, and the Richtersveld—stretch from the Orange River in the north to the Western Cape border in the south and from the small towns of Springbok and Port Nolloth in the west across 1,000 km (630 mi) with places named Pofadder and Hotazhel to the diamond capital, Kimberley, in the east. It is a province of grand and rugged beauty—a far cry from the verdant greenness of Mpumalanga and the Western Cape. The Northern Cape's appeal is in its sense of loneliness and its lunar landscapes, which would make an episode of *Star Trek* look tame. All told, it covers an area of 363,389 square km (225,665 square mi), roughly a third bigger than the entire United Kingdom, but it has a population of less than a million people (only about two per square km), and most are concentrated in a handful of towns.

Many of the Northern Cape's attractions are linked to mining, which has been the province's economic backbone for more than a century. First there was the copper mania of the 1840s in Namaqualand; the deepest copper mines in the world are still operating here, although they are now nearing the end of their productive lives. But the history of copper mining was eclipsed 30 years later by the frenzied scrabbling for diamonds on the other side of what is now the Northern Cape. Kimberley, known as the City of Diamonds, is the provincial capital and in the 1870s was the site of one of the world's greatest diamond rushes. Thousands of hopeful diggers trekked to the hot, dusty diamond fields sitting in what is more or less the geographical center of South Africa. In Kimberley five diamond-bearing volcanic pipes were eventually discovered within a few miles of one another—a phenomenon unknown anywhere else in the world. Apart from copper and diamonds, the province's mineral deposits range from manganese and zinc to lime, granite, gypsum, and other gemstones, and there are even oil and gas fields off the Namaqualand coast.

Although only a fraction of the province is regarded as arable because of low rainfall, the Orange River (known as the *!ariep*—the exclamation mark indicates a click of the tongue against the roof of the mouth—or "mighty river by the Nama") flows the breadth of the province, emptying into the Atlantic Ocean at Alexander Bay, on the Namibian border. South Africa's largest and longest river, the Orange supplies water to numerous irrigation schemes that sustain various farming activities, most noticeably in the "Green Kalahari." Agriculture employs the most people in the province, and you'll find varied agricultural production, from the second-largest date plantation in the world, at Klein Pella, near Pofadder (named after the highly poisonous puff adder snake), to thousands of acres of grapes under irrigation in the Orange River Basin around Upington. The province boasts the country's second-largest national park, Kgalagadi Transfrontier Park, the first transfrontier (i.e., crossing a national border) park in Africa. Together with an adjoining national park in Botswana, this park forms one of the largest conservation areas in the world. Ecotourism also draws an annual pilgrimage of thousands, who come to see the spectacular Namaqualand flowers.

The Northern Cape is not for the fainthearted. It's a harsh province that does not yet really cater to travelers, but therein lies its beauty. There's plenty to see if you're the type who's not afraid to ask questions and to go where your nose leads you. Don't expect luxurious accommodations, fine cuisine, or well-stocked gift shops. What you can expect, given a little time and patience, are sleepy villages still much like they were a century ago; charming locals who appreciate visitors tremendously, though in some places they may be able to communicate only in very broken English; natural wonders; evidence of human origins; and an unusual getaway that could well turn out to be the highlight of your trip to South Africa.

Exploring the Northern Cape

The Northern Cape's vastness makes it a difficult place to travel, and on a first trip you'll probably see only part of it, such as Namaqualand in flower season, the Kalahari, or Kimberley. Namaqualand is most easily visited from Cape Town and the Western Cape, whereas Kimberley and the Kalahari are far more accessible from Johannesburg. If you are planning to drive from Johannesburg to Cape Town or vice versa, Kimberley makes an ideal stopover. The Kimberley route (along the N12) is less than 100 km (63 mi) longer than the sterile N1 route with its huge gas stations and fast-food places. It's also more scenic and not as busy. Although Upington and the Kgalagadi Transfrontier Park are about the same distance from Cape Town as they are from Johannesburg, the roads from Johannesburg are far better.

About the Restaurants

The Northern Cape cannot be described as gastronomically exciting. In the larger towns of Kimberley, Upington, and Springbok there are one or two good restaurants, but they are the exceptions rather than the rule. Your most memorable meal might be the legendary delicacy Karoo lamb—often roasted on a *braai* (barbecue). It can be savored not only on the farms of the Karoo but also in restaurants in Kimberley, Upington, and the Kalahari. Vegetarians will find their needs very difficult to meet in large towns and almost unheard of in small villages. However, fresh fruits, especially grapes, are delicious and abundant in the summer months in the Orange River valley, from Upington to Kakamas. In winter look out for homemade preserves like peach chutney and apricot jam.

Other than the more sophisticated hotels and such national steakhouse chains as Spurs and Saddles, many restaurants are closed Sunday evenings. Unless you are a large group, reservations are not essential or even expected. Dining in the Northern Cape, even in Kimberley, is a casual affair in all but the few elegant and chic establishments. Wearing anything other than slip-slops (a.k.a flip-flops) and T-shirts is usually acceptable.

Numbers in the text correspond to numbers in the margin and on the Kimberley and Northern Cape & Namaqualand maps.

If you have
3 days

If you have three days, spend them soaking up the history and culture of ▦ **Kimberley** ❶–❽. On your first day, tour the town and its landmarks, perhaps starting your morning with one of the reasonably priced registered guides. Day 2 can be spent taking an underground tour of a working diamond mine followed by an afternoon of diamond-rush history at a mine museum. To rest your weary feet, ride on a historic restored tram. On your third day take a side trip, either northwest of town toward **Barkly West** ❾, where you can see alluvial diggings with a guide or view ancient rock engravings, or south of Kimberley to the evocative Anglo-Boer War battlefield Magersfontein. Take a picnic and have it under one of the ubiquitous thorn trees scattered across the battlefield.

If you have
5 days

If it's spring (August–September), it's worth staying five days in ▦ **Springbok** ❼ to see Namaqualand, but if it's between mid-May and late July (winter in South Africa), head for the huge spaces of the Kalahari via ▦ **Upington** ❿, perhaps squeezing in **Augrabies Falls National Park** ⓫. Next try a few days of roughing it in the ruggedly beautiful ▦ **Kgalagadi Transfrontier Park** ⓬, cooking your own meals and driving your own vehicle in search of the black-maned Kalahari lions and the beautifully symmetrical gemsbok. Then head for the decadent luxury of two nights at ▦ **Tswalu Kalahari Reserve** ⓭, where you'll appreciate the game drives, bush walks, and attention to detail all the more for having roughed it for the past few days. If you come between October and mid-May, ▦ **Port Nolloth** ⓰ makes an excellent entry point for the Richtersveld as well as simply being a quaint port town with good fish and interesting locals. ▦ **Upington** ❿ is a good base for day trips to Pella and Klein Pella, Witsand, and Augrabies Falls, but be sure to make your visits in early morning or late afternoon, leaving time for a rest or a swim in the midday heat.

If you have
7 or
more
days

If you enjoy huge, empty spaces, take a week to drive from ▦ **Kimberley** ❶–❽ to ▦ **Springbok** ❼—taking in the Kalahari en route. There are some memorable places to stop and stay along the way, but beware: this is a long and lonely trip, and really should be considered only if the flowers will be in bloom when you get to Namaqualand (July–mid-October). From Kimberley drive to ▦ **Upington** ❿, where you can spend a night in a guesthouse after taking a quick peek in the museum and a paddle in the Orange. Then head north for two nights in the vast ▦ **Kgalagadi Transfrontier Park** ⓬, and continue to ▦ **Augrabies Falls National Park** ⓫ for another night. On Day 5 drive to Springbok, the heart of Namaqualand. Stay two nights here or in nearby Okiep, using this area as your base for exploring the picturesque towns of Leliefontein (with nearby Namaqua National Park) to the south and **Port Nolloth** ⓰ to the northwest. Head south down the N7 to Cape Town, where the madding crowds will catch you by surprise after the loneliness of the beautiful Northern Cape.

WHAT IT COSTS In South African rand				
$$$$	**$$$**	**$$**	**$**	**¢**
RESTAURANTS over 125	100–125	75–100	50–75	under 50

Prices are per person for a main course at dinner, a main course equivalent, or a prix-fixe meal.

About the Hotels

Like good food, good hotels are hard to find in the Northern Cape. Accommodations range from the absolute basics of backpacker lodgings, available in most of the towns covered in this chapter, to a few highly rated and expensive hotels and lodges. There are, however, guesthouses in just about every little town, and the bigger centers like Kimberley and Upington are brimming with them—from basic units with cooking facilities to luxurious bed-and-breakfasts. There are also some comfortable farm accommodations, which offer overnight stays that can be a saving grace late at night on the province's long and lonely roads. In and near the parks and nature reserves, accommodations are in rest camps, lodges, bungalows, and cottages, which often sleep up to six people. Though the price categories given for each property reflect the cost for two people, these places are often a better value if you're traveling as a family or larger party.

The price categories in this chapter are applied differently to full-service safari lodges than they are to other accommodations. This is because safari lodges are typically all-inclusive experiences, with all meals, alcoholic beverages, and activities (like game-viewing) accounted for in the price. The chart below explains the differences in detail.

WHAT IT COSTS In South African rand				
$$$$	**$$$**	**$$**	**$**	**¢**
LODGING				
over 3,000	2,000–3,000	1,000–2,000	500–1,000	under 500
FULL-SERVICE SAFARI LODGING				
over 12,000	8,000–12,000	5,000–8,000	2,000–5,000	under 2,000

Prices are for a standard double room in high season, including 12.5% tax.

Timing

By South African standards the Northern Cape's climate is exceptionally hot in summer (late November–February), often rising to above 35°C (95°F). It's exceptionally hot in Kimberley and just about intolerable in Upington and the Kalahari. Conversely, the region can get quite cold in winter (mid-May–early August), commonly dropping below 0°C (32°F) at night. In fact, the province has the dubious honor of being home to the hottest town in South Africa in summer (Upington) and the coldest in winter (Sutherland, in the Karoo), so come prepared to sweat or shiver. Any other time of year is fine, though. The best time to see the flowers in Namaqualand is usually between the middle of August and the end

3

Made by Hand

Technology lags behind in the Northern Cape. Much of the province has no cell-phone reception, and a full range of TV channels is a rarity outside Kimberley. Perhaps because of technology's tenuous reach, many old traditions are still in place. All around the province it is possible to buy original and interesting handcrafts, including ostrich shells painted by San (Bushmen) and Na'ama reed matting. In Upington, for example, the store Kalahari Living sells various locally made crafts, including textiles and beadwork. And of course, all of those diamonds and semiprecious stones abundant in the province find their way into curios and jewelry.

Made by Mother Earth

Concealed by the area's association and obsession with diamonds, the region's other hidden treasures are a wealth of semiprecious stones. Local resident George Swanson discovered blue lace agate, though it's mined in Namibia. Other stones you'll see are tigereye, garnet, blue-gray iolite, aquamarine, pinkish morganite, and quartz, which comes in shades from pink rose quartz and deep orange-red river quartz to brown smoky quartz and purple amethyst. Red jasper and agates can be found in the Orange River. Away from the water, in the hills between Kuruman and Prieska, tigereye is sourced. The blue variety is more valuable; the brown is heat-treated to turn it red. (The interior of Kuruman's bank building is clad in the stone.) This area and Augrabies are home to exquisite crystals of quartz. It's worth stopping in the village of Pella for the amethyst and orange-red and smoky quartz varieties. You can buy them informally from the locals.

of September, depending on when and how much rain has fallen. The weather is generally milder in Namaqualand than in the rest of the province. The only other time to be aware of is the four-day Gariep Annual Festival (Gariep means "orange" in Tsetswana, the language of the Tswana people), in September, when Kimberley gets jam-packed. Sporting events also bring crowds to Kimberley, but dates change annually.

KIMBERLEY

Kimberley was born in the dust, dreams, and disappointments of a rudimentary mining camp that grew into a city of grace and sophistication in some quarters, still evident in many of its early buildings. Today Kimberley is a city of about 200,000 people spread out around its diamond mines—giant holes in the earth, like inverted *koppies* (hills). Kimberley has a host of comfortable guesthouses, a few good restaurants, and many historical attractions, making it a wonderful place to spend a few days. It's an easy trip of about 500 km (313 mi) from Johannesburg and is about 970 km (606 mi) from Cape Town. (In South Africa the term *easy driving* means driving on good roads—no potholes, gravel, or single lanes.)

Kimberley's colonial beginnings date to 1869, when diamonds were first discovered in the area. Through the late 1860s alluvial diamonds were mined on the banks of the Vaal River near Barkly West, about 30 km (19 mi) away. These were all but forgotten after the finds in Kimberley of five pipes bearing the diamondiferous Kimberlite, or "blue ground," so called because of its color. In 1871 the richest pipe of all, the Kimberley Mine (now known as the Big Hole), was discovered. Diggers from around the world flocked to stake claims in the mine, which produced more than 14.5 million carats before its closure in 1914, making it one of the richest diamond mines in history. At times there were as many as 30,000 people working in the hole, burrowing like a giant colony of termites. The history of the diamond fields is dominated by eccentric personalities, like Barney Barnato, who came to South Africa with so little he had to walk to the diamond fields, yet died a magnificently wealthy man. Then there was Cecil John Rhodes, the diamond magnate and colonizer who aspired to paint the map of Africa red for Britain and to build a railroad from Cape Town to Cairo.

Both Rhodes and Barnato were shrewd businessmen. They watched diggers toiling at their individual claims in Kimberley's five holes. When the miners met what they perceived to be bedrock, they would often give up and stop digging, but what they were actually hitting was unweathered, hard blue ground that was fabulously rich in diamonds. The two men then snapped up claims at bargain prices, all the time increasing their shares in the mines. Eventually Barnato and Rhodes merged their companies into the De Beers Consolidated Mines Ltd. Today De Beers is the world's most powerful diamond-mining company. Its historic headquarters is still on Stockdale Street in Kimberley.

In addition to the allure of diamonds, another central part of Kimberley's history was its attack by the Boers during the Anglo-Boer War (1899–1902). Kimberley's close proximity to the border of the then-Boer Republic of the Orange Free State and its international fame as a diamond town occupied by prominent British citizens (including Rhodes) made it an ideal siege target. For four months in the summer of 1899 the town's citizens suffered dwindling rations, disease, Boer shellfire, and other hardships. British efforts to relieve the town were thwarted by the Boers at the famous Battle of Magersfontein, but eventually a sustained cavalry charge led by Major-General John French broke through to the beleaguered town. Kimberley's part in the Anglo-Boer War is brought to life everywhere through monuments, buildings, and statues.

Exploring Kimberley

The hub of business activity, in the CBD (Central Business District), is defined by Jones Street, George Street, and Du Toitspan Road, with its small manufacturing concerns. Victorian-style architecture abounds in Belgravia, Kimberley's first residential suburb, which, beginning in the late 1880s, was associated with the town's mines. De Beers, another suburb that grew up around the De Beers mine, originally constituted part of Johannes Nicholas de Beer's farm. (Both the Kimberley and De Beers mines are now closed, leaving three remaining working mines.) Also on

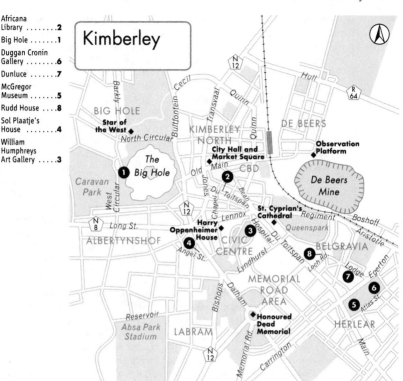

land originally owned by De Beers and of even greater historical interest, the residential area around the Civic Centre is similar to Cape Town's District Six (⇨ Chapter 1) in sociopolitical terms. Called Malay Camp, it was where freed Asian slaves (largely Muslim and erroneously lumped together under the name Cape Malays) settled. Given to the municipality as an open area in 1939, today it is a well-maintained, treed garden area stretching out from the base of the municipal building.

One of the two oldest townships in South Africa, Greenpoint, south of town, is populated by both coloured (a local term for people of mixed—white European, black African, or "Cape Malay"—heritage) and Africans (blacks). Despite its age, no standing buildings predate the 1930s. Galeshewe is the settlement to the west of town and is still where the majority of blacks in the area live.

a good walk

You can start your walk through history at the diamond-studded **Big Hole ❶** and the Kimberley Mine Museum. From here, hop the restored 1914 tram to City Hall, with its Corinthian columns. In the 1970s it was saved from demolition by referendum. Turn left into Jones Street, and follow it to Du Toitspan Road, where you turn left again. Cross Chapel Street and visit the reputedly haunted **Africana Library ❷**. Across the street is the elite Kimberley Club, one of whose first rules was "No dogs, women, and smoking." Established by Rhodes and his contemporaries, it is much as it was then and still has an invitation-only policy, reserved mainly for De Beers shareholders and their friends. St. Mary's Roman Catholic Cathedral is next door. Continue on Du Toitspan, turning right at Lennox Street and then left into Jonker Street; follow the curve into Jan Smuts Boulevard. Queen Elizabeth gazes haughtily down at you from the **William Humphreys Art Gallery** ❸. Across the way is the original site of the old Malay Camp, today the Civic Centre gardens with its Diggers Fountain. In the background is the Harry Oppenheimer House, an imposing 14-story building in which all diamonds mined in South Africa are sorted by the Diamond Trading Company and sold to cutters. (Public access is prohibited for security reasons.) The building was designed for diamond sorting under the correct light conditions—one side is concrete, the other almost completely glass. Follow the tourist info board to Angel Street, where you will see **Sol Plaatje's House** ❹ on the right. Retrace your steps to the Diggers Fountain, head back to Du Toitspan, turn right, and pass St. Cyprian's Cathedral. Note the statue of Sister Henrietta Stockdale, an Anglican nun honored for achieving recognition for nurses worldwide.

Pass the Halfway House Hotel, turn left into Atlas Street, and head to the Victorian **McGregor Museum** ❺, originally built by Rhodes as a sanatorium and now home to historical exhibits. Traverse the gardens to see the historical photographs of the **Duggan Cronin Gallery** ❻. Exit through the Egerton Road gates, cross the street, and make your way onto Lodge Road, which is in Belgravia, Kimberley's oldest suburb. No. 10 is **Dunluce** ❼, the home of the John Orr family. Continue up Lodge to Loch Road and **Rudd House** ❽, home to a Rhodes business partner. From here take Loch to a right turn on Elsmere Road and a left into Hemming Street, which brings you to Memorial Road and the Honoured Dead Memorial. It's a tribute to British soldiers who died defending Kimberley during the siege in the Anglo-Boer War, and under it 27 bodies are buried. The Byzantine synagogue on the left is the only one in the world to have a diamond-tipped pointer for reading the Torah. Assuming you're now tired and hungry, retrace your steps down Memorial Road and pick a café for a well-earned rest.

TIMING   It should take roughly three hours to walk this route at a leisurely pace, excluding stops.

What to See

❷ **Africana Library.** Housed in the old Kimberley Public Library, which was built in 1887, this is one of the country's premier reference libraries. Books are shelved from floor to ceiling, and an ornate wrought-iron staircase connects the floors. Included among the 20,000 books in the collection are such rarities as the Setswana Bible, the first-ever Bible in an African language, printed by Robert Moffat in the 1850s. The library also has four books dating from the 1400s and a good selection of locally published limited-edition books for sale. If there's enough interest on tours or when requested by researchers, books are removed from the safe, and visitors can—under surveillance—have hands-on contact with some literary jewels. The library is said to be haunted by the ghost of Bertram Dyer, the first qualified librarian in the country. After he was caught defrauding the library of money, he committed suicide. He now purportedly stacks files on the floor and rattles teacups in the kitchen. ⊠ *Du Toitspan Rd., CBD* ☎ *053/830–6247* ✍ *Donations accepted* ⊘ *Weekdays 8–12:45 and 1:30–4:30.*

★ ☾ ❶ **Big Hole.** If you do one thing in Kimberley, visit the Big Hole, at 2,690 feet deep, the largest hand-dug hole in the world. Although water and debris now fill most of its depth, it's still an impressive sight, particularly from the two observation posts. On the lip of the Big Hole is the extensive open-air **Kimberley Mine Museum,** comprising a host of authentic 19th-century buildings, many of which were moved here from the city center instead of being torn down. They include the first house erected in Kimberley (1877), which was brought piece by piece from Britain to the diamond fields by ship and ox wagon; Barney Barnato's boxing academy; and a bar reminiscent of a Wild West saloon. Replicas of the world's most famous diamonds, including the Eureka, a 21-carat yellow diamond that was South Africa's first recorded diamond discovery in 1866, are also on view. Kids can dig through gravel for a real diamond, and learn about 19th-century attire at the museum. At the time of writing, construction of an on-site restaurant and B&B had begun. Allow a few hours here, and wear comfortable shoes. ⊠ *Tucker St., CBD/Big Hole* ☎ *053/839–4901* ✍ *R25, including diamond dig* ⊘ *Daily 8–6.*

Bultfontein Mine. Kimberley is the only place in the world where you can take an underground tour of a working diamond mine—in this case the Bultfontein Mine, operated by De Beers. The tour starts with a short video on the history of Kimberley and diamond mining, after which you are outfitted with boots, hard hat, and gear. The underground experience is not at all claustrophobic, as the passages are fairly spacious and cool. You'll be awestruck if you're fortunate enough to be on a tour when miners do a working blast. The tour takes about 3½ hours and entails quite a lot of walking. It's best to book about two weeks in advance, although it's possible to get a place either the day before or the day of the tour. You must be over 16 but under 65 and in good health, and contact lenses are not advisable because of the dust. If you can't get on an underground tour, take the 1½-hour surface tour. ⊠ *Visitors' Reception Centre, Bultfontein Mine Gate, Molyneux Rd., Beaconsfield* ☎ *053/842– 1321* ✍ *R75 mine tour, R10 surface tour* ⊘ *Tours Mon. and Tues., and Thurs. and Fri. at 7:45, Wed. at 10.*

❻ **Duggan Cronin Gallery.** This gallery houses early photographs of Africa and its inhabitants taken by A. M. Duggan Cronin, an Irishman who arrived in 1897 to work as a night watchman for De Beers. A keen photographer, he traveled widely through southern Africa, capturing his impressions—mostly of African peoples—on film. ⊠ *Atlas St., adjacent to McGregor Museum, Belgravia* ☎ *053/839–2700* ⊕ *www.museumsnc. co.za* ✍ *Donations accepted* ⊘ *Weekdays 9–5.*

❼ **Dunluce.** A well-known Kimberley landmark, the family home of merchant John Orr has a colonial wraparound veranda painted a distinctive green and white. To see the house you need to take a personalized tour (run by the McGregor Museum), on which you'll hear about such details as the swimming pool (the first in Kimberley) and the red dining room, which took a shell through its ceiling during the siege. ⊠ *Lodge Rd., Belgravia* ☎ *053/839–2700* ⊕ *www.museumsnc.co.za* ⌦ *R15* ⊘ *Tours by appointment.*

en route

MAGERSFONTEIN BATTLEFIELD – Where this evocative, barren national monument now stands, the Boers resoundingly defeated British forces marching to relieve besieged Kimberley in December 1899. An excellent museum screens an 11-minute multimedia display that does such a good job of recalling the battle in pictures and sound that it will give you goose bumps. You can also visit several monuments dotted around the battlefield. A pleasant tearoom and the on-site Bagpipe Lodge (bagpipes not included) offer a place to refuel and recline. ⊠ *Magersfontein Rd., 31.5 km (20 mi) south of Kimberley* ☎ *053/839–2700* ⊕ *www. museumsnc.co.za* ⌦ *R5* ⊘ *Daily 9–5.*

❺ McGregor Museum. This graceful Kimberley landmark, built at Rhodes's instigation, was first used as a sanatorium, then an upscale hotel, and later as a girls' convent school. Rhodes himself stayed here during the siege, and you can see rooms he once occupied. Today the building houses a museum that focuses on Northern Cape history (prehistoric to early 20th century) within a global context. It contains quite a good display on the Anglo-Boer War and the even more impressive Hall of Ancestors—an extensive exhibition on the history of humanity that includes prehistoric human skulls dating back 3 million years. The natural history of the area can be seen in the EnviroZone, and a chapel once stood on what is today the Hall of Religion. ⊠ *Atlas St., Belgravia* ☎ *053/839–2700* ⊕ *www.museumsnc.co.za* ⌦ *R10* ⊘ *Mon.–Sat. 9–5, Sun. 2–5.*

❽ Rudd House. In the leafy suburb of Belgravia, Rudd House is the rambling home of Cecil John Rhodes's first business partner, the early diamond magnate Charles Dunnell Rudd. The house has been restored in the art-deco style of the 1920s, when the Bungalow, as the house was known, was in its heyday. Look for the croquet ground made out of kimberlite, and the massive snooker table surrounded by a multitude of animal heads from Rudd's trips north to Matabeleland. Like Dunluce, Rudd House can be seen only on a tour. ⊠ *Loch Rd., Belgravia* ☎ *053/839–2700* ⌦ *R15* ⊘ *Tours by appointment.*

❹ Sol Plaatje's House. Activist, author, and journalist Sol Plaatje (1876–1932) lived most of his multitalented life in this house. In addition to being the first general secretary of the African National Congress, he was the first black South African to publish a novel in English, an influential early black newspaper editor, and an energetic campaigner for human rights. His house is now a small reference library, publishing house, and museum with displays on his life and extracts from his diary. The reference library contains the works of previously exiled South Africans (in English) and a collection of Tsetswana literature; books are also for sale. ⊠ *32 Angel St., Albertynshof* ☎ *082/804–3266 or 053/833–2526* ⊕ *www.museumsnc.co.za* ⌦ *R5* ⊘ *Open by appointment.*

❸ William Humphreys Art Gallery. This renowned art museum in Kimberley's Civic Centre is at once sedate and lively. It's an air-conditioned haven of tranquillity on a hot summer day and an active site for community projects, such as the Whag Ubuntu Project, which teaches unemployed black women crafting skills. Come on a Monday, Wednesday, or Friday, and you'll see Tswana women embroidering and beading articles such as vests, pillowcases, and bags. The gallery's impressive collection features South African works as well as Dutch, Flemish, British, and French masters. One area is devoted to local work, and a very popular exhibit is a permanent display on rock art of the Northern Cape. Free guided tours (preferably booked two weeks in advance) cater to specific interests on request. Light meals are available in the gallery's downstairs tearoom, the Palette. ⊠ *Jan Smuts Blvd., Civic Centre* ☎ *053/831–1724 or 053/831–1725* ⊕ *www.museumsnc.co.za* ⊠ *R5* ☉ *Weekdays 8–4:45, Sat. 10–4:45.*

Where to Stay & Eat

$–$$$ ✕ **Barnato's.** Set in a picturesque old colonial home dating to around the turn of the 19th century, Barnato's offers plenty of atmosphere and well-presented, tasty food—although both come at a price, comparatively speaking in Kimberley. The meat dishes here are especially good; try the spareribs or, if you're really hungry, the Barnato's Challenge— a 1-kilo (more than 2-pound) fillet or rump steak (R130)—which will earn you a plaque on the wall. Fish is also a good choice, in particular the sole, which is prepared in a variety of ways. The Sole Diva (layered with smoked salmon and mussels in a creamy garlic sauce) is the signature dish. ⊠ *6 Dalham Rd.* ☎ *053/833–4110* ⚐ *Reservations essential* ⊟ *AE, DC, MC, V* ☉ *Closed Sun. No lunch Sat.*

¢–$$ ✕ **Mario's.** The relaxed atmosphere both in this historic Kimberley house and outside under a magical Japanese pagoda tree in summer make this one of the town's most popular restaurants. The extensive menu includes excellent pizza and pastas. Steaks (especially the panfried fillet), Karoo lamb chops, and fresh seafood flown up from Cape Town are recommended. ⊠ *159 Du Toitspan Rd., Belgravia* ☎ *053/831– 1738* ⚐ *Reservations essential* ⊟ *AE, DC, MC, V* ☉ *Closed Sun. No lunch Sat.*

$ ✕ **Spill the Beans.** This coffee shop is an excellent place to grab a bargain breakfast (R20), scones with biltong (air-dried meat) and cottage cheese, or a light lunch. Vegetarians might opt for a veggie burger or a *tramezzini* (an unusual toasted sandwich with a variety of fillings) and a Heavenly Coffee Shake. ⊠ *Checkers Centre, Sydney St.* ☎ *082/833– 2612* ⊟ *No credit cards* ☉ *Closed Sun. No dinner.*

¢–$ ✕ **Copacabana Sidewalk Cafe.** A laid-back, Continental atmosphere prevails at this restaurant, café, and bar. Caffeinoholics can get espressos and cappuccinos while contemplating the statue of Cecil John Rhodes on horseback outside. Cozy seating spills out onto the sidewalk, with reed screens for privacy. Dinner entrées range from pasta to surf 'n' turf: a 300-gram (10-ounce) rump steak bedecked with prawns and calamari. Several times monthly, jazz musicians strut their stuff, adding to the welcoming ambience. ✉ *15 D'arcy St.* 🖩 *053/832–3578* 🖃 *AE, DC, MC, V* ☺ *Closed Sun.*

¢ ✕ **Star of the West.** The oldest continuously operating bar in Kimberley, the Star is a national monument and worth a visit even if just for a drink. Typical pub fare such as steaks, salads, toasted sandwiches, and burgers makes it a good lunch option. Its sleepy, nostalgic atmosphere during the day is traded at night (it's open quite late) for noise and smoke, when it's frequented by locals. A lunch buffet (from R40) is available most Sundays, for which you should reserve in advance. Among regular menu items, ribs and *eisbein* (German pork knuckles) are very popular. Beware, though, that the attitudes of the regular clientele can make it unsafe for nonwhite travelers, particularly after a few drinks. ✉ *N. Circular and Barkly Rds., Big Hole* 🖩 *053/832–6463* 🖃 *AE, DC, MC, V.*

★ $$ ✕🖾 **Estate Private Hotel.** Built in 1907 as a wedding present to Lady Mary Oppenheimer, this exquisite guesthouse lets you see how the rich and famous lived it up at the turn of last century. The current owners successfully maintain the national monument's old English Victorian decor and atmosphere while imbuing each room with a different design. Small details include handmade chocolates (created by the in-house chef) on pillows, turndown service, and slippers and gowns laid out with care. The exclusive Butlers restaurant ($–$$$) and its tea garden have officially been demystified by locals, after having been the private domain of guests for many years. Fine dining accompanied by white linen and fine silverware makes this the place for the discerning diner who likes to linger over a meal. ✉ *7 Lodge Rd., Belgravia, 8300* 🖩 *053/832–2668* 🖶 *053/831–5777* ⊕ *www.theestate.co.za* 📨 *7 rooms* ♨ *Restaurant, in-room safes, minibars, pool, free parking* 🖃 *AE, DC, MC, V* ⑩ *BP.*

¢ 🖾 **Belgravia Bed and Breakfast.** In a 100-year-old house on leafy Elsemere Road, in the heart of historic Belgravia, this charming bed-and-breakfast is within easy walking distance of many of Kimberley's historic attractions, including the McGregor Museum, Dunluce, and the Rudd House. The furnishings are tasteful and homey and include antique wooden furniture, Persian carpets, and prints of Dutch masters and South African landscapes. In addition to two rooms in the main house, one of which has its bathroom outside the room, there is a self-catering cottage. ✉ *10 Elsemere Rd., Belgravia, 8300* 🖩 *053/832–5007 or 082/224–3605* 🖶 *053/833–1600* ✍ *belgraviabb@absamail.co.za* 📨 *2 rooms, 1 cottage* ♨ *Pool, free parking* 🖃 *No credit cards* ⑩ *BP.*

★ ¢ 🖾 **Langberg Guest Farm.** On the west side of the Magersfontein Battlefield, Langberg is far removed from the buzz of city life. Rooms here are all part of restored thick-walled, whitewashed farm buildings that date back to the days of the diamond rush. It's an operating game and cattle farm—raising buffalo and sable, roan, and 21 other antelope species—and hunting for kudu, gemsbok, and other antelope can be arranged. The atmosphere is relaxed, and the food is excellent. A three-course meal is served every night except Sunday, and typically includes such hearty dishes as homemade chicken pie and venison fillets stuffed with dried fruits. Meals aren't included in the lodging price—breakfast costs R35 and dinner another R65 per person—but Langberg is inexpensive considering the luxurious service. ⊠ *21 km (13 mi) south of Kimberley on the N12 and another 2.6 km (1.6 mi) on a farm road, Box 10400, Beaconsfield 8315* 🕿 *053/832–1001* 🕿 *082/926–0055* ⊕ *www.langberg.co.za* ✒ *13 rooms* ⚭ *Tennis court, pool, gym, bar; no room TVs* ⊟ *AE, MC, V.*

¢ 🏠 **Milner House.** Set in a tranquil part of the already-sedate Belgravia, this big old beautiful B&B offers all the comforts of home. Modern yet comfortable, Milner House has a cottagey feel with lots of wooden furnishings, and a location nestled amid huge trees. ⊠ *31 Milner St., Belgravia, 8301* 🕿 *053/831–6405 or 053/831–2878* 🖷 *053/831–6407* ⊕ *www.milnerhouse.co.za* ✒ *6 rooms* ⊟ *AE, DC, MC, V* ⦶ *BP.*

Nightlife

Cecil John Rhodes used to stop for a drink at **Halfway House** (⊠ 229 Du Toitspan Rd., Belgravia, 8301 🕿 053/831–6324), halfway between the Kimberley and Bultfontein mines. Because he was short and it was difficult for him to mount and dismount, he was served on his horse. Thanks to the building of a 6-foot wall to prevent people from drinking in public, this novel tradition still lives on. You can drive into the parking lot at "the Half," honk your horn, and a waiter will appear. Today, though, most of the action is inside, where the under-30 crowd gets rowdy at night. If you go on a drinking spree, you can even spend the night at the attached hotel (locals describe the rooms as "shabby"), at which point no amount of noise will wake you.

Shopping

In addition to a branch at Kimberley's airport, **Africa Now** (⊠ 37–39 Du Toitspan Rd., CBD 🕿 053/832–5522 or 082/413–6016) has a big warehouse in town, which is loaded with objects from just about every inch of Africa—in bone, bead, wood, and resin. **Big Hole Gift Shop** (⊠ W. Circular Rd., Big Hole 🕿 053/833–1557) has Kimberley's best assortment of postcards, slides, books, videos, and knickknacks as well as a wide range of ethnic souvenirs such as T-shirts and pillow covers. (Postcards mailed in the pre-1902 Victorian mailbox outside the shop will receive a Kimberley Mine Museum postmark.) You can also buy diamonds and diamond jewelry here, but it may be useful to compare pieces and prices with the Jewel Box, down the road. The **Jewel Box & Big Hole Diamond Cutting Factory** (⊠ 18 W. Circular Rd., Big Hole 🕿 053/832–1731) specializes in diamond jewelry and can custom-make a piece if you will be in town for a day or two. Although the Jewel Box doesn't boast about its prices, they are among the country's most reasonable, which draws customers from as far as Johannesburg. On weekdays you can watch goldsmiths at work in the on-premises factory. **Kimberley Jewellers** (⊠ 23 Jones St., CBD 🕿 082/413–6016), around the corner from and a sister store of Africa Now, carries Euro-African jewelry, specializing in tanzanite and antique jewelry.

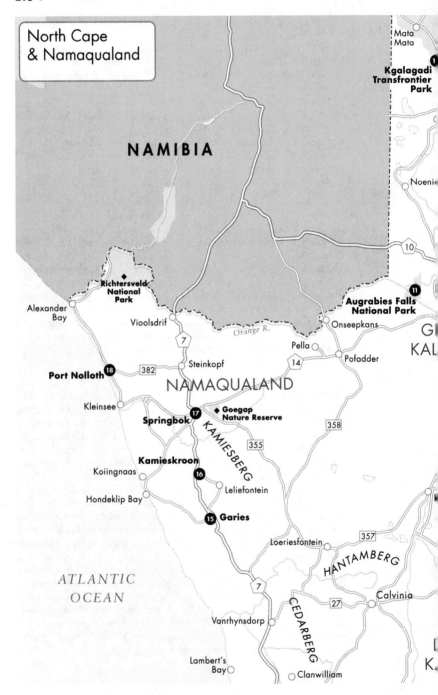

North Cape & Namaqualand

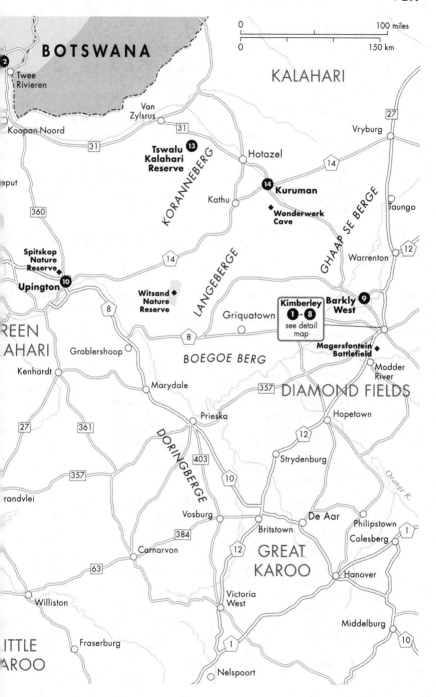

BOTSWANA

KALAHARI

0   100 miles

0   150 km

2

Twee Rivieren

Koopan-Noord

Van Zylsrus

Vryburg

27

31

Tswalu Kalahari Reserve 13

KORANNEBERG

Hotazel

14

eput

360

Kathu

14 **Kuruman**

Taungo

♦ **Wonderwerk Cave**

GHAAP SE BERGE

Spitskop Nature Reserve ♦

Upington 10

14

LANGEBERGE

Warrenton

12

GREEN
...AHARI

8

Groblershoop

Witsand ♦ Nature Reserve

Griquatown

8

BOEGOE BERG

Kimberley 1 - 8
see detail map

Barkly West 9

Magersfontein ♦ Battlefield

Modder River

Kenhardt

Marydale

357

DIAMOND FIELDS

27

361

...randvlei

357

Prieska

DORINGBERGE

403

10

12

Hopetown

Strydenburg

Orange R.

Vosburg

12

Britstown

De Aar

Philipstown

Colesberg

1

384

Carnarvon

10

GREAT KAROO

Hanover

63

Victoria West

Middelburg

10

Williston

Fraserburg

1

...ITTLE
...AROO

Nelspoort

Side Trip to Barkly West

❾ *32 km (20 mi) north of Kimberley on the R31.*

The town of Barkly West, on the Vaal River, was the site of some of the earliest alluvial diamond diggings in South Africa. Today you can visit the open-air **Canteen Kopje Archaeological Site** to view both archaeological and geological treasures, ranging from Stone Age artifacts over a million years old to rock axes, found in a recent excavation, that date from the late 1800s. Walk the 1-km (½-mi) trail to take in the exhibits. ⊠ *Follow signs* 🖭 *Free* ⊙ *Weekdays 7:30–4:15, weekends 8:30–4.*

Located in an old tollhouse, the **Barkly West Museum** tells of diamond diggers' history and the archaeology of the area. It includes artifacts discovered at Canteen Kopje, only ½ km (⅓ mi) away. ⊠ *Barkly West Resort* ⊙ *Daily 9–4.*

need a break? Finish off your tour with a drink or light snack at the **Pumphouse Bar** (⊠ Barkly West Resort ☎ 053/531–0867), within a stone's throw of the museum. It's a great place to meet locals, enjoy a good steak or other pub fare, and contemplate the waters of the Vaal River.

Fodor's Choice ★ At the **Wildebeest Kuil Rock Art Tourism Centre,** the ½-mi-long San Rock Art Trail takes you on a short walk back through time. Billed as "helping to protect the future of the past," this memorable rock art experience includes engravings made by ancestors of the Khoisan, dating between 1,000 and 2,000 years ago. (Ancestors of the Khoisan are believed to be some of the earliest humans to walk the face of the earth.) Listening to an audio player, you take a boardwalk to the best of more than 400 images—eland, elephant, rhino, wildebeest, hartebeest, ostrich, and dancing human figures—on a low ridge of ancient andesite rock. The center also offers a 20-minute introductory film and display on the subject and a crafts shop run by the !Xun and Khwe San (refugees from the Angolan and Namibian wars), whose land surrounds the site. ⊠ *15 km (9 mi) northwest of Kimberley on the R31, en route to Barkly West* ☎ *053/833–7079* ⊕ *www.museumsnc.co.za/wildebeestkuil.htm* 🖭 *R20* ⊙ *Tues.–Sun. 10–5.*

en route On your way from Kimberley to Upington, stop for half an hour or so in **Griquatown** (144 km [90 mi] from Kimberley; 252 km [158 mi] from Upington). The town, locally known as Griekwastad, was the center of a 19th-century state called Griqualand West, which had its own flag, coinage, and even language. The Griquas, a social group that came into being in the late 18th century, were at first a mixture of indigenous Khoisan and black peoples, runaway slaves, freebooters, adventurers, and criminals escaping the Cape Colony to the south. Some people still identify themselves as Griquas today. In 1803 the London Missionary Society established a mission here, and Mary Moffat, wife of explorer David Livingstone, was born here. The old mission house is now home to the **Mary Moffat Museum,** which has interesting displays and literature on the history of the Griquas, the missionaries, and the area. ⊠ *Main St., Griquatown* ☎ *053/ 343–0180* 🖭 *Donations accepted* ⊙ *Weekdays 8–1 and 2–5.*

ROCK ART

AN IMPORTANT KEY to understanding humankind's past, rock art is a fascinating aspect of South African and world heritage. In the Northern Cape, engravings (made by scratching into the rock surface), paintings, and finger paintings proliferate throughout the province and still carry an aura of mystique, since relatively little is known about them. Although some archaeologists have attributed the origins of rock art to ancient Egyptians, Phoenicians, and even extraterrestrial races, the rock art found here was created by ancestors of the San. Materials came from the immediate environment. Ocher (red iron-oxide clay) was used to obtain red, charcoal for black, and white clay for white. Blood, egg, and plant juices were used for binding, creating a paint with obvious staying power.

Most rock art illustrates the activities and experiences of the African medicine people, or shamans. Religious rituals, such as those for making rain and healing the sick, involved trances and inspired visions, from which rock-art images were created. The images included large animals, such as the highly regarded eland and rhino, which were believed to possess supernatural power. Half-animal, half-human representations and geometric patterns and grids are also featured. The shamans believed that when an image was drawn, power was transferred to the land.

Today some of the province's most significant examples of rock art are found at Wonderwerk Cave and Wildebeest Kuil. The former contains one of the country's oldest engravings—at 10,200 years old—as well as finger paintings, a method used by older-era painters. The latter is well known because its animal engravings are easily accessible to visitors.

Kimberley A to Z

AIR TRAVEL
Small and well-marked Kimberley Airport, 12 km (7½ mi) southwest of town, is served by South African Express, which connects to Johannesburg five times daily, and SA Airlink, with service from Cape Town twice a day on weekdays, less often on weekends. To book tickets, you can also contact Rennies Travel in Kimberley.

Taxis are not big business in Kimberley, and there are only two companies. Although Rikkis taxis try to meet most flights on arrival, they are not a guaranteed presence, and cabs should be reserved in advance. A ride in a Rikkis "fish tank" four-wheeler, with an open back and canvas, costs R45 from the airport to town. Service from AA Taxis, available 24 hours, costs about R30.

🛈 Airport **Kimberley Airport** ✉ N12 ☎ 053/838-3337.
🛈 Airlines **SA Airlink** ☎ 011/961-1700 ⊕ www.saairlink.co.za. **South African Express** ☎ 011/978-1111 ⊕ www.saexpress.co.za.
🛈 Airport Transfers **AA Taxis** ☎ 053/861-4015 or 083/283-0558. **Rikkis Taxis** ☎ 053/842-1764 or 083/342-2533.

🔝 Booking Agent **Rennies Travel** ✉ Shop 22b, Newpark Centre, Holland Park Ⓓ Box 512, 8300 ☎ 053/831-1825 or 053/831-1826 ⊕ www.renniestravel.co.za.

BUS TRAVEL

Daily bus service between Kimberley and both Cape Town (about 11 hours, R389–R422) and Johannesburg (about 6 hours, R227) is offered by Greyhound and Translux. The local company Tickets for Africa provides schedules, prices, and other information and sells tickets for all buses in and out of Kimberley.

🔝 Bus Lines **Greyhound** ⊕ www.greyhound.co.za. **Translux** ⊕ www.translux.co.za.
🔝 Bus Tickets **Tickets for Africa** ✉ Diamantveld Visitors' Centre, 121 Bultfontein Rd., ☎ 053/832-6040.

CAR TRAVEL

Having a car in Kimberley is a good idea, as it gives you more freedom, but it's not mandatory if you're staying only a day or two and you hire a good tour guide. Strategically placed monuments and good signage make this an easy town to find your way around in. Just remember to drive within the speed limits, as there are plenty of hidden cameras. Parking is no problem, and gas stations are visible and plentiful. Roads out of town are very straight and generally do not have shoulders.

🔝 Rental Companies **Alamo** ✉ 19a Smitsdrift St. ☎ 053/861-2508. **Avis** ✉ Kimberley Airport ☎ 053/851-1082. **Budget** ✉ Kimberley Airport ☎ 053/851-1182 or 053/851-1183. **Imperial Car Rentals** ✉ Kimberley Airport ☎ 053/851-1131 or 053/851-1132.

EMERGENCIES

The Curomed Private Hospital has an emergency room that is open 24 hours. The Kimberley Pharmacy is open weekdays 8–8, weekends 8–2 and 5–8.

🔝 Emergency Services **Ambulance** ☎ 10177 or 053/831-1954. **Police** ☎ 10111.
🔝 Hospital **Curomed Private Hospital** ✉ 177 Du Toitspan Rd. ☎ 053/838-1111 or 053/831-4730.
🔝 Pharmacy **Kimberley Pharmacy** ✉ Market Sq. ☎ 053/831-3035.

INTERNET

🔝 Internet Access **CyberZone** ✉ Sanlam Centre, between Sydney and Chapel Sts., CBD. **Small World Internet Café** ✉ 42 Sidney St., CBD ☎ 053/831-3484.

MONEY MATTERS

Typical banking hours are weekdays 9–3:30 and Saturday 9–11. You can exchange money efficiently at either the ABSA main office, at Long and Bultfontein roads, or at Nedbank, on Chapel Street. (At time of writing, ABSA provided the consistently cheapest exchange rate.) Other possibilities are the Rennies Exchange Bureau and the Holiday Inn on Du Toitspan Road. Though Kimberley is a very safe town, extra-safe ATM withdrawals can be made at the Standard Bank on Chapel Street, which has good security.

TOURS

GROUP TOURS Consider a tour by chartered township taxi (minibus), which will pick you up from wherever you wish. These tours focus on the history and culture of Galeshewe, Kimberley's largest township, named after an important Tswana chief. Places visited include the homes of legendary human-rights activists Sol Plaatje and Robert Sobukwe, as well as the Northern Cape legislature to observe the symbolism inside. The tours also take in a traditional *shebeen* (drinking place) and a restaurant serving traditional South African meals. Those wanting a longer township visit can stay at one of several guesthouses catering to tourists. Tour lengths and prices vary; book through the Diamantveld Visitors' Centre (*see* Visitor Information, *below*).

Something different, the Kimberley Ghost Route starts at night with sherry inside the Honoured Dead Memorial and then proceeds to several of Kimberley's (purportedly) haunted places, such as the Kimberley Club and Rhodes's boardroom. The tour ends with a visit to the historic Gladstone Cemetery, where a certain Mr. Frankenstein and his wife are buried. Price varies according to size of group. Book at least two days in advance through the Diamantveld Visitors' Centre, and make sure you specify that you want to go inside the haunted buildings, or the tour can be disappointing.

GUIDE SERVICES   Guide fees are not regulated, and guides therefore charge different rates. A half-day guide should not cost more than R350 per person, a full day not more than R640. This excludes transportation, entrance fees, and refreshments.

One of the town's most popular and informative guides, Janet Welsh is a mine of interesting information and asides. Offering specialized tours to sites relating to early nursing sister Henrietta Stockdale and another on human-rights activist Sol Plaatje, she is also registered to do Kimberley and battlefield tours.

Versatile Dirk Potgieter of Diamond Tours Unlimited offers diamond-themed tours and alluvial diamond diggings about 40 km (25 mi) from Kimberley. Claiming the most popular ghost-trail tours in town, he is also the only fly-fishing guide in Kimberley. Bird-watching, canoeing on the Vaal River, and visits to the Kalahari Desert constitute his other tours.

The culture of the indigenous people of the area (the San) and prehistoric people is clearly a passion for local archaeologist David Morris. Offering both an Archaeological Route tour and a Sacred Sites tour of precolonial history, his tours, which include superb deconstructions of the region's sites, are an awe-inspiring experience. Book early, because he's busy.

Galeshewe Township expert and rock-art and Kimberley guide Andries Mokgele gets you in touch with authentic African life, jive, history, food, and drink, such as *umqumboti* (corn beer). He also conducts a memorable historical walk through the township and can arrange meals at interesting restaurants and overnight township stays.

First-class Anglo-Boer War registered guide Scotty Ross concentrates on the Kimberley Battlefield Route or will home in on particular battles, such as Magersfontein or Paardeberg.

Local Guides Andries Mokgele ✉ 642 (19741) Nicolas St., Galeshewe 8335 ☎ 084-6897251. **David Morris** 🖉 McGregor Museum Archaeology Department, Box 316, 8300

☎ 053/839–2706, 053/832–8355, or 082/222–4777 ⊕ www.elsemere.itgo.com or www.driekopseiland.itgo.com. **Dirk Potgieter** ✆ Box 2775, 8300 ☎ 083/265–4795. **Scotty Ross** ✉ 115 Main Rd., 8301 ☎ 053/832–4083 or 082/320–4380. **Janet Welsh** ✉ 4 Camelot, Francey St., 8301 ☎ 053/832–8343 or 082/856–2280.

TRAIN TRAVEL

Trains between Kimberley and Johannesburg (eight hours) run daily, with extra trains on Wednesdays, Fridays, and Sundays. There are daily trains to Cape Town (seven hours), with an additional one on Thursdays. Sleepers are available only in first and second classes, but you'll want to travel first or second class for safety reasons anyway, and preferably with a companion. Make sure you book tickets together so that they are issued for the same compartment. First- and second-class passengers must reserve in advance. The one-way fare between Kimberley and Johannesburg is R170, R340 between Kimberley and Cape Town, but prices increase for the December–January school vacation. Information on these routes can be obtained from Shosholoza Meyl, the long-distance passenger division of Spoornet. A private security company (Spoornet Security), train assistants, and a manager are on every train.

🚆 Train Line **Shosholoza Meyl/Spoornet** ☎ 086/000–8888, 053/838–2731 or 053/838–2631 in Kimberley, 011/773–4555 or 011/773–3063 in Johannesburg, 021/449–4596 in Cape Town ⊕ www.spoornet.co.za.

🚆 Train Station **Kimberley Train Station** ✉ Florence Rd. ☎ 053/838–2420.

TRAM TRAVEL

A restored 1914 tram travels through Kimberley between the Big Hole and City Hall. The cost is R14 round-trip or R7 one-way. Trams leave from the Big Hole on the hour daily from 9 to 4 and from City Hall at quarter past the hour daily 9:15 to 4:15. (Kimberley was the first South African city to have tram service.)

VISITOR INFORMATION

The Northern Cape Tourism Authority, in Kimberley, has information on the entire province. The Diamantveld Visitors' Centre has maps and brochures on the Northern Cape and the Kimberley region in particular, and can make tour and travel bookings and referrals. Local guides can also provide good information (⇨ Tours, *above*).

🚆 Tourist Offices **Diamantveld Visitors' Centre** ✉ 121 Bultfontein Rd., Box 1976, 8301 ☎ 053/832–7298 ⊕ www.kimberley-africa.com. **Northern Cape Tourism Authority** ✉ 15 Dalham Rd., Private Bag x5017, 8300 ☎ 053/832–2657 ⊕ www.northerncape.org.za.

THE KALAHARI

With Namibia to its west and Botswana to its north, the Kalahari is an area of arid dunelands that rightfully conjures up images of desolation. Much of the area is vast, semidesert terrain with minimum rainfall, and it's largely uninhabited—by humans, that is. It is home to the oryx and black-maned lion.

Paradoxically, the southern Kalahari—stretching west along the R64 from Upington to Kakamas and beyond—turns that stereotype on its head. This is the Green Kalahari, the basin of the Orange River, South Africa's largest. Where the hunter-gatherer San (Bushmen) marked the dry Kalahari as their home, the area of the Orange was originally occupied by the farming Khoi people. Here irrigation has created a literal oasis that includes thousands of acres of vineyards and the largest date farm in the Southern Hemisphere. Along the roads, irrigation canals are punctuated with waterwheels, an old-fashioned irrigation technique that elevates water so it can be directed into the vineyards, particularly in Kakamas and Keimoes. In winter the fields and vineyards are brown and bare, but in spring they turn from the neon green of new growth into a deep, lush summer green that makes the area look like the Winelands of Paarl and Stellenbosch. Grapes are one of the province's major industries: 80% of South African sultanas are grown in the Northern Cape, and table grapes are a rapidly growing export.

Acting as a gateway to both these Kalaharis is the river town of Upington, known countrywide for its intense heat.

Upington

10 *411 km (257 mi) northwest of Kimberley.*

Home to about 74,000 residents, Upington is a thriving agricultural center on the north bank of the Orange River. In the 1870s a Koranna (a group within the Na'ama culture) captain named Klaas Lucas invited missionary Christiaan Schroder to come to *Olyvenhoudtsdrift* (Ford at the Olive-wood Trees), as Upington was first known. Construction on the first mission buildings, now part of the Upington museum complex, was started in 1873. The town was renamed after Sir Thomas Upington, a Cape attorney general who was responsible for ridding the area of its notorious bandits in the 1880s. Although convention has it that the first person to irrigate crops from the Orange was Christiaan Schroder himself, recent historical research has revealed that this honor should go to Abraham September, a freed coloured slave, who first led water from the Orange in about 1882.

The **Kalahari-Oranje Museum Complex** comprises simple whitewashed buildings that were erected by missionary Christiaan Schroder in the 1870s. It houses displays on agriculture and local history and collections of minerals and artifacts used by area San. Just outside the complex is the Donkey Monument, a bronze sculpture by Hennie Potgieter that is a testimony to the role played by the animal in developing the Lower Orange River valley. ⊠ *4 Schroder St.* ☎ *054/331–1373* ✉ *Donations accepted* ☉ *Weekdays 8–5, Sat. by arrangement.*

About 2 km (1 mi) from the museum, in front of the Upington police station, the **Camel Statue** (⊠ Schroder St.) stands as a bronze monument to the police who used camels as mounts when they patrolled the Kalahari in frontier days.

In Upington's industrial area is **Oranjerivier Cooperative Wine Cellars**, the second-largest wine cooperative in the world (the largest is in South America). Tastings of a variety of white wines—from the sweet and rich dessert wine Hanepoort to the lighter steens and chenin blancs—as well as grape juice are offered. Between January and March you can also take a tour of the cellars. ⊠ *Industrial Rd.* ☎ *054/337–8800* ⊠ *Tastings R5, tours R5* ☉ *Tours/tastings weekdays at 9, 11, and 3.*

If you're missing the sea, a sedate sunset cruise on the Orange River may be just the thing. **Sakkie se Aartjie** (Sakkie's Ark) offers a 1½-hour trip on a double-decker raft complete with cash bar. After dark you may see monkeys, fish eagles and other birds, and catfish. ⊠ *Park St., below O Hagans Restaurant* ☎ *054/334–0597 or 082/564–5447* ⊠ *R30* ☉ *Daily at sunset.*

en route

SPITSKOP NATURE RESERVE – An easy climb to the top of an overlook of granite boulders yields a good view of this small reserve. Here a telescope helps you spot the springbok, gemsbok, eland, Burchell's zebra, and odd camel that inhabit the park. The reserve has three walking trails, which range from a morning to a full-day hike, as well as braai and picnic facilities and a range of overnight facilities from basic backpacking style to a guesthouse, with more luxurious accommodation to be completed shortly. ⊠ *15 km (9 mi) north of Upington on the R360* ☎ *054/ 332–1336* ⊠ *R12* ☉ *Daily sunrise–sunset.*

Where to Stay & Eat

¢–$$ ✕ **Le Must.** It's for good reason that the likes of Presidents Nelson Mandela and Thabo Mbeki dine here when they're in town, and that one of South Africa's chicest magazines voted this among the country's best restaurants. With a focus on South African cuisine, a large selection of local and Cape wines, and an informal and intimate atmosphere, Le Must is easily the best restaurant in town, if not the province. The biltong and port soup, which originated here and remains the signature dish, has been exported to cities as far away as Hong Kong. Kalahari lamb cutlets served with a brandy cream reduction is a popular choice. Finish with a piece of delicious brandy-and-date tart. ⊠ *11 Schroder St.* ☎ *054/332–3971* ⊟ *AE, DC, MC, V* ☉ *No lunch Sat.*

¢–$ ✕ **Die Dros.** You can drop in for a meal or just a drink at the bar in this large and rowdy franchise steak house, which its owner has dubbed a "grill and wine cellar." Bottles are packed into the walls from floor to ceiling, and numerous archways give the place a Mediterranean feel. In addition to steak, specialties include hamburgers and pizza. There is seating outside and inside, and it's open daily from 9 AM until late. ⊠ *Pick 'n Pay Centre, Le Roux St.* ☎ *054/331–3331* ⊟ *AE, DC, MC, V.*

★ $ ▦ **La Boheme Guest House.** If you arrive here in the evening, it will be to candlelight, soft music, and a star-studded sky. Swiss owner Evelyne Meier's attention to detail and desire to pamper combine to create a haven of refined tranquillity where the town ends and desert begins. The hillside location provides for sweeping views over the Kalahari and the Orange, especially from the palm-fringed pool. You can opt for the Zen-like self-catering cottage or either of two double rooms, one of which has a large tub for two. Two units have a private garden and veranda, and interiors are both elegant and natural, thanks to earth-tone interiors and water features. Locals come for special dinners (and you can, too), but only if it doesn't bother the guests. ⊠ *172*

Groenpunt Rd., 8801 ☎ *054/338–0660* 🖷 *054/338–0661* 🖃 *labo-heme@mweb.co.za* ⮑ *2 rooms, cottage* ⚭ *Minibars, pool* ▤ *AE, MC, V* ▯◉ *CP.*

¢ ▦ **Kalahari Guest House.** A perfect overnight stop to or from the Kgalagadi National Park, this typical South African homestead, 50 km (31 mi) north of Upington, caters to all budgets. It comes complete with a farm stand and traditional *boere kos* (farm food) snacks such as ginger beer, biltong, and tipsy tart (a deliciously rich brandy-infused tart). In addition to the guesthouse, which sleeps six, and a double room (available MAP), you can opt for the two-person bush camp, which comprises a thatch roof and walls lovingly created from three thorn bushes, or get even closer to the earth by camping next to a rainwater dam that welcomes 145 bird species. Energy is generated by a solar system as well as a wind charger at night. ⊠ *R360* 🖭 *Farm Uitsig, Box 1717, 8800* ☎ *054/902 and ask for 918704 or 073/194–2864* ⊕ *www.upington. co.za/kalahariguesthouse* ⮑ *1 room, 1 guesthouse, 1 bush camp, campsites* ⚭ *Some a/c, fans, kitchen; no room TVs* ▤ *No credit cards.*

¢ ▦ **Le Must Guesthouse.** This Cape Dutch house is elegant without being pretentious; original artwork hangs in every room, and the beds are covered in Egyptian percale cotton. The house has a great view of the Orange River, and the garden—where you can sit and have a cup of tea or a gin and tonic—sweeps right down to the waterside. You can take a dip in the river or a lazy paddle in a canoe. There is also access to the neighboring pool. ⊠ *12 Murray Ave., 8801* ☎ *054/332–3971* 🖷 *054/ 332–7830* ⊕ *www.lemustupington.com* ⮑ *7 rooms, 5 with bath* ▤ *AE, DC, MC, V.*

¢ ▦ **Riviera Garden Lodge.** In the middle of a row of guesthouses, the Riviera is an oasis of personal attention, charm, and tasteful interiors. Hostess Anneke Malan loves to chat, and will readily tell you all there is to know about Upington and its environs, but she's sensitive enough to leave you alone if you want quiet. In summer, breakfast is served on the veranda in the award-winning garden, from which you can also embark on a river cruise. ⊠ *16 Budler St., 8801* ☎ *054/332–6554* 🖃 *www. upington@lantic.co.za* ⮑ *2 rooms* ▤ *No credit cards* ▯◉ *BP.*

¢ ▦ **Witsand Nature Reserve.** It's worth staying a few nights at this beautiful site in the southern Kalahari, 220 km (137 mi) east of Upington on the road to Griquatown and then another 45 km (28 mi) down a sometimes rocky road to Witsand. Owned by the provincial government, luxurious thatch-and-stone accommodations sit in thick bush under large camelthorn trees. They blend in well with the reserve, which covers vast white dunes, up to 200 feet high and stretching across an area 9 km (6 mi) long and 4 km (2½ mi) wide. In hot and dry conditions you can experience "roaring sands," dunes that produce a deep hum when walked on; as the sand moves, air escapes, producing a vibration. Although not easily seen in their natural state, fulgerites, glassy gray tubes reconstituted from melted silica that was struck by lightning, are on display at the information center, as are 500-year-old ostrich eggs that were buried by Bushmen. Different meal plans are available, as are different-size lodgings sleeping two to six people. 🖭 *Box 1474, Postmasburg 8420* ☎ *053/313–1061* ⊕ *www.witsandkalahari.co.za* ⮑ *10 lodges, 7 bun-*

galows, 10 campsites ⚑ *2 pools, bicycles, shop; no a/c in some rooms, no room TVs* ⊟ *DC, MC, V.*

Shopping

Community developer Estelle Visser's store, **Kalahari Living** (⊠ 29 Le Roux St., on the Pick 'n Pay corner ☎ 054/332–3141), reflects her passion to help the impoverished empower themselves. She trains the unemployed to make embroidered wall hangings, place mats, pillow covers, quilts, and *laslappie* textiles, used in the traditional dresses of the Na'ama people. Among the other popular wares are Themba Masala's colorful papier-mâché creations (fish, lizards, tortoises, and water birds), beadwork and other art of the Kalahari Khoisan, and Kalahari skins and leather goods.

Augrabies Falls National Park

⓫ *120 km (75 mi) west of Upington, 40 km (25 mi) northwest of Kakamas.*

The Khoi, who lived in this area for thousands of years before the arrival of Europeans, called these falls Aukoerabis (Place of Great Noise), and though Augrabies is a relatively small national park (696,850 acres), its falls are truly impressive. South Africa's largest falls in volume of water, Augrabies plunges 653 feet over terraces and into a gorge 18 km (11 mi) long, which was carved into smooth granite over millions of years. It is strangely otherworldly.

Reports of sightings of a river monster in the gorge have been made frequently but are probably fanciful accounts of shoals of giant barbels, which reach about 7 feet in length. Legend has it that an unplumbed hole beneath the main falls is filled with diamonds washed downriver over millennia and trapped there.

Depending on what you're looking for, you can hike in the park for an hour or several days. You don't need a guide. You can also drive around the park to its lookout points, which offer spectacular views of the gorge below the falls. Unfenced Ararat provides the best views. Oranjekom, which has a fence and shaded hut, is particularly welcome in the blistering summer heat, and the Swartrante lookout offers a view over the rugged, barren areas of the park. All are easily accessible and well marked. For the energetic, the Gariep 3-in-1 Adventure is a day trip that consists of canoeing down the Orange for 4 km (2½ mi), hiking another 4 km (2½ mi), and taking a 12-km (7½-mi) mountain-bike ride. During peak times, the park also offers worthwhile night drives (around R60 per person). Recently renovated, reception is at the main gate, and the visitor center, with an information office, shop, and restaurant, is a few miles down the road. ☎ 054/452–9200 ⊕ *www.SANParks.org* ⊠ *R15 South Africans, R60 foreigners.*

Where to Stay

¢ ▣ **Augrabies Rest Camp.** South African National Parks (SANParks) offers a variety of modern, clean, and recently renovated units near both the main visitor center and the falls. Clay-colored floors and natural materials such as stone, wood, and clay blend into the environment. All units have braai areas and fully equipped kitchens and sleep three or four people. A 20% discount is offered November through June, excluding the March/April school vacation. (Although putting off making a reservation is risky, especially during vacation times, the park does take last-minute bookings.) Campsites are also available. ⌂ *SANParks, Box 787, Pretoria 0001* ☎ *012/426–5000 parks board or 054/452–9200 park* 🖷 *012/343–0155* ⊕ *www.SANParks.org* ⤳ *40 chalets, 9 cottages, 10 bungalows, 40 campsites* ⌂ *Restaurant, kitchens, 3 pools, bar, shop; no room TVs* ⊟ *AE, DC, MC, V.*

Sports & the Outdoors

Located 25 km (15 mi) from Kakamas, the **Kham Kirri Private Game Reserve** (⌂ Riemvasmaak Rd. ☎ 054/451–0325) offers white-water rafting, abseiling (rappelling), and 4x4-ing. An inexpensive overnight stay at their chalets or campground adds the opportunity of a game drive.

Kgalagadi Transfrontier Park

★ ⓬ *260 km (162 mi) north of Upington on the R360.*

In an odd little finger of South Africa, jutting north and surrounded by Botswana in the east and Namibia in the west, lies South Africa's second-largest park after Kruger National Park. Kgalagadi was officially launched in 2000 as the first transfrontier, or "Peace Park," in southern Africa by merging South Africa's vast Kalahari Gemsbok National Park with the even larger Gemsbok National Park in Botswana. The Kgalagadi is now one of the largest protected wilderness areas in the world—an area of more than 38,000 square km (23,750 square mi). Of this awesome area 9,600 square km (6,000 square mi) falls in South Africa, and the rest falls in Botswana. Passing through the Twee Rivieren Gate, you will encounter a vast desert under enormous, usually cloudless skies and a sense of space and openness that few other places can offer.

The Kgalagadi Transfrontier is less commercialized and developed than Kruger. The roads aren't paved, and you will come across far fewer people and cars. There is less game on the whole than in Kruger, but because there is less vegetation, the animals are much more visible. Also, as the game and large carnivores are concentrated in two riverbeds (the route that two roads follow), the park offers unsurpassed viewing and photographic opportunities. Perhaps the key to really appreciating this barren place is understanding how its creatures have adapted to their harsh surroundings to survive—like the gemsbok, which has a sophisticated cooling system allowing it to tolerate extreme changes in body temperature. There are also insects in the park that inhale only every half hour or so to save the moisture that breathing expends.

The landscape—endless dunes punctuated with blond grass and the odd thorn tree—is dominated by two dry riverbeds: the Nossob (which forms the border between South Africa and Botswana), and its tributary, the Auob. The Nossob flows only a few times a century, and the Auob flows only once every couple of decades or so. A single road runs beside each riverbed, along which windmills pump water into man-made water holes, which help the animals to survive and provide good viewing stations for visitors. A third road traverses the park's interior to join the other two. The scenery and vegetation on this road changes dramatically from the two river valleys, which are dominated by sandy banks, to a more grassy escarpment. Two more dune roads have been added, and several 4x4 routes are being developed. From Nossob camp a road leads to Union's End, the country's northernmost tip, where South Africa, Namibia, and Botswana join. Allow a full day for the long and dusty drive, which is 124 km (77 mi) one-way. (At present no roads within the park join the South African and Botswana sides, although plans are afoot to change this. Visitors who wish to go to both sides must therefore cross into Botswana at the Bokspits border post 60 km [38 mi] south of Twee Rivieren and reenter the park on the Botswana side. The park infrastructure in Botswana is very basic, with just three campsites and mostly 4x4 terrain.)

The park is famous for its gemsbok and its large black-maned lions. It also boasts leopard, cheetah, eland, blue wildebeest, and giraffe, as well as meerkats and mongooses. Rarer desert species, such as the desert-adapted springbok, the elusive aardvark, and the tiny Cape fox, also make their home here. Among birders, the park is known as one of Africa's raptor meccas; it's filled with bateleurs, lappet-faced vultures, pygmy falcons, and the cooperatively hunting red-necked falcons and gabar goshawks.

The park can be super-hot in summer and freezing at night in winter. Autumn—from late February to mid-April—is perhaps the best time to visit. It's cool after the rains, and many of the migratory birds are still around. The winter months of June and July are also a good time. It's best to make reservations as far in advance as possible, even up to a year or more if you want to visit at Easter or in June or July, when there are school vacations.

The park's legendary night drives (R100) depart most evenings about 5:30 in summer, earlier in winter (check when you get to the camp), from Twee Rivieren Camp, Mata Mata, and Nossob. Reservations are essential and can be made when you book your accommodations. The drives use a 20-passenger open truck, and set out just as the park gate closes to everyone else. You'll have a chance to see rare nocturnal animals like the brown hyena and the bat-eared fox by spotlight. ⊠ *Reception at Twee Rivieren Rest Camp* ☎ *054/561–2000.*

Where to Stay

Accommodations within the park are in three traditional rest camps and several wilderness camps, which are spread around the park. All of the traditional rest camps have shops selling food, curios, and some basic equipment, but Twee Rivieren has the best variety of fresh fruit, vegetables, milk, and meat, and is the only camp with a restaurant. Twee Rivieren is also the only camp with telephone and cell-phone reception and 24-hour electricity; the other camps have gas and electric, but the electricity runs only part of the day, at different times in each camp. Rental

SAN CULTURE & LANGUAGE

THE NORTHERN CAPE has a long and rich human history. Also called the /Xam, the hunter-gatherer San (Bushmen) have a culture that dates back more than 20,000 years, and their genetic origins are more than 1 million years old, contemporary humans' oldest. Fast-forward a few years—about 2,000 years ago, to be inexact—when Korana or Khoi (Khoe) herders migrated south, bringing their livestock and settling along the Orange (Gariep/Garieb), Vaal, and Riet rivers. During the 18th and 19th centuries the Griquas—thought to be part Khoi and part slave—moved into the Northern Cape with their cattle and sheep.

At one time 20–30 languages pertaining to various clans flourished, but colonialism brought with it devastating results for the San's native tongue. It lost out to Tswana and Afrikaans. In the nick of time in the 1870s, British doctor Wilhelm Bleek (who spoke /Xam) and Lucy Lloyd recorded the

last activities of /Xam culture and tradition. (Some of these records can be found at the McGregor Museum in Kimberley.)

Still thousands of Northern Cape residents today acknowledge an ancestral connection to the largest San or /Xam group of the 18th and 19th centuries. The two biggest remaining groups are the !Xu and Khwe, who live at Schmidtsdrift, 80 km (50 mi) from Kimberley. Among the best-known groups in South Africa today are the Khomani San, some of whom still speak the ancient Nu. For a good overview on the languages, culture, and peoples who migrated to the Northern Cape, check out the McGregor Museum.

---

cars can be picked up from Twee Rivieren if reserved through a rental agency in Upington.

Although they sound like a contradiction in terms, the more luxurious wilderness camps have been kicking up a popular storm among wannabe desert nomads who can't do without a comfortable bed and showers. This most recent addition to Kgalagadi's accommodations consists of partially tented, unfenced desert camps with their own water holes for game viewing. All have the same facilities and are similarly priced but are somewhat different. The Kalahari Tented Camp, near the Mata Mata shop and gas station, has a wooden deck with braai facilities. Gharagab is in the dunes close to the Namibian border, and Urikaruus is on stilts, between Twee Rivieren and Mata Mata. Grootkolk is surrounded by camelthorn trees and close to the Nossob River bed. Bitterpan has a 4x4 trail, and Kieliekrankie is on a high sand dune.

For all reservations, contact **South African National Parks,** or you can reserve directly through the park (☎ 054/561–2000) if you happen to be there and would like to stay a night or add another night onto your stay. (Visitors are advised to take antimalarial drugs and use a mosquito repellent, especially during the summer months.) ⬧ Box 787, Pretoria

0001 ☎ *012/426–5000 Pretoria or 021/552–0008 Cape Town* 🖨 *012/ 343–0155 Pretoria or 021/246–2115 Cape Town* ⊕ *www.SANParks. org* 🖃 *AE, DC, MC, V.*

¢ 🏨 **Mata Mata.** This camp is 120 km (75 mi) from Twee Rivieren on the Namibian border. In fact, access to Namibia via Mata Mata is expected shortly. The camp's facilities are not as modern as those at Twee Rivieren, although there is a small shop stocking basics. Mata Mata has good game viewing due to the proximity of the water holes. ↪ *2 six-person cottages, 3 four-person cottages, 1 five-person mobile home, 2 three-person mobile homes* ⚭ *Kitchen, shop.*

¢ 🏨 **Nossob.** In the central section of the park, this camp is on the Botswana border, 166 km (104 mi) from Twee Rivieren. Basic brick chalets come with an outside braai and real bush atmosphere and sleep from three to six people. Guesthouses have showers but no tubs. A small shop sells the basics. There is no electricity in the camp, and the generators are turned off at 11 PM. ↪ *15 chalets, 1 cottage, 2 guesthouses* ⚭ *Kitchen, shop; no a/c.*

¢ 🏨 **Twee Rivieren.** On the Kgalagadi's southern boundary, this camp is home to the park's headquarters. It is the biggest of the camps and has the most modern facilities; all units have fully equipped kitchens, and the camp shop here is the best. Guests can choose between three types of accommodations, from a two-bedroom, six-bed family cottage to a bungalow with two single beds and a sleeper couch. There are educational exhibits on the Kalahari's animal and plant life. From Upington to Twee Rivieren is 260 km (162 mi) on a relatively good road; only the last 52 km (32 mi) is gravel. ↪ *1 cottage, 30 bungalows* ⚭ *Restaurant, kitchens, pool, bar, shop; no room TVs.*

Tswalu Kalahari Reserve

⑬ *250 km (155 mi) southeast of Kgalagadi Transfrontier Park.*

Fodor's Choice
★
At 1,000 square km (386 square mi), Tswalu is the biggest privately owned game reserve in Africa. It's also the perfect place to photograph a gemsbok against a red dune and an azure sky. Founded by the late multimillionaire Stephen Boler as a conservation project designed primarily to protect and breed the endangered desert black rhino, it is now owned by the Oppenheimer family. It spreads over endless Kalahari dunes covered with tufts of blond veld and over much of the Northern Cape's Korannaberg Mountain range. As South Africa's only private reserve with desert rhinos—it's home to a third of the country's total population—it is the best place in Africa to see them. Other rare species include roan and sable antelope, black wildebeest, and mountain zebra. There is not as much game as in some of the private reserves of the Lowveld because the land has a lower carrying capacity (the annual rainfall is only about 9¾ inches). But when you do see animals, the lack of vegetation makes sightings spectacular. Only three or so vehicles traverse the vast area, so it's easier than at most reserves to feel like a true pioneer.

Where to Stay

Nothing is left wanting at Tswalu, one of a dozen prestigious Relais & Châteaux properties in South Africa. Children are welcome and well catered to (children under 12 accompanied by an adult are free), and unlike most southern African bush lodges, Tswalu is malaria free. Road transfers from Kimberley or Upington can be arranged, and there are chartered flights from Johannesburg and Cape Town daily. ✑ *Box 1081, Kuruman 8460* ☎ *053/781–9311 or 053/781–9234* 🖷 *053/781– 9238* ⊕ *www.tswalu.com* 🖃 *AE, DC, MC, V.*

$$$$ 🏨 **Tarkuni.** If the famous (and wealthy) Oppenheimer family use this as their private getaway when in the Kalahari, you can imagine what kind of experience it offers. Tarkuni is an exclusive, self-contained house decorated similarly to Motse and offering comparable luxury. Perfect for small groups and families, Tarkuni sleeps 8–14 and comes with its own chef, Land Rover, and tracker. The food is almost as memorable as the scenery, and every meal is served in a different location—on a lantern-lighted dune or alongside a crackling fire in the lodge's *boma* (outdoor eating area). Apart from guided walks and drives, a stay at Tarkuni comes with horseback riding with a qualified guide, offering even closer encounters with wildlife. ⇨ *1 house* ♿ *Pool, archery, horseback riding, bar, airstrip* ¶◯¶ *FAP.*

$$$ 🏨 **Motse.** Tswalu's main lodge is made up of freestanding thatch-and-stone suites clustered around a large main building, with a heated, natural-color pool and a floodlighted water hole. The decor—in keeping with the emphasis on bringing the outside in—echos the landscape in colors and textures while remaining minimalist and modern. Meals are prepared in different nature spots—perhaps a dune dinner or a bush brunch. A forthcoming wellness center will even offer Kalahari mud-pack treatments. ⇨ *9 suites* ♿ *Pool, archery, horseback riding, bar, airstrip* ¶◯¶ *FAP.*

Kuruman

⑭ *250 km (156 mi) northeast of Upington.*

If you have a car while in the Kalahari region, it's worth stopping in Kuruman, the hub of a dairy-, cattle-, and game-farming area. With flat, wide streets, the town is a rush of green in the middle of the Kalahari. Camelthorn and stinkwood trees are everywhere, but cleanliness is not high on this municipality's priority list, so arrive without expectations. Follow signs to "The Eye" or "Die Oog," an amazing natural spring that bubbles out 5 million gallons of water daily and is the source of the Kuruman River.

Established in 1816, the **Kuruman Moffat Mission** is the most famous mission station in Africa. It was headed by Robert Moffat from 1820 until his retirement in 1870. The site, with stone-and-thatch buildings dating from the 1820s and 1830s and surrounded by huge trees, represents an interface between precolonial history and the present. A complete Setswana Bible was printed here in 1857—the first time the Bible was printed in its entirety in a previously unwritten African language. The mission served as a springboard for many early adventures into the interior, including David Livingstone's expeditions. It's a lovely and gentle place full of memories. It still functions as a mission and community center, and has an excellent curio shop. ⊠ *Moffat La., 5 km (3 mi) north of Kuruman on Hotazel Rd.* ☎ *053/712–2645* 🖃 *R5* ⊙ *Mon.–Sat. 8–5, Sun. 3–5.*

en route

WONDERWERK CAVE – This fascinating heritage site contains a spectacular 460-foot-long cave that shows evidence of 800,000 years of Stone Age occupation and early fire use. Some 10,000-year-old engravings were found in the deposit, and the cave has unusual rock paintings on its walls. A good museum adjacent to the cave provides detailed interpretation, and a resident guide will show you around. Kimberley's McGregor Museum can provide additional information, and advance reservations are advised. ⊠ *Off the R31, 50 km (31 mi) south of Kuruman* ☎ *053/839–2700 or 053/839–2706 and ask for the Archaeology Department* 🖃 *R7* ⊙ *Daily 9–5.*

Where to Stay

$ 🏨 **Livingstone Lodge.** This establishment is a classy dose of desert decadence. You're in the heart of meat-eating country, so take advantage of such traditional South African dishes as oxtail and T-bone steaks. The lodge has a huge treed garden that may inspire you to work off those calories afterward. Besides, you may want to acquaint yourself with the other permanent residents here: ponies, ducks, and antelope. ⊠ *283 Seodine Way, 8460* ☎ *083/285–1485* 🖷 *053/712–3930* ✒ *livingstone@donco.co.za* ⤢ *6 rooms* ⚭ *Minibars, pool, bar* 🖃 *AE, DC, MC, V* †⚬† *BP.*

Kalahari A to Z

AIR TRAVEL

A five-minute drive from the city center, Upington International Airport has the longest runway in the Southern Hemisphere (4.8 km [3 mi]). SA Airlink operates daily service between Upington and both Johannesburg and Cape Town. Many lodgings provide shuttle service. Alternatively, you can book on the Blue Line Shuttle, run by Grace Grey, which costs R40.

🏮 **Airport Upington International Airport** ☎ 054/332–2161.
🏮 **Airline SA Airlink** ☎ 054/332–2161 or 0861/359–722 ⊕ www.saairlink.co.za.
🏮 **Airport Transfers Blue Line Shuttle** ☎ 072/215-0479.

BUS TRAVEL

Intercape Mainliner runs daily service and night coach service three times a week between Upington and Johannesburg/Pretoria (approximately 10½ hours, R280) and Sunday–Friday service from Upington to Cape Town (about 12 hours, R250) and to Windhoek (approximately 12½ hrs, R330). The bus stop is in Lutz Street, opposite the Nedbank building.

🏮 **Bus Line Intercape Mainliner** ☎ 054/332–6091 or 0861/287-287 ⊕ www.intercape.co.za.

CAR TRAVEL

Upington and the Kalahari are usually approached from Kimberley along the scenic and winding R64—a distance of 411 km (257 mi). The N14, on the northern side of the Orange River, is a slightly longer alternative—450 km (313 mi)—but it's faster because it is straighter. Upington is 375 km (233 mi) from Springbok along an excellent paved road. You can rent a car or a 4x4 in Upington, but reserve well in advance. There are several 4x4 trails within the Kgalagadi at Bitterpan and Gharagab, but it is not necessary to have one to get there or for getting around inside the park.

Most towns, game parks, and even remote areas have gas, but use common sense and anticipate long distances by refueling when passing a gas station. Roadside car wrecks bear testimony to what locals say is the biggest danger on these roads: falling asleep at the wheel.

🚗 Rental Companies **Avis** ⊠ Upington Airport, Upington ☎ 054/332-4746 or 054/332-4747. **Budget Car Hire/Upington 4x4** ⊠ 53 Market St., Upington ☎ 054/337-5222 or 082/773-1050. **Europcar/4x4 Hire** ⊠ Near Desert Palace Hotel, Schroder St., Upington ☎ 082/426-8489 ⊕ www.europcar.co.za.

EMERGENCIES

De Duine Pharmacy's hours are weekdays 9–8, Saturday 9–2 and 7–8, and Sunday 10–1.

🚗 Emergency Services **Ambulance** ☎ 10177. **Police** ☎ 10111 or 054/337-3400.
🚗 Hospital **Upington Medi Clinic** ⊠ 4th Ave. and Du Toit St., Upington ☎ 054/338-8900 ⊕ www.mediclinic.co.za.
🚗 Pharmacy **De Duine Pharmacy** ⊠ Pick 'n Pay Centre, Le Roux St., Upington ☎ 054/331-1458.

MONEY MATTERS

Most banks in Upington have a *bureau de change,* and all have safe ATMs. The major banks—ABSA, First National Bank, and Nedbank—are clustered around Schroder Street. Hours of business are weekdays 9–3:30 and Saturday 9–11. Visa and MasterCard are widely accepted locally.

TOURS

Day trips from Upington to Augrabies Falls start at R630 per person. Kalahari Desert tours start at R2,500 per person for a few days. The latter are usually fully inclusive of entrance fees, food, and beverages.

"One of the last wildernesses," describes Pieter Hanekom of Kalahari Safaris. "People say if the sand of the Kalahari gets in your shoes you always come back." His intriguing perspective and tours take 2–10 people and cater to budgets across the board, with accommodation ranging from chalets to tent camps. "Reading the history of the previous night in the sand" is clearly an infectious passion, as he's often booked five months in advance.

Dantes Liebenberg of Kalahari Tours and Travel customizes trips to Kgalagadi Transfrontier Park from an afternoon to two weeks. Other specialties are the Witsand Nature Reserve, Augrabies Falls, the Kalahari, Namaqua flower tours (in season), and farther afield to Namibia and Botswana.

The all-inclusive three-day desert experience, which includes interacting with the San community, is a must. Tours range from the four-star variety to backpacker style.

Guide Hanspeter Meier of Magic of Desert appeals to those with an adventurous spirit. His unfenced sleeping arrangements in Botswana and Namibia mean lions sometimes walk into the camp and spend the night roaring outside tents. The exclusivity of the tours involves two 4x4 vehicles for two people and includes shower, toilet, and telephone to make for a supreme bushwhacking experience. Accident insurance is included.
🚩 Tour Operators **Kalahari Safaris** ✉ 3 Orange St., Upington 8801 ☎ 054/332-5653 or 082/435-0007. **Kalahari Tours and Travel** ✉ 12 Mazurka Draai, Upington 8800 ☎ 054/338-0375 or 082/493-5041 ⊕ www.kalahari-tours.co.za. **Magic of Desert** ✉ 5 Swartbas Ave., Upington 8800 ☎ 054/332-5787 ⊕ www.kalaharibudgettours.com or www.magicdesert.com.

TRAVEL AGENT
Le Must Travel can organize car rentals and accommodations, and makes referrals for other travel details.
🚩 Travel Agent **Le Must Travel** ✉ 11 Schroder St., Upington 8800 ☎ 054/332-3971.

VISITOR INFORMATION
Local guides (⇨ Tours, *above*) are often more reliable, knowledgeable, and helpful in disseminating information than the local government tourist office. This is especially true for off-the-beaten-track places in interesting locations and farm accommodations.

The Green Kalahari Tourism Centre provides information on Upington, the Kalahari, and beyond. In addition, Neil Stemmet, owner of Le Must Travel, Guesthouse, and Restaurant, is an unofficial but excellent source of assistance for many travel queries and itineraries around the Upington area. He can be located through his various businesses.

For information on the region's national parks, contact South African National Parks in Pretoria or Cape Town. Bookings for the Botswana side of Kgalagadi Transfrontier Park must be done through the Parks and Reserves Reservation Office in Gaborone.
🚩 Tourist Offices **Green Kalahari Tourism Centre** ✉ 26 Swartmodder Ave., Upington 8800 ☎ 054/337-2885. **Parks and Reserves Reservation Office** ☝ Department of Wildlife and National Parks, Box 131, Gaborone, Botswana ☎ 09267/318-0774. **South African National Parks** ☝ 643 Leyds St., Muckleneuk Pretoria 0001 ☎ 012/428-9111 ⊕ www.SANParks.org ✉ Cape Town Tourism Building, Castle and Burg Sts., Roggebaai 8001 ☎ 021/426-4260.

NAMAQUALAND

This huge, semidesert region extends north from the West Coast to Namibia, hundreds of miles north of Cape Town and west of Kimberley. It's a remote, unpopulated area, with few facilities and comforts. In spring, however, it puts on a spectacle that must be the greatest flower show on earth. Vast fields that seemed barren only a month before blush with blossoms. *Vygies* (a type of fynbos) and Namaqualand daisies brightly splash the hillsides and valleys with color. Known as the Succulent Karoo, the area is dependent on the right weather conditions—staggered and regular rainfall and particular temperature and light—to show off its full beauty. As with many South African village businesses, the flowers tend to open at 10 and close at 4. Unless it's flower season, think twice about trekking to Namaqualand. As in parts of the American West, distances are vast, and the landscape looks harsh, mostly hills dotted with giant boulders and swollen-trunked *kokerbooms* (quiver trees, so named because Bushmen cut arrow quivers from them).

Khoisan people have lived in Namaqualand for thousands of years. The first Europeans to venture into the area were Dutch settlers from the Cape, who came in search of the copper they knew existed here because the Khoi had used it in trade. Though Simon van der Stel, a governor of the Cape Colony, sank test shafts in 1685 and realized there were rich quantities of copper in the hills around Okiep and Carolusberg, it wasn't until the 1840s, when the Okiep Copper Mining Company came to Namaqualand, that copper was mined on a large scale. Today the region's commercial activity is clustered in the dorps (villages) of Okiep, Concordia, and Nababeep, and in the region's most prominent town, Springbok—all of whose roots lie in copper. The area is littered with heritage sites harking back to the early copper days, from the smokestack in Okiep to the Messelpad Pass, south of Springbok.

The life of the mines is now almost at an end, and most of Namaqualand is poverty-stricken but still intriguing. As the copper mines reach the end of their lives, tourism is becoming the region's great hope, and a tourism infrastructure is being put into place slowly. That said, hotels and restaurants are still basic, and Namaqualand isn't the easiest place to get to. It's 909 km (568 mi) from Kimberley and 375 km (233 mi) from Upington. Although Namaqualand is part of the Northern Cape Province, it's actually more accessible from Cape Town, and many travelers choose this approach. It's 544 km (340 mi) from Cape Town to Springbok, and a four- to five-hour drive from Cape Town just to reach Kamieskroon, the closest Namaqualand hamlet with a decent hotel. To do the area justice, you need to budget four days or more. The order of towns below maps out the best flower routes if you are driving up from Cape Town. If you are driving to Springbok from Upington, read the towns in reverse.

Garies

⓯ *58 km (36 mi) northeast of Vanrhynsdorp.*

Garies is a one-horse town cradled amid sun-baked hills, and one of the best flower routes runs just north of it for 100 km (60 mi) to Hondeklipbaai, on the coast. The road winds through rocky hills before descending onto the flat coastal sandveld. Flowers in this region usually bloom at the end of July and early August. If you're lucky, fields along this route will be carpeted with purple vygies, but also look for Namaqualand daisies, aloes, and orchids. Quiver trees are common along this route, too.

Kamieskroon

⑯ *49 km (30 mi) north of Garies; 72 km (45 mi) south of Springbok on the N7.*

Another base for exploring Namaqualand in spring, Kamieskroon is the closest decent place to stay to Namaqua National Park. The Kamieskroon Hotel, although no great shakes for accommodations, is probably the best source of information on wildflowers in Namaqualand.

Fodor'sChoice ★ During its flower season (August to October), **Namaqua National Park** can usually be counted on for superb wildflower displays, even when there are no flowers anywhere else. Covering an area of almost 200,000 acres, 21 km (11 mi) west of Kamieskroon, the park is the world's only arid biodiversity hot spot. Recent and planned upgrades include more routes and new rest camps, and game (tsetsebe, oryx, springbok, and eland) is slowly being reintroduced. Visitors look for Namaqua daisies in oranges and yellows as well as succulents, such as the many-colored vygies in hues of purple, magenta, and orange. Roads are good throughout the park. Driving from Soebatsfontein toward Springbok yields spectacular views over the coast from the top of the Wildeperdehoek Pass. Two short hiking trails take a few hours each. A visitor center is at the Skilpad entrance, and a *padstaal* (road stall) across the road can supply you with local eats and treats. ✉ *Skilpad Rd.* ☎ *027/672–1948* ⊕ *www.SANParks.org* 🎫 *R15* ☉ *Daily 8–5.*

en route **LELIEFONTEIN –** A 29-km (18-mi) detour from Kamieskroon brings you to this old Methodist mission station at the top of the Kamiesberg, which has spectacular views across the desert to the sea. The church, a national monument, was finished in 1855, but the adjacent parsonage is much older. The wildflowers in Leliefontein bloom much later than those on the coast, often lasting as late as the end of October. Even if there are no flowers, it's a beautiful drive back down the Kamiesberg to Garies, 72 km (45 mi) away.

Where to Stay & Eat

$ ✕🏠 **Cosy Mountain.** This intimate mountain hideout is as close as you can get to Namaqua National Park while maintaining a level of comfort and privacy. Even though it gets swelteringly hot in summer, the 200-year-old homestead's super-thick walls ensure that you'll keep cool. On the other hand, if you really love the cold and good snowball fights, this is the place to come in winter, as it's at the base of the Sneeukop (Snow Head) Mountain. Rooms have original clay floors and wooden ceilings taken from shipwrecks at nearby Hondeklip. If you like roughing it a little more, you can opt for one of the campsites separated by *koppies* (little rocky hills), which sleep up to 10. Unusual in these meat-eating parts, the restaurant *($$)* is getting a reputation for its vegetarian dishes, such as spring vegetable casserole and Grecian tomato pie. Carnivores aren't ignored, though. ✉ *Farm Windhoek, Skilpad Rd., 8241* ☎ *027/672–113* ✉ *cosymountain@mweb.co.za* 🛏 *3 rooms, 3 campsites* ⚐ *Pool, lounge, laundry service, Internet; no room TVs* ▤ *No credit cards* ⦿❘ *MAP.*

Springbok

 117 km (73 mi) north of Kamieskroon, 375 km (233 mi) southwest of Upington.

The capital of Namaqualand is set in a bowl of rocky hills that form part of the Klipkoppe, a rocky escarpment that stretches from Steinkopf, in the north, to Bitterfontein, in the south. Quiver trees proliferate in the area, and flower season brings the town alive with multicolored carpets. Though the town owes its existence to the discovery of copper, its architecture is mostly modern, with very few buildings dating from the 1800s. Compared with most of the dorps in the Northern Cape, Springbok is a buzzing little town, with a fair number of things to see in the area if you need to take a break from flower gazing.

Displays at the **Namaqualand Museum** tell the history of Namaqualand, the town of Springbok, and the people who lived here. Articles range from some 17th-century pieces to an old fridge and washing machine made from kokerboom wood. The museum is housed in an old synagogue, and pays tribute to the era when Jews lived in Springbok (180 Jews lived here until 1972, but there are none left today). ⊠ *Monument St.* ☎ *027/718–8100* ⊠ *Donations accepted* ☉ *July–mid-Oct., weekdays 8–5, Sat. 9–2, Sun. 10–1; mid-Oct.–June, weekdays 8–5.*

The now inactive **Blue Mine** deserves a peek, just for how large and bright blue it is. This copper mine was first mined in 1852 by Phillips and King, a local trading company based in Cape Town. The smokestack was built in 1880, and the Cornish Pumphouse in 1882 to house the steam-driven pump that "dewatered" the copper mines until the mid-1930s. One-hour guided tours are led daily (by request) from the Okiep Country Hotel, next door. ⊠ *Voortrekker Rd., opposite Agenbag gas station* ☎ *027/744–1000* ⊠ *Free* ☉ *Tours by request.*

The **Simon van der Stel Mine** is the most impressive of six shafts sunk by Simon van der Stel, governor of the Cape from 1679 to 1699, during his visit to the area in 1685 to prospect for copper. There is a steep climb up to the shaft, around which the rocks are blue with copper. Graffiti from van der Stel's trip is still visible at the mine's entrance. For guided tours contact Piet van Heerde of Virosa Tours or inquire at the Namaqua Regional Tourism Office (⇨ Namaqualand A to Z, *below,* for both). ⊠ *8 km (5 mi) east of Springbok and 3 km (2 mi) south of Carolusberg on the R64* ☎ *No phone* ⊠ *Free* ☉ *Tours by request.*

en route

GOEGAP NATURE RESERVE – Each spring this reserve transforms into a wildflower mosaic, which you can discover on either of two short (4 and 6 km [2½ and 4 mi]) walking trails. Goegap is also home to the Hester Malan Wildflower Garden, which displays an interesting collection of succulents, including the bizarre *halfmens,* or "half person" (*Pachypodium namaquanum*), consisting of a long, slender trunk topped by a passel of leaves that makes it resemble an armless person—hence the name. ⊠ *R355, 16 km (10 mi) southeast of Springbok via airport road* ☎ *027/712–1880* ⊠ *R10* ☉ *Daily 7–7 (last admission 3:30); office daily 8–4.*

Where to Stay & Eat

$ ✕ **Melkboschkuil Restaurant.** Traditional South African fare is prepared here by people who know what visitors want. Lovers of game are catered to with anything from crocodile to ostrich to kudu, depending on availability, but these options don't come cheap. Vegetarians have a good selection of dishes to choose from as well. In a tranquil old house, the restaurant manages to be homey, busy, and stylish all at the same time. ⊠ *15 Voortrekker St.* ☎ *027/718–1789* ▭ *DC, MC, V* ⊘ *No lunch Sun.*

¢ ✕ **Godfather's.** If it's been a while since you carbo-loaded, grab a pizza from Godfather's. Don't go expecting anything but good food (provided the owner is there) at reasonable prices. The restaurant is notorious for its bad service, linoleum-covered tables, and lack of atmosphere. Better still, wait for takeout, and find a spot with a pleasant view to enhance digestion. ⊠ *51 Voortrekker St.* ☎ *027/718–1877* ▭ *AE, DC, MC, V.*

$–$$ ✕🏠 **Naries Guest Farm.** Twenty-seven km (17 mi) west of Springbok along a dirt road, this Cape Dutch–style guesthouse looks out over the mountains of the Spektakelberg. Gracious hosts Johan and Denise Heydenrych make guests feel welcome and will take you out to a lovely overlook for evening cocktails. Large guest rooms are individually decorated, 1970s style. Dinner ($$$) is a three-course feast of robust Afrikaans home cooking, including such dishes as venison stew, pumpkin fritters, *bobotie* (a spicy ground-meat dish), and cabbage and beans. In the morning work it off with a walk through the flowers. A self-catering cottage is available. Reserve well in advance. ⊠ *Kleinzee Rd. (R355), Box 35, 8240* ☎🖨 *027/712-2462* ⊕ *www.naries.co.za* 🛏 *5 rooms, 1 cottage* ⑬ *Restaurant, kitchen* ▭ *AE, DC, MC, V,* ¶ *MAP.*

¢ ✕🏠 **Okiep Country Hotel.** About 8 km (5 mi) from Springbok, this hotel is one of the nicest places to stay in Namaqualand, not only for the above-average accommodations and dining (¢–$$), but also because owner Malcolm Mostert has created a homey atmosphere and goes out of his way to be helpful and friendly. The interior is basic but clean. Homemade curries, stews, and such meat dishes as spareribs and steaks are both popular and recommended. The hotel is right next door to the Cornish Pumphouse, a landmark on Okiep's main road. A lodge across the street is more basic. ⑩ *Main St., Okiep 8270* ☎ *027/744–1000 or 082/ 569–7158* 🖨 *027/744–1170* ⊕ *www.okiep.co.za* 🛏 *34 rooms, 1 self-catering unit* ⑬ *Restaurant, pool, billiards, bar* ▭ *AE, DC, MC, V.*

¢ 🏠 **Springbok Lodge and Restaurant.** People come here as much for the living museum that owner extraordinaire Jopie Kotze has created as for the rest of the establishment, which originated as private homes. The former tour guide's displays include a mineral collection, a photographic exhibit on the Richtersveld and historic Namaqualand, and floral and landscape paintings by local artists. The mammoth operation sleeps 200 people in a variety of accommodations: rooms that sleep two or three; family units that sleep four to six; self-catering suites; and houses that sleep up to 13 people. The complex also houses a restaurant, where breakfast and dinner are available. A gift, postcard, and curio shop carries a wide range of books. ⊠ *37 Voortrekker St., 8240* ☎ *027/712–1321* 🖨 *027/ 712–2718* 📧 *sbklodge@intekom.co.za* 🛏 *51 rooms, 19 suites, 2 houses* ⑬ *Restaurant, some kitchens, some refrigerators* ▭ *AE, DC, MC, V.*

Shopping

If you've grown frustrated driving past land you know contains quartz crystals quietly whiling away eternity, stop at **George Swanson Enterprises** (⊠ 28 van Riebeeck St. ☎ 027/712–2341 or 082/496–2484) to dig up some treasures without a permit. Swanson's yard is full of raw rock crystals, water sapphires, turquoise, and blue lace agate along with the entire gamut of semiprecious minerals found in Namaqualand. Even if you don't find a piece of rock that speaks to you, Swanson, who "turns rock into bread," will regale you with anecdotes from his "famous past with American presidents' wives," including his ecology award for the discovery of blue lace agate, which had remained hidden for more than 50 million years until he found it in the 1960s. Swanson's is primarily a working yard, and watching the splitting of the rock is fascinating. Having the option to buy something is a bonus.

en route

For an excellent **flower drive,** take a 320-km (200-mi) rectangular route that heads north on the N7 from Springbok to Steinkopf and then west on the paved R382 to Port Nolloth. From there a dirt road leads south through the Sandveld to Grootmis, then east along the Buffels River before climbing the Spektakel Pass back to Springbok. If the rains have been good, the route offers some of the best flower viewing in the region. Try to time your return to Springbok to coincide with the sunset, when the entire Spektakel Mountain glows a deep orange-red.

Port Nolloth

⑱ *110 km (69 mi) northwest of Springbok.*

Port Nolloth—a lovely drive from Springbok, particularly during flower time—started life as a copper port, but is better known today as a fishing and diamond center. With only one (decent) road leading into it, the flat, desertlike coastal town is, according to local residents, a ghost town at night, as the little life that exists by day dies completely after dark.

Port Nolloth is also the springboard to the Richtersveld, the vast region of mountains and desert to the north, which is well known for its exquisite succulents and other flora but which should be visited only on an organized tour or once you have armed yourself with a considerable amount of information. It's extremely remote, and you'll definitely need a 4x4 or *bakkie* (pickup truck) to avoid breakdowns.

Port Nolloth's bay is safe for swimming, although the water is freezing. Head over to the harbor to check out the diamond-vacuuming boats, with their distinctive hoses trailing astern. Divers use the hoses to vacuum under boulders on the seabed in search of any diamonds that have washed into the sea from the Orange River over many millennia. It's a highly lucrative endeavor but not without its dangers; at least one diver has been sucked up the vacuum hose to his death.

Where to Stay

¢ ▦ **Bed Rock Accommodation.** Across the street from the sea, these weathered old guesthouses look from the outside as though they've seen better days. The interiors, however, are delightful, decorated with an eclectic collection of Africana and antiques. Each room has its own bathroom, although not always in the room. ✉ *Beach Rd., 8280* 🖸🖸 *027/ 851–8865* ⤶ *5 cottages* 🖃 *MC, V.*

Namaqualand A to Z

AIR TRAVEL

The Springbok airport, about 12 km (7½ mi) away, is accessed by National Airlines charter service, which flies from Cape Town. Piet van Heerde of Virosa Tours runs a transfer service for R30 per person; book in advance.

🛂 **Airline National Airlines** ☎ 021/934-0350 ⊕ www.nac.co.za.

🛂 **Airport Transfer Virosa Tours** ☎ 027/712-3650 or 073/229-5014.

BUS TRAVEL

Intercape Mainliner operates bus service up the West Coast from Cape Town to Springbok (nine hours) on Sunday, Tuesday, Thursday, and Friday evenings, stopping en route at Piketburg and Vanrhynsdorp in the Western Cape and Garies in the Northern Cape. Return service to Cape Town runs Sunday, Monday, Wednesday, and Friday late at night. In addition to booking with the bus line, you can buy tickets at any Shoprite/Checkers supermarket in the region. The bus terminal is at Springbok Lodge in Voortrekker Street.

🛂 **Bus Lines Intercape Mainliner** ✉ Cape Town Station Office, 1 Adderley St., Cape Town ☎ 0861/287-287 or 027/386-4400 ⊕ www.intercape.co.za.

CAR TRAVEL

Namaqualand is more than 320 km (200 mi) north of Cape Town and 900 km (563 mi) west of Kimberley. With the great distances involved and the absence of any real public transportation, the only way to get around is by car. Roads are generally well paved, but signage to tourist attractions is not always good. From Springbok to Hondeklipbaai there is an 80 km (50 mi) stretch of sandy gravel road. Traffic to Springbok picks up on Fridays and Saturdays, when people from neighboring communities converge on the town.

If you arrive by bus or air, you can rent from Tempest/Imperial Car Rental or Namaqualand 4X4 Hire, which also rents camping equipment. Make your reservations early. If you're going to the Richtersveld, rent a bakkie or 4x4, as sedans are not permitted.

🛂 **Rental Companies Namaqualand 4X4 Hire** ✉ Voortrekker Rd., opposite information center, Springbok ☎ 072/171-3081 or 083/753-7246. **Tempest/Imperial Car Rental** ✉ 75 Voortrekker Rd., Springbok ☎ 072/171-3081.

EMERGENCIES

Springbok has the region's main and largest hospital. One pharmacy services the area and is open only during regular shopping hours. After-hours emergencies are handled by arrangement.

🛂 **Emergency Services Police** ☎ 10111 or 027/718-9100.

🛂 **Hospital Dr. van Niekerk Hospital** ✉ Hospital St., Springbok ☎ 10177 or 027/712-2019.

🗎 Pharmacy **Namaqualand Apteek (Pharmacy)** ✉ Voortrekker St., Springbok ☎ 027/
712-2091 or 027/712-3335 after hours.

INTERNET
Primarily a computer sales and repair shop, Something Online charges
R1 per minute for Internet services. It's open weekdays 7:30–5, week-
ends by arrangement.
🗎 Internet Access **Something Online** ✉ 57 Voortrekker Rd., Springbok ☎ 027/712-2561.

MONEY MATTERS
In Springbok, First National is at Namaqua and Monument streets, Standard Bank is on Voortrekker Road, and ABSA is on van der Stel Street.
They are open weekdays 9–3:30, Saturday 9–11:30. Note that foreign
exchange cannot be dealt with here on Saturday, so make sure you're
prepared in advance. Apart from Springbok, Port Nolloth, and Garies,
Namaqualand towns do not have banks.

TOURS
Local trips around Springbok lasting several hours start from R200 per
person. Three-day Richtersveld trips cost around R4,850 per person,
all inclusive, with a minimum of two people.

Guide and tour operator Piet van Heerde of Virosa Tours specializes in
off-the-beaten-track tours to Namaqualand, the Richtersveld, Kgalagadi,
and the West Coast. His very exclusive Land Cruiser trips are from 1
to 15 days and have a maximum of four people.

Photographer and tour and river guide Rey van Rensburg caters to adventure tourists on 4x4 trails to the mountainous desert of the Richtersveld,
Namibia, Namaqualand, and Kaokoland (home of the Himba), in
northern Namibia, one of the most remote and unspoiled areas left on
the continent. He has a good eye for spotting the unusual. He also does
botanical tours.
🗎 Tour Operators **Rey van Rensburg** ✆ Box 142, Springbok 8240 ☎ 027/712-1905.
Virosa Tours ✉ Farm Morea, Springbok Rd., off the N7, Springbok 8240 ☎ 027/712-
3650 or 073/229-5014 ⊕ www.virosatours.com.

VISITOR INFORMATION
The Namaqua Regional Tourism Office is across from the Agenbag gas
station. Springbok Lodge's tourist-friendly, welcoming approach often
makes it the first place visitors stop for information and free maps.
🗎 Tourist Offices **Namaqua Regional Tourism Office** ✉ Voortrekker Rd., Springbok
8240 ☎ 027/712-8035 or 027/718-2985. **Springbok Lodge/Tourist Information** ✉ 37
Voortrekker St., Springbok 8240 ☎ 027/712-1321.

The Garden Route & the Little Karoo

4

Updated by
Jennifer Stern

THIS REGION IS A STUDY IN CONTRASTS. The Outeniqua and Tsit-sikamma mountains, forested ranges that shadow the coastline, trap moist ocean breezes, which then fall as rain on the verdant area known as the Garden Route. Meanwhile, these same mountains rob the interior of water, creating the arid semideserts of the Little and Great Karoo. Even within these areas, however, there is significant variety.

The Garden Route, the 208-km (130-mi) stretch of coastline from Mossel Bay to Storms River, encompasses some of South Africa's most spectacular and diverse scenery, ranging from long beaches and gentle lakes and rivers to tangled forests, impressive mountains, and steep, rugged cliffs that plunge into the wild and stormy sea. It's the kind of place where you'll have trouble deciding whether to lie on the beach, lounge in a pretty pastry shop, or go on an invigorating hike. For most people the Garden Route is about beaches, which are among the world's best. Though the ocean may not be as warm as in KwaZulu-Natal, the quality of accommodations tends to be far superior, and you can take your pick of water sports.

A trip into the Little Karoo, on the other hand, offers a glimpse of what much of South Africa's vast hinterland looks like. This narrow strip of land wedged between the Swartberg and Outeniqua ranges, stretching from Barrydale in the west to Willowmore in the east, is a sere world of rock and scrub. The area is most famous for its ostrich farms and the subterranean splendors of the Cango Caves, but there is much more for the discerning visitor to see. However, unlike those found on the classic safari destinations, these treasures are not handed to you on a plate. You have to really look. Scour the apparently dry ground to spot tiny and beautiful plants. Or spend time walking in the sun to discover some of the many bird species. A fairly energetic hike into the hills will reward you with fascinating geological formations, numerous fossils, and extensive rock art. You can also just stand still and enjoy the space and the silence. Even if all this leaves you cold, it is still worth the effort to explore spectacular passes that claw through the mountains into the desert interior.

Exploring the Garden Route & the Little Karoo

There are two practical routes from Cape Town to Port Elizabeth. You can follow the N2 along the Garden Route or Route 62, which goes through the Little Karoo. These two roads are separated by the Outeniqua Mountains, which are traversed by a number of scenic passes. So it is possible—even desirable—to hop back and forth over the mountains, alternating between the lush Garden Route and the harsher Little Karoo. The inland border of the Little Karoo is formed by the Swartberg Mountains, on whose far side is the Great Karoo, which covers much of the interior of South Africa. Although it *is* possible to get from place to place by bus, the best way to explore this region is by car.

About the Restaurants

Most medium-size towns along the Garden Route offer a pretty good selection of restaurants, with Nature's Valley, which has only one restaurant, the exception. The smaller towns of the Little Karoo usually have one or two good restaurants and a handful of lesser eateries. If you look around in the region, you'll find some fabulous places to eat.

Not surprisingly, the emphasis is on seafood in general and oysters in particular. (Knysna has an oyster festival in July.) The farms of the Little Karoo provide fresh ostrich meat and organic mutton or lamb, which stand up to South African red wines. Ostrich *biltong* (jerky) is widely considered the best variety of this national treat. Be careful when ordering coffee in small towns. You may see espresso and cappuccino on the menu, but check that these are made with an espresso machine and not simply spooned out of a jar labeled "espresso" and mixed with hot water.

WHAT IT COSTS In South African rand				
$$$$	**$$$**	**$$**	**$**	**¢**
RESTAURANTS over 125	100–125	75–100	50–75	under 50

Prices are per person for a main course at dinner, a main course equivalent, or a prix-fixe meal.

About the Hotels

The region would not have such allure if it weren't for its exclusive seaside getaways and colonial manor houses, as well as its more rustic inland farms and national-park log cabins. Many of the better establishments are set on little islands of well-tended gardens within wild forests. Breakfast is included in many lodgings' rates, and if your guesthouse serves dinner, eating the evening meal in situ often has a welcome intimacy after a day of exploring. (Excellent little guesthouses open up every day, so it is almost impossible to keep track of them all.) On the flip side, some cottages are self-catering (with cooking facilities); pick up some local delicacies and make yourself a feast.

Note that the prices listed are for high season. In some cases these are significantly higher than low season, and they may go up higher still for the busiest month (mid-December to mid-January). If you're traveling during South Africa's winter, don't let high-season prices put you off before inquiring about seasonal specials.

WHAT IT COSTS In South African rand				
$$$$	**$$$**	**$$**	**$**	**¢**
LODGING				
over 3,000	2,000–3,000	1,000–2,000	500–1,000	under 500
FULL-SERVICE SAFARI LODGING				
over 12,000	8,000–12,000	5,000–8,000	2,000–5,000	under 2,000

Prices are for a standard double room in high season, including 12.5% tax.

4

Because of the compactness of the Garden Route, you can see much of it in as little as three days, but there's plenty to occupy you for a week or more. The essential places to see are Wilderness, Knysna, Plettenberg Bay, and Tsitsikamma, which run in a line along the coast, making them ever so easy to string together. Try to fit them into whichever itinerary you choose.

Numbers in the text correspond to numbers in the margin and on the Garden Route & Little Karoo map.

If you have 3 days

Choose a home base, either ▣ **Wilderness ③**, ▣ **Knysna ⑥**, or ▣ **Plettenberg Bay ⑦**, also called Plett. You'll encounter wonderful crafts shops and studios in all these towns, so keep your credit card handy. On Day 1, take a half-day walk, either at Robberg Nature Reserve, at the Garden of Eden (a shorter, wheelchair-friendly walk), at the Featherbed Nature Reserve, or through the deep forest, where you may see abandoned gold mines. In the afternoon take a boat trip to see the dolphins, seals, and whales at Plett. Dedicate Day 2 to your chosen activity—lounging on the beach, paddling, horseback riding, abseiling (rappelling), or scuba diving. If you're staying in Plett, drive out to **Storms River ⑨** on Day 3, and do the treetop canopy tour or, for the less adventurous, a tractor tour of the forest. If you're staying farther west, head over one of the scenic passes to **Oudtshoorn ⑫**, visit the **Cango Caves ⑬**, and take a different scenic drive back.

If you have 5 days

Using the other two itineraries as a guide, spend one or two days at ▣ **Sanbona Wildlife Reserve ⑪**; one or two at either ▣ **Plettenberg Bay ⑦**, ▣ **Knysna ⑥**, or ▣ **Wilderness ③**; and one or two at ▣ **Storms River ⑨**.

If you have 8 days

Spend the first day or two at ▣ **Sanbona Wildlife Reserve ⑪**, watching game, perhaps taking a balloon flight or horseback ride, and maybe even getting pampered at the spa. Then head along the R62, stopping at the Rose of the Karoo, in Calitzdorp, for lunch, and ending up in ▣ **Oudtshoorn ⑫**. The next day, drive a long scenic loop, stopping at wineries and visiting the **Cango Caves ⑬**. Then head over either the Montagu or Outeniqua Pass to ▣ **Plettenberg Bay ⑦**, ▣ **Knysna ⑥**, or ▣ **Wilderness ③**, where you will have no trouble filling the rest of your time with shopping, beach lounging, diving, kayaking, whale-watching, or any combination thereof. If you have an adventurous bent, spend the last two or three days at ▣ **Storms River ⑨**, where you can take the treetop canopy tour, go black-water tubing, hit a mountain-bike trail, or go for a long walk in the **Tsitsikamma National Park ⑩** from Storms River Mouth. Want still more adventure? En route to Storms River, make the world's highest bungee jump at the Bloukrans River Bridge.

Timing

There's no best time to visit the Garden Route, although the water and weather are warmest December through March. From mid-December to mid-January, however, the entire Garden Route is unbelievably crowded and hotel prices soar, so try to avoid visiting at this time. Between May and September the weather can be very cold and even rainy. But—and it's a big but—it makes all the more cozy the huge, blazing log fires and large bowls of steaming soup that local hostelries provide. And, of course, there are fewer tourists. Even in these colder months it's rarely cold for more than two or three days at a stretch, after which you'll get a few days of glorious sunshine. Wildflowers bloom along the Garden Route from July to October, the same time as the annual southern right-whale migration along the coast. The Little Karoo can be scorchingly hot in summer and bitterly cold at night in winter. Winter days are often warm and sunny. It really doesn't rain much in the Little Karoo.

GARDEN ROUTE

The Garden Route means different things to different people. The backpacking crowd loves it for the great beaches, exciting adventures, and parties, whereas more sophisticated visitors revel in the fantastic seafood, scenery, golf courses, and guesthouses and hotels—many with attached spas—where pampering is the name of the game. The Garden Route is also a fabulous family vacation destination, where little ones can frolic on the beach, visit Monkeyland and the Knysna Elephant Park, or go exploring in the forest. And almost no one passes up the opportunity to see whales and dolphins.

Mossel Bay

❶ *384 km (240 mi) east of Cape Town via the N2.*

Mossel Bay has the most highly developed industrial infrastructure of any of the Garden Route towns, so it can't compete with Knysna or Plett as a resort town, but it's pleasant nevertheless and has a number of interesting historic buildings. Its main attractions are an excellent museum complex, some of the best oysters along the coast, and good beaches with safe, secluded bathing. Mossel Bay has the only north-facing (read: sunniest) beaches in South Africa, but be warned: as it's very popular with local families, it is a writhing, seething mass of juvenile humanity every summer. Dolphins—as many as 100 at a time—frequently move through the bay in search of food, and whales swim past during their annual migration (July–October). If you're not going to Plett, you may want to take a cruise out to Seal Island, home to a breeding colony of more than 2,000 Cape fur seals. A slightly dubious operation offers the opportunity to crawl into a cage to view the numerous great white sharks (blue pointers) that hang around the seal colony.

★ The **Bartolomeu Dias Museum Complex** concentrates on the early history of Mossel Bay, when it was a regular stopover for Portuguese mariners en route to India from Europe. Probably the most interesting exhibit is the full-size (340-foot-long) replica of Dias's ship, which was sailed to Mossel Bay from Lisbon as part of the quincentenary celebrations in 1988. If you pay the extra fee to board it, you'll find it all pretty authentic, except for the modern galley and heads. Also here is the Post

4

Adventure Sports

The Garden Route is an outdoor adventurer's paradise. The long coastline offers loads of marine diversions, from excellent scuba diving off Knysna and Plettenberg Bay to surfing off Mossel Bay and Buffalo Bay (near Knysna). On land, some of the country's best backpacking, including guided trips, can be found here, and forests and beaches alike are crisscrossed with good day-hiking, mountain-biking, and horseback-riding trails. Thinking of something a little higher still? There are a number of commercial abseiling (rapelling) organizations, most notably in Wilderness, Knysna, and Storms River, as well as numerous paragliding and hang-gliding launch sites, a tandem skydiving operation in Plett, and two bungee-jumping operations, including the world's highest. The small town of Storms River has become an adventure destination of note, with a fabulous canyoning trip, mountain biking, hiking, and a unique treetop canopy tour. The Little Karoo has its own adventures. A tour of the Cango Caves can be either mild or wild (your choice), and there are good horse trails near Oudtshoorn and at the Sanbona Wildlife Reserve, near Barrydale.

Cetacean Central

From land, sea, and air, watching all the whales go by is a joy. And it's not just whales. Dolphins and seals are also prime viewing targets along the Garden Route. Around Plett, for instance, bottlenose dolphins frolic in the surf, Cape fur seals are plentiful, Bryde's whales are permanent residents, southern right whales come to calve from July to October (maybe longer), and humpback whales, which migrate between Antarctica and northern Mozambique, pass through and hang around a while from May to June and then again from November to February. Killer whales (orcas) are around all year, although they are not common. There are as many ways to see these big and not-so-big beauties as there are types of marine mammals to see. Traditional whale-watching boats let you see a number of species—three or four on most days, as many as seven on exceptional days. From a glider in Plett or a paraglider in Wilderness, you can see the scope of the whale's mammoth body and get an impressive view of the huge schools of up to 1,000 dolphins. Or you can paddle a kayak out into their world or simply gaze out at them from the beach.

Winning Wines

For many years skeptics said that the only things that grew in the Karoo were ostriches, and that the Boland was the only South African region producing high-quality wine. Well, the skeptics have been proved wrong. Wines grown in the Little Karoo are starting to muscle their way into the medals. Although for some time the area has been justly renowned for sweet varieties and fortified wines such as port, Karoo wine farmers have started producing a full range of wines. The reds, in particular, are more full bodied and tropical than those from the cooler and moister Boland. You can take a tasting trip along the Little Karoo's wine route, including two wineries between Oudtshoorn and De Rust.

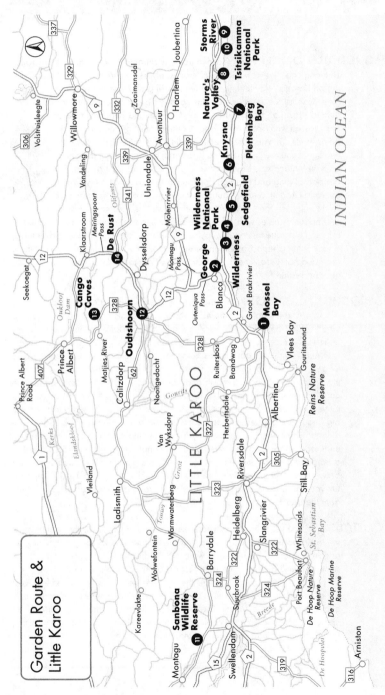

Garden Route &
Little Karoo

INDIAN OCEAN

Office Tree. In the 15th century a few sailors decided that the tree—then a lone tree on a deserted beach on an unexplored coast—stood out sufficiently and left some letters here in an old boot, under a stone, in the hope they would be found and delivered. They were. Pop a postcard into the shoe-shaped mailbox, and see if the service is still as good. Your mail will arrive with a special postmark. ⊠ *Church and Market Sts.* ☏ *044/691–1067* ⊕ *www.diasmuseum.co.za* ☒ *R6, caravel additional R10* ⊘ *Weekdays 9–4:45, weekends 9–3:45.*

Where to Stay & Eat

$–$$$ ✕ **Café Gannet.** Tour-bus crowds occasionally descend on this popular spot, but don't let that put you off. Justly renowned for its seafood—the oysters are superfresh and wild, not cultivated—it also has good general and vegetarian menus. Try a pizza from the wood-fired oven or something a bit more exotic, such as tempura goat cheese with blue-cheese-and-fig cigars drizzled with wild-forest-berry coulis, followed by skewered tuna cubes with mango and peppadew (a cross between a sweet pepper and a chili, usually served pickled) yogurt. The inevitable ostrich is here, best served up *cordon bleu* (filled with smoked ostrich and a tangy mustard-and-cheese sauce). In summer sit outside on the shaded terrace or inside with the eclectic collection of fish-themed African artifacts. ⊠ *Church and Market Sts.* ☏ *044/691–1885* ▤ *AE, DC, MC, V.*

¢–$ ✕ **Delfino's Espresso Bar and Pizzeria.** Good coffee, yummy pizzas and pastas, tables on the lawn, and a fantastic view of the bay and the Cape St. Blaize lighthouse make this a great place to spend a sunny afternoon. ⊠ *2 Point Village* ☏ *044/690–5247* ▤ *AE, DC, MC, V.*

$$ ✕🖭 **Diaz Strand Hotel.** This new multistory hotel has a fantastic location smack-dab on Diaz Beach, a few miles east of the town center. Standard decor makes rooms feel like they could be in almost any hotel in the world—that is, until you draw the curtains on the large sliding glass doors that lead to a tiny private balcony, revealing a fantastic view of the bay and nearby Seal Island. The resort offers loads of facilities, including some that were inherited from its previous incarnation as a self-catering resort. For a quick munch you can walk straight off the beach to the Rosebud (¢–$), which offers burgers, sandwiches, and pastas. If you have time to shower and put on shoes, you might try the Bahia dos Vaqueiros ($–$$$$) for a more formal experience, often accompanied by piano music. ⊠ *Beach Blvd. E, Box 2933, 6500* ☏ *044/692–8400* 🖨 *044/692–0049* ⊕ *www.diazbeach.co.za* ➷ *81 rooms, 5 suites* ♿ *2 restaurants, café, room service, in-room data ports, in-room safes, mini-bars, cable TV with movies, 9-hole golf course, miniature golf, 2 pools (1 indoors), gym, hot tubs, massage, sauna, beach, snorkeling, fishing, 2 bars, beer garden, sports bar, piano, babysitting, children's programs, playground, laundry service, Internet, business services, convention center, airport shuttle, helipad, travel services, free parking, no-smoking floors* ▤ *AE, DC, MC, V* ⍵ *BP.*

¢   ✕🖭 **Santos Express Train Lodge.** And now for something completely different. In a real train parked on the beach, accommodations are real train compartments. Though it's not exactly luxurious, the location is hard to beat. Book way ahead to secure the Conductor's Suite, which has its own bathroom and a private deck. Popular with both backpackers and local families, this place buzzes. The restaurant (¢–$) is almost always busy, and serves the usual fish, steak, and burgers, as well as a good range of traditional South African dishes, such as *bobotie* (a spicy ground-meat dish) and *waterblommetjiebredie* (water-flower stew)—don't knock it till you've tried it, especially if you can't pronounce it. Early-morning Pilates and yoga classes on the beach are complemented by beach massage. ✉ *Santos Beach, 6500* ☎📠 *044/691–1995* 🌐 *www.santosexpress.co.za* ⇨ *29 rooms, 1 with bath; dormitory* ♨ *Restaurant, beach, bar, laundry service, Internet, business services, meeting room, airport shuttle, travel services, free parking, some pets allowed, no smoking; no a/c, no room phones, no room TVs* ▭ *AE, DC, MC, V* 🍴 *CP.*

$ 🏨 **Protea Hotel Mossel Bay.** Previously called the Old Post Office Tree Manor, this comfortable hotel is conveniently situated just yards from the museum complex and close to most of what's happening. You can take in the great view of the harbor, beach, and sea while relaxing at the Blue Oyster Cocktail Bar, a delightfully colorful pub and terrace. Strange nooks and crannies and yard-thick stone walls testify to the building's status as the third-oldest in Mossel Bay. Self-catering apartments have all the modern conveniences and a great view. Breakfast is served at the attached Café Gannet. ✉ *Market St.* 📮 *Box 349, 6500* ☎ *044/691–3738* 📠 *044/691–3104* 🌐 *www.oldposttree.co.za* ⇨ *21 rooms, 1 suite, 7 apartments* ♨ *Restaurant, room service, in-room data ports, in-room safes, minibars, pool, hot tub, mountain bikes, bar, shops, babysitting, laundry service, airport shuttle, travel services, free parking; no a/c, no smoking* ▭ *AE, DC, MC, V* 🍴 *BP.*

Sports & the Outdoors

BUNGEE JUMPING & BRIDGE SWINGING — The Gouritz Bridge is about 35 km (20 mi) from Mossel Bay. It is only 220 feet high, but it offers a range of wacky adrenaline opportunities. **Face Adrenalin** (☎ 044/697–7001 🌐 www.faceadrenalin.com) offers bungee jumps for R170. **Wildthing Adventures** (☎ 021/423–5804 🌐 www.wildthing.co.za) operates a bridge-swinging operation. You jump from one bridge with climbing ropes and swing from the adjacent bridge. The first jump costs R160 for a single, and tandems and triples cost R110 per person, after which you get a "wild card," which entitles you to discounted jumps for the next two years.

HIKING ★ — The **Oyster Catcher Trail** (☎ 044/699–1204 🌐 www.oystercatchertrail.co.za) offers the best of both worlds, providing a multiday hiking experience while you carry only a day pack. Treks are both guided and catered. Walking along the beach and over rocky shorelines, you are met at midday with a delicious picnic lunch. Nights are spent in either a guesthouse or self-catering cottage, but you don't have to cook. Knowledgeable guides point out birds and plants and discuss local history and customs. Walking on the beach can be hard going if the tide is in, but most people of average fitness should manage. A typical trip is four days and starts at R3,500 per person (more for groups fewer than six), but shorter hikes can be arranged.

HORSEBACK RIDING — **Garden Route Equestrian Adventure Tours** (☎ 082/835–9110 🌐 www.great.co.za) offers rides ranging from an hour to a full day (advisable only for experienced riders). You can ride on the beach one day and head inland to the mountains the next. The cost ranges from R200 for an hour to R600–R800 for a full day, including lunch.

George

❷ *45 km (28 mi) northeast of Mossel Bay, 50 km (31 mi) southeast of Oudtshoorn.*

About 11 km (7 mi) from the sea, George is the largest town and the de facto capital of the Garden Route. Although the surrounding countryside is attractive and there is a thriving farming and crafts community on its outskirts, George itself is not particularly appealing unless you are a golfer.

If you're into country life, pick up a map from George Tourism and follow the **Outeniqua Hop,** a fun country route to hop farms (hops are used in beer making), strawberry farms, cheese farms, and numerous crafts outlets.

★ The **Outeniqua Choo-Tjoe** is an authentic narrow-gauge steam train that travels the scenic route between George and Knysna. You'll end up with a soot-blackened face if you succumb to the temptation of sticking your head out of the window to admire the crashing waves or the tranquil Knysna Lagoon, but it is so hard to resist. It's also fun to wave at by-standers who gather to watch the immense billows of steam as the driver obliges keen photographers with an extra blast when the train passes particularly scenic sections. Two trains do the round-trip in op-posite directions. In the off-season the train is also used to haul freight, but tourists are its main cargo. Unfortunately, when weather and veg-etation conditions are very dry, the steam engine poses a fire threat, so a diesel locomotive is used. Reservations are essential and should be made at least a day in advance at the station or from the George or Knysna tourism offices. ✉ *Station St.* ☎ *044/801–8288, 044/801–8289, or 044/801–8202* 💷 *R65 one-way, R75 round-trip* ⊙ *Mon.–Sat. 9:30–2.*

Where to Stay & Eat

$–$$ ✕ **Copper Pot.** Cream walls and candlelight set the tone at this elegant restaurant. Timbale of smoked salmon, baby spinach, guacamole, and tomato crowned with cream cheese and served with red caviar and mango sauce is just one of the great starters. Roasted duck breast served with peppers, cashew nuts, and dried-fruit couscous is an unusual main. Desserts include homemade ice cream, hot ginger pudding, and a no-table crème brûlée. ✉ *12 Montagu St., Blanco* ☎ *044/870–7378* 🍴 *Reservations essential* ▤ *AE, DC, MC, V* ⊙ *Closed Sun and Mon. in May–Sept. No lunch weekends.*

★ ¢–$ ✕ **Leila's Arms.** Part of a poverty-alleviation and permaculture (envi-ronmentally responsible) project, this friendly and informal restaurant offers fabulous lunches at a great price. The classic is a baked sweet potato smothered with cream cheese, olive oil, spinach, salsa, dates, and fresh herbs. There is always a slow-cooked lamb dish, either curry or *bredie* (stew), and most of the ingredients are organic. The crockery is from a local potter—and you won't find two matching plates. ⊠ *28 Montagu St., Blanco* ☎ *044/870–7613* ▤ *No credit cards* ⊘ *Closed Sun. No dinner.*

★ **$$$–$$$$** ✕▦ **Fancourt Hotel and Country Club Estate.** If you are one of those people who believes that people were created with opposable thumbs in order to hold a golf club, you'll *love* Fancourt. In the shadows of the Outeniqua Mountains, this luxury resort has a country-club feel and numerous sports, leisure, and business facilities. Elegant rooms are either in an old 1860 manor house or in villas nestled in landscaped gardens. Whereas the rooms in the manor house have a classical air, the newer rooms are sleek and modern, with cream walls and pale stone finishes. Of the five restaurants, Sansibar *($–$$$$)*, with its Africa-themed menu, is the most popular. A bonus if you are flying in or out, Fancourt has its own private airport lounge at George Airport. ⊠ *Montagu St., Box 2266, Blanco 6530* ☎ *044/804–0000* ▤ *044/804–0700* ⊕ *www. fancourt.com* ⮎ *32 rooms, 63 suites* ⟐ *5 restaurants, grocery, picnic area, room service, in-room data ports, in-room safes, minibars, cable TV, 2 driving ranges, 4 18-hole golf courses, 5 putting greens, 4 tennis courts, 3 pro shops, 4 pools (2 indoors), gym, health club, hair salon, sauna, spa, steam room, mountain bikes, billiards, croquet, hiking, lawn bowling, volleyball, 6 bars, cinema, piano, 2 recreation rooms, video game room, babysitting, playground, Internet, business services, convention center, airport shuttle, car rental, travel services, no-smoking rooms* ▤ *AE, DC, MC, V* ⦿ *BP.*

$ ▦ **Ambleside Country House.** One of the more reasonably priced options in town, this is a great base from which to play golf. The owner, a keen golfer himself, can book courses, arrange transportation, and generally make sure you play as much golf as you can handle. The lodge is totally unpretentious without compromising on comfort. The casual lounge, attractive pool area, and honor bar create a great home away from home for weary golfers. Although no dinner is served, many guests make use of the breakfast room and get food delivered. ⊠ *Upper Maitland St., Blanco, 6530* ☎ *044/870-8138* ▤ *044/870-7943* ⊕ *www. ambleside.co.za* ⮎ *7 rooms, 1 suite* ⟐ *Fans, putting green, saltwater pool, lounge, babysitting, Internet, no-smoking rooms; no a/c, no room phones, no children under 12* ▤ *AE, DC, MC, V* ⦿ *BP.*

★ **$** ▦ **Hoogekraal.** About 16 km (10 mi) outside George, this historic farm sits on a grassy hill with panoramic views of the Outeniqua Mountains and the Indian Ocean, and has been in the same family since the early 18th century. The public rooms are beautiful—filled with antiques and heirlooms—and just being in them makes a stay here worthwhile. Accommodations are in two sections, a building dating from 1760 and a newer one built in 1820. Although the buildings are characterful and there are many lovely old pieces of furniture, the rooms suffer from problems often encountered in historic buildings: the bathrooms are somewhat cramped and many rooms have unusual proportions. Suites have two bathrooms. Most guests choose to stay for the five-course dinner served on fine porcelain at a communal table in the magnificent dining room. Almost all the vegetables come straight from the garden, and the fish from the distantly glimpsed ocean; the milk and beef come from the cows in the field. ⊠ *Glentana Rd., off N2 between George and Mossel Bay* ⬠ *Box 34, 6530* ☎ *044/879–1277* 🖷 *044/879–1300* ⊕ *www. hoogekraal.co.za* ⤵ *3 rooms, 2 suites* ⚭ *Restaurant, lounge, laundry service, airport shuttle; no a/c, no room phones, no room TVs, no kids under 13* ⊟ *DC, MC, V* ❖| *BP.*

Sports & the Outdoors

Fancourt's Links, Montagu, and Outeniqua golf courses and the public George Golf Club are all regularly featured among South Africa's top 10 courses, and are never out of the top 20. Though you have to stay at **Fancourt Hotel and Country Club Estate** (⊠ Montagu St. ☎ 044/ 804–0000) to play on two of its Gary Player–designed championship courses (Montagu and Outeniqua), two others (Bramble Hill and the Links) are open to the public. The Links is particularly challenging and was the venue of the 2003 Presidents Cup. Greens fees for Bramble Hill fluctuate with the season; high-season rates are about R450 for 18 holes, R175–R200 for club rental, and the same for cart rental (compulsory). The Links is expensive—R1,000. There is also an on-site golf academy.

Expect to pay about R330 in greens fees and R150 for a golf cart or R80 for a caddy at the top-rated public **George Golf Club** (⊠ Langenhoven St. ☎ 044/873–6116). You can rent clubs (R100–R200 for 18 holes) and pull carts (R20) from **Logans Golf** (⊠ George Golf Club ☎ 044/874–7597).

en route The road from George descends steeply to the sea through a heavily forested gorge formed by the Kaaimans River. Look to your right to see a curved railway bridge spanning the river mouth. This is one of the most photographed scenes on the Garden Route, especially when the Outeniqua Choo-Tjoe steam train is puffing over it. As you round the point, a breathtaking view of mile upon mile of pounding surf and snow-white beach unfolds before you. There is an overlook from which you can often see dolphins and whales frolicking in the surf, and if you look up, you may see a colorful paraglider floating overhead.

Wilderness

❸ *12 km (7 mi) southeast of George.*

Wilderness is a popular vacation resort for good reason. Backed by thickly forested hills and cliffs, the tiny town presides over a magical stretch of beach between the Kaaimans and Touw rivers, as well as a spectacular system of waterways, lakes, and lagoons strung out along the coast, separated from the sea by towering vegetated dunes.

❹ Much of the area now falls under the control of **Wilderness National Park,** a 6,500-acre reserve that stretches east along the coast for 31 km (19 mi). This wetlands paradise draws birders from all over the country to its two blinds. Walking trails wend through the park, including the circular 10-km (6-mi) Pied Kingfisher Trail, which covers the best of what Wilderness has to offer: beach, lagoon, marsh, and river. ⊠ *Off N2* ☎ *044/ 877–1197* ⤳ *R60* ☉ *Daily 8–5.*

Where to Stay & Eat

★ **$–$$$** ✕ **Riverside Kitchen.** The name says it all. You can watch birds as you nibble, and canoeists wave as they paddle by. Main dishes are mostly meat- or fish-based—the line-fish duo is served with a sweet Thai chili sauce and a peach-and-ginger salsa. Starters include black mushroom topped with fresh pear and melted Roquefort. Among the nice touches are nonsweet desserts, such as ripe Camembert served with mascarpone, roasted almond flakes, fruit preserve, and crackers—not quite a cheese board, either. If you have a sweet tooth, though, fear not: the Bushmans River mud pie is a chocolate brownie served with fudge, melted chocolate, and ice cream. ⊠ *Pirates Creek, N2* ☎ *072/124–7375* ⌕ *Reservations essential* ⊟ *DC, MC, V* ⊘ *No dinner Mon.*

$–$$ ▦ **Dolphin Dunes.** This modern brick bed-and-breakfast is bright inside, but the main attraction is the view. Perched high on the dunes, it overlooks the sea, and a semiprivate boardwalk leads down to the beach. Spacious public rooms have clay-tile floors, and guest rooms are white and cream, light and airy. Room layout is clever; three rooms can be taken together to form an apartment with kitchen for several couples or a family. ⊠ *Buxton Close, Box 158, 6560* ☎ *044/877–0204* ⌕ *3 rooms, 2 apartments* ⌂ *Minibars, pool, Internet, business services; no a/c, no room phones* ⊟ *AE, DC, MC, V* ❙◎❙ *BP.*

¢ ▦ **Ebb and Flow Restcamp, Wilderness National Park.** The rest camp is divided into two sections, North and South. The South section is larger and consists of brick family cottages, which sleep up to six, as well as log cabins and forest huts, both of which sleep up to four. Of the cottages and log cabins, both with bedrooms, kitchens, and bathrooms with balconies, the log cabins are prettier, but both are bright and pleasant, furnished in a plain but adequate manner with floral or geometric curtains and upholstery. Forest cabins are smaller but cute. Campsites are set on a wide lawn under trees, some directly overlooking the river. The much smaller North section has a few grassy campsites and 15 not particularly attractive *rondawels* (round huts). As with all national park accommodations, the communal bathroom areas are well maintained, clean, and adequate. This is a good place from which to photograph the Outeniqua Choo-Tjoe. ⊠ *Off N2* ☎ *044/877–1197* ☎ *044/877–0111* ⊕ *www.SANParks.org* ⌕ *5 cottages; 8 log cabins; 10 2-bed and 10 4-bed forest cabins; 15 rondawels, 10 with bath; 100 campsites* ⌂ *Picnic area* ⊟ *AE, DC, MC, V.*

Sports & the Outdoors

Wilderness National Park and environs provide opportunities for lovely walks, fantastic paddling, and fishing that is more recreational than productive.

★ Based inside the park, **Eden Adventures** (☎ 044/877–0179 ⊕ www.eden. co.za) offers a canoeing and mountain-bike trip (R200), a kloofing (canyoning) trip (R200), and a fun abseiling (rappelling) trip on the Kaaimans River (R235). These are all half-day trips and include lunch, but they can be combined to form a full-day trip (R375–R425). Eden rents mountain bikes (R50 for two hours, R90 per day) and two-seater canoes for exploring the wetlands (R90 per day). Eden Adventures also supplies guides for four-day escorted hikes through the national park (about R600 per person). Accommodations are very rustic, you do all your own cooking, and the trail is due for upgrading. Booking is through the **Ebb and Flow Restcamp** (☏ 044/877–1197 ⊕ www. SANParks.org).

PARAGLIDING Wilderness is one of the best paragliding spots in the country, with loads
★ of launch sites. You can ridge-soar for miles along the dune front, watching whales and dolphins in the sea. If you've never done it before, don't worry: you can go tandem (R350) with an experienced instructor from **Cloudbase Paragliding** (☏ 044/877–1414 ⊕ www.cloudbase-paragliding.co.za). All you have to do is hang in there.

Sedgefield

❺ *20 km (12 mi) east of Wilderness.*

From Wilderness the road snakes through more lovely lakes and the town of Sedgefield, which is decidedly unattractive from the road. There are fabulous beaches and wetlands hidden behind the commercial facade, however, one of the best of which is the beach fronting the **Goukamma Nature Reserve.** (Take the Lake Pleasant and Groenvlei exit off the N2 and follow the unpaved road for 3 km [2 mi].) Backed by steep hills covered with dense bush, the reserve is deserted except for a few fishermen.

Knysna

❻ *20 km (12 mi) east of Sedgefield.*

Knysna (pronounced *nize*-nuh) is one of the most popular destinations on the Garden Route. The focus of the town is the beautiful Knysna Lagoon, ringed by forested hills dotted with vacation homes. Several walking and mountain-bike trails wind through Knysna's forests, many offering tremendous views back over the ocean. With luck you may spot the Knysna loerie, a brilliantly plumed and elusive forest bird, or the even more outrageously colored and even more elusive Narina trogon.

Towering buttresses of rock, known as the Heads, guard the entrance to the lagoon, funneling the ocean through a narrow channel. The sea approach is so hazardous that Knysna never developed into a major port, and now is very much a modern resort town, with the attendant hype, commercialism, and crowds, especially in summer. About the only aspect of the town that hasn't been modernized is the single-lane main road (the N2 goes straight through the middle of town), so traffic can be a nightmare. Walking is the best way to get around the town center, which is filled with shops, galleries, restaurants, and coffeehouses. Knysna's main claims to fame are edible and drinkable. The former are its famous—and abundant—oysters, and the latter is locally brewed Mitchell's beer, on tap at most bars and pubs.

Knysna Art Gallery is situated in the Old Gaol, a structure that dates back to 1859. As well as constantly changing exhibitions of a high standard, there is a permanent exhibit of mostly local artists, of which Knysna seems to produce an inordinate number. It must be the light on the lagoon. ⊠ *Queen and Main Sts.* ☎ *044/382-7124* ⤶ *Free* ⊙ *Weekdays 9:30–4:30, Sat. 9:30–1.*

★ You can't come to Knysna without making a trip out to the **Heads** at the mouth of the lagoon. These rock sentinels provide great views of both the sea and the lagoon. Only the developed, eastern side of the Heads is accessible by car, via George Rex Drive off the N2. You have two options: to park at the base of the Head and follow the walking trails that snake around the rocky cliffs, just feet above the crashing surf, or to drive to the summit, with its panoramic views and easy parking.

Unlike its eastern counterpart, the western side of the Heads, part of the **Featherbed Nature Reserve** (☎ 044/382–1693 ⊕ www.featherbed.co.za), is relatively unspoiled. In addition to a bizarre rock arch and great scenery, the reserve is home to various small mammals, more than 100 species of birds, and 1,000 plant species. A trip here consists of a ride on one of three ferries operated by the reserve, a tractor-trailer ride to the highest point, an escorted walk back, and an optional buffet lunch. In season or when a tour bus is in town, both the tour and the restaurant can be pretty crowded. The trip costs R110 without lunch or R220 with it.

One of the most interesting buildings in the area stands across the lagoon from Knysna, in the exclusive community of Belvidere. The Anglican **Holy Trinity Church,** built in 1855 of local stone, is a lovely replica of a Norman church of the 11th century. Holy Trinity was erected by Thomas Duthie, a young ensign of the 72nd Highland Regiment who settled in Knysna in 1834. The interior is notable for its beautiful stinkwood and yellowwood timber and stained-glass windows. ⊠ *N2 west out of Knysna to Belvidere turnoff just after bridge, then follow signs* ☎ *No phone* ⤶ *Free* ⊙ *Daily 8:30–5, except during services.*

need a break? If you visit Belvidere, be sure to stop at **Tapas at Crabs Creek** (⊠ Belvidere Rd. ☎ 044/386–0011), a fun tavern that sits on the bank of Knysna Lagoon. On a sunny day you may have to wait for an outside table, but it's worth it—the view across the water to Knysna is better than the food. The pint of prawns is very popular, or you can order a tapas platter.

Where to Stay & Eat

Of course there are restaurants that don't serve seafood, but very few of them are in Knysna. It's what the town's all about. There are more B&Bs than you can possibly imagine, as well as some fantastic guesthouses, self-catering resorts, and hotels, so you will not be short of choices.

★ $–$$$ ✕ **Drydock Food Company.** It's no surprise that you'll find oysters here. Six coastal, or wild, oysters will set you back R84. The seafood theme continues with tiger prawns, fusion fish curry, and the line fish Fontana: a grilled line fish layered with avocado, *brinjal* (eggplant), rocket (arugula), and smoked salmon trout and drizzled with balsamic vinegar and a creamy lemon coulis. The Caribbean blue cheese salad with roasted butternut is a big favorite, and meat eaters won't be disappointed with the chicken stir-fry or good old rump steak. ⊠ *Knysna Quays* ☎ *044/382–7310* ☐ *AE, DC, MC, V.*

¢–$ ✕ **Ile de Pain.** Watch bakers hand-mix dough in the background before

Fodor'sChoice consigning their huge assortment of European-style breads into wood-
★ fired ovens. All the meals on the seasonally changing menu are bread based, but they are definitely not your average sandwich. For breakfast try a rolled frittata with herbs, leeks, smoked salmon, horseradish sauce, cream cheese, and capers, or brioche French toast with caramelized pineapple, frozen yogurt, and passion-fruit syrup. Lunch favorites include a slice of ciabatta bread with sirloin steak, balsamic caramelized onions, and mustard butter, as well as a garden sandwich of mixed lettuce, avocado, pea-and-pistachio pesto, and tomato vinaigrette. All toppings are made on-site from fresh ingredients. And, of course, there is a selection of yummy pastries and good coffee. ⊠ *Boatshed, Thesen Island* ☎ *044/302–5707* ☐ *AE, MC, V* ☉ *Closed Mon. No dinner.*

¢–$ ✕ **Knysna Oyster Company.** If you love oysters, make a beeline for this tasting tavern attached to one of the world's largest oyster-farming operations. Diners sit at picnic tables next to the lagoon, with great views of the Heads. Each tasting consists of between six and eight fresh oysters and a basket of brown bread. Chase the oysters with excellent local Mitchell's beer—then do it all again. You'll pay about R40 for six medium oysters, R60 for six large ones. It's a good idea to order some coastal oysters, too, just to see what the fuss is about. They'll set you back R80 for six small ones and R100 for six large. If you're not into squishy mollusks, you can choose from a range of salads, fish, and meat dishes, such as chicken kebabs and ostrich steaks. ⊠ *Long St., Thesen Island* ☎ *044/382–6942 (ask for restaurant)* ☐ *DC, MC, V* ☉ *No dinner Sun.*

¢–$ ✕ **34° South.** Not a fishmonger, a bar, or a bistro; not a deli, a coffee shop, or a seafood restaurant—yet it's somehow all of these. Right on the water's edge in what appears to be a dolled-up warehouse, this place gives off a sense of abundance, with shelves, baskets, and display stands overflowing with all kinds of delicious goodies. Choose from the huge array of seafood or fresh fish, and enjoy your feast while sitting on the jetty looking at the boats. Try a delicious sandwich laden with avocados and peppadews. Or just fill a basket with delicious breads, pickles, cheeses, meats, and other delights. It's worth traveling halfway around the world just for the cilantro pesto. ⊠ *Knysna Quays* ☎ *044/382–7331* ⊟ *AE, DC, MC, V.*

★ $$$–$$$$ ✕⊞ **Phantom Forest Lodge.** Set on a private 300-acre nature reserve, this stunning lodge is built from sustainable natural materials. Accommodations are in luxury tree houses, and the living areas are joined by wooden walkways to protect the undergrowth. Rooms look straight out into the forest canopy. Though the original suites have natural tones and wood, thatch, and coir finishes, newer rooms are decorated in a vibrant North African style. Of the two restaurants, Chutzpah (*$$$$*), the newer one, focuses on North African/Moroccan food, with tasty tagines (meat stews) and couscous in a variety of guises, and the Boma (*$$$$*) produces contemporary classical cuisine. Try a peppered springbok loin with asparagus, roasted garlic mashed potatoes, and berry jus, or roasted butternut tortellini with apple, asparagus, and fennel salad. For dessert try a fresh fig, passion-fruit, and browned-butter pie with chili and vanilla ice cream. ⊠ *Phantom Pass, Box 3051, 6570* ☎ *044/386–0046* 🖷 *044/ 387–1944* ⊕ *www.phantomforest.com* ⌁ *14 suites* ♿ *2 restaurants, fans, minibars, pool, saltwater pool, gym, spa, mountain bikes, hiking, bar, laundry service, Internet, business services, airport shuttle, travel services, free parking, no-smoking rooms; no a/c, no children under 12* ⊟ *AE, DC, MC, V* ⏃⏃ *MAP.*

★ $$–$$$$ ⊞ **St. James of Knysna.** This elegant getaway is right on the edge of Knysna Lagoon. Outdoors you can enjoy a garden with tranquil koi ponds. Indoors the decor is light and bright, with some lovely antiques. Most of the individually decorated rooms have uninterrupted views of the water. Bathrooms range from a brick-tone retreat with a glass wall that leads to a private leafy garden with an outside shower to Victorian fantasies. Each room comes with an iron and ironing board, so you can unwrinkle a much-traveled shirt without the hassle of valet service. ⊠ *The Point, Main St., Box 1242, 6570* ☎ *044/382–6750* 🖷 *044/382–6756* ⊕ *www. stjames.co.za* ⌁ *2 rooms, 13 suites* ♿ *Restaurant, picnic area, room service, in-room safes, minibars, cable TV, 2 pools, boating, waterskiing, fishing, croquet, bar, dry cleaning, laundry service, Internet, business services, airport shuttle, parking (fee); no children under 12, no smoking* ⊟ *AE, DC, MC, V* ⏃⏃ *BP.*

★ $$ ⊞ **Belvidere Manor.** This attractive establishment has lovely views across the lagoon to Knysna, some 6½ km (4 mi) away. White, light, and airy cottages face each other across a lawn that slopes down to a jetty. Choose from one- and two-bedroom units, all with dining areas, sitting rooms with fireplaces, and fully equipped kitchens. The manor house, a lovely 1834 farmstead, has been converted into a restaurant and guest lounge. In summer breakfast is served on a wooden deck overlooking the lagoon. Sizable discounts are offered for long stays. ⊠ *Lower Duthie Dr., Belvidere Estate, Box 1195, 6570* ☎ *044/387–1055* 🖷 *044/387– 1059* ⊕ *www.belvidere.co.za* ⌁ *33 cottages* ♿ *Restaurant, room service, fans, pool, pub; no a/c* ⊟ *AE, DC, MC, V* ⏃⏃ *BP.*

$ ⊞ **Cunningham's Island Guest House.** This casual beach house—okay, it's not actually on the beach, but it feels like it is—gets many return guests. Decorated with light lime-washed pine and wicker furnishings, the guesthouse has an easy flow from the breakfast room to the sunny pool area. Owner Tim Cunningham will help make arrangements for golf, and can provide plenty of advice on other activities, too. Bathrooms don't have tubs, but the generously proportioned shower stalls make up for that. ⊠ *Kingsway and Church St., Leisure Isle 6570* 🕾 *044/384–1319* 🖷 *044/384–1327* ⊕ *www.islandhouse.co.za* ⤳ *8 rooms* ⟁ *Breakfast room, fans, saltwater pool, bar, laundry service, Internet, business services, airport shuttle, travel services, free parking, some pets allowed (fee), no-smoking rooms; no a/c, no room phones, no children under 10* ▭ *AE, DC, MC, V* ⦿| *BP.*

★ $ 🖾 **Lightleys Holiday Houseboats.** For a sense of freedom and adventure, take one of these fully equipped houseboats and cruise the lagoon. Inside is compact, light, and bright, and outside is an ever-changing vista of lagoon, forest, and mountain. This is self-catering at its very best. A four-berth boat costs R800 per day; a six-berth boat costs about R1,500 per day. If you don't fancy cooking, you can arrange to pick up meals or picnic baskets from the base or have them delivered to you at a mooring of your choice. ⊠ *Box 863, 6570* 🕾 *044/386–0007* 🖷 *044/386–0018* ⊕ *www.knysna.co.za/lightleys* ⤳ *9 4-berth boats, 5 6-berth boats* ⟁ *Kitchens* ▭ *MC, V.*

$ 🖾 **Wayside Lodge.** Offering good value for the money, this establishment is conveniently located right in the middle of town. Rooms are simply but pleasantly decorated with wrought-iron bedsteads and white linen. ⊠ *Pledge Sq., 6570* 🕾🖷 *044/382–6011* ⊕ *www.waysideinn.co.za* ⤳ *11 rooms, 4 suites* ⟁ *Cable TV, laundry service, airport shuttle, free parking; no a/c, no smoking* ▭ *MC, V* ⦿| *CP.*

Sports & the Outdoors

BEACHES Although Knysna is very much a seaside destination, there are no beaches actually in the town—unlike Plett or Mossel Bay—but there are some fabulous ones nearby. **Leisure Isle,** in the middle of the lagoon, has a few tiny strands. The beach at **Brenton-on-Sea,** past Belvidere, is a beautiful, long white-sand beach on which you can walk for 3½ km (2 mi) to Buffalo Bay. It's about a 10-minute drive; the turnoff from the N2 is about 12 km (7 mi) west of Knysna. Another lovely beach is **Noetzie,** 7 km (4 mi) east of town. It's a steep walk up and down from the parking lot, but it's worth it. While there, take a look at the fanciful vacation homes shaped like European castles.

BOATING Boating on the lagoon is a scenic experience, and going through the Heads is quite dramatic. It makes you think about how dangerous it once was for big sailing ships to maneuver through narrow passages such as these without auxiliary engines.

Deep South Eco-Ventures (⊠ Knysna Quays 🕾 044/382–2010 ⊕ www.deepsoutheco.com) leads interpretive boat trips on the lagoon, starting at R250. A boat trip can also be combined with a bike tour.

In addition to running the ferry to the nature reserve, the **Featherbed Company** (⊠ Ferry Terminus, Remembrance Ave. 🕾 044/382–1693 ⊕ www.featherbed.co.za) operates a number of sightseeing boats on the lagoon (trips start at R50 per person), as well as a Mississippi-style paddle steamer that does lunch and dinner cruises.

★ **Springtide Charters** (✉ Knysna Quays ☎ 082/470–6022 ⊕ www.
springtide.co.za) operates a luxury 50-foot sailing yacht for scenic
cruises on the lagoon and through the Heads (weather permitting). You
can have breakfast, lunch, or a romantic dinner on board—or even spend
the night. The boat takes a maximum of 12 passengers, and dinner and
overnight trips are limited to one party. Rates start at about R350 per
person for a 2½-hour sail with snacks.

GOLF   Perched on the cliff top of the Eastern Head, the challenging 18-hole
Pezula Championship Golf Course (☎ 044/384–1222 ⊕ www.pezula.
com) is one of South Africa's most scenic courses. Designed by Ronald
Fream and David Dale, it costs R700 per person, including a compulsory golf cart, at time of writing (a price increase is anticipated with the
opening of an on-site hotel in 2005). Also available are a comfortable
clubhouse with a great restaurant and lessons from resident pros.

HIKING   There are a number of nice day walks from **Diepwalle** (open 7:30–4),
about 40 km (23 mi) out of town on the unpaved R339, which continues to Prince Alfred's Pass and on to Uniondale. For more information,
contact the **Department of Water Affairs and Forestry** (☎044/382–5466.).

The two-day **Harkerville Trail** starts at the Garden of Eden, on the N2
about 15 km (9 mi) from both Plett and Knysna. Along the way you'll
pass the expected indigenous forests, pine plantations, and "islands" of
fynbos (a local plant), as well as fairly taxing sections on the coast. (This
is not a beginner's trail.) Homesick Californians can hug a tree in a small
stand of huge redwoods (*Sequoia sempervirens*), planted as part of a
forestry experiment years ago. Watch out for mountain bikers, who use
sections of the trail and usually shout a warning as they hurtle toward
you. The kiosk at the Garden of Eden is open daily 7:30–4, and the trail
costs R60 per person. If you don't want to do the whole hike, consider
a quick walk into the forest on the wheelchair-friendly wooden board-
walks. You'll see some big old trees, and you can bring a picnic, as there
are some tables.

If you don't fancy heading off on your own, take a guided walk with
Knysna Forest Tours (☎ 082/921–1480 ⊕ www.knysnaforesttours.co.
za). Prices are about R150–R250.

HORSEBACK   If you've ever dreamed of riding a horse along a deserted beach, this is
RIDING   your chance. **Garden Route Equestrian Adventure Tours** (☎ 082/835–9110
Fodor's Choice   ⊕ www.great.co.za) offers great horseback rides along the Goukamma
★   Beach. Experienced riders who go fast enough can opt to return through
the densely forested Goukamma Nature Reserve. Rides are 1½ hours
long and cost R200.

MOUNTAIN   Knysna is mountain-biking heaven. There are four circular trails of
BIKING   varying length and difficulty at **Harkerville** (✉ N2, 15 km [9 mi] east of
★   Knysna), all starting and ending at the Garden of Eden. If you're cycling without a guide, reservations are not necessary; just register when
you start and pay the nominal fee (R6 per person). All the trails are great,
but the last 6 km (4 mi) of the Petrus se Brand trail is widely considered to be the most fun (but not challenging) piece of single track in South

Africa. Petrus se Brand is not circular; it can be done either way between Diepwalle and Garden of Eden. It's tight and twisty, and you'll zip downhill (if you start at Diepwalle) over the springy forest floor, ducking enormous trees. You can rent bikes (R120) from **Outeniqua Biking Trails** (⊠ Harkerville ☎ 044/532–7644), which is conveniently located right on the forest edge and close to the trails. Guided trips start at R320.

Deep South Eco-Ventures (☎ 044/382–2010 ⊕ www.deepsoutheco.com) offers guided mountain-bike tours into the forests, starting at R240.

en route

Knysna Forest once harbored large herds of elephants, but first hunting and later development and habitat encroachment almost put an end to the wild population. At one time it was thought there was only one old matriarch left, so a few young elephants were relocated from Kruger to keep her company and—with luck—breed. The new ellies couldn't cope with the forest, however, and after they wandered into farmland, the project was abandoned. Since then, more elephants, including a few young ones, have been found deep in the forest, but since they're not venturing near the more-traveled areas, it's extremely unlikely that you'll see one. Still it's nice to know they're there. If you want to see an elephant, your best bet is the **Knysna Elephant Park,** where you can go on a guided forest walk with these amazing animals, touch them, and learn more about them. ⊠ N2, 22 km east of Knysna ☎ 044/532–7732 ⊕ www. knysnaelephantpark.co.za ⛟ R90 ☉ Daily 8:30–4:30; tours on the ½ hr.

Plettenberg Bay

❼ 32 km (20 mi) east of Knysna.

Plettenberg Bay is South Africa's premier beach resort, as the empty houses on Beachy Head Road (known as Millionaires' Mile) during the 11 months when it's not beach season will attest. But in December the hordes with all their teenage offspring arrive en masse. Even then you can find yourself a stretch of lonely beach if you're prepared to walk to the end of Keurboomstrand. Plett, as it is commonly known, is one of the best places in the world to watch whales and dolphins. Boat-based trips are run from Central Beach, as are sea-kayaking trips, which, although loads of fun, are not quite as efficient as the big motorboats. Aerial viewing is available from standard planes or gliders.

Monkeyland is a refuge for abused and abandoned primates, most of which were pets or laboratory animals. They now roam in a huge enclosed area of natural forest and are free to play, socialize, and do whatever it is that keeps primates happy. There are lemurs, gibbons, spider monkeys, indigenous vervet monkeys, howler monkeys, and many more. Guided walks are run throughout the day, and the tamer "inmates" often play with guests. ⊠ 16 km (10 mi) east of Plettenberg Bay along the N2, just before Nature's Valley turnoff ☎ 044/534–8906 ⊕ www.monkeyland. co.za ⛟ R80 ☉ Daily 8–5.

Where to Stay & Eat

As one of the most sophisticated destinations on the Garden Route, Plett has plenty of fabulous places to eat and overnight.

¢–$　✕ **Cornuti Al Mare.** Sibling to Cornuti the Cradle, in the Cradle of Humankind, outside of Johannesburg, this is Cornuti on vacation by the sea. Everything is far more casual and relaxed. Try the thin wood-fired pizzas or a nice solid pasta. In summer, get there early to get a seat on the veranda. ✉ *Oddlands and Perestrello Sts.* ☎ *044/533–1277* ⚞ *Reservations not accepted.* ▤ *AE, DC, MC, V.*

¢　✕ **Plett Ski Boat Club.** Want to know a secret? Plett fishermen, ski-boat skippers, surfers, kayak operators, and other locals frequent this very, very casual eatery. It's right on the beach where the ski boats launch, so there is a great view—especially from the outside tables. It offers really good value for the money; well-cooked, fresh but not fancy seafood; the usual burgers and fries; and full, hangover-busting breakfasts. Many locals can be reliably tracked down to the popular bar after 5 on weekdays—especially if there is a rugby match on TV. ✉ *Central Beach* ☎ *044/533–4147* ⚞ *No reservations* ▤ *AE, DC, MC, V* ⊘ *No dinner Sun.*

★ $$$$　✕▩ **Kurland.** On the road out of Plett toward Tsitsikamma, this magnificent 1,500-acre estate is centered on a lovely historic Cape Dutch homestead. Spacious guest suites are in separate buildings, and huge bathrooms, antique furniture, book-filled shelves, fireplaces, and private balconies give you the feeling you're staying in your own country home. A view of horse-filled paddocks makes it seem even more opulent. Ten rooms have staircases leading to charming children's attic rooms. The food in the restaurant ($$$$) is exactly what you would expect in such a refined atmosphere: well cooked, beautifully presented, and made from whatever's fresh. Guests have the use of a complimentary quad bike for exploring the huge estate, children's programs are offered during school breaks, and polo packages for tournaments or clinics for groups or individuals are available, too. ✉ *N2, about 20 km (12 mi) from Plett, Box 209, The Crags 6602* ☎ *044/534–8082* 🖷 *044/534–8699* ⊕ *www.kurland.co.za* ⇝ *12 suites* ⚭ *Restaurant, room service, in-room safes, minibars, cable TV, tennis court, pool, gym, spa, billiards, hiking, horseback riding, Ping-Pong, bar, babysitting, playground; no a/c* ▤ *AE, DC, MC, V* ⍩ *MAP.*

★ $$$–$$$$　✕▩ **Plettenberg.** High on a rocky point in Plettenberg Bay, this luxury hotel has unbelievable views of the bay, the Tsitsikamma Mountains, Keurbooms Lagoon, miles of magnificent beach, and, in season, whales frolicking just beyond the waves. Built around an 1860 manor house, the hotel is light and bright, decorated in shades of white and blue. Service is wonderfully attentive, with a front-desk staff that tries to anticipate your every need. Even if you don't stay here, treat yourself to lunch on the hotel terrace. Diners sit under large fabric umbrellas and look out over a pool that seems to extend right into the incredible views. The lunch menu is small: salads, sandwiches, a pasta dish, and catch of the day. Dinner in the restaurant ($$–$$$; reservations essential) is a fancier affair, focusing on local meat and seafood. Villas are self-catering. ✉ *Lookout Rocks, Box 719, 6600* ☎ *044/533–2030* 🖷 *044/533–2074*

⊕ *www.plettenberg.com* ↩ *24 rooms, 12 suites, 2 villas* ⚬ *Restaurant, 2 pools, spa, bar, airport shuttle, free parking; no kids under 12, no smoking* ▤ *AE, DC, MC, V* ⦿⊙ *BP.*

★ **$$–$$$$** ✕⊞ **Hunter's Country House.** Just 10 minutes from town, this tranquil property is set amid gardens that fall away into a forested valley. The heart of the lodge is an old farmstead, a lovely thatch building with low beams and large fireplaces. Guest rooms are in individual white thatch cottages, each with its own fireplace and veranda. Three suites have private plunge pools. Antiques grace the rooms, and claw-foot tubs are the centerpiece of many of the gigantic bathrooms. Service is outstanding. Most guests eat at the hotel's excellent table d'hôte restaurant (*$$$$*), which brings a French touch to local South African produce. Reservations are essential for nonguests. The lodge is very child-friendly, which makes it one of the few places where you don't have to sacrifice sophistication for family accommodations. ⊠ *Off N2, between Plett and Knysna, Box 454, 6600* ☎ *044/532–7818* 🖷 *044/532–7878* ⊕ *www. hunterhotels.com* ↩ *23 suites* ⚬ *Restaurant, in-room safes, minibars, cable TV, tennis court, pool, massage, bar, library, babysitting, children's programs, playground, laundry service, Internet, business services, meeting room, no-smoking rooms* ▤ *AE, DC, MC, V* ⦿⊙ *BP.*

$$$–$$$$ ⊞ **Tsala Treetop Lodge.** Built on the same property as Hunter's, and also run by the Hunter family, this lodge combines the best of sleek design with spectacular natural surroundings. Fabulous glass, stone, metal, and wood chalets are built on stilts overlooking a steep forested gorge and, in some cases, extending into the forest canopy. Suites have plunge pools with fantastic views, verandas, and fireplaces, and the unusual decor includes specially manufactured oval baths, hand-beaten brass plumbing fittings, and loads of glass. Suites are connected by raised timber walkways. ⊠ *Off N2, between Plettenberg Bay and Knysna, Box 454, 6600* ☎ *044/532–7818* 🖷 *044/532–7878* ↩ *10 suites* ⚬ *Restaurant, room service, in-room data ports, in-room safes, minibars, cable TV, massage, bar, library, laundry service, Internet, business services, airport shuttle, no-smoking rooms; no a/c, no children under 10* ▤ *AE, DC, MC, V* ⦿⊙ *BP.*

★ **$$$** ⊞ **Plettenberg Park.** The setting of this stylish, minimalist lodge—in splendid isolation on a cliff top in a private nature reserve on the western (wild) side of Robberg Peninsula—is one of the best anywhere, and the view of the open ocean across fynbos-clad hills is spectacular. Rooms are decorated in an understated African-colonial style in shades of white and cream; those that face the sea have dramatic views, and the others overlook a tranquil lily pond. A steep path leads to a private beach and natural tidal pool. On arrival, guests are invited to confer with the two resident chefs and decide on a menu for their stay. ⊲⎓ *Box 167, 6600* ☎ *044/533–9067* 🖷 *044/533–9092* ⊕ *www.plettenbergpark.co.za* ↩ *9 rooms* ⚬ *Restaurant, room service, in-room safes, minibars, cable TV, in-room VCRs, pool, gym, hot tub, spa, beach, snorkeling, hiking, lobby lounge, shop, laundry service, concierge, Internet, business services, airport shuttle; no a/c, no children under 12, no smoking* ▤ *AE, DC, MC, V* ⦿⊙ *FAP.*

$$ ⊞ **Buffalo Hills Game Reserve and Lodge.** Pockets of indigenous bush and tracts of fynbos alternate with old farmland on this fun property about

15 minutes outside Plett. It's not Mpumalanga—or even the Karoo or Eastern Cape—but it's a great place to see a variety of game, including buffalo and rhino. In this warm, friendly place, evening meals are taken around an enormous table, and outrageous stories are told. Try the game walk or even a multiday hike up into the hills. Even little ones can do short game walks near the lodge at this child-friendly lodging. ⊠ *Stofpad, Wittedrif, Box 1321, 6600* ☏ *044/535–9739* 🖷 *044/535–9480* ⊕ *www.buffalohills.co.za* ⇒ *4 rooms, 8 tented rooms, 1 cottage* ⚷ *Dining room, some in-room hot tubs, saltwater pool, hiking, bar, shop, laundry service, airport shuttle, travel services, no-smoking rooms; no a/c, no room phones, no room TVs* ☰ *AE, DC, MC, V* ⦿ *FAP.*

★ **$$** 🖭 **Hog Hollow Country Lodge.** This lovely, friendly lodge is set in a small island of gardens on the edge of a forested gorge. Vistas stretch into the misty green distance. Rooms are decorated in a modern African motif, with cast-iron furniture, white linen, and African artwork. In summer the private verandas with hammocks are as popular as the many fireplaces are in winter. The food is great, and meals are sociable affairs, taken around a huge table in the main house. Local seafood and ostrich are well represented on the menu, but vegetarian food is handled with flair. Especially good is the homemade pasta with butternut-squash filling. Breakfasts are taken on the patio to the accompaniment of varied birdsong. A one-hour walk through the forest brings you to Monkeyland. ⊠ *18 km (11 mi) east of Plettenberg Bay, The Crags, Box 1047, 6600* ☏🖷 *044/534–8879* ⊕ *www.hog-hollow.com* ⇒ *15 suites* ⚷ *Dining room, fans, minibars, pool, sauna, bar; no a/c, no room phones, no room TVs* ☰ *AE, DC, MC, V* ⦿ *BP.*

$ 🖭 **Bayview Hotel.** In the middle of town, this hotel offers good value for the money, and the self-catering penthouse suite, with fantastic views and an enormous deck, is an even better value. Only sea-facing rooms have air-conditioning, but since they also overlook the main road, they can be a tad noisy. ⊠ *Main Rd. and Gibb St., 6600* ☏ *044/533–1961* 🖷 *044/533–2059* 🖂 *bayviewplett@telkomsa.net* ⇒ *33 rooms, 3 suites* ⚷ *In-room safes, cable TV, bar, babysitting, laundry service, Internet, airport shuttle, free parking, no-smoking rooms; no a/c in some rooms* ☰ *AE, DC, MC, V.*

$ 🖭 **Bitou River Lodge.** Some places just seem to get everything right. This
Fodor$Choice lovely, quiet, restful B&B has a wonderful location on the bank of the Bitou
★ River, about 3 km (2 mi) upstream from the lagoon. Rooms overlook a pretty garden and a quiet bird-rich and lily-filled pond. The decor is understated and soothing, with neutral pastels dominating. Breakfasts are delicious affairs with freshly baked bread, muffins, and other goodies in addition to fruit, cereal, and eggs. Bitou feels like it's in the middle of nowhere, but it's only a 10-minute drive from the center of town. Don't pass up the opportunity to explore the river in one of the available canoes. ⊠ *About 3 km (2 mi) on the R340 to Wittedrif (off the N2), Box 491, 6600* ☏ *082/978–6164* ☏🖷 *044/535–9577* ⊕ *www.bitou.co.za* ⇒ *5 rooms* ⚷ *Breakfast room, fans, refrigerators, saltwater pool, boating; no a/c, no room phones, no children under 12, no smoking* ☰ *MC, V* ⦿ *BP.*

¢ 🖭 **Nothando Backpackers & Deios Guest House.** Half hostel and half guesthouse, this warm, friendly place is always buzzing. It's light and bright, and is conveniently near the middle of town. It's easy to find a sunny or shady spot in the garden to just relax with a book, and the lively bar is a great place to share adventures come evening. All in all, it's an excellent value. ✉ *5 Wilder St., 6600* ☎ *044/533–0220* ⊕ *www. deios.co.za, www.nothando.co.za* ⤴ *8 rooms, 6 with bath; dormitory* ⚐ *Dining room, fans, bar, laundry service, Internet, business services, travel services, free parking; no a/c, no room phones, no TV in some rooms, no smoking* ☰ *AE, DC, MC, V.*

Sports & the Outdoors

BEACHES Plett presides over a stretch of coastline that has inspired rave reviews since the Portuguese first set eyes on it in 1497 and dubbed it *bahia formosa* (the beautiful bay). Three rivers flow into the sea here, the most spectacular of which—the Keurbooms—backs up to form a large lagoon. For swimming, surfing, sailing, hiking, and fishing you can't do much better than Plett, although the water is still colder than it is around Durban and in northern KwaZulu–Natal.

All the dolphin-watching boats and kayak trips leave from **Central Beach**. A constant stream of tenders going out to the fishing boats moored in the bay makes this quite busy, but it's still a great spot. Just keep away from the boat-launching area, and swim in the southern section. **Keurboomstrand** is about 10 km (6 mi) from Plett—right on the eastern edge of the bay. If you're fit, you can walk all the way from here to Nature's Valley, but you need to watch both the tides and the steep, rocky sections. It's best to ask locals before tackling this. Even if you're unfit, you can still walk about a mile down the beach, chill out for a while, and then walk back. **Lookout Beach** was Plett's flagship Blue Flag beach, but as the lagoon mouth shifts, the beach is disappearing. Don't let that stop you from visiting, though. It should still be around for a few years, and it's great for swimming, body surfing, and sunbathing. There's even a nice little bar and restaurant where you can top up if you feel peckish or thirsty. Just on the other side of the Beacon Isle, the unmissable hotel on the island at the end of the tombolo, is **Robberg Beach**, a great swimming beach that continues in a gracious curve all the way to Robberg Peninsula. You can get pretty good sightings of dolphins and whales just behind the back break.

FLYING & **African Ramble Air Charter** (✉ Plettenberg Bay Airport ☎ 044/533–
SKYDIVING 9006 ⊕ www.aframble.co.za) runs half-hour flights over the bay for R440 per person as well as charter flights to the Eastern Cape game reserves. These particularly scenic trips start by flying over Robberg and out over the bay, where you may see whales or dolphins, and then hug the coast up to Nature's Valley before heading inland. If you want your views with a bit of adrenaline thrown in, consider a tandem skydive with **Skydive Plett** (✉ Plettenberg Bay Airport ☎ 082/905–7440 ⊕ www.skydiveplett. co.za). Tandem jumps cost about R1,300, and it's worth the extra R400 to get the DVD so you can show your friends back home. You get nearly half a minute of free fall, during which you get to see Robberg and the whole of the Tsitsikamma coast.

HIKING

★

Robberg Nature Reserve (⊠ Robberg Rd. (on way to airport) ☎ 044/ 533–2125) has three fabulous walks. The shortest circuit takes about a half hour and offers great views of the ocean. A longer walk (1½ hours) passes above a seal colony and connects to the "island" via a tombolo. At 2½ or more hours, the longest walk goes right to the end of the peninsula. You need to watch the tides on this one. In addition to great sea views, dolphins, whales, birds, and seals, you can see fantastic flowers and lovely swimming beaches. Admission is R20, and it's worth taking a picnic. A fascinating archaeological excavation at Nelson's Bay Cave has a display outlining the occupation of the cave over thousands of years. **Ocean Blue** (☎ 044/533–5083 ⊕ www. oceanadventures.co.za) leads guided walks on Robberg starting at R50 for the short walk.

KAYAKING

★

Kayaking on **Plettenberg Bay** is a great way to see the sights and possibly enjoy a visit from a whale or dolphin. Though you aren't likely to see as many animals as the people on the big boats, it's a far more intimate and exciting experience if you do. You also get to paddle past the Cape fur seal colony on Robberg. Trips cost about R200–R250 for three hours. **Dolphin Adventures** (⊠ Central Beach ☎ 083/590–3405 ⊕ www.dolphinkayak.com) offers regular trips in sleek but stable double sit-upon kayaks. **Ocean Blue** (⊠ Hopwood St., Central Beach ☎ 044/ 533–5083 ⊕ www.oceanadventures.co.za) runs regular paddling trips on which you may see whales and dolphins.

SCUBA DIVING

Diving off Plett is great. Rocky reefs are covered in colorful invertebrate life, and there is always a chance that a dolphin may swim past you while you're underwater. **Tsitsikamma Divers** (⊠ Central Beach ☎ 044/533–6260 or 082/558–9375 ⊕ www.stormsriver.com) runs charters ranging from a shore dive (R60) to a far-boat dive (R150); they also rent equipment and offer several PADI and NAUI courses.

WHALE-
WATCHING
🕭
Fodor'sChoice
★

Plettenberg Bay is truly one of the very best locations worldwide for boat-based whale- and dolphin-watching. Most days visitors see at least two cetacean species and Cape fur seals, as well as a variety of seabirds, including Cape gannets and African penguins. On some days people have seen up to six cetacean species in the course of a few hours.

Two similar operators have you board an open vehicle outside a shop and from there step directly onto a boat at the beach. Boats are fast, safe, and dry. Both operators offer a standard trip (about R300), in which the boat must stay 975 feet from the animals, and a close-encounter trip (about R500) on a boat that is licensed to approach within 162 feet. These trips are limited in order to minimize disturbance to the whales. **Ocean Blue** (⊠ Hopwood St., Central Beach ☎ 044/533–5083 ⊕ www. oceanadventures.co.za) runs trips from its shop on the beach, where it also sells terrific original African artworks with fishy motifs. Based near the beach, **Ocean Safaris** (⊠ Hopwood St., Central Beach ☎ 044/ 533–4963 or 082/784–5729 ⊕ www.oceansafaris.co.za) shares a shop with a dive school and sells a wide range of dolphin- and whale-motif goodies, from beautiful crafts to fun, kitschy gifts.

Shopping

Plenty of shops in and around town sell casual beachwear and various crafts, but for a good concentration in a small place, you can't beat **Old Nick** (⊠ N2, just east of town ☎ 044/533–1395). Originally just a pottery and weaving studio, it has grown to include a host of other crafts—so many that you could spend a whole day here. Included are a weaving museum, a shop selling lovely woven goods, a jeweler, and a small number of art galleries. **Earth-Sea Batiks** produces unbelievably delicate artworks using this ancient technique usually associated with rather crude images. A handmade-soap factory beckons with the scent of essential oils and fruits, and the **Pansy Shell Country Kitchen** competes for your olfactory attention with the heady aroma of freshly brewed espresso.

Nature's Valley

❽ *33 km (21 mi) east of Plettenberg Bay.*

Taking the N2 east from Plett, you cross a flat coastal plain of fynbos, with the forested Tsitsikamma Mountains on your left. Just after The Crags, turn off onto the R102, an alternative to the toll road and a far more interesting and scenic route. The road passes through farmland before dropping suddenly to sea level via the Groot River Pass. It's a great descent, with the road worming back and forth through a tunnel of greenery, impenetrable bush pressing in on either side. At the bottom of the pass, turn right into Nature's Valley, where the Groot River forms a magnificent lagoon hemmed in by bush-cloaked hills before crossing a long, beautiful beach to enter the sea. An almost fairy-tale settlement nestles beneath the trees. This is the end point of the Otter Trail. At a small restaurant-cum-shop near the beach, weary hikers give their boots a solemn resting place if they're not fit for another hike. A walk to Salt River is another great way to spend the day, and there is a reasonable chance of spotting a river otter.

Where to Stay & Eat

There is only one restaurant in Nature's Valley. It's fine for a light meal, but its prices reflect its market dominance. If you want really good food, you'll have to eat at your guesthouse.

★ $$ 🏨 **Lily Pond Lodge.** Almost Zen-like in its simplicity, this contemporary classic sits neatly at the edge of two enormous natural lily ponds. Long koi pools line the entrance, and clean lines and geometric shapes define the various spaces, extending into the rooms, all of which overlook the ponds. The food is great, and the menu changes daily, easily skipping between European, Asian, and African cuisines. Children under 12 are permitted by arrangement. ⊠ *Nature's Valley Rd. (R102), Box 158, The Crags 6602* ☎ *044/534–8767* 🖷 *044/534–8686* ⊕ *www.lilypond.co.za* ⇆ *4 rooms, 2 suites* ⚭ *Dining room, fans, minibars, cable TV, saltwater pool, massage, fishing, bar, laundry service, Internet, business services, airport shuttle; no a/c, no smoking* ▭ *AE, DC, MC, V* ⭗ *BP.*

$ 🏨 **Tranquility Lodge.** Just across from the Nature's Valley beach, this peaceful lodge is well situated for long walks, gentle swims, and general lazing around. Rooms are small and simply furnished, but beautifully finished in soothing neutrals and white. The garden—a slightly tamed version of the forest—is delightful. Some rooms have a tub and shower, but those with just a shower are much roomier and a better choice. The suite has its own hot tub, a spacious shower stall, and a private balcony. Each room is assigned a double kayak in which to explore the lagoon. This is a great place to spend a night after tackling the Otter Trail; chill out in the garden's covered hot tub, enjoy a delicious prearranged dinner, and then have a really good night's sleep in a comfy bed. ⊠ *130 St. Michael's Ave., Box 137, The Crags 6602* ☎ *044/531–6663* 🖷 *044/531–6879* ⊕ *www.tranquilitylodge.co.za* ⤷ *6 rooms, 1 suite* ☖ *Dining room, saltwater pool, hot tub, boating, fishing, mountain bikes, laundry service, airport shuttle; no a/c, no room phones, no room TVs, no children under 14, no smoking* ▭ *AE, DC, MC, V* ⊘ *BP.*

¢ 🏠 **De Vasselot Rest Camp.** On the banks of the Groot River, this rest camp is great if you're looking for a rustic place to escape. Though the huts are very basic, the setting—nestled under huge trees and close to the beach, lagoon, and lovely walks—is wonderful. This is definitely not one of those manicured campsites. As with all national park facilities, the communal bath and kitchen facilities are basic but clean and in good order. ⊠ *R102* ☎ *044/531–6700* 🖷 *044/531–6881* ⊕ *www.SANParks.org* ⤷ *10 huts, 45 campsites* ☖ *Boating, fishing, laundry facilities* ▭ *MC, V.*

Storms River

★ ❾ *35 km (22 mi) east of Nature's Valley, 62 km (39 mi) east of Plettenberg Bay.*

From Nature's Valley the R102 climbs out of the Groot River valley and crosses the N2. Here you can choose to take the N2 or stay on the R102 through the incredibly scenic Bloukrans Pass and rejoin the N2 13 km (8 mi) farther on. From this point it is another 9 km (6 mi) to the turnoff to Tsitsikamma National Park and the Storms River Mouth. The pretty and rather remote Storms River Village is another 4 km (2 mi) farther east on the N2. Although it's a really small, isolated village, Storms River absolutely buzzes with activity. A hotel, a couple of guesthouses, and a smattering of backpacker's lodges all cater to the numerous adrenaline junkies and nature lovers who frequent this hot spot for adventure and ecotourism activities.

> **need a break?**
>
> Don't expect anything fancy, but do expect good value for the money at simple **Trees Fine Foods** (⊠ Main Rd. ☎ 042/281–1836), which is part of a poverty alleviation and employment program. Conveniently located in the heart of Storms River Village, it serves burgers, sandwiches, and baked potatoes.

❿ **Tsitsikamma National Park,** a narrow belt of coastline extending for 80 km (50 mi) from Oubosstrand to Nature's Valley, encompasses some of the most spectacular coastal scenery in the country, including deep gorges, evergreen forests, tidal pools, and beautiful empty beaches. The best way to see the park is on the five-day Otter Trail, South Africa's most popular hike, or the somewhat easier Dolphin Trail. A less-stren-

Fodor's Choice
★

uous highlight is the Storms River Mouth, in the middle of the park. The river enters the sea through a narrow channel carved between sheer cliffs. Storms River was aptly named: when gale winds blow, as they often do, the sea flies into a pounding fury, hurling spray onto the rocks and whipping spume high up the cliffs. From the visitor center a trail descends through the forest (different tree species are all labeled) and over a narrow suspension bridge strung across the river mouth. It's a spectacular walk, a highlight of any trip to the Garden Route. On the other side of the bridge a steep trail climbs to the top of a bluff overlooking the river and the sea—the turning point of the Storms River MTB (mountain bike) Trail. Other trails, ranging from 1 to 3.2 km (½ to 2 mi), lead either to a cave once inhabited by hunter-gatherers or through the coastal forest. A basic restaurant with great views of the river and the ocean serves breakfast, lunch, and dinner. ☎ 042/281–1607 ⌂ R80 ⏾ Daily 5:30 AM–9:30 PM.

Where to Stay & Eat

$ ✕⊡ **Old Village Inn.** The guest rooms here are in pretty, colorful buildings that are neatly arranged around a village green, and the public rooms are in an old hunting lodge built in 1888. The inn is well known for its restaurant—De Oude Martha (¢–$)—which was named after the hotel's first cook; though she has retired, her influence lingers. Food is mostly dependable standbys such as grilled line fish, chicken, and pastas, but there's a new twist on the inevitable ostrich steak: creamy amarula (a native fruit) and gooseberry sauce. ⊡ Box 53, 6308 ☎ 042/ 281–1711 ⊟ 042/281–1669 ⊕ www.village-inn.co.za ⇆ 48 rooms, 8 apartments ⚐ Restaurant, fans, in-room safes, pool, pub, babysitting, laundry service, meeting rooms, some pets allowed; no a/c ⊟ AE, DC, MC, V ⏍⊙ BP.

¢–$ ⊡ **Tsitsikamma National Park–Storms River Mouth.** The lodgings here are pretty basic, but they are clean and comfortable, and the setting, almost within soaking distance of the pounding surf, is spectacular. Log cabins sleep either two or four people; forest huts are the cheapest option and very basic; and "oceanettes" are attractive seaside apartments with fully outfitted kitchens. ⊠ Off N2 ☎ 042/281–1607 or 012/428–9111 ⊕ www.SANParks.org ⚐ Restaurant, beach, dive shop, snorkeling, boating, fishing, shop, laundry facilities; no a/c, no room phones, no room TVs ⊟ AE, DC, MC, V.

Sports & the Outdoors

BOATING   **Storms River Adventures** (⊠ Storms River Mouth ☎ 042/281–1836 ⊕ www.stormsriver.com) offers boat trips on the *Spirit of Tsitsikamma* (R35), the easiest way to see the impressive gorge. The outfit also operates a dive facility in the park.

BUNGEE JUMPING   If you do only one bungee jump in your life, do it from the Bloukrans
★   River Bridge with **Face Adrenalin** (⊠ N2 ☎ 042/281–1458 ⊕ www. faceadrenalin.com). At 700 feet, it's the highest commercial bungee jump in the world. The span is the third-highest bridge in the world and the highest in the Southern Hemisphere. The jump costs R580, and the video to show your friends back home is an extra R80. If you want to

see what it's all about but have no intention of flinging yourself off the bridge, you can do a walking tour for R50, but even that's not for the faint of heart, as it is pretty high, exposed, and scary. The flying fox—a cable on which you slide under the bridge and above the bridge arch to the jump-off spot—is destined to be another thrill; the combo of fox and jump costs R680.

CANOPY TOUR
Fodor'sChoice
★

Want a loerie's-eye view of the treetops? **Storms River Adventures** (✉ Main Rd. ☎ 042/281–1836 ⊕ www.stormsriver.com) will take you deep into the forest, where you don a harness, climb up to a platform, clip in, and "fly" on long cables from platform to platform. You can even control your speed. The cost is R395.

HIKING

In addition to its more famous multiday hikes, the national park has numerous short, easy-to-follow walks. There are enough trails at Storms River Mouth to keep you amused for a couple of days, walking through the forest or along the coast.

Fodor'sChoice
★

The **Dolphin Trail** (☎ 042/280–3699 ⊕ www.dolphintrail.co.za) is the perfect marriage between exercise and relaxation, rugged scenery and comfort. Starting at Storms River Mouth, the trail continues east along the coast, with scenery similar to the Otter Trail's. Though the Dolphin is quite hard going, it covers just 20 km (12 mi) over two days, and the best part is that you carry only a day pack (your luggage is transported by vehicle to the next spot). Accommodations are in very comfortable cabins with private baths, and the food is great. It costs R2,500 per person, which includes a guide, all meals, transportation, and three nights' accommodation.

★

The most popular of South Africa's hiking trails, the **Otter Trail** (☎ 012/428–9111 ⊕ www.SANParks.org) runs along the coast from the mouth of Storms River to Nature's Valley, passing rocky cliffs, beaches, fynbos, rivers, and towering indigenous forest. The trail is only 42 km (25 mi) long, but there are a lot of steep uphills and downhills. It's billed as a five-day hike to give you time to swim and hang out. Accommodations are in overnight huts equipped with sleeping bunks, *braais* (barbecues), and chemical toilets. You must carry in all food and carry out all trash. Only 12 people are allowed on the trail per day, making it vital to book at least a year in advance. However, because people sometimes book all 12 slots and then arrive with only four or five others, there are often cancellations. If you really want to hike this trail but don't get a reservation, you can try hanging around for a few days to see if a spot opens up. The trail costs R450 per person.

The **Tsitsikamma Trail** (☎ 044/874–4363 ⊕ www.mtoecotourism.co.za) runs in the opposite direction from the Otter Trail, through the fynbos-clad mountains. It can be quite strenuous, as the distances between huts are longer than on the Otter, and there is very little shade in some places. It's a great hike, though, and energetic hikers may want to do both hikes back to back. The full trail takes six days and five nights, but you can choose to do a shorter version. The trail costs R54 per person per day.

MOUNTAIN
BIKING
The **Storms River Mountain Bike Trail** is a scenic, circular 22-km (13-mi) trail administered by the Department of Water Affairs and Forestry. It's free, and you don't need a reservation. Just go to the starting point, near the police station at Storms River, and fill out a form in a box at the gate to issue yourself a permit. Bikes can be rented (R90 for three hours) from **Storms River Adventures** (⊠ Main Rd. ☎ 042/281–1836 ⊕ www.stormsriver.com), which also will also provide a guide for R150.

TUBING
Fodor'sChoice
★
That ubiquitous adventure outfit, **Storms River Adventures** (⊠ Main Rd. ☎ 042/281–1836 ⊕ www.stormsriver.com) lets you flip and flop your way down the Storms River on a specially designed tube. The scenery is impressive: 300-foot-high cliffs tower overhead as you negotiate narrow canyons in deep, black water. The all-day trip costs R345, including lunch, snacks, and transportation.

LITTLE KAROO

The landscape of the Little Karoo—austere, minimal, and dry—stands in stark contrast to the Garden Route. In summer it resembles a blast furnace, whereas winter nights are bitterly cold. In its own way, however, it is absolutely beautiful. The Little Karoo, also called the Klein Karoo (*klein* is Afrikaans for "small"), should not be confused with the Great Karoo, a vast semidesert scrub on the other side of the Swartberg Mountains. The word *karoo* derives from the San (Bushman) word for "thirst."

Sanbona Wildlife Reserve

⑪ *27 km (17 mi) west of Barrydale.*

Fodor'sChoice
★
The Sanbona Wildlife Reserve was the first big-five reserve in the Western Cape. Considering that the Karoo is technically semidesert, it's amazing how many absolutely beautiful plants there are here. Game drives concentrate on mammals and birds, but it's impossible to drive past the magnificent flowering shrubs without at least stopping for a better look. In addition to the usual big game you can see springbok, bontebok, and other animals you won't see in Mpumalanga or farther north. Rugged gorges alternate with gently rolling plains to create an ever-changing vista. One of the more interesting options is to see the reserve on horseback, ranging from a half-day jaunt to a four-day adventure. Another big plus is that the reserve is entirely malaria-free.

Where to Stay

$$$$ ⌂ **Khanni Lodge.** Khanni Lodge is the lighter side of Sanbona. Well-appointed rooms with light-wood finishes flow into luxurious bathrooms with double-sided tubs, indoor and outdoor showers, and double vanities. A central Zen-like water feature mitigates the heat of the Karoo, and you can watch animals at the water hole from the infinity pool or shaded veranda. All rooms have private balconies that look out onto the reserve. Room layout—including interior connecting doors between rooms—is particularly family-friendly. ⊠ *Box 149, Montagu 6720* ☎ *028/572–1077* 🖶 *028/572–1810* ⊕ *www.sanbona.com* ⇔ *4 rooms*

⚘ *Dining room, room service, in-room safes, minibars, cable TV, salt-water pool, hiking, horseback riding, babysitting, children's programs, laundry service, Internet, business services, no smoking* ▤ *AE, DC, MC, V* ⦿ *FAP.*

$$$$ ▦ **Tilney Manor.** Accommodations here are spread out around an attractive lawn and garden and face the open Karoo. The spacious guest rooms are classically decorated with dark-wood finishes and neutral upholstery. Enormous bathrooms feature indoor and outdoor showers as well as freestanding, double-sided tubs. The public rooms are in an old manor house built in 1894 for a former district magistrate. Children under six are not permitted on game drives. ✉ *Box 149, Montagu 6720* ☎ *028/ 572–1365* 🖷 *028/572–1361* ⊕ *www.sanbona.com* ⤢ *6 rooms* ⚘ *Dining room, room service, in-room safes, minibars, cable TV, saltwater pool, spa, hiking, horseback riding, shop, babysitting, children's programs, laundry service, Internet, business services, meeting room, airport shuttle, airstrip; no smoking* ▤ *AE, DC, MC, V* ⦿ *FAP.*

> **need a break?**
>
> If you're heading down the R62 toward Oudtshoorn and you get a little peckish, stop at **Rose of the Karoo on Route 62** (✉ 21 Voortrekker St., Calitzdorp ☎ 044/213–3133). Options range from a light sandwich to a lamb- or ostrich-based Karoo specialty, and breakfast and tea are served here, too. And it's one of the few places in town where you can get really good coffee. Out back is a lovely vine-covered patio with a couple of gift shops, and a small deli section sells home-baked goods and local preserves. An added bonus in summer: it's air-conditioned.

Oudtshoorn

⑫ *201 km (125 mi) east of Sanbona Wildlife Reserve, 85 km (51 mi) north of Mossel Bay.*

Oudtshoorn has been famous for its ostriches since around 1870, when farmers began raising them to satisfy the European demand for feathers to adorn women's hats and dresses. In the years leading up to World War I, ostrich feathers were almost worth their weight in gold, and Oudtshoorn experienced an incredible boom. Many of the beautiful sandstone buildings in town date from that period, as do the "feather palaces," huge homes built by prosperous feather merchants and buyers. Although feathers are no longer a major fashion item, these huge birds are now bred for their tough and distinctive leather and almost completely fat- and cholesterol-free red meat. Almost as much of a moneymaker, though, is the tourist potential of these weird and wonderful birds. In addition to visiting an ostrich farm, you can buy ostrich products ranging from the sublime—feather boas—to the ridiculous—taxidermic baby ostriches emerging from cracked eggs. Several farms compete for the tourist buck, offering almost identical tours and a chance to eat an ostrich-based meal. Be warned—these can be real tourist traps: glitzy, superficial, and filled with horrendous crowds. As well as watching local "jockeys" racing on ostriches, you'll be offered the opportunity to ride one. Accept if you like, but this is pretty cruel; although the birds are incredibly strong, their legs are very thin, and many birds suffer broken legs when ridden. If this concerns you, visit instead the Cape Town ostrich farms, which do not allow this practice.

The **C. P. Nel Museum** focuses on the ostrich and Oudtshoorn's boom period at the beginning of the 20th century. The section on fashions of the feather-boom period are by far the most picturesque. The display that depicts the contribution of Lithuanian Jews to the economic development of Oudtshoorn and the feather industry contains a reconstruction of the town's first synagogue. ⊠ *Baron van Reede St.* ☎ *044/272-7306* ⊕ *www.cpnelmuseum.co.za* ⊠ *R10* ⊙ *Mon.–Sat. 8–5.*

The most interesting remnants of the glory of the boom period are the magnificent feather palaces built by successful farmers. Most are private homes, but you can visit the sandstone **Le Roux's Town House,** built in 1909 and furnished in period style, to see just how good they had it in those heady days. ⊠ *High and Loop Sts.* ☎ *044/272–3676* ⊠ *Free with ticket to Nel Museum* ⊙ *Weekdays 9–4.*

Ⓒ The name **Cango Wildlife Ranch** is a bit misleading, as this is really just a glorified zoo, crocodile farm, and cheetah-breeding center. As well as the crocodiles and cheetahs, you may see pumas, jaguars, and lions in large pens. A snake park, pygmy hippos, and a small museum are also here. For an extra R60 you can cuddle a cheetah, and you can "adopt" one for a minimum donation of R150. ⊠ *Caves Rd.* ☎ *044/272-5593* ⊕ *www.cango.co.za* ⊠ *R46* ⊙ *Daily 8–5.*

Ⓒ **Cango Ostrich Farm** is probably the least commercialized of the ostrich show farms. Guides take you through every step in the production of feathers, leather, and meat, and explain the bird's extraordinary social and physical characteristics. It's conveniently located, en route to the Cango Caves from town, for those exploring the area by car. ⊠ *R32, 14 km (9 mi) from Oudtshoorn* ☎ *044/272–4623* ⊕ *www.cangoostrich. co.za* ⊠ *R35* ⊙ *Daily 9–4:15.*

★ ⓭ Between Oudtshoorn and Prince Albert, the huge and stunningly beautiful **Cango Caves** are deservedly one of the most popular attractions in the area. Discovered in 1780 by Jacobus van Zyl, who was grazing his cattle in the area, the caves were opened to the public in 1964. Only a small fraction of the caves, which stretch for several miles through the mountains, is open, and the passage of countless people has turned the cave formations from milky white to red and brown because of a buildup of iron oxide and acid damage from human breath. You can choose between two tours: the hour-long standard tour and the aptly named adventure tour. Think long and hard before opting for the latter if you're overweight, very tall, claustrophobic, or have knee or heart problems. It's exhilarating, but the temperature and humidity are high, there's not much oxygen, and you'll be shimmying up narrow chimneys on your belly, wriggling your way through tiny tunnels, and sliding on your bottom. Wear old clothes and shoes with a good tread. Standard tours leave on the hour, adventure tours on the half hour. ⊠ *Off R328, 32 km (20 mi) from Oudtshoorn* ☎ *044/272-7410* ⊕ *www.cangocaves.co.za* ⊠ *Std. tour R40, adventure tour R55* ⊙ *Daily 9–4.*

BACK & FORTH

PART OF THE BEAUTY of the Garden Route and Little Karoo is found in the spectacular passes that connect the two, and in those between the Little and Great Karoo. Be sure to see at least one.

Between Oudtshoorn and George, choose between the Outeniqua Pass, via the paved N12, and the more historic Montagu Pass, off the N9 (after it diverges from the N12) on a narrow gravel road built in 1843 by Henry Fancourt White. The latter offers excellent views, picnic sites, and examples of Victorian road building, including a five-span arch bridge, railway viaduct, and expertly laid dry-stone embankments. An old tollhouse still sits at the bottom of the pass.

For a great loop between the Great and Little Karoo, drive counterclockwise from Oudtshoorn through De Rust and the spectacularly scenic Meiringspoort. The road runs along the bottom of a deep gorge, crossing the pretty Meirings River 25 times as it cuts through red cliffs. Halfway through the pass is a rest area, where a path leads to a 200-foot waterfall. Head west on the R407 to Prince Albert; then head south through the Swartberg Pass on the R328 back to Oudtshoorn. (The views are more dramatic from this direction.) The road through this pass was built between 1881 and 1886 by the legendary engineer Sir Thomas Bain. At times the road barely clings to the mountainside, held only by Bain's stone retaining walls. From the top, at 5,230 feet, you can look out toward the hot plains of the Great Karoo and the distant mountains of the Nuweveldberg or down at the huge gorge and sheer walls of deep-red rock.

---

need a break?

At the turnoff to the Cango Caves, **Wilgewandel Coffee Shop and Country Farmstall** (⊠ R328, 2 km [1 mi] from the caves ☎ 044/272–0878) serves well-cooked simple food such as hamburgers, toasted sandwiches, ostrich steaks, and a variety of sweet treats. The lemon meringue pie is naughty but nice. Shady outdoor tables overlook a big lawn and duck-filled pond, and camel and pony rides are offered for children.

Where to Stay & Eat

★ ¢–$$ ✕ **Kalinka Café.** Set in a lovely old stone house with a small but tranquil garden, this is a great place for a substantial meal, a light lunch, or just something to snack on at teatime. Try the Georgian chicken, done in a spicy walnut coriander sauce served with flat bread, or a pancake filled with salmon trout caviar and sour cream. Of course there has to be an ostrich meal; try the fillet baked with cheese and onions and served with roasted veggies and hash browns. Fabulous pastries are great for afternoon tea. ⊠ 93 Baron von Reede St. ☎ 044/279–2596 ☰ MC, V ☻ No lunch Mon.

¢–$ ✕ **Jemima's Restaurant.** Named after the mythical guardian angel of love, good taste, and good cooking, this restaurant would not disappoint its muse. All the ingredients are sourced locally from farmers in

Fodor'sChoice
★

the district, and the menu focuses on such local delicacies as olives, Karoo mutton, and, of course, ostrich. Meat lovers often opt for the Three Tenors—medallions of beef and ostrich and springbok fillet. Herbivores love the mushroom risotto. There is an extensive list of local wines. ⊠ *94 Baron von Reede St.* ☎ *044/272–0808* ⩟ *Reservations essential* ☰ *AE, DC, MC, V* ☾ *Closed Sun. No lunch Mon.*

$ ⌘ **Hlangana Lodge.** Conveniently situated on the edge of town on the road out to the caves, this great option strikes a nice balance between slick and stylish and warm and friendly. Superior rooms have baths and showers, whereas standard rooms have showers only. Though only breakfast is served on the premises, you can arrange for a plan that includes a shuttle to dinner at Jemima's, just down the road. In case you're wondering, it's pronounced *Shlung*-gahna. ⊠ *Baron von Reede and North Sts., 6625* ☎ *044/272–2299* ☎ *044/279–1279* ⊕ *www.hlangana.co.za* ⇲ *18 rooms, 1 suite* ⌂ *In-room data ports, in-room safes, minibars, cable TV, saltwater pool, gym, bar, shop, babysitting, airport shuttle, free parking, no-smoking rooms* ☰ *AE, DC, MC, V* �|◌| *BP.*

★ **$** ⌘ **La Plume Guest House.** This stylish guesthouse is situated on a working ostrich farm on the Calitzdorp side of Oudtshoorn. The rooms are all individually decorated with beautiful antiques, and some of the bathrooms feature Victorian claw-foot tubs. Guests meet for predinner drinks in the elegant lounge or on the veranda overlooking the valley. If you're keen on seeing what ostrich farming is all about, you can do an informal and informative tour with the owner of the farm—so much better than all the hype you'd get at the show farms. The turnoff to the farm is 7 km (4 mi) west of Oudtshoorn and is well marked from the R62. ⊠ *Volmoed, 14 km (9 mi) west of Oudtshoorn, Box 1202, 6620* ☎ *044/272–7516 or 082/ 820–4373* ☎ *044/272–3892* ⊕ *www.laplume.co.za* ⇲ *6 rooms, 1 suite, 1 2-bedroom cottage* ⌂ *Dining room, fans, in-room safes, minibars, saltwater pool, mountain bikes, hiking, shop, babysitting, laundry service, Internet, business services; no smoking* ☰ *AE, DC, MC, V* |◌| *BP.*

¢–$ ⌘ **Kleinplaas.** The name means "small farm," and although it isn't really a farm, there are sheep, goats, ostriches, ducks, and other animals in small pens, where children can pet or feed them. Comfortable, well-appointed cottages with fully equipped cooking facilities are neatly arranged in a huge shady lawn area. There's also a pretty campsite with laundromat. Prices are per chalet for a maximum of four or six people (depending on the chalet). Extra people can be accommodated on sleeper-sofas. ⊠ *171 Baron von Reede St., 6620* ☎ *044/272–5811* ☎ *044/279–2019* ⊕ *www.kleinplaas.co.za* ⇲ *54 chalets* ⌂ *Fans, pool, babysitting, playground, laundry facilities; no a/c in some rooms, no room phones, no smoking* ☰ *AE, DC, MC, V* |◌| *EP.*

Sports & the Outdoors

★ **Horse Trek Africa** (☎ 044/272–4509 or 082/552–1391 ⊕ www. horsetrekafrica.co.za) offers a number of day trips in the fantastic riding country surrounding Oudtshoorn. Guests generally camp or stay in a convenient guesthouse and take day rides from a central point. Trail rides can be tailored to suit and usually cost between R300 and R650 per day. Half-day rides are available on request.

Shopping

Oudtshoorn has loads of stores selling ostrich products, but it pays to shop around, as prices vary significantly. The smartest shops have a great variety but are a tad pricey. **Lugro Ostrich** (☎ 044/272–7012 or 082/788–7916) is a small factory on a farm 10 km (6 mi) south of Oudtshoorn (8 km [5 mi] off the R62). Here you'll find great handbags and wallets as well as a few feather products. The retractable, ostrich-leather-clad computer duster is a great buy and looks fabulous on a desk. The **Klein Karoo Co-op** (☎ 044/203–5155 ⊕ www.kleinkaroofeathers.com), which coordinates the marketing of ostrich products, has a boutique on its premises near the airport, on the western side of town. (This is really just an airfield, but it's called the airport.) Here you will find bags, feather boas, shoes, and other smaller items.

De Rust

⑭ *40 km (25 mi) northeast of Oudtshoorn.*

De Rust is a sleepy little Karoo village. The main road is lined with a number of crafts shops, coffee shops, restaurants, and wineshops.

★ While in the area, pop in to **Domein Doornkraal** for a wine tasting. The winery features a superb range of fortified wines and a fantastic, inexpensive chardonnay–chenin blanc blend, but the red wines are what it's really all about—particularly the cabernet sauvignon, which you sometimes have to fight for. You may be lucky and find a few jars of homemade olives, but the small stock usually sells out pretty quickly. ⊠ *N12, about 15 km (10 mi) southwest of de Rust* ☎ *044/251–6715* �ऀ *Free* ☉ *Weekdays 9–5, Sat. 8–1, later in Dec.*

Mons Ruber Estate is named after the Red Hills, which dominate the landscape and whose soil creates the perfect environment for growing grapes with a high sugar content. So it's not surprising that this winery specializes in dessert wines as well as a fine brandy. There is a lovely restored 19th-century kitchen, and an easy hiking trail stretches 1½ hours into the fascinating Red Hills. ⊠ *N12, about 15 km [10 mi] southwest of De Rust* ☎ *044/251–6550* 🗀 *Free* ☉ *Weekdays 8:30–5, Sat. 9–1.*

Where to Stay

★ $$ 🏠 **Oulap Country House.** Oulap is an eclectic mix of textures and colors, winding staircases and little book-filled nooks, antiques and impressive contemporary South African art. Guest rooms are individually decorated with original artworks, and the owners grow their own olives and fruit, which they preserve. But the show is stolen by the almost unbelievable star-studded Karoo sky; you haven't seen stars until you've spent a night in the Karoo. Four-course farmhouse suppers—Karoo lamb, hearty soups, and regional produce—are wonderful, and conversation around the huge dining table, which often carries on until late in the evening, is possibly even better. ⌂ *Box 77, 6650* ☎ *044/241–2250* 🖷 *044/241–2298* ⊕ *www.classicafrica.com/portfolio/oulap.htm* ⇨ *5 rooms* ⌂ *Dining room, pool, bar, babysitting, laundry service, Internet, airport shuttle, some pets allowed; no a/c, no room TVs, no smoking* ⊟ *AE, DC, MC, V* ⧀ *MAP.*

GARDEN ROUTE & LITTLE KAROO A TO Z

AIR TRAVEL

Two airports serve the Garden Route: Plettenberg Bay Airport, 6 km (4 mi) west of town, and George Airport, 10 km (6 mi) southwest of town, which also serves the Little Karoo. George is well served by South African Airways (SAA), Kulula.com, and Nationwide. Service between Plett and Johannesburg—one flight a day on SA Airlink—comes and goes.

🛪 **Airports George Airport (GRJ))** ☎ 044/876-9310 ⊕ www.acsa.co.za. **Plettenberg Bay Airport (PBZ)** ☎ 044/533-9026 ⊕ www.acsa.co.za.

🛪 **Airlines Kulula.com** ⊕ www.kulula.com. **Nationwide Airlines** ☎ 0861/737-737 ⊕ www.flynationwide.co.za. **SA Airlink** ☎ 044/533-9041 ⊕ www.saairlink.co.za. **South African Airways** ☎ 0861/359-722 or 011/978-5313 ⊕ www.flysaa.com.

BUS TRAVEL

The Intercape Mainliner offers regular service between Cape Town and Port Elizabeth, stopping at all major Garden Route destinations on the N2. Translux has a similar route, traveling on secondary roads from Cape Town to Mossel Bay; from there it stays on the N2. Neither of these services accesses out-of-the-way places like Barrydale, Oudtshoorn, Storms River, and Nature's Valley, however. For them you need the Baz Bus, which does go to Nature's Valley and Storms River and meets a shuttle in George that will get you to Oudtshoorn. The bus stops at all backpacker hostels along the Garden Route, so you don't have to arrange transportation from a bus station.

🚌 **Bus Lines Baz Bus** ☎ 021/439-2323 ⊕ www.bazbus.com. **Intercape Mainliner** ☎ 021/380-4400 ⊕ www.intercape.co.za. **Translux** ☎ 0861/589-282 ⊕ www.translux.co.za.

CAR TRAVEL

Mossel Bay, at the western end of the Garden Route, lies 384 km (240 mi) from Cape Town along the N2 highway. The road is in fantastic condition and well signposted. It usually takes about four hours from Cape Town to Mossel Bay—unless you stop to look at a view, have lunch, or browse in a roadside produce or crafts store. A few words of warning, however: there is a wide shoulder almost all the way, but pull onto it only when you can see a good few hundred yards ahead. The area between George and Wilderness is notorious for speed traps, especially in the Kaaimans River Pass, just west of Wilderness. And the fuel complex at the Storms River Bridge is your last eastbound chance to fill up before Port Elizabeth—more than 100 miles away.

An alternative to the N2 is the less traveled—some say more interesting—inland route, dubbed Route 62, even though some of it is on the R60. From Worcester, in the Breede River Valley (*see* Chapter 2), traveling on the R60 and R62 to Oudtshoorn provides a great view of the Little Karoo.

Avis, Budget, Europcar, and Hertz all have car-rental offices at George Airport. Budget also has an office in Plettenberg Bay. Europcar rentals include a cell phone.

🚗 **Rental Companies Avis** ✉ George Airport ☎ 044/876-9314 ⊕ www.avis.co.za ✉ Knysna ☎ 044/382-2222 ✉ Oudtshoorn ☎ 044/272-4727. **Budget** ✉ George

Airport 🕾 044/876-9204 ⊕ www.budget.co.za ✉ 9 Hill House, Main St., Plettenberg Bay 🕾 044/533-1858. **Europcar** ✉ George Airport 🕾 044/876-9070 ⊕ www.europcar. co.za ✉ Plett Airport 🕾 044/533-9006. **Hertz** ✉ George Airport 🕾 044/801-4700 ⊕ www.hertz.co.za.

EMERGENCIES

Most towns have late-night pharmacies, and if they don't, pharmacies usually have an emergency number on the door.

🖪 **Emergency Services Ambulance** 🕾 10177. **Police** 🕾 10111 from landline or 112 from mobile phone.

🖪 **Hospitals Knysna Private Hospital** ✉ Hunters Estate Dr., Knysna 🕾 044/384-1083. **Lamprecht Mediclinic** ✉ York St. and Gloucester Rd., George 🕾 044/803-2000. **Medsac Private Hospital** ✉ Marine Dr., Plettenberg Bay 🕾 044/533-0212.

🖪 **Late-Night Pharmacies Central Pharmacy** ✉ 19 Main St., Knysna 🕾 044/382-5222. **Link Pharmacy** ✉ Lamprecht Centre, York St. and Gloucester Rd., George 🕾 044/873-5752.

MAIL & INTERNET

Each town's main post office usually stays open from about 9 to 4:30 on weekdays and on Saturday mornings. There are Internet cafés all over, and most lodgings offer Internet access to their guests. Most bigger towns also have Postnets, a franchise that offers business, mail, and courier services.

🖪 **Internet Access Adventure Café** ✉ Waterfront Dr. and Gray St., Knysna 🕾 044/382-4959. **Computer Shop** ✉ First National Bank Bldg., Main Rd., Plettenberg Bay 🕾 044/533-6007. **Vsquare Internet Café** ✉ Harryman Sq., York St., George 🕾 044/884-0020.

MONEY MATTERS

There are ATMs all over, except in Nature's Valley and Storms River; the closest ATM to these towns is at the fuel complex at the Storms River Bridge on the N2. Banks are open from about 9 to 3 or 3:30 during the week and on Saturday mornings.

TRAIN TRAVEL

See George, *above,* for information on the Outeniqua Choo-Tjoe train, which runs between George and Knysna. The luxurious Blue Train travels between Port Elizabeth and Cape Town once a month, connecting with a shuttle at George for a day trip to Oudtshoorn.

🖪 **Train Line Blue Train** 🕾 021/449-2672 or 012/334-8459 ⊕ www.bluetrain.co.za.

VISITOR INFORMATION

Most area tourism offices are very helpful. In high season (generally October to April), you may find them open longer than their off-season hours, which are typically weekdays 8 or 8:30 to 5 or 5:30, Saturday 8 or 8:30 to 1 or 1:30. In very quiet periods the staff may close up shop early.

🖪 **Tourist Offices De Rust Tourism Bureau** ✉ 29 Schoeman St., De Rust 🕾 044/241-2109 ⊕ www.derust.org.za. **George Tourism Information** ✉ 124 York St., George 🕾 044/801-9295 ⊕ www.georgetourism.co.za. **Knysna Publicity Association** ✉ 40 Main St., Knysna 🕾 044/382-5510 ⊕ www.visitknysna.com. **Mossel Bay Tourism**

✉ Market Sq., Mossel Bay ☎ 044/691-2202 ⊕ www.visitmosselbay.co.za. **Oudtshoorn Tourism Bureau** ✉ 21 Baron von Reede St., Oudtshoorn ☎ 044/279-2532 ⊕ www. oudtshoorn.com. **Plettenberg Bay Tourism Association** ✉ Shop 35, Melville's Corner, Marine Dr. and Main St., Plettenberg Bay ☎ 044/533-4065 ⊕ www.plettenbergbay. co.za. **Wilderness Eco-tourism Association** ✉ Leila's La., Wilderness ☎ 044/877-0045 ⊕ www.wildernessinfo.co.za.

The Eastern Cape

5

WORD OF MOUTH

"I stayed at Addo Elephant National Park in a 'forest cabin' and it was terrific. No amenities or personnel, but complete freedom and privacy. Tea at dawn on the balcony before getting into the park as soon as it opened—and seeing an elephant close enough to touch within 30 seconds—was the greatest!"

—jenviolin

Updated by
Jennifer Stern

THE EASTERN CAPE IS SOUTH AFRICA'S MOST DIVERSE PROVINCE and has some of its best vacation destinations; yet it is perhaps the most glossed over by overseas visitors. Starting where the Garden Route stops, it includes much of the Great Karoo—a large, semidesert region of ocher plains, purple mountains, dramatic skies, and unusual, hardy vegetation—and abuts KwaZulu-Natal in the northeast and Lesotho's mountain lands in the north. But a glance at a map will reveal the region's main attraction: its coastline, largely undeveloped and running for some 640 km (400 mi) from temperate to subtropical waters.

The climate is mild across the region and throughout the year, with temperatures at the coast ranging between winter lows of 5°C (41°F) and summer highs of 32°C (90°F). It has many of the country's finest and least crowded beaches, African montane forests and heathlands, an ever-increasing number of fantastic malaria-free game reserves, and some of the most interesting cultural attractions in South Africa.

There are a few areas of note. Formerly known as Settler Country, the area that stretches from the outskirts of Port Elizabeth to Port Alfred in the east, Grahamstown in the northeast, and the Zuurberg Mountains in the north is now referred to as Frontier Country. It was here that the early-19th-century immigrants (colloquially called the 1820 Settlers) tried to set up farms, some successfully, some not. Toward the end of the last century, many of the unprofitable farms were bought up and redeveloped as game reserves, thus adding superb game viewing to the already existing cultural attractions. This area encompasses Addo Elephant National Park, Shamwari, Grahamstown, and Kwandwe. Towns are small and interesting, and the surrounding countryside alternates between hilly terrain, steep gorges, and gentle rolling hills.

The Wild Coast is aptly but perhaps a little unfairly named. Sure, it does get some monumental storms, when huge waves crash into the beach and cliffs, but it also has a gentler face. Lovely long beaches stretch as far as the eye can see, with only a few cows and a small herder to break the isolation. Strictly speaking, the Wild Coast originally stretched from the Kei River mouth to Port Edward, which were the borders of the then nominally independent Transkei, but today it has spread almost to the outskirts of East London.

Unfortunately, during the political uncertainty of the 1980s the Wild Coast lost a lot of its allure—more due to the perceived threat of violence than anything else. Hotels went out of business, the overnight huts on the fantastic Wild Coast Hiking Trail fell into disrepair, and the Transkei sank further into economic depression. For many years it was only die-hard locals with strong emotional ties and hordes of backpackers who frequented these still-lovely and little-known places. Today, however, the area is going through a revival. Coastal hotels are being renovated one by one, and community projects are being put in place to ensure that the tourist dollar goes where it is intended. In addition to long, lovely beaches, the Wild Coast has crystal-clear turquoise lagoons, some of which can be paddled for miles. The area is still virtually unspoiled, and the people who live here are mostly subsistence farmers and fishermen. It's not uncommon for a family who can't afford a loaf of bread to dine on oysters and lobster. It's just another of the Eastern Cape's contrasts and seeming contradictions.

Exploring the Eastern Cape

The Eastern Cape is a big space with many tiny gems. The towns, and even the cities, of the province are relatively small, often quaint, and the distances between them are fairly large. Since the only airports are in Port Elizabeth, East London, and Umtata, the best way to experience the region is on a driving tour, leaving yourself plenty of time to explore.

About the Restaurants

Generally speaking, the restaurants of the Eastern Cape are good but not great. Of course there are always a few serendipitous exceptions to every rule, but for really good food, choose a great guesthouse—some of which are noted for their cuisine. Not surprisingly, most restaurants are reasonably casual, and there are none where you would be expected to wear a tie.

WHAT IT COSTS In South African rand					
	$$$$	**$$$**	**$$**	**$**	**¢**
RESTAURANTS	over 125	100–125	75–100	50–75	under 50

Prices are per person for a main course at dinner, a main course equivalent, or a prix-fixe meal.

About the Hotels

Most hotels along the coast get pretty booked up over summer vacation (December–January), and the Wild Coast hotels are even busy over the winter school vacation, usually around June. Most establishments run winter specials, but there are exceptions. Grahamstown is packed the first week of July; every guesthouse is full, the campsite is bulging, and even school and university dorms rent out rooms—at double the regular price. Hotels on the Wild Coast often offer packages for the sardine run, usually in June or early July, but it's always a bit of a gamble. The sardines are just not as reliable as the artists of the Grahamstown Festival.

The price categories in this chapter are applied differently to full-service safari lodges than they are to other accommodations. This is because safari lodges are typically all-inclusive experiences, with all meals, alcoholic beverages, and activities (like game-viewing) accounted for in the price. The chart below explains the differences in detail.

WHAT IT COSTS In South African rand				
$$$$	**$$$**	**$$**	**$**	**¢**
LODGING				
over 3,000	2,000–3,000	1,000–2,000	500–1,000	under 500
FULL-SERVICE SAFARI LODGING				
over 12,000	8,000–12,000	5,000–8,000	2,000–5,000	under 2,000

Prices are for a standard double room in high season, including 12.5% tax.

Numbers in the text correspond to numbers in the margin and on the Eastern Cape map.

If you have 2 or 3 days Spend your first night in ⊞ **Port Elizabeth ❶**, perhaps taking a cultural history tour the next morning, and then drive to ⊞ **Shamwari Game Reserve ❸**, ⊞ **Kwandwe Private Game Reserve ❺**, or the elephant park at ⊞ **Addo ❷**, where you can stay at Gorah for luxury or the SANParks camp for the value. If your interests are more cultural than wild, spend a day in **Grahamstown ❹** en route to ⊞ **Graaff-Reinet ⓫**, where you can spend two days, taking a short drive to **Nieu-Bethesda ⓬**. Of course, if you really need to relax, you could spend two or three days in Port Elizabeth, soaking up the sun, playing a round of golf, and generally hanging out.

If you have 5 or 6 days Try a Wild Coast Meander (⇨ Tours in Eastern Cape A to Z, *below*)—your days filled with walking this wonderful coastline and each of your five nights spent at a different beach hotel. If you like the beach thing but don't fancy walking a few miles every day, you could spend a day in ⊞ **East London ❻** and then head up to one of the great Wild Coast beach destinations, stopping in at the Nelson Mandela Museum en route.

If you have 7 or more days Depending on whether you'd rather spend time on the Wild Coast or inland, choose one of the following options (both include a visit to a game reserve). Fly into **Port Elizabeth ❶** early in the morning, and immediately make the long but scenic drive to ⊞ **Graaff-Reinet ⓫**, where you stay two nights, visiting museums and **Nieu-Bethesda ⓬**. Then spend two or three nights at ⊞ **Addo ❷**, ⊞ **Shamwari Game Reserve ❸**, or ⊞ **Kwandwe Private Game Reserve ❺**. Give yourself one or two nights in ⊞ **Grahamstown ❹** before driving back to Port Elizabeth, where you can relax for a day before flying out. Alternatively, fly into ⊞ **East London ❻**, and head up the Wild Coast for several days. Take a leisurely drive back to either Kwandwe, Shamwari, or Addo, where you can spend two nights before driving back to Port Elizabeth or East London.

Timing

Although winters are pretty mild, especially farther north along the Wild Coast, summer—from September to April—is the most popular time to visit, especially for sun worshippers. But even winter has its attractions. The sardine run, usually in June or July, is becoming a major draw, and the Grahamstown Festival, in July, draws thousands of cultural pilgrims to this delightful university town.

Port Elizabeth

❶ *770 km (478 mi) east of Cape Town.*

Port Elizabeth, or PE, is probably South Africa's best-kept secret. Along with its almost perfect weather and wonderful beaches—from overdeveloped urban playgrounds to deserted snow-white sands—it has some fascinating cultural attractions, including beautifully preserved historic buildings. Most of these are in the older part of the city, called Central, some parts of which have become a tad unsafe in recent years. So it's not wise to wander around alone taking photos of these lovely old buildings with your expensive camera. Rather take a tour, or pop in the tourism office (also in Central, but a nice part) and ask advice.

PE is also a good base for exploring some other fantastic destinations, both wild and cultural, including Addo Elephant National Park. The suburbs can be a little confusing, however. Humewood and Summerstrand are PE's two main coastal suburbs, with Humewood closer to the city center. The Humewood Golf Course, one of South Africa's best, is in Summerstrand, not Humewood, though.

The **St. Croix Motor Museum** is an absolute must for car buffs. Port Elizabeth has long been the center of the automotive industry in South Africa, and this fun museum is a tribute to the city. Lined up in an aircraft hangar are more than 100 vintage cars, most of which still work and are regularly driven for special occasions. ⊠ *Old Government Garage, Mowbray St., Westview* ☎ *083/463–5286 or 041/392–5362* ☒ *Free* ☉ *Sat. 2–5 or by appointment.*

South End was the most vibrant part of Port Elizabeth until it was flattened by the apartheid-era government to "tidy up" the city and put everything and everyone in their places. At the **South End Museum** a map, photographs, and paintings give you an idea of what the old South End was like in its heyday. ⊠ *Humewood Rd. and Walmer Blvd., Summerstrand* ☎ *041/582–3325* ☒ *Donations welcome* ☉ *Weekdays 9–4, weekends 10–3.*

Where to Stay & Eat

The beachfront is lined with an enormous range of reasonably priced hotels and restaurants, as well as a few more-special ones.

★ **$$–$$$$**   ✕ **Mauro's on the Beachfront.** This justifiably popular eatery (previously Ristorante di Mauro) has moved from the suburbs to the beachfront, so now, in addition to great food, it serves up fabulous views over McArthur Baths and the beach. With constantly changing daily specials, there's always something new to try here. If they're available, order the prawns in a white-wine-and-onion sauce topped with mozzarella and baked, or the grilled sweet-and-sour ostrich steak. Linguine with creamy chicken sauce is one of the more-traditional choices. ⊠ *38 Newton St., Newton Park* ☎ *041/365–1747* ☖ *Reservations essential* ▭ *AE, DC, MC, V* ☉ *Closed Sun. No lunch Sat.*

¢–$$ ✕ **34° South.** Sibling to the fabulous deli-cum-restaurant-cum-fishmonger of the same name in Knysna, this is the most popular restaurant at the well-frequented Boardwalk. The line fish is always fresh, and the best way to try it is as a *kingklip espatada*—skewered chunks of firm, white fish grilled with roasted peppers and onions and drizzled with lemon butter. For an equally fishy experience, fill a huge platter from the seafood meze. Even the snack-type options, like sandwiches, are big

Beaches & Water Sports Whether in, on, or under the water, visitors to the Eastern Cape make good use of all that water to the south. From highly developed urban playgrounds to deserted stretches of wild littoral, there is a beach for every purpose. The coastal cities and towns all have a pretty well-developed beach culture, and tiny seaside resorts form islands of development along the otherwise aptly named Wild Coast.

5

The surfing is great here, with world-class waves at Jeffrey's Bay, some good beginner waves in Port Elizabeth, and numerous "secret" breaks along the Wild Coast—definitely only for the experienced. You can also find a range of guided adventure trips, some of which include surfing or canoeing. The diving is also great, but the only really dependable operators are in Port Elizabeth, mostly due to the fact that the conditions elsewhere are too erratic to support a permanent operation. During the sardine run (usually late June–early July), however, numerous dive operators base themselves on the Wild Coast to take advantage of the hordes of scuba enthusiasts who want to experience this spectacular phenomenon. Port Elizabeth has some excellent whale- and dolphin-watching too.

Cultural Attractions From unsullied Xhosa villages, where women still paint their faces with ocher clay and boys undergo circumcision ceremonies to become men, to colonial mansions, the range and depth of the Eastern Cape's cultural attractions is amazing. It was here that black and white first met face to face on equal terms, with black pastoralists going up against white settlers and the British military. Since the late 17th century, the Eastern Cape has been a frontier and focus of black resistance. It was here that many of the leading lights of the struggle against apartheid were born, nurtured, and educated. It was here, for instance, that Steve Biko came to prominence as the founder-leader of the Black Consciousness Movement. In almost every town you'll find some fascinating museums and art galleries and a good tour operator who can expose you to the history and culture of this heterogenous society. And, as they do everywhere else in Africa, people celebrate the arts here with music and dance. The cultural highlight of South Africa is the annual National Festival of the Arts, which runs for 10 action-packed days every July in Grahamstown and is purported to be second in size only to the festival in Edinburgh, Scotland.

Watching out for Wildlife The Eastern Cape has rich and varied topography and flora. Consequently, it supports a wide range of game, much of which was once hunted to the brink of extinction by farmers and settlers trying in vain to tame this recalcitrant land. The first initiative to reclaim this area for its original inhabitants was Addo Elephant National Park, established in the 1930s to protect the 11 remaining elephants in the area. In the early 1990s Shamwari was carved out of some unprofitable farms. Not only has this ambitious project proved a success, but it has inspired more conservation efforts in the area. Addo Elephant National Park is being expanded to include the sea, offshore islands, and the mountainous Zuurberg, and highly successful CC Africa, which runs many lodges in southern Africa, opened Kwandwe in 2001.

It's important to know what you're going to see here. This is not Kenya, Mpumalanga, or Limpopo. Instead of savannah, most of the terrain is hilly with thick bush, so you won't see vast herds of animals wandering across open plains, and there are some areas that bear visible scars from farming. But the game is here. Shamwari, Addo, and Kwandwe all support the big five. Black rhinos lurk in thick scrub, leopards hide out unseen, and bushbuck wander at ease in the thick undergrowth. In the open areas, herds of elephants wander, white rhinos graze peacefully, and buffalo roam. A huge bonus is the many interesting plants, such as bright orange aloes and countless flowering shrubs. The huge plains of the Karoo make the Eastern Cape reserves more scenically varied than those farther north. And best of all—it's malaria-free.

---

enough to qualify as a meal. ⊠ *Boardwalk, Marine Dr., Summerstrand* ☎ *041/583–1085* ▭ *AE, DC, MC, V.*

★ **$$** ✕⊞ **La Provence Country House.** Rooms look out over lovely gardens, rolling lawns, and horse-filled paddocks on this large property. It's a quiet, restful place to stay, and the garden suites, which were once very roomy stables, are particularly soothing, with monastically understated decor. It's a quick drive to the lovely Sardinia Bay Beach, where you can do a long, leisurely walk of up to 8 km (5 mi). It's worth staying for the delicious three-course dinners ($–$$), as this establishment is a member of Good Cooks and Their Country Houses. The menu changes constantly, and nonguests are accommodated if there is room. Four new rooms were due to debut in mid-2005. ⊠ *Old Seaview Rd., 6011* ☎ *041/368–1911* 🖷 *041/368–1982* ⊕ *www.laprovence.co.za* 🛏 *10 rooms* ⟐ *Restaurant, some fans, in-room data ports, in-room safes, minibars, cable TV, tennis court, pool, massage, Internet, business services, airport shuttle, travel services, free parking; no a/c, no kids under 10, no smoking* ▭ *AE, DC, MC, V* ⟐I *BP.*

★ **$$$$** ⊞ **Hacklewood Hill Country House.** For superbly comfortable and gracious lodgings, try this inn set in English-style gardens in the leafy suburb of Walmer. Rooms are spacious and furnished with beautiful antiques, such as four-poster beds. Some of the rooms are absolutely enormous, with a sofa and huge wardrobe, as are the Victorian baths, with separate shower and marble-top vanity. All rooms have balconies except one. ⊡ *Box 319, 6000* ☎ *041/581–1300* 🖷 *041/581–4155* 🛏 *8 rooms* ⟐ *Restaurant, room service, inroom safes, minibars, cable TV, tennis court, pool, bar, lounge, babysitting, laundry service, Internet, business services, meeting rooms, airport shuttle, free parking; no kids under 12, no smoking* ▭ *AE, DC, MC, V* ⟐I *BP.*

$–$$ ⊞ **Beach Hotel.** This light and airy hotel has fantastic views of the sea and is right next to the Boardwalk and across the road from Hobie Beach. The rooms are comfortable and attractive, but the only really inspiring aspect of the decor is the many prints of impressionist paintings of sea and beach scenes in both the rooms and the corridors. ⊠ *Marine Dr., Humewood* ☎ *041/583–2161* 🖷 *041/583–6220* ⊕ *www.pehotels.co. za/beach* 🛏 *57 rooms, 1 suite* ⟐ *3 restaurants, room service, in-room data ports, in-room safes, minibars, cable TV, saltwater pool, 3 bars,*

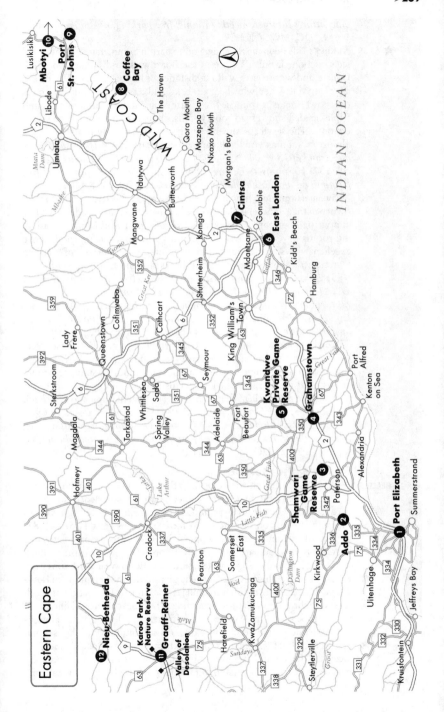

babysitting, Internet, meeting rooms, free parking, no-smoking rooms ⊟ AE, DC, MC, V ⊩⊙⊩ EP.

★ **$–$$** ⊞ **King's Tide Boutique Hotel.** In a quiet part of Summerstrand, this hotel feels cocooned, but it's close to the Boardwalk and Humewood Golf Course and within easy walking distance of Pollock Beach. The rooms are richly furnished with heavy fabrics and dark wood, but it's not as overpowering as it sounds. Most bathrooms have enormous tubs and triple-headed showers in roomy stalls, though four rooms have showers only. The service is super-friendly, so you're likely to feel at home almost as soon as you walk through the door. ✉ 16 10th Ave., Summerstrand 6013 ☎ 041/583–6023 ⊞ 041/583–3910 ⊕ www.kingstide. co.za ⇝ 10 rooms △ Dining room, fans, in-room data ports, bar, free parking; no a/c, no kids under 13 ⊟ AE, DC, MC, V ⊩⊙⊩ BP.

$ ⊞ **Summerstrand Inn.** A great value for the price, this large, comfortable, owner-managed hotel is close to the beach on the quieter side of the bay and virtually on top of the excellent Humewood Golf Course. Sea-facing rooms have lovely bay views, and golf course–facing rooms have excellent views of the fourth and fifth holes plus a glimpse of sea. The Summerstrand does one of the best breakfasts in PE—a huge buffet for R65. ✉ Marine Dr., Summerstrand ☜ Box 204, Port Elizabeth 6000 ☎ 041/583–3131 ⊞ 041/583–2505 ⇝ 175 rooms, 5 suites △ Restaurant, room service, pool, golf privileges, bar, babysitting, playground, laundry service, concierge, Internet, business services, meeting rooms, airport shuttle, free parking, no-smoking rooms ⊟ AE, DC, MC, V.

¢ ⊞ **Calabash Lodge.** This simple, comfortable bed-and-breakfast offers good value for the money. Rooms are clean and comfortable. One triple room (with three single beds) has a private, but not en-suite, bathroom and is ideal for a group of friends. This lodge is run by the same people who lead the excellent Calabash Tours (⇨ Eastern Cape A to Z, below). ✉ 8 Dollery St., Central, 6011 ☎ 041/585-6162 ⊞ 041/585-0985 ⊕ www.calabashlodge.co.za ⇝ 7 rooms △ Lounge, babysitting, airport shuttle, travel services, free parking; no a/c, no room phones, no smoking ⊟ AE, DC, MC, V ⊩⊙⊩ CP.

Sports & the Outdoors

BEACHES Within the bay and starting closest to the city center and harbor (which is best avoided), the first beach you come to is **King's Beach**, so named because King George VI slept in the Royal Train here during a visit to the city. The section of beach near **McArthur Baths** (☎ 041/582–2282) is great for swimming and very popular. If you'd rather swim in flat water, head for the stylish bath complex (R30, open September–April), which has a range of pools—some heated, some not. **Humewood Beach** runs from

★ King's Beach to Shark Rock Pier. The pier marks the beginning of **Hobie Beach**, where sailing catamarans and jet skis launch. The section of beach closest to the pier is great for swimming. These beaches are all lined with restaurants, shops, and coffee bars, and there are flea markets on weekends. Beyond Hobie Beach the seafront is still built up with houses and

★ apartments, but the frenetic commercialism is missing. **Pollock Beach**, adjacent to the suburb of Summerstrand, is one of the better swimming beaches, with a lovely small natural tidal pool. It also offers great surfing. (Generally the surfing in PE is not too challenging, unlike Jeffrey's Bay, just over an hour's drive to the west, which offers some pretty exciting waves.) The far end of Pollock Beach, like the far end of King's, is best avoided, as it can get crowded with somewhat boisterous, picnicking, partying crowds.

★ For a truly fantastic beach experience, very little can beat **Sardinia Bay Beach,** outside the bay and about a 20-minute drive from the main beaches. Here miles and miles of deserted, snow-white sand are great for long walks.

Port Elizabeth is the first South African city to supply off-road wheelchairs for use on the beach (either King's or Humewood). You can swap your regular street-legal chair for a "four-wheel-drive" model—and even get a lifeguard to help you in and out of the water. And, yes, it's free. Book
★ the chairs through **PE Beaches** (☎ 041/586–1040).

GOLF   Consistently listed as one of the country's top 10 courses, the challenging
★ championship **Humewood Golf Course** (✉ Marine Dr., Summerstrand ☎041/583–2137 ⊕ www.humewoodgolf.co.za) is set in undulating dunes on the edge of Algoa Bay, making it one of South Africa's few genuine links courses. The late Bobby Locke considered it the finest in the country and compared it favorably to the best of British links courses. At 6,800 yards (club 6,490 yards) and exposed to stiff sea breezes, it's not for the fainthearted. Greens fees are R310, cart fees R140, caddies R70, and club rental R150.

WHALE- &   **Ocean Safaris** (☎ 072/490–7842 ⊕ www.oceansafaris.co.za) offers boat-
DOLPHIN-   based whale- and dolphin-watching trips, on which you are likely to see
WATCHING   southern right whales and humpback whales in season, bottlenose dolphins, humpack dolphins, Bryde's whales, and a number of seabirds, including breeding colonies of roseate terns and African penguins. This operator holds a permit to approach within 165 feet of a whale, whereas all other boats must stay nearly 1,000 feet away. A 2½-hour "close encounter" cruise costs R360 per person, but other options are also available.

Nightlife

If you're looking for bright lights and sophisticated nightlife, PE is not the city for you—in fact, you should not be in the Eastern Cape. There is some good homegrown music, but the only way you'll find out where to catch it is to watch the papers. There are a couple of bars on Brooks Hill, opposite King's Beach, that rise and fall in popularity, but most nighttime places are filled with dazed and confused teenagers. For a really interesting night out you could do a *shebeen* (township bar) tour with Calabash Tours (⇨ Eastern Cape A to Z, *below*). If you like gambling, you could try the **Boardwalk Casino** (✉ Marine Dr., Private Bag 777, Humewood ☎ 041/507–7777), which also has a collection of shops, restaurants, and coffee bars as well as a five-screen cinema, adventure golf, and fun rides. It's an attractive space with a view of the sea and a winding artificial lake that's home to a sizeable population of ducks.

Addo

❷ *72 km (45 mi) north of Port Elizabeth.*

★ Undoubtedly, the greatest attraction in this area is **Addo Elephant National Park.** At present the park is about 300,000 acres, but it's expanding all the time. Current population figures are estimated at 374 elephants, 378 buffalo, 15 black rhino, hundreds of kudu and other antelopes, and six totally free-ranging lions, which were introduced quite recently. You can explore the park in your own vehicle or take a night or day game drive with a park ranger in an open vehicle from the main camp. A more adventurous option is to ride a horse among the elephants. Less-experienced riders may ride along the fence line. Warning: No citrus fruit may be brought into the park, as elephants find it irresistible and can smell it for miles. ☎ *042/233–0556* 🖷 *042/233–0196* ⊕ *www.addoelephantpark.com* 🖃 *R80* ☉ *Daily 7–7 (may vary with seasons).*

★ ☮ **Addo Elephant Back Safaris** offers you the opportunity to get really up close and personal to a small group of trained Africa elephants as you walk through the bush with them. You can touch them, feed them, and watch them as they bathe themselves with sand, water, or both (i.e., mud). Despite the name, riding is done only by very special request. You can also arrange for a fly-in day trip from Plett (⇨ Chapter 4). ☎ *042/235–1400 or 083/375–6514* ⊕ *www.addoelephantbacksafaris.co.za* 🖃 *R700 half day* ☉ *Visits by appointment.*

Where to Stay

★ **$$** 🏨 **Gorah Elephant Camp.** A private concession within Addo, this lodge centers on an old farmhouse, which has been restored and filled with antiques. Roaring log fires warm chilly winter nights, and the wide veranda offers cool shade in the heat of the day. The lodge overlooks a water hole where a variety of animals come to drink, the stars of which are the elephants. Accommodations are in huge tents with private baths, shaded under thick thatch. Mosquito nets are more for effect than necessity, as this is a malaria-free area. Be warned that, although this is a luxury lodge, there is no electricity, so you won't find hair dryers in the rooms. Meals are taken alfresco on the veranda or in the dining room. Cuisine and service are equal to the best in Africa. The lodge operates three game drives per day and/or escorted walks. ⊠ *Addo Elephant National Park* ✉ *Box 454, Plettenberg Bay 6600* ☎ *044/532–7818 reservations* 🖷 *044/532–7878* ⊕ *www.gorah.com* ➩ *11 tents* ⚘ *Dining room, in-room safes, pool, bar, lounge, laundry service, Internet, business services, airport shuttle, airstrip, no-smoking rooms; no a/c, no room TVs, no kids under 10* ☰ *AE, DC, MC, V* ❮⦿❯ *FAP.*

★ **$$** 🏨 **Hitgeheim Country Lodge.** This lovely lodge is set on a steep cliff overlooking the Sundays River and the town of Addo. Classically decorated rooms, graced with lovely antiques, are in separate thatch buildings, all with verandas overlooking the river. The bathrooms are spacious and luxuriously appointed with large tubs and enormous shower stalls. Some rooms have indoor and outdoor showers. Birds frolic in the natural vegetation that has been allowed to grow up to the edge of the verandas, and tame buck often wander around the garden. Hitgeheim (pronounced *hitch*-ee-hime) is a working ostrich, citrus, and game farm. Though it's been open a relatively short time, the lodge has already acquired a deserved reputation for fantastic food. ⌂ *Box 95, Sunland 6115* ☎ *042/234-0778* 🖷 *042/234-0787* ⊕ *www.hitgeheim-addo.co.za* ⤳ *5 rooms* ⚏ *Dining room, minibars, saltwater pool, hiking, lounge, laundry service, Internet, business services, meeting room, airport shuttle, airstrip, helipad, no-smoking rooms; no a/c, no room phones, no room TVs, no kids under 12* 🖃 *AE, DC, MC, V* ⦾ *BP.*

¢ 🖾 **Addo Elephant National Park Rest Camp.** This typical SANParks rest camp has comfortable self-catering (with cooking facilities) chalets and a shop that sells basic supplies as well as souvenirs. An à la carte restaurant is open for all meals, and a floodlighted water hole is nearby. Prices are calculated according to a complicated SANParks formula, which works out to anything from R120 to R165 per person sharing. Camping ranges from R30 to R50 per person. ✉ *Addo Elephant National Park* ⌂ *Box 787, Pretoria 0001* ☎ *042/233-0556* 🖷 *042/233-0196* ⊕ *www.addoelephantpark.com* ⤳ *53 chalets, 5 tents, 20 campsites* ⚏ *Restaurant, pool, shop; no a/c in some rooms, no room TVs* 🖃 *AE, DC, MC, V.*

Shamwari Game Reserve

❸ *72 km (45 mi) northeast of Port Elizabeth, 70 km (44 mi) west of Grahamstown.*

Shamwari is, in every sense of the word, a conservation triumph. Unusable land has been turned into a successful tourist attraction, wild animals have been reintroduced, and alien vegetation has been, and is still being, eradicated. The reserve is constantly being expanded and now stands at about 54,400 acres. Its mandate is to conserve not only the big impressive animals, but also small things: the plants, buildings, history, and culture of the area. Shamwari has been awarded the Global Nature Fund Award for Best Conservation Practice, and wildlife manager Dr. Johan Joubert was voted one of South Africa's top 10 conservationists by the Endangered Wildlife Trust.

★ About 7,400 acres have been set aside as **Wilderness Area,** where only self-supported walking safaris are allowed. You carry all your own stuff, including food and sleeping bags, which are supplied, and head off into the wilds in the company of a ranger to sleep under the stars. The first and last night are spent at the Wilderness Base Camp, which, though pretty rustic, has four rooms with en-suite bathrooms with showers. The four-night package runs Monday to Friday and costs R2,600 per person, all-inclusive.

☾ Part of the reserve has been set aside as the **Born Free Centre,** where African animals rescued from around the world are allowed to roam in reasonably large enclosures until they can be rehabilitated. If they can't be rehabilitated, they either stay and form part of the educational program or are moved to another protected environment. At the cultural center, called **Khayalendaba,** you can get a glimpse of African life through dancing, oral history, and material culture. If you are not staying at Shamwari, you can visit for a day tour, which includes a game drive, Khayalend-aba, the Born Free Centre, and a traditional African lunch at the Day Centre—all for R1,650 per person. ☎ *042/203–1111* 🖷 *042/235–1224* ⊕ *www.shamwari.com.*

Where to Stay

$$$ 🏨 **Bayethe Tented Lodge.** Huge air-conditioned safari tents under thatch create characterful but comfortable accommodations. Private decks with plunge pools offer views over the Buffalo River. One tent is wheelchair accessible. ⌂ *Box 91, Paterson 6130* ☎ *042/203–1111* 🖷 *042/235–1224* ⊕ *www.shamwari.com* ⤴ *9 rooms ₰ Dining room, in-room safes, minibars, pool, lounge, shop, laundry service, Internet, business services, airport shuttle, airstrip; no room TVs, no kids under 12* ▤ *AE, DC, MC, V* ⑪ *FAP.*

★ **$$$** 🏨 **Bushmans River Lodge.** This tastefully restored original settler cottage takes a maximum of eight guests in a homelike setting. A dedicated chef, hostess, and ranger make this a rather exclusive experience for small groups, who can book the whole house. ⌂ *Box 91, Paterson 6130* ☎ *042/203–1111* 🖷 *042/235–1224* ⊕ *www.shamwari.com* ⤴ *4 rooms ₰ 2 dining rooms (1 outdoor), cable TV, pool, lounge, laundry service, Internet, business services, airport shuttle, airstrip* ▤ *AE, DC, MC, V* ⑪ *FAP.*

$$$ 🏨 **Eagles Cragg.** Very different from the other Shamwari options, this

Fodor'sChoice sleek, modern lodge is decorated with light wood, pale sandstone, and

★ stainless-steel finishes. It's light and airy and gives a sense of space. All rooms have indoor and outdoor showers and private decks with plunge pools. Glass walls fold away to bring the feel of the bush into the room. ⌂ *Box 91, Paterson 6130* ☎ *042/203–1111* 🖷 *042/235–1224* ⊕ *www.shamwari.com* ⤴ *9 rooms ₰ Dining room, fans, in-room safes, minibars, spa, lounge, shop, laundry service, Internet, business services, airport shuttle, airstrip; no room TVs, no kids under 16* ▤ *AE, DC, MC, V* ⑪ *FAP.*

★ **$$$** 🏨 **Lobengula Lodge.** Though rooms are set around a central lawn and pool area, which makes the lodge compact, they face outward for privacy. Thatch roofs and muted earth tones create an African feel. All rooms have outdoor showers (as well as indoor) and open onto a private veranda. Two rooms and the suite have private plunge pools. Meals are served around a central fireplace, and guests may choose wines from the extensive cellar. ⌂ *Box 91, Paterson 6130* ☎ *042/203–1111* 🖷 *042/235–1224* ⊕ *www.shamwari.com* ⤴ *5 rooms, 1 suite ₰ Dining room, minibars, cable TV, pool, gym, spa, steam room, bar, shop, laundry service, Internet, business services, airport shuttle, airstrip; no kids under 16* ▤ *AE, DC, MC, V* ⑪ *FAP.*

$$$ 🏨 **Long Lee Manor.** Long Lee appeals to those looking for an *Out of Africa* romance, complete with four-poster beds, teak staircases, antique furniture, and manicured lawns. An authentic part of Eastern Cape history, this renovated salmon-pink Edwardian mansion was built in 1816 and served as the original farm owner's home. Ask for one of the designer-decorated suites in the main house. Other rooms are in a separate building at the bottom of the lawn. Every other night, supper is an opulent

African feast—corn on the cob, game stews, *mielie pap* (a gritslike corn porridge)—served in a period courtyard. ⓓ *Box 91, Paterson 6130* ☎ *042/203–1111* 🖷 *042/235–1224* ⊕ *www.shamwari.com* ⇱ *16 rooms, 2 suites ⓒ 2 dining rooms, room service, fans, minibars, cable TV, bar, lounge, shop, babysitting, laundry service, Internet, business services, meeting room, airport shuttle, airstrip* ▭ *AE, DC, MC, V* ⓘ❶ *FAP.*

★ **$$$** 🏨 **Riverdene Lodge.** The public areas are in a period farmhouse, and accommodations are in three enormous renovated barns, which are long, white buildings with rooms opening onto private balconies. A large open-air dining area is used whenever the weather allows. The walls are adorned with a collection of black-and-white photographs, all taken at Shamwari. ⓓ *Box 91, Paterson 6130* ☎ *042/203–1111* 🖷 *042/235–1224* ⊕ *www.shamwari.com* ⇱ *9 rooms ⓒ 2 dining rooms (1 outdoor), fans, minibars, cable TV, pool, bar, lounge, shop, laundry service, Internet, business services, airport shuttle, airstrip; no kids under 12* ▭ *AE, DC, MC, V* ⓘ❶ *FAP.*

Grahamstown

❹ *70 km (44 mi) east of Shamwari Game Reserve, 120 km (75 mi) northeast of Port Elizabeth.*

Although billed as a city, Grahamstown looks more like an English village than anything else—except, of course, for that alter ego of most South African towns, those desperately poor contiguous shanty townships. They're a big part of Grahamstown and contribute to the city's wealth of cultural history. As a garrison town, Grahamstown was the center of a lot of conflict over the last couple of centuries. A few local tour operators conduct fascinating area tours (⇨ Eastern Cape A to Z, *below*).

Home to Rhodes University and other top schools, Grahamstown is considered by many to be the seat of culture and learning in South Africa. This claim is given further credibility by its hosting of the country's premier cultural event—the **National Festival of the Arts** (☎ 046/622–4341 ⊕ www.nafest.co.za), which takes place in July. The festival includes local and international music, theater, ballet and modern dance, fine art, combinations of all of these, and then some. There's the formal program, an official fringe festival, and even a fringe of the fringe that gets seriously alternative. Events are staged throughout town but mainly at the **1820 Settlers National Monument,** a concrete edifice on Gunfire Hill, next to the old garrison, Fort Selwyn.

Grahamstown is an elastic city. Most of the year it's pretty small, but around festival time it expands to fit the tens of thousands of festival-goers, and in December it shrinks to a mere ghost of itself as the students and scholars go home. As befits a city of culture and learning, most of Grahamstown's attractions are a tad cerebral, but many are also just beautiful.

The **Cathedral of St. Michael and St. George** is Grahamstown's most prominent landmark, as much by virtue of its steeple—the highest in South Africa—as the strict geometry of the town. High Street runs in a straight line from the cathedral doors through the Drostdy Arch to the doors of the administration buildings of Rhodes University. Its eight bells, which you can hear ringing out on Sundays, were the first and still are the heaviest in Africa. Though started in 1824, the cathedral was only finally completed in 1952. ⊠ *High St.* ☎ *No phone* ▣ *Free* ☉ *Mon.–Sat. 9–3.*

The statue of the **Winged Angel of Peace** (⊠ Bathurst St.) commemorates the dead of the Anglo-Boer War (1899–1902). The site was chosen as one that was "in the midst of our daily work," so it would be seen often and would serve as a constant reminder of the dead and an inspiration for peace. Irreverent students can't help pointing out that it looks like the angel is supporting a drunk (not dying) soldier and pointing accusingly at one of the local pubs.

The **Observatory Museum** is an intriguing study of Victorian-era cutting-edge science. The building was constructed by a watchmaker and amateur astronomer, H. C. Gulpin, who built a cupola above his shop to house his instruments. The building contains a two-story pendulum and the only genuine Victorian camera obscura in the Southern Hemisphere. You can stand in the tower and watch what's happening in the town below—pretty useful if you've lost your companions. ⊠ *Bathurst St.* ☎ *046/622–2312* ⊕ *www.ru.ac.za/albany-museum/* ▣ *R8* ☉ *Weekdays 9:30–1 and 2–5, Sat. 9–1.*

The **National English Literary Museum** houses a comprehensive collection of books, articles, and press clippings on South African writers in the English language, including some unpublished works. There is also a bookshop. ⊠ *87 Beaufort St.* ☎ *046/622–7042* ▣ *Free* ☉ *Weekdays 9–12:30 and 2–4:30.*

When Grahamstown was a garrison town, the **Drostdy Arch** (⊠ High St.) was the original entrance to the military parade ground. Now it is the gateway through which thousands of Rhodes students pass when leaving campus for town. There is a small **crafts market** "under the Arch" on weekdays 9–5 and Saturday 9–1.

The **International Library of African Music** is a teaching and research center for indigenous music. It has a collection of more than 200 traditional African musical instruments, including *djembes* (drums), *mbiras* (thumb pianos), and *marimbas* (xylophones). ⊠ *Prince Alfred St., Rhodes University* ☎ *046/603–8557* ▣ *Free* ☉ *By appointment.*

Made famous by the identification here of the first specimen of a coelacanth, the **SA Institute for Aquatic Biodiversity** houses exhibitions relating to "old fourlegs," as this prehistoric fish was called, as well as other fishy topics. Take note of the magnificent carved hardwood and brass doors. ⊠ *Somerset St., Rhodes University* ☎ *046/636–1002* ▣ *Free* ☉ *Weekdays 8:30–1 and 2–5.*

en route

ALICEDALE – A tiny settlement west of Grahamstown, Alicedale was once an important railway town in the days of regular steam trains. After a long decline, its fortunes are turning around thanks to the development of a golf course and game lodge.

Where to Stay & Eat

Your best bet for help with lodging is the **Grahamstown Accommodation Bureau** (⌂ Box 758, 6140 ☎ 046/622–5777 or 082/758–4740 🖷 046/622–8949 ⊕ www.grahamstownaccom.co.za).

¢–$ ✕ **La Galleria.** Italian is South Africa's alternate gastronomic culture, and there's a good family *ristorante* in almost every town. Choose from a selection of starters presented on a trolley, then perhaps try the panfried fillet of beef in a red-wine-and-herb sauce or with blue cheese and brandy flambé. Naturally, all pastas are homemade. ⊠ *13 New St.* ☎ *046/622–2345* ⊟ *AE, DC, MC, V.*

¢ ✕🏠 **137 High St.** Conveniently located right on High Street, this warm, friendly coffee shop (¢) is popular with students. It serves the usual pastas, sandwiches, and salads—and arguably the best coffee in town. The B&B upstairs has fabulous yellowwood floors in the residents' lounge, but otherwise its main attraction is its good value. Rooms are small but clean and comfortable. One room has a tub; the others have showers only. ⊠ *137 High St., 6140* ☎ *046/622–3242* 🖷 *046/622–2896* ✉ *137highstr@xsinet.co.za* ⟿ *7 rooms* ⌂ *Restaurant, room service, fans, babysitting, laundry service, free parking; no a/c, no smoking* ⊟ *DC, MC, V* �*◎ BP.*

$ 🏠 **Bushman Sands Hotel.** Built around a demanding Gary Player–designed, links-style golf course and adjacent to the Bushman Sands Game Reserve, this hotel offers a number of leisure options—from golf and tennis to game drives and sunset cruises on the nearly 500-acre New Year's Dam. Rooms are in separate buildings that echo the style of the original Victorian school building, which forms the hotel's center. Decor is understated and classical, with black-and-white-tiled bathroom floors and claw-foot tubs. The suites, which are renovated railway cottages, have fabulous bathrooms, with shower stalls just big enough for you and your favorite baseball team. ⊠ *Alicedale* ☎ *042/231–1350* 🖷 *042/231–1312* ⊕ *www.bushmansands.com* ⟿ *34 rooms, 5 suites* ⌂ *2 restaurants, in-room safes, minibars, cable TV, driving range, 18-hole golf course, putting green, 2 tennis courts, pro shop, 2 saltwater pools, wading pool, gym, spa, boating, mountain bikes, squash, bar, pub, library, shops, babysitting, laundry service, Internet, business services, convention center, airport shuttle, car rental; no smoking* ⊟ *AE, DC, MC, V* ⁜◎ *BP.*

$ 🏠 **Cock House.** Over the years, this small hotel has been the home of distinguished citizens, most notably academic and novelist André Brink, so it's fitting that the individually decorated rooms are named after previous owners. The charming building suffers from (or is blessed by, depending on how you look at it) the rather haphazard improvements that have been made over time. It's worth staying here just for the food. Try the delicious lamb shank, served in a thyme-and-rosemary sauce, or feta cheese soufflé with peppadews (a cross between a sweet pepper and a chili). Dinner is usually a set menu (R115), and lunch is à la carte. ⊠ *10 Market St., at George St., 6140* ☎ *046/636–1295* 🖷 *046/636–1287* ⊕ *www.cockhouse.co.za* ⟿ *7 rooms, 2 suites* ⌂ *Dining room, fans, in-room data ports, cable TV, bar, babysitting, laundry service, meeting room, free parking; no a/c, no smoking* ⊟ *AE, DC, MC, V* ⁜◎ *BP.*

★ $ 🖼 **7 Worcester Street.** This magnificent stone mansion, built in 1888, has been meticulously restored and decorated with an eclectic mix of Thai and Indonesian artifacts. Rooms are elegantly proportioned and have high ceilings and large bathrooms. Dinner is by arrangement. ✉ 7 Worcester St., 6140 ☎ 046/622–2843 🖨 046/622–2846 ⊕ www. worcesterstreet.co.za 🛏 10 rooms ⚒ Dining room, fans, in-room safes, minibars, cable TV, saltwater pool, lounge, laundry service, Internet, business services, free parking, no-smoking rooms; no a/c ☰ AE, DC, MC, V ⍑⊙⍑ BP.

¢–$ 🖼 **8A St. Aidans.** A large contemporary home that has been converted into a small hotel, this offers quite varied accommodations. There is one standard suite, one suite that can be combined with two rooms that share a bath to form a wonderful family suite, and one ordinary room. It all overlooks a lovely garden. ✉ 8A St. Aidans Rd., 6140 ☎ 046/622–3242 🖨 046/622–2896 ⊕ www.137highstreet.co.za/8a.html 🛏 3 rooms, 1 with bath, 2 suites ⚒ Some minibars, lounge ☰ DC, MC, V ⍑⊙⍑ BP.

Kwandwe Private Game Reserve

⑤ 38 km (24 mi) northeast of Grahamstown.

Kwandwe is set in about 50,000 acres of Karoo scrubland, a mere 20 minutes from Grahamstown. Undulating hills, beautiful flowering plants, and endless vistas form a perfect backdrop for a good variety of game. Carved out of unusable farmland, this reserve has a number of beautifully renovated old buildings, including the world's first commercial ostrich farm. The Great Fish River, which runs through the reserve, offers a change in scenery as the riverine vegetation gets thicker and higher. At time of writing, Kwandwe was planning air-shuttle service from the Port Elizabeth airport.

Where to Stay

$$$$ 🖼 **Uplands Homestead.** This renovated farmhouse is a fabulous choice for a biggish family or two or three couples traveling together. You have to take the whole house, which, at R14,750 per day, is a good deal for two couples and a great one for three. You get your own chef, game ranger, and vehicle, so you can plan your day as you like—a real bonus for families. ♻ CC Africa, Box X27, Benmore 2010 ☎ 011/809–4300 🖨 011/809–4400 ⊕ www.kwandwereserve.co.za 🛏 3 rooms ⚒ Pool, exercise equipment, lounge; no room TVs ☰ AE, DC, MC, V ⍑⊙⍑ FAP.

$$$ · FodorsChoice · ★ 🖼 **Ecca Lodge.** If you believe a game lodge has to be thatch and decorated with African artifacts, the heads of dead animals, and zebra-skin rugs, you'll hate Ecca. But if you like clean lines, unusual materials, and a sense of place, you'll love it. Built largely from gabions (those caged rocks used to shore up roads), bare concrete, and glass and accented with bright orange, this is a masterpiece of design. It's different and vibrant. Huge, light rooms lead onto private decks with plunge pools and views of the surrounding bush. It's child-friendly, and a well-appointed activity center will keep the little ones amused between other activities. ♻ CC Africa, Box X27, Benmore 2010 ☎ 011/809–4300 🖨 011/809–4400 ⊕ www.kwandwereserve.co.za 🛏 6 rooms ⚒ Dining room,

fans, in-room safes, minibars, pool, massage, fishing, recreation room, shop, babysitting, children's programs, laundry service, Internet, business services, airport shuttle, airstrip; no room TVs 🖃 AE, DC, MC, V 🍽 FAP.

★ **$$$** 🏨 **Kwandwe Main Lodge.** Built on a slope overlooking the Great Fish River, Kwandwe consists of traditional-style, glass-fronted thatch rooms in individual buildings, with indoor and outdoor showers and every possible creature comfort. Each room has its own wooden boardwalk down to the river, where you can relax on a large, shaded deck next to a private plunge pool. A minibar and telephone for pool service ensure that you won't die of hunger or thirst. In summer you can go canoeing. 🏠 CC Africa, Box X27, Benmore 2010 ☎ 011/809–4300 🖶 011/809–4400 ⊕ www.kwandwereserve.co.za 🏨 9 rooms ⌕ Dining room, room service, fans, in-room safes, minibars, exercise equipment, massage, fishing, lounge, library, shop, laundry service, Internet, business services, airport shuttle, airstrip; no room TVs, no kids under 12 🖃 AE, DC, MC, V 🍽 FAP.

en route | If you're driving from Grahamstown or Kwandwe toward East London, you'll pass through King William's Town. As you enter town, stop at the gas station complex on your left, pick up a few goodies from the store, and then drive across the road for an impromptu picnic at the **Steve Biko Memorial Garden.** There isn't really much here—just a plaque and a few tables where you can sit and reflect on the life of one of the Black Consciousness's most illustrious martyrs. Steve Biko lived near King William's Town and was killed in detention in Port Elizabeth on September 12, 1977.

East London

❻ *150 km (90 mi) east of Grahamstown.*

A great place to spend a day or two on either side of a Wild Coast trip, East London was built around the mouth of the Buffalo River, which forms South Africa's only river port, and has expanded to include the mouth of the Nahoon River. About 20 minutes out of town to the northeast is the mouth of the Gonubie River, where a satellite suburb has formed around a beautiful beach. East London is the gateway to the Transkei, so it's pretty urban, but it's still really close to the rural heartland and so retains a pleasantly small-town air. You can take a half-day city tour, an escorted visit to a local township, or a full-day tour of a rural village (⇨ Eastern Cape A to Z, *below*).

There's definitely something fishy going on at the **East London Museum.** In addition to a whole section on the discovery of the coelacanth, the museum has a large display of preserved fish, including an enormous manta ray. For a different kind of fishy, check out what is claimed to be the world's only existing dodo egg. Jurassic Park, here we come! Probably the most worthwhile exhibit, though, is the extensive beadwork collection; it's both culturally interesting and just plain beautiful. ✉ 319 Oxford St. ☎ 043/ 743–0686 🎟 R5 🕐 Weekdays 9:30–5, Sat. 2–5, Sun. 11–4.

Where to Stay & Eat

$–$$ ✕ **Cape to Cairo.** The views are fantastic, and the food isn't half bad, either. The menu changes pretty regularly and includes some old favorites like rolled lamb with red-wine sauce and minted pea mash. The Thursday night curry buffet is very popular with locals. Join in and work your way through about 16 different curries, two starters, and a dessert for R135. There's live jazz on Wednesday nights. ⊠ *10 Seaview Terr.* ☎ *043/702–8630* ⌂ *Reservations essential* ⊟ *AE, DC, MC, V* ⊘ *No dinner weekends.*

★ **$** ▦ **Stratfords Guest House.** This stylish guesthouse is worth staying in just to see the building. A masterpiece of design, it uses unusual materials like corrugated iron, bare concrete, wood, and glass in incredibly innovative ways to create a comfortable environment. Built in 2000, it received a merit award from the SA Institute of Architects in 2001. The rooms are small but comfortable. Loft suites have microwaves, fridges, and combination tub-showers, whereas the other rooms have only showers. Centrally situated in the suburb of Vincent, Stratfords is particularly popular with business travelers. ⊠ *31 Frere Rd., Vincent 5247* ☎ *043/726–9765* 🖷 *043/726–9233* ⋈ *12 rooms, 4 suites* ⌂ *Dining room, some microwaves, some refrigerators, cable TV, pool, exercise equipment, bar, laundry service, Internet, business services, meeting room, free parking; no a/c, no smoking* ⊟ *MC, V* ⧄ *BP.*

¢ ▦ **White House B&B.** Originally built as a home for a large extended family, this local landmark consists of about four separate apartments. Some of the family are still around, but others have turned their share of the building into a B&B. It's furnished much like a suburban house with lots of pretty floral wallpaper and soft furniture, but the views are absolutely spectacular. Built at the top of a small hill, it overlooks the bay formed by the mouth of the Gonubie River on one side and the open ocean on the other. Not surprising, considering its origins, the accommodations are pretty flexible; four of the rooms can be taken together as a large self-catering apartment—much as it was in its previous existence. Guests can use a central kitchen. ⊠ *10 Whitthaus Rd., Gonubie* ☎ *043/740–0344* ⊕ *www.thewhitehousebandb.co.za* ⋈ *9 rooms, 1 apartment* ⌂ *Dining room, fans, in-room safes, kitchen, cable TV, pool, babysitting, playground, laundry service, Internet, business services, free parking, some pets allowed (fee); no a/c, no room phones, no smoking* ⊟ *AE, DC, MC, V* ⧄ *BP.*

Sports & the Outdoors

East London is just that little bit farther north than PE, so the water and the weather are just a little bit warmer. Close to the city, **Orient Beach & Pool Complex** (⊠ Beachfront ☎ 043/705–2538) offers stress-free, year-round bathing for just R5 (R7 mid-December–mid-January). **Nahoon Beach,** at the mouth of the Nahoon River, has some fantastic surf—but only for people who know what they're doing. Of course, it's also just a lovely beach for bathing, sunbathing, and watching surfers. **Gonubie Beach** is at the mouth of the Gonubie River, about half an hour northeast of the city. The riverbank is covered in dense forest, with giant *strelitzias* (wild banana trees) growing right to the water's edge. A lovely beach, tidal pools, and a 500-yard-long wooden walkway make this a fantastically user-friendly beach.

Cintsa

❼ *40 km (25 mi) northeast of East London.*

Just over half an hour's drive from East London, this lovely, quiet little seaside town is a winner. A long, lovely beach; pretty rock pools; and a beautiful lagoon on which to paddle make this a coastal paradise. Not much happens here, which is its main attraction. The town—if it can be called a town—is divided by the river mouth into an eastern and a western side. It's a drive of about 6 miles between them, although you can walk across the river at low tide (most of the time). The town has a couple of restaurants and small shops.

Where to Stay

$ 🏨 **Cintsa Lodge.** Clean lines, space, and fabulous sea views define this sleek, modern guesthouse. In fact, all rooms have a sea view. There are two beautifully appointed self-catering cottages in the garden next door, and a twisty path leads to the beach, five minutes away. Dinner, available on request, is usually an extensive barbecue. ⊠ *Fish Eagle Dr., Cintsa East 5275* ☎ *043/738–5146* 🖷 *043/738–5147* ⊕ *www.cintsalodge. com* ➭ *5 rooms, 2 cottages* ⚒ *Dining room, in-room safes, minibars, cable TV, saltwater pool, bar, playground, laundry service, Internet, business services, airport shuttle; no a/c, no room phones, no smoking* ▤ *No credit cards* ⊺⊙⊦ *BP.*

¢ 🏨 **Buccanneers Retreat and Backpackers.** This very casual establishment is a great value. Rustic chalets, six of which have cooking facilities, are scattered across a wooded slope leading to the beach. It's a shirts- and shoes-optional sort of place, and it does get quite lively. It *is* a backpackers' haven, so although you don't need to be young to stay here, you do need to be young at heart. The backpackers' dorms are separate from the cottages, but they share all facilties. There's something happening at 4 every afternoon—a volleyball game, free sundowner cruise, or some other spur-of-the-moment activity. It's a great base from which to undertake a whole range of reasonably priced cultural tours and excursions. If you don't fancy self-catering, breakfast is about R35, lunch—which is usually very simple—about R30, and a hearty supper will set you back about R50. Children are permitted, but be warned: this is a PG-13 kind of place. ⊠ *Cintsa West* ⌂ *Box 13092, Vincent 5217* ☎ *043/734–3012* 🖷 *043/734–3749* ⊕ *www.cintsa.com* ➭ *9 chalets, 3 dormitories* ⚒ *Dining room, pizzeria, pool, beach, mountain bikes, billiards, hiking, horseback riding, Ping-Pong, volleyball, bar, babysitting, laundry service, Internet, business services, meeting room, airport shuttle, car rental, travel services, some pets allowed; no a/c, no room phones, no room TVs, no smoking* ▤ *MC, V.*

> **need a break?**

The **H Nelson Mandela Museum** stands as evidence of the love and respect that this awesome statesman has inspired in people all over the world, from rural schoolchildren to royalty. The many gifts Mandela has received through his life say more about the givers than the receiver, and the Long Walk to Freedom display shows the political and personal journey of this beloved politician. In addition to the building in Umtata, there are two other sites. **QUNU,** where Mandela spent his childhood and where he now has his permanent residence, is on the N2, 32 km (about 20 mi) south of Umtata. You can see his home—a rather ordinary brick-face house—from the highway. **MVEZO,** Mandela's birthplace, is more a place of pilgrimage than a museum as such, because there are no displays. It's best to get directions from the museum in Umtata, as it is not easy to find. ⊠ Owen St. and Nelson Mandela Dr. (N2), Umtata ☏ 047/532–5110 ☐ Free ☉ Weekdays 9–4, Sat. 9–noon.

Coffee Bay

❽ *295 km (180 mi) northeast of East London.*

The village of Coffee Bay is a bit run-down, but the beaches and the scenery are great. Though the surf is fantastic, don't head out there if you don't know what you're doing. What makes Coffee Bay stand out from all the other lovely destinations, though, is its proximity—only 9 ★ km (about 5 mi)—to the spectacular **Hole-in-the-Wall,** a natural sea arch through a solid rock island. You can go here on a rather adventurous road from Coffee Bay, and it's included on almost any tour of the Wild Coast. The Xhosa name, Esikaleni, means "place of the water people," and it is believed to be a gateway to the world of our ancestors. If you try swimming through it in rough seas, it certainly will be, but some intrepid souls have made it on calm (very calm) days.

Where to Stay & Eat

★ $ ✕⊡ **Ocean View Hotel in Coffee Bay.** This old Wild Coast hotel has been well renovated. It's light and bright, with white walls and blue fabrics with marine motifs. A resident tour operator can arrange for anything from day walks and gentle cruises to abseiling (rappelling), mountain biking, and canoeing. Activity prices range from R50 for a half day of mountain biking to R80 for a full day of hiking or abseiling (including lunch). Like all Wild Coast resorts, it's child-friendly. The food ($$) is good, well cooked, and unpretentious. However, bear in mind that here huge platters of seafood are considered unpretentious, and you may well find wild coastal oysters offered as bar snacks. ⊠ *Main Beach, Coffee Bay* ☝ *Box 566, Umtata 5100* ☏☏ *047/575–2005 or 047/575–2006* ⊕ *www.oceanview.co.za* ➲ *30 rooms* ⚲ *Restaurant, fans, in-room safes, beach, snorkeling, fishing, hiking, Ping-Pong, volleyball, bar, recreation room, shop, babysitting, children's programs (ages 3–12), laundry service, Internet, business services; no a/c, no room phones, no room TVs* ☰ *AE, DC, MC, V* ❍⧮ *MAP.*

¢ ⊡ **Coffee Shack on the Beach.** The main (but certainly not only) attraction of this vibey backpackers' lodge is the free surfing lessons—from ex–South African surfing champion Dave Malherbe, who has moved here so he can surf the perfect wave whenever he wants . . . at least when he isn't running one of the better backpackers on the coast. You need to book pretty far ahead to secure the room with the private bathroom, or you may end up jostling for shower space or even sleeping in a dorm.

As at all backpackers, you don't need to be young to stay here, but an open mind and a sense of fun is a prerequisite. Guided trips include abseiling (R80), canoeing (R70), cultural tours (R60), and hikes (R50). ⌂ *Box 54, Umtata 5100* ☎ *047/575–2048* ⊕ *www.coffeeshack.co.za* ⤳ *7 rooms, 1 with bath, 6 dormitories, 15 campsites* ⌘ *Dining room, beach, hiking, billiards, volleyball, laundry service, Internet, airport shuttle, travel services; no a/c, no room TVs* ⊟ *No credit cards.*

Port St. Johns

❾ *320 km (200 mi) northeast of East London.*

This is by far the largest of the Wild Coast towns. In fact, it's the only one that even remotely aspires to be more than a village. Once the playground of the coast, it enjoyed an enormous boom in the late 1970s and early '80s. Today it's somewhat run-down, and it truly is a black African town, with the attendant lively street life. Perhaps it's this, as much as the fantastic beaches, surfing, and history, that attracts successive waves of alternative people. Some have never left and are still "parking off" here. Port St. Johns is just a little removed from reality. Though it is a favorite backpackers' destination, there are a few more comfortable options as well. There are also fabulous hikes through indigenous forest and to lovely beaches. But you could easily get lost, and it is quite lonely out there, so it's best to take a guide. Street signs are not big in Port St. Johns, so addresses mean little. However, when you get into the town, you will see signs directing you to the resorts.

Where to Stay & Eat

$ ✕⊞ **Cremorne Estate.** This friendly and unpretentious resort is in a scenic location on the banks of the Umzimvubu River across from Port St. Johns, so it's conveniently close but removed in feeling. Hotel rooms are in a long wooden building, and self-catering chalets can be used as regular rooms by simply locking the door to the central kitchen units. The resort is a favorite with families. Children gambol on the emerald lawn and try their hand at fishing in the river. This is one of the better options during the sardine run, because of the ease of launching. Food at the restaurant (¢–$; reservations essential for nonguests) is plentiful, well cooked, and nicely presented, but not exactly haute cuisine—mostly fish, seafood, steaks, burgers, pastas, and salads. ⌂ *Box 104, 5120* ☎ *047/564–1110* 🖷 *047/564–1113* ⊕ *www.cremorne.co.za* ⤳ *6 rooms, 10 self-catering units, 15 campsites* ⌘ *Restaurant, fans, in-room safes, some kitchens, putting green, pool, gym, dock, boating, fishing, mountain bikes, billiards, hiking, horseback riding, bar, babysitting, playground, laundry service, meeting room, airport shuttle, helipad, no-smoking rooms; no room phones, no room TVs* ⊟ *DC, MC, V* ❙⌾❙ *BP.*

$$$ ⊞ **Umngazi River Bungalows.** One of the most popular destinations on the Wild Coast, this lovely resort is about 20 km (12 mi) from Port St. Johns on a paved road. Set in its own nature reserve, it offers lots of water sports, other outdoor activities, and children's and family programs. The bungalows are attractively decorated and provide all the necessities for a relaxed vacation. Request a water-facing location so as to be able to watch the dolphins right from your doorstep. Umngazi has fly-in

CloseUp

THE FOOD CHAIN UP CLOSE

HAILED BY LOCALS *as "the greatest shoal on earth," the sardine run is, in terms of biomass, the world's largest animal migration. Cold water moving up the coast moves closer to shore and brings with it untold millions of sardines (actually pilchards). These tiny fish are, of course, highly edible, so they have quite a following. Cape gannets, Cape fur seals, common and bottlenose dolphins, shark, and Bryde's whales all follow this movable feast. The run coincides with the northern migration of the humpback whales, so the sea is teeming with life. Local fishing folk revel in the huge catches to be had simply by wading into the shallows with makeshift nets, and sightseers can watch for the bubbling water and attendant cloud of seabirds that signal shoals moving past.*

There are boat trips aplenty to take you out for a closer look, but the real thrill is in diving the run. It's awesome just being amid all those fish, but you often are also among a thousand-strong common dolphins. What everyone is really hoping for, though, is a baitball—when dolpins herd a big school of sardines into a circle, keep them there by swimming around them, and pick them off at will. Sharks almost always join in, and an acrobatic seal or two might take advantage of the free lunch. Bryde's, and even humpback, whales have been known to take a (rather large) passing bite out of the ball, and the sight of Cape gannets from underwater as they divebomb the fish is memorable. Of course, while you're watching this feeding frenzy, you're hovering on the edge of the food chain—ideally to stay there.

packages from Durban. ☎ *047/564–1115* 🖷 *047/564–1210* ⊕ *www. umngazi.co.za* 🖈 *65 bungalows* ⌂ *Dining room, tennis court, pool, spa, boating, fishing, mountain bikes, billiards, hiking, Ping-Pong, volleyball, bar, lounge, library, recreation room, shop, babysitting, playground, laundry service, Internet, business services, meeting room; no a/c, no room phones, no room TVs, no smoking* 🖃 *AE, DC, MC, V* Ⅰ⊙Ⅰ *FAP.*

¢ ▦ **Gwynneth's Barn Ekuphumleni.** This friendly, very casual establishment is a great option if you're counting pennies. It's deep in the residential areas of Port St. Johns and about a five-minute walk from the beach. Simple wooden huts are built among indigenous trees on a sloping plot set back from the road. A small kitchen and communal bath facilities lead onto a communal deck. Whereas the huts are pretty rustic—almost glorified tree houses—the self-catering cottages are quite basic but comfortable. This place is well suited to a family or other group. ⊠ *1st Beach, Port St. Johns* ☎ *083/920–4278* 🖷🖷 *047/564–1506* 🖈 *3 huts, 1 cottage* ⌂ *Kitchen, laundry service, free parking, some pets allowed, no-smoking rooms; no a/c, no room phones, no room TVs* 🖃 *No credit cards.*

Shopping

★ At **Pondo People** (⊠ On the way to Cremorne ☎ 047/564–1274), you'll find the usual pottery, basketwork, and local paintings, which are all very nice—but the *pièce de résistance* is the beadwork. Pillow covers, skirts, bustiers, and vests are made elsewhere and beaded by local women, who spend hours creating intricate, colorful patterns. Whether you shop here to dress a couch or yourself, you'll be making a serious style statement. The store, open every day but Sunday, doesn't accept credit cards, so take lots of cash.

Mbotyi

⑩ *67 km (42 mi) northeast of Port St. Johns.*

As you go farther north, the coast becomes wilder, and the scenery becomes more and more dramatic. Here you'll find waterfalls plunging down sheer cliffs into the sea, lovely river walks, quiet lagoons, and beaches that seem to go on forever. Quiet thatch homesteads perch high on hillsides, their aqua-blue walls contrasting with the emerald-green hills of summer or the blond grass of winter. Mbotyi (pronounced Mm-*boy*-key) is a tiny village not far from the small but bustling town of Lusikisiki. The road is good, with only about 20 km (12 mi) unpaved.

Where to Stay

$$ ⊞ **Mbotyi River Lodge.** This resort was, literally, abandoned overnight in the slightly paranoid early 1990s because of a perceived threat of violence to the hotel managers. Not only did the violence not materialize, but the unguarded hotel was left untouched, unlooted, and unvandalized for eight years. When the new owners bought it, the beds were made and the tables laid for dinner—the *Marie Celeste* of Wild Coast resorts. Today varnished timber bungalows and thatch chalets surround a central lawn and pool. Many balconies feature fantastic banana tree–framed views of the lagoon and beach. Not surprisingly, the menu leans heavily toward seafood, with wild oysters and lobsters featuring prominently. You can take your shoes off as you enter the gate and put them on again only when you leave. ⌂ *Box 645, Lusikisiki 5200* ☎ *039/253–8822* 🖷 *039/253–8253* ⊕ *www.mbotyi.co.za* 🛏 *48 rooms* ⌃ *Dining room, fans, in-room safes, pool, beach, fishing, billiards, hiking, horseback riding, volleyball, bar, babysitting, children's programs, playground, laundry service, meeting room; no a/c, no room phones, no TV in some rooms* ⊟ *AE, DC, MC, V* ⊺⊙⊺ *FAP.*

Graaff-Reinet

⑪ *420 km (250 mi) north of Port Elizabeth.*

Founded in 1786, Graaff-Reinet is the fourth-oldest town in South Africa and is unique in that it is situated entirely within the Karoo Park Nature Reserve. The town has more than 200 listed national monuments, so a casual walking tour will be greatly rewarded. (The tourism office has maps, or you can take one of several guided tours of the area.) Four museums—Urquart House, Reinet House, the Old Library, and Die Ou Pastorie—are administered together. You can buy a ticket for all four for R16, or one for any three for R12, but only the Old Library and Reinet House are open on weekends.

The **Reinet House,** one of the oldest homes in the country, provides a good example of what life in the Cape Colony was like for early settlers. Take a look at the biggest grapevine in the world, planted in 1870, with a stem circumference of about 10 feet. ⊠ *Naude and Murray Sts.* ☎ *049/892–3801* 🖼 *R7* ⊘ *Weekdays 8–12:30 and 2–5, Sat. 9–3, Sun. 9–4.*

The **Hester Rupert Art Museum,** in a renovated Dutch Reformed mission church, houses an excellent collection of contemporary South African art. ⊠ *Church St.* ☎ *049/892–2121* 🖼 *R5* ⊘ *Weekdays 10–noon and 3–5, weekends 9–noon.*

The **Dutch Reformed Church,** built in 1886 along the same lines as Salisbury Cathedral, is a fine example of Gothic architecture. It's made of local sandstone that was transported by the congregation free of charge. The ecclesiastical silver is of exceptional value and is still in use today, but you'll have to take communion if you want to see more than a photograph. ⊠ *Church St.* ☎ *No phone* 🖼 *Free* ⊘ *Weekdays 9–noon and 2–4.*

☾ The **Old Library** showcases rock-art reproductions and other artifacts, but is best known for its large collection of Karoo fossils—dinosaurs and the like. ⊠ *Church and Somerset Sts.* ☎ *049/892–3801* 🖼 *R5* ⊘ *Weekdays 8–noon and 2–5, Sat. 9–3, Sun. 9–4.*

★ In a restored missionary church, the **Pierneef Museum** houses a semi-permanent exhibition of the works of J. H. Pierneef, one of South Africa's most renowned artists. Pierneef is best known for the panels he painted for the Johannesburg Station building in 1932. Depicting South African scenes, they illustrate his characteristic style of painting clouds, rocks, and mountains. The exhibition should remain until at least mid-2006. ⊠ *Middle St.* ☎ *049/892–6107* 🖼 *R5* ⊘ *Weekdays 9–12:30 and 2–5, weekends 9–noon.*

en route   **VALLEY OF DESOLATION** – It's a drive of about 14 km (9 mi) from Graaff-Reinet to this overlook, where you can see for miles. Most people, though, find it hard to look beyond the enormous pinnacles that rise up from the valley floor to a height equal to the overlook. It's a wild and dramatic place, but there are nice walks among the fragrant flowering plants.

Where to Stay & Eat

¢ ✕🖭 **Kliphuis Restaurant and B&B.** This is primarily a restaurant (¢–$), but the two spacious, minimally furnished garden rooms are a good value. One upstairs, one downstairs, they both look out onto the small but prolific vegetable and herb garden that supplies the restaurant. And that's what it's really all about. You can try Karoo lamb and venison in many guises, but pastas and salads offer a lighter alternative. The restaurant serves tea; mostly pastas, salads, sandwiches, and soup at lunchtime; and pretty much what you'd expect for breakfast. ⊠ *46 Bourke St., 6280* ☎ *049/892–2345* 🛏 *2 rooms* ⏃ *Restaurant, fans, laundry service, free parking, some pets allowed; no a/c, no room phones, no room TVs, no smoking* ▤ *MC, V* 🍽 *BP.*

$$ 🏠 **Andries Stockenström Guest House.** A typical town house built in 1819,
Fodor'sChoice this small, homey guesthouse was named for an anti-imperialist district
★ commissioner. It's furnished simply but elegantly with old Cape furni-
ture and Persian rugs strewn about the glowing yellowwood floors. Being
a member of Good Cooks and Their Country Houses means it's really
all about the food, however. Beatrice Barnard personally oversees each
and every meal, and her passion for good food shows. The daily chang-
ing menu almost always features Karoo lamb, ostrich, and/or venison
(picture lightly smoked kudu salad), but they certainly don't dominate,
and Beatrice loves cooking for vegetarians. Starters may include such
delights as artichokes filled with prawns with avocado and carrot coulis,
and soups are usually vegetarian. ✉ *100 Cradock St., Box 55, 6280*
☎ *049/892–4575* ⊕ *www.stockenstrom.co.za* ⇱ *6 rooms* ⚹ *Dining
room, in-room safes, pool, 2 lounges, laundry service, free parking; no
room phones, no room TVs, no kids under 12, no smoking* ▤ *AE, DC,
MC, V* ☉ *Closed June and late Dec.–early Jan.* �{○⟩ *MAP.*

$ 🏠 **Avondrust Guest House.** The rooms of this friendly guesthouse are set
in the oasislike gardens of a beautiful Victorian villa. Clay-tile floors and
simple finishes make them cool and comfortable. Breakfast is taken under
cover around the pool or in the lush garden. ✉ *40 Somerset St., 6280*
☎ *049/892–3566* 🖷 *049/892–3577* ✉ *avondrust@elink.co.za* ⇱ *5
rooms* ⚹ *Dining room, pool, bar, lounge, babysitting, laundry service,
Internet, business services, free parking; no room phones, no room
TVs, no kids under 12, no smoking* ▤ *AE, DC, MC, V* ⫶○⟩ *BP.*

Nieu-Bethesda

⑫ *70 km (44 mi) north of Graaff-Reinet.*

This little hamlet would have been forgotten but for the life and works
of Helen Martins. From a life of darkness and suffering she reached deep
into her soul and pulled out a creation of light and transcendence she
Fodor'sChoice called her **Owl House.** Huge and fantastical glass-decorated concrete sculp-
★ tures of mythical figures, owls, lions, camels, and other animals crowd
out the garden of this once ordinary country cottage. Inside, the walls
are painted in bright colors and covered with ground glass and mirrors.
The whole effect is one of light, reflected and refracted, and is as fine
an example of outsider art as the world has ever been privileged to see.
Athol Fugard's play and the subsequent film *The Road to Mecca* (with
Kathy Bates) focused on Martins's fear of the darkness, which drove
her to create a world of light; hence the mirrors, glass, and many pools
in the garden. After her death by suicide in 1976, ironically inspired by
her impending blindness, the house was left abandoned until it was opened
as a museum. ☎ *049/841–1603* ⊕ *www.owlhouse.co.za* 🎟 *R12*
☉ *Apr.–Sept., daily 9–5; Oct.–Mar., daily 8–6.*

There are a number of interesting accommodation options in Nieu-
Bethesda, most of which are self-catering cottages that double as vaca-
tion homes for their absentee owners. You can book these through
either the Graaff-Reinet Publicity Association or the Nieu-Bethesda
Community Tourism Forum (⇨ *Eastern Cape A to Z, below*).

Eastern Cape A to Z

AIR TRAVEL

Port Elizabeth (PLZ) and East London (ELS) airports, which are both small and easy to navigate, are served daily by South African Airways and SA Airlink. SA Airlink also flies between the tiny airport at Umtata (UTT)—for travel to the Wild Coast—and Johannesburg. Though East London and PE have all the expected facilities, Umtata doesn't; it's really small.

🛈 **Airports East London Airport** ☎ 043/706-0304 ⊕ www.acsa.co.za. **Port Elizabeth Airport** ☎ 041/507-7348 ⊕ www.acsa.co.za. **Umtata Airport** ☎ 047/536-0023.

🛈 **Airlines SA Airlink** ☎ 0861/359-722 or 011/978-5313 ⊕ www.saairlink.co.za. **South African Airways** ☎ 0861/359-722 or 011/978-5313 ⊕ www.flysaa.com.

BUS TRAVEL

Greyhound and Intercape Mainliner operate pretty reliable and reasonably priced bus service, but the distances are long. Always arrange a shuttle ahead of time, as bus stations are not great places to hang around. If you are concerned about your budget, consider saving money by staying at a backpackers' lodge and spending a bit more on the Baz Bus (which goes door-to-door at backpackers). At least that way you won't have to wander around town with your luggage, which is not a good idea.

🛈 **Bus Lines Baz Bus** ☎ 021/439-2323 ⊕ www.bazbus.com. **Greyhound** ☎ 011/276-8500 or 083/915-9000 ⊕ www.greyhound.co.za. **Intercape Mainliner** ☎ 021/380-4400 ⊕ www.intercape.co.za.

CAR TRAVEL

It's easiest and best to tour by car. The major rental agencies have offices at the airports and downtown. Generally, roads are in good condition, but the Transkei roads, including the N2, are potholed in places and not fenced, so cattle, dogs, horses, and sheep cross at will. It's also not uncommon to find spectacularly unroadworthy vehicles in this area, so be alert and don't drive here at night. You will need to travel on unpaved roads to get to some game lodges and to Mbotyi.

🛈 **Rental Companies Avis** ☎ 043/736-1344 in East London, 046/622-8233 in Grahamstown, 041/363-3014 in PE, 047/536-0066 in Umtata ⊕ www.avis.co.za. **Budget** ☎ 043/736-1084 in East London, 041/581-4242 in PE, 047/501-2800 in Umtata ⊕ www.budget.co.za. **Europcar** ☎ 043/736-3092 in East London, 041/581-1547 in PE. **Hertz** ☎ 043/736-2116 in East London, 041/508-6600 in PE ⊕ www.hertz.co.za.

EMERGENCIES

Where pharmacies don't stay open late, such as in Grahamstown, they are generally on call for emergencies.

🛈 **Emergency Services General Emergencies** ☎ 10111 from landline or 112 from mobile phone.

🛈 **Hospitals Greenacres Hospital** ⊠ Rochelle and Cape Rds., Greenacres, Port Elizabeth ☎ 041/390-7000. **St. Dominic's Hospital** ⊠ 45 St. Mark's Rd., Southernwood, East London ☎ 043/743-4303.

🛈 **Pharmacies Berea Pharmacy** ⊠ 31 Pearce St., Berea, East London ☎ 043/721-1300. **Mount Road Pharmacy** ⊠ 559 Govan Mbeki Ave., Port Elizabeth ☎ 041/484-3838. **RET Butler Pharmacy** ⊠ Bathurst St., Grahamstown ☎ 082/568-8784.

MAIL & INTERNET

There are post offices in all towns except really small places like Nieu-Bethesda and the Wild Coast towns. In most of the bigger towns you will also find Postnets—a franchise that offers business, mail, and courier services—in shopping malls or other convenient places. There are Internet cafés all over. In Grahamstown the Makana Tourism office (⇨ Visitor Information, *below*) offers a handy e-mail facility.

Internet Access Cyber Link ✉ 53 Beach Rd., Nahoon, East London ☎ 083/375-9040. **Funtasia** ✉ Greenacres and the Bridge Shopping Centre, Greenacres, Port Elizabeth ☎ 041/363-4681.

MONEY MATTERS

You will find ATMs in even really small towns—but not tiny villages like Nieu-Bethesda, Coffee Bay, or Mbotyi—and full-service banks in PE, East London, Grahamstown, and Graaff-Reinet.

TOURS

African Heartland Journeys, based in Cintsa, offer tours into the Transkei and Wild Coast. They range from a one-day jaunt for about R330–R375 to a six-day Wild Coast tour utilizing self-catering accommodations, villages, and tented camps for about R6,500 to a seven-day hotel-hopping adventure for about R9,000.

Grahamstown oral historian Alan Weyers offers full- and half-day tours of the surrounding countryside, including a visit to the Valley of the Ancient Voices, which is rich in rock art. Prices range from about R350 per person for a half-day trip to about R670 for a full day.

Calabash Tours offers the best cultural, township, and shebeen tours in Port Elizabeth. In recognition of its commitment to community development, this operator has been awarded a Fair Trade in Tourism, SA accreditation—one of only a few. You can choose between a tour of the local townships (R275) or, for the more adventurous, an evening shebeen tour (R325), during which you'll visit a couple of township taverns and, almost certainly, hear some good music. Calabash also offers multiday tours to the game reserves near PE and three- to five-day African heritage tours.

Camdeboo Adventure Tours offers half-day trips to the Valley of Desolation, Karoo Park Nature Reserve, or Umazazaki Township for R120. Guided historic walks are R75 for 2½ hours; quad (ATV) trips to see small game and fabulous scenery, including the Sundays River Gorge, cost R400 for 2½ hours; and a microlight flight will set you back R300 for 15 minutes or R500 for a half-hour flight that takes you over the Valley of Desolation.

One of South Africa's most seminal historical incidents is the 1819 Battle of Grahamstown, when the Xhosa chief Makana tried to rid his area of British colonizers. Makana was arrested and sent to Robben Island, where he died trying to escape. You can relive this battle from the point of view of young Xhosa historians with Egazini Tours. The cost varies according to the number of people on the tour, but should be about R200 if you have a rental car and are prepared to drive the guide around. The tour usually includes a visit to the Masikhule Craft Co-operative, where you can see and buy local artworks, screen-printed fabric, T-shirts, and bags. The co-op is administered in concert with Egazini Tours.

Ganora Excursions, based on a farm just outside Nieu-Bethesda, offers guided walks to rock engravings and paintings (R30), and vehicle and walking tours to in situ fossils (R40). There is also a small private fossil and stone-tool museum (R15).

Based in East London, Imonti Tours offers a three- to four-hour tour through the local township, including a visit to a *sangoma* (traditional healer) for about R180. On Sundays the same tour lasts an hour or two longer and includes a visit to a church; you get to see how people spend their leisure time. A tour of a rural village takes the whole day and costs R385. Imonti also leads full-day tours to Coffee Bay, Hole-in-the-Wall, Port St. Johns, and the Nelson Mandela Museum in Umtata.

The Wild Coast has been a favorite hiking destination for years, but the huts have practically disintegrated. Perhaps they will be repaired, but until then you can take advantage of some good options—perhaps better than the original—offered by Wild Coast Holiday Reservations: the Wild Coast Meander and the Wild Coast Amble. On five- or six-day guided hikes, you walk between hotels and/or resorts. The trips are all catered, and you can arrange to have your luggage driven or portered. Costs are R2,700–R6,500 per person, depending on package and number of people. Shorter trails can be organized on request. This really is the best of both worlds: walking on deserted beaches during the day and staying in comfy hotels with all the modern conveniences at night. But you do have to walk.

If you dive and you think you've done it all, think again. The sardine run is the ultimate adrenaline dive. Blue Wilderness runs mobile, dynamic charters along the coast, using air support to find out where the little guys (and the big guys) are and then heading out to the appropriate spot. You really need to spend a good couple of days at sea if you want a chance of hitting the big time—a baitball. Seven-night, six-day packages cost about R15,000, all-inclusive. Experienced divers only.

🔳 Tour Information **African Heartland Journeys** ☎ 043/734-3012 or 082/269-6421 ⊕ www.africanheartland.co.za. **Alan Weyers Tours** ☎ 046/622-7896 or 046/622-7897 ⊕ www.alanweyerstours.co.za. **Blue Wilderness** ☎ 039/973-2348 ⊕ www.bluewilderness.co.za. **Calabash Tours** ☎☎ 041/585-6162 ⊕ www.calabashlodge.co.za. **Camdeboo Adventure Tours** ☎ 049/892-3180 or 082/579-1789 ⊕ www.camdeboo.co.za. **Egazini Tours** ☎ 046/637-1500 or 083/428-9424. **Ganora Excursions** ☎ 049/841-1302 or 082/698-0029 ⊕ www.ganora.co.za. **Imonti Tours** ☎ 083/487-8975 ☎☎ 043/741-3884. **Wild Coast Holiday Reservations** ☎ 043/743-6181 ⊕ www.wildcoastholidays.co.za.

VISITOR INFORMATION

The Graaff-Reinet Publicity Association, which can arrange accommodations in Graaff-Reinet and Nieu-Bethesda, is open weekdays 8:30–5, Saturday 8:30–1, and Sunday 9–noon. In Grahamstown, Makana Tourism is open weekdays 8–5 and Saturday 9–1. Port Elizabeth's Nelson Mandela Bay Tourism is open weekdays 8–4:30 and weekends 9:30–3:30. Nieu-

Bethesda Community Tourism Forum handles bookings for a range of accommodations in Nieu-Bethesda. Tourism Buffalo City, in East London, is open weekdays 8–4:30, Saturday 9–2, and Sunday 9–1.

🚩 Tourist Offices **Graaff-Reinet Publicity Association** ✉ 13 Church St., Graaff-Reinet ☎🖥 049/892-4248 ⊕ www.graaffreinet.co.za. **Makana Tourism** ✉ 63 High St., Grahamstown ☎ 046/622-3241 ⊕ www.grahamstown.co.za. **Nelson Mandela Bay Tourism** ✉ Donkin Reserve, Belmont Terr., Central, Port Elizabeth ☎ 041/585-8884 ⊕ www.nelsonmandelabaytourism.co.za. **Nieu-Bethesda Community Tourism Forum** ☎ 072/558-4883 ⊕ www.nieubethesda.info. **Tourism Buffalo City** ✉ King's Tourism Centre, Aquarium Rd., Esplanade, East London ☎ 043/722-6015 ⊕ www.visitbuffalocity.co.za.

Durban & KwaZulu-Natal

WORD OF MOUTH

"Durban is rich in its cultural heritage, mixing Zulu, British, and Indian cultures with a vast range of points of interest—and you won't run into other tourists day in and day out. The area also has much to offer in terms of military history, the last outpost of the British empire, the Zulu empire, and the Anglo-Boer War."

—traci_local_in_sa

By Bronwyn
Howard and
Peta Lee

Updated by
Kate Turkington
and Tara
Turkington

KWAZULU-NATAL IS A PREMIER VACATION AREA for South Africans, though it's a comparatively small province. Here lie the highest and most beautiful mountains in southern Africa (the Drakensberg), some of the finest game reserves, and a landscape studded with memorials commemorating the great battles between Briton, Boer, and Zulu. The main draws, though, are the subtropical climate and the warm waters of the Indian Ocean. In fact, the entire 480-km (300-mi) coastline, from the Wild Coast in the south to the border with Mozambique in the north, is essentially one long beach, attracting hordes of swimmers, surfers, and anglers.

Durban, South Africa's third-largest city, is Africa's busiest port (chiefly cargo). It's from here that many of South Africa's exports—from sugar to cars—set sail, and it's here that many of the country's imports—including petroleum, electronic goods, industrial machinery, and textiles—arrive. Durban's chief appeal to tourists is its long strip of high-rise hotels and its popular promenade—known as the Golden Mile (though it's actually several miles long)—fronting its beaches. To find beaches unmarred by commercial development, you need to travel northeast to Zululand, where much of the coastline is protected. In addition, the area is becoming more and more tourist-friendly.

Three hours northeast of Durban, in Zululand, lies a collection of game parks and nature reserves easily rivaling Kruger National Park. One of these, Hluhluwe-Umfolozi Game Reserve, is the jewel in the crown of the KwaZulu-Natal Nature Conservation Service and is responsible for bringing the white rhino back from the brink of extinction. It is also one of the best places to see the even rarer black rhino. It would be a mistake to visit Hluhluwe (pronounced shloo-*shloo*-ee) without also exploring the nearby St. Lucia Greater Wetland Park, an enormous estuary where crocodiles, hippos, and sharks all share the same waters.

Zululand, the region north of the Tugela River and south of Swaziland and Mozambique, is the traditional home of the Zulu people. In the early 19th century the Zulus established themselves under King Shaka as one of the preeminent military powers in the region. At the Battle of Isandlwana, Zulu *impis* (regiments) inflicted one of the most famous defeats on the British army in history, before being ultimately crushed in 1879 at Ulundi. A visit to Zululand would be incomplete without learning something of the Zulus' fascinating culture, and a tour of the old battlefields will enthrall history and battle buffs.

KwaZulu-Natal's two-part moniker is just one of the many changes introduced since the 1994 democratic elections. Previously the province was known simply as Natal (Portuguese for "Christmas"), a name bestowed by explorer Vasco da Gama, who sighted the coastline on Christmas Day, 1497. KwaZulu, "the place of the Zulu," was one of the nominally independent homelands created by the Nationalists (1948–94) to deprive blacks of their South African citizenship. The Nationalists' strategy entailed declaring most of the country the province of whites, while carving out a tiny portion of the least arable and desirable land as "homelands" for black "tribes" (a term now politically incorrect). Black South Africans were then relegated to these homelands (which often had never been their homes previously), where they had to live except when they were working in the "white" areas, such as the cities. KwaZulu was carved out of the old Natal Province, but with the arrival of democratic South Africa the two were merged to form KwaZulu-Natal.

KwaZulu-Natal has long been politically volatile. Its people's loyalties are split between the national juggernaut (the African National Congress) and the Inkatha Freedom Party (IFP), which appeals strongly to a sense of Zulu nationalism. In the run up to the 1994 elections, there were certain "no-go" areas for the less dominant party, and many people were killed by rivals from the opposing side. Today, however, political violence is the exception rather than the rule, and the IFP seems to be losing its grip, even in some of its rural strongholds.

During the years of white rule, parts of Natal were seen as a bastion of English-speaking South Africans and were known, rather derogatorily by outsiders, as the "Last Outpost" (of the British Empire). There are still relatively few whites here who speak Afrikaans, and Zulu is the lingua franca of black KwaZulu-Natalians. Natal's first white settlers—a party of British officers seeking trade with the Zulu in ivory—established themselves in Port Natal (now Durban) in 1824. The colony of Natal was formally annexed by the British in 1843. Cities like Durban and Pietermaritzburg present strong reminders of the colonial past in their Victorian architecture and public monuments. The province's huge Indian population is another reminder of Britain's imperial legacy. In the 1860s the British brought thousands of Indians to South Africa to work as indentured laborers cutting sugarcane, which grows abundantly on the coastal hills. Today the Indian population of Durban alone numbers 1 million, and it plays a major part in the economic, political, and cultural life of the province.

Warning: It is essential that visitors to the northern parts of the province, including Zululand, take antimalarial drugs, particularly during the wet summer months.

Exploring Durban & KwaZulu-Natal

For tourism purposes, KwaZulu-Natal can generally be divided into eight areas: Durban (including the outlying Valley of a Thousand Hills), the Dolphin (also called North) Coast, the South Coast, Pietermaritzburg and the Midlands, the Drakensberg, Zululand, the Battlefields, and the Elephant Coast.

Travel 20 minutes northwest of bustling downtown Durban and you'll be in the rural Valley of a Thousand Hills, so called because of the hundreds of steep valleys that cut into the rolling countryside. This region is home not only to traditional Zulu people but also to many artists, who have shops and studios here. On weekends many Durbanites drive out into the country to enjoy the quaint restaurants, hotels, and rural activities of this region.

As you head north of Durban along the coast, you will pass through small coastal villages, fields of sugarcane (which give it the name the

If you have

2 days

Two days doesn't give you much time for an in-depth experience of all this province has to offer, but you can get a good idea of it by basing yourself at the 🖼 **Durban ❶–㉜** beachfront. Take an early morning walk along the Golden Mile to watch the surfers and later wander around the Indian District. (Leave jewelry and valuables in your hotel safe before venturing into this area.) Spend the afternoon on a township tour. A 50-minute drive on the N3 the next morning will get you to **Pietermaritzburg ㉝–㊷** with its Victorian architecture and maze of small shopping lanes. On your way back to Durban take a detour into the beautiful rolling countryside of the **Valley of a Thousand Hills** where, just minutes from the city, you can still experience rural Africa.

6

If you have

5 days

You can make a circuit to many places of interest in KwaZulu-Natal. Pick one of two options: the Drakensberg and Zululand or Zululand and the more northern section, which takes in the coastal strip and some of the northern game parks and private lodges. If you opt for the mountains, plan a day or two hiking and walking, overnighting in one of the reserves or small establishments in the 🖼 **Northern or Central Drakensberg ㊸–㊾**; then head toward the battlefield sites of **Isandlwana,** 🖼 **Rorke's Drift ㉒**, and the **Talana Museum,** at Dundee. If battlefields aren't your scene, try the 🖼 **Southern Drakensberg ㊾–㊿**, where you can make your way up the spectacular Sani Pass to the very roof of Africa. Afterward, travel north and take the R103 to pick up the 🖼 **Midlands Meander,** which stretches north all the way to Mooi River, through the tranquil Natal Midlands. Within three hours of the battlefields or the Drakensberg, you can be in 🖼 **Durban ❶–㉜** and at the coast. Spend at least one day in Durban, wandering around the Indian District and its markets or going on a township tour.

If you decide to head up the north coast, spend a night at 🖼 **Shakaland** or 🖼 **Simunye Zulu Lodge** to get the total Zulu cultural experience. Then continue to 🖼 **Hluhluwe-Umfolozi Game Reserve ㉕** or 🖼 **Phinda Private Game Reserve ㉙**, scheduling at least two days in the area to see some of the big game for which these reserves are known. A trip to **Greater St. Lucia Wetland Park ㉖** to see hippos and crocodiles in the wild is another great experience. Again, allow a day for 🖼 **Durban ❶–㉜**, either at the beginning or the end of your trip.

If you have

7–10 days

Don't pass by 🖼 **Durban ❶–㉜** altogether, but once you have spent a day or two exploring the area, shake off the city and head up to Zululand to start your grand loop. Visit **Greater St. Lucia Wetland Park ㉖** on your way to the incredible wildlife of 🖼 **Hluhluwe-Umfolozi Game Reserve ㉕** or 🖼 **Phinda Private Game Reserve ㉙**. A three-day trail in the wilderness of Umfolozi could be the high point of your trip. For something more sedate, spend three days at Rocktail Bay Lodge in the 🖼 **Maputaland Coastal Reserve ㉓**, close to the Mozambique border; it's especially interesting during turtle-breeding season, from November to early March. Another distant park near the edge of the province is the delightfully less-visited 🖼 **Itala Game Reserve ㉗**. On your way back to Durban, drive through the battlefields.

Sugar Coast), and commercial forestry plantations. One of the key Durban suburbs here for surf, sand, and sun is Umhlanga (pronounced M-*shlang*-gah), which has a host of decent restaurants, movie theaters, and shops. The coastal strip from Zimbali (south of the bigger town of Ballito) north to Zinkwazi Beach (about an hour's drive from Durban) is the Dolphin Coast, a popular local vacation spot that gets busy during school and public holidays. The many beaches here are protected by shark nets and lifeguards, making them safe for swimming.

Stretching south of Durban for 100 miles or so to Port Edward is the similarly popular South Coast, also known as the Hibiscus Coast, which spans vacation towns like Scottburgh, Margate, and Ramsgate and boasts terrific beaches that have garnered Blue Flag status (awarded for excellence in safety and security, environmental management, and water quality). However, swimming along the coast is often banned during the annual sardine run (a few weeks between June and September), when the area's shark nets are lifted to prevent injury to the dolphins, sharks, and other big-game fish that follow the sardines up the coast. Not surprisingly, the angling at this time is generally very good.

Moving inland takes you to the Natal Midlands, just off the N3 between Durban and Johannesburg. Here racehorse and dairy farms stud rolling green hills and lush pastures that are reminiscent of England. The area has attracted numerous artists, bohemians, and those who make their living from herb farming, cheese making, leather working, weaving, knitting, and pottery. For a wonderful way to experience this part of the province, follow the Midlands Meander (a route set up by the local tourism board), which starts north of Pietermaritzburg (about an hour from Durban) and takes you to farms and crafts shops. You can stop for coffee and cakes or lunch at some of the charming hotels and restaurants along the way.

Just a couple of hours northwest of Durban—and also easily accessible from the N3—are the Drakensberg Mountains (aka the Berg), a spectacular wilderness national park offering tremendous hiking amid some of the country's most spectacular unspoiled scenery. Restaurants and hotels catering to all tastes are spread along the base of the range. Sharing the lowlands areas on the approach to the Drakensberg are white farmers, some of whose families settled in the area more than 100 years ago, and a number of sprawling villages and subsistence farms populated by Zulus, many of whom were displaced by the system of forced removals during the apartheid years.

Zululand begins at the Tugela River, but it is only after you have crossed the Umfolozi River farther north that you really begin to feel the magic of old Zululand; it is here that the great Zululand game reserves are located. Prominent towns (though these are all relatively small) in this region are the industrial towns of Empangeni and Richards Bay, Babanango, Eshowe, Melmoth, Phongola, and Ulundi. The farther north you go, the less populated and more rural the area becomes, with traditional Zulu huts and herds of long-horned brown-and-white and black-and-white Nguni cattle tended by boys or young men scattering over the hills. In fact, the farther north you go across the whole province, the more con-

6

Fabulous Fishing
The Drakensberg and its low-lying areas are not only famous for spectacular scenery, but are also popular with fly fishermen. The crystal-clear Drakensberg streams are good for rainbow and brown trout, and many farmers stock their dammed ponds specifically for fly-fishing. With its long stretch of coastline, saltwater fly-fishing is growing as a sport, and an early morning or an evening on the long, empty beaches of the north coast can provide some wonderfully rewarding fishing. Bear in mind, however, that most resorts require anglers to bring their own tackle. In winter, when huge shoals of sardines pass along the KwaZulu-Natal coast, rock and surf anglers follow flocks of seabirds in the hopes of catching some of the accompanying game fish. Obtain permits from the KwaZulu-Natal Nature Conservation Service or at post offices in larger cities and towns.

A Walk on the Wild Side
The warm climate and magnificent scenery of KwaZulu-Natal are conducive to just about any outdoor activity you can imagine, and the variety of environments allows for hikes and walks to suit nearly everyone. Most game reserves have guided day walks, if you don't have time for an overnight hike. The landscapes of the Drakensberg wilderness are fantastic. The province also has hundreds of equally enjoyable but less dramatic hikes and walks along beaches, through coastal forests, and around the area's many nature reserves.

Wildlife-Watching
Big-game viewing in KwaZulu-Natal is superb, if not on the scale of Kruger National Park. Top wildlife-watching is found at Hluhluwe-Umfolozi, Phinda, Itala, and the Greater St. Lucia Wetland Park, a Natural World Heritage Site in the northeastern corner of the province. The experience of seeing a rhino or a pride of lions in their natural environment while walking in one of the few true wilderness areas left is unforgettable. But don't forget the armed guide!

---

servative the population, whether traditional Zulu, obstinate Afrikaner, or staunch English-speaking folk.

The Battlefields (Anglo-Zulu and Anglo-Boer) are inland, to the north of the Midlands and northeast of the Drakensberg. The towns dotted among the Zululand battlefields tend to be a little ugly and dusty during the dry winter months, but this is an area to visit more for its historic than its scenic value, and for its opportunities to meet the salt-of-the-earth rural people who have made the country what it is.

The Elephant Coast, in the province's northeast corner, is home to the Hluhluwe and Mkuze game reserves, St. Lucia National Park, and Kosi Bay.

About the Restaurants
Durban's dining public is fickle by nature, and restaurants tend to change hands fairly often. This means that what is popular today may

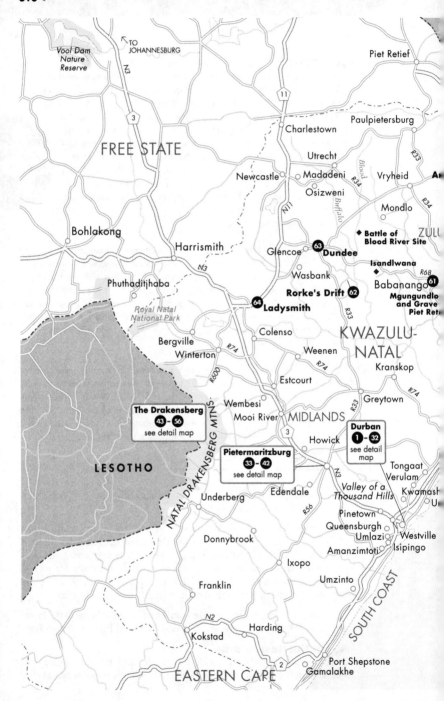

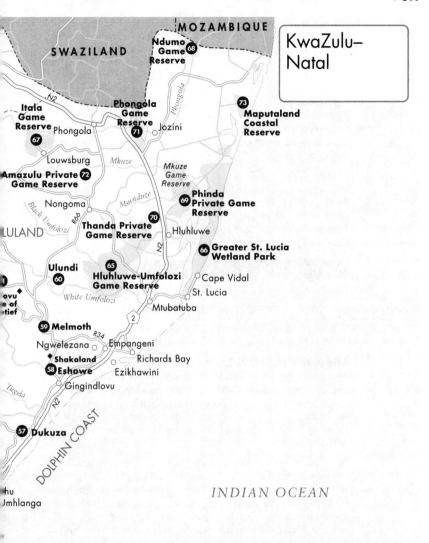

KwaZulu–Natal

MOZAMBIQUE

SWAZILAND

Ndumo Game Reserve ⑥⑧

Itala Game Reserve ⑥⑦
Phongola

Phongola Game Reserve ⑦①
Jozini

Maputaland Coastal Reserve ⑦③

Louwsburg

Mkuze

Amazulu Private Game Reserve ⑦②

Msunduze

Mkuze Game Reserve

Phinda Private Game Reserve ⑥⑨

Nongoma

Black Umfolozi

R66

Thanda Private Game Reserve ⑦⑩

Hluhluwe

ZULULAND

Ulundi ⑥⓪

Hluhluwe-Umfolozi Game Reserve ⑥⑤

Greater St. Lucia Wetland Park ⑥⑥

Cape Vidal

White Umfolozi

St. Lucia

Mtubatuba

Melmoth ⑤⑨

R34

Ngwelezana

Empangeni

Richards Bay

Shakaland

Eshowe ⑤⑧

Ezikhawini

Gingindlovu

Tugela

N2

Dukuza ⑤⑦

DOLPHIN COAST

Umhlanga

INDIAN OCEAN

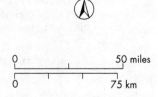

| 0 | | 50 miles |
| 0 | | 75 km |

often be totally out tomorrow. However, there are a couple of old favorites whose food is consistent. Durban offers some superb dining, provided you eat to its strengths. Thanks to a huge Indian population, it has some of the best curry restaurants in the country. Durban's other great gastronomic delight is fresh seafood, especially prawns and langoustines, brought down the coast from Mozambique. LM prawns (LM stands for Lourenço Marques, the former Portuguese name for Maputo) are a revered delicacy in South Africa. Served with *peri-peri* (a spicy Portuguese marinade of chilies, olive oil, garlic, and sometimes tomatoes), they are a real taste sensation. Apart from the food, some of the dining locales—including many with spectacular sea views—are among the best in the world.

Durbanites eat lunch and dinner relatively early, because they're early risers, particularly in summer, when it's light soon after 4. Perhaps because of the warm and humid weather, they're also generally casual dressers. You won't need a jacket and tie in even the fanciest of restaurants, and jeans are rarely frowned upon.

WHAT IT COSTS In South African rand					
	$$$$	**$$$**	**$$**	**$**	**¢**
RESTAURANTS	over 125	100–125	75–100	50–75	under 50

Prices are per person for a main course at dinner, a main course equivalent, or a prix-fixe meal.

About the Hotels & Lodges

Apart from the Royal and Hilton hotels, many of Durban's main hotels lie along the Golden Mile, Durban's beachfront. Southern Sun, the giant chain that operates Sun and Holiday Inn hotels in South Africa, has had a virtual monopoly on Durban accommodations, but this is changing as many outstanding, smaller boutique hotels and excellent B&Bs open.

Places to stay in the Berg include expensive hotels, lodges, and guesthouses, campgrounds, self-catering (with cooking facilities) cottages, and bed-and-breakfasts. The older Berg resorts tend to be family-oriented establishments that encourage guests to participate in outdoor activities and sports, including daily guided hikes, horseback rides, tennis, lawn bowling, even golf. Not to be left out, many area farmers have opened B&Bs, which range from the warm and welcoming to the just plain mediocre. And speaking of quaint, many Midlands and Valley of a Thousand Hills lodgings can be described with that adjective.

In northern Zululand and Maputaland, game reserves and lodges, both publicly and privately owned and managed and smaller than what you'd find in Mpumalanga, offer delightful game-viewing experiences. Many are all-inclusive (or nearly so), though some have self-catering options.

Prices, especially along the coast, tend to rise with the heat (and crowds) of summer.

WHAT IT COSTS In South African rand				
$$$$	**$$$**	**$$**	**$**	**¢**
LODGING				
over 3,000	2,000–3,000	1,000–2,000	500–1,000	under 500
FULL-SERVICE SAFARI LODGING				
over 12,000	8,000–12,000	5,000–8,000	2,000–5,000	under 2,000

Prices are for a standard double room in high season, including 12.5% tax.

Timing

The best time to tour KwaZulu-Natal is early autumn through winter and into spring (April to October), with the coast particularly pleasant in winter. Even in the middle of winter people swim at Durban's beaches. April is a lovely time to visit the city (avoid Easter weekend if you can), though most of this time is pleasant enough, with warm air and sea temperatures. The Ocean Action festival, 10 days of outdoor and water sports–related activities held in July on Durban's Golden Mile, centers on the world-famous surfing championships, known as the Mr. Price Pro. There's night surfing, music fills the air, and market stalls stay open late on the promenade. In September—springtime—the Celebrate Durban Festival offers similar activities minus the surfing.

Game-viewing is also better during winter (late June, July, and August), when the grass is shorter, many trees have lost their leaves, and animals tend to congregate around water holes. Northern parts of the province are dry and dusty in winter, but the frosty mornings, crisp late afternoons, and reduced risk of malaria make up for it. Cold weather doesn't deter thousands of folk-music lovers from congregating at the annual folk-music festival held at Splashy-Fen Farm, in the Drakensberg. During this four-day celebration on a long weekend close to Easter both local and international folk musicians perform.

The height of summer (December and January) brings heat, humidity, higher prices, and crowds, who pour into "Durbs," as it's fondly known, by the millions. Locals know never to brave the beach on holidays or over the Christmas season except for an hour or two from 6 AM—one of the nicest times there. Some facilities in the Zululand game reserves close in summer because of the extreme and unpleasantly high temperatures.

DURBAN

No city in South Africa feels more African than Durban. Cape Town could be in the Mediterranean, and Johannesburg's endless suburbs could be anywhere in the United States. Durban alone has the pulse, the look, the complex face of Africa. It may have something to do with the summer heat, a clinging sauna that soaks you with sweat in minutes. You don't need to take a township tour here to see the emerging new South Africa. Hang out in Farewell Square in the city center and rub shoulders with Zulus, Indians, and whites. Wander into the Indian District or drive through the Warwick Triangle—an area away from the sea around Warwick Road—and the *real* Africa rises up to meet you. Traditional healers tout animal organs, vegetable and spice vendors crowd the sidewalks, and minibus taxis hoot incessantly as they trawl for business. It is by turns colorful, stimulating, and hypnotic.

It's a place steeped in history and culture. Gandhi lived and practiced as a lawyer here, and Winston Churchill visited as a young man. It's home to the largest number of Indians anywhere in the world outside India, many of them descendants of the indentured laborers brought to Natal by the British to work at the docks and in the sugarcane fields. The massive Indian townships of Phoenix and Chatsworth stand as testimony to the harsh treatment Indians received during apartheid, though now thousands of Indians are professionals and businesspeople in Durban.

By no means should you plan an entire vacation around Durban, because there is so much more to see beyond the city. Nevertheless, it's definitely worth a stopover. To get the most from a city visit, get ready to explore its different areas—perhaps the city center; the lovely, shady Berea, where Durban's wealthier residents live, on a ridge overlooking the sea behind the Golden Mile; or the vibrant markets of the Indian District. In fact, the metro area breaks down easily into five sections: the city center around Francis Farewell Square down to the bayfront; the Indian District; the Beachfront; Umhlanga, to the north, which is popular for its beach, hotels, and mall; and outlying attractions. Remember that Durban is a large port city with all the negative baggage that implies. For security reasons it's advisable to walk around the Farewell Square area and the Indian District with a guide, don't wander around the city center or outside your hotel alone at night, and keep expensive cameras concealed. The Durban Beachfront, Umhlanga, and the outlying areas are safe to explore on your own, however, though you'll need a taxi or car to get between them.

Numbers in the text correspond to numbers in the margin and on the Durban map.

City Center & the Bayfront

a good
walk

Though this walk will give you an excellent feel for the soul and history of Durban, it's advisable for security reasons that you take it with a tour guide from the local tourism authority, Durban Africa (also known as Tourism Durban), based at **Tourist Junction ❶**, the city's main tourist information center. From Tourist Junction, cross Pine Street to the early-20th-century **St. Paul's Church ❷** and follow the pedestrian thoroughfare to West Street. Cross the street to **Francis Farewell Square ❸** in front of the imposing **City Hall ❹**, also built in the early 20th century. Walk down the Smith Street side of City Hall and up the steps leading into the **Durban Natural Science Museum ❺** and, above it, the **Durban Art Gallery ❻**. Directly opposite is the entrance to the Playhouse, Durban's major cultural center. Continue to the end of the block on Smith Street to reach the **Old Court House Museum** ❼. From outside the museum's front entrance on Aliwal Street, turn right and walk toward the bay.

Durban's city center borders on the sea to the east and adjoins the harbor to the south in a neighborhood called the Victoria Embankment (also referred to as the Esplanade). Cross the Esplanade and pass through the walkway under the railway line to reach the **Bartle Arts Trust (BAT) Centre** ❽, on the quayside. Wander around the center's small shops and cluster of galleries, where all sorts of visual and performing artists are at work; you can also get a light bite to eat here while tugs and ships move in and out of the harbor. If you end up here in the late afternoon, you may catch local jazz musicians playing out on the deck. The Maydon Wharf, a large section of the harbor, adjoins Victoria Embankment to the southwest; here you find **Wilson's Wharf** ❾ and the **S. A. Sugar Terminal** ❿.

TIMING   The center of the city can get horribly humid from December through February, so if you visit then, avoid walking too much during the midday heat. Browse the air-conditioned museums when it's hot, and save walking outside for later in the afternoon, making sure you get to the museums and galleries before they close, around 4:30.

What to See

★ ❽ **Bartle Arts Trust (BAT) Centre.** To some, this arts center resembles a giant flying bat when viewed from above—as from the Roma Revolving restaurant (⇨ Where to Eat, *below*)—though this takes some stretch of the imagination. The vibrant center is abuzz with Durban's trendy set: artists, musicians, and other hipsters. Most days—and some nights— you can watch sculptors, dancers, musicians, and painters at work, and at night the BAT theater comes alive with plays, music, and African film or video festivals. The center is home to three small galleries—the Bayside, Democratic, and Menzi Mchunu—which showcase the work of local artists. The center contains a restaurant, a coffee bar overlooking the bay, a nightspot with live music, and shops that sell both bric-a-brac and artwork, including an excellent selection of high-quality African crafts, fabrics, and ceramics. ⊠ *45 Maritime Pl., Small Craft Harbour, Victoria Embankment* ☎ *031/332–0468* ⊕ *www.batcentre.co.za* ⊠ *Free* ⊙ *Daily 8:30–4:30.*

need a break?

TransAfrica Express (⊠ BAT Centre, 45 Maritime Pl., Victoria Embankment ☎ 031/332–0804) specializes in traditional African dishes, from *samp* (coarsely ground corn) and beans to tender lamb cutlets. Local seafood includes Amatikulu prawns, named after the place on the province's north coast where they are caught.

❹ **City Hall.** Built in 1910 in Edwardian neo-Baroque style, the hall looks as if it has been shipped straight from London column by column—hardly surprising, since it's an exact copy of the Belfast City Hall. The main pediment carries sculptures representing Britannia, Unity, and Patriotism, and allegorical sculptures of the Arts, Music, and Literature adorn the exterior. City Hall still houses the mayor's parlor and other government offices, the Durban Art Gallery and Natural Science Museum, and the City Library. Ask the guard to let you in to see the huge theater's or-

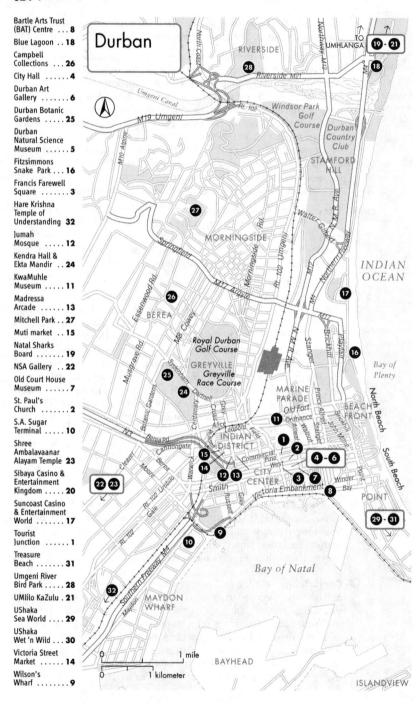

Durban

nate molding and grand parterre boxes, or join an official tour run by Durban Africa. ✉ *West and Church Sts., city center* ☎ *031/304–4934* ⊕ *www.cityofdurban.co.za* ✉ *Free* ☉ *Daily 8:30–3:30.*

need a break? The **Royal Coffee Shoppe** (✉ 267 Smith St., city center ☎ 031/304–0331), in the Royal Hotel, is a popular meeting place for Durban society and pre- and post-theater crowds. Crystal chandeliers, etched glass, formally dressed staff, and live piano music in the nearby lounge at lunchtime create a rich atmosphere of old-time colonial Durban. The café serves a light breakfast as well as coffees, teas, cakes, quiches, salads, and sandwiches.

❻ Durban Art Gallery. The gallery presents a vibrant mix of both local and international work, and many pieces have a distinct feel of African patriotism. Recent exhibits have included a show focusing on the cultural diversity of handicrafts in South Africa, large-scale photographs and videos about forensic investigation, a fatherhood project celebrating the paternal instinct, and a multimedia display highlighting Durban's annual events, with work by artists from Mozambique, Botswana, and Angola. Look out, too, for the traditional, patterned *hlabisa* baskets, regularly displayed at the gallery. Exhibits change every few months. The first Friday of every month is set aside for Red Eye, an initiative aimed at attracting younger audiences to the gallery. It showcases Durban's latest entertainment talent, with bands, African drummers, other musicians, and dancers performing among the exhibitions. ✉ *City Hall, Smith and Church Sts., 2nd fl., city center* ☎ *031/311–2264* ⊕ *www.durbanet.co.za/exhib/dag/dagmain.htm* ✉ *Free; small fee for Red Eye* ☉ *Mon.–Sat. 8:30–4 (1st Fri. of month to 10), Sun. 11–4.*

❺ Durban Natural Science Museum. Despite its small size, this museum provides an excellent introduction to Africa's numerous wild mammals (including a stuffed elephant, a leopard, and smaller mammals like wild dogs and vervet monkeys), plants, birds, reptiles, and insects. It's a great place to bring the kids or to familiarize yourself with the local wildlife before heading up to the game parks in northern KwaZulu-Natal. At one popular gallery, the KwaNunu Insect Arcade, giant insect replicas adorn the wall; another, the bird gallery, showcases a variety of stuffed birds, including flamingos, ostriches, eagles, and penguins. The museum also offers Internet access at a minimal charge. ✉ *City Hall, Smith and Church Sts., 1st fl., city center* ☎ *031/311–2256* ⊕ *www.durban.gov.za/naturalscience* ✉ *Free* ☉ *Mon.–Sat. 8:30–4, Sun. 11–4.*

need a break? At the **Waterhole** coffee shop, in the Durban Natural Science Museum, you can sip cappuccino and have a snack in the middle of a re-created mangrove swamp. For a more authentic experience of the city center, try the roasted *mielies* (corn on the cob), prepared and sold by vendors on most street corners.

❸ Francis Farewell Square. In the heart of Durban, the square is a lovely shady plaza bordered by some of the city's most historic buildings, like City Hall, the Central Post Office, and the Royal Hotel. Walkways lined with stately palms and flower beds crisscross the square and lead to monuments honoring some of Natal's important historic figures. The square stands on the site of the first European encampment in Natal, established by Francis Farewell and Henry Fynn in 1824 as a trading station to purchase ivory from the Zulus. A statue representing Peace honors the Durban volunteers who died during the Second South African War (1899–1902), also known as the Boer War or Anglo-Boer War. The Cenotaph, a large stone obelisk, commemorates the South African dead from the two world wars. Pay attention to your valuables while walking in the square. ⊠ *Bounded by Smith, West, and Gardiner Sts. and the Church St. pedestrian mall, city center.*

⓫ KwaMuhle Museum. Pronounced kwa-moosh-le (with a light *e,* as in *hen*), this small museum, housed in what used to be the notorious Department of Native Affairs, tells of Durban's apartheid history. During apartheid the department was responsible for administering the movement of black people in and out of the city, dealing with the dreaded passes that blacks had to carry at all times, and generally overseeing the oppressive laws that plagued the black population. Ironically, the name means "place of the good one," after J. S. Marwick, the manager of the municipal native affairs department from 1916 to 1920. Exhibits provide the often heartbreaking background on this period through old photographs and documents, replicas of passbooks, and lifelike models of people involved in the pass system, including *shebeen* (an informal bar) queens, who had to apply for permits to sell alcohol. ⊠ *150 Ordnance Rd., city center* ☎ *031/311–2223* ⊕ *www.durban.gov. za⁄museums⁄localhistory* ☞ *Free* ⊙ *Mon.–Sat. 8:30–4, Sun. 11–4.*

❼ Old Court House Museum. This old courthouse was built in 1866, and during the Zulu War of 1879, when Durban was in danger of attack, the building's exterior was temporarily provided with loopholes so defenders could fire their rifles from inside. Today it's a museum whose exhibits focus on Natal's colonial past, including a reconstruction of Henry Fynn's original 1824 wattle-and-daub hut, as well as simulated shopfronts of a turn-of-the-20th-century apothecary and department store. Upstairs is a display of miniature dolls, replicas of important people in Durban's history and development, including Zulu King Shaka. Local artists showcase mixed-media work at the museum, and a recent display comprised T-shirts celebrating 10 years of democracy. ⊠ *Smith and Aliwal Sts., city center* ☎ *031/311–2229* ☞ *Free* ⊙ *Mon.–Sat. 8:30–4, Sun. 11–4.*

❷ St. Paul's Church. One of Durban's main Anglican churches, built in 1909 in Gothic Revival style, St. Paul's stands on the site of a previous church dating from 1847. From the outside it's not much to look at, but the interior is beautiful: notice the lovely wood ceiling and the stained-glass chancel windows. ⊠ *Church and Smith Sts., city center* ☎ *031/305–4666.*

❿ S. A. Sugar Terminal. Much of Durban's early economy was built on the sugar industry, and even today the hills and fields around the city and along the north and south coasts are covered with sugarcane. It is not surprising then that Durban's Sugar Terminal is the largest in southern Africa and one of the most advanced in the world. A short video presentation gives you background about the sugar industry, and then you'll be taken on a walking tour of the terminal. Together, the tour and video presentation take 45 minutes. It is extraordinary to see the terminal's three enormous silos piled high to the domed ceiling with tons of raw sugar. The architectural design of the silos has been patented and used in other parts of the world. ✉ *25 Leuchars Rd., Maydon Wharf* ☎ *031/365–8100 or 031/365–8153* 🔖 *R12* ☉ *Tours weekdays at 8:30, 10, and 11:30, plus Mon.–Thurs. at 2.*

❶ Tourist Junction. The city's principal tourist information outlet occupies Durban's old railway station, an attractive brick building constructed in 1894 in Flemish Revival style. The NGR above the main entrance stands for Natal Government Railways. Durban Africa, the city's tourist authority, is here, as well as a reputable jewelry store selling locally made pieces and an excellent African crafts shop that sells intricate bead and basket work by women, many of whom live in rural communities in KwaZulu-Natal. ✉ *160 Pine St., at Soldier's Way, city center* ☎ *031/ 304–4934* ☉ *Weekdays 8–5, weekends 9–2.*

❾ Wilson's Wharf. Near the BAT Centre and on the edge of the harbor, this pleasant, privately developed section of waterfront is a lovely place to while away a few hours, soaking up the atmosphere, admiring the harbor view, and maybe having a meal or drink at one of the open-air restaurants on the expansive wooden deck. It's reminiscent of the incipient V&A Waterfront in Cape Town 20 years ago. In addition to restaurants and fast-food outlets, there are boat rentals and a market with 65 stalls, some selling classy local crafts, others selling cheaper trinkets from India and China. ✉ *Boatman's Rd., Maydon Wharf, Victoria Embankment* ☎ *031/307–7841* ⊕ *www.durbanswaterfront.co.za* ☉ *Market daily 9–6, some restaurants daily 8:30–midnight.*

need a break? The popular **Zack's** (✉ Wilson's Wharf ☎ (031/305–1677) often hosts live music, including jazz on Saturday afternoons and open mike on Monday evenings. It serves breakfast until late.

Indian District

a good walk This is one of Durban's most fascinating neighborhoods, but like the city center, it's best enjoyed, and safest, when visited on an official tour with Durban Africa, based at the **Tourist Junction ❶**. From Tourist Junction, walk west up Pine Street or Commercial Road, away from the Beachfront. Three blocks up, turn right on Grey Street, generally considered the heart of the district. Here you'll find an intoxicating mix of Africa and Asia. Narrow doorways lead into fascinating spice shops, and traders touting saris compete with vendors selling vegetables, hair weaves, and fake Rolexes. A little farther along, near the junction of Queen and Grey streets, is the **Jumah Mosque ⓬**; right next door is the **Madressa Arcade ⓭**. At the corner of Queen and Russell streets you'll reach the most-hyped part of the Indian District, the bustling **Victoria Street Market ⓮**. From Victoria Street, turn right onto Russell Street, go one block, and turn left onto Market, where you'll see the **muti market ⓯** spread out in front of you.

TIMING   The best time of day to do this tour is in the morning. Set off before 9, when it's relatively cool. This also gives the street sellers time to set up their stalls. Their part of town can be quite grubby, and in the midday summer heat it can get unpleasantly humid. The walk should take between two and three hours.

What to See

⑫ **Jumah Mosque.** Built in 1927 in a style that combines Islamic and colonial features, this is the largest mosque in the Southern Hemisphere. Its colonnaded verandas, gold-domed minaret, and turrets give the surrounding streets much of their character. Tours (the only way to visit) are free and can be arranged through the Islamic Propagation Center, in a room at the entrance of the mosque, or through Durban Africa. If you plan to go inside, dress modestly, as in most mosques around the world. Women should bring scarves to cover their heads out of courtesy, wear skirts below the knees, and cover their shoulders. Men should not wear shorts. A good idea is to keep a *kikoi* (a lightweight African sarong readily available in local markets) in your bag to use as a skirt or scarf. Men can use them, too, to cover bare legs. You'll have to take off your shoes as you enter, so wear socks if you don't want to go barefoot. No tours are offered during Islamic holidays, including Ramadan, which varies but lasts a whole month in the latter part of the year. ⊠ *Grey and Queen Sts.* ☎ *031/ 306–0026* ⊑ *Free* ⊘ *Weekdays 9–4:30.*

⑬ **Madressa Arcade.** The thoroughfare has a Kiplingesque quality, recalling the bazaars of the East. Built in 1927, it's little more than a narrow, winding alley perfumed by spices and thronged with traders. You can buy everything from plastic trinkets to household utensils and recordings of Indian music. Bursts of colors—from bright yellow material to dark red spices—create a refreshing and photogenic sight. You can buy striking costume jewelry that would cost three times more at major shopping centers, but be wary of pickpockets while browsing through the stores. ⊠ *Entrances on Queen and Cathedral Sts.* ⊘ *Daily 9–5.*

⑮ **Muti market.** For a uniquely African experience, hire a guide to take you to southern Africa's largest and most extensive *muti* (traditional medicine, pronounced moo-tee) market. The market also serves as a distinctive traditional-medicine facility, where *sangomas* (traditional healers) offer consultations to locals in a bustling, urban atmosphere. If you're feeling bold, you might wish to consult a sangoma on matters of health, wealth, or personal problems. (But don't go without a guide.) ⊠ *Warwick Junction* ☎ *No phone* ⊘ *Weekdays 8–6, Sat. 8–1.*

★ ⑭ **Victoria Street Market.** Masses of enormous fish and prawns lie tightly packed on beds of ice while vendors competing for your attention shout their respective prices. In the meat section, goat and sheep heads are stacked into neat piles, and butchers slice and dice every cut of meat imaginable. The noise is deafening. The place pulsates with life, and even if you have no kitchen in which to cook, it's tough to resist joining the fray. In an adjacent building—where all the tour buses pull up—you'll discover a number of curio shops whose proprietors are willing to bargain over wood

BUNNY CHOW

CONTRARY TO WHAT YOU MIGHT THINK, bunny chow is not about lettuce and carrots. This Durban specialty, prevalent in the Indian District, is a hollowed-out loaf of bread traditionally filled with bean curry, although mutton and sometimes beef and chicken are also used. The dish was popularized in the 1940s, during apartheid, when blacks were prohibited from entering Kapitan's Restaurant, in the city center, where traditional Indian beans in roti (pancakelike bread) were sold. The manager, known fondly as Bhanya, started offering takeout on the pavement, but the rotis often fell apart. So he started using a hollowed-out quarter loaf of bread as a small pot for the beans, and the soft bread was used to soak up the gravy. "Bhanya's chow" became bunny chow, and meat was soon added as fillings.

Good bunnies can be found at several Indian District eateries. **Patel Vegetarian**

Refreshment (✉ Rama House, 202 Grey St. ☎ 031/306–1774), in existence for almost 90 years, has built a family legacy of good traditional food. **Victory Lounge** (✉ Grey and Victoria Sts. ☎ 031/306–1906) puts meat in its bunny chow and is therefore busy. In a quieter part of town, the vegetarian **Little Gujarat** (✉ 43 Prince Edward St. ☎ 031/305–3148) has simple wooden decor. Wherever you sit, you can watch people walk by as you chow down on your bunny chow.

and stone carvings, beadwork, and basketry. You'll also find shops selling spices, recordings of African music, and Indian fabrics. The current structures stand on the site of an original, much-loved market, a ramshackle collection of wooden shacks that burned down during the years of Nationalist rule. Watch your belongings closely. ✉ *Queen and Russell Sts.* ☎ *031/306–4021* ✆ *Weekdays 8–5, weekends 10–2.*

Beachfront

Either you will hate the Durban Beachfront for its commercial glitz, or you will love it for its endless activity. It extends for about 12 km (7½ mi) from South Beach, at the base of Durban Point, all the way past North Beach and the Suncoast Casino to Blue Lagoon. The section of beachfront between South Beach and the Suncoast Casino is safe, as police patrol often. It's lovely to take a stroll along here early or late in the day, when it's less busy. Walk out onto one of the many piers and watch surfers tackling Durban's famous waves. Of anyplace in Durban, the Beachfront most defines the city.

The busiest area of the Beachfront is the 5-km (3-mi) stretch between South Beach and the Suncoast Casino. Since it was turned into a pedestrians-only walkway about 20 years ago, Durbanites have taken to this promenade in droves—strolling, jogging, rollerblading, cycling, or just sitting in the sun to watch the surfers and body-boarders.

The Beachfront is a bit of a hike from the city center; it's best to take a taxi or drive to the end of West Street or Commercial Road. Start at Joe Kool's restaurant (a good place to park), between Durban's two most famous beaches, North and South beaches. Amble to the end of North Beach Pier, directly in front of you, where you can watch surfers and body-boarders in action, or one of the other piers, where professional anglers regularly cast their lines. Then decide whether to walk north or south. If you go south for about 1 km (½ mi), you come to a large open area where vendors sell corn to feed hundreds of pigeons, which will eat right out of your hand (popular with kids). If you walk away from the beach toward the road here, you'll find some of the best street stalls the Beachfront has to offer. They're packed with wooden carvings, beadwork, and baskets, though the quality is not as high as at the African Art Centre. If you go north instead, you pass the **Fitzsimmons Snake Park** 🔟 on your right and then the **Suncoast Casino and Entertainment World** 🔟. On the way, perhaps take in a rickshaw ride (beware, you'll need to pay for photos, too) and browse among the crafts stalls on the road above the promenade. Beyond this, there is a popular flat running and walking route all the way to **Blue Lagoon** 🔟, 5 km (3 mi) from Joe Kool's.

TIMING   Depending on the weather, parts of the Beachfront can be quite busy, especially on weekends. There is always something to see, even in the early mornings, when people come to surf or jog before going to work. Head off early, but try to time your walk so that you visit the snake park during feeding times or when there is a demonstration. Whether you go south or north as far as Suncoast, a round-trip should take about an hour, longer if you go all the way to Blue Lagoon. End with a cool drink in one of the open-air restaurants at Suncoast.

What to See

🔟 **Blue Lagoon.** About 3 km (2 mi) north of Suncoast, Durban's Umgeni River flows out to sea at the legendary Blue Lagoon, and on weekends local Indian families in particular gather for picnics and traditional South African *braais* (barbecues). The mood is often festive; cricket games and volleyball matches abound, and music plays on car stereos. There's also a mini-golf course for those who want to engage in a quieter activity. 📞 *No phone* 🎫 *Free* 🕐 *24 hrs.*

en route   **Coconut Grove** (✉ Blue Lagoon), opposite the mini-golf course, is a fast-food outlet famous for spicy burgers and excellent bunny chow—even at 4 AM. Young people who've been out at nightclubs in the city head here for a quick and pleasing meal. Pop in to experience a lively expression of modern South African Indian culture you won't find anywhere else.

🔟 **Fitzsimons Snake Park.** The zoo houses a slithery collection of snakes, crocodiles, and other reptiles from around the world. Live snake demonstrations are held in a small amphitheater; on weekends these shows are followed by a feeding. There is also a snake breeding center and rehabilitation lab. ✉ *Snell Parade* ☎ *073/156–9606* ☉ *Weekdays 9–4:30, weekends 9–5; snake demonstrations daily at 10, 11:30, 1, 2:30, and 3:30; crocodile feedings Wed. and Sat. at 2.*

🅲 ⑰ **Suncoast Casino and Entertainment World.** Part of the rejuvenation of Durban's Golden Mile, this casino is done in the art-deco style for which Durban is famous. Colorful lights make it a nighttime landmark, but it's established itself as a daytime hot spot as well. There are deck chairs beneath umbrellas on a grassy sundeck, and a pretty beach. A paved walkway dotted with benches is a pleasant place to sit and watch cyclists, rollerbladers, and joggers. There's often a band playing directly in front of the complex, which you can listen to from the stairs. If you prefer swimming pools to salt water, visit **Waterworld** (☎ 031/ 337–6336 ✆ R30 ☉ Weekdays 9–5), a water park with pools, slides, and a picnic area. ✉ *20 Suncoast Blvd.* ☎ *031/328–3000* ⊕ *www. suncoastcasino.co.za* ✆ *Pedestrians free, cars R5, sundeck R5* ☉ *24 hrs.*

> **need a break?**
>
> Of the 20 or so restaurants, fast-food outlets, and coffee shops at Suncoast Casino, two are good for a respite. Durban's only **Mugg & Bean** (☎ 031/368–1848), a popular chain, is open 24 hours a day near the west entrance. Besides excellent coffee and refreshing almond margaritas, it turns out huge servings for a good value, from chocolate cake to well-roasted beef. Sit inside or on the terrace, with its beautiful view of the ships on their way to the harbor. At **Mozart's** (☎ 031/332–9833), you can choose from up to nine flavors of smooth ice cream, including mint chocolate chip, granadilla, and blueberry.

Umhlanga

Also known as Umhlanga Rocks, this used to be a small vacation town, but Durban's northward sprawl has incorporated it into a popular and upscale residential and business suburb, much like Sandton is to downtown Johannesburg (⇨ Chapter 7). Umhlanga is just 15 km (9 mi) from the city center along the M4 (Northern Freeway)—close enough for those staying in the center of town to come here for a meal or a walk on the vibey promenade, which runs for a mile or so along the beach. To the north are the nicest sea views; to the south is Umhlanga's lighthouse. Umhlanga remains a popular vacation destination and boasts many of Durban's top hotels.

What to See

★ 🅲 ⑲ **Natal Sharks Board.** Most of the popular bathing beaches in KwaZulu-Natal are protected by shark nets maintained by this shark-research institute, the world's foremost. Each day, weather permitting, crews in ski boats check the nets, releasing healthy sharks back into the ocean and bringing dead ones back to the institute, where they are dissected and studied. The Natal Sharks Board offers one-hour tours that include a shark dissection (sharks' stomachs have included such surprising objects as a boot, a tin can, and a car license plate!) and an enjoyable and fascinating audiovisual presentation on sharks and shark nets. An exhibit area and good curio shop are also here. You can also join the early morning trip out to sea on a Sharks Board ski boat and watch the staff service the shark nets off Durban's Golden Mile. Depending on the season, you will more than likely see dolphins and whales close at hand. ⊠ *M12* ☎ *031/566–0400* ⊕ *www.shark.co.za* ☜ *Tours R20; other times free* ☉ *Weekdays 8–4, Sun. 1–4; tours Tues.–Thurs. at 9 and 2, Sun. at 2.*

⑳ Sibaya Casino & Entertainment Kingdom. Opened late in 2004, Sibaya is overwhelming—in size, decor, and number of activities—but is worth seeing for its grandiose architecture and decor, all styled along a Zulu theme. The buildings themselves, for example, echo a giant and opulent Zulu *kraal* (traditional village). Huge bronze statues of Zulu warriors and buffalos at the entrance provide a truly African welcome. Wherever you are at Sibaya, all 119 acres of it, a breathtaking view of the ocean is only a window or a balcony away. As you might expect, it's loaded with dining options, and a 120-room hotel is scheduled to open in 2006. ⊠ *1 Sibaya Dr.* ☎ *031/580–5000 or 0860/742–292* ⊕ *www.sibaya.co.za* ☜ *Free.*

㉑ UMlilo KaZulu. Adjoining the Sibaya Casino, this cultural village, whose name means "circles of fire," was inspired by the history of the Biyela clan, a branch of the Royal Zulu House. The young warrior prince Mkhosana, who fought against the British in the Battle of Isandlwana and lost his life in the clash, is honored here. Two-hour tours take you on a journey through the village that includes stick fighting and storytelling. There's an art gallery with traditional paintings and a curio shop with locally made beadwork and sculptures, and the village's Sondela Tavern dishes up African specialties. ⊠ *1 Sibaya Dr.* ☎ *031/580–5000 or 0860/742–292* ⊕ *www.sibaya.co.za* ☜ *Free* ☉ *Daily 11–9.*

Outlying Attractions

Directly west of city center is Glenwood, an old leafy suburb with wide streets, big homes, and the NSA gallery. Farther west, over the ridge, is Cato Manor (home to the Shree Ambalavaanar Alayam Temple) and then Westville (and, if you keep heading northwest, Pietermaritzburg, the Midlands, and ultimately Johannesburg). North of Glenwood is the Berea, also an old and well-to-do suburb, built on a ridge overlooking the sea, and home to the Durban Botanic Gardens. To the east—toward the sea—are Greyville and the Kendra Hall & Ekta Mandir. Heading north toward Morningside you'll find the Campbell Collections and Mitchell Park, and farther north still, on the other side of the Umgeni River, are Durban North and the Umgeni River Bird Park. (Even farther north you reach Umhlanga and eventually the Dolphin Coast.) The neighborhood that's directly south of the main Durban beachfront and borders the north side of the harbor is called Point. Here is Durban's finest tourist attraction, uShaka Marine World, a large entertainment complex comprising four components—Sea World, Wet 'n Wild, uShaka Beach, and Village Walk—that's modeled on a mixture of Zulu, wider African, and maritime themes. On the south side of the harbor is a giant strip of dune covered by vegetation on which the suburb of Bluff is built, and where you find Treasure Beach. Surrounding

Durban, many Indian and black "townships" are largely racially homogenous and mostly poor, a holdover from apartheid. Chatsworth, one such large township, to the southwest, has the Hare Krishna Temple of Understanding.

What to See

★ ❷❻ **Campbell Collections.** In the middle of bustling, suburban Berea, Muckleneuk is a tranquil Cape Dutch home in a leafy garden. It's much as it was when it was built in 1914 upon the retirement of Sir Marshall Campbell, a wealthy sugar baron and philanthropist who lived here with his wife, Ellen, and daughter, Killie. Today Muckleneuk houses a museum administered by the University of KwaZulu-Natal, including the **William Campbell Furniture Museum.** (William was the son of Sir Marshall.) The house is furnished much as it was when the Campbells lived here, and contains some excellent pieces of Cape Dutch furniture that belonged to the family, an extensive collection of works by early European traveler artists, such as Angas, as well as paintings by prominent 20th-century black South African artists, including Gerard Bhengu, Daniel Rakgoathe, and Trevor Makhoba. The **Mashu Museum of Ethnology** displays perhaps the best collection of traditional Zulu glass beadwork in the country; African utensils, like tightly woven wicker beer pots; weapons such as assegais dating from the Bambatha Uprising of 1906, during which blacks in Natal rebelled against a poll tax and were brutally put down; carvings; masks; pottery; and musical instruments. Paintings of African tribespeople by artist Barbara Tyrrell, who traveled around South Africa from the 1940s to 1960s capturing people in their traditional costumes and gathering valuable anthropological data, add vitality to the collection. The **Killie Campbell Africana Library,** which is open to the public though it is not a lending library, is a treasure trove of historical information on KwaZulu-Natal. It includes the papers of James Stuart, a magistrate and explorer during the early 20th century; the oral tradition of hundreds of Zulu informants; a collection of pamphlets produced by the Colenso family in their struggle for the recognition of the rights of the Zulu people; and a good collection of 19th-century works on game hunting. ✉ *220 Marriott Rd., at Essenwood Rd., Berea* ☎ *031/207–3432 or 031/260–1722* ⊕ *khozi2.nu.ac.za* ✉ *Muckleneuk tours R25, library free* ☉ *Muckleneuk by appointment; library weekdays 8:30–1 and 2–4:30, Sat. 9–noon.*

❷❺ **Durban Botanic Gardens.** Opposite the Greyville Racecourse, Africa's oldest surviving botanical garden is a delightful 150-year-old oasis of greenery interlaced with walking paths, fountains, and ponds. The gardens' orchid house and collection of rare cycads are renowned. The Garden of the Senses caters to the blind, and the tea garden enjoys a sylvan setting far from the city's hustle and bustle. It's a great place to take a load off your feet and settle back with a cup of hot tea and cakes. ✉ *Sydenham Rd., off the M8, Berea* ☎ *031/201–1303* ⊕ *www.durbanbotgardens.org.za* ✉ *Free* ☉ *Mid-Apr.–mid-Sept., daily 7:30–5:15; mid-Sept.–mid-Apr., daily 7:30–5:45.*

❸❷ **Hare Krishna Temple of Understanding.** This magnificent lotus-shaped temple opened in 1985 and is at the heart of activities run by the city's

International Society for Krishna Consciousness. Gold-tinted windows adorn the outside of the temple, and the interior has floors made of imported Italian marble. Colorful laser drawings depicting the life of the Hindu god Krishna cover the ceiling, and statues of Krishna and his consort Radha are elaborately dressed in traditional Indian attire. You need to remove your shoes when entering the temple. ⊠ *50 Bhaktivedanta Swami Circle, off Higginson Hwy., Unit 5, Chatsworth* ☎ *No phone* 💳 *Free* ☉ *Mon.–Sat 10–1 and 4–8, Sun. 10–3:30; traditional singing and dancing Mon.–Sat. 4–6.*

need a break? **Govinda's** (⊠ Hare Krishna Temple of Understanding ☎ 031/ 403–4600) is an inexpensive yet excellent vegetarian restaurant. Hare Krishna devotees do not use onions, garlic, or mushrooms in their food. The traditional Indian *biryani*, a rice dish, is a favorite.

㉔ Kendra Hall & Ekta Mandir. One of the most easily accessible and opulent temples in the city center, the Kendra, adjacent to the Durban Botanic Garden, opened in 2001 after two years of intricate work by sculptors in India. The structure is unmistakably Eastern, with golden domes that tower above a palm tree supported by ornately decorated columns and arches that give the temple an East-meets-West look. Inside are two halls: a small one on the ground level and a larger one upstairs, which is a popular venue for weddings and leads to the temple. Huge statues of Hindu gods, notably Ganesha, Krishna, and Ram, are garlanded and clothed in exquisite Indian fabric. You can join an early morning or evening prayer daily at 6:30 AM and PM. ⊠ *5 Sydenham Rd. Greyville* ☎ *031/309–1824* 💳 *Free* ☉ *Daily 6–noon and 3–6.*

㉗ Mitchell Park. The magnificent rose garden, colorful floral displays, and leafy lawns here are real treats on a hot summer day. Attached to the park is a beautiful small zoo, named after Sir Charles Mitchell, an early governor of Natal. It was opened at the turn of the 19th century, and the Aldabra tortoises that were donated to the park in the early 1900s, now massive, are still in residence. There are also a number of small mammals, reptiles, tropical fish, and birds in large aviaries. The park has a popular playground, and the leafy terrace of the park's Blue Zoo Restaurant is a great place for breakfast or a light lunch. ⊠ *6 Nimmo Rd., off Musgrave Rd., Morningside* ☎ *031/303–3568* 💳 *Gardens free; zoo R3* ☉ *Gardens daily 7:30–8; zoo daily 7:30–4.*

need a break? From the bottom of Mitchell Park, stroll over Innes Road to **Mozart's** (⊠ 467 Innes Rd., Morningside ☎ 031/303–3294) for one of the finest ice creams you might ever taste.

㉒ NSA Gallery. The National Society of the Arts' Gallery complex houses four exhibition areas, in addition to a crafts shop, the Durban Center for Photography, and a classy open-air restaurant. The center does not have a particular focus, but is committed to promoting emerging talent in the province. Recent exhibits have included a collection of handmade jewelry and furniture and intriguing miniature works on wooden panels, including a carving of Nelson Mandela. The center's clean architectural lines and leafy setting make this a popular venue with Durban's trendy set, and it's a lovely place to cool off after a hot morning touring the town. The gallery and crafts shop support and promote local art, so it's worth hunting for tasteful souvenirs. ☒ *166 Bulwer Rd. off the M8, Glenwood* ☎ *031/202–3686* ⊕ *www.nsagallery.co.za* ☒ *Free* ⊙ *Tues.–Fri. 9–5, Sat. 9–4, Sun. 10–3.*

㉓ Shree Ambalavaanar Alayam Temple. One of Durban's most spectacular Hindu shrines is in Cato Manor. The temple's facade is adorned with brightly painted representations of the Hindu gods, notably Ganesha, Shiva, and Vishnu. The magnificent doors leading to the cellar were salvaged from a temple built in 1875 on the banks of the Umbilo River and subsequently destroyed by floods. During an important Hindu festival held annually in March, unshod fire walkers cross beds of burning, glowing coals. There are no set visiting hours; however if the temple is open, you'll be welcome to go inside. If not, the exterior of the building is still worth seeing. ☒ *890 Bellair Rd., Cato Manor, take M13 (from Leopold St.) out of the city; at major fork in road after Westridge Park and high school, veer left onto Bellair Rd.* ☎ *No phone* ☒ *Free* ⊙ *Hrs. vary.*

㉛ Treasure Beach. A visit to the Wildlife Society of South Africa's coastal reserve and environmental education center, on the Bluff, will give you an idea of what this section of the coast looked like before it was commercially developed. This is not a swimming beach but rather a good example of a rocky shore and narrow, sandy beach, accessed down a flight of almost 200 stairs and through a tropical dune forest. The center organizes night walks along the beach once or twice a month, after a new or full moon; they're very popular, especially with kids. The evening begins with a traditional braai at around 5:30 in the picnic area above the beach (bring your own meat, salad, and utensils). You're then led down to the shore, where society staff help you look for octopus, eels, mussels, oysters, crabs, and other sea creatures. Bring your own flashlight and shoes that don't come off easily but that you don't mind getting wet. ☒ *835 Marine Dr., Bluff* ☎ *031/467–8507 or 031/467–8508* ⊕ *www.wildlifesociety.org.za/Treasure.htm* ☒ *R22.*

★ ㉘ Umgeni River Bird Park. This bird park, ranked among the world's best, is built under high cliffs next to the Umgeni River and has various walk-through aviaries. The variety of birds, both exotic and indigenous, is astonishing. You'll be able to take close-up photographs of macaws, giant Asian hornbills, toucans, pheasants, flamingos, and eight species of crane, including the blue crane, South Africa's national bird. Try to time your visit to take in the bird show, which is a delight for both children and adults, and afterward have your photo taken with Otis, a white-faced owl. Drinks and light lunches are served at the park's kiosk. ☒ *Riverside Rd., off the M4, Durban North* ☎ *031/579–4600* ⊕ *www. umgeniriverbirdpark.co.za* ☒ *R25* ⊙ *Daily 9–4:30; bird shows daily at 11 and 2.*

★ ㉙ UShaka Sea World. The world's fifth-largest aquarium and the largest in the Southern Hemisphere, Sea World has a capacity of nearly 6 million gallons of water, more than four times the size of Cape Town's aquarium. The innovative design is as impressive as the size. You enter through the side of a giant ship and walk down several stories, past the massive skeleton of Misty, a southern right whale that died near Cape Town after colliding with a ship, until a sign welcomes you to the BOTTOM OF THE OCEAN. Here you enter a "labyrinth of shipwrecks"—a jumble of five different fake but highly realistic wrecks, from an early-20th-century passenger cruiser to a steamship. Within this labyrinth are massive tanks, housing more than 200 species of fish and other sea life and the biggest variety of sharks in the world, including ragged-tooth and Zambezi sharks (known elsewhere as bull sharks), responsible for more attacks on humans than any other species. Don't expect to see great whites, though; they don't survive in aquariums. While inside the aquarium, try to catch a fish-feeding. The best is the open-ocean feed in the afternoon, when divers hand-feed the fish. Look out for the interesting bottom feeders, like rays and sand sharks.

On dry land, 20-minute dolphin and seal shows, held in adjacent stadiums twice a day (three times during busy seasons), are both well worth attending. Up to four dolphins perform impressive tricks (leaping into the air, waving their tails, and "kissing" their trainers) at a time. Watch for Gambit, the biggest dolphin in any dolphinarium in the world; the over-30 dolphin jumps out of the water and perches on the side of the pool. Seals strut their stuff in humorous shows held just after the dolphin performances. For the best views of dolphin and seal shows, sit in the middle of the stadium toward the back.

Add-ons include a 20-minute shark dive in an acrylic capsule, with instruction (R100 weekdays, R120 weekends; no children under 12); a snorkeling experience in the fish tanks (R60); and ocean walking (R120 weekdays, R160 weekends; no children under 12), where you descend in a large bubblelike helmet in a fish tank, with the assistance of a guide. Ocean walking and shark dives don't take place on Monday. ⊠ *1 Bell St., Point* ☎ *031/328–8000* ⊕ *www.ushakamarineworld.co.za* ✉ *R80, R110 with Wet 'n Wild* ☼ *Daily 9–6.*

★ ☾ ㉚ **UShaka Wet 'n Wild.** This extensive water fun park, run in tandem with Sea World, comprises slides, pools, and about 10 different water rides. There's something for everyone, from toddlers to adrenaline junkies. As you walk into uShaka Marine World, you'll see people lazily floating on giant red tubes in the Duzi Adventure River, a ride that circles the aquarium, descends down a long slide, and runs under waterfalls and past fish tanks in a nearly 1,500-foot loop that takes about 15 minutes. The giant, almost vertical Plunge is the most exciting slide, and the Zoom-Zoom, a five-lane racer, is also popular. You can easily spend the better part of a day here, and a combo ticket with Sea World lets you go back and forth between the two. ⊠ *1 Bell St., Point* ☎ *031/328–8000* ⊕ *www. ushakamarineworld.co.za* ✉ *R55, R110 with Sea World* ☼ *Daily 9–6.*

Where to Eat

★ $$$$ ✕ **Chefs on Stage.** For a reality-TV-style dining experience, put on your chef's hat, and prepare to entertain as well as be entertained at this fun establishment. The restaurant here is adjacent to a theater, outfitted with

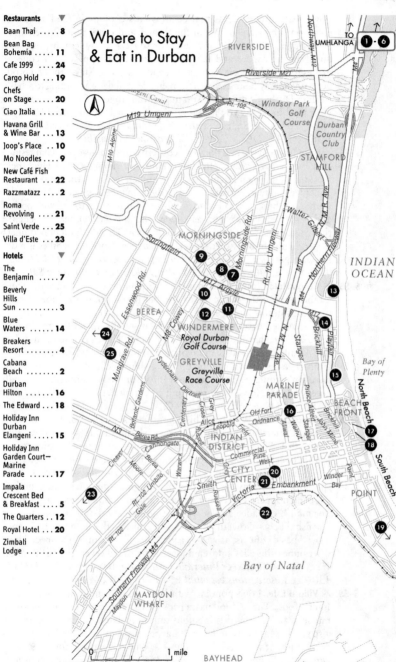

Where to Stay & Eat in Durban

Restaurants ▼

Baan Thai **8**

Bean Bag Bohemia **11**

Cafe 1999 .... **24**

Cargo Hold ... **19**

Chefs on Stage **20**

Ciao Italia **1**

Havana Grill & Wine Bar ... **13**

Joop's Place .. **10**

Mo Noodles **9**

New Café Fish Restaurant .. **22**

Razzmatazz **2**

Roma Revolving **21**

Saint Verde ... **25**

Villa d'Este ... **23**

Hotels ▼

The Benjamin **7**

Beverly Hills Sun **3**

Blue Waters **14**

Breakers Resort **4**

Cabana Beach **2**

Durban Hilton **16**

The Edward ... **18**

Holiday Inn Durban Elangeni **15**

Holiday Inn Garden Court— Marine Parade **17**

Impala Crescent Bed & Breakfast **5**

The Quarters .. **12**

Royal Hotel ... **20**

Zimbali Lodge **6**

stage, seats, and cameras that beam what's cooking in the kitchen directly onto big-screen TVs in the theater and restaurant. Professional chefs might ask you to stir a sauce or squeeze a few lemons, but they do all the dirty work and leave the fun stuff for the guests. The concept makes for a highly sociable occasion, and make no mistake: the end product is unfailingly fantastic, with the menu devised daily according to what's fresh in Durban's markets. You might want to save Chefs on Stage for your final night, as you'll find no finer fun or food in town. ⊠ *Royal Hotel, 267 Smith St., city center* ☎ *031/333–6002* ⌂ *Reservations essential* ⊟ *AE, DC, MC, V* ⊘ *Closed Sun. No lunch.*

$–$$ ✕ **Baan Thai.** On the 2nd floor of a converted town house, this Thai restaurant brings a refreshing flavor to Durban's dining scene. Thai chefs working in an open kitchen whip up authentic dishes that make heady use of lemongrass, coriander, and *galangal* (a type of ginger). Among the starters, the beef waterfall salad (thinly sliced grilled beef tossed with onions and coriander) is excellent, as are pad thai noodles. Other winners are the whiskey prawns, Thai crab, and the Baan Thai duck (deboned fillets basted in an almost-sweet sauce). *Brinjal* (eggplant) with chilies is a delicious vegetarian option. ⊠ *138 Florida Rd., Morningside* ☎ *031/303–4270* ⊟ *AE, DC, MC, V* ⌂ *BYOB* ⊘ *Closed Sun. No lunch Sat.*

★ **$–$$** ✕ **Cargo Hold.** You'll need to book several months in advance to secure a table next to the shark tank here, but if you do, it'll be one of your most memorable dining experiences ever. You can enjoy a trio of carpaccios—smoked ostrich, beef, and salmon—while 13-foot ragged-tooth and Zambezi sharks drift right by your table. There are also meat dishes like oxtail, a South African favorite; and rosemary-and-rock-salt leg of lamb. The restaurant is done up like a shipwreck; of three floors, two have tank frontage. The restaurant is part of the Phantom Ship; though access costs R20, you can recoup it by eating here. ⊠ *1 Bell St., Point* ☎ *031/328–8065* ⊟ *AE, DC, MC, V.*

★ **$–$$** ✕ **Havana Grill & Wine Bar.** This upmarket restaurant is one of Durban's finest. It offers spectacular sea vistas (ask for a table with a view) and minimalist Afro-Cuban decor, with richly upholstered chairs, some leather couches, and antelope horns on the walls. Steak—aged on meat hooks in a giant fridge integrated into the decor—and seafood are both specialties. Try Havana's tasting platter for starters: nachos, crumbed jalapeno poppers stuffed with cheese, grilled calamari, and spring rolls. For mains, consider a fillet with a Dijon-mustard-and-cream sauce or line fish (likely yellowtail or swordfish) grilled with Cajun spices. There's a good basic wine list as well as a walk-in cellar from which special bottles can be ordered. Children under 12 are not allowed after 6. ⊠ *Shop U2, Suncoast Casino & Entertainment World, Beachfront* ☎ *031/337–1304* ⌂ *Reservations essential* ⊟ *AE, DC, MC, V.*

$–$$ ✕ **Villa d'Este.** Long popular with locals, this restaurant has excellent Italian food. The seafood pasta packed with fish, prawns, langoustines, mussels, and calamari is fabulous, but roast lamb and pork shank are also good. As at many of the city's Italian restaurants, the chef's or owner's description of the specials is almost as enjoyable as the food. ⊠ *Davenport and Bulwer Rds., Glenwood* ☎ *031/202–7920* ⌂ *Reservations essential* ⊟ *AE, DC, MC, V* ⊘ *Closed Mon.*

¢–$$ ✕ **Bean Bag Bohemia.** One of the city's most intimate restaurants, Bohemia serves a mix of cosmopolitan and Mediterranean food. It's abuzz with Durban's young and trendy, especially late at night, when you can get a good meal after movies or the theater. Cocktails and lighter meals are served at the bar downstairs, where live musicians often play jazz or the piano. Up rickety wooden stairs at the main restaurant, the most popular starter is the meze platter, with Mediterranean snacks such as hummus, baba ghanoush (an eggplant spread), olives, and pita. Bohemia is well known for its vegetarian meals, but dishes such as lamb shank and duck are also good. You can finish your meal with the baked pecan praline and then relax and get some fresh air on the terrace in back after your hearty meal. ⊠ *18 Windermere Rd., Windermere* ☎ *031/309–6019* ⊟ *AE, DC, MC, V.*

¢–$$ ✕ **Cafe 1999.** Trendy this restaurant may be, but the food is even more memorable than the scene. The husband-and-wife owners encourage you to celebrate taste with a menu of dishes that are meant for sharing, from the "titbits" (small servings) to the "bigbits." Let your fork and fingers wander between dishes like breaded olives stuffed with ricotta cheese and chicken kebabs with coriander-and-lemon pesto. The macadamia-nut-and-honey tart makes for a sweet finish. ⊠ *Shop 2, Silvervause Centre, 117 Vause Rd., Musgrave* ☎ *031/202–3406* ⌂ *Reservations essential* ⊟ *AE, DC, MC, V* ⊗ *Closed Sun. No lunch Sat.*

¢–$$ ✕ **Joop's Place.** No trip to South Africa would be complete without a good traditional steak, and without a doubt, Joop's (pronounced yopes) is the best and most popular steak house in Durban. Most customers are regulars. The specialty here is panfried steak, but the pepper steak and the Hollandse (Dutch-style) *biefstuk* (a center-cut fillet panfried in black butter and flambéed in brandy) are tasty, too. For the exceptionally hungry, try the 800-gram (about 21-ounce) T-bone. ⊠ *Shop 14, Avonmore Centre, Morningside* ☎ *031/312–9135* ⌂ *Reservations essential* ⊟ *AE, DC, MC, V* ⊗ *Closed Sun. No lunch Sat.–Thurs.*

¢–$ ✕ **Ciao Italia.** Don't expect anything traditional at this "modern trattoria" with its friendly, family atmosphere. The food is "zooped-up" Italian; for example, penne Oriental—a multi-culti mix of pasta, chicken breast, ginger, garlic, curry powder, coriander, and chutney. The most exciting dishes are often on the extensive specials list, which changes daily. Both branches are superb, though the decor at Durban North is more stylish and the sea views from the outside deck make it particularly attractive for a sunny lunch. ⊠ *12a Broadway, Durban North* ☎ *031/564–4245* ⊠ *Shop 7A, Multichoice Centre, Westville Rd., Westville* ☎ *031/267–1762* ⌂ *Reservations essential* ⊟ *AE, DC, MC, V* ⊗ *Closed Sun. No lunch Sat.*

★ ¢–$ ✕ **Mo Noodles.** Don't let the name or outside location fool you: this is one of Durban's best restaurants, known for its huge portions and reasonable prices. The decor is chic and minimalist, but unpretentious and comfortable. Opt for a starter of prawn skewers in peanut-dipping sauce or chicken teriyaki salad with a peanut dressing; then move on to chicken, prawn, and beef panfried noodles; a seared, marinated sesame fillet of beef; or any of the excellent Thai-style curries. Homemade ice cream comes in flavors like ginger, coconut, and honey and cashew. Because they don't take reservations, go early, especially on weekend nights. ☒ *Shop 5, Florida Centre, 275 Florida Rd., Morningside* ☎ *031/ 312–4193* ⚍ *Reservations not accepted* ▤ *AE, DC, MC, V* ⊘ *Closed Sun. No lunch Sat.*

¢–$ ✕ **New Café Fish Restaurant.** This long-popular eatery juts out into the Durban Yacht Basin between the BAT Centre and Wilson's Wharf. Here the city's vertical lines—towering skyskrapers along the embankment and the slender masts of vessels anchored alongside the restaurant—tie sky and sea together. The food is tasty, though not superb. Try the mild Thai prawn curry or the pesto line fish, or ask your waiter to bring out the array of uncooked seafood and make up your own platter from individually priced items. The bar upstairs (⇨ Nightlife & the Arts, *below*) is pleasant for sundowners (cocktails) and also serves light meals and snacks. ☒ *31 Yacht Mole, Victoria Embankment* ☎ *031/305– 5062 or 031/305–5063* ▤ *AE, DC, MC, V.*

¢–$ ✕ **Razzmatazz.** The ocean view is reason enough to enjoy an afternoon here—but so is the food. Weather permitting, book a sea view on the deck and dig into an order of fresh oysters or the line fish beurre blanc, grilled and served with a white-wine-and-butter sauce. The chef is well known for his game dishes, so the more adventurous might want to try the springbok carpaccio or the crocodile kebab for starters, and for mains either the kudu gently simmered in red wine or an ostrich fillet in gooseberry sauce. There's also usually a wide array of specials, too. ☒ *Cabana Beach, 10 Lagoon Dr., Umhlanga* ☎ *031/561–5847* ⚍ *Reservations essential* ▤ *AE, DC, MC, V.*

¢–$ ✕ **Roma Revolving.** In business since 1973, this slowly revolving restaurant continues to be one of Durban's most venerable establishments. It is still run by the original Italian owners and staff, and its breathtaking views over the entire city, especially the harbor, are complemented by its Italian charm, service, and menu. Many ingredients are imported, but where possible, local products are used, such as fresh north-coast oysters, fish purchased straight off the boats, and veal sourced from a monastery near Pietermaritzburg. Pasta comes from even closer; it's made on the premises. ☒ *John Ross House, 32nd fl., Victoria Embankment* ☎ *031/337–6707* ⚍ *Reservations essential* ▤ *AE, DC, MC, V* ⊘ *Closed Sun.*

¢–$ ✕ **Saint Verde.** The atmosphere in this eatery (pronounced Saint Verd) buzzes as much as its origins as an old power station. It's a good spot for breakfast (open from 7), a light lunch, dinner, or even a sundowner in the upstairs cocktail bar. It's also the perfect place to plop after a morning of heavy shopping at the Essenwood Flea Market, held in the park next door. For breakfast, feast on an omelet, for lunch, on rare roast fillet on a bagel or ciabatta bread. Alternatively, come for morning or afternoon tea and enjoy the wide selection of cakes and pastries. ☒ *199 Essenwood Rd., Berea* ☎ *031/201–9176* ▤ *AE, DC, MC, V* ⊘ *No dinner Sun.*

Where to Stay

Durban

$–$$$ 🏨 **Royal Hotel.** Durban's best hotel and a cherished city center institution, the aptly named Royal has often hosted British royals. Dating from **Fodor'sChoice** ★ 1842—the city's infancy—the original Royal was replaced by a high-rise in 1978, and all that remains of the old building is the grand Royal Grill. Nevertheless, the hotel maintains some classic touches, such as a butler for every floor and traditional shoe-shine service. Recently refurbished rooms are decorated with a mix of African and Indian influences in a classic, modern look. Bedrooms have dark-wood furniture with red cushions and white cotton bedding, and bathrooms have separate shower and tub. Request a room on an upper floor for a spectacular view of the harbor, which you can also get from the Top of the Royal, a great place for breakfast or Sunday lunch. ✉ *267 Smith St. Box 1041, city center 4000* ☎ *031/333–6000* 🖷 *031/333–6002* ⊕ *www.theroyal. co.za* ⤙ *196 rooms, 16 suites* ⚴ *6 restaurants, room service, in-room data ports, pool, health club, hair salon, squash, 2 bars, travel services* ▤ *AE, DC, MC, V* ⫶⊙⫶ *BP.*

★ **$$** 🏨 **Durban Hilton.** This massive luxury hotel adjacent to the International Convention Centre is within relatively easy walking distance of city center and Beachfront. Rooms, tastefully decorated with an African influence, have sprawling views of either beach or city. Executive floors have a small club room, where guests can get breakfast and free Internet access. Vast and impressive public areas come complete with marble pillars and a pianist tinkling away on a baby grand. The Rainbow Room restaurant has an excellent buffet and an unusual à la carte menu. The Hilton also boasts impeccable service, making it one of the top hotels in this chain in Africa. Though expensive by Durban standards, rates can vary significantly based on how full the hotel is. ✉ *12–14 Walnut Rd., Box 11288, Marine Parade 4056* ☎ *031/336–8100* 🖷 *031/ 336–8200* ⤙ *327 rooms, 16 suites* ⚴ *2 restaurants, in-room data ports, pool, health club, hair salon, bar, shops, Internet, business services* ▤ *AE, DC, MC, V.*

$$ 🏨 **The Edward.** Built in 1939 in classic colonial style, the Edward is one of Durban's oldest hotels and has changed hands a few times. Although it's almost been restored to its former elegance, it seems to have lost a little of its soul. Nevertheless, service is excellent, and the stylish cut-glass chandeliers, molded ceilings, and subtle art-deco details bring to mind Durban's more refined past. Rooms are tastefully furnished; 10 have balconies overlooking the sea, and the others have bay windows with sea views. The hotel faces beautiful South Beach, just a 10-minute walk from the city center. ✉ *149 Marine Parade, Box 105, Beachfront 4000* ☎ *031/337–3681* 🖷 *031/332–1692* ⊕ *www.proteahotels.com* ⤙ *101 rooms, 10 suites* ⚴ *Restaurant, room service, pool, hair salon, 2 bars, shop, business services* ▤ *AE, DC, MC, V.*

$$ 🏨 **Holiday Inn Durban Elangeni.** One of the best hotels on the Beachfront, this 21-story high-rise overlooks North Beach, a two-minute drive from the city center. It attracts a mix of business, conference, and leisure travelers. Though all rooms have views of the water, request a room on an upper floor for a full ocean view. Rooms are small and narrow and have a beachlike seaside feel at odds with the formality of the marbled lobby and public rooms. The hotel has one of the few Japanese restaurants in the city as well as a first-class Indian restaurant. ✉ *63 Snell Parade, Box 4094, Beachfront 4000* ☎ *031/362–1300* 🖷 *031/332–5527* ⊕ *www. southernsun.com* ⤙ *446 rooms, 10 suites* ⚴ *3 restaurants, room ser-*

vice, 2 pools, health club, hair salon, 2 bars, business services 🖃 *AE, DC, MC, V.*

★ **$$** 🖾 **The Quarters.** Four converted Victorian homes compose the city's most intimate boutique hotel, a contemporary European-style property with a colonial African feel. Rooms have mahogany furniture, cream damask-covered beds, and sunken tubs in luxurious bathrooms. Many of the rooms have small verandas facing onto Florida Road, with its swaying palm trees and sometimes busy traffic, but double-glazed windows keep it quiet. ✉ *101 Florida Rd., Berea 4001* ☎ *031/303–5246* 🖷 *031/303–5269* ⊕ *www.quarters.co.za* 🛏 *25 rooms* ⌂ *Restaurant* 🖃 *AE, DC, MC, V* ⦿ *BP.*

$ 🖾 **Holiday Inn Garden Court—Marine Parade.** You can't beat the location of this pleasant hotel midway between South and North beaches and only a five-minute drive from the city center. Rooms are attractive and modern, with textured wallpaper, bold floral bedspreads, and a small sitting area. All face the sea, but request an upper-floor room. Views from the pool deck on the 30th floor are superb. ✉ *167 Marine Parade, Box 10809, Beachfront 4056* ☎🖷 *031/337–3341* ⊕ *www.southernsun.com* 🛏 *340 rooms, 6 suites* ⌂ *Restaurant, indoor pool, bar* 🖃 *AE, DC, MC, V* ⦿ *BP.*

$ 🖾 **The Benjamin.** In one of Durban's transformed historic buildings, this small hotel offers excellent value for the money. Its location is ideal—perched on trendy Florida Road, with its excellent restaurants and nightlife, and approximately five minutes from both the beaches and the city center. The residents' lounge is quiet and elegant but still warm and comfortable, as are the stylish rooms. The breakfast room has big glass doors opening out onto a small pool. ✉ *141 Florida Rd., Morningside, 4001* ☎ *031/303–4233* 🖷 *031/303–4288* ⊕ *www.benjamin.co.za* 🛏 *45 rooms* ⌂ *In-room data ports, pool* 🖃 *AE, DC, MC, V* ⦿ *BP.*

¢ 🖾 **Blue Waters.** A Durban landmark, the family-owned Blue Waters stands right at the end of the Golden Mile. This means it's quieter than most of the other Beachfront hotels. The circular residents' lounge, with its floor-to-ceiling windows, is a wonderful place to enjoy the stunning sea views and elegant tea and scones. The '60s-style mosaic indoor pool is also delightful. Rooms are comfortable, and all have balconies—which few of the other Beachfront hotels do. ✉ *175 Snell Parade, Beachfront 4056* ☎ *031/332–4272* 🖷 *031/332–5817* ⊕ *www.bluewatershotel.co.za* 🛏 *250 rooms, 14 suites* ⌂ *Dining room, room service, indoor pool, hair salon, sauna, squash, lounge* 🖃 *AE, DC, MC, V.*

Umhlanga

$$$$ 🖾 **Zimbali Lodge.** One of only two luxury lodges in the province with direct access to the beach, Zimbali's setting is in one of only three remaining coastal forests in the province. The decor is a stylish mix of colonial Malaysian/African, with lots of glass, dark wood, and rough woven fabrics. Rooms have crisp white linen, wood carvings, and balconies that look out onto the forest and the lake beyond. It's a wonderful place to laze around one pool, play a round of golf, or swim in the private Mauritian-style pool on the beach. The service is warm and friendly. ✉ *M4, 20 km (12 mi) north of Umhlanga, Box 404, Umhlali 4390* ☎ *032/538–1007* 🖷 *032/538–1019* ⊕ *www.sunint.co.za* 🛏 *76 rooms, 8 lodges* ⌂ *Room* service, 18-hole golf course, 2 tennis courts, 2 pools, health club, hair salon, steam room, beach, horseback riding, playgrounds ⊟ AE, DC, MC, V.

$$$–$$$$ ▦ **Beverly Hills Sun.** In a high-rise building right on the beach, this up-scale hotel is popular with both vacationers and businesspeople. The service is excellent and the facilities superb. However, if you're the sort of beachgoer who likes to loll about in a bathing suit, you may find this hotel too formal. The public lounge, festooned with huge floral arrangements and yards of gathered drapes, serves a full silver-service tea in the afternoon, and a pianist plays in the evening. Guest rooms are fairly small, but all have terrific sea views, particularly those on the upper floors. The decor makes extensive use of bleached-wood furniture and bold floral fabrics. For a more open, beachlike feel, take one of the cabanas, large duplex rooms that open onto a lovely pool deck. ⊠ *Lighthouse Rd., Box 71, Umhlanga 4320* ☎ *031/561–2211* 🖷 *031/561–3711* ⊕ *www.interconti.com* ⤵ *90 rooms, 5 suites, 10 cabanas* ⚲ *2 restaurants, room service, pool, hair salon, 2 bars* ⊟ *AE, DC, MC, V* ⦿ *CP.*

$$ ▦ **Breakers Resort.** This property enjoys an enviable position at the northern tip of Umhlanga, surrounded by the wilds of the Hawaiian Forest and overlooking the unspoiled wetlands of Umhlanga Lagoon. Of all the resorts in Umhlanga, this one suffers the least from crowds—amble north along the beach and you will see scarcely another soul and no buildings. The disadvantage is that you probably need a car to get into town, and you can't swim directly in front of the resort because the surf's too dangerous. The building is unattractive, with long, depressing corridors, but the rooms themselves are fine, with fully equipped kitchens and great views of the beach and lagoon. ⊠ *88 Lagoon Dr., Box 75, Umhlanga 4320* ☎ *031/561–2271* 🖷 *031/561–2722* ⊕ *www.southernsun.com* ⤵ *80 rooms* ⚲ *2 restaurants, kitchens, tennis court, pool, bar, playground* ⊟ *AE, DC, MC, V* ⦿ *CP.*

★ $$ ▦ **Cabana Beach.** Families who want a traditional beach vacation can't do better than this large resort, where children under 18 stay free, the bathing beach is directly in front of the hotel, and there are tons of activities to keep kids happy. Room decor is simple, comfortable, and appropriate for the beach. Each cabana comes with a fully equipped kitchen, a dining-living area, and a veranda with great sea views. Request a tower or beachfront apartment for the most attractive and practical space configuration. Out of season, the tariffs are about half price. ⊠ *10 Lagoon Dr., Box 10, Umhlanga 4320* ☎ *031/561–2371* 🖷 *031/561–3522* ⊕ *www.cabanabeach.southernsun.co.za* ⤵ *217 rooms* ⚲ *4 restaurants, kitchens, 2 tennis courts, 2 pools, health club, squash, bar* ⊟ *AE, DC, MC, V* ⦿ *CP.*

$ ▦ **Impala Crescent Bed & Breakfast.** If you prefer a more personal guesthouse over a hotel, Mari and Steve Pete's welcoming B&B in La Lucia—near Umhlanga, Gateway, the Zimbali Lodge, Sibaya, and Suncoast—is a good choice. The Petes will offer you a welcoming margarita or cappuccino on their beautiful wooden deck overlooking the sea and surrounded by tropical indigenous bush that is home to monkeys, mongeese, and abundant birdlife. They'll also take you on a personal orientation tour of the area and will make special dinners on request, like a traditional South African braai, at R100 per person. The private suite is large enough for two adults and one or two small children. ⊠ *24 Impala Crescent, La Lucia 4051* ☎ *083/296–9433* ✒ *mpete@dit.ac.za* ⤴ *1 suite* ⚫ *Kitchenette, pool, babysitting, laundry service, airport transfers; no smoking* ⊟ *No credit cards* ⊖*l BP.*

Nightlife & the Arts

What's on in Durban, a free monthly publication put out by the tourism office and distributed at popular sites, lists a diary of upcoming events. The "Entertainment" section of the Durban-based *Sunday Tribune* and the *Mail & Guardian,* a weekly tabloid, are good information sources. *The Mercury* and *Daily News,* both published weekdays, also contain entertainment sections.

Tickets for shows, movies released by Nu Metro, concerts, and other events can be obtained through **Computicket** (☎ 083/915–8000 or 083/ 915–1234) ⊕ www.computicket.com). Note, though, that Computicket does not accept foreign credit cards. Tickets for movies released by Ster Kinekor can be obtained from **Ticketline** (☎ 0861/300–444 or 082/ 16789 ⊕ www.sterkinekor.com), which accepts foreign credit cards. Both ticket agencies have outlets in major shopping centers.

Nightlife

BARS   You can sip a cocktail watching the sun go down over Durban's harbor at the **New Café Fish Bar** (⊠ 31 Yacht Mole, Victoria Embankment ☎ 031/305–5062 or 031/305–5063), in the Durban Yacht Basin. **Zansi Bar** (⊠ 45 Maritime Pl., Small Craft Harbour, city center ☎ 031/ 368–2029) promotes local bands and shows off a breathtaking view of the harbor.

Durban's young and fashionable relax at the **Café Vacca Matta** (⊠ 20 Suncoast Blvd., Beachfront ☎ 031/368–6535), on the upper level of the Suncoast Casino. California-style **Joe Kool's** (⊠ 137 Lower Marine Parade, Beachfront ☎ 031/332–9697) is popular with younger crowds.

Huge lava lamps give a sophisticated feel to the DJs, live bands, and cabaret shows at **Krakatoa Show Bar** (⊠ 1 Sibaya Dr., Umhlanga ☎ 031/580– 5555), at the Sibaya Casino.

Both Florida and Windermere roads, near each other in Berea and adjacent Morningside, are known for their bars, cafés, and restaurants, which often flow out onto the pavement. **Billy the BUMS** (⊠ 504 Windermere Rd., Morningside ☎ 031/303–1988) hums from the early evening until late. **Wanda Bar** (⊠ 258 Florida Rd., Morningside ☎ 031/ 312–9436) is a popular place for a pre- or post-dinner drink. The refurbished **Zeta Bar** (⊠ 258 Florida Rd., Berea ☎ 031/312–9436) has a comfortable cocktail lounge and attracts a mixed-race crowd.

CASINOS   The omnipresent sound of slot machines makes your ears ring at **Sibaya Casino** (⊠ 1 Sibaya Dr., Umhlanga ☎ 031/580–5000 or 0860/742–292 ⊕ www.sibaya.co.za). The casino area has more than 900 slot machines and 37 betting tables, among them roulette and poker. **Suncoast Casino** (⊠ 20 Suncoast Blvd., Beachfront ☎ 031/328–3000 ⊕ www. suncoastcasino.co.za), a hub of dining, drinking, and gambling activity, has 1,250 slot machines and 50 gaming tables, including blackjack, roulette, and poker.

DANCE CLUBS **Bonkers** (⊠ Hotel California, 17 Florida Rd., Berea ☎ 031/303–1146) has regular karaoke evenings and offers the latest commercial dance tunes. Rated as one of the country's best dance clubs, **330** (⊠ 330 Point Rd., Point ☎ 031/337–7172) attracts a hip crowd of models and glitterati with loud techno music and also brings in the older set. The club is synonymous with Durban's rave scene. One of the oldest and best-known downtown clubs, **Zoom** (⊠ 19 Dick King St., city center ☎ 031/337–6916) attracts a mixed-race crowd that keeps coming back for the red-hot DJs and occasional live music, including rock, pop, and reggae.

LIVE MUSIC CLUBS Alternative rock bands play at **Burn** (⊠ Clark and Umbilo Rds., Glenwood ☎ 031/201–0076), and crowds love the heavy-metal music. **Rivets** (⊠ 12 Walnut Rd., Marine Parade ☎ 031/336–8110), at the Hilton, is a smaller venue that offers some of the best jazz in Durban and lets you rub shoulders with the city's rich and wanna-be famous.

The Arts

The **Playhouse** (⊠ Smith St., across from City Hall, city center ☎ 031/369–9555) stands at the heart of Durban's cultural life. The complex encompasses five performing arts venues, and the Playhouse Company stages productions of music, ballet, drama, opera, and cabaret. The Playhouse is also home to the Natal Philharmonic Orchestra.

Located at the University of KwaZulu-Natal, the **Elizabeth Sneddon Theatre** (⊠ King George V Ave., Glenwood ☎ 031/260–2296) hosts music and drama productions on a smaller scale than those at the Playhouse. Famous local, national, and international poets, writers, dramatists, and filmmakers gather at the Sneddon for annual festivals, such as the Durban International Film Festival in June and Poetry Africa in October.

Regular musical shows, such as those celebrating the music of the 1960s or the development of South African music, as well as cabaret performances are staged at the large, multitiered **Barnyard Theatre** (⊠ Gateway mall, 1st fl., Gateway Rd. and Sugar Close, Umhlanga Ridge ☎ 031/566–3045). There's always something theatrical happening at the **BAT Centre** (⊠ 45 Maritime Pl., Small Craft Harbour, Victoria Embankment ☎ 031/332–0468), from a drumming session to a live poetry festival. The intimate **Catalina Theatre** (⊠ Wilson's Wharf, 18 Boatman's Rd., Victoria Embankment ☎ 031/305–6889) specializes in comedy. Sibaya's **iZulu Theatre** (⊠ 1 Sibaya Dr., Umhlanga ☎ 031/580–5555), which can seat more than 600 people, opened with the internationally acclaimed *African Footprint,* a colorful and elaborate African musical. A short distance from the restaurants at Florida Road, the small but popular **KwaSuka Theatre** (⊠ 50 Stamford Hill Rd., Greyville ☎ 031/309–3326) stages mostly local musicals and dramas. Suncoast's cinema complex, **Supernova** (⊠ 20 Suncoast Blvd., Beachfront ☎ 031/328–3333) has the largest screen in the province but is still cozy. It screens the latest releases from both Hollywood and Bollywood (and is the only movie house in Durban to show midnight movies, on Saturdays) and occasionally stages local dramas.

Sports & the Outdoors

Beaches

The sea near Durban, unlike that around the Cape, is comfortably warm year-round: in summer the water temperature can top 27°C (80°F), whereas in winter 19°C (65°F) is considered cold. All of KwaZulu-Natal's main beaches are protected by shark nets and staffed with lifeguards, and there are usually boards stating the wind direction, water temperature, and the existence of any dangerous swimming conditions. Directly in front of uShaka Marine World, **uShaka Beach** is an attractive public beach. The **Golden Mile,** stretching from South Beach all the way to Snake Park Beach, is packed with people, who enjoy the water slides, singles bars, and fast-food joints. A little farther north are the **Umhlanga beaches,** and on the opposite side of the bay are the less commercialized beaches on **Durban's Bluff.** Another pretty beach and coastal walk, just north of the **Umhlanga Lagoon,** leads to miles of near-empty beaches backed by virgin bush. Please note: you should not walk alone on deserted beaches or carry any jewelry or other valuables.

Boating & Dolphin-Watching

It's easy to charter all manner of boats, from a paddleski (a flat fiberglass board that you paddle) for a few rand to a deep-sea fishing vessel for a few thousand. Inexpensive harbor tours lasting a half hour, booze cruises, and dinner cruises can all be booked from the quayside at Wilson's Wharf. Shop around to find something that suits your budget, taste, and time frame.

 If you'd like to catch a glimpse of Durban at first light from the sea while dolphins jump softly around your small boat, take a tour with **Durban Marine Safari** (✉ Wilson's Wharf, Victoria Embankment ☎ 073/269–9316 or 084/725–6638 ⊕ www.dolphinviewing.co.za). The boat travels a half-mile or so out to sea through the harbor and along the Durban Beachfront and visits the Natal Sharks Board workers as they check the nets. You may be lucky enough to see a shark, but if not, there are plenty of other things to see, especially from June to November, when you might well come across whales. Owner-skipper David Phillips is knowledgable about both marine biology and the history and goings-on in the harbor. Two-hour tours (R200) depart daily at 6:30, if there are enough people.

Cricket

Kingsmead Cricket Ground (✉ 2 Kingsmead Close, Marine Parade ☎ 031/335–4200) is home to the KwaZulu-Natal provincial team, the Dolphins, and is a frequent venue for international test matches between South Africa and touring teams from abroad. Cricket is played in Durban mostly between September and March.

Fishing

Deep-sea fishing is a popular activity, as there's almost always something biting. Summer (November–May) brings game fish like barracuda, marlin, sailfish, and dorado, whereas winter is better for the bottom fishes, like mussel crackers, salmon, and rock cod. Sharks are present year-round. Depending on the wind and conditions, charters are likely to head north, toward Tongaat, where the fishing is often better than south of the city.

Casea Charters (⊠ 1 Manderley Mews, 6 Newlands Dr., Umhlanga ☎ 031/561–7381 or 083/690–2511 ⊕ www.caseacharters.co.za) offers trips on a ski boat from Granny's Pool, in front of Cabana Beach, that vary from two to eight hours (R250–R3,000). Fish for dorado, yellowfin tuna, king and queen mackerel, garrick, rock cod, salmon, and other species. Bait and equipment are supplied, but bring your own food and drinks. **Lynski Charters** (✆ Box 2262, Mount Edgecombe 4300 ☎ 031/539–3338 or 082/445–6600 ⊕ www.lynski.com) offers deep-sea fishing for barracuda, sailfish, marlin, shark, and reef fish out of Durban's harbor. Trips, in a 35-foot game-fish boat, cost R3,800 for up to six people fishing, although the boat can take nine people altogether. The price includes equipment, tackle, bait, and cold drinks. **Swissroll Charters** (✆ 246 Gray Park Rd., Brighton Beach, 4052 ☎ 031/467–2185 or 082/451–6567 ⊕ www.swissroll.co.za) offers similar deep-sea fishing trips from the harbor. For R3,800, skipper-owner Ralph Nussbaumer takes a maximum of six people for a day on his 30-foot boat with cabin. Sometimes he sets up a gas cooker and fries some fresh fish.

Golf

Durban Country Club (⊠ Walter Gilbert Rd., Stamford Hill ☎ 031/313–1777) has hosted more South African Opens than any other course, and is regularly rated the best in South Africa. Tees and greens sit atop large sand dunes, and trees add an additional hazard. Visitors can play Monday–Saturday, and fees for the 18-hole, par-72 course are R425. The first tee-off at 6:55 is popular because of the heat. Rental clubs are available. Inside the Greyville Racecourse, the **Royal Durban Golf Club** (⊠ 16 Mitchell Crescent, Greyville ☎ 031/309–1373) offers no protection from the wind, which makes hitting the narrow fairways very difficult, but the surroundings are attractive and the venue is central. Fees for the 18-hole, par-72 course are R150, rental clubs are available, and reservations are essential. **Zimbali Country Club** (⊠ M4, between Umdloti and Ballito ☎ 032/538–1041 ⊕ www.sun-international.com) incorporates one of the three remaining coastal forests in the province. The world-class 18-hole course was designed by Tom Weiskopf and lies amid sand dunes above a secluded beach, natural springs, and a lake. There is a fully stocked pro shop. Greens fees for 18 holes are R210 weekdays, R240 weekends. Compulsory cart rental is R160; rental clubs are available for R150–R300.

The **Roger Manning Golf Shop** (⊠ Windsor Park Golf Course, N.M.R. Ave., Stamford-Hill ☎ 031/303–1728) rents clubs for R50–R100 per day.

Horse Racing

The main horse-racing season extends from May to August. Meets are usually held Wednesday and Saturday and tend to consist of 9 or 10 races. The area's racecourses, including Pietermaritzburg's Scottsville (⇨ Side Trips from Durban, *below*), take turns holding meets. **Greyville**

Racecourse (✉ 106 Avondale Rd., Greyville ☎ 031/309–4545), almost in the city center, is the only course in the province to hold night meets, usually midweek. At the Durban July—probably the country's most famous horse-racing event—the outrageous fashions worn by racing fans attract almost as much attention as the horses themselves.

Those with a passion for horse racing may enjoy Greyville Racecourse's **Stud Farm Tours** (☎ 031/314–1640). These relaxing one-day trips to the beautiful Midlands run mid-May–August. Kick off the day with a trainer's breakfast at Summerveld, about a half hour from the city center, before you amble up to three of the top stud farms in the country. The R100 tour also includes a fabulous lunch at Hartford House or Greenfields Manor.

Rock Climbing

At around 79 feet, the **Gateway mall's rock-climbing wall** (✉ Gateway Rd. and Sugar Close, Umhlanga Ridge ☎ 031/566–4955) is the world's tallest indoors. Rock-climbing sessions for beginners and experts are available daily 9–9. Halfway up the rock costs R25, to the top of the rock is R35, and an unlimited session for experienced climbers is R60.

Rugby

KwaZulu-Natal's Sharks play at **Kings Park Rugby Stadium** (✉ Jacko Jackson Dr., Stamford Hill ☎ 031/312–6368). The Sharks are strong contenders in the annual Super 12 Tournament, held between Australian, South African, and New Zealand teams between February and July, and in the South African round-robin Bankfin Currie Cup competition, held from July to October. International rugby test matches are often played here, too.

Surfing

KwaZulu-Natal's coastline is blessed with a warm-water current and world-class surfing spots. Surfing has a fanatical following in Durban, and several international tournaments are staged on the city's beaches, at nearby Umhlanga, or on the Bluff. Crowds of more than 10,000 are not unusual for night surfing competitions or the annual Mr. Price Pro championship (formerly the Gunston 500), a top World Qualifying Series event on the world surfing circuit and the longest-running event of its kind in the world. The Mr. Price Pro is held at Durban's most famous beaches, North Beach and New Pier. When the conditions are right, New Pier is one of the best beach breaks in the world.

Just the other side of Durban's protected bay, Cave Rock, on the Bluff, offers a seething right-hander that can handle big swell. It can be a tough paddle and is not for amateurs. Farther down the South Coast, surfers head for Scottburgh, Green Point, Park Rynie, or Southbroom. North of Durban, popular spots include Umhlanga, Ballito, Richard's Bay, and Sodwana Bay.

The more popular spots can get crowded, and locals are known to be territorial about certain sections. Be sure to obey the laws of surfing etiquette. Usually the best waves are found at dawn and dusk. If the southwester blows, the Durban beaches are your best bet. In the winter months look out for an early-morning northwester to set up good waves along the whole coastline.

You can rent a surfboard (R80) or body board (R50) from the ideally positioned **North Beach Surf Shop** (✉ North Beach, Beachfront ☎ 031/ 368–4649). You can also arrange for surfing lessons (R100 per hour). At the well-stocked **Pirana Surf Shop** (✉ 65 Brickhill Rd., Beachfront ☎ 031/337–6666 ✉ uShaka Marine World, 1 Bell St., Point ☎ 031/ 337–0281), you can buy surf gear like sunglasses, wet suits, swimsuits, surfboards, and body boards. The shop also organizes surfing lessons and rents surfboards (R100) and body boards (R80). You can arrange for surfing lessons (R150 per hour, including all equipment) with **Eli DeNysschen** (☎ (084/686–3923) on North Beach or South Beach.

You'll find the world's first constantly rolling wave at the **Wavehouse** (✉ Gateway mall, Gateway Rd. and Sugar Close, Umhlanga Ridge ☎ 031/570–9200 ⊕ www.wavehouse.co.za), whose outdoor wave pools are excellent for learning how to surf.

Shopping

Durban offers a great array of shopping experiences, from the Beach-front, where you can buy cheap beadwork and baskets, to enormous Western-style malls. In general, bargaining is not expected, though you might try it at the Beachfront. Look out for goods indigenous to the province: colorful Zulu beadwork and tightly handwoven baskets.

Malls

One of the biggest malls in the Southern Hemisphere, **Gateway** (✉ Gateway Rd. and Sugar Close, Umhlanga Ridge ☎ 031/566–2332 ⊕ www. gatewayworld.co.za) contains almost 300 stores ranging from clothing to music to jewelry, outdoor and indoor restaurants, the province's only Imax theater, the live Barnyard Theatre, 23 movie screens, an adventure golf course, a skate park, the Wavehouse, and a rock-climbing wall. **La Lucia Mall** (✉ 90 William Campbell Dr., La Lucia ☎ 031/562–8420), between the city and Umhlanga, is smaller and somewhat more expensive than the big malls. **Musgrave Centre** (✉ Musgrave Rd., Berea ☎031/21–5129 ⊕www.musgravecentre.co.za) has everything from pharmacies to banks, travel agents, restaurants, and movie theaters. It's smaller but more elegant than most malls, it's only about a seven-minute drive from city center. Until Gateway opened, **Pavilion** (✉ Jack Martens Dr., Westville ☎ 031/265–0558) was by far the biggest and best mall in the metro area. All the popular chain stores have outlets here, like Woolworths and Mr. Price, both good for clothing and gifts. The Exclusive Books here is one of the best in Durban. Look & Listen is a great place to buy music—whether your fancy runs to traditional African, jazz, classical, or pop. The mall also has an Internet café, an indoor mini-golf course, bowling, and movie theaters showing the latest releases.

Village Walk (✉ 1 Bell St., Point ☎ 031/328–8000 ⊕ www. ushakamarineworld.co.za), part of uShaka Marine World, is an upmarket shopping and restaurant mall containing about 100 stores, including photo, surf-gear, art, and curio shops (the best of these are Juluka Curios, Bits of Africa, and Forest Village Curios). The main buildings are thatch, and eye-catching mosaics of lizards and snakes are inlaid into the walkways and echoed in the ceilings. Village Walk also has an American Express currency exchange, an Internet café, and a provincial Zulu Kingdom tourism office. A short walk from the International Convention Centre and Durban Hilton, the busy **Workshop** (⊠ 99 Aliwal St., city center ☎ 031/304–9894) is a slick renovation of the city's cavernous old railway workshops. Here you'll find everything from expensive clothing stores to curio shops, cinemas, and fast-food restaurants.

Markets

One of the nicest and most popular of Durban's many flea markets, the **Essenwood Flea Market** (⊠ Essenwood Rd., Berea ☎ 031/208–9916) is held every Saturday until 2. Classy stalls sell handmade clothes and crafts, leather work, stained glass, and restored wooden furniture in a beautiful park setting. **Farepark Market** (⊠ West and Farewell Sts., city center ☎ 031/368–2190) is open daily 8–5. Permanent stalls in rustic cabins sell the usual flea-market fare: clothes, crafts, and curios. The **Open Air Amphitheatre Market** (⊠ Amphitheatre Gardens, North Beach, Beachfront ☎ No phone), open Sunday 8:30–4, sells traditional African crafts, cotton candy, samosas, and cheap plastic goods made in the Far East. **South Plaza Market** (⊠ Durban Exhibition Centre, city center ☎ 031/301–9900) has more than 500 indoor and outdoor stalls selling everything from clothes to candles; it's open Sunday 9–4. The **Stables** (⊠ Newmarket horse stables, Jacko Jackson Dr., next to King's Park Rugby Stadium ☎ 031/312–3752) carries cheap imports from the East as well as an interesting selection of local crafts, such as beaded and leather goods. It's open Wednesday and Friday evenings 6–10 for a moonlight market and Sunday 10–5, except for June and July. The most exciting market in the city is the **Victoria Street Market** (⊠ Queen and Russell Sts. Indian District ☎ 031/306–4021), where you can buy everything from recordings of African music to curios and curry spices. Bargaining is expected here.

Specialty Stores

ART & CRAFTS The classy, nonprofit ★ **African Art Centre** (⊠ Old Station Bldg., 1st fl., Pine St., city center ☎ 031/304–7915 ⊕ www.afriart.org.za) acts as a sales outlet for the work of rural artisans. It carries an excellent selection of original African arts and crafts, including Zulu beadwork, ceramics, wood sculptures, and beautifully crafted wire baskets. The store will ship purchases overseas.

The small **Elizabeth Gordon Gallery** (⊠ 120 Florida Rd., Morningside ☎ 031/303–8133), in trendy and vibrant Florida Road, carries a wide selection of work (including prints) by local and international artists and photographers. You might meet local artists at collaborative exhibitions. The crafts shop at the **NSA Gallery** (⊠ 166 Bulwer Rd., Glenwood ☎ 031/202–3686) carries hand-crafted furniture, beaded stationery, and toys.

SPICES If you don't want to go all the way to the Indian District for your spices, stop in at the **Haribhai & Sons Spice Emporium** (⊠ 31 Pine St., city center ☎ 031/332–6662), near the beachfront. You can select from a tantalizing array of fresh spices, as well as hand-mixed curry powders.

The shop also sells mixes for creating your own vegetable *atchars* (Indian relishes), tea masala, and chili bites.

Side Trips from Durban

Valley of a Thousand Hills
45 km (27 mi) northwest of Durban.

In the early part of the 19th century, before cars were introduced, wagons traveled from the port of Durban up along the ridge of this region of plunging gorges, hills, and valleys into the hinterland, where the mining industry was burgeoning. Today the Old Main Road (M103) still runs between Durban and Pietermaritzburg, winding through a number of villages and offering stunning views of hills and valleys dotted with traditional Zulu huts. It is along this route that the Comrades Marathon—South Africa's most famous road race—is run.

For purposes of exploring, the area has been organized into routes by the local tourism office. A favorite with Durbanites, the routes wind through villages and past coffee shops, art galleries, restaurants, quaint pubs, small inns, farms, and nature reserves. There are a number of excellent B&Bs, small inns, and lodges in the area, often with fantastic views of the gorges.

The main route is called the T1. It follows the M13 out of Durban, up Field's Hill, through the village of Kloof, and past Everton, Gillits, and Winston Park; it then joins the Old Main Road (M103) at Hillcrest. A number of small shopping centers along the M103 sell a variety of goods, from crafts to old furniture, and there are some excellent coffee shops, restaurants, and small hotels as well as cultural attractions. At the end of the M103 is the small town of Monteseel. Drive along the dirt roads to the signposted overlook for one of the best uninterrupted views of the Thousand Hills. Other well-marked routes in the area are the Kranzkloof, Assagay Averston, and Isithumba routes and the Shongweni Shuffle, which all make for scenic drives.

WHAT TO SEE **Assagay Coffee.** You can take a tour to see how this homegrown coffee, very popular with locals, is grown, roasted, and packaged. ☒ *Off Old Main Rd., before Heidi's Farm Stall, Bothas Hill* ☎ *031/765–2941* ☒ *Tours R10* ☉ *Weekdays 8–4, Sat. 10–4.*

PheZulu Safari Park. Popular with big tour buses, PheZulu is the equivalent of fast-food tourism, good for people who want a quick-fix African experience. A tour of the cultural village with its traditional beehive huts gives some insight into African traditions, and there are performances of traditional Zulu dancing, but the operation is not as vibrant or professional as the cultural villages up north in Zululand. An old-fashioned crocodile farm and snake park is fairly interesting, if a little tacky. The curio shop is enormous; you can probably get just about any type of African memento or booklet imaginable. ☒ *Old Main Rd., Drummond* ☎ *031/777–1000* ⊕ *www.phezulusafaripark.co.za* ☒ *R40* ☉ *Daily 8–4:30; shows daily at 10, 11:30, 1:30, and 3:30.*

Rob Roy Hotel. This is probably one of the best lookout points for a view of the Valley of a Thousand Hills. On the lawns is a tea garden where you can enjoy tea and scones, and though the service is not always great, the view makes up for it. Also here are a children's animal farmyard and the Izintaba Cultural Village, which has fairly lackluster performances of traditional Zulu dancing and cultural celebrations. ⊠ *Old Main Rd., Bothas Hill* ☎ *031/777–1305* ⊕ *www.robroyhotel.co.za* ⊠ *Cultural village R25* ☉ *Performances daily at 10, 11:30, 1:30, and 3:30.*

WHERE TO EAT
¢–$ ✗ **Tree House.** On the banks of the Sterkspruit River, this small wooden restaurant is built on stilts so that you have a unique view of birds flitting among the tree leaves. Summer and fall are the best times to come and sample the small menu—only two starters, two entrées, and two desserts—which changes weekly. Choices might include roast vegetables with polenta or roast lamb with rosemary and farm vegetables. ⊠ *Follow signs through Hillcrest to Assagay and then on to Shongweni, or take Shongweni/Summerveld/Assagay exit off the N3, then 7 km (4½ mi) into valley* ☎ *031/769–1406 or 082/655–5931* ⊟ *AE, MC, V* ☉ *Closed Mon.–Sat.*

¢ ✗ **Chantecler Hotel.** Eating outside in the garden of this atmospheric old brick, stone, and thatch hotel is a Sunday tradition for Durbanites. In the winter there's a roaring fire to gather around. Breakfast is served until 11, and there's a buffet along with the regular menu. Try the soup of the day and the foot-long garlic roll for starters. The peri-peri chicken and the curries are also good. ⊠ *27 Clement Stott Rd., Bothas Hill* ☎ *031/765–2613* ⊟ *AE, DC, MC, V.*

¢ ✗ **Sprigs.** Durbanites make the 20-minute drive just to eat here. Breakfast is à la carte, but lunch is a buffet that's something of a favorite for locals. The buffet changes daily but always includes two hot dishes, one of which is usually vegetarian, two hot quiches or savory tortes, and a variety of delicious salads. ⊠ *Shop 34, Fields Shopping Centre, Kloof* ☎ *031/764–6031* ⊟ *AE, DC, MC, V* ☉ *Closed Sun. No dinner.*

SPORTS & THE   One of the best ways to see the Valley of a Thousand Hills is on a kayak-
OUTDOORS   ing trip on the Umgeni River—through the actual valleys of the hills. Oscar Chalupsky, of **Chalupsky Paddling and Adventure School** (☎ 031/303–7336 ⊕ www.chalupsky.com), is a bit of a national celebrity, having won South Africa's version of an Iron Man–style kayaking competition almost every year it's been held. Chalupsky's professional and attentive staff, including many local Zulu guides whom Chalupsky has trained, can help even the most novice paddler feel at ease. Rates start at R400 for a half-day trip.

SHOPPING   Most shopping centers do not post hours, as individual stores set their own opening and closing times. For the most part, hours are daily from 9 to 4:30.

The **Fainting Goat** (⊠ Old Main Rd., Bothas Hill ☎ 031/765–5731), a fairly ordinary-looking shopping center, has a very good secondhand furniture shop, a coffee roaster, and a lively restaurant serving German specialties. Stop in at the fiber design shop for good-quality woven rugs and tapestries. A long windy road up to **Heidi's Farm Stall** (⊠ Old Main

Rd., Bothas Hill ☎ 031/765–3024), open daily 7–5, gets you to your first real sighting of the Thousand Hills. Along with fruit and vegetables, Heidi's sells everything from homemade cheese and farm milk to preserves and honey. The pseudo-Victorian **Heritage Market** (⊠ Old Main Rd., Hillcrest ☎ 031/765–2500) is charming and colorful, if a little contrived. It has more than 100 specialty stores dotted around a wonderful little central bandstand with rose gardens and twirling vines. There are a number of good coffee shops and restaurants, as well as secondhand bookstores and numerous crafts shops. Just before you start the steep ascent to Bothas Hill from Hillcrest and Assagay, you'll see the fairly scrappy-looking little **Sugar Loaf Centre** (⊠ Old Main Rd., Assagay ☎ No phone) on your left. Despite its appearance, it has some interesting shops selling handwoven rugs and fresh farm produce, all from the district, and some woodwork and furniture shops.

KwaZulu-Natal South Coast

Vacation towns like Scottburgh, Margate, Ramsgate, Trafalgar, and Palm Beach dot KwaZulu-Natal's southern coast, which stretches for more than 200 km (125 mi) from Durban in the north to Port Edward in the south. The area has some of the country's best beaches, set against a tropical background of natural coastal jungle and palm trees. In fact, Blue Flag status has been conferred on the Uvongo, Lucian, and Scottburgh beaches, and those at Hibberdene, Margate, Ramsgate, and Marina are also top-notch.

The South Coast is also famous for the annual sardine run, in late winter and early spring (sometime between July and September). Colder currents in Antarctica at this time bring millions of sardines to local waters, and they often wash up right on the beach. Dolphins, seabirds, sharks, and whales follow in a feeding frenzy.

WHERE TO STAY & EAT

$$

✕⌂ **Lynton Hall.** This majestic castlelike country house sits on 160 acres of gardens and coastal forests that extend down to the Indian Ocean. Built by sugar baron brothers Charles and Sir Frank Reynolds in the late 1800s, it nestles next to the picturesque Umdoni Park golf course and has hosted royalty, prime ministers, and well-known literary figures. Each suite is different, boldly decorated with a mix of Victorian, Indian, and Southeast Asian furnishings. Large Victorian bathrooms have modern fittings, and even chandeliers. Lynton Hall's multi-award-winning "deconstruction cuisine" (R215 prix-fixe dinner) is offered on a frequently changing menu—which might include tempura of line fish, red roast quail, or beef fillet with truffle oil jus, followed by Gorgonzola ice cream with poached pears and red-wine jelly. ⊠ *Umdoni Park, Old South Coast Rd., Box 272, Pennington 4184* ☎ *039/975–3122* 🖷 *039/975–3333* ⊕ *www.hartford.co.za* ⇥ *9 suites* ⚬ *Restaurant, room service, minibars, refrigerators, cable TV, golf privileges, tennis court, pool, pond, beach, snorkeling, windsurfing, boating, fishing, mountain bikes, croquet, hiking, horseback riding, lounge, dry cleaning, laundry service, Internet, business services, convention center, airport shuttle, helipad, free parking, no-smoking rooms; no kids under 12* ▤ *AE, DC, MC, V* ⋈*◎⋈ BP.*

$–$$$$ 🖼 **San Lameer.** This exclusive self-catering resort is a great getaway from noisy city life for a group of friends or a family. Spacious one- to five-bedroom Tuscan-style villas, many with breathtaking views of the sea or the bird-filled lagoons, are set among gardens and indigenous forest. At night it's lighted up by hundreds of twinkling lights. Stroll down paved walkways to the private beach, or meander through the woods, and you'll likely see small antelope and monkeys. Golf enthusiasts enjoy the championship course, which hosts major tournaments, and there's also a mashie (tiny) course. If DIY is not your style, opt for the recently refurbished on-site Mondazur Resort Estate Hotel. **Heleen Fouche** (📠 011/896–3544 ✉ info@sanlameer.com) handles bookings for privately owned villas at reduced rates. ⊠ *Lower South Coast Main Rd., between Ramsgate and Palm Beach* ⌂ *Box 88, Southbroom 4277* ☎ *039/313–0011* 🖶 *039/313–0157* ⊕ *www.sanlameer.com* ⇨ *60 rooms, 400 villas* ⚐ *2 restaurants, kitchens, 18-hole golf course, 3 tennis courts, 2 pools, beach, fishing, mountain bikes, hiking, lawn bowling, squash, 3 bars, library, shops, playground, dry cleaning, laundry service, Internet, airport shuttle, helipad* 🖃 *AE, DC, MC, V.*

Pietermaritzburg
80 km (50 mi) northwest of Durban.

In a bowl of hills in the Natal Midlands, this city is the current capital of KwaZulu-Natal, and the legislature is in the busy city center. It's a pleasant town, with wide tree-lined streets and a temperate climate that escapes the worst of the coastal heat and humidity. Its redbrick colonial architecture offers tangible reminders of Natal's and South Africa's British past; dozens of late-19th-century buildings line the streets in the center of town. It's worth visiting just to see this slice of Victorian England.

The town is often referred to as the "Last British Outpost," even though it was first settled in 1838 by Voortrekkers—hardy Dutch farmers who sought new frontiers to escape British rule in the Cape. The city takes its name from two Voortrekker leaders, Gert Maritz and Piet Retief, who was murdered by the Zulu king Dingane.

Numbers in the text correspond to numbers in the margin and on the Pietermaritzburg map.

A GOOD TOUR   Pietermaritzburg's city center is small, and most of the places worth visiting are within easy access of each other. Start your tour at the **Pietermaritzburg Tourism** ㉝, on Commercial Road, before crossing the street to the **Tatham Art Gallery** ㉞ in the old Supreme Court building. The **Supreme Court Gardens** ㉟ are right next to the gallery. Across Commercial Road from the gardens stands the imposing **City Hall** ㊱. From here, head down Church Street to reach the **Voortrekker Museum** ㊲. Walk back up Church Street, cross Commercial Road, and stroll along the Maritzburg Mall, a mostly pedestrian thoroughfare lined with some superb examples of Victorian architecture. Fronting the Colonial Building is the **statue of Gandhi** ㊳. Next, turn left down Greys Inn Lane, and then take another left toward Change Lane, continuing on to the **Natal Parliament Building** ㊴ on Longmarket Street. Back on Commercial Road, turn right and then right again onto Loop Street to reach the eclectic **Natal Museum** ㊵. To

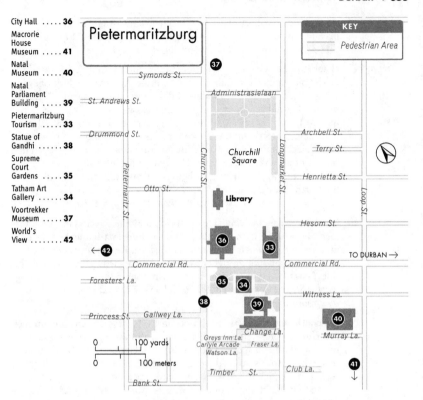

visit the **Macrorie House Museum** ④, a little more than 1 km (½ mi) southwest of Commercial Road on Loop Street (at the corner of Pine Street), you probably need a car. For a good view of Pietermaritzburg, drive back down Loop Street and turn left on Commercial Road, which after a while becomes Old Howick Road. Follow the signs to **World's View** ⑫.

TIMING Even though many of the sidewalks are shaded and the mall is quite leafy, it is wise to get any serious walking done either in the cooler earlier morning hours or in late afternoon, particularly in summer. Set aside a few hours in the morning to do this walk, and when the heat begins to settle in, take a drive out to World's View for a panoramic view of the town.

WHAT TO SEE **City Hall.** Built in 1900, this grand building is the largest all-brick structure in the Southern Hemisphere. It's a classic Victorian edifice, notable for its stained-glass windows, soaring clock tower, and ornate gables and domes. You can take a self-guided tour; brochures are available at the reception desk. ☒ *Church St. and Commercial Rd.* ☎ *033/395–1167* ☒ *Free* ☉ *Weekdays 8:30–4:30.*

④ **Macrorie House Museum.** This lovely residence with a corrugated-iron roof and ornate ironwork is typical of old Pietermaritzburg. Bishop Macrorie lived in the house from 1870 to 1892, and it's been furnished to reflect that period. A collection of dolls in Victorian costume and the bishop's private chapel, dating back to 1869, are displayed. ⊠ *11 Loop St.* ☎ *033/394–2161* ⊡ *R5* ⊘ *Mon. 11–4, Tues.–Fri. 9–1.*

🐧 ❹⓿ **Natal Museum.** One of five national museums in South Africa and the largest museum in KwaZulu-Natal, this museum contains a little of everything. You'll find lifelike models of dinosaurs as well as stuffed African mammals, snakes, other marine creatures, and local birds. The city's human history is revealed through a re-creation of an 1880s Pietermaritzburg street, complete with settler's cottage, shops, a pharmacy, and a blacksmith. Original San (Bushman) paintings are displayed in a replica of a Drakensberg cave. The exhibit on sub-Saharan cultures is quite interesting, highlighting religious, ceremonial, military, and household artifacts from across Africa. ⊠ *237 Loop St.* ☎ *033/345–1404* ⊕ *www.nmsa.org.za* ⊡ *R4* ⊘ *Weekdays 9–4:30, Sat. 10–4, Sun. 11–3.*

❸❾ **Natal Parliament Building.** This redbrick building, erected in 1889, formerly housed the twin chambers of the colonial parliament and is now used for the provincial legislature's sessions. Recent works promoting democracy and human rights by South African artists are displayed inside. A statue of Queen Victoria stands in front of the building. ⊠ *Longmarket St. and Commercial Rd.* ☎ *033/355–7720* ⊡ *Tours free* ⊘ *Tours by appointment.*

🐧 **National Botanic Gardens.** Established in 1870, these gardens contain such colorful flowers as bougainvilleas and azaleas and provide a sanctuary for more than 100 species of birds. Rare and indigenous plants are conserved here, so it's no surprise that there is a muti garden. Small game, such as buck (antelope), who have made the garden their home, can be spotted during guided tours. ⊠ *Mayors Walk, Prestbury* ☎ *033/344–3585* ⊡ *R8* ⊘ *Daily 6–6.*

❸❸ **Pietermaritzburg Tourism.** The office distributes detailed pamphlets and maps of the town. It's in a classic redbrick building erected in 1884 to house the Borough Police. In those days the bell tower signaled a curfew for blacks at 9 each night. ⊠ *177 Commercial Rd.* ☎ *033/345–1348* ⊕ *www.pmbtourism.co.za* ⊘ *Weekdays 8–5, Sat. 8–1.*

❸❽ **Statue of Gandhi.** On his arrival in the city in 1893, Gandhi, then a young lawyer, was thrown out of a whites-only first-class train compartment. A statue of the Indian pacifist leader was erected in 1993 to mark the centenary of that day, and he later said: "My active nonviolence began from that date." Gandhi lived in South Africa for 21 years before returning to India. ⊠ *Church Street Mall.*

❸❺ **Supreme Court Gardens.** The gardens are the city's memorial park. Several monuments commemorate those who died in wars that raged in this country and abroad: the Zulu War of 1879, the Second South African War (1899–1902), and World War I. The monuments all have a very English feel, emphasized by the legends on the commemorative stones extolling Queen, Country, and Empire. ⊠ *Commercial Rd. at Church St.*

❸❹ **Tatham Art Gallery.** Completed in 1871, the old Supreme Court building that houses this gallery is yet another of Pietermaritzburg's fine redbrick colonial structures. The museum is first-rate, with a solid collection of 19th- and 20th-century English and French paintings, including works by Picasso, Matisse, and Renoir. Of keenest interest, though, is the South African collection, which displays works by contemporary artists, including linocuts and such traditional crafts as beadwork, baskets, and tribal earplugs. The museum also presents temporary exhibits, including traveling displays from larger museums and collections, such as the prestigious Standard Bank Young Artist of the Year exhibition. The art gallery shop, though small, sells high-quality, locally produced contemporary crafts, such as baskets woven from fabric and plastic, beaded evening jewelry, African beaded Fabergé-style eggs, copper bracelets, carved wooden angels, and embroidered panels. ⊠ *Commercial Rd., near Church St.* ☎ *033/342–1804* 🕮 *Free* ☿ *Tues.–Sun. 10–6.*

37 **Voortrekker Museum.** The museum occupies the Church of the Vow, an immensely important monument in the eyes of many Afrikaners. After the murder of Voortrekker leader Piet Retief in 1838, the Voortrekkers sought revenge on the Zulus and their king, Dingane. A Boer commando under the leadership of Andries Pretorius vowed to build a church if God granted them victory. The result was the Battle of Blood River, in which 3,000 Zulus died and the Boers managed to emerge without a single casualty. Constructed in 1841 in typical Cape Dutch style, the church now houses a variety of Voortrekker artifacts, including an old wagon, flintlock rifles, and Piet Retief's prayer book. Next door, the thatch home of Andries Pretorius is also open to the public. ⊠ *333 Longmarket St.* ☎ *033/394–6834* 🕮 *R5* ☿ *Weekdays 9–4, Sat. 9–1.*

42 **World's View.** This spectacular overlook provides panoramic views of the city and surrounding countryside. The viewpoint lies on the route used by the Voortrekkers on their long migration from the Cape in the 19th century. A large diagram traces their route and labels the major landscape features. ⊠ *Off Old Howick Rd. (R103).*

WHERE TO EAT   ✕ **Tatham Coffee Shop.** On the 2nd floor of the Tatham Art Gallery, this pleasant café serves a wonderful selection of teas and coffees as well as light meals, including South African specialties like samp and beans, and desserts. If the weather's fine, sit outside on the narrow veranda overlooking Commercial Road. ⊠ *Commercial Rd., near Church St.* ☎ *033/342–8327* 🖃 *No credit cards* ☿ *Closed Mon.*

$ ✕ **Botanic Gardens Tea Shop.** One of the more pleasant places to spend an hour in town is the tea shop in the botanic gardens. You can relax over breakfast or a light lunch on a shady patio overlooking the enormous old trees and gardens. The shop has a great selection of teatime cakes. ⊠ *Mayors Walk, Prestbury* ☎ *033/344–2207* 🖃 *MC, V* ☿ *Closed Tues. No dinner.*

NIGHTLIFE   Pietermaritzburg's answer to a gaming facility, the **Golden Horse Casino** (⊠ 45 New England Rd., Scottsville ☎ 033/395–8136 ⊕ www.golden-horse-casino.co.za) has 450 slot machines and 18 gaming tables, including blackjack and roulette. A 46-foot-high sandstone statue of Pegasus stands at the entrance. The casino also has a food court and three restaurants, including an enormous buffet with 140 dishes.

Scottsville (⊠ New England Rd., off N3 ☎ 033/145–3405) is a pretty horse-racing track in pleasant surroundings.

The large, upscale **Liberty Midlands Mall** (⊠ 50 Sanctuary Rd., Chase Valley ☎ 033/342–0062), a relatively new addition to Pietermaritzburg, is in the same vein as Durban's Pavilion and Gateway shopping centers, but it offers many smaller clothing stores and shoe shops you won't find at either of these malls. There's also an extensive food court and banking facilities.

Midlands Meander

Set amid the rolling green foothills of the Drakensberg, the Midlands Meander—actually a series of meandering routes—provides opportunities to shop for authentic South African arts and crafts, often made on the premises, while enjoying the tranquillity and beauty of the countryside and top accommodations. The N3 bisects the Meander, with the towns of Curry's Post and Howick to the northeast and Nottingham Road, Balgowan, the Dargyle District, Lion's River, and Midmar to the southwest.

The most popular time to do the Meander is in the autumn (March to May), when it's not too hot or too cold. Many South Africans love the winters here; it often snows, particularly on the higher ground, and many establishments burn cheery log fires. No matter the time of year, though, there's always something to see and do, most of which involves shopping. However, **Howick Falls,** a waterfall in the town of Howick that plunges an impressive 312 feet, is definitely worth a 10-minute stop.

$–$$ ✕⌂ **Granny Mouse Country House.** One of the best-loved hotels on the Meander, Granny Mouse has cozy thatch rooms, all slightly different, with a river view, fireplace, and homey, though upmarket, atmosphere. Freestanding rooms offer privacy and peace, and the main hotel building—formerly an unusual farmhouse with doors and windows from an old church—offers conviviality and warmth in its several lounges. The onsite Mouse & Lion pub is locally famous for its lavish breakfasts and afternoon teas. Some of the best places on the Meander are within easy reach. ⊠ *R103, 25 km (15½ mi) south of Nottingham Road exit of N3* ⌂ *Box 22, Balgowan 3275* ☎ *033/234–4071* 🖷 *033/234–4429* ⊕ *www. grannymouse.co.za* ⇆ *16 suites* ⌂ *Restaurant, 2 pools, massage, mountain bikes, croquet, hiking, bar, 4 lounges, convention center* ▭ *DC, MC, V* ⦵⌊ *BP.*

★ **$–$$** ✕⌂ **Hartford House.** Built in 1875, this inn is steeped in history and misty beauty. High up on the Meander, in the foothills of the Drakensberg, and adjacent to the Summerhill racing stud, it is a deliciously luxurious, if rather formal, escape for the lucky few. A few of the suites are in the original house, whereas others front an ethereal, lovely lake. Each suite is different, decorated in a gloriously eclectic collision of fabrics and furnishings from Africa, Europe, and the East. The food, which has garnered top honors, is just as rich, spectacular, and eclectically surprising. Dinner (R180 for five courses; reservations essential), which the chefs start preparing at dawn, is an unforgettable five-course event with wines to match. ⊠ *Hlatikulu Rd., off road to Giant's Castle, Mooi River 3300*

☎ *033/263–2713* 🖷 *033/263–2818* ⊕ *www.hartford.co.za* ⤙ *13 suites* ☖ *Restaurant, some fans, in-room data ports, in-room safes, minibars, cable TV, tennis court, spa, boating, fishing, mountain bikes, hiking, horseback riding, bar, 11 lounges, dry cleaning, laundry service, convention center, airport shuttle, airstrip, no-smoking rooms; no kids under 12* 🖃 *AE, DC, MC, V* ¡○¡ *BP.*

$ 🖼 **Brookdale Health Hydro.** Eat delicious, healthful (but small) meals; pamper yourself with the included massages and beauty treatments; and relax for three nights (minimum stay) in this collection of comfortable, country-style cottages. Superb personal attention, professional treatments, lectures on topics ranging from stress management to dietary supplementation, late-night soaks in a whirlpool, early-morning walks over the mountains, and aquacise in the heated pool will get you into shape for the rest of your vacation—or cap it off with a feeling of rejuvenation. ⊠ *R103, opposite Rawdons Hotel, Box 109, Nottingham Road, 3280,* ☎🖷 *033/266–6208* ⊕ *www.brookdale.co.za* ⤙ *21 rooms, 2 suites* ☖ *Pool, gym, hot tubs, spa, steam room, hiking* 🖃 *AE, DC, MC, V* ¡○¡ *FAP.*

SHOPPING
You can find some high-quality South African arts and crafts along the Midlands Meander. You can also find many more establishments that are not up to the same standards. If you've only a limited time, head for the concentration of outlets, some of them excellent, on the R103 between Nottingham Road and Lion's River. If you have a couple of days, base yourself at one of the great hotels and explore the Meander using the large-format, free guide available at most Meander stops. Many of the better establishments offer shipping services for those unusual items large and small.

Kingdom Weavers (⊠ 5 km [3 mi] from Balgowan/Curry's Post exit off the N3, toward Curry's Post ☎ 033/234–4205) specializes in woolen and cotton-knit rugs hand-woven on site and sold at reasonable prices. A great place to buy handmade leather goods, especially shoes and beautiful bags and briefcases, is **Groundcover** (⊠ Curry's Post Rd., past Kingdom Weavers ☎ 033/330–6092 ⊕ www.groundcover.co.za). The **Rosewood Embroidery Shoppe** (⊠ 9 km [6 mi] northwest of the Curry's Post/Lion's River exit off the N3, then 5 km [3 mi] on the Dargyle Rd. ☎ 033/234–4386 ⊕ www.rosewoodshoppe.co.za) sells beautiful handstitched, pure cotton linens; upholstery; night wear; and gifts. The shop's signature is a pink-and-pale-green hand-stitched rose. At the **Woodturner** (⊠ 6 km [4 mi] from Rosewood, down the Dargyle Rd. ☎ 033/234–4548 ⊕ www.sculpturalwood.co.za), father and son Andrew and John Early specialize in making elegant bowls, modern wood sculptures, and one-of-a-kind furniture pieces using salvaged, exotic woods like jacaranda and local woods like African mahogany and stinkwood. Their pieces are often snapped up by studios in New York and elsewhere. The studio is a delight; ask to see the Earlys at work in their workshop behind the sprawling farmhouse. Near the Woodturner is the **Dargyle Valley Pottery** (⊠ 1 km [½ mi] on the D666 off the Dargyle Rd. ☎ 033/234–4377), where renowned potter Ian Glenny, whose work is in private collections and galleries worldwide, founded the Meander 20 years ago. Choose from porcelain, stoneware, or terra-cotta pots, bowls, and vases—or indulge in a fireplace. **Culamoya Chimes** (✉ 3 km [2 mi] off the R103 ☎ 033/234–4503 or 083/627–6195), in the Dargyle District, has a 13-foot chime as well as other chimes that boom the sounds of Big Ben and St. Paul's Cathedral down to gentle tinkles of fairy magic. Near Culamoya and Granny Mouse, **Mole Hill** (✉ R103, 8 km [5 mi] south of Nottingham Rd. ☎ 033/234–4352 ⊕ www.molehill.co.za) has a good reputation for high-quality men's and women's shirts with an African twist, such as a guinea-fowl motif. Back toward Durban, How-ick is worth a visit for the impressive falls and the **Weaver's Hut** (✉ 4 km [2½ mi] from the Howick/Midmar exit off the N3 ☎ 033/330–4026 ⊕ www.weavershut.com), where you'll find beautiful handmade eth-nic rugs in russets, creams, and blues. Farther south, **Peel's Honey** (✉ N3, below the Midmar Dam ☎ 033/330–3762) sells an assortment of honey, brittle, and other tasty treats.

Durban A to Z

AIR TRAVEL

Durban International Airport (DUR), formerly known as Louis Botha Airport, is 16 km (10 mi) south of town along the Southern Freeway. South African Airways (SAA) flies to Durban via Johannesburg. Domestic airlines serving Durban include SAA, BA/Comair, Kulula, 1Time, and SA Airlink.

The most inexpensive transfer into town and back is the Airport Shut-tle Service, which costs R30 and departs a half hour after incoming flights arrive and leaves the city center every hour. Call ahead and the bus will pick you up at any hotel in the city; there's no need to reserve for the trip into Durban. If you want to go farther afield, call Mozzie Cabs or the Magic Bus.

🛪 Airport **Durban International Airport** ☎ 031/408–1155.

🛪 Airlines **BA/Comair** ☎ 031/450–7000 ⊕ www.britishairways.com. **Kulula** ☎ 0861/585–852 ⊕ www.kulula.com. **1Time** ☎ 086/134–5345 ⊕ www.onetime.com. **SA Air-link** ☎ 031/408–1029 ⊕ www.saairlink.co.za. **South African Airways** ☎ 031/450–2336 ⊕ www.flysaa.com.

🛪 Airport Transfers **Airport Shuttle Service** ☎ 031/465–5573. **Magic Bus** ☎ 031/561–1096. **Mozzie Cabs** ☎ 0860/669–943.

BUS TRAVEL

Greyhound and Translux Express offer long-distance bus service to cities all over South Africa. A cheaper company, Golden Wheels, offers daily service to Johannesburg only. All intercity buses leave from New Durban Station (off N.M.R. Avenue, between Old Fort Avenue and Argyle Road). Nowadays, though, you can often fly for much the same prices as trav-eling by bus, especially if you book well in advance or find a discount.

Durban Transport operates two types of bus service, but you need con-cern yourself only with the Mynah buses. These small buses operate fre-quently on set routes through the city and along the Beachfront and cost R2 a ride. Bus stops are marked by a sign with a mynah bird on it. The main bus depot is on Pine Street between Aliwal and Gardiner streets. You pay as you board; exact change is not required. Route information is also available at an information office at the corner of Aliwal and Pine streets.

Cheetah runs a minibus service twice daily between Durban and Pieter-maritzburg, and is probably the most convenient way to travel between the two cities.

🚌 Bus Lines **Cheetah** ☎ 033/342-2673. **Golden Wheels** ☎ 031/307-3363. **Grey-hound** ☎ 031/309-7830. **Mynah buses** ☎ 031/307-3503. **Translux Express** ☎ 031/308-8111.

CAR TRAVEL

You'll be much freer to explore Durban and its surroundings if you have a car. It's relatively easy to find your way around, because the sea is a constant reference point. Downtown Durban is dominated by two parallel one-way streets, West Street (going toward the sea) and Smith Street (going away from the sea, toward Berea and Pietermaritzburg); together they get you in and out of the city center easily. Parking in downtown Durban is a nightmare; head for an underground garage whenever you can. As with the rest of South Africa, wherever you go you'll be beset by self-appointed car guards, who ask if they can watch your car. The going rate for a tip—if you want to give one—is R2–R5, depending on how long you're away. The guards directly outside Joe Kool's, between North and South beaches, are particularly good, and it's safe to leave your keys with them while you go for a swim, but don't leave your keys with other guards.

The M4, which stretches north up to the Dolphin Coast—from Umhlanga to Ballito, about 40 km (25 mi), and beyond—is a particularly pretty coastal road, offering many views of the sea through lush natural vegetation and sugarcane fields. It's much nicer than the sterile N2 highway, which takes a parallel path slightly inland and offers no sea views.

The easiest way to reach Pietermaritzburg from Durban is along the N3, a direct 80-km (50-mi) run. Far more interesting and scenic, however, is the route that follows Old Main Road (R103) through the Valley of a Thousand Hills and rejoins the N3 east of Pietermaritzburg. Allow for an hour from Durban to PMB if you take the highway and add another half hour for the R103.

KwaZulu-Natal is particularly strict about speeding, and there are always either camera traps or police traps on the Durban–PMB road, so don't go more than 10 kph above the speed limit. On the whole, you'll find KZN drivers a lot slower, friendlier, and more accommodating than drivers from Gauteng.

Avis, Budget, EuropCar, Imperial, and Tempest have rental offices at the airport. The cheapest car costs about R250 per day, including insurance, plus R1.06 per kilometer (per half mile). Avis offers unlimited mileage to international visitors, as long as you can produce your return ticket as proof. Another major car-rental agency in Durban is Berea Car & Bakkie Hire.

🚗 Rental Companies **Avis** ✉ Ulundi Pl., city center, Durban ☎ 031/304-1741 ⊕ www. avis.co.za. **Berea Car & Bakkie Hire** ✉ 331 Berea Rd., Berea, Durban ☎ 031/202-8410.

Budget ✉ Durban International Airport ☎ 031/408-1809. **EuropCar Hire** ✉ Durban International Airport ☎ 031/469-0667. **Imperial Car Rental** ✉ 52 Stanger St., Morningside, Durban ☎ 031/337-3731. **Tempest Car Hire** ✉ 47 Victoria Embankment, Victoria Embankment, Durban ☎ 031/368-5231.

EMBASSIES

🔢 **United Kingdom** U.K. Embassy ✉ The Marine, Gardiner St., city center, Durban ☎ 031/305-2929.

🔢 **United States** U.S. Embassy ✉ Durban Bay House, 333 Smith St., city center, Durban ☎ 031/304-4737.

EMERGENCIES

The best hospitals in central Durban are Entabeni and St. Augustine's, both private hospitals in the Glenwood area with 24-hour emergency rooms. Umhlanga Hospital is the best north of the city. Addington Hospital, a massive public hospital on the Beachfront, operates a 24-hour emergency room; though it's cheaper, it's not recommended. Daynite Pharmacy is open daily until 10:30.

🔢 **Emergency Services** Ambulance ☎ 10177. Fire ☎ 031/361-0000. **General Emergencies** ☎ 082911. Police ☎ 10111.

🔢 **Hospitals** Addington Hospital ✉ Erskine Terr., South Beach, Beachfront, Durban ☎ 031/327-2000. Entabeni Hospital ✉ 148 S. Ridge Rd., Glenwood, Durban ☎ 031/204-1300. **St. Augustine's** ✉ 4 Cato Rd., Glenwood, Durban ☎ 031/268-5000, 031/268-5559 trauma. Umhlanga Hospital ✉ 323 Umhlanga Rocks Dr., Umhlanga ☎ 031/560-5500, 080/033-6967 trauma.

🔢 **Late-Night Pharmacy** Daynite Pharmacy ✉ West St., city center ✉ Point Rd., Point, Durban ☎ 031/368-3666.

INTERNET

Most hotels provide access to the Internet through business centers or Internet cafés. Outside of hotels, Internet cafés seem to come and go quickly, so ask around. An Internet café at uShaka Marine World is open 8 AM–10 PM.

MONEY MATTERS

There are plenty of ATMs in and around Durban—at shopping centers, large attractions like Suncoast and uShaka, and even some of the smaller supermarkets. Most bank branches exchange money, and the airport and uShaka have money exchanges, as do Rennies and the AmEx foreign-exchange bureau. Shops in the bigger malls like Gateway, Pavilion, Musgrave, and La Lucia often take traveler's checks. Though you will need cash at the markets, don't carry too much. Use credit cards where you can.

🔢 **Exchange Services** AmEx foreign-exchange bureau ✉ 350 Smith St., city center, Durban ☎ 031/301-5562. Rennies ✉ Durban Bay House, 333 Smith St., city center, Durban ☎ 031/304-1511.

SAFETY

Durban has not escaped the crime evident in every South African city. Particularly in the city center but also elsewhere, smash-and-grab thieves roam the streets, looking for bags or obvious valuables in your car, even while you're driving, so lock any valuables in the trunk and keep your car doors locked and windows up at all times. Don't walk downtown with expensive equipment like cameras clearly visible, and carry only small amounts of cash. Ask your hotel or guesthouse for safety tips about specific areas, because levels of crime can vary within a few streets. The Golden Mile is fairly safe and is regularly patrolled by police, but watch out for the street kids, who sometimes hunt in gangs.

At the beach, swim where lifeguards are on duty and between the beacons, and make sure you have plenty of sunscreen. When you swim in the sea, ask a neighbor or lifeguard to keep an eye on your belongings, or put them in a locker—available between North and South beaches.

TAXIS

Taxis are metered and start at R2.50, with an additional R5 per kilometer (per half mile). Expect to pay about R50 from City Hall to North Beach and R150 to the airport. The most convenient taxi stands are around City Hall and in front of the beach hotels. Some taxis display a "for-hire" light, whereas others you simply hail when you can see they're empty. Major taxi companies include Aussie's Cabs (often yellow, with East Coast Radio branding), Bunny Cabs, Checker Radio Taxis, Deluxe Radio Taxis, and Morris Radio Taxis. Eagle Radio Taxis is a little more expensive than other companies. If you're headed to the Indian Market on a weekend, consider having your taxi wait for you, as it can be difficult to flag a taxi in this neighborhood.

🚖 **Taxi Companies Aussie's Cabs** ☎ 031/309-7888. **Bunny Cabs** ☎ 031/332-2914. **Checker Radio Taxis** ☎ 031/465-1660. **Deluxe Radio Taxis** ☎ 031/337-1661. **Eagle Radio Taxis** ☎ 031/337-8333. **Morris Radio Taxis** ☎ 031/337-2711.

TOURS

Durban Africa has a series of city walking tours for R25 per person. Tours depart from the Tourist Junction weekdays at 9:45 and return at 12:30. The Oriental Walkabout explores the Indian District, including Victoria Market and several mosques. The Historical Walkabout covers the major historic monuments in the city, and the Feel of Durban Walkabout explores some of the city's military past, including the Old Fort, Warrior's Gate, and the original armory. Durban Africa offers other tour options as well.

Strelitzia Tours offers daily minibus tours of Durban for about R200. The three-hour tours touch on all the major historic and scenic points in the city, including Beachfront and the harbor, exclusive residential areas like Morningside, the National Botanic Gardens, and the Indian District. Its specialty is the township tour, which is a must for anyone who has an interest in contemporary South African history.

Trips 'n Transport has standard sightseeing tours of Durban, including the National Botanic Gardens, as well as tours to the Thousand Hills area. They can tailor trips to any interest. Zulwini Safaris provides standard tours (including the Drakensberg, the battlefields, game parks, and adventure travel) and designs custom tours to anywhere in the province; it also does tours for small groups. Its specialties are unusual, adventure, and off-the-beaten-path trips.

Sarie Marais Pleasure Cruises and Isle of Capri offer sightseeing cruises around Durban Bay or out to sea. Tours, which last about 90 minutes and cost about R50 per person, depart from the jetties next to the Natal Maritime Museum, on the Victoria Embankment at Aliwal Stand, the Point.

Tours of the Jumah Mosque can be arranged through the Islamic Propagation Center, inside the mosque, or through Durban Africa.

Durban-based Shiney Bright and Urmilla Singh are both award-winning guides.

⚑ Tour Operators Durban Africa ✉ Tourist Junction, 160 Pine St., city center, Durban ☎ 031/304-4934. **Islamic Propagation Center** ✉ Grey and Queen Sts., Indian District ☎ 031/ 306-0026. **Isle of Capri** ☎ 031/337-7751. **Sarie Marais Pleasure Cruises** ☎ 031/305-2844. **Shiney Bright** ☎ 031/303-9158 or 083/726-4413. **Strelitzia Tours** ☎ 031/266-9480. **Trips 'n Transport** ☎ 031/337-0230. **Urmilla Singh** ☎ 031/337-7879 or 083/560-9999. **Zulwini Safaris** ☎ 033/347-1579.

TRAIN TRAVEL

The Durban railway station is a huge, ghastly place that is difficult to find your way around in. It's dirty and crowded, and petty theft is a problem. Spoornet's *Trans-Natal* train runs daily between Durban and Johannesburg, stopping at Pietermaritzburg, Estcourt, and Ladysmith. The trip to Jo'burg takes 13 hours and costs about R250 one-way.

⚑ Train Station Durban Railway Station ✉ N.M.R. Ave., city center, Durban ☎ 031/ 308-8118.

⚑ Train Line Spoornet ☎ 031/361-3388 ⊕ www.spoornet.co.za.

TRAVEL AGENCIES

Rennies is the South African representative of Thomas Cook. It is open weekdays 8:30–4:30 and Saturday 8:30–noon. American Express is open weekdays 8–5 and Saturday 8:30–11, and has a full range of client services (no client mail pickup on Saturday).

⚑ Travel Agents American Express ✉ 2 Durban Club Pl., off Smith St., city center, Durban ☎ 031/301-5541. **Rennies** ✉ Durban Bay House, 333 Smith St., city center, Durban ☎ 031/304-1511.

VISITOR INFORMATION

The Tourist Junction, in the restored Old Station Building, houses a number of tourist-oriented companies and services, where you can find information on almost everything that's happening in Durban and KwaZulu-Natal. Among the companies represented are Durban Africa, the city's tourism authority; an accommodations service; an intercity train reservations office; a KwaZulu-Natal Nature Conservation Service booking desk; regional KwaZulu-Natal tourist offices; and various bus and transport companies. It is open weekdays 8–5 and weekends 9–2. Sugar Coast Tourism (covering the Umhlanga and nearby Umdloti areas), is open weekdays 8–4:30 and Saturday 9–noon. Thousand Hills Tourism Association, not surprisingly, covers the Valley of a Thousand Hills.

An excellent Web site for all areas in KwaZulu-Natal is the official provincial tourism site Zulu Kingdom.

⚑ Tourist Offices Sugar Coast Tourism ✉ Chartwell Dr., off Lighthouse Rd., Umhlanga 4320 ☎ 031/561-4257. **Thousand Hills Tourism Association** ✉ Old Main Rd.,

Botha's Hill 3660 ☎ 031/777-1874 ⊕ www.tourism.1000hills.com. **Tourist Junction**
⊠ 160 Pine St., city center, Durban 4001 ☎ 031/304-4934.
📘 **Web Site** **Zulu Kingdom** ⊕ www.zulu.org.za.

THE DRAKENSBERG

Afrikaners call them the Drakensberg: the Dragon Mountains. To Zulus
they are uKhahlamba (pronounced Ooka–hlamba)—"Barrier of Spears."
Both are apt descriptions for this wall of rock that rises from the Natal
grasslands, forming a natural fortress protecting the mountain kingdom
of Lesotho. The Drakensberg is the highest range in southern Africa and
has some of the most spectacular scenery in the country. It's a hiker's
dream, and you could easily spend several days here just soaking up the
awesome views. uKhahlamba/Drakensberg Park, a World Heritage Site,
is the first site in South Africa to be recognized for its combination of
natural and cultural attractions.

The blue-tinted mountains seem to infuse the landscape, cooling the
"champagne air"—as the locals refer to the heady, sparkling breezes that
blow around the precipices and pinnacles. The mountains, with names
like Giant's Castle, Cathedral Peak, and the Sentinel, seem to have a special atmosphere, as well as a unique topography. It's no surprise that
South African–born J. R. R. Tolkien—legendary author of *The Lord of
the Rings*—was inspired by the fantastic shapes of the Drakensberg mas-
sif when he created the phantasmagorical settings of his Middle Earth.

The Drakensberg is not a typical mountain range—it's actually an escarpment separating a high interior plateau from the coastal lowlands
of Natal. It's a continuation of the same escarpment that divides the
Transvaal Highveld from the hot malarial zones of the Lowveld in
Mpumalanga. However the Natal Drakensberg, or Berg, as it is commonly known, is far wilder and more spectacular than its Transvaal counterpart. Many of the peaks—some of which top 10,000 feet—are the
source of crystalline streams and mighty rivers that have carved out myriad valleys and dramatic gorges. The Berg is a natural watershed, with
two of South Africa's major rivers, the Tugela and the Orange, rising
from these mountains. In this untamed wilderness you can hike for days
and not meet a soul, and the mountains retain a wild majesty missing
in the commercially forested peaks of Mpumalanga.

Besides the hiking opportunities and the sheer beauty of the mountains, the other great attraction of the Berg is the San (Bushman)
paintings. The San are a hunter-gatherer people who once roamed the
entire country from 8,000 years ago to the 1800s. More than 40,000
of their paintings are sprinkled in scores of caves and on rock overhangs throughout the Berg in more than 550 known San rock-art sites—
probably the finest collection of rock paintings in the country. They
tell the stories of bygone hunts, dances, and battles and touch on the
almost mystical relationship of the San with the animals they hunted.
With the arrival of the Nguni peoples from the north and white settlers from the southwest in the 18th century, the San were driven out
of their traditional hunting lands and retreated into the remote fast-

nesses of the Drakensberg and the Kalahari Desert. San cattle raiding in Natal in the late 19th century occasioned harsh punitive expeditions by white settlers and local Bantu tribes, and by 1880 the last San had disappeared from the Berg. Today only a few clans remain in the very heart of the Kalahari Desert.

The best times to visit the Berg are spring (September–October) and late autumn (late April–June). Summer sees the Berg at its greenest and the weather at its warmest—and wettest, so don't forget to pack your rain gear. Vicious afternoon thunderstorms and hailstorms, which can put a severe damper on long hikes, are an almost daily occurrence. In winter the mountains lose their lush overcoat and turn brown and sere. Winter days in the valleys, sites of most resorts, are usually sunny and pleasant, although there can be cold snaps, usually accompanied by overcast, windy conditions, depending on the severity of the winter. Nights are chilly, however, and you should pack plenty of warm clothing if you plan to hike high up into the mountains or camp overnight. Snow is common at higher elevations. Hikers heading above the 10,000-foot level are obliged to sign the mountain register at the nearest Natal Parks Board/ KwaZulu-Natal Nature Conservation Service office in case of emergency. Don't forget to sign out again on your return. It's also a good idea to check the weather forecast beforehand, particularly in winter (June–September), as extreme cold conditions may be experienced, many roads are closed, and hiking is dangerous and prohibited.

The Natal Drakensberg is not conducive to traditional touring. The nature of the attractions and the limited road system make a connect-the-dots tour impractical and unrewarding. Although there are a number of small towns in the area, it's best to check into a hotel or resort for two or three days instead and use it as a base for hiking and exploring the immediate area. If you decide to stay at one of the self-catering camps, you probably won't find all your supplies at the resort or camp shops, which tend to be a little basic. Shop in one of the bigger towns, such as Winterton or Harrismith for Tendele, and Bergville or Estcourt for Giant's Castle, Kamberg, and Injasuti.

Numbers in the margin correspond to points of interest on the Drakensberg map.

Northern Drakensberg

43 Access to **Royal Natal National Park** is via the R74, north of Bergville. The park contains some of the most stunning mountain scenery in the Drakensberg. The highlight is the Amphitheatre, a sheer rock wall measuring an unbelievable 5 km (3 mi) across and more than 1,500 feet high. Another showstopper is the Tugela River, which flows off Mont-aux-Sources (10,836 feet) and plunges nearly 3,000 feet over the plateau in a series of five spectacular falls that make up the Tugela Falls, the longest in South Africa. The park's most popular and scenic walk winds up the Tugela Gorge, a six-hour hike that crosses the river several times and passes through a tunnel before emerging into the Amphitheatre. Hikers often turn back at the first fording of the river,

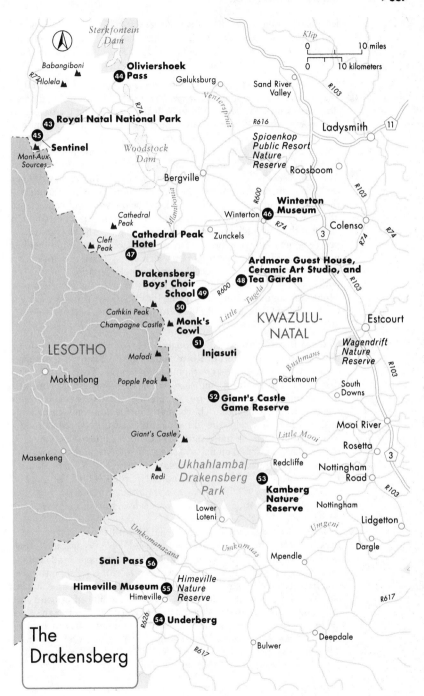

Sterkfontein Dam

Klip

0 _____ 10 miles

0 _____ 10 kilometers

Babangiboni

R74 Hlolela

44 **Oliviershoek Pass**

Geluksburg

Sand River Valley

R103

Ventersprit

43 **Royal Natal National Park**

R74

R616

Ladysmith

11

45 **Sentinel**

Mont-Aux-Sources

Woodstock Dam

Spioenkop Public Resort Nature Reserve

Roosboom

R103

Bergville

Mlambonja

R600

Winterton

46 **Winterton Museum**

R74

Colenso

R74

Cathedral Peak

Cathedral Peak Hotel

Zunckels

47

Cleft Peak

Little Tugela

Drakensberg Boys' Choir School **49**

R600

48 **Ardmore Guest House, Ceramic Art Studio, and Tea Garden**

R103

50

Monk's Cowl

KWAZULU-NATAL

Estcourt

Cathkin Peak

Champagne Castle

51

Injasuti

Bushmans

Wagendrift Nature Reserve

R103

LESOTHO

Mafadi

Popple Peak

Rockmount

South Downs

Mokhotlong

52 **Giant's Castle Game Reserve**

Little Mooi

Mooi River

Rosetta

3

Giant's Castle

Masenkeng

Redi

Ukhahlamba/ Drakensberg Park

Redcliffe

Nottingham Road

R103

53

Kamberg Nature Reserve

Nottingham

Lidgetton

Lower Loteni

Dargle

Umkomanazana

Umkomaas

Umgeni

Mpendle

Sani Pass **56**

Himeville Nature Reserve

R617

Himeville Museum **55**

Himeville

R826

54 **Underberg**

Deepdale

R617

Bulwer

The Drakensberg

because the hike looks difficult. Persevere, for the scenery gets better and better, and the walk's not as tough as it appears. ✉ *N. Berg Rd., 19 km (8 mi) off R74* ☎ *036/438–6303* 🔲 *R10* ☉ *Apr.–Sept., daily 6–6; Oct.–Mar., daily 5 AM–7 PM.*

Just past the turnoff to Royal Natal National Park, the northbound R74 begins a twisty ascent up the **Oliviershoek Pass** (6,912 feet), offering tremendous views over the plains and hills. If these views don't satiate you, continue on the R74 past the Sterkfontein Dam until the road ends at a T. Turn left onto the R712 and head into Qwa Qwa, also known as Phuthaditjhaba. Follow signs to the Witsieshoek Mountain Resort. Just before the resort, the road splits and continues for about 13 km (8 mi) to the **Sentinel** (8,580 feet), where a path takes you to the very edge of the Drakensberg escarpment. The views from here are breathtaking—the entire Royal Natal National Park lies below you, and you can see all the way to Estcourt. You will need to purchase a permit from the guard at the parking lot before venturing onto the path. The number of people going to the overlook is restricted; it's not a specific number but is rather based on the number of cars, so it's best to arrive before noon to avoid disappointment, especially during popular vacation periods. The parking lot is also the starting point for a strenuous hike to the top of Mont-aux-Sources. From the parking lot it's an easy drive back down the R712 to Harrismith and the N3 to Johannesburg and Durban.

Where to Stay

$ 🏨 **Orion Mont-Aux-Sources.** Although this hotel is more than 8 km (5 mi) from the hiking trails of Royal Natal National Park, it more than compensates with its views—stunning panoramas of the Drakensberg that take in the grand Amphitheatre, the Eastern Buttress, and miles of the escarpment. These views are the hotel's greatest asset, so be sure to request a front-facing room. The rooms themselves are nondescript, reminiscent of chain hotels around the world. Likewise, the public rooms lack warmth, seeming more suited to the hotel's midweek conference business. Breakfast and dinner are served buffet-style, with extensive selections ranging from roasts to vegetarian curries. ✉ *N. Berg Rd., off R74* ⌂ *Private Bag X1670, Bergville 3350* ☎🖨 *036/438–6230* ⊕ *www. orion-hotels.co.za* 🛏 *75 rooms* ⚐ *Restaurant, room service, miniature golf, tennis court, 2 pools, horseback riding, squash, volleyball, bar* ▤ *AE, DC, MC, V* ⭐ *MAP.*

¢ 🏨 **Tendele Hutted Camp.** Smack in the middle of Royal Natal National Park, this camp makes a great base for long hikes into the mountains. Accommodations are in a variety of bungalows, cottages, and chalets, each with excellent views of the sheer rock face of the Amphitheatre. You must bring all your own food, although you can purchase staples and frozen meat at the main visitor center. In the bungalows and cottages all food is prepared by camp staff, but you can do your own cooking in the chalets. There is one lodge, which accommodates six people. ⌂ *KwaZulu-Natal Nature Conservation Service, Box 13069, Cascades 3202* ☎ *0331/845–1000* 🖨 *0331/845–1002* 🛏 *26 chalets, 2 cottages, 1 lodge* ⚐ *Some kitchens, shop* ▤ *AE, DC, MC, V.*

Central Drakensberg

46 The small but fascinating **Winterton Museum** provides a nice overview of the Berg. Most exhibits in this delightful and informative museum were donated, made, or built by people from the Winterton and other nearby communities. If you are planning to hike to see any San (Bushman) paintings later in the day, first take a look at the museum's San Art Gallery, the most extensive photographic record of Berg San paintings, consisting of 10 panels of 180 photographs. If you are planning a tour of the battlefields, pop into the reading room, where an outstanding private collection of books on the South African War is available for perusal. These volumes are used as reference sources by many of the professional battlefield tour guides. ✉ *Winterton Village* ☎ *036/488–1885* 🖘 *Free* ☉ *Weekdays 9–3, Sat. 9–noon.*

47 The **Cathedral Peak Hotel,** accessible from Winterton or via dirt roads off the R600, is a tremendous base for hikes—and drives—into the mountains. Although KZN Wildlife levies a fee to enter the area, the hotel acts as the de facto center for hikers heading into the surrounding mountains. Leaflets, available at reception, give information on area trails—from easy strolls to demanding hikes. A scale model in the hotel lobby gives you the lay of the land before you set off. Cathedral Peak (9,900 feet) is the easiest of the major peaks to scale. Anyone who is fit and accustomed to long hikes can make the 19-km (12-mi) round-trip from the hotel to the summit and back; only the last portion near the summit is difficult. Budget 9 to 10 hours to get up and down, allowing plenty of time to drink in the view from the top, surely one of the highlights of the region. Another recommended route is the hike to Rainbow Gorge, about a six-hour trip, encompassing indigenous forest, pools, streams, and panoramic views. If you're traveling by car, drive up Mike's Pass (the road is a little rough, so take it slowly) to experience a magnificent vista of the entire Champagne Range and valley. ✉ *Cathedral Peak Rd.* ☎ *036/488–1000* ⊕ *www.cathedralpeak.co.za* 🖘 *R20* ☉ *Daily 7–sunset.*

The R600, accessible from the N3 via Winterton, leads to many of the resorts and attractions in the Central Berg. Seventeen km (8 mi) down
48 the R600 from Winterton is the turnoff to the **Ardmore Guest House, Ceramic Art Studio, and Tea Garden.** Started on a farm by artist Fée Berning in 1985, the studio is now home to nearly 40 Zulu and Sotho artists, each pursuing his or her own artistic visions in clay. Their colorful ceramics, which incorporate zebras and giraffes as handles on teapots, bowls, and platters, have won national and international awards and are displayed in galleries around the world. You can watch artists at work or just browse through the collection, which is housed in a converted farm shed. The studio ships purchases overseas. Have tea and scones in the tea garden or stay a night in the old farmhouse, now a guesthouse. ✉ *D275, off R600, Central Berg* ☎ *036/468–1314* 🖘 *Free* ☉ *Weekdays 9–4:30.*

★ **49** A couple of miles farther down the R600 is the turnoff to the **Drakensberg Boys' Choir School.** Mentioned in the same breath as the Vienna and

Harlem boys' choirs, this is one of the most famous choral groups in the world. It's worth coming for one of the weekly performances in the auditorium, which run the musical gamut from the classics to ethnic songs. Reservations are essential. There are no performances during school vacations. ⊠ *Off R600* ☎ *036/468–1012* ☉ *Performances Wed. at 3:30.*

50 The R600 runs directly into the mountains, ending at **Monk's Cowl**, a Natal Parks Board/KwaZulu-Natal Nature Conservation Service station. This is the gateway to several day and overnight hikes into the high Drakensberg. Among the highlights are a one-hour walk to Sterkspruit Falls, the largest waterfall in the area, and a 3½-hour walk to the top of the Little Berg. On this walk you pass the Sphinx (a rock formation that looks like the famous Egyptian monument) and Breakfast Falls before joining the Contour Trail for panoramic views of the spectacular formations Champagne Castle, Cathkin Peak, Dragon's Back, and Sterkhorn. Hikers who wish to camp out in the mountains must sign the mountain register and pay R25 per person for the first night and R16 per person for each night thereafter. ⌂ *Private Bag X2, Winterton 3340* ☎ *036/ 468–1103* 🖃 *R20* ☉ *Daily 6 AM–7 PM.*

51 **Injasuti**, 32 km (20 mi) down a dirt road off the Central Berg/Loskop Road, is a collection of huts set in the northern section of the Giant's Castle Game Reserve. A number of spectacular hikes start from here, including a guided 5-km (3-mi) walk (R35) up the Injasuti Valley to **Battle Cave**, which holds one of the most fascinating collections of San paintings in the country. Some 750 paintings cover the rock walls of the cave, but it's the subject matter that is most enthralling: one clearly depicts two Bushman clans at war—with some figures falling, others running away. Tours of Battle Cave leave daily at 8:30 from the camp office, which is 5 km (3 mi) from the gate and well marked, and return around 1. There's drinkable water all the way, but wear good shoes—hiking boots if possible—and take a hat and rain gear, as there are frequent thunderstorms. Reservations are essential. ⌂ *Private Bag X7010, Estcourt 3310* ☎ *036/431–7848* ⊕ *www.kznwildlife.com* 🖃 *R15* ☉ *Apr.–Sept., daily 6–6; Oct.–Mar., daily 5 AM–7 PM.*

52 South of Monk's Cowl is **Giant's Castle Game Reserve**, an 85,500-acre reserve encompassing rolling grasslands as well as some of the highest peaks in the Drakensberg. A host of trails, ranging in length from two hours to overnight, start at the main visitor center. The most popular tourist attraction is the **Main Caves**, which have the finest collection of San paintings in the Drakensberg. More than 500 paintings, some now barely discernible, adorn the faces of two huge rock overhangs just a 40-minute walk from the camp office. Many paintings depict eland hunts, as the huge antelope held a special religious significance for the San. Guided tours start from the caves themselves. Take binoculars if you can; some of the paintings are hard to see with the naked eye.

☾ **Lammergeyer Hide,** set high on a cliff, is where bird-watchers can observe the endangered lammergeyer, or bearded vulture, and other birds of prey. On weekend mornings between May and September, rangers put out meat and bones for these birds below the hide (blind). In addition to giving birders a close-up view of the vultures, the feeding program is intended to draw the birds away from nearby farmland, where they might eat poisoned carcasses. Afrikaner farmers erroneously believe that the birds kill their young livestock, hence the name *lammergeyer,* or "lamb killer." The hide accommodates a maximum of six people. If you don't have a 4x4, take one of the hide tours, which are extremely popular and are sometimes fully booked six months in advance. Make sure you reserve a spot before leaving home, or call to see if there is availability the minute you arrive in the country. A ranger drives you up to the blind, and you're on your own for the walk back. ⊠ *Mooi River or Central Berg/Giant's Castle exit off N3, near EstCt.* ⬠ *Hide bookings, Giant's Castle Game Reserve, Private Bag X7055, Estcourt 3310* ☎ *036/353–3718* 💲 *R20; cave tours R25; hide tours R150* ⊙ *Apr.–Sept., daily 6–6; Oct.–Mar., daily 5 AM–7 PM; cave tours daily 9–3 hourly; hide tours May–Sept. at 7:30 AM.*

㊳ **Kamberg Nature Reserve,** in the foothills of the uKhahlamba/Drakensberg Park, is best known for its superb collection of San rock-art paintings.

Fodor'sChoice Visit the **Kamberg Rock Art Centre** (wheelchair-friendly) to learn about
★ the hunter-gatherer world of the San before taking a 2½- to 3-hour guided walk to **Game Pass Shelter,** along the same routes taken by the San to their rock shelters. One of the first rock-art sites recorded by Europeans and subsequently written up in a 1915 issue of *Scientific American,* Game Pass Shelter and its paintings are sometimes called the Rosetta Stone of San rock art, because it was here that archaeologists first came to understand the spiritual significance of rock paintings. ⊠ *Mooi River or Central Berg/Giant's Castle exit off N3, near EstCt.* ⬠ *KZN Wildlife, Box 13053, Cascades, Pietermaritzburg 3202* ☎ *033/267–7251 or 031/845–1000* 💲 *R15* ⊙ *Daily.*

Where to Stay & Eat

¢–$ ✕ **St. Anton's Restaurant & Bar in the Mountains.** Close to the Drakensberg Boys' Choir School and with outstanding views of Champagne Castle and Cathedral Peak, St. Anton's has superfriendly service, a wonderfully warm mountain atmosphere, and alfresco dining beside a tranquil lake. Start your meal with Thai pumpkin soup with lemongrass or the popular mushrooms St. Anton—button mushrooms in a creamy garlic cheese sauce with flaked almonds. Seafood creole and the Drakensberg trout are excellent main courses, and the chicken and prawn curry, oxtail, and pub lunches are also highly recommended. ⊠ *Off R600, Winterton* ☎ *036/468–1218* ⬠ *Reservations essential* ☰ *MC, V.*

$ ✕▥ **The Nest.** Most guests at this well-run resort seem content to park themselves on the sun-drenched lawns, soak in the dazzling mountain views, and await the next round of tea, drinks, or meals. Few manage to muster the energy to drive the 8 km (5 mi) to the trailheads at Monk's Cowl. The hotel, built by Italian prisoners of war, is one of the most attractive and appealing of the Berg resorts. Many rooms have pine ceilings, heated towel racks, and under-floor heating (there are no TVs). Be sure to request a mountain-facing room. All meals are table d'hôte, with an emphasis on traditional South African cuisine, including home-cooked specialties like roasts, oxtail, and cottage pie. The quality of the food is much higher than that at most other Berg resorts. ☒ *R600, Central Berg* ✑ *Private Bag X14, Winterton 3340* ☏ *036/468–1068* 🖶 *036/ 468–1390* ⊕ *www.thenest.co.za* ☞ *52 rooms* ⚘ *Restaurant, tennis court, pool, mountain bikes, croquet, horseback riding, bar, playground; no room TVs* ▭ *AE, DC, MC, V* ¶ *FAP.*

$$$ 🏨 **Cleopatra Mountain Farmhouse.** It would be difficult to find better lodg-
Fodor'sChoice   ing or dining anywhere in southern Africa than at this enchanting hide-
★   away tucked away at the foot of the Drakensberg Range. The lodge
overlooks a trout-filled lake and is encircled by mountains and old
trees. Richard and Mouse Poynton, legendary South African chefs and
hosts, have renovated the 1936 family fishing farm and created a per-
fect combination of comfort, tranquillity, style, and exceptional food.
Homemade biscuits, hand-painted and stenciled walls, lovingly em-
broidered cushions and samplers, fluffy mohair blankets, and heated towel
racks are just a few of the details you'll find here. For meals you'll eat
with ceremony but no pretension in an intimate dining room warmed
on cold days by a blazing log fire. ✑ *Box 17, Balgowan 3275* 🖶 *033/ 267–7243* ⊕ *www.cleomountain.com* ☞ *6 rooms, 3 suites* ⚘ *Dining room* ▭ *AE, DC, MC, V* ¶ *MAP.*

$$ 🏨 **Drakensberg Sun Resort.** This hotel and resort is part of the Southern
Sun Hotel Group but retains the ambience of a country hotel. The
grounds are spectacularly set in a valley at the foot of the Champagne
Range, with wonderful views of Champagne Castle and Cathkin Peak
from most rooms and public areas. There are huge log fires everywhere,
and the deck off the main dining area is very popular, even when the
sun isn't shining. Decor is reminiscent of a country lodge, with brass
lamps, pastel colors, and lots of wood. Activities focus on a range of
sporting options and excursions, including horseback riding and brief
helicopter sightseeing trips. The resort is extremely family oriented,
something to keep in mind during school vacations and other peak periods. ☒ *R600, Champagne Valley, Central Berg* ✑ *Box 335, Winter-
ton 3340* ☏ *036/468–1000* 🖶 *036/468–1224* ⊕ *www.southernsun. com* ☞ *71 rooms* ⚘ *Restaurant, 9-hole golf course, tennis court, pool, gym, fishing, hiking, horseback riding, squash, volleyball, 2 bars* ▭ *AE, DC, MC, V* ¶ *MAP.*

★ **$**   🏨 **Cathedral Peak Hotel.** Few hotels in South Africa can rival the exquisite
setting of this large resort, high above the Ulamboza River and ringed
by towering peaks. Hiking trails start right from the hotel and wend their
way through a dozen mountains and valleys. Choose from luxury or
standard rooms or thatch bungalows. French doors open onto private
verandas overlooking the gardens or the mountains, and pine furnishings give the rooms a pleasant, rustic feel. The hotel has a 9-hole golf
course and daily helicopter sightseeing trips. Food is served buffet-style
and is fairly standard Drakensberg hotel fare, with an emphasis on
roasts and carved meats, fresh salads, and desserts such as trifle and cream
cakes. ☒ *Cathedral Peak Rd., 43 km (18 mi) from Winterton 3340* 🖶 *036/488–1888 or 036/488–1889* ⊕ *www.cathedralpeak.co.za* ☞ *94 rooms* ⚘ *Restaurant, room service, 9-hole golf course, tennis court, pool, gym, sauna, horseback riding, squash, 2 bars, playground* ▭ *AE, DC, MC, V* ¶ *MAP.*

$ ⌖ **Champagne Castle.** Along with Cathedral Peak, this old family-style hotel enjoys one of the best settings of any of the Berg resorts. It lies right in the mountains, with magnificent views down Champagne Valley to the towering massifs of Champagne Castle and Cathkin Peak. A host of hiking trails begin practically on the hotel's doorstep, and the trailheads at Monk's Cowl lie just minutes away. There's nothing remotely fancy about the hotel itself, but it's a peaceful haven where genteel traditions linger—gentlemen are still required to wear ties to dinner. It also has a family-oriented bent, so expect to encounter South African families en masse during school vacations. Rooms, in thatch *rondawels* (traditional round huts) and bungalows scattered through the gardens, are pleasantly furnished and comfortable. Meals are served buffet-style, with an emphasis on traditional South African roasts and vegetables. ⊠ *R600, Central Berg* ⌖ *Private Bag X8, Winterton 3340* ☎ *036/468–1063* 🖷 *036/468–1306* ⊕ *www.champagnecastle.co.za* ↘ *56 rooms* ⌂ *Restaurant, putting green, tennis court, pool, horseback riding, volleyball, 2 bars* ⊟ *AE, DC, MC, V* ⏃⎪ *FAP.*

¢ ⌖ **Giant's Castle.** This luxurious camp not only offers comfortable and

Fodor'sChoice well-equipped accommodations but is also ideally situated in Giant's Cas-

★ tle Game Reserve. Hidden away in a beautiful valley close to the sheer face of the High Drakensberg, it is an ideal base for viewing the San paintings in the main caves and bearded vultures from the Lammergeyer Hide. Accommodations are either in chalets, which share communal kitchens, or in self-contained cottages, with either four or six beds. There is also a lodge accommodating seven people. If you choose this option, you must provide your own food, which is then cooked by camp staff. A store in the main office sells staples like milk, bread, charcoal, and packs of meat, and some good curios and souvenirs. ⊠ *Mooi River exit off the N3 KZN Wildlife, Box 13053, Cascades, Pietermaritzburg 3202* ☎ *031/845–1000* 🖷 *031/845–1002* ↘ *37 chalets, 6 cottages, 1 lodge* ⌂ *Restaurant, some kitchens, shop* ⊟ *MC, V.*

¢ ⌖ **Injasuti.** At the head of Injasuti Valley in the northern section of the Giant's Castle Game Reserve, this camp has great views of Cathkin Peak, Monk's Cowl, and Champagne Castle. Cabins sleep up to six people, and all have kitchens and dining-living rooms. Electricity is available only from 5:30 to 10 each night. ⊠ *1 McKenzie Dr., Cascades, Pietermaritzburg* ⌖ *KZN Wildlife, Box 13069, Cascades, Pietermaritzburg 3200* ☎ *033/845–1000* 🖷 *033/845–1001* ⊕ *www.kznwildlife.com* ↘ *18 cabins* ⌂ *Kitchens* ⊟ *AE, MC, V.*

¢ ⌖ **Kamberg Camp.** Deep in the mountains of the Kamberg Nature Reserve, these rustic self-catering accommodations are a good base from which to see the famous San rock paintings. Options range from two- and six-bed chalets to an eight-bed cottage, all with bathrooms and kitchenettes. A small café serves tea, coffee, muffins, and toasted sandwiches. ⊠ *Mooi River or Central Berg/Giant's Castle exit off N3, near EstCt.* ⌖ *KZN Wildlife, Box 13053, Cascades, Pietermaritzburg 3202* ☎ *033/267–7251 or 031/845–1000* 🖷 *031/845–1002* ✉ *kamberg@kznwildlife.com* ↘ *6 chalets, 1 cottage* ⌂ *Café, picnic area, kitchenettes, hiking, lounge* ⊟ *AE, DC, MC, V.*

Southern Drakensberg

This attractive region is a ways south of the main Drakensberg Range, about a two-hour drive from Pietermaritzburg along pretty country roads. Its slightly remote location keeps it far from the madding tourist crowds. Much of the area is accessed by a network of rough dirt roads. Although most are suitable for regular cars, drive carefully and slowly. If you should get a flat, stop and fix it immediately; you could severely damage your tire rims on pebbles if you don't.

54 The tiny town of **Underberg** is accessed via the R617, a long but very pretty road from the town of Howick on the N3. Underberg comes as a surprise, set in a fertile green valley with views of the Drakensberg on the horizon. The Tourist Information Centre can provide details on the tourist route known as the Sani Saunter, which covers most area restaurants, accommodations, and attractions; not all are recommended, however.

55 Another 5 km (3 mi) farther along the road to Sani Pass brings you to Himeville, where you might want to stop for a pint at the Himeville Arms Hotel or drop by the **Himeville Museum,** across the street. Built as a fort on Natal Crown Colony lands in 1899 to protect the region's pioneer farmers, the building was later converted to a prison and used as such until the early 1970s. It became a museum in 1976, and the premises were subsequently declared a national monument. One of the best rural museums in the region, it houses an open-air display on the early European settlers in Himeville, Underberg, and Bulwer as well as traditional weapons and ornaments of the San and other African tribes who once lived here. There are also displays on the area's fauna and flora, geography, and topography. ⊠ *Main St., Himeville* ☎ *033/702–1184* 🖃 *Free* ☉ *Tues.–Sun. 8:30–12:30.*

56 **Sani Pass** attracts local 4x4 enthusiasts who test man and machine all the way into Lesotho. The pass, one of the traditional routes over the Drakensberg into the Lesotho highlands, ascends an incredible 5,730 feet through the upper valley of the Mkomazana River. From the top, the view of row upon row of tall peaks is truly stupendous. Just inside the Lesotho border is a mountaineer's chalet known as Sani Top, the highest pub in Africa. The pass is accessible only by 4x4 vehicle, and most accommodations in the nearby country towns of Himeville and Underberg can arrange tours to the top with qualified guides. Remember to take your passport with you, as you will enter Lesotho on these excursions. The cost is approximately R160 per person for a full day, which usually includes lunch and teas. The beautiful Giant's Cup Hiking Trail (⇨ Sports & the Outdoors, *below*) begins halfway up the pass.

Where to Stay

¢–$ 🏨 **Sani Pass Hotel.** Just 11 km (57 mi) from Himeville at the base of the spectacular Sani Pass, this attractive country hotel is close to the Roof of Africa and so is a favorite with international guests. The tranquil valley setting offers spectacular mountain views. Accommodations are either in attractive garden cottages or larger, more luxurious rooms in the main building. The latter rooms all have mountain views. The food is delicious country fare, and candlelit dinners are a hotel specialty. Activities include scenic walks and drives, a choice of horseback rides (including plateau and sunset rides), and, of course, regular trips up that fabulous pass. ⊠ *Sani Pass Rd., 11 km (7 mi) north of Himeville* ✆ *Box 44, Himeville 3256* ☎ *033/702–1320* 🖷 *033/702–0220* ⊕ *www. sanipasshotel.co.za* ➩ *43 rooms, 44 cottages* ⚭ *Restaurant, 9-hole golf course, tennis court, pool, badminton, horseback riding, squash, volleyball, 2 bars; no a/c* ▤ *AE, DC, MC, V* ⍾ *MAP.*

¢ 🏨 **Taylor's B&B.** A delightful respite is just off the R617, 2 km (1 mi) from Underberg on the Swartberg road (look for the sign to the Banks, on the left). All rooms are attractively and individually decorated; upstairs units have lovely views across the surrounding countryside. Each room has snack-making facilities, including a toaster and a *skottelbraai* (gas wok). A huge farm breakfast is included, and dinners can be arranged beforehand on request. Hosts Edith and John Taylor are extremely friendly and helpful and can arrange trips to Sani Pass as well as tennis, fishing, canoeing, and horseback-riding excursions. ✆ *Box 33, Underberg 3257* ☎🖷 *033/701–2011* ⊕ *www.taylorsguesthouse.com* ➩ *3 suites* ⚭ *Fans, refrigerator, no-smoking rooms; no a/c* ▤ *No credit cards* ⍾ *BP.*

Sports & the Outdoors

If you're into backpacking and want to see this beautiful region on foot, don't miss the **Giant's Cup Hiking Trail** (✆ KZN Wildlife, Box 13069, Cascades, Pietermaritzburg 3202 ☎ 033/845–1000 ⊕ www.kznwildlife. com). Although actually a five-day hike, the trail is never so far from civilization that you can't shorten it by a day or two. Giant's Cup winds through the Little Berg, as this part of the southern Drakensberg is known, with incredible views of the escarpment at every turn. It passes by a petrified forest, San paintings, rock shelters, streams, and deep blue pools. If you like swimming, definitely come in summer. Accommodations are in old foresters' houses. The supply of firewood is plentiful, and roaring log fires will warm you. There aren't any comforts, though—water is usually heated by a donkey boiler, bunks have mattresses but no bedding, and only one hut has electricity, so don't forget your flashlight. You'll need to carry your own food, sleeping bag, hiking stove and fuel, eating utensils, and clothing. If you're equipped for backpacking and are reasonably fit, this is a real treat, beginning halfway up Sani Pass and ending near the Lesotho border post at Bushman's Neck. The trail costs approximately R65 per person per night.

Drakensberg A to Z

BUS TRAVEL

On request, most resorts will pick up guests at the Greyhound or Translux terminal in Estcourt or Ladysmith or at the Montrose Service Area, one of the busiest gas stops on the N3, halfway between Johannesburg and Durban. Buses from both lines stop at these towns at least once a day on their runs between Durban and Johannesburg. Ladysmith to Jo'burg costs about R175 and takes roughly six hours, and Ladysmith to Durban is about R140 and takes roughly three hours.

🚌 Bus Stations **Estcourt terminal** ✉ Municipal Library, Victoria St., Estcourt 🕾 No phone. **Ladysmith terminal** ✉ Murchison St., Ladysmith 🕾 No phone. **Montrose Service Area** ✉ City Shell Complex, Swinburne 🕾 058/672-1044.

🚌 Bus Lines **Greyhound** 🕾 083/915-9000, 011/830-1400, or 031/309-7838 ⊕ www.greyhound.co.za. **Translux** 🕾 031/361-7461.

CAR TRAVEL

The main resort area of the Drakensberg lies 380 km (250 mi) from Johannesburg and 240 km (150 mi) from Durban—an almost direct shot along the N3. A car is not strictly necessary for a trip to the Berg, although it is certainly a convenience, and though a 4x4 would be an advantage, it, too, is not a necessity. Gas stations can be found in Bergville, Winterton, and at the foot of Champagne Castle. Driving in this area is time consuming. Trucks often slow up traffic, and you should be vigilant of animals on and attempting to cross the road.

EMERGENCIES

A dispensary and health-care clinic can be found at the Winterton Pharmacy. For health care in Ladysmith, *see* Zululand & the Battlefields A to Z, *below*. For mountain rescue, contact the Search & Rescue Section of the Mountain Club of South Africa.

🚑 Emergency Services **Police** 🕾 036/448-1095 Bergville, 036/352-2280 Estcourt, 036/488-1502 Winterton. **Search & Rescue Section of the Mountain Club of South Africa** 🕾 082/990-5877.

🚑 Hospital **Estcourt Hospital** ✉ Old Main Rd., Estcourt 🕾 036/342-7000.

🚑 Pharmacies **Estcourt Pharmacy** ✉ 126 Victoria St., Estcourt 🕾 036/352-3506. **Winterton Pharmacy** ✉ Springfield Rd., Winterton 🕾 036/488-1177, 036/468-1303 after hours.

MONEY MATTERS

Most larger towns have ATMs and banks, but don't count on finding one everywhere. Make sure you travel with enough cash. Both Winterton and Estcourt have a First National Bank, ABSA, and Standard Bank. Bergville has ABSA and FNB ATMs. Hours for all banks are weekdays 9–3:30 and Saturday 8:30–11.

VISITOR INFORMATION

Drakensberg Tourism is open weekdays 9–4. Underberg Tourist Information is open Monday–Saturday 8:30–4:30.

🛈 Tourist Offices **Drakensberg Tourism** ✉ Tatham St., Bergville 🕾 036/448-1296 ⊕ www.drakensberg.org.za. **Underberg Tourist Information** ✉ Main St. 🕾 Box 230, Underberg 3257 🕾 033/701-1419.

ZULULAND & THE BATTLEFIELDS

Zululand stretches north from the Tugela River all the way to the border of Mozambique. It's a region of rolling grasslands, gorgeous beaches, and classic African bush. It has also seen more than its share of bloodshed and death. Modern South Africa was forged in the fiery crucible of Zululand and northern Natal. Here Boers battled Zulus, Zulus battled Britons, and Britons battled Boers. The most interesting historic sites, however, involve the battles against the Zulus. Names like Isandlwana, Rorke's Drift, and Blood River have taken their place in the roll of legendary military encounters.

Indeed, no African tribe has captured the Western imagination quite like the Zulus. A host of books and movies have explored their warrior culture and extolled their martial valor. Until the early 19th century the Zulus were a small, unheralded group, part of the Nguni peoples who migrated to southern Africa from the north. King Shaka (1787–1828), the illegitimate son of a Zulu chief, changed all that. Before Shaka, warfare among the Nguni had been a desultory affair in which small bands of warriors would hurl spears at one another from a distance and then retire. Shaka introduced the assegai, a short stabbing spear, teaching his warriors to get close to the enemy in hand-to-hand combat. He also developed the famous chest-and-horns formation, a cattle analogy for a classic maneuver in which you outflank and encircle your enemy. In less than a decade Shaka created a military machine unrivaled in black Africa. By the time of his assassination in 1828, Shaka had destroyed 300 tribes and extended Zulu power for 800 km (500 mi) through the north, south, and west.

Fifty years after Shaka's death, the British still considered the Zulus a major threat to their planned federation of white states in South Africa. The British solution, in 1879, was to instigate a war to destroy the Zulu kingdom. They employed a similar tactic 20 years later to bring the Boer republics to heel and the rich goldfields of the Witwatersrand into their own hands.

Recently, interest in the battlefields has been growing, particularly in light of the Boer and Zulu War centenary celebrations, which started in 2000. The best way to tour the battlefields is with an expert guide, who can bring the history to life. However, unless you've done extensive research or have a vivid imagination, you may find it difficult to conjure up the furious events of a century ago. Many of the battle sites are little more than open grassland, graced with the occasional memorial stone. If you're not a history buff, it's better to head straight to the game reserves and natural wonders of northern Zululand.

Towns and sights on this tour appear on the KwaZulu-Natal map.

Dukuza

57 *75 km (47 mi) north of Durban on the N2.*

Though today Zululand starts on the north side of the Tugela River, in Shaka's day the Zulu empire was much larger, encompassing much of present-day KwaZulu-Natal. Shaka called his royal settlement of a thousand huts Dukuza, for which the north-coast town formerly known as Stanger was renamed. Amafa AkwaZulu Natali (formerly the KwaZulu Monuments Council) has opened the **KwaDukuza Interpretive Center,** which houses displays and information on the Shaka period, including

CloseUp

BOERS, BRITS & BATTLEFIELDS

THE BOER WAR (1899–1902), now referred to as the South African War, was the longest, bloodiest, and most costly war fought by Britain for nearly 100 years. The Brits and the Boers, Afrikaner descendants of 17th-century Dutch settlers fighting for independence from Britain, engaged in numerous battles in which the little guys (the Boers) often made mincemeat of the great British colonial army sent out to defeat them. Britain marched into South Africa in the spring of 1899, confident that it would all be over by Christmas. However, the comparatively small bands of volunteers from the republics of the Transvaal and the Orange Free State were to give Queen Victoria's proud British army, as Kipling wrote, "no end of a lesson." Today history has also revealed the part played by hundreds of thousands of black South Africans in the war as messengers, scouts, interpreters, and laborers—hence the renaming of the war.

The most famous—or infamous—of the battles was fought on top of Spion Kop, in KwaZulu-Natal, where the mass grave of hundreds of British soldiers stretches from one side of the hill to the other. Of interest is that three men who were to change the course of world history were there on that fateful day: Winston Churchill, Mahatma Gandhi (who was a stretcher bearer), and Louis Botha, the first prime minister of the Union of South Africa.

— Kate Turkington

a slide show on Shaka. There's also a crafts shop and a bookshop. ✉ *King Shaka St.* ☎ *032/552-7210* 🖬 *Free* 🕙 *Weekdays 8–4, weekends 9–4.*

Eshowe

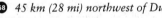 *45 km (28 mi) northwest of Dukuza on the N2 and R66.*

High up in the hills, this oldest town in Zululand has great views of the Dhlinza Forest and fields of sugarcane. The town is the birthplace of King Cetshwayo, the son of King Shaka's half brother Mpande. Eshowe is the site of **Fort Nongqayi**, which houses the Zululand Historical Museum, the Vukani Basket Museum, and Sharpel's Church, with a display and artifacts relating to the Norwegian missionary Bishop Schreuder, who built 22 churches in the area in the 1800s. The fort was built in 1883 and served as the headquarters of the Nongqai Police, a black police contingent under British command. Museum displays trace the role of the fort in the Bambata Rebellion of 1906, when Chief Bambata took up arms to protest a £1 poll tax on every African male. A particularly interesting exhibit deals with John Dunn (1834–95), the son of settler parents, who was fluent in Zulu, Afrikaans, and English. He became Chief Cetshwayo's political adviser in 1856, and was given the status of a Zulu chief. Dunn observed Zulu customs and laws, going so far as to marry 49 Zulu wives, by whom he had 117 children. Periodically, the descendants of John Dunn stage reunions. ⊠ *Nongqayi Rd.* ☎ *035/ 474–1141* 🖃 *Tours, including 3 museums R20* ☉ *Weekdays 7:30–4, weekends 9–4.*

Shakaland, a living museum of Zulu culture, is one of the most popular tourist stops in the region. Originally the movie set for *Shaka Zulu,* Shakaland consists of a traditional Zulu kraal, with thatch beehive huts arranged in a circle around a central cattle enclosure. The emphasis here is on Zulu culture as it existed under King Shaka in the 19th century. You can watch Zulus dressed in animal skins or beaded aprons engaged in everyday tasks: making beer, forging spears, and crafting beadwork. Opt for a three-hour day tour or spend the night. A Zulu cultural adviser leads you through the kraal, explaining the significance of the layout and the roles played by men and women in traditional Zulu society. A highlight of the visit is a half-hour dance performance, featuring a variety of Zulu and other traditional dances. The whole setup is touristy, and some critics have labeled it a Zulu Disneyland, but you learn a great deal about Zulu culture nevertheless. A buffet lunch is included in the tour. ⊠ *Off R66, 13 km (8 mi) north of Eshowe* ☎ *035/460–0912* ⊕ *www.shakaland.com* 🖃 *R195* ☉ *Tours daily at 11 and 12:30.*

Where to Stay & Eat

$ ✕🏨 **Protea Shakaland.** Staying overnight at Shakaland is far more rewarding than the three-hour daytime tour. Overnight guests see a more extensive program of cultural events (from 4 PM to 11 AM the next day) and get to experience a night in a quasi-traditional Zulu dwelling. The rooms here are attractive and luxurious Africa-inspired accommodations. Enormous thatch beehive huts supported by rope-wrapped struts are decorated with African bedspreads, reed matting, and interesting African art, creating an appealing ethnic elegance. All have modern bathrooms and superb views. All meals are included in the price, though day-trippers can purchase lunch or dinner ($$; reservations essential), which feature a selection of Western-style dishes and some Zulu specialties. ⊠ *Off R66, 13 km (8 mi) north of Eshowe* 🖂 *Box 103, Eshowe 3815* ☎ *035/ 460–0912* 🖷 *035/460–0824* ⊕ *www.proteahotels.com* 🛏 *48 rooms, 45 with bath* 🖫 *Restaurant, pool, bar* ▤ *AE, DC, MC, V* ⑩ *FAP.*

Melmoth

❺❾ *30 km (19 mi) north of Eshowe.*

As you drive along the R66, follow signs for the **Nkwalini Pass.** The road snakes up and over the mountains, revealing knockout views of valleys and hills dotted with Zulu kraals.

Where to Stay

★ $ 🏨 **Simunye Zulu Lodge.** If Shakaland is too commercial for your tastes, consider this small settlement tucked away in a remote valley of Zululand. Like Shakaland, Simunye attempts to introduce you to traditional Zulu culture, but the emphasis here extends to contemporary Zulu lifestyles, too. You'll reach the camp on an ox wagon or on horseback, and the one-hour ride into the valley is one of the highlights of a visit. During a stay you'll watch Zulu dancing and visit a working kraal, complete with traditional beehive huts, where you'll learn about Zulu culture and meet the kraal's residents. You can opt to sleep overnight in one of the guest beehive huts or stay in the more luxurious main camp, built into the side of a hill overlooking the Mfule River. The rooms, built of stone and thatch, are a classy mix of Zulu and pioneer cultures. You'll sleep in a wooden bed handmade by local villagers in a room decorated with Zulu cooking pots, cow-skin rugs, and handmade wooden African chairs. Only the lodges have electricity; in the rooms, light is provided by candles and hurricane lanterns. Unfortunately, the stone bathrooms were designed more for their aesthetic value than any practical purpose: awkward steps lead to a hand-filled stone bath, and just getting in and out requires balance and agility. Most people stay only one night, but try to book for two nights over a weekend and arrange to attend a wedding or coming-of-age ceremony in a neighboring village (if one is happening while you're there). These ceremonies are purely local affairs, and you won't experience a more authentic celebration of rural Zulu culture elsewhere. ⊠ *D256, off the R34, 6 km (4 mi) south of Melmoth* 🖅 *Box 248, Melmoth 3835* 🕾 *035/450–3111 or 035/450–7103* 🖷 *035/ 450–2534* 🛏 *6 rock rooms, 5 lodge rooms, 5 huts* ⚷ *Bar* ▤ *AE, DC, MC, V* ⦿*❘ FAP.*

Ulundi

60 *35 km (22 mi) north of Melmoth.*

Ulundi is the joint capital—with Pietermaritzburg—of KwaZulu-Natal. Except for a huge legislative complex, however, it's a small, unremarkable town with a shopping complex and not much more. Two kilometers (1 mi) south of town, you'll see the turnoff to the **Battle of Ulundi Memorial.** A stone temple with a silver dome marks the site of the battle on the sunbaked uplands surrounding Ulundi. The Battle of Ulundi marked the culmination of the Zulu War of 1879. Lord Chelmsford, smarting from his defeat at Isandlwana, personally led the march on Ulundi and King Cetshwayo's royal kraal, Ondini. Cetshwayo, already disheartened by heavy losses at Kambula and Gingindlovu, sent messengers to the British seeking peace. In reply, Chelmsford demanded the disbandment of the Zulu regiment system and the surrender of the royal cattle herd. To the Zulu, for whom cattle are the very thread of the social fabric, such terms were unacceptable.

On July 4, 1879, a British force of 5,317 crossed the White Umfolozi River, marched onto the open plain near Ondini, and formed an infantry square. Mounted troops then harassed the 15,000-strong Zulu force into making an undisciplined attack. None of the Zulu warriors got within 100 feet of the British square before being cut down by rifle and artillery fire. Within 45 minutes the Zulus were in flight, and the British 17th Lancers and a flying column were giving pursuit, spearing the fleeing Zulus from horseback. The Zulu dead numbered 1,500. British losses amounted to a mere 13.

The British burned Ondini to the ground, and King Cetshwayo fled into the Ngome Forest. He was captured two months later and exiled to Cape Town and, finally, to England. Although he was restored to the throne as a puppet in 1883, the Zulu empire had been shattered. ⊠ *Cetshwayo Hwy.* ☎ *No phone.*

Continue down the dirt road to the **KwaZulu Cultural Museum—Ondini,** the original site of King Cetshwayo's royal kraal. Ondini was modeled after the kraal of Shaka's younger brother, Dingane, at Mgungundlovu (*see below*). At the time of its destruction in 1879, the kraal consisted of 1,500 huts and was home to some 5,000 people. Today only the royal enclosure has been restored, but a stroll among the deserted beehive huts gives you a feel for the kraal's size and scope. A site museum at the entrance traces the history of the Zulu kings and displays the silver mug and Bible presented to King Cetshwayo by Queen Victoria in 1882. The Cultural Museum, in a separate building, houses a superb collection of beadwork from various tribes, plus detailed exhibits on Zulu life. ⊠ *Cetshwayo Hwy.* ☎ *035/870–2051* 🕾 *R15* ☉ *Weekdays 8–4, weekends 9–4.*

<table>
<tr><td>en route</td><td>From Ulundi retrace your route back down the R66 and turn right onto the R34 toward Vryheid. The turnoff to Mgungundlovu and the Grave of Piet Retief lies just a couple of miles farther on. Mgungundlovu was the site of Dingane's royal kraal and home to his 500 wives. Dingane, Shaka's younger brother, killed Shaka in 1828 to seize power for himself. During Dingane's rule (1828–40) the Zulu came under increasing pressure from white settlers moving into the area. In 1837 Piet Retief and a party of Voortrekkers petitioned Dingane for land. The king agreed on condition that Retief retrieve some Zulu cattle stolen by a rival chief. Retief duly recovered the cattle and returned to Mgungundlovu with nearly 100 men. Dingane welcomed the Voortrekkers into the royal kraal, instructing them to leave their guns and horses outside. Once they were inside, Dingane shouted, "Kill the wizards!" and 8–10 warriors seized each of the unarmed men. The Voortrekkers were dragged to Execution Hill and murdered. A monument now stands on the hill where Piet Retief and his men are buried. The beehive huts of the royal enclosure have been reconstructed on their original foundations, and a guide leads short tours of the kraal. There's also a small site museum. ⊠ R34 ☎ No phone 🕾 R15 ☉ Daily 8–4.</td></tr>
</table>

Babanango

61 *38½ km (24 mi) northwest of Mgungundlovu and the Grave of Piet Retief.*

A dirt road connecting the R34 to Babanango passes through some of the most beautiful countryside in Zululand, with seemingly endless views over rolling grasslands. The road ends at the tarred R68. Turn right and drive less than 2 km (1 mi) into the pleasant hamlet of Babanango.

From Babanango follow the R68 for 48 km (30 mi) to the turnoff to **Isandlwana.** The Battle of Isandlwana, on January 22, 1879, was a major defeat for the British army. Coming as it did at the very beginning of the Zulu War, the defeat sent shudders of apprehension through the corridors of Whitehall and ultimately cost Lord Chelmsford his command. Chelmsford was in charge of one of three invasion columns that were supposed to sweep into Zululand and converge on Cetshwayo's capital at Ulundi. On January 20 Chelmsford crossed the Buffalo River into Zululand, leaving behind a small force at Rorke's Drift to guard the column's supplies, and encamped at Isandlwana.

Unknown to Chelmsford, the heart of the Zulu army—20,000 men—had taken up a position just 5 km (3 mi) away. Using Shaka's classic chest-and-horns formation, the Zulus swept toward the British positions. The battle hung in the balance until the Zulus' left horn outflanked the British. The fighting continued for two hours before the British fled the field, with the Zulus in triumphant pursuit. About 1,000 Zulus perished in the attack, as did 1,329 British troops. Today the battlefield is scattered with whitewashed stone cairns and memorials marking the resting places of fallen soldiers. The visitor center houses a small but excellent museum of mementos and artifacts, following the course of the battle in marvelous detail—a good place to start if you're here without a guide. Allow at least two or three hours for a visit. ⊠ *Off R68* ☎ *034/271–8165* 🖂 *R15* 🕙 *Daily 8–4.*

Where to Stay & Eat

$ ✕🏠 **Babanango Hotel.** In the small Babanango Hotel you can relax in one of the country's most famous watering holes. It's a tiny place decorated in country style, with lots of wood and earthy colors. The pub serves a variety of inexpensive meals (¢–$) including grilled rump steak and french fries. ⊠ *16 Justice St., Babanango* ☎ *035/835–0029* 🖂 *035/835–0322* ❑ *5 rooms* 🖒 *Restaurant, bar* ▭ *No credit cards* ⦿I *MAP.*

$$ 🏠 **Isandlwana Lodge.** This American-owned lodge is built on Nyoni Rock and has sweeping views of the entire Isandlwana battlefield. Shaped like a Zulu shield, the building commemorates Isandlwana. The comfortable rooms are named for Zulus significant in the war, and bathrooms contain shield-shape sink pedestals. Decor is modern yet Afrocentric, with African prints and wooden furniture. Picture windows in public areas make the most of the incredible battlefield views. Trips to the local battlefields (R300) are the main activity at this lodge. 🏠 *Box 30, Babanango 3005* ☎ *034/271–8301* 🖂 *034/271–8306* ⊕ *www.isandlwana.co.za* ❑ *13 rooms* 🖒 *Pool, bar* ▭ *AE, DC, MC, V* ⦿I *MAP.*

$ 🏠 **Babanango Valley Lodge.** This tiny guest lodge lies at the end of a rutted dirt road on an 8,000-acre cattle farm. Obviously, it's not the sort of place where you constantly pop in and out, but that's okay—you probably won't want to leave anyway. The lodge sits at the head of a steep valley, far from any other buildings and with tremendous views of acacia-studded grasslands and hills. John and Meryn Turner, the charming hosts, and their very hospitable team, go out of their way to make you feel at home. John is a registered guide, and many people stay at the lodge as part of his battlefield tour. Rooms are decorated in contemporary style with fluffy white duvets and raw-silk lamp shades—simple, comfortable, and elegant. The four-course table d'hôte dinner focuses on traditional South African fare, including fresh farm produce.

Battlefield tours, including a picnic lunch, cost R695. ⊠ *15 km (9 mi) off R68, near Babanango* ☐ *Box 160, Dundee 3000* ☎ *035/835–0062* 🖷 *035/835–0160* ↩ *9 rooms* ☖ *Dining room, pool* ▤ *MC, V* ⦿ *MAP.*

Rorke's Drift

★ ⑥ *35 km (22 mi) west of Isandlwana.*

Rorke's Drift is by far the best of the Zulu War battlefields to see without a guide. An excellent museum and orientation center retells the story of the battle, with electronic diagrams, battle sounds, and dioramas. From the British perspective this was the most glorious battle of the Zulu War, the more so because it took place just hours after the disaster at Isandlwana. The British force at Rorke's Drift consisted of just 141 men, of whom 35 were ailing. They occupied a Swedish mission church and house, which had been converted into a storehouse and hospital. The Zulu forces numbered some 3,000–4,000 men, composed of the reserve regiments from Isandlwana. When a survivor from Isandlwana sounded the warning at 3:15 PM, the tiny British force hastily erected a stockade of flour bags and biscuit boxes around the mission. The Zulus attacked 75 minutes later, and the fighting raged for 12 hours before the Zulus faltered and retreated. To this day, historians cannot figure out why the Zulus failed to press their huge advantage. When the smoke cleared, 500 Zulus and 17 Britons lay dead. ⊠ *Rorke's Drift Rd., off the R68* ☎ *034/ 642–1687* 🖷 *R15* ⊙ *Daily 8–4.*

Where to Stay

\$\$ 🏨 **Fugitives' Drift Lodge.** Set on a 4,000-acre game farm, this attractive lodge lies just a couple of miles from the site of the famous engagement at Rorke's Drift and overlooks the drift where survivors of the British defeat at Isandlwana fled across the Buffalo River. Even more important, the owner is the legendary David Rattray, the best battlefield guide in the country. Rooms, in individual cottages that open onto gardens, have fireplaces and wood furniture. You can rent a room in a cottage or the whole cottage, depending on your group size. The focal point of the lodge is the lounge and dining room, decorated with old rifles, British regimental flags, Zulu spears, and antique military prints. Battlefield tours cost R600 per person. ⊠ *Rorke's Drift Rd.* ☐ *Rorke's Drift 3016* ☎ *034/271–8051* 🖷 *034/271–8053* ⊕ *www.fugitives-drift-lodge.com* ↩ *8 chalets, 2 cottages* ☖ *Dining room, pool, bar, lounge* ▤ *AE, DC, MC, V* ⦿ *FAP.*

\$\$ 🏨 **ISibindi Lodge.** This lodge within the iSibindi Eco Reserve combines game viewing and an optional Zulu cultural experience with battlefield tours (R460) led by excellent local guides and historians. Game drives might encounter antelopes, giraffes, zebras, or wildebeests, and during cultural evenings Zulu dancers from a local school perform for guests. You can also have the bones read by a traditional sangoma to reveal your past, present, and future. In summer, river rafting is possible on the Buffalo River. Rooms, in elevated Zulu-style huts with private decks, face glorious vistas of hill and valley. An attractive lounge-bar area shows off African prints and Zulu artifacts, and an outdoor bar and sunken pool also look out at the view. ⊠ *9 km (4 mi) from Rorke's Drift* ⬧ *Box 275, Umhlali 4390* ☎ *034/642–1620* ⬧ *035/474–1490* ⊕ *www. zulunet.co.za* ↝ *6 huts* ♦ *Pool, bar, lounge* ⊟ *AE, DC, MC, V* ⦿ *MAP.*

Shopping

Rorke's Drift is still a mission station, run by the Evangelical Lutheran Church. The **Rorke's Drift ELC Art and Craft Centre** (⊠ Rorke's Drift Rd., off R68 ☎ 034/642–1627), at the mission, sells wonderful pottery, handwoven rugs, and linocuts, all created by mission artists.

Dundee

63 *35 km (22 mi) north of Rorke's Drift.*

Once a busy coal-mining town, Dundee still has straight roads wide enough for the ox wagons of pioneer days to turn in, but today it's just a small commercial center in an area of subdued farming activity. The first-rate **Talana Museum,** on the outskirts of Dundee, encompasses 10 buildings. Fascinating exhibits trace the history of the area, from the early San hunter-gatherers to the rise of the Zulu nation, the extermination of the cannibal tribes of the Biggarsberg, and, finally, the vicious battles of the South African War. The museum stands on the site of the Battle of Talana (October 20, 1899), the opening skirmish in the South African War, and two of the museum buildings were used by the British as medical stations during the battle. The military museum here is an excellent starting point for the Battlefields Route, along which you follow in the footsteps of the Zulus, Brits, and Boers as they battled it out for territory and glory. ⊠ R33, 2 km (1 mi) east of Dundee ☎ 034/212–2654 ⬧ R15 ☉ Weekdays 8–4:30, weekends 10–4:30.

need a break?

The **Miner's Rest Tea Shop,** in a delightfully restored miner's cottage at the Talana Museum, serves refreshments as well as more substantial dishes like peri-peri chicken livers and spinach, feta, and chicken pie in phyllo pastry. The food is good and the atmosphere most welcoming. Alternatively, you can take advantage of the braai and picnic facilities on the museum grounds.

Off the R33 northeast of Dundee is the **site of the Battle of Blood River,** one of the most important events in the history of South Africa. This battle, fought between the Boers and the Zulus in 1838, predates the Anglo-Zulu War by more than 40 years. After the murder of Piet Retief and his men at Mgungundlovu in February 1838, Dingane dispatched Zulu impis to kill all the white settlers in Natal. The Voortrekkers bore the brunt of the Zulu assault. For the next 10 months their future hung in the balance: entire settlements were wiped out, and a Boer commando was smashed at the Battle of Italeni. By November a new commando of 464 men and 64 wagons under Andries Pretorius had moved out to challenge the Zulus. On Sunday, November 9, the Boers took a vow that should God grant them victory, they would forever remember that day as a Sabbath and build a church in commemoration. They repeated the vow every night for the next five weeks. On December 16 an enormous Zulu force attacked the Boers, who had circled their wagons in a strategic position backed by the Blood River and a deep *donga,* or gully. Armed with only spears, the Zulus were no match for the Boer riflemen. At the end of the battle 3,000 Zulus lay dead, but not a single Boer had fallen. The immediate effect of the victory was to open Natal to white settlement, but the long-term effects were far more dramatic. The intensely religious Voortrekkers saw their great victory as a confirmation of their role as God's chosen people. This deeply held conviction lay at the spiritual heart of the apartheid system that surfaced more than a century later, in 1948. Indeed, when you see the monument here, there's no mistaking the gravity and importance that the Nationalist government ascribed to its erection. The laager, a defensive circle of 64 wagons, has been reconstructed in exacting detail, made from a mix of cast steel and bronze. It's a truly haunting monument, made even more so by its position on empty grasslands that seem to stretch for eternity. ⊠ *Off R33, between Dundee and Vryheid* ☎ *034/632–1695* ⊠ *R8* ⊙ *Daily 8–4.*

Where to Stay

¢ ▣ **Lennox Cottage.** This active farm is owned and run by ex-Springbok rugby center Dirk Froneman and his wife, Salomé. After a day touring the battlefields, if you've still got some energy left you can ride, swim in the large pool, play tennis or snooker, or go on an evening game drive around the farms before sinking into a comfortable bed in your country-style room. Salomé's home cooking is superb, and each evening she serves such traditional Afrikaans dishes as butternut soup, *bobotie* (a spicy ground-meat dish), and local venison on an antique dining table as guests discuss the day's doings over a *dop* (drink) or two. ⊠ *R68, Box 197, 3000* ☎ *082/574–3032* ☎☎ *034/218–2201* ✎ *lennox@dundeekzn.co.za* ⇥ *10 rooms* ⚑ *Tennis court, pool, horseback riding, bar* ⊟ *AE, DC, MC, V* ⧄ *MAP.*

Ladysmith

64 *60 km (37 mi) southwest of Dundee.*

Ladysmith became famous around the world during the South African War, when it outlasted a Boer siege for 118 days. Nearly 20,000 people were caught in the town when the Boers attacked on November 2, 1899. During the next four months there was little fighting around Ladysmith itself—the Boers seemed content to shell the town with their Long Tom siege guns—but the town's food supply steadily dwindled. By the end of the siege the desperate residents were slaughtering half-starved horses to supplement their diets, and each day 28 people died from sickness and malnutrition.

Much of the early part of the war revolved around British attempts to end the siege. The incompetence of British general Sir Redvers Buller became apparent during repeated attempts to smash the Boer lines, resulting in heavy British losses at Spionkop, Vaalkrans, and Colenso. Finally, the sheer weight of numbers made possible the British defeat of the Boers in the epic 10-day Battle of Tugela Heights and ended the siege of Ladysmith on February 28, 1900.

Today Ladysmith is a small provincial town with a haphazard mix of old colonial and newer buildings and the same inhospitable climate (scorchingly hot in summer, freezing in winter). Some of the beautiful old buildings that remain include the white Soofie Mosque, on the banks of the Klip River, and on Murchison Street (the main street), Surat House, a shop built in the 1890s, where Ghandi used to shop on his way through Ladysmith.

The **Ladysmith Siege Museum** brings the period of the siege skillfully to life, with the use of electronic mapping, artifacts from the period, and black-and-white photos. The museum can arrange guided tours, but it also sells two pamphlets that outline self-guided tours: the "Siege Town Walkabout" and the "Siege Town Drive-About." ⊠ *Murchison St., next to Town Hall* ☎ *036/637–2992* ⊠ *R2* ☉ *Weekdays 9–4, Sat. 9–1.*

Next to the Siege Museum, directly in front of Town Hall, stands a replica of a Long Tom, the 6-inch Creusot gun used by the Boers during the siege. Also in front of Town Hall are two howitzers used by the British and christened Castor and Pollux.

Where to Stay & Eat

$ ╳▦ **Royal Hotel.** The Royal will suffice if you find yourself in Ladysmith at the end of the day. It's a typical South African country hotel that has seen more glorious days. The hotel was built in 1880, just 19 years before the town was attacked by the Boers during the war. During the siege a shell from a Long Tom gun exploded on the hotel veranda, killing a doctor. Expect small rooms, although TVs and air-conditioning are standard features. The hotel serves a buffet for lunch and dinner at R66 a head and offers an à la carte menu on weekends. ⊠ *140 Murchison St., 3370* ☎ *036/637–2176* ⊕ *www.royalhotel.co.za* ⟆ *71 rooms* ⌂ *Restaurant, 3 bars* ▤ *AE, DC, MC, V* ⁙◯⁙ *BP.*

Zululand & the Battlefields A to Z

CAR TRAVEL

Unless you're on a tour, it's almost impossible to see this part of the country without your own car. Your best bet is to rent a car in Durban and perhaps combine a trip to the battlefields with a self-drive tour of KwaZulu-Natal's game reserves. Roads are in good condition, although some of the access roads to the battlefields require more careful and slower driving, as dirt roads can be bumpy and muddy when wet.

EMERGENCIES

Of Ladysmith's two hospitals, the state-run Ladysmith Provincial Hospital and the Netcare's private Laverna Hospital, the latter, which has full emergency services and a pharmacy that's open 8–5, is probably a better bet. Elsewhere, call the general police number to be put in touch with the nearest hospital.

🛂 Emergency Services **Police** ☎ 036/638-3300 Ladysmith or 10111.

🛂 Hospitals **Ladysmith Provincial Hospital** ⊠ 36 Malcolm Rd., Ladysmith ☎ 036/637-2111. **Laverna Hospital** ⊠ 1 Convent Rd., Ladysmith ☎ 036/631-0065.

🛂 Pharmacy **Ladysmith Pharmacy** ⊠ 262 Murchison St., Ladysmith ☎ 036/631-0648 or 082/542-7677, 036/637-3516 after hours.

MONEY MATTERS

There are plenty of banks and ATMs in all towns and at the larger filling stations. Ladysmith has branches of all the main banks, with ABSA, FNB, Standard Bank, and Nedbank ATMs on Murchison Street.

TOURS

The visitor information offices at Dundee's Talana Museum and in Ladysmith have lists of registered battlefield guides. At the Talana Museum you can also rent or buy cassette tapes describing the events at Rorke's Drift and Isandlwana. Of all the battlefield guides in the region, David Rattray is widely considered to be the finest. His accounts of the action at Rorke's Drift, Isandlwana, and Fugitives' Drift sometimes move listeners to tears. Many combine one of David's tours with a stay at his lodge, just a couple of miles from Rorke's Drift. David is slowly losing his voice, so part of the tour now includes David-trained guides or his taped narrative. Other reputable guides to the Zulu battlefields are John Turner of the Babanango Valley Lodge and Neville Worthington. Bethuel and Dudu Manyathi specialize in ethnic and cultural tours, and Commander Jim Parker is known for Berg, bush, and battlefield tours. For information about battlefield guides and guides specializing in authentic Zulu culture, contact any of the information centers or tourism offices.

🛈 Tour Operators **Bethuel and Dudu Manyathi** ☎ 034/271-9710. **Commander Jim Parker, Parker Tours** ☎ 033/263-2280 or 033/263-2886. **David Rattray** ☎ 034/271-8051. **John Turner** ☎ 035/835-0062. **Neville Worthington** ☎ 034/212-1347.

VISITOR INFORMATION

Battlefields Route is a good source for information on the battlefields. Dundee's Regional Information Tourism Office is open weekdays 7:30–4. The Talana Museum visitor information office is open weekdays 8–4:30 and weekends 10–4:30. The Ladysmith Information Bureau is open weekdays 9–4, Saturday 9–1, and Sunday by request. For information on Ulundi, check with the Ulundi Tourism Office, weekdays 9–4, or the KZN Wildlife office. For a good overview covering this area, go to Tourism KwaZulu-Natal's Web site.

🛈 Tourist Offices **Battlefields Route** ✆ Box 3330, Ladysmith 3370 ☎ 082/802-1643 ⊕ battlefields.kzn.org.za. **Regional Information Tourism Office** ⊠ Main St. and Osborn Rd., Dundee ☎ 035/474-1141. **KZN Wildlife** ⊠ Prince Mkabayi St., Ulundi ☎ 035/870-0552. **Ladysmith Information Bureau** ⊠ Siege Museum, Town Hall, Murchison St., Ladysmith ☎ 036/637-2992. **Talana Museum** ⊠ R33, 2 km [1 mi] east of Dundee ☎ 034/212-2654. **Ulundi Tourism Office** ⊠ Kulani Park, 93 Princess Mkabayi St., Ulundi ☎ 035/870-0034.

🛈 Web Site **Tourism KwaZulu-Natal** ⊕ www.zulu.org.za.

HLUHLUWE-UMFOLOZI GAME RESERVE

🌙 ⑥⑤ *264 km (165 mi) northeast of Durban.*

Reputedly King Shaka's favorite hunting ground, Zululand's Hluhluwe-Umfolozi (pronounced Shloo-*shloo*-ee Im-fuh-*low*-zee) incorporates two of Africa's oldest reserves: Hluhluwe and Umfolozi, both founded in 1895. In an area of just 906 square km (325 square mi), Hluhluwe-Umfolozi delivers the Big Five plus all the plains game as well as species like nyala and red duiker that are rare in other parts of the country. Equally important, it boasts one of the most biologically diverse habitats on the planet, a unique mix of forest, woodland, savanna, and grassland. You will find about 1,250 species of plants and trees here—more than in some entire countries.

The park is administered by Ezemvelo KZN Wildlife, the province's official conservation organization, which looks after all the large game reserves and parks as well as many nature reserves. Thanks to its conservation efforts and those of its predecessor, the highly regarded Natal Parks Board, the park can take credit for saving the white rhino from extinction. So successful was the park at increasing white rhino numbers that in 1960 it established its now famous Rhino Capture Unit to relocate rhinos to other reserves in Africa. The park is currently trying to do for the black rhino what it did for its white cousins. Poaching has decimated Africa's black rhino population from 14,000 a decade ago to a saddening 2,250. Twenty percent of Africa's remaining black rhinos live in this reserve, and you won't get a better chance of seeing them in the wild than here.

Until 1989 the reserve consisted of two separate parks, Hluhluwe in the north and Umfolozi in the south, separated by a fenced corridor. Although a road (R618) still runs through this corridor, the fences have been removed, and the parks now operate as a single entity. Hluhluwe and the corridor are the most scenic areas of the park, notable for their bush-covered hills and knockout views, whereas Umfolozi is better known for its broad plains.

Compared with Kruger, Hluhluwe-Umfolozi is tiny—less than 6% of Kruger's size—but such comparisons can be misleading. You can spend days driving around this park and still not see everything, or feel like you're going in circles. Probably the biggest advantage Hluhluwe has over Kruger is that game viewing is good year-round, whereas Kruger has seasonal peaks and valleys. Another bonus is its proximity to Mkuze Game Reserve and the spectacular coastal reserves of Greater St. Lucia Wetland Park. The park is also close enough to Durban to make it a worthwhile one- or two-day excursion.

Bush Walks

Armed rangers lead groups of eight on two- to three-hour bush walks departing from Hilltop Camp. You rarely see much game on these walks, but you do learn a great deal about the area's ecology and tips on how to recognize the signs of the bush, including animal spoor. Walks leave daily at 5:30 AM and 3:30 PM (6 and 3 in winter) and cost R100. Reserve a few days in advance at Hilltop Camp reception.

Game Drives

A great way to see the park is on game drives led by rangers. These drives (R150 per person) hold several advantages over driving through the park yourself: you sit high up in an open-air vehicle, with a good view and the wind in your face; a ranger explains the finer points of animal behavior and ecology; and your guide has a good idea where to find animals like leopards, cheetahs, and lions. Game drives leave Monday–Saturday at 5:30 in summer, 6:30 in winter. The park also offers three-hour night drives, during which you search for nocturnal animals with powerful spotlights. These three-hour drives depart at 7, and you should make advance reservations at Hilltop Camp reception.

Wilderness Trails

The park's wilderness trails are every bit as popular as Kruger's, but they tend to be tougher and more rustic. Led by an armed ranger, you must be able to walk 16 km (10 mi) a day for a period of three days and four nights. All equipment, food, and baggage are carried by donkeys. The first and last nights are spent at Mndindini, a permanent tented camp. The other two are spent under canvas in the bush. While in the bush, hikers bathe in the Umfolozi River or have a hot bucket shower; toilet facilities consist of a spade and toilet-paper roll. Trails, open March–November, are limited to eight people and should be reserved a year in advance (R2,340 per person).

If that sounds too easy, you can always opt for the **Umfolozi Primitive Trail.** On this trek hikers carry their own packs and sleep out under the stars. A campfire burns all night to scare off animals, and each participant is expected to sit a 90-minute watch. A ranger acts as guide. The cost is R2,580 per person.

A more genteel wilderness experience is **Weekend Trails,** based out of the tented Dengezi Wilderness Camp, where you're guaranteed a bed and some creature comforts. The idea behind these trails is to instill in the participants an appreciation for the beauty of the untamed bush. The weekend begins on Friday at 2:30 and ends on Sunday at 3. Participation is limited to eight people and costs about R1,320 per person.

Where to Stay

In Hluhluwe-Umfolozi
National parks and lodges appear on the KwaZulu-Natal map.

Hluhluwe-Umfolozi offers a range of accommodations in government-run rest camps, with an emphasis on self-catering (only Hilltop has a restaurant). Unfortunately, most foreign visitors can't avail themselves of the park's secluded bush lodges and camps, as each of them must be reserved in a block, and the smallest accommodates at least eight people. At Hilltop you can expect to pay R345 per person for a rondawel and R699 for a chalet with private bath and cooking facilities.

¢–$ 🏠 **Hilltop Camp.** It may be a government-run camp, but this delightful lodge in the Hluhluwe half of the park matches some of the best private lodges. Perched on the crest of a hill, it has panoramic views over the park, the Hlaza and Nkwakwa hills, and Zululand. Thatch and ocher-colored walls give it an African feel. Scattered across the crown of the hill, self-contained chalets have high thatch ceilings, rattan furniture, and small verandas. If you plan to eat all your meals in the restaurant or sample the evening braai, forgo the more expensive chalets with fully equipped kitchens. If you're on a tight budget, opt for a basic rondawel with two beds, a basin, and a refrigerator; toilet facilities are communal. There's an à la carte restaurant, an attractive pub, and a convenience store. Take a stroll along a forest trail rich with birdsong, or take a bottle of wine to Hlaza Hide and join the animals as they come for their sundowners. There is a gas station on the premises. ⌂ *KZN Wildlife, Box 13069, Cascades, Pietermaritzburg 3202* ☎ *033/845–1000* 🖷 *033/845–1001* ⊕ *www.kznwildlife.co.za or www.rhino.org. za* 🛏 *20 rondawels, 49 chalets* ♿ *Restaurant, some kitchens, bar, shop* ▭ *AE, DC, MC, V.*

Near Hluhluwe-Umfolozi

$$ 🏨 **Hluhluwe River Lodge.** Overlooking False Bay Lake and the Hluhluwe River flood plain, this luxurious, spacious, family-owned lodge set in indigenous gardens is the ideal base for visiting the game reserves and the Greater St. Lucia Wetland Park. After a day spent game-viewing, canoeing, bird-watching, boating, fishing, or walking in the pristine sand forest, you can relax in a terra-cotta-colored A-frame chalet with cool stone floors, wood and wicker furniture, and cream-and-brown decor and furnishings. Alternatively, sit out on your wooden deck overlooking the bush, the floodplain, and the lake. This lodge is the only one with direct access to the lake, and as you chug along through bird-filled papyrus channels decorated with water lilies en route to the broad expanses of the main body of water, you might easily feel as though you were in Botswana's Okavango Delta. Water activities are dependent on the seasonal rains, so check with the lodge in advance. The food is excellent—wholesome country cooking with lots of fresh vegetables and good roasts. ✉ *Follow signs from Hluhluwe village* ⌂ *Box 105, Hluhluwe 3960* ☎ *035/562–0246* 🖷 *035/562–0248* ⊕ *www.hluhluwe.co. za* 🛏 *12 chalets* ♿ *Restaurant, pool, boating, bar* ▭ *AE, DC, MC, V* ¶○¶ *MAP.*

$$ 🏨 **Zululand Tree Lodge.** Sixteen kilometers (8 mi) from the park, this lodge lies in a forest of fever trees on the 3,700-acre Ubizane Game Reserve, a small park stocked with white rhinos and plains game. It makes a great base from which to explore Hluhluwe, Mkuze, and St. Lucia. Built of thatch and wood, the open-sided lodge sits on stilts overlooking the Mzinene River. Rooms are in separate cottages, also on stilts, along the riverbank. The rooms themselves are small, but tastefully decorated with mosquito nets covering old-fashioned iron bedsteads made up with fluffy white duvets, African-print cushions, wicker, and reed matting. If you want the experience of sleeping alfresco, fold back the huge wooden shutters dividing the bedroom from the open deck. A qualified ranger will take you for a bush walk or a game drive through the small reserve or a little farther afield for a game drive in the nearby Hluhluwe-Umfolozi reserve. ✉ *Hluhluwe Rd.* ⌂ *Box 116, Hluhluwe 3960* ☎ *035/ 562–1020* 🖷 *035/562–1032* 🛏 *24 rooms* ♿ *Restaurant, pool, bar* ▭ *AE, DC, MC, V* ¶○¶ *MAP.*

Side Trips from Hluhluwe-Umfolozi

Mkuze Game Reserve

48 km (30 mi) north of Hluhluwe-Umfolozi.

This 88,900-acre reserve lies in the shadow of the Ubombo Mountains, between the Mkuze and Msunduze rivers. In the process of being incorporated into the Greater St. Lucia Wetland Park, Mkuze is famous for birds and rhinos. More than 400 bird species have been spotted here, including myriad waterfowl drawn to the park's shallow pans in summer. Several blinds, particularly those overlooking Nsumo Pan, offer superb views. Don't miss out on the awesome 3-km (2-mi) walk through a spectacular, rare forest of towering, ancient fig trees, some as big as 82 feet tall and 39 feet around the base. Although only a fraction of Kruger's size, this is the place to find rhinos; there's a healthy population of both black and white rhinos. You won't find lions, buffalo, or elephants, but the low-lying thornveld supports lots of other game, including zebras, giraffes, kudus, and nyalas. ⊠ *Off the N2* ☎ *035/573–9004* 🖃 *R70 per vehicle, R35 per person* ⊗ *Daily 6–6.*

WHERE TO STAY

⌂ **Ghost Mountain Inn.** Swathes of scarlet bougainvillea run riot in the lush gardens of this family-owned country inn near Mkuze. It was here that Rider Haggard wrote some of his adventure stories, inspired perhaps by the mysterious lights and elusive flickering flames that give the mountain its spooky name. Rooms, each with a small veranda, are tastefully furnished in understated creams and browns with interesting historical prints. Large, invitingly restful public areas have terra-cotta tiles and comfortable cane furniture, and the cozy African lounge makes you feel like you've slipped back to the past. Don't miss the enthusiastic Zulu dancing before a succulent barbecue under the stars. At first light, wander down to the lake and watch the waterbirds wake up, or, later in the day, sit in the blind and watch them come home to roost. There is an excellent curio shop. The friendly staff can arrange tours to the neighboring game reserves and cultural sights, or will fix you up to go bird-watching or fishing. ⊠ *Fish Eagle Rd, Mkuze* ⋈ *Box 18, Mkuze 3965* ☎ *035/573–1025* 🖷 *035/573–1025* ⊕ *www.ghostmountaininn.co.za* 🖃 *33 rooms* ⌂ *Restaurant, pool, bar, shop, meeting rooms,* ▤ *AE, DC, MC, V* ⫴ *BP.*

Greater St. Lucia Wetland Park

66 *133 km (83 mi) from Mkuze Game Reserve.*

This huge park, a Natural World Heritage Site, is one of the most important coastal and wetland areas in the world. The focal point is Lake St. Lucia, a broad 95,545-acre lake dotted with islands and populated by crocodiles and hippos. Bird-watchers rave about the avian life, too—at times the lake is pink with flamingos. KZN Wildlife offers guided trips up the estuary aboard the *Santa Lucia,* an 80-seat motor launch that makes the 90-minute voyage three times daily (reservations are essential). KZN Wildlife maintains an office and self-catering camp in the small but rapidly expanding fishing resort of St. Lucia, near the mouth of the estuary. The village is also the access point to the thin strip of land that runs up the coast between Lake St. Lucia and the Indian Ocean, with terrific beaches as well as the highest vegetated dunes in the world. There's a small KZN Wildlife base at Cape Vidal, 20 km (12 mi) north of St. Lucia, where you can visit privately owned whale-watching towers to spy on southern right whales and humpbacks, which drift south on the warm Aghulas current around October each year. ✉ *24 km (15 mi) east of Mtubatuba exit off the N2* ✆ *Officer-in–Charge, Cape Vidal, Private Bag X04, St. Lucia Estuary 3936* ☎ *035/590–1340* 🖷 *035/590–1300* 💻 *Boat tours R80* ☉ *Tours daily at 8, 10:30, and 2:30 plus Fri. and Sat. at 4.*

Hluhluwe-Umfolozi A to Z

AIR TRAVEL

The closest airport to the park is at Richards Bay, about 100 km (60 mi) south of Hluhluwe-Umfolozi. The airport is served by SA Express Airways, which has daily flights from Johannesburg.

✈ **Airline SA Express Airways** ☎ 035/786–0301.

CAR TRAVEL

From Durban, drive north on the N2 to Mtubatuba; then cut west on the R618 to Mambeni Gate. Otherwise, continue up the N2 to the Hluhluwe exit and follow the signs to the park and Memorial Gate. The whole trip takes about three hours, but watch out for potholes.

Avis and Imperial have car-rental offices at the Richards Bay airport.

🚗 **Rental Companies Avis** ☎ 035/789–6555. **Imperial** ☎ 035/786–0309.

TOURS

Umhluhluwe Safaris is by far the largest tour operator in Zululand and offers a full range of half- and full-day game drives in Hluhluwe-Umfolozi, as well as night drives and bush walks. The company also leads game drives into the nearby Mkuze Game Reserve and guided tours to the bird-rich wetlands and beaches of St. Lucia.

🚗 **Tour Operator Umhluhluwe Safaris** ✆ Box 273, Hluhluwe 3960 ☎🖷 035/562–0414.

ITALA GAME RESERVE

67 *221 km (138 mi) northwest of Hluhluwe-Umfolozi.*

In northern KwaZulu-Natal, close to the Swaziland border, Itala, at 296 square km (107 square mi), is small even compared with the relatively compact Hluhluwe-Umfolozi. Its size and its dearth of lions are probably why this delightful park is usually bypassed, even by South Africans—although they clearly don't know what they're missing. The other four of the Big Five are here—it's excellent for black and white rhinos—and the park is stocked with cheetahs, hyenas, giraffes, and an array of antelopes among its 80 mammal species. It's also an excellent spot for birders. The stunning landscapes and the relaxed game-viewing make this area a breath of fresh air after the Big Five melee of Mpumalanga.

Founded in 1972, the reserve, run by KZN Wildlife, is a rugged region that drops 3,290 feet in just 15 km (9 mi) through sandstone cliffs, multicolored rocks, granite hills, ironstone outcrops, and quartz formations. Watered by nine small rivers rising in its vicinity and covered with rich soils, Itala supports a varied cross section of vegetation, encompassing riverine thicket, wetland, open savanna, and acacia woodland. Arriving at its Ntshondwe Camp is nothing short of dramatic. The meandering road climbs from open plains to the top of a plateau dotted with granite formations, which at the last minute magically yield the rest camp at the foot of pink and russet cliffs.

Self-Guided Trails

An unusual feature of Itala is its self-guided walking trails, in the mountainside above Ntshondwe Camp. It gives you a chance to stretch your limbs if you've just spent hours cooped up in a car. It also has the advantage of giving you the chance to get really close to the euphorbias, acacias, and other fascinating indigenous vegetation that festoon the hills. Ask at the camp reception for further information.

Where to Stay

Although Itala has several exclusive bush camps, these are booked up months in advance by South Africans, making the chalets at its main camp the only practical accommodations for foreign visitors. Two people sharing a two-bed unit at Ntshondwe will pay about R352 per person per night.

★ ¢ 🏨 **Ntshondwe Camp.** In architecture, landscaping, and style, this beautiful government-run rest camp, 69 km (43 mi) from Vryheid, comes closer than any other in the country to matching the expensive private lodges. Built around granite boulders and vegetation lush with acacias, wild figs, and giant cactuslike euphorbias, airy chalets with steep thatch roofs blend perfectly with the surroundings. Its two-, four-, and six-bed units can accommodate a total of 200 guests. Each self-catering chalet has a spacious lounge simply furnished with cane chairs, a fully equipped kitchen, and a large veranda surrounded by indigenous bush. Keep an eye open for eagles soaring above the pink and russet sandstone cliffs. A magnificent game-viewing deck juts out over a steep slope to provide views of a water hole and extensive panoramas of the surrounding valleys. Take a guided game drive (R86) or guided walk (R65), hike a self-guided trail, or follow one of the well-laid-out drives with markers at points of interest. Picnic at one of the many scenic picnic spots, all of which have barbecue facilities and toilets. There's a gas station, a store (with great curios), and a good restaurant on the premises. ⌂ *KZN Wildlife, Box 13069, Cascades, Pietermaritzburg 3202* ☎ *033/845–1000 or 034/983–2540* 🖷 *033/ 845–1001* 🛏 *39 chalets* 🍴 *Restaurant, kitchens, pool, bar, shop, airstrip* ▭ *AE, DC, MC, V.*

Itala Game Reserve A to Z

AIR TRAVEL

The closest airport to the park is at Richards Bay, about 224 km (140 mi) south of Itala. The airport is served by SA Express Airways, which has daily flights from Johannesburg.

✈ Airline **SA Express Airways** ☎ 035/786-0301.

CAR TRAVEL

From Durban drive north on the N2 to Empangeni, and then head west on the R34 to Vryheid. From here cut east on the R69 to Louwsburg. The reserve is immediately northwest of the village, from which there are clear signs. The journey from Durban takes around five hours and from Hluhluwe-Umfolozi about 2½ hours. Roads are good, and there are plenty of gas stations along the way.

Avis and Imperial have car-rental offices at the Richards Bay airport.

🚗 Rental Companies **Avis** ☎ 035/789-6555. **Imperial** ☎ 035/786-0309.

NDUMO GAME RESERVE

68 *80 km (50 mi) north of Jozini.*

In Maputaland, this game reserve lies in a remote northern region of KwaZulu-Natal, near the Mozambique border. The 24,700-acre park does not have the Big Five, and visitors wanting to see big game should head elsewhere. What makes Ndumo famous are its birds. Along with Mkuze, the park is probably the premier bird-watching locale in the country. More than 400 species of birds—60% of all the birds in South Africa—have been spotted here, including the gorgeous purple-crested lourie, the green coucal, the elusive narina trogon, the African broadbill, and the bird-watchers' mega-sighting, the splendid Pel's fishing owl. Myriad waterfowl also flock to the reserve's Nyamiti and Banzi pans, and summer migrants take up residence from October until April.

Ndumo has no lions or elephants, but it supports a healthy population of black and white rhinos, rare Suni antelopes, and red duikers, as well as the usual plains animals. And even though it may not have the Big Five, it is one of the most beautiful reserves in the country. Forests of yellow-fever trees are mirrored in glassy lakes, and giant sycamore figs provide shelter for crowned eagles and those rare fishing owls. Crocodiles numbering in the hundreds bask on the grassy banks, and hippos honk and blow in deep pools. In addition to leading the usual game drives, rangers often take guests on extended bush walks. The best time to visit is October, when migrant birds return and antelope start bearing their young.

Where to Stay

¢ 🏠 **Ndumo Camp.** This lovely little KZN Wildlife camp has twin-bedded chalets set in grassy open areas shaded by marula trees. You can sit on the veranda of your air-conditioned chalet and look out across the

Phongola River floodplain, go for a bird walk around the pans and through the spectacular fig forest with some of the best bird guides in South Africa, or take a game drive. There's a well-equipped communal kitchen to do your own thing, or the camp cook will whip up meals for you from your own food. Either way, it's cheap and cheerful. ✑ *KZN Wildlife, Box 13069, Cascades, Pietermaritzburg 3202* ☎ *033/845–1000* 🖷 *034/ 907–5190* ⌨ *7 chalets* ⚒ *Kitchen, pool* ▤ *AE, DC, MC V.*

Ndumo Game Reserve A to Z

For information on getting here, *see* Itala Game Reserve A to Z.

PRIVATE GAME RESERVES & LODGES

KwaZulu-Natal's best private lodges lie in northern Zululand and Maputaland, a remote region close to Mozambique. With one exception, the lodges reviewed here do not offer the Big Five. However, they are sufficiently close to one another and Hluhluwe-Umfolozi Game Reserve to allow you to put together a bush experience that delivers the Big Five and a great deal more, including superb bird-watching opportunities and an unrivaled beach paradise. Malaria does pose a problem, however, and antimalarial drugs are essential. Summers are hot, hot, hot. If you can't take heat and humidity, then autumn, winter, and early summer are probably the best time to visit.

Phinda Private Game Reserve

Established in 1991, this flagship CC Africa reserve is a heartening example of tourism serving the environment with panache. Phinda (*pin*-duh) is Zulu for "return," referring to the restoration of 42,000 acres of overgrazed ranchland in northern Zululand to bushveld. It's a triumph. You'll find it impossible to believe the area wasn't always the thick bush you see all around you. The Big Five have established themselves firmly, and Phinda can claim a stunning variety of ecosystems: sand forest (which grows on the fossil dunes of an earlier coastline), savanna, bushveld, open woodland, and verdant wetlands.

Phinda can deliver the Big Five, although not as consistently or in such numbers as its sister lodge, Londolozi, in Mpumalanga. Buffalo, leopards, lions, cheetahs, spotted hyenas, elephants, white rhinos, hippos, giraffes, impalas, and the rare, elusive tiny Suni antelope are all here, and rangers work hard to find them for guests. Birdlife is prolific and extraordinary, with some special Zululand finds: the pink-throated twin spot, the crested guinea fowl, the African broadbill, and the crowned eagle. Where Phinda also excels is in the superb quality of its rangers, who can provide fascinating commentary on everything from local birds to frogs. You'll be amazed at just how enthralling the love life of a dung beetle can be! There are also adventure trips (optional extras) down the Mzinene River for a close-up look at crocodiles, hippos, and birds; big-game fishing or scuba diving off the deserted, wildly beautiful Maputaland coast; and sightseeing flights over Phinda and the highest vegetated dunes in the world.

Where to Stay

For all reservations, contact **CC Africa** ✆ *Private Bag X27, Benmore 2010* ☎ *011/809–4300* 🖷 *011/809–4400* ⊕ *www.phinda.com* 🖃 *AE, DC, MC, V* ⦿ *FAP.*

$$$$ 🏠 **Phinda Zuka Lodge.** An exclusive spot for a family or group of friends, Phinda Zuka (Zuka means "sixpence" in Zulu) is a couple of miles from the bigger lodges. (The land was recently added to Phinda to accommodate black rhinos.) Thatch cottages overlook a busy water hole, and you'll be looked after by the camp's personal ranger/host, butler, and chef. Kids are welcome. ⟿ *4 cottages* ⚲ *Pool, bar, airstrip.*

★ $ 🏠 **Forest Lodge.** Hidden in a rare sand forest, this fabulous lodge overlooks a small water hole where nyalas, warthogs, and baboons frequently come to drink. The lodge is a real departure from the traditional thatch structures so common in South Africa. It's very modern, with a vaguely Japanese feel thanks to glass-paneled walls, light woods, and a deliberately spare, clean look. The effect is stylish and very elegant, softened by modern African art and sculpture. Suites use the same architectural concepts as the lodge, where walls have become windows, and rely on the dense forest (or curtains) for their privacy. As a result, you feel very close to your surroundings, and it's possible to lie in bed or take a shower while watching delicate nyalas grazing just feet away. ⟿ *16 suites* ⚲ *Pool, bar, airstrip.*

$ 🏠 **Mountain Lodge.** This attractive thatch lodge sits on a rocky hill overlooking miles of bushveld plains and the Ubombo Mountains. Wide verandas lead into the lounge and bar, graced with high ceilings, dark beams, and cool tile floors. In winter guests can snuggle into cushioned wicker chairs next to a blazing log fire. Brick pathways wind down the hillside from the lodge to elegant split-level suites with mosquito nets, thatch roofs, and large decks overlooking the reserve. African baskets, beadwork, and grass matting beautifully complement the bush atmosphere. Kids are welcome, although those under 5 are not allowed on game drives and 6- to 11-year-olds are permitted only at the manager's discretion. ⟿ *15 suites, 7 chalets* ⚲ *Pool, bar, airstrip.*

$ 🏠 **Rock Lodge.** If you get tired of the eagle's-eye view of the deep valley below from your private veranda, you can write in your journal in your luxurious sitting room or take a late-night dip in your own plunge pool. All of Phinda's activities are included, including twice-daily game drives, nature walks, riverboat cruises, and canoe trips along the Mzinene River. Scuba diving, deep-sea fishing, and spectacular small-plane flights are extras. Don't miss out on one of Phinda's legendary bush braais, when hundreds of lanterns light up the surrounding forest and bush and the food is unforgettable. ⟿ *6 suites* ⚲ *Pool, bar, airstrip.*

$ 🏠 **Vlei Lodge.** Accommodations at this small and intimate lodge are nestled in the shade of the sand forest and are so private it's hard to believe there are other guests. Suites—made of thatch, teak, and glass—have a distinct Asian feel and overlook a wet marshland on the edge of an inviting woodland. The bedrooms and bathrooms are huge, and guests have private plunge pools (a recent visitor found a lion drinking from his) and outdoor decks. The lounge/living area of the lodge has two fireplaces on opposite glass walls, a dining area, and a large terrace under a canopy of trees, where breakfast is served. The bush braai, with its splendid food and fairy-tale setting, is a memorable occasion after an evening game drive. ➚ *6 suites* ♦ *Dining room, pool, bar, airstrip.*

$ 🏕 **Phinda Walking Safari.** This unusual experience is a really delightful way to get close to the bush. Your home for three nights is a spacious safari tent (with bathroom) in the middle of a rare sand forest. Here crowned eagles may survey you as you take a postprandial nap in a hammock under giant fig trees, or a fishing owl may call as you swap safari stories under the stars. An armed ranger makes sure you get home safely, and the camp cook keeps the calories coming. Each morning (depending on the consensus of the group) you amble through the forest or over the plains for four or five hours; then it's back to camp until a pre-sunset walk and game drive. The walking safari is not offered in summer because of the heat. ➚ *4 tents* ♦ *Bar, airstrip; no kids under 16* ⊗ *Closed Dec.–Feb.*

Thanda Private Game Reserve

70 Located in a wildly beautiful part of northern Zululand, Thanda is KwaZulu-Natal's newest game reserve, and, like its neighbor Phinda did more than a decade ago, it is restoring former farmlands and hunting grounds to their former pristine state. The reserve currently occupies more than 12,000 acres of rehabilitated land, but that will soon become 37,000, thanks to a joint venture with local communities and the king of the Zulus, His Majesty Goodwill Zweletini, who is offering some of his royal hunting grounds to the project. Game that used to roam this wilderness centuries ago has been reestablished, including the Big Five. Thanda (tan-duh) is Zulu for "love," and its philosophy echoes just that: "for the love of nature, wildlife, and dear ones." You won't see game with the frequency and in the numbers that you would at some of the Mpumalanga lodges, because the animals are not yet habituated to vehicles and some are still skittish. Rangers often have to work hard to find game, but the rewards of seriously tracking lions or rhinos with your enthusiastic and very experienced ranger and tracker are great. Because its owner is passionately committed not only to the land but also to the local people, there are many opportunities to interact with them. Don't miss out on Vula Zulu, one of the most magical and powerful Zulu experiences offered in South Africa. After exploring the village, from the sangoma's hut (have the bones thrown and read) and visiting the chief's kraal, you'll be treated to the Vula Zulu show, a memorable blend of narration, high-energy dance, song, and mime that recounts Zulu history. The lodge can also arrange golf, scuba diving, snorkeling, whale-watching, and fishing expeditions.

Where to Stay

For all reservations, contact **Thanda.** Both the tented camp and the main lodge offer kids' programs and a customized Junior Ranger's course. 📫 *Box 652585, Benmore 2010* ☎ *011/704–3115* 📠 *011/462–5607* 🌐 *www.thanda.com* 🖃 *AE, DC, MC, V* 🍴 *FAP.*

★ $ 🏕 **Thanda Main Lodge.** There's a palpable feeling of earth energy in this magical and exquisite lodge that blends elements of royal Zulu with an eclectic pan-African feel. Beautiful domed, beehive-shape dwellings perch on the side of rolling hills and overlook mountains and bushveld. On the inside it's contemporary Scandinavian meets pan-African chic. Both are works of art, from the "eyelashes" of slatted poles that peep out from under the thatch roofs to the embedded mosaics in royal Zulu red and blue that decorate the polished, honey-colored stone floors. Check out the creative light fixtures—no two are alike—from chandeliers made of handcrafted Zulu beads or twisted wire to lamps made of straw or filmy cotton mesh. A huge stone fireplace divides the bedroom area—which has drawn threadwork bed linens and a curtain of river pebbles and wire behind the bed—from the comfortable and roomy lounge. Each chalet has a different color scheme and is decorated with beaded, hand-embroidered cushions and throws. Dip in your personal plunge pool after an exciting game drive; then sunbathe on your private deck or commune with the surrounding bushveld in your cool, cushioned *sala* (outdoor covered deck). Later, after a meal that many a fine restaurant would be proud to serve, come back to your chalet to find a bedtime story on your pillow, marshmallows waiting to be toasted over flickering candles, and a glass of Amarula cream. Or dine alone with your loved one in your private *boma* (outdoor eating area) by the light of the stars and the leaping flames of a fragrant wood fire. The spacious, uncluttered public areas—dining decks, bomas, library, and lounge—are decorated in restful earth tones accented by royal Zulu colors, beads from Malawi, Ghanaian ceremonial masks, and Indonesian chairs. ➥ *9 chalets ⚒ Pool, spa, bar, library, children's programs (ages 5–15), airstrip.*

$ ⊞ **Thanda Tented Camp.** Perfect for a family or friends' reunion, this intimate camp deep in the bush brings you into even closer contact with your surroundings. Wake up in your spacious safari tent with en-suite bathroom and private veranda to find a warthog or nyala or three grazing outside. The camp has its own vehicle, ranger, and tracker, and a huge sala with pool and sundeck. ➥ *4 tents ⚒ Pool, spa, bar, children's programs (ages 5–15), airstrip.*

Phongola Game Reserve

One of the largest inland bodies of water in Zululand, the Jozini Dam covers an area of some 39,520 acres along the Phongola (also called Pongola) River, close to the southern Swaziland border. Some 200 km (120 mi) of its pristine shoreline is bounded by the Phongola Game Reserve, today only a part of the original area declared a reserve in 1894 by President Paul Kruger. The dam (lake), built in the 1960s to provide irrigation to sugarcane farmers and hydroelectric power to the region, was never used for those purposes, and for many years was something of a white elephant. Today it has found its niche, becoming a magnet for tourists to northern KwaZulu-Natal. Surrounded by pristine bushveld and scrub, the lake provides sanctuary to a large number of crocodiles and hippos. Tiger fish that had nowhere to swim to after the river was dammed stayed put, and now fish of up to 24 pounds have been caught in the lake's waters. The region hosts an annual tiger-fishing competition in late September, drawing fishing enthusiasts from around the country. The lake has also ensured that the area is a birding hot spot, with more than 300 species of bushveld and waterbirds recorded. The purple-blue Lebombo Mountains looming behind the lake add majesty to the landscape.

Game here includes four of the Big Five (except lions), all of which have been reintroduced. The most interesting are the elephants, to the south of the reserve. It is the first time in more than 100 years that the great beasts have populated the region, and their effect on bushveld ecology is being monitored by a dedicated team. In addition, you may see warthogs, wildebeests, giraffes, zebras, and a variety of antelopes, including nyalas.

Phongola Game Reserve is definitely not for the armchair wildlife enthusiast. Activities include traditional game drives in open safari vehicles, as well as guided bush walks, fishing, big-game tracking, and boat trips on the Phongola River and Jozini Dam.

Where to Stay

NORTHERN SECTION To access the northern part of the reserve, travel north on the N2, past Umfolozi and Hluhluwe, toward the town of Phongola. Approximately 30 km (19 mi) south of Phongola, look for the sign to Golela and take this road to the right. After about 4 km (2 mi) you will see a sign to Phongola Game Reserve. The gate is on the right-hand side. *Note: Do not take the first right-hand turn, also signposted* PHONGOLA GAME RESERVE, *off the N2. This accesses the southern part of the reserve only.*

$ ▦ Mvubu Lodge. This beautiful and affordable lodge is high on the banks of the Phongola River and has endless, unspoiled views of silver river, blue sky, and rolling green hills. Attractive thatch-and-wood chalets face the magnificent panorama, but bathrooms are rather small, containing only a sink, toilet, and shower. A stone-walled communal lounge-bar area, attractively furnished with huge basket chairs, has sliding doors that open onto a wooden deck. Breakfasts are usually served on a thatch deck, and a traditional boma is the place for dinner, where, if you're adventurous, you can try such meats as kudu rumps or impala schnitzel. There's also a swimming pool—a must during summer, when temperatures soar beyond 38°C (100°F). ⊠ *Golela Rd., off the N2, Box 767, Phongola 3170* ☎ *034/435–1123* 🖷 *034/435–1104* ⊕ *www.pongolagamereserve.co.za* ⤙ *11 chalets* ♻ *Kitchen, pool, bar, lounge* ⊟ *MC, V* ⊙ *MAP.*

¢ ▦ Mhlozi Camp. Comfortable, simply furnished, self-catering thatch rondawels are grouped around a communal boma in attractive bushveld and face riverine bush and a seasonal stream. The catch is that you either have to book the whole camp or have a minimum of seven people. (The camp can hold up to 14 people.) The camp has a fully equipped communal kitchen where you can do your own cooking, dining and lounge-bar facilities, and a swimming pool. You can purchase food and drinks in Phongola. ⊠ *Golela Rd., off the N2, Box 767, Phongola 3170* ☎ *034/435–1123* 🖷 *034/435–1104* ⊕ *www.pongolagamereserve.co.za* ⤙ *7 rondawels* ♻ *Kitchen, pool, bar, lounge* ⊟ *AE, DC, MC, V.*

SOUTHERN
SECTION

To access the southern part of the reserve, travel north on the N2, past Umfolozi and Hluhluwe, toward the town of Phongola. Fifty kilometers (28 mi) from Phongola, look for the brown sign to Phongola Game Reserve and turn right.

★ $$ ▦ **White Elephant Lodge.** Built in the 1920s, White Elephant is a lovely lodge that captures the elegance of colonial Africa, with white furniture, African prints, sepia photographs of local historical scenes, and antiques. The lounge and dining room are in a historic farmhouse, with wide verandas providing sweeping views of the bushveld and Lebombo Mountains. Behind the house, sheltered from the prevailing winds, a traditional Zulu boma is the site of dinners and Zulu dancing. Accommodations are in luxurious East African safari tents—airy, cool, and perfect for hot subtropical nights. Each tent has a private bathroom with a claw-foot tub, an outdoor shower surrounded by canvas screens, and a private veranda. Paths link the tents and the main house. You can choose between taking part in the lodge's elephant monitoring program or going rhino tracking (no kids under 12), viewing game from an open vehicle, or fishing for a whopping tiger fish or two. Once you are in the Phongola Game Reserve, follow the Pongolwane signs (painted on rocks) and white arrows (*do not turn off to Mpelane*) and the logos of white elephants. ⊠ *Off the N2, south of Phongola* ✉ *Box 792, Phongola 3170* ☎ *034/413–2489* 🖷 *034/413–2499* ⊕ *www.whiteelephantlodge.co.za* 🛏 *8 tents* ⚖ *Dining room, minibars, pool, lounge* ▤ *AE, DC, MC, V* ⏉ *FAP.*

$ ▦ **White Elephant Bush Camp.** If you're watching pennies and want a back-to-nature experience, then this lovely little camp will hit the spot. Thatch chalets have private verandas, ceiling fans, and the ubiquitous mozzie nets. Chill out at the swimming pool, sit quietly in the blind, or watch the passing show at the water hole. Go for a bush walk or game drive, catch a tiger fish or two, or go "elephanting" (no kids under 12). ⊠ *Off the N2, south of Phongola, Box 792, Phongola 3170* ☎ *034/413–2489* 🖷 *034/413–2499* ⊕ *www.whiteelephantlodge.co.za* 🛏 *7 chalets* ⚖ *Fans, pool* ▤ *AE, DC, MC, V* ⏉ *FAP.*

Amazulu Private Game Reserve & AmaKhosi Lodge

🄕 Forty kilometers (21 mi) south of Phongola lies AmaKhosi Lodge, in the Amazulu Private Game Reserve, which covers some 25,000 acres of pristine wilderness on the perennial Mkuze River. Different habitats range from rocky hillsides to thick bushveld, tamboti forests to broad wetlands. AmaKhosi has all of the Big Five, in addition to wildebeests, zebras, giraffes, and a variety of antelopes, including the shy nyala. Most animals have been reintroduced, with the exception of leopards, which remain secretive and very difficult to spot. In addition, a wide variety of bird species will delight birders.

★ ▦ **AmaKhosi Lodge.** In the heart of northern KwaZulu-Natal, amid coun-
$$$ tryside that Alan Paton would have described as beautiful beyond any singing of it, this gorgeous new lodge overlooks the Mkuze River, which carves its way through mountains, rolling hills, open plains, thick

thornveld, and riverine bush. Bird-life is abundant, the Big Five are all here, and rangers work hard to find game, instead of relying on animals habituated to vehicles, as at some of the older camps. Superb air-conditioned suites (big enough to swing a pride of lions) have huge decks from which you can survey the river below. The staff excels, from management right down to the friendly gardeners, and the food would put many a posh restaurant to shame. Dine under the stars on a sprawling deck overlooking the river, in a gracious dining room if the weather is inclement, or in the staff-built branch-enclosed boma, entertained by local schoolchildren who practice their singing and dancing hard to help pay their school fees. For something very different, try a frog safari: after a bush braai, you'll be supplied with gum boots and miners' lamps, and led on a hunt for more than 30 species of these fascinating and little-known creatures with the resident frog expert. ⊠ *Off the N2, south of Phongola* ✆ *Box 354, Phongola 3170* ☎ *034/414–1157* ⊠ *034/414–1172* ⊕ *www.amakhosi.com* ⤶ *6 suites* ♨ *Dining room, in-room safes, minibars, cable TV, pool, bar, library* ⊟ *AE, DC, MC, V* ⫶◯⫶ *FAP.*

Maputaland Coastal Reserve

If Robinson Crusoe had washed ashore on the pristine coastline of Maputaland, he wouldn't have found anybody to call Friday—and he certainly wouldn't have cared what day of the week it was. It's that empty and that magnificent. No other buildings lie within 16 km (10 mi) of **73** Rocktail Bay Lodge, tucked away in **Maputaland Coastal Reserve,** a narrow strip of wilderness that stretches from St. Lucia all the way to Mozambique. If you love exploring along untouched beaches, fishing, scuba diving, snorkeling, and walking, coming here will be one of the highlights of a visit to South Africa. Rocktail Bay is not a game lodge—the only animals you're likely to see are loggerhead and leatherback turtles. It is included in this section because it lies far from any other major tourist destination and operates much like a game lodge. In fact, unless you have a four-wheel-drive vehicle, the lodge must pick you up for the final 11-km (7-mi) journey along deep sand tracks carved through coastal dune forest.

Rocktail Bay *does not offer traditional game-viewing,* although you can combine a visit here with a trip to Phinda, about 95 km (60 mi) to the south. Besides glorious beaches, its major attraction is the annual arrival of giant loggerhead and leatherback turtles to lay their eggs. The beaches here are one of the few known egg-laying areas of these endangered animals, and the season extends from the November through early March. During these months rangers lead after-dinner walks down the beach to look for turtles, and you can expect to cover as much as 16 km (10 mi) in a night. From a weather standpoint, the best times to visit the lodge are probably spring (September–October) and autumn (March–May). In summer the temperature regularly soars past 38°C (100°F), and swimming during winter is a brisk proposition. August is the windiest month, and it's in summer that the turtles come ashore to dig their nests and lay their eggs—an awesome spectacle.

Where to Stay

$$ □ **Rocktail Bay Lodge.** The lodge lies in a swale formed by enormous dunes
Fodor'sChoice fronting the ocean. Walkways tunnel through the dune forest to a golden
★   beach that sweeps in a gentle arc to Black Rock, several miles to the north.
There are no lifeguards or shark nets, but the swimming and snorkel-
ing are fabulous. The lodge consists of simple A-frame chalets raised on
wooden platforms above the forest floor. Wood and thatch create a rus-
tic ambience, complemented by solar lighting and basic furnishings. A
large veranda and adjoining thatch bar provide the backdrop for alfresco
meals under a giant Natal mahogany tree. Activities include great surf
fishing (tackle provided), snorkeling, and walking through the forest or
along the beach. Rangers lead excursions to see hippo pools, the rich
bird-life of Lake Sibaya, and Kosi Bay, where the local Tembe people
catch fish using the age-old method of basket netting, and Tsonga de-
scendants also use ancient woven fish traps. For many people, though,
a trip to Rocktail Bay is a chance to kick back and just soak in the atmo-
sphere of an unspoiled coastal wilderness. ⌂ *Box 78573, Sandton
2146* ☎ *011/883–0747* 🖷 *011/883–0911* ⊕ *www.rocktailbay.com*
⮌ *10 chalets* ⚲ *Pool, bar* ▭ *AE, DC, MC, V* ⦿ *FAP.*

Sports & the Outdoors

At Manzengwenya, 11 km (7 mi) south of the camp, you'll find some
of the best (some say the best) scuba-diving sites in the country. This is
the only diving concession in the marine reserve, so you'll be diving from
the only boat in the area and should have the pristine reefs all to your-
self (R350 for the first dive, R300 for the second). The **Rocktail Bay Dive
Centre** (☎ 035/574–8557) is fully outfitted, and you can dive reefs that
have never been dived on before. In December and January pregnant
ragged-tooth sharks migrate to the area and rest placidly in reef caves.

Johannesburg & Environs

WORD OF MOUTH

"Must-sees on my trips [to Johannesburg] are the daily craft markets in Bruma and the Sunday craft market in the Rosebank Mall parking garage. Hyde Park also has a nice craft market."

—Lisa

"After of good deal of searching, we ultimately booked a scientist-led tour of Sterkfontein and The Cradle of Humankind. At these sites (Sterkfontein, Drimolen, Kromdraai and Swartkrans), they unearthed the fossilized remains of 'Little Foot,' a pre-human believed to be 4 million years old. I recommend these dig sites as a 'must.'"

—jrruff

By Andrew
Barbour

Updated by
Matthew
Burbidge and
Riaan
Wolmarans

JOHANNESBURG, EGOLI, JOZI: THE PLACE WHERE THE GOLD IS. This is
where you come to seek your fortune.

Nobody wanted Johannesburg. It was just a triangular, rocky piece of
Highveld land left over after the surrounding farms had been surveyed
in November 1886. Judged to be without good water, it remained government land—until something better than water was found. Although
substantial deposits were recorded as early as 1881, gold was officially
discovered here in 1886 by an Australian, George Harrison, who stum-
bled on a surface deposit while prospecting on the Witwatersrand
(White-Water Ridge). Unknown to him, he was standing atop the world's
richest gold reef, and his discovery sparked a gold rush unrivaled in history. Prospectors flocked to the area. Since then the area has probably
produced about half the world's gold.

The land was carved into tiny plots and, later, into city blocks, somewhat smaller than those of other major cities—the better to fit more bars
on the corners. Foreigners, or *uitlanders,* arrived by the thousands, and
prostitutes followed to the rough mining town. Everything was dusty
and dirty, and water was in short supply. It's difficult to overstate the
effect of these goldfields on the development of Johannesburg and modern South Africa. In 1899 Britain engineered a war with the Boer republic just to get its hands on them, and the entire cultural and political
fabric of black South Africa has been colored by gold. Over the last century British and Irish fortune hunters, many of whom became wealthy
mining magnates and settled in today's Parktown suburb, together with
millions of blacks from South Africa, Mozambique, Zimbabwe, and
Botswana, made the long journey to Egoli (a Zulu name meaning "the
place of gold") to work in the mines.

Johannesburg became a modern, bustling metropolis that powers the
country's economy. It is the center of a vast urban industrial complex
that covers most of the province of Gauteng (writer Paul Theroux recommends using "the soft deep throat clearing and gargled 'g' of the
Dutch"), which is Sotho for "place where the gold is." Home to more
than 7 million people, it sprawls across the featureless plains of the mile-
high highveld, spawning endless suburbs that threaten even Tshwane
(formerly Pretoria), more than 50 km (30 mi) distant.

In the late 1980s, big business decided it didn't want Johannesburg, and
so it fled north, not quite as far as what was then called Pretoria, but
far enough away from the grit of the mine dumps. Lately, business has
been coming back. Derelict buildings are being demolished, and old ones
are being restored. It seems the whole city is being reorganized. The
diminutive but beautiful Nelson Mandela Bridge spans the railway
tracks close to the Newtown Cultural Precinct, which has been decorated with wonderful street sculpture. Even the street names in downtown Johannesburg have been renamed: Bezuidenhout Street is now called
Miriam Makeba Street, which is next to Dolly Rathebe Street, named
for the 1950s singer from the Jazz Pioneers. Unfortunately, she died in
2004, shortly before the renaming. In 1952, so the story goes, the young
Rathebe and a young, white German photographer, Jürgen Schadeberg,

If you have 1 or 2 days

If you have only one day in Jo'burg, take a tour of Soweto or Alexandra, see the Apartheid Museum, go shopping, and then head out to Muldersdrift for a wild and wacky African dinner at the Carnivore restaurant. If you have a second day, focus on what interests you most: perhaps a day trip to the Cradle of Humankind, where you'll explore the sites of some of the latest and most significant paleontological discoveries in the world, or a jaunt to Sun City. You could start the day off with a balloon ride and then amble through the Magaliesberg area, wandering from coffee shop to art studio. Other options include a tour of the Cullinan Diamond Mine, near Tshwane, or a visit to Gold Reef City and the Apartheid Museum. Each of these options could take up a half or full day.

If you have 3 or 4 days

Spend Days 1 and 2 as first described above, overnighting, perhaps, at the Misty Hills Country Hotel after your visit to the Cradle of Humankind. En route back to Johannesburg on Day 3, visit the Cullinan mine and do a short walking tour of central Pretoria. On Day 4 do some shopping in the morning, visiting the Bruma flea market or the African market outside Rosebank Mall. Alternatively, if you'd rather mix your energy with some peace and quiet, you can stay in a chalet at Mountain Sanctuary Park, in the Magaliesberg, for a night or two, and go for long walks.

---

scrambled to the top of a mine dump for a *Drum* magazine photo shoot. The photograph looks like it was taken on some strange beach: Rathebe smiles, posing in a bikini. They were spotted by the police and arrested as they descended. They were charged under the Immorality Act, which forbade extramarital intercourse between blacks and whites.

The gold-mine dumps are still there, just visible from the edge of town. There are more than 200 of these massive mounds of discarded earth; some close to 300 feet high, they march east and west along the seam of gold. Many people are fond of them—it's one of the city's defining characteristics—but those who live near them are blinded by the dust, and very little grows on them. Since they are also rich in minerals, they're slowly being chipped away and remined.

There's something in the higgledy-piggledy way the city was founded and built that survives to this day. City planners cleared city blocks and often replaced them with something new, for no other reason than that it *was* new. This has made for an interesting city, with myriad styles of architecture, from quietly rotting pre-1900 structures to restored art-deco buildings. Johannesburg, in fact, is said to have the greatest number of art-deco buildings in South Africa, but an international conference on the style took place in Cape Town instead. This may have been because of Johannesburg's infamous crime problem. For reasons of their own, the police no longer release crime statistics, and street crime such as muggings, hijackings, and pickpocketing are almost a way of life. According to the police, however, things are getting better, and most serious crimes are in decline. Visitors and residents, as in any large city, need to keep their wits about them.

If there is a symbol of Johannesburg, it's Ponte City: a massive, hollow, 50-story cylinder of apartments perched on the edge of the central business district with a flashing cell-phone ad on top—one of the biggest in the Southern Hemisphere. Visitors from other African cities are apparently surprised to find that it's only a building; they were expecting an entire township.

Johannesburg is South Africa's most African city. Traders hawk *skop* (boiled sheep's head, split open and eaten off newspaper) in front of polished glass buildings, as taxis jockey for position in rush hour. *Sangomas* (traditional healers) lay out herbs and roots next to the pavement tents of roadside barbers, and you never seem to be far from a woman selling *vetkoek* (dollops of deep-fried dough).

People have moved to, in, and around Johannesburg driven by need, greed, or just plain unbridled ambition. The miners' shacks gave way to the skyscrapers of downtown, and the rude dwellings of upwardly mobile adventurers became the opulent mansions of Parktown and Houghton. Black mine workers, whose presence was deemed undesirable in the midst of the nouveau riche, were moved away to the southwest fringes of the rapidly expanding city to what is now Soweto, an acronym for *South Western Townships*. The city grew up and out as the wealth poured in, and Hillbrow, near the city center, became the most happening place in South Africa from the 1950s through the 1980s.

Johannesburg is caught in this endless dance, as people pour in from all over the country and the continent following the lure of lucre. People come here to work, and it seems at times as though no one actually comes *from* Johannesburg. Many thought they would just come to make some money and then leave, but they stayed and put down roots. The city is full of immigrants: Italians, Portuguese, Chinese, Hindus, Swazis, English, Xhosa—all in the same boat, sink or swim. But most Jo'burgers tend to be generous and gregarious. They'll show you the ropes, give you advice, and show you their favorite bar. Just heaven help you if you're in the wrong traffic lane.

Exploring Johannesburg & Environs

Johannesburg is a huge urban sprawl, and though all the hotels and major malls have moved to the northern suburbs, some of the city center is enjoying a renaissance. The area near City Hall and the Newtown Cultural Precinct has been completely overhauled. The streets have been gentrified with stylish lighting, paving, and small wooden sculptures on concrete plinths. Soweto, too, is well worth a visit, although you should take a guided tour. Jo'burg is a sprawling city that can seem rather boring if you don't know what to look for, where to go, and how to interpret what you're seeing.

Arts & Crafts

Johannesburg is a great city for art lovers. Galleries and crafts outlets offer African and Western art, both classic and modern. In addition to indigenous crafts, Jo'burg is a good place to buy artifacts from the rest of Africa, and many a tourist goes home with local crafters' wire animals or tall wooden giraffes. In the countryside on Johannesburg's northwestern side, the region's creative talent hosts the wonderful Crocodile Ramble close to the large Hartbeespoort Dam. Drive down farm roads to visit the galleries and studios of painters, sculptors, potters, woodworkers, and others. Trips to Soweto, which can be arranged with a tour operator, may include stops at crafts stalls. The Magaliesberg is also an increasingly good spot to shop for art, as artists who want to leave the urban hustle often take refuge here.

7

Culture & History

If you are remotely interested in the adventure of being human, or in the history of South Africa, this is the place for you. The Cradle of Humankind, where some of the world's most important remains of early civilizations have been found, is an absolute must-see if you are curious about your origins. A visit to Soweto or Alexandra is a window onto a totally different world for many people, and a number of museums and historical buildings in these townships and in the city itself may also provide insight into the South African psyche. The Apartheid Museum is one of the most important of these, providing an up-close, harrowing look at South Africa's apartheid history and road to democracy.

Outdoor Adventures

Although Johannesburg and its environs are decidedly urban, there are plenty of opportunities for adventure. The Melville Koppies, near the suburb of Northcliff, have good places to walk, which can be enhanced by the company of a member of the botanical society. Hikers and climbers also revel in the Magaliesberg region, where a magnificent geologic fault runs northwest of Johannesburg. Most of the lodges in the area offer hiking, mountain biking, and fly-fishing, and within an hour or so of the city you can go horseback riding, do a tandem skydive, go hot-air ballooning, explore caves, go white-water rafting, or fly in a vintage plane.

Though Johannesburg is rarely associated with the great outdoors, it has its share of pleasant parks and nature reserves hugging the outskirts of the city. In the outer areas it's possible to envision how the inland plateau must have appeared to the region's first settlers. Beyond this to the north lies the largely unspoiled Magaliesberg region. Here you can get a restful break amid lovely mountain scenery, farmlands, and quiet country roads. Also close by is the fascinating Cradle of Humankind, a World Heritage Site with a spectacularly rich fossil record. It was here that the remains of the first hominid, *Australopithecus*, were found, as well as records of the earliest known use of fire.

Less than an hour north of Johannesburg, Tshwane, formerly known as Pretoria, is the country's pleasant capital. Though it was once a bastion of hard-line Afrikanerdom, the town now has a refreshing cosmopolitan breeze blowing through its streets. In addition to its several historic buildings, the city is renowned for its jacaranda trees, whose purple blossoms blanket the city in September and October.

You have to travel 90 minutes beyond the borders of Gauteng to reach Sun City, a rather crass entertainment and gambling resort set amid the arid beauty of the North West Province bush. Here are Las Vegas–style hotels, championship golf courses, and water rides, as well as lovely Pilanesberg, a pocket-size game reserve.

It is virtually impossible to see anything of the Johannesburg area without a car. Your best bet is to rent one, decide what you want to see, get a good road map, and work from there. Service-station attendants should also be able to point you in the right direction. If you're staying only a day or two, you could also just stick to escorted trips.

About the Restaurants

If there's one thing that Jo'burgers love doing, it's eating out. There are thousands of restaurants scattered throughout the city. Dining in Johannesburg is usually a casual affair, and "smart casual" dress is fine at most restaurants. Reservations are generally a good idea. Most restaurants are open for lunch and dinner, and many are closed on Mondays. Many restaurateurs also close over Christmas.

Some notable destinations for food include Melrose Arch, Parkhurst, Sandton, the South (for its Portuguese cuisine), Melville, and Chinatown in the CBD (Central Business District). There is also a new Chinatown—a strip of restaurants and Asian grocery stores in Cyrildene, just above Bruma Lake. Also check out the restaurants recommended on the official Johannesburg Web site ⊕ (www.johannesburg.gov).

WHAT IT COSTS In South African rand					
	$$$$	$$$	$$	$	¢
RESTAURANTS	over 125	100–125	75–100	50–R75	under 50

Prices are per person for a main course at dinner, a main course equivalent, or a prix-fixe meal.

About the Hotels

Most, if not all, of the good hotels are now in the northern suburbs. Many of the hotels are linked to nearby malls and are well policed. The Melrose Arch enclave is worth visiting; it's effectively a separate city, with its own restaurants and business district. Boutique hotels have sprung up everywhere, as have bed-and-breakfasts from Melville to Soweto. Hotels are quieter in December and January, and their rates are often cheaper over this period. Generally the busy months are from June to August. However, if there is a major conference, some of the smaller hotels can be booked months in advance.

	$$$$	**$$$**	**$$**	**$**	**¢**
WHAT IT COSTS In South African rand					
HOTELS	over 3,000	2,000–3,000	1,000–2,000	500–1,000	under 500

Prices are for a standard double room in high season, including 12.5% tax.

Timing

To residents, Johannesburg seems a bit of a ghost town over the December holidays. It's high summer and it's hot, and there's often a thunderstorm in the afternoon. The city empties out as all the factories close down and families head for the seaside or the bush. There is little or no rain in winter (from March to September), and it gets bitterly cold. Johannesburg seems stark, with the cold reflecting off the concrete, but at least the aloes flower, some a deep red. Then the city starts to thaw. Jacaranda trees bloom, carpeting the streets with purple blossoms, and a local arts festival, Arts Alive, makes things festive.

JOHANNESBURG

The Greater Johannesburg metropolitan area stretches out over a massive area and now incorporates the large and formerly separate municipalities of Randburg and Sandton to the north. Most of the sights are just north of the city center, which degenerated badly in the 1990s but is being revamped along with the Newtown neighborhood right next to it. Just to the south, in Ormonde, are the Apartheid Museum and Gold Reef City, and the impressive Standard Bank Gallery and Johannesburg Art Gallery are in the city itself. Diagonal Street runs—you guessed it—diagonally through the city center. Not far away, MuseuMAfricA and the SAB World of Beer are in Newtown, which is connected via the gracious Nelson Mandela Bridge to Braamfontein, home to Constitution Hill and the Johannesburg Planetarium. Sprawling Soweto is to the southwest, as its name implies, and the more affluent side of Johannesburg is its northern suburbs. On the way to the shopping mecca of Rosebank you'll find the Johannesburg Zoo and the South African Museum of Military History.

Numbers in the margin correspond to numbers on the Johannesburg and Soweto maps.

What to See

① **Apartheid Museum.** Johannesburg's most important museum leaves no stone unturned, black or white, as it takes you on a journey through South African apartheid history—from the entrance, where you pass through a turnstile according to your skin color, to the myriad historical, brutally honest, and sometimes shocking photographs, video displays, films, documents, and other exhibits. It's an emotional journey second to none. As you walk chronologically through the apartheid years and eventually reach the country's first steps to freedom, with democratic elections in 1994, you experience a taste of the pain and suffer-

Fodor'sChoice
★

ing with which so many South Africans had to live. A room with 121 ropes with hangman's knots hanging from the ceiling—one rope for each political prisoner executed in the apartheid era—is especially chilling. ⊠ *Northern Pkwy. and Gold Reef Rd., Ormonde* ☎ *011/309–4700.* ⊕ *www.apartheidmuseum.org.* 🎫 *R25.* ☉ *Tues.–Sun. 10–5.*

★ ❾ **Constitution Hill.** Overlooking Jo'burg's inner city and suburbs, Constitution Hill houses the new Constitutional Court as well as the austere Old Fort Prison Complex (also called Number Four), where thousands were incarcerated before the advent of democracy, including Nelson Mandela and Mahatma Gandhi. Tours and exhibitions in the visitor center portray the country's journey to democracy. You can walk along the prison ramparts (built in the 1890s), read messages of democracy on the We the People Wall (and add your own), or view the court itself, in which large, slanting columns represent the trees under which African villagers traditionally met to discuss matters of importance. A restaurant, a coffee shop, and a museum shop are found on Constitution Square, a central piazza, as well as a children's room with special programs. Future plans for Constitution Hill include restaurants, apartments, and hotels. ⊠ *Joubert and Kotze Sts. (entrance on Sam Hancock St.), Braamfontein* ☎ *011/274–5300* ⊕ *www.constitutionhill.org.za* 🎫 *R15, Tues. free* ☉ *Daily 9–5 (last entry at 4).*

❺ **Diagonal Street.** This street in the city center is lined with African herbalists' shops, where you can acquire a mind-boggling array of homeopathic and traditional cures for whatever ails you. If you're lucky, a sangoma might throw the bones and tell you what the future holds. This is also the site of the old Johannesburg Stock Exchange building (the modern version is in Sandton).

🐾 ❷ **Gold Reef City.** This theme park lets you step back in time to the Johannesburg of the 1880s and see why it became known as the City of Gold. One of the city's most popular attractions for both visitors and locals (don't go on public holidays or weekends if you can avoid it), it has all the usual rides and kitschy amusements and is based on the real history of Jo'burg. In addition to riding the Anaconda, a scary roller coaster on which you hang under the track, feet in the air, you can descend into an old gold mine (additional fee), see molten gold being poured, or watch a gumboot dance, a riveting dance developed by black miners. The reconstructed streets are lined with operating Victorian-style shops and restaurants. And for those with money to burn, the large, glitzy Gold Reef Village Casino beckons across the road. ⊠ *Gold Reef Rd., 6 km (4 mi) south of the city center, Ormonde* ☎ *011/248–6800* ⊕ *www.goldreefcity.co.za* 🎫 *R55–R70* ☉ *Tues.–Sun. 10–4:40; dancing at 11:30 and 3; mine tours 10–5 every 30 mins.*

❸ **Johannesburg Art Gallery.** This three-story museum, the biggest in southern Africa, hosts top-notch local and international exhibitions in 15 halls and has collections of 17th-century Dutch art, 18th-century French art, and, of course, paintings by great South African artists such as Pierneef, Ezrom Legae, Walter Battiss, Irma Stern, Gerard Sekoto, and Anton van Wouw. It exhibits only about 10% of its treasures at a time. You can also admire a large selection of traditional African objects, such as headrests, tree carvings, and beadwork. ⊠ *King George and Klein Sts., Joubert Park* ☎ *011/725–3130* ⍯ *Free* ☉ *Tues.–Sun. 10–5.*

❿ **Johannesburg Planetarium.** This centrally located planetarium, dating from 1960, has entertaining and informative programs on the African skies and presentations that range from space travel to our neighboring planets. Phone ahead to find out what's on. ⊠ *Yale Rd., University of the Witwatersrand, Braamfontein* ☎ *011/717–1392 or 011/717–1390* ⊕ *www.wits.ac.za/planetarium* ⍯ *Varies by event, average R25* ☉ *Usually Fri.–Sun.*

⓫ **Johannesburg Zoo.** Smaller than its Tshwane (Pretoria) counterpart but no less impressive, the city's zoo makes for a pleasant day trip, with plenty of lawns and shade—good for a picnic. The large variety of animals includes rare white lions and highly endangered red pandas. The polar-bear enclosure has a viewing tunnel where you can see the bears cavorting underwater (the zoo has the only two polar bears in Africa). Afterward, stroll past Zoo Lake in the large peaceful park across the road. ⊠ *Opposite Zoo Lake, Jan Smuts Ave., Parkview* ☎ *011/646–2000* ⊕ *www.jhbzoo.org.za* ⍯ *R30* ☉ *Daily 8:30–5:30.*

★ ❻ **MuseuMAfricA.** Founded in 1935, this was the first major museum to acknowledge black contributions to the city's development. The museum houses plenty of geological specimens, paintings, and photographs relating to South Africa's complex history. You can step into a re-creation of a 1950s *shebeen* (informal bar) or view the ever-changing exhibits of pottery, photography, and other arts and crafts. Seven permanent displays include a look at the history of gold mining in Johannesburg and a journey through the history of South African music, such as township jazz, kwela, and *mbaqanga,* a form of driving township pop-jazz. Another display illustrates the life of Mahatma Gandhi, who lived in Jo'burg before becoming an important Indian political hero. Upstairs, the Bensusan Museum examines the art, development, and technology of photography with fun, hands-on exhibits. ⊠ *121 Bree St., Newtown* ☎ *011/833–5624* ⍯ *R7* ☉ *Tues.–Sun. 9–5.*

❽ **Nelson Mandela Bridge.** This modern, 931-foot-long bridge with sprawling cables spans the bleak Braamfontein railway yard, connecting Constitution Hill and Braamfontein to the revamped Newtown Cultural Precinct. A symbol of the renewal process going on in the city, the bridge is especially beautiful at night, when it is lighted in white and blue. ⊠ *Take Queen Elizabeth St. from Braamfontein, or follow signs from central Newtown or from M1 south, Braamfontein and Newtown.*

❼ **SAB World of Beer.** This unusual museum is dedicated to a great South African favorite—beer! South African Breweries (SAB) is the country's—and Africa's—largest. You'll find out all about the history of beer brewing in South Africa and the process of beer making, including African brewing traditions. After a 90-minute tour you can enjoy two complimentary beers in the tap room. ⊠ *15 President St., Newtown* ☎ *011/836–4900* ⊕ *www.worldofbeer.co.za* ⍯ *R10* ☉ *Tues.–Sat. 10–6.*

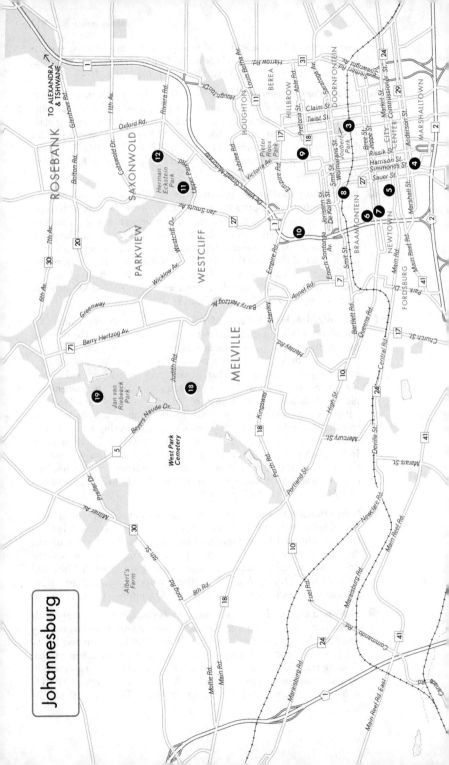

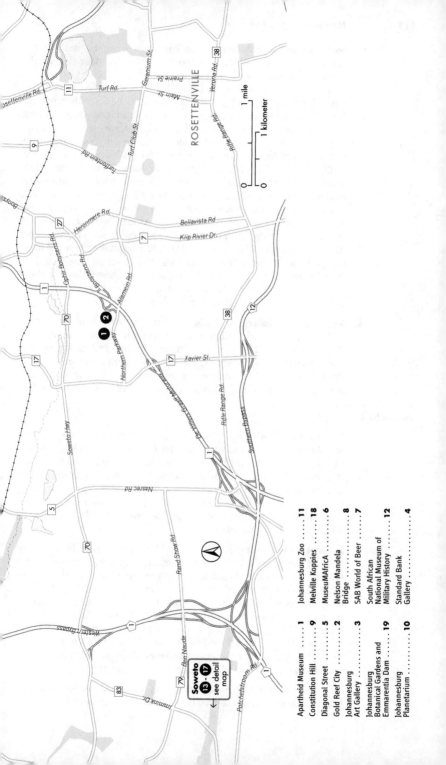

ROSETTENVILLE

1 mile
1 kilometer

Apartheid Museum **1**
Constitution Hill **9**
Diagonal Street **5**
Gold Reef City **2**
Johannesburg
Art Gallery **3**
Johannesburg
Botanical Gardens and
Emmarentia Dam **19**
Johannesburg
Planetarium **10**

Johannesburg Zoo **11**
Melville Koppies **18**
MuseuMAfricA **6**
Nelson Mandela
Bridge **8**
SAB World of Beer **7**
South African
National Museum of
Military History **12**
Standard Bank
Gallery **4**

⑫ South African National Museum of Military History. Set in a park, this museum has two exhibition halls and a rambling outdoor display that focus on South Africa's role in the major wars of the 20th century, with an emphasis on World War II. On display are Spitfire and Messerschmidt fighters (including what is claimed to be the only remaining ME110 jet night fighter), various tanks of English and American manufacture, and a wide array of artillery. Among the most interesting objects are the modern armaments South Africa used in its war against the Cuban-backed Angolan army during the 1980s, including highly advanced artillery, French-built Mirage fighters, and Russian tanks stolen by the South Africans from a ship en route to Angola. More recent exhibits include the national military art collection, memorabilia from the Anti-Conscription Campaign, and an exhibit on the history of Umkhonto we-Sizwe (Spear of the Nation, or MK, the African National Congress's military arm), from inception until its incorporation into the South African National Defence Force. The tall, freestanding South African (Anglo-Boer) War memorial, which looks like a statue-adorned mini Arc de Triomphe, is the most striking landmark of the northern suburbs. ✉ *20 Erlswold Way, Saxonwold* ☎ *011/646–5513* ⊕ *www. militarymuseum.co.za* ▧ *R10* ☯ *Daily 9–4:30.*

❹ Standard Bank Gallery. At the home of the Standard Bank African art collection, you can also admire examples of other contemporary South African artwork. The gallery hosts high-quality, ever-changing local and international exhibitions, including the annual traveling World Press Photo show. ✉ *Frederick and Simmonds Sts., City Center* ☎ *011/ 636–4231* ⊕ *www.sbgallery.co.za* ▧ *Free* ☯ *Weekdays 8–4:30, Sat. 9–1.*

Soweto

Soweto was founded in 1904, when city councilors used an outbreak of bubonic plague as an excuse to move black people to a location outside the town. Today it's home to more than a million residents. What it lacks in infrastructure, it more than makes up for in soul and energy. The largely working-class population here knows how to live for today, and Soweto seethes with streetwise music, jive, and humor. What other place on Earth can boast of having had two Nobel laureates living within a block of each other?

For most of his adult life, Anglican archbishop Desmond Tutu lived on Vilakazi Street, in the Orlando West neighborhood, and for most of that time his close neighbor would have been an attorney named Nelson Rolihlahla Mandela, except that the latter spent most of *his* adult life incarcerated on Robben Island, in Cape Town (⇨ Chapter 1). (South Africa has two other Nobel Peace Prize winners—the first was African National Congress [ANC] founder Albert Luthuli, and the fourth is ex-president F. W. de Klerk.) Close to the Holy Cross Church, Tutu's home parish, the archbishop's home is a gray, two-story affair, not open to the public, whereas the nearby Mandela house is a museum.

Other Soweto neighborhoods worth touring include old-town neighborhood Diepkloof, just beyond Orlando West, and its neighbor, the new

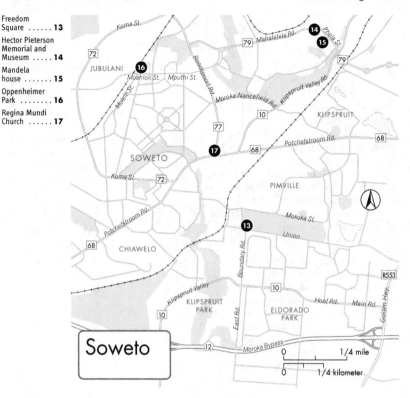

Soweto

Diepkloof Extension, which dates from the mid-1970s, when bank loans first became available to black property owners. The difference between the two is startling: the dreary prefabricated "matchbox" houses of Diepkloof next to what looks like a middle-class suburb anywhere. In nearby Dube, many of the evicted residents of Sophiatown—a freehold township west of the city and a melting pot of music, bohemianism, crime, and multiracialism that insulted Afrikaner Calvinism and nationalism—were resettled in 1959. At the time they brought an exciting vibe to the dreary, homogenous dormitory town. This can be seen today in the relative variety of houses here.

On the whole, however, Soweto is a chaotic, virtually indistinguishable sprawl that, even if you found your way in, you'd probably struggle to find your way out of—let alone around in. It's best, therefore, to take a guided tour (⇨ Johannesburg & Environs A to Z, *below*). Bus tours are offered by various companies, but it's better to hire a private guide or join a smaller group tour. You can ask for a special-interest tour, such as art, traditional medicine, restaurants, nightlife, or memorials. Standard tours usually include some or all of the following.

CloseUp

HECTOR PIETERSON & THE SOWETO UPRISING

ON JUNE 16, 1976, hundreds of schoolchildren in Soweto marched to protest the use of Afrikaans as the primary language of education in the overcrowded, much neglected Bantu schools in the townships. This was a highly charged political issue. Not only was Dutch-based Afrikaans considered the "language of the oppressor" by blacks, but it also made it more difficult for students to learn, as most spoke an African language and, as a second language, English.

The march turned nasty quickly. The protesters, mostly young students, became overexuberant, and so, too, did the police. The police started firing into the youthful crowd. One of the first people of more than 500 to die, in what was the beginning of a long and protracted struggle, was 12-year-old Hector Pieterson. A picture of the dying Pieterson in the arms of a crying friend, taken by photographer Sam Nzima, put a face on apartheid and sent it around the globe.

Pieterson was just a schoolboy trying to ensure a better life for himself and his friends, family, and community, but his name lives on. He and the many students who joined the liberation movement strengthened the fight against apartheid. Eventually Afrikaans was dropped as a language of instruction, and more schools and a teaching college were built in Soweto. Today Hector Pieterson's name graces a simple memorial and museum about the conflict, and June 16 is Youth Day, a public holiday.

What to See

⓭ **Freedom Square.** In 1955 the Freedom Charter was adopted here by the Congress Alliance—a gathering of political and cultural groups trying to map a way forward in the repressive 1950s. The charter, the guiding document of the African National Congress, envisaged an alternative nonracial dispensation in which "all shall be equal before the law." It has the same significance in South Africa as the Declaration of Independence has in the United States. ⊠ *Close to Union St. and Boundary Rd., Kliptown.*

⓮ **Hector Pieterson Memorial and Museum.** Opposite Holy Cross Church, a stone's throw (literally, in those days) from the Tutu and Mandela homes, the Hector Pieterson Memorial and Museum is a crucial landmark for the city. Pieterson, a student, was the first victim of police fire on June 16, 1976, when schoolchildren rose up to protest their second-rate *Bantu* (black) education system. The memorial itself is just an inscribed stone slab, but in the museum you can look at grainy photographs and films of that fateful day. Small granite blocks in the museum courtyard are a tribute to the 350 children among the more than 500 people who died during this violent time. ⊠ *Khumalo and Phela Sts., Orlando West* ☎ *011/536–0611* ⊠ *R10* ☉ *Mon.–Sat. 10–5, Sun. 10–2.*

⓯ **Mandela House.** The former president lived in this small house, until his arrest in 1961, with his now disgraced ex-wife Winnie Madikizela-Mandela, who owns a high-security mansion higher up the street. The house is now a museum containing Mandela memorabilia from the 1960s. ⊠ *Vilakazi St., Orlando West* ☎ *011/936–7754* ⊠ *R20* ☉ *Daily 9:30–5.*

⓰ **Oppenheimer Park.** Named after mining magnate Ernest Oppenheimer, this park is one of the only official green spaces in Soweto (as opposed to stream courses and wetlands). It's dominated by a large tower built as a tribute to Oppenheimer, who helped resettle people displaced by the apartheid government in the 1950s. Here you can also see **Kekhayalendaba,** a cultural village built in the 1970s by South Africa's best-known traditional healer, artist, and oral historian, Credo Mutwa. Some of his statues here portray African gods, warriors, and mythical figures, even sculptures of prehistoric African animals. It's best to visit the park with a guide in daytime for safety reasons. ⊠ *Majoeng St., Central Western Jabavu* ☎ *No phone* ⊠ *Free* ☉ *24 hrs.*

⓱ **Regina Mundi Church.** Central to the liberation struggle, this Catholic church was a refuge of peace, sanity, and steadfast moral focus for the people of Soweto throughout the harshest years of repression (1976–1990). Archbishop Desmond Tutu often delivered sermons in this massive church during the apartheid years. It has a black Madonna and child inside and an art gallery upstairs. ⊠ *1149 Khumalo St., Rockville* ☎ *011/986–2546* ⊠ *Donations requested* ☉ *Weekdays 9–5.*

Northern Suburbs

Alexandra

Less well known than Soweto, Alexandra (commonly called Alex) is a small bustling suburb right on Sandton's doorstep. Black people have been able to buy freehold land here for decades, and it's here that the famous bus boycotts of the 1940s took place. Protesting a hike in the city's bus ticket prices, workers walked to work and back every day for six months—sometimes a journey of two hours or more. Alex has developed into a vibrant community and seems to have less emotional baggage than "planned" locations, which were usually forced on unwilling residents. It was here that Nelson Mandela had his first home in Johannesburg. It is recommended that you visit Alexandra with a guide, for safety reasons. Contact the Alexandra Tourism Forum (⇨ Johannesburg & Environs A to Z, *below*) to arrange tours.

Melville

The trendy suburb of Melville essentially grew around the South African Broadcasting Corporation (SABC) in nearby Auckland Park. It was once an average middle-class enclave but has become one of the hippest places around Johannesburg; here you might just see a television or radio personality walking the street or eating at one of the many small restaurants. Seventh Street has a number of pleasant shops and sidewalk cafés. Although you may not find anything uniquely African here, you'll see how suburban South Africa entertains itself, particularly on weekends, when coffeehouses and shops buzz.

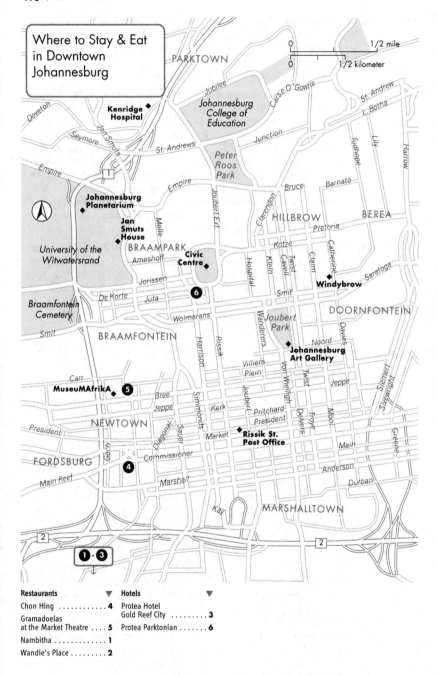

Where to Stay & Eat in Downtown Johannesburg

PARKTOWN

1/2 mile
1/2 kilometer

Jubilee

Doveton

Kenridge Hospital

Johannesburg College of Education

Carse O'Gowrie

St. Andrew
L. Botha

Seymore
Jan Smuts
St. Andrews
Empire
Junction

Tudhope
Lily
Harrow

Empire

Peter Roos Park

Johannesburg Planetarium

Jan Smuts House

Empire

Joubert Ext.

Bruce

Barnato

Clarendon

HILLBROW

BEREA

Pretoria

Melle

Kotze

BRAAMPARK

University of the Witwatersrand

Ameshoff

Civic Centre

Twist
Cavell
Catherine
Saratoga

Jorissen

De Korte

Juta

6

Hospital
Klein

Smit

Windybrow

DOORNFONTEIN

Braamfontein Cemetery

Smit

Wolmarans

Joubert Park

Davies

BRAAMFONTEIN

Harrison

Rissik

Wanderers

Noord

Johannesburg Art Gallery

Siemert
Sivewright

Villiers
Plein

Jeppe

Mooi

Greene

Carr

MuseuMAfricA

5

Bree

Jeppe

Simmonds

Kerk

Joubert

Pritchard

Twist

Delvers

Troye

President

Diagonal

Sauer

Market

President

NEWTOWN

Rissik St. Post Office

Main

FORDSBURG

Gogh

Commissioner

Main Reef

4

Marshall

Anderson

Durban

Kay

MARSHALLTOWN

2

2

1 · 3

Restaurants ▼

Chon Hing **4**

Gramadoelas
at the Market Theatre **5**

Nambitha **1**

Wandie's Place **2**

Hotels ▼

Protea Hotel
Gold Reef City **3**

Protea Parktonian **6**

A small nature reserve on the southern side of the Johannesburg Botanical Gardens, **Melville Koppies** has guided ecology walks; many of the guides are members of the local botanical society and can introduce you to the rich diversity of highveld flora found here. Bird-watching is also excellent. Expect to see more than 200 varieties of grassland and highveld birds as well as suburban garden species and small mammals. An archaeological site contains a furnace dating from the Iron Age. The reserve is managed by volunteers, hence the strange opening times, but you can also book a special tour outside these times. A paved brick path is wheelchair-friendly. ⊠ *Judith Rd. and Beyers Naude Ave., Melville* ☎ *011/788–7571, 011/482–4797 special tours* ⊕ *www.veld.org.za* ⊡ *Free* ☽ *1st 3 Sun. of month, times vary.*

The large and beautiful **Johannesburg Botanical Gardens and Emmarentia Dam** are actually five minutes down the road from Melville, in the nondescript suburb of Roosevelt Park. This gigantic parkland is a wonderful haven amid the city bustle. You can relax on benches beneath weeping willows surrounding the dam (lake), where canoeists and windsurfers brave the water, or wander across to the 24-acre rose and herb gardens, filled with arbors, statues, fountains, and ponds. On weekends you will likely bump into bridal parties using the gardens as a backdrop for photographs. ⊠ *Thomas Bowler St., Roosevelt Park* ☎ *011/407–6111* ⊕ *www.jobot.co.za* ⊡ *Free* ☽ *Daily sunrise–sunset.*

Parktown

A superb way to introduce yourself to the colonial history of early Johannesburg is to stroll through this suburb perched on the Braamfontein Ridge. The city's early mining magnates, such as the Oppenheimers and the Cullinans, settled here and commissioned renowned architects—most notably Sir Herbert Baker, one of South Africa's premier architects during the late 1800s and early 1900s—to build their magnificent houses, many of which are national monuments. Baker studied classical Italian, Greek, and Egyptian architecture and adapted these to his own style. His Parktown buildings are clean and stately, constructed with locally quarried stone. In many cases interiors have been converted to modern uses, but exteriors remain authentic. The Parktown–Westcliff Heritage Trust, with which you can take guided weekend tours of the area (⇨ Johannesburg & Environs A to Z, *below*), fought to preserve these old mansions, many of which were almost demolished to make way for the ubiquitous office buildings that cover much of southern Parktown.

Perhaps the cream of the suburb's architectural treasures is **Northwards** (⊠ Rock Ridge Rd., near Oxford Rd.), designed by Baker. For many years it was the home of socialite Jose Dale Lace, whose ghost is said to still grace Northwards's Mistral's Gallery. Now Wits Business School, the mansion **Outeniqua** (⊠ St. David's Pl.) was built in 1906 for the managing director of Ohlssons Breweries. Across the road, **Eikenlaan** (⊠ St. David's Pl.) was built in 1903 for James Goch, a professional photographer and the first to use flash photography in South Africa. In 1985 the home was turned into a rather garish franchise of the Mike's Kitchen steak-house chain.

Rosebank

This suburb linking Parktown and Sandton is attractive, but it lacks the old-world charm of places like Melville. Large shopping malls have lots of chrome and glass, catering to everyone from punk youths to fussy grandmothers. You can, however, find quiet squares away from the constant hive of activity. On sunny days (of which there are many), you can dine alfresco at one of Rosebank's sidewalk cafés.

Where to Eat

There is no way to do justice to the sheer scope and variety of Johannesburg's restaurants in a few pages. What follows is a (necessarily subjective) list of some of the best. Try asking locals what they recommend; eating out is the most popular form of entertainment in Johannesburg, and everyone has a list of his or her favorite spots.

Downtown

$ ✕ **Gramadoelas at the Market Theatre.** Crossing the threshold here is like stepping into some strange museum from another time. African artifacts and mirrors litter the huge room. Gramadoelas specializes in the food of ordinary South Africans but also has a few dishes from farther north in the continent. Try *umngqusho* (beans and whole corn) or, if you're feeling adventurous, *mogodu* (unbleached ox tripe) or *moroho* (mopane worms). Cape Malay food is the mainstay, such as rich *bredie* (lamb casserole in a tomato sauce) and *bobotie* (a casserole of minced lamb). Meat lovers will like the selection of game meats such as the kudu panfried with dried fruit and spices. ✉ *Market Theatre, Wolhuter St., Newtown* ☎ *011/838–6960* ▤ *AE, DC, MC, V* ⊘ *Closed Sun. No lunch Mon.*

¢–$ ✕ **Chon Hing.** Tucked away in a side street and looking a little world-weary, this Chinese restaurant is still one of the best-kept secrets of the cognoscenti. No tablecloths mask the Formica tabletops, and the chairs are upholstered in red plastic, but in a place like this it's the food that keeps people coming back. You can order one of the set menus, but you're better off selecting dishes from the two pages at the back of the menu. Good choices are beef flank served with noodles or rice, prawns stuffed with minced chicken, and calamari in black-bean sauce. For a real treat order the steamed rock cod. ✉ *26 Alexander St., at John Vorster Sq., Ferreirastown* ☎ *011/834–3206* ▤ *AE, DC, MC, V* ⌕ *BYOB.*

Soweto

★ $ ✕ **Wandie's Place.** Wandie's isn't the only good township restaurant, but it is the best-known and one of the most popular spots in Jo'burg. The decor is eclectic township (i.e., a bit makeshift), the waiters are smartly dressed in bow ties, and the food is truly African. Meat stews, *imifino* (a wild-spinach dish), sweet potatoes, beans, corn porridge, traditionally cooked pumpkin, chicken, even some tripe are laid out in a buffet in a motley selection of pots and containers. A selection of salads is the only concession to Western tastes. The food is hot, the drinks are cold, and the conversation flows. You may be unlucky and end up here with a tour bus, but it's big enough to cope. It's not that difficult to find and parking is safe, but it's probably better to organize a visit here on a guided trip. ✉ *618 Makhalamele St., Dube* ☎ *011/982–2796* ▤ *AE, DC, MC, V.*

¢ ✕ **Nambitha.** Though you can't actually see Nelson Mandela's old house from this trendy restaurant, it also means that you're less likely to run into a tour bus. Many people seek out the restaurant for its mogodu (ox tripe)—something, according to a waiter, "that you're not going to find in Sandton." Meaty "good morning Soweto" breakfasts include, for the brave, a dish of *uputhu* (porridge) with *inkomazi* (sour cream). Delicious mutton stew is served in a rich tomato gravy and little piles of spinach, pumpkin, and potato salad. ⊠ *Vilakazi St., Orlando West* ☎ *011/936–9128* ☱ *MC, V.*

Northern Suburbs

$$$–$$$$ ✕ **Linger Longer.** Ever since the annual Top Ten restaurant awards were
Fodor'sChoice initiated by *Wine* magazine in the early '90s, this restaurant has stood
★ among the top three. Set in the spacious grounds of a grand home in Wierda Valley, near Sandown, it has an air of gracious elegance. Some rooms have a Wedgwood-like quality—deep green walls with pale trim and striped curtains—whereas others glow in salmon pink. Diners can also reserve a table in the garden. Chef Walter Ulz is famous for duck; other specialties include quail stuffed with mushroom risotto, seared tuna with Asian vegetables, and ostrich fillet with roast vegetables and an Amarula (a sweet creamy liqueur) sauce. ⊠ *58 Wierda Rd. E, Wierda Valley* ☎ *011/884–0465* ☱ *AE, DC, MC, V* ☉ *Closed Sun. No lunch Sat.*

$–$$$$ ✕ **Moyo.** Now with four locations (Melrose Arch, the Market Theatre, Zoo Lake, and the Spier wine estate, outside Cape Town), Moyo has taken the concept of the Africa-themed restaurant by the horns and has been wildly successful. The focus of the rich and varied menu is pan-African, incorporating tandoori cookery from northern Africa; Cape Malay influences such as bobotie, available in both lentil and venison versions; tasty *tagines* (stews with lamb, chicken, fish, or seven vegetables); ostrich burgers; flaked, smoked *snoek* (a South African game fish); and excellent line fish. There are also storytellers, face painters, and musicians, some of whose CDs are available for sale. This is the kind of place where if you tell the waiters you're cold, they'll wrap you in a blanket. ⊠ *Melrose Arch, Shop 5, High St., Melrose North* ☎ *011/684–1477* ⌨ *Reservations essential* ☱ *AE, DC, MC, V.*

$–$$$ ✕ **Vilamoura.** This is the place to go if you want an excellent Portuguese meal. The restaurant made its name in Rosebank and has reopened, under new ownership, in Sandton City as well as in Bryanston. Vilamoura serves fresh oysters, crayfish, prawns, and line fish with garlic-and-lemon-butter sauce as well as a spectacularly hot peri-peri sauce. It also turns out a very good fillet and marinated chicken. On Friday and Saturday nights you can dance under a mirror ball to a Latin American band. ⊠ *Sandton City, 5th St. and Alice La., Sandton* ☎ *011/884–0360* ☱ *AE, DC, MC, V.*

$$ ✕ **La Cucina di Ciro.** This is one of the best Italian restaurants in Johan-
Fodor'sChoice nesburg. The owner, Ciro, says the cuisine is "very much my own," which
★ means you'll find truly inventive dishes on his constantly changing menu. For summer starters there's chilled gazpacho with mint and chili, or prawn-and-calamari salad with fresh coriander, roast cashews, and avocado. Main courses might include a fillet of Scottish salmon baked

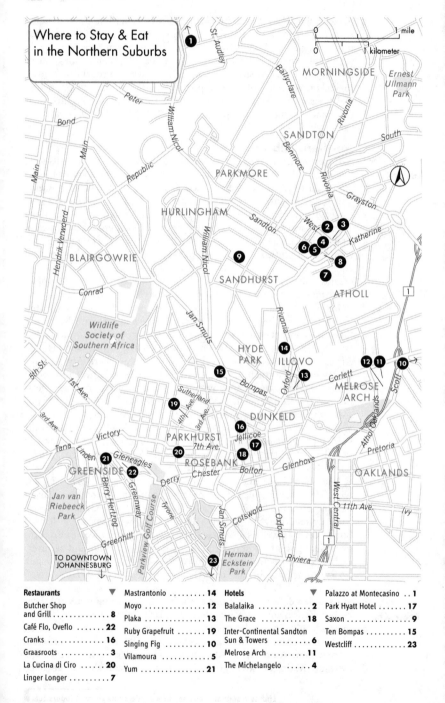

Where to Stay & Eat
in the Northern Suburbs

Restaurants ▼		Hotels ▼
Butcher Shop and Grill **8**	Mastrantonio **14**	Palazzo at Montecasino . . **1**
Café Flo, Oveflo **22**	Moyo **12**	Park Hyatt Hotel **17**
Cranks **16**	Plaka **13**	Balalaika **2**
Graasroots **3**	Ruby Grapefruit **19**	The Grace **18**
La Cucina di Ciro **20**	Singing Fig **10**	Inter-Continental Sandton Sun & Towers **6**
Linger Longer **7**	Vilamoura **5**	Melrose Arch **11**
	Yum **21**	The Michelangelo **4**
		Saxon **9**
		Ten Bompas **15**
		Westcliff **23**

in a *harissa* (a hot North African chili sauce) crust and lamb loin with a pepper-and-rosemary crust. There's always a great fresh pasta selection: spinach fettuccine with olives and roasted eggplant, or ravioli stuffed with roasted butternut, chickpea, ricotta, and fresh herbs. Ciro has that rare quality of making you feel instantly at home. He'll chat with complete strangers as if they had been friends for years. ⊠ *17 4th Ave., Parkhurst* ☎ *011/442–5346* ⚱ *Reservations essential* ⊟ *AE, DC, MC, V* ⊗ *Closed Sun. No dinner Sat.*

$$ ✕ **Yum.** The toast of Johannesburg for the last few years, this restaurant has won more awards than most other places see in their lifetimes.
Fodor's Choice The self-trained chef and owner, Dario De Angeli, makes food that is
★ new and exciting, a product of his single-minded dedication to produce something unique. His "new South African cuisine" is basically a fusion of classic French with an Asian twist made in South Africa—or something like that. Best picks on the extensive menu are the roast duck, served over dried brandied fruits and dusted with lemon zest; smoked-salmon-and-strawberry salad; and fried squid salad served with mixed Asian greens, pickled ginger, and caramelized garlic salsa. All the food is intelligently paired with an appropriate wine by the glass. ⊠ *26 Gleneagles Rd., Greenside* ☎ *011/486–1645* ⚱ *Reservations essential* ⊟ *AE, DC, MC, V* ⊗ *No lunch Mon. No dinner Sun.*

$–$$ ✕ **Café Flo, Oveflo.** This pair of easygoing, unpretentious restaurants always seems to be busy, perhaps because they're right on a corner on a busy restaurant street in Greenside, but more likely because the food is good and cheap. Once Café Flo is full, you "oveflo" next door. You can order from both menus in either one. Café Flo serves unusual pizzas, like roast lamb, or *peri-peri* (a hot chili sauce) prawn. Favorites at Oveflo are prawn-stuffed calamari and duck confit. Oveflo also serves breakfast. ⊠ *116 Greenway, Greenside* ☎ *011/646–6817* ⊟ *AE, DC, MC, V* ⊗ *Closed Sun.*

¢–$$ ✕ **Mastrantonio.** This is the original (and still the best) of the chain of Mastrantonios in Jo'burg. Although it's always packed, the service is surprisingly quick and the food superb. This is *the* place to go for great pastas and unbelievably light, melt-in-your-mouth gnocchi—considered by some locals to be the best in town. Try them with the *forestier* sauce (finely chopped mushrooms in cream) or—an old standby—sage and butter. ⊠ *5c Illovo Centre, Rivonia Rd., Illovo* ☎ *011/268–0901* ⊟ *AE, DC, MC, V* ⊗ *No dinner Sun.–Mon.*

¢–$$ ✕ **Ruby Grapefruit.** This unpretentious little fusion sushi restaurant hasn't run out of customers since it opened in 2000. Dining here is a casual affair and you're never rushed. Besides popular dishes like Thai chicken curry and spring rolls, you can opt for prawn-and-pumpkin soup or fresh oysters from Knysna. There are bagels—*prego* (a Portuguese-inspired steak flavored with garlic) and peppadew (a cross between a sweet pepper and a chili), prawn and avocado—and irreverent spins on sushi, including salmon, cream cheese, and cucumber or avocado and pecan. Ruby Grapefruit serves a good strawberry daiquiri and, usually, live music on Thursday and Friday nights. ⊠ *24c 4th Ave., Parkhurst* ☎ *011/880–3673* ⊟ *DC, MC, V.*

$ ✕ **Butcher Shop and Grill.** This is the best place in town for serious carnivores, with prime South African meat aged to perfection by Alan Pick, the butcher/owner. Game—such as kudu, springbok, and ostrich—appears regularly on the list of specials, and for lighter appetites there are chicken and line fish. Pick also has an excellent cellar. ⊠ *Nelson Mandela Sq., Sandton* ☎ *011/784–8676* ▤ *AE, DC, MC, V.*

$ ✕ **Plaka.** Greek music floats above the buzz of conversation, a souvlaki spit turns slowly near the door, and a refrigerated case displays an array of meze (small appetizers) at this Greek taverna. Most people sit on the roofed terrace or at the few street-side tables; the surprisingly spacious inside dining area has a slightly more formal feel. Start with a couple of glasses of ouzo (an anise-flavor liqueur) and share a platter of souvlaki, feta, olives, cucumber, and tomato. Follow that with a platter of meze, a Greek salad, and a carafe of wine. On weekend evenings belly dancers mingle between the tables, and Greek dancers do the Zorba to a backdrop of ouzo and "controlled" plate breaking. ⊠ *3 Corlett Dr., Illovo* ☎ *011/788–8777* ▤ *AE, DC, MC, V.*

★ ¢–$ ✕ **Cranks.** This funky Thai/Vietnamese restaurant has been a Jo'burg favorite since it opened in the mid-'80s. Brightly colored cloths cover tables that spill out onto the square, and the eclectic decor usually raises an eyebrow or two among passersby. The food is fresh and spicy. Green curries are a classic, but a more interesting choice is the mussels in tamarind sauce. There are also good vegetarian options such as K-B-2, crispy fried baby potatoes with cashews and chili. There's live music on Friday and Saturday nights. ⊠ *Rosebank Mall, Rosebank* ☎ *011/880–3442* ▤ *AE, DC, MC, V.*

¢–$ ✕ **Graasroots.** The surname of the owner is Graas, hence the name. Fresh, innovative vegetarian fare is the order of the day here: vegetable *biryani* (a rice dish) with spicy potatoes; pasta with artichokes, pine nuts, and olive-and-balsamic sauce; and sweet-potato-and-butternut soup. The mango-and-avocado salad is a favorite in summer. Graasroots also makes some of the best smoothies in town, with mango and orange or a velvety papaya. All the cakes are sugar and egg free. ⊠ *Village Walk, Maude St., Sandton* ☎ *011/883–6020* ▤ *AE, DC, MC, V.*

¢–$ ✕ **Singing Fig.** The decor at this extremely popular neighborhood restaurant can only be described as Karoo meets Tuscany, with apricot walls, white tablecloths, and beautiful old globe chairs. The menu, scribbled on a blackboard, changes daily. For starters try the mussels steamed in white wine and flavored with orange and fennel. The duck à l'orange and oxtail are two classics that have regulars coming back time and again. But for something a little different, try the Norwegian salmon skewered with pickled ginger, crusted with lime and wasabi, and grilled. For dessert, indulge in the signature homemade fig-and-vanilla ice cream, made with dried figs cooked in port. ⊠ *44 The Ave., Norwood* ☎ *011/728–2434* ⌕ *Reservations essential* ▤ *AE, DC, MC, V* ☉ *Closed Mon. No dinner Sun.*

Where to Stay

Downtown

$$ ▥ **Protea Hotel Gold Reef City.** Small buildings with Victorian-style wrought-iron trim make up this hotel spread over a large part of the

Gold Reef City theme park. All rooms are furnished in Victorian period style, with claw-foot tubs and reproduction furniture. Since the entire hotel is within the theme park, it's safe to walk around at night—even across the highway on the pedestrian bridge to the nearby casino. ⊠ *Shaft 14, Northern Pkwy., Ormonde* ⬦ *Box 25, Gold Reef City 2159* ☎ *011/248–5700* ⊞ *011/248–5791* ⊕ *www.proteahotels.com* ⌁ *74 rooms* ♿ *Restaurant, pool, bar, casino* ⊟ *AE, DC, MC, V* ⏲*BP.*

$ 🏨 **Protea Parktonian.** Close to the Rotunda (the city's main transportation hub) and the Civic Theatre and just a three-minute drive from the central business district, this Braamfontein property offers the best value in the city as well as a view of the cityscape. Suites are all air-conditioned, and each has a separate lounge and balcony. You can enter the hotel directly from a secure parking garage, and there's a free shuttle to Gold Reef City, Rosebank, and the northern suburbs. A word of warning: though whole city blocks have been gentrified, the neighborhood still isn't safe to walk in at night. ⊠ *120 De Korte St., Braamfontein* ⬦ *Box 32278, Braamfontein 2017* ☎ *011/403–5740* ⊕ *www.proteahotels.com* ⌁ *294 suites* ♿ *2 restaurants, room service, minibars, cable TV, pool, health club, bar* ⊟ *AE, DC, MC, V* ⏲ *BP.*

Northern Suburbs

$$$$ 🏨 **Saxon.** Located in the exclusive suburb of Sandhurst, Saxon was voted
Fodor'sChoice the World's Leading Boutique Hotel by World Travel Awards in 2003.
★ Heads of state stay here, including Nelson Mandela, who came here after his release from prison and to work on his autobiography, *Long Walk to Freedom.* A staff of butlers pride themselves on keeping files on their guests, right down to what they order from the bar. There's a sense of anticipation as you pass through the imposing gates, where you park. You're then driven through what is almost a mini-estate to the hotel. An azure pool adjoins the sleek modern building. Inside, the feeling is calm and classical. Rooms are huge, light, and airy and have big bay windows overlooking gardens or pool; large-screen TVs, DVD players, and surround sound; and a workstation with an ISDN line. The delightful restaurant has a wonderful setting and tasteful African decor. In fact, an extensive African art collection is on display throughout the hotel. ⊠ *36 Saxon Rd., Sandhurst 2132* ☎ *011/292–6000* ⊞ *011/292–6001* ⊕ *www. thesaxon.com* ⌁ *32 suites* ♿ *Restaurant, in-room data ports, minibars, 2 pools, gym, spa, lounge, cinema, library, concierge, meeting rooms* ⊟ *AE, DC, MC, V* ⏲ *BP.*

$$$ 🏨 **The Grace.** Most of the visitors to the Grace are businesspeople, who
Fodor'sChoice are drawn to the old-world elegance behind the towering brick facade
★ and concrete columns. It's also conveniently located in the center of Rosebank and is linked to the nearby mall and African crafts market. Travelers rave about the breakfast, and indeed the restaurant, called simply the Dining Room, has established itself as one of Johannesburg's culinary centers. One of the hotel's finest features is the rooftop garden and pool area, which has amazing views of the northern suburbs' greenery. Another is the service. Thoughtful extras include transportation within a 10-km (6-mi) radius, tea and cake served in the lounge, and separate children's accommodations. ⊠ *Bath and Tyrwhitt Aves., Rosebank*

2196 ☎ *011/280–7200* 🖷 *011/280–7474* ⊕ *www.grace.co.za* ⇗ *60 rooms, 15 suites* ⚷ *Restaurant, pool, gym, hair salon, lounge, airport shuttle* ▤ *AE, DC, MC, V* ⏐◌⏐ *BP.*

$$$ ▥ **Melrose Arch.** Colorful, cool, and trendy, this stylish modern hotel has discreet lighting and odd works of art dotted about. Standard rooms—compact and luxurious—have minibars and coffee stations that fold away into cabinets as well as an entertainment center with a large-ish TV, a DVD player with surround sound, and a tray of free movies. The hotel also furnishes free high-speed Internet access. There's also a wi-fi hot spot in a bar that is set in a library, and in keeping with the modern theme, the restaurant, March, serves fusion food. The pool and deck area looks like something out of *Alice in Wonderland.* Trees are planted in huge steel buckets, and tables and chairs are set in a few inches of water. The pool is heated and has piped underwater music. ⊠ *1 Melrose Sq., Melrose North, 2196* ☎ *011/214–6666* 🖷 *011/214–6600* ⊕ *www. africanpridehotels.com/melrosearch* ⇗ *117 rooms, 1 suite* ⚷ *Restaurant, minibars, pool, bar, library, Internet* ▤ *AE, DC, MC, V.*

$$$ ▥ **The Michelangelo.** As though taken from a street in Florence, this hotel forms the northern facade of much-touted piazza-inspired Sandton Square, now renamed Nelson Mandela Square. But whereas the hotel is unusually tasteful, even grand, the square—to quote a local architect—is to an Italian piazza what Donald Duck is to Swan Lake. Still, this hotel has all the class, comforts, and facilities you'd expect from a top establishment. The atrium-style pool area is notable. The restaurant, Piccolo Mondo, focuses on Mediterranean cuisine, which means plenty of seafood from Mozambique, such as rock cod, prawns, lobsters, langoustines, and mussels. ⊠ *West St., Nelson Mandela Sq., Sandton* ⏍ *Box 784682, Sandton 2146* ☎ *011/282–7000* 🖷 *011/282–7171* ⊕ *www.michelangelo.co.za* ⇗ *242 rooms* ⚷ *Restaurant, room service, cable TV, pool, health club, sauna, 2 bars* ▤ *AE, DC, MC, V.*

★ **$$$** ▥ **Ten Bompas.** This boutique hotel has consistently been voted one of the best places to stay in Johannesburg. There are other boutique hotels and guesthouses in the northern suburbs, but none quite match the élan of this eclectic hotel-cum-restaurant and art gallery. It's small and luxurious, and the decor is minimalist, with carefully chosen African art. Suites, each done by a different interior designer, have separate lounges and bedrooms, fireplaces, complimentary minibars, satellite TV, and sound systems. You can also ogle brochures for the hotel's luxurious game lodges in the far north of Kruger National Park. Sides, the restaurant, turns in consistently good reviews. Its seasonal menu changes four times a year. The food is exciting and fresh: roasted artichoke, mozzarella, and olive salad and roast-duck-and-orange risotto, for example. It also has a well-stocked cellar. ⊠ *10 Bompas Rd., Dunkeld West* ⏍ *Box 786064, Sandton 2146* ☎ *011/325–2442* 🖷 *011/341–0281* ⊕ *www.tenbompas. com* ⇗ *10 suites* ⚷ *Restaurant, in-room fax, minibars, pool, bar, meeting rooms* ▤ *AE, DC, MC, V* ⏐◌⏐ *BP.*

★ **$$$** ▥ **Westcliff.** This hotel was built on a steep hill and it has amazing views of the northern suburbs. You are ferried to your destination by a shuttle service, winding your way up twisting lanes. Bedrooms are in multistory villas, each with its own balcony. The feeling is cozy Mediterranean, courtesy of soft pink buildings that blend with the sandstone foundations. Enormous bathrooms have marble vanities and huge soaking tubs. The cuisine, service, and facilities are all top-notch. ⊠ *67 Jan Smuts Ave., Westcliff 2193* ☎ *011/646–2400* 🖷 *011/646–3500* ⊕ *www. westcliffhotel.orient-express.com* 🛏 *104 rooms, 14 suites* ⚭ *2 restaurants, room service, in-room data ports, in-room fax, tennis court, pool, gym, hair salon, bar, business services* ▤ *AE, DC, MC, V.*

$$–$$$ 🏨 **InterContinental Sandton Sun & Towers.** These two high-rise hotels are right next to Johannesburg's favorite mall, Sandton City, and the adjoining Nelson Mandela Square. The focal point of each hotel is a central atrium soaring the height of the building. Guest rooms are small but superbly laid out, with understated lighting and elegant decorative touches. There is little to recommend one hotel over the other, although the towers are smaller and farther removed from the bustle of Sandton City. The towers also have two full floors of executive suites, which have their own bar, breakfast room, and full-time staff. ⊠ *Sandton City, 5th St. and Alice La., Sandton 2146* ☎ *011/780–5000* 🖷 *011/780–5002* ⊕ *www.southernsun.com* 🛏 *Sun: 311 rooms, 22 suites; Towers: 214 rooms, 17 suites* ⚭ *5 restaurants, room service, minibars, cable TV, health club, hair salon, sauna, laundry service, concierge floor, Internet, business services* ▤ *AE, DC, MC, V.*

$$ 🏨 **Balalaika.** The large garden here—a rarity in Jo'burg—sets this hotel apart from other similar northern suburb properties. It's conveniently located in the middle of Sandton and connected to the Village Walk shopping mall by a pedestrian walkway. It is actually two hotels run as one, each with its own character. The Crown Court is somewhat smarter, with bigger rooms, separate showers in all the bathrooms, and in-room dedicated modem lines. ⊠ *20 Maude St., Sandton* 🖃 *Box 783372, Sandton 2146* ☎ *011/322–5000* 🖷 *011/322–5023* ⊕ *www.proteahotels.com* 🛏 *301 rooms, 24 suites* ⚭ *2 restaurants, in-room data ports, minibars, 2 pools, bar, meeting rooms* ▤ *AE, DC, MC, V.*

★ $$ 🏨 **Palazzo at Montecasino.** Built in the style of a Tuscan villa, the hotel is set among formal herb gardens. Public rooms are on a grand scale, and the whole is decorated in gilt, marble, and terra-cotta, with small touches of trompe l'oeil. The rooms are spacious, with rich tapestry-style draperies, canopied beds, and gilt-framed mirrors and prints. Large picture windows and light terra-cotta tiles lighten the effect. The hotel is done with so much more style, attention to detail, and class than the adjacent casino and mall that it's almost impossible to believe they're connected. This is a good choice for a business stay. Service is impeccable. ⊠ *Montecasino Blvd., Fourways* 🖃 *Private Bag X125, Bryanston 2021* ☎ *011/510–3000* 🖷 *011/510–4000* ⊕ *www.ichotelsgroup.com* 🛏 *246 rooms, 12 suites* ⚭ *Restaurant, in-room data ports, in-room fax, cable TV, pool, gym, bar, casino, business services, meeting rooms* ▤ *AE, DC, MC, V.*

$$ 🏨 **Park Hyatt Hotel.** This Hyatt gleams with lots of black, gold, and glass. Enormous picture windows reveal stunning views of the northern suburbs. Should you book one of the Regency Club suites, you'll have complimentary cocktails and even more glorious views. Local art lines the walls in discreetly lighted passageways, and there's an ultramodern restaurant, a wine bar, and a solar-heated pool on the roof. Sunday brunch is a favorite with guests and local families alike. ⊠ *191 Oxford Rd., Rosebank* ⬧ *Box 1536, Saxonwold 2132* ☎ *011/280–1234* 🖨 *011/280–1238* ⊕ *www.johannesburg.park.hyatt.com* ⟿ *244 rooms* ⬧ *2 restaurants, room service, in-room data ports, pool, health club, bar, babysitting, laundry service, airport shuttle, car rental* ▤ *AE, DC, MC, V.*

Nightlife & the Arts

The best place to find out what's going on in town is in the "Tonight" section of *The Star,* Johannesburg's major daily. For a comprehensive guide, get the "Friday" supplement of the weekly *Mail & Guardian* (⊕ www. mg.co.za). *Time Out* publishes a useful Johannesburg guide in magazine format, which includes information on Tshwane (Pretoria), too. A useful Web site for event details is **JHBLive** (⊕ www.jhblive.com). Almost all major performances and many smaller ones can be booked through **Computicket** (☎ 083/915–8000 ⊕ www.computicket.com).

Nightlife

Johannesburg comes alive after dark, and whether you are a rebellious punk rocker or a suave executive in search of a classy lounge, there is always something to do. Rivonia has become a trendy spot for advertising executives and their style-conscious friends, and the old neighborhood of Melville still has streets filled with comfortable, lively little bars and restaurants and the odd club or two. The Newtown Cultural Precinct, an old area that started as a produce market, has undergone a successful rejuvenation. Now clean and brightly lighted, it's home to the Market Theatre complex, Carfax, and other entertainment venues. The largely Jewish suburb of Norwood also has a central street with a good selection of small restaurants and bars. Rosebank used to have clubs, but rezoning put an end to that. To dine and dance in one go, you should venture to the classy Melrose Arch or visit one of the casino complexes, such as the popular Montecasino in Fourways or Caesars Gauteng next to the Jo'burg airport.

BARS & PUBS   Dress stylishly for **Café Vacca Matta** (⊠ Montecasino, William Nicol Dr., Fourways ☎ 011/511–0511), a trendy bar and restaurant where a ★ sometimes snobbish crowd dances to top-40 hits. **Capitol Music Café** (⊠ Tyrwhitt and Keyes Aves., Rosebank ☎ 011/880–0033) is a hip and happening vinyl shop and bar, where DJs play what they have just bought and an eclectic crowd gathers to sip cocktails. It's a good place ★ to find out where the hottest parties will be. **Color Bar** (⊠ 44 Stanley Ave., Auckland Park ☎ 011/482–2038) is a fun, trendy hangout with a courtyard and an indoor section where DJs play Thursday–Saturday. Now and then a band pops up to entertain the media types and their creative friends who frequent the bar. Wednesdays are jazz nights, and food is served until 10. **Cool Runnings** (⊠ 4th Ave., Melville ☎ 011/482–4786) is a lively, reggae-themed Gauteng chain of bars, where rock bands and stand-up comedians often perform. The huge Jo'burg branch has excellent stand-up comedy on Sunday nights.

KWAITO

KWAITO IS A UNIQUELY SOUTH AFRICAN *music genre, rooted in house, ragga, hip-hop, and local rhythms. It emerged from the* country's townships post-apartheid and gets its name, some say, from township slang for "cool talk." Its hard-pumping bass beats, lightly slowed down from a house rhythm, are topped with rambled-off lyrics in which you might hear a dash of American rap. It's as much a lifestyle as it is a music genre, with its own ways of dancing and dressing.

The best-selling kwaito musicians (and kwaito DJs) have superstar status in South Africa, but they have a less unsavory reputation than their American hip-hop equivalents. Though some kwaito acts stand accused of sexism and vulgar lyrics, the kwaito attitude is generally respectable. Lyrics are often about banning guns or respecting women, or they comment on murder, rape, AIDS, and unemployment. One kwaito star, Zola—named after an impoverished Soweto community—has his own long-running TV series, in which he works to improve people's lives. Other chart-topping kwaito stars include Mandoza, whose catchy, powerful songs have earned him several awards and crossover appeal; Arthur; South African Music Award–winning group Mafikizolo; Mdu; the Brothers of Peace; and Mzekezeke, an enigmatic masked singer.

Unfortunately, many up-and-coming kwaito acts don't get much further than one-hit-wonder status due to a lack of creative support in the fast-moving industry. Once ignored by major record labels, kwaito has spawned several smaller independent labels.

— *Riaan Wolmarans*

Designer venue **88** (⊠ 114 Ivy Rd., Norwood ☎ 011/728–9283) has a retro feel to the beat of drum 'n' bass, funk, soul, and jazz Tuesday–Saturday. **Katzy's** (⊠ The Firs, Cradock Ave., Rosebank ☎ 011/447–5162) is a stylish cigar lounge where the wealthy and connected get together over a stogie or an expensive single-malt whiskey. Often a jazz or cover band plays. **Merely Mortal** (⊠ 356 Jan Smuts Ave., Craighall ☎ 011/501–3385) plays dub, electro, world funk, and more Thursday–Saturday. You can admire the funky local art while chatting with the interesting characters who frequent this gallery-cum-restaurant-cum-bar. The upscale **Mo's** (⊠ Grant Ave., Norwood ☎ 011/728–8256) offers not-too-hectic music—chilled lounge beats, drum 'n' bass, R&B, and deep house—all week long to go with a glass of red wine.

Fodor'sChoice ★ Lounge, bar, and restaurant **Ninetysix** (⊠ Witkoppen and Main Rds., Fourways ☎ 011/467–6696) has a stylish interior and a simple but stunning menu. It's open Wednesday–Saturday, with DJs playing easy house and jazz most nights. **Oh!** (⊠ 4th Ave. and Main Rd., Melville ☎ 011/482–4789) is the city's busiest gay bar. On summer weekend nights an entertaining and stylish crowd gathers on the balcony, which is also perfect for sundowners (cocktails) while watching the sun set over Melville.

At the Westcliff, one of Jo'burg's most stylish hotels, the **Polo Lounge** (✉ 67 Jan Smuts Ave., Westcliff ☎ 011/646–2400) is a sexy spot with an excellent view from up high across the city's northern suburbs. It's a good spot for pricey sundowners, and you might just run into a music or movie star. The **Radium Beer Hall** (✉ Louis Botha Ave. and 9th St., Orange Grove ☎ 011/728–3866) opened in 1929, and is one of the oldest pubs still operating in the city. It's got spicy Portuguese food accompanied by blues and jazz on Wednesday, Friday, and Saturday.

★ Melville's **7th Street** brings together several blocks of small restaurants, shops, bars, and lounges. If you're feeling up for a night of pub-crawling, this is the place to go. It varies from stylish spots, such as the Mozambique-style Xai Xai Lounge to glitzy, vibey bars, such as Unplugged on 7th, Six, Trans.Sky, gay lounge Statement, psychedelic trance hangout Trance Sky, Buzz 9, and the kitsch-but-cool Tokyo Star, which is frequented by an energetic twentysomething crowd.

CLUBS Jo'burg's clubs are usually not too expensive, depending on what events are taking place. On a normal club night, or for B-list local bands, you will pay between R20 and R50 to get in. When dance parties or bigger events take place (or big-name DJs and musicians appear), you will have to pay R60 to R150. Below are just some of the city's established clubs.

Yeoville and Hillbrow used to be hot spots for nightlife in the 1980s and 1990s; this is true no more. Crime is rife in these areas, and they are best avoided. Though the Newtown Cultural Precinct has been much enhanced, it is still not an entirely safe area at night, so take care, especially if you are unaccompanied.

★ **Back 2 Basix** (✉ Perth and Lancaster Rds., Westdene ☎ 011/726–6857) is a comfortable restaurant and music venue with top local folk, pop, and rock musicians performing weekends and most weeknights. Best of ★ all, you can have a beer with the band afterward. **Back o' the Moon** (✉ Gold Reef City Casino, Ormonde ☎ 011/496–1423) is a sophisticated re-creation of a 1950s-style nightclub. There's good live jazz to counter the clanging slot machines outside. It's closed Monday. The **Blues Room** (✉ Village Walk, Sandton ☎ 011/784–5527) is one of the city's most stylish and dependable blues, rock, and jazz venues. It serves good food and is open Tuesday–Sunday with music on most nights. At **Café Vogue** (✉ 9th and Wessels Sts., Rivonia ☎ 011/234–9515), DJs play R&B and hip-hop on Thursdays and soulful house on weekends for the ever-so-stylish Rivonia crowd, made up of advertising executives and wannabe software millionaires. Dress in smart casual or stay outside.

Fodor'sChoice Some of the city's biggest parties happen at **Carfax** (✉ 39 Pim St., New-★ town ☎ 011/834–9187), a converted factory building. Performance art, dance events with guest DJs, and rock shows draw an eclectic selection of the town's more interesting people. After many years and a move into the suburbs, **the Doors** (✉ 19 Van Riebeeck Ave., Edenvale ☎ 011/453–7673) still delivers solid rock, alternative, and metal classics and current favorites to a twentysomething crowd, especially on Fridays and Saturdays. Bands often play. The atmospheric **Horror Café** (✉ 15 Becker St., Newtown ☎ 011/838–6735) is decked out with horror, sci-fi, and B-movie memorabilia over three stories. Thursdays bring reggae, ragga, and dance-hall nights, and Fridays and Saturdays have eclectic events. Sundays often see traditional and modern African music and poetry.

Close to the Jo'burg airport, **Monsoon Lagoon** (⊠ Caesars Gauteng, 64 Jones Rd., Kempton Park ☎ 011/928–1280) is a glittery upscale casino hangout with weekend party nights ranging from bhangra (Punjabi folk music) bashes to commercial R&B, kwaito, and dance events. **115** (⊠ 115 Anderson St., City Center ☎ 011/331–2878) is a small, vibrant club playing drum 'n' bass and deep house on Fridays, now and then with a dash of hip-hop. Since the late 1980s, **Roxy's** (⊠ 20 Main Rd., Melville ☎ 011/726–6019) has brought the country's best new and old rock bands to a rowdy, energetic student crowd. The best bands play on the weekend. Rascasse cocktail bar, in the same complex, has good cocktails and sometimes stand-up comedy or music. A bit farther afield, **Who Zoo** (⊠ 16 Alexander Rd., Midrand ☎ 083/283–4916) attracts a fashionably dressed crowd for kwaito, R&B, and house on Saturday nights, sometimes live.

The Arts

CLASSICAL MUSIC The **Linder Auditorium** (⊠ St. Andrews Rd., Wits Education Campus, Parktown ☎ 011/643–6413) hosts classical performances by top-notch singers, instrumentalists, and orchestras almost every week. It's the home of the Johannesburg Philharmonic Orchestra's seasonal series. At the restaurant **Montpellier de Tulbagh** (⊠ 7th and 3rd Aves., Parktown ☎ 011/880–1946) you can drink a glass of wine in style and splendor to the accompaniment of the country's best opera singers on Sundays. A bit far out of town, the **Pro Musica Theatre** (⊠ Christiaan de Wet Rd., Florida Park, Roodepoort ☎ 011/672–2217) has a year-round program of classical music and dance and its own orchestra, the Sasol Pro Musica Orchestra.

FILM The best art-house and foreign-language films from around the world Fodor'sChoice are shown at the large **Cinema Nouveau** (⊠ Rosebank Mall, Bath Ave., ★ Rosebank ☎ 011/445–7000, 083/915–8000 Computicket ⊕ www. sterkinekor.com). Movies change every Friday, and several film festivals, such as the glamorous Gay and Lesbian Film Festival (usually in March), run every year.

THEATER The **Civic Theatre** (⊠ Loveday St., Braamfontein ☎ 011/877–6800 ⊕ www.showbusiness.co.za) is Jo'burg's main cultural venue. Housed in a slick, modern complex, the Civic contains the enormous Nelson Mandela Theatre as well as the smaller People's and Tesson theaters. Many productions have a South African focus, such as works by local talents Pieter-Dirk Uys and playwright and actor Paul Slabolepszy.

Occupying an old produce market that dates from the early 1900s, the **Market Theatre** (⊠ Bree and Wolhuter Sts., Newtown ☎ 011/832–1641 ⊕ www.markettheatre.co.za) has a delightful vintage look and feel. Now completely refurbished, the three-theater complex keeps the flag of high-quality and experimental theater flying, attracting a cosmopolitan crowd of theater fans, art lovers, and jazz aficionados. Theater productions encompass everything from plays by Athol Fugard and Gibson Kente to comedies imported from London's West End. The theater occasionally features traditional African music and jazz performances. Experimental plays test audience approval at the Market Theatre Laboratory, just across Bree Street. The complex also has a great bar and restaurant, an art gallery with changing exhibits, and an interesting collection of antiques stores and African art shops.

The **Liberty Theater on the Square** (⊠ Nelson Mandela Sq., Maude and West Sts., Sandton ☎ 011/883–8606) is a smaller theater, easily accessible from the restaurants on Nelson Mandela Square. It often stages high-quality productions that run for some time. **Pieter Toerien's Montecasino Theatre** (⊠ Montecasino, William Nicol Dr., Fourways ☎ 011/511–1988), a large casino venue, often hosts famous playwright and satirist Pieter-Dirk Uys's satirical shows, comedies, and appearances by international theater stars.

The city has many smaller venues that cater to experimental and amateur productions, such as the stately **Windybrow Theater** (⊠ 161 Nugget St., city center ☎ 011/720–7009), built in 1896. The **Wits Theater Complex** (⊠ University of the Witwatersrand, Jorissen St., Braamfontein ☎ 011/717–1732) is a center of student drama. All the town's casino complexes have a cabaret venue or two hidden among the slot machines.

Sports & the Outdoors

Adventure Sports

There are all sorts of adventures available around Jo'burg on land, water, and in the air. Many outfitters offer several options and even combination trips. **Air Routes** (☎ 011/768–6822 ⊕ airroutesadventures.co.za) offers scenic flights in a vintage DC-3 Dakota aircraft—mass produced for transport during World War II—over Johannesburg and the Hartbeespoort Dam, followed by a buffet breakfast at Wings, the restaurant at Lanseria Airport. Sparkling wine and orange juice are served during the flight, which costs R760. **Icarus Skydiving School** (☎ 011/452–8858 ⊕ www.icarus.co.za) has first-jump courses and tandem jumps for beginners and regular jumps for experienced skydivers. It's expensive, though, with prices from about R1,500. **Pure Rush Industries** (☎ 082/605–1150 ⊕ www.purerush.co.za) will take you sand-boarding down a mine dump for R200 or abseiling (rappelling) off a building (R200 for three jumps). **River Tours and Safaris** (☎ 011/803–9775 ⊕ www.rafting.co.za) offers one-day rafting trips through some small rapids on the Vaal River near Johannesburg, as well as rappelling and other thrilling activities at a river camp. The cost for a day trip is R300, including breakfast and lunch. **Sunwa Ventures** (☎ 056/817–7107 ⊕ www.sunwa.co.za) is based at Parys, on the Vaal River, about an hour's drive from Johannesburg. It offers short, easy white-water trips, helicopter rides, paintball, and fly-fishing, among other activities.

Cricket

South Africa loves cricket, and many South Africans take off work to watch tests against other nations. The **Wanderers Club** (⊠ 21 North St.,

Illovo ☎ 011/788–5010) is the country's premier cricket ground and the site of many international contests between South Africa and touring sides from England and its former colonies. Unfortunately, a fire in 2003 destroyed much of the club's old, impressive buildings.

Fishing

SA Fly Fishing Safaris (☎ 082/885–0589 or 082/881–5789) can show you where and how to catch indigenous yellow fish or trout. It offers weekend clinics (from R1,200) and one-day clinics (from R500), as well as countrywide guided tours and safaris (from R1,700).

Golf

Johannesburg's finest golf courses are open to foreign visitors, although weekend play is sometimes restricted to members only. Expect to pay R300–R400 for a round. You can rent clubs for about R160–R350, depending on the set, from **Allan Henning Golf Shop** (☎ 011/485–4899 or 011/640-3021) at the Royal Johannesburg Golf Club.

The beautiful, par-73 **Bryanston Country Club** (⊠ Bryanston Dr., Bryanston ☎ 011/706–1361) has water hazards on 13 of its 18 holes. **Glendower Club** (⊠ Marais Rd., Bedfordview ☎ 011/453–1013) is within a bird sanctuary. The 85 bunkers, numerous water hazards, and extra length (6.7 km [4.1 mi]) make this one of the most challenging courses in the country. The **Houghton Golf Club** (⊠ 2nd Ave., Lower Houghton ☎ 011/728–7337) is a good-quality course that used to host the South African Open. Near the Houghton Golf Club is the 18-hole **Killarney Golf Club** (⊠ 60 5th St., Lower Houghton ☎ 011/442–7411). The **Royal Johannesburg and Kensington Golf Club** (⊠ Fairway Ave., Linksfield North ☎ 011/640–3021) is more than 100 years old and a favorite of golfing legend Gary Player. It has two courses, each more than 6 km (nearly 4 mi) long. The East Course is the more popular of the two and has hosted the South African Open seven times. The club has a golf academy and a driving range. The scenic 18-hole **Wanderers Golf Club** (⊠ Corlett and Rudd Rds., Illovo ☎011/447–3311) was designed in 1939 and counts many local celebrities among its members.

Horseback Riding & Horse Shows

At the **Inanda Club** (⊠ 1 Forest Rd., Illovo ☎ 082/489–8208), beginners and experienced riders can sometimes clock in for an afternoon gallop, depending on the availability of horses.

Midway between Johannesburg and Tshwane, the **Lipizzaner Centre** (⊠ 1 Dahlia Rd., Kyalami, Midrand ☎ 011/702–2103) is home to the stunning white Lippizaner stallions, distinguished purebred horses with a centuries-old lineage. The horses are trained in the classic Spanish riding style, and during their weekly dressage shows (Sundays at 10:30, R70) perform a complex ballet of exercises to the strains of Verdi, Mozart, and Handel.

Rugby

South Africa's showcase rugby stadium is **Ellis Park** (⊠ Staib St., Doornfontein ☎ 011/402–8644), where the Springboks beat New Zealand's All Blacks to win the 1995 World Cup, a crowning moment in South

African rugby history. It's a magnificent stadium, capable of seating nearly 65,000 people. **SA Rugby** (⊕ www.sarugby.net) has details on matches.

Soccer

Soccer has a far bigger following in South Africa than either rugby or cricket. The most popular teams in the country are legendary Johannesburg rivals: the Orlando Pirates and the Kaizer Chiefs. Though soccer fans rarely resort to hooliganism, matches do get very loud, with many fans blowing hard on their *vuvuzelas* (a long, thin, and very loud trumpet) to signal their excitement. Games are played all over the city, but the biggest matches are at Ellis Park (⇨ Rugby, *above*) and the large **FNB Stadium** (⊠ Nasrec Rd., Nasrec ☎ 011/494–3640). Ticket prices depend on the match, and most tickets can be booked through **Computicket** (☎ 083/915–8000 ⊕ www.computicket.com).

Shopping

Whether you're after designer clothes, the latest books or DVDs, high-quality African art, or glamorous gifts, Johannesburg offers outstanding shopping opportunities. Dozens of galleries and curio shops are scattered throughout the city, often selling the same goods at widely different prices. It's best to shop around.

Malls

Johannesburg has more malls than seems healthy, especially in the northern suburbs, where new ones appear almost overnight. Most are quite exclusive, with shops selling the latest from Italy, France, and the States, but you might get it cheaper at home. Most malls also have department stores, such as Edgars and Woolworths (which stocks good-quality food and clothes), as well as movie theaters and plenty of restaurants and fast-food outlets. Mall hours are usually Monday–Saturday 9–5, 9–2 on Sunday.

In the city center, the towering **Carlton Centre** (⊠ Commissioner and Von Weilligh Sts., city center ☎ 011/308–1331) houses a large mall of 200-odd shops that has recently been renovated and attracts plenty of attention again. A bonus is that you can go to the top of the center for an unparalleled view of the city.

You can eat a spicy samosa and haggle over the massive selection of textiles, clothes, and the like at the maze of little shops in the **Oriental Plaza** (⊠ Bree St., Fordsburg ☎ 011/838–6752), where you're sure to find a bargain.

Rosebank is a lively suburb surrounding a cluster of shopping centers. The **Rosebank Mall** (⊠ Bath Ave., Rosebank ☎ 011/788–5530) has a good selection of shops as well as Cinema Nouveau, Jo'burg's art-house complex. Across the street, the **Zone** (⊠ Oxford Rd., Rosebank ☎ 011/788–1130) is a bright, trendy mall aimed at under-25s (not as classy as the Rosebank Mall). It contains clothing stores, a cinema, Exclusive Books, bowling, and the massive CD Wherehouse. It's also where hip youth radio station Yfm, with about 2 million listeners, has its headquarters. The Zone runs into **Mutual Gardens** (⊠ Oxford Rd., Rosebank ☎ 011/

788–1130), another center in the block defined by Biermann Avenue, Baker Street, Oxford Road, and Bath Street. Here you can safely walk among boutiques and outdoor cafés. On the other side of the Zone, the **Firs** (✉ Cradock Ave., Rosebank ☎ 011/448–3800) has more small shops, a deli, secondhand bookstores, and the like.

Hyde Park Corner (✉ 6th and Jan Smuts Aves., Hyde Park ☎ 011/325–4340) is an upscale shopping center where fashion victims sip cappuccinos and browse in Exclusive Books, a major branch of the country's best chain of bookstores.

Melrose Arch (✉ 32 Melrose Blvd., Melrose North ☎ 011/684–0000) is a shopping, residential, and business district where you can walk among sidewalk cafés and specialty shops. When night falls, savor North African flavors at Moyo.

The major mall in Johannesburg is **Sandton City** (✉ Sandton Dr. and Rivonia Rd., Sandton ☎ 011/217–6000), which has almost 300 stores, a rather confusing layout, and a tax refund center for tourists. The wing of shops leading to the neighboring Sandton Sun hotel has some worthwhile African art galleries. Adjoining Sandton City is **Nelson Mandela Square** (✉ 5th St., Sandton ☎ 011/217–6000), which vaguely resembles an Italian piazza, complete with expensive Italian shops, an ice-cream parlor, sushi joints, and restaurants surrounding a 20-foot bronze statue of Mandela.

Montecasino (✉ William Nicol Dr., Fourways ☎ 011/510–7777) is a reproduction of a Tuscan village with a ceiling painted to resemble the sky. Some hate it, some love it, but it's a favorite tourist destination nonetheless, attracting up to a million people a year. It contains many restaurants, movie theaters, and a central casino.

Markets

At the city's several markets, bargaining—although not expected as much as in some other countries—can still get you a bargain price. But watch out for inferior goods, pirated DVDs and CDs, and fake designer clothes.

The **African Craft Market**, between the Rosebank Mall and the Zone, has more African crafts and curios than you can shake a wooden giraffe at, all to the beat of traditional African music. ✉ *Bath Ave., Rosebank* ☎ *011/880–2906* ⊘ *Daily 9–5.*

Bigger is better at **Bruma Market World**, one of the biggest flea markets in South Africa. You'll find anything you can imagine here—and probably a whole lot you can't. Search for it between the West African wood crafts, "designer" clothing (but check the quality before you buy), wire sculptures, cheap plastic gadgets, home crafts, homemade toys, and the like. African dancers perform twice daily. ✉ *Ernest Oppenheimer and Marcia Sts., Bruma* ☎ *011/622–9647* ⊘ *Tues.–Fri. and Sun. 9:30–5, Sat. 8:30–5.*

For a selection of crafts, you can venture north to the **Crafters Market**, which also sells a range of African goods. ✉ *Fourways Crossing, William Nicol Dr., Fourways* ☎ *011/705–2125* ⊘ *Mon.–Sat. 9–5:30, Sun. 9–2:30.*

Into healthful living? Then visit the **Michael Mount Organic Market,** where a variety of homemade and organically grown food, flowers, and other products clamor for your clean-living attention. Remember to taste the cheeses. ✉ *Bryanston and Culross Aves., Bryanston* ☎ *011/706–3671* ⊘ *Thurs. 9–1, Sat. 9–2.*

Newtown Market Africa, across the street from the Market Theatre, is a good option for African art and artifacts. Craftspeople from as far away as Cameroon and Zaire sell their masks, wooden artworks, decorative cloths, and blankets, often at prices that are cheaper than elsewhere in town. This is a good place to try to bargain a little. ✉ *Bree and Wolhuter Sts., Newtown* ☎ *083/732–0302* ⊘ *Sat. 9–5.*

Rosebank's **Rooftop Market** has become a Sunday tradition in the city. More than 500 stalls sell African and Western crafts, antiques, books, food, art, trinkets, CDs, and clothes. Frequently African musicians, dancers, and other entertainers delight the roving crowds. ✉ *Rosebank Mall, 50 Bath Ave., Rosebank* ☎ *011/442–4488* ⊘ *Sun. 9–5.*

Specialty Stores

AFRICAN ARTS &
CRAFTS

Art Africa brings together a dazzling selection of ethnic arts, crafts, and artifacts from across the continent, and also sells funky items produced in self-help projects, such as tin lizards and wooden animals. ✉ *62 Tyrone Ave., Parkview* ☎ *011/486–2052.*

The **Bus Factory** is an old bus depot that's now a busy hub of South African craft, with workshops and displays that don't always seem to be in any particular order. The Beautiful Things shop is a good source of indigenous work, from beadwork to baskets to wooden objects. ✉ *President and Goch Sts., Newtown* ☎ *011/834–9569.*

The **Everard Read Gallery,** established in 1912, is one of the largest privately owned galleries in the world. It acts as agent for several important South African artists as well as a number of international contemporary artists. The gallery specializes in wildlife paintings and sculpture. ✉ *6 Jellicoe Ave., Rosebank* ☎ *011/788–4805.*

The highly successful, three-decade-old **Goodman Gallery** presents exciting monthly exhibitions by the stars of contemporary South African art, including Norman Catherine, William Kentridge and Deborah Bell. ✉ *163 Jan Smuts Ave., Parkwood* ☎ *011/788–1113.*

The **Kim Sacks Gallery,** in a lovely old home, has a superb collection of authentic African art. Displayed throughout its sunny rooms are Zairian raffia cloth, Mali mud cloth, Zulu telephone-wire baskets, wood sculptures, and original masks and carvings from across the continent. It's also a good place to find ceramic art. Prices are high. ✉ *153 Jan Smuts Ave., Parkwood* ☎ *011/447–5804.*

Go to **Rural Craft** for Xhosa and Ndebele beadwork, including wedding aprons and jewelry. It also sells fabrics made by rural Ndebele, Xhosa, and Zulu women. ✉ *Mutual Gardens, 31 Tyrwhitt Ave., Rosebank* ☎ *011/788–5821.*

Totem Gallery specializes in artifacts from west and central Africa, including Kuba cloth from Zaire, Dogon doors from Mali, glass beads, masks from Burkina Faso, and hand-painted barbershop signs. Some pieces come with detailed descriptions of their history. Prices are high. ⊠ *U17 Sandton City, Sandton* ☎ *011/884–6300* ⊠ *The Firs, Rosebank* ☎ *011/447–1409.*

Warren Siebrits Modern and Contemporary Art is a respected gallery for the country's best contemporary artists, such as Gerard Sekoto, Lucas Sithole, and Dumile Feni, as well as the art of local printmakers. The gallery's shows are well curated and accompanied by high-quality catalogs. ⊠ *140 Jan Smuts Ave., Parkwood* ☎ *011/327–0000.*

BOOKS If you're just looking for something cheap to read on vacation or for out-of-print books at rock-bottom prices, go to one of the **Bookdealers** chain of secondhand bookstores for an excellent selection. ⊠ *Mutual Gardens, Rosebank* ⊠ *011/442–4089* ⊠ *12 7th St., Melville* ☎ *011/ 726–4054* ⊠ *Rivonia Sq., Rivonia* ☎ *011/234–0486.*

Exclusive Books is the best chain of bookstores in the country, with an impressive selection of African literature, history, travel, and culture. You can select a book, order a designer coffee from the in-store Seattle Coffee Company, and read in comfort all day. ⊠ *Sandton City, Sandton* ☎ *011/883–1010* ⊠ *Hyde Park Corner, Hyde Park* ☎ *011/325–4298* ⊠ *The Zone, Rosebank* ☎ *011/327–5736* ⊠ *Rosebank Mall, Rosebank* ☎ *011/784–5419.*

GOLD & Krugerrands, which carry images of President Paul Kruger and a springDIAMONDS bok on either side, are among the most famous gold coins minted today. They lost some of their luster during the apartheid years, when they were banned internationally. Krugerrands are sold individually or in sets containing coins of 1 ounce, ½ ounce, ¼ ounce, and ¹⁄₁₀ ounce of pure gold. You can buy Krugerrands through most city banks, and several branches of First National Bank sell them over the counter. The most convenient branches are in Sandton City and Rosebank.

South Africa is also diamond country The world's biggest diamond, the 3,106-carat Cullinan, was found in the town of the same name (near present-day Tshwane) in 1905, and is now among the British crown jewels. For a comprehensive list of diamond retailers, contact the **Shining Light of South Africa** (☎ 011/880–0230 ⊕ www.sadiamond.com).

Charles Greig (⊠ Hyde Park Corner, Jan Smuts Ave., Hyde Park ☎ 011/ 325–4477) is an upmarket jeweler selling a dazzling array of diamonds.

Schwartz Jewellers (⊠ Sandton City, Sandton ☎ 011/783–1717) is a diamond wholesaler and manufacturing jeweler. It offers a large range of classical and ethnic African pieces as well as a custom design service.

For something shiny but less expensive, try **De Klerk's Coppersmith** (⊠ 24 Currey St., Doornfontein ☎ 011/402–7644). The only remaining authentic coppersmith in South Africa, it turns out coal scuttles, candlesticks, brass products, and even bathtubs.

TSHWANE (FORMERLY PRETORIA)

Tshwane is overshadowed by Johannesburg, 48 km (30 mi) to the south, and few people outside South Africa know that it's the country's administrative capital. It's a pleasant city, with many historic buildings and a city center that is easily explored on foot.

Founded in 1855, the city was originally named after Afrikaner leader Andries Pretorius, the hero of the Battle of Blood River (1838) and one of the Voortrekkers who moved from the Cape to escape British rule. For many years the city remained a bastion of Afrikaner culture. In 1860 Pretoria was named the capital of the independent Transvaal Voortrekker Republic, and in the late 1870s the Transvaal war of independence was successfully waged against the British, who wished to annex the area (the proclamation of annexation was read on Church Square). The British withdrew—temporarily. After the South African War of 1899–1902 (also called the second Anglo-Boer War), however, the city became the capital of the then British colony, and in 1910 it was named the administrative capital of the Union of South Africa. Jumping ahead to 1948, when the National Party came to power, Pretoria also became the seat of the apartheid government, and the city developed a reputation for hard-line insularity. In 1964 the Rivonia treason trial (named for the Johannesburg suburb where 19 ANC leaders had been arrested in 1963) was held here, and Nelson Mandela and seven of his colleagues were sentenced to life imprisonment.

Early in 2005 the Tshwane metropolitan council, which is responsible for all the areas within the municipality (including not just the city but also nearby Centurion; the sprawling townships of Atteridgeville, Mamelodi, and Soshanguve; and other neighboring areas), decided to rename the entire city structure Tshwane. The name is a reference to the indigenous people who lived in the area before the first white Afrikaners arrived. The name Pretoria is still used for the city center, however, which is now basically a neighborhood of Tshwane. At time of writing, the council was planning to change the names of most of the city center's major streets.

Much has changed in recent years, and the country's democratically elected president now occupies the stately Union Buildings overlooking the city. Tshwane is also home to many foreign embassies and personnel, bringing a refreshing cosmopolitan air to the city, which also boasts the glossy South African Reserve Bank building. One thing that doesn't change is the many clusters of jacaranda trees, which blanket the city with their purple blossoms in spring (September–October).

Numbers in the text correspond to numbers in the margin and on the Tshwane (Pretoria) map.

a good tour

If you're coming from Johannesburg, your first stop should be the **Voortrekker Monument and Museum** ⓴. To get there, take the N1, and, where it branches, take the R28 to the Eeufees Road exit. At the traffic light at the bottom of the exit, turn left. (Alternatively, you can turn right first to relax at **Fountains Valley** ㉑.) Turn right at the next lights,

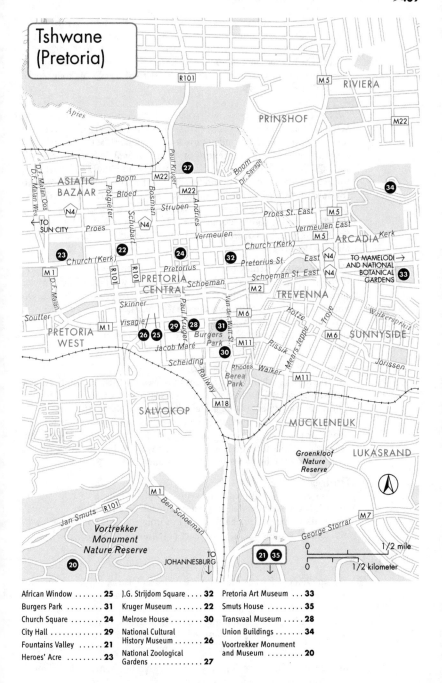

Tshwane (Pretoria)

and look for the monument's entrance gates on the right. Return to the R28, and drive north into the city. The R28 becomes Potgieter Street (a one-way street north) going into Pretoria central. Turn right on Church Street. The **Kruger Museum** ② is on your left. Street parking is available. About two blocks west down Church is the **Heroes' Acre** ㉓ and four blocks east is **Church Square** ㉔.

Go back and collect your car, drive one block east, and turn right onto Schubart Street (one-way south). Drive four blocks to Visagie Street, and turn left. Park in the grounds of the **African Window** ㉕, the cultural history museum. Practically next door is the **National Cultural History Museum** ㉖. From there walk two blocks east to Paul Kruger Street. (If you turned left and drove to Boom Street, you'd find the **National Zoological Gardens** ㉗.) Turn right. On your left is the **Transvaal Museum** ㉘, the best natural science museum in the country. Across the street stands **City Hall** ㉙. Continue south down Paul Kruger, and turn left on Jacob Maré Street. Walk until you reach the high-Victorian national monument **Melrose House** ㉚. Cross the street to beautiful **Burgers Park** ㉛.

You can then backtrack to your car and do the following as a drive, or, if you're feeling energetic, you can continue down Jacob Maré Street, turn left on Van der Walt Street, and follow it to Pretorius Street. On your right are **J. G. Strijdom Square** ㉜ and the awe-inspiring South African State Theatre. Walk west on Pretorius Street past Church Square; turn left into Bosman Street and right into Visagie to get back to the African Window and your car.

Return to Potgieter Street, and turn right on Schoeman Street. Continue for about 10 blocks, and turn right into Wessels Park to visit the **Pretoria Art Museum** ㉝. From here take Wessels Street across Schoeman to Church Street, where you turn right. The **Union Buildings** ㉞, home to the government, are on your left. Still heading east on Church, take the first available road to the right, and then turn left on Schoeman until you reach the N1 to Johannesburg. On your way back to Jo'burg, detour by following the brown tourist signs to **Smuts House** ㉟.

Timing
It takes about 30 minutes to travel from Johannesburg to Tshwane on the N1. If you want to see everything, schedule an entire day in Tshwane. The walk alone will probably take a morning. A side trip to the Cullinan diamond mine will take at least half a day.

What to See

㉕ **African Window.** Part of the National Cultural History Museum, this cultural center offers song and dance programs, a traditional crafts shop, exhibitions (including Bushman, or San, art), and an archaeology program. Don't miss the stunning, full-color Ndebele mural along the entrance wall. ✉ *Visagie St., between Bosman and Schubart Sts.* ☎ *012/324–6082* ⊕ *www.nfi.org.za/NCHM/nchmindex.htm* ☞ *R8* ◷ *Daily 8–4.*

Atteridgeville. This township outside the city has not been developed much as a tourist destination. However, it does have Moroe Park, which sometimes hosts concerts, and Ga-Mothakga Park, home to a memorial to 607 black South Africans who died when the transport ship SS *Mendi* sank off the coast of France in 1917. You should come here with a guide, not on your own.

🐾 ㉛ **Burgers Park.** This lovely park, the oldest in the city, is a tranquil midtown spot and an example of a formal Victorian botanical garden design. The gates are all that remain of a Victorian mansion that lost out to developers. You can wander between fragrant rose gardens and flower beds filled with indigenous plants to reach the center of the park, where a converted Victorian house contains a delightful restaurant. ✉ *Jacob Maré St., between van der Walt and Andries Sts.* ☎ *012/308–0452* ☎ *Free* ☼ *May–Aug., daily sunrise–sunset; Sept.–Apr., daily 6 AM–10 PM.*

㉔ **Church Square.** Anton van Wouw's statue of President Paul Kruger, surrounded by sentries, dominates this pleasant square, which is flanked by some of the city's most historic buildings: the Old Raadsaal (Council Chamber), designed by Dutch architect Sytze Wierda; the Palace of Justice (used as a military hospital during the South African War), built in early Italian Renaissance style; and the modern Provincial Administration Building. On Wednesday mornings you can watch a military parade and flag-raising. ✉ *Bordered by Paul Kruger and Church Sts.*

need a break? In a building dating from 1904, **Café Riche** (✉ Church Sq. ☎ 012/328–3173) is one of the better coffee shops in the center of town. In addition to excellent coffees, it serves *tramezzini* (toasted sandwiches), other sandwiches, and salads. You can sit outside and watch the informal parking attendants and car washers waving their trademark white(ish) cloths in a circle to attract clients.

㉙ **City Hall.** This imposing structure has a semi-Italian style that borrows freely from classical architecture. A tympanum on the front, by Coert Steynberg, one of South Africa's most famous sculptors, symbolizes the growth and development of the city. Statues of Andries Pretorius and his son Marthinus, the city's founder, stand in the square fronting the building, and relief panels depict the founding in 1855. ✉ *Visagie and Paul Kruger Sts.* ☎ *012/308–8949* ⊕ *www.museumpark.co.za/cityhall.htm* ☎ *Free* ☼ *Weekdays 8–4.*

en route **CULLINAN DIAMOND MINE –** About 48 km (30 mi) north of the city on the N1, this fully operational mine is three times the size of the famous hole at Kimberley. The world's largest diamond, the 3,106-carat Cullinan, was unearthed here in 1905. Machinery extracts 12 tons of kimberlite and 6,000 carats of diamonds each day. About 80% of these are for industrial use, but the rest are high-grade gems. On the standard mine tour you'll see the big hole, watch a 12-minute video, pass through a typical mine security check, view replicas of the most famous diamonds, and travel through a mock-up of an underground tunnel. There's also a three-hour underground tour. You can buy diamonds and custom-made pieces from the resident jeweler. You must reserve in advance for tours, and no children under 10 are permitted. Cullinan's delightful old Victorian mine director's house has been turned into a guesthouse and tea garden, **Oak House** (✉ 103 Oak Ave. ☎ 012/305–2364) – It serves breakfast, home-cooked lunches, and afternoon teas from 8 daily. ✉ *Mine: Oak Ave., west of Olienhout Ave.; Cullinan Tours: 95 Oak Ave., Cullinan* ☎ *012/734–0260* 🎫 *Standard tours R35, underground tours R75* ⊙ *Standard tours weekdays at 10 and 2:30, weekends at 10; underground tours daily at 8.*

☾ ❷ **Fountains Valley.** The Apies River, which flows through Tshwane, originates in this 24-acre park with a game and bird sanctuary. The springs drew early humans to the area and was one of the reasons this river valley was originally chosen as the site for Pretoria. You can hike, swim, or picnic here while the kids enjoy the play area and miniature locomotive. There is also a restaurant. ✉ *Christina de Wit Dr. and Eeufees Rd.* ☎ *012/440–2121* 🎫 *Free* ⊙ *Daily 7–7.*

❷ **Heroes' Acre.** The central part of the historic Church Street Cemetery, established in 1867, contains the graves of many South African statesmen and celebrities. The walkways are lined with trees planted in the 19th century. ✉ *Church St. and D. F. Malan Dr.*

❷ **J. G. Strijdom Square.** This square was once dominated by a huge bust of former pro-apartheid prime minister J. G. Strijdom. However, on May 31, 2001—exactly 40 years to the day after the government declared South Africa a republic—the supporting structure of the whole edifice crumbled, and Strijdom fell unceremoniously into the parking garage under the square. All that remains is a statue by Danie de Jager of charging horses atop a high column along with informal stalls selling bric-a-brac. ✉ *Church and van der Walt Sts.*

❷ **Kruger Museum.** This was once the residence of Paul Kruger, president of the South African republic between 1883 and 1902 and one of the most revered figures in South African history. The home, still fully furnished, is humble and somber, befitting this deeply religious leader who loved to sit on the front *stoep* (veranda) and watch the world go by. Exhibits in the adjoining museum trace Kruger's career, culminating in his exile by the British and eventual death in Switzerland in 1904. Of particular interest are the letters of support that Kruger received from all over the world, including the United States, when Britain instigated the Second South African War (1899–1902). Across the road is the Dutch Reformed Church (a national monument), where Kruger's wife is buried. ✉ *60 Church St. W, at Potgieter St.* ☎ *012/326–9172* ⊕ *www.nfi.org.za/KM/khindex.htm* 🎫 *R16; guided tours R20* ⊙ *Weekdays 8:30–5:30, weekends 8:30–5.*

Mamelodi. At the entrance to this nearby township, the Solomon Mahlangu Freedom Square, dating from 1991, is one of the country's first monuments to honor an African National Congress cadre hanged by the apartheid government. Moretele Park hosts music festivals, especially large daytime jazz festivals with some of the country's top acts. It is best not to visit Mamelodi without a guide.

❸ **Melrose House.** Built in 1886, this opulent structure is one of South Africa's most beautiful and best-preserved Victorian homes, furnished in period style. It has marble columns, mosaic floors, lovely stained-glass windows, ornate ceilings, porcelain ornaments, and richly colored carpets. On May 31, 1902, the Treaty of Vereeniging was signed in the dining room, ending the Second South African War. You can view a permanent exhibit on the war or arrange for a guided tour (R30 for a group of 20 or fewer). ✉ *275 Jacob Maré St.* ☎ *012/322–2805* ⊕ *www.melrosehouse.co.za* 🎫 *R5* 🕙 *Tues.–Sun. 10–5.*

☺ **National Botanical Gardens.** A ridge separates the flora of Tshwane's cooler south from that of the warmer north. Here, some 8 km (5 mi) east of the city center, you can wander along a 2-km (1-mi) circular trail to see indigenous trees from a range of climatic regions. Aloes bloom in winter, and in summer you can rest on the lush lawns. ✉ *2 Cussonia Ave., off Church St., Brummeria* ☎ *012/843–5000* 🎫 *R12* 🕙 *Daily 8–5.*

★ ㉖ **National Cultural History Museum.** This museum offers an insightful look at the country's indigenous cultures. You can marvel at San rock art, African headdresses, clay sculptures, and several permanent collections of archaeological material dealing with Tshwane, South Africa, and the many people who call this country home. The museum also has a restaurant. ✉ *149 Visagie St., between Bosman and Schubart Sts.* ☎ *012/324–6082* ⊕ *www.nfi.co.za/NCHM/nchmindex.htm* 🎫 *R10* 🕙 *Daily 8–4.*

☺ ㉗ **National Zoological Gardens.** The city's zoo, covering nearly 200 acres,
FodorśChoice is considered one of the world's best, with about 4,300 animals from
★ almost every continent (including rare Komodo dragons). The animal enclosures here are much larger than those of most zoos. However, like any modern zoo worth its name, this is just the public facade for a much larger organization that specializes in the research and breeding of endangered species. It includes an aquarium (with Africa's largest collection of freshwater fish) and reptile park, where the king crocodiles won't fail to intimidate you. A cable car transports you high above the zoo to a hilltop lookout. ✉ *Boom St.* ☎ *012/328–3265* ⊕ *www.zoo. org.za* 🎫 *R32* 🕙 *Daily 8–5:30.*

㉝ **Pretoria Art Museum.** Despite its dull exterior, this gallery houses an impressive collection of South African art in constantly changing exhibitions, including touring shows like the massive Leonardo da Vinci exhibit. The more than 5,000-piece collection includes works by Pierneef and Anton van Wouw and such international maestros as Salvador Dalí and Pablo Picasso, collections of 17th-century Dutch art, and international graphic art. Guided tours are available for an extra R5. The museum also has a sculpture garden. ✉ *Schoeman and Wessels Sts., Arcadia* ☎ *012/344–1807* ⊕ *www.pretoriaartmuseum.co.za* 🎫 *R5* 🕙 *Tues. and Thurs.–Sun. 10–5, Wed. 10–8.*

> **en route**

SAMMY MARKS MUSEUM – About 23 km (14 mi) outside Tshwane, this furnished Victorian mansion and its outbuildings, surrounded by gardens, were built in 1884 for mining and industrial magnate Sammy Marks, who wielded much influence in the Zuid-Afrikaansche Republiek. You can relax at the restaurant after visiting the 48 rooms (in a mixture of grand styles) or have a picnic on the grounds. Guided tours take place every

90 minutes on weekdays; for the brave, there are ghost tours at night. ✉ *Off Centurion exit of N4; follow signs* ☎ *012/802–1150* ⊕ *www. nfi.org.za/sammy* ✉ *R20* ⊙ *Tues.–Fri. 10–5, weekends 10–4.*

㉟ Smuts House. This small wood-and-iron country house was the residence of Jan Christian Smuts, who played active roles in the South African War and World Wars I and II and was instrumental in setting up the League of Nations (forerunner of the United Nations). Despite his military background, he was committed to working for peace and remains one of South Africa's most interesting historical characters. His home illustrates the simple manner in which he lived until his death in 1950. There is a tea garden on the large grounds; an adjacent campsite; and easy trails up a nearby hill. Ask about guided bird-watching and other tours. On the second and last Saturdays of each month a crafts market takes to the grounds. ✉ *Off Nelmapius Rd., Irene* ☎ *012/667–1176* ▣ *R10* ⊙ *Weekdays 9:30–4:30, weekends 9:30–5.*

㉘ Transvaal Museum. This massive natural history museum has an extensive collection of land and marine animals from around the world, with an emphasis on African wildlife. The beautiful building also contains the Austin Roberts Bird Collection, the most comprehensive display of taxidermied African birds in southern Africa. Much of the museum is laid out with students in mind, and exhibit descriptions are exceptionally informative. Of particular interest are the Genesis exhibits, tracing the evolution of life on Earth, and the geology section, with displays of weird and wonderful rocks and minerals. Mrs. Ples, the famous australopithecine fossilized skeleton found at Sterkfontein (in the Cradle of Humankind), resides here. Tours cost an extra R3 per person. ✉ *Paul Kruger St., across from City Hall* ☎ *012/322–7632* ⊕ *www.nfi.org.za/ tmpage.html* ▣ *R10* ⊙ *Daily 8–4.*

en route

TSWAING CRATER MUSEUM – This huge meteorite crater with a salt lake was formed about 220,000 years ago and today is home to 320 bird species and even more plant species. You can browse through the crater's eco-museum (guided or unguided) to learn more about the area and explore a Ndebele cultural village. A three-hour guided tour (R80 a guide) includes a walk to the crater. ✉ *Old Soutpan Rd. (M35), about 40 km (25 mi) outside Tshwane* ☎ *012/790–2302* ⊕ *www.nfi. org.za/Tswaing/Index.htm* ▣ *R15* ⊙ *Daily 7:30–4.*

㉞ Union Buildings. Its foundations laid in 1901, this impressive cream-sandstone complex—home to the administrative branch of government—was designed by Sir Herbert Baker, one of South Africa's most revered architects. It is his masterpiece. The complex incorporates a hodgepodge of styles—an Italian-tile roof, wooden shutters inspired by Cape Dutch architecture, and Renaissance columns—that somehow works beautifully. Expansive formal gardens step down the hillside in terraces, dotted with war memorials and statues of former prime ministers. There is no public access to the building, but the gardens are perfect for a picnic lunch. ✉ *Off Church St., Meintjeskop* ⊙ *Gardens open 24 hours.*

② **Voortrekker Monument and Museum.** It is indicative of the tolerance of the democratically elected South African government that this tribute to the ideals at the heart of apartheid remains. Completed in 1949, the monument honors the Voortrekkers, Boer families who rejected British rule in the Cape and in 1835–38 trekked into the hinterland to found their own nation. The Hall of Heroes traces in its marble frieze their momentous Great Trek, culminating in the Battle of Blood River (December 16, 1838), when a small force of Boers defeated the Zulu army without losing a single life. The Voortrekkers considered this victory a confirmation of their special relationship with God. An adjoining museum displays scenes and artifacts of daily Voortrekker life, as well as the Voortrekker Tapestries, 15 pictorial weavings that trace the historical high points of the Great Trek. The monument is situated in a nature reserve, which has a picnic area and hiking and biking trails. You can dine in the restaurant and tea garden if you don't like to rough it. Also on the site is **Fort Schanskop**, the best-preserved of four area forts commissioned by President Paul Kruger in about 1897. The fort houses a South African (Anglo-Boer) War museum and gift shop. ⊠ *Off R28* ☎ *012/326–6770* ⊕ *www.voortrekkermon. org.za* ⊠ *R25* ⊙ *May–Aug., daily 8–5; Sept.–Apr., daily 8–6.*

Where to Stay & Eat

Befitting Tshwane's diverse residents, its restaurants offer a wide variety of food, from the inevitable well-done steak to fancier, more experimental food. The town has experienced somewhat of a restaurant boom in recent years, so old favorites, such as La Madeleine, are facing fresh competition with new ideas.

$–$$$$ ✕ **O'Galito's.** You'll find it hard to believe you're nearly 500 km (300 mi) inland at this seafood restaurant. Of course there's no sea view, but if you have an enormous imagination, the big airy spaces and white tables bring to mind the beach. The Galito platter is the most expensive and most popular dish on the menu, with langoustines, king prawns, small crayfish (lobster), mussels, grilled calamari, baked oysters, and french fries and rice. There is a limited vegetarian menu, too. ⊠ *367 Hilda St., Hatfield* ☎ *012/342–6610* ▤ *AE, DC, MC, V.*

$–$$$ ✕ **Cynthia's Restaurant and Art Gallery.** This bistro-style restaurant is a good place to try some local game or seafood. Locals flock here for the line fish cooked on an open grill. ⊠ *Maroelana Centre, Maroelana St.* ☎ *012/460–3220* ⚄ *Reservations essential* ▤ *AE, DC, MC, V.*

★ $$ ✕ **La Madeleine.** Noted for its classic and creative French cuisine, this restaurant ranks among the country's top 10 on most critics' lists. The wine list, too, is exceptional. The menu changes daily, depending on what's available at the market. For starters expect calamari tubes stuffed with ratatouille or oysters and mussels in a curry cream sauce. For a main dish, try to select between rack of lamb with fresh vegetables and olives, line fish in champagne sauce, ostrich fillet with cranberry sauce, and veal in muscat sauce. In season try the strawberries in black pepper and balsamic vinegar with mascarpone ice cream. ⊠ *122 Priory Rd., Lynnwood* ☎ *012/361–3667* ⚄ *Reservations essential* ▤ *AE, DC, MC, V* ⊙ *Closed Sun. and Mon. No lunch Sat.*

$–$$ ✕ **La Perla.** Your food will not come stacked into a pile at this restaurant, but you will get a square meal. Before it moved, this restaurant was part of the furniture of central Pretoria for 22 years, but now all those government ministers have to make their way to its new home on an out-of-the-way side street in Brooklyn. Swiss chef and owner Marco Balmelli says he cooks "with a Spanish slant." This being Tshwane, home to the big appetite, you'll find plenty of meat here, like saddle of lamb or carpaccio made from at least 10 different kinds of game. The menu has an extensive seafood component, such as fresh line fish and prawns. ⊠ *Bronkhurst St., Brooklyn* 🕾 *012/460–1267* ✍ *Reservations essential* ⊟ *AE, DC, MC, V* ⊘ *Closed Sun. No lunch Sat.*

¢ ✕ **Delicious Carlton Cafe.** If you weren't looking for it, this little café might just disappear into the facade of suburban mall shops. If you're hungry at lunchtime, however, make a point of seeking it out. The home-style food is fastidiously prepared by owner and chef Rachel Botes and her all-woman team. Some of the more popular dishes include leg-of-lamb pies, massive deli sandwiches, cashew-and-chicken salad, and salmon cured in tequila. Botes says she's a chocoholic, and the array of desserts includes good cheesecake. ⊠ *13th St., Menlo Park* 🕾 *012/460–7996* ⊟ *AE, MC, V* ⊘ *Closed Sun.*

★ $$$ ▥ **Illyria House.** Although there are grander hotels in town, sheikhs and presidents have been known to request this small but special suburban guesthouse on Muckleneuk Hill, overlooking the city bowl. The house takes its name from the setting of Shakespeare's romantic comedy *Twelfth Night,* and the house and gardens feel as though they're part of an elaborate stage set for the play. Presiding over the array of French antiques and over-the-top Venetian light fixtures is vivacious owner and host Marietjie van der Walt. There is a dining room but no set menu; the butler and chef will discuss options with you each day and then shop just for you. Nothing is too much, which explains something of the lodge's appeal. If it's available, ask for the Katarina Suite, with its view of the Union Buildings. Horseback riding, golf, tennis, and hiking can also be arranged. ⊠ *327 Bourke St., Muckleneuk 0002* 🕾 *012/344–5193 or 012/344–4641* 🖷 *012/344–3978* ⊕ *www.illyria.co.za* ↩ *7 suites* ♧ *Dining room, spa* ⊟ *AE, DC, MC, V* ⋈ *MAP.*

$ ▥ **Sheraton Pretoria.** The first five floors here consist of standard or classic rooms, all decorated in shades of cream with Italian marble tiles. The top two floors are towers: 36 executive rooms and 7 suites, each with a personal computer and decorated in a subtle African theme with shades of green, brown, and ocher. Ask for a room overlooking the Union Buildings' gardens. Sunday brunches are long, leisurely affairs with live jazz on the terrace. ⊠ *643 Church St., at Wessels St., 0002* 🕾 *012/429–9999* 🖷 *012/429–9300* ⊕ *www.sheraton.com/pretoria* ↩ *168 rooms, 7 suites* ♧ *3 restaurants, pool, health club, massage, sauna, 2 bars* ⊟ *AE, DC, MC, V.*

¢ ▥ **Pretoria Backpackers.** This backpackers' hostel is run more like a family guesthouse. There is a dormitory, but there are also 14 rooms and wooden cabins in the lush, tropical garden. The owner, Francois Van Rooyen, can take you on a daylong sightseeing tour to Johannesburg, Soweto, and the Apartheid Museum, and will also pick you up from the Johannesburg airport. ⊠ *425 Farenden St., Clydesdale 0002* ☎ *012/343–9754* 🖷 *012/343–2524* ⊕ *www.pretoriabackpackers.net* ➪ *14 rooms, 1 dormitory* ♨ *Kitchens, pool, bar* ⊟ *MC, V* ⑩ *CP.*

¢ 🖽 **Ted's Place.** Situated in a sleepy cul-de-sac on the spectacular Bronberg mountain, Ted's Place looks like a large, smart suburban home with a lived-in appeal. From a large veranda you can watch the abundant birdlife that has taken sanctuary on the mountain. Annemarie, Ted's wife, serves a full bacon-and-egg breakfast, sometimes with pancakes, too. Ted is a registered tour guide and can show you the sights, such as the hulking Voortrekker Monument or the Cullinan Diamond Mine. ⊠ *Wagon Wheel Ave., Wapadrand 0050* ☎ *012/807–2803* 🖷 *012/807–2741* ⊕ *www.teds-place.za.net* ➪ *4 rooms* ♨ *Lounge* ⊟ *DC, MC, V* ⑩ *BP.*

Nightlife & the Arts

Nightlife

For such a large city, Tshwane is on the quiet side, and has far fewer nightspots than Johannesburg. Hatfield—the area defined by Burnett, Hilda, and Festival streets and just off Duncan Street—is the liveliest area at night. It's a hodgepodge of bars, coffeehouses, and restaurants and is reasonably safe to walk in at night. You'll find an interesting mix of slightly rowdy students, young professionals, diplomats, politicians, and a few creative types.

The clubs and bars rubbing shoulders in Hatfield's Burnett Street range from commercial to comfortable. They are all within walking distance in a three-block area of continuous clubs, shops, and restaurants. **Cool Runnings** (⊠ Burnett St., Hatfield ☎ 012/362–0100) is one of a chain of lively, reggae-themed bars in Gauteng. Rock bands, DJs, and stand-up comedians often perform, and meals are good, too. **Recess** (⊠ Burnett St., Hatfield ☎ 012/362–2776) plays commercial dance tunes, R&B, and hip-hop to student clubbers. Continuing down the street, **Good4Fellas** (⊠ Burnett St., Hatfield ☎ 012/362–4122) is another rather commercial club that gets loud and rowdy as the night wears on. **Times Four** (⊠ Burnett St., Hatfield ☎ 012/362–5520) is a somewhat generic venue, playing pop, house, R&B, and hip-hop, with a student crowd loudly supporting the many drink specials. **Tings an' Times** (⊠ Hatfield Galleries, Burnett St., Hatfield ☎ 012/362–5537) is Hatfield's most atmospheric student eatery, with a reggae theme, tasty and cheap food, and bands or DJs playing regularly. The two-story **Cuban Café** (⊠ 129 Duxbury Rd., Hatfield ☎ 012/362–1800) is a Cuban-themed cocktail haven that also serves excellent food. The upstairs balcony is perfect for a relaxing afternoon with friends.

Pop in at the chilled-out **Jazztime Café** (⊠ Brooklyn Mall, Veale St., Brooklyn ☎ 012/346–4296) to chat with friends over a slow drink. **Legends** (⊠ President Arcade, Schoeman and Pretorius Sts. ☎ 084/400–1271) is Tshwane's biggest gay club, but it attracts a very mixed crowd of straight and gay. On Fridays, resident DJs play funky house, and on Saturdays the music is commercial. Gay party bunnies can look out for drag

★ shows. **Lucit Restaurant** (⊠ 42 Belrene St., Rietondale ☎ 012/329–4180)

is one of Tshwane's best spots for weekend performances of classical music, jazz, and cabaret—all in a garden surrounded by a legion of candles. The restaurant is open Tuesday to Sunday. At the **Nile Crocodile** (⊠ 60 Glenwood Rd., Lynnwood Glen ☎ 012/361–2025) the country's best rock bands and promising newcomers play on weekends and some weeknights to an appreciative young audience. **Zeplin's** (⊠ 384 Pretorius St. ☎ 082/869–8894) is the city's largest and darkest venue for rock lovers, with separate areas for gothic, industrial, and metal beats. Rock bands often perform on weekends.

The Arts

The **South African State Theatre** (⊠ Church St. ☎ 012/322–1665 ⊕ www. statetheatre.co.za) is the largest theater in Africa. It hosts world-class local and international touring productions in its two large venues, one smaller theater, and one intimate cabaret theater. The Gorona restaurant serves African fare and buffet meals on theater nights.

Sports & the Outdoors

Horseback Africa (⊠ De Tweede Spruit, Cullinan ☎ 012/735–1531 ⊕ www.colin.co.za) has well-organized rides in a game reserve near Cullinan. Trips are about R660 for a full day, but prices vary according to the activity you choose (and they do an airport transfer, too, for R300). They're particularly well suited for beginners or nervous people, but experienced riders can have a fun canter, too. There are also overnight accommodations, ranging from R90 per person sharing in a 12-bed cottage to R450 per person sharing in a luxury lodge.

Shopping

Gallery

At the **Association of Arts Pretoria** (⊠ 173 Mackie St., Nieuw Muckleneuk ☎ 012/346–3100 ⊕ www.art.co.za) you can admire or buy contemporary paintings, prints, and sculpture. The gallery regularly plays host to important national art competitions.

Malls

The **Brooklyn Mall** (⊠ Fehrsen and Lange Sts., Nieuw Muckleneuk ☎ 012/346–1063), with more than 170 stores, is classy but vibrant. Many shoppers are students from the nearby University of Pretoria. The **Centurion Lake** (⊠ Heuwel Ave., Centurion ☎ 012/663–1702) is a rather standard shopping center, but its claim to fame is its musical fountain, one of the largest in the country. Water streams move to lights and music Wednesday and weekend nights from about 6. Tshwane's most impressive mall is **Menlyn Park** (⊠ Atterbury Rd. and Lois Ave., Menlo Park ☎ 012/348–8766). Over the years it has grown into a labyrinthine complex with just about every major chain as well as plenty of smaller shops, a rooftop drive-in movie theater, the only Imax theater in the province, and an arena.

Markets

The **Hatfield Flea Market** (⊠ Burnett St., Hatfield ☎ 012/342–3769) spreads out over a central parking lot in Hatfield all day every Sunday.

Hundreds of stalls sell crafts, toys, goldfish, food, secondhand books, and other tidbits. The **Irene Village Market** (✉ Nelmapius Rd., Irene ☎ 012/667–1659) appears on the second and last Saturdays of the month from 9 to 2. You can stroll through about 300 stalls of art, fresh produce, flowers, hand-painted African fabrics, and toys. When you're tired, head for the tea garden. **Magnolia Dell** (✉ Queen Wilhelmina Dr., Nieuw Muckleneuk ☎ 072/836–2446) comes alive on the first Saturday of each month from 9 to 3, when it is home to a large arts and crafts market. On the last Saturday of the month, shop for bargains when up-and-coming artists show their work at Art in the Park. At the busy **Ubuntu Market** (✉ Boschkop and Donkerhoek Rds. ☎ 012/802–0333) you can buy souvenirs in the form of handmade items from different South African cultures the second Saturday of the month from 9 to 3.

CRADLE OF HUMANKIND

South Africa's most famous and important paleontological site is the Cradle of Humankind, an area of about 100,000 acres just outside Johannesburg that was declared a World Heritage Site in 1999. Among the many Stone Age and Iron Age fossils and artifacts found here, the most significant are the hominid remains, which provide important information about humankind's earliest forebears. The explored sites are not open to the public, but a tour of the Sterkfontein Caves and the Visitor Centre provides an excellent overview of the archaeological work in progress. Special tours to the explored sites can be booked at the Visitor Centre.

The impressive **Cradle of Humankind Visitor Centre** comprises displays, interactive exhibits, storytellers, and even an underground boat ride for the brave. It's a one-stop tourist destination with a restaurant, lodge, arts-and-crafts market, and interpretative center, and you can attend cultural events in its amphitheater. ✉ *Sterkfontein Caves Rd., Kromdraai* ☎ *011/956–6342 or 0800/204–177* ⊕ *www.coh.co.za and www.cradleofhumankind.co.za* ☉ *Tues.–Sun. 9–4.*

★ Just down the road from the Visitor Centre, the **Sterkfontein Caves** are the best known of the Cradle's sites. It was here, in 1936, that Dr. Raymond Dart discovered his now famous Mrs. Ples, as she is popularly known—part of a fossilized skeleton of an *Australopithecus africanus.* This first identified "missing link" provided evolutionary evidence of the connection between humans and apes. Another important find, Little Foot is the near-complete skeleton of an early australopithecine child. Unfortunately, early limestone miners broke off most of the caves' stalactites and stalagmites, but the rock formations and underground lake with albino shrimp are still awe-inspiring. Guided tours last an hour and leave on the half hour. (Wear comfortable shoes.) ✉ *Sterkfontein Caves Rd., Kromdraai* ☎ *011/956–6342.* 🎟 *R20* ☉ *Tues.–Sun. 9–4.*

For more recent history you can tour the **Old Kromdraai Gold Mine,** one of the country's oldest gold mines, where gold was found in 1881. Frankly, it's a little spooky. You don a miner's helmet and wander into the mine's murky depths as part of one-hour guided tours, which leave on the hour. It's not a difficult walk though. ⊠ *Ibis Ridge Farm, Kromdraai Rd., Kromdraai* ☎ *011/957–0205 or 011/957–0211* ⊡ *R40* ⊙ *Weekends 9–5 (last tour at 4), weekdays by appointment.*

Rhinos, lions, wild dogs, cheetahs, hippos, and crocodiles are among the animals you can see at the **Rhino and Lion Park.** You can spot about 600 head of game; visit the lion, wild dog, and cheetah enclosures (be careful of lions approaching vehicles) or vulture blind; or be thrilled by live snake shows on weekends and holidays. You can also visit the endangered species breeding center (and the magnificent white lions) or cuddle a baby animal at the nursery for young orphaned animals. In addition to the self-driving tour, you can book an escorted game drive or horseback ride. The visitors area has a kiosk, pool, the Croc Pub and Diner, 4x4 trails, and a curio shop, as well as a small rest camp with three self-catering chalets. ⊠ *Kromdraai Rd., Kromdraai* ☎ *011/957–0109* ⊕ *www.rhinolion.co.za* ⊡ *R70* ⊙ *Weekdays 8–5, weekends 8–6.*

The **Wonder Cave** is a huge single-chamber cave—2 billion years old—with a number of intact stalagmites and stalactites and formations up to 50 feet high. An elevator takes regular guided tours all the way down, but if you're feeling adventurous you can rappel down (by prior arrangement only). You can also book evening tours. ⊠ *Kromdraai Rd., Kromdraai* ☎ *011/957–0106* ⊕ *www.rhinolion.co.za* ⊡ *R50* ⊙ *Weekdays 8–5, weekends 8–6.*

Where to Stay & Eat

★ **$$$$** ✕ **The Carnivore.** Don't come expecting a quiet romantic dinner, as the huge space lends itself to a loud and sometimes frenetic scene. Game meat such as warthog, impala, and crocodile vies for space around an enormous open fire with tamer fare such as pork and mutton. Great hunks of meat are brought around to your table on Masai spears and carved directly onto your plate until you (literally) surrender by lowering the flag on your table. It's an eat-as-much-as-you-can set menu for R125. Vegetarians won't feel left out, with an excellent vegetarian à la carte menu with such African delicacies as *aviyal* (a spicy mixed vegetable dish cooked in coconut milk) and *kumbi baji* (mushrooms and peas cooked in a spicy yogurt sauce). ⊠ *Misty Hills Country Hotel, 69 Drift Blvd., Muldersdrift* ☎ *011/950–6000* ⊟ *AE, DC, MC, V.*

$$$$ ✕ **Hotel Aloe Ridge.** The restaurant at this hotel complex is all about the view. In the daytime you can gaze out over a dramatic river gorge with a pleasant-sounding little waterfall. At night you can see, literally, to the ends of the universe, as the restaurant has a 16-inch Cassegrain telescope with an Apogee 7 camera, which enables the resident astronomer to project the real-time night sky onto a screen in the dining room. (If it's cloudy, they use images from sometime during the previous week.) The star shows cost R100, and an informative talk is followed by a session of comet or supernova hunting—you may even get to name one. The food is good, although not particularly imaginative, composing an à la carte menu of *braais* (barbecue), stir-fries, carved meats, salads, and other standards. ⊠ *Off M5, Muldersdrift* ☎ *011/957–2070* ⊟ *AE, DC, MC, V.*

¢ ✕⊡ **The Cradle.** Located in the Cradle conservation area, the forest camp has eight self-catering thatch A-frame cottages on the banks of a stream. Each cottage is comfortable and fully equipped with a fridge, stove, dishes, and other necessities. Game drives, fly-fishing trips, and guided walks can be arranged. The Cornuti restaurant ($$$–$$$$) has tables overlooking a 6,600-acre game reserve. The overall impression is one of light, space, and silence. The frequently changing menu is pretty impressive, too. Choices may include ostrich medallions with vegetable ratatouille, beef fillet on buttered spinach, or loin of lamb with butternut and sweet potato. The extensive wine list has many local specialties. ⊠ *Cradle Nature Reserve, Kromdraai Rd., Box 792, Lanseria 1748* ☎ *011/659–1622* ⊕ *www.thecradle.co.za* ⇨ *8 cottages* � ⌂ *Restaurant, kitchens* ⊟ *AE, DC, MC, V.*

$–$$ ⊡ **Toadbury Hall.** This small country hotel is peaceful and pretty, set in lovely spacious grounds. The rooms are predominantly white, enlivened with bold, framed botanical prints; two rooms are decorated French Quarter–style, à la New Orleans. All rooms have under-floor heating, and bathrooms have separate showers and two sinks. It's a great place to escape the city. ⊠ *M5, Elandsdrift* ⋑ *Box 746, Muldersdrift 1747* ☎ *011/659–0335* 🖷 *011/659–0058* ⊕ *www.toadburyhall.co.za* ⇨ *8 rooms, 2 suites* ⌂ *Restaurant, 2 tennis courts, pool, bar, meeting rooms; no kids under 12* ⊟ *AE, DC, MC, V* � ⎁⎧ *BP.*

¢–$$ ⊡ **Glenburn Lodge.** Hot-air balloons launch here, making this a good spot to stay if this early-morning activity is on your agenda. Comfortable chalets are built in something approaching a suburban subdivision style, but the rooms are bright and cheerful, decorated in warm, earthy colors and patterned in stripes, geometrics, and, befitting the Scottish theme, tartans. ⊠ *Off Beyers Naude Dr.; follow signs to Kromdraai and turn off on dirt road for 2 km (1 mi)* ⋑ *Box 492, Muldersdrift 1747* ☎ *011/668–1600* 🖷 *011/668–1620* ⊕ *www.glenburn.co.za* ⇨ *48 rooms, 3 suites, 32 chalets* ⌂ *Restaurant, miniature golf, tennis court, pool, gym, hot tub, fishing, hiking, horseback riding, volleyball, bar, meeting rooms* ⊟ *AE, DC, MC, V* ⎁⎧ *BP.*

★ $ ⊡ **Misty Hills Country Hotel.** This attractive hotel is spread over a huge expanse of landscaped gardens with banks of white roses and African sculptures. The rooms are predominantly white with African artwork. Suites have outside showers in an enclosed garden, and royal suites have a plunge pool. There is an excellent on-site spa offering the whole range of massage, beauty, and health therapy treatments. ⊠ *Drift Blvd., off M5* ⋑ *Private Bag 1, Muldersdrift 1747* ☎ *011/957–2099* 🖷 *011/957–3212* ⊕ *www.rali.co.za* ⇨ *138 rooms, 13 suites* ⌂ *2 restaurants, tennis court, 3 pools, sauna, spa, volleyball, bar, meeting rooms* ⊟ *AE, DC, MC, V* ⎁⎧ *BP.*

Sports & the Outdoors

Ballooning

Flying Pictures (☎ 011/957–2322) offers hot-air balloon trips at sunrise, weather permitting. The flight costs between R1,100 and R1,700, lasts about an hour, and includes sparkling wine and a full English breakfast.

Horseback Riding

Danielsrust Horse Trails (☎ 011/957–0115) operates in the Krugersdorp area and offers horseback rides (R120 for an hour, R180 for two hours) on game farms in the Cradle of Humankind area. All levels of experience are accommodated.

Shopping

The **Crocodile Ramble** (☎ 011/957-3745 ⊕ www.theramble.co.za) is an arts, crafts, attraction, and restaurant route set up by local artists, potters, sculptors, and other craftspeople. It meanders extensively through the Cradle of Humankind area on up to the Hartbeespoort Dam in the Magaliesberg. Whether you are shopping for jewelry, antiques, or art, or just looking for restaurants or pubs to visit, it's all on the Ramble. The Web site has a handy interactive road map.

THE MAGALIESBERG

The Magaliesberg hill range stretches 120 km (74 mi) between Tshwane and the town of Rustenburg, about a 90-minute drive northwest of Johannesburg. The South African War once raged here, and the remains of British blockhouses can still be seen. However, the region is most remarkable for its natural beauty. Grassy slopes cleft by ocher cliffs, streams adorned with ferns, waterfalls plunging into pools, and superb rock formations contribute to the Magaliesberg's unique beauty.

It's an outdoor lover's paradise: go hiking, mountain biking, or horseback riding; swim in crystal streams; take a picnic lunch to one of the natural hideaways; or take a dawn balloon flight over the area followed by a champagne breakfast. It is also home to the large Hartbeespoort Dam, a water-sports hot spot. The mountains and the town of Magaliesburg are popular with locals and tourists alike (also due to the various roadside crafts stands and old shops), and the main areas and attractions become extremely crowded on weekends.

The internationally renowned **De Wildt Cheetah Centre,** respected for its conservation and breeding programs, offers three-hour guided tours in vehicles (included in the price of admission) as well as a guided walking trail. You need to book visits to the center in advance. A beautiful stone lodge has nine guest rooms, if you should wish to stay over. No children under six are permitted. ⊠ *R513, near Hartbeespoort Dam* ☎ *012/504–1921* ⊕ *www.dewildt.org.za* ☟ *R150* ⊙ *Tours Tues., Thurs., and weekends at 8:30 and 1:30.*

The **Elephant Sanctuary** is home to 10 of the big mammals. You can take a ride lasting about 2½ hours, or you can simply touch and feed them, which is less expensive. Booking is essential. A small lodge sleeps up to 10. ⊠ *Rustenburg Rd. (R104), about 2 km (1 mi) from Hartbeespoort Dam* ☎ *012/258-0423* ⊕ *www.hartbeespoortdam.com* ☟ *R295–R495* ⊙ *Rides daily at 7, 10, and 2.*

The **Snake and Animal Park** is not big (you can walk through in less than two hours) but has more animals than you might think, including rare white lions, gray wolves, many primate species, and birds of prey. Its selection of reptiles is overwhelming. Snake cages line the walkways, containing anything from harmless little garden snakes to poisonous cobras and giant pythons. Keep an eye out for snake shows, especially on weekends. The park also runs a ferry restaurant on the dam and a tea garden. ⊠ *1 Scott St., Hartbeespoort* ☎ *012/253–1162* ⊕ *www.hartbeespoortdam.com* ⊠ *R40* ⊙ *Daily 8–5.*

You can see freshwater fish, birds, and animals at the **Hartbeespoort Aquarium.** It's a small and slightly run-down park, but it's home to a fascinating selection of fish species, some from local waters and some from as far afield as the Amazon and Australia. Open-air enclosures have some crocodiles and tortoises as well as ducks, geese, pelicans, and a couple of seals. ⊠ *Plot 97, Melody, on R511, just before Hartbeespoort coming from Johannesburg* ☎ *012/259–0080* ⊕ *www.hartbeespoortdam.com* ⊠ *R25* ⊙ *Daily 8:30–5.*

For a panoramic view from the top of the mountain range running alongside the Hartbeespoort Dam, step onto the **Hartbeespoort cableway.** The view—of the dam on one side and the North West Province on the other— is worth the trouble. You can pack a picnic basket to enjoy on the mountain, where there's a small shop selling beer and snacks as well as a few picnic tables, or have a bite to eat afterward at the base station restaurant. ⊠ *1 km (½ mi) from Brits turnoff on R511, Hartbeespoort* ☎ *012/253–1706* ⊕ *www.hartbeespoortdam.com/cableway* ⊠ *R30* ⊙ *Weekdays 9:15–3:30, weekends 9:15–5.*

Where to Stay & Eat

$$–$$$ ✕🏠 **Mount Grace Country House Hotel.** This peaceful, village-style bed-and-breakfast country hotel near the town of Magaliesburg has accommodations in delightful buildings of different height. All have glorious views of the mountains, valley, and 10 acres of landscaped gardens. The Mountain Village is the most luxurious lodging, with sunken baths and heated towel bars. If you're looking for more privacy, you might prefer to stay at Grace Village, which is a little more secluded and farther down the mountain. The most reasonable lodging is the Thatchstone Village. Thatch, wood, and wicker create a delightful country-style ambience. The food ($$$$) is wholesome country fare, and the Mount Grace is famous for its Sunday lunches. ⊠ *R24 to Hekpoort, near Magaliesburg* ⌂ *Private Bag 5004, Magaliesburg 1791* ☎ *014/577–1350* ⌨ *014/577–1202* ⊕ *www.grace.co.za* ⌦ *81 rooms* ⌕ *2 restaurants, some minibars, tennis court, 2 pools, spa, fishing, mountain bikes, billiards, bowling, croquet, hiking, bar, library* ▭ *AE, DC, MC, V* ⊙❘ *BP.*

$ ✕🏠 **Budmarsh Country Lodge.** In the heart of the Magaliesberg, this lodge has rooms with beautiful antique furniture, all surrounded by a lush garden. It's a good place for a river ramble or a mountain hike. Even if you don't stay overnight, drive through for dinner or a light lunch. It's a beautiful drive, and the always-changing food is prepared by a master chef. Dinner (reservations essential) is a contemporary six-course set menu (R150). ⊠ *T1, off R24, Magaliesburg* ⌂ *Box 1453, Highlands*

North 2037 ☎ *011/728–1800* 🖷 *011/728–1001* ⊕ *www.budmarsh.co. za* ⤳ *11 rooms* ⚹ *Restaurant, pool, fishing, billiards, hiking, library* ⊟ *AE, DC, MC, V* ⦿ *BP.*

$ ✕⌧ **De Hoek Country House.** In France this exclusive establishment would be called an *auberge,* and its dressed stone-and-heavy-timber construction would not be out of place in Provence. De Hoek is set in semi-indigenous gardens in the exquisite Magalies River valley. In a two-story stone building along the river, the quiet rooms have deep golden-yellow walls and dark mahogany furniture. Superior suites have fireplaces, and all rooms have under-floor heating. However, the food is what brings most people here. Classic French techniques applied to contemporary ingredients result in an eclectic menu, with dinner (reservations essential) costing R200 for a semi-set menu with several choices. ⊠ *Off the R24, north of Magaliesburg* ⬭ *Box 117, Magaliesburg 2805* ☎ *014/577–1198* 🖷 *014/577–4530* ⊕ *www.dehoek.com* ⤳ *4 rooms, 16 suites* ⚹ *Pool, fishing, archery, croquet, hiking, library* ⊟ *AE, DC, MC, V* ⦿ *BP.*

$ ✕⌧ **Goblin's Cove.** You will find this delightful little restaurant ($$$–$$$$), the creation of sculptor Charles Gotthard, between green trees next to a river. It's decorated as a fantasy fairy world, with three stories of little rooms, winding passageways, and stairs leading to colorful private alcoves and balconies. The restaurant has tasty, eclectic, and creative cuisine, such as South African sushi (made with springbok carpaccio), Thai chicken salad, and lime-marinated chicken breasts. A set menu (about R170) is offered on Sundays and holidays. A small shop sells dream catchers, small fairy statues, and the like, and the Gobble D'Gook coffee shop serves homemade cakes on weekends and holidays. There are three B&B units in a restored vintage train car and two forest cabins. (Less than 10 km [6 mi] away and also operated by Gotthard are the smaller Out of Africa Guest Lodge, which has five two-story thatch cottages, and La Provence, which has seven suites, each with a lovely antique Victorian bath, in an old stone sculptor's studio.) ⊠ *Off R24, Bekker School Rd., Box 98, Magaliesburg 1991* ☎ *014/576–2143* ⊕ *www.goblins.co.za* ⤳ *3 rooms, 2 cabins* ⚹ *Restaurant* ⊟ *AE, DC, MC, V* ⦿ *BP.*

¢–$ ✕⌧ **Lesedi Cultural Village.** This is not just a place to stay and eat, though you can do both here. It's a place to learn more about the cultures and history of South Africa's Basotho, Ndebele, Pedi, Xhosa, and Zulu nations. Daily shows of dancing and singing, tours of traditional homesteads, and a crafts market complement the dining, lodging, and conference facilities. The large Nyama Choma restaurant ($$$–$$$$) serves food from all over the continent, so you can taste North African fare, choose East African cuisine, or opt for a South African barbecue. Most of the Africa-themed guest rooms have two beds, but five have space for more. You can arrange packages that include breakfast, dinner, and the tours. ⊠ *R112, 12 km (7½ mi) north of Lanseria* ☎ *012/ 205–1394 or 012/205–1395* ⊕ *www.lesedi.com* ⤳ *30 rooms* ⚹ *Restaurant, pub, meeting rooms* ⦿ *BP.*

¢–$ ⌧ **Valley Lodge.** Although it's a bit too big to be called a hideaway, this B&B has a great country feel attributable to the bird sanctuary, 240-acre nature reserve, and stream that runs through the grounds. The lodge is very popular with corporate groups, but it's big enough to find a quiet spot away from it all. Rooms have small sitting areas and are decorated with country accents. Some have four-poster beds and fireplaces; all have covered patios. ⊠ *Jennings St.* ☍ *Box 13, Magaliesburg 1791* ☎ *014/ 577–1301 or 014/577–1305* ☒ *014/577–1306* ⊕ *www.valleylodge.co. za* ⇨ *70 rooms* ♨ *Restaurant, in-room data ports, putting green, 3 tennis courts, pool, gym, fishing, hiking, horseback riding, volleyball, bar, library, recreation room* ⊟ *AE, DC, MC, V* �"O" *BP.*

★ ¢ ⊞ **Green Hills.** This peaceful and romantic B&B is just right for a break from the bustle of the city. Rooms are in three separate cottages in a lovely garden. Attractive ceramic fireplaces glow on cold winter nights. The bathrooms are spacious, with large showers and separate baths. Nothing is too much trouble for hosts Peter and Etaine, who will make dinner, picnic hampers, or braais by arrangement. ⊠ *T1, 11 km (7 mi) from Magaliesburg, near Bekker School* ☍ *Box 286, Magaliesburg 1791* ☎ *014/577–2063* ⊕ *www.greenhills.co.za* ⇨ *3 cottages* ♨ *Fishing, hiking; no room TVs* ⊟ *No credit cards* �"O" *BP.*

¢ ⊞ **Jameson Country Cottages.** These pretty, well-appointed self-catering cottages can sleep four or six people and have stoves, fridges, TVs, and a good selection of culinary appliances. Set in an attractive garden around a pool and adjacent to a cane-furniture factory and shop, they offer excellent value for the money. A tea garden serves breakfast and lunch. ⊠ *R509 (Koster Rd.), 10 km (6 mi) from Magaliesburg* ☍ *Box 96, Magaliesburg 1791* ☎ *014/577–1361 or 083/301–5791* ☒ *014/577– 4621* ⊕ *www.westcane.co.za* ⇨ *6 cottages* ♨ *Café, kitchens, driving range, pool, shop* ⊟ *AE, DC, MC, V.*

★ ¢ ⊞ **Mountain Sanctuary Park.** Don't let the rather terse list of rules at the entrance put you off this place, but do heed it as a warning that the owners are fiercely protective of their little piece of paradise—and justly so. This is a simple campsite, with spotless bath facilities, on-site trailers, and some basic but clean and comfortable self-catering cottages with electricity, hot water, and cooking facilities. The emphasis here is on the surrounding 2,200 acres of mountains, pools, waterfalls, and streams, where you can hike a different route every day—each more beautiful than the last. Pets and radios are forbidden, but the sound of children's laughter is welcome. ⊠ *40 km (25 mi) from Magaliesburg on a dirt road, 15 km (9 mi) from the N4* ☎ *014/534–0114 or 082/371–6146* ☒ *014/ 534–0568* ⊕ *www.mountain-sanctuary.co.za* ⇨ *3 chalets, 3 trailers, 30 campsites* ♨ *Pool* ⊟ *No credit cards.*

Sports & the Outdoors

Ballooning

A fun and fascinating way to start the day is with an early-morning balloon ride. **Bill Harrop's Original Balloon Safaris** (☎ 011/705–3201 ⊕ www. balloon.co.za) flies daily at sunrise from a site close to the Hartbeespoort Dam for about an hour, weather permitting. A flight costs R1,995, including breakfast and sparkling wine.

Horseback Riding

Roberts Farm Horse Trails (⊠ R24, 30 km [19 mi] from Magaliesburg ☎ 014/577–3332) is a working farm that offers horseback rides in addition to the more serious business of growing crops and raising cattle. Monday through Saturday you can choose from beginner rides or faster rides for experts, farming schedules permitting; longer rides are available on Sunday. The cost is R150 for an hour, R450 for a full day.

Paragliding

There is better paragliding and hang gliding than you would think close to Johannesburg, and one of the most popular launch sites is at Hartbeespoort Dam. It's controlled by **1st Paragliding Club** (☎ 083/306–2804 ⊕ www.1stpara.co.za), which will put you in contact with the right instructors and gliding operators.

Shopping

Stretching from the Cradle of Humankind to the Magaliesberg area, the **Crocodile Ramble** (☎ 011/957–3745 ⊕ www.theramble.co.za) includes many restaurants, shops, and attractions. Most visitors just amble around the area exploring the many crafts shops and studios and nibbling away in coffee shops.

The **Chameleon Village Lifestyle Junxion** (✉ Hartebeespoort Dam ☎ 012/253–1451 ⊕ www.chameleonvillage.co.za) has shops, fast-food outlets, and restaurants lined up alongside art studios. You can visit an ostrich show farm, a Bushman village, pet a pony (and put the kids on one), browse through the Crafters Junxion market, or enjoy live music on weekends. **Crystal Feeling** (✉ Akasha Centre, 15 Rustenburg Rd., Magaliesburg ☎ 014/577–2182) has many fascinating decorative and healing crystals, dream catchers, books, and jewelry. Check out the fantastic handmade wood and steel furniture with an African theme, from Zimbabwe and Botswana, at **Delcardo** (✉ Hartleys Guest House, Shop No. 1, Rustenburg Rd., Magaliesburg ☎ 014/577–3509). The **Welwitschia Country Market** (✉ R104 [Rustenburg Rd.], 2 km [1 mi] from Hartbeespoort Dam, at Doryn four-way stop ☎ 083/302–8085 ⊕ www.countrymarket.co.za) sells arts and crafts among other goodies at 38 little shops and three restaurants. At **Western Cane Trading** (✉ R509, 10 km [6 mi] from Magaliesburg ☎ 014/577–1361 ⊕ www.westcane.co.za) you can browse through a huge warehouse of cane, wood, and iron furniture. There's a good tea garden here and even a driving range.

PILANESBERG & SUN CITY

The 150,000-acre **Pilanesberg National Park,** 150 km (93 mi) northwest of Jo'burg, is centered on the caldera of an extinct volcano dating back about 100 million years. Concentric rings of mountains surround a lake filled with crocodiles and hippos. Open grassland, rocky crags, and densely forested gorges provide ideal habitats for a wide range of plains and woodland game, including rare brown hyenas, sables, and gemsbok. Since the introduction of lions in 1993, Pilanesberg can boast the Big Five—lions, elephants, rhinos, leopards, and buffalo. It is a bird-watcher's paradise, with a vast range of grassland species, waterbirds, and birds of prey. You can drive around the park in your own vehicle or join guided safaris of various types with Pilanesberg Safaris (⇨ Johannesburg & Environs A to Z, *below*).

Sun City is a huge entertainment and resort complex in the middle of dry bushveld, close to Pilanesberg and 177 km (110 mi) northwest of Johannesburg. It's the dream child of Sol Kerzner, the South African entrepreneur who first saw the possibilities of a casino in the rocky wilds of the Pilanesberg mountains. The area was in the then Bantustan of Bophuthatswana—one of several areas in apartheid South Africa set aside for black ethnic groups, with a semblance of self-government. (No one was given the choice of becoming a member of a homeland, however, and those who did no longer had even basic rights as South African citizens.) As such, it was exempt from South Africa's then strict anti-gambling laws. Today Sun City comprises four luxurious hotels, two casinos, major amphitheaters, and a host of outdoor attractions. The complex is split into two parts: the original Sun City and Lost City, a project anchored by the magnificent Palace Hotel.

The resort burst onto the international scene in the apartheid era, when a few American and British music stars broke the cultural boycott to play Sun City. Today Bophuthatswana forms part of South Africa's North West Province.

Almost like Las Vegas, Sun City relies on such entertainments as slot machines and other gambling, topless revues, and big-time extravaganzas. It stages rock concerts, major boxing bouts, the annual Sun City Golf Challenge, and the occasional Miss World pageant. It also displays that familiar Vegas sense (or lack) of taste—with the Palace a notable exception—doling out the kind of ersatz glitter and glare that appeals to a shiny polyester crowd. Whatever your feelings about the complex, you have to admire Kerzner's creativity when you see the Lost City, where painted wild animals march across the ceilings, imitation star-spangled skies glitter even by day, lush jungles decorate the halls, and stone lions and elephants keep watch over it all.

Sun City's genuine appeal lies not in the slots but in nearby Pilanesberg National Park and a full round of outdoor sports and activities, including two Gary Player–designed golf courses and an artificial lake where visitors can water-ski, parasail, sailboard, or surf in the Valley of the Waves, a water park with a giant pool that creates perfect waves for bodysurfing, waterslides, a fake beach, and swimming pools.

Where to Stay

Accommodation in Sun City is generally expensive, and only the Palace can justify its rates. You may opt to stay instead in the nearby rest camps and private lodges of Pilanesberg National Park.

★ $$$$ **Palace of the Lost City.** Given the tackiness of Sun City, you would think any hotel based on the concept of a lost African palace would suffer from theme-park syndrome, but happily that's not the case here. Sculpted cranes and leaping kudu appear to take flight from the hotel towers, elephants guard triumphal stairways and bridges, and graceful reminders of ersatz Africa strike you at every turn. No expense has been spared, and the attention to detail is mind-boggling. All rooms have hand-carved doors and furnishings, the jungle paintings on the ceiling of the lobby's rotunda took 5,000 hours to complete, and the hand-laid mosaic floor is made up of 300,000 separate tiles. Guest rooms, done in rich earth tones, blend African motifs with delicate Eastern touches. ☐ *Box 308, Sun City 0316* ☎ *014/557–3131, 011/780–7800 reservations* 🖷 *014/557–4302* 🌐 *www.suninternational.com* ⤺ *338 rooms* ♨ *2 restaurants, room service, pool, 2 bars, meeting rooms* ☰ *AE, DC, MC, V* ⫯❶ *BP.*

★ **$$$$** 🏨 **Tshukudu Game Lodge.** By far the most stylish option in the area, Tshukudu is built into the side of a steep, rocky hill and overlooks open grassland and a large water hole where elephants come to bathe. If you watch long enough, you'll probably see most of the Big Five from your veranda. Winding stone stairways lead up the hill to thatch cottages with private balconies, wicker furniture, bold African materials, and black-slate floors. Fireplaces and mosquito nets are standard, and sunken bathtubs have spectacular views of the water hole. It's a long, 132-step climb to the main lodge on the summit, making this an impractical choice for those with mobility problems. At night you can use a spotlight to illuminate game at the water hole below. ✉ *Pilanesberg National Park, Box 6805, Rustenburg 0300* ☎ *014/552–6255, 011/806–6888 reservations* 🖷 *014/522–6266* 🌐 *www.legacyhotels.co.za* ⤺ *6 chalets* ♨ *Dining room, minibars, pool* ☰ *AE, DC, MC, V.*

$$$ 🏨 **The Cascades.** The lavish use of mirrors, brass, and black marble in the lobby sets the tone for this rather overpriced hotel only yards from Sun City's massive entertainment center. Rooms are decorated in soothing rust tones highlighted with bold blues and yellows. All overlook the Gary Player golf course, the gardens, and an artificial waterfall. The restaurant serves an excellent breakfast. For the best views request a room on an upper floor. ☐ *Box 7, Sun City 0316* ☎ *014/557–1020, 011/780–7800 reservations* 🖷 *014/557–3442* ⤺ *243 rooms* ♨ *2 restaurants, room service, pool, hot tub, 2 bars* ☰ *AE, DC, MC, V* ⫯❶ *BP.*

$$-$$$ 🏨 **Bakubung.** Abutting the national park, this lodge sits at the head of a long valley with terrific views of a hippo pool that forms the lodge's central attraction—it's not unusual to have hippos grazing 100 feet from the terrace restaurant. Despite this, the lodge never really succeeds in creating a bush feel, perhaps because it's such a big convention and family destination. Its brick buildings also feel vaguely institutional. Nevertheless, the guest rooms, particularly the executive studios, are very pleasant, thanks to light pine furniture, colorful African bedspreads, and super views of the valley. The lodge conducts game drives in open-air vehicles, as well as ranger-guided walks. A shuttle bus (R30 round-trip) runs to Sun City, 10 km (6 mi) away. ✉ *Bakunbung Gate, Pilanesberg National Park* ☐ *Box 294, Sun City 0316* ☎ *014/552–6000, 011/806–6888 reservations* 🖷 *014/552–6300* 🌐 *www.legacyhotels.co.za* ⤺ *76 rooms, 66 chalets* ♨ *Restaurant, tennis court, pool, volleyball, bar, shop* ☰ *AE, DC, MC, V* ⫯❶ *BP.*

$$-$$$ 🏨 **Kwa Maritane.** Unfortunately, this hotel fails to take advantage of its setting in a bowl of rocky hills on the edge of the national park—definitely its greatest asset. Many hotel buildings look inward onto swimming pools and lawns. And as at Bakubung, the bustle of convention goers and children tends to drown out the mesmerizing sound of the bush. The big exception is the resort's terrific blind, overlooking a water hole and connected to the lodge via a tunnel. Guest rooms, with high thatch ceilings and large glass doors that open onto a veranda, are comfortable. You can pay to go on day or night game drives in open-air vehicles or to go on guided walks with an armed ranger. ⊠ *Pilanesberg National Park* ⌂ *Box 39, Sun City 0316* ☎ *014/552–5100, 011/806–6888 reservations* 🖷 *014/552–5333* ⊕ *www.legacyhotels.co.za* ⤣ *155 rooms* ⚴ *Restaurant, miniature golf, 2 pools, volleyball, bar, playground* ▤ *AE, DC, MC, V* ⧈ *BP.*

$–$$ ▦ **Manyane.** Offering affordable accommodations in the Sun City area, the resort sits in a thinly wooded savanna east of the Pilanesberg's volcanic ridges. Manyane is short on charm but long on functional efficiency and cleanliness. Thatch roofing helps soften the harsh lines of bare tile floors and brick. You can choose either a two- or four-bed chalet, all with fully equipped small kitchens and bathrooms. Self-guided nature trails lead from the chalets, providing interesting background on the geology and flora of the park. You can also take advantage of the outdoor chess and trampoline. ⊠ *Pilanesberg National Park, Box 6651, Rustenburg 0300* ☎ *014/555–1000* ⊕ *www.goldenleopard.co.za* ⤣ *40 chalets* ⚴ *Restaurant, kitchens, miniature golf, 2 pools, bar, playground, meeting rooms* ▤ *AE, DC, MC, V* ⧈ *BP.*

$ ▦ **Sun City Hotel and Casino.** This is the original Sun City property, and it still houses the gaming casino, banks of slot machines, and a topless extravaganza. If gambling and nonstop action are your scene, this will appeal to you, but most people find its tackiness overwhelming. The main room is decked out like a Tarzan jungle, with palms, artificial waterfalls and rope walkways. The sound of rushing water drowns out the jangle of the slots somewhat, but nothing can conceal the jarring glitter of this lurid spectacle. Thankfully, rooms—in cream and white—are more sedate. ⌂ *Box 2, Sun City 0316* ☎ *014/552–1001, 011/780–7800 reservations* 🖷 *014/557–4210* ⤣ *340 rooms* ⊕ *www.suninternational. com* ⚴ *4 restaurants, room service, pool, 2 bars, casino* ▤ *AE, DC, MC, V* ⧈ *BP.*

JOHANNESBURG & ENVIRONS A TO Z

To research prices, get advice from other travelers, and book travel arrangements, visit www.fodors.com.

AIR TRAVEL

Johannesburg International Airport is Africa's busiest airport. About 13 million travelers pass through every year. It's about 19 km (12 mi) from Johannesburg and is linked to the city by a fast highway, which gets busier at 5 PM, as commuters leave the city and stream east. Most international flights depart from this airport, which has been refurbished in the last several years and now looks a bit like an upscale mall. There is a tourist information desk in the international arrivals terminal, and the domestic terminal offers a slew of restaurants and coffee shops. There's also a duty-free mall and VAT refund office. You can also leave your bags at Lock-Up Luggage, which is one level below international departures. It costs about $5 per bag per day. Information and airport maps can be obtained from the ACSA Web site. Flight and general information is available from the airport itself. There are a number of hotels near the airport as well as one within the airport precinct.

Expect long lines at check-in counters in the early evening, when many long-distance flights depart, but the lines move quickly; it shouldn't take more than a half hour to get through. Baggage claim usually takes about 15 minutes. The precinct is well protected by security guards, and the airport has its own police station.

Major airlines serving Johannesburg include Air Namibia, British Airways, KLM Royal Dutch Airlines, Qantas, Singapore Airlines, South African Airways, and Virgin Atlantic. In addition to South African Airways, the major domestic carriers serving Johannesburg are British Airways, operated by Comair, and SA Airlink.

Magic Bus operates a minibus service that connects to all the major hotels in Sandton. It runs all day on the half hour, costs R95, and takes 30 minutes to an hour. Airport Link will ferry you anywhere in Johannesburg in a Toyota Camry or Mercedes minibus for R230 for the first person, R50 each additional person. Wilro Tours charges R390 to Sandton for three people. In addition, scores of licensed taxis line up outside the airport terminal. By law they must have a working meter. Expect to pay about R250–R350 for a trip to Sandton. If you're transferring directly between a train or an intercity bus and the airport, head to the Rotunda; the main hub for airport shuttles, it's outside the Johannesburg train station at Leyds and Loveday streets.

🚊 Airport **ACSA** ⊕ www.acsa.co.za. **Johannesburg International Airport** ☎ 011/975-9963, 086/727-7888 help line.

🚊 Airlines **Air Namibia** ☎ 011/390-2876. **British Airways** ☎ 011/441-8600. **KLM Royal Dutch Airlines** ☎ 011/881-9696. **Qantas** ☎ 011/441-8600. **SA Airlink** ☎ 011/978-1111. **Singapore Airlines** ☎ 011/880-8566. **South African Airways** ☎ 011/978-1111. **Virgin Atlantic** ☎ 011/340-3400.

🚊 Airport Transfers **Airport Link** ☎ 011/792-2017. **Magic Bus** ☎ 011/548-0822. **Wilro Tours** ☎ 011/789-9688.

BUS TRAVEL

Intercity buses depart from Braamfontein's Rotunda, the city's principal transportation hub, opposite the main train station at Leyds and Loveday streets. It's a reasonably well run operation, but it gets quite busy. Be attentive at all times, as tourists are sometimes mugged here. Greyhound and Translux operate extensive routes around the country. Intercape Mainliner runs to Cape Town. The Baz Bus does not depart from the Rotunda but operates a hop-on, hop-off door-to-door service, stopping at backpackers' hostels between Johannesburg and Durban or Jo'burg and Cape Town on two routes—via the Drakensberg or via Swaziland.

🚌 Bus Lines **Baz Bus** ☎ 021/439-2323 ⊕ www.bazbus.com. **Greyhound** ☎ 083/915-9000, 083/915-8000 Computicket ⊕ www.greyhound.co.za. **Intercape Mainliner**

☎ 0861/287-287, 083/915-8000 Computicket ⊕ www.intercape.co.za. **Translux** ☎ 0861/589-282, 083/915-8000 Computicket ⊕ www.translux.co.za.

CAR TRAVEL

Traveling by car is the easiest way to get around Johannesburg, as the city's public transportation is not as reliable or extensive as those of other world cities. The general speed limit for city streets is 60 kph (37 mph), for main streets it's often 80 kph (50 mph), and for highways it's 100 kph or 120 kph (62 mph or 75 mph). Be warned, though: Jo'burgers are known to be the most aggressive drivers in the country, and minibus taxis are famous for not obeying the rules of the road. Most city roads are in good condition, with plenty of signage, and main roads in the countryside are also very passable. Street names are sometimes visible only on the curb, however. Try to avoid driving in rush hours, 6:30–8:30 AM and 4–6 PM, as the main roads become terribly congested. Gas stations are plentiful in most areas.

Some areas of town have parking meters, and almost everywhere there are security guards who look after parked cars, as street parking is always risky because of car burglaries. It is customary to give these guards a small tip when you return to your car. Most big shopping centers have parking garages, where you will pay anything from R4 to R15.

Most visitors need concern themselves only with the city center and the northern suburbs. The city center is laid out in a grid, making it fairly easy to get around if you can keep track of the many one-way streets. (It's not advisable to tour the area on foot, however, except in groups or with a local guide.) Jan Smuts Avenue runs north from the city center through the major suburbs of Parktown, Rosebank, Dunkeld, Hyde Park, Craighall, and Randburg. William Nicol Drive splits off and runs toward Sandton, another business hub. An easier way to get from the city center to Sandton is up the M1, which intersects the N1. To the south the N1 leads to Roodepoort and the southern suburbs, to the north, toward Tshwane, where it in turn intersects the R28, which continues to Tshwane going east and to Krugersdorp, Magaliesburg, and the Cradle of Humankind to the west. The N1 continues north to Pietersburg and Zimbabwe. If you plan to drive yourself around, get a *good* map. MapStudio prints excellent complete street guides, available at bookstores, and tourism operators often have maps of the area.

Major rental agencies have offices in the northern suburbs and at the airport. Most are open 24/7.

🚗 **Rental Companies Avis** ⊠ 167A Rivonia Rd., Sandton ☎ 011/884-2221 ⊠ Johannesburg International Airport ☎ 011/394-5433 ⊕ www.avis.co.za. **Budget** ⊠ Holiday Inn Crowne Plaza, Rivonia Rd. and Grayston Dr., Sandton ☎ 011/883-5730 ⊠ Johannesburg International Airport ☎ 011/394-2905 ⊕ www.budget.co.za. **Europcar** ⊠ Sandton Holiday Inn Garden Court, Maude and West Sts., Sandton ☎ 011/883-8508 ⊠ Johannesburg International Airport ☎ 011/394-8832 ⊕ www.europcar.ca.za. **Hertz** ⊠ Sandton Hilton, Rivonia Rd. at Chaplin St., Sandton ☎ 011/322-1598 ⊠ Johannesburg International Airport ☎ 011/390-9700 ⊕ www.hertz.co.za. **Imperial** ⊠ Sandton Sun hotel, 5th St. and Alice La., Sandton ☎ 011/883-4352 ⊠ Johannesburg International Airport ☎ 011/390-3909 ⊕ www.imperialcarrental.co.za. **Tempest Car Hire** ⊠ Village

Walk, Maude St., Sandton ☎ 011/784-3343 ✉ Johannesburg International Airport ☎ 011/394-8626 ⊕ www.tempestcarhire.co.za.

EMBASSIES & CONSULATES

Tshwane is the capital of South Africa, and most embassies are there; however, some countries also maintain consulates in Johannesburg.

🗷 Australia **Australian High Commission** ✉ 292 Orient St., Arcadia, Tshwane ☎ 012/342-3740.

🗷 Canada **Canadian Embassy** ✉ 1103 Arcadia St., Hatfield, Tshwane ☎ 012/422-3000.

🗷 United Kingdom **British High Commission** ✉ 255 Hill St., Arcadia, Tshwane ☎ 012/483-1200 🖷 012/433-3207. **U.K. Consulate** ✉ 275 Jan Smuts Ave., Dunkeld West ☎ 011/327-0015 🖷 011/325-2131.

🗷 United States **U.S. Embassy** ✉ 877 Pretorius St., Arcadia, Tshwane ☎ 012/342-1048.

EMERGENCIES

In the event of a medical emergency, seek help at one of the city's private hospitals. Among the most reputable are Milpark Hospital and Sandton Medi-Clinic.

🗷 Emergency Services **Ambulance** ☎ 999 or 011/375-5911. **General Emergencies** ☎ 10111 from landline or 112 from mobile line. **Police** ☎ 10111.

🗷 Hospitals **Helen Joseph Hospital** ✉ Perth Rd., Auckland Park ☎ 011/489-1011. **Milpark Hospital** ✉ 9 Guild Rd., off Empire Rd., Parktown ☎ 011/480-5600. **Sandton Medi-Clinic** ✉ Main St. and Peter Pl., off William Nicol Dr., Lyme Park ☎ 011/709-2000.

🗷 Pharmacies **Brug Pharmacy** ✉ Jacob and Frads Sts., Rietfontein, Tshwane ☎ 012/329-2664. **Bruma Pharmacy** ✉ Bruma Boardwalk, Bruma ☎ 011/622-1453.

MAIL & INTERNET

🗷 Internet Café **Milky Way** ✉ Rosebank pedestrian boulevard, Rosebank ☎ 011/447-1295.

🗷 Post Offices **Johannesburg** ✉ Jeppe and Small Sts., City Center 2000 ☎ 011/336-1361. **Sandton** ✉ 5th Ave., Sandton 2146 ☎ 011/783-7364. **Tshwane** ✉ Church Sq., Pretoria 0001 ☎ 012/339-8000.

MONEY MATTERS

You can exchange currency at Johannesburg International Airport or at the larger branches of South Africa's banks, such as ABSA, Standard Bank, and Nedbank's operations in Rosebank and Sandton. Look for the BUREAU DE CHANGE signs at these banks. ATMs are scattered all over the city, especially at shopping centers. Be careful when using them, though. Don't let anybody distract your attention, and try to avoid using ATMs in quiet spots at night. Traveler's checks are welcome, but increasingly people simply use credit cards, as most shops and restaurants accept them.

TAXIS

The city has a great number of minibus taxis, which form the backbone of Jo'burg's transportation. They are very cheap and run on main routes; often, however, they are not roadworthy, and drivers have a reputation for being irresponsible. Also, there's no real way to know where these taxis go without stopping one and asking. Car taxis, which are much more expensive, have taxi stands at the airport, the train station, and the Rotunda, but otherwise you must phone for a cab. They don't tend to drive around waiting for a fare. Taxis should be licensed and have a working meter. Ask the taxi company how long it will take the taxi to get to you. Many taxis are radioed while on call, and the time to get to your area may vary considerably, depending on whether there is a taxi in the vicinity already. The meter starts at R2.50 and clicks over at a rate of R6 per kilometer. Expect to pay about R150–R240 to the airport from town or Sandton and about R120 to the city center from Sandton. The charge for waiting time is about R50–R60 per hour.

🗂 Taxi Companies **City Taxis** 🕾 011/339-4608. **Rose Taxis** 🕾 011/403-9625 or 011//403-0000 ⊕ www.rosetaxis.com.

TOURS

GENERAL-INTEREST TOURS Springbok Atlas and Gold Reef City Tours both offer two- to three-hour tours (including self-drive tours) of Johannesburg, which may include visits to the city center, Soweto, the Apartheid Museum, Gold Reef City, and some of the city's more interesting parks and suburbs. Other tours explore Tshwane; Cullinan, including a working mineshaft; Sun City; and Pilanesberg National Park. Tour fees start at about R310 per person for half-day tours. Wilro Tours conducts various tours to Soweto, Johannesburg, and the Pilansberg. The Johannesburg Tourism Company has customized tours, including visits to Alexandra, the Apartheid Museum, the Tswaing Meteorite Crater, Soweto, and even a golf tour. The company also has plenty of information and brochures on the city's accommodations, sights, nightlife, and restaurants. Observer Tours will do tailor-made, chauffeur-driven tours for one or two people or small groups, costing up to R1,250 for an eight-hour tour of the city. It also has shorter tours to Soweto and Tshwane. JMT Tours and Safaris can arrange trips to Soweto, Sun City, the Lesedi Cultural Village in Magaliesburg, or Kruger National Park, and other destinations. Guided weekend tours of the area's gardens and homes (the exteriors, anyway) can be arranged through the Parktown–Westcliff Heritage Trust, which also offers tours of the rest of Johannesburg with such themes as mining and the South African (Anglo-Boer) War.

The Adventure Bus is an excellent way to see Johannesburg's main sights in about three hours, with plenty of stops. Tours leave several times a day from Sandton (except Mondays). Your ticket is valid for 24 hours, so you can jump on and off as many times as you like. For something completely different, try the Mystery Ghost Bus Tour, which stops at haunted houses (and lively pubs).

Africa Explore offers full-day and half-day tours of the Cradle of Humankind area; the full package (from R600 per person) includes the Kromdraai Gold Mine, Sterkfontein Caves, and Rhino and Lion Park. Palaeo-Tours runs full- and half-day trips to many of the local paleontological sites along with informed, user-friendly interpretation.

If you choose not to drive around Pilanesberg National Park on your own, you can join a 2½-hour escorted safari with Pilanesberg Safaris for R230. Or you can embark on an elephant safari, offered three times daily for R990. The outfit also offers balloon safaris. A one-hour flight

(R2,500 per person) includes a game drive, sparkling wine, and a full English breakfast at the Bakubung game lodge.

📷 Tour Operators **Adventure Bus** ☎ 011/975-9338. **Africa Explore** ☎ 011/917-1999 ⊕ www.africa-explore.co.za. **Gold Reef City Tours** ☎ 011/496-1400. **JMT Tours and Safaris** ☎ 011/980-6038 ⊕ www.jmttours.co.za. **Johannesburg Tourism Company** ☎ 011/214-0700 ⊕ www.joburg.org.za/travel/travel_tours.stm. **Mystery Ghost Bus Tour** ☎ 083/915-8000 Computicket ⊕ www.mysteryghostbus.co.za. **Observer Tours** ☎ 011/609-4752 or 082/410-0209 ⊕ www.observertours.co.za. **Palaeo-Tours** ☎ 011/726-8788 ⊕ www.palaeotours.com. **Parktown–Westcliff Heritage Trust** ☎ 011/482-3349 ⊕ www.home.intekom.com/parktown. **Pilanesberg Safaris** ☎ 014/552-1561. **Springbok Atlas** ☎ 011/396-1053 ⊕ www.springbokatlas.com. **Wilro Tours** ☎ 011/789-9688.

DIAMOND & GOLD TOURS
For information on a tour of a working diamond mine, *see* the Cullinan Diamond Mine in Tshwane, *above*. Mynhardts Diamonds, which sells diamonds and jewelry, gives audiovisual presentations by appointment. It covers the diamond industry, the cutting of diamonds, and jewelry manufacturing, including a talk on diamond certification—all aimed more at prospective diamond buyers than curious tourists. Schwartz Jewellers conducts one-hour tours of its workshops in Sandton by appointment. You can see stone grading, diamond setting, and gold pouring, and, of course, you can buy the finished product. Tours are free and include refreshments, but you need to take your passport or other identity document along for security reasons. Schwartz Jewellers also offers a daily guided diamond tour of Cullinan (R30), which includes a video on diamond-mining history, a walk in the mine to see how it all works, and a visit to the Cullinan big hole, where the famous Cullinan diamond was found. (Transportation to Cullinan can be arranged for an additional fee.) There is also a store and a jewelry school, where you can see how diamond crafters are trained.

📷 Tour Operators **Mynhardts Diamonds** ✉ 27 Ridge Rd., 2nd fl., west wing, Parktown ☎ 011/484-1717. **Schwartz Jewellers** ☎ 011/783-1717 ⊕ www.schwartzjewellers.com.

TOWNSHIP TOURS
Tours of Soweto and/or Alex are offered by many of the operators listed above as well as Jimi's Face to Face Tours. Information on Soweto tours can also be obtained from the Soweto Tourism Association and Soweto.co.za. Contact the Alexandra Tourism Forum for information about tours to and in Alexandra.

📷 Tour Information **Alexandra Tourism Forum** ☎ 011/882-0673. **Jimi's Face to Face Tours** ☎ 011/331-6109. **Soweto.co.za** ☎ 011/326-1600 ⊕ www.soweto.co.za. **Soweto Tourism Association** ☎ 011/938-3337.

WALKING TOURS
Walk Tours has a range of walking tours of the city center, Kensington, Parktown, Melville Koppies, and Alexandra, among other areas, as well as "dinner hops," a dinner tour with stops all over town. Group tours can be arranged for eight or more, and electronic self-guiding systems are available.

📷 Tour Operator **Walk Tours** ☎ 011/444-1639 ⊕ www.walktours.co.za.

TRAIN TRAVEL

Johannesburg's train station is opposite the Rotunda in Braamfontein, at Leyds and Loveday streets. The famous, luxurious *Blue Train,* which makes regular runs to Cape Town, departs from here, as do Shosholoza

Meyl trains to cities around the country, including the *Trans-Karoo* to Cape Town, the *Komati* to Nelspruit in Mpumalanga, and the *Trans-Natal* to Durban. Many of these trains have overnight service and are acceptable, but they're not terribly comfortable because they can get crowded. There is also no air-conditioning, but you can always just open the window.

⛉ Train Lines *Blue Train* ☎ 012/334-8459 ⊕ www.bluetrain.co.za. **Shosholoza Meyl** ☎ 086/000-8888 ⊕ www.spoornet.co.za/ShosholozaProject/index.jsp.

VISITOR INFORMATION

The helpful Gauteng Tourism Authority is responsible for information on the whole province, but you often find more detailed information at each town or city's own tourism association. The Johannesburg Tourism Company has an excellent Web site with tons of useful information. The Soweto Accommodation Association lists more than 20 lodging options. Covering Pretoria, Centurion, Atteridgeville, Mamelodi, and surrounds, the Tshwane Tourism Information Centre has friendly staff, plenty of pamphlets and printed guides, and a 24-hour info line. Cullinan Excursion provides information about tours and attractions in and around Cullinan. Magalies Reservations covers accommodations and attractions in the Magaliesberg area. For inquiries about the Cradle of Humankind and Magaliesberg areas—including suggestions for restaurants, small lodges and routes to take—contact the Crocodile Ramble Information Centre.

⛉ Tourist Offices **Crocodile Ramble Information Centre** ☎ 011/957-3745 ⊕ www.theramble.co.za. **Cullinan Excursion** ☎ 012/734-2665 ⊕ www.cullinantourism.co.za. **Gauteng Tourism Authority** ☎ 011/340-9000 ⊕ www.gauteng.net. **Johannesburg Tourism Company** ☎ 011/214-0700 ⊕ www.joburg.org.za. **Magalies Reservations** ☎ 014/577-1733 ⊕ www.magaliesinfo.co.za. **Soweto Accommodation Association** ☎ 011/936-8123 ⊕ www.sowetobedandbreakfast.co.za. **Tshwane Tourism Information Centre** ☎ 012/358-1430, 082/239-2630 24 hrs ⊕ www.tshwane.gov.za.

Mpumalanga & Kruger National Park

WORD OF MOUTH

"As you head south in Kruger, the environment changes, getting drier and more savanna-like. We saw lots and lots of game on the drive from Satara south, including hyenas, elephants, a whole troop of baboons with juveniles playing in the trees, jumping around and being lovingly teased by older ones."

—Celia

Updated by
Kate Turkington

MPUMALANGA ("WHERE THE SUN RISES") spreads east from Gauteng to the border of Mozambique. In many ways it's South Africa's wildest and most exciting province. The 1,120-km (700-mi) Drakensberg Range, which originates in KwaZulu-Natal, divides the high, interior plateau from a low-lying subtropical belt that stretches to Mozambique and the Indian Ocean. The lowveld, where Kruger National Park alone covers a 320-km (200-mi) swath of wilderness, is classic Africa, with as much heat, dust, untamed bush, and big game as you can take in.

Larger than Israel and approximately the same size as Wales, Kruger National Park encompasses diverse terrain ranging from rivers filled with crocodiles and hippos to rocky outcrops where leopards lurk and thick thorn scrub sheltering lions and buffalo. Roaming this slice of quintessential Africa are animals in numbers large enough to make a conservationist squeal with delight: in all, there are nearly 150 mammal species and more than 500 species of birds.

With credentials like these, it's no surprise that Kruger and the private game reserves abutting its western borders provide the country's best and most fulfilling game experience; in fact, it's highly probable that you will see all of the Big Five—buffalo, leopards, lions, elephants, and rhinos—during an average two- to three-night stay at one of the private game reserves.

The Drakensberg Escarpment rises to the west of Kruger and provides a marked contrast to the lowveld; it's a mountainous area of trout streams and waterfalls, endless views, and giant plantations of pine and eucalyptus. Lower down, the forests give way to banana, mango, and papaya groves. People come to the escarpment to hike, unwind, soak up its beauty, and get away from the summer heat of the lowveld. Touring the area by car is easy and rewarding, and you can reach many of the best lookouts without stepping far from your car.

Mpumalanga's local history is action-packed, from local wars and international battles to a gold rush every bit as raucous and wild as those in California and the Klondike. Legend has it that you can still find a few old-time prospectors panning for gold in the rivers and streams of the Pilgrim's Rest area. Today, however, it's the luxury game and guest lodges that are the modern-day gold rush.

Warning: The lowveld area, which stretches from Malelane (east of Nelspruit) to Komatipoort, on the Mozambique border, and up throughout Kruger National Park, is a malarial zone, and you should take antimalarial drugs. Consult your doctor when planning your trip.

Exploring Mpumalanga & Kruger National Park

Mpumalanga offers a wealth of activities, from poking around cultural villages and hiking on mountain trails to driving through game reserves. The best way to get around Mpumalanga is by car, either from Johannesburg or from the airport at Nelspruit, Hoedspruit, or Phalaborwa (if you're going into the central section of Kruger). Plan your road trip with booked-in-advance accommodations (there are superb options all over the province), and stop at at least one farm stall, dotted along country roads, for superb fresh fruit and veggies (in season), nuts, and creamy farm milk.

About the Restaurants

Because Mpumalanga is a sought-after tourist destination, its culinary scene keeps getting better and better, both in *larney* (South African slang for "posh") restaurants and attractive cafés. Cuisines range from Mediterranean to Pan-African, and many places serve local delicacies such as fresh trout, venison, Cape Malay favorites such as *bobotie* (a spicy meat-and-egg dish), and curries. Food is cheap and cheerful in Kruger's cafeterias and restaurants, and usually excellent in the private game lodges. Dinner is eaten 7:30-ish, and it's unlikely you'll get a meal in a restaurant after 9. The more larney the restaurant, the more formal the dress, with "smart casual" the norm. In Kruger you might put on clean clothes for an evening meal in a restaurant, but that's how formal it gets. After an exciting night game drive in a private reserve, you'll want to change or at least freshen up, but keep the clothes very casual. Wear long sleeves and long pants because of mosquitoes. Many higher-end restaurants close on Monday, and it's always advisable to make reservations at these in advance.

WHAT IT COSTS In South African rand				
$$$$	**$$$**	**$$**	**$**	**¢**
RESTAURANTS over 125	100–125	75–100	50–75	under 50

Prices are per person for a main course at dinner, a main course equivalent, or a prix-fixe meal.

About the Hotels & Lodges

You may be in Darkest Africa, but you'll be amazed by the very high standards you'll encounter for both service and accommodations. The latter range from fairly basic in the Kruger Park huts to the ultimate in luxury at most of the private camps. You may forget that you are in the bush until an elephant strolls past your chalet or suite. The advantage of a private lodge (apart from superb game viewing) is that often everything is included—lodging, meals, beverages including excellent house wines, game drives, and other activities. There are, of course, several other options, including regular hotels and, if you're watching your pennies, B&Bs and self-catering (with cooking facilities) places. The price categories used for lodging in this chapter treat all-inclusive lodges differently than other lodgings; see the price chart below for details. It's essential to book well in advance and, if possible, avoid July and December, which are South African school vacations.

At most guest establishments on the escarpment, prices include a three-to five-course dinner plus a full English breakfast. Most places now have at least one vegetarian course on the menu. Many lodges and hotels offer

If you have more than a handful of days in the area, split them between the mountain scenery of the escarpment and wildlife viewing in the lowveld. You could complete a tour of the Drakensberg escarpment area in two days, but you're better off budgeting three or more if you plan to linger anywhere. To take in parts of Kruger National Park or one of the private game lodges, which are simply a must, add another three days or more.

Numbers in the text correspond to numbers in the margin and on the Mpumalanga map.

8

If you have 3 days

One of the prime reasons for visiting Mpumalanga is for big game, so fly into the airport nearest your destination and either rent a vehicle and take off into Kruger or get picked up by the private game lodge of your choice. Driving anywhere else in such a short time is not really an option.

If you have 5 days

Your biggest decision will be how much time to spend wildlife watching and how much to spend exploring the escarpment and its historic towns. A good suggestion is two days for the mountains and three in Kruger. Driving from Johannesburg, you can stop for a trout lunch at **Dullstroom** ❶, famous for its superb trout fishing. Continue through **Lydenburg** ❷ and overnight in 🏨 **Sabie** ❺ after driving the awesome **Long Tom Pass** ❸. The next day, head to the former mining town of **Pilgrim's Rest** ❽ and soak up some of the colorful local history. After taking in some of the province's most gorgeous views around **Graskop** ❾, head for Kruger or to a private lodge, making sure you get there in time for the afternoon game drive, followed by dinner. Otherwise, spend the night at 🏨 **Pilgrim's Rest** ❽ or in the vicinity, and start out early the next morning for Blyde River Canyon, with its hiking trails and magnificent escarpment scenery. Alternatively, you can drive to **Nelspruit** ❷⓿—stopping at Hall's Gateway to the lowveld, just south of Nelspruit, for great fresh fruit, veggies, bush clothes, and curios—and continue on to 🏨 **White River** ❶⓽, which has some enchanting overnight places nearby. Then it's off to Kruger, Sabi Sands, Manyeleti, or Timbavati game reserves.

If you have 7 to 10 days

Spend four or more days in the bush—half at Kruger and half at a private lodge, perhaps. A minimum of two nights at either one is non-negotiable. Then split the rest of your time between the escarpment and the lowveld outside Kruger, as in the previous itinerary.

---

special midweek or winter low-season rates. If you're opting for a private game lodge, find out whether they accept children (many specify only kids over 12), and stay a minimum of two nights, three if you can.

In Kruger National Park you have the choice between budget self-catering huts from R250 per couple per night and much more expensive (but worth it) self-catering cottages in the more remote and exclusive bushveld camps, which average R850.

WHAT IT COSTS In South African rand				
$$$$	$$$	$$	$	¢
LODGING				
over 3,000	2,000–3,000	1,000–2,000	500–1,000	under 500
FULL-SERVICE SAFARI LODGING				
over 12,000	8,000–12,000	5,000–8,000	2,000–5,000	under 2,000

Prices are for a standard double room in high season, including 12.5% tax.

Timing

Where you stay on the escarpment may well dictate the kind of weather you get. High up, around Pilgrim's Rest, Graskop, and Sabie, the weather can be chilly, even in summer. Pack a sweater whatever the season. At these elevations fog and mist can be a hazard, especially while driving. On the other hand, the lowveld, especially in summer, is downright sultry.

Kruger National Park is hellishly hot in midsummer (November–March), with afternoon rain a good possibility, though mostly in the form of heavy short showers that don't interfere with game viewing for long. If you plan your drives in the early morning (when the gates first open) or in the late afternoon, you will manage even if you are extremely heat sensitive. In summer the bush is green, the animals are sleek and glossy, and the bird-life is prolific, but high grasses and dense foliage make spotting animals more difficult. Also, because there's plenty of surface water about, animals don't need to drink at water holes and rivers, where it's easy to see them. There are also more mosquitoes around then, but you'll need to take malaria prophylactics whatever time of year you visit.

In winter (May through September), the bush is at its dullest, driest, and most colorless, but the game is much easier to spot, as many trees are bare, grasses are low, and animals congregate around the few available permanent water sources. Besides, watching a lion or leopard pad across an arid but starkly beautiful landscape could be the highlight of your trip. It gets very cold in winter (temperatures can drop to almost freezing at night and in the very early morning), so wear layers of warm clothes you can shed as the day gets hotter. Lodges sometimes drop their rates during winter (except July) because many foreign tourists prefer to visit in the South African summer months, which coincide with the Northern Hemisphere winter.

Spring (September and October) and autumn (March to early May) are a happy compromise. The weather is very pleasant—warm and sunny but not too hot—and there are fewer people around. In October, migratory birds will have arrived, and in November many animals drop their young. In April some migrating birds are still around, and the annual rutting season will have begun, when males compete for females and are often more visible and active.

Big-Game Adventures

There's nothing quite like tracking rhinos on foot—with an armed ranger leading the way, of course—or having an elephant mock-charge to within yards of your Land Rover. The slow-motion gallop of a giraffe, the sinister slouch of a hyena, and the interactions of the smaller creatures of the bush, such as the dwarf mongoose or the bush baby, are all Mpumalanga musts. If you don't stay in one of the area's private game lodges, be sure to go out with a park ranger on a bush walk.

Splendor in the Grass & Bush

If you can afford it, a splurge on a Kruger SKI (spend the kids' inheritance) vacation could be the experience of a lifetime. Staying for a couple of nights at a private game lodge combines superb accommodations, service, and food with equally excellent game-viewing opportunities. Exclusivity on game drives (most lodges put only six people per vehicle with a dedicated ranger and tracker) almost guarantees sightings of the Big Five. Words like *elegance, luxury,* and *privacy* are overused when describing the accommodations, but the lodges are not all the same. One place might feature chalets done in modern chic, another lodges with an African-colonial feel, and a third open-air safari tents whose proximity to the bush makes up for what they lack in plushness. And you'll be treated like royalty, with whom you may well rub shoulders.

8

MPUMALANGA

In addition to Cape Town and the Winelands, Mpumalanga should be high on any South African list. Nowhere else in the country can you spend one day seeing spectacular wildlife, the next climbing or gazing over the escarpment, and a third poking around some of the country's most historic towns—all with a minimum amount of time spent getting from place to place. The local history is fascinating. In the late 1800s skirmishes and pitched battles pitted the local Pedi against the Boers (who had been trekking up from the Cape for decades to escape British oppression) as well as the Brits against the Boers (in the First South African War). At the turn of the 20th century, the Brits and Boers fought again (the Second South African War), when England's Queen Victoria brought some of her finest troops from all corners of the British Empire to South Africa, hoping for a final victory over the Boers. Gold and diamonds had been discovered in South Africa, and there was more at stake than political games. The Pilgrim's Rest gold strike of 1873 was minor compared with those in and around Johannesburg, but it nevertheless provided inducement for gold-hungry settlers hoping to strike it rich.

Although the safest route to these goldfields was the 800-km (500-mi) road from Port Natal (now Durban), many opted for a 270-km (170-mi) shortcut from Lourenço Marques (now Maputo), in Mozambique, through the wilds of the lowveld, where malaria, yellow fever, lions, and

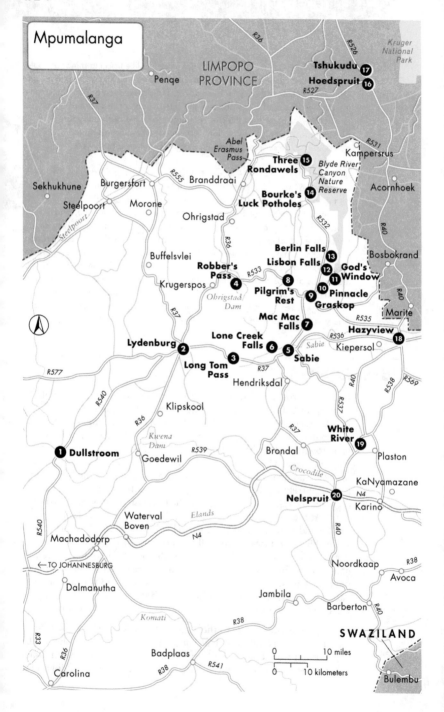

Mpumalanga

LIMPOPO PROVINCE

Penqe

Tshukudu **17**
Hoedspruit **16**

Kruger National Park

R36

R526

R527

Abel Erasmus Pass

Kampersrus

Three Rondawels **15**

Blyde River Canyon Nature Reserve

Acornhoek

Sekhukhune

Burgersfort

Branddraai

Bourke's Luck Potholes **14**

R555

Steelpoort

Morone

Ohrigstad

R532

R531

Bosbokrand

Buffelsvlei

Berlin Falls **13**

R40

Robber's Pass **4**

Lisbon Falls **12**

God's Window **11**

Krugerspos

R533

8

Pilgrim's Rest

9 **10** Pinnacle

Marite

Ohrigstad Dam

Graskop

R535

Mac Mac Falls **7**

Hazyview **18**

R36

R37

Lydenburg **2**

Lone Creek Falls **6**

5 Sabie

Sabie

R536

Kiepersol

3

Long Tom Pass

R37

Hendriksdal

R577

R540

Klipskool

R40

R538

R569

Kwena Dam

R539

White River **19**

Plaston

1 Dullstroom

Goedewil

Brondal

Crocodile

KaNyamazane

Nelspruit **20**

N4

Karino

Waterval Boven

Elands

Machadodorp

← TO JOHANNESBURG

N4

R40

Noordkaap

R38

Avoca

Dalmanutha

Jambila

Barberton

R33

R36

Komati

R38

Badplaas

R541

SWAZILAND

Carolina

0   10 miles

0   10 kilometers

Bulembu

crocodiles exacted a dreadful toll. Part of that route still survives (though it is not quite so hazardous) in the form of Robber's Pass, a scenic route winding down from Lydenburg to Pilgrim's Rest. Those early gold-mining days have been immortalized by Sir Percy Fitpatrick in *Jock of the Bushveld*, a classic of South African literature. (*Bushveld* is the generic term for the wild indigenous vegetation of the lowveld.) Jock was a Staffordshire terrier whose master, Percy (he was later knighted by the British crown), worked as a transport rider during the gold rush. Sir Percy entertained his children with tales of his and Jock's adventures braving leopards, savage baboons, and all manner of dangers. Rudyard Kipling, who wandered this wilderness as a reporter covering the First South African War in the early 1880s, encouraged Fitzpatrick to write down the stories. Jock is still a household name in South Africa today. You'll see lots of Jock of the Bushveld signs all over Mpumalanga, seemingly wherever he cocked a leg.

Dullstroom

❶ *260 km (162 mi) east of Johannesburg on the N4 and R540.*

The tiny hamlet of Dullstroom—the trout-fishing capital of Mpumalanga—sits amid rolling, grass-covered mountains and sparkling streams. At 6,600 feet it's one of the coldest towns in South Africa, and sweaters and roaring fires are common comforts, sometimes even in midsummer. Trout were introduced into the streams of the Mpumalnga Drakensberg at the turn of the 20th century, and trout fishing is now one of the major moneymakers of the region, along with timber and tourism. The village has very good dining and lodging options.

Where to Stay & Eat

$ ✕ **Fibs.** Look out from the main road for this well-signposted, detourworthy restaurant. Choose from the blackboard lunch or dinner menu, which might suggest warm salads or smoked trout as a starter, an adventurous main course of quail or guinea fowl (if you're unadventurous, fall back on the fresh-baked quiches and homemade pasta), and wicked desserts such as rich chocolate pudding. ✉ *567 Voortrekker St.* ☎ *013/254–0059* ▭ *AE, DC, MC, V* ☉ *Closed Mon. and Tues.*

$$$ ✕▦ **Walkersons.** Set in a valley on a 1,500-acre farm of grass-covered hills laced with trout streams, this classy country-house hotel is famous for its food and hospitality. The main lodge, built of stone and thatch, overlooks a small lake and offers 2 km (1 mi) of river fishing as well as eight well-stocked trout ponds, all of different size and character. Owners Howard and Ingrid Walker pride themselves on their fine collection of 19th-century English oil paintings, Persian rugs, and French tapestries, which adorn the public rooms. Horse trails and paved walking trails meander through the forest and beside streams, and game drives through the surrounding game reserve in an open Land Rover to spot several species of antelope are another relaxing option. All rooms face the lake, and in winter and on chilly nights you can sit in front of your own open log fire before snuggling under your electric blanket after a relaxing massage at the in-house spa. The lodge's five-course dinner (R135) is flaw-

lessly presented. Get the taste buds going with broccoli and pear soup or a sweet corn fritter layered with brie cheese and sun-dried tomato. Follow with the house specialty, panfried, deboned whole trout set on gooseberry risotto; and finish up with apple crumble with crème anglaise. Children under 12 are only accepted by prior arrangement. ⊠ *Off R540, 13 km (8 mi) north of Dullstroom* ☏ *Box 185, 1110* ☎ *013/254–0999* 🖷 *013/254–0262* ⊕ *www.walkersons.co.za* ➩ *18 rooms, 2 suites* ⌂ *Restaurant, in-room safes, minibars, pool, spa, fishing, hiking, horseback riding* ▭ *AE, DC, MC, V* ⏣ *MAP.*

$$ ✕⊡ **Critchley Hackle Lodge.** Staff in Scottish kilts, rolling mists, antiques, crackling log fires, and trout streams might make you think you're in Scotland instead of in the heart of the village of Dullstroom. It's a perfect stop on the way to Kruger or a great weekend getaway from Johannesburg. The interiors of the stone-and-brick cottages, which nudge a trout pond, are decorated in gentle shades of cream and beige with an occasional splash of red in a Persian rug. Touches of luxury include heated towel bars, electric blankets, and open fires. A large, informal dining room overlooking the trout lake is a great place to savor the delicious four-course dinners (R110), which could start with green asparagus with truffle cream drizzled with wasabi paste, followed by rack of lamb served with ratatouille, and finished with chocolate tart with chocolate sorbet. Children under 12 are only accepted by prior arrangement. ☏ *Box 141, 1110* ☎ *013/254–0999* 🖷 *013/254–0262* ⊕ *www. critchleyhackle.co.za* ➩ *23 rooms* ⌂ *Restaurant, in-room safes, fishing, bar* ▭ *AE, DC, MC, V* ⏣ *MAP.*

$$ ✕⊡ **Stonecutters Lodge.** Situated in a valley between Dullstroom and Lydenburg, with magnificent views of the surrounding mountains, this classy, comfortable lodge is an exceptional value for the money. The main reception area is in the Stone Manor House, where a large open fireplace dominates the lounge and dining room, furnished in an eclectic fusion of original African art and earth tones. This understated, attractive African theme is carried through all the accommodations: Trout House (sleeps six and is wheelchair-friendly), Stone Cottage (sleeps four), and Cobbles Studios (sleep two). Some accommodations are self-catering, although the delicious meals served up by the Cordon Bleu chef are difficult to resist. The three-course dinner (R140) could include smoked trout; fillet medallions with red wine *jus*; and the house specialty, lemon meringue pie. If you need to work off the calories, go walking, jogging, bird-watching, or trout fishing along 3 km (2 mi) of river frontage in the lodge's tranquil surroundings. ⊠ *R540, 30 km (19 mi) northeast of Dullstroom* ☏ *Box 515, Lydenburg 1120* ☎ *013/235–4225* 🖷 *013/235–4254* ⊕ *www.stonecutters.co.za* ➩ *22 rooms* ⌂ *Restaurant, some kitchenettes, bar, lounge* ▭ *AE, DC, MC, V* ⏣ *MAP.*

Lydenburg

❷ *58 km (36 mi) northeast of Dullstroom on the R540.*

In an open plain between the Drakensberg and Steenkampsberg mountains, Lydenburg was founded in 1849 after the early Boer settlers (Voortrekkers) were forced to abandon their original homestead at Andries-Ohrigstad, where many of them died from malaria. Shaken by those years of death and misery, the survivors named the new town Lydenburg, which means "town of suffering." Ironically, Lydenburg prospered so much that in 1857 its citizens seceded from the Transvaal because of incessant bickering between Voortrekker factions; it remained an independent "country" for three years before rejoining the Transvaal. Today Lydenburg is the bustling, fast-growing center of the surrounding region, its prosperity fueled by the growth of the burgeoning mining industry in platinum, chrome, and coal.

❸ As spectacular as **Long Tom Pass** is, this mountain pass is more famous for its historical associations than its scenic beauty. For it was here, September 8–11, 1900, that one of the last pitched battles of the Second South African War (1899–1902) was fought. Lydenburg had fallen easily to the British on September 7, but the retreating Boers reformed on the heights above town and began shelling the British with their two remaining Creusot siege guns. Known as "Long Toms" because of their long barrels and range, these guns could hurl a 90-pound shell a distance of nearly 9½ km (6 mi). The guns were a tremendous headache for the British, who could not match their range. The Boers, struggling to get these monsters up the pass, can hardly have felt more kindly toward them; at least 16 oxen were required to pull each gun. It took the British two days to push the Boers out of their positions on the pass and drive them over the steep wall of the escarpment. Even then, the Boers managed to set up a gun position on the other side of the valley to shell the British as they maneuvered down the Staircase, a series of switchbacks zigzagging down the pass. You can still see shell holes in the Staircase as you drive along the R37 (toward Sabie) as it begins its winding ascent to the pass.

If you're bypassing Sabie and want to go straight to Pilgrim's Rest from ❹ Lydenburg, try **Robber's Pass,** another spectacular mountain drive. The pass was originally the road linking Lydenburg with Pilgrim's Rest and Delagoa Bay (now Maputo), and was called the Berg (Mountain) Road. During the gold rush the region attracted its share of thieves and desperate men, and highway robberies became common; in fact, so many stagecoaches were held up by highwaymen that the Berg Road was dubbed "Robber's Pass," a name it bears to this day. The scenic pass gives panoramic vistas of high, rolling hills and deep, green valleys. Small farms abound, and eucalyptus and wattle plantations alternate with open grassland. A number of overlooks enable you to get your fill of the scenery. Shortly after entering the pass you'll see the turnoff to Ohrigstad Dam on your right. The lake is a favorite with bird-watchers, as a wide variety of grassland and mountain species have been seen there. To reach Robber's Pass, take the R36 from Lydenburg toward Ohrigstad; approximately 29 km (18 mi) from town, turn right on the R533 toward Pilgrim's Rest. The road winds some 27 km (18 mi) down to its final destination.

The 1,225-acre **Mount Sheba Nature Reserve** contains one of the last stands of indigenous forest in the Transvaal Drakensberg. Fourteen trails of varying difficulty run through the reserve, each taking from 1½ to 2½ hours. Some walks lead to waterfalls hidden in the forest or to fresh mountain pools where you can swim. A map is available from reception at the Mount Sheba Hotel, which is a good place to stop for lunch (R40–R60) or for the six-course dinner (R130). ⊠ *Off R533, follow signs from Robber's Pass* ☎ *013/768–1241* ⊕ *www.mountsheba.co.za* ✉ *Free* ⊙ *24 hrs.*

Where to Stay & Eat

$ ✕🏠 **Hops Hollow.** This combination B&B and pub is at the highest point of Long Tom Pass, at milestone 22/2 from Lydenburg. Here you can sit in the pub and watch through a huge picture window as the beer is brewed. (Theo and Sarie de Beer have four different beers on tap: Digger's Draught, Old Bull Bitter, Mac's Porter, and Blacksmith's Brew.) The ambience is more country house than pub, however. Log fires add to the glow of warm hospitality, and the guest rooms have furnishings in soft country colors enhanced by a mix of charming prints and originals on the walls. The food (R95 prix fixe) is superb. Sarie uses mainly local ingredients, with beer and malted barley in most of the delicately flavored dishes. The spinach quiche is so light it is almost ethereal. Chicken cooked in Old Bull Bitter or beef casserole cooked with Mac's Porter are both excellent choices. ⊠ *Long Tom Pass, 22 km (14 mi) from Lydenburg* ⬧ *Box 430, 1120* ☎ *013/235–2275* 🖷 *083/118–627–6940* ⊕ *www.hopshollow.com* ⤴ *3 rooms* ♨ *Bar* ▭ *MC, V* ℗ *BP.*

Sabie

⑤ *30 km (19 mi) east of Lydenburg.*

As you descend Long Tom Pass, the town of Sabie (sah-bee) comes into view far below, in a bowl formed by the surrounding mountains. It's by far the pleasantest and most enjoyable town in the region, with restaurants, shops, and bars. The name Sabie is derived from the Shangaan word *uluSaba,* which described the "fearful river," home to many crocodiles. Today it makes a great base for exploring.

Gold was first discovered in appreciable amounts in Mpumalanga in the area around present-day Sabie. On November 6, 1872, a prospector named Tom McLachlan located deposits of gold in a creek on the farm known as Hendriksdal, now a small hamlet about 16 km (10 mi) from Sabie. Sabie itself owes its origins to an altogether luckier strike. In 1895 Henry Glynn, a local farmer, hosted a picnic at the Klein Sabie Falls. Loosened up by a few drinks, his guests started to take potshots at empty bottles arrayed on a rock ledge. The flying bullets chipped shards of rock off the cliff face, revealing traces of gold beneath. Fifty-five years later, when mining operations closed down, more than 1 million ounces of gold had been taken from the Klein Sabie Falls.

Today timber has replaced gold as the community's livelihood, and Sabie sits in the heart of the world's largest man-made forest—more than a million acres of exotic pine and eucalyptus. The first forests were planted in 1876 to provide the area's mines with posts and supports. Today much of the timber is still used to prop up shafts in the Gauteng gold mines.

Sabie itself is a busy little town with a farming feel. It boasts some of the biggest traffic humps in South Africa, ensuring that farmers' and visitors' tractors and cars drive slowly through the broad, shady, tree-lined streets. It's easy to walk from one end of the central part of town to the other, taking in sights like **Market Square,** the commercial hub of Sabie in its early days. Here St. Peter's Anglican Church, designed by the famous architect Sir Herbert Baker and built by Italians in 1913, stands in its own pleasant gardens. Just outside the First National Bank you can see the hitching rail (1911) where travelers would tether their horses. Also in the square is a Jock of the Bushveld sign, said to commemorate Jock and Percy's arrival in 1885. Make time to visit the **Sabie Forestry Museum,** which not only details the history of this attractive and friendly small town but also provides a wealth of information on wood and the timber industry. ⊠ *Between 10th Ave. and 4th St.* ☎ *013/764–1958* 🎫 *R5* ☉ *Weekdays 8–1 and 2–5, Sat. 8–noon.*

❻ **Lone Creek Falls** is the prettiest, most peaceful, and last of three local waterfalls on a dead-end road (the others are Bridal Veil Falls and Horseshoe Falls). An easy paved walkway leads to the falls, which plunge 225 feet from the center of a high, broad rock face framed by vines and creepers. The path crosses the river on a wooden bridge and loops through the forest back to the parking lot. If you're feeling energetic, follow the steep steps leading up to the top of the falls. Lone Creek is accessible to the elderly and those with disabilities because of its easy approach. ⊠ *6½ km (4 mi) down Old Lydenburg Rd., off Main Rd.* ☎ *No phone* 🎫 *R5* ☉ *Daily 8–5.*

❼ Set in an ampitheater of towering cliffs, **Mac Mac Falls** is arguably the most famous waterfall in Mpumalanga. The water plunges 215 feet into a pool, and rainbows dance in the billowing spray. It's worth the small entry fee to go through the gate to get a closer look. The falls owe their name to President Thomas Burger, who, while visiting some nearby gold diggings in 1873, noticed that many miners' names began with "Mac," revealing their Scottish background. He promptly dubbed the area Mac Mac. At the gate a number of peddlers sell very cheap curios. ⊠ *R532, 15 km (9 mi) northeast of Sabie* ☎ *No phone* 🎫 *R5* ☉ *Daily 8–5.*

Where to Stay & Eat

¢–$ ✕ **Loggerhead Restaurant.** Heavy wooden furniture here is brightened by sparkling glass- and tableware, and lounge furniture arranged around the fireplace makes a relaxing spot for a cocktail. Local delicacies such as fresh trout feature on the menu alongside standard dishes such as grilled steak, fresh line fish, and schnitzels. ⊠ *Old Lydenburg Rd. and Main St.* ☎ *013/764–3341* ▤ *AE, DC, MC, V* ☉ *Closed Mon.*

¢–$ ✕ **Wild Fig Tree Restaurant and Pub.** This pleasant eatery serves breakfast, a light lunch, and dinner either indoors or on a deck shaded by a huge wild fig tree. There is also a coffee shop with homemade scones, tarts, and pies. Game dishes such as crocodile and saddle of warthog are among the specialties, and trout features strongly on the menu. Friendly, prompt service, reasonable prices, and a pleasant ambience with an open log fire in the lounge make this a popular venue. A good range of wines and spirits is available, as are Internet and tourist-information services. After your meal, pop into the adjoining Wild Fig Tree shops, where arts, crafts, jewelry, and hand-made clothing are for sale. ✉ *Main and Louis Trichardt Sts.* ☎ *013/764–2239* ▭ *AE, DC, MC, V.*

$ 🏠 **Sabie Town House.** Built of local Sabie stone, this beautifully appointed bed-and-breakfast has sweeping views over the Sabie Gorge. The attractive atrium entrance, with skylight and plants, sets the scene for the rest of the establishment, which has spacious guest rooms, including one for families. Four rooms have separate entrances, and all have a minibar-fridge and tea/coffeemaker. Guests have free use of the lush garden, guest lounge, swimming pool, and patio. Barbecue facilities are available, and by special arrangement hosts Frikkie and Louma Van Rooyen will arrange a complete evening *braai* (barbecue) for guests in the *boma* (outdoor eating area) overlooking the gorge. Breakfast is served in the breakfast room or on the patio. ⇥ *5 rooms, 1 suite* ✉ *Power St., 2060* ☎ *013/764–2292* 📠 *013/764–1988* ⊕ *www. sabietownhouse.co.za* ♿ *Minibars, refrigerators, pool, lounge, Internet* ▭ *AE, DC, MC, V* ⊙ *BP.*

Pilgrim's Rest

❽ *16 km (10 mi) north of Sabie on R533.*

Pilgrim's Rest has become a rather shabby reminder of gold-rush days, when it was the first proper gold-mining town in South Africa, centered on the richest gold strike in Mpumalanga. Alec "Wheelbarrow" Patterson, a taciturn Scot who had struck out on his own to escape the hordes of new miners at Mac Mac, discovered gold here in 1873. Mining operations ceased only in 1972, and since then the entire town has been declared a national monument. Many of the old corrugated-iron houses have been beautifully restored and now serve as museums, hotels, gift shops, and restaurants. It's definitely worth a visit, even for a few hours, although it's very touristy, a bit seedy, and you will be besieged by beggars, car washers, and general layabouts.

The old houses you see today date from the more staid years after 1900, when Pilgrm's Rest became a company town. During the mad years 1873–1875, when most of the alluvial gold was panned by individual prospectors, the town consisted of nothing more than a collection of tents and mud huts. Rumors about the richness of the strike carried quickly around the world, and miners homed in from California, Australia, and Europe. By January 1874 more then 1,500 diggers were working Pilgrim's Creek. Only a few struck it rich; the rest spent their earnings in local hostelries until their claims played out and they drifted off.

Your first stop should be the **Pilgrim's Rest Information Centre** (✉ Main St. ☎ 013/768–1080 or 013/768–1471), in the middle of town, opposite the Royal Hotel. Browse through the various tours offered, such as panning for gold and the Prospector's Hiking Trail, as well as maps and tickets for all the museums in the village.

Start your walking tour at the top end of this tiny town (at the top of the hill), and make your way down the main street, where most of the attractions are. The first stop is **St. Mary's Anglican Church** (✉ Main St.). Built in 1884, the iron-roofed stone building replaced the original makeshift wattle-and-daub structure. It was an uphill battle for the early ministers to lure miners from the town's 18 canteens. After a backbreaking week spent on the sluices, Holy Communion just didn't pack the punch of a belt of Cape brandy or Squareface gin.

The tiny **Pilgrim's and Sabie News Printing Museum** is full of displays of antique printing presses and old photos. The building, constructed in the late 19th century as a residence, later served as the offices of the weekly *Pilgrim's and Sabie News*. The first newspaper in Pilgrim's Rest was the *Gold News*, published in 1874 and notable for its libelous gossip. The editor, an Irishman by the name of Phelan, felt obliged to keep a pair of loaded pistols on his desk. ⊠ *Main St., Uptown* ☎ *No phone* 🎫 *R5* ◷ *Daily 9–1 and 1:30–4.*

The town's focal point, the **Royal Hotel** (⊠ Main St.) is well worth a visit for its history. The hotel is made up of 10 different Victorian-style buildings with 50 bedrooms, a lounge, and the Church Bar, formerly a chapel at a girls' school in Cape Town. The chapel was dismantled in 1870, shipped to Lourenço Marques, and then carried by ox wagon to Pilgrim's Rest, where it ministered a different kind of spirit to thirsty miners. The bar retains much of its gold-rush atmosphere, with wood-paneled walls, an antique cash register, a wonderful old bar counter, and a fascinating display of photographs depicting the historical life of the village. If you're hungry, you can order fish-and-chips or a hamburger.

The **House Museum,** across and up the street from the Royal Hotel, re-creates the way of life of a middle-class family in the early part of the 20th century. The house was built in 1913 of corrugated iron and wood and is typical of buildings erected at the time. ⊠ *Main St., Uptown* ☎ *No phone* 🎫 *R5* ◷ *Daily 9–12:45 and 1:15–4:30.*

The **Pilgrim's Rest Cemetery** sits high on the hill above Main Street. The fascinating inscriptions on the tombstones evoke the dangers and hardship of life in Mpumalanga a century ago. That of Fred Sanders, for example, tells how he was "shot in a skirmish on the 27th August, 1878, aged 24." Tellingly, most of the dead were in their twenties and thirties and hailed from Wales, Scotland, and England. The cemetery owes its improbable setting to the Robber's Grave, the only grave that lies in a north–south direction. It contains the body of a thief who was banished from Pilgrim's Rest for stealing gold from a tent, after which he was tarred and feathered and chased out of town; the man foolishly returned and was shot dead. He was buried where he fell, and the area around his grave became the town's unofficial cemetery. To get here, follow the steep path that starts next to the picnic area, near the post office.

In 1930, 16 general stores lined the streets of Pilgrim's Rest. By 1950 mine production had taken a nosedive, and most of the businesses had shut down. The **Dredzen Shop and House Museum** re-creates the look of a general store during those lean years, with shelves displaying items that would have been on sale in the early days, from jams and preserves to candles and matches. The attached residence focuses on life in Pilgrim's Rest in the years immediately following World War II. After you come down the hill from the cemetery, turn left on Main Street to get to the museum. ✉ *Main St., Uptown* ☎ *No phone* 🖅 *R5* ⊙ *Daily 9–1 and 1:30–4.*

Guided tours, including refreshments, are offered at **Alanglade,** the beautiful home of the Transvaal Gold Mining Estates' mine manager, set in a forested grove 2 km (1 mi) north of town. The huge house was built in 1916 for Richard Barry and his family and is furnished with pieces dating from 1900 to 1930. Look carefully at the largest pieces—you will see that they are segmented, so they could be taken apart and carried on ox wagons. Tour tickets are available at the information center and should be reserved 30 minutes in advance. ✉ *Vaalhoek Rd., off R533* ☎ *No phone* 🖅 *Tours R20* ⊙ *Tours Mon.–Sat. at 11 and 2.*

At the **Diggings Museum,** in the creek where the alluvial gold was originally panned, you'll find displays of a water-driven stamp battery and some of the tents and wattle-and-daub huts typical of the early gold-rush years. The tour lasts about an hour and is more of an enjoyable experience than an informative one. The retired prospector who conducts the tours enlivens the proceedings with yarns about the old days. You'll also see a display of gold panning and get to poke around in some of the old diggings. Tickets are available at the information center. ✉ *R533, 2 km (1 mi) south of Pilgrim's Rest* ☎ *No phone* 🖅 *R5* ⊙ *Tours daily at 10, 11, noon, 2, and 3.*

Where to Stay & Eat

¢ ✕ **Scott's Café.** Dozens of varieties of crepes—both savory (stir-fried chicken) and sweet (fried nuts and cinnamon with chocolate sauce)— are the draw at this restaurant. Also on the menu are sandwiches and salads. Meals can be eaten outside on the pleasant wide veranda. There's also an interesting little arts-and-crafts gallery, which, like the café, is open from 9 to 6. ✉ *Main St.* ☎ *013/768–1061* ▭ *DC, MC, V.*

¢ ✕ **Vine Restaurant and Pub.** In a former trading store dating from 1910, the Vine uses antique sideboards, sepia photos, and country-style wooden furniture to capture a gold rush–era feeling. The food is straightforward and hearty. Try traditional South African *bobotie* (curried ground mutton topped with egg), *potjiekos* (lamb stew), digger's stew (beef and veggies) served in a digger's gold-prospecting pan, or *samp* (corn porridge). The pub is a good place to sit outside and watch the world go by. ✉ *Main St., Downtown* ☎ *013/768–1080* ▭ *DC, MC, V.*

$$ 🛏 **Royal Hotel.** Established in 1873, this hotel dates from the very beginning of the gold rush in Pilgrim's Rest—you'll see its corrugated-iron facade in sepia photos displayed around town. The hotel is spread out over 10 quaint wood-and-tin buildings, and rooms are decorated with reproduction four-poster beds, wood ceiling fans, sumptuous deep baths, and marble-and-oak washstands. Activities arranged by the hotel include horseback riding, gold panning, hiking, golf, museum visits, and trout fishing. ✉ *Main St., Uptown* ✑ *Box 59, 1290* ☎ *013/768–1100* 🖷 *013/768–1188* ⊕ *www.royal-hotel.co.za* ➽ *50 rooms* ⌂ *Restaurant, bar; no a/c, no room TVs* ▭ *AE, DC, MC, V* ⦿ *BP.*

¢–$ 🛏 **District 6 Miners' Cottages.** On top of a hill a few minutes' walk from the center of town, these self-catering cottages are a very good value.

The cottages are all miners' homes dating from 1920, and they're delightful. From their verandas are spectacular views of the town and surrounding mountains. Interiors are furnished with period reproductions, complete with wooden floors, brass bedsteads, and claw-foot tubs. Each cottage consists of a small living room, two double bedrooms, a fully equipped kitchen, and a bathroom. Phone reservations can be made only weekdays 9–4, and if you arrive after hours, you'll pick up keys from the Royal Hotel. ⊠ *District 6* 🖃 *Private Bag X516, 1290* ☎ *013/768–1211* 🛏 *6 cottages* ⚬ *Kitchens* ☰ *No credit cards.*

Sports & the Outdoors

Ranging from two nights to five days, several area hiking trails are part of the **Prospector's Hiking Trail.** You follow in the footsteps of the old miners as you walk through indigenous forest and over rolling hills. Overnight accommodations are very basic 16-bunk huts, good if you're hardy and love unspoiled countryside. The birdlife is superb, and you may even see a small antelope or two. Book trails well in advance through the **Komatiland Forest Ecotourism Office** (🖃 Box 1771, Silverton, Pretoria 0127 ☎ 012/481–3615 ⊕ www.komatiecotourism.co.za).

Graskop

9 *25 km (16 mi) northeast of Sabie, 15 km (9 mi) southeast of Pilgrim's Rest.*

Graskop (translation: "grass head") was so named because of the vast tracts of grassveld and singular lack of trees in the area. Like so many of the little towns in this area, it started as a gold-mining camp in the 1880s on a farm called Graskop that was owned by Abel Erasmus, who later became the local magistrate. After the gold mines closed down, the town served as a major rail link for the timber industry. Today the main features of this rather featureless little town are its curio shops and eateries. Perched on the edge of the Drakensberg/Mpumalanga Escarpment, Graskop considers itself the Window on the lowveld, and several nearby lookouts do have stunning views over the edge of the escarpment. It's an ideal base for visiting scenic hot spots, including Mac Mac Falls and the beauties in and around the Blyde River Canyon Nature Reserve.

Traveling east toward Hazyview, you enter the lovely Koewyns Pass, named for a local Pedi chief. Unfortunately, there are few scenic overlooks, but you'll still get sweeping views of the Graskop gorge. Look for the turnoff to Graskopkloof on your left as you leave town, and stop to get a closer view into this deep, surprisingly spectacular gorge, where in the rainy season two waterfalls plunge to the river below.

Where to Stay & Eat

¢ ✕ **Harrie's Pancakes.** A huge selection of delectable pancakes (crepes) comes with both sweet and savory fillings. You might start with sausage and sauerkraut, chicken and mushroom with cashew nuts, or tomato confit, rocket (arugula), and mozzarella, followed by a delicious bitter chocolate mousse or black cherries in liqueur. Traditional fillings, such as plain cheese and cinnamon and sugar with lemon, satisfy the not so adventurous. Also available are muffins, scones, and a variety of salads. Harrie's has a liquor license, and is noted for its quick, friendly, and efficient service. Because it serves the best pancakes in Graskop, Harrie's is the most popular eatery. Though you may have to wait for a table, it's worth it, but be warned: it closes at 5. ⊠ *Louis Trichardt Ave. and Kerk St.* ☎ *013/767–1273* ▭ *MC, V* ⊘ *No dinner.*

$ ▣ **Lisbon Hideaway.** In a peaceful meadow overlooking a small stream (fun for swimming), this self-catering establishment makes a great base from which to explore the escarpment. Graskop, several waterfalls, and the magnificent views of God's Window are minutes away. Accommodations are in modern, comfortable wood cabins done in wicker and bright colors. Each cabin sleeps a maximum of six, with two bedrooms, a living-dining room, and a fully equipped kitchen. Friendly Gerda Flischman, the owner, will stock your fridge for you if you call her in advance. ⊠ *Lisbon Falls Rd., off R532, 10 km (6 mi) from Graskop* ⊕ *Box 43, 1270* ☎ *013/767–1851 or 083/438–2714* ⇆ *3 cabins* ⚲ *Kitchens* ▭ *No credit cards.*

$ ▣ **West Lodge.** This attractive Victorian-style B&B is set in a delightful garden bursting with roses. Luxurious bedrooms are decorated in pastels and have crisp white linens, both bath and shower, satellite TV, and tea/coffeemakers. The two rooms on the first floor of the main building are completely private but share a balcony and lounge; they look out over an area known as Fairyland, a communal farm area where Sir Percy Fitzpatrick set up camp on his way to Lydenburg. Two garden suites are in a detached building and have private entrances. Guests can use a visitors' lounge as well as a fridge in the main house. A small chapel in the garden is the spot for tying the knot, renewing wedding vows, or just meditating quietly. A wide choice of eateries and the town center are only minutes away. ⊠ *12/14 Huguenot St.* ⊕ *Box 2, 1270* ☎ *013/767–1390 or 082/429–2661* ⊕ *www.westlodge.co.za* ⇆ *4 rooms* ⚲ *Dining room, lounge, library, no smoking; no kids under 16* ▭ *AE, MC, V* ⑪ *BP.*

Blyde River Canyon Nature Reserve

15 km (9 mi) northeast of Graskop.

As you head north from Graskop, the dense plantations of gum and pine fall behind, and the road runs through magnificent grass-covered peaks. This lush land is fed by two rivers, the Treur and the Blyde; how they came to be named is part of Mpumalanga lore. The story goes that Pioneer (Voortrekker) leader Hendrik Potgieter led an expedition to Lourenço Marques in 1840, leaving the womenfolk behind near Graskop. The men took so long to return that the women gave them up for dead, named the river beside which they camped the Treur (sorrow), and set off for home. As they were about to wade across another river, they were met by the returning men and were so overjoyed that they named the river the Blyde (joy). This is the setting for the Blyde River Canyon, nearly 30 km (19 mi) long, and the nature reserve of the same name, which stretches for 60 km (37 mi) from its entrance just north of Graskop up to the Abel Erasmus Pass. One of South Africa's great scenic highlights, the reserve has gigantic rocks, deep gorges, and high mountains. ✉ *Along the R532* ☎ *013/761–6019* 🖾 *R25 (payable at Bourke's Luck Potholes)* ⏲ *Reserve daily 7–5, visitor center daily 7:30–4.*

❿ **Pinnacle** is a 100-foot-high quartzite "needle" that rises dramatically out of the surrounding fern-clad ravine, as it has for countless millennia. Way down below, beneath and to the right of the viewing platform, you can see the plateau beneath the escarpment. The watercourse drops down some 1,475 feet in a series of alternating falls and cascades. From Graskop take the R532 north and turn right after 2½ km (1½ mi) onto the R534, marked GOD'S WINDOW. To reach the Pinnacle, continue 1½ km (1 mi) and look out for the brown sign marked PINNACLE.

⓫ **God's Window** is the most famous of the lowveld lookouts. It got its name because as you peer through the rock "window" at the sublime view below, or gaze out into seeming infinity from the edge of the escarpment (which drops away almost vertically), you feel you're on top of the world. Geared to tourists, it has toilet facilities, paved parking areas, curio vendors, and paved, marked walking trails leading to various lookouts. The God's Window lookout has a view back along the escarpment framed between towering cliffs. For a broader panorama, make a 10-minute climb along the paved track through the rain forest to a small area with sweeping views of the entire lowveld. The altitude here is 5,700 feet, just a little lower than Johannesburg. If you're traveling from the Pinnacle, turn right on the R534, pass two overlooks, and travel another 4½ km (nearly 3 mi).

⓬ Set in a bowl between hills, **Lisbon Falls** cascades 120 feet onto rocks below, throwing up spray over a deep pool. You can hike down to the pool on a path from the parking area. From God's Window turn right on the R534 and continue 6 km (4 mi). At the T with R532, turn right onto the road marked LISBON FALLS.

⓭ A small stream, Waterfall Spruit, runs through a broad expanse of grassland to **Berlin Falls**. A short walk takes you to the cascade, which is a thin stream that drops 150 feet into a deep-green pool surrounded by tall pines. Berlin Falls is a little over 2 km (1 mi) north of Lisbon Falls off the R532.

⓮ Another 27 km (17 mi) north of Berlin Falls on the R532 are **Bourke's Luck Potholes** and the nature reserve visitor center. Named after a gold prospector, the cylindrical and rather alien-looking deep potholes filled with green water are carved into the rock by whirlpools where the Treur and Blyde rivers converge. The visitor center has interesting information on the flora, fauna, and geology of the canyon. Several long canyon hiking trails start from headquarters, as do shorter walks and trails. A three-hour walk, for example, could take you down into the bottom of the canyon, where you follow a trail marked by rocks painted with animal or bird symbols as the gorge towers above you.

⓯ Continuing north from Bourke's Luck Potholes, you get occasional glimpses of the magnificent canyon and the distant cliffs of the escarpment. Nowhere, however, is the view better than from the **Three Ron-**

dawels (Drie Rondawels), 14 km (9 mi) from the potholes. This is one of the most spectacular vistas in South Africa—you'll find it in almost every travel brochure. Here the Blyde River, hemmed in by towering buttresses of red rock, snakes through the bottom of the canyon. The Three Rondawels are rock formations that bear a vague similarity to the round, thatch African dwellings of the same name. Before Europeans moved into the area, the indigenous local people named the formations the Chief and His Three Wives. The flat-top peak to the right is Mapjaneng (the Chief), named in honor of a Mapulana chief, Maripe Mashile, who routed invading Swazi at the battle of Moholoholo (the very great one). The three wives, in descending order from right to left, are Maseroto, Mogoladikwe, and Magabolle.

Where to Stay

$ 📺 **Belvedere Guest House.** A good place for overnighting in the canyon, this grand old house completed in 1915 originally served as quarters for the workers of the now-inoperative Belvedere power station. Today it's a self-catering guesthouse that sleeps nine. You can relax in the spacious lounge with fireplace and prepare your meals in the roomy farmhouse-style kitchen. Three of the bedrooms, the lounge, and kitchen open onto a broad veranda that sweeps around all four sides of the house and has breathtaking views dominated by the awesome canyon walls. There are some short but fascinating walks from the house; don't miss the marked trail to Dientjie Falls. ⊠ *Off the R532, 5 km (3 mi) north of Bourke's Luck Potholes* 🄳 *Mpumalanga Parks Board, Central Reservations, Box 1990, Nelspruit 1200* ☎ *013/759–5432* 🖷 *013/755–3928* 🛏 *1 house* ☖ *Kitchen, lounge* ▤ *MC, V.*

Sports & the Outdoors

The **Blyde River Canyon Trail** is a 29-km (18-mi) three-day hike that runs from God's Window right along the edge of the escarpment to the Sybrand van Niekerk Resort. The mountain scenery is spectacular, making it one of the most popular trails in the country. Several shorter trails explore the canyon from trailheads at Bourke's Luck Potholes. The number of hikers on the multiday trails is controlled, so it's essential to reserve far in advance (contact the nature reserve).

en route   The descent out of the nature reserve, down the escarpment, and through **Abel Erasmus Pass** is breathtaking. (From the Three Rondawels, take the R532 to a T, and turn right onto the R36.) Be careful as you drive this pass. The local African population has taken to grazing cattle and goats on the verges, and you may be surprised by animals on the tarmac as you round a bend. The J. G. Strijdom Tunnel serves as the gateway to the lowveld. At the mouth of the tunnel are curio and fruit stands where you can buy clay pots, African masks, wooden giraffes, and subtropical fruit. As you emerge from the dark mouth of the tunnel, the lowveld spreads out below, and the views of both it and the mountains are stunning. On the left, the Olifants River snakes through the bushveld, lined to some extent by African subsistence farms.

Hoedspruit

⓰ *63 km (39 mi) northeast of Graskop.*

Hoedspruit (hoot-sprate), best known for its proximity to Kruger and private game reserves and for its attractive little Africa-themed airport, is an ideal jumping-off place for the surrounding game lodges. It's also the center of the area's burgeoning tourist industry. Have a cup of tea or coffee, surf the Net, or browse in the stores at the Kamogelo shopping center.

⟲ ⓱ North of town, **Tshukudu** is a 12,350-acre farm that bills itself as a safari lodge, but it's more like an animal park. Go somewhere else for a genuine safari experience, but stop here for a day visit where you can do a bush walk (no kids under 12) followed by breakfast. You can, however, take the kids on a morning or afternoon game drive followed by lunch (R90) or dinner (R100). The highlight of the day is meeting some of the farm's orphaned animals; you can get up close with a lion cub, nudged by a wildebeest, or accompanied by a young female elephant and her baby on your bush walk. Children under 12 pay half price for all activities and meals. ⊠ *R40, 4 km (2½ mi) north of Hoedspruit* ☎ *015/793–2476 or 015/793–1886* 🎫 *Bush walk R120, game drive R150* ⊙ *By appointment.*

Where to Stay

$$ 🏨 Otters Den. If you fancy something more adventurous than eyeballing game from an open Land Rover, try the Otters Den, where owner Wynand Uys offers white-water kayaking or rafting (both short and long trips), abseiling (rappelling), and hot-air ballooning over the nearby game lodges. (All activities cost extra.) You get to this stone, timber, and thatch lodge on an island in the Blyde River by crossing a swing bridge. The whole camp—from rustic chalets on stilts to the bar, dining area, and wooden deck—is sheltered by indigenous trees. All the chalets have showers and ceiling fans. After a dawn flight over the African wilderness in a hot-air balloon, cool off in the natural rock pool. Dinner is usually a traditional meal: a potjiekos or barbecue with homegrown vegetables. ⊠ *Off the R531* ⌀ *Box 408, 1380* ☎ *015/795–5488* ⊕ *www.ottersden.co.za* 🛏 *4 chalets* ⚲ *Fans, pool, bar* ☰ *AE, DC, MC, V* ⑩ *FAP.*

¢ 🏨 Mohlabetsi Safari Lodge. In Balule (an area adjoining Kruger National Park), this small, relaxed game lodge offers a true hands-on bush experience. It's unlikely you'll see all the Big Five—although elephants, lions, and buffalo have been known to wander through camp—but you *will* experience true Africa. Experienced game rangers lead game drives and long bush walks. The public areas of the lodge have informal cane furniture and a bar area on a wide thatch veranda, where you can relax and look out over surprisingly green lawns to a water hole. Spacious thatch *rondawels* (round lodging huts modeled after traditional African dwellings) have a decor that echoes the colors and themes of the bushveld. Although informal, the lodge is extremely personal: rangers and staff are always on hand to offer you a drink or identify a bird you've seen.

✉ *On R40, north of Hoedspruit* ☎ *Box 862, 1380* ☎ *015/793–2166*
⊕ *www.mohlabetsi.co.za* ⇄ *7 rondawels* ⌂ *Pool, 2 bars, 2 lounges;*
no a/c, no room TVs ⊟ *AE, DC, MC, V* ⏐⊙⏐ *FAP.*

Hazyview

⑱ *93 km (57 mi) south of Hoedspruit.*

Named for the heat haze that rises from the fruit plantations and bush
in the surrounding area, Hazyview is a boomtown. Situated in the center of the prime tourist attractions, it's also the gateway to Kruger
through the nearby Phabeni, Numbi, and Kruger gates. There are plenty
of good places to stay and eat, and Hazyview is also the adventure mecca
of the region. Here you can try your hand at horseback riding, helicopter
trips, river rafting, hiking, ballooning, quad biking, golf, and game-viewing safaris.

The **Shangana Cultural Village** is a genuine Shangaan village and is
presided over by Chief Israel Ngobeni, who has lived here for more than
35 years. After your hour-long tour of the *kraal* (traditional rural village), visit the crafts market and crafts school for good-quality local handicrafts and curios, followed by a traditional lunch of *pap* (corn porridge)
and stew. During the evening festival the chief hosts a firelit song-and-
dance performance portraying the history of the Shangaan people in his
royal kraal. It is truly memorable, and a traditional dinner is included.
Reservations are essential for all meals. ✉ *R535, 5 km (3 mi) northwest of Hazyview* ☎ *013/737–7000* ⊕ *www.shangana.co.za* ⇄ *Tour
and meal R120* ⊙ *Daily 9–5, to 8 for evening shows.*

At **Sabie Valley Coffee** you can take a coffee tour, led by owner Tim Buck-
land, through the whole coffee-making process—from orchards to roast-
ing to packaging. Challenge your taste buds with a tasting of homegrown,
100% pure Arabica specialty coffees, before sampling some of the cof-
fee-related goodies for sale: coffee liqueur, cake, and candies. Reservations are essential. ✉ *R536, 18 km (11 mi) west of Hazyview* ☎ *013/
737–8169* ⇄ *Tours with tastings R25* ⊙ *Wed. at 3, Sat. at 10.*

Where to Stay & Eat

★ **$$$** ✕⚎ **Cybele Forest Lodge and Spa.** An ideal honeymoon or couples' re-
treat, Cybele, which celebrated its silver anniversary in 2004, is set in
the forests of the lowveld. Cottages and suites are private, and the main
lodge, separate from guest rooms, has two lounges, a country pub, out-
door relaxing spaces, and two dining rooms. In winter you can play
backgammon by any number of fireplaces, and in summer you can sit
on large shaded verandas. Cottages all have private outside areas, fire-
places, heated towel bars, and under-floor heating. Larger Courtyard
and Paddock suites have private heated pools and outdoor showers. Cy-
bele's Forest Suite, set in a garden, has a heated natural rock pool, mul-
tiple TVs and fireplaces, a full bar and coffee area, surround-sound music,
and a luxurious bathroom with a champagne-stocked fridge. You can
unwind in the spa or get fit at the small, well-equipped gym before brows-
ing in Therapy, comprising a cocktail bar, gift shop, and modest gallery.

All meals are prepared using only organic or free-range foods. A typical five-course dinner (R195; reservations essential) could include Emmenthaler crepes, followed by panfried Atlantic salmon in hollandaise sauce, and fig pâté and passion-fruit brûlée tart. ☒ *Off R40, between Hazyview and White River* ✆ *Box 346, White River 1240* ☎ *013/764–9500* 🖷 *013/764–9510* ⊕ *www.cybele.co.za* 🛏 *12 rooms* ⚹ *2 dining rooms, in-room safes, minibars, 3 pools, gym, spa, hiking, horseback riding, bar, 2 lounges, shops, Internet; no kids under 10* ▤ *AE, DC, MC, V* ⋈ *MAP.*

$$ ✕🖭 **Rissington Inn.** Well off the main road, this relaxed, charming, reasonably priced lodge offers not only fine food and superb hospitality but also all the facilities you'd expect at a top lodge. Whitewashed walls, thatch roofs, and panoramic views over the rolling Sabie River Valley make for a country-house atmosphere. Gaily colored checked or striped bedspreads, pine furniture, and rush mats add to the rustic ambience, and—a special bonus—all rooms have verandas. Not surprisingly, the inn gets lots of repeat visitors. At the restaurant (¢–$) you can dine à la carte on venison stew or tarragon trout and then indulge in chocolate mousse or apple crumble. ☒ *Off the R40, 1 km [¾ mi] from Hazyview and down dirt rd.* ✆ *Box 650, 1242* ☎ *013/737–7700* 🖷 *013/737–7112* ⊕ *www.rissington.co.za* 🛏 *14 rooms* ⚹ *Restaurant, pool, bar* ▤ *AE, DC, MC, V* ⋈ *BP.*

$$ ✕🖭 **Umbhaba Lodge.** You can chill out at this haven of tranquillity set in a lush, subtropical garden with numerous streams, waterfalls, and splashing water features. Earthy colors and timbered ethnic decor give the rooms a real sense of Africa. The main complex overlooks a rock pool, and a walkway leads to a hide and hippo pool. Dine à la carte on the open terrace ($) on almond-and-feta crepes, followed by creamy Amarula (a local liqueur) sirloin schnitzel. For dessert, try black cherries flamed with brandy. ☒ *R40, east of Hazyview* ✆ *Box 1677, 1242* ☎ *013/737–7636* 🖷 *013/737–7629* 🛏 *22 suites* ⚹ *Restaurant, pool, bar; no a/c* ▤ *AE, DC, MC, V* ⋈ *BP.*

★ $ ✕🖭 **Böhm's Zeederberg Country House.** Expect a warm, sincere welcome at this owner-run guesthouse situated on spacious grounds with verdant lawns shaded by fever trees and indigenous chestnuts. Chalets are fully equipped, with bathrooms, minibar-fridges, tea/coffeemaker, a heater, air-conditioning, and hair dryers. Take time to sit on your private veranda and gaze at the spectacular view of the Sabie River Valley and the prolific bird-life. A four-course dinner (R100) includes Sabie trout, venison, and local mushrooms served with fresh herbs and vegetables from the lodge's own garden. ☒ *R536, 18 km (11 mi) west of Hazyview* ✆ *Box 94, Sabie 1260* ☎ *013/737–8101* 🖷 *013/737–8193* ⊕ *www.bohms.co.za* 🛏 *10 rooms* ⚹ *Restaurant, minibars, refrigerators, pool, bar* ▤ *AE, DC, MC, V* ⋈ *BP.*

$$ 🖭 **Tanamera.** The mountain aerie of Tanamera sits in an indigenous forest overlooking the rushing Sabie River. Thatch chalets have sliding glass doors that lead out to a deck, where forest birds skim and dart only yards away. The views are gorgeous. Wash the travel dust off in a huge oval stone bath or "waterfall" shower as you gaze out at the forest canopy. Meals are served either in your chalet or at the main lodge. Start with mushrooms stuffed with brie and feta, followed by a springbok shank with mint sauce and minted peas. At dinner's end, you could tap your inner anglophile and finish with blue cheese and port. A generous wine list offers a good choice of local wines. You can also stay in the self-catering lodge, which has a private plunge pool; the tariff here does not include meals. ⊠ *R536, 20 km (12½ mi) west of Hazyview* ⬧ *Box 383, 1242* ☎ *013/764–2900* 🖷 *013/764–3517* ⊕ *www.tanamera.co.za* ⇆ *4 chalets, 1 lodge* ⚘ *Dining room, kitchen, pool, bar* ☰ *AE, DC, MC, V* ⏉❘ *MAP.*

Shopping

Stop in at the **Windmill Wine Shop** (⊠ R536, 18 km [11 mi] west of Hazyview ☎ 013/737–8175), on the same property as Böhm's Zeederberg, to pick up excellent Cape wines, ports, and brandies, local beer made by Hops Hollow Brewery, and local cheeses, olives, olive oil, and coffee grown and processed at nearby Sabie Valley Coffee. You can also get a light meal of local cheese, cold meats, pâté, and olives.

White River

❶⁹ *35 km (22 mi) southeast of Sabie.*

This green, pleasant little town is set amid nut and tropical-fruit plantations and is one of the gateways to the Panorama Route, which links the major sights of the escarpment. Settled by retired British army officers in the early 20th century, it still has a colonial feel, although there's plenty of new development.

If you're into automobiles and their history, travel to the Casterbridge Farm shopping and entertainment center for the **White River Motor Museum.** It has an impressive collection of more than 60 vehicles, dating from as early as 1911, including a 1936 Jaguar SS100, one of only 314 ever built. ⊠ *R40 and Numbi Rd.* ☎ *013/750–2196* ⊕ *www.casterbridge. co.za* 🗺 *Free* ⏲ *Weekdays 9–4:30, weekends 9:30–4:30.*

Where to Stay & Eat

$–$$ ✕ **Salt Restaurant.** If you fancy African fusion food, there's no better place in the lowveld than this trendy restaurant. Owners Brian Doke and Dario De Angeli have successfully translated their hugely successful formula from their Johannesburg restaurant, Yum, to these lush rolling hills. Enjoy carpaccio of blesbok or ostrich fillets with Moroccan spice rub from the splendid à la carte menu, served on mosaic tables on a veranda surrounded by pink bougainvillea. Salt has a blend of rustic and modern architecture in warm earthy tones, which contribute to a sexy and sophisticated atmosphere. ⊠ *R40, 2 km (1 mi) north of White River* ☎ *013/751–1555* ⚘ *Reservations essential* ☰ *AE, DC, MC, V* ⏲ *Closed Mon.*

★ $$$ ✕🖩 **Highgrove House.** On a hillside overlooking avocado and banana orchards, this former farmhouse is considered one of the very best lodges in the country. Rooms are in white cottages scattered about lovely gardens, and each has a veranda, sitting room, and fireplace. The decor has colonial overtones, with plenty of gathered curtains and floral upholstery. The atmosphere here tends to be rather formal. Highgrove serves an excellent Anglo-French dinner; a typical meal might be a mélange of Knysna oysters, quail eggs, and caviar followed by slivers of guinea fowl and foie gras with a port-and-cranberry sauce. One heavenly dessert is tartlets of fresh figs and almonds. Weather permitting, lunch and breakfast are served in the gazebo by the pool. Nonguests must reserve at least a day ahead for meals at the restaurant (R180). ⊠ *R40, between Hazyview and White River* ⌦ *Box 46, Kiepersol 1241* ☏ *013/764–1844* 🖶 *013/764–1855* ⊕ *www.highgrove.co.za* ⏎ *8 suites* ⚘ *Restaurant, in-room safes, pool, bar; no a/c, no room TVs, no kids under 14* ⊟ *MC, V* ⏐◯⏐ *MAP.*

$$$ ✕▦ **Jatinga Country Lodge and Restaurant.** Situated in magnificent gardens with river frontage on the outskirts of White River, only 38 km (24 mi) from Kruger, this lodge is an original 1920s homestead. Rooms are individually furnished in colonial, Victorian, Provençal, or English-country style. Some have open fireplaces, others private outdoor showers. Complimentary fresh-baked scones are served in the afternoon, sparkling wine with canapés in the privacy of your room at sundown. The superb à la carte restaurant ($–$$) offers house specialties such as crab curry, loin of impala, and homemade Jatinga ice cream in flavors of crème brûlée, passion fruit, and Kahlua. Jatinga offers fly-in guests complimentary transfers to Kruger Mpumalanga International Airport, only 4½ km (3 mi) from the lodge. ⊠ *Jatinga Rd.* ⌦ *Box 3577, 1240* ☏ *013/751–5059 or 013/751–5108* 🖶 *013/751–5119* ⊕ *www.jatinga. co.za* ⏎ *14 rooms* ⚘ *Restaurant, in-room safes, minibars, pool, bar, airport shuttle* ⊟ *AE, DC, MC, V* ⏐◯⏐ *MAP.*

$–$$ ✕▦ **Oliver's Restaurant and Lodge.** This large, white-walled, red-roofed country house situated among pine trees and lush forest is an excellent touring base for both Kruger and the escarpment. Wildflower prints and motifs and white and pastel embroidered linen decorate each room, and brick-red couches and red-checked cushions enliven the lounge and eating areas. Soak up spectacular views of the White River Estate championship golf course, or treat yourself to a soak of another kind at the in-house Wellness and Beauty Clinic. Oliver's is known for its superb food; the excellent à la carte menu ($–$$) might lead you from marinated beef or ostrich carpaccio to the grilled scallops or venison platter and finally to baked chocolate-and-almond pudding. ⊠ *R40, between Hazyview and White River* ⌦ *Box 2809, White River 1240* ☏ *013/ 750–0479* 🖶 *013/751–5555* ⊕ *www.olivers.co.za* ⏎ *9 rooms* ⚘ *Restaurant, in-room safes, minibars, pool, health club, spa, bar* ⊟ *AE, DC, MC, V* ⏐◯⏐ *BP.*

Shopping

You can browse in White River's noted art and crafts galleries or venture to **Casterbridge Farm** (⊠ R40 and Numbi Rd. ☏ 013/750–2196 ⊕ www.casterbridge.co.za), a shopping and entertainment center that was once a rambling mango estate. It now houses stores selling designer clothing, jewelery, local pottery, and art, as well as a range of excellent restaurants offering everything from Portuguese cooking to wood-oven pizza.

Nelspruit

 19 km (12 mi) southwest of White River on the R40.

Nelspruit (nel-sprate), the capital of Mpumalanga and home of the provincial government, is a modern, vibrant city of just over 250,000 people. On the main east–west route between Gauteng and Maputo, Mozambique, it's a notable stop on this route as well as a gateway town to the lowveld and Kruger. The compact town sits in the middle of a prosperous agricultural community, which farms citrus, subtropical fruit, tobacco, and vegetables. It has an international airport and excellent hospitals. You'll probably drive straight through it in search of more exotic destinations. If you have time, it's worth having a look at the **Lowveld National Botanical Gardens,** where more than 500 plant species indigenous to the valley are on display, including a spectacular collection of cycads and ferns. ⊠ *White River Rd., 3 km (2 mi) outside Nelspruit* ☎ *013/752–5531* 🖅 *R7.50* ☉ *May–Sept., daily 8–5:15; Oct.–Apr., daily 8–6.*

Mpumalanga A to Z

AIR TRAVEL

Three airlines—SA Airlink, SA Express, and Nationwide—link Johannesburg to KMIA (Kruger Mpumalanga International Airport), at Nelspruit, which is equipped to handle the largest and most modern aircraft. KMIA has a restaurant, curio shops, banking facilities, car-rental agencies, VIP lounges, information desks, and shaded parking. SA Airlink has daily flights, SA Express flies on Saturday and Sunday, and Nationwide has flights on Wednesday, Friday, and Sunday.

Hoedspruit is an attractive little Africa-themed airport with a restaurant and curio shop. Connected to Johannesburg by SA Express daily, it is close to Kruger's Orpen Gate and serves the Timbavati Game Reserve. SA Airlink has daily flights between Johannesburg and Phalaborwa, a mining town on the edge of central Kruger.

Nelair Charters and Travel, one of the largest privately owned aviation companies in South Africa, is operational 24 hours a day. It operates out of KMIA and does lodge hops within the Sabi Sands, Manyeleti, and Timbavati reserves as well as flights to and from Johannesburg. 🗗 **Airlines Nationwide** ☎ 011/390-1660 ⊕ www.flynationwide.co.za. **Nelair Charters and Travel** ☎ 013/751-1870 or 013/751-1873 ⊕ www.nelair.co.za. **SA Airlink** ☎ 015/781-5823 or 015/781-5833 ⊕ www.saairlink.co.za. **SA Express** ☎ 011/978-5578 ⊕ www.flysax.com.

BUS TRAVEL

Greyhound runs daily between Johannesburg and Nelspruit, stopping at the Promenade Hotel, on Louis Trichardt Street, on the N4 toward Malelane. (The Greyhound office is opposite the hotel in the Old Mutual Building.) The direct trip takes five to six hours, but there are also buses that stop along the way. A round-trip ticket is R330, one-way R165.

Public bus service is limited or nonexistent in Mpumalanga. If you don't have your own car, you're dependent on one of the tour companies to get around the escarpment and into the game reserves. Many of these companies also operate shuttle services that transfer guests between the various lodges and to the airport. It's usually possible to hire these chauffeured minibuses at an hourly or daily rate.

🚌 Bus Line **Greyhound** ☎ 013/753-2100.

CAR TRAVEL

The road system in Mpumalanga is excellent, and the well-maintained roads make it a great place to travel by car. Three principal routes—the N4, N11, and R40—link every destination in the province. From Johannesburg drive north on the N1, and then head east on the N4 to Nelspruit, which is close to many of Kruger's well-marked gates. It's best to arm yourself in advance with up-to-date maps, available at most large gas stations or bookstores, and plan your route accordingly.

The N4 is an expensive toll road (approx R150 for the one-way trip between Johannesburg and Kruger). You can use plastic or cash at the toll booths, where tolls vary between R16 and R40. Though it's a very good, well-maintained road, always look out for the ubiquitous, often reckless taxi drivers in their overcrowded *combis* (vans). Traffic jams are most common on weekends and at the beginning and end of school vacations. Secondary roads are also well maintained and often more scenic, but watch out for goats and donkeys that stray from the villages.

The best places to pick up rental cars are at the KMIA, Hoedspruit, and Phalaborwa airports. Avis, Budget, and Imperial all have desks at KMIA and Phalaborwa, whereas Hoedspruit offers Avis and Budget.

🚗 Rental Companies **Avis** ✉ KMIA, Nelspruit ☎ 013/750-1015 ✉ Hoedspruit Airport ☎ 015/793-2014 ✉ Phalaborwa ☎ 015/781-3169. **Budget** ✉ KMIA, Nelspruit ☎ 013/751-1774 ✉ Hoedspruit Airport ☎ 015/793-2806 ✉ Phalaborwa ☎ 015/781-5822. **Imperial** ✉ KMIA, Nelspruit ☎ 013/750-2871 ✉ Phalaborwa ☎ 015/781-0376.

EMERGENCIES

In case of an emergency, contact the police. In the event of a serious medical emergency, contact Med Rescue International (MRI) or Netcare. Nelmed Forum provides a 24-hour GP service and an emergency service. Nelspruit Medi-Clinic is an excellent, well-equipped hospital with a 24-hour pharmacy.

🚑 Emergency Services **Police** ☎ 10111.

🏥 Hospitals and Medical Services **MRI** ☎ 011/752-3930. **Nelmed Forum** ✉ Nel and Rothery Sts., Nelspruit ☎ 013/755-5000. **Nelspruit Medi-Clinic** ✉ Louise St., behind West End Shopping Centre, Nelspruit ☎ 013/759-0645. **Netcare** ☎ 911/082-911 or 013/741-1620.

INTERNET

Most hotels, guesthouses, and some game lodges have Internet facilities. Check with the tourist office in each town for Internet cafés.

MONEY MATTERS

There are plenty of banks and ATMs in lowveld towns and at KMIA.

TOURS

All tour operators offer an assortment of trips and tours that cover the Panorama Route, which links the major escarpment sights, as well as game-viewing trips into Kruger National Park and the private reserves. Fausto Carbone of Matsimba Safaris is a superb personal tour guide. Springbok Atlas, Trips SA, Welcome Tours, and Cybele Tours and Transfers are just some of the many operators that lead trips in the area. It's pricey, but worth it, to take Cybele's Magic Mountain helicopter trip (R6,275). The helicopter journeys from one sight (including waterfalls) to another, stopping off at the Pinnacle, near Graskop, for a picnic champagne breakfast.

Expressions of Africa, the leisure division of SA Express Airways, has more than 25 years of tour-operating experience in South Africa as well as good access to the most exclusive game lodges. Packages range from standard to luxurious, and Expressions also customizes packages.

🚩 Tour Operators **Cybele Tours and Transfers** ☎ 013/764-1823 ⊕ www.cybele.co.za. **Expressions of Africa** ☎ 011/978-3552 or 011/978-6384. **Matsimba Safaris** ☎ 072/159-4180 or 083/226-6239. **Springbok Atlas** ☎ 011/396-1053 ⊕ www.springbokatlas.com. **Trips SA** ☎ 013/764-1177. **Welcome Tours** ☎ 011/328-8050 ⊕ www.welcome.co.za.

TRAIN TRAVEL

Shosholoza Meyl/Spoornet's *Komati* train travels between Johannesburg and Nelspruit via Tshwane daily, and although it's comfortable and has a dining car, it's very slow (10 hours). It departs from Johannesburg at 5:45 PM and arrives in Nelspruit at 3:32 AM, so make sure there's somebody to meet you at that early hour. A one-way, first-class ticket costs R175, round-trip R350.

The luxurious *Blue Train* also makes occasional runs from Tshwane to Nelspruit; Rovos Rail, the Edwardian-era competitor of the *Blue Train,* travels from Tshwane to Komatipoort, just outside Kruger National Park. Most passengers combine a journey on Rovos Rail with a package trip to a game reserve or one of the exclusive lodges on the escarpment.

🚩 Train Lines **Blue Train** ☎ 012/334-8459 ⊕ www.bluetrain.co.za. **Rovos Rail** ☎ 012/315-8242 or 012/323-6052 ⊕ www.rovos.co.za. **Shosholoza Meyl/Spoornet** ☎ 011/773-2944 ⊕ www.spoornet.co.za.

VISITOR INFORMATION

Mpumalanga Tourism Authority has a host of information. There are also tourist information offices for Hoedspruit, Nelspruit, and White River. The Golden Monkey offers a free booking service for places to stay and things to do in the lowveld and escarpment. Sabie and Lowveld Info have Web sites for additional information.

🚩 Tourist Offices **Golden Monkey** ✉ Hazyview ☎ 013/737-8191 ⊕ www.big5country.com. **Hoedspruit tourist information** ✉ Unit 1, Maroela Park, Kudu St., Hoedspruit ☎ 015/793-2996. **Mpumalanga Tourism Authority** ✉ Box 679, Nelspruit 1200 ☎ 013/752-7001 ⊕ www.mpumalanga.com. **Nelspruit tourist information** ✉ The Crossing shopping center, N4, Nelspruit ☎ 013/750-2136. **White River tourist information** ✉ Casterbridge Farm, White River ☎ 013/750-1073.

🚩 Web Sites **Lowveld Info** ⊕ www.lowveld.info. **Sabie** ⊕ www.sabie.co.za.

KRUGER NATIONAL PARK

Visiting Kruger is likely to be one of the great experiences of your life. You'll be delighted and amazed not only with the diversity of life forms, from trees, amphibians, and fish to reptiles, birds, and mammals, but also its San (Bushman) rock paintings and major archaeological sites. (There is ample evidence that prehistoric humans—*Homo erectus*—roamed the area between 500,000 and 100,000 years ago.) Founded in 1898 by Paul Kruger, president of what was then the Transvaal Republic, the park is a place to safari at your own pace, choosing from upscale private camps or simple campsites as you wish.

Kruger lies in the hot lowveld, a subtropical section of Mpumalanga and Limpopo provinces that abuts Mozambique. The park cuts a swath 80 km (50 mi) wide and 320 km (200 mi) long from Zimbabwe and the Limpopo River in the north to the Crocodile River in the south. It is divided into 16 macro ecozones, each supporting a great variety of plants, birds, and animals, including 145 mammal species and almost 500 species of birds, some of which are not found elsewhere in South Africa. In the next few years, although no final date has yet been arrived at, the fences between Kruger, the Gonarezhou National Park in Mozambique, and the Limpopo National Park in Zimbabwe will come down to form the Great Limpopo Transfrontier Park, which will then be the largest wildlife reserve in Africa.

Exploring Kruger National Park

The southern and central sections of the park are where you will probably see the most game. Riverine forests, thorny thickets, and large, grassy plains studded with knobthorn and marula trees are typical of this region and make ideal habitats for a variety of animals, including black and white rhinos (once on the verge of extinction), leopards, giraffes, hyenas, numerous kinds of antelope, lions, and the rare "painted wolf"— a wild dog. One of the most consistently rewarding drives in the park is along the H4, running along the Sabie River from Skukuza to Lower Sabie. It can be crowded, however, particularly on weekends and public holidays and especially (read: avoid the park then!) during the July and December school vacations.

As you drive north to Olifants and Letaba, you enter major elephant country, although you're likely to spot lots of other game, too, including lions and cheetahs. North of Letaba, however, the landscape becomes a monotonous blur of *mopane* (bushwillow) trees, the result of nutrient-poor land that supports smaller numbers of animals, although the lugubrious-looking *tsessebe* (sess-a-bee) antelope and the magnificent and uncommon roan antelope, with its twisty horns, thrive here. Elephants love mopane, and you'll certainly see plenty of them. The Shingwedzi River Drive is one of the park's most rewarding drives, with elephants, leopards, giraffes, and other game regularly seen. Park your vehicle underneath the lovely hide on this drive, and take in life on the river, including waterbirds, hippos, and basking crocs. To experience the

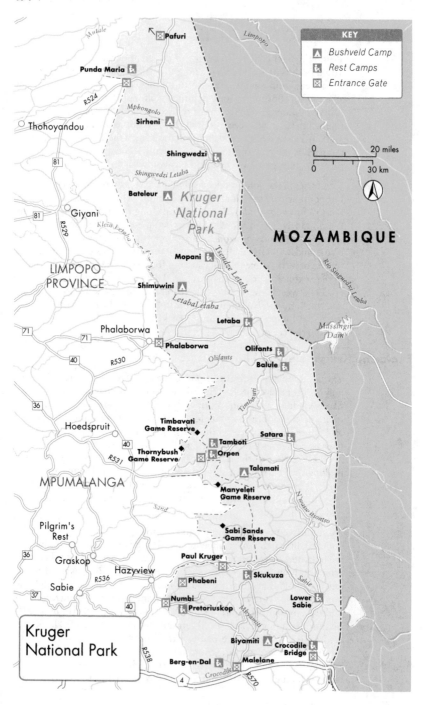

KEY

△ Bushveld Camp
🏕 Rest Camps
⊠ Entrance Gate

0   20 miles
0   30 km

Pafuri

Punda Maria

Mutale

Limpopo

R524

Mphongolo

Sirheni △

Thohoyandou

Shingwedzi 🏕

Shingwedzi Letaba

Bateleur △   *Kruger*
                 National
                 Park

81

Giyani   *Klein Letaba*

81

R529

LIMPOPO
PROVINCE

Mopani 🏕

Tsendze Letaba

MOZAMBIQUE

Shimuwini △

LetabaLetaba

Letaba 🏕

Massingir
Dam

71

71

Phalaborwa

R530

Phalaborwa ⊠

Olifants

Olifants 🏕

Balule 🏕

Rio Singwedzi Letaba

40

36

Timbavati
Game Reserve ◆

Timbavati

Satara 🏕

Hoedspruit

Tamboti 🏕
Orpen ⊠

Thornybush ◆
Game Reserve

R531

Talamati △

MPUMALANGA

Manyeleti
Game Reserve ◆

Sand

N'waswitsontso

Pilgrim's
Rest

Sabi Sands
Game Reserve ◆

36

Graskop

Hazyview

Paul Kruger ⊠

Skukuza 🏕

Sabie

37

Sabie

R536

Phabeni ⊠

40

Numbi ⊠

Pretoriuskop 🏕

Lower
Sabie 🏕

Mbyamiti

Kruger
National Park

Biyamiti △

Crocodile
Bridge 🏕 ⊠

R538

Berg-en-Dal 🏕

Malelane ⊠

4

Crocodile

R570

full richness of the northern Kruger, visit the Pafuru Picnic Site (hot water and braais available), where ancient massive leadwood and jackalberry trees lean over the often dry Luvuvhi River, the haunt of the scarlet-and-green Narina trogon and the much-sought-after Pel's fishing owl. But don't leave your picnic unattended while you look for more special birds, such as the wattle-eyed flycatcher, because the vervet monkeys will have it in a flash.

Since the bush is unpredictable, you may get some of your best sightings where and when you least expect them: a pack of wild dogs lying in the road just outside the Skukuza camp gate or a cheetah and two cubs sitting in the middle of the tar road 100 yards inside the Orpen Gate. If you have a week in Kruger, it's worth driving north, as there are always fewer people here. However, if you are short on time, then stick to the south or central sections of the park. But wherever you go, **don't get out of your vehicle** except at certain well-marked picnic sites or view sites, unless you want to make an international headline.

There are nine entrance gates to Kruger, namely (counterclockwise from the north) Pafuri, Punda Maria, Phalaborwa, Orpen, Paul Kruger, Phabeni, Numbi, Malelane, and Crocodile Bridge. National access roads to all the entrance gates are tarred. You can arrange for a late-entry escort (R150) until 9 PM for the following gates (and their nearby camps): Paul Kruger (Skukuza), Numbi (Pretoriuskop), Malelane (Berg-en-Dal and Malelane), Crocodile Bridge (Crocodile Bridge), Punda Maria (Punda Maria), and Orpen (Orpen). Always check at your entry gate for visitor-friendly pamphlets, maps, and books (also available in the camp shops).

There is a daily conservation fee, but WildCards, available at the gates or online, are more economical for stays of more than a few days. Reservations for all accommodations, bush drives, wilderness trails, and other park activities must be made through South African National Parks. ⌂ *Box 787, Pretoria 0001* ☎ *012/343–1991* 🖷 *012/343–0905* ⊕ *www. SANParks.org* 💳 *R120* ☉ *Gates Apr.–Sept., daily 6–5:30; Oct.–Mar., daily 5:30* AM*–6:30* PM*, but sometimes vary.*

Bush Drives
First-time visitors sometimes feel a little lost driving themselves through the park. They don't know what to look for, and they can't always identify the animals they see. Besides, not everyone knows what to do when a herd of elephants blocks the road. An affordable solution is to hire a game ranger to show you the park and its animal and bird inhabitants. All the major rest camps offer ranger-led bush drives in open-air vehicles (minimum of two people). Not only can rangers explain the finer points of what you're seeing, but they can also take you into areas off-limits to the public. They may even take you on short walks through the bush, something else you can't do on your own. Day excursions cost about R600 per person, R300 per child. Book drives at least two weeks in advance or when you make your park reservations.

Day & Night Drives
Even if you tour the park by yourself during the day, don't miss out on a ranger-led night drive, when the park is closed to regular visitors.

CloseUp
SPOTTING KRUGER'S BIG GAME

WATCHING GAME in the bush is very different from watching it on the Discovery Channel with its nonstop action. The former demands energy, concentration, patience, and luck, and with these you'll probably see wonderful game at Kruger, including the Big Five. The easy option is to visit a private game reserve, where knowledgeable rangers take you out in open vehicles or on foot and find game for you. You might spend two or three nights at a private reserve and then rent a vehicle and strike out on your own into Kruger's unknown territory. There's nothing quite like the thrill of finding your "own" elephant or identifying that psychedelic turquoise-and-lilac bird for yourself. Bring a couple of good field guides, available at bookstores and Kruger camp shops.

Drive slowly, stop at water holes, and keep your eyes and ears open. Talk to other visitors, and read the "game sightings" notice board and visitor's book at each camp. If other vehicles are stopped on the road, be courteous. Don't drive in front or beside them and block their view, but edge along and find out what's being looked at. Don't forget to absorb the total bush experience—big and little creatures, trees, plants, sounds, colors, shapes, and smells. Look for the Little Five: the elephant shrew, lion ant, leopard tortoise, buffalo weaverbird, and rhinoceros beetle. You'll often find these in camp along with hundreds of birds that are habituated to visitors, good for up-close pictures.

You'll sit in a large open-air vehicle, scanning the bush with the ranger, who uses a powerful spotlight to pick out animals, including nocturnal creatures that you would never see otherwise. You might see bush babies (enchanting furry, big-eared, big-eyed little primates that leap from bush to bush), servals (mini leopard-looking felines), civets (black and white possum look-alikes), genets (spotted catlike creatures with bushy tails), or an aardvark ambling along in the moonlight. Scrutinize branches of big trees for the giant eagle owl, with its sexy pink eyelids, or a leopard chewing on its kill. Night is also the time when hyenas and lions hunt. These opportunities alone make a night drive an unforgettable experience. The three- to four-hour trip leaves the rest camps half an hour before the gates close. Book as far in advance as possible. Night drives cost R140–R190 per person (depending on the size of the vehicle—smaller vehicles cost more), half price for kids. Don't forget your binoculars, a snack or drink, and a warm jacket whatever the season.

Day drives follow the same format as night drives. Choose between dawn, midmorning, and sunset drives. The cost is approximately the same as for night drives.

Wilderness Trails

Spend a few days hiking through the wilds of Africa and you may never again be satisfied with driving around a game reserve. On foot you gain an affinity for the animals and the bush that's impossible in the confines of a vehicle. Kruger has seven wilderness trails, each accommodating eight people. You need to be walking-fit and reasonably adventurous. Led by an armed ranger and local tracker, you'll go out in the morning for a few hours, come back at lunchtime for a meal and a siesta, and go out again in the early evening before returning to the same trail camp to relive the day's adventures around a cheerful campfire. These are not military-style marches but slow meanders, the point being to learn about your surroundings: the medicinal uses of trees and plants, the role of dung beetles and wasps in the ecology, and how to recognize animals by their spoor. In general, you don't get as close to animals on foot as you can in a vehicle. You will see animals, though, and many hikers can recount face-to-face encounters with everything from rhinos to elephants and lions.

Hikes last three nights and two days (starting on Sunday and Wednesday), and you should be prepared to walk as far as 19 km (12 mi) a day, although this will depend on the consensus of the group. Don't be afraid to make your wishes heard; have a group chat with your ranger on the first night and decide on the walking agenda. No one under 12 or over 60 is allowed, although if you book the whole trail and produce a doctor's certificate, over-60s are allowed. Hikers sleep in rustic A-frame two-bed huts and share a reed-wall bathroom with flush toilets and bucket showers. Meals are simple bush fare, including stews and barbecues; you provide your own booze and soft drinks (which you can purchase from the camp where you meet before the trail). In summer the trails are often cheaper (it is uncomfortably hot to walk at this time), and in winter, nights can be freezing, so take very warm clothes and an extra blanket. These trails are incredibly popular; try to reserve 13 months in advance, when bookings open. The cost is approximately R2,150 per person per trail.

Bushman Trail. In the southwestern corner of the park, this trail takes its name from the San rock paintings and sites found in the area. The trail camp lies in a secluded valley dominated by granite hills and cliffs. Watch out for white rhinos, elephants, and buffalo. Check in at Berg-en-Dal.

Metsimetsi Trail. The permanent water of the nearby N'waswitsontso River makes this one of the best trails for winter game viewing. Midway between Skukuza amd Satara, the trail camp hunkers in the lee of a mountain in an area of gorges, cliffs, and rolling savanna. Check in at Skukuza.

Napi Trail. Sightings of white rhinos are common on this trail, which runs through mixed bushveld between Pretoriuskop and Skukuza. Other frequent sightings include black rhinos, cheetahs, leopards, and elephants. If you're lucky, you may also see the nomadic wild dogs. The trail camp is tucked into dense riverine forest at the confluence of the Napi and Biyamiti rivers. Check in at Pretoriuskop.

Nyalaland Trail. If it's pristine wilderness and remoteness you're after, then this camp in the far north of the park is for you. The camp is situated among ancient baobab trees near the Luvuvhu River, and you'll walk at the foot of huge rocky gorges as well as in dense forest. Some highly sought-after birds, such as Bohm's spinetail, crested eagle, and Pel's fishing owl, can be found in this birding mecca of huge baobabs and sinister-looking slime-green fever trees. You're almost certain to see hippos, crocodiles, elephants, buffalo, and the strikingly colored nyala antelope, with its dark fur, white spotted nose, and yellow "soccer stockings." Check in at Punda Maria.

Olifants Trail. With one of the most spectacular sites of all trail camps, this camp commands a great view of the Olifants River and affords regular sightings of elephants, lions, buffalo, and hippos. You'll walk through landscape varying from riverine forest to the rocky foothills of the Lebombo Mountains. Check in at Letaba.

Sweni Trail. East of Satara, this trail camp overlooks the Sweni Spruit and savanna dotted with marula and knobthorn trees. The area attracts large herds of zebras, wildebeests, and buffalo with their attendant predators: lions, spotted hyenas, and, if you're very lucky, wild dogs. Check in at Satara.

Wolhuter Trail. If you want to come face-to-face with a white rhino, choose this trail midway between Berg-en-Dal and Pretoriuskop. The undulating bushveld, interspersed with rocky *kopjes* (small hills), is ideal habitat for these tremendous, somehow anachronistic beasts, but you're also likely to see elephants, buffalo, and lions. Check in at Berg-en-Dal.

Where to Stay in Kruger National Park

Rest Camps

Rest camps include a variety of accommodations with prices to match—from R100 for a campsite for two people through basic two-person huts at R220 up to R1,700 for a luxury guesthouse for up to four people. Options include rondawels (round beehive huts), huts, cottages, bungalows, safari tents, guest cottages, and guesthouses. As a rule of thumb, here's what's meant by these terms (keeping in mind that each camp is different): Rondawels and huts consist of one room with electricity; you'll share a communal bathroom facility (always clean and with hot and cold running water) and communal kitchen with hot plates, sinks, and fridge. Cottages comprise at least one bedroom, a living room, bathroom, and a partially equipped kitchen or kitchenette, and a family cottage will have one, two, or three bedrooms with kitchenette. Bungalows have one room and a bathroom; some have their own kitchenettes, whereas others share communal kitchen facilities. Units with cooking facilities have basic kitchen equipment, dishes, and cutlery. Guest cottages and guesthouses are secluded units within a rest camp and have three or four bedrooms, most of which have private bathrooms. Each has a fully equipped kitchen, a communal lounge/living room, or an open veranda. Permanent, comfortable, large walk-in East African–style safari tents with insect-proof flaps and windows sleep one or two people. Very popular, they give an *Out of Africa* feel and are equipped with beds, a cupboard, table and chairs, fridge, and electric fan. Communal kitchen and bathroom facilities are provided. In all accommodations, beds are comfortable, linens are always impeccable, soap and towels are provided, and units are serviced on a daily basis. A site to pitch your own tent costs approximately R100 for up to two people throughout the park. All campsites have excellent cooking and bathroom facilities.

All the major rest camps have electricity; a first-aid center; a shop selling food, drink (including alcohol—local wine is particularly good), curios, wildlife books, videos, and DVDs; barbecue and communal kitchen facilities; a self-service laundry or laundry tubs; public telephones (cell-phone reception is usually possible at most of the major rest camps and environs); a gas station; and a restaurant and/or self-service cafeteria. However, most people bring their own food and drink (or buy it), and the evening braai (most rooms have individual open-air barbecue facilities) is a friendly park ritual; visitors build their fires as night falls and lions and hyenas start their nocturnal choruses. Holiday programs and evening shows on wildlife and conservation are arranged at many of the rest camps. Nature trails have been laid out in Punda Maria, Berg-en-Dal (also accessible to blind/visually impaired visitors), and Pretoriuskop. There are no age limits on kids except for on the walking trails.

All rest camps have their own individual character and charm. However, Skukuza, the hub of the park, is more like a small town than a rest camp. Avoid it if you dislike crowds, particularly in summer. There are swimming pools for residents only at Berg-en-Dal, Lower Sabie, Pretoriuskop, Mopani, Shingwedzi, and Skukuza. Skukuza also has a post office and a bank. There is an additional pool for day visitors at the Skukuza Day Visitor Area (to be avoided if possible, as it is nearly always packed). All rest camps are protected and enclosed by electrified fences, which are highly functional but don't prevent good game viewing through the wire. It's always worth a dawn patrol or sunset stroll around your camp fence; you never know what you may spot.

The golden rule when booking your accommodation is to get as much information as possible about the different types before you make your decision. It's often necessary to reserve a year in advance if you want to come during peak seasons (December–January and July). Reservations should be made with the **South African National Parks.** ✑ *Box 787, Pretoria 0001* ☎ *012/343–1991* 🖷 *012/343–0905* ⊕ *www.SANParks. org* 🖃 *AE, DC, MC, V.*

¢ 🏠 **Balule.** On the banks of the Olifants River, this rustic camp differs radically from the others, appealing to those who don't mind roughing it a bit and want to experience the true feel of the bush. There are no shops or restaurants, and there's no electricity either—only lanterns—so bring your own food. Accommodations are in basic three-bed huts with no windows (vents only) and shared bathroom facilities with running water. You must check in at Olifants, 11 km (7 mi away). ➥ *15 campsites, 6 huts.*

¢ ▦ **Berg-en-Dal.** This rest camp lies at the southern tip of the park, in a basin surrounded by rocky hills. Berg-en-Dal is known for its white rhinos, leopards, and wild dogs, but it lacks the tremendous game intensity of some of the camps to its north. A small pond by one side of the perimeter fence offers good game viewing, including a close look at cruising crocodiles. One of the more attractive camps, it has thoughtful landscaping, which has left much of the indigenous vegetation intact, making for more privacy. One slight disadvantage here is that the lights of a timber and paper mill are visible at night, which destroys the illusion that you are deep in the wilderness. ↪ *63 chalets, 23 family cottages, 2 guesthouses, 70 campsites* ⌂ *Restaurant, cafeteria, grocery, kitchens, pool, shop, laundry facilities.*

¢ ▦ **Crocodile Bridge.** In the southeastern corner of the park, this superb small rest camp (it's won awards for good service three years running) doubles as an entrance gate, which makes it a convenient stopover if you arrive near the park's closing time and thus too late to make it to another camp. Although the Crocodile River provides a scenic backdrop, any sense of being in the wild is quickly shattered by views of power lines and farms on the south side. The road leading from the camp to Lower Sabie is famous for sightings of general game as well as buffalo, rhinos, cheetahs, and lions, but it's often crowded on weekends and holidays and during school vacations. A hippo pool lies just 5 km (3 mi) away. ↪ *20 bungalows (2 for disabled), 8 safari tents, 12 campsites* ⌂ *Grocery, kitchens, shop, laundry facilities.*

¢ ▦ **Letaba.** Overlooking the frequently dry Letaba River, this lovely camp sits in the middle of elephant country in the central section of the park. There's excellent game viewing on the roads to and all around the Englelhardt and Mingerhout dams. The camp itself has a real bush feel: all the huts are thatch (ask for one overlooking the river), and the grounds are overgrown with apple-leaf trees, acacias, mopane, and lala palms. The restaurant and snack bar, with attractive outdoor seating, look out over the broad, sandy riverbed. Even if you're not staying at Letaba, stop at the superb elephant exhibit at the Environmental Education Centre. Campsites, on the camp's perimeter, offer lots of shade for your tent or trailer. ↪ *8 bungalows, 5 huts, 10 guest cottages, 2 guesthouses, 20 safari tents, 35 campsites* ⌂ *Restaurant, cafeteria, kitchens, shop, laundry facilities.*

¢ ▦ **Lower Sabie.** This is one of the most popular camps in Kruger for good reason: it has tremendous views over a broad sweep of the Sabie River and sits in one of the best game-viewing areas of the park (along with Skukuza and Satara). White rhinos, lions, cheetahs, elephants, and buffalo frequently come down to the river to drink, especially in the dry winter months when there is little surface water elsewhere. The vegetation around the camp is mainly grassland savanna interspersed with marula and knobthorn trees, and there are also lots of animal drinking holes within a few minutes' drive. After a devastating fire, the camp was rebuilt, and long wooden walkways that curve around the restaurant and shop are particularly attractive; you can sit here looking out over the river. Half the safari tents have a river view. ↪ *30 huts, 62 bungalows, 24 safari tents, 1 guest cottage, 1 guesthouse, 33 campsites* ⌂ *Restaurant, cafeteria, kitchens, pool, shop, laundry facilities.*

¢ ⊡ **Mopani.** Built in the lee of a rocky kopje overlooking a lake, this camp in the northern section is one of Kruger's biggest. The lake and the camp are an oasis for both animals and people amid not very attractive surrounding mopane woodlands. If it's hippos you're after, sit on your veranda overlooking the lake and feast your eyes on a cavalcade of these giants mating, frolicking, or just mooching about. Constructed of rough stone, wood, and thatch, the camp blends well into the thick vegetation. Shaded wooden walkways connect the public areas, all of which overlook the lake, and the view from the open-air bar is awesome. The à la carte restaurant (reserve before 6 PM) serves better food than most of the other camps, and the cottages are better equipped and larger than their counterparts elsewhere in Kruger. Ask for accommodations overlooking the lake when you book. Mopani lacks the intimate charm of some of the smaller camps, but it's a really comfortable camp to chill out in for a night or two if you're driving the length of the park. ⟿ *45 bungalows, 12 cottages, 45 guest cottages, 1 guesthouse ⟁ Restaurant, cafeteria, kitchens, pool, bar, shop, laundry facilities.*

¢ ⊡ **Olifants.** In the central section of the park, Olifants has the best setting of all the Kruger camps, high atop cliffs on a rocky ridge with panoramic views of the distant hills and the Olifants River below. A lovely thatch-sheltered terrace allows you to sit for hours with binoculars and pick out the animals below. Lions often make kills in the river valley, and elephants, buffalo, giraffes, kudu, and other game come to drink and bathe. Try to book one of the thatch rondawels overlooking the river for at least two nights (you'll need to book a year in advance) so you can hang out on your veranda and watch Africa's passing show below. Olifants offers more than a good view, however. It's a charming old camp, graced with wonderful indigenous trees like sycamore figs, mopane, and sausage trees—so called because of the huge, brown, sausage-shape fruits that weigh down the branches. A big drawback, particularly in the hot summer months, however, is that it has no pool. ⟿ *97 rondawels, 2 guesthouses ⟁ Restaurant, cafeteria, kitchens, shop, laundry facilities.*

¢ ⊡ **Orpen.** Don't dismiss this tiny Cinderella rest camp in the center of the park because of its proximity to the Orpen Gate. It may not be a particularly attractive camp—the rooms, arranged in a rough semicircle around a large lawn, look out toward the perimeter fence, about 150 feet away—but there's a permanent water hole, where animals come to drink, and plenty of game in the vicinity, including cheetahs, lions, and rhinos. The two-bedroom huts are a bit sparse, with no bathrooms or cooking facilities (although there are good communal ones), but there are three comfortable family cottages with bathrooms and kitchenettes. And it's a blissfully quiet camp, as there are so few accommodations. ⟿ *12 huts, 3 guest cottages ⟁ Some kitchenettes, shop.*

¢ ⊡ **Pretoriuskop.** This large, rather bare-looking camp, conveniently close to the Numbi Gate in the southwestern corner of the park, makes a good overnight stop for new arrivals. The rocky kopjes and steep ridges that characterize the surrounding landscape provide ideal habitat for mountain reedbuck and klipspringers—antelope not always easily seen elsewhere in the park. The area's sourveld (so named because its vegetation is less sweet and attractive to herbivores than other kinds of vegetation) also attracts browsers like giraffes and kudu, as well as white rhinos, lions, and wild dogs. There's not a lot of privacy in camp—accommodations tend to overlook each other—but there is some shade. ⟟ *82 rondawels, 52 bungalows, 6 cottages, 45 campsites ⅏ Restaurant, cafeteria, kitchens, pool, shop, laundry facilities.*

¢   ▦ **Punda Maria.** Few foreign visitors make it to this lovely little camp in the far end of the park near Zimbabwe. If you have time, however, try to get there, because in some ways it offers the best bush experience of any of the major rest camps. It's a small enclave, with tiny whitewashed thatch cottages arranged in terraces on a hill. The camp lies in sandveld, a botanically rich area notable for its plant and birdlife. At a tiny, saucer-shape, ground-level, stone birdbath, just over the wall from the barbecue site, dozens of really special birds come and go all day. A few hours sitting on the bench overlooking this birdbath can be a highlight for birders. A nature trail winds through and behind the camp—also great for birds. Two-bed huts all have bathrooms, and many have fully equipped kitchenettes. There are also two very private six-bed cottages up on a hill above the camp, visited by an amazing variety of not-often-seen birds and some friendly genets. Reservations are advised for the restaurant, and only some of the campsites have power. ⟟ *22 huts, 2 cottages, 50 campsites ⅏ Restaurant, some kitchenettes, shop.*

¢   ▦ **Satara.** Second in size only to Skukuza, this camp sits in the middle of the hot plains between Olifants and Lower Sabie, in the central section of Kruger. The knobthorn veld surrounding the camp provides the best grazing in the park and attracts large concentrations of game. That in turn brings the attendant predators—lions, cheetahs, hyenas, and wild dogs—which makes this one of the best areas in the park for viewing game. If you stand or stroll around the perimeter fence, you may see giraffes, zebras, and waterbucks and other antelopes. Despite its size, Satara has far more appeal than Skukuza, possibly because of the privacy it offers (the huts aren't all piled on top of one another) and possibly because of the tremendous bird-life. The restaurant and cafeteria are very pleasant, with shady seating overlooking the lawns and the bush beyond. Accommodations are in large cottages and two- or three-bed thatch rondawels, some with kitchenettes (no cooking utensils). The rondawels, arranged in large circles, face inward onto a central, open, grassy area. Campsites are secluded, with an excellent view of the bush, although they don't have much shade. ⟟ *153 rondawels, 10 guest cottages, 3 guesthouses, 74 campsites ⅏ Restaurant, cafeteria, some kitchenettes, shop, laundry facilities.*

¢   ▦ **Shingwedzi.** This camp lies in the northern section of the park, amid monotonous long stretches of mopane woodland. The camp benefits enormously from the riverine growth associated with the Shingwedzi River and Kanniedood (Never Die) Dam. As a result, you'll probably find more game around this camp than anywhere else in the region. Thatch and rough tree trunks that serve as roof supports give the camp a rugged, pioneer feel. Both the à la carte restaurant and the outdoor cafeteria have views over the Shingwedzi River. Accommodations are of two types: A and B. Try for one of the A units, whose steeply pitched thatch roofs accommodate an additional two-bed loft; some also have fully equipped kitchenettes. The huts face one another across a fairly barren expanse of dry earth except in early spring, when the gorgeous bright pink impala lilies are in bloom. *24 huts, 54 bungalows, 1 cottage, 1 guesthouse, 50 campsites △ Restaurant, cafeteria, some kitchenettes, pool, laundry facilities.*

¢ ▦ **Skukuza.** It's worth popping in to have a look at this huge camp. More like a small town than a rest camp, it has a gas station, police station, airport, post office, car-rental agency, grocery store, and library. It's nearly always crowded, not only with regular visitors but with busloads of noisy day-trippers, and consequently has lost any bush feel at all. Skukuza is popular for good reason, though. It's easily accessible by both air and road, and it lies in a region of thorn thicket teeming with game, including lions, cheetahs, and hyenas. The camp itself sits on a bank of the crocodile-infested Sabie River, with good views of thick reeds, dozing hippos, and grazing waterbuck. Visit the worthwhile museum and education center to learn something about the history and ecology of the park. However, if you're allergic to noise and crowds, limit yourself to a stroll along the banks of the Sabie River before heading for one of the smaller camps. *199 bungalows, 16 cottages, 15 guest cottages, 7 guesthouses, 20 safari tents, 80 campsites △ Restaurant, cafeteria, grocery, pool, library, shop, car rental.*

¢ ◬ **Tamboti.** Kruger's first tented camp (very near the Orpen Gate) is superbly sited on the banks of the frequently dry Tamboti River, among sycamore fig and jackalberry trees. Communal facilities make it a bit like an upscale campsite, but nevertheless it's one of Kruger's most popular camps, so book well ahead. From your tent you may well see elephants digging in the riverbed for water just beyond the barely visible electrified fence. Each of the walk-in, permanent tents has its own deck overlooking the river, but when you book, ask for one in the deep shade of large riverine trees—worth it in the midsummer heat. All kitchen, washing, and toilet facilities are in two shared central blocks. Just bring your own food and cooking and eating utensils. *30 safari tents.*

Bushveld Camps

Smaller, more intimate, more luxurious, and consequently more expensive than regular rest camps, Kruger's bushveld camps are in remote areas of the park that are often off-limits to regular visitors. Access is limited to guests only. As a result you get far more bush and fewer fellow travelers. Night drives and day excursions are available in most of the camps. There are no restaurants, gas pumps, or grocery stores, so bring your provisions with you, though you can buy wood for your barbecue. All accommodations have fully equipped kitchens, bathrooms, ceiling fans, and large verandas, but only Bateleur has air-conditioning and TV, the latter installed especially for a visit by South Africa's president. Cottages have tile floors, cheerful furnishings, and cane patio furniture and are sited in stands of trees or clumps of indigenous bush for maximum privacy. Many face directly onto a river or water hole. There are only a handful of one-bedroom cottages (at Biyamiti, Shimuweni, Sirheni, and Talamati), but it's worth booking a four-bed one and paying the extra, even for only two people. The average cottage price for a couple is R850, with extra people (up to five or six) paying R180 each.

Reservations should be made with **South African National Parks.** ⊙ *Box 787, Pretoria 0001* ☎ *012/343–1991* 🖨 *012/343–0905* ⊕ *www. SANParks.org* 🖃 *AE, DC, MC, V.*

$ 🏕 **Bateleur.** Hidden in the northern reaches of the park, this tiny camp, the oldest of the bushveld camps, is one of Kruger's most remote destinations. Shaded by tall trees, it overlooks the dry watercourse of the Mashokwe Spruit. A raised platform provides an excellent game-viewing vantage point, and it's only a short drive to two nearby lakes, which draw a huge variety of animals, from lions and elephants to zebras and hippos. The main bedroom in each cottage has air-conditioning. 🛏 *7 cottages.*

$ 🏕 **Biyamiti.** Close to the park gate at Crocodile Bridge, this larger-than-average bush camp overlooks the normally dry sands of the Biyamiti River. It's a very popular camp because it's close to the southern gates, and because the game is usually prolific. The vegetation is mixed combretum woodland, which attracts healthy populations of kudu, impalas, elephants, lions, and black and white rhinos. 🛏 *15 cottages.*

$ 🏕 **Shimuwini.** Birders descend in droves on this isolated camp set on a lovely lake on the Letaba River. Towering jackalberry and sycamore fig trees offer welcome shade, as well as refuge to a host of resident and migratory birds. Away from the river, the riverine forest quickly gives way to mopane woodland, not typically known for supporting large quantities of game. Even so, the outstandingly beautiful roan antelope and handsome, rare black and white sable antelope, which has back-sweeping scimitarlike horns, move through the area. Resident leopards patrol the territory, and elephants are usually browsing in the mopane. Cottages have one, two, or three bedrooms. 🛏 *15 cottages.*

$ 🏕 **Sirheni.** The most remote of all the bushveld camps and one of the loveliest, Sirheni, another major bird-watching camp, sits on the edge of the Sirheni Dam, in the far north of the park. Because there is permanent water, game—including lions, leopards, and white rhinos—can often be seen at the lake, particularly in the dry winter months. A rewarding drive for birders and game spotters alike runs along the Mphongolo River. Watch the sun set over the magnificent bush from one of two secluded viewing platforms at either end of the camp, but be sure to smother yourself with mosquito repellent. 🛏 *15 cottages.*

$ 🏕 **Talamati.** On the banks of the normally dry N'waswitsontso River in Kruger's central section, this peaceful camp offers excellent game viewing. Grassy plains and mixed woodlands provide an ideal habitat for herds of impalas, zebras, and wildebeests, as well as lions, cheetahs, and elephants. You can take a break from your vehicle and watch birds and game from a couple of raised viewing platforms inside the perimeter fence. 🛏 *15 cottages.*

Concessions Within Kruger

Among the privately operated areas within the boundaries of the park is the 37,000-acre wilderness area of the N'wanetsi concession. Here two lodges, Singita Lebombo and Sweni, are located at the confluence of the N'wanetsi and Sweni rivers. The area was once the base for the park's foot and horse patrols, and until the building of the lodges, it had never been traversed by vehicles. Today it's home to the Big Five as well as zebras, giraffes, wildebeests, hippos, hundreds of bird species, and varied flora. Twice-daily game drives (dawn and late afternoon) in an open vehicle are led by a highly experienced and knowledgeable ranger. You can also take a bush nature walk, camp out under the stars, or try your hand at archery.

The camps of Rhino Walking Safaris, Rhino Post Safari Lodge and Plains Camp, are situated in about 30,000 acres of pristine bushveld in the Mutlumuvi area of Kruger, 10 km (6 mi) northeast of Skukuza. The concession shares a 15-km (9-mi) boundary with Mala Mala, in the Sabi Sands Game Reserve, and game moves freely between the two. The environmental impact of the lodge and tented camp is minimal; no concrete was used in buildings, battery power is used for lighting, and a special Reedbed System processes bathroom waste. The area is home to the Big Five as well as many other mammals, birds, trees, and other plants. Activities include twice-daily game drives with professional guides in specially adapted open Land Rovers (the camps have access to some of Kruger's public roads at night), a sleep-out on an elevated wooden platform overlooking a water hole, a guided bush walk, a half- or full-day drive on public roads (with picnic lunch), or a game of golf, which can be arranged at the 9-hole Skukuza course. Trail packages, which include lodging, encourage a sense of companionship among the group (maximum eight), which decides together on speed and length of walks; feats of endurance are not the name of the game. Often, in fact, when you move very slowly you see far more in the way of not only game, but also of the smaller facets of bush life.

★ $$$$ 🏨 **Singita Lebombo Lodge.** Taking its name from the Lebombo mountain range and eco-driven in concept, Singita Lebombo, winner of numerous international accolades, has been built "to touch the ground lightly." It hangs seemingly suspended on the edge of a cliff, like a huge glass box in space. Wooden walkways connect the aptly named "lofts" (suites), all which have an uncluttered style and spectacular views of the river and bushveld below. Outdoor and indoor areas fuse seamlessly. Organic materials—wood, cane, cotton, and linen—are daringly juxtaposed with steel and glass. This is Bauhaus in the bush, with a uniquely African feel. Soak in perfumed luxury in a big sunken tub in your outsize bathroom while you gaze at the river. Public areas, built around stately candelabra euphorbias endemic to the area, are light, bright, and airy, furnished with cane furniture, crisp white cushions, comfy armchairs, and recliners. Service is superb, as is the food, and nothing is left to chance. At the classy Trading Post, you can buy African art and artifacts or treat yourself to a beauty treatment at the spa. 📪 *Box 650881, Benmore 2010* ☎ *011/234–0990* 🖷 *011/234–0535* 🌐 *www.singita.co.za* 🛏 *15 suites* 🛎 *In-room safes, minibars, pool, gym, spa, bar, library, shop, Internet, airstrip* 🚫 *AE, DC, MC, V* 🍽 *FAP.*

$$$$ 🏨 **Sweni Lodge.** Unlike Singita Lebombo, which hangs over the edge of a cliff, Sweni is cradled on a low riverbank amid thick virgin bush and ancient trees. More intimate than its sister camp, it has six huge river-facing suites glassed on three sides, wooden on the other. At night khaki

floor-to-ceiling drapes lined with silk divide the living area from the bedroom, which has a king-size bed with weighted, coffee-colored mosquito netting and a cascade of ceramic beads. Hanging fishtrap lampshades of brown netting, cream mohair throws, and brown leather furniture enhance the natural feel and contrast daringly with the gleam of stainless steel in the living room and bathroom. Chill out in a wooden rocking chair on your large reed-shaded deck while watching an elephant herd drink, or spend the night under the stars on a comfy, mosquito-net-draped mattress. A fully stocked bar and your own library of bird and mammal books, wildlife magazines, and board games are available if you decide to do your own thing for an hour or three. ⌂ *Box 650881, Benmore 2010* ☎ *011/234–0990* 🖷 *011/234–0535* ⊕ *www.singita. co.za* ⇝ *6 suites* ⅙ *In-room safes, minibars, pool, gym, spa, bar, library, shop, Internet, airstrip* ☰ *AE, DC, MC, V* ⦿ *FAP.*

$$ ⛺ **Rhino Post Safari Lodge.** The lodge comprises eight spacious suites on stilts overlooking the Mutlumuvi riverbed. Open-plan suites built of canvas, thatch, wood, and stone each have a bedroom, private wooden deck, bathroom with a deep freestanding bath, his-and-her sinks, a separate toilet, and an outdoor shower protected by thick reed poles. ⌂ *Box 1881, Juskei Park 2153* ☎ *011/467–1886* 🖷 *011/467–4758* ⊕ *www.zulunet. co.za* ⇝ *8 suites* ⅙ *Fans, pool, bar* ☰ *AE, DC, MC, V* ⦿ *FAP.*

$ ⛺ **Rhino Post Plains Camp.** Overlooking a water hole amid an acacia knobthorn thicket deep in the heart of the Timbitene Plain, Plains Camp has comfortably furnished tents with wooden decks and great views of the plains. A deck with bar and plunge pool are great for post-walk get-togethers, and there's a small tented dining area. Simple, unpretentious, and very friendly, the camp has great food. ⌂ *Box 1881, Juskei Park 2153* ☎ *011/467–1886* 🖷 *011/467–4758* ⊕ *www.zulunet.co.za* ⇝ *4 tents* ⅙ *Fans, bar* ☰ *AE, DC, MC, V* ⦿ *FAP.*

Where to Stay Near Kruger National Park

The hotels and lodges reviewed below lie in private game reserves adjoining Kruger National Park, and game roams freely between the reserves and the park.

Lodges are substantially more expensive than the rest camps and bushveld camps in Kruger, but there's a reason. Service is more personalized, accommodations are more plush, the food is quite tasty, game-viewing opportunities are excellent, and generally everything's included. Don't worry if you are averse to venison or are a vegetarian; there are tempting, creative dishes for all tastes. Most accommodations have air-conditioning, minibars, room safes, a ceiling fan, tea/coffeemakers, and bathrooms offering the most gorgeous "smellies"—shampoo, body lotion, shower gels—plus insect repellent. If reception is available, there are room telephones. Cell-phone reception is patchy (depending on the area), but never take your cell phone on a game drive for obvious reasons. All camps have radio telephones if you need to make contact with the outside world. Chartered flights to and from the camps on shared private airstrips are available, or lodges will collect you from Hoedspruit Airport or KMIA. Most lodges recommend a two- to three-night stay (try for three nights) so that you can experience as much as possible, from starlit dinners to ranger-led bush walks.

The daily program at each lodge rarely deviates from a pattern, starting with tea, coffee, muffins, or rusks (toast) before an early morning game drive (usually starting at dawn, later in winter). At 10, when you get back to the lodge, you get a full English breakfast or brunch. You can then choose to go on a bush walk with an armed ranger, where you learn about some of the minutiae of the bush (including the Little Five), although you could also happen on giraffes, antelopes, or any one of the Big Five. But don't worry, you will be well briefed in advance on what you should do if you come face-to-face with a lion, for example. The rest of the day, until the late-afternoon game drive, is spent at leisure, so read up on the bush in the camp library, snooze, or have a swim. A sumptuous afternoon tea is served at 3:30 or 4 before you head off back into the bush for your night drive. During the drive, your ranger will find a peaceful spot for sundowners (cocktails), and you can sip the drink of your choice and nibble snacks as you watch one of Africa's spectacular sunsets. As darkness falls, your ranger will switch on the spotlight so you can spy nocturnal animals: lions, leopards, jackals, porcupines, servals, civets, and the enchanting little bush babies. You'll get back to the lodge around 7:30, in time to freshen up before a three- or five-course dinner in an open-air boma around a blazing fire. Often the camp staff entertains after dinner with local songs and dances—an unforgettable experience. Children under 12 are not allowed at some of the camps (unless the whole camp is booked), and if they are, those six years or under are not allowed to take part in game activities; they make too easy a take-out snack for hungry predators!

$$ 🏨 **Protea Hotel Kruger Gate.** Set in its own small reserve only 110 yards from the Paul Kruger Gate, this comfortable hotel gives you a luxury alternative to the sometimes bare-bones accommodations of Kruger's rest camps. The hotel has two major advantages: fast access to the south-central portion of the park, where game viewing is best, plus the impression that you are in the wilds of Africa. Dinner, heralded by beating drums, is served in a boma, a traditional open-air reed enclosure around a blazing campfire. Rangers lead guided walks through the surrounding bush, and you can even sleep overnight in a tree house. Rooms, connected by a raised wooden walkway that passes through thick indigenous forest, are not very imaginative. They have Spanish-tile floors and standard hotel furniture, as well as air-conditioning, TV, minibar, and tea/coffeemakers. There are also self-catering chalets that sleep six. Relax on the pool deck overlooking the Sabie river, have a cocktail in the cool bar, or puff on a cheroot in the sophisticated cigar bar while the kids take part in a fun-filled Prokidz program (during school vacations only). ✉ *Kruger Gate, Skukuza* 🕿 *013/735–5671* 🖷 *013/735–5676* ⊕ *www.proteahotels.co.za* ⤺ *96 rooms, 7 chalets* ⚐ *Restaurant, minibars, pool, bar* ⊟ *AE, DC, MC, V.*

Sabi Sands Game Reserve

This is the most famous and exclusive of the private reserves. Collectively owned and managed, the 153,000-acre reserve is home to dozens of private lodges, including the world-famous Mala Mala and Londolozi.

The Sabi Sands fully deserves its exalted reputation, boasting perhaps the highest game density of any private reserve in southern Africa.

Although not all lodges own vast tracts of land, most have traversing rights over most of the reserve. With an average of 20 vehicles (from different camps) watching for game and communicating by radio, you're bound to see an enormous amount of game and almost certainly the Big Five, but since only three vehicles are allowed at a sighting at a time, you can be assured of a grandstand seat. Expect to see large herds of elephants, particularly in the fall (March–May), when they migrate from Kruger in search of water and better grazing. The Sabi Sands is also the best area for leopard sightings. (In fact, the Londolozi leopards are world famous.) It's a memorable experience to see this quite beautiful, powerful, and often elusive feline—the most successful of all feline predators—padding purposefully through the bush at night, illuminated in your ranger's spotlight. There are many lion prides, and occasionally, the increasingly rare wild dogs will migrate from Kruger to den in the Sabi Sands. You'll also see white rhinos, zebras, giraffes, wildebeests, and most of the antelope species, plus birds galore. Before you go on your first game drive, if there's a special animal or bird you would really love to see, tell your ranger, who will try to find it for you.

DJUMA Shangaan for "roar of the lion," Djuma is in the northeast corner of the Sabi Sands Game Reserve. It was the first game reserve in Africa to place permanent cameras at water holes and on a mobile vehicle so that Web surfers (www.africam.com) can watch the goings-on in the African bush without leaving home. Your hosts are husband-and-wife team Jurie and Pippa Moolman, who are passionate about their work (Jurie has a B.S. in ecology). Although there's a good chance of seeing the Big Five during the bush walk after breakfast and the twice-daily game drives, Djuma also caters to those with special bushveld interests, such as birdwatching or tree identification. Djuma's rangers and trackers are also adept at finding seldom-seen animals, such as wild dogs, spotted hyenas, and genets. You'll find none of the formality that sometimes prevails at the larger lodges. For example, members of the staff eat all meals with you and join you around the nighttime fire. In fact, Djuma prides itself on its personal service and feeling of intimacy. Your dinner menu is chalked up on a blackboard (try ostrich pâté with cranberry sauce for a starter), as is the evening cocktail menu (how about a Screaming Hyena or African Sunrise?). 🖃 *Box 338, Hluvukani 1363* 🕾 *013/735–5118* 🖷 *013/735–5070* 🌐 *www.djuma.com* 🖃 *AE, DC, MC, V* 🍴*FAP.*

$$ 🏠 **Bush Lodge.** Sitting in a lush grove of tamboti trees and overlooking a water hole, this homey safari camp contains thatch chalets with rugged wooden furniture and faux-animal-skin fabrics. Don't miss out on a trip to the local villages (the real thing—not tourist traps) of Dixie and Utah, where you'll be introduced to the families of the people looking after you at camp. 🛏 *8 chalets* ⚙ *Pool, bar.*

$$ 🏠 **Vuyatela.** Djuma's vibey, most upscale camp mixes contemporary African township culture with modern Shangaan culture. Bright colors, trendy designs, hand-painted napkins, and candy-wrapper place mats combine with traditional leather chairs, thatch, and hand-painted mud walls. Look out for some great contemporary African township art, both classic and "naïf" artifacts, and especially for the chandelier made with old Coca-Cola bottles above the dining table. The camp is unfenced, and it's quite usual to see kudu nibbling the lawns or giraffes towering above the rooftops. Accommodations are in beautifully decorated chalets with private plunge pools. For something different in between drives, why not have your hair braided in funky African style at the Comfort Zone, the in-camp spa? ⟑ *8 suites* ⟑ *Spa, bar.*

$ ▦ **Galago.** A delightful and affordable alternative to the upscale lodges, Galago, which means "lesser bush baby" in Shangaan, is a converted U-shape farmhouse whose five rooms form an arc around a central fireplace. There's a big, shady veranda where you can sit and gaze out over the open plain before cooling off in the plunge pool. You can bring your own food and do your own cooking for less than half the all-inclusive price, or you can bring your own supplies and hire the camp's chef (R300 per day) to cook it for you. Game drives and walks are led by your own ranger. This is a perfect camp for a family safari or friends' reunion. ⟑ *5 rooms* ⟑ *Pool.*

INYATI ▦ **Inyati Lodge.** Set on a hillside overlooking green rolling lawns that lead
$ down to the Sand River and a hippo pool, Inyati offers incredible value for the money. Sit out on the thatch veranda or on the shady viewing deck by the river itself, and scan the banks for animals coming to drink. Like its glitzier competitors, Inyati ("buffalo" in Shangaan) delivers the Big Five and often more. The service is superlative, a welcome mix of professionalism and friendliness. The food is excellent, as are the rangers, some of whom have been with the lodge for more than 10 years. Simple thatch cottages have rustic log furniture and Africa-themed materials and curios. ✑ *Box 38838, Booysens 2016* ☏ *011/880–5950* 📠 *011/788–2406* ⊕ *www.inyati.co.za* ⟑ *10 rooms* ⟑ *Pool, gym, bar, airstrip; no kids under 8* ▤ *AE, DC, MC, V* ⏧ *FAP.*

LEOPARD HILLS ▦ **Leopard Hills Lodge.** Renowned for its relaxed and informal atmosphere,
$$$ Leopard Hills is one of the premier game lodges in the Sabi Sands area. Set on a rocky outcrop with panoramic views of the surrounding bushveld, this small lodge offers privacy and luxury. Its main draw is its spectacular game viewing; during a two-night stay guests can almost be guaranteed to see the Big Five at close quarters. Rangers are eager to share their knowledge and quick to rush guests off to see big game. Decor has an authentic bush theme, which gels well with the surroundings. Each double room has its own private pool (in addition to the main pool) and deck overlooking the bushveld. Bathrooms have his-and-her showers both indoors and out. Attention to detail is manifested in the leopard tracks and similar African motifs that appear in walkways, bedrooms, and bathrooms; check out the ceramic chameleon around the dressing table. ✑ *Box 612, Hazyview 1242* ☏ *013/737–6626 or 013/737–6627* 📠 *013/737–6628* ⊕ *www.leopardhills.com* ⟑ *8 rooms* ⟑ *In-room safes, minibars, pool, gym, spa, bar, Internet; no kids under 10* ▤ *AE, DC, MC, V* ⏧ *FAP.*

LION SANDS Guests of the Lion Sands Private Game Reserve can take direct scheduled flights to the Mala Mala airfield through SA Airlink (⇨ Mpumalanga

A to Z, *above*). ⟨𝒟⟩ *Box 30, White River 1240* ☎ *013/735–5330* ⊕ *www. lionsands.com* ▭ *AE, DC, MC, V* ⟨𝍠⟩ *FAP.*

$$$$ ⊞ **Ivory Lodge.** Ultraluxurious yet simple and uncluttered, this lodge has a contemporary, Afro-European elegance. Each of the six suites offers absolute exclusivity, operating as a private villa where you can chill out with intimate dinners and on-the-spot spa treatments. Alternatively, opt for game drives in a private game vehicle with your own personal ranger. You also have a personal butler and plunge pool. ↘ *6 suites* ⌂ *In-room safes, minibars, spa, shop.*

$$ ⊞ **River Lodge.** This friendly lodge is set on one of the longest and best stretches of river frontage in Sabi Sands. You can watch the passing animal and bird show from your deck or from the huge tree-shaded wooden viewing area that juts out over the riverbank facing Kruger National Park. Although the guest rooms are small, they are comfortable and attractively Africa themed, with honey-colored stone floors with pebble inlays, cream wooden furniture, embroidered white bed linens, and lamps and tables of dark indigenous wood. The food is imaginative and tasty (try kudu stuffed with peanut butter with a mushroom and Amarula sauce), the young staff cheerful and enthusiastic, and the rangers highly qualified. After an exhilarating game drive, take a leisurely bush walk, go fishing, sleep out under the stars, or relax with a beauty treatment at Lalamuka Spa (*Lalamuka* means "unwind" in Shangaan). Public spaces are large and comfortable and lack the African designer clutter that mars some other lodges. There's a resident senior ecologist and a classy and interesting curio shop. ↘ *20 rooms* ⌂ *In-room safes, minibars, pool, spa, bar, shop, airstrip.*

LONDOLOZI Since its inception in 1974 (it was a family farm and retreat before that), Londolozi has become synonymous with South Africa's finest game lodges and game experiences. (*Londolozi* is the Zulu word for "protector of all living things.") Dave and John Varty, the charismatic and media-friendly grandsons of the original owner, Charles Varty, put the lodge on the map with glamorous marketing, superb wildlife videos, pet leopards and lions, visiting celebrities, and a vision of style and comfort that grandfather Charles could never have imagined. Game abounds, and the leopards of Londolozi are world famous. There are four camps: Bateleur, Tree, Pioneer, and Founders. Each is totally private, hidden in dense riverine forest on the banks of the Sand River. The central reception and curio shop are at Bateleur camp. ✉ *CC Africa, Private Bag X27, Benmore 2010* ☎ *011/809–4300* ⊟ *011/809–4400* ⊕ *www.londolozi.com* ▭ *AE, DC, MC, V* ⟨𝍠⟩ *FAP.*

$$$$ ⊞ **Pioneer Camp.** Pioneer Camp and its suites are a loving tribute to the early days and legendary characters of Sparta, the original name of the Londolozi property. Channel into a past world through faded sepia photographs, old hunting prints, horse-drawn carts, and scuffed safari treasures, taking you back in time to the day when it took five days by ox wagon to get to Londolozi. In winter sink deeply into your leather armchair in front of your own blazing fireplace; in summer sit outside in your outdoor dining room and listen to Africa's night noises. ↘ *3 chalets* ⌂ *Pool, bar.*

★ **$$$$** ▣ **Tree Camp.** The first Relais & Chateaux game lodge in the world, this gorgeous camp shaded by thick riverine bush is built into the riverbank and makes clever use of the natural rock and indigenous forest. The main living area consists of a huge, thatch A-frame with a wooden deck on stilts jutting out over the river. Guest rooms are an exquisite blend of modern luxury and *Out of Africa* chic: track lighting captures the glow of burnished Rhodesian teak; mosquito nets drape languidly over snow-white beds; and old railway sleepers, skillfully crafted into furniture and window frames, add to the room's rich textures. All suites have their own plunge pools. You may choose to dine with others, swapping bush stories with fellow guests and rangers, or alone on your private *sala* (outdoor covered deck). From the central wraparound deck you look out onto a world of cool green forest dominated by an ancient African ebony tree. ⌁ *6 suites ⌂ In-room safes, minibars, pool, bar.*

$$$ ▣ **Bateleur Camp.** Named for the endangered Bateleur eagle, the largest of Londolozi's camps is centered on a thatch A-frame lodge, which houses a dining room and lounge. Meals are also served on a broad wooden deck jutting over the riverbed and under an ancient jackalberry tree. The thatch rondawels that once made up the original Varty family hunting camp now do duty as a library, a wine cellar, and an interpretive center, where you can listen to history and ecotourism talks or try your hand at wood carving. If you're looking for romance, have a private dinner on your veranda and go for a moonlight dip in your own plunge pool. In suites, the pool leads right to the riverbed. All rooms are decorated in African ethnic chic—in creams and browns and with local carvings and artifacts—and have great bushveld views. ⌁ *8 chalets, 4 suites ⌂ Dining room, in-room safes, minibars, pool, bar, library.*

$$$ ▣ **Founders Camp.** This camp takes you back to the early days of Londolozi, before ecotourism was invented—when it was more important to shoot a lion than to take the perfect shot of it. Each stone-and-thatch chalet, in thick riverine bush and linked to others by meandering pathways, has its own wooden viewing deck, and each is warmly decorated in cream, brown, and other neutral shades with African artifacts. Relax on the thatch split-level dining and viewing decks that jut out over a quiet backwater of the Sand River, and watch the mammal and bird worlds go by. After your game drive or walk, cool off in the tree-shaded swimming pool, which also overlooks the river. ⌁ *5 chalets, 1 suite ⌂ In-room safes, minibars, pool, bar.*

MALA MALA Fodor's Choice ★ This legendary game lodge, which along with Londolozi put South African safaris on the international map, has been tops in its field for more than 40 years, delighting visitors with incomparable service, superb food, and elegant, comfortable accommodations. Mike Rattray, a legend in his own time in South Africa's game lodge industry, describes Mala Mala as "a camp in the bush," but it's certainly more than that, although it still retains that genuine bushveld feel of bygone days. Both the hospitality and the game-viewing experience keep guests coming back. Mala Mala constitutes the largest privately owned Big Five game area in South Africa, and includes an unfenced 30-km (19-mi) boundary with Kruger National Park, across which game crosses continuously. The variety of habitats ranges from riverine bush, favorite hiding place of the leopard, to open grasslands, where cheetahs hunt. Mala Mala's animal-viewing statistics are probably unbeatable: the Big Five are spotted almost every day. At one moment your well-educated, friendly, articulate ranger will fascinate you with the description of the sex life of a dung beetle, as you watch the sturdy male battling his way along the road pushing his perfectly round ball of dung with wife-to-be perched perilously on top; at another, your adrenaline will flow as you follow a leopard stalking impala in the gathering gloom. Along with the local Shangaan trackers, whose eyesight rivals that of the animals they are tracking, the rangers ensure that your game experience is unforgettable. ⬤ *Box 55514, Northlands 2116* ☎ *011/268–2388* 🖷 *011/268–2399* ⊕ *www.malamala.com* ⊟ *AE, DC, MC, V* ⏏⃝ *FAP.*

$$$ ⬚ **Sable Camp.** This fully air-conditioned, exclusive camp at the southern end of Main Camp also overlooks the Sand River and surrounding bushveld. With its own pool, library, and boma, it's smaller and more intimate than Main Camp, although sharing the same magnificent all-around bush and hospitality experience. ⤳ *5 rooms, 1 suite* ⬧ *In-room safes, minibars, pool, gym, bar, library; no kids.*

$$ ⬚ **Main Camp.** Ginger-brown stone and thatch air-conditioned rondawels with separate his-and-her bathrooms are decorated in creams and browns and furnished with cane armchairs, colorful handwoven tapestries and rugs, terra-cotta floors, and original artwork. Public areas have a genuine safari feel, with plush couches, animal skins, and African artifacts. A huge deck is shaded by ancient jackalberry trees and overlooks the Sand River and its passing show of animals. Browse in the air-conditioned Monkey Room for books and wildlife videos, sample the magnificent wine cellar, sun yourself by the pool, or stay fit in the well-appointed gym. The food (among the best in the bush) is tasty, wholesome, and varied, with a full buffet at both lunch and dinner. Children are welcome, but children under five are not allowed on game drives unless with their own family group. ⤳ *18 rooms* ⬧ *In-room safes, minibars, pool, gym, bar, library.*

SABI SABI Founded in 1978 at the southern end of Sabi Sands, Sabi Sabi was one of the first lodges, along with Londolozi, to offer photo safaris and to link ecotourism, conservation, and community. Superb accommodations and the sheer density of game supported by its highly varied habitats draw guests back to Sabi Sabi in large numbers. There's a strong emphasis on ecology: guests are encouraged to look beyond the Big Five and to become aware of the birds and smaller mammals of the bush. ⬤ *Box 52665, Saxonwold 2132* ☎ *011/483–3939* 🖷 *011/483–3799* ⊕ *www.sabisabi.com* ⊟ *AE, DC, MC, V* ⏏⃝ *FAP.*

$$$ ⬚ **Bush Lodge.** This large lodge overlooks a busy water hole (lions are frequent visitors) and the dry course of the Msuthlu River. The thatch, open-sided dining area, observation deck, and pool all have magnificent views of game at the water hole. Thatch suites are connected by walkways that weave between manicured lawns and beneath enormous shade trees where owls and fruit bats call at night. All have a deck overlooking the dry river course (where you may well see an elephant padding along) and outdoor and indoor showers. Chalets are older and smaller—although more intimate in a way—but still roomy; they are creatively decorated with ethnic designs and have a personal wooden deck. ⤴ *21 chalets, 5 suites ⚭ In-room safes, minibars, pool, spa, bar.*

$$$ ⊞ **Earth Lodge.** Don't expect designer chic here. There's not a knickknack or bit of clutter anywhere in this avant-garde, ecofriendly lodge. It's a cross between a Hopi cave dwelling and a medieval keep, but with modern luxury. On arrival, all you'll see is bush and grass-covered hummocks until you descend a hidden stone pathway that opens onto a spectacular landscape of boulders and streams. The lodge has rough-textured, dark brown walls encrusted with orange seeds and wisps of indigenous grasses. The mud-domed suites are hidden from view until you are practically at the front door. Surfaces are sculpted from ancient fallen trees, whereas chairs and tables are ultramodern or '50s style. Huge living spaces contain a sitting area, mega bathroom, private veranda, and plunge pool. A personal butler takes care of your every need, and there's a meditation garden. Dine in a subterranean cellar or in the boma, fashioned from roots and branches and lighted at night by dozens of lanterns. ⤴ *13 suites ⚭ In-room safes, minibars, pool, spa, bar, library.*

★ $$$ ⊞ **Selati Lodge.** Formerly the private hunting lodge of a famous South African opera singer, Selati is an intimate, stylish, colonial-style camp. The early-1900s atmosphere is created by the use of genuine train memorabilia—old leather suitcases, antique wooden chairs, nameplates, and signals—that recall the old Selati branch train line, which once crossed the reserve, transporting gold from the interior to the coast of Mozambique in the 1870s. At night the grounds of this small, secluded lodge flicker with the lights of the original shunters' oil lamps. Members of the glitterati and European royalty have stayed at the spacious Ivory Presidential Suite. ⤴ *8 chalets, 1 suite ⚭ In-room safes, minibars, pool, bar; no kids under 10.*

SINGITA   Although Singita (Shangaan for "the miracle") offers much the same bush experience as the other lodges, its huge public areas, extravagant megasize accommodations, and superb dining options help set it apart. Enjoy a riverside breakfast, picnic lunch, or starlit supper in the bush; browse in the reading rooms and wine cellar, which has a superb stock of vintage wines; relax in your huge, private suite; or shop at the Trading Store for African artifacts, bush clothes, handmade jewelry, and ostrich-skin purses. ⌂ *Box 650881, Benmore 2010* ☎ *011/234–0990* 🖷 *011/234–0535* ⊕ *www.singita.co.za* ⊟ *AE, DC, MC, V* ⊚⫯ *FAP.*

★ $$$$ ⊞ **Boulders Lodge.** The style is traditional African at this ultraluxurious camp, whose exterior echoes the great Zimbabwe ruins. Large ponds guard the entrance to the public areas, where decor combines modern with bushveld. An entrance hall with fully stocked bar and pantry welcomes you into your enormous suite, where a glass-sided lounge is dominated by a freestanding fireplace. Dark brown, cream, and pale blue fabrics complement leather and wicker armchairs, a zebra-skin ottoman, and antique pieces from owner Luke Bailes's original family home. Occasional touches of steel—candleholders, mirrors, and lamps—provide a nice contrast. A herd of impalas could easily fit into the bathroom, which has dark stone floors, a claw-foot tub, his-and-her sinks, and massive indoor and outdoor showers. All the doors in the suite lead directly onto a wooden deck with mattresses, chairs, and a bubbling infinity pool with views of the surrounding bushveld. ➥ *9 suites ⚘ In-room safes, minibars, pool, spa, bar.*

$$$$ 🏠 **Castleton Camp.** The original home of owner Luke Bailes is ideal for a family vacation or reunion (children of all ages welcome), as the whole place must be taken together. Each of the comfortable, air-conditioned thatch chalets has sweeping views across the plains to a large, busy water hole. Family antiques, brown-and-white-striped fabrics, and dark wooden furniture provide a homey colonial atmosphere, transporting you back to a gracious pre-condominium era. ➥ *6 chalets ⚘ Pool, bar.*

$$$$ 🏠 **Ebony Lodge.** Gardens, well-worn polished terra-cotta tiles and mud floors, deep comfy armchairs and sofas, and antiques give this lodge an intimate feel—like staying in somebody's old family lodge. The cozy library with its leather-bound books, period prints, leather armchairs, and silver trophies is a little gem. The bright yellow-and-orange walls in the suites contrast surprisingly well with the soft colors of the bush outside. Each suite has a double-sided fireplace, separate living room, enormous veranda, and bathroom with indoor and outdoor showers, plus a personal deck and plunge pool. ➥ *9 suites ⚘ In-room safes, minibars, pool, spa, bar, library.*

Manyeleti Game Reserve

North of the Sabi Sands, Manyeleti ("the place of the stars" in Shangaan) is a public park covering 59,280 acres adjoining Kruger, but it's something of a Cinderella reserve compared with its more famous neighbors. Away from the major tourist areas, it's amazingly underused; you'll probably see very few vehicles while you're here. The park's grassy plains and mixed woodland attract good-size herds of general game and their attendant predators. You have a strong chance of seeing the Big Five, but the Manyeleti lodges focus more on providing an overall bush experience than simply rushing after big game. You'll learn about trees, birds, and bushveld ecosystems as you go on guided bush walks.

HONEYGUIDE TENTED SAFARI CAMPS ★ Honeyguide Tented Safari Camps offer some of the best value in Mpumalanga, achieving the delicate balance of providing professional service with a casual atmosphere, a welcome relief if the over-attentiveness of some of the more upscale lodges isn't to your taste. Because the camps are small, an added bonus is that there are only six people per game vehicle. 🖂 *Box 781959, Sandton 2146* ☎ *011/341–0282* 🖷 *011/ 341–0281* ⊕ *www.honeyguidecamp.com* 🖃 *AE, DC, MC, V* ⍾ *FAP.*

$ 🏠 **Khoka Moya.** This delightful, value-priced camp is situated on both sides of a riverbed. Simply designed and built of corrugated iron, the large lounge and dining areas overlook green lawns leading to the pool and outside bar. There's a private space in front of each tent, where you can chill out and take in the sights and sounds of the surrounding bush. Each open-air bathroom has a concrete tub, double shower, and separate toilet. Nice touches in your tent include a leather couch, cotton sheets, and damask linen bedspreads. As part of the Children's Safari program, kids can make clay footprints, learn about the little bugs and critters they see on their guided walks, play soccer, swim, relax in the playroom, and then dig into a special kids' menu. ⏚ *12 tents ⟁ Pool, bar, children's programs (ages 4–14).*

$ ⊞ **Mantonbeni.** This tented camp, minimalist but with surprising luxury touches, gives you the total bush experience without some of the bells and whistles of more upscale camps and at half the price. Designed to reflect Hemingway's Africa, it sits in a tamboti grove overlooking a riverbed. You'll feel very close to the bush (but quite safe and secure) in your large, comfortable tent with its leather couch and open-air bathroom with concrete bath, double shower, and separate toilet. Spot game as you lounge on the swimming pool deck, or browse in the temperature-controlled wine cellar. Tea or coffee is served in your tent at dawn, and meals are served in a big safari tent around a long wooden table, where you can swap animal war stories with your fellow guests in an intimate, relaxed atmosphere. ⏚ *12 tents ⟁ Pool, bar.*

TINTSWALO ⊞ **Tintswalo Safari Lodge.** This gorgeous new lodge, which aims to re-
$$$ capture the mid-19th century, is sited under huge jackalberry and fig trees overlooking a seasonal river, where game come down to drink and bathe. Each suite is themed for one of the great African explorers, including Burton, Speke, Livingstone, and Stanley, who would undoubtedly be amazed by such modern conveniences as air-conditioning, hair dryers, en-suite bathrooms, and personal plunge pools. The suites are warmed by Persian rugs and honey-colored velvet chairs and ottomans. Dining is under the stars or in an elegant thatch dining room with open fireplace and sparkling chandelier. Although it's great to have a personal butler, sometimes it's rather disconcerting to be offered something every time you move a muscle. Stargaze by telescope, enjoy a complimentary spa treatment, visit a local Shangaan village, or, if you're both adventurous and romantic, opt for a moonlight sleep-out in the bush. Children are allowed only in the Presidential Suite. ⌖ *Box 70378, Bryanston 2021* ☎ *011/706–7207* 🖷 *011/463–8251* ⊕ *www.tintswalo.com* ⏚ *7 suites ⟁ Dining room, in-room safes, minibars, pool, spa, bar* 🍽 *AE, DC, MC, V* ⦿ *FAP.*

Timbavati Game Reserve

The 185,000-acre Timbavati, the northernmost of the private reserves, is collectively owned and managed and famed for its rare white lions, the product of a recessive gene that surfaces occasionally. (If you miss them here, see them at the National Zoological Gardens in Tshwane.) Timbavati also has a large population of "regular" lions, and there's a good chance of finding leopards, elephants, buffalo, and spotted hyenas. Rhinos are scarcer, however. Rumor has it that they keep crossing back into Kruger. You might get lucky and see wild dogs, as they migrate regularly to this region from Kruger.

NGALA *Ngala* means "the place of the lion" and certainly lives up to its name. There's wall-to-wall game, and you'll almost certainly see the King of the Beasts as well as leopards, rhinos, elephants, and buffalo, among others. Ngala lies in Timbavati's mopane shrubveld, and its main advantage over Sabi Sands is its proximity to four major ecozones—mopane shrubveld, marula combretum, acacia shrub, and riverine forest—which provide habitats for a wide range of animals. As this camp is unfenced, always be sure to walk with a guide after dark,. Ngala welcomes kids and puts on a range of activities for them. Ngala rangers, trackers, and general staff are specially trained to look after children and their needs, and, what's more, they seem to delight in their company. After the morning game drive, the kids are whisked away to go on a bug hunt, visit a local village, or bake cookies. ⊠ *CC Africa, Private Bag X27, Benmore 2010* ☎ *011/809–4447* ☒ *011/809–4525* ⊕ *www.ngala.co.za* ▤ *AE, DC, MC, V* ⦿ *MAP.*

★ **$$$** ⊡ **Ngala Tented Safari Camp.** It seems that the marula seeds softly falling on the tents are applauding this gorgeous little tented camp shaded by a canopy of giant trees. You'll feel like a sultan as you lie beneath your billowing, honey-colored canvas roof, which acts as a ceiling for your basket-weave handmade bed and headboard. Polished wooden floors, gauze-screened floor-to-ceiling windows, and a dressing area with his-and-her stone washbasins and gleaming old-fashioned bath create a feeling of such roominess and elegance that it's hard to believe you're in a tent. The camp's dining area and lounge have an almost nautical feel. Huge wooden decks are tethered by guy ropes and stout poles on the very edge of the Timbavati River. It seems as if at any moment you could be gently blown into the sky over the surrounding bushveld. ⇔ *6 tents* ⛱ *Pool; no kids under 12.*

$$ ⊡ **Main Camp.** This camp has Mediterranean style and a sophistication that is refreshing after the hunting-lodge decor of some other lodges. Track lighting and dark-slate flooring and tables provide an elegant counterpoint to high thatch ceilings and African art. A massive, double-sided fireplace dominates the lodge, opening onto a lounge filled with comfy sofas and chairs on one side and a dining room on the other. Dinner at Ngala is quite formal (kids on their best behavior, please!); it's served in a reed-enclosed boma or a tree-filled courtyard lighted by lanterns with crystal and silver. Air-conditioned guest cottages, in mopane shrubveld with no views, comprise two rooms, each with its own thatch veranda. Rooms make extensive use of hemp matting, thatch, and dark beams to create an appealing, warm feel. ⇔ *20 rooms, 1 suite* ⛱ *Pool, bar.*

TANDA TULA ★ **$$** ⊡ **Tanda Tula Safari Camp.** With a well-deserved reputation as one of the best bush camps in Mpumalanga, Tanda Tula is very professional, yet makes you feel at home. When lions roar nearby, the noise sounds like it's coming from under the bed. The reason is simple: you sleep in a large safari tent with huge window flaps that roll up, leaving you gazing at the bush only through mosquito netting. Tanda Tula is decorated with colorful Africa-themed furnishings. Each thatch tent has electricity, a freestanding fan, a private bathroom with a Victorian-style tub and outdoor shower, and a private wooden deck overlooking the Nhlaralumi River. You'll eat breakfast and lunch in a large, open, thatch lounge, but for dinner enjoy one of Tanda Tula's famous bush braais in the dry riverbed, with the moon reflecting off the dry sand. Although the lodge can sleep 24, it usually keeps numbers down to 16, which makes for added intimacy. First-class rangers give you a very thorough understanding of the environment, local history, and animals without concentrating solely on the Big Five. If you want real privacy, book the luxurious two-person lodge next to the tented camp; it comes with its own butler, vehicle, plunge pool, and in-house catering. ⌂ *Box 32, Constantia, Cape Town 7848* ☎ *021/794–6500* ⌨ *021/794–7605* ⊕ *www.tandatula.co.za* ⬌ *12 tents, 1 lodge* ⚭ *Fans, pool, bar; no kids under 12* ▤ *AE, DC, MC, V* ¶⚫¶ *FAP.*

Thornybush Game Reserve

This small game reserve is similar to Timbavati, whose western boundary it abuts.

$ ▦ **Jackalberry Lodge.** This lodge offers understated luxury, excellent food, superb guiding, and the Big Five at half the price of some of the better-known lodges. The air-conditioned thatch-and-stone chalets face the purple Drakensberg Mountains and lie in pristine bushveld that nudges the public areas and pool. It's commonplace to watch a warthog munching while you do, or a giraffe wander past as you sun yourself. Chalets have stone floors, braided straw rugs with leather bindings, deep armchairs, and beaded cushions in soft earth tones, all echoing a simple but elegant African theme. Spacious bathrooms have his-and-her sinks, a tub with a bushveld view, and indoor and outdoor showers. The rangers are terrific, the staff friendly and efficient, and a particular bonus is that kids of all ages are welcome. Trained babysitters keep them occupied while you are off on game drives. For a little extra you can book the two-bedroom family chalet or one of the two large rooms where the bush comes right up to your doorstep. Don't be surprised if a herd of curious zebras eyeballs you as you sit on your large, private stoop. ⌂ *Box 798, Northlands 2116* ☎ *015/793–2980* ⌨ *015/793–2750* ⊕ *www. jackalberrylodge.co.za* ⬌ *7 rooms, 1 suite* ⚭ *Pool, bar, library, shop, babysitting* ▤ *AE, DC, MC, V* ¶⚫¶ *FAP.*

Kruger National Park A to Z

AIR TRAVEL

For information on the airports in Nelspruit, Hoedspruit, and Phalaborwa and the airlines that fly into them, *see* Mpumalanga A to Z, *above.* SA Airlink also flies directly to Mala Mala airstrip, which serves the Sabi Sands lodges.

BUS TRAVEL

For information about bus transportation to Nelspruit, 50 km (31 mi) from Kruger's Numbi Gate and 64 km (40 mi) from Malelane Gate, *see* Mpumalanga A to Z, *above.* Only tour-company buses actually go through Kruger, but they're not recommended. Being in a big tour bus in the park is like being in an air-conditioned bubble, totally divorced from the bush. Also, the big tour buses aren't allowed on many of Kruger's dirt roads and have to stick to the main paved roads.

CAR TRAVEL

For information on car rentals and the routes to Kruger, *see* Mpumalanga A to Z, *above.* Maps of Kruger are available at all the park gates and in the camp stores, and gas stations are available at the park gates and at the major camps. Once in the park, observe the speed-limit signs carefully (there are speed traps): 50 kph (31 mph) on paved roads, 40 kph

(25 mph) on dirt roads. Leave your vehicle only at designated picnic and view sites, and if you do find animals on the road, allow them to pass before moving on. Sometimes you have to be very patient, especially if a breeding herd of elephants is blocking your way. Animals always have the right-of-way. Always be cautious. Kruger is not a zoo; you are entering the territory of wild animals, even though many may be habituated to the sights and sounds of vehicles.

If you are planning to go into Kruger or one of the private reserves, it's worth renting an eight-seater combi (van) or SUV. Though more expensive than a car, they provide more leg room and you'll probably spot more game and see it better from your lofty perch. It's best to reserve well in advance, particularly if you want a bigger vehicle. Opt for the "super-cover" insurance; it's not that much more expensive, but if you do get bumped by an elephant, you'll be covered.

HEALTH & SAFETY

Malaria is endemic in the park, making it essential to take malaria prophylactics. Consult your doctor well in advance of your trip. Although you see many families with small kids in the park, doctors recommend against it, as malaria prophylactics are unsuitable for children under six. Prevention is the best medicine: at dawn and dusk, smother yourself with insect repellent, and wear long sleeves, long pants, socks, and covered shoes.

MONEY MATTERS

There is a bank at Skukuza. Kruger accepts credit cards, which are also useful for big purchases, but always have some small change for staff tips (tip your cleaning person R20 per hut per day) and for drinks and snacks at the camp shops.

TOURS

For information on tours and tour operators for Kruger National Park, *see* Mpumalanga A to Z, *above.*

TRAIN TRAVEL

For information about arriving by train, *see* Mpumalanga A to Z, *above.*

VISITOR INFORMATION

There are information centers at the Letaba, Skukuza, and Berg-en-Dal rest camps.

Victoria Falls

9

WORD OF MOUTH

"The whitewater rafting trip at the Falls was definitely somewhat risky, but it was incredible. We picked a raft with an oarsman. We sat clinging on for our lives on the back of the raft (which we had been assured was the safest location) and were thrown out several times into the churning river! It's definitely frightening but they have expert kayakers following the rafts to make sure anyone who is thrown out is fine. It was great, incredibly exhilarating."

—welltraveledbrit

Revised by
Sanja Cloete-
Jones

ROMANCE, INTRIGUE, MYTH, DECADENCE, AWE, AND TERROR: the largest curtain of falling water known to humankind reveals itself like an irresistible read. Roughly 1,200 km (750 mi) from its origin as an insignificant spring, the Zambezi River has grown more than a mile wide. Suddenly there's a bend to the south, the current speeds up, and a few miles downstream the entire river is forced into a fissure created in the Jurassic age by the cooling and cracking of molten rock. Nearly 2½ million gallons of water disappear over a vertical drop 300 feet high in a matter of seconds. The resulting spray is astounding, the force splashing drops of water up into the air to form a smokelike cloud that is visible 40 miles away on a clear day. Dr. David Livingstone, a British medical doctor and missionary, visited the area in 1855 and is widely credited with being the first European to document the existence of this natural wonder. He named it Victoria Falls in honor of his queen, although the Makololo name, Mosi-oa-Tunya (literally, "the Smoke that Thunders"), remains popular.

Livingstone fell madly in love with the falls, describing them in poignant prose. Other explorers had slightly different opinions. E. Holub could not contain his excitement and spoke effusively of "a thrilling throb of nature," and A. A. de Serpa Pinto called them "sublimely horrible" in 1881 and L. Decle (1898) expected "to see some repulsive monster rising in anger." The modern traveler can explore all of these points of view. There is so much to do around the falls that your only limitations will be your budget and sense of adventure (or lack of sense!).

The settlements of Livingstone, Zambia, and Victoria Falls, Zimbabwe, both owe their existence to the falls. In different countries and intriguingly different in character, they nevertheless function like two sides of one town. Crossing the border is a formality that generally happens with a minimum of fuss. Although the Zimbabwean town of Victoria Falls remains perfectly safe, far away from the documented strife, Livingstone, on the Zambian side, is currently the favored destination. Not only are visitors spoiled with choices in Zambia, which has a plethora of top-class safari lodges along the Zambezi, but strong competition places the emphasis on individualized service, which enables you to tailor your visit. In Zimbabwe the general mood is not always upbeat, but the absence of throngs of travelers is lovely, and it currently provides excellent value for the money. The region deserves its reputation as an adventure center and offers adrenaline-inducing activities by the bucketful. The backdrop for any of these is stunning and the safety record superb.

Exploring the Victoria Falls Area

The fissure containing the falls stretches over a mile, roughly from southwest to northeast. Livingstone lies to the north and the town of Victoria Falls immediately to the south.

The border between the countries at the falls is within walking distance of the compact town of Victoria Falls. Livingstone was settled 10 km (6 mi) from the falls in an attempt to avoid malaria, believed to be caused by the swampy Zambezi. The stretch between the falls border and town

SO, TO ZIM OR TO ZAM?

The Zimbabwe side is currently a buyer's market, with hotel prices negotiable up to 20% less than the advertised price. Service is still superb. Until recently this was the preferred destination, so the people here are definitely comfortable with anticipating visitors' needs. The majority of operators are all one-stop shops, which makes booking activities straightforward. The view of the falls can be a little overwhelming in the flood season, an experience similar to being caught in a blizzard, and the climb out of the gorge following rafting is also pretty daunting, with no plans for any automated aids at the moment. Finally, although the town is perfectly safe, the atmosphere can be understandably negative, as inhabitants struggle to cope with the tyrannical rule of President Mugabe, which affects their access to basics such as bread and milk.

Zambian lodge owners are quite used to coping with limited supply, and their knack for innovation is tangible, from the fabulously unusual decor finishes to astoundingly inspired food. Individual attention is the norm, and you can expect to have a lot of control over your schedule. Service in Zambia can be infuriating, however, as it tends to be slow and unimaginative. As for the falls themselves, the view is spectacular year-round, though it does vary based on time of year. If you travel halfway across the world for a lot of water, come during the wet season. During the dry season you see fantastic rock formations, as the basalt gorge is exposed. It's also possible to walk across a large part of the falls on this side during the drier months—an awe-inspiring activity. The climb down into the gorge for your rafting trip happens at the Boiling Pot (the first bend of the river after the falls), which gives you an interesting view of the bridge. The new Ecolift means no more walking out of the gorge at the end of a hard day's rafting.

center should not be attempted on foot, because of the dangers of wandering elephants, the African sun, and the occasional opportunistic thief.

About the Restaurants

Welcome to carnivore country! Superior free-range beef and chicken are available everywhere, and the portions can be daunting. In Zimbabwe, game meat can be found on almost any menu, but it is something of a delicacy in Zambia. The local bream, filleted or whole, is quite good, and the staple starch, a thick porridge similar to polenta and called *sadza* in Zimbabwe and *nsima* in Zambia, is worth a try. Expect to be given a finger bowl, as the initiated roll the corn into a ball and eat it with their fingers. More adventurous travelers can try *macimbi* or *vinkuvala* (sun-dried mopane worms) and, in the flood season, *inswa* (flash-fried flying ants).

Meals are taken at regular hours, with breakfast from 7 on, lunch around midday, and dinner served at 8 in most lodges. During the week, restaurants close around 10. Dress tends to be extremely casual, although you will never be out of place in something more formal, as Africa is definitely suited to a bit of glamour. The local brews are Mosi in Zambia and Zambezi in Zimbabwe, both crisp, light, and thirst-quenching beers. Following your meal, order an Amarula on ice. Not unlike Baileys Irish Cream, this liquor is made from the fruit of the marula tree, a well-documented delicacy for elephants.

Livingstone has seen a dining boom in recent years, with culinary options ranging from wasteland to worth making that reservation for. Service is slow, as the town comes to grips with the increase in tourist volume, and it is a good idea to ask your waiter to repeat your order to avoid communication errors. The lodges all take their cuisine seriously and spoil guests with freshly prepared and beautifully presented meals. Though breakfast and dinner buffets at the Zambezi Sun are awe inspiring, hotel restaurants are exorbitantly priced. The culinary focus has shifted into town. Local restaurants use regionally grown ingredients and serve both local and international fare with panache.

WHAT IT COSTS In U.S. dollars				
$$$$	**$$$**	**$$**	**$**	**¢**
RESTAURANTS over $25	$15–$25	$10–$15	$5–$10	under $5

Prices are per person for a main course at dinner, a main course equivalent, or a prix-fixe meal.

About the Hotels

Sun International has excellent package deals to Zambia from South Africa, although the cost of eating and drinking at the hotels is exorbitant and could easily double the price of a three-night stay. Lodge reservations can be made at any time, but flight availability can be a problem, especially traveling from South Africa on a Friday and to South Africa on a Sunday (due to those special packages at the Sun hotels). Lodges tend to have fully inclusive packages, whereas the hotels generally include only breakfast. All hotels and lodges quote in U.S. dollars and accept payment in other currencies only at unfriendly exchange rates. Though hotels in Zimbabwe have set rates, they are currently desperate for business, and you can bargain them down 20% in many instances. A 10% service charge is either included or added to the bill (as is the value-added tax) in both countries, which frees you to include an extra tip only for exceptional service.

Although air-conditioning can be expected in the hotels, lodges tend to have fans. During very hot months it is advisable to travel with a sarong (locally available as *achitenge*), which you can wet and wrap around you for a cooler siesta.

WHAT IT COSTS In U.S. dollars				
$$$$	**$$$**	**$$**	**$**	**¢**
HOTELS over $350	$200–$350	$100–$200	$50–$100	under $50

Prices are for a standard double room in high season, including 12.5% tax.

Timing

If you are at all sensitive to heat and humidity, visit from May through August, when it is dry and cool, with pleasant days and cool to cold nights. Although the bush can resemble a wasteland, with short brown stubble and bare trees, it does improve game viewing, and most other adventure activities are more comfortable in the cooler weather. This is also the time when the mosquitoes are less active, although it remains a malaria area year-round, and precautions should always be taken. (Consult your medical practitioner a minimum of four weeks prior to your trip.)

The rainy season starts sometime around late October and generally stretches well into April. Following the first rains, the *mopane* (bush-willow) forests are clad in a shiny, psychedelic light green as they come into new leaf, which becomes an intense emerald green by the end of the rains. With the first rains also comes the "time of the bugs," with tsetse flies, mosquitoes, and the harmless but aptly named stink bug seemingly running the show for a couple of months. Of course, the abundance of insect life also leads to great bird-watching. Although the rain showers tend to be of the short and spectacular kind, they can interfere with some activities, especially if your visit is a short one. As a rule of thumb, try to arrange your activities for the early hours, as the rain generally falls in the late afternoon.

The water plunging over the falls relies on the rainfall in Angola, and therefore the Zambian side dries up almost completely at the beginning of the year (in the middle of the rainy season). Peak flow is achieved in late April and May, when rafting and visiting Livingstone Island might not be possible. If you would like to see a lunar rainbow, plan your trip to coincide with the full moon; Victoria Falls park areas are accessible only at night during the days surrounding a full moon. Finally, make sure your visit does not coincide with school vacations in South Africa, as the area tends to get uncomfortably full of 4x4 enthusiasts.

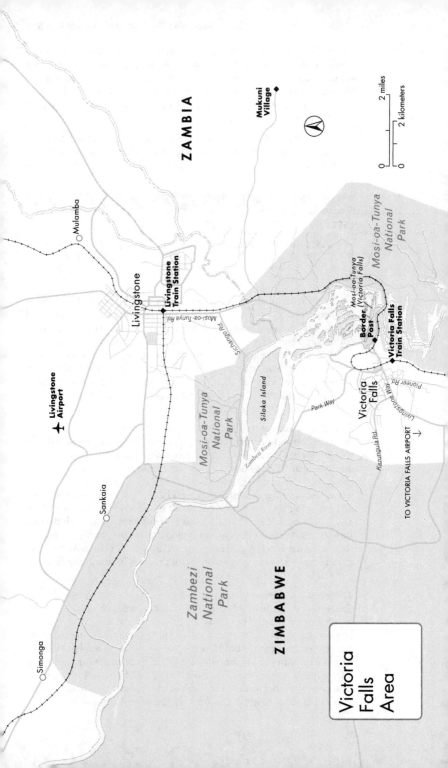

VICTORIA FALLS, ZIMBABWE

The town of Victoria Falls enjoys the happy coincidence of being a shopper's paradise inside a national park. This means you can buy an elephant carving while watching the real McCoy march past the shop window. The town is extremely compact. Almost all the hotels are within walking distance, and the falls themselves are only 10 minutes away on foot. The main road that runs through town and goes to the falls in one direction and to the airport in the other is called Livingstone Way. Park Way is perpendicular. Most of the shops, banks, and booking agents can be found on these two streets, and this part of town is also where most of the hawkers operate. Give them a clear berth, as their wares are cheap for a reason (the boat cruise is substandard, it is illegal to change money, etc.).

The town started with a little curio shop and slowly expanded until the 1970s, when it became the preferred falls destination. The political problems following independence have been well documented in the world press and have certainly taken their toll. At night the town is plunged into symbolic darkness, with little or no street lighting. (The bulbs are stolen on a regular basis.) Even sadder, the Zambezi National Park, to the northwest, has seen significant poaching. (If you really want to have the African game experience, take a day trip to Chobe National Park, 70 km [44 mi] away in Botswana; ⇨ Livingstone A to Z, *below.*)

What to See

Numbers in the margin correspond to numbers on the Victoria Falls (town) map.

❶ Falls Craft Village. The village consists of 35 life-size constructions, typical of six main ethnic groups living in Zimbabwe in the 19th century. All artifacts are genuine. A free pamphlet and on-site guide explain the living arrangements, various crafts, and the uses of different tools. At the back of the village you can watch artisans carving the stone and wood sculptures that are sold in the adjoining shop. For a small fee you can have a *n'anga* (witch doctor) "throw the bones" to tell your fortune. There is traditional dancing every night (about US$20). ⊠ *Stand 206, Soper's Crescent, off Livingstone Way, behind banks* ☎ *013/4–4309* ☒ *US$8* ☉ *Daily 8:30–5.*

> **need a break?**
>
> For a light lunch, visit **Three 10 Tea Garden** (⊠ 310 Pkwy. ☎ 013/4–3468) to investigate their claim to the best cappuccino in town. The **River Cafe** (⊠ Landela Centre, off Livingstone Way ☎ No phone) is a popular lunch venue.

❷ Victoria Falls Bridge. A monument to Cecil Rhodes's dream of completing a Cape-to-Cairo rail line, this graceful structure spans the gorge formed by the Zambezi River, 360 feet below. It would have been far easier and less expensive to build the bridge upstream from the falls, but Rhodes was captivated by the romance of a railway bridge passing over this natural wonder. A net was spanned across the gorge under the construc-

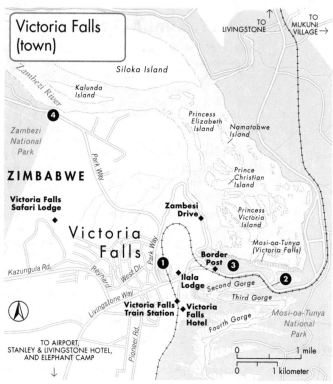

tion site, whereupon the construction workers went on strike for a couple of days. They resumed work only when it was explained that they would not have to leap into it at the end of every workday. Although the workers did not share the current adrenaline-fueled obsession with jumping into the abyss, the net probably had a lot to do with the miraculous fact that only two people were killed during construction. The bridge was completed in only 14 months, and the last two cross-girders were defiantly joined on April 1, 1905.

To get onto the bridge, you first have to pass through Zimbabwean immigration and customs controls, so bring your passport. Unless you decide to cross into Zambia, no visa is necessary. Depending on crowds, the simple procedure can take from five minutes to a half hour. The border posts are open daily from 6 AM to 10 PM, after which the bridge is closed to all traffic. From the bridge you get a knockout view of the river raging through Batoka Gorge (the fissure containing the falls) as well as a section of the falls on the Zambian side. An added bonus is watching adrenaline junkies hurling themselves off the bridge in the second-highest and one of the most scenic bungee jumps in the world. ⊠ *Livingstone Way.*

3 **Victoria Falls National Park.** Plan to spend at least two hours soaking in the splendors of this park. Bring snacks and water, and supervise children extremely well, as the barriers are by no means safe. Babies and toddlers can be pushed in a stroller. If you visit the falls during the high-water peak, between April and June, you'd do well to carry a raincoat or umbrella (you can rent them at the entrance) and to bring along a waterproof, disposable camera, because you *will* be drenched in the spray from the falls, which creates a permanent downpour. Photo opportunities are very limited due to the mist. Leave expensive cameras, cell phones, and wristwatches in your hotel or lodge safe.

The constant drizzle has created a small rain forest that extends in a narrow band along the edge of the falls. A trail running through this dripping green world is overgrown with African ebony, Cape fig, Natal mahogany, wild date palms, ferns, and deep red flame lilies. A fence has been erected to keep non-fee-paying visitors at bay. Clearly signposted side trails lead to viewpoints overlooking the falls. The most spectacular is **Danger Point,** a perilous rock outcropping that overlooks the narrow gorge through which the Zambezi River funnels out of the **Boiling Pot,** but be careful, as this viewpoint is hazardously wet and precarious. In low-water months (September–November) most of the water goes over the falls through the **Devil's Cataract,** a narrow and mesmerizingly powerful section of the falls visible from **Livingstone's statue.** Around the full moon the park stays open late so you can see the lunar rainbow formed by the spray—a hauntingly beautiful sight. Early morning and late afternoon are popular visiting times, as you can see the daylight rainbows then. A booklet explaining the formation and layout of the falls is available from the Victoria Falls Publicity Association for a small fee. ⊠ *Off Livingstone Way* 📞 *No phone* 💵 *US$20* ⊙ *Daily 6–6, later around full moon.*

4 **Zambezi Wildlife Sanctuary.** Originally a crocodile farm, this place also has several wildcats in cages as well as ostriches, making it an interesting stop. During late December you can watch baby crocodiles hatch—an almost continuous process. Feeding times are 11:15 and 3:45. There's shuttle service from Ilala Lodge in Vic Falls, but if you don't use it, you can drive down a short bush track about 200 feet before the entrance to the sanctuary, where you can spy large numbers of vultures preying on the leftovers from the croc feedings. The sanctuary also has a tea garden. ⊠ *Park Way* 📞 *013/4-3576 or 013/4-4604* ⊕ *www.ilalalodge. com* 💵 *US$3, US$10 with shuttle* ⊙ *Daily 8–5.*

Where to Stay & Eat

¢–$ ✕ **Mama Africa Eating House.** Painted a wild lime green, Mama Africa wraps you in her vibrantly colored bosom and stimulates your senses. Place mats are old Zimbabwean newspapers, funky sculptures abound, and a live township quartet provides toe-tickling local jazz from 7 until late. Humorously named for its size, the Elephant Turd T-Bone Steak competes with Sadza Ndiraye ("the meal that kills you") and other dishes from all over Africa, many served in traditional black cast-iron, three-legged pots. Ground nuts, mild Mozambique *peri-peri* (a chili-based sauce), and slow-cooked local sadza flavors the air. Game meat is available in individual portions cooked to order. Alternatively, have a selection on a platter with the evening barbecue. Mama Africa provides a courtesy shuttle, which you can book when you make your reservation. ⊠ *Back of Trading Post Shopping Centre, Livingstone Way* ☎ *013/4–1725* ⌲ *Dinner reservations essential* ☷ *No credit cards.*

$$$$ ⊞ **Elephant Camp.** Miss Ellie, named after the soap-opera matriarch, is one of eight African elephants, including four youngsters, that will be your transportation—and friends—at this bush camp near the falls. The camp takes only eight guests, which is how many can ride at a time. The experience is larger than the ride. You'll be encouraged to bond with your beast by helping to feed and wash it, and game walks in the bush with the largest guide you'll ever have is quite a memorable experience. Rooms here are spacious brick, canvas, and thatch structures, with wood furniture and muted colors. The central lounge area has a vaulted thatch roof and beautiful views of the sweeping green lawn and nearby water hole, where many animals, including wild elephants, come to drink. Transfers to Victoria Falls are extra. ⌂ *Wild Horizons, Box 159* ☎ *013/ 4–2313* ☐ *013/4–2004* ⊕ *www.wildhorizons.co.zw* ⇜ *4 tents* ⌂ *Pool, bar; no a/c, no room TVs* ☷ *No credit cards* ☉ *FAP.*

$$$$ ⊞ **Stanley and Livingstone at Victoria Falls.** This painstakingly composed small hotel is set on its own 6,000 acres of game reserve 10 minutes out of town. Public rooms are furnished with some spectacular antiques and have verandas overlooking a water hole where elephants and other animals come to drink. Spacious suites are decorated with dark wood, and bathrooms are a stylish study in white tile, green marble, and gold trim. All suites share the view of the water hole. The rate includes game drives and all on-site activities except elephant rides and transfers to the airport or to town. ⌂ *Box 160* ☎☎ *013/4–1003 through 013/4–1009* ⊕ *www.stanley-livingstone-hotel.com* ⇜ *15 suites* ⌂ *Restaurant, pool, bar; no kids* ☷ *AE, MC, V* ☉ *FAP.*

$$$–$$$$ ✕⊞ **Victoria Falls Hotel.** Hotels come and go, but this landmark built in
Fodor'sChoice   1904 has retained its former glory as a distant, stylish outpost in empire
★   days, while pandering to today's modern tastes, needs, and wants. Such grandeur can be a little overwhelming, and especially surprising if you've just been on safari. The hotel's manicured lawns are perched on the falls' edge, with a view of the bridge, and soothing sounds permeate the gardens (and the rooms if you leave the windows open). Cool cream walls form the backdrop for elegant mahogany and wicker furniture. In the bathroom an old-fashioned drench shower will wash away the most stubborn African dust. Halls are filled with sepia-tone photos from throughout the hotel's history and animal trophies so old they are going bald. After checking your e-mail in the E-Lounge, visiting the salon, and dragging your fancy clothes out of your bag, you can dine and dance at the elegant Livingstone Room ($$$$). Two far less formal restaurants include the Terrace ($–$$$), with an à la carte menu, daily high tea, and a beautiful view of the bridge, and Jungle Junction (US$25), which has a huge barbecue buffet and traditional dancers. ⊠ *Mallet Dr., Box 10* ☎ *013/ 4–4751 through 013/4–4759* ☐ *013/4–4586* ⇜ *174 rooms, 6 suites* ⌂ *3*

restaurants, room service, tennis court, pool, hair salon, bar, business services, travel services ⊟ *AE, DC, MC, V* |○| *BP.*

$$$-$$$$ ╳▥ **Victoria Falls Safari Lodge.** Award-winning architecture, superb service, beautiful decor, and a magnificent view all set this lodge apart. About 4 km (2½ mi) outside town, it sits on a hilltop overlooking Zambezi National Park. A water hole below the lodge attracts herds of game, including buffalo and elephants. Soaring thatch roofs, huge wooden beams, and reed ceilings envelop you in a luxurious African atmosphere. The sides of the lodge are completely open to admit cooling breezes. All rooms face out, and you can fold back the glass-and-wood screens leading to your private veranda. The Makuwa-Kuwa Restaurant ($-$$$) makes full use of the view. Carniverous options include prime Zimbabwe beef, warthog, and ostrich grilled to perfection. For dessert, dare to resist the Bavarian Tower, an exquisite combination of chocolate cake and ice cream. The Boma, also on the premises, offers prix-fixe dining (US$30). There is a courtesy shuttle to and from town and Victoria Falls. ⊠ *Off Park Way, 4 km (2½ mi) from Victoria Falls* ⌖ *Box 29* ☎ *013/ 4–3211 through 013/4–3220* 🖷 *013/4–3205* ✉ *saflodge@saflodge.co. zw* 🛏 *72 rooms, 6 suites* ♨ *2 restaurants, room service, 2 pools, bar, travel services; no room TVs* ⊟ *AE, MC, V* |○| *BP.*

★ $$$ ╳▥ **Ilala Lodge.** Near the center of town, this small gem is just 10 minutes from the falls on foot. Thatch roofs give the lodge an elegant yet African look. Dining outside under the night sky at the Palm Restaurant ($$), with the falls thundering 300 feet away, is a particularly enticing way to while away a Zimbabwean evening. The Palm also serves a great terrace lunch overlooking the bush. Guest rooms are hung with African paintings and tapestries and filled with delicately caned chairs and tables and with dressers made from old railroad sleepers. French doors open onto a narrow strip of lawn backed by thick bush. Unlike most hotels in town, Ilala Lodge has no fence around it, so at night it's not uncommon to find elephants browsing outside your window or buffalo grazing on the lawn. ⊠ *411 Livingstone Way, Box 18* ☎ *013/4–4737* 🖷 *013/4–4740* ⊕ *www.ilalalodge.com* 🛏 *30 rooms, 2 suites* ♨ *Restaurant, room service, pool, bar* ⊟ *DC, MC, V* |○| *BP.*

$ ▥ **Jingle Bells.** A comfortable and spacious residential house, Jingle Bells is a great option for a quiet stay in Victoria Falls. Decor is fresh and simple. Mariolina De Leo, the very friendly and helpful host, is fluent in Italian, English, and French. Of the rooms, two have double beds and nine have twins; all have private bathrooms. The entire house can be rented fully serviced with a cook and cleaners. ⊠ *591 Manyika Rd., Box 289* ☎ *013/4–3242* ✉ *marcla@mweb.co.zw* 🛏 *11 rooms* ♨ *Pool* ⊟ *No credit cards* |○| *BP.*

¢ ▥ **Victoria Falls Backpackers.** Rooms at this inexpensive and jolly backpacker's lodge are named after animals, with decor to match. The owners have created a child-friendly environment (the pool has a small fence, for example), offer great booking services, and claim to get the best activity prices in town. Overland trucks are not allowed. ⊠ *357 Gibson Rd., Box 151* ☎ *013/4–2209 or 013/4–2248* 🖷 *013/4–2209* ⊕ *www.victoriafallsbackpackers.com* 🛏 *6 rooms* ♨ *Pool, bar, travel services* ⊟ *No credit cards* |○| *CP.*

Sports & the Outdoors

You can book all the adventures listed below (and many others) through your hotel or one of the major booking offices along Park Way:

Safari Par Excellence (⊠ Shop 4, Phumula Centre, off Park Way ☎ 013/4–4726 ⊕ www.zambezisafari.com). **Shearwater Adventures** (⊠ Shops 1 and 2, Sopers Arcade, Park Way ☎ 013/4–5806 ⊕ www.shearwateradventures.com). **Wild Horizons** (☎ 013/4–2313 ⊕ www.wildhorizons.co.zw).

Boating

A cruise on the Upper Zambezi is a relaxing way to take in game and scenery. Hippos, crocs, and elephants are spied fairly regularly, and your captain will stop and comment whenever something noteworthy rears its head. **Shearwater Adventures** (☎ 013/4–5806 ⊕ www.shearwateradventures.com) has sunset and dinner cruises at prices ranging from about US$25 to US$35. Shearwater also offers a 30-minute white-water jetboat ride below the falls. This activity is a great adventure for the not so bold, since all you do is hang on. Children over seven can jetboat if accompanied by an adult. Beer and other cold drinks are included in the price (US$70).

Bungee Jumping

As the second-highest bungee jump in the world, the 340-foot leap from the bridge is a major magnet for adrenaline junkies. The view, if you can stomach it, is pretty spectacular, too. A jump with **Shearwater Adventures** (☎ 013/4–5806 ⊕ www.shearwateradventures.com) costs US$75, and you must produce your passport to get a bridge pass.

Canoeing

Shearwater Adventures (☎ 013/4–5806 ⊕ www.shearwateradventures.com) offers half- and full-day canoe trips and a very gentle "wine route" trip, on which you don't even paddle; you just watch the view while your guide does the work and hands you drinks and snacks (US$45). **Wild Horizons** (☎ 013/4–2313 ⊕ www.wildhorizons.co.zw) leads canoe trips on the Zambezi River above the falls. The river here is mostly wide and flat, with the occasional tiny rapid. As the river winds around islands and splits into myriad channels, you might view crocodiles, hippos, or elephants. The one-hour game drive through Zambezi National Park to reach the launch point is an added bonus. Most trips provide a bush breakfast before you start, a brief coffee or tea break, and a casual lunch on an island in the river. You can select either a half- or full-day trip or two- to three-night expeditions. No experience or physical prowess is required. Expect to pay about US$65 for a half day and US$85 for a full day.

Elephant-Back Riding

The **Shearwater Elephant Company** (☎ 013/4–5806 ⊕ www.shearwateradventures.com) has morning and evening rides accompanied by breakfast or snacks and sunset drinks (US$90). You can also book a lunchtime interaction activity called Jumbo Junction (US$60). A light lunch (salad, chicken, or quiche, for example) is included, but the main attraction is the elephants. You get to touch them, talk to them, and ask the guide all kinds of questions about their history, biology, and personal quirks. **Wild Horizons** (☎ 013/4–2313 ⊕ www.wildhorizons.co. zw) offers elephant rides (US$90), including transfers and either a full breakfast or drinks and snacks. They have recently acquired four baby elephants, so be prepared to fall in love.

Flying & Parasailing

Flying over the falls, called the Flight of Angels, is a better option from the Zambian side, as the Vic Falls airport is a long way from the Zimbabwean side of the falls. Still, there are some options available. **Shearwater Adventures** (☎ 013/4–5806 ⊕ www.shearwateradventures.com) runs a helicopter flight from the Elephant Hills Hotel and gets you over the falls in a couple of minutes. It costs US$85 for 12–13 minutes. **Zambezi Parasailing** (☎ 013/4–2209 ⊕ www.victoriafallsbackpackers.com) provides 10-minute parasails for US$40, including transfers from anywhere in town. And yes, you land back in the boat.

Horseback Riding

Riding a horse through Zambezi National Park is an unforgettable experience. You get to sneak up on unsuspecting antelopes and even buffalo, giraffes, and elephants, especially during the rainy months. Safari Par Excellence is the booking agent for **Zambezi Horse Trails** (☎ 091/ 131–3270), run by Alison Baker, a Vic Falls legend. She knows the bush like the back of her hand, rides hard, and can shoot straight. Even more important, though, she knows how to avoid having to. Experienced riders may go on game-viewing rides that range anywhere from 2½ hours to one, two, or three days. Novice riders can go for 1½ hours but will not be allowed close to animals such as elephants and lions. Costs range from US$35 for 1½ hours to US$90 for a full-day ride, including lunch, drinks, and park fees. Multiday trail rides are available by request.

Rafting & River Boarding

The Batoka Gorge is reputed to offer the world's best one-day white-water rafting, with commercial rapids class 5 and down. To include river boarding, stop at suitable rapids on the rafting trip and (still clad in helmet and life jacket) hop on a body board and surf the standing waves (US$115). The walk in and out of the gorge is quite strenuous, but as long as you are reasonably fit and looking for adventure, you need no experience. The safety briefing is extensive. Bring a baseball cap to wear under your helmet, water-friendly shoes that grip well, and dry clothes to change into at the end of the day.

Shearwater Rafting (☎ 013/4–5806 ⊕ www.shearwateradventures.com) runs a full-day trip for US$95—lunch, drinks, and transfers included. Half-day trips are also available. **Wild Horizons** (☎ 013/4–2313 ⊕ www. wildhorizons.co.zw) leads full- and half-day rafting trips, as well as a 2½-day trip, starting at US$95.

Rappelling & Swinging

Wild Horizons (☎ 013/4–2313 ⊕ www.wildhorizons.co.zw) lets you swing off steel cables in the gorge. Take your pick from the flying fox, rap jump, abseil (rappel), or the big gorge swing. For descriptions of what these crazy activities are, *see* Rappelling & Swinging under Livingstone, Zambia, *below.* The cost is US$60 for a single activity, US$85 for a half day, and US$100 for a full day.

Shopping

Several curio and crafts shops lie just beyond the Falls Craft Village, including the stylish **Elephant Walk Mall** (⊠ Sopers Crescent, behind banks and post office). At the sprawling **Trading Post** (⊠ Livingstone Way) you can buy a variety of crafts, from an 8-foot-tall wooden giraffe to soapstone carvings and brightly colored Zimbabwean batiks. To get your acquisitions back home, visit the international shipping agent sandwiched between the curio shops.

Victoria Falls A to Z

AIR TRAVEL

Victoria Falls Airport (VFA) lies 22 km (14 mi) south of town. South African Airways, Air Zimbabwe, and British Airways all fly direct between Johannesburg and Victoria Falls daily.

Most hotels send free shuttle buses to meet incoming flights and provide free airport transfers for departing guests; arrange this in advance with your hotel. Taxis, at time of writing, could get you to or from the airport for about US$20, payable in local or foreign currency, but taxi fares fluctuate drastically. Be prepared for local drivers to accost you with offers of rides into town.

🛪 Airport **Victoria Falls Airport** ⊠ Livingstone Way ☎ 013/4–4250.

🛪 Airlines **Air Zimbabwe** ☎ 013/4–4316. **British Airways–Comair** ☎ 013/4–5825 or 011/405–282 ⊕ www.british-airways.com. **South African Airways** ⊠ Takura House, 2nd fl., 69–71 Union Ave. ☎ 011/808–678.

BUS TRAVEL

Most of the outlying hotels have shuttle buses that run into town hourly. Inquire at your hotel in advance.

EMERGENCIES

MARS (Medical Air Rescue Services) is on standby for all emergencies. Dr. Nyoni is a trauma specialist and operates a hospital opposite the Shoestring lodge. The well-stocked Victoria Falls Pharmacy is the place to go if you need prescription medicines.

🏥 Emergency Services **Police** ☎ 013/4–4206 or 013/4–4681. **MARS** ⊠ West Dr., opposite Shoestring ☎ 013/4–4646.

🏥 Hospital **Dr. Nyoni** ⊠ West Dr., opposite Shoestring ☎ 013/4–3356.

🏥 Pharmacy **Victoria Falls Pharmacy** ⊠ Phumula Centre, off Park Way ☎ 013/4–4403.

HEALTH & SAFETY

For tips on health and safety *see* Livingstone A to Z, *below.*

INTERNET

Internet prices can vary wildly, as the telephone rates keep climbing. The average cost at time of writing is US$5 for 15 minutes.

🔲 Internet Access **E-world** ⊠ Victoria Falls Hotel ☎ 013/4-4751. **Shearwater** ⊠ Park Way ☎ 013/4-5806.

MONEY MATTERS

If you limit your Zimbabwe visit to Vic Falls, it's not absolutely necessary to change money into Zimbabwean dollars, because everyone from taxi drivers to curio vendors accepts foreign currency (the same applies on the Zambian side of the falls). However, you will be given change in Zimbabwean dollars—probably at a pretty bad exchange rate.

It's expected that tour operators will soon accept only U.S. currency; check before you go. If the trip is run by a Zambian operator—even if you book it in Zimbabwe and are picked up at your Zimbabwean hotel—you *must* pay in foreign currency. Credit card facilities are either not available or carry very stiff fees.

Change your money only at banks, located around Livingstone Way and Park Way, and generally open only during the morning. It is illegal to change money on the black market, and street vendors are world-class con artists who will rip you off in ways you never would have believed possible. All official *bureaux de change* have been closed down by the government.

PASSPORTS & VISAS

Plan your trip carefully to avoid having to pay repeated visa fees to Zimbabwe. A multiple-entry visa might save you money if you plan to cross the border more than once. If you cross the river to do a one-day trip with a recognized Zambian-registered tour operator, your day visa costs might be included in the cost of the activity. Visit Zambia on your own, and you will need to buy a day visa, which costs US$10 at the border. You do not need another visa for Zimbabwe if you are out of the country only for the day.

TAXIS

Taxis are a cheap and convenient way to get around town. Hotels can summon reputable taxis quickly and advise you on the cost. Tipping is not usual, but change is always appreciated.

VISITOR INFORMATION

The Victoria Falls Publicity Association is fairly well stocked with brochures. It's open weekdays 8–1 and 2–4 and Saturday 8–1. It's also a good idea to seek advice from the many safari companies in town.

🔲 Tourist Office **Victoria Falls Publicity Association** ⊠ 412 Park Way ☎ 013/4-4202.

LIVINGSTONE, ZAMBIA

This marvelous old town has a wealth of natural beauty and a glut of activities. It was the old colonial capital, and after a few decades of neglect it is now recasting itself as Zambia's tourism and adventure capital. There is a slight air of the past here. Historic buildings outnumber

ZIMBABWE ESSENTIAL INFO

Electricity
To use electric-powered equipment purchased in the United States or Canada, bring a converter and adapter. If your appliances are dual voltage, you'll need only an adapter. The electrical current is 220 volts, 50 cycles alternating current (AC); wall outlets in most of the region take 15-amp plugs with three square prongs.

Embassies
🏠 Canada **Canadian High Commission** ✉ 45 Baines Ave., Box 1430, Harare ☎ 04/25–2181 through 04/25–2185 🖷 04/25–2186.

🏠 United Kingdom **British High Commission** ✉ Corner House, Samora Machel Ave. and Leopold Takawira St., 7th floor, Harare ☎ 04/77–2990 or 04/77–4700 🖷 04/77–4605.

🏠 United States **U.S. Embassy** ✉ 172 Herbert Chitepo Ave., Box 3340, Harare ☎ 04/70–3169 🖷 04/79–6488.

Gay & Lesbian Travelers
Homosexuality is not illegal in Zimbabwe but can be a practical problem. Although attitudes are improving, it is advisable to be extremely circumspect.

Language
Zimbabwe's official language is English. Chishona and Sindebele and their dialects are widely spoken.

Money Matters
Zimbabwe's currency is the Zimbabwe dollar. There are Z$100, Z$500, and Z$1,000 bills, and bearer notes for Z$5,000, Z$10,000, and Z$20,000 denominations. This currency remains particularly volatile, and although the rate of exchange at the time of writing was around Z$6,000 to the US$, you can expect any number of surprises from one day to the next.

Passports & Visas
Americans can buy point-of-entry visas for US$35 for a single entry. Visas for British citizens cost US$55 for a single entry. If you leave Zimbabwe for more than 24 hours, you will need to buy another (unless you bought a multiple-entry visa), so think before you save those dollars. To cross the border into Zambia for a day, Britons, Canadians, and Americans need to purchase a Zambian day visa for US$10, unless you have booked an activity that includes this cost. Visas can be purchased from an embassy before departure, but generally cost more than buying them at the border. Multiple-entry visas are available only from Harare.

🏠 Zimbabwean Missions Abroad **United Kingdom** ✉ 429 Strand London ☎ 0870/005–6710 🖷 0207/379–1167.

Telephone
The country code for Zimbabwe is 263. When dialing from abroad, drop the initial 0 from local area codes. Operator assistance is 962 for domestic and 965 for international inquiries, but it's better to ask a hotel or restaurant owner.

Zimbabwe has card-operated pay phones. Phone cards are available in several denominations, and a digital readout tells you how much credit remains while you're talking. Telephone cards are available at newsstands and convenience stores.

Time
Zimbabwe operates on CAST (Central African Standard Time), which is two hours ahead of Greenwich mean time. That makes it seven hours ahead of North American eastern standard time (six hours ahead during eastern daylight saving time).

new ones, and many inhabitants live a life not unlike that of their ancestors 100 years ago. Livingstone handles the surge of tourists with equal parts grace, confidence, African mischief, and nuisance.

Many visitors to this side of the falls opt to stay in one of the secluded safari-style lodges on the Zambezi River. The Zambian experience offers a tranquil respite from the noise and crowds at hotels across the border in Zimbabwe.

What to See

Numbers in the margin correspond to numbers on the Livingstone map.

⑤ Livingstone Museum. The country's oldest and largest museum contains history, ethnography, natural history, and archaeology sections and includes materials ranging from newspaper clippings to photographs of the queen dancing with Kenneth Kaunda (Zambia's first president) to historical information dating back to 1500. Among the priceless David Livingstone memorabilia is a model of the mangled arm bone used to identify his body and various journals and maps from the period when he explored the area and claimed the falls for his queen. ⊠ *Mosi-oa-Tunya Rd., between civic center and post office; temporary building off Mosi-oa-Tunay Rd., behind National Milling* ☎ *03/32–0495* 🎫 *US$3 or ZK9,000* ☉ *Daily 9–4:30.*

⑥ Mosi-oa-Tunya. The Smoke that Thunders more than lives up to its reputation as one of the world's greatest natural wonders. No words can do these incredible falls justice, and it's a difficult place to appreciate in just a short visit, as it has many moods and aspects. Though the Zimbabwean side may offer more panoramic views, the Zambian side—especially the **Knife Edge** (a sharp headland with fantastic views)—allows you to stand virtually suspended over the Boiling Pot, with the deafening water crashing everywhere around you. From around May to August the falls are a multisensory experience, though you'll get absolutely drenched if you venture onto the Knife Edge, and there may be too much spray to see the bottom of the gorge. If you get the sun behind you, you'll see that magic rainbow. A network of paths leads to the main viewing points; some are not well protected, so watch your step and wear good, safe shoes, especially at high water, when you are likely to get drenched. You will have dramatic views of the full 1½ km (1 mi) of the ironstone face of the falls, the Boiling Pot directly below, the railway bridge, and Batoka Gorge. At times of low water it is possible to take a guided walk to Livingstone Island and swim in the **Devils Pool,** a natural pond right on the lip of the abyss. ⊠ *Entrance off Mosi-oa-Tunya Rd., just before border post* ☎ *No phone* 🎫 *US$10* ☉ *Daily 6–6, later at full moon.*

⑦ Mosi-oa-Tunya National Park. This park is a quick and easy option for viewing plains game. In fact, you are almost guaranteed to spy white rhinos. You can also visit the Old Drift graveyard, as the park includes the location of the original settlement here. Many park guides are knowledgeable, but the ultimate park experience is the three-hour guided walking safari offered by Livingstone Safaris (⇨ *Tours, below*). You can visit the park without a guide, but the roads get seriously muddy in the

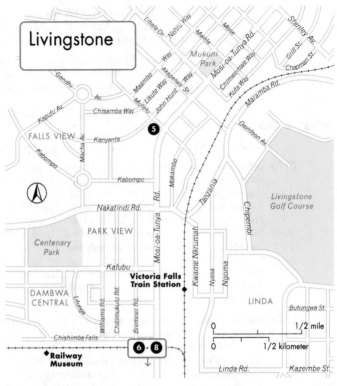

rainy season, and a guide who knows where to drive becomes a near-necessity. ⊠ *Sichanga Rd., off Mosi-oa-Tunya Rd., 3½ km (2 mi) from Livingstone* ⊠ *US$6, US$3 Zambian-registered car* ⊙ *Apr.–Nov., daily 6 AM–6:30 PM; Dec.–Mar., daily 6 AM–7 PM.*

8 Mukuni Village. Fascinated by the history, customs, and traditions of the area? Local guides can escort you on an intimate visit inside a local house and explain the customs of the village. This is not a stage set but a very real village, so your tour will be different depending on the time of the day you go. For example, at mealtimes you can see how local delicacies are prepared. It is customary to sign in the visitor book and to pay a small fee to your guide. Bushtracks (⇨ Livingstone A to Z, *below*) conducts organized visits. ⊙ *Daily 6–6.*

Where to Stay & Eat

$$$$ ✕ **Livingstone Island Picnic.** Available throughout the year except for a
Fodor'sChoice   couple of weeks when the water level is too high, this is a spectacular,
★   romantic dining option. Livingstone Island is perched right on the edge of the abyss, where you'll sit around a linen-decked table while being plied with a delicious buffet lunch (with salads) and drink by liveried waiters. You get here by boat (two engines, just in case). Brunch and

afternoon tea are US$40 and US$55, respectively, and lunch is US$95, including transfers. The trips are run by Tongabezi Lodge, and there is a maximum of 12 guests. ⊠ *Livingstone Island* ⌂ *Box 31* ☎ *03/ 32–4450* ⊟ *MC, V* ☯ *Closed a few weeks Feb.–Mar., depending on water level. No dinner.*

$–$$ ✕ **Rite Pub and Grill.** This place is an African jazz club, English pub, and American steak house all rolled into one. The menu is unassuming, the service is good, portions are huge, and the food is mostly marinated and grilled, accompanied by fries or nsima. With live music twice a week, this is the busiest restaurant in Livingstone and a good choice if you would like to meet local characters. While you get down and sticky with a full rack of ribs, watch the lead guitarist do a solo with his teeth à la Jimmy Hendrix. ⊠ *Mosi-oa-Tunya Rd.* ☎ *03/32–2597* ⌕ *Reservations accepted only until 7* ⊟ *No credit cards.*

¢–$$ ✕ **Kamuza.** The Moguls themselves might declare a meal here a feast. Spicy but not hot, the curries are lovingly prepared from ingredients imported from India. The chicken Tikka Masala is a house specialty, and the hand-made saffron Kulfi is a great way to end a hot day in Africa. ⊠ *Ngolide Lodge, Mosi-oa-Tunya Rd.* ☎ *03/32–1091* ⊟ *MC, V* ☯ *No dinner Mon.*

¢–$ ✕ **Funky Munky.** Cheap and cheerful, this small pizzeria offers thin-crust pizzas baked in a traditional wood-fired oven and named after primates. Try the popular bacon and mushroom Baboon or Chimpancheese four-cheese extravaganza, or build your own. If you seek lighter fare, have a fresh French baguette stuffed with various traditional lunch fillings. ⊠ *Mosi-oa-Tunya Rd.* ☎ *03/32–0120* ⊟ *No credit cards.*

¢–$ ✕ **Zig Zag Coffee House.** First came this coffee shop, which still serves the best coffee in town, including a choice of flavored espresso and cappuccino. Then its owners added the Warehouse complex, with a swimming pool, crafts market, children's play area, plant nursery, and B&B. Meals are simple and good—soups, ciabatta bread, nachos, muffins, and all-day breakfasts, which you can eat while catching up on all the scandalous gossip Livingstone town can provide. ⊠ *Mosi-oa-Tunya Rd.* ☎ *03/ 32–4081* ⊟ *No credit cards.*

★ $$$$ ☷ **River Club.** With split-level rooms that cling to the edge of the great Zambezi, the River Club puts a modern spin on a Victorian house party. It is hard to beat the view from the infinity pool, until you watch the sun set from your claw-foot tub. Clever cooling mists of water draw flocks of birds to the massage tent, and the library begs for a glass of port and a serious book. History clings to the structure, built to the plans of the original house, but decorations have been lovingly collected from past and present. You could spend an entire day reading interesting anecdotes, old maps, Punch cartoons, and updates about the River Club's support of the local village. A candlelight dinner is followed by croquet on the floodlighted lawn before you retire to your partially starlit room. You approach the lodge from the river—purely for the spectacular effect— but it necessitates negotiating some steep stairs. If you think you'll struggle, ask to be transferred by vehicle. ⌂ *Box 60469* ☎ *03/32–3672* 🖷 *03/32–3659* ⇥ *10 rooms* ⌕ *Dining room, pool, massage, croquet* ⊟ *MC, V* ⊕ *www.wilderness-safaris.com* ⚏ *FAP.*

$$$$ ⌕ **Royal Livingstone.** This upmarket hotel has an incredibly gorgeous sundowner deck, arguably on the best spot on the river, just upstream from the falls. The attractive colonial safari-style buildings are set amid sweeping green lawns and big trees and have fantastic views, but enough guest traffic passes by rooms that privacy is nonexistent. The decor of both the guest rooms and public rooms is deliberately ostentatious. Don't look too closely though; the old library books are painted onto the shelves, making it all seem slightly phony. Staff are friendly and try to be helpful, but numerous communication problems, omissions, and errors can infuriate guests expecting service to match the high costs. Vervet monkeys are an entertaining nuisance, so hang on to your expensive cocktail. ⌂ *Mosi-oa-Tunya Rd.* ☎ *03/32–1122* 🖷 *03/32–1128* ⊕ *www. suninternational.co.za* ⇨ *173 rooms* ⅋ *Restaurant, room service, pool, hair salon, bar, shop* ▤ *AE, DC, MC, V* �⊙1 *CP.*

$$$$
Fodor'sChoice
★
⌕ **Tongabezi and Sindabezi Island.** Never formal but flagrantly romantic, Tongabezi and Sindabezi, its satellite 4 km (2½ mi) downriver, do not upstage Africa. Instead they are the frame around the picture. At Tongabezi, standard rooms are spacious cream-and-ocher *rondawels* (round thatch huts) featuring private verandas that can be enclosed in a billowing mosquito net. Three suites are built into a low cliff and incorporate the original riverine forest canopy. King beds set in tree trunks and covered by curtains of linen netting, oversize sofas in the sitting area, and giant bathtubs on the private decks are all unashamedly romantic. Every room has a local guide who acts as a personal valet and delights in decadently catering to your every whim. Room service is ordered via antique telephones, and the lodge has an in-house holistic therapist. Small **Sindabezi Island** (eight-guest maximum) is separated by a stretch of river from Zambezi National Park. Each island hut has a private view, and your every need is anticipated. (Sindabezi guests get a valet and a guide.) Dinner is served by lantern and candlelight on a sandbank under the stars. ⌂ *Box 31* ☎ *03/32–4450, 097/77–0917, or 097/77–0918* 🖷 *097/ 84–0920* ⊕ *www.tongabezi.com* ⇨ *5 suites, 5 cottages* ⅋ *Tennis court, pool, boating* ▤ *MC, V* �⊙1 *FAP.*

$$$$ ⌕ **Zambezi Sun.** Part of the same complex as the Royal Livingstone, this hotel is less expensive, less pretentious, and a whole lot more welcoming than its pricier cousin. The design borrows freely from a variety of (mostly African) cultures and is vibrantly colorful, sparkly, and fun. Buildings are earth red and round cornered, blending in with the surroundings. Rooms are decorated with bright primary-color murals, and the spacious bathrooms have colorful tiles and handmade sinks. The hotel is child-friendly, with family rooms and a play center. The buffet breakfasts and dinners are gastronomic feasts, but all food and drink are exorbitantly priced. Although the Zambezi Sun doesn't share the Livingstone's fantastic view, it's even closer to the falls—within walking distance. ⌂ *Mosi-oa-Tunya Rd.* ☎ *03/32–1122, 27/11/780– 7444 reservations (South Africa)* 🖷 *27/11/780–7449 or 27/11/780– 7061 (South Africa)* ⊕ *www.suninternational.co.za* ⇨ *208 rooms, 4 suites* ⅋ *2 restaurants, pool, wading pool, bar, cabaret, babysitting, children's programs (all ages), playground, meeting rooms* ▤ *AE, DC, MC, V* �⊙1 *CP.*

$$ 🏨 **Waterfront.** There's a hive of happy activity here ranging from opportunistic monkeys relieving unsuspecting tourists of their lunch to serious late-night boozing to adventure enthusiasts (hangover optional) being whisked off to do their thing at all hours of the day. Curiously, the spacious family rooms can be reached only via a steep exterior wooden staircase, but this is also a popular spot for camping. Restaurant service is notoriously slow and mediocre. ⊠ *Sichanga Rd., just off Mosi-oa-Tunya Rd.* ☎ *03/32–0606* ⊕ *www.zambezisafari.com* ↪ *21 chalets, 30 tents, 9 campsites* ⌂ *Restaurant, 2 pools, 2 bars, travel services* ☰ *MC, V* ⍥ *BP.*

¢ 🏨 **Bovu.** For the vibe of California and Marrakesh in the '60s and '70s, head to this satellite camp of Jungle Junction (which has camping only). Set on the banks of the Zambezi 52 km (32 mi) upstream of the falls, this is the place to chill out. Take a good book or an excellent companion. Accommodations are in basic but somehow quite perfect huts with gorgeous river views, and there are hot showers and flush toilets. The food is good, and the coffee better than most of the upscale lodges serve. You can swim in a shallow section of small rapids naturally protected from crocodiles or hippos (or this is the theory). Warning: "island time" operates here and anything goes, so the staid or conservative are likely to find it unsuitable. The rates include transfers and two activities; choose from a sunset cruise in a *mokoro* (an African canoelike boat), guided walks, and village visits. Meals are provided but cost extra. ✉ *Box 61122* ☎ *03/32–3708* ⊕ *www.junglejunction.info* ↪ *8 huts* ⌂ *Dining room, bar.*

¢ 🏨 **Fawlty Towers.** An old textile factory has had a revamp and become the most popular backpacker's lodge in the area. This centrally located lodging has a big lawn with a pool and a popular restaurant and bar. Very comfortable rooms with private bath are available, as are dorm rooms. ⊠ *Mosi-oa-Tunya Rd.* ☎ *03/32–3432* 🖷 *03/32–1338* ⊕ *www.adventure-africa.com* ↪ *23 rooms, 6 dormitories* ⌂ *Restaurant, pool, bar* ☰ *MC, V* ⍥ *EP.*

Sports & the Outdoors

Livingstone can compete with the best as far as indulging the wildest fantasies of adrenaline junkies and outdoor enthusiasts goes. You can reserve activities directly with the operators, let your hotel or lodge handle it, or book through a central booking group. **Safari Par Excellence** (☎ 03/32–1629 ⊕ www.safpar.com) runs kayaking and rafting as well as booking trip combinations, good if your time is limited or you just want to go wild. One of the most popular—and an excellent value—is the Raft-Heli (US$170–US$210), which saves you a bit of a walk and offers a spectacular view of the gorge. You can substitute tandem kayaking or river boarding for rafting (at a greater cost). Heli-Jet (US$210) involves no strenuous walking. You helicopter in, jetboat, and then helicopter out. **Livingstone's Adventure** (☎ 03/32–0058 ⊕ www.livingstonesadventure.com) offers a central booking service as well as operating Batoka Sky, *African Queen,* and Livingstone Quad Company.

ATVing

Riding a quad through the mopane forest, seeing local villages, and playing in Batoka Gorge is possible courtesy of **Livingstone Quad Company** (☎ 03/32–0058 ⊕ www.livingstonesadventure.com). A one-hour eco-trail adventure costs US$55. The minimum age is 16, but even absolute beginners are welcome.

Boating

Truly the monarch of the river, the *African Queen* (☎ 03/32–1513) is an elegant colonial-style riverboat. Sunset cruises offer the maximum style and splendor. Costs start at US$48 for a 1½-hour lunch cruise. **Victoria Falls River Safaris** (☎ 03/32–1513) operates a doubly silenced, propeller-free, water-turbine boat (from US$57), which can access areas no other boats can get to. It's excellent for game and bird spotting.

Bungee Jumping

Bungee jumping off the 340-foot-high Victoria Falls Bridge with **African Extreme** (☎ 03/32–4231) is a major adrenaline rush, with 65 feet and three seconds of free fall and a pretty spectacular view. The jump costs US$75, but it's worth getting the US$40 video, complete with *Top Gun* music track.

Canoeing

A gentle canoeing trip on the upper Zambezi is a great opportunity to see birds and a variety of game. Many of the lodges upriver have canoeing as an inclusive activity, but trips are also run by a number of companies, which are all reputable and provide similar value for your money. Most companies require a minimum of two clients. **Bundu Adventures** (☎ 03/32–4407) runs half-day canoe trips for US$80 and full-day trips including lunch and soft drinks for US$85. **Chundukwa Adventure Trails** (☎ 03/32–4452) leads half-day trips (US$75) and full-day trips including lunch (US$95), as well as multiday canoeing safaris (US$175 per night, all inclusive) on request. **Makoro Quest** (☎ 03/32–4253) is one of the oldest upper Zambezi canoe operators on the Zambian side. Half-day trips are US$76, and a full day costs US$95, including an island lunch.

Flying

Batoka Sky (☎ 03/32–0058 ⊕ www.livingstonesadventure.com) offers weight-shift Aerotrike twin-axis microlighting (flying jargon for what resembles a motorized hang glider) and helicopter flights over the falls and through the gorges. There's a minimum of three passengers for helicopters. For microlighting you are issued a flightsuit (padded in winter) and a helmet with a headset, but you may not bring a camera for safety reasons. Batoka Sky has been operating since 1992, and has a 100% microlighting safety record. Flights are booked for early morning and late afternoon, and are dependent on the weather. Prices run US$80–US$170, depending on length of flight and aircraft. Your transfer and a day visa, if you are coming from Victoria Falls, are included. The Helicopter Gorge picnic (US$170) includes lunch and drinks for a minimum of four people.

Fodor's Choice
★

Sitting in the front of an open-cockpit biplane, your pilot shouting "Swing the prop" and "Contact" it is difficult not to get swept up in the romance of times gone by. **Tiger Moth Flight of the Angels** (✉ Livingstone Airport, Airport Rd. ☎ 03/32–3095 ⊕ www.uaczam.com) provides the ultimate prop-driven viewpoint for an overview of the falls and the gorges that mark its ancient trail. A 20-minute flight goes for US$120; a flight including the gorges runs US$160.

Horseback Riding

You can take a placid horseback ride through the bush along the banks of the Zambezi with **Chundukwa Adventure Trails** (☎ 03/32–4452). If you are comfortable enough to keep your riding cool while a herd of elephants approaches, you may want to watch game from horseback or do a multiday trail ride. Costs are US$40 for 1½ hours to a full day including lunch and drinks for US$100.

Jetboating

If you want some thrills and speed but rafting seems a bit daunting, or you can't face the walk in and out, you'll probably enjoy jetboating with **Jet Extreme** (☎ 03/32–1375). A new cable-car ride, included in the cost of the jetboat ride (US$70 for 30 minutes), will mean no more strenuous walking out of the gorge. Jetboating can be combined with a rafting excursion, as the jetboat starts at the end of the rafting run, or with a helicopter trip out of the gorge. (Please note that the rafting and heli must be booked separately, although big operators like Safari Par Excellence and Livingstone's Adventure offer combinations.) Children over seven can jetboat if they are accompanied by an adult.

Kayaking

If you're feeling brave, try tandem kayaking. You do the same stretch of river as the rafting trips but in a two-seat kayak with a guide. Although you don't need previous experience, you have to be a fast study, as it entails getting a crash course in steering a kayak through serious grade-5 rapids. It's not for the faint of heart or, strangely, the big and macho—there's a weight limit of 175 pounds. The trip costs US$135 and is run by **Safari Par Excellence** (☎ 03/32–0606 ⊕ www.safpar.com).

Rappelling & Swinging

For something completely different, **Abseil Zambia** (☎ 03/32–1188) has taken some specially designed heavy-duty steel cables, combined them with various pulleys and rigs, one dry gorge, and a 100% safety record to entertain both the fainthearted and the daring. The full day (US$95) is a great value, as it includes lunch, refreshments, and as many repeats of the activities as you like. (Keep in mind that you will have to climb out following the gorge swing and the rappel; a half day, US$80, is advised during the hot months of October–December.) Work up an appetite for more daring drops by starting on the zip line (or flying fox). You run off a ramp while attached to the line, and the sensation is pure freedom and surprisingly unscary, as you are not moving up or down. Next rappel down into the 175-foot gorge, and, after you climb out, try it again facing forward. It's called a rap run. You're literally walking down the cliff face. End the day with the king of adrenaline activities, a whopping 175-foot, 3½-second vertical free-fall swing into the gorge (US$60 for two swings). Three-two-one-hoooo-ha!

Rafting & River Boarding

The Batoka Gorge below the falls has the best one-day white-water rafting in the world. Rapids are classed at grades 4 and 5, and a "long swim" (falling out of the raft at the start of a rapid and body surfing through) will redefine the word *scary*. Guides do this every day and know the river intimately. Theoretically, there are easy and more exciting options on most rapids, and guides will offer to run the rapids to suit your mood. Of course, there is no guarantee that you will not flip. You can also decide to try river boarding (US$125), in which you hop off the raft onto a body board and surf suitable rapids. Most operators offer rafting excursions that cost US$95 for either a full- or half-day trip, including a one-day visa if you're crossing the border to do it. The new Ecolift transports rafters out of the gorge, so you only have to climb down. You can also do a combination helicopter-and-rafting trip. Bring secure shoes, dry clothes for the long drive home, a baseball cap to wear under your helmet, and plenty of sunscreen.

Safari Par Excellence (☎03/32–0606), operating from the Waterfront lodge, is the biggest operator.

Shopping

If you fall in love with the furniture in your lodge, visit **Kubu Crafts** (✉ 133 Mosi-oa-Tunya Rd. ☎03/32–4093 ⊕www.kubucrafts.com), a stylish home decor shop. Locally made furniture in hardwood and wrought iron is complemented by a selection of West African masks and weavings and the work of numerous local artists, including the fantastic oil paintings of Stephen Kapata. Prices can be ridiculously inflated. It's worth having a look through Mukuni Park before you buy the same article at a 500% markup. Kubu Crafts also sells tea, coffee, and cakes to enjoy in the garden.

Although the park at the entrance to the falls overlook has stalls where you can find stone and wood carvings and simple bead and semi-precious-stone jewelry, the real gem of an African bazaar lies in the center of town, at **Mukuni Park Market** (✉ Mosi-oa-Tunya Rd. and Libala Dr. ☎ No phone). This is the place to bargain. You'll be quoted top dollar initially, but shop around and watch the prices drop to roughly one-third of the original quote. Walk through the entire market before you commence buying. This will not only ensure that you get the best price but will give you the opportunity to gauge the level of craftsmanship that can be expected. Look out for individual and unusual pieces, as it is occasionally possible to find valuable antiques. The market is open daily approximately 7–6.

Livingstone A to Z

AIR TRAVEL

Nationwide and Comair/British Airways fly regularly from Johannesburg into Livingstone International Airport, 5 km (3 mi) out of town.

The flight is a comfortable hop, just over two hours long, and the airport is small and friendly, with helpful staff to speed you on your way. If at all possible, do not check your luggage through from Johannesburg International, and always lock suitcases securely, as luggage theft in South Africa is an everyday occurrence.

🛪Airlines **Comair/British Airways** ☎03/32-2827 or 03/32-2873 ⊕www.british-airways. com. **Nationwide** ☎ 03/32-2251 ⊕ www.flynationwide.co.za.

CAR TRAVEL

There is a perfectly reasonable traffic code in Zambia. Unfortunately, not many people have ever heard of it. You would do well to leave the driving to your guides or negotiate an all-inclusive rate with a taxi driver recommended by your hotel or lodge for the duration of your stay. Note that taxis are generally not allowed to cross the border, so if you want to visit Zimbabwe, you will have to book a tour that includes transfers. Once at the border, it is feasible to walk into and around Victoria Falls town, or rent a bicycle.

If you insist on renting a car, you should know that some of the roads have more potholes than tar. You don't need four-wheel drive, but it's not a bad idea, especially if you want to travel farther afield. Imperial Car Rental operates from the offices of Voyagers at the Day Activity Center near the Zambezi Sun. Foley's 4x4 Hire rents out Land Rovers, fully equipped with tents and other camping equipment.

🚗 Rental Companies **Foley's 4x4 Hire** ☎ 01/25-4096 or 097/46-2048 ⊕ www. hireafrica.com. **Imperial Car Rental** ☎ 03/32-1122.

EMERGENCIES

For minor injuries, a test for malaria, or the treatment of non-life-threatening ailments, you can go to the Rainbow or Southern medical centre or the Mwenda or Shafik clinic. For serious emergencies, contact SES (Speciality Air Services). Musamu Pharmacy is open weekdays 8:30–8, Saturday 8:30–3, and Sunday 9–1.

🚑 Emergency Services **General Emergency** ☎ 999. **Police** ☎ 992. **Fire** ☎ 993. **SES** ☎ 01/27-3302 through 01/27-3307 or 097/77-0303.

🏥 Hospitals **Mwenda clinic** ✉ 1907 Kabila St., off Lusaka Rd. ☎ 03/32-3519 or 097/ 88-2391. **Rainbow Medical Centre** ✉ 1905 Kabila St. ☎ 03/32-3519. **Shafik clinic** ✉ Akapelwa St. ☎ 03/32-1130. **Southern Medical Centre** ✉ House 9, 1967 Makombo Rd. ☎ 03/32-3547.

💊 Pharmacy **Musamu Pharmacy** ✉ 116A Mosi-oa-Tunya Rd. ☎ 03/32-3226.

INTERNET

The Activity Centre is a friendly Internet stop open daily 7–7; it charges around US$2.55 an hour.

💻 Internet Access **Activity Centre** ✉ Fawlty Towers, Mosi-oa-Tunya Rd. ☎ 03/32-3432 or 097/43-6262 ⊕ www.adventure-africa.com.

MONEY MATTERS

At the time of writing, K4,700 was equivalent to US$1. Kwacha and U.S. dollars are both welcomed everywhere from street vendors to big hotels. It is a good idea to travel with plenty of small U.S. denomina-

ZAMBIA ESSENTIAL INFO

Electricity

To use electric-powered equipment purchased in the United States or Canada, bring a converter and adapter. If your appliances are dual voltage, you'll need only an adapter. The electrical current is 220 volts, 50 cycles alternating current (AC); wall outlets in most of the region take 15-amp plugs with three straight-edge prongs. Power cuts are a way of life in Livingstone. Do not leave anything plugged in that can be damaged by a power outage or fluctuating current.

Embassies

🇨🇦 Canada **Canadian Embassy** ✉ 5119 United Nations Ave., Box 31313, Lusaka ☎ 01/25-0833 🖷 01/25-4176.

🇪🇺 European Union **European Union Delegation** ✉ Plot 4899, Los Angeles Blvd., Lusaka ☎ 01/25-0711, 01/25-1140, 01/25-5586, or 01/25-5587 🖷 01/25-0906 or 01/25-2336.

🇬🇧 United Kingdom **British Embassy** ✉ Independence Ave., Box 50050, Lusaka ☎ 01/25-1133 🖷 01/25-3798 ⊕ www.britishhighcommission.gov.uk/zambia.

🇺🇸 United States **U.S. Embassy** ✉ United Nations Ave. and Independence Ave., Box 31617, Lusaka ☎ 01/25-0955 🖷 01/25-2225 ⊕ http:/www.zambia.usembassy.gov.

Gay & Lesbian Travelers

Homosexuality is technically illegal in Zambia, although it is widely accepted and presents no real problem.

Language

Zambia has more than 70 dialects, but there are only four main languages: Lozi, Bemba, Nyanja, and Tonga. English is the official language and is widely spoken, read, and understood.

Money Matters

Zambia's currency is the Zambian kwacha, which comes in denominations of ZK20, ZK50, ZK100, ZK500, ZK1,000, ZK5,000, ZK10,000, and ZK50,000 bills, necessitating carrying huge wads of notes. The kwacha is theoretically divided into 100 ngwees, but as you can buy nothing for one kwacha, an ngwee exists in name only and any bill including ngwees will simply be rounded off. At time of writing the conversion rate was ZK4,700 to the US$.

In Zambia MasterCard and Visa are preferred by business owners and banks to American Express or Diners Club because of substantial charges levied to proprietors. Business owners in Zambia always prefer cash (or traveler's checks) to credit cards, and some smaller hotels levy fees up to 10% to use their credit card facilities. Bank ATMs accept only Visa.

Passports & Visas

All U.S., British, and Canadian citizens, even infants, need a valid passport and visa to enter Zambia. A single-entry or transit visa costs US$25 for Americans and Canadians and US$65 for British citizens. Canadians and Americans pay US$40 for a double/multiple-entry visa, and Britons pay US$80 for double/multiple entry. It is very simple to purchase a visa as you enter the country and not advisable to go to the trouble of getting one ahead of time.

The lodging where you are planning to stay can enter information about you on a manifest, so that your visa fee will be waived. The visa waiver manifest needs to be stamped at least 24 hours before your arrival, so you should forward your name as it appears in your passport, your nationality, passport number, and expiration date well in advance. The manifests are kept at the point of entry. Simply give the immigration official the name of your lodging. Day-trip visas cost US$10 (this is often included in the cost of prebooked activities, so check with your booking agent). If you leave Zambia for less than a day, you need a reentry visa (ZK5,000), or you'll have to buy a new visa—at the full price. You must get this before you leave for the trip or as you leave Zambia. If you're doing an organized tour, the operator should take care of it, but double-check anyway.

🔢 Zambian Missions Abroad **United Kingdom** ✉ *2 Palace Gate, Kensington, London* ☎ *087/0005–6987 or 087/ 0005–6987* 🖷 *020/7581–1353.* **United States** ✉ *2419 Massachusetts Ave., NW, Washington, DC* ☎ *202/265–9717* 🌐 *www.zambiaembassy.org.*

Taxes
Zambia has a 17.5% V.A.T. and a 10% service charge, which is included in the cost or itemized on your bill.

Telephone
The country code for Zambia is 260. When dialing from abroad, drop the initial 0 from local area codes. Note that all telephone numbers are listed as they are dialed from the country that they are in. Although the number for operator assistance is 100, you will be much better off asking your local lodge or restaurant manager for help. If you can't live without a telephone, get international roaming on your cell phone. Although reception is patchy, you will be surprised at how far the networks now cover this destination. Alternatively you could purchase a local Sim card with pay-as-you-go fill-ups. Pay phones are not a reliable option, and the costs of all telephone calls out of the country can be exorbitant.

Time
Zambia operates on CAST (Central African Standard Time), which is two hours ahead of Greenwich mean time. That makes it seven hours ahead of North American eastern standard time (six hours ahead during eastern daylight saving time).

tions for tips and small purchases. If you plan to exchange money, try to have large-denomination notes, as the exchange rates are far better. Make sure you have only "big head" dollars, as the older, "small head" ones are no longer accepted. International banks, located along Mosi-oa-Tunya Road, have ATMs and exchange services. Banking hours are generally weekdays 8–2 (although they can open the last Saturday of the month).

You may be invited to do a little informal foreign exchange by persuasive street financiers, who will offer you excellent rates. Resist the temptation—it's not worth the risk of being ripped off or caught and arrested. There are many reputable exchange bureaus dotted throughout town, although they are sometimes flooded with dollars and low on kwacha, generally toward the end of the month. Most hotels accept credit cards, and you can get advances in local currency on your credit card from most banks. Traveler's checks are also widely accepted, but your change is likely to be in Zambian kwacha.

HEALTH & SAFETY

It is always a good idea to leave ample space in your luggage for common sense when traveling to Victoria Falls. Wild animals abound throughout this area and must invariably be given a lot of room and respect. Zimbabwe and Zambia are relatively poor. Both countries have tourism police, but opportunistic thieving still happens occasionally. Although crime is generally nonviolent, losing your money, belongings, or passport will result in spending the remainder of your trip with various officials in stuffy, badly decorated offices instead of sitting back on the deck of your sunset cruise with a gin and tonic in hand.

As for the water, it is always advisable to drink bottled water, although the tap water in Zambia is generally considered safe. Should you develop any stomach upset, be sure to contact a physician, especially if you are running a fever, in order to rule out malaria or a communicable disease.

Finally, confirm that your insurance covers you for a medical evacuation should you be involved in a serious accident, as the closest intensive-care facilities of international standard are in South Africa.

PASSPORTS & VISAS

For all entries into Zambia, make sure you are included on a visa manifest by the lodge or hotel where you will be staying. As a courtesy, the Zambian government waives visa fees for overnight visitors. If you cross the border into Zimbabwe you will need to obtain a reentry permit (ZK5,000, or a bit more than US$1) before leaving so you can return without incurring new visa costs.

TELEPHONES

Livingstone telephone rates are much cheaper and more stable than the rates in Zimbabwe. Check numbers very carefully, as some are Zimbabwean mobile phones (numbers starting with 011). Zambia and Zimbabwe now both have cell coverage, and there are certain areas where the networks overlap and mobile telephones work in both countries. If you have any trouble dialing a number, check with a hotel or restaurant owner, who should be able to advise you of the best and cheapest alternative. International roaming on your standard mobile phone is an option, as coverage is quite extensive.

Tipping

Tipping is less common in Zambia, since service charges are included, but it is always appreciated. Small notes or 10% is appropriate. Gas station attendants can be tipped, but you will generally tip a taxi driver only on the last day if you have used the same driver for a number of days.

Tours

If it is serious game viewing you desire, join a one-day excursion to Chobe National Park in Botswana with **Bushtracks** (☎ 03/32–3232). The trip costs US$147 and includes transfers from Livingstone, a game drive, a boat cruise, and all meals. Bushtracks is also your best bet for a visit to the Mukuni Village (US$26). Reservations must be in writing and prepaid for both.

Livingstone Safaris (☎ 03/32–2267) offers a three-hour guided walking safari of Mosi-oa-Tunya National Park. Not only can you see the endangered white rhino and other plains game, but your professional guide and park scout will impart detailed information on birding, flora, and the modern use of plants by local people. Walks are conducted early in the morning and late in the afternoon and cost US$45, including transfers within Livingstone. A game drive (US$38) is also offered.

VISITOR INFORMATION

Although the Zambia National Tourist Board (open weekdays 8–1 and 2–5, Saturday 8–noon) is very helpful and friendly, you might be better off visiting the Activity Centre for serious unbiased advice, including a free cup of percolated coffee. It's open daily 7:30–7:30.

🄵 Tourist Offices **Activity Centre** ✉ Fawlty Towers, Mosi-oa-Tunya Rd. ☎ 03/32–3432 or 097/43–6262 ⊕ www.adventure-africa.com. **Zambia National Tourist Board** ✉ Mosi-oa-Tunya Rd. ☎ 03/32–1404 ⊕ www.zambiatourism.com.

Botswana & Namibia's Best Safari Destinations

10

By Kate
Turkington

LOOK NORTH OF SOUTH AFRICA, and you find two of Africa's most beautiful and dramatic safari destinations: Botswana and Namibia. Although both contain some of the last true wilderness areas left in the world, both are accessible to tourists and have excellent infrastructures. Your first night in Botswana's legendary Okavango Delta—an inland water wilderness of crystal-clear waters, perfumed water lilies, papyrus channels breaking into open stretches of sky-reflecting calm waters, hippos, crocs, elephants, and rare, shy water antelope—will linger with you forever, as will your eyeball-to-eyeball encounters with wall-to-wall big game in Moremi Wildlife Reserve. Namibia's unbelievably wide-open spaces—deserts stretching to an ever-vanishing horizon, jagged mountain peaks, flat gravel plains glistening with garnets—cannot fail to stir your soul. In the Great White Place of Etosha National Park or the Place of Mirages, your camera will click nonstop as golden lions pad over white sand, crimson-breasted shrikes flit among dry trees, and herds of black-faced impalas slake their thirst at water holes in the heat of day, watched by a crouching leopard.

BOTSWANA

In Botswana superlatives are unavoidable—and never quite adequate. Some of the last great wilderness areas left in the world are here, all remarkable in their diversity. A short plane ride can whisk you from scorching desert to water wonderlands, from great salt pans to fertile floodplains.

Once upon a time—a mere 25 or so years ago—Botswana was a Cinderella among nations, one of the world's poorest countries. Then the Fairy Godmother visited and bestowed her gift: diamonds. The resulting economic boom transformed Botswana into one of Africa's richest countries as measured by per capita income.

The 1960s were a decade of self-determination all over Africa, led by Uganda, Ghana, and Nigeria. The British Protectorate of Bechuanaland was granted independence in 1966 and renamed Botswana. Where other nations' celebrations quickly turned sour, Botswana's independence brought an enduring tide of optimism. The country sidestepped the scourge of tribalism and factional fighting that cursed much of the continent—including bordering South Africa and Zimbabwe—and is considered one of Africa's most stable democracies. The Batswana (singular: Motswana) are renowned for their courteousness and dignity.

Roughly the size of France or Texas, Botswana, once relatively unknown on the tourist map, is now a popular safari destination. Although cities such as Gaborone (pronounced *ha*-bo-ronee), the capital, have been modernized, Botswana has little in the way of urban excitement. Outside the cities it's a land of amazing variety: the Kalahari Desert is in stark contrast to the lush beauty of the Okavango Delta, one of Botswana's most magnificent and best-known regions. A vast area of tangled waterways and aquatic, bird, and mammal life, it's sometimes referred to as the Swamps, but this gives a false impression. There are no murky mangroves here, no sinister everglades, just open tranquil waters of breathtaking beauty leading into narrow, papyrus-fringed channels.

Nearly 18% of this very flat country's total land area is reserved for conservation and tourism. The Moremi Wildlife Reserve, the first such reserve in southern Africa to have been created by an African community (the BaTawana people) on its own tribal lands, is a major draw. Here, as in other parts of northern Botswana, you'll see elephants, lions, buffalo, wild dogs, cheetahs, leopards, giraffes, kudus, wildebeests, hippos, and hundreds of awesome birds. One hundred km (62 mi) west of Victoria Falls in Botswana's northeast corner is Chobe National Park, another of Africa's fine game sanctuaries, known for its elephants. The wide and tranquil Chobe River is surrounded by a natural wilderness of floodplain, dead lake bed, sand ridges, and forest. Downstream it joins the mighty Zambezi on its journey through Zimbabwe and Mozambique to the Indian Ocean. Upstream, where it's known as the Linyanti, it forms the border between Botswana and Namibia. In this area the Linyanti Reserve, which borders Chobe National Park, is a huge private concession, as is the Kwando Reserve, to the west, named for the river of the same name—the lifeblood of the Linyanti, Savuti, and Chobe systems.

About the Camps & Lodges

Botswana has some of the most diverse safari accommodations in the world, where you are guaranteed exclusivity and a true wilderness experience. Whether you choose to stay in a wooden cabin or a rustic tent with bucket showers or a five-star, air-conditioned chalet or safari tent with your own romantic outdoor shower and personal plunge pool, you are guaranteed some of the best game-viewing in Africa. And you won't be crowded out by other visitors. Most camps are very small, accommodating only about 12–16 people, which means that there are never more than three vehicles at that memorable leopard or cheetah sighting and the only traffic you'll encounter among the waterways of the delta are grazing hippos and dozing crocodiles. Even in the northern part of Chobe, around Chobe Game Lodge, where there are more vehicles than elsewhere, early-morning and late-afternoon rush hour usually consists of large buffalo and elephant herds trekking down to the rivers for their sundowners.

A word about terminology: "Land camps" are in a game reserve or contiguous concession and offer two daily game drives, morning and evening. If you're not in a national park, you'll be able to go out for night drives off-road with a powerful spotlight to pick out nocturnal animals. "Water camps" are deep in the Okavango Delta and often accessible only by air or water. Most of the newer camps now offer both a land and a true water experience, so you get the best of both worlds.

Don't come to Botswana expecting a profound gastronomic experience. There is little or no local cuisine, so the food in the camps and lodges is designed to appeal to a wide variety of international visitors. Nevertheless, it is quite tasty—soups, roasts, pies, quiches, curries, vegetables, and lots of lovely fresh fruit. Most camps bake their own excellent bread, muffins, and cakes and often make desserts such as meringues, eclairs, and homemade ice cream. And you'll find plenty of tasty South African wine and beer. Don't expect TVs either, even at very expensive camps, and air-conditioning is the exception rather than the rule. It's mentioned in reviews only when it is present.

Most lodging prices are quoted in U.S. dollars, and you can use dollars as tips wherever you stay. The average price per person per night at private lodges is US$500–US$600, which includes accommodations, all meals, soft drinks, and good South African wine. Camps arrange transfers from the nearest airport or airstrip.

WHAT IT COSTS In U.S. dollars				
$$$$	**$$$**	**$$**	**$**	**¢**
SAFARI CAMPS AND LODGES				
over $800	$700–$800	$600–$700	$500–$600	under $500

All prices refer to an all-inclusive per-person rate including tax, assuming double occupancy.

Timing

The best time to visit Botswana is in the autumn and winter months (April through September), although if you don't mind heat, then any time is a good time. In the delta during the winter months the water has come in from the Angolan highlands, and the floodplains, channels, lakes, and inland waterways are literally brimming with sparkling fresh water. Elsewhere, as it's the dry season, the grass and vegetation are sparse, and it's much easier to see game, which often have no choice but to drink at available water holes or rivers. But be warned: it can be bitterly cold, particularly early in the morning and at night. Dress in layers (including a thigh-length thick jacket, hat, scarf, and gloves), which you can discard or add to as the sun goes up or down. From October through February it gets very hot—up to 35°C (95°F)—so unless you're in a lodge with air-conditioning, can stand great heat, or are a keen bird-watcher—for it's then that the migrants return—stick with fall and winter.

The Okavango Delta

The Okavango Delta is in Ngamiland, the tribal land of the BaTawana tribe. It's the legendary hunting area that, with the help of Dr. David Livingstone's accounts of his explorations, fueled the 19th-century European imagination. The delta is formed by the Okavango River, which descends from the Angolan highlands and then fans out over northwestern Botswana. It's made up of an intricate network of channels and crystal-pure quiet lagoons, papyrus- and reed-lined backwaters.

The *mokoro* boat, synonymous with the Okavango, was introduced to the area in the mid-18th century, when the Bayei tribe (the river bushmen) moved down from the Zambezi. Previously, the nomadic Bayei, who drifted the waterways looking for food and game, used papyrus rafts, but they invented the mokoro as a more controllable craft that could be maneuvered up- or downstream. These boats were traditionally made from the trunks of the great jackalberry, morula, and sausage trees. Today, because of the need to protect the trees, you may find yourself in the modern equivalent: a fiberglass canoe. Your skilled poler—who would put any tightrope walker to shame—is always on the alert for the ubiquitous hippos but is quite laid-back about the mighty crocs lying smiling in the sun. (In deeper waters powerboats are an option.) Bird-watching from these boats is a special thrill: the annual return of thousands of gorgeous carmine bee-eaters to the Swamps in August and September is a dazzling sight, as is a glimpse of the huge ginger-color Pel's fishing owl, the world's only fish-eating owl and one of its rarest birds. This is a water wilderness experience above all others, so don't miss the chance to go on a guided walk on one of the many islands.

There *is* big game, but it's more elusive and difficult to approach than in the game reserves. You'll almost certainly see elephants, hippos, crocs, and red lechwes (a beautiful antelope endemic to the Swamps) and may catch a glimpse of the rare, aquatic sitatunga antelope. You'll almost certainly hear lions but may not always see them; if you're very lucky, you may see a pride swimming between islands. On the other hand, you might see lots of game. Just remember that you're not in the delta for the big game—you'll see plenty of that elsewhere in Botswana. You're here for the unforgettable beauty of this amazing wilderness area.

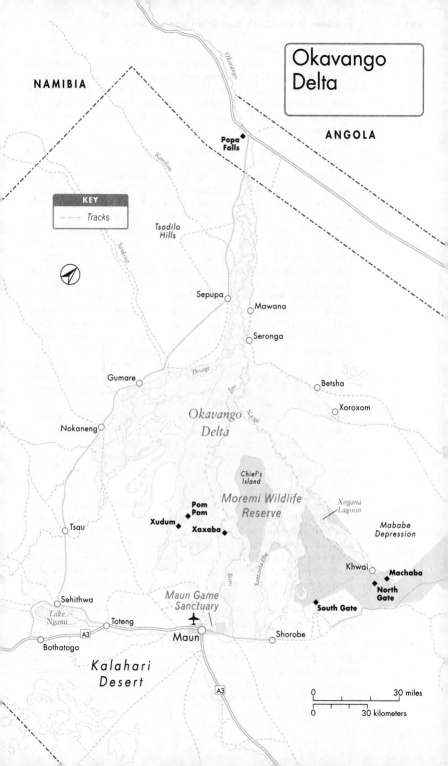

Camp Okavango

An electric fence around the camp keeps the elephants out but not the smaller animals (like hippos!); though whatever is in the area might stroll around at night, you're quite safe within your canvas walls. The major experience here is the water. In season, fishing is good; and because the camp is so well established, the bird-life is prolific. There's no dawn chorus quite like it.

WHERE TO STAY | ☒ **Camp Okavango.** Most people involuntarily draw a breath when
★ $ | they walk from the airstrip into this sprawling campsite. On remote Nxaragha Island in the heart of the permanent delta, it's accessible only by plane or water. Built by an eccentric American millionaire many years ago (she used to jet off to L.A. to get her hair done), it combines style, comfort, and a year-round water wilderness experience. Huge old trees arch over an outdoor lounge area with sweeping lawns leading down to the water, where hippos snort all night. Your super luxury tent with private bathroom, built on a raised wooden platform overlooking the delta, is set among groves of ancient trees and is so well separated from the others that you might believe yours is the only one in camp. Cool pastel linens, handcrafted wood furniture, and colorful handwoven rugs make up the spacious interior. Common areas with worn flagstones have comfortable colonial-style furniture and carved elephant stools on which you can watch hundreds of birds feed, bathe, and drink—aided and abetted by a few cheeky squirrels. Dinners are served in the high-thatch dining area, where an original sycamore fig mokoro is suspended over the long wooden dining table. Don't miss out on a spectacular sunset view from your fiberglass mokoro as you sip chilled drinks from a bar set up in the middle of a water-lily-studded lagoon tended by a wading barman. If you're going to the sister camp, Camp Moremi, go by water transfer, a three-hour trip with an island coffee stop on the way. *Desert & Delta Safaris, Box 130555, Bryanston 2125, South Africa* ☎ *27/11/706–0861* ⊟ *27/11/706–0863* ⊕ *www.desertdelta.co.za* ⏦ *11 tents* ⚐ *Pool, bar* ⊟ *MC, V* ⚑ *FAP.*

Xugana Island

On a big, permanent waterway, Xugana (pronounced *koo*-gana) lets you do all the things the Okavango Delta does best: lap up tranquillity as you glide in a mokoro through the papyrus, get the adrenaline going as you fight a tiger fish, listen to an elephant midnight snacking next to your *mesasa* (the Setswana word for "dwelling"), walk on a lovely island searching for a Pel's fishing owl, and watch tiny jewel-like sunbirds sip nectar from flowering trees. The island also has the Mokoro Trail, a three-night accompanied camping excursion by canoe that slowly follows the river and goes on to the next camping site (not offered in January, February, and March).

WHERE TO STAY | ☒ **Xugana Island Lodge.** The lodge consists of stylish reed-and-thatch
$ | mosasa perched high on stilts, under massive ebony and jackalberry trees overlooking the wide Xugana lagoon. In fact, in this camp everything is on the very edge of the lagoon. Each mesasa has a private bathroom. They're spacious, with wooden floors, high roofs, colorful blinds, sturdy

wooden furniture, and a ceiling fan. Huge mosquito-proof windows provide one of the best views in the delta. Early-morning tea and coffee are brought to your own wooden deck, where you can sit and watch a wading elephant or listen to the tumultuous birdsong. Enjoy a drink at the cozy thatch bar that overlooks the lagoon, then dine on excellent food alfresco under the stars. This is a classy, well-established, gracious camp with a wonderfully intimate atmosphere, the result of years of experience and professionalism. ⌾ *Desert & Delta Safaris, Box 130555, Bryanston 2125, South Africa* ☎ *27/11/706–0861* 🖷 *27/11/706–0863* ⊕ *www.desertdelta.co.za* ↩ *18 mosasa* ⚬ *Fans, pool, bar* ▭ *MC, V* ↯ *FAP.*

Delta Camp

Activities from the camp include guided mokoro trails into the maze of waterways and game walks on adjacent islands with a professional licensed guide. Your walks will teach you about the African environment, ranging from the habits of dung beetles and warthogs to superb birdspotting and how to dodge a charging elephant. A major conservation plus for Delta Camp is that motorboats are not used, as the emphasis is on preserving the pristine purity of the environment. This adds immeasurably to the relaxed, peaceful atmosphere that pervades this lovely camp. Hikes on the Sitatunga Trail can be arranged for select groups of at least four who wish to further explore this wondrous place for six nights or more. You may meet big or little game; in the delta there's no way of knowing.

WHERE TO STAY ⚐ **Delta Camp.** This enchanting traditional camp is set deep on an is-
$ land in the Okavango. Reed chalets, each with private bathroom, are furnished with wood furniture and upturned mokoros; they look like something straight out of *The Swiss Family Robinson.* Each chalet faces northeast to catch the first rays of the sun as it rises above the palm trees, and below your windows are shallow, bird-filled pools, with deeper waterways only paces from your front door. Family-owned for many years, the camp has an intimate, relaxed atmosphere; the goal is to experience the tranquillity of the environment. Sit under the stars at dinner, listen to the haunting calls of Okavango's birds, go for a guided walk around the island, chill out on the extended deck with its spectacular views of the surrounding waterways, and at night sip tea or coffee around a blazing fire. ⌾ *Lodges of Botswana, Box 39, Maun, Botswana* ☎ *267/686–1154* 🖷 *267/666–0589* ⊕ *www.lodgesofbotswana.com* ↩ *7 chalets* ▭ *MC, V* ↯ *FAP.*

Duba Plains

This tiny, intimate camp deep, deep in the delta is built on an island shaded by large ebony, fig, and garcinia trees and surrounded by horizon-touching plains that are seasonally flooded, usually from late April to early October. It's one of the best-kept secrets in the Okavango, tucked into the delta's farthest reaches. When the water is high in winter, the game competes with the camp for dry ground, and lions and hyenas become regular dusk-to-dawn visitors. You'll hear the roar of lions pervading the camp as night falls. There's wall-to-wall game, including herds of hundreds of buffalo, leopards, lions, cheetahs, elephants, hippos, lechwes, and the most beautiful of all the antelopes—the sable—all of which you can watch from one of only two 4x4 open game vehicles in the reserve. Duba Plains is also a birder's paradise, with an abundance of waterfowl. The Duba lion prides are among the few to hunt by day; they specialize in taking down buffalo. If you're really lucky, you might find yourself and your vehicle bang in the middle of one of these spectacular hunts.

WHERE TO STAY

$$

Fodor'sChoice

★

Duba Plains. Big, cool, tented rooms are built on raised decks and have ceiling fans and gleaming furniture of Rhodesian teak that's complemented by the subtle grays and greens of the fabrics. A lattice screen divides each bedroom/sitting area from the private bathroom, which has a ceramic sink, glass shower, and plenty of storage space. The lodge's lounge and dining area is small and inviting, with comfortable chairs and couches, a bar, and a stupendous view. There's a poolside gazebo where you can relax and watch the plains after a refreshing dip, as well as a bird blind tucked behind the camp. Now rivaling its oh-so-luxurious sister camp, Mombo, for wall-to-wall game and abundant birdlife, Duba also draws guests for its remoteness, simplicity, and solitude. ☞ *Wilderness Safaris, Box 5219, Rivonia 2128, South Africa* ☎ *27/11/807–1800* 🖷 *27/11/807–2110* 🌐 *www.dubaplains.com* 🔊 *6 rooms* � *Fans, pool, bar* ▭ *MC, V* 🍴 *FAP.*

Chitabe Camp

Chitabe is in an exclusive photographic reserve bordered by the Moremi Wildlife Reserve to the north, the Gomoti Channel to the east, and the Santantadibe River in the west. It's a lovely and popular camp whose big, comfortable tents on stilts are connected by environmentally friendly raised wooden walkways that put you safely above the ground and give you a Tarzan's-eye view of the surrounding bush—you might come eyeball to eyeball with a wandering elephant. Not only elephants, but also buffalo, lions, leopards, and cheetahs are among the main attractions of this area, as well as a host of small nocturnal game such as porcupines, civets, and bush babies. Chitabe lies within a study area of the Botswana Wild Dog Research Project, which has up to 160 dogs in packs of 10 to 12, so you're almost certain to see these fascinating "painted wolves." Night drives are particularly rewarding. The area has a good variety of habitats, from marshlands and riverine areas to open grasslands and seasonally flooded plains, but although it's on one of the most beautiful islands in the delta and has classic Okavango scenery, it's not a water camp as such and doesn't offer water activities.

WHERE TO STAY

$

Chitabe Camp. This very attractive and popular camp has luxurious twin-bedded, East African–style tents with wooden floors, woven lala palm furniture, wrought-iron washstands, and private bath. Tents are reached by walking along raised wooden walkways that wind their way through palms and mopane trees. A separate thatch dining room, bar, and lounge area, also linked by wooden walkways, looks out over a floodplain. However, the shallow water that surrounds the camp is hidden by the long grass, so it's difficult to believe that you're actually in the Okavango Delta; there are no vistas of water. For groups that would like a camp to themselves, Chitabe Trails Camp, often used by overland safaris, accommodates eight guests in similar tents built on the ground with private bathrooms, private dining room, bar, and lounge area. 🖉 *Wilderness Safaris, Box 5219, Rivonia 2128, South Africa* 🕾 *27/11/807–1800* 🖷 *27/11/807–2110* ⊕ *www.wilderness-safaris.com* 📞 *8 tents at Main Camp, 4 tents at Trails Camp* 🕭 *Dining rooms, pool, bars, lounges* ☰ *MC, V* ¶❂¶ *FAP.*

Nxabega Camp

The gorgeous Nxabega (pronounced *na*-becka), a sister camp to Okavango and Moremi, is in the very heart of the delta. Renowned for its beauty, this 17,000-acre private concession encompasses all the vegetation types of the Okavango—mopane, riverine, mixed, palm and acacia woodland, terminalia sandveld, perennial swamp, and seasonally flooded grassland. This means you can have both a water and a land experience—viewing from a mokoro or an open 4x4. You could well see most of Botswana's 550 species of birds, or follow the lions or wild dogs as they hunt at dusk. Because this is a private concession, you can thrill to a night drive in an open Land Rover and by spotlight pick out not only the big predators but also some of the smaller ones: civets, bush babies, genets, or—if you get really lucky—a pale prehistoric aardvark or scaly pangolin. A special bonus is the resident naturalist on hand to complement the team of knowledgeable and friendly guides.

WHERE TO STAY   ▦ **Nxabega Camp.** One of only two camps in the delta run by CCA (of
$ South Africa's Londolozi and Phinda fame), this beautiful camp offers both a land and a water experience. Safari tents are on raised teak platforms, each with a private veranda overlooking idyllic water and bush views. The main lodge is of thatch and wood with dark-wood paneling inside. Animal-skin rugs, fine woven cane furniture, cushions in various ethnic designs, hand-carved wooden tables, wooden bowls full of ostrich eggs, and lamps fashioned out of guinea fowl feathers and porcupine quills give the lounge an exotic African ambience, while the high-roofed, paneled dining room has an almost medieval banquet-hall feel. Be sure to zip up your tent at night (there's lots of game around) before you retire to your comfortable bed with its leather headboard and fresh white linen. Zip your way through to the dressing room and bathroom area with its big wooden wardrobe, glass-enclosed shower, and reed walls. Tea or coffee is brought to your tent so that you can watch the early morning delta world go by in splendid seclusion. The food is excellent, so make sure you lose some of those calories by taking a guided walk on one of the nearby islands to track game and marvel at the different varieties of bird-life. 🖉 *CC Africa, Private Bag X27, Benmore 2010, South Africa* 🕾 *27/11/809–4300* 🖷 *27/11/809–4400* ⊕ *www.ccafrica.com* 📞 *10 tents* 🕭 *Dining room, pool, bar* ☰ *MC, V* ¶❂¶ *FAP.*

Sandibe Camp

Sandibe, the sister camp to Nxabega Camp, is also run by CC Africa of Londolozi and Phinda fame. It's absolutely gorgeous. Both a land and a water camp, Sandibe clings to the edge of one of the delta's beautiful pristine channels. You can step into your mokoro at the campsite and switch off stress and modern-day living as you cocoon yourself in another, gentler world. Sandibe's guides are superb, thrilling you with campfire tales at night, fishing with you in the open water spaces, poling your mokoro through tunnels of interlacing feathery papyrus, walking with you on one of the many palm-studded islands, and tracking big game in an open Land Rover or on foot, depending on which you prefer. You might see hippos, lions, cheetahs, buffalo, wild dogs, leopards, elephants, and some Okavango specials: the aquatic tsessebe antelope, fastest of all antelope, and the secretive sitatunga antelope.

WHERE TO STAY ★ $ 🔲 **Sandibe Camp.** The camp has a fairy-tale feel, as if a giant had fashioned an idyllic tiny village out of adobe and thatch and set it down amid an enchanted forest full of birds nestled beside a papyrus-fringed secret lagoon. Honey-colored cottages with stepped and fringed thatch roofs add to the unusual visual effect of this spectacular camp. The cottages are open and airy and decorated with a lavish use of wood; each contains a huge carved bed covered with a woven leather bedspread, colorful kilims, skillfully chosen African artifacts, and lamps fabricated of woven metal and ostrich eggs. Sit on your stone veranda or tiny personal deck that overlooks the waterways, shaded by huge old African ebony trees, or walk along the elephant dung paths to the main lodge area, where "curtains" of tattered russet bark waft in the breeze. This is a wonderful place to sit and relax or swap big-game stories with your fellow guests. Climb up to the secluded wooden decks with their comfortable sitting areas above the main sitting and dining area, and catch up on your reading or game and bird lists, or just sit and relax in the outdoor *boma* (hut) around a crackling fire and stargaze as you sip your after-dinner coffee or liqueur. 🔲 *CC Africa, Private Bag X27, Benmore 2010, South Africa* 🕾 *27/11/809–4300* 🖶 *27/11/809–4400* ⊕ *www.ccafrica.com* ➴ *8 cottages* ⚒ *Pool, bar* ▭ *MC, V* ⦿ *FAP.*

Jao Camp

This spectacular and stunning camp, a pure Hollywood-meets-Africa fantasy, is in a private concession bordering the Moremi Wildlife Reserve west of Mombo, on a densely wooded island overlooking vast plains. The landscape includes a great variety of habitats, including permanent waterways and lagoons, open floodplains, and thick Kalahari soils. The place is teeming with creatures of all kinds—fish, fowl, and game. Jao can offer both land and water activities, depending on the seasonal water levels, so you can take a day or night game drive in an open 4x4, glide in a mokoro through rippling meadows of water lilies in possibly the most beautiful setting in the whole of the delta, chug along hippo highways in a motorboat, or go on a guided walk. You'll see lots of predators, especially lions, who live here in the highest concentration in the country, according to a recent wildlife census.

WHERE TO STAY $$$$ 🔲 **Jao Camp.** If you love the fanciful and have an exotic imagination, then Jao (Jow as in "now") will delight you. You'll be one of only 16 pampered guests when you sleep in your own spacious tree house with superb views over the vast floodplains. You can lie in your canopy bed and watch the sun rise or recline on megacushions, pasha style, and watch the translucent waters beyond the lush palms below. Private bath facilities include an indoor shower, flush toilet and sink, Victorian claw-foot tub, and outdoor shower. Rare and fascinating African artifacts decorate the wood, multitier interior of the main building. The food is delicious, and the superb standard of service can best be appreciated as you dine in the cool thatch dining area under a canopy of trees alive with birdsong. After a night drive, eat under the night sky in the outdoor boma and watch the sparks from the roaring fire compete with the dazzling stars. ⊕ *Wilderness Safaris, Box 5219, Rivonia 2128, South Africa* ☎ *27/11/807–1800* 🖷 *27/11/807–2110* 🛏 *8 chalets* ⚲ *Pool, bar* ▤ *MC, V* ⦿ *FAP.*

$ 🛏 **Kwetsani Camp** A mere eagle's flight from its more sumptuous neighbor, Jao, Kwetsani is one of the loveliest of the delta camps. It's perched on high wooden stilts amid a forest canopy of ancient trees on Kwetsani Island, 2 km (1 mi) long by nearly 1,000 yards wide, surrounded by enormous open plains. The deck and lounge areas overlooking the floodplains are built around a massive sycamore fig and huge marula tree, and a giant jackalberry dominates the bar. The pool lies in a wooden platform below the deck, looking as if at any moment it will sail out like a raft into the surrounding water in the wet season or away into the yellow grasses in the dry season. Each spacious room, made of canvas, wood, and slatted poles, is set like a child's building block in the middle of a large wooden deck built high into the trees. Polished wooden floors; coir mats; cane armchairs; butlers' tables with tea, coffee, and biscuits; billowing mosquito nets; twinkling ostrich-egg lamps, which light up his and her sinks; and indoor and outdoor showers all contribute to a warm, homey atmosphere. After enjoying a game drive or mokoro trip, end your day with a sundowner (cocktail) party by the lagoon lighted by flickering lanterns, with entertainment by top local groups—hippos snorting, hyenas whooping, lions roaring, and waterbirds keening. ⊕ *Wilderness Safaris, Box 5219, Rivonia 2128, South Africa* ☎ *27/11/807–1800* 🖷 *27/11/807–2110* ⊕ *www.kwetsani.com* 🛏 *5 chalets* ⚲ *Pool, bar* ▤ *MC, V* ⦿ *FAP.*

Kanana Camp

Set deep in the delta among grass-covered islands dotted with fig, palm, ebony, and sausage trees, Kanana is simpler and more rustic than many of the other delta camps. Its natural charm puts you in close touch with your surroundings, so you feel part of the delta, not cocooned away from it. Game drives, mokoro-ing, boating, and bush walks (there are resident Pel's fishing owls on nearby islands) are all part of the experience, but a visit to the Thapagadi Lagoon is a must. The lagoon is home to a fantastic heronry, where open-billed, maribou, and yellow-billed storks all nest, together with herons of all kinds, cormorants, pelicans, darters, and egrets. You won't forget the sounds of this avian community—squawks, squeals, honks, belches, and gargles.

WHERE TO STAY 🛏 **Kanana Camp.** Safari tents (where tea and coffee are brought at dawn **¢** by a cheerful staff member) have their own wooden decks overlooking dense reed beds and a papyrus-thick floodplain; water laps almost to the front steps. Simple cane furnishings and dark-wood cabinetry are complemented by colorful rugs and a white curtain, which separates the gaily decorated bathroom from the bedroom. You'll fall asleep to the sound of hippos munching, squelching, and splashing outside your tent and awake to tumultuous birdsong. Public areas are built around a massive ancient fig tree, where green pigeons feast as you enjoy imaginative food on the dining deck overlooking the delta. The emphasis is on service and comfort rather than OTT (over-the-top) clutter and style. *Ker & Downey, Box 27, Maun Botswana ☎ 267/686–0375 ⚏ 267/686–1282 ⊕ www. kerdowney.com ⤴ 8 tents ⚐ Bar, shop ⊟ MC, V ⦿ FAP.*

Footsteps across the Delta

This interpretive safari experience is the ultimate in back to nature. The emphasis is on learning the secrets of the Okavango—on foot and by mokoro. Because this is a mobile camp that moves with the seasons, there is no electricity, but you'll be more than rewarded for the lack of luxury by the surrounding bird and animal life. The night sounds are awesome, from lions roaring to raucous hippos partying to a Pel's fishing owl emitting ghostly screams every five minutes or so. Walking with outstanding guides is the main activity; you might track lions on foot or absorb the habits of insects and plants. Game drives, night drives, boat trips, and fishing are also offered.

WHERE TO STAY ¢ ⚠ **Footsteps across the Delta.** If you need hair dryers and other modern conveniences, this is not for you. You'll sleep in one of three tents with insect-proofing and sewn-in floors; two iron bedsteads, some wooden shelves, and a small table are the only furnishings. You'll wash in a canvas washstand outside your tent (where there are also two deck chairs), and your personal "bathroom" tent consists of a long drop (bush toilet) and a bucket shower. *Ker & Downey, Box 27, Maun Botswana ☎ 267/686–0375 ⚏ 267/686–1282 ⊕ www.kerdowney.com ⤴ 3 tents ⚐ Bar ⊟ MC, V ⦿ FAP.*

Shinde Camp

Ker & Downey's oldest camp, and possibly its loveliest, Shinde lies in a vast palm-dotted area in the heart of the northern delta. Surrounded by lagoons and waterways encrusted with white, yellow, and purple water lilies, and home to hundreds of birds, it's also home to lots of game. Here superb guides and other friendly, well-trained staff take you under their expert wings. As you sip sundowners on a boat ride on the horseshoe-shape lagoon, cruising hippos serenade in a comic chorus.

WHERE TO STAY $ ▦ **Shinde Camp.** Large tents have polished wooden floors both inside and out on your viewing deck. They're outfitted with furniture in cane and Rhodesian teak, complemented by fabrics in brown, teal, terra-cotta, and white. Spacious bathrooms have flower-painted ceramic sinks, and a sturdy door leads to a separate outside toilet. A spiraling wooden ramp connects the dining area, built high in the trees at the top of the lodge, with a lookout deck and lounge in the middle and a boma under huge old trees at the bottom. If you want even more exclusivity and private pampering, opt for Shinde Enclave, which accommodates up to six guests with a private guide and waiter/barman. *Ker & Downey, Box 27, Maun Botswana ☎ 267/686–0375 ⚏ 267/686–1282 ⊕ www. kerdowney.com ⤴ 9 tents ⚐ Pool, bar, shop ⊟ MC, V ⦿ FAP.*

Eagle Island Camp

On Xaxaba (pronounced ka-*ka*-ba) Island, deep in the central delta, this camp is surrounded by pristine waterways, islands of tall palm trees, and vast floodplains. All the ingredients of a classic Okavango experience are present, from seeing myriad floating water lilies—white by day, purple by night—from your viewing deck to hearing the ubiquitous call of Africa's fish eagle. At dawn and dusk hippos sing their fascinating chorus of belches, snorts, grunts, squelches, and the occasional squeal.

WHERE TO STAY **$$$** ▦ **Eagle Island Camp.** Activities here are water-based: gliding through high, emerald-green papyrus tunnels in a mokoro; boating on wide lagoons; and enjoying sundowners as you float on crystal-clear water (go on and drink it—it's pure) as the sun sets in a blaze of red and gold. Or have a front-row seat for the same nightly spectacle in the Fish Eagle Bar, which juts out over the water. There's plenty of animal life, too; if you're very lucky, you might even catch a glimpse of one of the world's rarest antelopes, the aquatic sitatunga. ⌂ *Orient-Express Safaris, Box 786432, Sandton 2146, South Africa* ☎ *27/11/481–6052* 🖷 *27/11/481–6065* ⊕ *www.orient-express-safaris.com* ⇨ *15 tents* ⚐ *A/c, pool, bar, meeting rooms* ▤ *MC, V* ❏ *FAP.*

Moremi Wildlife Reserve

In the northeastern sector of the Okavango lies the spectacular Moremi Wildlife Reserve. In 1963 Chief Moremi III and the local BaTawana people proclaimed 1,800 square km (about 1,100 square mi) of pristine wilderness—ancient mopane forests, lagoons, islands, seasonal floodplains, and open grassland—as a game sanctuary, a first in southern African conservation history. Here, where the life-giving waters of the Okavango meet the vast Kalahari, is one of Africa's greatest parks, teeming with game and birds and, unlike the Masai Mara or Kruger Park, with hardly any people. You'll love the Garden of Eden atmosphere even if you do encounter the odd snake or two.

As there are no fences, the big game—and there's lots of it—can migrate to and from the Chobe park in the north. Sometimes it seems as if a large proportion of Botswana's 70,000 elephants have made their way here, particularly in the dry season. Check off on your game list lions, cheetahs, leopards, hyenas, wild dogs, buffalo, hippos, dozens of different antelopes, zebras, giraffes, monkeys, baboons, and more than 400 kinds of birds. Although during the South African school vacations (around July) there are more vehicles than normal, traffic is mostly light, and at this one, unlike many of Africa's other great reserves, you'll often be the only ones watching the game.

There are three main camp areas in the reserve. At Camp Moremi you get the best of both water and land. Early-morning and evening game drives with excellent rangers pretty much ensure that you see lions galore, elephants, giraffes, zebras, all kinds of antelopes, and often the elusive leopard, cheetah, and wild dog. The rare Pel's fishing owl regularly plummets down to the shallow pool below Tree Lodge to snag a fish and carry it away to the only spotlighted tree. Bird-watching is excellent throughout the year; marabou and yellow-billed storks, pelicans, and cormorants nest here in the summer months. You can take a power-boat to the heronries on Gadikwe and Xakanaxa lagoons. You'll see similar game at Xigera, which overlooks the floodplain and has access to water year-round. The camp offers mokoro and boat trips, ranger-led walking safaris, and driving safaris if conditions aren't too wet (summer is your best bet for this). Mombo Camp is strictly a land-activity camp. Although there is plenty of surface water in the area (marshes and floodplains), it's not deep enough for water activities. Mombo is set deep within the Moremi and has exclusive use of a large area of the reserve, so privacy is assured. Because of its great wildlife, including all of the large predators, several well-known documentaries have been filmed here. Though not actually within Moremi, Khwai River is close enough to get the benefit of excellent game-viewing.

WHERE TO STAY ★ $$$$

Mombo Camp and Little Mombo. On Mombo Island, off the northwest tip of Chief's Island, this legendary camp surrounded by wall-to-wall game is sometimes linked to land, depending on the ebb and flow of the water. The excellent game at Mombo has made this area Botswana's top wildlife documentary location—*National Geographic* and the BBC have both filmed here. The stunning camp has identical guest rooms divided into two distinct camps: Mombo has nine rooms, Little Mombo only three. These camps are among the best known, most expensive, and most sought after in Botswana, so be sure to book months in advance. Each spacious room is built on a raised wooden platform with wonderful views over the open plains, and although rooms have a tented feel, they are luxurious, with padded chaise longues, comfortable sofas, interesting lamps, woven rugs, and polished wooden floors. You can wash off the day's dust in your private bathroom or cool off in your outdoor shower. The dining room, lounge, and bar are also built on big wooden decks overlooking the magnificent animal-dotted savanna. The atmosphere is friendly, and the personal attention, food, and guides all excellent. The camp isn't fenced, so make sure you are escorted back to your room after dinner and then just lie back in your comfortable bed and listen to the sounds of the African night, from the haunting call of the fiery-necked night jar ("Good Lord, deliver us!") to the dry cough of a leopard as it patrols its territory. ⌂ *Wilderness Safaris, Box 5219, Rivonia 2128, South Africa* ☎ *27/11/807–1800* 🖷 *27/11/807–2110* ⊕ *www.mombo.co.za* ➥ *12 rooms* △ *Dining room, pool, bar, lounge* ⊟ *MC, V* ⊙ *FAP.*

$$$

Khwai River Lodge. As you sit on the wooden deck jutting out over the clear delta waters, munching brunch or just chilling out, you may just forget the outside world. Floating water lilies, tiny bejeweled kingfishers dipping and swooping in front of you, and the sounds of gently lapping water relax even the most driven work junkie. Bigger than some of the other safari lodges and one of the oldest, Khwai is renowned for its personal attention and friendly service. The location, 8 km (5 mi) northwest of the north gate of the Moremi Wildlife Reserve, means that you will see lots of game, not only on your drives but also from the lodge itself. The excitement of seeing a hippo or elephant stroll past the viewing deck outside your deluxe tent is not something you'll easily forget. The lodge is also the stuff of bird-watchers' dreams. ⌂ *Orient-Express*

Safaris, Box 786432, Sandton, 2146 South Africa ☎ *27/11/481–6052*
🖷 *27/11/481–6065* ⊕ *www.orient-express-safaris.com* ⊐ *15 tents*
⚗ *A/c, pool, bar, meeting rooms* ▤ *MC, V* ⦿ *FAP.*

$ ⊞ **Camp Moremi.** This is the luxurious sister camp to the delta's Camp
Okavango, so expect the same high level of service, food, and accommodations. Huge old African ebony trees, home to two-legged, four-legged,
winged, and earthbound creatures, dominate the campsite on the edge
of a lovely lagoon. From the high viewing platform in the trees you can
look out on a limitless horizon as the sun sets orange and gold over the
smooth, calm waters. Tastefully decorated, comfortable tents are well
spaced to ensure privacy. Camp Moremi's attractive timber-and-thatch
tree lodge has a dining area, bar, main lounge, small library, and sundeck with great views of Xakanaxa Lagoon. ⊕ *Desert & Delta Safaris,
Box 130555, Bryanston 2125, South Africa* ☎ *27/11/706–0861* 🖷 *27/
11/706–0863* ⊕ *www.desertdelta.co.za* ⊐ *11 tents* ⚗ *Pool, bar, lounge,
library* ▤ *MC, V* ⦿ *FAP.*

★ $ ⊞ **Xigera Camp.** The cry of the fish eagle permeates this exceptionally
lovely camp (pronounced *kee*-jer-a). It's set on aptly named Paradise Island amid thickets of old trees in one of the most beautiful parts of the
delta deep in the Moremi Wildlife Reserve. Huge airy rooms of timber
and canvas are built on a high wooden platform overlooking a floodplain. Reed walls separate the sleeping area from the spacious dressing
room, which in turn leads into a reed-floored shower and separate toilet. Or you can choose to shower under the stars as hippos and frogs
compete in the loudest-noises-of-the-night competition. Raised wooden
walkways connect the rooms to the main lodge, which sprawls beside
a lagoon where a small wooden bridge joins the island to the mainland.
At night this bridge becomes a thoroughfare for lions and hyenas, and
it's not uncommon to see one of these nocturnal visitors walk by as you
sip your postprandial coffee or liqueur by the blazing fire. This camp
does not concern itself with designer ethnic chic but concentrates on old-
fashioned comfort and elegance. The food is varied and excellent, and
the staff all seem to be chosen for not only their superb sense of service
but also for their great sense of humor. ⊕ *Wilderness Safaris, Box
5219, Rivonia 2128, South Africa* ☎ *27/11/807–1800* 🖷 *27/11/807–
2110* ⊕ *www.xigera.com* ⚗ *Pool, bar* ⊐ *5 rooms* ▤ *MC, V* ⦿ *FAP.*

Vumbura Camp

Deep in the delta, this spacious yet delightfully intimate tented camp
nestled among stands of ancient African ebony trees offers both land
and water activities. Go drifting through watery carpets of day and night
water lilies in a mokoro; catch your fish supper from a motorboat; or
look for lions, elephants, and wild dogs on your early-morning or spot-
lighted night drive in an open 4x4 vehicle. The privacy of the area, about
25 km (15 mi) north of Mombo, is one of its greatest attractions. The
surrounding Botswana communities work in concert with the camp, de-
riving direct benefits from the wildlife through significant concession
fees, jobs, and training, and contributing with their detailed local knowledge and exceptional friendliness and helpfulness. Sit on your private
wooden deck and watch a spectacular sunset over the floodplain, or after
dark listen to the mournful sounds of the night birds, the Kermit ca-

cophony, and the omnipresent hippos swishing through the shallow water in front of your tent.

🏕 **Little Vumbura.** You hardly notice this tiny, charming camp as you walk
$ along a wooden jetty after your boat transfer through a winding waterway. That's because it's hidden among, and part of, a fantasy forest of African ebony, marula, knobthorn, and fig trees. The sitting and dining area is built of canvas and reeds, and living trees form part of the structure. Cool blues predominate, and this color scheme is carried right through to the beaded salt cellars, indigo pottery, and blue cushions. Blue dominates your tented and timber bedroom with terra-cotta-tile veranda and floor, rush mats, and blue tie-dyed bedspreads. White-linen curtains and blinds and a comfortable wicker armchair complete your forest hideaway. Outside one room, wooden steps lead up to an enchanting open-air shower built around two huge jackalberry trees—you can exfoliate your back on the rough bark in true rhino style. The public areas include a reed-enclosed deck for alfresco dining by firelight and a reed-shaded sundeck, where you can lie by the small pool and look out over the never-ending waterways. Although Little Vumbura offers all the activities of its bigger neighbor, Vumbura, it's a delightful small world that seems to grow organically out of the surrounding trees and gently lapping water—a cross between Hans Christian Andersen and the Swiss Family Robinson. ✉ *Wilderness Safaris, Box 5219, Rivonia 2128, South Africa* ☎ *27/11/807–1800* 🖷 *27/11/807–2110* ⊕ *www. littlevumbura.com* 🛏 *5 tents* ⚲ *Pool, bar* 🚭 *MC, V* ⊙I *FAP.*

$ 🏕 **Vumbura Camp.** There's nothing quite like sleeping in a tent, however luxurious and comfortable, for getting the real feel of Africa. The large tents here are so privately situated you might feel you're alone in the camp. Remember, however, that even though elephants may be making the ground tremble right outside the wooden door of your tent, you are perfectly safe between your canvas walls. Sit tight and enjoy the experience. Wood wicker screens and a sturdy wooden-top low wall separate your comfortable bedroom area from the private bathroom. Laze in a deck chair on your small tiled deck and listen to the cries of the brightly colored parrots and green pigeons chattering in the huge trees encircling your tent. Tasty meals are served in an open-sided dining area tucked beneath a canopy of indigenous trees with a superb view across the floodplain. ✉ *Wilderness Safaris, Box 5219, Rivonia 2128, South Africa* ☎ *27/11/807–1800* 🖷 *27/11/807–2110* ⊕ *www.vumbura.com* 🛏 *8 tents* ⚲ *Pool, bar* 🚭 *MC, V* ⊙I *FAP.*

Chobe National Park

This 12,000-square-km (7,440-square-mi) reserve is home to nearly 40,000 elephants. In addition to spotting Chobe's great pachyderm herds, however, you should see lions, leopards, hyenas, possibly wild dogs, impalas, waterbucks, kudus, zebras, wildebeests (gnus), giraffes, and warthogs. Watch closely at the water holes when prey species come down to drink and are most vulnerable—they are so palpably nervous that you'll feel jumpy, too. Lions in this area are often specialized killers; one pride might target giraffes, another zebras, another buffalo, or even

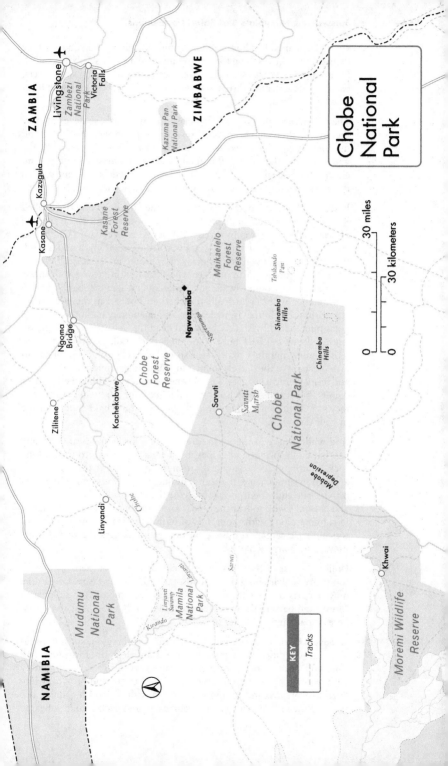

Chobe National Park

KEY
— Tracks

30 miles
30 kilometers

ZAMBIA

Livingstone
Zambezi National Park
Victoria Falls

Kazugula

ZIMBABWE

Kazuma Pan National Park

Kasane

Kasane Forest Reserve

Maikaelelo Forest Reserve

Tshikando Pan

Ngwezumba

Ngwezumba

Shinamba Hills

Chinamba Hills

Ngoma Bridge

Chobe Forest Reserve

Kachekabwe

Zilitene

Savuti

Savuti Marsh

Chobe National Park

Mababe Depression

Chobe

Linyandi

Savuti

Mudumu National Park

Linyanti Swamp
Mamila National Park
Linyanti

Kwando

NAMIBIA

Khwai

Moremi Wildlife Reserve

young elephants. But lions are opportunistic killers, and you could see them pounce on anything from a porcupine to a lowly scrub hare. Bird-life along the river is awesome: rarely seen birds including slaty egrets, rock pratincoles, pink-throated longclaws, and lesser gallinules get bird-watchers excited.

The northern section of park comprises riverine bush, so devastated by the hordes of elephants coming down to the perennial Chobe to drink that in winter it looks like a World War I battlefield. Fortunately, the wide sweep of the Caprivi floodplains, where hundreds of buffalo and elephants graze silhouetted against almost psychedelic sunsets, softens this harsh, featureless landscape where it faces neighboring Namibia.

In the southwestern part of the park lies the fabled Savuti (also spelled Savute) area, famous for its predators. Savuti offers a sweeping expanse of savanna brooded over by seven rocky outcrops that guard a relic marsh and the dry Savuti Channel, Africa's Stolen River of myth and legend. (It's "stolen" because it mysteriously disappeared in the early 1980s and has never returned.) You may see wild dogs hunting where only a few decades ago crocodiles swam and basked on the channel banks. Savuti is dramatically different from elsewhere in Botswana; there are open spaces, limitless horizons, wide skies, and unending miles of waving tall grass punctuated by starkly beautiful dead trees—the legacy of the relentless drought. Like Chobe National Park overall, Savuti is famed for its elephants, but the female of the species is rarely seen here, for Savuti is the domain of the bull elephant: old grandfathers, middle-aged males, and feisty young teenagers. The old ones gaze at you with imperturbable dignity, but it's the youngsters who'll make your adrenaline run riot as they kick up the dust and bellow belligerently as they make a mock charge in your direction.

And while you're in the Savuti area looking for leopards and the tiny acrobatic klipspringer antelopes, be sure to pay a visit to the striking rock paintings, early humans' attempts to represent the wildlife all around. In summertime thousands of migrating zebras and wildebeests provide the equivalent of fast food for the lion prides, hungry hyenas, and cheetahs who follow the herds. The Cape buffalo herds also arrive in summer along with thousands of returning bird migrants. The raptors are spectacular. You'll see falcons, eagles, kestrels, goshawks, ospreys, and sparrow hawks.

Unlike the rest of Botswana, Chobe can be crowded; there are simply too many vehicles on too few roads, particularly in season. One of the quieter parts of the park is around the Ngwezumba River, an area of forests and pans in the more remote middle of the park; the drawback here is that game is harder to find.

WHERE TO STAY   ☑ **Savute Elephant Camp.** In the semi-arid Savuti region, splendid, spa-
$$$ cious, air-conditioned, twin-bedded tents are elegantly furnished with cane and dark-wood furniture, an impressive overhead bed canopy with attendant mosquito net, woven rugs in creams and browns, white linen bedspreads, and a roomy bathroom with his and her sinks. For those cold winter mornings and evenings, there's even a built-in heater.

Your private viewing deck overlooking one of the busiest elephant water holes in the world has comfortable chairs and an inviting hammock. As the camp is in Chobe National Park, night drives and walking are against regulations, but you will see plenty of game and birds. If you can manage to be here at full moon, the sight of hundreds of great, gray shapes gleaming in the moonlight, jostling, rumbling, and coming and going at the water hole is truly unforgettable. ⌂ *Orient-Express Safaris, Box 786432, Sandton 2146, South Africa* ☎ *27/11/481–6052* 🖷 *27/11/481–6065* ⊕ *www.orient-express-safaris.com* ⇨ *12 tents* ⚷ *A/c, pool, bar* ⊟ *MC, V* ⦿ *FAP.*

$ 🏨 **Chobe Game Lodge.** The only permanent lodge set in Chobe National Park, this grand old dame—Liz Taylor and Richard Burton got married for the second time here in the '70s—still offers one of Botswana's most sophisticated stays, although the feel is more hotel-like than lodge-like. Terra-cotta tiles, Rhodesian teak furniture, African artifacts, and the ubiquitous beautiful handwoven Botswana baskets give the feel of the Dark Continent. The solid Moorish-style buildings—with their graceful high arches and barrel-vaulted ceilings—insulate the not-so-intrepid traveler from too-close encounters of the animal kind: baboon mothers have been known to teach their young how to turn a doorknob! The gorgeous gardens are a riot of color and attract lots of small fauna. There's a well-stocked curio shop with great clothes and wildlife books. Don't miss out on the well-run daily activities from game drives to river cruises. An early-morning canoe ride is also a must. ⌂ *Desert & Delta Safaris, Box 130555, Bryanston 2125, South Africa* ☎ *27/11/706–0861* 🖷 *27/11/706–0863* ⊕ *www.desertdelta.co.za* ⇨ *46 rooms, 4 suites* ⚷ *Pool, billiards, bar, shop* ⊟ *MC, V* ⦿ *FAP.*

$ 🏨 **Chobe Savanna Lodge.** This luxury lodge lies on the banks of the Chobe River, overlooking Chobe National Park. Each North Africa–inspired stone-and-thatch cottage has a private deck, air-conditioning, and a private bathroom. Cream textured linen, vases of dried grasses, ethnic-design cushions, polished wooden floors, handcrafted furniture, and handwoven cream-and-brown rugs provide a comfortable and elegant haven. Cruise the wide river game-spotting, bird-watching, or just soaking up an awesome sunset; take a guided game walk through the unspoiled bush; or just sit out on the viewing deck with its magnificent views of the floodplains and river and watch scores of elephants and buffalos mooching about. ⌂ *Desert & Delta Safaris, Box 130555, Bryanston 2125, South Africa* ☎ *27/11/706–0861* 🖷 *27/11/706–0863* ⊕ *www.desertdelta.co.za* ⇨ *12 cottages* ⚷ *Pool, bar* ⊟ *MC, V* ⦿ *FAP.*

$ 🏨 **Savute Safari Lodge.** As your small plane arrives at this attractive lodge, you can see the wide swathe the dry riverbed makes through the surrounding countryside. The exterior of the main building and the safari suites are traditional thatch and timber; however, when you enter your spacious suite, it's a bit like walking out of Africa into a Scandinavian design center—blond wood, dazzling white bed linens, comfortable furniture in bright primary colors, gaily colored handwoven rugs, and lots of glass. Outside on your spacious wooden deck it's back to Africa; by full moon watch the gray, ghostly shapes of elephants drinking from the water hole in front of the camp, or if the moon is not yet full, marvel at the myriad stars in the African night sky. Excellent safari guides can reveal the secrets of the African bush to you on game drives. When you're not watching the abundant game, there's a large elegant dining room where you can enjoy scrumptious late-morning brunches and candlelit silver-service dinners, a lounge with a huge fireplace, and an upstairs viewing deck. ⌐ *Desert & Delta Safaris, Box 130555, Bryanston 2125, South Africa* ☎ *27/11/706–0861* ⊟ *27/11/706–0863* ⊕ *www.desertdelta. co.za* ⤴ *12 suites* ⚅ *Dining room, a/c, pool, bar, lounge, library* ⊟ *MC, V* ⍢ *FAP.*

Linyanti Reserve

The Linyanti Reserve, which borders Chobe National Park, is one of the huge concession areas leased to different companies for up to 15 years by the Department of Wildlife and National Parks and the Tawana Land Board. It's a spectacular wildlife area comprising the Linyanti marshes, open floodplains, rolling savanna, and the Savuti Channel. Because it's a private concession, open vehicles can drive where and when they like, which means superb game-viewing.

Basic choices for viewing wildlife are game drives (including thrilling night drives with spotlights), boat trips, and walks with friendly and knowledgeable Motswana guides. Even in peak season there is a maximum of only six game vehicles driving around at one time, allowing you to see Africa as the early hunters and explorers might have. The Savuti Channel, once a huge river, but dry now for more than two decades, has starred in several *National Geographic* documentaries, and it's not hard to see why. Stock up on film, and for once you won't bore your friends with the results: hundreds of elephants drinking from pools at sunset, hippos and hyenas nonchalantly strolling past a pride of lions preparing to hunt under moonlight, and thousands of water and land birds everywhere.

WHERE TO STAY   ⊡ **Duma Tau.** This classy camp, with imaginatively decorated and fur-
$ nished raised tent chalets under thatch and overlooking the water, lies at the very heart of the concession. The spacious chalets have African fabrics; clever cane furniture decorated with plaited reeds, brass, and local beadwork; wood floors with handwoven rugs; an indoor shower and another one on your outside deck so you can wash as you view; and personal touches such as a guinea-fowl feather or dried seedpod placed artistically among your towels. The lounge and dining area of the main lodge are open on all sides (a bit cold in winter); the toilet at the end of the deck must have the best view of any in the world. The food is simple but superb. Before you set out on your early morning game drive, try a plate of piping hot porridge, a Danish straight from the oven, or a freshly baked muffin. ⌐ *Wilderness Safaris, Box 5219, Rivonia 2128, South Africa* ☎ *27/11/807–1800* ⊟ *27/11/807–2110* ⊕ *www.dumatau. com* ⤴ *8 chalets* ⚅ *Pool, bar, lounge, library* ⊟ *MC, V* ⍢ *FAP.*

★ $ ⊡ **Savuti Bush Camp.** If you really want to get down with elephants, this is the place. In front of the rustic lodge of large and comfortable tents is an elephant blind made of piled logs. You'll be escorted into the blind (where the elephants can't see you), and then hold on to your hat, your breath, and your camera as you watch from the closest possible quarters. You'll be almost under their trunks, looking up at their huge yellow teeth and wise old long-lashed eyes and feeling diminutively human. You may well get an impromptu shower as an elephant blows water over you or find yourself eyeball to eyeball with a "tiny" baby. Although neither glamorous nor showy, and without the finery of some of its sister camps (if you need hair dryers and air-conditioning, stay away), Savuti has a simple, laid-back charm that's irresistible. Being a guest here is like being a member of a small, intimate house party. Other game is spectacular, too, with resident wild dogs, lions galore, and cruising cheetahs. ☝ *Wilderness Safaris, Box 5219, Rivonia 2128, South Africa* ☎ *27/ 11/807–1800* 🖷 *27/11/807–2110* ⊕ *www.savuticamp.com* ⤳ *7 tents* ☼ *Pool, bar* ▭ *MC, V* ⴲ *FAP.*

Kwando Reserve

Like the Okavango, the Kwando River comes down from the wet Angola highlands and then meanders through a few hundred kilometers of wilderness. The 2,300-square-km (900-square-mi) private Kwando concession has more than 80 km (50 mi) of river frontage. It stretches south from the banks of the Kwando River, through huge open plains and mopane forests to the Okavango Delta. It's an area crisscrossed by thousands of ancient game trails traversed by wildlife that move freely between the Okavango Delta, Chobe, and the open Namibian wilderness to the north. As you fly in to the reserve, you'll see this web of thousands of interlacing natural game trails—from hippo highways to the tiny paths of smaller animals. This should clue you in to Kwando's diverse animal life: wall-to-wall elephants, crowds of buffalo, zebras, antelope of all kinds including roan and sable, wild dogs, lions, and wildebeests. Experienced rangers—who learned their animal ethics at South Africa's Londolozi and Phinda camps—and their San (Bushman) trackers have already managed to habituate what is truly wild game to vehicles and cameras. Participants on one night drive came upon a running battle between a pack of 14 wild dogs and two hyenas who had stolen the dogs' fresh kill. The noisy battle ended when a loudly trumpeting elephant, fed up with the commotion, charged the wild dogs and drove them off. There's a sheer joy in knowing you are one of only four vehicles in a half million acres of wilderness.

If you'd like to take a safari with children, there's no better place than Kwando, where under the special care of top rangers you'll not only have a truly memorable time but also learn lots about the bush. The safari starts with a safety briefing, and kids get their own tents next to Mom and Dad or you can share one. Kids learn to track and take plaster casts of spoor (to show their friends at home), sit up in the tracker's seat on the vehicle to follow game, cook marshmallows over the boma fire, tell stories, catch and release butterflies, make bush jewelry, and learn about ecology. Kids can eat on their own or with you, and if you want an afternoon snooze, they'll be supervised in the pool or at some other fun activity. This program is available at both Kwando camps; the price is the same per night as for an adult.

★ **$$** ⊞ **Kwando Lagoon Camp.** The camp perches on the banks of the fast-flowing Kwando River, quite literally in the middle of nowhere. Comfortable walk-through tents with private bathrooms and verandas nestle on grassy slopes under the shade of giant jackalberry trees that are hundreds of years old. After a night spent next to one of these mighty trees, a major source of natural energy, people say you wake up rejuvenated, your body buzzing with new life. From the thatch dining and bar area you can watch herds of elephants only yards away as they come to drink and bathe or hippos snoozing in the sun. You might also spot a malachite kingfisher darting like a bejeweled minijet over the water. Go for a morning or evening game drive, drift along the river in a small boat, or go spinner- or fly-fishing for tiger fish and bream. The emphasis in the camp is on informality, simplicity, and soaking up the wilderness experience. ⌐*Kwando Wildlife Experience, Box 550, Maun, Botswana* ☎ *267/686–1449 or 267/686–4388* 🖷 *267/686–1457* ⊕*www.kwando.co.za* ⤳*6 tents* ⌂*Pool, bar* ⊟*DC, MC, V* ⦿*FAP.*

$ ⊞ **Kwando Lebala Camp.** Lebala Camp is 30 km (18 mi) south of Lagoon Camp and looks out over the Linyanti wetlands. The secluded tents, built on raised teak decks, are magnificent. All have private bathrooms with Victorian claw-foot tubs. If you want to get even closer to nature, bathe in your own outdoor shower or just sit on your sundeck and look out at the endless vistas. On morning or evening game drives you'll see loads of game, and if you fancy a freshly caught fish supper, try your hand at spinner fishing. ⌐ *Kwando Wildlife Experience, Box 550, Maun, Botswana* ☎ *267/686–1449 or 267/686–4388* 🖷 *267/686–1457* ⊕ *www.kwando.co.za* ⤳ *8 tents* ⌂ *Pool* ⊟ *DC, MC, V* ⦿ *FAP.*

Botswana A to Z

AIR TRAVEL

In this huge, often inaccessible country, air travel is the easiest way to get around. Sir Seretse Khama Airport, 15 km (9½ mi) from Gaborone's city center, is Botswana's main point of entry. Kasane International Airport is 3 km (2 mi) from the entrance to Chobe National Park, and small but very busy Maun Airport is 1 km (½ mi) from the city center of this northern safari capital. All three are gateways to the Okavango Delta and Chobe; they're easy to find your way around in and rarely crowded.

Air charter companies operate small planes from Kasane and Maun to all the camps. Flown by some of the youngest-looking pilots in the world, these flights, which your travel agent will arrange, are reliable, reasonably cheap, and average between 25 and 50 minutes. Maximum baggage allowance is 12 kilograms in a soft, squashable sports/duffel bag (no hard cases allowed), excluding the weight of camera equipment (within reason). Because of the thermal air currents over Botswana, and because most flights are around midday, when thermals are at their strongest, flights can sometimes be very bumpy—take air-sickness pills if you're susceptible to motion sickness; then sit back and enjoy the fabulous bird's-eye views. You're sure to spot elephants and hippos from the air.

Air Botswana has scheduled flights from Johannesburg to Gaborone and Maun on a daily basis, and from Cape Town to Maun on Monday,

Wednesday, and Friday, returning to Cape Town Tuesday, Thursday, and Sunday. The airline also flies Johannesburg to Kasane on Thursday and Sunday. SA Express Airways also has daily flights between Johannesburg and Gaborone.

Mack Air, Northern Air, Sefofane Air, Swamp Air, and Delta Air/Synergy Seating fly directly between Johannesburg's Grand Central Airport and Maun on private charters.

🛂 Airports **Kasane International Airport** ☎ 267/625-0161. **Maun Airport** ☎ 267/686-762. **Sir Seretse Khama Airport** ☎ 267/391-4518.

🛂 Airlines **Air Botswana** ☎ 267/390-5500 or 267/395-1921 🖷 267/395-3928 ⊕ www.airbotswana.co.bw. **Delta Air/Synergy Seating** ✒ Box 39, Maun ☎ 267/686-0044 🖷 267/686-1703. **Mack Air** ✒ Private Bag 329, Maun ☎ 267/686-0675 🖷 267/686-0036. **Northern Air** ✒ Box 27, Maun ☎ 267/686-0385 🖷 267/686-1559. **SA Express Airways** ☎ 27/11/978-1111. **Sefofane Air** ✒ Private Bag 159, Maun ☎ 267/686-0778 🖷 267/686-1649. **Swamp Air** ✒ Private Bag 33, Maun ☎ 267/686-4607.

CAR TRAVEL

All the main access roads from neighboring countries are paved, and cross-border formalities are user-friendly. Maun is easy to reach from South Africa, Namibia, and Zimbabwe, but the distances are long and not very scenic. Gaborone is 360 km (225 mi) from Johannesburg via Rustenburg, Zeerust, and the Tlokweng border post. Driving in Botswana is on the left-hand side of the road. The "Shell Tourist Map of Botswana" is the best available map. Find it at Botswana airports or in airport bookstores.

Forget about a car in the Okavango Delta unless it's amphibious. Only the western and eastern sides of the delta panhandle and the Moremi Wildlife Reserve are accessible by car; but it's wisest to always take a 4x4 vehicle. The road from Maun to Moremi North Gate is paved for the first 47 km (29 mi) up to Sherobe, when it becomes gravel for 11 km (7 mi) and then a dirt road.

It's not practical to reach Chobe National Park by car. A 4x4 vehicle is essential in the park itself. The roads are sandy and/or very muddy, depending on the season.

Electricity

To use electric-powered equipment purchased in the United States or Canada, bring a converter and adapter. If your appliances are dual-voltage, you'll need only an adapter. The electrical current is 220 volts, 50 cycles alternating current (AC); wall outlets usually take 15-amp plugs with three round prongs, but some take the straight-edged three-prong plugs, also 15 amps. Most of the lodges and camps have their own generators, so you're able to charge your cameras and other electronic equipment. Bring a reading light if you intend to read in bed at night, as tent and chalet lights tend to be dim.

EMBASSIES

British High Commission (✉ 1079 Queen's Rd., Private Bag 0023, Gaborone ☎ 267/395-2841 🖷 267/395-6105).

U.S. Embassy (✉ Government Enclave, Embassy Dr., Gaborone ☎ 267/ 395–3982 🖷 267/395–6947).

EMERGENCIES

Most safari companies include medical insurance in their tariffs. Medical Rescue International has 24-hour emergency help.

🛈 Emergency Services **Medical Rescue International** ☎ 267/390-1601.

LANGUAGE

Although Botswana's national language is Setswana, English is the official one, and it is spoken nearly everywhere.

MONEY MATTERS

The pula (the Setswana word for "rain") and the thebe constitute the Botswana currency; one pula equals 100 thebe. You will need to change your money or traveler's checks into pula, as this is the only legally accepted currency. (The currency rate fluctuates marginally.) However, you can use U.S. dollars or euros as tips at lodges and camps, and most camp prices are quoted in U.S. dollars.

There are no restrictions on foreign currency notes brought into the country as long as they are declared. Travelers can carry up to P10,000, or the equivalent in foreign currency, out of the country without declaring it. Banking hours are weekdays 9–3:30, Saturday 8:30–11. Hours at Barclays Bank at Sir Seretse Khama International Airport are Monday–Saturday 6 AM–10 PM.

PASSPORTS & VISAS

All visitors, including infants, need a valid passport to enter Botswana for visits of up to 90 days.

TELEPHONE NUMBERS

Both Botswana and South African telephone numbers appear in this section. Botswana numbers begin with the 267 country code, which you shouldn't dial within the country. (There are no internal area codes in Botswana.) South African numbers begin with that country code (27) followed by the area code—e.g., 11 for Johannesburg.

TIME

Botswana is on CAST (Central African Standard Time), which is two hours ahead of Greenwich mean time. That makes it seven hours ahead of North American eastern standard time (six hours ahead during eastern daylight saving time).

TOURS

Most operators offer ready-made safaris to many different destinations or will customize one for you.

CC Africa Safaris and Tours is a highly experienced tour operator and has ready-made trips and tours to all parts of Botswana or can tailor one to your needs, from the budget-conscious to the lavish. Desert & Delta Safaris has inclusive fly-in safari packages to its own camps, as well as other destinations, such as Victoria Falls. Ker & Downey is one of the oldest and most respected safari companies in Botswana. Utilizing its four exclusive camps, it offers traditional safari experiences that range from rustic to deluxe. Orient-Express Safaris, a member of Small Luxury Hotels of the World, owns three strategically located camps in some of Botswana's most diverse ecosystems and most desirable destinations: Chobe National Park, Moremi Wildlife Reserve, and the Okavango Delta. All camps have identical thatch tented lodging with identical furnishings and plenty of bells and whistles. Watch the night sky with a state-of-the-art telescope before reading the ancient Botswana folk story placed on your bed each night, from "The Origin of People" to "Squirrel's Guilt-stained Coat." Wilderness Safaris, which owns the majority of lodges in Botswana, offers all kinds of packages, including a choice of "premier," "classic," "vintage," or "camping wild" camps in a great variety of locations and ecosystems, from the delta to the Kalahari Desert. It also offers mobile safaris and custom tours for all Botswana destinations.

🛈 Tour Operators **CC Africa Safaris and Tours** ✉ Private Bag X27, Benmore 2010, South Africa ☎ 27/11/809-4300 🖷 27/11/809-4514 ⊕ www.ccafrica.com. **Desert & Delta Safaris** ✉ Box 130555, Bryanston 2125, South Africa ☎ 27/11/706-0861 🖷 27/11/706-0863 ⊕www.desertdelta.co.za. **Ker & Downey** ✉Box 27, Maun, Botswana ☎267/686-0375 🖷 267/686-1282 ⊕ www.kerdowney.com. **Orient-Express Safaris** ✉ Box 786432, Sandton 2146, South Africa ☎ 27/11/481-6052 🖷 27/11/481-6065 ⊕ www.orient-express-safaris.com. **Wilderness Safaris** ✉ Box 5219, Rivonia 2128, South Africa ☎ 27/11/807-1800 🖷 27/11/807-2110 ⊕ www.wilderness-safaris.com.

TRAVEL AGENCIES

Harvey World Travel (✉ Box 1950, Gaborone ☎ 267/390–4360 🖷 267/390–5840). **Kudu Travel** (✉ Private Bag 00130, Gaborone ☎ 267/397–2224 🖷 267/397–4224). **Travelwise** (✉ Box 2482, Gaborone ☎ 267/390–3244 🖷 267/390–3245).

VISITOR INFORMATION

Department of Tourism (✉ Private Bag 0047, Main Mall, Gaborone ☎ 267/395–3024 🖷 267/318–0991 ⊕ www.botswanatourism.org).

NAMIBIA

Many countries in Africa boast teeming wildlife and gorgeous scenery, but few, if any, can claim such limitless horizons; such huge, untamed wilderness areas; such a pleasant sunny climate; so few people (fewer than two per square mi); the oldest desert in the world; a wildly beautiful coastline; one of Africa's greatest game parks; plus—and this is a big bonus—a First World infrastructure and tourist facilities that are among the best in Africa. But you'll find all these—and more—in Namibia.

A former German colony, South West Africa, as it was then known, was a pawn in the power games of European politics. Although the Portuguese navigators were the first Europeans to arrive in 1485, they quickly abandoned the desolate and dangerous Atlantic shores of the "Coast of Death," as they called it. By the late 1700s British, French, and American whalers were using the deepwater ports of Lüderitz and Walvis

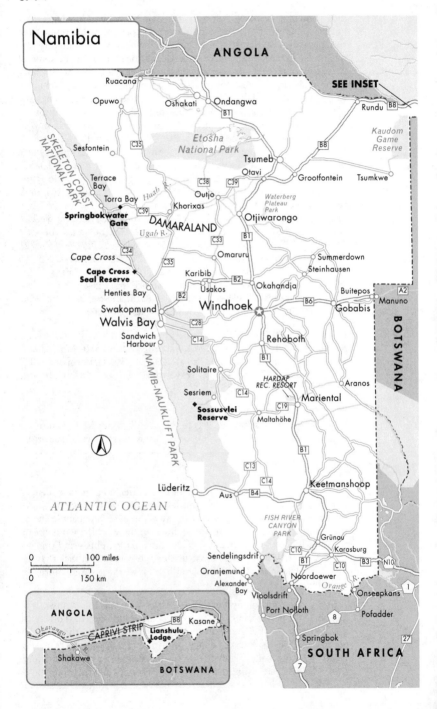

Namibia

ANGOLA

Ruacana

Opuwo

Oshakati   Ondangwa

SEE INSET   Rundu   B8

B1

SKELETON COAST NATIONAL PARK

Sesfontein

Etosha National Park

Kaudom Game Reserve

C35

B8

Terrace Bay

C38   C39

Tsumeb

Torra Bay

Otavi   Grootfontein   Tsumkwe

Springbokwater Gate   C39

Outjo   *Waterberg Plateau Park*

Khorixas

Huab R.

DAMARALAND   Otjiwarongo

Ugab R.   C33   B1

Cape Cross   C34

Omaruru   Summerdown

Cape Cross Seal Reserve   C35   Karibib   Steinhausen

B2   Usakos   B2   Okahandja   Buitepos   A2

Henties Bay   **Windhoek**   B6   Gobabis   Manuno

Swakopmund   C28

Walvis Bay   Rehoboth   BOTSWANA

Sandwich Harbour   C14

B1

Solitaire   *HARDAP REC. RESORT*   Aranos

Sesriem   C14

Sossusvlei Reserve   C19   Mariental

Maltahöhe

NAMIB-NAUKLUFT PARK

B1

C13

C14

Lüderitz   Keetmanshoop

Aus   B4

ATLANTIC OCEAN

FISH RIVER CANYON PARK

Grünau

Sendelingsdrif   C10   Karasburg   B3   N10

Oranjemund   B1   C10

Alexander Bay   *Orange R.*   Onseepkans

Vioolsdrift   Noordoewer

Port Nolloth   8   Pofadder

Springbok   27

SOUTH AFRICA

7

0   100 miles
0   150 km

ANGOLA

Okavango   B8   Kasane

CAPRIVI STRIP   **Lianshulu Lodge**

Shakawe   BOTSWANA

(Whalefish) Bay, which the Dutch, now settled in the Cape, then claimed as their own. A few years later, after France invaded Holland, England seized the opportunity to claim the territory together with the Cape Colony. Then it became Germany's turn to throw its hat into the ring. In the wake of its early missionaries and traders, it claimed the entire country as a German colony in 1884, only to surrender it to South African forces, who were fighting on the Allied side during World War I. South Africa was given a League of Nations mandate to administer the territory after the war, and despite a 1978 UN resolution to revoke the mandate, South Africa held on to Namibia for a further stormy 10 years. A bitter and bloody bush war with SWAPO (South West African People's Organization) freedom fighters raged until Namibia finally won its independence on March 21, 1990, after 106 years of foreign rule. Although most of the earlier colonial influences have now vanished, everywhere you go in Namibia today you'll find traces of the German past—forts and castles, place-names, cuisine, and German efficiency.

Bounded by the icy Atlantic on the west, the Kalahari Desert on the east, the Kunene River on the north, and the Orange River on the south, this land, harsh and often inhospitable yet full of rare beauty, has been carved out by the forces of nature. The same savage, continuous geological movements produced not only spectacular beauty but also great mineral wealth: alluvial diamonds, uranium, platinum, lead, zinc, silver, copper, tungsten, and tin—still the cornerstone of Namibia's economy. Humans have lived here for thousands of years; the San (Bushmen) are the earliest known people, although their hunting-gathering way of life is now almost extinct. Today most Namibians are employed in the agricultural sector, from subsistence farms to huge cattle ranches and game farms. It's a big country, four times as large as the United Kingdom and bigger than Texas, but its excellent road network means you can get around very easily. As you travel through the changing landscapes of mountains and plains, lush riverine forests, and high sand dunes, marvel at the amazing diversity of light and shade, color and contrast, and soak up the emptiness and isolation, the silence and the solitude. Far from crowded polluted cities, you could easily imagine yourself on another planet or in a land where time has stood still—a land you will never forget.

About the Camps & Lodges

Namibia's private camps, lodges, and other accommodations are up to high international standards. Even deep in the desert, at the tented camps, tents have en-suite bathrooms and private verandas, but don't expect TVs. Air-conditioning is the exception, rather than the rule. It's mentioned in reviews only when it is present. Most prices at private lodges are all-inclusive (aka Full American Plan), including transfers, meals, activities, and usually drinks. Camps offer at least two activities a day, from morning and evening game drives to riding moon buggies over the desert dunes, or from picnics on one of the wildest coasts in the world to visiting a traditional Himba settlement.

At the national-park camps, self-catering (with cooking facilities) accommodations are basic, clean, comfortable, and much cheaper than the private lodges outside the park. They're often more fun, too. After all, you're in the very midst of the big-game action. Each camp has a restaurant with adequate, if not memorable, food; a shop selling basic foodstuffs and curios; a post office; gas station; and swimming pool. Most rooms have private toilets, baths or showers, air-conditioning, a refrigerator, and a *braai* (barbecue). Linen and towels are provided. Some of the bigger bungalows have a full kitchen with cutlery and dishes.

You won't find much truly Namibian food (although local venison, seafood, and Namibian oysters are superb); instead, cuisine is mainly European, often German. Lodges usually serve good home-style cooking—pies, pastries, fresh vegetables, lots of red meat, venison, mouthwatering desserts, and the traditional braai. Because of its past as a German colony, Namibia is known for its superb lagers, and it's well worth trying a Hansa or a Windhoek Export. South African wine, which is excellent, is readily available.

WHAT IT COSTS In Namibian dollars				
$$$$	$$$	$$	$	¢
SAFARI CAMPS AND LODGES				
over 1,500	1,000–1,500	700–1,000	400–700	under 400

All prices refer to an all-inclusive per-person rate including tax, assuming double occupancy.

Timing

Namibia has a subtropical desert climate with nonstop sunshine throughout the year. It's classified as arid to nonarid, and, generally speaking it gets wet only in the northwest and then only during the rainy season (October–April). The south is warm and dry, although temperatures vary dramatically between night and day, particularly in the desert.

In the Namib Naukluft the air is sparkling, and pollution practically unheard-of, and although nights always come early with dramatic suddenness, days are crystal clear and perfect for traveling. The hottest season, the rainy season, is from December to March, but unless you're in the north you're unlikely to see much rain or experience much humidity. Sometimes there's no rain at all in the southern Kalahari and the Namib Desert, where it can get very hot indeed (top temperature 104°F). From September through April (summer) the region's weather is clear, dry, crisp, and nearly perfect, averaging 77°F during the day, but in the desert areas it can drop to freezing at night, especially in winter. (Bring warm clothes for after the sun goes down.) If it's game you're after, then winter (April through August) is the best because the lack of surface water ensures that animals congregate around water holes.

Along the Skeleton Coast the climate can be breathtakingly varied. Because of the pounding, fierce Atlantic and its cold Benguela Current, thick fog and mist roll over the beaches and into the nearby interior in the early morning and at night, bringing precious moisture to all the desert creatures and plants but making it chilly and damp for humans. The day that follows will be bright and sunny, and in summer, extremely hot, so dress in layers.

Etosha's best season is winter (May–September), when the weather is cooler, the grass shorter, and the game easier to see. But if you can stand the heat, summer sees the return of thousands of waterbirds to the flooded pan, as well as the great annual migration of tens of thousands of zebras, wildebeests, giraffes, and springbok and other antelopes from their winter feeding grounds on the Andoni Plains to the new, lush feeding grounds around Okuakuejo. Summer is the hottest season (top temperature 104°F), and the rainy season is from December to March, with dramatic afternoon thunderheads building up followed by heavy but short rainstorms. But almost any time is a good time to visit Etosha, because game depends on the man-made water holes distributed throughout the park.

Namib Naukluft Park

Namib Naukluft Park, south of Walvis Bay, is the fourth-largest national park in the world, and is renowned for its beauty, isolation, tranquillity, romantic desert landscapes, and rare desert-adapted plants and creatures. Covering an area of 12.1 million acres, stretching 400 km (250 mi) long from Swakopmund in the north to Lüderitz in the south and 150 km (93 mi) wide, it accounts for a tenth of Namibia's surface area. To examine the park properly, it's best to think of it as five distinct areas: the Northern Section—between the Kuiseb and Swakops rivers—synonymous with rocky stone surfaces and granite islands (*inselbergs*) and dry riverbeds; the Middle Section, the 80-million-year-old heart of the desert and home of Sesriem Canyon and Sossusvlei, the highest sand dunes in the world; Naukluft (meaning "narrow gorge"), some 120 km (74½ mi) northwest of Sesriem, which has wall-to-wall game and birds and is the home of the Kuiseb Canyon; the Western Section, with its lichen-covered plains, prehistoric plants, and bird sanctuaries of Walvis Bay and Sandwich Harbour; and the Southern Section, where, if you're traveling up from South Africa by road, it's worth having a look at Duwisib Castle, 72 km (46 mi) southwest of Maltahöhe beside the D286—an anachronistic stone castle built in 1909 by a German army officer who was later killed at the Somme. The park's southern border ends at the charming little town of Lüderitz.

The kind of wildlife you'll encounter will depend on which area of the park you visit. In the north look out for the staggeringly beautiful gemsbok (oryx), believed by some to be the animal behind the unicorn myth. Also visible are springboks, spotted hyenas, black-backed jackals, and the awesome lappet-face vultures, the biggest in Africa. In Naukluft you'll see the most game, more than 50 species of mammals, including leopards, caracals, Cape and bat-eared foxes, aardwolves, and klipspringers. There are almost 200 species of birds, from the startlingly beautiful crimson-breasted boubou shrike to soaring falcons and buzzards. You'll notice huge haystacks weighing down tall trees and telephone poles. These are the condominiums of the sociable weavers, so called because they nest communally, sometimes with thousands of fellow weavers; yet each tiny bird has its own exit and entrance.

Where there are sand dunes you'll be able to observe some of the earth's strangest creatures: the dune beetle, which collects condensed fog on its

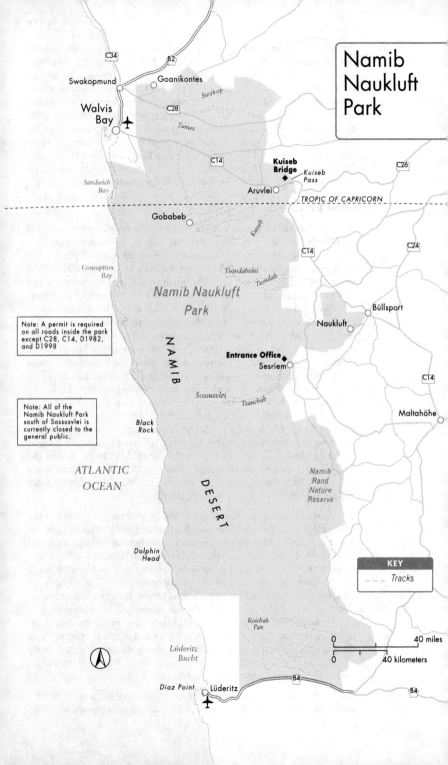

back into a single droplet that it then rolls down its back into its mouth; a beetle that digs a trench to collect moisture; the golden mole (thought until recently to be extinct), which spends its whole life "swimming" beneath the sand, ambushing beetles and grubs on the surface; the sidewinding adder, a sand-diving lizard that raises one foot at a time above the hot sand in a strange stationary dance to nonexistent music.

Don't overlook the amazing desert-adapted plants. Ask your guide to point out a dollar bush (so called because its leaves are dollar size) or an ink bush, both of which can survive without rain for years; the gold, frankincense, and myrrh of the Commiphora plants; the Namib's magic plant, the nara melon, still harvested and eaten by the locals; and the baffling geophytes, plants that disguise themselves as stones. Watch for withered-looking desert lichens—if you pour a tiny drop of water onto one you will see it seemingly rise from the dead. Last, but by no means least, is the mind-boggling *Welwitschia mirabalis,* a fleshy green plant that spreads its long waxy stems like so many huge, fat tendrils over the surrounding desert. The older the plant, the bigger and longer the leaves. This is the Namib's most famous, and the world's oldest, living plant.

Sesriem & Sossusvlei

Even if you're not a romantic, the Sossusvlei's huge, star-shape desert dunes, which rise dramatically 1,000 feet above the surrounding plains and sprawl like massive pieces of abstract sculpture, are guaranteed to stir your soul and imagination. You might even dash off a sonnet or two. The landscape has continuously shifting colors—from yellow-gold and ocher to rose, purple, and deep red—which grow paler or darker according to the time of day. The dunes have their own distinctive features, ranging from the crescent-shape *barcan* dunes—which migrate up to 2 or 3 yards a year, covering and uncovering whatever crosses their path—to the spectacular, stationary star-shape dunes, formed by the multidirectional winds that tease and tumble the sands back and forth. Park gates open an hour before sunrise, so if you can, try to be among the dunes as the sun comes up—it's a spectacular sight. If you're in good shape, you can hike to the top of Big Daddy, the highest sand dune in the world. If you haven't been eating all your Wheaties, you can climb halfway up and sit and admire the stupendous views. And if you just don't feel up to any physical exertion, simply walk up to see the stark beauty of Dead Vlei and then leisurely make your way down to sit in the shade of camel-thorn trees and watch the bird life. Never walk in the desert without water, a sun hat, and sunblock.

About 4 km (2½ mi) from Sesriem Gate, your entry point to Sossusvlei, is Sesriem Canyon, named after the six *rieme* (thongs) that were tied to the buckets of the early Dutch settlers when they drew up water from the canyon. If you have time, cool off in the cold water and climb the towering Elim Dune, about 5 km (3 mi) away; it will take you well over an hour, but the superb views of the surrounding desert and gravel plains are worth the effort. Be warned: Dune climbing is exhausting, so make discretion the better part of valor. If you're driving yourself, check with your car-rental company for distances and times, which can vary according to the state of the roads. It's more than an hour's very hot walk (4 km

[2½ mi]) to climb the major route up to Dead Vlei and Big Daddy, the hub of Sossusvlei, from the parking area. With a four-wheel-drive vehicle you can park just below Dead Vlei.

WHERE TO STAY   🏨 **Kulala Desert Lodge.** In the heart of the Namib and bordering the Namib

$$$$ Naukluft Park, this lodge offers magnificent views of the famous red dunes of Sossusvlei, superb mountain scenery, and vast open plains. Tented, thatch-roofed chalets (*kulala*) have a wooden platform overlooking the dry riverbed. In summer you can move your mattress onto a private stargazing platform on your rooftop to sleep under the stars. The veranda at the main lodge overlooks a water hole and is the perfect place to watch or photograph the magnificent desert sunset. Activities include desert excursions, morning and evening game drives, trips to Sossusvlei, birding, and guided walks. You can splurge on a hot-air balloon trip over the desert (extra cost)—a once-in-a-lifetime opportunity. 🏛 *Wilderness Safaris, Box 5219, Rivonia 2128, South Africa* 📞 *27/11/807–1800* 🖨 *27/11/807–2110* ⊕ *www.wildernesskulalalodge.com* 🛏 *12 chalets* ♨ *Pool, bar* ▤ *AE, DC, MC, V* ⊚ *FAP.*

$$$$ 🏨 **Sossusvlei Lodge.** If you want to be on the spot when the park gates open at first light, then this hotel right at the Sesriem entrance is the right choice for you. Its decor in shades of terra-cotta, burnt sienna, and apricot blends perfectly with the desert surroundings. You'll feel like an upmarket bedouin in your spacious and luxurious tented room, imaginatively constructed of concrete, ironwork, canvas, and leather. After a hot, dusty day in the desert, wallow in the swimming pool, which faces the dunes, and later gaze at the dazzling brilliance of the night skies. There's a good restaurant serving light meals. 🏛 *Box 6900, Windhoek, Namibia* 📞 *264/63/69–3223* 🖨 *264/63/69–3231* 🛏 *45 rooms* ♨ *Restaurant, pool, bar* ▤ *AE, MC, V* ⊚ *MAP.*

$$$$ 🏨 **Sossusvlei Mountain Lodge.** This gorgeous lodge has a spectacular setting in the heart of the Namib Desert in the NamibRand Nature Reserve. Its ultraluxurious desert villas, facing a vast golden yellow plain with misty mountains on the horizon, are built of natural rock and look out over a plain ringed by peaks. Huge desert-facing suites have private patios and sundecks and big open fireplaces to keep you warm on chilly desert nights. Shower in your megasize bathroom (even your toilet has an incomparable view) or outside in your own little walled garden. You can lie in bed and watch the stars through the skylight overhead or climb up to the observatory behind the lodge. It has its own state-of-the-art telescope through which an astronomer/ranger will guide you through the heavens. The food is as creative as the lodge itself—try tandoori-baked *kingklip* (a delicious southern African fish) served with mango salsa—and there's a super wine cellar. You can explore the area on an eco-friendly quad bike, go for guided nature walks or drives, spot some native desert birds and animals, or just sit and gaze at the incredible views. 🏛 *Africa Leisure Travel, Swakopmund, Namibia* 📞 *264/64/46–3812 or 264/64/46–3813* 🖨 *264/64/40–0216* ⊕ *www.ccafrica.com* 🛏 *10 villas* ♨ *A/c, pool* ▤ *AE, DC, MC, V* ⊚ *FAP.*

$$$$ 🏨 **Sossusvlei Wilderness Camp.** In one of the most dramatic settings in Africa, exquisitely appointed rock, timber, and thatch bungalows cling to the side of a mountain with spectacular views of the desert as it stretches away to the horizon. You'll enjoy breakfast under spreading camel-thorn trees at the foot of Sossusvlei after the bumpy 20-km (12½-mi) drive to the dunes before returning to camp at midday via the Sesriem Canyon. Then cool off in your private plunge pool as you watch the sun set over awesome desert scenery to the calls of barking geckos. ⌖ *Wilderness Safaris, Box 5219, Rivonia 2128, South Africa* ☎ *27/11/807–1800* 🖷 *27/11/807–2110* ⊕ *www.sossusvleicamp.com* ⮎ *9 bungalows* ⌂ *Restaurant, a/c, pool, bar* ⊟ *AE, DC, MC, V* ⦿ *FAP.*

$$ 🖾 **Namib Naukluft Lodge.** This pinkish-brown desert-toned lodge sits in the middle of a wide plain of desert and looks like children's building blocks set down by a giant hand in the middle of nowhere. Awesome views go with the territory. You can choose to sit on your private veranda and watch the fiery desert sunset, sip a sundowner by the pool, or enjoy a meal in the open-air restaurant. The lodge will arrange outings and activities for you—don't miss out on an easy walk in the world's oldest desert. ⌖ *Elena Travel Services, Box 3127, Windhoek, Namibia* ☎ *264/61/24–4443* 🖷 *264/61/24–4558* ✉ *info@namibweb. com* ⮎ *16 rooms* ⌂ *Restaurant, pool, bar* ⊟ *AE, DC, MC, V* ⦿ *FAP.*

$ 🖾 **Zebra River Lodge.** From this delightful lodge, where personal attention and friendly service are outstanding, you can drive yourself to Sesriem and Sossusvlei (90 km [56 mi] to the gate) or to Naukluft, or take a full-day excursion with Rob Field, the friendly and knowledgeable owner (book this when you reserve your room). The comfortable and unpretentious lodge has its own canyon, hiking trails, perennial springs, and superb cooking. The seven guest rooms all have views of the plunge pool and green garden. ⌖ *Box 11742, Windhoek, Namibia* ☎ *264/63/ 69–3265* 🖷 *264/63/69–3266* ⊕ *www.zebrariver.com* ⮎ *7 rooms, 1 cottage* ⌂ *Pool, bar* ⊟ *MC, V* ⦿ *FAP.*

SPORTS & THE OUTDOORS A stupendous, not-to-be-missed view of the desert can be had in a hot-air balloon piloted by the legendary Belgian Eric Hefemans. You ascend at dawn and watch the sun come up over the breathtaking, silent landscape, followed by a champagne breakfast amid the dunes. Contact **Namib Sky Adventures** (⌖ Box 5197, Windhoek, Namibia ☎ 264/63/29–3233 ⊕ www.namibsky.com).

The Skeleton Coast

This wildly beautiful but dangerous shore, one-third of Namibia's western coastline, stretches from the Ugab River in the south to the Kunene River, the border with Angola, in the north. The Portuguese, facing the coast in tiny, frail caravels, called this treacherous coast with its cold Benguela Current and deadly crosscurrents the "Coast of Death." Its newer, no-less-sinister name, the Skeleton Coast, testifies to innumerable shipwrecks, to lives lost, to bleached whale bones, and to the insignificant, transient nature of puny humans in the face of the raw power of nature. Still comparatively unknown to tourists, this region has a stark beauty and an awesomely diverse landscape—gray gravel plains, rugged wilderness, rusting shipwrecks, desert wastes, meandering barcan dunes, distant mountains, towering walls of sand and granite, and crashing seas. You'll rarely see more than a handful of visitors in this inaccessible and rugged coastal area. This is not an easy ride, as distances are vast, amenities scarce or nonexistent, and the roads demanding.

Skeleton Coast National Park extends along this rugged coast and about 40 km (25 mi) inland. The southern part is open to tourists up to Terrace Bay, and the northern part is managed by the government as a wilderness area. If it's lush green pastures and abundance of game you want, then this raw, rugged, harsh, and uncompromising landscape is not for you. What you will find is dramatically different scenery, an absence of tourists (crowds around here mean one or two vehicles), and some wildlife: brown hyenas, springbok, oryx, jackals, and, if you're really lucky, a coastal lion. (The sight of a majestic oryx silhouetted against towering sand dunes or a cheeky jackal scavenging seal pups on the beaches is extremely rewarding.) The best activity, however, is just concentrating on the freedom, beauty, and strange solitude of the area. You can drive (a 4x4 gives you more flexibility) from Swakopmund north through Henties Bay via the Ugab Gate with its eerie painted skulls and crossbones on the gates or from the more northerly Springbokwater Gate. You must reach your gate of entry before 3 PM. Always stick to the marked roads and avoid driving on treacherous salt pans. Look out for an unusual wreck lying next to the road between the Ugab River and Terrace Bay; it's an abandoned oil rig, now home to a huge colony of cormorants. If you are only passing through, you can buy a permit (N$20 per adult, N$20 per car) at the gate. For a longer trip you must obtain a permit in advance from Namibia Wildlife Resorts (⇨ Visitor Information in Namibia A to Z, *below*).

WHERE TO STAY

★ **$$$$** ⊡ **Skeleton Coast Camp.** If you long for a remote wilderness area, consider a three-night safari into this desolate camp in 660,000 acres of the northern part of Skeleton Coast National Park. You sleep under canvas in an elegantly furnished tent with your own small deck and awesome desert view and eat in the open-air dining room under an ancient leadwood tree. You visit an authentic Himba settlement, picnic beside the crashing Atlantic, visit the loneliest grave in the world, and drive through oryx-studded plains and shifting sand dunes with their desert birds. The days are long—you leave camp after breakfast as the morning mists drift from the coastline into the interior and don't return till after sunset—but they are packed so full of excitement and beauty that your head will still be spinning as you fall into your comfortable bed after a splendid dinner. Departures are from Windhoek every Wednesday and Saturday. ⌾ *Wilderness Safaris, Box 5219, Rivonia 2128, South Africa* ☎ *27/11/807–1800* 📠 *27/11/807–2110* ⊕ *www.skeletoncoast.com* ⇱ *5 tents* ⚴ *Dining room* ▤ *AE, DC, MC, V* ⦿ *FAP.*

$$$$
Fodor'sChoice
★ ⊡ **Serra Cafema.** This astonishingly different and dramatically sited camp in the extreme northwest of Namibia, on the Angolan border, is the most remote camp in southern Africa. After a dry, dusty, but magnificently beautiful drive from the airstrip, you are guaranteed to gasp with awe as you first catch sight of the camp from a high sand dune. Built amid a grove of ancient Albida trees on the banks of the wide Kunene River, it seems like a desert mirage. Only the nomadic Himba people

share this area, and a visit to a local village is a must. Another day, ride a quad bike over the billowing sand dunes and spot the Atlantic from a high vantage point. Although tents (on raised platforms) are ultra-luxurious and have private bathrooms, don't come here if you are a sissy. The flight from Windhoek is long and bumpy, and the terrain harsh and demanding, but the experience—staying by a wide river in the midst of the oldest desert in the world—is almost surreal. This is one-of-a-kind Africa. Stay for three nights to make the most of the experience: go walking, boating, birding, or quad biking; do a nature drive; or just sit by the rushing river and contemplate. ⌖ *Wilderness Safaris, Box 5219, Rivonia 2128, South Africa* ☎ *27/11/807–1800* 🖷 *27/11/807–2110* ⊕ *www.serracafema.com* ⬅ *8 tents* ⚭ *Pool, bar* ⊟ *AE, DC, MC, V* ⦿ *FAP.*

$$$ ⊡ **Terrace Bay.** This isolated outpost and government resort is the northernmost point in the park to which you can drive. Surrounded by gravel plains, it's a popular spot for anglers and people who want to get to know the desert. Don't miss the surprising Uniab River delta—a lush green oasis in a miniature canyon a couple of miles from Terrace Bay. It's also a good stop if you're going on into Damaraland. The accommodations, once part of a diamond-mining operation, are simple and basic, though each bungalow has a refrigerator, shower, and toilet. The four-room Presidential Suite has all the modern conveniences, including air-conditioning and a fully equipped kitchen. All meals are provided, and there's a small shop that stocks basics. The resort does not accommodate day visitors. ✉ *Namibia Wildlife Resorts, Independence Ave., opposite Zoo Park, Windhoek, Namibia* ☎ *264/61/23–6975 through 264/61/23–6978* 🖷 *264/61/22–4900* ⊕ *www.nwr.com.na* ⚭ *Restaurant, refrigerators, bar, shop; no a/c in some rooms* ⊟ *MC, V* ⦿ *FAP.*

Damaraland

Stretching 600 km (370 mi) from just south of Etosha to Usakos in the south and 200 km (127 mi) from east to west, this stark, mountainous area is just inland from Skeleton Coast National Park. You can drive into Damaraland from the park via the Springbokwater Gate, or drive from Swakopmund to Uis, where you can visit the Daureb Craft Centre and watch the craftspeople at work, or make it part of your customized safari. A good base for touring southern Damaraland is the little town of Khorixas. From here you can visit the Organ Pipes, where there are hundreds of angular rock formations, or watch the rising or setting sun bathe the slopes of Burnt Mountain in fiery splendor. You'll find yourself surrounded by a dramatic landscape of steep valleys; rugged cliffs of red, gray, black, and brown; and towering mountains, including Spitzkoppe (Namibia's Matterhorn), where Damara guides will show you the Golden Snake and the Bridge—an interesting rock formation—and the San (Bushman) paintings at Bushman's Paradise. There are more spectacular Bushman rock paintings at the Brandberg, especially the famous White Lady of Brandberg, at Tsisab Gorge, whose depiction and origin have teased the minds of scholars for decades. Other stops of interest are the Petrified Forest, 42 km (25 mi) west of Khorixas, and Twyfelfontein, 90 km (56 mi) west of Khorixas, the biggest outdoor art gallery in the world, where thousands of rock paintings and ancient rock engravings are open to the sky. It's extremely rare for this many paintings and engravings to be found at the same site. Give yourself a full day here, start early (it's hard to pick out some of the art in full sun), take binoculars, wear sturdy shoes, and take water (at least a gallon) and a hat.

Northern Damaraland consists of concession areas that have been set aside for tourism, with many tourist operators working hand in hand with the local communities. It's a mountainous landscape dotted with umbrella-shape camel-thorn trees; candelabra euphorbias raising their prickly, fleshy arms to the cloudless sky; salt bushes; and the ubiquitous shepherd's tree. Look out for black rhinos and the first traces of the amazing desert elephants, their huge footprints trodden over by the herds of goat and sheep belonging to the local farmers. Ask your guide to point out the *welwitschia* (fossil plant) and the "enchanted" *moringa* tree. The Kaokoveld, north of Damaraland, although enticing because it is pristine and rarely visited, is also inhospitably rugged. If you're driving yourself, it's only for the intrepid, do-it-yourself explorer.

WHERE TO STAY 🔲 **Wilderness Damaraland Camp.** A joint community venture with the
$$$$ local *riemvasmakers* (thong makers), this desolate camp is on the Huab River in central Damaraland, midway between Khorixas and the coast. From your large, comfortable walk-in tent you can look out over a landscape of craggy beauty formed by millions of years of unending geological movement: brick-red sediments complement gray-lava slopes punctuated by black fingers of basaltic rock creeping down from the rocky horizons. You'll drive with an experienced ranger in an open 4x4 to see Namibia's famous fossil plant—the welwitschia—and go tracking desert elephants. After a day in the desert, cool off in the natural rock pool and watch the desert birds. 🖃 *Wilderness Safaris, Box 5219, Rivonia 2128, South Africa* 🕾 *27/11/807–1800* 🖷 *27/11/807–2110* ⊕ *www.damaraland.com* 🛏 *8 tents* ⚲ *Pool, bar* ▭ *AE, DC, MC, V* ⑩ *FAP.*

$$ 🔲 **Vingerklip Lodge.** In a dramatic locale in Damaraland's Valley of the Ugab Terraces, this lodge is set against the backdrop of a mighty stone finger pointing toward the sky. Take time while you're here to listen to the silence. The 360-degree views from the Sundowner Terrace are magnificent. The friendly and knowledgeable staff organize tours to the well-known sights in the vicinity. Bungalows cling to the side of a rocky hill and are clean and comfortable, but it's the remarkable views that you'll always remember. 🖃 *Box 443, Outjo, Namibia* 🕾 *264/61/25–5344* 🖷 *264/61/22–1432* ⊕ *www.vingerklip.com.na* 🛏 *11 bungalows* ⚲ *Restaurant, pool, bar* ▭ *MC, V* ⑩ *MAP.*

$ 🔲 **Khorixas Restcamp.** Grayish stone-and-tiled bungalows, some of which face a seasonally flowing river, are scattered among trees and flowering shrubs. Although this spot is hardly the last word in luxury, it is clean, budget priced, unpretentious, and very handy for exploring the major attractions of the area. 🖃 *Box 2, Khorixas, Namibia* 🕾 *264/67/33–1196* 🖷 *264/67/33–1388* 🛏 *38 bungalows, campsite* ⚲ *Restaurant, pool, bar* ▭ *MC, V* ⑩ *BP.*

Etosha National Park

This incredibly photogenic and startlingly beautiful park takes its name—meaning "Great White Place"—from the vast, flat depression that 12 million years ago was a deep inland lake. Although the park is never crowded with visitors like some of the East African game parks, the scenery here is no less spectacular: huge herds of animals that dot the plains and accumulate at the many and varied water holes, the dust devils and mirages, terrain that changes from densely wooded thickets to wide-open spaces and from white salt-encrusted pans to blond grasslands.

The game's all here—the Big Five—large and small, fierce and gentle, beautiful and ugly. On the road from the Von Lindequist Gate to the well-restored white-wall German colonial fort that is now Namutoni rest camp, look out for the smallest of all African antelopes, the Damara dik-dik. If you see a diminutive Bambi sheltering under a roadside bush, that's it. The Namutoni area and the two Okevi water holes—Klein Namutoni and Kalkheuwel—probably provide the best chances to see leopards. Don't miss the blackface impala, native to Etosha. But the real secret of game-watching in the park is to settle in at one of the many water holes, most of which are on the southern edges of the pan and each with its own unique personality and characteristics, and wait. Repeat, wait. Even if the hole is small and deep, like Ombika, on the western side, you'll be amazed at what may arrive. Old Africa hands maintain you should be up at dawn for the best sightings, but you can see marvelous game at all times of day; one visitor was lucky enough to see a leopard and her cubs come to drink at high noon. The plains, where you should spot cheetahs, are also home to huge herds of zebras, wildebeests, and springboks, and you may see the silhouettes of giraffes as they cross the skyline in stately procession. Salvadora, a constant spring on the fringe of Etosha Pan near Halali, is a favorite watering point for some of these big herds. And where there's water, there's always game. Predators, especially lions, lurk around most of the water holes looking for a meal. Plan to spend at least half a night sitting on a bench at the floodlighted Okuakuejo water hole. You'll be amazed at the game that comes down to drink: black and white rhinos, lions, jackals, and even the occasional leopard. Don't overlook the more than 340 dazzling varieties of birds—the crimson-breasted shrike is particularly gorgeous—and watch for ostriches running over the plains or raptors hunting silently overhead.

Although many tour companies offer safaris, it really is best to drive yourself, so you can stop and start at your leisure (but stick to marked roads). In addition to patience, you'll need drinks, snacks, and your camera. There are more than 40 water holes, with Rietfontein, Okuakuejo, Goas, Halali, Klein Namutoni, and Chudob regarded as the best for game-watching and taking pictures, but nothing is certain in the bush. Keep your eyes and ears open all the time, and you may come across game at any time, in any place.

The park gates are open from sunrise to sunset, and the daily entrance fee is N$30.

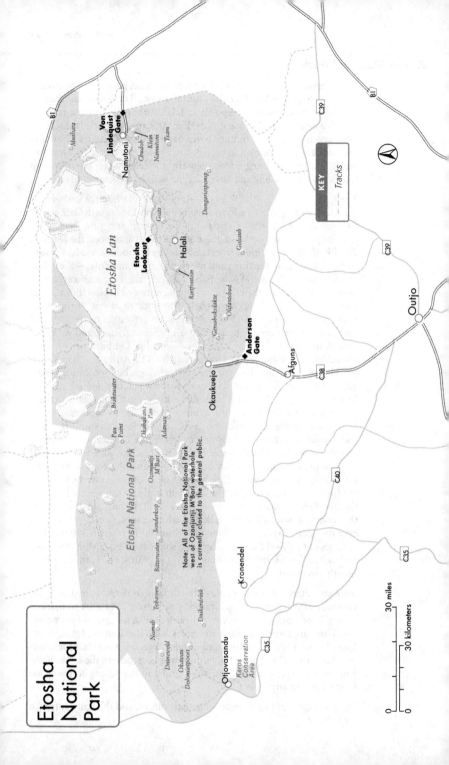

WHERE TO STAY

★ $$$$ **Ongava Lodge.** Set on the southern boundary of Etosha close to the Andersson Gate, the lodge has its own surrounding game reserve as well as its own entrance into the park. It's one of Namibia's most luxurious lodges, with accommodations in private, spacious thatch chalets with handmade wood furniture—and gold faucets in the bathrooms. Chalets also have wood decks, which cling to the side of a steep, rocky outcrop overlooking a couple of busy water holes. The stunning main area has stone floors and sweeping thatch roofs, as well as myriad spots from which to gaze at the never-ending plains beyond. Take a guided walk and sneak up on some zebras and wildebeests, or sit in the bird blind just before sunset and listen to the soft twittering calls of hundreds of sand grouses as they come to drink. Lions often stray in from Etosha and join the evening party. If you want to be more on the wild side, you can stay at Ongava's Tented Camp, a small, intimate site nestled deep in the bush. You'll sleep in a walk-in tent on a slate base under a thatch awning with a private bathroom. After a day spent game-watching (tracking rhinos on foot is a highlight), it's great to cool off in the outside shower or in the plunge pool. If you want even more exclusivity and luxury, then go for Little Ongava, which has three gorgeous suites all with their own plunge pool and *sala* (outdoor covered deck). *Wilderness Safaris, Box 519, Rivonia 2128, South Africa 27/11/807–1800 27/11/807–2110 www.ongavalodge.com 10 chalets, 6 tents, 3 suites Restaurant, pool, bar AE, DC, MC, V FAP.*

$$$ **Etosha Aoba Lodge.** This small, family-owned and ultrafriendly lodge is 10 km (6 mi) east of the Von Lindequist Gate—about a 30-minute drive from the park. You can slip into crisp, white bed linens in your cool, thatch chalet after a hot, dusty day in the park, or sip a cocktail on your mini-veranda while listening to the noises of the night. The owners put a lot of emphasis on excellent cuisine, which you'll enjoy under the thatch roof of the main building. Most visitors have their own vehicles, but the lodge can arrange trips into the park for you. *Box 21783, Windhoek, Namibia 264/61/22–9106 264/61/22–9107 mushara@iafrica.com.na 10 chalets Restaurant, a/c, pool, bar; no kids under 13 MC, V BP.*

$$$ **Mokuti Lodge.** Since it's in its own park a stone's throw from the Von Lindequist Gate, the eastern entrance to Etosha, you may well wake up and find an antelope or warthog munching the grass outside your room. This was Namibia's first lodge, and it is also its largest, and the experience is obvious in the impeccable service and good food. The smallish rooms are rather sparsely furnished, but you'll be out most of the day game-spotting. You can take a walk, either guided or on your own, and be quite safe. Follow the paths, and you may come face to face with a giraffe or any number of gorgeous birds. Don't miss the amazing reptile park, where you can meet pythons, scorpions, tortoises, and the odd crocodile. To catch sight of the bigger game, take an early-morning or afternoon tour into Etosha from the lodge. Air Namibia flies to and from Mokuti five days a week. *Namib Sun Hotels, Box 2862, Windhoek, Namibia 264/61/23–3145 264/61/23–4512 www.namibsunhotels.com.na 92 rooms, 8 suites, 8 family units Restaurant, a/c, tennis court, pool, horseback riding, bar MC, V BP.*

$ ▦ **Halali.** Etosha's smallest national-park camp, roughly halfway between Okuakuejo and Namutoni, is rather barracklike and dusty, but if you're a bird-watcher, it merits a giant check mark on your list. Rare violet wood-hoopoes and bare-cheeked babblers frequent the camp, and if you walk up the rocky path to the pleasant floodlighted water hole and are prepared to sit and wait, there's a good chance you'll spot lions, elephants, and black rhinos. Halali is in the only area of the park with hills. Meals are not included. ✉ *Namibia Wildlife Resorts, Independence Ave., opposite Zoo Park, Windhoek, Namibia* ☎ *264/61/23–6975 through 264/61/23–6978, 264/67/22–9400 Halali* 🖷 *264/61/22–4900* ⊕ *www.nwr.com.na* ⤴ *60 huts, 2 cottages* ♨ *Restaurant, a/c, pool, shop* ▤ *MC, V* ☾ *Closed Nov.–mid-Mar.*

$ ▦ **Namutoni.** On the eastern edge of the park, this restored colonial camp is the most picturesque of the national-park camps. Hearing the bugle call from the watchtower at sunrise and sunset, you almost expect to see the French Foreign Legion come galloping over the horizon. The historic rooms are tiny—the troops didn't live all that well—so if it's comfort rather than history you're after, don't choose a fort room; opt instead for one of the fully equipped bungalows, built at a respectful distance from the fort so as not to destroy the ambience. Directly behind the fort is a floodlighted water hole for game-viewing. Meals are not included. ✉ *Namibia Wildlife Resorts, Independence Ave., opposite Zoo Park, Windhoek, Namibia* ☎ *264/61/23–6975 through 264/61/23–6978, 264/67/22–9800 Namutoni* 🖷 *264/61/22–4900* ⊕ *www.nwr.com.na* ⤴ *18 bungalows, 10 rooms, 1 apartment, 4 cottages, 4 dormitories* ♨ *Restaurant, a/c, pool, shop* ▤ *MC, V.*

¢ ▦ **Okuakuejo.** On the western side of Etosha, this is the biggest and noisiest national-park camp (the noise comes from the staff quarters), and the staff could certainly do with a few workshops on how to deal with the public in a pleasant way. But its floodlighted water hole—regarded as one of the finest in Africa—more than makes up for any inconvenience. Climb the spiral staircase to the top of the round tower for a good view of the surrounding countryside, and then settle down to an all-night game-watching vigil. Pleasantly furnished, spotlessly clean accommodations range from basic two-bed huts with communal facilities to large, fully equipped eight-bed cottages. Meals are not included. ✉ *Namibia Wildlife Resorts, Independence Ave., opposite Zoo Park, Windhoek, Namibia* ☎ *264/61/23–6975 through 264/61/23–6978, 264/67/22–9800 Okuakuejo* 🖷 *264/61/22–4900* ⊕ *www.nwr.com.na* ⤴ *97 cottages* ♨ *Restaurant, a/c, some kitchens, pool, shop* ▤ *MC, V.*

Namibia A to Z

AIR TRAVEL

Namibia's main point of entry is Hosea Kutako International Airport. It's a small, bustling, modern airport that's a splendidly scenic 45-km (27-mi) drive from Windhoek. The smaller Eros Airport handles local flights and charters. Once in the country you can make use of scheduled flights or charter flights that service all domestic destinations.

Walvis Bay is the nearest airport for Namib Naukluft and the Skeleton Coast and has daily flights from Windhoek.

The national carrier is Air Namibia, which operates international flights between Windhoek and London, Frankfurt, Johannesburg, and Cape Town, and internal flights to most of Namibia's major tourist destinations. South African Airways (SAA) operates links to Johannesburg and Cape Town. Air Botswana links Maun with Windhoek, and SA Express Airways flies between Johannesburg and Walvis Bay.

There's frequent bus service from Hosea Kutako International Airport to Windhoek's city center; the pickup and drop-off point is opposite the Kalahari Sands Hotel, on Independence Avenue. Expect to pay N$70 each way. Many larger hotels run a courtesy shuttle service to and from the airport. Taxis are available, but negotiate the price before you get in. Check on current fares at the airport information counter.

All camps in Etosha National Park have their own landing strip. Have your tour operator arrange charters or fly-in safaris for you. Air Namibia flies directly to Mokuti on the regularly scheduled flight between Windhoek and Victoria Falls. Chartered flights and fly-in safaris also use the Ongava airstrip.

🛪 Airports **Eros Airport** ☎264/61/23–8220. **Hosea Kutako International Airport** ☎264/62/54–0315 or 264/62/54–0229. **Walvis Bay Airport** ☎ 264/64/20–2867.

🛪 Airlines **Air Botswana** ☎ 27/11/447–6078 Johannesburg. **Air Namibia** ☎ 264/61/298–2605 🖷 264/61/22–1382. **SA Express Airways** ☎ 27/11/978–5577 Johannesburg. **South African Airways** ☎ 27/11/778–1111 Johannesburg.

CAR TRAVEL

Driving to Namibia from South Africa is possible, and there's an excellent road network for all in-country tourist attractions, but be warned that the trip is tiring and time-consuming because of the huge distances involved. The Trans-Kalahari Highway links Johannesburg to Windhoek and Gaborone. From Johannesburg to Windhoek on this road is 1,426 km (885 mi). To allow free access to game, there are no fences in the Kalahari, so don't speed, and look out for antelope as well as donkeys and cows on the road. You can also drive from Johannesburg to Windhoek (1,791 km [1,237 mi]) via Upington, going through the Narochas (Nakop) border post (open 24 hours). This is a good route if you want to visit the Augrabies Falls and Kgalagadi Transfrontier Park in South Africa first. You can also drive from Cape Town to Namibia along the N7, an excellent road that becomes the B1 as you cross into Namibia at the Noordoewer border post (open 24 hours). It's 763 km (474 mi) from Cape Town to Noordoewer, 795 km (493 mi) from Noordoewer to Windhoek. Border posts are efficient and friendly—make sure you have all your paperwork to hand over. You will need a current international driver's license.

To reach Etosha National Park you can drive from Windhoek, via Otjiwarongo and Tsumeb, and arrive at the park on its eastern side by the Von Lindequist Gate (near Namutoni rest camp), 106 km (65 mi) from

Tsumeb and 550 km (330 mi) north of Windhoek. Alternatively, you can drive from Windhoek via Otjiwarongo and Outjo and come in the Andersson Gate, south of Okuakuejo, 120 km (74½ mi) from Outjo, 450 km (280 mi) north of Windhoek. The latter is the more popular route. Both drives are long, hot, and dusty, so you might want to fly if you're short on time. Travel time will depend on your driving and choice of vehicle, so check with your car-rental company. Etosha's gates open at sunrise and close just before sunset. You pay for your vehicle entry permit at the gate (N$30 for most small vehicles) and for any balance remaining on your prebooked accommodations (which include personal entry fees) at the reception area.

If you're not staying at a private lodge that provides transportation, you will need to rent your own vehicle. Air-conditioning is a must at any time of the year, as are spare tires in good condition. You can pick up rental cars at the town nearest whichever park you are visiting or at Etosha itself, but it's better to book them before you leave home. For driving on the main roads, a two-wheel-drive vehicle is fine. In some areas, though, including parts of the Namib Naukluft Park and Damaraland, four-wheel-drive is essential. In Etosha a two-wheel-drive car is fine (although you get better views in a van or SUV because you sit higher up); don't exceed the speed limit of 60 kph (37 mph). Always check the state of the roads with the nearest tourist office before you set off, and never underestimate the long distances involved. Don't drive at night unless you absolutely have to. Roads are unlighted, and animals like to bed down on the warm surfaces. If you hit an animal, even a small one, it could be the end of you and your vehicle. Never speed on gravel roads (80 kph [50 mph] is reasonable), which can often be very slippery. It's very easy to skid or roll your vehicle—at least one tourist per year is killed this way. And make sure you have plenty of water and *padkos,* Afrikaans for "road food."

Electricity

To use electric-powered equipment purchased in the United States or Canada, bring a converter and adapter. If your appliances are dual-voltage, you'll need only an adapter. The electrical current is 220 volts, 50 cycles alternating current (AC); wall outlets usually take 15-amp plugs with three round prongs, but some take the straight-edged three-prong plugs, also 15 amps. The more inaccessible lodges have their own generators, but if you want to read at night in your tent, bring a good reading light.

EMBASSIES

🔳 Canada **Canadian Consulate** 🔲 Box 239, Windhoek ☎ 264/61/25-1254 📠 264/61/25-1686.

🔳 United Kingdom **British High Commission** ✉ 116 Robert Mugabe Ave., Box 22202, Windhoek ☎ 264/61/27-4800.

🔳 United States **U.S. Embassy** ✉ 14 Lossen St., Box 12029, Windhoek ☎ 264/61/22-1601 📠 264/61/22-9792.

EMERGENCIES

For a general emergency, you can dial a standard number from your mobile phone (where there's service), the police, or International SOS. Call Netcare for any medical emergency.

There's a high standard of medical care in Namibia. Consult your hotel about particular doctors or consult the white pages of the telephone directory under *M* for medical practitioners. If you get sick, go to a private clinic rather than a government one. Windhoek and Otjiwarongo both have excellent private clinics. Windhoek has the Medi-Clinic and the Catholic Mission Hospital. In Otjiwarongo there is a Medi-Clinic. Be sure you have comprehensive medical insurance before you leave home.

🚩 Emergency Services **International SOS** ☎ 112 from mobile phone, 264/61/23-0505 Windhoek ☎ 264/64/40-0700 Swakopmund ☎ 264/81/28-5501 Tsumeb ☎ 264/64/20-0200 Walvis Bay. **Netcare** ☎ 264/61/22-3330. **Police** ☎ 10111.

🚩 Hospitals **Catholic Mission Hospital** ✉ 92 Stubel St., Windhoek ☎ 264/61/23-7237. **Medi-Clinic** ✉ Heliodoor St., Eros Park, Windhoek ☎ 264/61/22-2687 ✉ Son St., Otjiwarongo ☎ 264/67/30-3734 or 264/67/30-3735.

LANGUAGE

Namibia's official language is English, which, although widely spoken in the cities, lodges, national parks, and resorts, is usually spoken as a second language. Afrikaans is spoken by many residents of various races, and there is a large population of German-speaking people. The most widely spoken indigenous languages are Kwanyama (a dialect of Owambo), Herero, and a number of Nama (San) dialects, which are spoken by almost no one other than native speakers.

MONEY MATTERS

Namibia's currency is the Namibian dollar, which is linked to the South African rand. (Namibia's currency is not usable in South Africa, except unofficially at border towns.) In Namibia, MasterCard and Visa are preferred by business owners to American Express because of substantial charges levied by AmEx to proprietors. No credit cards are accepted at gas stations. Bank hours are weekdays 9–3:30 and Saturday 9–11. *Bureau de change* offices at the airports often stay open until late.

PASSPORTS & VISAS

All U.S., Canadian, New Zealand, Australian, and British citizens—in fact, all non-nationals, including infants—need a valid passport to enter Namibia for visits of up to 90 days. Business visitors to Namibia need visas.

TIME

Namibia is on CAST (Central African Standard Time), which is two hours ahead of Greenwich mean time. That makes it seven hours ahead of North American eastern standard time (six hours ahead during eastern daylight saving time).

TOURS

African Extravaganza specializes in shuttle services, scheduled safaris, charter tours and fly-ins, self-drive options, day excursions, and transfers. For instance, it offers a three-day Windhoek/Sossusvlei shuttle for N$3,200 per person, which includes minibus transport via the scenic, serpentine Spreetshoogte Pass, accommodations at the Namib Naukluft Lodge, your own guide, all meals, and an excursion to Sesriem and Sossusvlei. African Kirikara Safaris, whose base of operations is the family-owned farm Kiripotib, 160 km (100 mi) southeast of Windhoek in the Kalahari Desert, offers small, exclusive, tailor-made safaris throughout Namibia—even for as few as two people. Dune Hopper Air Taxis, operated by NatureFriend Safaris, offers flexible fly-in packages from Windhoek or Swakopmund to the Sossusvlei area. Pasjona Safaris offers tented safaris, guided tours, accommodations in lodges or hotels, and self-drive tours. Wilderness Safaris has a seven-day fly-in safari from Windhoek, which covers most of the main tourist destinations. Elena Travel Services offers transfers to guest farms, lodges, the coast, and other towns in Namibia. Skeleton Coast Fly-In Safaris offers superb four- and six-day trips to this starkly beautiful wilderness. Included is a visit to the remarkable Himba people who with their red-ocher body coverings, elaborate plaited hair, and intricate bead necklaces and leather aprons live much as they have for centuries. You'll fly to the park from Windhoek over the impressive Kuiseb Canyon and its surrounding sea of red dunes, staying at tented camps throughout and experiencing the desert from open Land Rovers.

NACOBTA (Namibia Community Based Tourism Association) promotes community-based tourism projects throughout Namibia benefiting both the indigenous people and the tourist. There are 45 established community-based tourism enterprises, which include campsites, crafts centers, traditional villages, indigenous tour guides, tourism information centers, and museums.

Guided rock-art safaris, including a fully inclusive six-day hike in the Brandberg (you need a doctor's certificate of fitness), are conducted by Joe Walter of Damaraland Trails and Tours. Few people know the Brandberg as intimately as Joe, who also has a wealth of knowledge on the rock art and flora of the mountain range.

🎫 Tour Operators **African Extravaganza** ⌂ Box 22028, Windhoek, Namibia ☎ 264/ 61/37-2100 📠 264/61/21-5356 ⊕ www.natron.net/afex. **African Kirikara Safaris** ⌂ Private Bag 13036, Windhoek, Namibia ☎ 264/62/57-3319 📠 264/61/22-3617. **Damaraland Trails and Tours** ⌂ Box 3073, Windhoek, Namibia ☎ 264/61/23-4610 ⊕ www.natron. net/tour/dtat/dtte.htm. **Dune Hopper Air Taxis** NatureFriend Safaris ⌂ Box 5048, Windhoek, Namibia ☎264/61/23-4793 📠264/61/25-9316 ⊕www.dunehopper.com. **Elena Travel Services** ⌂ Box 3127, Windhoek, Namibia ☎ 264/61/24-4443 📠 264/61/24-4558. **NACOBTA** ⌂ Box 86099, 18 Liliencron St., Windhoek, Namibia ☎ 264/61/25-0558 📠 264/ 61/22-2647 ⊕ www.nacobta.com.na. **Pasjona Safaris** ⌂ Box 90485, Windhoek, Namibia 📠📠 264/61/22-3421. **Skeleton Coast Fly-In Safaris** ⌂ Box 2195, Windhoek, Namibia ☎ 264/61/22-4248 📠 264/61/22-5713 ⊕ www.orusovo.com/sksafari. **Wilderness Safaris** ⌂ Box 5219, Rivonia 2128, South Africa ☎ 27/11/807-1800 📠 27/11/807-2110.

TRAVEL AGENCIES

Namibia-Direkt (✉ Box 2766, Windhoek ☎ 264/61/23–3691 🖷 264/61/24–8718). **Namib Travel Shop** (✉ Box 6850, Windhoek ☎ 264/61/22–6174 🖷 264/61/23–9455). **Sand Rose** (✉ Box 40263, Windhoek ☎ 264/61/24–5455 🖷 264/61/24–5454).

VISITOR INFORMATION

Namibian Tourism can provide details on camps, a free map, and a free copy of *Welcome to Namibia—Official Visitors' Guide,* which gives lots of useful information plus accommodation lists. It's open weekdays 8–1 and 2–5. Namibia Wildlife Resorts dispenses information on the national parks.

🚹 Tourist Offices **Namibian Tourism** ✉ Sanlam Centre, Independence Ave., Windhoek ✉ Private Bag 13244, Windhoek ☎ 264/61/290–6000 🖷 264/61/25–4848 ⊕ www. namibiatourism.com.na. **Namibia Wildlife Resorts** ✉ Independence Ave., opposite Zoo Park, Windhoek ☎ 264/61/23–6975 through 264/61/23–6978 🖷 264/61/22–4900 ⊕ www.nwr.com.na.

🚹 Web Site **Namibia information** ⊕ www.namibweb.com.

UNDERSTANDING SOUTH AFRICA

CHRONOLOGY

Prehistoric South Africa

South Africa had no written history until the Europeans arrived. Fossils and artifacts suggest that the first humans in South Africa, and perhaps the world, lived more than 3 million years ago.

The First Known Inhabitants

AD 100   For thousands of years the San, descendants of the prehistoric Africans, have been the only inhabitants of South Africa. A related group called the Khoikhoi, indigenous nomadic herders, settle in communities and raise cattle and sheep.

AD 200   People speaking various Bantu languages move into the area that is now eastern South Africa, bringing with them Iron Age culture. They grow grain, make tools and weapons out of iron, and trade among themselves.

AD 500–   The Khoikhoi settle in what is now western South Africa, and Bantu-
1300s   speaking peoples inhabit much of the eastern part of the country. Some Bantu speakers begin to group together and form large and powerful chiefdoms, especially the Sotho-Tswana people in the Highveld and the Nguni farther east.

European Exploration and Colonization

1487   At the command of King John II, Portuguese explorer Bartolomeu Dias sets sail to explore the African coast in search of gold and a sea route to India. A storm blows his fleet around the Cape of Good Hope, setting them back nearly two weeks. With their food supply now depleted, the men steer their ships back to Portugal. Later that year Vasco de Gama is commanded by the monarch to expand upon Dias's discoveries. He reaches India, and the Portuguese establish a monopoly on the trade route to India. The first detailed information on the indigenous inhabitants of South Africa is transmitted to Europe the following year.

1580   Compelled by Portuguese success in the East, the English begin to make voyages of trade and exploration. Sir Francis Drake sails around the world, passing the Cape of Good Hope. The same year, Spain occupies Portugal and begins to take over Portuguese ports.

1600s   The first Europeans settle in South Africa as convoys of the Dutch East India Company. Headed by commander Jan van Riebeeck, they set up camp in Cape Town in 1652. The base serves as a way station for ships traveling to and from the East Indies. In 1657 the company allows some employees to start their own farms east of Table Mountain and calls them free burghers (citizens) or Boers (farmers). The growing free burgher population wages war on the Khoikhoi (referred to as Hottentots by the Dutch), ending in the defeat of the Khoikhoi in 1677. The Dutch East India Company offers free passage and land to new settlers from Europe in 1679. In 1688 French Huguenots escaping religious persecution also settle at the Cape.

Early 1700s   Europeans now occupy most of the fertile farmland around Cape Town. The Khoikhoi and San populations begin to decline. Khoikhoi living near areas of European settlement are forced into service for the colonists. Dutch spoken in the area begins to incorporate words and sounds from the languages of other European settlers, Southeast Asian slaves, and San and Khoikhoi servants. A new language, called Afrikaans, develops, and those who speak it are called Afrikaners.

1770s   White settlers spread into the area occupied by the Xhosa, a Bantu-speaking people, in what is now the Eastern Cape. In 1778 Dutch Governor Joachim van Plettenberg tours the colony to redefine its boundaries, which triggers frontier wars between the Xhosa and Trekboers (white cattle and sheep herders) who occupy the disputed area. The white population spreads about 480 km (300 mi) north and more than 800 km (500 mi) east of Cape Town. This area becomes known as Cape Colony. Out of a total population of about 60,000, nearly 20,000 are whites; the rest are Khoikhoi, San, and slaves.

1795   France conquers the Netherlands, and British troops occupy the Cape Colony to keep it out of French control.

1803–1814   The British return the Cape Colony to the Dutch, only to reoccupy it three years later. A treaty between the British and the Dutch formally recognizes the Cape as a permanent British colony.

The Mfecane and the Great Trek

1818–1828   The Bantu-speaking Zulu clan, ruled by Shaka, evolves into the most powerful black African kingdom in southern Africa and occupies most of what is now KwaZulu-Natal. Less powerful chiefdoms flee to other parts of southeastern Africa. This period of forced migration and battles becomes known as the Mfecane (or Difaqane). The British government declares English the Cape Colony's only official language in 1828, though the Khoikhoi and coloureds are allowed the same legal rights as whites.

1834   In 1833 the British free all slaves in the empire, devastating those Boers who depend on slaves to work their fields. Though this is not the majority of Boers, several thousand Boers leave the Cape Colony to escape British rule in a historic journey called the Great Trek. They become known as the Voortrekkers (pioneers) and travel into lands occupied by Bantu-speaking peoples, including the Zulu kingdom, hoping to establish an independent republic.

1837–1838   Afrikaner farmer and businessman Piet Retief leads a party of Voortrekkers and their servants into Zulu-dominated Natal and attempts to negotiate a land agreement with the Zulu king, Dingane. The following year the Zulus kill Retief and more than 500 Voortrekkers. In December 1838 a Boer raiding party led by the Afrikaner pioneer Andries Pretorius defeats the Zulu at the Battle of Blood River. The

Voortrekkers then settle in Natal and set up the independent Republic of Natalia, now roughly the state of KwaZulu-Natal.

1843   The British annex Natalia and rename it Natal.

Early 1850s   The British recognize the independence of two other Boer republics: the Transvaal (1852) and the Orange Free State (1854). In Natal and the Boer republics whites claim the best land and extend their control over black Africans and coloureds. Meanwhile, in 1853 the British government grants the Cape Colony a constitution. Colonists of all races who pass certain wage or property qualifications can vote for members of the legislature.

1856   The British government grants a constitution similar to that of the Cape Colony, effective for whites only, to Natal.

1858–1859   The Boers in the Transvaal name their government the South African Republic (SAR). Both the Transvaal and the Orange Free State then set up their own exclusively white governments.

1860–1864   The growing of sugarcane in Natal makes its mark on the economy, and the British import Indians to work as indentured laborers on sugar plantations. Under this system, the Indians work in exchange for payment of their voyage, food, clothing, shelter, and a small wage from the British.

Diamonds and War

1867–1877   The discovery of diamonds and gold changes everything, and the emphasis of the economy shifts from agriculture to mining. Investment and profits flow in, and new money makes possible the development of a modern transportation and communication network. A coal-mining industry is established to supply fuel for the railways. After ousting several rival claimants, the British annex the diamond fields. The Cape Colony is granted self-government in 1872. Bantu-speaking farmers are required to remain in homelands, or Bantustans, outside Cape Colony borders. The British take advantage of a financial crisis in the SAR, annex the republic, and rename it the Transvaal in 1877.

1879   The British see the Zulu kingdom, now the region's only major African state, as a threat to their plan for a confederation of South Africa's colonies. They successfully invade the territory in what becomes known as the Zulu War, and the Zulu state falls under imperial control.

1880–1881   The Transvaal Boers rise in revolt in the First South African War (also called the Boer War, Anglo-Boer War, and Anglo-Transvaal War). They defeat the British, who agree to withdraw from the Transvaal under the Pretoria Convention. The Boers regain independence in the Transvaal and again name it the South African Republic.

1888   The consolidation of diamond claims leads to the creation of De Beers, headed by Cecil Rhodes, who becomes prime minister of the Cape Colony (1890–1896).

1897   Zululand is incorporated into Natal.

1899–1902   The SAR and the Orange Free State declare war on the United Kingdom and fight what is now called the Second South African War (also referred to as the Anglo-Boer or Boer War). In 1902 the Boers surrender to Great Britain, the two Boer republics become British colonies, and the SAR is once again declared the Transvaal.

1907   The United Kingdom grants self-government to the Transvaal and to the Orange River Colony (the colonial name of the Orange Free State). Representatives from both colonies and from the Cape Colony and Natal meet at a national convention to protest the exclusion of blacks from government in the proposed union constitution—without success.

1909–1910   At a national convention held in Durban, white delegates pass the South Africa Act, which unites the British colonies of Cape Colony, Natal, Transvaal, and Orange River, thereby establishing the nation of South Africa. In 1909 a new constitution for a united South Africa is promulgated with British acceptance. The constitution agreed upon is largely the work of Jan Smuts, colonial secretary of the Transvaal, and his English secretary, R. H. Brand. Louis Botha, a former Transvaal premier, becomes the new Union of South Africa's first prime minister and founds the South African Party in 1910.

The Rise of Afrikaner Nationalism

1912–1913   In response to the discriminatory nature of the South Africa Act, black political leaders set up the South African Native National Congress (SANNC). In keeping with the segregationist principles of the South African Native Affairs Commission, the first Union government establishes the Natives Land Act, which defines the borders of ancestral lands and declares illegal all land purchases and rent tenancy outside these reserves by blacks.

1914   In a breakaway from the ruling South African Party, James Barry Munnik Hertzog, a Boer general who had fought the British, founds the National Party to reflect Afrikaner nationalism.

1920   The League of Nations, a forerunner of the United Nations, gives South Africa control of South West Africa (now Namibia).

1923   The SANNC shortens its name to the African National Congress (ANC) and becomes the main political voice for blacks. That same year the Natives (Urban Areas) Act establishes the tenets of urban segregation and controls African mobility by means of pass laws.

1924–1925   Hertzog makes a pact with Labour Party leader Frederick H. P. Creswell for the upcoming general election. The two win and form the Pact government, of which Hertzog becomes prime minister in 1924. The Pact government makes Afrikaans, instead of Dutch, an official language along with English in 1925.

1931   South Africa gains full independence as a member of the Commonwealth of Nations, an association of the United Kingdom.

1933 Hertzog, who has lost some prestige due to the Great Depression, accepts a proposal from Jan Smuts to form a government of national unity with Hertzog as prime minister and Smuts as deputy.

1934 The National Party and the South African Party merge to form the United Party. In revolt, Afrikaner nationalist Daniel Malan forms a new National Party.

1945 South Africa becomes a founding member of the United Nations (UN).

1948 The National Party wins the general election.

Apartheid and the State of Emergency

1950 The National Party, under the leadership of Malan, begins to implement an apartheid program, coordinated by the white-male Afrikaner group the Broederbond. The cornerstone of apartheid is the Population Registration Act, under which all South Africans are classified according to race. The government establishes separate schools, universities, residential areas, and public facilities for each racial group.

1955 Opposition to apartheid grows swiftly under the leadership of ANC presidents James Moroka and later Albert Luthuli. The ANC, the Congress of South African Trade Unions, and other groups representing coloureds, Indians, and whites join to form the Congress Alliance, which meets at the Congress of the People in Kliptown (now part of Johannesburg). The alliance sets out a statement of goals called the Freedom Charter, which emphasizes equality of races, liberty, and human rights.

1959 Members of the ANC leave to form the Pan-Africanist Congress (PAC) in opposition to the ANC's participation in the multiracial Congress Alliance. The PAC first targets the pass laws, which require all people classified as black to carry identity papers. PAC leaders encourage blacks to appear at police stations without their passes in protest.

1960 South Africa leaves the Commonwealth and becomes a republic. A new currency (the rand), flag, anthem, and coat of arms are formally introduced. Prime Minister H. F. Verwoerd introduces the homeland policy, which delineates separate areas for each racial group. Though the government grants limited self-rule—and, in some cases, full independence—to black African homelands, also called Bantustans, the policy uproots black Africans and denies them South African citizenship. With all avenues of peaceful protest closed to them, the ANC and PAC begin waging armed struggle against the state. Police shoot and kill 69 anti-pass demonstrators in Sharpeville. To prevent further insurgencies, a state of emergency is declared, and detention without trial is introduced.

1964 Nelson Mandela, a prominent ANC leader, is sentenced to life imprisonment for sabotage and conspiracy against the South African government. While in prison Mandela becomes a symbol of the black struggle for racial justice.

1970s The Black Consciousness Movement, led by Steve Biko, reawakens a sense of pride in black Africans. Opposition to white rule increases both inside and outside the country. In 1976 several thousand black African schoolchildren march through the township of Soweto (now part of Johannesburg) to protest the use of Afrikaans as a medium of instruction in schools. During what becomes known as the Soweto Uprising, police kill more than 500 people, almost all of them black. In 1977 Steve Biko is killed in detention, and in 1978 P. W. Botha becomes prime minister.

1980s A new constitution restructures parliament to include representation for whites, coloureds, and Indians but makes no provisions for black representation. The constitution also calls for a state president and eliminates the office of prime minister. A series of violent protests carried out by the military branches of the ANC and PAC end in guerilla attacks on government targets (1983–1984). In opposition to apartheid, the European Community (the forerunner of the European Union), the Commonwealth of Nations, and the United States enact bans on certain kinds of trade with South Africa. In response the South African government begins to repeal apartheid laws, including the pass law, and more than 1 million black Africans move to cities in 1986.

1989–1990 F. W. de Klerk succeeds Botha as state president and abolishes most apartheid restrictions. He orders the release, in 1990, of Nelson Mandela, after nearly 26 years of imprisonment. De Klerk also lifts the ban on the ANC and ends South Africa's state of emergency.

1991 The South African government repeals most of the remaining laws that had formed the legal basis of apartheid. The government, the ANC, and other groups begin holding talks on a new constitution.

1993 The government adopts an interim constitution that allows South Africa's blacks full voting rights.

A Decade of Democracy

1994 The country holds its first elections open to all races. The ANC wins nearly two-thirds of the seats in parliament, which then elects Nelson Mandela president. South Africa resumes full participation in the UN and rejoins the Commonwealth. An interim constitution divides South Africa into nine provinces in place of the previous four provinces and 10 homelands.

1995 The government appoints a panel called the Truth and Reconciliation Commission (TRC), headed by Desmond Tutu, a former Anglican archbishop and winner of the 1984 Nobel Peace Prize, to probe human rights violations during the apartheid years.

1996 South Africa adopts a new constitution, guaranteeing freedom of religion; freedom of expression, including freedom of the press; and freedom of political activity. It also establishes the right to adequate housing, food, water, education, and health care.

1997   Mandela resigns as head of the ANC and is replaced by South Africa's deputy president, Thabo Mbeki.

1998   The TRC issues a report accusing the apartheid-era government of committing "gross violations of human rights," including kidnapping and murder. The report also criticizes anti-apartheid groups, including the ANC.

1999   Mandela retires as president of South Africa. The ANC wins a majority in parliament, which elects Mbeki president in the second democratic national election.

2002   In his annual address to parliament, President Thabo Mbeki defines as national goals black economic empowerment, poverty eradication, and nation building driven by volunteerism. The organization of implementation is called the African Union.

2003   Parliament accepts the government's response to the TRC's final report. Out of the 22,000 people who appeared before the commission, 19,000 receive interim reparations.

2004   On the 10th anniversary of democracy in South Africa the ANC wins a landslide victory, assuring a second five-year term for Mbeki. Mandela retires from public life and praises Mbeki while advising him to address the crisis of the country's rising AIDS epidemic.

2004   It's announced that the 2010 World Cup soccer tournament will be hosted in South Africa. It's the first time the tournament has gone to an African nation.

— By Audra Epstein

BOOKS & MOVIES

Books

The issue of language weighs heavily in the history of South African literature. Until the 18th century, Dutch was mandated. By 1925, with the legal recognition of Afrikaans that resulted from growing nationalism, several authors begin writing in that language, and interest in English-language literature lagged. But as the British population increased, a strong literary community developed, and many African writers, divorced from their ethnic heritage, began to write in English.

Fiction, Drama, & Poetry

Olive Schreiner's *The Story of an African Farm* (1883) follows three childhood friends as they strive for individuality in the face of strict Boer conventions. Though initially controversial, it was eventually accepted as the first great South African novel. Also set in the late 19th century, a time not unlike America's Wild West—an untamed frontier filled with marauding animals, gold rushes, skirmishes with locals, and desperadoes of all kinds—Sir Percy Fitzpatrick's classic *Jock of the Bushveld* (1907) documents this pioneer excitement. It follows the exploits of Jock, a fearless and lovable Staffordshire bull terrier, in the untamed bush in the area around today's Kruger National Park. The short stories of Herman Charles Bosman (1905–1951) capture the slow, measured life of Afrikaner farmers and early settlers. Laced with humor and irony, Bosman's stories recapture a time in South Africa when survival was a triumph and religion and peach brandy were necessary crutches.

South African writers have drawn steadily from the well of racial injustice to produce some of the finest literature of the last century. One of the first such novels is also one of the best: Alan Paton's *Cry, the Beloved Country* (1948), the story of a simple, dignified black pastor who heads from his rural Zululand parish to Egoli—Johannesburg, City of Gold—to save his son from execution for murder. With the rise of the Black Consciousness movement, led by the legendary Steve Biko, the 1970s saw a literary revival of black voices. Poetry became a vehicle for social unrest, and a group known as the Soweto Poets (Soweto is an abbreviation for South Western Townships) underscored Biko's appeal for racial solidarity. The most notable writers from this period are Mongane (Wally) Serote, Sipho Sepamla, Oswald Joseph Mbuyiseni Mtshali, Christopher van Wyk, Mafika Gwala, and Don Mattera, who often performed their work at political rallies. *Soweto Poetry,* an anthology of these poems edited by Michael Chapman, is now out of print but well worth the search.

Nadine Gordimer, who won the Nobel Prize for literature in 1991, is known both for her short stories and her novels. *The Conservationist* and *July's People* provide insights into South Africa, its peoples, their strife, and their history. Other major writers include J. M. Coetzee (*Life and Times of Michael K, Waiting for the Barbarians, Disgrace*), the first author to win the Booker Prize twice and also the 2003 Nobel Prize for literature; Athol Fugard (*Master Harold and the Boys, Boesman and Lena*), South Africa's most famous playwright; and André Brink, whose accessible novels make for compulsory reading. Try his historical novel *A Chain of Voices* or the magical realism of *Devil's Valley* for a start.

Since the end of apartheid, another generation of writers has arisen. Zakes Mda is credited with bringing magical realism into South African literature. *The Madonna of Excelsior* (2004) reimagines the events surrounding an actual South African court case. Marlene van Niekerk's *Triomf* (2004) takes place in a white, working-class neighborhood in west Johannesburg from which hundreds of black families were banned in the 1950s. Both Ivan Vladislavic and K. Sello Duiker experiment with the literary conventions of fiction while confronting the realities of contemporary South Africa. The characters in Phaswane Mpe's *Welcome to Our Hillbrow* (2001) illustrate the ongoing struggle of moving from poverty to prosperity in a democratic South African.

History, Politics, & Sociology

As its title implies, *A History of South Africa, Third Edition* (2001) is a comprehensive, but penetrating, exploration of the country's history, from the first documented evidence of human existence to life as it stands in the era of Thabo Mbeki's presidency.

South African journalist Allister Spark's *Tomorrow Is Another Country* (1996) chronicles the mostly clandestine meetings that eventually led to majority rule and the end of apartheid. The book begins with details of the collaboration between Nelson Mandela and South Africa's minister of justice and continues with talks between the ANC and top leaders of the Broederbond. For a lyrical, impassioned, and disturbing account of the TRC hearings, try poet Antje Krog's *Country of My Skull* (2000). Equally compelling reading for visitors is *Indaba, My Children* (1999) by Credo Mutwa, the most famous and best loved of all African *sangomas* (healers, prophets, and shamans). Described by the *London Sunday Times* as "a work of genius," it's a compilation of African tribal history, legends, customs, and religious beliefs by a master storyteller.

Lost World of the Kalahari (1977), by Laurens van der Post, mentor to Britain's Prince Charles, is a fascinating mix of fact and fantasy, recalling the author's expedition into the Kalahari Desert after World War II to study the San (Bushmen). The book has a mystical, spiritual quality befitting a people who lived in complete harmony with nature and each other. A classic and very readable study of the San, Elizabeth Marshall Thomas's *The Harmless People* (1989) describes the traditional ways of this hunting-gathering culture, which has become endangered and made almost extinct by the intrusion of industrial civilization. Thomas Pakenham's reader-friendly, fascinating, and definitive study *The Boer War* (1992) explains an important and evocative part of South Africa's colonial history, when thousands of British soldiers died fighting for a cause they didn't understand in a country they barely knew. Their enemy? The brave, independent Boers, the founders of fierce and innovative guerilla warfare, who were fighting for the fatherland they had carved out of the African wilderness.

Memoir & Biography

For 45 years South Africa's political and historical writing focused on the issues of apartheid. The best way to put the record straight is to hear the personal observations and histories of the people who have lived and worked through "the struggle"—as South Africa's stormy passage to democracy is known. Foremost among these is *Long Walk to Freedom* (1995), by Nelson Mandela. An inspiring account of the triumph of idealism, the book looks back over Mandela's life and also takes a pragmatic view of the political road ahead. It should be required reading for South Africans and visitors alike. *In His Own Words* (2004) collects and thematically organizes more than 100 of Mandela's speeches. *Mandela: The Authorized Biography* (1999), by Anthony Sampson, is the definitive biography of the man who changed South African politics; it assesses the years before, during, and after his imprisonment.

Rainbow People of God (1994) tells the story of another of the heroes of the struggle, Archbishop Desmond Tutu, through his speeches, sermons, and letters from 1976 to 1994. *No Future Without Forgiveness* (2000), his poignant personal account of the proceedings, stories, and people he presided over as chairman of the Truth and Reconciliation Commission (TRC), is remarkable for its sense of balance and lack of bitterness, in spite of the accounts of the horrors and trauma he heard on a daily basis for months.

Afrikaner poet, artist, and leftist exile Breyten Breytenbach's most renowned work is a four-volume memoir—*A Season in Paradise* (1973), *The True Confessions of an Albino Terrorist* (1983), *Return to Paradise* (1991), and *Dog Heart: A Memoir* (1999)—that chronicles nearly three decades in the life of a South African "traitor," including seven years in prison for his involvement in the liberation movement. Breytenbach's poetic political rants and bittersweet nostalgia for his homeland embody the fierce dissonance felt throughout the Afrikaner apartheid state.

Nobel Prize for literature nominee Professor Es'kial Mphahlele's classic *Down Second Avenue* (1985) is the story—moving, sad, funny, painful—of his upbringing in the black slums outside what was then Pretoria, in the mountains of South Africa's then Northern (now Limpopo) Province.

Nature

For armchair orientation before your trip and reference throughout it, *The Wildlife of South Africa: A Field Guide to the Animals and Plants of the Region* is indispensable. The more than 2,000 species contained in the volume are also the most likely to be encountered on nature treks and safaris. *Birds of Southern Africa* is the most comprehensive and authoritative guide to the region's rich ornithological treasury. With more than 4,000 illustrations depicting southern Africa's approximately 950 species, no birder will tread unprepared. *The Safari Companion: A Guide to Watching African Mammals Including Hoofed Mammals, Carnivores, and Primates* is the result of more than eight years of fieldwork focusing on animal behavior. Included are loads of tried-and-true tips on using binoculars and photographic equipment and pages of drawings for easy identification. Also recommended are any bird guide by Ken Newman or the *Sasol Guide to Birds*.

Wine

Wines and Vineyards of South Africa includes a brief history of the South African wine industry, followed by information on cellar techniques, soils, climates, main grape varieties, and the wines they yield as well as fantastic photos. Other well-researched options are *The Wines of South Africa* and *New World of Wine from the Cape of Good Hope: The Definitive Guide to the South African Wine Industry*. A concise but thorough pocket book, *John Platter South African Wine Guide* lists the major players in South Africa's wine country along with culinary and tourist hot spots.

Movies

Most movies about South Africa have traditionally focused on the tragedy of apartheid. Among these is the remake of *Cry, the Beloved Country* (1995), starring James Earl Jones. *Cry Freedom* (1987), starring Denzel Washington and Kevin Kline, follows the story of white South African journalist Donald Woods and Steve Biko, a prominent black activist who died in 1977 after being beaten in police custody in Port Elizabeth. *Breaker Morant* (1979), a superbly crafted and acted Australian movie about the Second South African War (1899–1902), looks at British military hypocrisy through the eyes of three Australian soldiers on trial for shooting Boer prisoners.

The South African movie industry, though relatively small, has produced one major hit, *The Gods Must Be Crazy* (1980), the enchanting story of a San clan in the Kalahari Desert. Try to get your hands on the 1980s movie version of *Jock of the Bushveld*, starring Jonathan Rand, with music by Johnny Clegg and Savuka—it's delightful. Gavin Hood's fine movie *A Reasonable Man* (1999) tells the story of a simple Zulu cowherd on trial for killing a child whom he believed to be an evil spirit. With a superb performance by Sir Nigel Hawthorne as the trial judge, this groundbreaking and thought-provoking movie, based on an actual case in South African law, attempts to answer the questions, Who is a reasonable man? Which standards do we apply—those of Western law or traditional African belief? And which, if either, is right?

The 2003 documentary *Amandla: A Revolution in Four Part Harmony* celebrates the vital role music played during the apartheid era. *Africa: The Serengeti,* a swooping IMAX documentary narrated by James Earl Jones, follows South Africa's annual migration, during which 2 million wildebeests, zebras, and antelope travel 500 miles across the plain to ensure their survival; it's a great pre-safari fix well worth tracking down.

Winner of the 2004 human rights prize at the 54th Berlin International Film Festi-val Special, *In My Country* was based on Antje Krog's *Country of My Skull.* It stars Samuel L. Jackson as a *Washington Post* journalist sent to South Africa to cover the post-apartheid Truth and Reconciliation Commission hearings. There he meets an Afrikaans poet (played by Juliette Binoche) reporting for the South African state media, and the shared experience of recording the trial's gruesome testimonials draws them together, despite their clashing ideals concerning a country recovering from its inherent social fragmentation.

— By Audra Epstein

VOCABULARY

South African Glossary

South Africa has 11 official languages, including 9 indigenous African languages. English is the lingua franca; in its everyday use it includes a rich assortment of terms from the other languages. Afrikaans, originally a Dutch dialect, has a shadowed history because of its role in apartheid politics, but it's still a very common language. Zulu is the most widely spoken indigenous African language; it doesn't hurt to know a few polite phrases if you're traveling to a Zulu-speaking area like KwaZulu-Natal. Below we've listed common terms, followed by some essential terms in Zulu and a menu guide. *See also* the safari-specific vocabulary list in the Safari Primer.

Ablution blocks	public bathrooms
Abseil	rappel
Backpackers	hostel
Bakkie	pickup truck (pronounced "bucky")
Banda	bungalow or hut
Berg	mountain
Boma	enclosure, sometimes used as the term for a dining area in lodges
Boot	trunk (of a car)
Bottle store	liquor store
Bra/bru/my bra	brother (term of affection or familiarity)
Buck	antelope
Burg	city
Cape Malay/Malay	referring to descendants of Asian, largely Muslim, slaves, brought to the Cape starting in the 1600s and erroneously lumped together under the term Malay
Coloured	a locally non-offensive term for people of mixed-race descent, representing Malay, Khoi-San, other black African, and/or European descent
Dagga	marijuana, sometimes called *zol*
Djembes	drums
Dorp	village
Fanagalo	a mix of English and various South African languages, used often by guides and trackers
Fynbos	the collective name for a variety of bush plants, which can be divided into 4 basic types (proteas, ericas or heather, restios or reeds, and ground flowers)
Highveld	the country's high interior plateau, including Johannesburg
Howzit?	literally, "how are you?" but used as a general greeting
Indaba	literally, a meeting but also a problem, as in "that's your indaba."

Jol	a party or night on the town
Kloof	river gorge
Kokerbooms	quiver trees
Koppies	hills (also *kopjes*)
Kraal	traditional rural settlement of huts and houses, village
Lekker	nice
Lowveld	land at lower elevation, including Kruger National Park
Marula	tree from which amarula (the liquor) gets its name
Mokoro	dugout canoe, pluralized as *mekoro*
Mopane	nutrient-poor land
Moppies	vaudeville-style songs
More-ish	so good you will want more, mouth-watering
Muthi	traditional (non-Western) medicine
Petrol	gasoline
Robot	traffic light
Rondawel/rondavel	a traditional, round dwelling with a conical roof
Sala	outdoor covered deck
Sangoma	traditional healer or mystic
Self-catering	with cooking facilities
Shebeen	a place to drink, often used for taverns in townships
Sis	gross, disgusting
Sisi or usisi	sister (term of affection or respect)
South African War	the more inclusive name for the Boer War or Anglo-Boer War and actually referring to either of two South African Wars (1880–1881 and 1899–1902)
Spaza shop	an informal shop, usually from a truck or container
Stoep	verandah
Takkie	(pronounced tacky) sneaker
Veld	open countryside

Zulu Essentials

Yes or hello	yebo
No	cha
Please	uxolo
Thank you	ngiyabonga
You're welcome	nami ngiyabonga
Good morning/hello	sawubona
Excuse me	uxolo
Goodbye	sala kahle
Do you speak English?	uya khuluma isingisi?

Menu Guide

Biltong	spiced air-dried (not smoked) meat, made of everything from beef to kudu
Bobotie	spiced minced beef or lamb topped with savory custard, a Cape Malay dish
Boerewors	Afrikaaner term for a spicy farmer's sausage, often used for a braai (pronounced "*boo-rah-vorse*")
Braai	roughly, a barbeque or grill, with sausages, fish etc.
Bredie	a casserole or stew, usually lamb with tomatoes
Bunny chow	not a fancy name for salad—it's a half loaf of bread hollowed out and filled with meat or vegetable curry
Chakalaka	a spicy relish
Gatsby	a loaf of bread cut lengthwise and filled with fish or meat, salad, and fries
Kabeljou	one of the varieties of line fish
Kingklip	a native fish
Koeksister	a deep-fried braided, sugared dough
Malva	pudding
Melktert	a sweet custard tart
Mogodu	beef or ox tripe
Moroho	mopane worms
Pap	also called *mielie pap,* a maize-based porridge
Peppadews	a patented vegetable, so you may see it under different names, usually with the word *dew* in them; it's a sort of a cross between a sweet pepper and a chili and is usually pickled.
Peri-peri	a spicy chili marinade, Portuguese in origin, based on the searing hot *piri-piri* chili; some recipes are tomato-based, while others use garlic, olive oil, and brandy
Potjie	pronounced "*poy*-key" and also called *potjiekos,* a traditional stew cooked in a 3-legged pot
Rocket	arugula
Rooibos	an indigenous, earthy-tasting red-leaf tea
Samp	corn porridge
Snoek	a barracuda-like fish, often smoked, sometimes used for *smoorsnoek* (braised)
Sosaties	local version of a kebab, with spiced, grilled chunks of meat
Waterblommetjie	water lilies, sometimes used in stews
Witblitz	moonshine

INDEX

NOTES

NOTES

NOTES

FODOR'S KEY TO THE GUIDES

AMERICA'S **GUIDEBOOK LEADER** PUBLISHES GUIDES FOR **EVERY KIND OF TRAVELER**. CHECK OUT OUR MANY SERIES AND FIND YOUR **PERFECT MATCH**.

FODOR'S GOLD GUIDES
America's favorite travel-guide series offers the most detailed insider reviews of hotels, restaurants, and attractions in all price ranges, plus great background information, smart tips, and useful maps.

COMPASS AMERICAN GUIDES
Stunning guides from top local writers and photographers, with gorgeous photos, literary excerpts, and colorful anecdotes. A must-have for culture mavens, history buffs, and new residents.

FODOR'S 25 BEST / CITYPACKS
Concise city coverage in a guide plus a foldout map. The right choice for urban travelers who want everything under one cover.

FODOR'S AROUND THE CITY WITH KIDS
Up to 68 great ideas for family days, recommended by resident parents. Perfect for exploring in your own backyard or on the road.

SEE IT GUIDES
Illustrated guidebooks that include the practical information travelers need, in gorgeous full color. Perfect for travelers who want the best value packed in a fresh, easy-to-use, colorful layout.

FODOR'S FLASHMAPS
Every resident's map guide, with 60 easy-to-follow maps of public transit, parks, museums, zip codes, and more.

FODOR'S LANGUAGES FOR TRAVELERS
Practice the local language before you hit the road. Available in phrase books, cassette sets, and CD sets.

THE COLLECTED TRAVELER
These collections of the best published essays and articles on various European destinations will give you a feel for the culture, cuisine, and way of life.